| CHAPTER | Parenting, Policy, and Practice | Focus O… Research In… | | | …ng |
|---|---|---|---|---|---|
| 9 Cognitive Development in Early Childhood | **Practice:** Piaget's Theory and Preschool Classrooms • Vygotsky's Theory and Preschool Classrooms • Information Processing Theory and Preschool Classrooms<br>**Parenting:** Helping Preschool Children Become Readers<br>**Policy:** The Personal Responsibility and Work Opportunities Reconciliation Act | **Focus On:** Barbara Rogoff<br>**Research Insights:** Can We Teach Executive Function Skills to Young Children?<br>• Young Children and Board Games | Culture and Learning Numbers | The Role of Executive Function<br>Language Delays | A Growth Spurt in Executive Function<br>What Happens in the Brain?<br>Beginning to Read |
| 10 Psychosocial Development in Early Childhood | **Practice:** How Can Preschool Teachers Support Play?<br>**Policy:** The Individuals with Disabilities Act (IDEA) • The Federal Child Abuse Prevention and Treatment Act<br>**Parenting:** Spanking | **Focus On:** Albert Bandura<br>**Research Insights:** Do Children with Autism Lack a Theory of Mind? • The Effects of Extreme Emotional Neglect | Culture and Showing Pride and Shame | Developing a Theory of Mind | Self-Representation and the Brain |
| 11 Physical Development and Health in Middle Childhood | **Policy:** Dealing with Childhood Obesity<br>**Parenting:** Family Mealtime<br>**Practice:** The Coordinated School Health Program (CSHP) Model | **Focus On:** Michelle Obama and Let's Move!<br>**Research Insights:** Degrees of Freedom | Culture and Body Weight | Why the Incidence of Overweight and Obesity Has Increased | The Developing Brain in Middle Childhood |
| 12 Cognitive Development in Middle Childhood | **Practice:** Helping Children Develop Their Cognitive Skills in the Classroom • Vygotsky in the Classroom • Teaching Effective Memory Strategies<br>**Policy:** English Language Learners<br>**Parenting:** Parent Engagement in Children's Schooling | **Focus On:** Eric Kandel<br>**Research Insights:** Children with Problems with Attention | Culture and Views on Intelligence | Mathematical Skills and Executive Functioning | Attention |
| 13 Psychosocial Development in Middle Childhood | **Parenting:** Building Self Esteem • Supporting Children's Well-Being After Divorce<br>**Policy:** Anti-Bullying Legislation<br>**Practice:** Making Moral Principles Meaningful | **Focus On:** Antonio Damasio<br>**Research Insights:** Do Violent Video Games Promote Aggression? | Culture and Children's Evaluations of Truths and Lies | Coping with Stress | The Social Brain<br>What Happens in the Brain? Emotional Self-Regulation in Middle Childhood |
| 14 Physical Development and Health in Adolescence | **Policy:** Cervical Cancer, Human Papillomavirus, and a Vaccine<br>**Parenting:** The Role of Parents in Adolescent Sexual Behavior<br>**Practice:** Treating Concussions in Adolescents | **Focus On:** G. Stanley Hall<br>**Research Insights:** Survey Data | Culture and Menarche | Adolescent Brain Development<br>An Uneven Playing Field | Brain Development<br>What Happens in the Brain? Having a Conversation while Driving a Car |
| 15 Cognitive Development in Adolescence | **Practice:** Peer Tutoring<br>**Parenting:** Promoting School Achievement<br>**Policy:** No Child Left Behind and High School Completion | **Focus On:** Claude Steele<br>**Research Insights:** Can Knowledge About Income Differences Motivate Students?<br>• Can You Grow Your Intelligence? | Culture and Learning Models | The Effects of Experience<br>School Completion | The Brain and Adolescent Cognition |
| 16 Psychosocial Development in Adolescence | **Parenting:** Psychological Control<br>**Policy:** Trying Juveniles as Adults<br>**Practice:** Positive Youth Development | **Focus On:** Janet E. Helms<br>**Research Insights:** Impulsivity and Reward Seeking<br>• Treatment for Adolescents with Depression | Culture and the Immigrant Paradox | Identity Achievement and Cognitive Skills<br>Risk for Depression | Moral Judgments |

# The Development of Children and Adolescents

**Penny Hauser-Cram**
*Boston College*

**J. Kevin Nugent**
*Boston Children's Hospital, Division of Developmental Medicine; Harvard Medical School; University of Massachusetts Amherst*

**Kathleen M. Thies**
*Graduate School of Nursing, University of Massachusetts Worcester*

**John F. Travers**
*Boston College*

WILEY

| | |
|---|---|
| Vice President and Executive Publisher | George Hoffman |
| Executive Editor | Christopher T. Johnson |
| Senior Developmental Editor | Marian Provenzano |
| Content Editor | Brian Kamins |
| Editorial Program Assistant | Marie Dripchak |
| Editorial Operations Manager | Yana Mermel |
| Senior Marketing Manager | Margaret Barrett |
| Product Designer | Beth Tripmacher |
| Senior Production Editor | William A. Murray |
| Media Specialist | Anita Castro |
| Senior Photo Editor | Billy Ray |
| Senior Designer | Maureen Eide |
| Cover Designer | Thomas Nery |
| Cover Photo Credits | Image 1: xefstock/E+/Getty Images<br>Image 2: Fuse/Getty Images<br>Image 3: JGI/Jamie Grill/Blend Images/Getty Images<br>Image 4: Norah Levine Photography/Brand X Pictures/ Getty Images<br>Image 5: Rubberball/Mike Kemp/Getty Images |
| Design Element Photo Credits | Woman wondering: Winston Davidian/Photodisc/ Getty Images, Inc.<br>Man wondering: IMAGEMORE Co, Ltd./Getty Images, Inc.<br>Mosaic tile: Getty Images, Inc. |

This book was set in 10/12 Janson Text by Aptara and printed and bound by Courier/Kendallville.

Founded in 1807, John Wiley & Sons, Inc. has been a valued source of knowledge and understanding for more than 200 years, helping people around the world meet their needs and fulfill their aspirations. Our company is built on a foundation of principles that include responsibility to the communities we serve and where we live and work. In 2008, we launched a Corporate Citizenship Initiative, a global effort to address the environmental, social, economic, and ethical challenges we face in our business. Among the issues we are addressing are carbon impact, paper specifications and procurement, ethical conduct within our business and among our vendors, and community and charitable support. For more information, please visit our website: www.wiley.com/go/citizenship.



ISBN: 978-0-470-40540-6
BRV ISBN: 978-1-118-76764-1

Printed in the United States of America
10 9 8 7 6 5 4 3 2 1

# ABOUT THE AUTHORS

**Penny Hauser-Cram** is Professor of Developmental and Educational Psychology at Boston College in the Lynch School of Education. She received her EdD in Human Development from the Graduate School of Education at Harvard University. Her research focuses on the importance of the family system and effects of early education on children's optimal development. She has conducted longitudinal studies on the developmental pathways of children living in poverty and on the experiences of children and adolescents with developmental disabilities and their families.

**J. Kevin Nugent** is the Director of the Brazelton Institute in the Department of Developmental Medicine at Boston Children's Hospital. He is on the faculty of the Harvard Medical School and is also Professor Emeritus of Children, Families and Schools at the University of Massachusetts at Amherst. His research focuses on newborn behavior and development, the study of parent-child relationships in different cultural settings, and neurobehavioral assessment and early intervention.

**Kathleen M. Thies** received her PhD from Boston College in developmental psychology. She chaired the Department of Nursing at Colby–Sawyer College, and was program director of the Graduate School of Nursing at the University of Massachusetts Medical School, where she maintains an academic affiliation. Most recently, as the researcher for the Elliot Health System in New Hampshire, Dr. Thies has developed research studies on perinatal mood disorders, and in adult and neonatal intensive care. This is her third book with John F. Travers.

**John F. Travers** received his EdD from Boston College and was a professor at Boston College in the Lynch School of Education for more than 50 years. He was the author and coauthor of 19 books and numerous publications in the fields of educational and developmental psychology. He passed away in May 2011, but his legacy lives on through his students, colleagues, and family.

*To John Travers—an extraordinary colleague, mentor, and friend, a teacher and scholar who inspired generations of students, and a man who unequivocally bequeathed good to all who were fortunate enough to meet him.*

# Brief Contents

# Contents

# Preface

When the four of us came together as authors to write *The Development of Children and Adolescents*, we shared a deep personal conviction about the importance of understanding development in our contemporary world. At the same time, we brought four quite different perspectives to the task. Our backgrounds encompassed research, clinical practice, and teaching, and our specialties ranged from the prenatal period through adolescence, and included the vital intersection of development and health. We believed that this breadth of perspective would enable us to create a unique offering in the field.

As we wrote the book, we had several key goals in mind. We intended our book primarily for students pursuing careers in psychology, education, health, and human services, as well as for those taking a child development course because they expect to be parents someday. First and foremost, we wanted to help these students understand how children develop, from conception through adolescence. We especially wanted them to appreciate the dynamic and integrative nature of this development. We also wanted to enable them to apply what they learn in their lives, both professional and personal. We brought these goals to life in the three major themes running through this book.

## THEMES OF THE BOOK

Three major themes shape the organization of *The Development of Children and Adolescents*: understanding the concepts, integrating the concepts, and applying the concepts.

### Understanding the Concepts

To help students *understand* the fundamental concepts, we present research that supports the state of today's knowledge about children's development. In addition, our book uses some special features to guide learning.

**A Focus on Research.** As students begin the absorbing task of following children's developmental journey, they will encounter a great deal of research data. This research is at the core of developmental psychology, and students need to understand its importance. To help them do this, we have made sure that the many studies highlighted in our text have been carefully selected, clearly explained, and directly applied to practical situations. Our examples include both classic and current research studies, and we believe students will find them both interesting and enlightening.

In addition, new research and remarkable brain imaging studies have broadened our knowledge of children's brain development. Therefore, based on current insights gained from the neurosciences, we include an exciting and accessible teaching tool that graphically illustrates what happens in children's brains when they perform such common behaviors as reading and walking. This feature, *What Happens in the Brain*, relies on the most recent scholarly information and includes clear descriptions of the central brain mechanisms involved.

**A Guided Learning Approach.** To foster understanding, we take a guided learning approach within each chapter. Following an opening narrative (called *Making a Difference*) that focuses on improving children's lives, we pose *Key Questions* to guide readers through the chapter. These questions are keyed to the major sections in the chapter and to the end-of-chapter summary. *Check Your Progress* questions at the end of each major section give students the opportunity to review their understanding of the section contents; and *Critical Thinking* questions at the end of each chapter encourage students to reflect on issues discussed in the chapter.

### Integrating the Concepts

Understanding individual concepts is important, of course, but to truly appreciate how children develop, students need to *integrate* these concepts. Our approach to the relationship between nature and nurture, between maturation and learning, is holistic. We assume a complex, dynamic relationship between the changing individual child and the ever-changing environment—each transforming and being transformed by the other.

**A Systems Approach to Development.** In describing how child and environment interact, we assume that each aspect of development—physical, cognitive, and psychosocial—is dynamically related to the others. Learning to walk or learning to go up or down stairs, for example, is a landmark motor milestone in children's lives, but it is important, too, because it transforms their sense of competence and sense of self. These motor milestones give infants a new sense of satisfaction and a growing awareness of themselves as independent and autonomous beings.

The developmental systems approach that we follow in the book is necessarily multidisciplinary. Therefore, in integrating concepts, we touch on a number of diverse areas. Because biology is an essential part of understanding child behavior, we discuss the biological underpinnings of development in Chapter 2 and in sections throughout the book labeled *The Developing Brain*, as well as in the *What Happens in the Brain* features mentioned earlier. We highlight cultural influences on development in special *Culture and . . .* features and through integrate coverage of this topic throughout the text. Developmental science inevitably produces results related to the promotion of healthy child and family development. For that reason, we discuss various aspects of national policy concerning children, and advocacy for children in our opening features, titled *Making a Difference*, and our *Policy* sections, described further below.

**Children's Health—A Key Developmental Issue.** Worthy of special note is our emphasis on the critical intersection of health and children's cognitive and psychosocial development. Normative development has its foundations in the biology of good health, and we cannot take health for granted. Consistent with our systems approach, we emphasize the roles of families and communities in promoting children's health. For example, we address how lack of access to prenatal and well-child care, and lack of health-related services in the community or at school, can undermine children's ability to grow and develop normally.

Given the increased incidence of chronic illness among children, we help future child professionals and parents to understand how medications, disease processes, and nutrition affect learning and behavior. We also suggest ways to promote children's health and safety at home, at school, and in their communities.

## Applying the Concepts

Today's students need to *apply* what they have learned to their chosen occupations—education, psychology, nursing and other health-care fields, child care, behavioral pediatrics, and social work, among others. Furthermore, many will become parents. To emphasize the relationship between research and theory on the one hand, and application on the other, we have integrated applications throughout the chapters that focus on three themes—Parenting, Policy, and Practice. This unique feature highlights our efforts to offer readers not only pertinent theories and research but also examples of how these ideas affect the daily lives of children.

**Parenting** A child's parents, of course, play a central role in the child's development. Children thrive in the context of close and dependable relationships that provide love, nurturance, and security. In our book, parenting is presented as a dynamic process influenced by the parents' child-rearing goals and practices, and shaped by the powerful influence of the child and by the social and cultural context in which development takes place. Our *Parenting* sections discuss many issues parents face—from writing a birth plan, to encouraging their young children to become readers, to dealing with sexual behavior in their teenagers—and offer research-based ideas about how best to face these issues.

**Policy** Students who become teachers, health-care providers, social workers, psychologists, nurses, and other service providers will quickly find themselves immersed in decision making related to public policy. Their understanding of key laws and other public policies will affect how they do their jobs. We therefore introduce in each chapter a critical piece of federal legislation, such as the Individuals with Disabilities in Education Act, or some other policy issue, such as public health concerns about childhood obesity. Our *Policy* sections serve as another reminder to students that child development occurs within a broad context with many influences—one of them at the level of policy making.

**Practice** An important feature of our book is the emphasis that we place on practice in settings such as education and health, as well as at home. In our *Practice* sections, we discuss, for example, how teachers can use the ideas of theorists like Piaget and Vygotsky to promote learning in their classrooms and explain what kinds of education work best for English-language learners. *Practice* sections in several chapters deal with preschool child-care environments; we also discuss such diverse topics as baby-friendly hospitals, developmental screening, and treatment of concussions in children and adolescents.

# Chapter-by-Chapter Coverage

*The Development of Children and Adolescents* is divided into 6 parts and 16 chapters. Part One comprises an introductory chapter, and Part Two deals with "biological beginnings," including the biological foundations of child development, prenatal development, and birth and the newborn. Parts Three through Six describe, in turn, physical development and health, cognitive development, and psychosocial development in each of four age periods, presented chronologically: infancy and toddlerhood, early childhood, middle childhood, and adolescence. The chronological approach encourages students to recognize how the different domains of development are related to each other within each age period, as well as to appreciate how development builds and changes throughout these periods.

A summary of the chapter contents follows.

### Chapter 1: A CHILD'S JOURNEY

The book's introductory chapter examines what development is, how it differs from change, and what kinds of issues the study of development involves. It presents a brief glimpse of a child's development at home and in the community, and touches on the relationship between children and technology. After explaining the major theories currently influencing the study of children's development, the chapter describes the research methods psychologists use to study development and the ethics of such research.

### Chapter 2: BIOLOGICAL FOUNDATIONS OF CHILD DEVELOPMENT

Chapter 2 reviews the essential biology of life to underscore how molecules and cells form the building blocks of development. It examines how genes and the environment interact over the course of development, discusses the implications of the brain and nervous system for child development, and introduces some health-care issues that will be revisited throughout the book. The chapter emphasizes a key theme: that nature and nurture work together, from "neurons to neighborhoods."

### Chapter 3: PRENATAL DEVELOPMENT

Chapter 3 describes conception and normal fetal development in the womb. The chapter also discusses agents outside the womb that can affect a child's development for a lifetime. It covers women's health during pregnancy, and begins several discussions on health, parenting, and culture that will continue throughout the book. As part of these discussions, the chapter delves into the science and policy of fertility, infertility, and reproductive assistance.

### Chapter 4: BIRTH AND THE NEWBORN

Chapter 4 begins by describing childbirth, including its life-changing effects on parents. It goes on to discuss the effects of birth complications, such as prematurity and low birth weight, on future development, and addresses the question of what can be done to prevent infant mortality. The chapter then focuses on the remarkable capacities of the newborn and the newborn's ability to engage caregivers. Finally, it discusses the emergence of the parent-infant bond and the developmental challenges facing the infant as the newborn period comes to an end.

## Chapter 5: PHYSICAL DEVELOPMENT AND HEALTH IN INFANCY AND TODDLERHOOD

Chapter 5 introduces the framework for the book's chapters on physical development and health. The framework, developed by the Center on the Developing Child at Harvard University, underscores the vital relationship between health and development. The chapter goes on to examine physical, motor, and perceptual development in infancy and toddlerhood. It explains why these first years are so critical for health and development. It also discusses what happens when physical abilities are compromised, and stresses the importance of early intervention.

## Chapter 6: COGNITIVE DEVELOPMENT IN INFANCY AND TODDLERHOOD

Chapter 6 focuses on the remarkable cognitive abilities of infants and toddlers. It begins by examining various theories of early cognitive development. It then reviews the ingenious research methods and technological advances that allow today's scientists to study cognitive development in infants and toddlers in ways that once could scarcely have been imagined. The chapter also discusses how language emerges and develops in the first years of life. It ends with a review of educational programs specifically designed for infants and toddlers.

## Chapter 7: PSYCHOSOCIAL DEVELOPMENT IN INFANCY AND TODDLERHOOD

In describing psychosocial development in infants and toddlers, Chapter 7 starts by looking at how the major theories of psychosocial development view these early years. Next, the chapter discusses the lifelong importance of infants' attachment relationships with caregivers. It also explains how changes in the brain affect psychosocial development, and how emotional and social growth are interwoven. The chapter goes on to address the developing sense of self. It concludes by analyzing how caregivers, on the one hand, and the child's own temperament, on the other, play vital roles in early psychosocial development.

## Chapter 8: PHYSICAL DEVELOPMENT AND HEALTH IN EARLY CHILDHOOD

Chapter 8 opens with a discussion of physical growth, brain development, and motor development during early childhood. It then describes various ways of promoting health in young children. Because young children's immune systems are immature, making them vulnerable to infection, immunization is one aspect of health promotion, along with nutrition and dental health. After discussing these issues, the chapter reviews the role of caregivers and community resources in keeping children healthy and safe. It concludes with coverage of asthma and ear infections—two of the most common health disruptions in young children.

## Chapter 9: COGNITIVE DEVELOPMENT IN EARLY CHILDHOOD

Chapter 9 covers children's cognitive growth during the early childhood years. It begins with two contrasting views of how young children develop cognitively: those of Jean Piaget and Lev Vygotsky. It next discusses the central aspects of language development during this period and then examines developments in cognitive processes, especially those related to executive function, such as paying attention. These processes serve as a foundation for school readiness skills. Finally, the chapter looks at the role of preschool programs in influencing children's cognitive development and school readiness.

## Chapter 10: PSYCHOSOCIAL DEVELOPMENT IN EARLY CHILDHOOD

Erik Erikson's view of the psychosocial tasks of early childhood opens Chapter 10. The chapter goes on to discuss two important aspects of emotional development—recognizing and regulating emotions. It also examines how young children gradually acquire a sense of self. Next, in describing children's relationships with peers, the chapter covers play, prosocial and antisocial behaviors, and theory of mind. It then explores how children begin to make moral judgments. Finally, it examines parenting practices and their importance during early childhood.

## Chapter 11: PHYSICAL DEVELOPMENT AND HEALTH IN MIDDLE CHILDHOOD

Chapter 11 reviews the physical changes of middle childhood and discusses their implications for school readiness, physical fitness, and participation in sports. The chapter also notes various problems that can arise for many children during this period: poor nutrition, obesity, illness, and the unrelenting pressure to succeed, which can lead to emotional stress and physical injuries. The chapter goes on to discuss the role of school health services in improving and maintaining children's health. It ends with a review of the potential effects of disease and treatment on learning and behavior.

## Chapter 12: COGNITIVE DEVELOPMENT IN MIDDLE CHILDHOOD

Chapter 12 opens its examination of how children develop cognitively in the middle-childhood years by revisiting the theories of Piaget and Vygotsky. Next, it turns to information processing theory, focusing on recent research into attention and memory. It continues by considering the meaning of intelligence, the role of IQ tests, and different perspectives on what it means to be intelligent. It ends by discussing language development, including the need for many children to learn a second language, and the school-related skills of literacy and mathematics acquired during middle childhood.

## Chapter 13: PSYCHOSOCIAL DEVELOPMENT IN MIDDLE CHILDHOOD

The middle-childhood years are significant and exciting times in psychosocial development. To explain why, Chapter 13 first covers emotional development, discussing how children are increasingly aware of their emotions and increasingly able to regulate them as they move through this period. Children's greater understanding of their emotions is related to their understanding of themselves, and the chapter next describes growth in self-understanding during middle childhood. It goes on to explore the development of friendships and the social cognition necessary to understand the perspectives of others—an important skill in children's expanding social world. Finally, the chapter considers moral development and how children of this age think about and reason through moral dilemmas.

## Chapter 14: PHYSICAL DEVELOPMENT AND HEALTH IN ADOLESCENCE

Chapter 14 examines various physical aspects of puberty and growth, including brain development in adolescence. It then covers several topics important in adolescent health, including nutrition and physical activity, sleep and stress, and such health behaviors as sexual activity and substance use. Motor vehicle safety, access to health care, and sports injuries are also important health issues in adolescence, and the chapter examines these areas before concluding with a discussion of managing a chronic illness—diabetes—during the teen years.

## Chapter 15: COGNITIVE DEVELOPMENT IN ADOLESCENCE

A discussion of Piaget's theory opens Chapter 15, which covers cognitive development in adolescence. The chapter also examines in some detail the more recent perspectives provided by the information processing theorists, as well as the sociocultural perspective of Vygotsky. Next, the chapter examines changes in the adolescent brain that relate to cognitive development. Finally, because cognitive development during adolescence is closely related to educational experiences, it considers the role of schooling during the adolescent years.

## Chapter 16: PSYCHOSOCIAL DEVELOPMENT IN ADOLESCENCE

Chapter 16 considers the major psychosocial changes occurring during adolescence—a time of enormous psychosocial change. It begins with the central question of identity development. It then turns to ways in which adolescents relate to others who are important in their lives, including parents and peers. Adolescents often face situations that involve moral decisions, and the chapter next discusses this important aspect of adolescents' lives. The final section considers one of the most frequent risk factors of the adolescent period: the risk of developing mental health difficulties, including major depressive disorder and eating disorders. It also examines the role of resilience in protecting against risk factors.

# Pedagogical Features

To achieve the objectives we have just described, and to help students engage in meaningful learning, we include the following pedagogical features in our book:

### Chapter-Opening Vignettes

*Chapter-opening vignettes, entitled Making a Difference*, describe how a particular individual or organization has worked to improve the status of children in our society in a way that reflects the content of the chapter.

Cognitive Development in Early Childhood

MAKING A difference

The Harlem Children's Zone

Geoffrey Canada became an activist for children because of his own experiences growing up in the South Bronx in New York. He knows firsthand the struggles of children and families living in poverty. His father left the family after his mother had given birth to four sons. His mother often had trouble finding work, and she sometimes lacked enough money to feed and clothe Geoffrey and his brothers. But he recalls that despite these struggles, his mother took the time to emphasize the importance of getting an education, encouraging her boys to read and taking them to museums. "My mother was famous for finding out when things were free" (Quoted in Tough, 2008, p. 101). His first-grade teacher introduced him to books that told stories through rhymes, and many years later, at a talk he gave at Syracuse University, Geoffrey emphasized that "poetry saved my life" (Stevens, 2004). As early as age 9, he decided he wanted to help children like himself who live in the inner city.

Now a public advocate, Geoffrey Canada has established the Harlem Children's Zone, a 60-block area that offers a range of educational, social, medical, and support programs to families, wrapping children in a safety net of supportive programs. Those programs include a preschool program, a family support center, classes for new parents, an after-school program, and a charter school. He reflects that his motivation "is all based on a personal understanding of what these kids go through and what the rest of the world doesn't see" (quoted in Tough, 2008, p. 123).

The Harlem Gems, the preschool program in the Harlem Children's Zone, has elements similar to other preschools in its strong support of children's psychosocial development, but it differs in substantial ways as well. It is a full-day program, has a low teacher–child ratio, and operates 11 months of the year. Although the activities are similar to those in any preschool, including imaginative play, music, and block-building, it differs in its emphasis on language. Because studies indicate that children from the lowest socioeconomic group enter school with little knowledge about letter names and letter–sound associations and a limited range of vocabulary, Canada worked with teachers to develop a preschool program that introduces language skills in all activities, essentially making the classroom a verbal "hothouse." In addition, the staff at the Harlem Children's Zone encourages parents to read to their preschool-aged children every night.

CHAPTER OUTLINE

## Guided Learning

Chapter-opening **Key Questions** highlight the most important material for students to consider while reading each section. We return to these questions throughout the chapter as a guided review for readers in our **Check Your Progress** features, which help students assess their understanding of key topics and concepts. We also connect the questions to the main headings under **Chapter Summary**, which provides an integrated review of the chapter. At the end of each chapter, we pose a set of **Critical Thinking** questions to challenge readers to think more deeply about topics discussed in the chapter.

**[KEY QUESTIONS] *for* READING CHAPTER 9**

1. What are the characteristics of children's thinking during the preoperational stage, according to Piaget?
2. In what ways do others assist children in learning, according to Vygotsky?
3. What are examples of executive function displayed in early childhood?
4. What changes occur in children's language development during early childhood?
5. What are some important skills that help prepare children for formal schooling?

**✓CHECK YOUR PROGRESS**

1. According to Piaget, what are three limitations to children's thinking in the preoperational stage?
2. Give an example of how children's egocentrism might affect their communication with other children or adults.
3. Suppose you hear a 3-year-old girl say "It's a rose, it's not a flower." In what way would her thinking be typical of children in the preoperational stage?

### CHAPTER SUMMARY

**Piaget's Theory and Preoperational Thought**

**[ KEY QUESTION ] 1.** What are the characteristics of children's thinking during the preoperational stage, according to Piaget?

- Piaget emphasized that during early childhood, children are preoperational (that is, prelogical) and are not yet able to reason with logical mental operations. As a result, they tend to provide human qualities to inanimate objects (animism), have difficulty considering perspectiv... on one, ra...
- Piaget de... that is, fo... derstand ... favor of n...

Children improve in their executive functioning during early childhood, especially in their ability to focus and shift attention, to purposefully remember, to inhibit responses, and to show cognitive flexibility.

**Language Development**

**[ KEY QUESTION ] 4.** What changes occur in children's language development during early childhood?

- Children's vocabulary growth increases rapidly through a process called fast mapping.

### CRITICAL THINKING QUESTIONS

1. **Piaget's Theory.** What do you consider to be the most important criticism of Piaget's theory and why?
2. **Vygotsky's Sociocultural Theory.** Do you think it is possible for classroom teachers to instruct all children in a classroom based on knowledge of each child's ZPD? Why or why not?
3. **Information Processing Theory.** What are some predictions you would make about the different behaviors you might see in children on a playground based on whether they had strong or weak response inhibition skills?
4. **Language Development.** Do you think that all children should learn to speak more than one language? Discuss your response, using research.
5. **School Readiness.** Why do you think that learning to say the alphabet is a necessary but not sufficient aspect of learning to read?
6. **Cultural Perspectives.** Vygotsky proposed that culture affects the tools children learn to become full participants in society. Consider how the tools necessary to learn in American society today might differ from those of a different cultural group, such as a nomadic society. How might the process of learning those tools be in some ways similar, and in other ways different in these different cultural groups?

**Everyday Stories** appear in each section of every chapter. These stories present interesting real-world examples of the concepts and topics being covered. **What if...?** questions ask students to think about how they would respond to various scenarios, and help them to deepen and apply their understanding of developmental concepts. Instructors also may find these questions useful in initiating class discussions.

*Everyday stories*

DRAWING A STAR WITH SELF-TALK Isabella is working on drawing a star for a picture she is making of the night sky. Her friend has shown her a way of making a five-pointed star, and she is trying to remember and follow the directions the friend gave her. As she draws the star, she says out loud, "You start here. Then it goes down to here, then up to here, then over to here, then down, then up. And you're done!" Repeating these directions to herself out loud has helped her remember how to draw the star in the way her friend taught her. Eventually she will be able to make this kind of drawing without saying the directions out loud, but she still may say them to herself silently.

**what if...?**

Suppose you are a day-care provider at a neighborhood center. You notice that Ben, who is usually upbeat, seems quite gloomy and distracted today, and then you see that he has a burn on his arm. When you ask him about the burn, he covers it up by pulling his shirt sleeve down, and then he runs away from you. You are concerned about him but don't want to make him uncomfortable in the classroom. What would you do?

**Parenting, Policy, and Practice**

*Parenting, Policy,* and *Practice* applications are integrated throughout each chapter. These highlight knowledge that will help students both as parents and in their chosen occupations, such as education, health care, child care, psychology, and social work, among others.

## Implications of Piaget's Theory for Preschool Classrooms

**Practice**

Piaget's emphasis on children's construction of knowledge has many implications for educational settings. You can see from the following suggestions that this orientation often involves providing young children with opportunities to learn by engaging in activities.

1. Children learn best by being engaged in an activity, not by simply being told information or being asked to memorize information. For example, encourage children to discover what happens when they blend primary colors in their painting rather than telling them that "blue and yellow make green."

### Helping Preschool Children Become Readers

**Parenting**

Even if parents are not strong readers themselves, they can promote preliteracy skills in their preschool children. Parents can integrate many of these tasks into their daily routines with their children. Epstein (2002) lists 12 ways in which parents can help young children become readers:

1. Have daily conversations with children. This can involve looking at family pictures together and discussing them, as well as playing word games like, "I'm thinking of something in the refrigerator that begins with the sound '*m*'.
2. Keep lots of printed and written materials in the home.

### The Individuals with Disabilities Education Act (IDEA)

**Policy**

In 1975, federal legislation was enacted to ensure that the more than 6 million children with disabilities in the United States would receive the education they needed from birth to early adulthood. The law, now known as the Individuals with Disabilities Education Act (IDEA), has been revised several times since it was first enacted in 1975 as Public Law 94-142. The law currently has three major provisions, which apply to individuals from ages 3 to 21:

1. *Children with disabilities are entitled to receive a free and appropriate public education.* The interpretation of what "appropriate" means is usually made at the district and

WHEN SYSTEMS CONNECT

## Developing a Theory of Mind

Communicating well with others requires children to understand that others may think differently than they do and have a different perception of a situation. This type of thinking requires a "theory of mind." **Theory of mind** is a term used to refer to children's understanding of the mental states (that is, the "minds") of themselves and of others (Tager-Flusberg, 1999). Theory of mind is an aspect of social cognition, because it in-

**When Systems Connect** discussions, integrated throughout the text, highlight coverage of developmental systems theory. Similarly, special headings identify **The Developing Brain** discussions, which explain how new findings in brain development add to our understanding of children's behavior.

THE DEVELOPING BRAIN

**A Growth Spurt in Executive Function.** Adele Diamond (2001) proposes that a growth spurt occurs in executive function from ages 3 to 6, making the early childhood period a critical time for changes in this area of functioning. As we mentioned in Chapter 8, studies in neuroscience indicate that much of this growth occurs in the prefrontal cortex, as stronger networks are created between this area of the brain and other regions of the cortex in which language, mathematical, and spatial skills are represented (see Figure 9.7).

## Culture

Discussions of culture appear throughout the chapters. In addition, a *Culture and . . .* feature in each chapter highlights both cross-cultural and multicultural examples, such as *Culture and Medical Beliefs, Culture and Learning Numbers,* and *Culture and Showing Pride and Shame.*

### Culture and Learning Numbers

Many studies have found that children in East Asian countries tend to outperform children in North America on assessments of mathematics skills (Göbel, Shaki, & Fischer, 2011; Organisation for Economic Co-operation and Development, 2006). Although there are many reasons for this difference, one involves the way that math ideas are represented by language. For example, in Chinese the term for a triangle is "sao jiao xing" which means "three corner shape." Although in English the word "triangle" describes the meaning of the shape, which has three angles, to a young child this is a complex term because the child needs to understand that "tri" means "three" and needs to know

| Language | Number 1 | Number 10 | Number 11 |
|---|---|---|---|
| Japanese | ichi | juu | juu-ichi |
| Korean | ii | ship | ship ii |
| Chinese | yi | shi | shi-yi |

Best View Stock/Getty Images, Inc.

**Focus On** features spotlight important individuals in child development, such as Albert Bandura, Eric Kandel, and Barbara Rogoff. **Research Insights** features highlight a pertinent research study, such as a study examining the question *Do Violent Video Games Promote Aggression?* or the question *Can You Grow Your Intelligence?*

### Focus On: Barbara Rogoff

*In referring to cultural processes I want to draw attention to the configurations of routine ways of doing things in any community's approach to living. I focus on people's participation in their communities' cultural practices and traditions, rather than equating culture with the nationality or ethnicity of individuals. (Rogoff, 2003, p. 3)*

Barbara Rogoff contributes to our understanding of child development by recognizing the importance of everyday routines and showing us how children's participation in those activities is shaped by culture. Inspired by the work of Lev Vygotsky, she has studied how children are guided by older children and adults in the communities in which they live. For example, young girls in a Mayan community in Guatemala often learn various tas dren migh

Rogoff's work draws on examples from many cultural groups and shows how we make assumptions about what is "normal" from experiences within our culture. For example, she describes how views of praising a child differ in different cultural groups. We may think that praising a child by saying "good job" or "good for you" is a normal part of good parenting. In some cultures, however, such praise is avoided because it is seen as making chil-

Rose Cartwright

### Research Insights: Do Children with Autism Lack a Theory of Mind?

As we noted in Chapter 7, autism spectrum disorders are developmental disorders marked by severe deficits in social interaction, communication, and imagination, as well as repetitive and restricted patterns of interests and behaviors (DSM-5, 2013; Volkmar, Lord, Baily, Schultz, & Klin, 2004). Children with autism fail to orient to social stimuli when they are young and have difficulties with social reciprocity and communication skills (Tager-Flusberg, 2010). Current estimates from the Centers for Disease Control and Prevention (2012) indicate that approximately 1 in 88 children in the United States have been diagnosed with the disorder. This is an estimated 350% increase in the last 10 years, and the difficulties with false-belief tasks (Peterson, Wellman, & Liu, 2005). Researchers conclude that children with autism most likely process these types of tasks in a different way than do typically developing children and that such differences also lead to the social aloofness seen in children with autism (Peterson et al., 2005).

One type of current neuropsychological research is focusing on specific neurons, called *mirror neurons* because they react when an individual observes an action as well as produces one. (You may recall that we discussed mirror neurons in Chapter 4.) Some studies have found that the mirror neurons in specific brain regions (e.g., the medial prefron-

## Real Development

Wiley's *Real Development* provides the basis for an active learning project at the end of each chapter. The activities focus on developing and assessing higher-order thinking skills. Students will be asked to analyze, critically evaluate, synthesize, and reflect on the information presented.

### REAL Development

### Psychosocial Development in Early Childhood

In the accompanying Real Development activity, you are interested in learning more about the development of peer interactions. A developmental psychologist at your university, Dr. Jones, has researched extensively on different types of play. You will read about different types of play described below and then use these descriptions to help Dr. Jones identify different forms of play in Adeline's pre-school classroom.

© John Wiley & Sons, Inc.

**WileyPLUS** Go to WileyPLUS to complete the *Real Development* activity.

# What Happens in the Brain

## Beginning to Read

Think about learning to read. It is different from learning to talk, as it requires explicit instruction as well as much practice. Thus, studying children as they learn to read provides a unique opportunity for researchers to learn more about the influence of experience on the developing brain.

When we learn to read, at the most elementary level—the level of the beginning reader—we translate a set of written letters into a meaningful word. This may seem like a simple task, but it's actually very complex. Moving from looking at a series of symbols to understanding a word requires transmitting nerve impulses over a specific brain pathway.

Here's a simplified sketch of some key things that must happen for a young child to look at, for example, the letters C-A-T and end up thinking of a furry little animal with whiskers and a long tail.

- First, the child perceives the written letters as light rays entering her eyes. The rays are changed to electrical nerve impulses, which travel to the visual cortex. The visual cortex is in the occipital lobe and recognizes previously learned simple visual patterns like lines.
- The impulses travel from the visual cortex to the Visual Word Form area located in the left occipital-temporal cortex in the middle region called the fusiform gyrus. This region is involved in translating the simplistic pattern of the written word into recognizable previously learned words.
- Then the impulses travel to the angular gyrus, which matches the visual word with the sounds of the word.
- Next, the impulses move to Wernicke's area, responsible for language comprehension. This area processes the word as if it has been heard.
- If the word C-A-T were part of a sentence, like "The cat sat," then the impulses would also travel to Broca's area, which is involved in processing syntax, such as word order and grammar.

In beginning readers, this pathway becomes stronger with practice, and the pathway becomes more focused in the left hemisphere of the brain. As reading becomes more complex—for example, as young readers must remember the words they've already read and decode unknown words—many other areas of the brain also come into play.

Alex Mares-Manton/Asia Images/Getty Images, Inc.

### Recognizing Visual Patterns

Nerve impulses representing visual patterns travel from the primary visual cortex to the visual word form area of the fusiform gyrus. If this area hasn't learned the visual patterns of our alphabet, it won't recognize them. Children generally need explicit training to learn letter patterns—which explains why we see so many letter shapes and activities in preschools.

warrengoldswain/Age Fotostock America, Inc.

This fMRI image shows increased activity (yellow areas) in the fusiform gyrus in kindergarten children after several sessions of instruction in associating sounds with letters.



Bruce D. McCandliss, "Educational Neuroscience: The Early Years" PNAS, Vol. 107, no. 18, pages 8049–8050.

### Linking Visual Patterns with Sound Patterns

The angular gyrus translates the visual pattern of the word to the sounds of the word when spoken. The angular gyrus is responsible for phonological processing. Activity in this area is stronger in children (who are learning to read) than in adults (who are skilled readers).

### Comprehending Meaning

Once the brain has made the connection between the alphabetic symbols and the word sounds, Wernicke's area provides an interpretation of the sound pattern—the familiar word that describes a furry little animal.

Jose Luis Pelaez Inc./Blend Images/Getty Images, Inc.

**C-A-T**

Light rays entering the eyes are changed to electrical nerve impulses. → The visual cortex recognizes the visual patterns these impulses represent. → The fusiform gyrus translates a simple visual pattern into a known word. → The angular gyrus translates the word to the sounds of the word. → Wernicke's area is involved in comprehension of the word. → Broca's area processes syntax.

iStockphoto

### What Happens in the Brain

*What Happens in the Brain* is a key teaching feature that helps bring neuroscience directly into the lives of readers. Visual and accessible two-page layouts appear throughout the book illustrating what happens in children's brains when they are performing everyday activities, such as reading or walking. These layouts provide students with up-to-date, understandable information about the neural mechanisms at work in the child's developing brain.

### Milestones

*Milestones* at the ends of Parts Three, Four, Five, and Six summarize important accomplishments in the physical, cognitive, and psychosocial domains for each period of development.

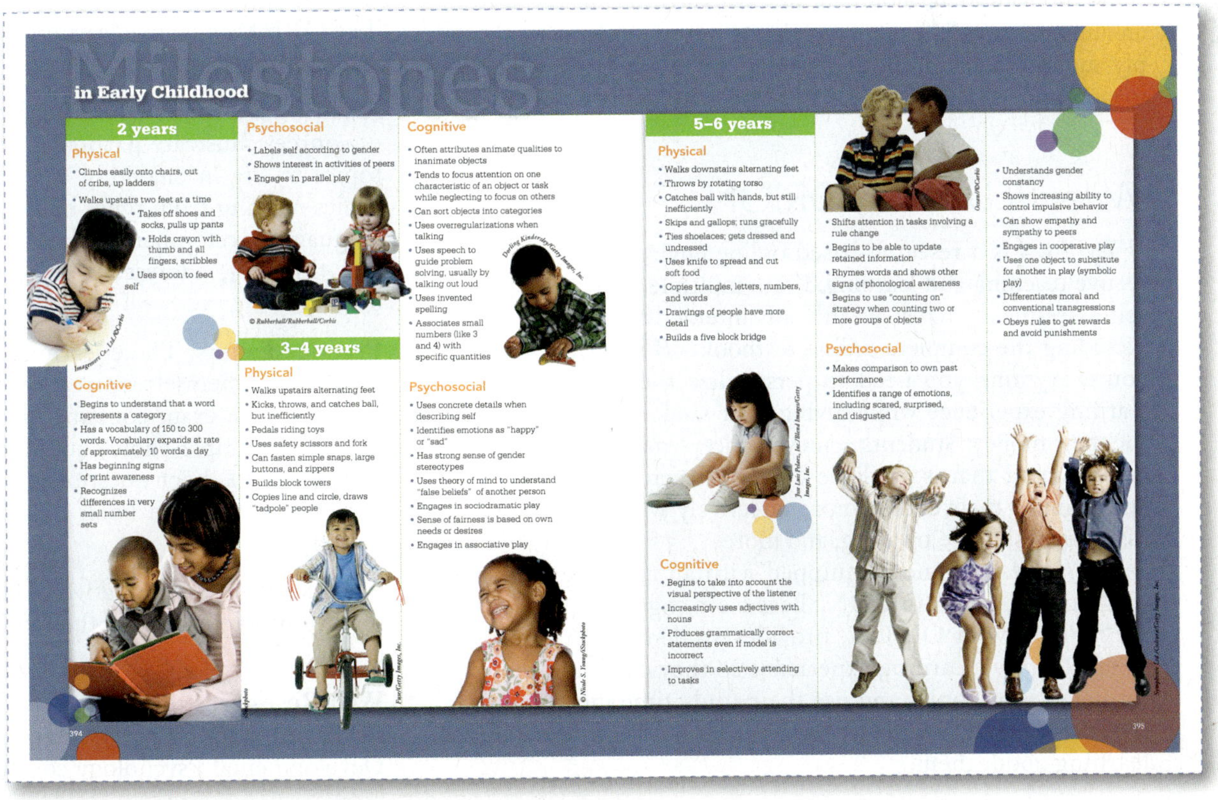

# Milestones in Early Childhood

## 2 years

### Physical

- Climbs easily onto chairs, out of cribs, up ladders
- Walks upstairs two feet at a time
- Takes off shoes and socks, pulls up pants
- Holds crayon with thumb and all fingers, scribbles
- Uses spoon to feed self

Imagemore Co., Ltd./Corbis

### Cognitive

- Begins to understand that a word represents a category
- Has a vocabulary of 150 to 300 words. Vocabulary expands at rate of approximately 10 words a day
- Has beginning signs of print awareness
- Recognizes differences in very small number sets

### Psychosocial

- Labels self according to gender
- Shows interest in activities of peers
- Engages in parallel play

© Rubberball/Rubberball/Corbis

## 3–4 years

### Physical

- Walks upstairs alternating feet
- Kicks, throws, and catches ball, but inefficiently
- Pedals riding toys
- Uses safety scissors and fork
- Can fasten simple snaps, large buttons, and zippers
- Builds block towers
- Copies line and circle, draws "tadpole" people

### Cognitive

- Often attributes animate qualities to inanimate objects
- Tends to focus attention on one characteristic of an object or task while neglecting to focus on others
- Can sort objects into categories
- Uses overregularizations when talking
- Uses speech to guide problem solving, usually by talking out loud
- Uses invented spelling
- Associates small numbers (like 3 and 4) with specific quantities

Dorling Kindersley/Getty Images, Inc.

### Psychosocial

- Uses concrete details when describing self
- Identifies emotions as "happy" or "sad"
- Has strong sense of gender stereotypes
- Uses theory of mind to understand "false beliefs" of another person
- Engages in sociodramatic play
- Sense of fairness is based on own needs or desires
- Engages in associative play

Fuse/Getty Images, Inc.

© Nicole S. Young/iStockphoto

394

## 5–6 years

### Physical

- Walks downstairs alternating feet
- Throws by rotating torso
- Catches ball with hands, but still inefficiently
- Skips and gallops; runs gracefully
- Ties shoelaces; gets dressed and undressed
- Uses knife to spread and cut soft food
- Copies triangles, letters, numbers, and words
- Drawings of people have more detail
- Builds a five block bridge

Jose Luis Pelaez, Inc./Blend Images/Getty Images, Inc.

### Cognitive

- Begins to take into account the visual perspective of the listener
- Increasingly uses adjectives with nouns
- Produces grammatically correct statements even if model is incorrect
- Improves in selectively attending to tasks
- Shifts attention in tasks involving a rule change
- Begins to be able to update retained information
- Rhymes words and shows other signs of phonological awareness
- Begins to use "counting on" strategy when counting two or more groups of objects

### Psychosocial

- Makes comparison to own past performance
- Identifies a range of emotions, including scared, surprised, and disgusted
- Understands gender constancy
- Shows increasing ability to control impulsive behavior
- Can show empathy and sympathy to peers
- Engages in cooperative play
- Uses one object to substitute for another in play (symbolic play)
- Differentiates moral and conventional transgressions
- Obeys rules to get rewards and avoid punishments

395

# Teaching and Learning Environment: Learn More at www.wileyplus.com

## Wiley's Real Development

**REAL Development**

Child development does not happen in isolation. It happens in larger familial, interpersonal and cultural contexts. Capturing these powerful dynamics in a child development course was a challenge—until now.

Wiley's *Real Development* is an innovative multimedia product that uses authentic video capturing moments from four real families, allowing students to view the pivotal stages of child development within larger interpersonal and cultural contexts. In each *Real Development* activity, created by Nicole C. DiDonato of Montclair State University and Christine J. Hatchard of Monmouth University, students analyze and evaluate concepts—demonstrated in a variety of naturalistic and professional settings—through assessment activities grounded in real-world applications. Through this active engagement with visual media, pictures and artifacts, students will gain a deeper understanding of developmental theories and concepts.

*Real Development* also includes a filterable topic-based library with dozens of selections by Shawn Guiling of Southeast Missouri State University. It includes observational footage and interviews with children and professionals to help further illustrate key concepts central to the understanding of child development in today's world. The result is an authentic media experience that prompts students to apply and interact with the course material in ways that will be meaningful in their personal and professional lives.

## *WileyPLUS* with ORION

*WileyPLUS* is a research-based online environment for effective teaching and learning. From multiple study paths, to self-assessment, to a wealth of interactive resources—including the complete online textbook—*WileyPLUS* gives you everything you need to personalize the teaching and learning experience while giving your students more value for their money. Students achieve concept mastery in a rich environment that is available 24/7. Instructors personalize and manage their course more effectively with assessment, assignments, grade tracking, and more.

*WileyPLUS* is now equipped with an adaptive learning module called ORION. Based on cognitive science, *WileyPLUS* with ORION, provides students with a personal, adaptive learning experience so they can build their proficiency on topics and use their study time most effectively. *WileyPLUS* with ORION helps students learn by learning about them.

## *WileyPLUS* with ORION is great as:

- an adaptive **pre-lecture tool** that assesses your students' conceptual knowledge so they to come to class better prepared,
- a **personalized study guide** that helps students understand both strengths and areas where they need to invest more time, especially in preparation for quizzes and exams.

Unique to ORION, students **begin** by taking a quick **diagnostic** for any chapter. This will determine each student's baseline proficiency on each topic in the chapter. Students see their individual diagnostic report to help them understand where they need to do additional work.

## What do students receive with *WileyPLUS*?

- A **digital version** of the complete textbook with integrated media and quizzes.
- **Real Development** Students are able to complete activities based on viewing these authentic videos. Each activity is assignable and gradable. Students can view the videos and complete the activities in class or at home.
- The **ORION** adaptive learning module that maximizes students' study time.
- **Additional Videos.** Excerpts selected from a variety of sources illustrate particular concepts, bringing the topics to life in engaging ways. The videos focus on topics ranging from types of and places for childbirth, language development, school readiness, intelligence and thinking, adolescent sexual health, autism, and others.
- **Practice Exams.** These learning features give students a way to test themselves on course material before exams. Each practice exam contains fill-in-the-blank, application, and multiple-choice questions that provide immediate feedback. Each question is also linked to a learning objective within the book to aid students in concept mastery.
- **Flashcards.** This interactive module gives students the opportunity to easily test their knowledge of vocabulary terms.
- **Web Resources.** Annotated web links put useful electronic resources for psychology into the context of your Developmental Psychology course.

## What do instructors receive with *WileyPLUS*?

Pre-created teaching materials and assessments help instructors optimize their time:

- A wealth of brief **video segments** perfect for classroom use.
- The **Instructor's Manual,** prepared by Eugene Geist of Ohio University is designed to help instructors maximize student learning. It presents teaching suggestions for each chapter of the text, including lecture starters, lecture extensions, classroom discussions and activities, out of the classroom assignments, Internet and print resources, and more!
- Every chapter contains a **Lecture PowerPoint presentation,** prepared by Lee Ann Jolley of Tennessee Tech University and Janette Kopp of Mississippi Gulf Coast Community College, with a combination of key concepts, figures and tables, and examples from the textbook.
- **Media Enriched PowerPoint presentations,** available in *WileyPLUS*, contain embedded links to multimedia sources and can be easily modified according to your needs.
- The **Test Bank,** prepared by Betsye Robinette of Indiana Wesleyan University, is available in a word document format or through Respondus or Diploma. The questions are available to instructors to create and print multiple versions of the same test by scrambling the order of all questions found in the Word version of the test bank. This allows users to customize exams by altering or adding new problems. The test bank has over 100 multiple choice, true-false, text-entry, and essay questions per chapter. Each question has been linked to a specific, student learning outcome, and the correct answer provided with section references to its source in the text.

**Gradebook:** ***WileyPLUS*** provides instant access to reports on trends in class performance, student use of course materials, and progress toward learning objectives, helping inform decisions and drive classroom discussions.

# Acknowledgments

While it is the authors' names that appear on the cover of this book, its publication would not have been possible without the combined efforts of a large number of people—among them, the professionals at John Wiley & Sons, our colleagues from the academic community, our families and friends, the many children we have known, and our mentors and students. We are deeply indebted to each of them, in particular the following:

We first want to express our sincere thanks to our spouses and children. We realize that we could not have completed the work on this book without their love, patience, and unfailing support. We would especially like to pay tribute John Travers's wife, Barbara, who has been an inspiration to us from the time the idea of this book came into being. She sacrificed her time and energy to host our meetings, and gave us her unstinting backing as the planning and writing of the manuscript progressed.

We were very fortunate to have been able to work with a remarkable group of professionals, assembled by Wiley, in the development and production of this book. We are especially indebted to those with whom we have worked so closely throughout the writing and editing process: Marian Provenzano, Senior Development Editor; Beverly Peavler, Freelance Development Editor; Robert Johnston, Senior Acquisitions Editor; and Bill Murray, Senior Production Editor. We were impressed by their judicious editing in terms of form, style, and continuity, clarifying what was muddy and often suggesting revisions or rewrites of whole sections—a necessary part of that miraculous transformation that occurs when a manuscript becomes a book. That we were able to develop a collaborative working relationship with them made the back-and-forth editing process both positive and productive, and for that we are immensely grateful.

We also want to thank Chris Johnson, Executive Editor; Margaret Barrett, Senior Marketing Manager; Maureen Eide, Senior Designer; Beth Tripmacher, Product Designer; Brittany Cheetham, Assistant Editor; Marie Dripchak, Editorial Program Assistant; and photo researchers Billy Ray and Lisa Passmore.

We want to thank and acknowledge the contributions of Lisa S. Scott and Matt Davidson, both of the University of Massachusetts, Amherst, for their expert reviews of the brain development content throughout the chapters. We greatly appreciate the significant help provided by graduate students Amanda Cannarella, Miriam Heyman, Terese J. Lund, Sandra Tang, Miriam Tillinger, and Ashley Woodman, and by undergraduate students Brigitte Butler, Meghan Cannavina, and Molly McMullan.

We offer a special word of thanks to the reviewers, focus group, workshop participants, and class testers, whose willingness to review and critique the book, videos, and activities at various stages was instrumental in the quality of the final product. Finally, we acknowledge the contributions made by the following individuals:

## Reviewers

Anne Acker, Saginaw Valley State University
Denise Adkins, Roanoke College
Lin Agler, University of Southern Mississippi Gulf Coast
Alicia Alvero, Queens College, City University of New York
Patricia Bellas, Irvine Valley College
Denise Berg, Santa Monica College
Melina Bersamin, California State University, Sacramento
Karl Blendell, The College of Saint Rose
Heather Bouchey, University of Vermont
Gina Brelsford, Pennsylvania State University, Harrisburg
Eileen Brittain, Jamestown Community College
Diane Buffington, California University of Pennsylvania
Stephen Burgess, Florida State University
Gustavo Carlo, University of Nebraska, Lincoln
Tammy Carroll, The University of Alabama
Richard Coelho, Lansing Community College
Irene Cook, California State University, Bakersfield
Victoria Cooke, Erie Community College, City Campus in New York
Mary Cordell, Navarro College
Trina Cowan, Northwest Vista College
Kathleen Cummings, Suffolk County Community College
Carrie Dale, Eastern Illinois University
Hobart Davies, University of Wisconsin, Milwaukee
Michelle Demaray, Northern Illinois University
David Donnelly, Monroe Community College
Petra Duran, Kent State University
Tina Durand, Wheelock College
Lori Ellingford, Arizona State University
Ronald Fannin, Texas Woman's University
Linda Fayard, Mississippi Gulf Coast Community College, Jackson
Meredyth Fellows, West Chester University of Pennsylvania
Laura Fiorenza, West Chester University of Pennsylvania
Catherine Forestell, The College of William and Mary
Christopher France, Wright State University, Dayton
Teresa Galyean, Wytheville Community College
Eugene Geist, Ohio University, Athens
Vivien Geneser, Texas A&M University, San Antonio
Andrew Getzfeld, New York University

Kimberly Glackin, Metropolitan Community College, Blue River
Michael Glassman, The Ohio State University
Donna Greene, College of the Desert
Suzanne Gurland, Middlebury College
Vivian Harper, San Joaquin Delta College
Myra Harville, Holmes Community College
James Higley, Brigham Young University
Lisa Huffman, Ball State University
Nancy Hughes, State University of New York at Plattsburgh
Alishia Huntoon, Oregon Institute of Technology
Jamie Hurst, Texas Christian University
Virginia Huynh, California State University, Northridge
Jessica Jablonski, Richard Stockton College of New Jersey
Peggy Jessee, The University of Alabama
Julia Grace Jester, Harrisburg Area Community College
Virginia Johnson, Biola University
Lee Ann Jolley, Tennessee Tech University
Jeffrey Kaplan, University of Central Florida
Jason Kaufman, Inver Hills Community College
Kerry Kazura, University of New Hampshire
Mumbe Kithakye, Oklahoma State University, Stillwater
Laura Knight, Indiana University of Pennsylvania
Janette Kopp, Mississippi Gulf Coast Community College
Deborah Laible, Lehigh University
Judith Levine, Farmingdale State College
Amanda Lipko-Speed, The College of Brockport
Martina Marquez, Fresno City College
Jennifer Marshall, Raymond Walters College
Lisa Matthews, Georgia State University
Kathie McAfee, Butte College
Daniel McConnell, University of Central Florida
Ann Merriwether, Binghamton University
Mary Beth Miller, Fresno City College
Nancy Miodrag, California State University, Northridge
Darcy Mitchell, Colby Sawyer College
Nanci Monaco, Buffalo State College
Elizabeth Morin, Southern Connecticut State University
Nancy Nolan, Vanderbilt University
Wendy Orcajo, Mt. San Jacinto Community College
Robert Pasnak, George Mason University
John Prange, Irvine Valley College
Christine Raches, University of Indianapolis
Nicole Reiber, Coastal Carolina Community College
Mary Ann Remsen, Middle Tennessee State University
Sandra Richardson, The University of Virginia's College at Wise
Sabrina Rieder, Rockland Community College
Betsye Robinette, Indiana Wesleyan University
David Rudek, Aurora University
Marie Saracino, Stephen F. Austin State University
Bob Sasse, Palomar College
Matthew Schlesinger, Southern Illinois University, Carbondale
Candace Schulenburg, Cape Cod Community College
Shannon Shepard, Lewis & Clark Community College
Lawrence Sidlik, Arizona State University
Maureen Smith, San Jose State University
Patrick Smith, Thomas Nelson Community College
Jane Spruill, Pensacola State College
Becky Stoffel, West Liberty State College
Amy Strimling, Sacramento City College
Dennis Thompson, Georgia State University
Steven Toepfer, Kent State University
Holli Tonyan, California State University, Northridge
Paula Tripp, Sam Houston State University
Dana Van Sinden, Long Beach City College
Haley Vlach, University of Wisconsin, Madison
Paul Vonnahme, New Mexico State University, Las Cruces
Anja Wagner, Pennsylvania State University
Eric Walle, University of California, Merced
Henriette Warren, University of Minnesota
Karen Watts, Snead State Community College
Jeannine White, California State, San Diego
Lona Whitmarsh, Fairleigh Dickinson University, Madison
Clancie Wilson, University of Arkansas, Fort Smith
Gina Wilson, Palomar College
Denise Winsor, University of Memphis
Melissa Wright, Northwest Vista College
Jennifer Zosh, Pennsylvania State University, Brandywine

## Content Consultants

Denise Adkins, Roanoke College
Denise Berg, Santa Monica College
Melina Bersamin, California State University, Sacramento
Eileen Brittain, Jamestown Community College
Richard Coelho, Lansing Community College
Mary Cordell, Navarro College
Kathleen Cummings, Suffolk County Community College
Carrie Dale, Eastern Illinois University
Laura Fiorenza, West Chester University
Myra Harville, Holmes Community College
Nancy Hughes, State University of New York at Plattsburgh
Alishia Huntoon, Oregon Institute of Technology
Virginia Huynh, California State University, Northridge
Lee Ann Jolley, Tennessee Tech University
Judith Levine, Farmingdale State College
Nanci Monaco, Buffalo State College
Nicole Reiber, Coastal Carolina Community College
Sabrina Rieder, Rockland Community College
David Rudek, Aurora University
Shannon Shepard, Lewis and Clark Community College
Patrick Smith, Thomas Nelson Community College
Dana VanSinden, Long Beach City College
Lona Whitmarsh, Fairleigh Dickinson University
Gina Wilson, Palomar College

## Focus Group Participants

Eileen Brittain, Jamestown Community College
Jarrod Calloway, Northwest Mississippi Community College
David Donnelly, Monroe Community College
Christopher France, Cleveland State University
Melissa Garvin, Sonoma State University
Andrew Getzfeld, New York University
Donna Green, College of the Desert
Lisa Huffman, Ball State University

Mary Hughes, Stone San Francisco State University
Nancy Hughes, State University of New York at Plattsburgh
Virginia Huynh, California State University, Northridge
Lee Ann Jolley, Tennessee Tech University
Kimberly Kinsella, Middlesex Community College
Maurice Malone, Nova Southeastern University
Darcy Mitchell, Colby–Sawyer College
Kristie Morris, Rockland Community College
Caroline Olko, Nassau Community College
Nicole Reiber, Coastal Carolina Community College
Greg Reynolds, University of Tennessee
Sabrina Rieder, Rockland Community College/Westchester Community College
Claire Rubman, Suffolk County Community College
David Rudek, Aurora University
Matthew Schelesinger, Southern Illinois University, Carbondale
Paula Tripp, Sam Houston State University
Haley Vlach, University of Wisconsin, Madison
Herman Walston, Kentucky State University
Sharon Ward, California State University, San Bernardino
Henriette Warren, University of Minnesota
Jennifer Zosh, Pennsylvania State University, Brandywine

# Real Development Reviewers

Robin Arkerson, University of Massachusetts, Dartmouth
Patricia Bellas, Irvine Valley College
Karl Blendell, The College of Saint Rose
Richard Coelho, Lansing Community College
Carrie Dale, Eastern Illinois University
Rachel Dinero, Cazenovia College
Daracie Donegan, Whatcom Community College
David Donnelly, Monroe Community College
Linda L. Dunlap, Marist College
Warren Fass, University of Pittsburgh at Bradford
Lisa Fozio–Thielk, Waubonsee Community College
Kim Glackin, Metropolitan Community College, Blue River
Suzanne Gurland, Middlebury College
Sidney Hardyway, Volunteer State Community College/Tennessee Regents Online Degree Programs
Myra Harville, Holmes Community College
Julia Heberle, Albright College
Sharon Hirschy, Collin College
Lisa Huffman, Ball State University
Nancy Hughes, State University of New York at Plattsburgh
Virginia Huynh, California State University, Northridge
Lee Ann Jolley, Tennessee Tech University
Jean Kubeck, New York City College of Technology
Cindy Lahar, York County Community College
Dennis A. Lichty, Wayne State College
T. Darin Matthews, The Citadel
Jennifer O'Riordan, Joliet Junior College
Sharon Shepard, Lewis and Clark Community College
Timothy Sisemore, University of Tennessee at Chattanooga
Francis Staskon, Saint Xavier University
Patricia Twaddle, Moberly Area Community College

## Class Testers

Denise Adkins, Roanoke College
Diane Buffington, California University of Pennsylvania
Mary Cordell, Navarro College
Patrick Smith, Thomas Nelson Community College
Cecil Jane Spruill, Pensacola State College
Karen Watts, Snead State Community College

## Wiley Child Development Summit

Irene Cook, California State University, Bakersfield
Tina Durand, Wheelock College
Laura Fiorenza, West Chester University
Eugene Geist, Ohio University
Vivian Geneser, Texas A&M University, San Antonio
Shawn Guiling, Southeast Missouri State University
Virginia Huynh, California State University, Northridge
Lee Ann Jolley, Tennessee Tech University
Janette Kopp, Mississippi Gulf Coast Community College

# The Development of Children and Adolescents

# Chapter 1

© drbimages/iStockphoto, © Johnny Greig/iStockphoto, © Steve Ross/iStockphoto, © jo unruh/iStockphoto, © Steve Ross/iStockphoto

# A Child's Journey

## CHAPTER OUTLINE



MAKING A

## difference

### All Children Have Birthdays

Two young sisters, Makayla and Joy, are celebrating their birthdays in grand style. The girls join their friends in getting their faces painted with fanciful designs, collecting treats from a birthday piñata, playing games for prizes, and feasting on cupcakes and candy. What's different about Makayla and Joy's birthday party is that it's taking place in a homeless shelter.

Most children look forward to celebrating their birthdays. For many children, a birthday is a time to have a party where friends and family pay lots of attention to them and give them gifts—a day to feel really special. But children living in homeless shelters, like Makayla and Joy, seldom have the chance for such an experience. Their parents or guardians generally do not have the funds for a party, and most shelters do not have a big enough budget or staff to sponsor parties for children. A birthday for these children is just another day.

*Fuse/Getty Images, Inc.*

To three women volunteering in homeless shelters in Massachusetts, this situation looked like a problem that needed solving. In 2002, these three volunteers—Lisa Vasiloff, Karen Yahara, and Carol Zwanger—formed Birthday Wishes, Inc., to hold birthday parties for children living in shelters. Today, the organization serves more than 165 shelters and other, similar living facilities in Massachusetts, Rhode Island, and New York. (You can find out more about this organization at www.birthdaywishes.org.)

Volunteers working with Birthday Wishes plan each party based on the child's choice of a theme. They supply materials for craft projects and other activities like games and musical entertainment, along with goodie bags for all the children, a cake that fits the party theme, and a special gift. In planning, the volunteers pay attention to the family's cultural traditions concerning birthday celebrations, as described by the child's parents. Knowledge of child development also helps, because parties for 2-year-olds must be different from parties for 10-year-olds.

Sometimes all it takes is a simple observation—like the lack of birthday parties—to find an important way to make a difference for children. Throughout this book, we will be introducing different ways in which students, parents, teachers, health-care professionals, and others have made a difference in the lives of children. You may find that you, too, can make a difference.

## [KEY QUESTIONS] *for* READING CHAPTER 1

1. What are some of the key issues in understanding development?
2. How has modern society affected child development and its study?
3. How would you describe the major theories of child development?
4. What specific research methods do psychologists use to learn about children's development?

**IN THIS CHAPTER,** you will embark on learning about an exciting field, one that is relevant to the everyday lives of most people: child development. Many of us study child development because we want to improve the lives of children, like the volunteers in our chapter-opening feature. As you will see, however, there are many different ideas about how children develop and what helps them develop optimally. We begin this chapter by examining what development is, how it differs from change, and what kinds of issues the study of development involves. Then, to introduce some significant influences on a child's life, we present a brief glimpse of a child's development at home and in the community. We also discuss the relationship between children and technology. Next, we describe the major theories currently influencing the study of children's development. From there we turn to the research methods psychologists use to study development. We conclude with a summary of guidelines for ethical practices in conducting research with children.

# Children and Their Development

### [ KEY QUESTION ] 1. What are some of the key issues in understanding development?

How thoughts about children and childhood have changed over time! More than a hundred years ago, William James, a famous American psychologist, described the newborn's world as "one great blooming, buzzing confusion" (1890, p. 488). James, in other words, felt that infants come into the world helpless and unable to make any sense at all of what is going on around them. Contrast that view with those of the noted pediatrician T. Berry Brazelton (1973), who designed a way to assess the capabilities of newborn infants (Brazelton & Nugent, 1995). According to Brazelton, the newborn—far from simply reacting to a "blooming, buzzing confusion"—behaves in a way that is complex and competent. Most psychologists today, informed by genetic research, neuroscientific evidence, and sophisticated environmental studies, agree with Brazelton.

Still, there is no doubt that the competent newborns Brazelton writes about develop rapidly into ever more competent toddlers, then children, then adolescents as they journey through childhood and into adulthood. How this occurs leads us to the definition of development that will guide our work.

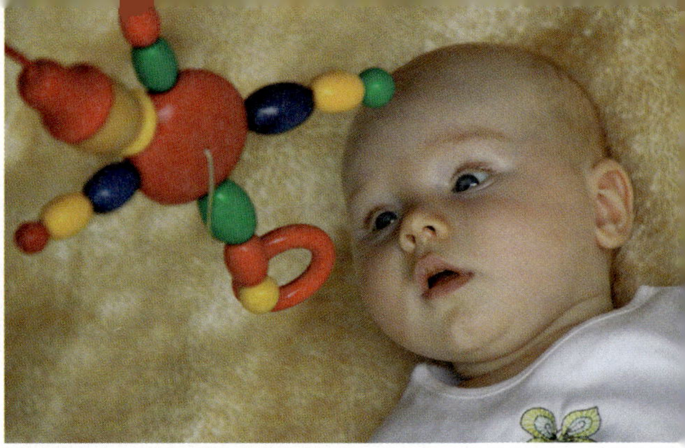
Altrendo Images/Getty Images, Inc.

Young infants are fascinated by patterns and movement. Psychologists today know that newborns are capable of far more than people once believed.

## What Is Development?

If we are going to consider how children develop, we need to start by defining what development is. To do that, we need to think about the relationship between development and change. Ask yourself these two questions: Does development mean change? Does change mean development? The answer to the first question is yes, and the answer to the second is no.

That said, the answers to these questions aren't as contradictory as they may first seem. In answering yes to the first question, we agree with most psychologists who study child development that development is about change (Overton, 2006). Such psychologists are concerned with changes in size, behavior, thinking, and personality during any age period. Thus, development, in a general sense, refers to change (Lerner, 2010; Rutter & Rutter, 1993).

In no way, however, does this mean that development and change are the same thing. Many changes in children have nothing to do with development. A young girl may be grumpy, complaining that her cereal is not sweet. Her father adds fruit to the cereal, and the child is now happy. The change in the child's mood has little to do with development. Clearly, development involves a very specific kind of change.

For change to be developmental, it must be *systematic*, it must be *organized*, and it must have a *successive* character (Lerner, 2002; Lerner, 2010; Overton, 2006; Rutter & Rutter, 1993; Travers & Travers, 2008). For example, most very young children walk with assistance, usually by holding the hands of a brother, sister, or parent, before they can walk on their own. By the time these children enter school just a few years later, they are not only walking but also running, hopping, and skipping with ease. Changes like this are developmental because they are *systematic*; that is, they occur in an orderly and predictable way. Walking with assistance occurs before walking independently, and walking independently occurs before skipping. Such changes are *organized* in that many systems work together in a specific way to support a child's first attempts at walking, including brain organization and muscle strength, which you will read about in Chapter 5. Finally, changes are *successive* in that those occurring at a later time have been influenced by those that occurred at an earlier time, as the ability to skip is influenced by the ability to walk and hop.

## The Study of Development

**Development**, then, is change that is systematic, organized, and successive in character. As we discuss children's development throughout this book, we will often cite the work of developmental psychologists. **Developmental psychology** is a field concerned with describing and understanding how people grow and change systematically over their lifetimes. In studying development, psychologists focus on *what* developmental changes are, *how* they occur, *how* they are maintained, and *how* the course of development varies among individuals (Rutter & Rutter, 1993). Next, we look at a few of the basic issues that arise in the study of development.

WHEN SYSTEMS CONNECT

## Developmental Domains

Developmental psychologists typically divide their analyses into three general domains: physical, cognitive, and psychosocial. The **physical domain** relates to patterns of change in children's biology and health, including sensory abilities and motor skills.

**Development** Change that is systematic, organized, and successive in character.

**Developmental psychology** The field of psychology concerned with describing and understanding how people grow and change over their lifetimes.

**Physical domain** An area of development that involves patterns of change in children's biology and health, including sensory abilities and motor skills.

**Cognitive domain** An area of development that involves patterns of change in children's intellectual abilities, including reasoning, learning, attention, memory, and language skills.

**Psychosocial domain** An area of development that involves patterns of change in children's personalities as well as their social and emotional skills, including relationships with others and the ability to regulate their own emotions.

**Table 1.1** Examples of Elements of Developmental Domains

| Physical | Cognitive | Psychosocial |
|---|---|---|
| Genetics | Language acquisition | Attachment |
| Brain development | Information processing | Temperament |
| Pregnancy and birth | Problem solving | Emotions |
| Physical growth | Memory | Self-regulation |
| Health | Perception | Relationships with peers |

The **cognitive domain** involves patterns of change in children's intellectual abilities, including reasoning, learning, attention, memory, and language skills. The **psychosocial domain** relates to patterns of change in children's personalities, as well as their social and emotional skills, including relationships with others and their ability to regulate their own emotions.

Table 1.1 lists selected elements from each domain. Of course, simply listing these elements tells us little about development. We must consider how the various elements interact. For example, genetic damage (in the physical domain) may negatively affect various ways of reasoning (in the cognitive domain), and immature reasoning may lead to poor relationships with peers (in the psychosocial domain) (Chang et al., 2010; Travers & Travers, 2008). The interactions among these domains, though generally complex and multidirectional, illustrate that aspects of children's development seldom occur in isolation but instead are part of a developmental system (Lerner, Easterbrooks, & Mistry, 2013). As you will see, we pay a great deal of attention to such system connections throughout this book.

## Developmental Epochs: Is Age the Answer?

We can also use a framework based on age to organize information about development. The childhood and adolescent years are typically divided into the age periods, often called epochs, listed in Table 1.2: the prenatal period, infancy and toddlerhood, early childhood, middle childhood, and adolescence. These periods make up the organizational frame of this book.

Age is useful as a general standard to assess a child's developmental status; but age by itself says little about the specific *causes* of a child's behavior (Rutter, 2006). As you continue to read this book, remember these important points:

- *Age by itself tells us about expected biological maturation*, but actual maturation varies from one individual to the next. For example, two children of the same age may differ widely in their skills.
- *Different aspects of development proceed at different rates.* For example, intellectual and physical development may follow quite divergent developmental paths, and a child may be more advanced in one area than in another.
- *Age alone reveals little about the underlying mechanisms of development.* For example, knowing a child is 9 years old and a skilled reader does not tell us how that child developed that skill.

## Issues in Development

As developmental psychologists observe children's development, they speculate about the forces that produce it and conduct experiments in search of explanations. In this process, they are guided by certain questions. Two of these questions—or issues—have remained important over the history of developmental psychology:

1. What is the relationship between nature and nurture?
2. Does development proceed in a continuous or discontinuous manner?

There are good reasons why these issues have guided, puzzled, and frustrated psychologists as long as they have.

**Table 1.2** Developmental Epochs

| Period | Characteristics |
|---|---|
| Prenatal | During the prenatal period—the nine months from conception until birth—the developing organism grows from a single cell to a fetus ready to be born. 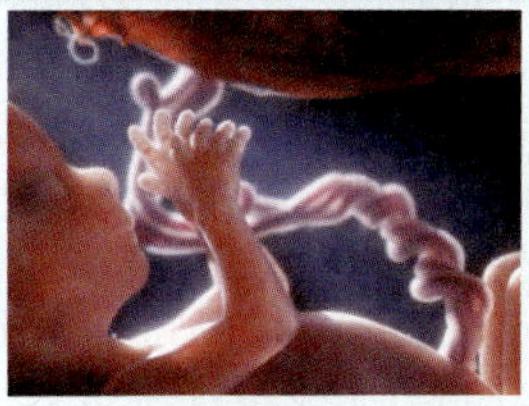 *Nestle/Petit Format/Science Source* |
| Infancy and toddlerhood (0–2 years) | From birth to about 2 years is the period of most rapid growth. Remarkable physical and cognitive changes occur—for example, walking and talking—and the nature of a child's personality becomes apparent.  *Hilary Helton/Photolibrary/Getty Images* |
| Early childhood (2–6 years) | During the years from 2 to about 6, children's bodies continue to change, language develops at a staggering rate, children's thinking edges into the symbolic world, and their personalities begin to shape the nature of their developing relationships.  *JGI/Jamie Grill/Blend Images/Getty Images, Inc.* |
| Middle childhood (6–12 years) | The years from 6 to 12 comprise a period of exciting change. Children's talents in all phases of development begin to flourish. Their bodies become more coordinated, they become more involved in the symbolic world especially after they begin school, and their relationships expand briskly as their environment continues to broaden.  *PhotoAlto/Sigrid Olsson/Getty Images* |
| Adolescence (12–18 or 19 years) | The years from 12 to 18 or 19 are a period of rapid growth, when children begin to leave the comfortable surroundings of childhood and prepare to enter the world of adults. Bodies change; sexual maturity beckons; and society's expectations for children mount as they prepare mentally, physically, and emotionally for adulthood.  *Lisa Petkau/First Light/Getty Images, Inc.* |

**Nature** The biological factors, including genes, that contribute to development.

**Nurture** The environmental factors and experiences that contribute to development.

**Continuity** The idea that development is a slow and steady process.

**Discontinuity** The view that development is characterized by abrupt changes in behavior; often associated with stage theories of development.

**Stage theories** Theories proposing that development proceeds in a discontinuous manner; each stage is qualitatively different from the ones that precede and follow it.

**NATURE AND NURTURE.** In learning about child development, you will see that a complex relationship exists between **nature**, which includes biological factors, such as the genes we inherit from our parents, and **nurture**, which includes environmental factors and experience. For a long time, there were arguments about whether nature or nurture is more important in children's development. We can trace the roots of the nature-nurture debate in Western philosophy and in more modern science (Dobbs, 2007; Meaney, 2010; Price, 2009; Sameroff, 2010). The prevailing view has changed from period to period. During the middle of the 20th century, for example, behaviorists strongly argued that environment is dominant. The prominent behaviorist B. F. Skinner (1953, 1983) believed that it is the *consequences of behavior* that shape learning and development. (You will read more about the behaviorists later in this chapter.)

Today, most psychologists reject any separation of nature and nurture to explain development. They prefer to focus on the interaction between these two critical forces (Diamond, 2009; Lenroot & Giedd, 2011; Lerner, 2010). Nevertheless, some psychologists still give relatively more emphasis to either nature or nurture. For example, Elizabeth Spelke (de Hevia & Spelke, 2010; Spelke, Gilmore, & McCarthy, 2011; Spelke & Kinzler, 2007) has argued that babies are born with a certain amount of innate knowledge, called *core knowledge*, a view that emphasizes the role of nature. In contrast, Betty Hart and Todd Risley (1995) believe that young children's vocabulary growth relates to the ways in which parents interact with them, a view that focuses more on the role of nurture.

## what if...?

Your cousin and your uncle are watching your sister, Elena, practice playing basketball. Your uncle says, "See how great Elena's aim is? That shows she has inherited my genes for good eye-hand coordination, which will make her a successful basketball player!" Your cousin points out that Elena spends hours every weekend practicing basketball and watching others play it and that is why she is so good at it. You listen to their conversation and claim, "You're both right." What might you say to them to explain how they both could be right?

**CONTINUITY AND DISCONTINUITY.** The issue of continuity versus discontinuity concerns *how* developmental changes occur. **Continuity** in development means that developmental change occurs smoothly, gradually, and predictably over time. A basic question about continuity is: Are you the same person now as you were in infancy or early childhood? Those who hold that development is continuous would say that you are. Maybe you were a shy toddler and you are still shy today. In contrast, **discontinuity** means that development is marked by periods of relative quiet and periods of rapid change. The idea that development is discontinuous is often associated with **stage theories,** such as that of Piaget, which we discuss later in this chapter. Stage theories are based on the idea that development proceeds through a series of distinct stages over time, with each stage qualitatively different from the last.

*Everyday stories*

CONTINUITY VERSUS DISCONTINUITY An illustration of the difference between continuity and discontinuity can be seen in Figure 1.1. An often-used example of continuous development is the growth of an evergreen tree, which offers few surprises or major transformations. It begins as a small shoot and gradually adds branches. Although it becomes taller and more branches develop, its overall configuration does not dramatically change. The mature tree very closely resembles the immature one. In contrast, consider the change in configuration that occurs when a tadpole turns into a frog. The adult frog bears little resemblance to the tadpole. The transformation from tadpole to frog is an example of discontinuous development.

**Continuous Development**–A sapling grows bigger and adds branches.

**Discontinuous Development**–An adult frog seems like an entirely different animal from a tadpole.

FIGURE 1.1 **An Example of Continuity and Discontinuity** Continuity in development means that change occurs smoothly, gradually, and predictably over time, as when a sapling grows to a mature tree. In contrast, discontinuity means that development is marked by periods of relative quiet and periods of rapid change, as when a tadpole turns into a frog.

It is not always easy to distinguish continuity and discontinuity in children's development, however. What may appear to be discontinuous—such as an infant's apparently sudden ability to roll over—actually occurs because of a series of small gains in motor skill acquisition (Dacey, Travers, & Fiore, 2009; Lerner, 2002). Nevertheless, the theories of development that we discuss later in this chapter differ somewhat in the extent to which they focus on development as a continuous or discontinuous process.

### ✓CHECK YOUR PROGRESS

1. Explain the differences between development and change.
2. Describe several reasons why knowing a child's age is not sufficient to understand that child's development.
3. What is the nature-nurture debate?
4. Explain the difference between continuity and discontinuity in development.

# A Child's Journey in the 21st Century

**[ KEY QUESTION ] 2. How has modern society affected child development and its study?**

The journey that children commence in the 21st century is a complicated one. Changes in family structure, society, and technology affect development in many ways (Bass, & Warehime, 2011; Thompson, 2012; Wooldridge & Shapka, 2012). The Research Insights feature gives an example of one way children have changed over the years. At the same time, new ideas, experimental methods, and knowledge from the neurosciences have altered the way developmental psychologists study and describe development. To understand how children develop in the midst of change, we must pay particular attention to the contexts in which children live and learn. We will do so throughout this book. At this point, we look briefly at three important contexts of development in the 21st century: home, culture, and technology.

## Research Insights: Are Today's Children More Imaginative?

Pretend play is important to the development of young children, because it relates to creative problem solving, divergent thinking, and emotional regulation (Berk, Mann, & Ogan, 2006; Elkind, 2007; Hoffmann & Russ, 2012; Russ, 2009). In pretend play, children develop characters and storylines. They also use one object, such as a block, to represent another, such as a truck. These tasks involve imagination because they require children to think beyond the concrete objects they are using.

Susanna Price/Dorian Kindersley/Getty Images

Children today are exposed to more novelty than children in the past, which may enhance their imaginative skills.

Recently, two researchers compared the results of 14 studies conducted over the course of 25 years (Russ & Dillon, 2011; Miller, 2012). In each study, children ages 6 to 10 were observed for 5 minutes playing with neutral-looking puppets and several colored blocks. Because the observers had used the same method of rating children's play, the results could be compared over the years.

The researchers found that some aspects of pretend play have not changed. For example, the amount of emotion children express when playing has remained about the same. Other aspects of pretend play have changed, however. In particular, children today are more comfortable engaging in pretend play, and they show greater imagination in their make-believe scenes. For example, they are more likely to create characters who are involved in unusual activities, such as exploring the oceans, rather than more everyday activities like going to school. The authors of the study speculate that although children may have less time for pretend play today than in the past, they may have greater exposure to novelty in the games they play and the everyday challenges they face. These experiences may in turn enhance their imaginative skills.

## Children in the Home   Parenting

Children benefit from close and dependable relationships that provide them with love, nurturance, and security (Collins, Maccoby Steinberg, Hetherington, & Bornstein, 2000; Grady, Karraker, & Metzger, 2012; Kovan, Chung, & Sroufe, 2009; Parade, Supple, & Helms, 2012). Complicating this simple truth is the realization that parenting is a dynamic process—a series of developmental challenges. Indeed, both parents and children develop throughout their relationship. This development is influenced by many factors: the parents' child-rearing goals and practices, the changes occurring in the child, and the social and cultural context of the times (Pluess & Belsky, 2010). Given the complexity of modern society, the possible influences on how the family develops seem almost endless.

To meet the demands of growing complexity, researchers have changed the way they analyze relationships between children and their parents, often referred to as the *under-the-roof culture*. Many studies have shifted from concentrating solely on parents or children to looking at the family as a social system (Parke & Buriel, 2006; Whiteman, McHale, & Crouter, 2011). The family system approach recognizes that there are many relationships within the family and that each relationship affects the others and is affected by all of them (Minuchin, 1988). Thus, the mother-child relationship is quite different from the father-child relationship, and both of those differ from each of the sibling relationships. Therefore, just studying, say, the mother-child relationship will not give researchers the complete picture of the family's dynamics.

Finally, today's researchers recognize that relationships among family members are *bidirectional* (for example, parent to child and child to parent), not solely *unidirectional*

Paul Simcock/Corbis

David Sacks/Lifesize/Getty Images, Inc.

Michael Hanson/Corbis

Daniel Hurst Photography/Getty Images

In today's complex society, families take many different forms.

(for example, only parent to child) (Gault–Sherman, 2012; Padilla-Walker, Carlo, Christensen, & Yorgason, 2012). Will you treat your children in the same way your parents treated you? Is there any proof that parenting styles are transmitted from one generation to another? The topic of intergenerational transmission of parenting has long fascinated developmental psychologists (Belsky, Conger, & Capaldi, 2009). Several studies have confirmed that both positive and negative parenting practices can indeed be passed from generation to generation (Beaver & Belsky, 2012; Capaldi, Pears, Patterson, & Owen, 2003; Chen & Kaplan, 2001; Conger, Neppl, Kim, & Scaramella, 2003; Neppl, Conger, Scaramella, & Ontai, 2009; Xing, Zhang, & Wang, 2011). Parents can break a cycle of negative parenting, however. For example, researchers of one study found that when low-income mothers increased their education after the birth of their first child, they showed more positive methods of responding to their child (Magnuson, Sexton, Davis–Kean, & Huston, 2009). The Parenting section in each chapter describes issues such as these involving parenting and family relationships.

The family system includes other influences as well—influences from outside the family. These include both direct influences, such as the community or neighborhood, and indirect influences, such as the policies developed by government agencies like the U.S. Department of Education. In the Policy section in each chapter, we discuss many of the policies that affect children and families.

**Culture** The customs, values, and traditions inherent in one's environment.

**Enculturation** The transmission of culture across generations.

## Children and Their Cultural Communities

People and their social worlds are inseparable (Markus & Hamedani, 2007). It isn't surprising, then, that children's cultural communities are important in their development (Cohen, 2009; Cole & Packer, 2011). The importance of culture in development is not a new idea. Still, today's psychologists have awarded it a more central role than ever before in their explanations of how development occurs—as you will see later in this chapter when we discuss theories of development.

You can think of **culture** as the customs, values, and traditions inherent in a person's environment (Markus & Hamedani, 2007; Nikapota, 2002). In addition, culture includes these three characteristics (Triandis, 2007):

1. Culture emerges from adaptive interactions between humans and their environments.
2. Culture consists of shared elements such as language, time, and place.
3. Culture is transmitted across time periods and generations, a process known as **enculturation.**

*Everyday stories*

STARTING SCHOOL IN DIFFERENT CULTURES Consider how culture influences the rituals developed for the beginning of the school year in elementary schools. In some Asian countries, parents go to school with their child on the first day and stay in the building so that a photograph can be taken of all the parents, children, and teachers together. In many Eastern European countries, children bring flowers to the teacher on the first day of school, and the youngest and oldest child together lead the other children into the building, with the parents watching and cheering. Both of these rituals contrast with those in the United States, which show wide individual variation. Some parents take their child to the classroom and meet the teacher. Other parents simply accompany their child to a bus stop.

Educator and researcher Barbara Rogoff (2003; Rogoff, Correa-Chavez, & Silva, 2011) has noted that human learning and development are cultural processes. A great deal of research has supported this view. For example, children from different cultural communities interpret physical punishment differently. Rogoff (2003) explains that many North American adolescents associate firm parental control with rejection and hostility, whereas Korean adolescents have been found to interpret strictness as a sign of parental warmth and concern. In other words, the children's perception of their parents' behavior

Families transmit culture across generations and time.

Stephen Simpson/Getty Images

© Alexander Rybka/Demotix/Corbis

Matt Henry Gunther

REUTERS/CARLOS BARRIA/LANDOV

On the first day of school, varying rituals are carried out in different countries.

makes a difference in how the children react to it, and often that perception varies by cultural group. Parents in different cultures also hold distinct views about children's development, as we discuss in Culture and Parents' Views on Children's Disabilities.

Researchers have also found differences in what young people from different cultures focus on—for example, in photographs. In a study investigating cultural differences between Chinese and American students, the students were shown photos of objects on a complex background—a tiger in a jungle, for example. The American students focused more on the objects, while the Chinese students turned their attention to the background (Chua, Boland, & Nisbett, 2005; Norenzayan, Choi, & Peng, 2007). Studies such as these appear throughout this text to illustrate the powerful impact of culture on development and to demonstrate that we cannot assume that all children think, feel, see, and perceive the behavior of others in the same way, even when they are placed in what appear to be identical situations (Nisbett, 2007).

## Children in a Technological World

Many children today are developing in a world that provides technological tools at their fingertips: television, computers, cell phones, video games, electronic tablets, and so forth. Indeed, a recent analysis of media use by 8- to 18-year-olds in the United States says that on average they spend more than 7½ hours a day, 7 days a week, involved with various forms of media (Rideout, Foehr, & Roberts, 2010). Members of

## Culture and Parents' Views on Children's Disabilities

Children with disabilities are born in all cultures. But families look at these disabilities differently depending on their cultural perspectives (Hauser–Cram, Cannarella, Tillinger, & Woodman, 2013). Researchers who study parenting across cultures stress the importance of parents' *ethnotheories*, their culturally shared belief systems about children's development and parents' roles (Harkness & Super, 2005; Harkness et al., 2011). In the United States, many parents take a scientific approach. They discuss a child's disability in terms of its biological causes, such as genes, physical trauma at birth, or early exposure to toxins like cigarette smoke or lead paint.

Even in the United States, though, subcultural groups may not share the dominant view. In one U.S. study, researchers asked mothers with a Mexican or Puerto Rican background about their children with a disability (Skinner, Bailey, Correa, & Rodriguez, 1999). Many of the mothers viewed the child as a gift from God. They believed they had received this gift because they were worthy of such parenting or because they would benefit from its challenges.

A different view is evident in a narrative about Lia, a child whose parents lived in the United States but were part of the Hmong culture from Cambodia (Fadiman, 1997). Lia had a seizure disorder that resulted in many developmental problems. Members of her cultural group, however, viewed her seizure disorder as "an illness of some distinction" (Fadiman, p. 21) because they considered that the seizures might allow her to see into the spiritual world.

Variations such as these can affect how parents of children with disabilities seek treatment and support from their communities. We might expect, for example, that parents who take a scientific view would more likely seek medical intervention than parents who view the disability as a gift from God or as a window into the spiritual world.

Manny Crisostomo/Sacramento Bee/MCT via Getty Images

Foua Yang, Lia Lee's mother, holds a photo of Lia, who had a seizure disorder. The Hmong culture, to which the family belonged, believed that the seizures might enable Lia to see into the spiritual world.

this age group spend more time involved with media than in any other activity except (maybe) sleeping.

### The Expanding Media World

The introduction of each new medium has been accompanied by concerns about its appropriateness (Paik, 2001). Nevertheless, technological improvements have made the expanding media world almost irresistible to children. Let's look at a few examples.

- *Television and children.* Today's young people watch television about 4½ hours per day, which includes time spent watching TV content on other platforms, such as laptops, smart phones, and tablets (Rideout et al., 2010). Researchers have found that television viewing begins before the age of 3 and peaks at about the age of 12. At the same time, interest changes from cartoon and educational programs such as *Sesame Street* to shows of greater complexity and violence (Comstock & Scharrer, 2006). Later chapters in this text discuss many effects of children's television and video viewing, both negative and positive.

- *Cell phones and children.* An image of an older child or teen typically includes a cell phone. Thirty-one percent of 8- to 10-year-olds, 69% of 11- to 14-year-olds, and 85% of 15- to 18-year-olds have their own phones and use them for talking, texting, listening to music, playing games, watching videos, and accessing other sites on the Internet (Rideout et al., 2010).
- *Video games and children.* There has been a steady increase in video gaming over the past few years, mainly because such games can now be played on a variety of platforms (Rideout et al., 2010). On a typical day, 8- to 18-year-olds spend more than an hour playing video games. Violence in video games, along with violence on television and in films, has come in for a great deal of criticism, as you will see in later chapters. This criticism stems from the fact that studies have identified negative effects of exposure to media violence (Brocato, Gentile, Laczniak, Maier, & Ji-Song, 2010; Gentile, Mathieson, & Crick, 2011).
- *Social networking and children.* Internet-based social networking through such sites as Facebook and Twitter is a well-known phenomenon. Also well known are abuses of these sites. "Using anonymity to avoid face-to-face contact, misrepresenting oneself on a social network, and even participating in libelous or fraudulent activities are increasingly common practices of teens in social network situations" (Lamb, 2010, p. 63). And the problem isn't limited to teens. Although some sites require users to be 13 or older, they have no practical way to verify ages, and many young users pretend to be older when signing up. Young people's use of social networking raises several concerns, including the important issue of teaching young people to use social networking ethically. Later chapters address this issue in more detail.

This brief overview of the technological world of children sheds light on some of the environmental complexity in which they develop. Children's use of technology has many implications. It has expanded ways in which children can access and learn information, but it also presents challenges to the development of their decision-making skills. As noted, you'll read more in the chapters to come about the issues we have raised here. There, we will consider them within the context of specific age groups.

© Sergey Novikov/Alamy

Children—even toddlers—find the expanding media world almost irresistible.

**what if...?**

A friend of yours has been encouraging you to give your 3-year-old daughter a smartphone. Your reaction is a stunned "Are you out of your mind?" look. But wait: Is the suggestion as absurd as it seems? You may have read an article in a respected newspaper (Swidey, 2010) that presented logical reasons for being so generous with a 3-year-old. The size of the phone is ideal for small hands, and the colorful icons immediately attract their attention. Toddlers touch all the buttons, run their hands over the screen, and promptly become fascinated. Companies have discovered this new market and have rushed to provide applications for toddlers and preschoolers, arguing that smartphones are good for children's development because they can provide "anywhere, anytime learning." Will you be tempted to buy your 3-year-old a smartphone? In future chapters you will read how 3-year-olds think and learn about the world, after which you might reconsider this question and see if you have the same response.

## Video Games and Learning **P**ractice

Can children learn from playing video games? Although many researchers have studied violent video games and their effects on children's aggression (Anderson et al., 2010), fewer have focused on the potential learning that can result from playing certain types of video games. One group of researchers, though, wondered whether children could improve their spatial skills by playing certain video games. Spatial skills involve imagining how a two- or three-dimensional object or array of objects would appear if rotated. You use spatial skills, for example, in completing a jigsaw puzzle, in order to imagine how a piece would look if it were rotated to be placed in a specific location. Such skills are related to the ability to solve some mathematical problems (Ganley & Vasilyeva, 2011).

Some researchers (De Lisi & Wolford, 2002) studied third-grade students as they played a video game that involved mental rotation of pieces on the screen. The students showed improvement in their mental rotation skills on other tasks after playing the game for approximately a half hour each day for 11 days. It appears, then, that playing certain types of video games can enhance the skills children use in solving problems in math. Other researchers have considered other aspects of video games, such as requiring children to use different strategies to solve a problem, that make them useful learning tools (Boyan & Sherry, 2011). Such research suggests that although many video games are violent and offer little value to teach children, it is possible to design video games that result in productive learning.

✓CHECK YOUR PROGRESS

1. Explain why asking only a mother or a father to report on the way a family operates would provide incomplete information.
2. Give an example of a bidirectional relationship between a parent and a child.
3. Discuss the meaning of *enculturation* as a guide to understanding children's development.

# Explaining Development: The Theories

**[ KEY QUESTION ] 3. How would you describe the major theories of child development?**

Developmental psychologists are scientists. As such, they have formed theories of development—frameworks for understanding observations and making predictions. Why are such theories valuable? Theories are important because they help guide us in investigating and understanding how children develop. Theories also help us to structure educational and psychosocial interventions to support children's learning and development. Kurt Lewin, a well-known psychologist of the 1930s and 1940s, claimed that there is nothing as practical as a good theory, and many psychologists today continue to agree with that claim.

In this section, we briefly discuss the major features of several important developmental theories, as summarized in Table 1.3. In later chapters, we analyze them further and apply them to various developmental issues. Some of the traditional theories we discuss are criticized today as being too *unidimensional* to explain the complexity of development; that is, they focus on only one aspect of development. For example, Freud spent his lifetime delving into the secrets of personality development, while Piaget focused exclusively on cognitive development. Nevertheless, each theory has valuable insights to offer.

## Psychoanalytically Based Theories

Both Sigmund Freud and Erik Erikson proposed stage theories of development that focused on personality formation. In each stage, children face conflicts that they must resolve to move on successfully to the next stage. In terms of the issues we discussed earlier, recall that stage theories like Freud's and Erikson's consider development discontinuous. Each stage marks a qualitative change from the one before. Psychoanalytic theories consider both nature and nurture to be important, as children have natural innate impulses that need to be controlled or directed through the nurture of parenting.

**Psychoanalytic theory** Freud's view of personality development, which attributes it largely to unconscious sources in the human mind. Psychoanalytic theory includes the idea that children pass through five stages of psychosexual development that affect their adult personalities.

### Sigmund Freud and Psychoanalytic Theory

Sigmund Freud (1856–1939) is the father of **psychoanalytic theory,** which attributes personality development largely to unconscious sources in the human mind. Freud, a

**Table 1.3** Major Theories of Child Development

| Theory: Major Theorists | Characteristics | Is Development Driven by Nature or Nurture? | Is Development Continuous or Discontinuous? |
|---|---|---|---|
| Psychoanalytically based theories: Freud, Erikson | Focus on personality formation; children must resolve conflicts to progress through stages | Both nature (innate impulses) and nurture (early experiences with caregiver) | Both Freud and Erikson propose a stage theory: discontinuous |
| Cognitive theories:<br>Constructivist: Piaget, Vygotsky<br>Information Processing: Siegler | Focus on the way children think | Both nature (innate desire to learn) and nurture (stimulating environment) | Piaget's stage theory: discontinuous<br>Vygotsky's sociocultural theory: elements of both<br>Information processing: continuous |
| Learning theories: Pavlov, Watson, Skinner, Bandura | Focus on how experiences affect learning and behavior | Nurture drives development | Continuous |
| Ethological theories: Lorenz, Bowlby | Focus on biology and the role of early experiences during specific periods | Both nature (biology) and nurture (early experiences) important but emphasis on early experiences | Elements of both: critical periods suggest discontinuous aspects of development |
| System theories: Bronfenbrenner, Gottlieb, Lerner, Sameroff | Focus on how interacting environmental and biological systems shape development | Both nature (biology) and nurture (multiple contexts) and their interaction | Continuous but may incorporate discontinuous elements |

physician who spent most of his life in Vienna, based his theories on observations of patients he saw in his practice—upper-class members of Viennese society. His ideas were particularly influential in the early 20th century. Although Freud's ideas no longer dominate psychology, his insistence on the decisive role of children's early years, and especially their early relationships, has remained a potent and controversial concept (Cairns & Cairns, 2006).

© Corbis

Sigmund Freud's psychoanalytic theory attributes personality development largely to unconscious sources. Freud was particularly interested in the early years of children, especially their early relationships.

**Personality Structure.** Freud (1940) viewed personality as composed of three parts: the id, the ego, and the superego, which appear at different stages of a child's development. The *id*, which is present at birth, contains all of our basic instincts, such as the need for food, drink, and sex. It seeks simply to secure pleasure, and so it often clashes with society's rules, thus leading to conflict. As this occurs, the *ego*, which begins to develop early in childhood, attempts to reconcile the id's drives with society's expectations. The ego is the key element in our personality—the (usually) rational part that does all the planning and keeps in touch with reality. Freud believed that the stronger the ego becomes, the more realistic, and usually the more successful, a person is likely to be (Lerner, 2002). The *superego*, the moral component of personality, is the arbiter of right and wrong—our conscience. The desires of the id and the demands of the superego are in constant conflict, with the ego struggling mightily to enact compromises between these two powerful forces. Because these forces are in such a dynamic struggle, this theory is often referred to as *psychodynamic*.

**Stages of Development.** For Freud, personality development meant moving through five psychosexual stages. Each stage is distinct from the others and has a major function, which is based on a pleasure center. This pleasure center must be stimulated appropriately (not too much, not too little). If it is not, the person becomes fixated (remains at that stage) and is unable to move successfully to the next stage (Kahn, 2002). Freud's stages are summarized in Table 1.4.

Freud's work, as important as it was, has been criticized on many grounds. Freud was a physician who based his ideas on his work with patients in his medical practice. Therefore, his ideas may not apply to people in general. Perhaps more importantly, his

**Table 1.4** Freud's Psychosexual Stages

| Stage | Approximate Age | Description |
|---|---|---|
| Oral | Birth–1½ years | The mouth is the main source of pleasure. |
| Anal | 1½–3 years | The anus is the pleasure center, and toilet training is the major task. |
| Phallic | 3–5 years | The genitals are the main source of pleasure. |
| Latency | 5–12 years | Repression of sexual desire occurs. Such desires are considered to be "latent" during this stage. |
| Genital | 12-plus years | This is the time of a reawakening of sexual desires. It should lead to sexual maturity. |

ideas are difficult, if not impossible, to test. As you will see, whether a theory can be tested is an important consideration among psychologists today.

### Erikson's Psychosocial Theory of Development

**Psychosocial theory** Erikson's explanation of development, which focuses on the effects of social influences. Erikson believed that individuals pass through eight stages of development. In each stage, they must resolve a crisis that determines their continuing healthy psychological development.

Erik Erikson (1902–1994), although his theoretical orientation was strongly psychoanalytic, became critical of Freud's emphasis on psychosexual stages. He became a leading proponent of a **psychosocial theory** of development, which focuses on the effects of social interactions. He believed that children interact with an ever-widening circle of individuals, beginning with their mothers and ending with all of humanity (Erikson, 1950). Erikson is well-known for his focus on the development of the ego, in particular. According to Erikson, individuals pass through eight stages of development, as listed in Table 1.5. In each stage, they experience a "crisis" in their emotional equilibrium. In Erikson's work, the term *crisis* refers to a challenge that pushes for resolution. The resolution occurs through processes provided by the family and culture in which a child lives. Although resolutions do not always occur, they are necessary to the continuing psychosocial strength of the developing ego.

*Everyday stories*

TWO PSYCHOANALYTIC VIEWS Suppose two psychologists are observing 3-month-old Ari, who is in the arms of his mother. As Ari starts to fuss, his mother smiles at him warmly and gives him a pacifier to suck on. Ari settles down. Both psychologists witness the same behavior, but each interprets it differently. The first psychologist discusses how much Ari enjoys sucking on objects, and attributes it to his innate need for oral pleasure. The second comments on the way Ari's mother responds warmly and positively to her son, which will serve to address his need to establish trust during this life stage.

Although both psychologists follow the psychoanalytic tradition, the first adheres more closely to Freud's interpretations, whereas the second is more closely aligned with Erikson's view. You can see how two professionals observing the same behavior might interpret it differently based on the theoretical perspective each has taken.

© Ted Streshinsky/Corbis

Erik Erikson's psychosocial theory focuses on how children's success with the fundamental tasks or "crises" related to each life stage affect their development.

Like Freud's five-stage theory, Erikson's eight stages of psychosocial development are difficult to test scientifically. Nevertheless, Erikson's views remain popular, and most psychologists agree that his ideas capture many of the important challenges for each life phase. You will read more about Erikson's stages in several later chapters.

## Cognitive Theories

Moving from the world of personality development to that of cognitive development requires us to consider how children know and learn. In this section, we discuss two distinct types of theories. The first, termed *constructivism*, takes us first to the ideas of

**Table 1.5** Erikson's Psychosocial Stages of Development

| Stage | Approximate Age (years) | Psychosocial Stage | Description |
|---|---|---|---|
| Infancy | Birth–age 1 | Trust vs. mistrust | Infants develop a basic trust in others. If their needs are not met by their caregivers, mistrust develops. |
| Toddler | 2–3 | Autonomy vs. shame, doubt | Children exercise their new motor and mental skills. If caregivers are encouraging, children develop a sense of autonomy, versus shame and doubt. |
| Early childhood | 4–5 | Initiative vs. guilt | Children enjoy initiating activities and mastering new tasks. Supportive caregivers promote feelings of power and self-confidence, versus guilt. |
| Middle childhood | 6–11 | Industry vs. inferiority | Children learn productive skills and develop the capacity to work with others; if not, they feel inferior. |
| Adolescence | 12–18 | Identity vs. identity confusion | Adolescents seek to develop a satisfying identity and a sense of their role in society. Failure may lead to a lack of stable identity and confusion about their adult roles. |
| Young adulthood | 19–35 | Intimacy vs. isolation | Young adults work to establish intimate relationships with others; if they cannot, they face isolation. |
| Middle age | 36–65 | Generativity vs. stagnation | Middle-aged adults seek ways to influence the welfare of the next generation. If they fail, they may become self-absorbed. |
| Old age | Over 65 | Integrity vs. despair | Older people reflect on the lives they have lived. If they do not feel a sense of accomplishment and satisfaction, they live in fear of death. |

Jean Piaget and then to the views of Lev Vygotsky. Both theorists are considered constructivists because they focused on the ways in which children construct knowledge. The second approach, *information processing theory*, focuses on how children pay attention to, remember, and develop strategies about information. Both types of theories share the view that nature and nurture interact in shaping development. They are also similar in assigning children active roles in their own development. Where they differ is in their orientation toward the continuity-versus-discontinuity issue. Piaget's stage theory proposes discontinuous development, while information processing theory assumes continuous development; Vygotsky's theory has elements of both.

Jean Piaget's influential stage theory of cognitive development is based on the idea that children construct knowledge, rather than having it "poured" into them.

## Piaget's Theory of Cognitive Development

Jean Piaget (1896–1980) was a biologist who became fascinated with studying how children think and how their thinking changes (Gruber & Vonèche, 1977). Why do infants who drop a toy from their high chair seem to lose interest in it immediately? Why do young children think there is more milk in a tall, thin container than in a short, wide one? Searching for insights into such behaviors led Piaget (1952, 1965, 1969, 1973) to devise a theory of cognitive development that has strongly influenced our appreciation of the growth of children's thinking.

Jean Piaget's theory is based on **constructivism**, the view that children *construct* knowledge, rather than having it "poured" into them. This theory emphasizes the importance of children's active engagement with objects and events. According to Piaget, in infancy, children begin to develop *schemas*, or schemes—mental structures that represent things they have experienced. For example, a 2-month-old might have a scheme to represent grasping an object. Once a mental structure is formed (for example, grasping an object), it is linked to others (such as bringing an object to the mouth), a process Piaget called *organization.*

Schemes change over time through *adaptation*, which in turn consists of assimilation and accommodation. When children *assimilate* something, they fit it into a mental structure they have already formed. You can see an example of assimilation and accommodation in Figure 1.2. Imagine a 2-year-old boy who sees a cow for the first time. If he is familiar with dogs, he may say "doggie" when he sees the cow. The child is adapting the new object, the cow, into his current scheme for dogs. Eventually, though, the child will learn that cows differ from dogs (they moo instead of bark, their ears and tail have different shapes, and so on). Thus, the structure will have to be changed, a process called *accommodation.* Children (and adults) continually search for *equilibrium* as they try to discover the balance between assimilation and accommodation.

Organization and adaptation are inseparable; they are two complementary processes of a single mechanism. Through these processes, children pass through four stages of cognitive development, which are described in Table 1.6. All children pass through the same stages, in the same order. Each stage involves thought processes that are qualitatively different from those of the previous stage. Piaget also maintained that children do not regress in their stage development. Once they have achieved a new

a. Assimilation

b. Accommodation

**FIGURE 1.2 A Simple Example of Assimilation and Accommodation**
A toddler who is familiar with dogs but not with cows may refer to a cow as a dog in an attempt to assimilate new information into a mental structure he has already formed. When he learns that cows are different from dogs, he will form a new structure to accommodate this new understanding.

**Table 1.6** Piaget's Stages of Cognitive Development

| Stage | Approximate Age | Features |
|---|---|---|
| Sensorimotor | Birth–2 years | Infants understand the world through actions. |
| Preoperational | 2–7 years | Preschoolers begin to use representations, including words and pictures, rather than actions to understand the world. |
| Concrete operational | 7–11 years | Children develop the ability to reason about concrete objects. |
| Formal operational | 11-plus years | Adolescents begin to use abstract thinking and reasoning with more complex symbols. |

stage of thinking, they may stay at that stage or move on to the next one, but they will not move backward. As you look at Table 1.6, keep in mind that the ages are approximate.

**Sociocultural theory** Vygotsky's theory that children's cognitive growth depends on their interactions with adults and more knowledgeable peers, which in turn are based on broad cultural values.

Piaget has been very influential in the study of child development, especially in regard to his attention on how children's thinking differs from that of adults. Nevertheless, he has come in for criticism. Some believe that change takes place more gradually than Piaget's stage theory implies—in other words, that development is more continuous than discontinuous (Courage & Howe, 2002). Others offer evidence that Piaget underestimated the abilities of young children (Baillargeon, 2004; McCarty & Keen, 2005; Moore & Meltzoff, 2004). Still others point out that he based his conclusions on observation of a very limited sample made up largely of his own three children. Thus, he failed to take possible social and cultural differences into account (Case & Okamoto, 1996).

## Vygotsky's Theory of Cognitive Development

Whereas Piaget focused on processes occurring within the developing child, the Russian psychologist Lev Vygotsky (1896–1934) turned his attention to social and cultural processes. Like Piaget, Vygotsky believed that children construct knowledge, but unlike Piaget, he emphasized *co-constructivism*. That is, Vygotsky (1962, 1978) claimed that children construct knowledge with the assistance of others, especially with the assistance of skilled adults and more knowledgeable peers. These people interact with the children in a way that emphasizes the things that their culture values. For this reason, Vygotsky's theory is often referred to as **sociocultural theory**. The social emphasis of Vygotsky's view highlights the cultural context in which children are developing.

Vygotsky was familiar with the writings of Piaget. Like Piaget, he believed that children are active in their construction of knowledge. Whereas Piaget focused on how an individual child reasons, however, Vygotsky emphasized that a child advances in concept formation primarily through interactions with others. He believed that children learn first at the social level through such interactions and then gradually internalize that learning. Because of the social importance of language, Vygotsky focused on how children develop language and how language skills promote children's dialogues with others. Through such interaction, Vygotsky maintained, children advance their cognitive development.

From his studies of development, Vygotsky introduced the notion of the *zone of proximal development (ZPD)*. He defined the ZPD as the distance between a person's actual developmental level, as determined by independent problem solving, and the higher level of development that could be achieved under the guidance of an adult or a more capable peer (see Figure 1.3). Psychologists and educators have used the zone of proximal development as a basis for the concept of *scaffolding*. Scaffolding offers support to children as they attempt to learn—an example of a practical application of the zone of proximal development.

*Michael Cole, University of California, San Diego*

Lev Vygotsky believed that children construct knowledge with the assistance of skilled adults and more knowledgeable peers.

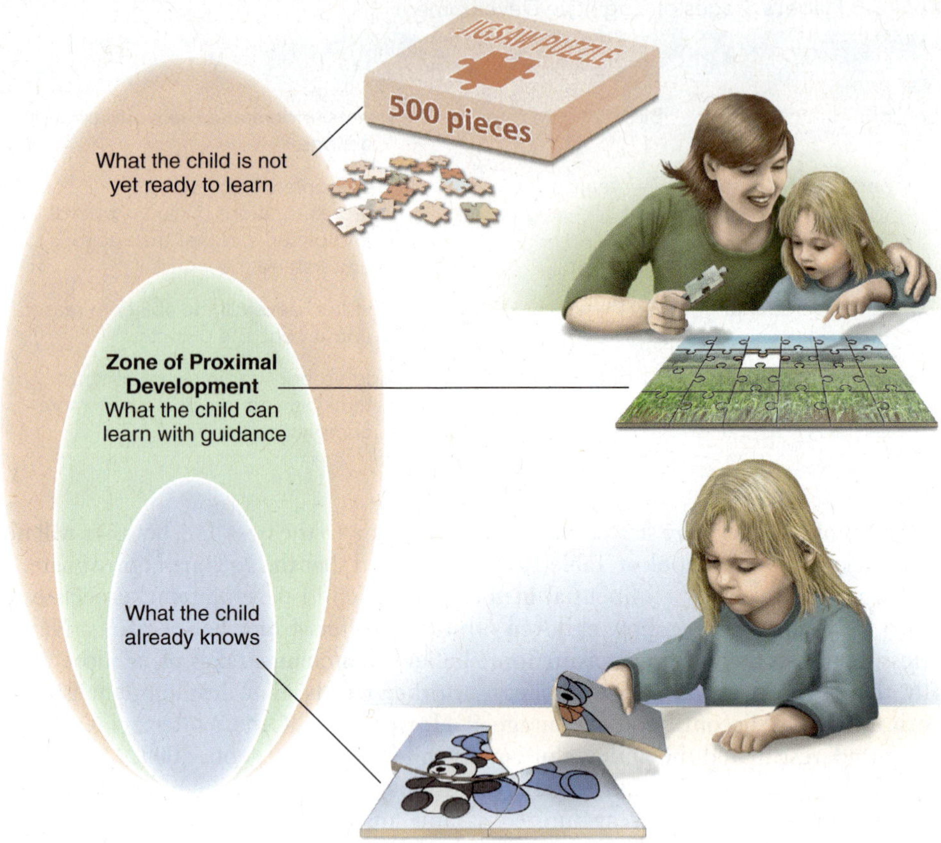


**FIGURE 1.3 The Zone of Proximal Development** Vygotsky introduced the notion of the zone of proximal development, which he defined as the distance between a person's actual developmental level, as determined by independent problem solving, and the higher level that the person can achieve under the guidance of an adult or a more capable peer.

## what if...?

Suppose your 7-year-old cousin is trying to figure out how to complete a 100-piece jigsaw puzzle for the first time. She dumps the pieces out of the box but then cannot figure out what to do next. Eventually, she selects one piece, looks at it, and then selects another to see if it fits with the first one. When it doesn't, she puts it back in the pile of pieces. She is quickly getting frustrated and asks for your help. What would you do to scaffold her actions as she works on the puzzle?

Developmental psychologists have generally embraced Vygotsky's theory. It provides a broad view of development by considering the importance of the social and cultural context. It is also appealing because of its emphasis on the role of instruction in the learning process. It is a broad theory, however, and so is somewhat vague about how children actually develop. Despite the importance attributed to instruction from teachers and more skilled peers, for example, the nature of how instruction actually advances children's development has not been fully described (Eun, Knotek, & Heining-Boynton, 2008).

### Information Processing Theory

The information processing perspective is often said to have taken its inspiration from the way computers work. Like computers, our brains receive input, process it, store it, and produce output (see Figure 1.4). Probably the most productive way of

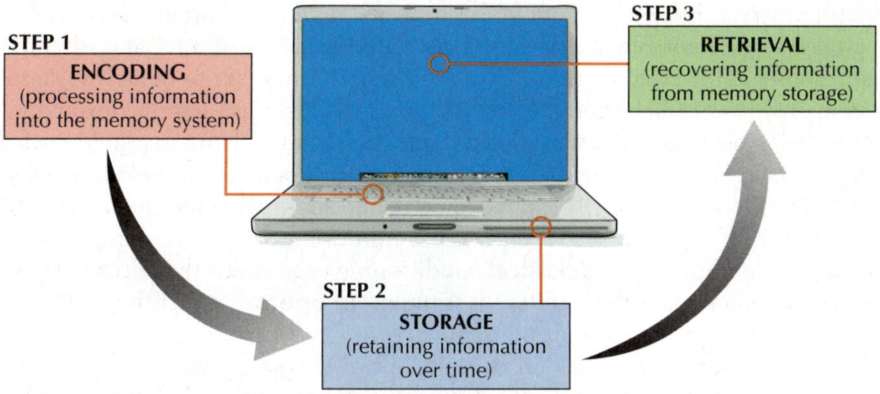


**FIGURE 1.4 The Information Processing Model** The information processing model can be said to have taken its inspiration from the way computers work. Like computers, our brains receive input, process it, store it, and produce output.



understanding **information processing theory** is to think of it as an attempt to explain what's going on in the human mind as it acquires, processes, retains, and comprehends information. Information processing theorists focus on *what* information children represent; *how* children represent, store, and retrieve this information; *how* these representations guide their behaviors; and *which* mechanisms lead to changes in these processes across development (Munakata, 2006). (Chapter 12 presents a more detailed discussion of attention and memory.)

Information processing theory offers specific and practical guidance to teachers and others who are helping children to learn, one of its key benefits. It provides a useful framework for analyzing the various processes involved in learning new information and for understanding difficulties children encounter in learning. Another advantage of this theory is the rigorous scientific approach favored by information processing researchers.

## Learning Theories

*Learning theory* is a general term for theories that focus on the importance of learned behaviors in development. The leading proponents of the learning tradition in psychology are John Watson and B. F. Skinner, who introduced and developed behaviorism, and Albert Bandura, who created social learning theory. As you will see, all these theorists describe development more in terms of nurture rather than nature. In addition, all tend to view development as continuous.

### Behaviorism

**Behaviorism** emphasizes observable behavior. The roots of behaviorism can be found in the work of Ivan Pavlov (1849–1936), a Russian physiologist. Pavlov (1927) was originally studying digestive processes in dogs when he noticed that the dogs salivated when a lab worker brought them food. Later he observed that the dogs also salivated when the lab worker was present even when he brought no food. The dogs had learned to associate one stimulus (food) with another (lab worker) and to respond in the same way to both. Pavlov later produced the same association using food and the sound of a bell. This association came to be known as **classical conditioning**.

The American psychologist John B. Watson (1878–1958) was intrigued with Pavlov's work. Watson believed that classical conditioning answered all our questions about human development and behavior. In Watson's eyes, humans are bundles of stimulus-response connections. He claimed that if adults turn their attention to infants early enough, the infants can become anything the adults want (Watson, 1930). He demonstrated this by teaching an infant, named Little Albert, to fear rats and other furry animals, even though Albert did not initially fear them. Watson did this by

**Information processing theory** A perspective that attempts to explain the mechanisms by which the human mind acquires, processes, retains, and comprehends information.

**Behaviorism** A theoretical orientation that emphasizes learning and focuses on observable behavior.

**Classical conditioning** A type of learning in which a neutral stimulus (such as the sound of a bell) comes to evoke a response (such as salivation) originally evoked by a different stimulus (such as the presence of food).

Nina Leen/Time & Life Pictures/Getty Images, Inc.

B. F. Skinner, in his theory of operant conditioning, proposed that organisms—including people—learn or change their behavior based on the consequences of that behavior.

associating furry animals with loud noises, unusual masks, and other events that naturally evoked fear. Eventually, Little Albert also developed fear of furry animals, a conditioned response. However, Watson's view of learning turned out to be far too simple to explain many forms of behavior. (Note that the experiment just described would not be approved today, because it is now considered unethical to cause harm to a child, such as by making a child fearful. You will read more about the ethics of research later in this chapter.)

B. F. Skinner (1904–1990) expanded Watson's ideas with his theory of operant conditioning (1953, 1974, 1983). Operant conditioning is a more complex concept than classical conditioning. In classical conditioning, a stimulus that already leads to a response is simply replaced by a different stimulus. In **operant conditioning,** behavior is learned or changed based on its consequences.

Operant conditioning relies on the concept of *reinforcement*, a consequence of a response that makes the original behavior more likely to occur in the future. Skinner identified two types of reinforcement: positive and negative. *Positive reinforcement* refers to a consequence *presented* after a response that makes that response more likely to happen in the future. For example, 4-year-old Natalia picks up her toys, and her father praises her warmly. His praise reinforces her action positively and makes it more likely that she will repeat picking up her toys in the future. *Negative reinforcement* refers to a consequence *removed* after a response that makes a desired response more likely to appear in the future (Skinner, 1953). This occurs, for example, when a teacher tells a class that if students complete all their assignments, they will not be required to take a test. In this example, the suggestion of the removal of the test makes it more likely that students will complete their assignments. (For a discussion of some practical applications of reinforcement, see the discussion of spanking in Chapter 10.)

Negative reinforcement is not the same as punishment. *Punishment* refers to an aversive action occurring after an undesired response (see Figure 1.5). For example, a teenager who stays out beyond an agreed-upon time might be punished by being "grounded." Thus, one type of punishment, called *negative punishment,* involves the removal of something that the person being punished finds pleasant, such as going out with friends. In contrast, *positive punishment* involves the introduction of something a person finds unpleasant; for example, instead of being grounded, the teenager might be given additional chores.

As suggested earlier, Skinner's version of behaviorism was very influential in the mid- to late- 20th century, and it is still important today in many areas. For example, operant conditioning principles are used effectively in both educational and therapeutic settings. One approach derived from this theory, *applied behavioral analysis*, is often used to teach children with autism spectrum disorders (Ahearn, & Tiger, 2013; Korn-Bursztyn, 2011; Matson, Tureck, Turygin, Beighley, & Rieske, 2012). A common criticism of behaviorism, however, is that behavior is often more complex than this theory

**Operant conditioning** A form of learning in which a behavior elicits certain consequences, which in turn make the behavior more or less likely to occur in the future.

**The action causes the child's behavior to.....**

| | | Increase | Decrease |
|---|---|---|---|
| **A child engages in a behavior. Afterward, something is...** | **Added** | **Positive Reinforcement** Parents praise a child who picks up toys. | **Positive Punishment** Parents scold a child who rides a bike without a helmet. |
| | **Taken Away** | **Negative Reinforcement** Teacher lets students who complete all homework in a unit skip the unit quiz. | **Negative Punishment** Parents "ground" or take away the privilege to go out, from a teen who stays out past curfew. |

FIGURE 1.5 **Reinforcement and Punishment** Positive reinforcement is a consequence presented after a response that makes that response more likely to repeat in the future. Negative reinforcement is a consequence removed after a response that makes a desired response more likely to repeat in the future. In contrast, punishment is an aversive action that occurs after an undesired response.

suggests (Seligman, 1970). Therefore, many aspects of behavior, such as the development of language, cannot be adequately explained according to its principles. Also, this theory fails to explain individual differences in behavior and disregards cultural influences (Escala, & Sánchez, 1977).

### Social Learning Theory

Albert Bandura's (b. 1925) **social learning theory** broadened Skinner's ideas by introducing the idea of *modeling*. Bandura's expansion of learning theory has made it more powerful as a way to understand children's behavior. In Bandura's view, a child can learn a behavior by observing it in someone else (the *model*). He called this *observational learning*. Indeed, learning occurs through observing others even when the observers do not imitate the model's responses immediately and even when they obtain no reinforcement (Bandura & Walters, 1963).

Jon Brenneis/Time & Life Pictures/Getty Images, Inc.

Albert Bandura's social learning theory introduced the idea of *modeling*, in which a child learns a behavior by observing it in someone else—the model.

In some of his more recent work, Bandura (1997, 2006) has focused on *self-efficacy*, one's belief that one can succeed in a given situation. Bandura's work in this area testifies to the power of children's belief that their actions will produce desired goals. A feeling of mastery and competence, based on successful performance, is a powerful motivational device that improves children's performance and makes them more willing to face riskier challenges (Fast et al., 2011; Mercer, Nellis, Martinez, & Kirk, 2011; Wang & Barrett, 2013). We discuss this work further in Chapter 10.

## Ethological Theories

Still another perspective emphasizes biological forces in development. This perspective was stimulated by the work of European zoologists during the mid-20th century. In a well-known experiment, Konrad Lorenz (1903–1989) studied the behavior of geese, which follow their mothers as soon as they hatch. Do the goslings actually know their mother? Lorenz (1965) developed a creative experiment to answer this question. He separated the eggs laid by one goose into two groups. The first group remained with the mother goose while the second was put into an incubator. When the goslings in the first group hatched, they followed their mother, as predicted. When the goslings from the second group hatched, the first moving object they saw was Lorenz, and they began to follow him. Even when the two groups were put together, the first group continued to follow the mother goose and the second continued to follow Lorenz. He termed this process **imprinting**, which is an innate form of rapid learning that involves attachment.

Nina Leen/Time Life Pictures/Getty Images

Konrad Lorenz discovered that baby geese follow the first moving object they see after they hatch—in this instance, Lorenz himself. He called this innate form of learning *imprinting*.

Lorenz believed that imprinting occurs during a **critical period**, a specific period of time during which a particular type of development must happen. If the development does not occur during the critical period, it will not occur at all. As you will see in later chapters, in humans there is little evidence of critical periods after birth. There are, however, **sensitive periods**, times when a particular experience (or lack of it) has a profound effect on development (Bagner, Pettit, Lewinsohn, & Seeley, 2010; Bruer, 2001). For example, the first few years of life appear to be a sensitive period for language development. During these years, most children readily develop the language to which they are regularly exposed. In contrast, children who have little or no exposure to language in their first few years have difficulty developing it fully at a later age (Newport, 1990).

How does Lorenz's insight into the behavior of geese relate to humans? John Bowlby (1907–1990) studied how human infants relate to their caregiver during their first few months of life. Drawing from Lorenz's work, he proposed that infants have a sensitive period for bonding with their caregivers. Bowlby (1980, 1989) proposed that

**Social learning theory** Bandura's version of learning theory, which emphasizes the role of modeling, or observational learning, in behavior.

**Imprinting** An innate form of rapid learning that involves attachment.

**Critical period** A particular period of time in which a biological or environmental event must happen, for typical development to occur.

**Sensitive period** A portion of time during which a particular experience (or lack of it) has a strong effect on development.

**Bioecological model** Bronfenbrenner's approach, in which the individual develops within and is affected by a set of nested environments, from the family to the entire culture.

**Microsystem** In Bronfenbrenner's bioecological model, the innermost environmental level (for example, home and school).

**Mesosystem** In Bronfenbrenner's bioecological model, the relationship among microsystems (for example, the interactions between home and school).

**Exosystem** In Bronfenbrenner's bioecological model, a system in which the developing child is not actually present but that influences the child's development (for example, social policies created by the government).

**Macrosystem** In Bronfenbrenner's bioecological model, the outermost environmental level, consisting of the child's culture and society.

**Chronosystem** In Bronfenbrenner's bioecological model, changes in ecological systems that are caused by time.

if the relationship between the caregiver and infant is positive during that period, the child will develop in an optimal way; but if the relationship is not positive, the child will likely have difficulty with social relationships later in life. We discuss this idea more in Chapter 7.

## Systems Theories

So far, we have looked at four kinds of child development theories: psychoanalytic, cognitive, learning, and ethological. Of these, only Vygotsky's theory of sociocultural development takes much account of the influence of society and culture on development. We turn next to a more interactionist view in which children's development is seen as a result of interacting systems.

Systems operate according to particular principles. One of these principles is that the same developmental task can be reached by different routes. As you will see in Chapter 5, for example, not all toddlers learn to go down stairs in the same way, but they all do learn to go down stairs. A second principle is that when change occurs in one system, changes occur in other systems. The result is a new type of organization. For example, when children are first learning to write words, they focus on which letters make up each word. As they become practiced at writing words, a cognitive skill, they use writing to communicate with others and to learn about the ideas and feelings of others, a psychosocial skill. Thus, both systems have been changed.

Here we discuss two systems theories: Bronfenbrenner's bioecological model and developmental systems theory. The first focuses on the contexts that affect children's lives and, in turn, their development. The second places more emphasis on how children's genetic and biological makeup interacts with these various contexts. Both approaches, however, view children as agents in their own development. They are not simply passive recipients of the effects of the environment; rather, they interact with the environment (including other people) in ways that affect their development.

### The Bioecological Model

Uri Bronfenbrenner (1917–2005) proposed a **bioecological model** of development in which individuals interact with five environmental systems. Bronfenbrenner visualized the environment as a set of nested structures, one inside the other, centered on the child, as shown in Figure 1.6:

- The **microsystem** includes the immediate settings in which children are nurtured and learn (including, for example, home, school, and peer groups).
- The **mesosystem** is the system of relationships among microsystems (for example, the interactions between home and school).
- The **exosystem** includes settings in which the child is not actually present but which influence a child's development. School boards are one example of such settings, as they enact social policies constructed at the federal, state, and local levels that affect children's experiences in schools. We discuss some of the most important of these social policies throughout this text.
- The **macrosystem** is the subculture and culture in which the child lives and which influence the child through broad social customs, attitudes, ideology, values, and so on.
- The **chronosystem** represents the passage of time. This element of Bronfenbrenner's model reminds us that changes occur in the other systems as time passes and the child grows and develops. For example, peers exert little influence on infants but a great deal on adolescents, so as time passes the influence of the microsystem of peers on the child expands.

Each system affects how the child develops, but the systems do not act independently. Rather, development emerges from the interactions *among* the systems (Bronfenbrenner & Morris, 2006). Furthermore, in later versions of his model,

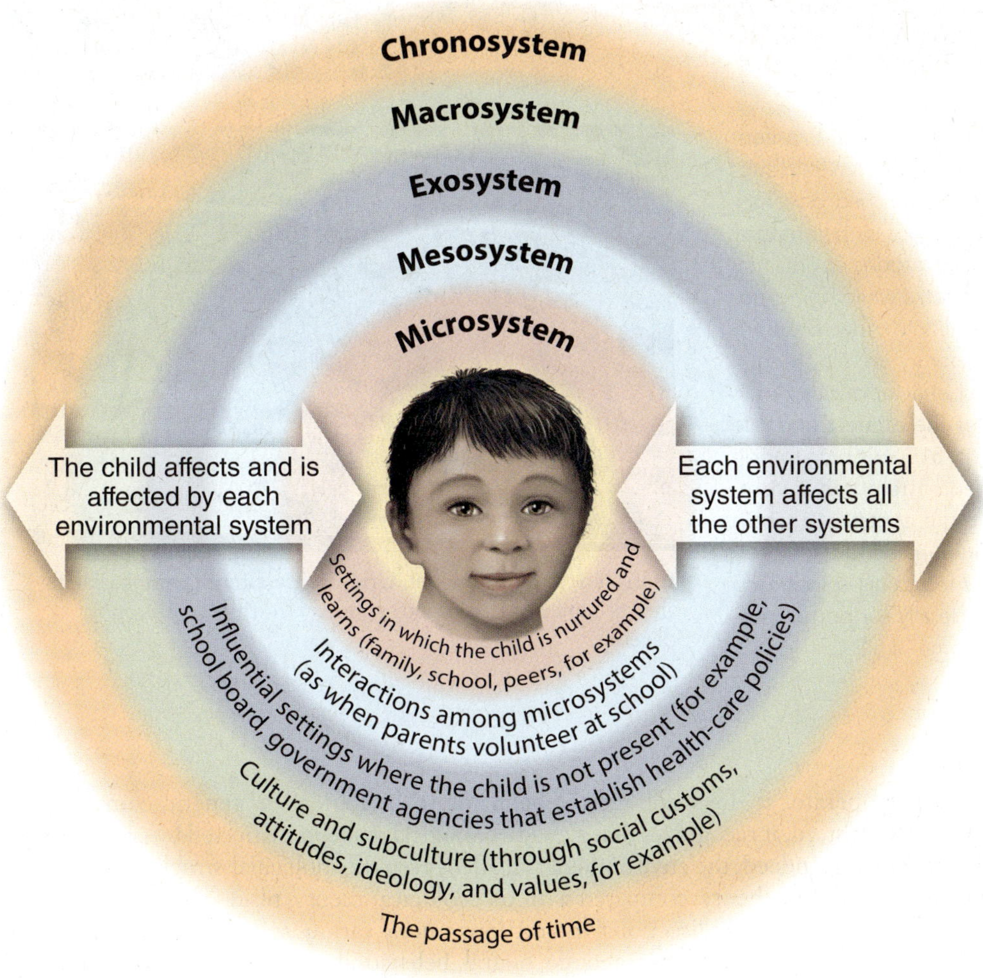


**FIGURE 1.6 The Bioecological Model** Bronfenbrenner visualized the environment as a set of nested structures centered on the child. Each element, including the child, affects and is affected by all the others.

Bronfenbrenner also discussed the child's own biological makeup (Bronfenbrenner & Morris, 2006), although the environmental contexts maintain a predominant role in this model (Gauvain & Parke, 2010).

Bronfenbrenner has given us a rich and complex vision of children's development. In particular, his model has emphasized examining the combination of *person*, *context*, and *process* to understand how children develop. In recent years, his theory has become increasingly important as developmental psychologists have become more interested in investigating cultural influences on development and in understanding how environmental differences affect children's well-being. His theory cannot be fully tested, however, due to its complexity. Instead, it is useful as a way to understand the many influences on children's development. (For more about Urie Bronfenbrenner, see the Focus On feature.)

## Developmental Systems Theory

**Developmental systems theory** is a relatively new area based on the work of several theorists, including Gilbert Gottlieb (1997; Gottlieb, Wahlsten, & Lickliter, 2006), Richard Lerner (2006), and Arnold Sameroff (2009, 2010). Developmental systems theory is similar to the bioecological model in its recognition of the importance of multiple contexts in affecting children's development, but it differs from the bioecological model in at least two ways. First, it places more emphasis on the way biological

**Developmental systems theory** A theory emphasizing reciprocal interactions between the individual and multiple levels of the individual's environment; work based on developmental systems theory that examines interactions at four levels: genetic, neural, behavioral, and environmental.

## Focus On: Urie Bronfenbrenner

In evaluating child development research, Urie Bronfenbrenner offered a crucial criticism that changed the field substantially. He argued that most researchers in child development studied children in artificial conditions, not in their natural daily lives. Children were brought into laboratories at universities, where they were asked to complete tasks while being observed or assessed by researchers they didn't know. Bronfenbrenner claimed that "much of contemporary developmental psychology is the science of the strange behavior of children in strange situations with strange adults for the briefest possible periods of time" (Bronfenbrenner, 1977, p. 513). His bioecological model derived from such concerns and attempted to remedy them by placing a greater focus on the contexts in which children live. He had a special interest in enhancing the development of children living in poverty. This led to his cofounding of the national Head Start program, a federally supported preschool program for children from low-income families.

*Cornell University Photography*

In his bioecological model, Urie Bronfenbrenner emphasized the influence of the various contexts in which children develop.

systems operate. It does not reduce behavior to biological or genetic components, however. Instead, it recognizes that a child's biological makeup is affected by environmental influences. Indeed, the environment can affect even the molecular structure of a child's cells. Second, this theory, compared with bioecological theory, places more emphasis on *transactions*, which are bidirectional interactions among various systems. The theory identifies interactions at four levels: genetic, neural, behavioral, and environmental. Transactions begin to affect children's development very early in life. As a result of these constant transactions, all of us—children, adolescents, and adults—experience continual reorganization as we move through the life cycle (Lerner, 2006; Sameroff, 2009).

The developmental systems approach has stimulated much current work on gene-environment interactions. For example, some individuals have a particular gene associated with the development of depression, but not all of them become depressed as adolescents or adults; instead, they tend to become depressed only when they experience certain levels of stress (Caspi et al., 2003). Therefore, neither the presence of the gene nor the presence of stress alone predicts depression; their interaction does. We discuss this approach in greater detail in several later chapters.

Developmental systems theory is a general theory and, like bioecological theory, is difficult to test as a whole due to its complexity. Nevertheless, the idea that systems connect to each other in different ways and reorganize throughout development is a powerful one that we discuss throughout this text.

### ✓ CHECK YOUR PROGRESS

1. What are some differences between Freud's and Erikson's theories of development?
2. Explain the difference between assimilation and accommodation according to Piaget.
3. How does scaffolding relate to the ZPD from the perspective of Vygotsky?
4. What is a major difference in the way children's development is viewed from the perspectives of learning theories and ethological theories?
5. Give an example of each of the systems affecting a child's development according to bioecological theory.

## Asking Questions, Examining Answers

**[ KEY QUESTION ] 4. What specific research methods do psychologists use to learn about children's development?**

As you have just read, theoretical perspectives help guide us in understanding how children develop. Psychologists use theory as they formulate the important questions to research, but they also use the results of research to test and advance theory. For example, researchers studying Piaget's theory have often found that children understand certain concepts about objects and abstract concepts much earlier than Piaget suggested (Baumard, Mascaro, & Chevallier, 2012), an issue we discuss in later chapters. These research findings have led to refinements in Piaget's theory. Thus, theory and research work together in advancing our knowledge of child development.

In this section, we discuss how psychologists conduct research. By research, we mean *empirical* investigations, systematic approaches that can be verified and replicated. We begin by discussing the scientific method. We follow by describing how researchers design their studies and gather data. The research discussed in these parts of the section generally involves *quantitative data*, data that can be converted into numbers. Some research, in contrast, yields *qualitative data*, information expressed in words. We discuss this type of research later in the section. Next, we consider how research findings are reported. We conclude with a discussion of ethical issues regarding research on children and adolescents.

### The Scientific Method

Most studies in child development follow the scientific method, which is a standard way of conducting studies in all scientific fields. The scientific method follows six steps:

1. Formulate a question, usually based on a theoretical perspective.
2. Develop a *hypothesis*, or possible explanation, about the question (usually in the form of a prediction).
3. Choose a method for testing the hypothesis.
4. Analyze the data collected by the method to test the hypothesis.
5. Draw conclusions about the hypothesis.
6. Disseminate the results of the study so the study can be replicated or the hypothesis revised.

To illustrate, let's consider some research mentioned earlier in this chapter. Recall the study described previously in which psychologists compared how two groups of students perceived the same photographs (Chua et al., 2005; Norenzayan et al., 2007). In this study, the researchers formulated a question about whether individuals from different cultural groups would focus on the same aspects of photographs. The researchers' hypothesis (prediction) was that they would find differences between American and Chinese students. The method they chose to investigate their hypothesis involved showing all the students the same series of photographs under the same conditions and measuring their eye movements as they looked at them.

All the photographs contained a central object (such as a tiger) and a complex, realistic background (such as a jungle). Studying the eye movements of the students, the researchers found that the Americans focused more on the objects, whereas the Chinese looked more at the background. These results indicate that there are cultural differences in how individuals look at a photograph, and thus support the researchers' hypothesis.

Why might such differences matter? The researchers suggest that such differences in perception might explain what someone remembers about a scene or event.

**Cross-sectional study** A study that compares groups of children of different ages at a single point in time.

**Longitudinal study** A study that follows the same group of children over a substantial period of time.

## Designing Research Studies

Researchers must design their studies based on the specific questions they plan to investigate. This decision involves two issues. First, the researchers must decide whether the participants in their research will be studied at one point or over time. Then they must decide on the specific research design to use.

### Three Approaches to the Study of Age-Related Developmental Differences

One of the first questions child development researchers ask is: Should our study compare children of different ages, or should it follow the same group of children over time? This is an especially important question because child development research often focuses on understanding developmental differences and what accounts for them. Clearly, comparing, say, 5-year-old Ernesto with 10-year-old Kofi might yield different results than comparing what Ernesto was like at 5 with what he is like at 10. There are three major research approaches to studying age-related differences in children: cross-sectional studies, longitudinal studies, and cross-sequential studies.

**Cross-Sectional Studies.** A **cross-sectional study** compares children of different ages. For example, suppose we want to study whether children's patterns of friendship change at different ages. One way to study this is simply to compare and analyze the friendships of 4-year-olds, 7-year-olds, and 10-year-olds. Cross-sectional studies are efficient because they allow researchers to make age-related comparisons with only one sample of data from each age point. They lack the capability, however, to determine how stable individual differences might be or how individual change might occur. For example, do young children who are outgoing have different friendship patterns in adolescence from young children who are shy?

**Longitudinal Studies.** A **longitudinal study** follows the same group of children over a lengthy period of time, often several years. The same elements of development are recorded at specific intervals during the study.

*Everyday stories*

A LONGITUDINAL STUDY OF COMMUNICATION SKILLS One longitudinal study followed a group of children with biologically based disabilities (Hauser–Cram, Warfield, Shonkoff, & Krauss, 2001). The researchers assessed children's communication skills (for example, their ability to communicate with others through talking, using sign language, and writing) at five age points over a 10-year period. They found that, as they expected, the children's communication skills improved over time. They also found that communication skills increased at a greater rate for children whose mothers had interacted with them in more positive ways during early childhood. This finding suggests that paths of development (that is, patterns of change over time) may differ for children based on the ways mothers interact with them when they are young.

Because they involve following the same participants over time, longitudinal studies are usually more time-consuming than cross-sectional ones. They may take many years to complete and involve the complexities of finding and assessing the same individuals over that period of time. They may also suffer from *cohort effects*. A cohort is a group of people of the same age growing up during the same time period. Sometimes large-scale events—such as a war, famine, natural disasters, economic changes, and even technological advances—can affect an entire cohort, but the effects are not known unless the cohort can be compared with a similar cohort growing up at a different time period. That said, longitudinal studies, do offer two advantages over cross-sectional studies: (1) They enable researchers to assess whether children stay the same or change in relation to particular characteristics, such as skills in communicating. (2) They allow researchers to examine hypotheses about what might predict change to occur—for example, mother-child interactions.

**Cross-sequential study** A study that combines the cross-sectional and longitudinal approaches. In a cross-sequential study, two or more age groups are tested at two or more points in time.

**Cross-Sequential Studies.** Psychologists sometimes combine longitudinal and cross-sectional approaches into a single study called a **cross-sequential study.** The framework is similar to a cross-sectional study in that it involves studying groups of children of different ages—for example, three groups of children, at ages 4, 7, and 10. It is like a longitudinal design in that it involves following those children for several years (see Figure 1.7).

An advantage of this approach over a longitudinal study is that it can take fewer years yet answer the types of questions examined in both longitudinal and cross-sectional studies. In the preceding example, suppose you are interested in learning about children's tendency to be shy or outgoing. You could study each group of children for only six years but still produce information on children from ages 4 to 16 (a span of 12 years). If you are interested in examining individual differences, you

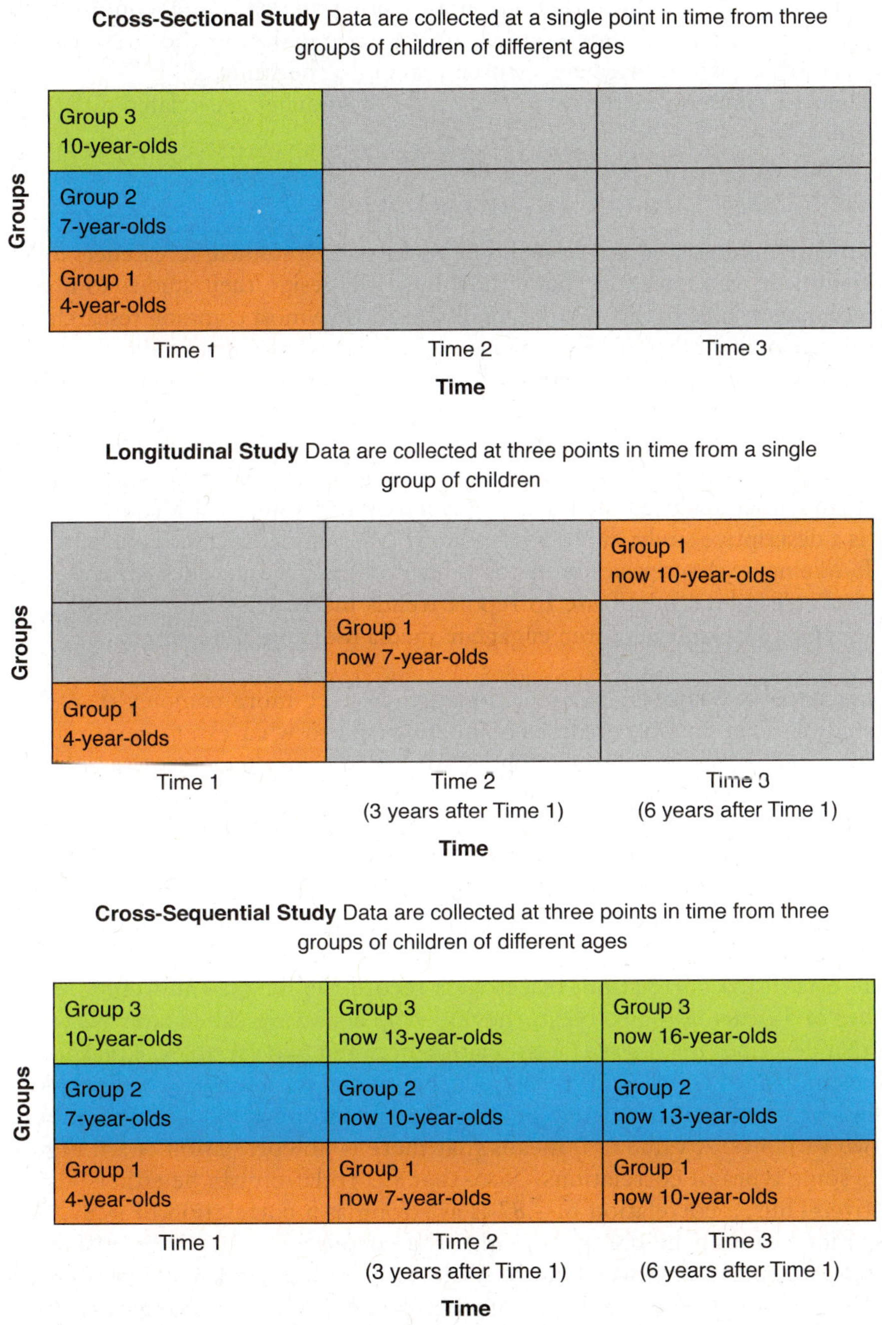


**FIGURE 1.7 Three Research Designs** Cross-sectional, longitudinal, and cross-sequential studies represent three different ways to make age comparisons among research participants. (Gray areas in the figures indicate times when no data are collected.)

**Table 1.7** Ways of Studying Age-Related Differences in Children

| Approach | Description | Strengths | Weaknesses |
|---|---|---|---|
| Cross-sectional | Children of different specific age groups are compared. | Efficient; less costly than the other two approaches; can investigate age-group comparisons. | Cannot investigate how individual children change. |
| Longitudinal | Children of one initial age group are followed over time. | Can track how children change and investigate predictors of change. | Expensive; cannot detect cohort effects. |
| Cross-sequential | Children of different specific age groups are followed over time. | More efficient than longitudinal approaches; can investigate how children change, as well as age-group and cohort differences. | More expensive than a cross-sectional study. |

could ask whether a child who is shy at age 4 is also shy at ages 7 and 10. If you are interested in making age comparisons, you could see whether children are more outgoing at certain ages. Another advantage is that you can study cohort effects by comparing children who, for example, turned age 7 during the first year of the study with those who turned age 7 three years into the study.

Table 1.7 summarizes the three main ways of studying age-related differences in children.

## Research Designs Using Quantitative Data

Beyond determining how age-related differences will be studied, researchers following the scientific method need to choose how they will design their studies to obtain the most accurate results. In this section, we discuss the five most common research designs in child development that make use of quantitative data: descriptive studies, correlational studies, experimental studies, quasi-experimental studies, and microgenetic studies.

**Descriptive Studies.** Descriptive studies simply record behavior. They do not aim to discover what causes the behavior. For example, earlier in this chapter, we cited a recent study that analyzed media use by children ages 8 to 18 (Rideout et al., 2010). This is a descriptive study, as it documents the types of media children of various ages use. It, like many descriptive studies, is valuable because it provides general information that researchers might use to report trends in behavior and to develop future studies about why some children engage in media use more than others.

**Correlational Studies.** Correlational studies are more complex than descriptive studies. They involve analyses of whether and to what extent certain variables are associated. *Variables*, in psychological studies, are the characteristics or behaviors that are being studied. Associations between variables allow us to make predictions. For example, suppose we know of two 5-year-old boys, Pedro and Eric, and we know that Pedro is taller than Eric. Now suppose we need to make a prediction about which one weighs more, without knowing anything else about them. To make this prediction, we can use the fact that a child's height and weight are often *correlated*, or associated.

To establish a correlation, researchers record the height and weight of a large number of 5-year-old boys. Next, they develop a statistic called a *correlation coefficient* that describes the degree of association between two variables. The correlation coefficient ranges from –1.00 to +1.00; the higher the numerical correlation, regardless of whether it is positive or negative, the stronger the association between the two variables. A value of 0 means that there is no correlation at all. Figure 1.8 shows some types of correlations. Note that a correlation can be either positive or negative. Thus, a correlation of –.87 is as strong as a correlation of +.87. For the association between height and weight, the correlation is positive, which means that taller people tend to weigh more. What is an example of a negative correlation? Research has identified a negative correlation between maternal cigarette smoking

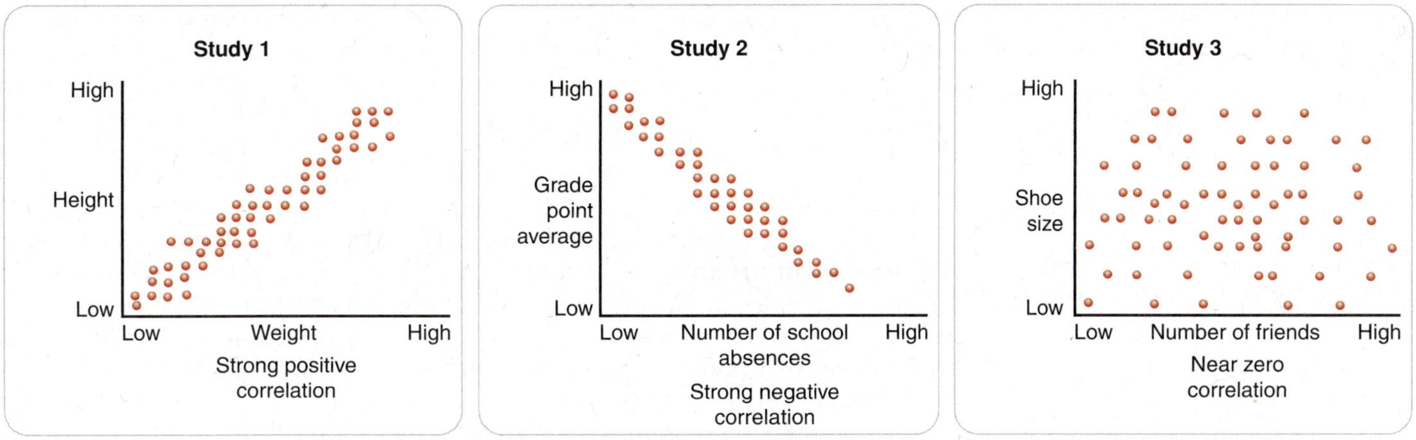


**FIGURE 1.8 Examples of Correlations** The graphs show three different types of correlation between scores on variable A (say, height) and variable B (say, weight). The variables display a strong positive correlation in study 1, a strong negative correlation in study 2, and no correlation in study 3.

Adapted with permission of John Wiley & Sons, Inc., from Comer, R., & Gould, E. (2013). *Psychology Around Us* (2nd ed.). Hoboken, NJ: Wiley, p. 50, Figure 2.5.

during pregnancy and infant birth weight (Centers for Disease Control, 2007; Tayie & Powell, 2012): As the number of cigarettes mothers-to-be smoke during pregnancy increases, children's birth weight decreases (Dalenius, Brindley, Smith, Reinold, Grummer-Strawn, 2012; Kramer et al., 1990).

You may be thinking that the research just mentioned indicates that cigarette smoking during pregnancy *causes* low birth weight. But that is not the case. A correlational study cannot tell us whether one variable causes another, because it cannot rule out other explanations. For example, women who smoke cigarettes during pregnancy may also drink alcohol or make other lifestyle choices that affect their newborns. Based only on the correlational study, we just can't tell. Thus, as you read about studies in which correlations have been found, keep in mind that there may be multiple explanations for that correlation. It is also important to keep in mind that correlation does not equal causation.

## what if...?

A friend of yours really enjoys exercising, although you exercise only grudgingly. He makes many claims about the value of exercise, including arguing that it improves his grades. He decides to do a study to investigate this hypothesis. He creates an online survey for college students in which he asks a series of questions, including the number of hours each respondent exercises each week and his or her grade point average. Using the responses he receives, he calculates a correlation between these two variables and finds it to be +.30, which means that students who reported exercising more also reported having higher grades. He shows you these results and says, "See! That proves my point. If you exercise more, you will get higher grades, so you better start exercising." What do you say to him?

**Experimental Studies.** The only way researchers can study causation is through an experimental study. An *experiment* is a carefully controlled study in which the variable of interest is manipulated while other factors are held constant. Among experimental studies, the **randomized controlled trial** is considered the "gold standard." In this type of study, researchers randomly assign individuals to groups. One group, called the *experimental group*, is exposed to the manipulated variable of interest, while the other, called the *control group*, is not. If the researchers then observe differences between the groups, they can assume that the manipulated variable caused these differences.

Let's consider some of the elements of the randomized controlled trial. First, what does it mean to assign individuals to groups randomly? Random assignment simply means that every person in the pool of possible participants has an independent and

**Randomized controlled trial** An experimental study in which researchers randomly assign individuals to either an experimental or a control group and expose the experimental group to the manipulated variable of interest.

**Independent variable** The variable that a researcher expects to cause changes in the dependent variable.

**Dependent variable** The variable measured to determine whether it is affected by the independent variable in an experiment.

**Quasi-experiment** An experimental study in which participants are not randomly assigned to groups but in which one group is exposed to the manipulated variable of interest.

**Microgenetic studies** Studies in which researchers observe the same children over a short period of time to document how their behavior is changing.

equal chance of being assigned to either group. An independent chance means that the selection of one person from the group will not affect the probability that another person might be selected. This practice is meant to ensure that the two groups are equivalent at the beginning of the study in terms of all other variables that might affect the study's outcome (even those a researcher might not be aware of), since these variables should be randomly distributed across the two groups.

Experiments involve two types of variables: an independent variable and a dependent variable. The **independent variable** is the one that the researchers manipulate. The **dependent variable**, often called the *outcome* or *criterion variable*, is the one that they measure to determine whether it is affected by the independent variable. For example, suppose you are interested in how children develop reading skills. You want to determine whether reading stories with an adult is a more effective intervention in helping children to develop reading skills than watching a video of the same story, another possible intervention. As illustrated in Figure 1.9, the independent variable in this study is assignment to the intervention—either the reading group or the video group. You will want to make sure that children are randomly assigned to these groups. Next, you will implement the experimental *intervention*; that is, you will in some way treat the two groups differently. In this case, you will have parents read a story with their children, or have children watch a video of the same story with their parents. Next, you will assess all the children's reading skills. Then you will analyze the difference in the skills for the children in the two groups. Finally, you will state a conclusion based on the analysis.

If randomized controlled trials are so effective in studying causation, why don't we use this research design all the time? For one thing, it is often not feasible to do so. We cannot randomly expose individuals to many of the conditions that we suspect have significant influences. Specifically, it is not ethical to expose individuals to situations that may harm them, even if we do not have data proving that the situations actually *cause* the harm. For example, we would not want to randomly assign pregnant women to a group and instruct them to smoke cigarettes just to determine whether smoking cigarettes causes low birth weight. We discuss such ethical issues later in this chapter.

**Quasi-Experiments.** Because random assignment is often unethical or infeasible, researchers sometimes use a design called a **quasi-experiment** that has some, but not all, characteristics of experimental studies. In a quasi-experiment, two or more groups are compared on the dependent variable, but participants are not randomly assigned to the groups. For example, suppose you are interested in comparing a new reading curriculum with the one currently used. For practical reasons, you may not be able to randomly assign individual students to the new curriculum model (the independent variable). You may, however, be able to try these approaches in two different existing classrooms. At the end of the study, you would measure reading scores in the two classrooms—the dependent variable.

The problem with this approach is the absence of random assignment. One group may begin the study higher or lower on the dependent variable than the other. Researchers conducting a quasi-experimental study use statistical means to take into account any lack of equivalence in the groups' initial characteristics. Still, such approaches are not as strong as those in which the study starts out with equivalent groups. Thus, we cannot say with certainty that these studies establish cause and effect.

**Microgenetic Studies.** **Microgenetic study** designs provide an in-depth description of a process that involves change (Flynn & Siegler, 2007; Siegler & Jenkins, 1989). In microgenetic studies, researchers observe the same children many times over a short period of time, usually days or weeks, to document their process of change (Benigno, Byrd, McNamara, Berg, & Farrar, 2011). The method is particularly well suited to study detailed changes in children's strategies when they are learning a new task. For example, some researchers have studied how young children learn that plants, like animals, are living things (Opfer & Siegler, 2004). At first, many children think that only some plants are living things—flowers, for example, but not trees. As children learn that all plants need water, can grow, and are capable of movement, they begin to realize that plants are living things. The microgenetic approach is helpful for documenting the

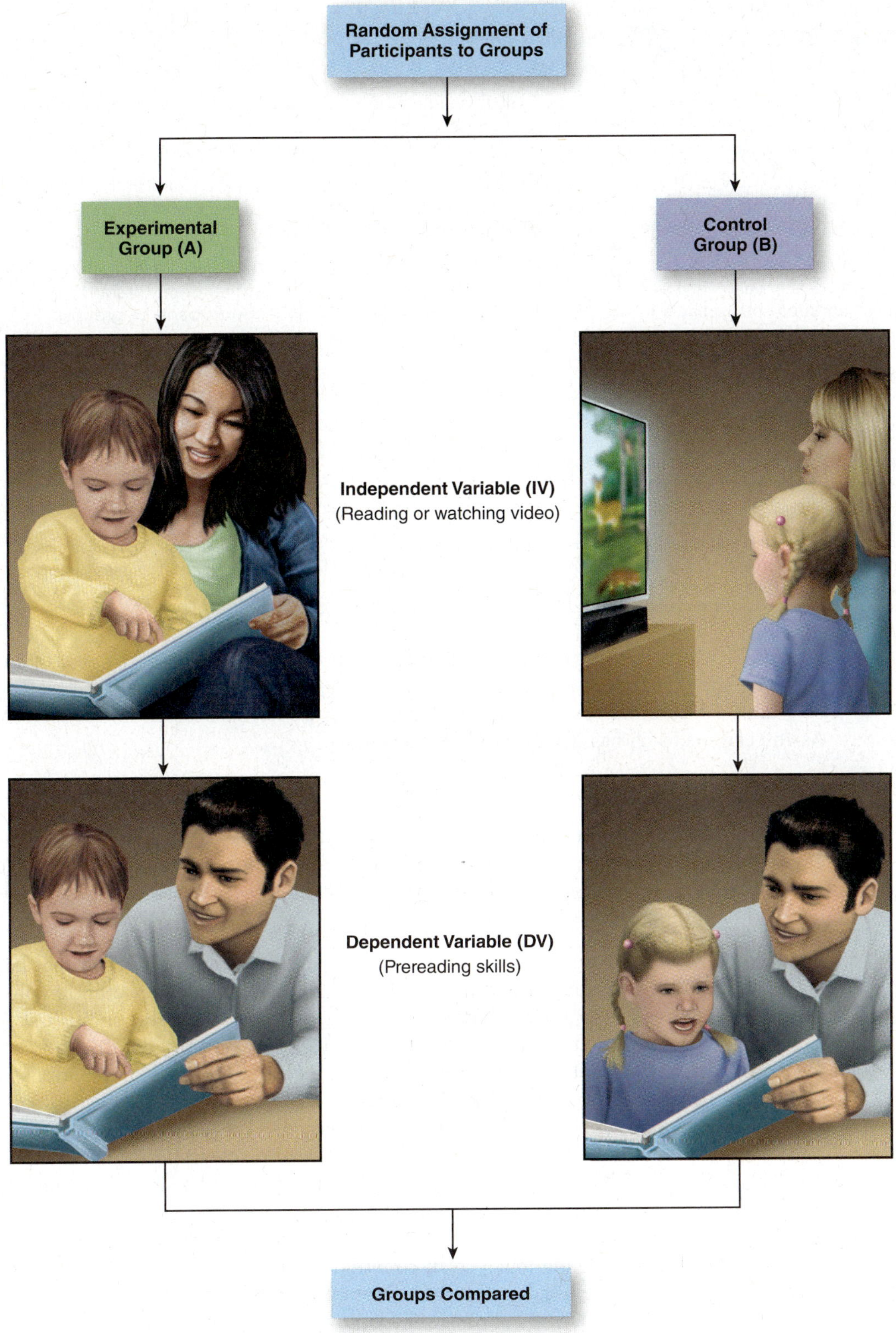


**FIGURE 1.9 Steps in Randomized Control Trials** To test whether reading a story with an adult is more effective in helping children to develop reading skills than watching a video of the same story, researchers would follow these steps: (1) Randomly assign child-parent pairs to group A (parent reads story to child) or group B (parent and child watch video of story). (2) Instruct the groups either to watch the video or read the story. (3) Have the children's reading skills assessed by a researcher who does not know which group the children are in. (4) Compare the results for the two groups. (5) Conclude whether the story-reading group had higher reading skills, as hypothesized.

Adapted with permission of John Wiley & Sons, Inc., from Carpenter, S., & Huffman, K. (2010). *Visualizing Psychology.* Hoboken, NJ: Wiley, p. 17, Figure 1.10.

**Table 1.8** Strengths and Weaknesses of Major Research Designs

| Design | Features | Strengths | Weaknesses |
|---|---|---|---|
| Descriptive study | Records basic information with no attempt to determine how variables relate. | Can provide baseline information about an aspect of development. | Does not provide information that can be used to make predictions. |
| Correlational study | Examines how two or more variables are associated. | Can yield predictions concerning one variable based on information concerning the other variable. | Cannot establish that one variable causes another. |
| Experimental study | Using randomly assigned participants in experimental and control groups, manipulates an independent variable and measures the effect on a dependent variable. | Enables researchers to assess whether the independent variable causes differences in the dependent variable. | Is not always ethical or possible to randomly assign participants to groups. |
| Quasi-experimental study | Examines differences in a dependent variable based on group membership, but does not randomly assign participants to groups. | Enables researchers to examine group differences when random assignment is not possible. | Does not allow causal conclusions to be made about group differences. |
| Microgenetic study | Examines changes in a small group of children over a short period of time. | Provides a detailed analysis of the sequence of developmental change. | Does not reach conclusions about what causes change. |

process by which learning occurs and is useful in providing suggestions of how to enhance learning. However, it does not address the causes of the changes being observed.

Table 1.8 summarizes the research designs that we have discussed in this section. As you can see, each has strengths and weaknesses.

## Research Designs Using Qualitative Data

Although many studies in child development use quantitative data and follow the scientific method, approaches using qualitative data are also important and add valuable information to our understanding of children and families. We discuss two approaches here: ethnographic studies and case studies.

**Ethnographic Studies.** **Ethnography** is a qualitative research approach that has given us important insights into various cultural groups. In general, ethnographic methods are derived from anthropology. Researchers may, for example, conduct open-ended interviews and then write narrative reports summarizing the themes and patterns that they have found. Their aim is to capture the experiences and perceptions of the people being studied and to understand the meaning these people give to daily activities. Ethnographers focus on understanding people's experiences in everyday life, rather than on creating experimental conditions. Because researchers employing an ethnographic approach do not begin with a hypothesis, they are open to exploring and understanding the experiences of individuals in a holistic way.

One example of this type of research was conducted by Barbara Rogoff. Rogoff (2003) studied children living in a Mayan community in Guatemala and detailed how they participated in the everyday routines of community life. In a rich description of the community and its routines, she chronicled how mothers simplified various tasks, like making tortillas, so children of various ages could participate in them. Studies like this one are useful in exploring how the ideologies and values of a cultural group relate to patterns of child rearing. They are usually rich in detail and suggest questions for further analysis. We discuss Rogoff's study further in Chapter 9.

**Case Studies.** The **case study** method is often used to gather in-depth information about a particular individual. A case study combines a range of data sources, such as interviews, test results, and observations. Clinical psychologists often use this method to develop an intervention or treatment plan. Research psychologists might use it to understand individuals with unusual traits or diagnoses. Although case studies have provided

**Ethnography** A qualitative research approach that aims to capture the experiences and perspectives of the people being studied, and to understand the meaning these people give to daily activities.

**Case study** Detailed information gathered about a particular individual.

remarkable insights, they are limited by their focus on a single individual. They lack external validity because we can't generalize from that individual to a whole group.

**Validity** The extent to which an instrument measures what it claims to measure.

**Reliability** The extent to which an instrument produces consistent measurements.

## Collecting Data

Psychologists use a range of techniques to collect data about children's development. Three frequently used approaches are observational studies, self-reports, and assessments.

### Observational Studies

Psychologists often use techniques of observation; that is, they gather information about children by observing what children do. In some cases, psychologists, especially those using ethnography, observe children in a natural setting, such as home or school (Puroila, Estola, & Syrjala, 2012). In other cases, they bring children into the laboratory for observation.

Wherever observation takes place, it is important that it be systematic so it can be replicated. If more than one observer is collecting data, it is essential that all observers collect data in the same way from all participants. Otherwise, of course, the data will not be comparable. One way to keep observation systematic is to use a written form that specifies the information observers should collect. Observers are trained to use the form before the observation takes place. For example, trained observers might use a form to record observations of how parents teach toddlers to put on a jacket. Observational studies like this one often provide findings that relate to children's typical everyday experiences. One weakness of observational studies, however, is that children behave differently when they know they are being observed.

### Self-Reports

You have probably been asked to relate information at some point, perhaps in a school or job application, using the technique of self-report. There are several types of self-reports, including various types of interviews and questionnaires. Let's consider questionnaires here as a common example of a self-report. Psychologists often use questionnaires that have been developed to measure a construct such as self-esteem or behavior problems. Parents may report on young children's attributes in such questionnaires. In middle childhood and adolescence, however, subjects are increasingly asked to complete the questionnaires themselves.

Questionnaires—as well as certain other instruments, such as assessments—are analyzed to make sure that they have good validity and reliability. **Validity** refers to the degree to which an instrument measures what it is intended to measure. If a questionnaire is said to measure children's self-esteem but only asks questions about children's reading skills, it would have poor validity. **Reliability** refers to consistency. A questionnaire might be considered reliable if, say, a child filled it in several times over a period of a few days and gave very similar responses each time.

One problem with self-reports is that individuals sometimes are not completely honest (Bekkers, & Wiepking, 2011; Hoza, Vaughn, Waschbusch, Murray–Close, & McCabe, 2012; Sintov & Prescott, 2011). Children responding to questionnaires may, for example, give the answer they believe will be most socially acceptable to adults. Moreover, as you will read in Chapter 14, adolescents may actually exaggerate such behavior as their level of sexual activity.

© Spencer Grant/Alamy Limited

This psychologist is gathering information about children by observing them in their classroom. Psychologists often use observation in their studies.

### Assessments

Another way to collect data from children is to assess their performance using a test. Assessments are often *standardized*, meaning that they have a uniform set of procedures for administration and scoring. This allows researchers to compare the performance of one child on the assessment with that of another child.

**Table 1.9** Strengths and Weaknesses of Three Methods of Gathering Information

| Method | Description | Strengths | Weaknesses |
|---|---|---|---|
| Observation | Children's behavior is watched and recorded based on pre-determined categories. | Provides a direct source of information about children's typical behavior. | Children may alter their typical behavior when they know they are being observed. |
| Self-report | Participants are asked to report on various aspects of their behavior using interviews or questionnaires. | Allows individuals to present their perspectives on how they think or feel. | Participants sometimes are not truthful or are reluctant to answer certain types of questions. |
| Assessment | Children are asked to perform a task or respond to a set series of questions. | Allows the performance of individuals to be compared. | Children's performance on any assessment may differ from their typical behavior in a natural setting. |

Assessments need to be developed carefully so they are valid. For example, as we discuss in Chapter 12, many psychologists claim that some intelligence tests are not valid because they do not assess all aspects of intelligence. Like questionnaires, assessments also need to be reliable, or consistent. If you assess a child on reading skill today and again tomorrow, you would expect the child's results on the test to be about the same on those two days.

Physiological measures are increasingly being used in conjunction with assessments (Nelson, 2011; Urion, 2009). *Neuroimaging*, like functional magnetic resonance imaging (fMRI), is one type of physiological measure. Researchers use it to construct images of a person's brain and biochemical activity. Neuroimaging is often used in combination with a cognitive assessment to show which parts of the brain have increased activity when undertaking certain tasks (Cédric, Koolschijn, & Crone, 2013; Prat, 2013 Sowell, Thompson, & Toga, 2007; Wilcox, Stubbs, Hirshkowitz, & Boas, 2012).

Table 1.9 summarizes the observation and self-report methods of gathering information.

## Reporting Research Results

After completing a study, it is important that researchers report the results, even when the results do not support their hypotheses. One reason to publish findings from a study is so that others can replicate, or reproduce, and extend that study. In this section, we first look briefly at the publication of research. Next, we consider how researchers summarize the results of an entire set of studies on a particular topic.

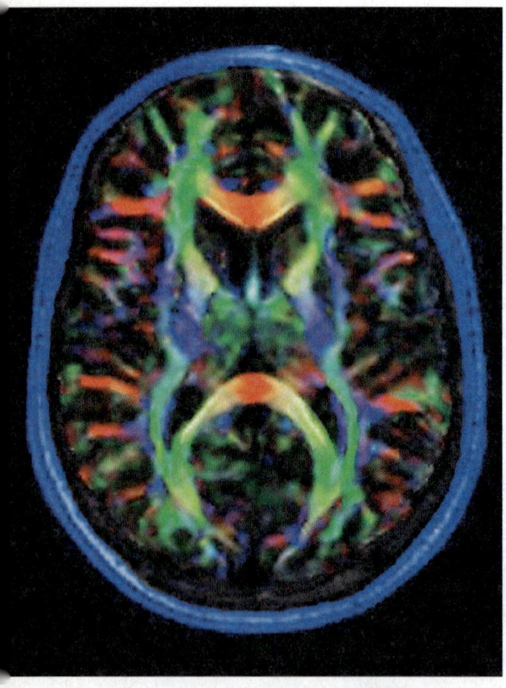

ISM/Phototake

Psychologists today often use neuroimaging techniques, like the fMRI shown here, to investigate which parts of the brain are active during certain tasks. This image shows connections between brain regions.

### Publication of Research Studies

Many research studies are published in journals, published by professional organizations such as the American Psychological Association, the Society for Research in Child Development, the American Educational Research Association, and the American Academy of Pediatrics, to name only a few. Many journals can be accessed online through PsychINFO (for studies in psychology) and MEDLINE (for studies on health) or at the library in most colleges and universities.

Most journals established by professional organizations are overseen by an editorial board of experts who evaluate submitted research articles before sending them on to additional experts for *peer review*. Peer review means than an article is being evaluated by others in the same field of research. Such a review is usually "blind," meaning that the reviewers do not know who wrote the article, a process intended to prevent bias in the review process.

The articles must be written in accordance with a particular structure. First, there is an *abstract*, a brief summary of the article. It is helpful to read the abstract first, to determine whether the article is of interest to you. The *introduction* follows, describing the main questions the research is addressing, along with prior research relevant to those questions. Third is the *methods* section, where the authors describe their research design, participants, and data collection, including the measures they used. Fourth is the *results* section, where the researchers report their analyses of the data. Finally, in the *discussion* section, the researchers offer their conclusions and integrate them with prior research. They also acknowledge limitations of the research, and make suggestions for future research studies on this topic. At the end of the article are the *references*, a list of the bibliographic sources the researchers consulted for the article.

### Summaries of Research Studies

Research journals often contain summaries of research results; we refer to such summaries in this book. The literature review and the meta-analysis are two methods that psychologists use to summarize a group of studies on the same topic.

A *literature review* provides a narrative discussion of the various studies. It summarizes what is known, discusses gaps in the research evidence, describes the limitations of the various studies (such as use of correlational rather than experimental designs), and offers suggestions for future work. Such reviews are useful because they provide an opportunity to learn about an entire area of research. Even a well-constructed literature review, however, is limited by the quality of the studies reviewed.

A *meta-analysis* is similar to the literature review in that it focuses on the compilation of a series of studies on a particular topic. It differs from a literature review in that it involves combining the quantitative results of each study and results in a quantitative summary of the entire set of studies. Meta-analysis has the advantage of providing quantitative information on a large group of studies. Like the literature review, however, it is limited by the quality of the individual studies themselves.

## Ethical Considerations Policy

Any psychologist who conducts research on individuals needs to consider ethical issues. This is especially true when the research involves children. Researchers need to consider both the potential risks and the potential benefits to children and make sure that the benefits outweigh the risks. Two professional organizations, the American Psychological Association (2002) and the Society for Research in Child Development (2007), are among many that have developed guidelines for ethical practices. Three of the most important principles are the following:

1. *Do no harm.* Be sure that the research will not harm children, either physically or psychologically.
2. *Obtain informed consent.* All participants should be told about all aspects of the research in language that is appropriate for them. When children are participants, parents need to be informed and asked to approve their child's participation, in writing. When children are old enough to understand the purpose of the research, generally around 7 years of age, assent needs to be gained from them, too (Sibley, Sheehan, & Pollard, 2012). Children also need to be told that they can quit the research project or refuse to participate in any part of it at any time without consequence.
3. *Ensure the confidentiality of information gathered from participants.* Individual anonymity must be preserved in all writings about the research process or findings.

The importance of conducting research in ethical ways has led universities and hospitals to convene committees, called institutional review boards (IRBs), that review research for ethical concerns. Research at colleges or universities must be approved by the IRB before faculty or students may conduct any aspect of a study. IRBs also require researchers to report any negative consequences that occur during the research process. The report of such consequences may cause the IRB to require that the research be stopped or changed significantly.

### ✓ CHECK YOUR PROGRESS

1. In what ways is a cross-sequential design preferable to either a cross-sectional or longitudinal design?
2. Explain the following statement: "Correlation does not mean causation."
3. Why might a researcher need to conduct a quasi-experimental study rather than an experimental study?
4. Why is it important to select measures that are both valid and reliable?
5. Describe three principles for conducting ethical research studies.

# CHAPTER SUMMARY

## Children and Their Development

**[ KEY QUESTION ] 1.** What are some of the key issues in understanding development?

- Developmental psychologists have been careful to distinguish development from change. Development is change that is systematic, organized, and successive in character.
- Developmental psychologists typically divide their analysis into three domains: biological, cognitive, and psychosocial. Interactions among the elements of these domains are generally complex and multidirectional.
- Age alone reveals little about the underlying mechanisms of development.
- Two of the most important and persistent issues in development have concerned nature-nurture interaction and continuity versus discontinuity. In the case of nature and nurture, most psychologists today agree that these two critical forces interact at every level.

## A Child's Journey in the 21st Century

**[ KEY QUESTION ] 2.** How has modern society affected child development and its study?

- Families, and parenting itself, are in a state of flux today. To understand the steady development of children's abilities and accomplishments in the midst of change demands an analysis of the many interactions that are at the heart of the developmental process.
- Research on the influence of families on development has shifted from focusing solely on individual parents to studying the family as a social system.
- The important effect of a child's cultural community on development is widely recognized today. A great deal of research supports the idea that human development is a cultural process.
- Children today live in an expanding technological world, one that reaches into every aspect of development.

## Explaining Development: The Theories

**[ KEY QUESTION ] 3.** How would you describe the major theories of child development?

- In their attempts to explain how children develop, psychologists and others have proposed many and varied theories of development.
- Freud's psychoanalytic theory explains personality development in terms of five psychosexual stages. Erikson's psychosocial theory proposes eight stages of development and focuses on the effects of social interactions. Freud's theories are less influential than there were in the early 20th century, whereas Erikson's ideas remain popular.
- Cognitive theories of development include those of Piaget, Vygotsky, and information processing theorists. Piaget's stage theory of cognitive development describes how children construct knowledge through adaptation and organization. Piaget had a significant influence for many years on studies of children's thinking. Vygotsky was interested in social and cultural influences on development, especially how children construct knowledge with the help of others. This perspective remains important today. Information processing theorists focus on how the human brain receives input, processes it, and produces output. Information processing theory has produced specific and practical guidance in many areas of cognition.
- Learning theories have a long and rich tradition in American psychology. John Watson's ideas about classical conditioning proved too simple to explain much about behavior in children. B. F. Skinner, in contrast, expanded and enriched learning theory by introducing the idea of operant conditioning, in which behavior depends on consequences. Skinner's ideas were very influential in the mid- to late- 20th century, and they are still important today, especially in educational and therapeutic settings. Albert Bandura's social cognitive learning theory broadened Skinner's ideas by introducing the idea of modeling—that is, learning by observing others.
- Bronfenbrenner's bioecological theory of development focuses on how individuals interact with five environmental systems as they develop. In recent years, his ideas have become increasingly important.
- Developmental systems theory focuses on reciprocal interactions between the individual and the environment. Work based on this theory examines interactions at four levels: genetic, neural, behavioral, and environmental. Like bioecological theory, it offers a rich and complex view of development.

## Asking Questions, Examining Answers

**[ KEY QUESTION ] 4.** What specific research methods do psychologists use to learn about children's development?

- When conducting quantitative research, developmental psychologists follow the scientific method, which includes six steps: formulating a question, developing a hypothesis, choosing a method for testing the hypothesis, analyzing the collected data, drawing conclusions about the hypothesis, and disseminating the results.
- In designing a study, researchers must decide how to study age-related differences and which specific research methodology to use. Ways to study age-related differences in children include the cross-sectional, longitudinal, and cross-sequential approaches. The typical research methodologies incorporating quantitative data that are used in developmental psychology are descriptive studies, correlational studies, experimental studies, quasi-experimental studies, and microgenetic studies. Two types of studies that use qualitative data are the ethnographic study and the case study.
- Research information can be gathered in a variety of ways. Three of the most commonly used data collection methods are observational studies, self-reports, and assessments. Summaries of a set of research studies can be presented in a narrative literature review or a meta-analysis, which includes a quantitative analysis of findings. The value of either type of summary depends on the quality of the individual studies being summarized. Researchers must follow a professional code of ethics in conducting all aspects of psychological research.

## KEY TERMS

Behaviorism 23
Bioecological model 26
Case study 36
Chronosystem 26
Classical conditioning 23
Cognitive domain 6
Continuity 8
Critical period 25
Cross-sectional study 30
Cross-sequential study 31
Culture 12
Dependent variable 34
Development 5
Developmental psychology 5
Developmental systems theory 27
Discontinuity 8
Enculturation 12
Ethnography 36
Exosystem 26
Imprinting 25
Independent variable 34
Information processing theory 23
Longitudinal study 30
Macrosystem 26
Mesosystem 26
Microgenetic studies 34
Microsystem 26
Nature 8
Nurture 8
Operant conditioning 24
Physical domain 5
Psychoanalytic theory 16
Psychosocial domain 6
Psychosocial theory 18
Quasi-experiment 34
Randomized controlled trial 33
Reliability 37
Sensitive period 25
Social learning theory 25
Sociocultural theory 21
Stage theories 8
Validity 37

## CRITICAL THINKING QUESTIONS

1. **Children and Their Development.** Describe and use examples to explain what is meant by the claim that "development implies change but change does not necessarily imply development."
2. **A Child's Journey in the 21st Century.** Analyze ways in which the use of media technology can be detrimental and, conversely, ways in which it can be advantageous to a child's development.
3. **Explaining Development: The Theories.** We have compared the major child development theories in this chapter. Which theories do you consider to have greater value for understanding children's learning? Why?
4. **Asking Questions, Examining Answers.** In examining the different approaches to conducting research on children's development, it is apparent that each is better suited to a different type of question. In what ways do experimental studies differ from other approaches in relation to the questions they address?
5. **Cultural Perspectives.** Contrast the various types of assistance and support two different families might seek in parenting their child with a disability based on their ethnotheories about their child's disability.

## REAL Development

### A Child's Journey

Welcome to Wiley's Real Development! This media program, based on the experiences of four real-life families, invites you to observe the pivotal stages of child development through the eyes of family members. Over the course of the term, your instructor may assign activities from this program that you will complete online. After viewing the video, you will engage in activities that will allow you to take on various roles and tasks related to children and their development.

In this module, you will have the opportunity to meet our families and learn a little about them and their lives.

Anthony and Lynn Borelli and their three children, Mikayla (age 15), Jenna (age 14), and Anthony Jr. (age 9)

Matt and Julianne Gray, their 4-year-old daughter Adeline, and their (soon-to-be-born) daughter Olivia

Barry and Tia Wagner and their six children, Terrell (age 11), Tocarri (age 9), Olivia (age 7), Benjamin (age 5), Brandon (age 1), and Shyairah (age 2 months)

Erica Ramirez, who is expecting her first child

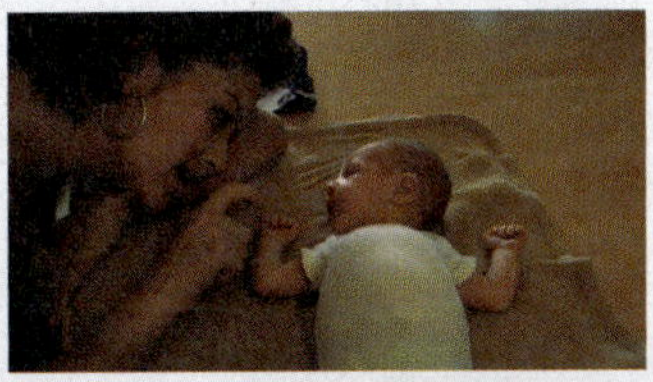

*All images © John Wiley & Sons, Inc.*

**WileyPLUS** Go to WileyPLUS to complete the *Real Development* activity.

# Chapter 2

# Biological Foundations of Child Development

## CHAPTER OUTLINE



## MAKING A difference

### It Can Start with Cells

Making life better for children can start at the cellular level. A good example involves phenylketonuria, or PKU. PKU is a genetic disorder in which the body lacks the enzyme phenylalanine hydroxylase, which breaks down phenylalanine. (*Enzymes* break down food so that it can be used by the body for energy or removed as waste.) Today, children with PKU can grow up to be healthy, but only a few decades ago, a diagnosis meant intellectual disability. How can the lack of a single enzyme have such an effect?

Phenylalanine is an amino acid that is an important building block for proteins. It is found in animal meats, dairy products, artificial sweeteners (aspartame), and soft drinks. In a child who lacks the enzyme and whose diet includes these foods, phenylalanine is not broken down but instead builds up in the brain. The eventual result is severe intellectual disability. The history of the identification and treatment of PKU shows us how detecting abnormalities at the cellular level led to public health policies through the combined efforts of scientists, physicians, and legislators (Paul, 1997).

PKU was first identified in 1934 by Asbjorn Folling, a Norwegian physician and chemist. Folling traced a strange odor he found among several intellectually disabled patients to a very high level of a chemical called "phenylketone" in their urine. Because he saw this disorder in siblings, he thought that it might be inherited. In 1951, Horst Bickel, a German scientist, developed a low-phenylalanine diet to treat people with PKU. Ten years later, he noted that cognitive improvement was greatest in youngest patients and recommended that the diet start in infancy. In 1960, an American microbiologist, Robert Guthrie, developed a simple blood test to detect PKU a few days after birth. Massachusetts, in 1963, became the first state to pass a law requiring that all newborns be tested for PKU. By 1975, 43 states had enacted such laws, and today all 50 states screen newborns for PKU. Now, special diets can start immediately after a diagnosis is confirmed.

This story appears to represent a steady march of progress. Along the way, however, opposition was strong, and skepticism was high. Early versions of the screening test did not always give accurate results, for example. And at first, there were no long-term population-based studies of how well dietary therapy worked, leading some to suggest that it was too soon to require universal screening.

Today, studies indicate that diet alone cannot *cure* PKU. Individuals with PKU do have difficulties with some cognitive functions, such as processing speed and attention (Anderson, et al., 2007; Moyle, Fox, Arthur, Bynevelt, & Burnett, 2007). But they can receive help with these functions, and most children treated for PKU can lead a normal life. To meet some children with PKU, go to http://www.pku.com.

## [KEY QUESTIONS] *for* READING CHAPTER 2

1. How does the biology of life at the cellular level affect human development?
2. How are traits passed from generation to generation?
3. What are some explanations for how genes and the environment interact?
4. What are the main components of the nervous system and the brain?
5. How does health-care policy affect children's well-being?

THE BOOK *From Neurons to Neighborhoods* (Shonkoff & Phillips, 2000)—an important work on early childhood development—begins with this point: "Human development is shaped by a dynamic and continuous interaction between biology and experience" (p. 3). As we noted in Chapter 1, contemporary systems theories of development emphasize dynamic interactions among the physical, cognitive, and psychosocial. Nevertheless, it is easy to overlook the role of the biological sciences when studying normal development, and we need to resist the temptation to do so. We cannot fully understand how children develop cognitively and socially if we do not understand the physiology of development and health.

In this chapter, we review the essential biology of life, a subject with which you are likely familiar, to emphasize how molecules and cells are the building blocks of development. We also examine how our genes and the environment interact to produce who we are, discuss the implications of the brain and nervous system for child development, and introduce some health-care issues that we will continue to discuss throughout this book. In addition, we continue to remind you that nature and nurture work together from "neurons to neighborhoods."

## The Biology of Life

**[ KEY QUESTION ] 1. How does the biology of life at the cellular level affect human development?**

Most of what we recognize as normal cognitive and psychosocial development is based on normal physiology. Often, we may best appreciate "normal" by studying what is atypical. For example, earlier we noted that one missing enzyme causes PKU, which can in turn result in intellectual disability. Yet we know there is no single gene or enzyme that causes normal cognition, and there are wide variations in intellectual disabilities as well. One enzyme is just a tiny piece in a huge puzzle.

*Everyday stories*

THE COMPLEXITY OF "NORMAL" What we think of as "normal" is actually quite complex. Toddlers in pursuit of cookies on the kitchen counter use cognitive planning skills when they climb up on a chair to reach the desired sweets. The act of climbing, in turn, represents a highly integrated system of nerve and motor pathways, muscles and bones, large and fine motor skills, depth perception, and brain development. We take it for granted that multiple physiological systems will work together to support the seemingly simple act of a child climbing on a chair to get a cookie.

The more we learn about human biology, the more amazing human development becomes. So, to help you better appreciate how development occurs, this section briefly addresses the basics: atoms, molecules, cells, and DNA.

**gametes** The cells of sexual reproduction: eggs, or ova, in females and sperm in males.

**somatic cells** Body cells, such as skin, muscle, bone, and so on.

## The Functions of Cells

Six atomic elements make up about 99% of our bodies: oxygen, carbon, hydrogen, nitrogen, calcium, and phosphorus. Most of the oxygen and hydrogen are tied up in $H_2O$—water. We are, in fact, more than 60% water, most of it in the bloodstream and muscles. Other elements appear in smaller amounts. *All* of these elements are critical for growth and development and for sustaining human life because they contribute to how our cells use energy, make proteins, and multiply. We will refer to some of these elements throughout this text.

You *are* your cells, and there are a lot of them. In fact, your body is made up of about 50 to 100 trillion cells. You have two types of cells: gametes and somatic cells. **Gametes** are the cells of sexual reproduction: eggs or ova in females and sperm in males. We discuss these later in this chapter and in Chapter 3. Most of your cells are **somatic cells**, or body cells—skin, muscle, bone, and so on. Somatic cells consist of an outer membrane and are filled with fluid called cytoplasm (see Figure 2.1). Within the cytoplasm are various bodies, including the cell nucleus. The nucleus controls reproduction of the cell, among other things, and contains the cell's DNA (Heuther & McCane, 2004).

Cells must perform a number of basic functions to sustain life and to make development possible. They take in nutrients and get rid of waste products, absorb oxygen, and conduct electrical charges. Conducting electrical charges, as we will see, is especially important in the nervous system. Cells generate forces that allow the parts of our bodies to move, and they secrete certain substances, such as hormones. Finally, they communicate with one another and reproduce themselves, so that worn-out cells can be replaced. Disease, and to some extent normal aging, is a breakdown in cellular function millions of times over. Children grow because their cells reproduce at a rapid rate. This explains why children heal from injury more easily than do adults: Young cells reproduce and repair more quickly than do aging ones.

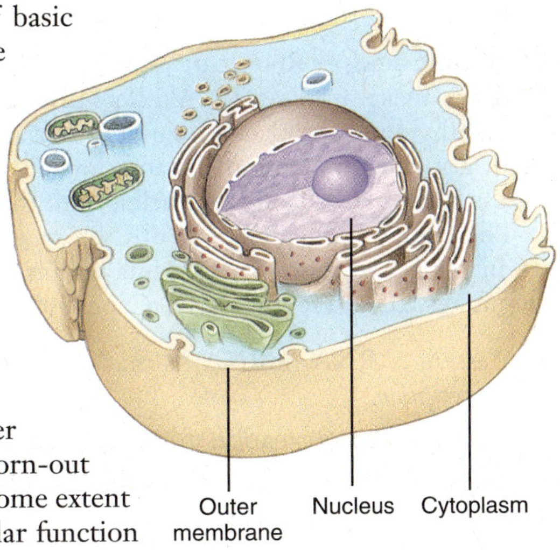


**FIGURE 2.1 A Somatic Cell** Somatic cells consist of an outer membrane and are filled with fluid called cytoplasm. Within the cytoplasm are various bodies, including the cell nucleus, which contains the cell's DNA.

## DNA, RNA, and Protein

To carry out their functions, cells need certain substances from their environments. While water, carbon dioxide, and oxygen pass through cell membranes easily, most molecules cannot. These substances must be transported across the cell membrane by proteins that the cell makes for this purpose. And that brings us to DNA, the master code for running our bodies. Information from DNA is copied into RNA, and that information is used as a template to make the proteins our bodies must have. As you review the structure and function of DNA and RNA on the following pages, think of DNA as books on a library shelf. Without a reader—RNA—the information in those books is useless (Champagne & Mashoodh, 2009).

deoxyribonucleic acid (DNA) The genetic material of cells; made of chemical building blocks called nucleotides arranged in a double-stranded helix, DNA contains all of the instructions needed to direct the activities of cells.

**genome** The complete sequence of DNA, genes, and chromosomes in an individual.

**ribonucleic acid (RNA)** A single-stranded substance made of nucleotides that transcribes and translates instructions from DNA in order to make proteins.

## DNA

Within the cell nucleus, as noted earlier, is the cell's **deoxyribonucleic acid**, or **DNA**. DNA contains all of the instructions needed to tell cells what to do. DNA is made of chemical building blocks called *nucleotides* that consist of three types of chemical subunits: (1) a sugar molecule (deoxyribose), (2) a phosphate group, and (3) one of four chemical units called *nucleotide bases*. Those four bases are adenine (A), thymine (T), guanine (G), and cytosine (C). In DNA, A and T always link together, as do G and C, creating four possible base pairs: AT, TA, GC, and CG.

A DNA molecule resembles a twisted ladder, called a double helix (see Figure 2.2). Each side of the ladder consists of long strands of the nucleotide base pairs—AT, TA, GC, and CG—arranged side by side. The sequence of approximately 3 billion base pairs is the DNA that makes up one person's **genome**.

The structure of DNA was discovered only in 1952; and its discoverers, James Watson, Francis Crick, and Maurice Wilkins earned the 1962 Nobel Prize for Physiology and Medicine. (Note: Because the Nobel Prize can be awarded only to the living, their colleague Rosalind Franklin, who had died, was not honored.) Forty-two years later, the International Human Genome Sequencing Consortium published the complete sequence of the human genome; that is, an identification and mapping of all human DNA (Rubin, Lucas, Richardson, Rokhsar, & Pennacchio, 2004). For more about the Human Genome Project and "turning off" genes, see the Research Insights feature on the following page.

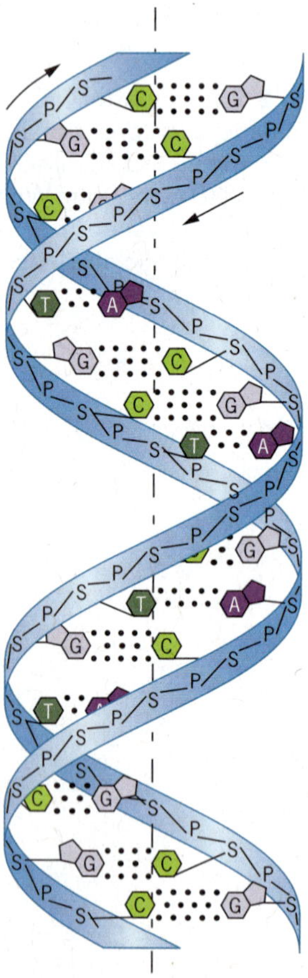

**FIGURE 2.2 The Structure of DNA** In this diagram of DNA, the S and P on the strands indicate sugar and phosphate units, with (A), thymine (T), guanine (G), and cytosine (C) forming the bonds between the strands.

Adapted with permission of John Wiley & Sons, Inc., from Snustad D. P., & Simons, M. J. (2012). *Principles of Genetics* (6th ed.). Hoboken, NJ: Wiley, p. 201, Figure 9.10.

## RNA

**Ribonucleic acid**, or **RNA**, carries, transcribes, and translates instructions from DNA in order to make proteins. RNA differs in several respects from DNA. For one thing, the base thymine is replaced by uracil. For another, RNA usually occurs as a single strand, not a double strand. In addition, DNA remains in the nucleus of the cell, whereas RNA moves from the nucleus into the cytoplasm.

There are three main types of RNA: *messenger, transfer*, and *ribosomal*. All participate in the manufacture of proteins within cells. The process includes these steps (Cummings, 2006; Heuther & McCane, 2004):

1. Messenger RNA (mRNA) is made in the cell nucleus through a process called *transcription*.
2. It carries the information it has received from the DNA into the ribosomes.
3. Ribosomal RNA (rRNA) reads the instructions on the mRNA.
4. Transfer RNA (tRNA) brings required amino acids to the ribosomes.
5. In a process called *translation*, mRNA directs the synthesis of a protein by interacting with tRNA.
6. The protein is released into the cytoplasm, where it performs its required function.

Sometimes, RNA misreads the information in DNA. Such errors in transcription and translation in RNA are increasingly recognized as playing a role in heritable diseases. PKU, for example, may be the result of an inborn error in transcription from DNA to mRNA.

## Proteins

You may have thought of proteins mostly as components of your diet. It is worth noting here that our cells cannot use the proteins we eat in the form in which we eat them. Instead, our bodies break down dietary protein into amino acids and then rearrange them to produce the kinds of protein that we, as humans, need to function.

The proteins that our bodies make do all of the work of the cell. They move needed substances across the cell membrane; they allow cells to adhere to one another;

and they make important chemical reactions possible. Proteins also act as receptors of signals in the brain and as antibodies that defend us against bacteria, viruses, and allergens. Hormones such as insulin and human growth hormone, as well as the hemoglobin that carries oxygen in the lungs, are proteins. Enzymes that break down food are proteins manufactured by the body. We cannot live without protein.

## what if...?

Think about how proteins do all of the work of cells. Recall, too, that we must have protein in our diets so that our bodies can use it to make the proteins we need. What if a child does not have enough protein in his or her diet? What do you think will happen to that child? Do you think a child could have enough calories in his or her diet to gain weight but not enough protein to develop? How would you prevent protein deficiency?

WHEN CELLULAR SYSTEMS CONNECT

## PKU as an Example

Why do we need to think about processes that take place at the level of the individual cell to understand human development? To illustrate, recall that PKU may be the result of an inborn error in transcription from DNA to mRNA, so the cells of people with this error are unable to manufacture the enzyme phenlyalanine hydroxylase (PAH) (Dobrowolski, Andersen, Doktor & Andresen, 2010). PAH converts the amino

## Research Insights: "Turning Off" Genes

Humans share many genes with other living creatures. We also suffer from some of the same diseases, such as cancer. One of the surprises of the Human Genome Project (HGP) a study launched in 1990 by the U.S. Department of Energy and the National Institutes of Health to analyze the DNA of human beings, was that the human genome has only 20,000 to 25,000 genes across 23 pairs of chromosomes. By comparison, dogs have 39 pairs of chromosomes and more than 25,000 genes, while the roundworm has 19,000 genes on 6 chromosomes. (We discuss genes and chromosomes in more detail later.) Scientists had expected the more complex human being to have many more chromosomes than other animals. What scientists are finding, instead, is that while humans and other animals have much the same set of protein-coding genes, the human set is regulated in a much more complicated way through RNA (Powner, Gerland & Sutherland, 2009).

In 1998, two American scientists, Andrew Fire of the Stanford University School of Medicine and Craig Mello of the University of Massachusetts Medical School, published their discovery of RNA interference (RNAi), which silences genes that instruct mRNA to make protein (Fire et al., 1998). These researchers were able to "turn off" a gene responsible for a protein involved in movement in the roundworm, essentially paralyzing it. For this discovery, they won the Nobel Prize in Medicine in 2006.

Why is the ability to turn off a gene important? If we know that specific genes cause particular diseases, then by turning those genes off, we might be able to prevent or treat the diseases. Identifying just which genes cause common diseases is turning out to be a lot more complex than expected, however. Unlike rare diseases caused by only one gene, such as PKU, more common diseases, like cancer and diabetes, are caused by multiple genetic variations in each person. While some of these variations have been identified, most of the genetic link remains unexplained (Goldstein, 2009).

Nevertheless, scientists are working on gene therapy for selected disorders. As of 2007, over 1,340 gene-therapy clinical trials in humans, involving 200 different genes, had been completed, were ongoing, or had been approved worldwide (Edelstein, Abedi, & Wixon, 2007). A major risk for patients, and a major challenge for researchers, concerns the fact that viruses are used to transport the new gene into the cells. Some viruses work better than others, and some have caused serious health complications for the patients (Flotte, 2007; Human Genome Project, 2009). The work is experimental, and results have been mixed, but efforts are slowly showing promise.

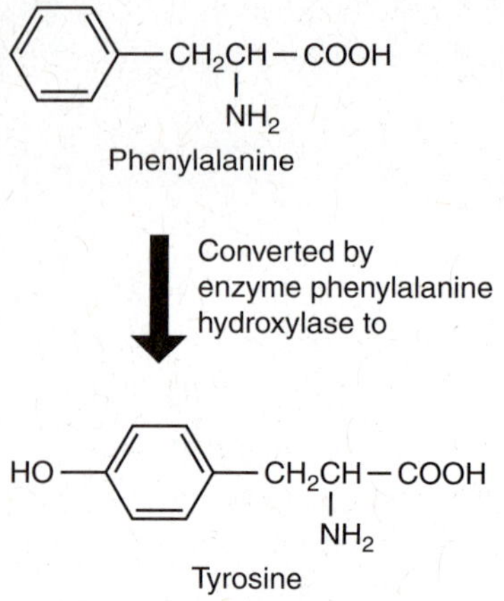


**FIGURE 2.3 Molecular Structures of Phenylalanine and Tyrosine** You can see in this figure that the enzyme phenlyalanine hydroxylase (PAH) adds one molecule to phenylalanine to make tyrosine. Without PAH, this transformation cannot occur. Phenylalanine then builds up in the body and brain, and the cell is starved of tyrosine, which it needs to function.

acid phenylalanine into tyrosine, another amino acid that is involved in the structure of almost every protein in the body. Without PAH, phenylalanine builds up in the body and brain and the cell is starved of tyrosine. The result is that children with PKU become intellectually disabled unless treatment begins early.

Figure 2.3 compares phenylalanine and tyrosine. You need not try to memorize these structures. You need only note that the difference between them is one molecule—OH—made up of one atom of oxygen (O) and one atom of hydrogen (H). The enzyme PAH transfers this one molecule onto phenylalanine to make tyrosine. One molecule—repeated millions of times in millions of cells—is the difference between normal cognitive development and possible intellectual disability for this particular group of children.

Note, too, that PKU gives us a clear example of one kind of relationship between nature and nurture. Children with PKU inherited it, a clear "nature" effect. But with the "nurture" interventions of correct diet, supportive medical care, and educational assistance, they can lead normal lives.

✓CHECK YOUR PROGRESS

1. What are the major functions of cells?
2. How are DNA and RNA similar, and how are they different?
3. What are some of the things protein does in the body?
4. What is the role of the enzyme PAH in PKU?

# Genes and Heredity

[ KEY QUESTION ] 2. How are traits passed from generation to generation?

We noted earlier that the complete sequence of the human genome has been mapped. But identifying the genome sequence has turned out to be the easy part! Understanding how it works is far more difficult. Indeed, about 41% of our genes have no known function. What we do know, though, is that DNA is the mechanism of heredity—the "nature" part of nature and nurture. To discuss heredity, we need to look at DNA in terms of genes and chromosomes. In this section, we start with a basic overview of these structures. We next explain how variations in genes can lead to disorders that compromise development, and then discuss genetic counseling and ethical and legal questions related to genetic testing.

## Genes and Chromosomes

Think of DNA's nucleotide base pairs—AT, TA, GC, and CG—as letters in the genetic language. A **gene** is a segment of DNA. It is like a word, a string of nucleotides that occur in a specific sequence. The human genome has 3 billion nucleotide base pairs (letters) arranged into about 20,000 to 25,000 genes (words). Some of these gene words overlap so that a single base pair may end the gene before it and begin the gene after it. These so-called gene words contain the critical instructions that direct the function of cells.

**gene** A segment of a DNA molecule; genes are the basic building blocks of inheritance.

**chromosome** A strand of DNA containing a number of genes.

**mitosis** The process by which somatic cells duplicate themselves to promote growth and repair; mitosis results in genetically identical cells, each containing 46 chromosomes.

Genes are arranged in **chromosomes**, with each gene occupying a specific place on the chromosome. In humans, there are 46 chromosomes in each somatic (body) cell. Clearly, then, each chromosome contains many genes. In somatic cells, the 46 chromosomes are arranged in 23 pairs. These cells duplicate themselves to promote growth and repair through the process of **mitosis** (shown in Figure 2.4), during which one cell splits into two *identical* cells.

*Gametes*—ova and sperm—differ from somatic cells. Instead of 23 pairs of chromosomes, each contains 23 single chromosomes. These cells divide through *meiosis*,

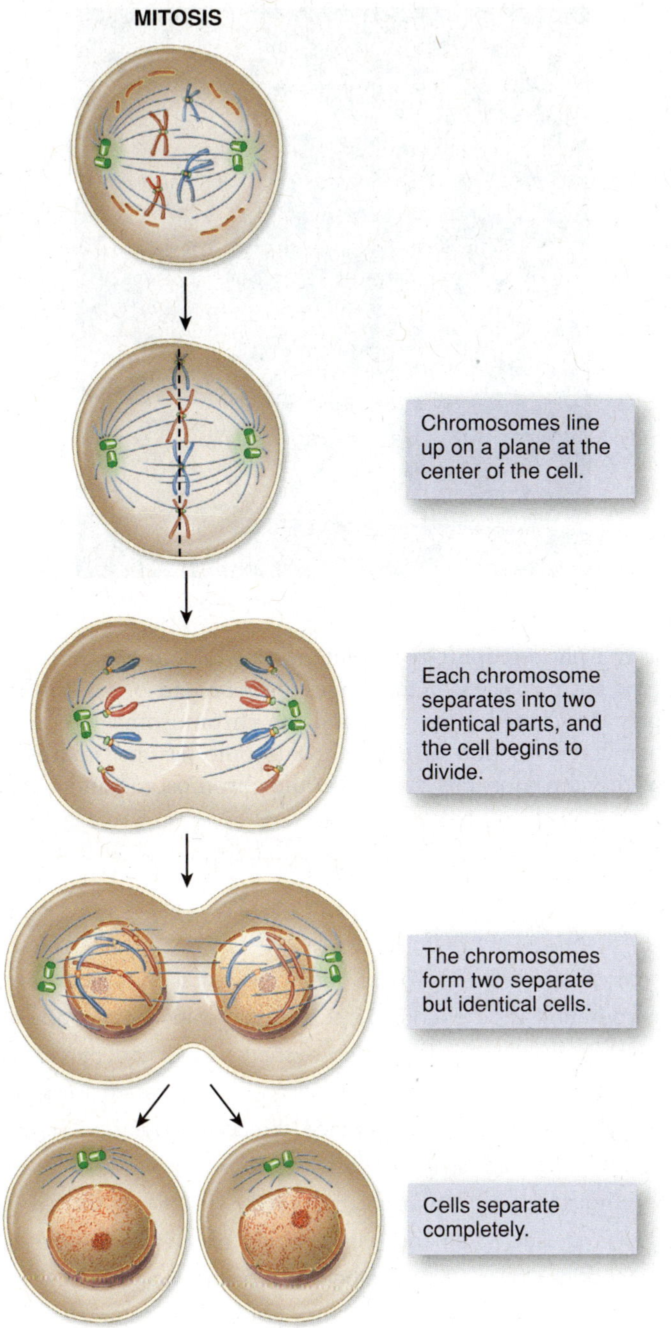


FIGURE 2.4 **Mitosis** In mitosis, a cell duplicates itself. The chromosomes in the original nucleus separate into two identical sets, each set in its own nucleus. These two nuclei, along with other cell contents, divide into two new cells, both identical to the original.
Adapted with permission of John Wiley & Sons, Inc., from Freudenrich, C. C., & Tortora, G. J. (2011). *Visualizing Anatomy and Physiology*. Hoboken, NJ: Wiley, pp. 68–69, Figure 3.20.

which we describe in more detail in Chapter 3. As you will see, when one sperm fertilizes one ovum, the 23 chromosomes from each gamete intertwine to make a cell with 46 chromosomes arranged in 23 pairs. The result is a one-of-a-kind human organism. (If this cell splits into two or more identical cells, the result is identical twins or triplets who have the same DNA.)

The 23 chromosome pairs in somatic cells include 22 pairs called *autosomes*, which control most inherited characteristics, and one pair of sex chromosomes: XX (female) and XY (male). In gametes, one of the 23 single chromosomes carries either an X or a Y. Female ova carry only the X sex chromosome, whereas male sperm can carry either the X or Y sex chromosome.

**FIGURE 2.5 A Human Karyotype** A karyotype like this one shows the 23 pairs of chromosomes that make up an individual's inheritance. Each of the individual's parents contributed one chromosome for each pair. The bands in the karyotype result from stains used in the laboratory to make the structure of the chromosomes more evident.

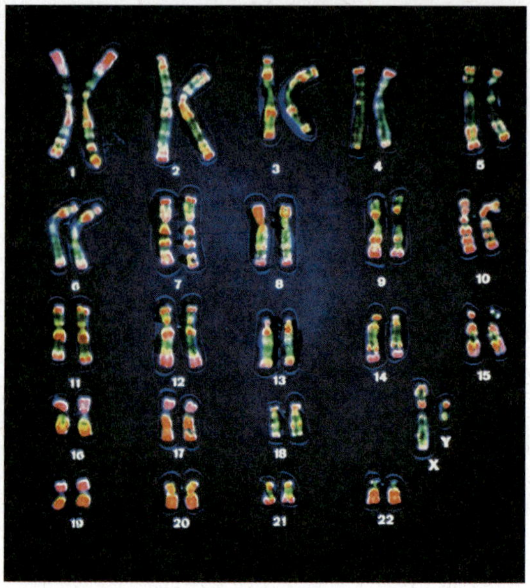


CNRI/Science Source

A *karyotype* is a photographic representation of human chromosomes. Figure 2.5 shows a karyotype with 22 pairs of autosomes and one pair of sex chromosomes. Each chromosome pair is assigned a number, and the chromosomes are arranged by their assigned number. Every section of each chromosome has an "address," based on its number, arm of the chromosome, region on the chromosome and band: for example,

## Culture, Genetics, and Human Migration

Modern humans began migrating out of Africa tens of thousands of years ago, cooperating in groups to increase their chances for survival in often-hostile environments. Eventually, some populations became isolated geographically and genetically, creating ancestral genetic clans called *haplogroups*. Members of these clans share a unique variation in a single base nucleotide, which genetic anthropologists have used to trace early human migrations across continents. Such variations have been found on the Y chromosome, passed from father to son, and on mitochondrial DNA, passed from mother to child (Behar et al., 2008; Human Genome Project, 2010; National Geographic Society, 2012; National Human Genome Research Institute, 2005; Wells, 2002). You can see on the accompanying map, for example, how Y haplogroups vary in different parts of the world.

These genetic ancestral clans produced variations in phenotype, such as skin color, through adaptation or natural selection—variations that continue to influence how we think and feel about who we are as a species. Furthermore, over time, the clans developed the shared beliefs, symbols, social structures, and rituals that we think of as comprising culture. But genetically, there is only one race among the peoples of the Earth—the human race. Culture, ethnicity, and what we call "race" are not based on biology. They are social constructions based on patterns of human behavior and beliefs about similarities within groups and differences among them. Our social constructions come from individual experiences and from the collective experiences of families and social groups passed on to us over time. They provide humankind with great *cultural* diversity, but the human species has far less *genetic* diversity than many other species.

1q2.4 means chromosome 1, arm q, region 2, band 4. Examining karyotypes for variations in shape, size, or gene construction is critical in the study of genetics, heredity, and disease.

**alleles** Pairs of corresponding genes located at specific positions on specific chromosomes.

## Patterns of Heredity

In thinking about heredity, we need to keep two things in mind. First, certain characteristics of a species remain constant from generation to generation. Second, there are variations in those characteristics among the individuals within a species (Cummings, 2006). The vast majority of our genes are designed for constancy. Constancy directs how cells function, how proteins and enzymes are made, how we exchange oxygen and metabolize food into energy, how brain cells communicate, and so on—everything that is life. We tend to take constancy for granted, and so perhaps it is not surprising that differences attract our attention more than similarities do. In addition, though, as we have seen in the example of PKU, small differences can have far-reaching effects, which can give us information about normal development. For that reason, we focus on differences in much of the remainder of this section. The feature Culture, Genetics, and Migration, also discusses genetic variation and genetic diversity.

### Alleles and Traits

Remember that genes occupy specific locations on chromosomes. Thus, when chromosomes pair up during fertilization, genes occur in corresponding pairs, one on each chromosome. (This is true of 22 of the 23 pairs—the autosomes; the sex chromosomes are exceptions.) The two corresponding genes are called **alleles**, and particular alleles control particular traits. When the two alleles in a pair are identical, we say that the

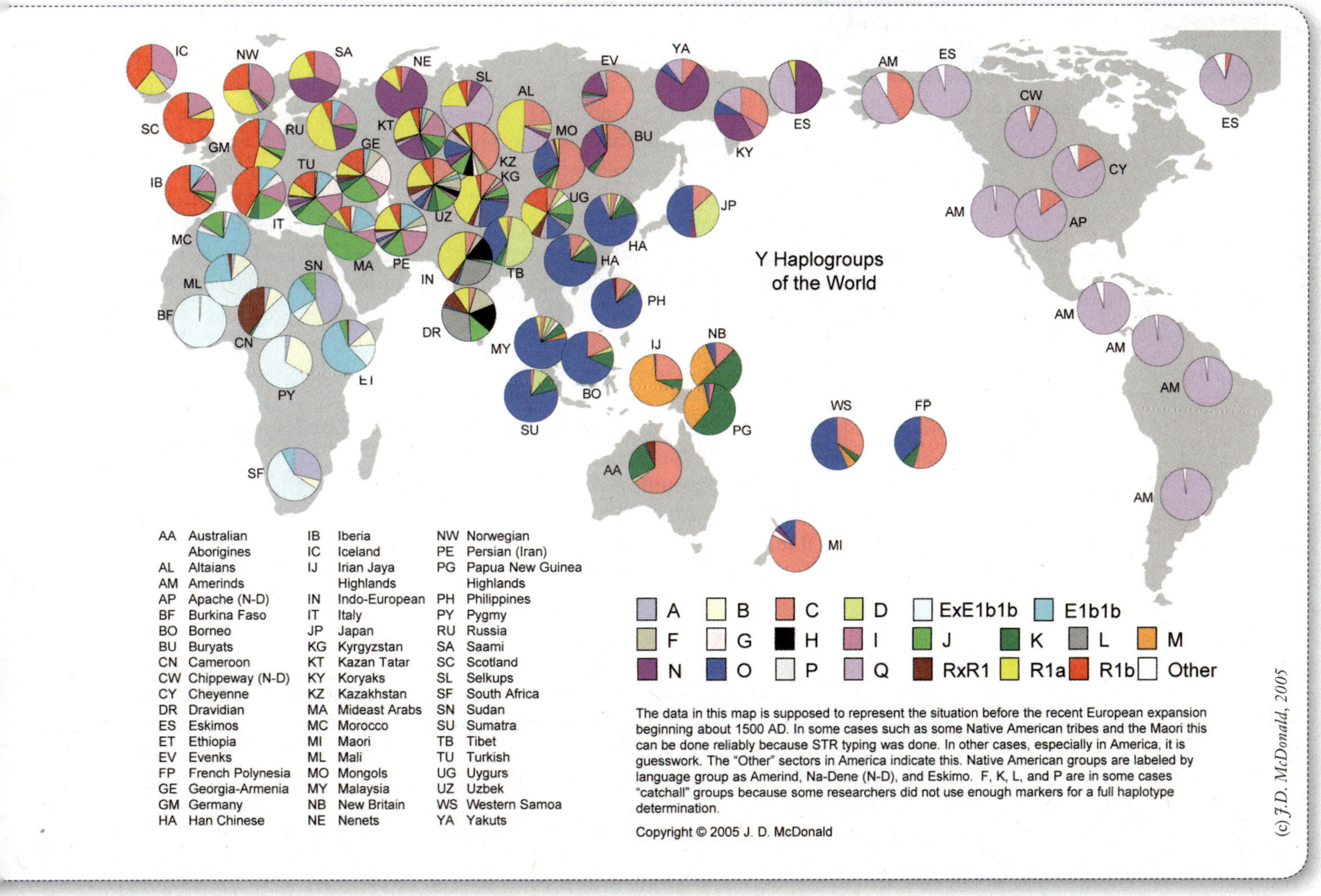

**homozygous** A condition in which an individual has a pair of identical alleles at a particular position.

**heterozygous** A condition in which an individual has a pair of nonidentical alleles at a particular position.

**genotype** A person's genetic makeup as determined at the moment of fertilization.

**phenotype** The observable expression of a person's genotype.

person is **homozygous** for that trait. When the alleles are different, the person is **heterozygous** for that trait. In this case, which trait the person will display depends on various factors.

Alleles can be dominant or recessive. When one allele in a heterozygous pair is dominant and the other is recessive, the dominant allele cancels out the effect of the recessive one. Often, however, neither allele is completely dominant nor completely recessive, and so the relationship is more complex. Further complicating the picture is the fact that most traits are affected by more than one gene, and one gene may have alleles that contribute to multiple traits.

Liza McCorkle/Vetta/Getty Images

Freckles are an inherited, dominant trait. This little boy's freckles would not have surfaced, though, if he had not been exposed to sunlight.

*Everyday stories*

GENES, ENVIRONMENT, AND FRECKLES As a relatively simple example, consider freckles. Freckles are an inherited, dominant trait. We'll call the dominant freckle allele *F* and the recessive no-freckle allele *f*. A child who inherits an *F* allele from both parents will be *FF* and will be inclined to have freckles. A child who inherits an *f* allele from both parents will be *ff* and will not. A child who inherits an *F* and an *f* will be *Ff* and will also tend to have freckles, since *F* is dominant. Note, though, that the actual appearance of freckles on the *FF* or *Ff* child's face will require exposure to sunlight—another example of how genes and environment interact (Online Mendelian Inheritance in Man [OMIM] 155555, 2012).

Your genetic makeup as it was determined at the moment of fertilization—with all its sets of homozygous and heterozygous alleles—is called your **genotype**. Your genotype, then, is your hard-wired potential. However, the self that you are today is your **phenotype**, how your genotype has been expressed. Some differences between genotype and phenotype are due to environmental influences on development: A child may be born with the potential, determined by genotype, to be 6 feet tall but may end up several inches shorter because of poor nutrition. Other differences are due to patterns of heredity. Let's look at some patterns of heredity, as well as chromosomal abnormalities that occur spontaneously at conception.

## Autosomal Patterns

As noted, relationships between corresponding alleles may be complicated, and in this section we look at several ways in which alleles work together to produce certain traits in the autosomal chromosomes—that is, chromosomes 1 through 22. In the examples that follow, these traits are health disorders that are inherited or that occur because of an accidental genetic error. Table 2.1 lists additional examples of some of the better-known genetic disorders.

**Autosomal Recessive Trait: Phenylketonuria (PKU).** As we've seen, in PKU, the protein phenylalanine builds up in the body because there is no enzyme to break it down. PKU is an example of a health disorder caused when a *recessive* allele from each parent is passed along to the child. Here is what happens: Each parent has one recessive allele and one dominant allele, so both are heterozygous for the trait. In this case, the dominant allele cancels the effects of the recessive one, so the parents do not have PKU. If, however, a child inherits a recessive allele from each parent, the child is homozygous for the trait and develops the disorder.

**Table 2.1** Patterns of Genetic Inheritance in Selected Disorders*

| Type of Genetic Pattern | Trait | Description | Prevalence | Treatment |
|---|---|---|---|---|
| Autosomal recessive pattern | Phenylketonuria (PKU) | Excess accumulation of phenylalanine in bloodstream; if untreated, causes intellectual disability. | Caucasians and East Asians, 1 in 2,600 births; Africans, ~1 in 100,000 births | Special diet, supplemental enzymes. Life expectancy: normal with treatment. |
| | Cystic fibrosis | Mucus production blocks ducts carrying enzymes from pancreas to small intestine and lungs; causes digestive and respiratory problems. | Caucasians, 1 in 2,000 births; Africans, 1 in 18,000 births; Asians, 1 in 90,000 births | Special diet, supplemental enzymes, treatment of respiratory problems. Life expectancy: 30s. |
| | Tay–Sachs disease | Degeneration of central nervous system, beginning in infancy. | 1 in 3,600 births among Ashkenazi Jews and the French-Canadian Cajun community of Louisiana | No treatment. Life expectancy: usually 4 years or less. |
| Autosomal incomplete dominance pattern | Sickle-cell anemia | Abnormal hemoglobin; blood vessels become clogged, causing pain and swelling during crisis. | 1 in 500 births among African Americans; 1 in 1,000–1,400 births among Hispanic Americans | Blood transfusions; pain and other medications; prevention of infection and stroke. Life expectancy: 40s. |
| Autosomal dominant pattern | Marfan syndrome | Defect in connective tissues of heart, lungs, muscles, tendons, eyes; death usually results from rupture of the aorta. | 7 to 17 in 100,000 births | Treatment depends on organ system affected. Life expectancy: from 30s in 1996 to 60s by 2009. |
| | Huntington's disease | Degenerative brain disorder that begins at ages 30–45; leads to total incapacitation and death. | 5 to 7 in 100,000 people | No treatment. Death occurs about 17 years after onset. |
| Chromosome X-linked recessive pattern | Duchenne muscular dystrophy (males) | Degenerative muscle disorder; leads to inability to walk and heart problems. | 1 in 3,500 males in United States | No treatment. Life expectancy: 20s. |
| | Hemophilia (males) | Bleeding disorder caused by a deficiency in a blood-clotting factor. | Affects 1 in 5,000 to 10,000 males in most populations | Blood transfusions, safety precautions. Life expectancy: normal. |
| Chromosomal abnormalities | Down syndrome | A common form of intellectual disability, also associated with higher risk for malformations of the heart, leukemia, and Alzheimer's disease. | Based on maternal age: 1 in 900 births at age 30; 1 in 400 at age 35; 1 in 105 at age 40; 1 in 20 at age 46 | Treatment for health problems are the same as for those without Down syndrome. Life expectancy: 50% die before age 50. |
| | Turner syndrome (females) | Short stature, joint problems, various other symptoms. Most girls with Turner syndrome do not have normal reproductive capacity, but do have normal intelligence. | 1 in 2,500 births | Sex and growth hormones can help symptoms. Life expectancy: normal. |
| | Fragile X syndrome | Major cause of intellectual disability; associated with various facial characteristics, as well as anxiety, attention deficits, and epilepsy. | 1 in 4,000 males; 1 in 6,000 females | Medications to manage symptoms. Life expectancy: normal. |

**Note:* For an extensive catalog of patterns of genetic heredity, and related diseases, visit the Online Mendelian Inheritance in Man (OMIM), which is managed by the National Center for Biotechnology Information and Johns Hopkins University: http://www.ncbi.nlm.nih.gov/omim.

*Sources*: Bender & Hobbs, 2003; Cummings, 2006; Kaback, 2006; Mitchell & Scriver, 2007; Moskowitz, Chmiel, Sternen, Cheng, & Cutting, 2008; National Fragile X Foundation, 2010; National Institute for Child Health and Human Development, 2010; Online Mendelian Inheritance in Man, 181500, 190685, 155555, 300624 www.ncbi.nlm.nih.gov/omim; von Kodolitsch, Raghunath, & Nienaber, 1998; World Health Organization, 2011.

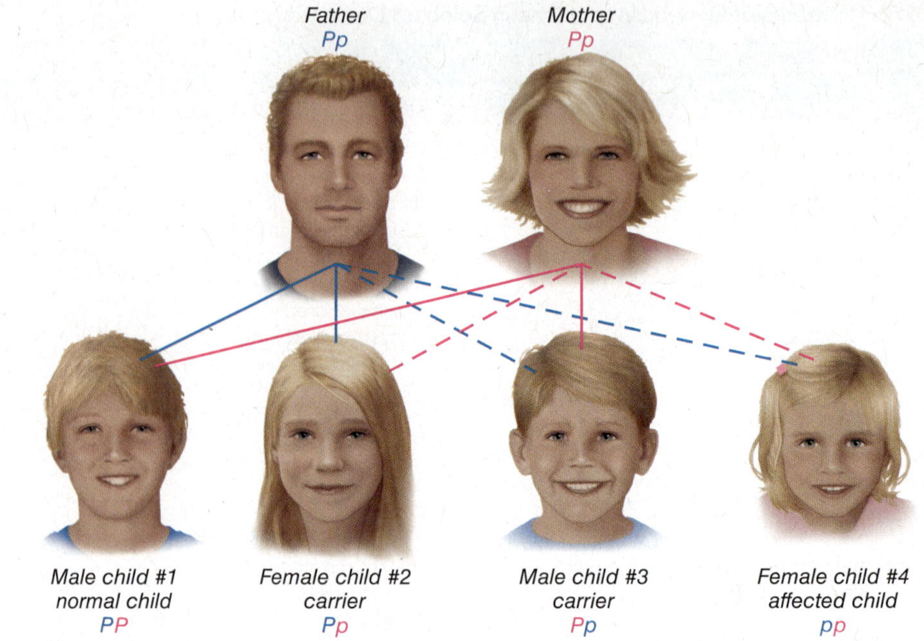


**FIGURE 2.6 The Pattern of Inheritance for PKU** In the figure, *P* represents the normal gene for making phenylalanine hydroxylase, and *p* represents the recessive gene that causes PKU. You can see that both parents have a *Pp* genotype, which means they are carriers for PKU. For each child, there is a 1 in 4 (25%) chance of having PKU (*pp*), a 1 in 4 chance of not having the recessive trait at all (*PP*), and a 2 in 4 (50%) chance of being a carrier (*Pp*).

Let's use *P* to indicate a normal gene for making the enzyme phenylalanine hydroxylase and *p* for the recessive gene that causes PKU. Figure 2.6 shows two parents, both of whom have a *Pp* genotype. Neither parent has PKU, but both are *carriers* for PKU because both carry *p*, the recessive gene. Each pregnancy has a 25% chance of having a child who will have the *pp* genotype and express the autosomal recessive trait PKU.

*Teresa Tamura KRT/Newscom*

People with Marfan syndrome are tall and thin, and they may suffer health problems related to a lack of fibrillin, a major component of connective tissue.

**Autosomal Dominant Trait: Marfan Syndrome.** Not all health problems are related to recessive traits. The allele responsible for *Marfan syndrome* is dominant. Thus, a person with two recessive alleles for this trait is disease free, whereas the person with two dominant ones has the disease. People with Marfan syndrome do not make fibrillin, a main component of connective tissue, which is part of blood vessels, cartilage, tendons, and muscles. The lack of fibrillin, especially in the aorta, results in a cardiovascular system that cannot support human body size, causing health problems and contributing to early death (Cummings, 2006; Dietz, 2009). People with the syndrome are also tall and thin.

**Autosomal Incomplete Dominance: Sickle Cell Disease.** Sometimes, neither allele is completely dominant, resulting in *incomplete dominance*. A good example of incomplete dominance is found in sickle cell disease. Homozygous recessive individuals have sickle cell disease; heterozygous individuals exhibit a mild version of the disease; and homozygous dominant individuals are normal. In people who have the disease, the red blood cells may collapse into a crescent shape (like a sickle; hence the name) and break apart. They fail to carry oxygen, and they also clog the bloodstream, especially the smaller capillaries, causing swelling and severe pain. People who are heterozygous may have mild symptoms when they are not getting sufficient oxygen—for example, during exercise (Stuart & Nagel, 2004).

Sickle cell anemia is most often associated with black Africans and their descendants. Interestingly, people who are heterozygous and homozygous for sickle cell disease are also more resistant to malaria than those who are homozygous for normal red blood cells. This suggests that the allele that causes sickle cell disease represents a useful adaptation in parts of the world where malaria is common, such as western Africa, because that same allele helps people resist malaria (Aidoo et al., 2002).

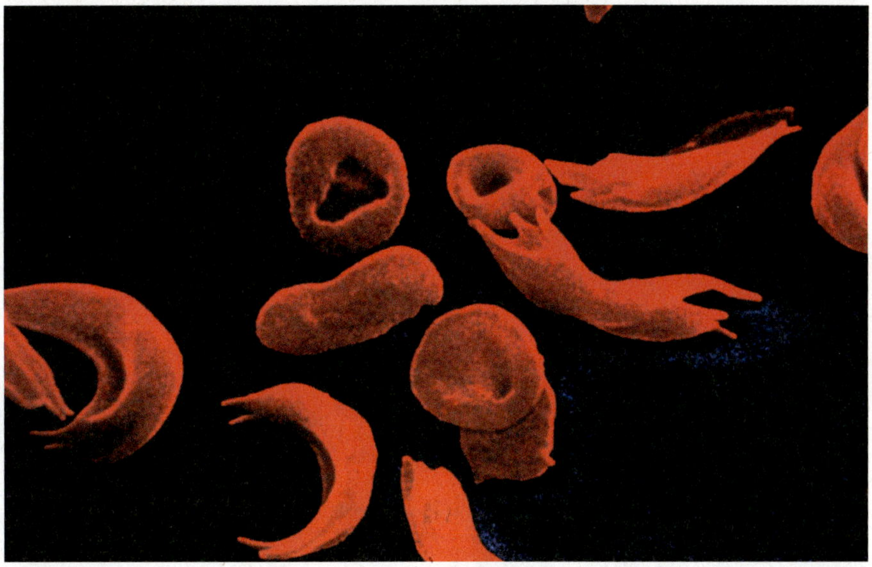
Omikron/Photo Researchers

In people with sickle cell disease, red blood cells take on a crescent shape. These cells fail to carry oxygen; they also clog blood vessels, causing swelling and severe pain.

**Autosomal Codominance: Blood Type.** Somewhat similar to incomplete dominance is *codominance*. Here again, neither allele is completely dominant nor completely recessive, but both are expressed. An example is blood type. The determination of blood type involves three alleles—alleles A, B, and O. Alleles A and B are codominant, and allele O is recessive. Pairings of these alleles result in six genotypes but four phenotypes, as shown in Table 2.2. A child who receives allele A from both parents will have blood type A, as will a child who receives allele A from one parent and allele O from the other, since allele O is recessive. The same is true with allele B. But a child who receives allele A from one parent and allele B from the other will have type AB blood. In Chapter 3, we will discuss another characteristic of blood type, the Rh factor. Rh-negative blood is an autosomal recessive trait that causes complications during pregnancy.

## Sex-Chromosome Linked Disorders

Disorders carried on the sex chromosomes create a very different pattern from those carried on the 22 autosomal chromosomes. Recall that the sex chromosomes make up the 23rd set and that the female chromosome is X and the male chromosome Y. The X chromosome is larger than the Y chromosome, which means the female carries more genes on the 23rd chromosome than does the male. In females, the 23rd set of chromosomes is a matched pair: XX. Thus, a female could carry a recessive gene on one X chromosome and a dominant one on the other X chromosome. When this happens, the dominant gene can mask the effect of the recessive one, preventing it from being expressed. But a male carries an unmatched pair: XY. If he carries a recessive gene on the X chromosome, he lacks a matching chromosome to neutralize its effect. For this reason, males have more sex-linked inherited disorders (Cummings, 2006).

**Table 2.2** Codominance for Blood Type

| | Allele A | Allele B | Allele O |
|---|---|---|---|
| Allele A | Genotype: AA<br>Phenotype: Type A blood | Genotype: AB<br>Phenotype: Type AB blood | Genotype: AO<br>Phenotype: Type A blood |
| Allele B | Genotype: AB<br>Phenotype: Type AB blood | Genotype: BB<br>Phenotype: Type B blood | Genotype: BO<br>Phenotype: Type B blood |
| Allele O | Genotype: AO<br>Type A blood | Genotype: BO<br>Type B blood | Genotype: OO<br>Type O blood |

Perhaps the most famous case of hemophilia was Alexis, the young son of Czar Nicholas II of Russia, who was killed with his family in 1918 during the Russian Revolution. Intermarriage among the royal families of Europe contributed to a higher incidence of hemophilia in their families over time.

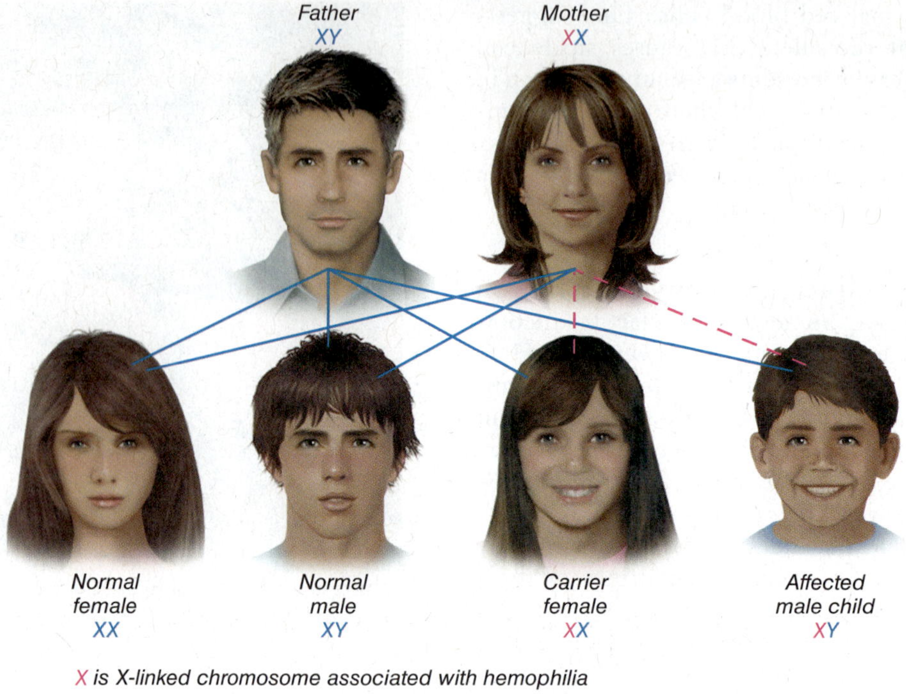


**FIGURE 2.7 The Pattern of Inheritance for Hemophilia** Sons of carrier mothers have a 50% chance of inheriting the X chromosome that carries the recessive gene for hemophilia, and thus of expressing the recessive trait. It is possible that no male child of a carrier mother will develop hemophilia, and daughters may carry the X-linked trait for generations without knowing it.

A male with an X-linked disorder will pass the recessive gene on his X chromosome to all of his daughters, who become heterozygous carriers for the recessive gene. Sons of heterozygous mothers have a 50% chance of inheriting the X chromosome that carries the recessive gene, and thus of expressing the recessive trait. Carriers may also develop a milder form of the illness. Figure 2.7 demonstrates how this works using hemophilia, discussed below, as an example.

Examples of X-linked recessive conditions include hemophilia and Duchenne muscular dystrophy. Hemophilia is a bleeding disorder caused by a deficiency in a blood-clotting factor. Males with hemophilia bleed easily, especially into joints and muscles, causing pain and damage. Treatment involves transfusions with human blood products and artificial substitutes for the deficient clotting factor (Brower & Thompson, 2008). In Duchenne muscular dystrophy, the recessive gene alters the structure of a protein that helps to stabilize muscles, including the muscles of the heart and lungs. Muscle cells without this protein become damaged, weaken, and die over time. Boys with this disease are often unable to walk by adolescence (Darras, Korf & Urion, 2008).

Probably the most famous case of hemophilia was Alexis, the young son of Czar Nicholas II of Russia. The 19th-century British queen Victoria, a carrier of this trait, passed it on to her many descendants among the royal families of Europe. Alexis was 14 years old when he, his parents, and his sisters were executed in 1918 during the Russian Revolution.

## Chromosomal Disorders

Sometimes, problems involve not just a gene but an entire chromosome. Chromosomal abnormalities fall into one of two categories: abnormalities of number (too many or too few) and abnormalities of structure. Some chromosomal abnormalities are inherited, such as Fragile X syndrome, but most are naturally occurring irregularities that occur spontaneously at conception or shortly after.

## Down Syndrome

Individuals with Trisomy 21, better known as *Down syndrome*, have an extra chromosome 21, for a total of 47 chromosomes instead of 46. The condition is not inherited through either parent. Most cases are due to abnormalities in the ovum, and the incidence of the syndrome is associated with increased maternal age. Individuals with Down syndrome have distinctive facial features, including a small mouth, small hands, and varying degrees of intellectual disability. Many different genes on chromosome 21 contribute to this phenotype. Some of these genes also carry a higher risk for leukemia, heart and thyroid disorders, and early Alzheimer's disease—common health problems in people with Down syndrome (National Institute for Child Health and Human Development [NICHD], 2010; OMIM 190685, 2013).

## Fragile X Syndrome

*Fragile X syndrome* involves a region of DNA on the long arm of the X chromosome. In some people, this arm is longer than usual. With each generation, the DNA lengthens, finally expanding to a critical length. At this critical point, gaps occur in the chromosome, and the production of a protein called FMRP stops. This protein regulates many genes, and the lack of it results in a characteristic phenotype, which can include a long face with a high forehead, a prominent chin, and softened muscles around the mouth, as well as attention deficits and epilepsy. Fragile X is the most common cause of intellectual disability in males (D'Hulst & Kooy, 2009; National Fragile X Foundation, 2010; OMIM 300624, 2013).

## Turner Syndrome

Females with *Turner syndrome* have 45 chromosomes instead of 46. The syndrome is not inherited genetically but is an error that occurs during meiosis of either the sperm cell or egg cell. An X chromosome gets lost, leaving the female child with only one

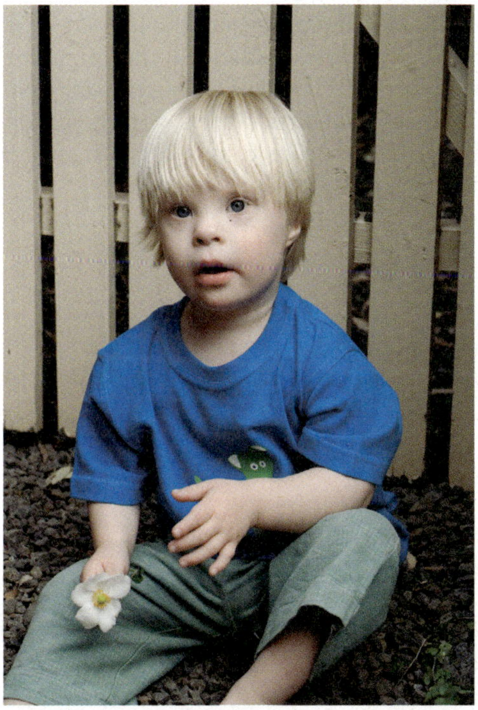

*Leanne Temme/Getty Images*

Along with varying degrees of intellectual disability, children with Down syndrome have distinctive facial features, including wide-set, almond-shaped eyes.

*FRAXA Research Foundation*

Often, a child with Fragile X syndrome has a long face with a high forehead, a prominent chin, and softened muscles around the mouth. Fragile X is the most common cause of intellectual disability in males.

sex chromosome, a single X. The absence of one X chromosome results in a range of features, with some girls having more than others. These include short stature (about 4 feet 8 inches in adults), irregular rotations of the wrist and elbow joints, heart problems, and blockages in the lymph system, resulting in swelling of hands and feet.

In most girls with Turner syndrome, the ovaries stop functioning in childhood. When this happens, girls can have a normal puberty only if treated with hormones. The affected ovaries usually do not produce ova. Although of normal intelligence, some of these girls experience difficulty with visual-spatial coordination tasks (such as mentally rotating objects in space) and math. These cognitive abilities have often been thought to be stronger in males. Perhaps the second X chromosome in females plays more of a role in these abilities than previously thought (NICHD, 2010).

## Genetic Counseling Parenting

Genetic counseling provides guidance for parents about the possibility of genetic disorders in their future children. Couples most often seek genetic counseling if: one of them knows there is a family history of an inherited disorder, the mother is older than 35, they have already had one child with a genetic disorder or other birth defect, or they have lost two or more pregnancies or had a baby who died. Sometimes couples seek counseling in response to a screening test during pregnancy that suggests there may be a problem.

During the consultation, the genetic counselor, a specially trained professional, prepares an extensive health history of both the mother's and father's families for as many generations as possible. This information is mapped to a pedigree. The counselor asks about education, employment, insurance, housing, family and friends, lifestyle preferences, religious affiliations, and so on, resources that will be helpful should the couple have a child with a disorder. A physical exam, including genetic testing using a blood test, can be done on the couple and other family members. If the couple has not yet conceived and the tests are positive for an inherited disorder, the counselor will discuss the chances of having a child with the disorder, as well as alternatives such as adoption.

If a woman is already pregnant, testing can be done on the developing fetus. A small sample of either amniotic fluid (fluid that surrounds the fetus) or chorionic villi (tissue from the developing placenta) is obtained via a thin probe and then tested. The sample will contain fetal cells. If tests confirm that the fetus is affected, the counselor will tell the couple what the child will be like, what the course of the disease may be, and how it can be managed. It is not possible to test for all birth defects, as tests are not available for some conditions. So while normal results from testing are reassuring, they are not a 100% guarantee that a baby will have no health problems.

### what if...?

What if your partner has a family member who has Duchenne muscular dystrophy? You don't know if this illness has ever occurred in your family. You are considering having a baby together. Your partner has not mentioned genetic testing, but you are thinking about it. How will you decide what to do? What trade-offs might be involved in your decision?

### ✓ CHECK YOUR PROGRESS

1. What are genes, alleles, and chromosomes?
2. What is the difference between genotype and phenotype?
3. What are examples of autosomal dominant and recessive patterns of genetic heredity?
4. Why are males more vulnerable to X-linked disorders?

# Gene-Environment Interactions

**[ KEY QUESTION ] 3. What are some explanations for how genes and the environment interact?**

We've been telling you that development is a result of the relationship between genes and environment, between nature and nurture. While this may seem obvious to you, it was not always considered so. In the 19th century, Charles Darwin (1859) wrote about the two key variables of evolution—inherited characteristics and environment—leading to the nature/nurture debate that we first mentioned in Chapter 1. During the 20th century, one school of thought favored the role of environment (nurture), while the other favored the role of inborn characteristics (nature).

The environment was easier for psychologists to study than were inherited characteristics, contributing to the emphasis placed for a very long time on the role of the environment. Knowledge about genes, and statistical methods for studying them, came later. In this section, we review some explanations for how the relationships between person and environment, and between genetic heredity and experience, shape development.

## Mechanisms of Interaction Between Genes and Environment

Earlier, we talked about genotype and phenotype. We also talked about genes in terms of constancy and individual differences. We begin this section by looking at how genetic constancy shapes early development in the human species. We then look at different theories about how genes and environment interact to shape phenotypical differences.

### Experience-Expectant Development and Experience-Dependent Development

Normally developing babies and toddlers worldwide achieve the same fundamental milestones—such as rolling over, grasping, and talking—at about the same age. Given a normal course of development in a typical physical and social environment, we expect children to achieve these milestones within a predictable period. We call this *experience-expectant development* (Greenough & Black, 1992).

*Experience-dependent development* (Greenough & Black, 1992), in contrast, occurs in response to more unique opportunities that may vary from one environment to another, with the potential to affect each individual differently. These opportunities may refine existing areas of expected development or foster the growth of new abilities that integrate several areas of development. For example, talking is experience-expectant, but learning a specific language is experience-dependent.

### Canalization

*Canalization* proposes that early on in development, heredity plays a greater role than environment in development (Waddington, 1957). In this view, a species-specific developmental path—or *canal*—provides a buffer from all but the most extreme environmental influences, lending stability to early development. An example of experience-expectant development is that children sit up at about the same age, worldwide. Severe circumstances, such as starvation, would be needed to derail this development.

Over time, however, development becomes more experience-dependent, according to this view. The environment exerts greater influence, and people have more control over their environments and behavior, and so individual paths branch off. For example, we don't expect every child to learn to ride a bicycle. Children have to be physically ready to learn this skill, and they need the experience of the bicycle itself. Hence, developmental paths become more individualized over time, so that infants who started out with more similarities than differences may come to look quite different from one another as they get older.

## Genotype-Environment Correlations

In the relationship between person and environment, the effects are bidirectional. Not only does the environment influence the child, but the child influences the environment. Children shape their environments simply by being in them. Thus, children affect how the environments shape them (Scarr 1992, 1996; Scarr & McCartney, 1983). When the effects of heredity and environment work to reinforce each other in such interactions, we have what some theorists call *genotype-environment correlations.* We look next at three types of correlation: passive, evocative, and active.

**Passive Gene-Environment Effect.** Have you ever noticed that musical talent seems to "run in families"? This is an example of a *passive gene-environment effect,* which results from a natural fit between genotype and environment. Parents who are musically talented pass along some of their genes to their children. In addition, they create home environments that foster any musical talent their children have inherited. As a result, the effects of heredity and environment complement one another, and children develop phenotypes that match their genotypic potential.

**Evocative Effect.** In the *evocative effect,* a child's inborn traits evoke responses from others in the environment that reinforce the child's genetic predisposition. A common example is temperament, which you will learn more about in Chapter 7. A baby with an easygoing temperament smiles readily, eats and sleeps regularly, and is easily soothed. As you can imagine, these behaviors are quite welcome to those around the baby, who respond with positive attention. That, in turn, reinforces the baby's easygoing style. In contrast, the difficult baby is not easily soothed, can't settle into sleep, and is fussy about food. Those around this baby will likely feel some frustration, which can end up adding to the baby's fussiness. Furthermore, the easygoing baby makes even insecure parents feel successful, whereas the difficult baby may make them more anxious. Both children are shaping their environments by being part of them.

**Active Effect.** With the *active effect*—also called *niche picking*—children actively seek out the environments, or niches, that provide the best fit for their inborn tendencies (Scarr & McCartney, 1983). The older a child gets, the more choices he or she is free to make. Each choice a child makes, however, may close off some pathways while opening others.

*Time & Life Pictures/Getty Images*

Ellis Marsalis (right) and three of his sons—Jason, Branford, and Wynton. Gifted and successful musicians, all the Marsalis brothers no doubt inherited musical ability, but they also were surrounded by music and musicians as they grew up.

Monica and Michael Sweet/Flickr/Getty Images

A baby with a cheerful, easygoing temperament is likely to get positive feedback from caregivers—an example of the evocative effect.

*Everyday stories*

NICHE PICKING A child whose genotype suits him well to be physically active may choose to play sports and to choose his friends from among his team members. A child of the musical parents we mentioned earlier may instead take music lessons, join the school band, and make friends with those whose interests are similar to hers. By choosing certain activities and friends, children choose their field of influence. In later chapters, you will read more about how children tend to choose friends who have similar families, interests, and relational styles.

### Range of Reaction

Another explanation of how heredity and environment affect one another involves the theory of *range of reaction* (Gottesman, 1963). Here, the genotype sets the upper and lower limits for possible outcomes. Where a person falls within this genetic range depends in part on environmental conditions. A given environment, however, can have different effects on different genotypes. To illustrate, consider Figure 2.8, which shows the scores of three fictional children on intelligence (IQ) tests over time and in environments ranging from extremely deprived to extremely enriched (Gottlieb, 2007; Gottlieb, Wahlsten & Lickliter, 2006; Wahlsten, 1994).

In the figure, we have taken the liberty of assigning the three children a range of intelligence, although in fact researchers can't say just what a range would be. Joe's range is deliberately designed as the widest. We can see that he is most sensitive to environmental conditions, because his performance improves the most as the environmental conditions improve. Mary improves, too, but not as much; her range is narrower. In fact, in an enriched environment, Mary performs as well as Joe does in an average one. Tom's range is not as wide as Joe's, but his upper and lower limits are higher than both Joe's and Mary's. Even in a poor environment, he performs almost as well as Joe performs in an enriched environment.

### Probabilistic Epigenesis

Another theory of how genes and environment interact over the course of development is *probabilistic epigenesis. Epigenesis* refers to a process of gradual differentiation, and *probabilistic* indicates that this differentiation is based on elements of probability

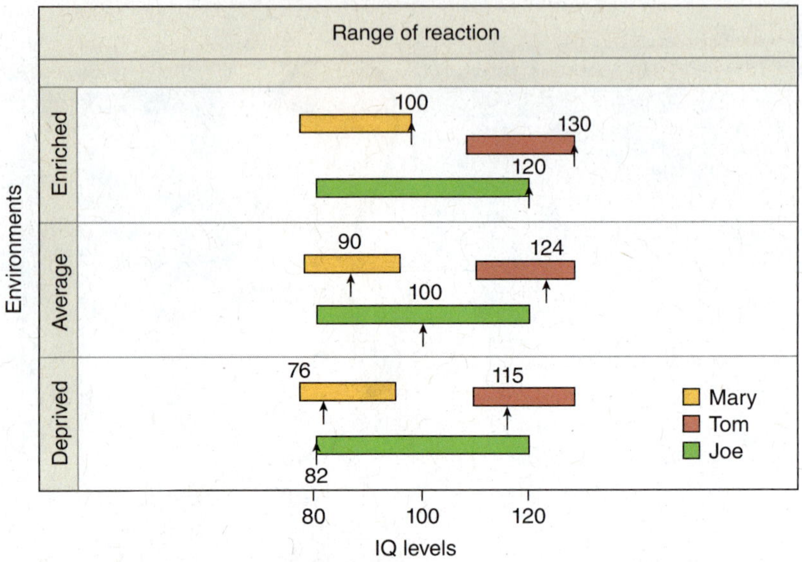


**FIGURE 2.8 Range of Reaction on IQ Tests for Three Fictional Children** This figure shows how three fictional children might perform on IQ tests over time and in different environments. You can see that they do not respond equally: Joe's range of reaction is much wider than Mary or Tom's, meaning that he is the most sensitive to environmental conditions.

and chance, rather than being predetermined. This view emphasizes the increasing complexity of interactions between genes and environments over time, so that each successive interaction further differentiates the developmental path, making it more distinct. The interactions between genes and environment are bidirectional and occur across multiple levels: genetic, neural, behavioral, and environmental. What does all this mean? In simple terms, it means that what we might predict based on genotype may differ considerably from what actually occurs (Gottlieb, 2003, 2007; Gottlieb et al., 2006).

Let's consider a fairly simple example involving aggressive, violent behavior. The enzyme monoamine oxidase A (MAOA) breaks down certain neurotransmitters in the brain after they have been used to communicate between brain cells. (We discuss neurotransmitters later in this chapter.) One behavior these neurotransmitters affect is aggression. The gene responsible for the manufacture of MAOA has a long and a short form. The shorter form results in low activity of MAOA; that is, the neurotransmitters are not broken down as needed, and the neurotransmitters remain in place instead. This increases the likelihood of violent behavior.

Researchers found that when boys with the short form of the gene are severely maltreated, 85% of them will develop aggressive behaviors; but 15% will not. Conversely, boys with the long form are far less likely to develop aggressive behaviors, even under conditions of severe maltreatment (Caspi et al., 2002). Girls do not appear to be affected in the same way, for a reason we discussed earlier: The gene is found on the X chromosome, and whereas boys have only one X chromosome, girls have two, so that the effect of one can be masked by the other.

In sum, we cannot really say that the MAOA gene "causes" aggressive, violent behavior. Only the short form of the gene increases risk, and only in the presence of severe maltreatment, and only in boys, and not in every boy who has the short form of the gene and has been mistreated. The interactions of genes, environment, experience, and perhaps other variables produce different results for different children, as the environments shape the children and the children shape their environments through multiple interactions back and forth over time.

## Quantitative Genetics

We've been exploring various theories of how genes and environment work together. We now turn to a field that tries to separate these influences. *Quantitative genetics,* sometimes also called *behavior genetics*, attempts to estimate how much of a trait or characteristic in a population can be attributed to genes and how much to environmental influences. Let's say we're looking at shyness in preschool children. In quantitative genetics, the answer to the question "How much?" is *not*, for example, "60% of shyness in a particular preschooler is attributable to inheritance." Instead, it is "60% of the variability in shyness among all preschoolers can be attributed to genes" (Rutter, 2006). It is an important distinction. Variability in this sense is a measure of differences within a specific group of people. The statistical term that is used to describe genetic variability is the *heritability estimate*. Heritability estimates are based on correlations. They are usually expressed as a range from 0 to 1.00—0 meaning no correlation and 1.00 meaning a perfect correlation.

Another measurement used to express the contribution of heredity to a particular trait is *concordance*. Concordance is based on studies of twins, which we discuss in the next section. Concordance is the extent to which twins share a particular trait. Concordance rates are expressed as percentages, ranging from 0 to 100%, with 0 indicating neither twin has the trait, and 100% indicating both have the trait.

**monozygotic twins** Genetically identical twins who developed from the same fertilized egg.

**dizygotic twins** Twins who developed from two different eggs released and fertilized at the same time.

## Research on Gene-Environment Interactions: Kinship Studies

To examine genetic and environmental contributions to phenotype, researchers often use kinship studies, which compare differences and similarities among members of the same family. These studies involve not only biological parents and siblings who share the same environment but also adopted children. Twins in particular have been studied extensively—both those reared together and those reared apart. The Minnesota Twin Family Study at the University of Minnesota has been studying about 8,000 pairs of twins of the same gender over time, beginning in 1989. Researchers from Australia, the Netherlands, the United Kingdom, and the United States have collaborated on studies involving 11,000 twin pairs (Haworth et al., 2009).

There are two types of twins. Identical twins come from the same fertilized egg, called the *zygote*, which divides into two separate but genetically identical zygotes. They are referred to as **monozygotic twins**—that is, one zygote. Fraternal twins are not identical but come from two different eggs released and fertilized at the same time. They are called **dizygotic twins**—that is, two zygotes—and are no more similar than nontwin siblings. Because monozygotic twins come from the same fertilized egg, they have the same genetic structure. It follows that if monozygotic twins are more similar to one another on a trait, such as intelligence, than are dizygotic twins, then this similarity may be attributed to their identical genetic structure. Accordingly, researchers often interpret higher concordance between monozygotic twins compared with dizygotic twins as evidence of heritability.

Note that a concordance rate cannot be 100%, and a heritability rate cannot be 1.00; that is, traits are not completely genetic. Environment plays a role. In assessing environmental contributions to development, researchers distinguish between shared and nonshared environments. Siblings typically share family environments, school environments, and so on. We would expect that these *shared environments* would make siblings more similar. However, there is also a *nonshared environment* that can make them more different. Nonshared factors include each child's unique position within the family—for example, the youngest, the oldest, the only girl—and his or her unique experiences—for example, having different teachers and friends (Rutter, 2006).

Next we look at some of the traits that have attracted interest in studies of genes and environment. First, though, we should note that the results of heritability studies should be interpreted with caution. Researchers may use different definitions and measures for the behaviors under study, and studies vary in sample size and quality. In addition, even when identical twins are separated at birth and reared apart, they are often placed by social service agencies into similar socioeconomic circumstances within the same culture. Parsing out what is truly inherited is difficult when environments are similar (Rutter, 2006).

## Intelligence

The heritability estimate for intelligence in identical twins is high—.86—supporting the case for heritability of intelligence. Of course, identical twins raised together also share an environment.

Intelligence is the subject of more genetic research than any other topic. In fact, the search for an "intelligence gene" has been described as the holy grail of behavior genetics (Rutter, 2006). It is unlikely such a gene will be found, however. In fact, the definition of intelligence itself is open to interpretation. A broad range of cognitive abilities have been identified as contributing to what we think of as intelligence. Furthermore, it appears that interactions among multiple genes are associated with some of these abilities. For example, we know there are about 300 genes associated with intellectual disabilities (Deary, Johnson, & Houlihan, 2009).

Nevertheless, to briefly summarize the extensive research, intelligence has a heritability estimate of about 0.5, with a range from 0.3 to 0.8, depending on the tests and cognitive abilities used in the studies and the age of the subjects. (See Figure 2.9 for some findings.) That is, on average, about 50% of the variability in the broad range of cognitive abilities called "intelligence" can be attributed to heredity and 50% to environmental resources and influences (Deary et al., 2009; Deary, Penke & Johnson, 2010; Plomin, DeFries, McClearn & McGuffin, 2007; Plomin & Spinath, 2004; Rutter, 2006).

Let's look at how the inherited component of intelligence might play out among twins. The heritability estimate for monozygotic twins is 0.86, and for dizygotic twins 0.6 (Plomin et al., 2007; Plomin & Spinath, 2004). Furthermore, over time, the difference between monozygotic and dizygotic twins increases (Plomin & Spinath, 2004). In addition, adopted children are more similar in intelligence to their biological parents than to their adoptive parents. The correlation between mothers and their biological children is seven to eight times stronger than that between mothers and their adoptive children (Petrill & Deter-Deckard, 2004).

Although these findings seem to support the case for heritability of intelligence, it is still important to account for those shared and nonshared environments. Research suggests that while the shared environment is an important factor in intelligence earlier in childhood, the nonshared factors have more influence over time, especially after adolescence (Plomin & Spinath, 2004). That is, biological siblings become more different as they get older. Nevertheless, as adults, biological siblings still are somewhat more like one another than are biological and adoptive siblings reared together in the same household (Loehlin, Horn & Ernst, 2007).

The issue of the heritability of intelligence has caused political as well as scientific controversy. The idea that intelligence is largely inherited has been used to explain why black children as a group have lower scores on intelligence tests than do white children, a gap that has persisted over 30 years of research (Jensen, 1969, 1998; Rushton & Jensen, 2005). However, most scientists disagree that genes are responsible for this effect. They point out that the gap has closed with better education and other opportunities. For example, a study of disadvantaged black children adopted into middle-class white

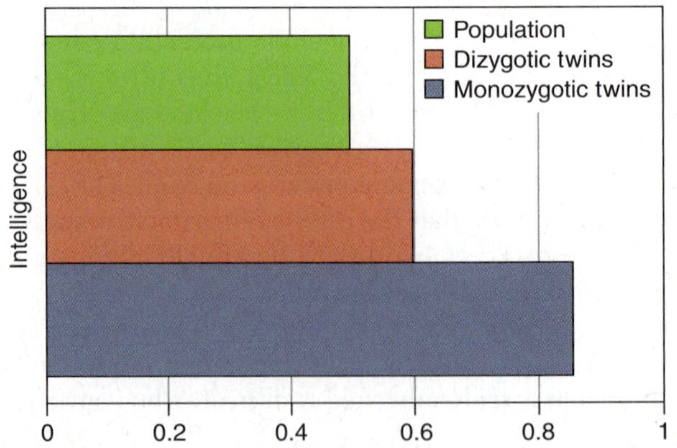


**FIGURE 2.9 Estimates of Heritability for Intelligence** In general, intelligence has a heritability estimate of about 0.5. This figure shows various estimates based on studies of twins and of the general population.

(Based on information from McGuffin, Riley, & Plomin, 2001; Plomin, DeFries, McClearn, & McGuffin, 2007; Plomin & Spinath, 2004; Rutter, 2006; and Cummings, 2006.)

homes when they were young found that these children scored as well as their adoptive siblings and better than black children raised in poverty (Nisbett, 2005, 2009). That is, a middle-class environment can nurture the genetic potential of children born without advantages.

**what if...?**

What if identical twins were separated at birth and placed in different families in different countries and in different socioeconomic and educational circumstances? As toddlers, both children are highly sociable and full of curiosity. What factors in their environments might support the full development of their intellectual potential? What factors might counter it?

### Mental Health and Behavioral Disorders

Studies of twins have generated concordance and heritability values for schizophrenia and some forms of depression, among other conditions. Here, we consider schizophrenia as an example. Schizophrenia is a severe mental illness that affects about 1% of the population. It is characterized by hallucinations, delusional thinking (such as belief that one is being persecuted by government spies), and self-neglect. The first episode of the illness usually occurs in young adulthood and requires medical management throughout life. Dozens of genes are associated with schizophrenia (OMIM 181500, 2012), making it very complex.

The concordance rate for schizophrenia among monozygotic twins, even those raised apart, is about 46%, about the same as for a child of two parents with schizophrenia. For dizygotic twins, the rate is 14%, about the same as for a child with one parent who has schizophrenia. For researchers, this suggests that the heritability estimate for schizophrenia is may be as high as .82 to .84 (Cardno & Gottesman, 2000; Cummings, 2006; Gottesman, 1991; Rutter, 2006). How it is inherited is not known.

### Physical Health: Obesity

Do genes cause overweight or obesity? In the United States, obesity in children and adolescents has increased threefold over the past 30 years. Such a large increase cannot be attributed to genetics; human evolution does not work that quickly. Too little exercise and high-calorie diets are major factors. Nevertheless, heredity does seem to play a role in body weight and risk for obesity. The concordance among monozygotic twins for the total mass of fat in one's body is reported to be 70 to 90%, and for dizygotic twins 35 to 45%. Researchers consider that in the general population, heritability for fat mass could range from 30 to 70% (Grant et al., 2008).

There are 135 different genes that have been associated with obesity, and 20 to 30 of them might contribute to the risk of obesity in humans. These candidate genes can be found on all chromosomes except Y. Researchers have yet to find the combination of genes that are associated with increased risk and do not understand how environmental factors interact with the gentoype for this risk to be realized (Raninken et al., 2006). We will return to the subject of obesity later in this text.

**✓ CHECK YOUR PROGRESS**

1. What are some mechanisms for gene-environment interactions?
2. What is probabilistic epigenesis, and how might it be related to violent behavior?
3. What are kinship studies?
4. Why is the heritability of intelligence controversial?

ntral nervous system The part of the rvous system that consists of the brain d the spinal cord.

ripheral nervous system The part of nervous system that connects the tral nervous system to sensory and other organs, muscles, blood vessels, and glands; it consists of the somatic nervous system and the autonomic nervous system.

# The Physiology of Thinking and Feeling

**[ KEY QUESTION ] 4. What are the main components of the nervous system and the brain?**

Earlier in the chapter, we discussed human biological makeup in terms of cells and genes. We're going to turn now to biology on a larger scale. We first describe the brain and nervous system and then explain how they, together with parts of the endocrine system, control how we deal with stress. Why do you need to learn about these systems? Because they provide the underlying anatomy and physiology for all of our thinking and feeling. Research over the past 20 years has vastly increased our appreciation of their implications for child development.

## The Brain and Nervous System

We refer to the critical role of the brain in child development throughout this book. In this section, we provide you with a basic understanding of how the brain and nervous system work across vast networks of cells. Here, we describe your brain—that is, the adult brain. The brain's development through childhood will be discussed separately, in later chapters. We begin by outlining the overall structure of the nervous system.

### Components of the Nervous System

The nervous system has two basic components: the central nervous system and the peripheral nervous system. The **central nervous system** consists of the brain, which sits inside the skull, and the spinal cord, which runs through the vertebrae of the spine. The **peripheral nervous system** lies outside of the central nervous system and connects it to sensory organs (such as the eyes and ears), other organs, muscles, blood vessels, and glands.

**The Central Nervous System (CNS).** We discuss the brain in more detail later. For now, think of the *spinal cord* as being like a major highway. It conducts sensory information from the peripheral nervous system to the brain, and motor information from the brain to the peripheral nervous system. The off-and-on ramps of this highway are 31 pairs of spinal nerves, each consisting of both sensory and motor pathways, which branch off from the spinal cord and go to different parts of the body via the peripheral nervous system.

The spinal cord is also the center for reflexes that protect us from harm: When you touch something hot, your hand automatically pulls back. We do not have to consciously tell our hand to move; in fact, we would need to consciously tell it to stay put. In Chapter 4, you will learn that babies are born with reflexes that disappear as their nervous systems mature. Try this: Using the tip of a regular key, quickly stroke the bottom of a friend's bare foot, from the heel to the toes. The toes will curl forward. But in babies, the toes would fan out and go upward because the sensory and motor nerves into the foot have not yet developed. In fact, if the toes had fanned out on your friend's foot, that would indicate damage to those nerves.

**The Peripheral Nervous System (PNS).** The peripheral nervous system consists of the somatic nervous system and the autonomic nervous system. The *somatic nervous system* gathers sensory information from all over the body and routes it to the spinal cord, which takes it to the brain. At the same time, the somatic nervous system conducts information from the brain through the spinal cord to muscles, telling them to move. Together, these activities are referred to as the *sensorimotor pathway*. They work closely together and with the spinal cord and brain.

In Chapter 4, you will read about the sensorimotor period of child development described by Jean Piaget. Early learning in babies occurs through their senses and

© KidStock/Blend Images/Corbis

Altrendo Images/Getty Images

A newborn may wave his arms and even appears to reach out purposefully to grasp things, but he cannot yet succeed because his sensorimotor pathways are incomplete. As his nervous system matures, and with practice, he develops the ability to reach for and grab things that attract him.

through movement of the muscles in their hands, feet, arms, legs, eyes, and so on. At first, these movements are not under the baby's control because the sensorimotor pathways are incomplete. As the nervous system matures, and with practice, the baby is able to reach, grab, and turn over on purpose.

The second part of the PNS is the *autonomic nervous system*, which is made up of the sympathetic nervous system and the parasympathetic nervous system. Unlike the somatic nervous system, the autonomic nervous system is not a two-way street of information exchange. Instead, it tends to operate more or less on its own, without our awareness or control. The *parasympathetic nervous system* controls normal body maintenance functions, such as digestion. The *sympathetic nervous system* is responsible for the freeze-fight-flight response, which we address in more detail shortly.

## Cells of the Nervous System

There are two types of cells in the nervous system: neurons and glia. **Neurons** are the fundamental units of the nervous system. They are like other somatic cells in many ways. However, they differ in that they have dendrites and axons—structures through which they communicate with other neurons. *Dendrites* receive information from other neurons and bring it into the cell body, and *axons* send the information out to other neurons. Dendrites (receivers), as shown in Figure 2.10, are multiple short branches that extend from the neuron's cell body. In contrast, a neuron typically has only one axon, often a very long thread. However, a single axon (sender) can have many branches at the tip. Each branch has an axon terminal that connects it to many other cells. Dendrites and axons create a vast network among the 100 billion or so neurons in the adult brain (Ropper & Samuels, 2009). The process of developing new neurons is called **neurogenesis.**

**Glia** comes from a Greek word meaning "glue." Glial cells are so called because they were long thought to be the glue that insulated neurons and held them together. Glia, which make up 90% of the brain, were not considered to be involved in the communication among neurons that supposedly constitutes thought. You may have heard someone say that we use only 10% of our brains. This misconception came from the idea that we use only our neurons and not our glia. More recently, research suggests that glial cells do communicate with neurons after all, as well as with each other (Koob, 2009).

The neurons and glia that make up the brain and spinal cord of the central nervous system are differentiated into white and gray matter. Gray matter is made up of the neurons' cell bodies and dendrites. White matter is made up of bundles of axons that are wrapped in *myelin sheaths*, which are made of glial cells. Myelin sheaths act very much like insulation on an electric cord. **Myelination** is the process of laying

**neurons** Nerve cells; neurons have dendrites and axons through which they communicate with each other.

**neurogenesis** The process of developing new neurons.

**glia** Cells in the nervous system that insulate neurons and hold them together.

**myelination** The process of laying down myelin sheaths to insulate the axons of neurons; it begins before birth and occurs in spurts throughout childhood.

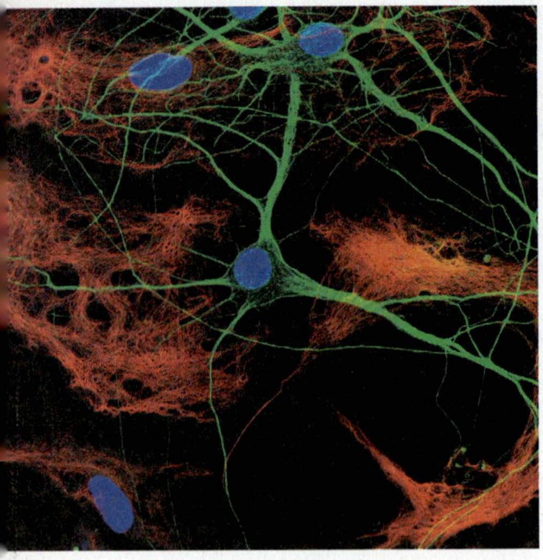

Claire E. Cockcroft - Babraham Hall, Babraham Research Campus

In this photo, the neuron's cell body is shown in blue; its axons and dendrites are shown in green.

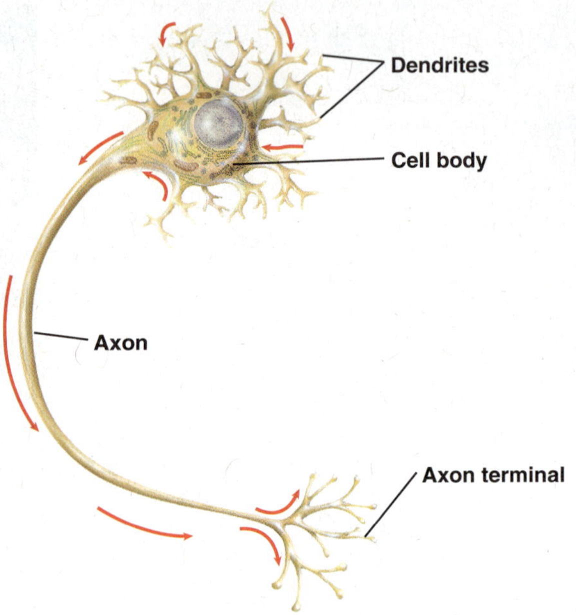


**FIGURE 2.10 The Anatomy of a Neuron** A neuron consists of a cell body, an axon, and dendrites. The arrows in the figure indicate the flow of information.

Reprinted with permission of John Wiley & Sons, Inc., from Comer, R., & Gould, E. (2013). *Psychology Around Us* (2nd ed.). Hoboken, NJ: Wiley, p. 116, Figure 4.1.

down myelin sheaths, which begins before birth, but occurs at a rapid pace thereafter and through adolescence. In later chapters, you will see that spurts in myelination are associated with some critical milestones in physical and cognitive development.

## Neuron Communication

We've said that neurons communicate with each other. How does this happen? First, through an electrochemical process called the *action potential*, an outgoing charge passes down a neuron's axon. When it reaches the axon terminal, though, it can't be sent directly to the dendrites of the next neuron. The message must instead go across a tiny space called a **synapse** (see Figure 2.11). Communication across synapses depends in part on chemicals called **neurotransmitters.** When a charge reaches the end of an axon, it triggers a release of neurotransmitters from the axon terminal into

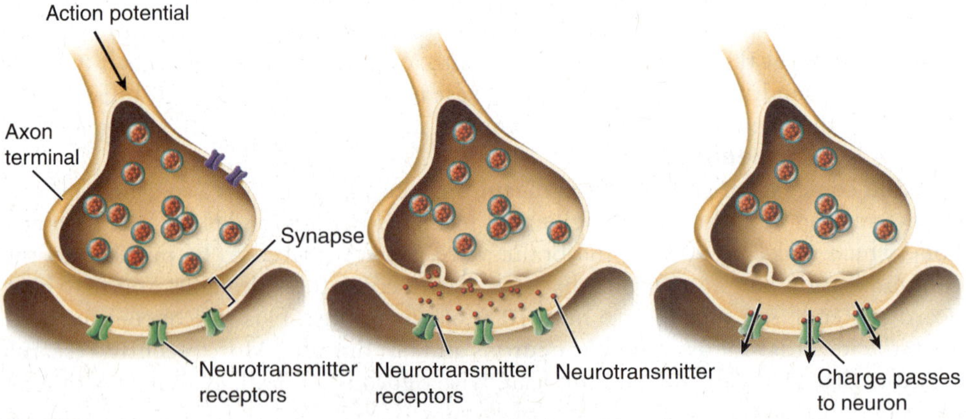


**FIGURE 2.11 Communication Across a Synapse** A positive charge travels down the axon and stimulates the release of neurotransmitters into the synapse. The neurotransmitters bind to receptors on the next neuron, allowing the charge to travel into that neuron.

Adapted with permission of John Wiley & Sons, Inc., from Comer, R., & Gould, E. (2013). *Psychology Around Us* (2nd ed.). Hoboken, NJ: Wiley, p. 120, Figure 4.4.

**Table 2.3** Examples of Neurotransmitters

| Neurotransmitter | Some Actions |
|---|---|
| Norepinephrine (adrenaline) | Increases heart rate, blood pressure, breathing, and oxygen intake; causes the freeze-fight-flight response. |
| Gamma aminobutyric acid (GABA) | Inhibits release of norepinephrine and so dampens the anxiety we feel in the freeze-fight-flight response. |
| Acetylcholine | Stimulates muscle movement and the gastrointestinal system; is necessary for learning and memory. |
| Dopamine | Required for smooth and coordinated movement. Too little causes rigid muscle movement, whereas too much is associated with schizophrenia and hallucinations. |
| Serotonin | Involved in mood, depression, emotion, sleep, and possibly appetite. |
| Endorphin | An opiate synthesized in the body; associated with pain relief, pleasure, and a sense of well-being. |

the synapse. On the receiving dendrite of the next neuron are receptors, each built to recognize only a specific kind of neurotransmitter. The binding of a neurotransmitter to a receptor creates an electrical signal. Most neurotransmitters have an *excitatory* effect—they make it more likely that the next neuron will fire, passing along the message. Some, however, have an *inhibitory* effect, making firing less likely.

There are many kinds of neurotransmitters, with many different functions; a few are listed in Table 2.3. And every day, we can see the effects of neurotransmission gone awry. For example, one reason for the learning and memory problems associated with intellectual disability may be that neurotransmitters are not properly synthesized due to a genetic defect in how RNA reads DNA—that is, a transcription problem (Johnston, Alemi, & Harum, 2003). In fact, Nobel laureate Eric Kandel once described the process of memory storage as a "dialogue between genes and synapses" (Kandel, 2001). That is, both need to work correctly.

Other problems relate to how neurotransmitters are passed from neuron to neuron. After a neurotransmitter is released into a synapse, the releasing neuron eventually reabsorbs what's left—a kind of recycling. This process is called *re-uptake*. On the one hand, failure to re-uptake the neurotransmitter leaves too much in the synapse, overstimulating the receptor. On the other hand, re-uptaking too quickly leaves insufficient amounts. In either case, the message isn't transmitted as it should have been. Various physical and mental conditions result from too much or too little of a neurotransmitter.

## Structures Within the Brain

As we mentioned, the brain is part of the central nervous system, sitting at the top of the spinal column. Next, we briefly describe the structures of the brain from the inside out, beginning with the most primitive neurological structures (Ropper & Samuels, 2009). Figure 2.12 shows a cross-section of the brain, indicating those structures, which we describe here.

- *Brainstem, Pons, and Reticular Formation.* The *brainstem*, also called the *medulla*, is sometimes referred to as the "primitive brain" because it regulates survival functions, especially breathing and heart rate, automatically and outside of our awareness. For example, if you pass out, the brainstem will immediately trigger the lungs to breathe for you. Injuries to the brainstem are usually fatal. The *pons* is important for attention, and the *reticular formation* is associated with sleep and mood.

**synapse** A tiny space between neurons, across which the neurons communicate.

**neurotransmitters** Chemicals released into the synapse by neurons to enhance communication between neurons.

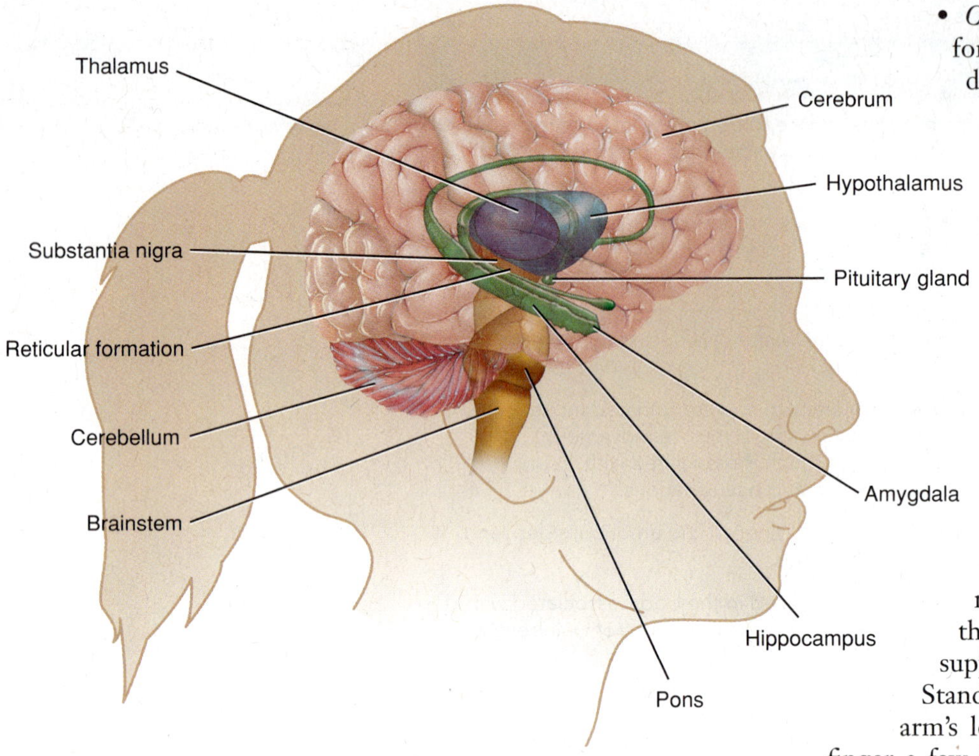


**FIGURE 2.12 Cross-Section of the Brain** The brain includes several major structures, each with its own special functions.

Adapted with permission of John Wiley & Sons, Inc., from Comer, R., & Gould, E. (2013). *Psychology Around Us* (2nd ed.). Hoboken, NJ: Wiley, p. 125, Figure 4.7.

- *Cerebellum.* The *cerebellum* is best known for its role in motor and spatial coordination, but it also plays a role in cognition (Strata, 2009), especially learning math (Feng, Fan, Yu, Lu, & Tang, 2008). In addition, it is involved in tasks requiring verbal working memory, planning, and shifting from one task to another, as well as spatial cognition (Ackermann, Mathiak & Riecker, 2007; Schmahmann & Caplan, 2006). Spinning around on the playground really is helping children learn in the classroom!
- *Substantia Nigra.* The *substantia nigra* is located in the midbrain and, like the cerebellum, is important for movement. This structure produces the neurotransmitter dopamine, which supports fluidity of movement. Try this: Stand face to face with a friend, at about an arm's length distance. Hold up your index finger a few inches in front of your face and ask your friend to first touch her nose and then touch your finger. People with disorders related to these areas of the brain, such as Parkinson's disease, cannot smoothly and precisely make this movement.
- *Thalamus, Hypothalamus, and Pituitary Gland.* The thalamus and hypothalamus are collections of neurons, rather than discrete structures. The *thalamus* is the major relay station of the nervous system. All sensory information, except smell, is routed through the thalamus. The hypothalamus is connected to the *pituitary gland*, and together they regulate hormones for growth and puberty. The *hypothalamus* plays a major role in the stress response and is also involved in motivation for basic human functioning, such as eating and sex.
- *Amygdala and Limbic System.* The *limbic system* is a set of individual structures surrounding the thalamus that form a network of connections often referred to as the seat of emotions (Andrews, 2001). In addition to the thalamus, these structures include the hypothalamus, amygdala, and hippocampus, as well as the prefrontal lobe. The *amygdala*, an important part of the limbic system, triggers a fear response when we encounter something we have learned to fear (Davis, 1992), even if we are not consciously aware of sensing it. The amygdala is especially sensitive to human facial expressions. Not surprisingly, the amygdala plays a significant role in emotional stress. In Chapter 10, you will learn that children who have been abused are more sensitive to angry faces, even when they don't remember seeing them, than are children who have not been abused (Pollak, Cicchetti, Klorman, & Brumaghim, 1997).
- *Hippocampus.* The *hippocampus* is important for memory and learning. There are three basic types of memory: sensory, short-term, and long-term. The hippocampus is essential for new learning, stored temporarily in short-term memory (Andrews, 2001; Squire, Stark & Clark, 2004). The hippocampus and the amygdala work closely together for memories of specific events that carry personal meaning, often called episodic memory.
- *Cerebrum.* The *cerebrum* is by far the largest part of the brain, and consists of four lobes. It is responsible for all of our higher thought processes. The cerebrum and cerebellum are covered by a thin layer of gray matter (neuronal cell bodies) called the **cerebral cortex**. With maturation, the cerebral cortex becomes very convoluted, with many peaks and furrows. As you will see throughout this book, brain maturation depends in large part on the child's interactions with the environment.

**cerebral cortex** The cerebral cortex is the thin layer of gray matter (neuronal cell bodies) that covers the cerebrum and cerebellum.

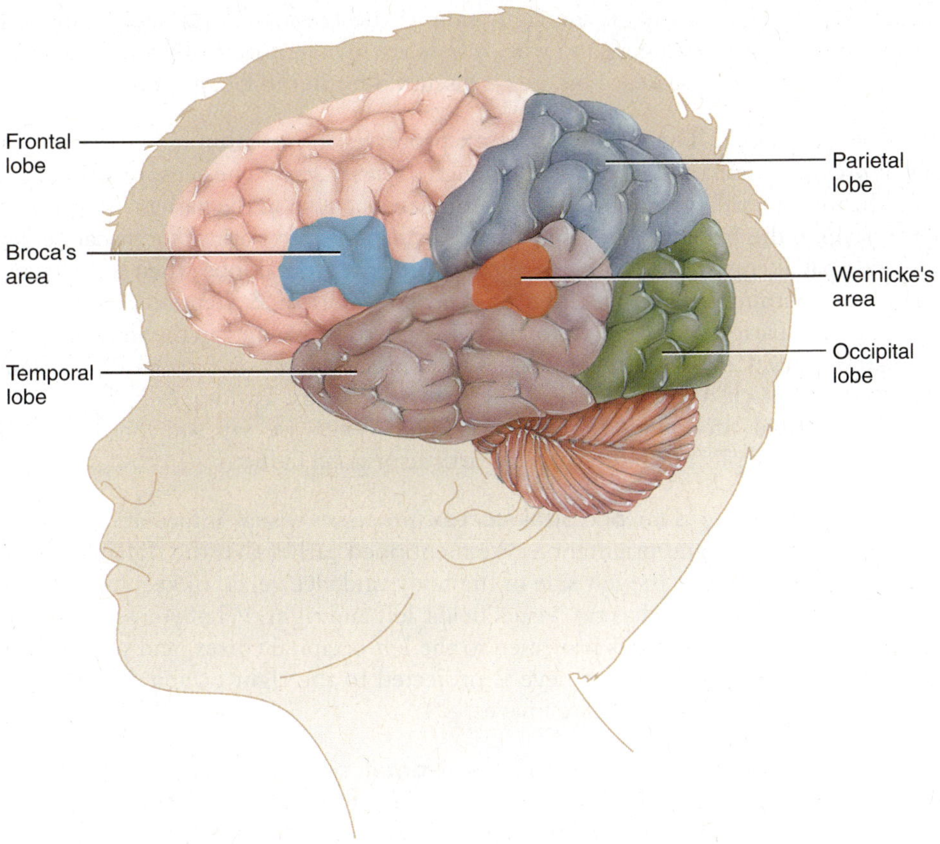


**FIGURE 2.13 The Lobes of the Cerebrum** The cerebrum is generally subdivided into four lobes: frontal, parietal, occipital, and temporal. Also shown in the figure are Broca's area, located in the frontal lobe, and Wernicke's area, located in the temporal lobe. Both are important for speech and language.

Adapted with permission of John Wiley & Sons, Inc., from Comer, R., & Gould, E. (2013). *Psychology Around Us* (2nd ed.). Hoboken, NJ: Wiley, p. 129, Figure 4.9.

## The Lobes of the Cerebrum

Let's look at the cerebrum more closely, because it is what we think of when we talk about our brains. The cerebrum is divided into four lobes: frontal, parietal, occipital, and temporal, as shown in Figure 2.13. When we talk about the lobes in this section, we focus on the gray matter that makes up the cerebral cortex.

The cerebrum has two hemispheres, left and right. Accordingly, each lobe also has a left and right side. The left side, in general, controls the right side of the body. When you raise your right hand, for example, the message to do that comes from the left hemisphere of your brain. The two hemispheres are connected by the *corpus callosum* (Latin for "tough body"), a large area of white matter that allows sensory and motor information to be communicated between the hemispheres.

The two hemispheres are also marked by asymmetry. That is, their functions aren't exactly the same—a characteristic called **lateralization**. Table 2.4 gives a very general outline of some functions that have been associated with each hemisphere.

TEMPORAL CORTEX. The **temporal cortex** processes information about sound. It also is involved in consciously remembering past events and in recognizing faces (Eichenbaum, Yonelinas, & Ranganath, 2007; Squire, Wixted, & Clark, 2007). Where the left temporal cortex meets the left parietal cortex is *Wernicke's area*, a region that is involved in language comprehension. (This is true for right-handed people; in left-handed

**Table 2.4** Functions Associated with the Right and Left Hemispheres of the Brain

| Functions Often Associated with Left Brain | Functions Often Associated with Right Brain |
|---|---|
| Language and speech | Visual-motor tasks |
| Analytic thought | Holistic thought (seeing the "big picture") |
| Logic | Intuition |
| Math and science | Creativity |
| | Art and music |

**lateralization** The extent to which certain brain functions are associated with either the right or left hemisphere of the brain.

**temporal cortex** Brain region that processes information about sound and is involved in consciously remembering past events, and for facial recognition.

**l c** ... in region that ses ... ion about sensation.

**al** ... ain region that ses ... ormation.

**cc** ... n region in which most us ... takes place.

**executive function** The capacity to regulate one's thinking and behavior.

people, Wernicke's area is on the right side of the brain.) People with damage to Wernicke's area do not understand what others are saying, nor can they monitor what they say for possible mistakes. This area is discussed further in Chapters 6 and 9.

Parietal Cortex. The **parietal cortex** processes information about sensation—touch, pressure, pain, and vibration—through a *sensory strip.* The sensory strip and its twin, the motor strip, lie side by side, with the sensory strip in the parietal lobe and the motor strip in the frontal lobe. The parietal cortex is also important for visual perception and spatial cognition, and it coordinates with the frontal lobe when we decide to reach for something that we see (Johnson, Ferraina, Bianchi, & Caminiti, 1996).

The right parietal cortex in particular is associated with ability in the visual arts, music, mathematics (Cohen Kadosh, Cohen Kadosh, Kaas, Henik, & Goebel, 2007; Tsang, Dougherty, Deutsch, Wandell, & Ben–Shachar, 2009; Varga, Pavlova, & Nosova, 2010), and visual-spatial processing (Klingberg, 2006). When we say someone is "right-brained," we generally mean the person is artistic or good in math.

Occipital Cortex. The **occipital cortex** processes visual information, such as lines, color, patterns, and orientation. We mentioned earlier that the right side of the brain sends its signals to the left side of the body, and vice versa. In keeping with this principle, each of our eyes has two visual fields, left and right. What you see with your right visual field in each eye is projected to the left occipital cortex, and what you see with your left visual field in each eye is projected to the right occipital cortex. The frontal cortex makes sense of these images.

Frontal Cortex. As already noted, the **frontal cortex** contains the *motor strip,* which controls voluntary movement. In addition, the left frontal cortex (in right-handed people) contains *Broca's area,* which is important for speech production, such as putting the right words in the right order. Recall that Wernicke's area, too, is generally on the left side of the brain. That explains why people who are good at language may be described "left-brained." As with Wernicke's area, we discuss Broca's area further in Chapters 6 and 9.

The part of the frontal cortex closest to the forehead is the *prefrontal cortex.* This area works as part of the limbic system because it ascribes meaning to emotion. In much the same way, the prefrontal correct is also is associated with **executive function**—our capacity to regulate our own thinking, feeling, and behavior (Garon, Bryson, & Smith, 2008). Executive behaviors include the ability to focus attention, shift attention, plan ahead, make decisions, solve problems, and hold information in working memory. Executive behaviors also include emotional self-regulation—for example, inhibiting the impulse to strike out and thinking before speaking. As you will see in later chapters, executive function improves throughout childhood and adolescence as the brain continues to develop.

### Brain Development and the Environment

Today, we understand that the brain develops in response to environmental conditions and stimuli. We also know there are sensitive periods of brain development, both before and after birth, as mentioned in Chapter 1. Interference with development during these periods can mean that certain abilities will not develop. Interference can involve either the presence of an adverse influence or the absence of a positive one. The effects may be permanent, or the brain may reorganize to recover some or all of the compromised abilities. You will learn more about these topics in later chapters.

## The Endocrine System and the Physiology of Stress

We conclude this section with a discussion of how the nervous system and the endocrine system work together to create the experience we call stress. Stress is a physiological state that comes from the meaning we ascribe to events. Stress in manageable doses can be good for us, as it allows us to exercise our responses to life's ups and downs. Unfortunately, chronic stress can have serious consequences for developing children.

## The Endocrine System

The endocrine system, which we discuss in greater detail elsewhere in this book, consists of several hormone-producing glands located throughout the body. The hypothalamus and pituitary gland are located in the brain; the thyroid gland, in the neck; the adrenal glands, at the top of the kidneys; and the pancreas deep in the abdomen. The reproductive glands are the testes in males and ovaries in females.

## Allostasis and Allostatic Load

Our bodies need to maintain physiological stability as events and activities produce day-to-day changes in our lives. We do this through a process called *allostasis*. The autonomic nervous system is responsible for allostasis through a system referred to as the HPA axis, so called because it involves the hypothalamus, the pituitary gland, and the adrenal glands. The HPA axis allows our blood pressure, heart rate, hormone production, and so on to increase or decrease as needed. Sometimes, though, it becomes overloaded. To understand how this happens, we need to return to the freeze-fight-flight response, which we mentioned earlier.

The freeze-fight-flight response is an immediate and automatic reaction to perceived threat that is controlled by the sympathetic nervous system (Gray, 1988; McEwen & Lasley, 2002). The freeze response makes us stop, look, and listen as we assess the threat. We attempt to flee from harm if we can, or fight if we cannot. The freeze-fight-flight response was designed to deal with short-term stressors. You can imagine, for example, how helpful it might have been to our human ancestors as they faced physical threats, such as wild animals. The response should shut off once the stressors are gone, returning us to normal.

*Everyday stories*

THE FREEZE-FIGHT-FLIGHT RESPONSE IN ACTION Let's say you oversleep on the morning of an exam. You take a look at the clock, and your adrenal glands release the hormone epinephrine (adrenaline). Perception narrows as you freeze momentarily. You jump into some clothes, run out the door, and dash down the street. Your heart rate increases and sends blood to major muscle groups in the arms and legs while diverting blood from your digestive system. Your lungs dilate to take in more oxygen. Glucose stores around your body are released, providing an immediate source of energy. If more energy is needed, the pituitary gland releases cortisol, a hormone that converts other sources of fuel, such as fat, into energy. You get to the bus on time, climb aboard, and calm down as the freeze-fight-flight response turns off.

But when stress becomes chronic, the stress response does not shut off. The result is **allostatic load**. The same hormones—adrenaline and especially cortisol—that are helpful in responding to short-term stressors remain at higher than normal levels in the blood stream, potentially damaging glands, organs, and the brain. Chronic stress is associated with high blood pressure, heart disease, type 2 diabetes, loss of protein, compromised immunity, depression, fatigue, memory problems, and behavior changes.

WHEN SYSTEMS CONNECT

## Stress and Child Development

Now let's consider how chronic stress can affect children's development. As with so many other aspects of development, the effect occurs through complex relationships between children and their environments. Thus, the combined effects of biology, environment, and stress can affect children differently. For example, some children may be more genetically vulnerable to the physiological changes associated with chronic stress than are others (McEwen & Wingfield, 2003). We also know that deprived environments contribute to allostatic load, which becomes associated with other problems.

**allostatic load** The physiological cost of chronic stress.

For example, an association between allostatic load and problems with health, academics, and behavior has been found in research on homelessness (Worthman & Panter–Brick, 2008) and in research on accumulated psychosocial stress, such as poverty along with crowded living conditions (Evans, Kim, Ting, Tesher, & Shannis, 2007). Chronic stress related to poverty during childhood has been found to compromise working memory in adults, suggesting that some changes to the brain may be permanent (Evans & Schamburg, 2009). Of course, not all children who grow up in poverty experience chronic stress, and not all children who experience chronic stress grow up in poverty. Unrelenting family conflict irrespective of socioeconomic circumstances can contribute to allostatic load as well (Davies, Sturge–Apple, Cicchetti & Cummings, 2007).

Children who have been maltreated are especially vulnerable to the physiological effects of allostatic load. They experience significant changes in the brain that interfere with learning and emotional self-regulation. In addition, their physiological reactions to stress may be reprogrammed, permanently altering the stress response (Grassi–Oliveira, Ashy, & Stein, 2008; Gunnar, Fisher, & Early Experience, Stress, and Prevention Network, 2006; Gunnar & Quevedo, 2007). But again, these changes do not necessarily happen in all maltreated children, nor are they always manifested in the same way (Caspi et al., 2002).

We can see how chronic stress involves all biological and social systems in a true "neurons to neighborhoods" fashion. You will learn in later chapters that there are factors that can protect children from some of the more negative consequences of chronic stress, making them more resilient in the face of adversity.

**what if...?**

Let's say you are a schoolteacher and one of your students is having difficulty managing his anger at school, and is not doing well academically. You suspect there is a lot of strife at home. How would you talk with the child's parents at your parent-teacher conference about your concerns? What if they say they don't see how problems at home would affect their child at school? What could you do to help this child?

**CHECK YOUR PROGRESS**

1. What are the components of the nervous system?
2. How do neurons communicate?
3. What are the lobes of the brain, and what are some functions of each?
4. Which structures in the brain are responsible for emotion and memory?
5. What is allostasis? What are the implications of allostatic load for child development?

## Children's Well-Being in Society

**[ KEY QUESTION ] 4.** How does health-care policy affect children's well-being?

We began the chapter by citing the book *From Neurons to Neighborhoods.* We started by describing neurons and noted that the "neighborhood" is the environment, from family to school to society in general. Consistent with the lessons of *From Neurons to Neighborhoods*, in this book we often ask you to think about the connections between development, health, and the environment. Accordingly, we end this chapter with a discussion of children's health and well-being in society.

In the United States, we tend to take our health for granted. Most of us are too young to remember the scourges of smallpox, measles, polio, and whooping cough. Today, American children are more likely to die from accidents than from disease. In this section, we provide a brief overview of the well-being of American children and some of the issues that affect their health. We will return to these topics throughout this book, because normal child development is predicated on good health, and that good health is achieved through good nutrition, exercise, clean air and water, education, and preventive health care.

## Indicators of Children's Well-Being in the United States

The U.S. government tracks six dimensions of children's well-being: family and social environment, economic circumstances, health, health care, physical environment and safety, and education. A sampling of the most recent findings appears in Table 2.5. In compiling these statistics, the government uses 23 sources of national data, many of which are based on self-report surveys. Data on education are taken from school records. Air and water quality are measured by the Environmental Protection Agency.

Is there anything in the table that surprises you? Are you wondering how the United States compared with other developed countries? The United Nations Children's Fund (UNICEF) compared children's well-being in 21 developed countries based on comparable dimensions. The United States ranked last for child health and safety, and 18th overall. Its highest ranking—12—was in education (UNICEF, 2007). Next, we focus on one aspect of well-being that we will revisit throughout this book: health care.

## Health Care among American Children

Health care is a complicated issue in the United States. Among 13 industrialized nations, ours is the only one that does not provide universal coverage for our citizens—or that, until March 2010, did not require its citizens to purchase health-care insurance (Squires, 2010). The Institute of Medicine (2001, 2003) reports that our system of health care is fragmented; that is, it consists of many different, unrelated parts, with wide gaps in quality and access. How do these factors affect our children?

**Table 2.5** Selected Indicators of U.S. Children's Well-Being, 2010

| Indicators | Percentage in 2010 |
|---|---|
| Children ages 0–17 living with two married parents | 66% |
| Children ages 5–17 who speak a language other than English at home and who have difficulty speaking English | 4.9% |
| Related children ages 0–17 living in poverty | 20% |
| Children ages 0–17 in households classified by USDA as "food insecure"* | 23% |
| Children ages 0–17 covered by health insurance at some time during the year | 90% |
| Children ages 0–17 with no usual source of health care | 6% |
| Children ages 19–35 months who have had the recommended series of vaccinations | 70% |
| Infants weighing less than 5 lb 8 oz at birth | 8.2% |
| Deaths before first birthday | 6.4 per 1,000 |
| Children ages 0–17 living in counties where levels of one or more air pollutants were above allowable levels | 59% |
| Children served by community water systems that did not meet all applicable health-based drinking water standards | 7% |
| Injury deaths of children ages 1–4 | 11 per 100,000 |
| Injury deaths of children ages 5–14 | 5.7 per 100,000 |
| Injury deaths of adolescents ages 15–19 | 39 per 100,000 |
| Children ages 3–5 who were read to every day in the previous week by a family member | 55% |
| Young adults ages 18–24 who have completed high school | 90% |
| Youth ages 16–19 who are neither enrolled in school nor working | 9% |

*Food-insecure households are those in which either adults, children, or both are unable to acquire sufficient nutrition to support active, healthy living because they lack the money or other resources (such as access to transportation) needed to acquire food.

*Source: America's Children: Key National Indicators of Well-Being, 2011,* http://childstats.gov/americaschildren/glance.asp.

## Who Is Covered by Insurance, and How? Policy

The vast majority of U.S. children are covered by health insurance through a parent's employer. The poorest children are covered by the government program called Medicaid. However, children of working parents who have no employee health benefits and who do not qualify for Medicaid have often been left without insurance. Although the number of children without insurance has declined since the 1990s, a report from the Robert Wood Johnson Foundation indicates that in 2008 about 7.3 million American children lacked health insurance (Lynch, Phong, Kenney, & Macri, 2010). Many of these children may be eligible for private insurance through State Child Health Insurance Programs (SCHIP)—more commonly called CHIP.

CHIP began in 1998 and was reauthorized by Congress in 2012. It makes health insurance available to uninsured children through government subsidies to private insurance companies. The program is financed jointly by the federal and state governments but is administered by the states. Each state determines the design of its program, including who is eligible, what the benefit packages are, how much money families pay based on their income, and so forth. The states budget for a certain amount and then receive matching funds from the federal government.

*Everyday stories*

NEW YORK'S CHIP New York State offers Child Health Plus, a managed-care program for uninsured children who are not poor enough to qualify for Medicaid. Health-care providers who participate in the program are located throughout the state to ensure that all eligible children have access to a provider. Parents choose one of the providers to manage their children's health care. Benefits include physician visits, medical equipment, hospital visits, prescription medication, mental health visits, speech therapy, and hospice care. Cost depends on household income, and eligible families pay between $9 and $60 a month to participate. (To learn more, visit http://www.health.ny.gov/health_care/child_health_plus/.)

In March 2010, Congress passed the Patient Protection and Affordable Care Act (Public Law 111–148), which will be rolled out in phases through 2015. Provisions of the law apply to all ages and socioeconomic groups, but some are specific to youth. The new law prevents insurance companies from denying coverage to children due to a preexisting condition, such as asthma or cancer. Additional funding will be provided for CHIP programs. And young adults are allowed to stay on their parent's plan until they turn 26 years old. Starting in 2014, people who do not have insurance from their employer will be able to buy it directly in an Affordable Insurance Exchange established in participating states. (To learn more about Public Law 111–148, go to http://www.healthcare.gov.)

The law, which was upheld as constitutional by the United States Supreme Court in 2012, remains controversial. Opponents cite the cost of covering so many Americans at government expense. There is also concern that employers may stop offering health insurance as a benefit, forcing their employees into publicly supported systems and further increasing government costs. The primary opposition to the bill, however, centers on the fact that purchasing health insurance is mandatory, which many consider a violation of personal rights.

### Access, Quality, and Disparities

Having insurance does not guarantee equitable care. There are disparities in care, and these disparities are based on access and quality. *Access* means having a health-care provider. *Quality* involves such components as seeing medical and dental health-care providers for routine preventive care, being up to date on immunizations, and receiving the latest standard of care for an illness. A *disparity* exists when a particular group has less access to care or receives care that is lower in quality than would be expected based on accepted standards. Sometimes the disparity is based on a patient's personal choice—for example, a decision to not have children immunized against communicable diseases. More often, disparity is related to barriers such as out-of-pocket costs for care and transportation to a clinic, as well as lack of education about how the health system works and what questions to ask during a medical appointment (Institute of Medicine, 2003, 2008; United States Department of Health and Human Services, 2003).

Unfortunately, racial and ethnic disparities continue to exist even when access to care and patients' preferences are not factors. For example, we know that the incidence of diabetes, heart disease, HIV/AIDS, cancer, stroke, and infant mortality are higher among persons of color than white Americans. Why? Many social and economic issues are involved, including lack of trust in the health-care system (Institute of Medicine, 2003, 2008). You will read in Chapter 11 how school-based clinics have begun to close the disparity gap for African American children.

what if...?

What if every child in the United States were guaranteed the same standard of health care, without regard to health or to social or economic status? What differences do you think it would make in the long run to children, their families, and society? Why do you think there are disparities in health care? What are some different ways in which these disparities could be addressed?

## A Hmong Child in the American Health-Care System

Practice

Cultural beliefs can also affect access to and quality of health care for children. The following true story presents the complex challenges of integrating health care, child development, and culture.

A mother brought her 4-year-old son to a local clinic because a deep cut on his finger had become infected. She was Hmong, a people that migrated for centuries throughout Asia before settling in Laos and relocating to the United States. They are known for their adamant refusal to assimilate into local cultures. The clinic was familiar with the case of another Hmong child, named Lia Lee, whose story we mentioned in Chapter 1. Her parents had refused to administer anti-seizure medications to their child based on their belief that the seizures were evidence of a divine spirit. Subsequently, the doctors were obligated to report the family to social services, resulting in yet more conflict about the child's care (Fadiman, 1998).

In the case of the boy with the infected finger, the doctors explained to his mother through an interpreter that they needed to perform surgery to clean the wound and repair damaged ligaments. She became quite upset, refused to accept treatment for her son, and left. Fortunately, the interpreter was also a cultural mediator for the clinic, and visited the mother and child at home. The mediator learned that before visiting the clinic the mother had taken her son to a Hmong healer. The healer had performed several rituals and advised that the hand not be touched until it had healed. The interpreter then met with the local Hmong leader, and together they arranged a meeting of the family, the doctors, and the Hmong healer. The Hmong healer listened, consulted with the Hmong leader, and then explained to the mother that the doctors were also healers. He gave permission for the surgery, the mother immediately agreed, and the boy recovered (Homer, 2005).

In health care, there is an increasing emphasis on culturally competent care. That means the family's cultural beliefs are integrated into safe and effective care for children. Research in child development has contributed to the understanding that children's physical well-being rests on an alignment of biological, family, community, and cultural systems—from "neurons to neighborhoods" (Shonkoff & Phillips, 2000). We will refer to this broader perspective on child health and development throughout this book.

CHECK YOUR PROGRESS

1. What are some of the indicators of child well-being in the United States?
2. How do most children in the United States get health insurance coverage? What are some other sources of insurance coverage?
3. What are the relationships between access to health care, quality of care, and health-care disparities?

# CHAPTER SUMMARY

## The Biology of Life

**[ KEY QUESTION ] 1. What aspects of the biology of life at the cellular level matter in human development?**

- Cells perform essential functions to sustain life and make development possible.
- DNA contains all of the instructions needed to direct the activities of cells.
- RNA carries, transcribes, and translates those instructions in order to make proteins.
- Proteins do the work of the cells.

## Genes and Heredity

**[ KEY QUESTION ] 2. How are traits passed from generation to generation?**

- Genes are segments of DNA. They are arranged in chromosomes, with each gene occupying a specific place. In humans, there are 46 chromosomes in each somatic cell and 23 in each germ cell. During meiosis, germ cells combine to form a cell with 46 chromosomes, 23 from each germ cell. This is where heredity is determined.
- Traits are controlled by alleles. When a person inherits an identical pair of alleles, one from each parent, the person is homozygous for the trait. When the alleles are different, the person is heterozygous for the trait.
- A person's inherited potential is his or her genotype; how that potential is ultimately manifested is the person's phenotype.
- Autosomal patterns of inheritance include recessive, dominant, incomplete dominant, and codominant patterns.
- Some inherited disorders are carried on the sex chromosomes instead of the autosomal chromosomes.
- Chromosomal disorders, such as Down syndrome, generally are not inherited but are naturally occurring irregularities.
- Parents concerned about having a child with a hereditary disorder may receive genetic counseling.

## Gene-Environment Interactions

**[ KEY QUESTION ] 3. What are some explanations for how genes and the environment interact?**

- Experience-expectant and experience-dependent development focus on how children become more different as they experience the unique aspects of their environments. Canalization makes similar assumptions.
- Genotype-environment correlations stress the bidirectional nature of the relationship between child and environment, and include passive, evocative, and active effects.
- In the range of reaction concept, the genotype sets upper and lower limits, and the environment helps to determine the ultimate outcome.
- Probabilistic epigenesis refers to a process of gradual differentiation that is based on elements of probability and chance, meaning that predictions based on genotype may be inaccurate.
- Quantitative genetics tries to separate the influence of genetics from that of environment to estimate how much of a trait is inherited. Measures used in quantitative genetics include heritability estimates and concordances.
- Researchers in quantitative genetics often study members of the same family, especially twins.
- Intelligence (as measured by an Intelligence Test) has a heritability estimate of about 0.5. Certain health problems, such as depression, schizophrenia, and obesity, have some genetic components but cannot be explained by genes alone.

## The Physiology of Thinking and Feeling

**[ KEY QUESTION ] 4. What are the main components of the nervous system and the brain?**

- The two basic components of the nervous system are the central nervous system, which includes the spinal cord and the brain, and the peripheral nervous system.
- The peripheral nervous system consists of the autonomic nervous system and the somatic nervous system. The autonomic nervous system, in turn, consists of the sympathetic nervous system and parasympathetic nervous system.
- There are two types of cells in the nervous system: neurons and glia.
- Neurons communicate with each other across synapses. Communication across synapses depends in part on chemicals called neurotransmitters.
- Structures of the brain include the brainstem, pons, reticular formation, cerebellum, substantia nigra, thalamus, hypothalamus, pituitary gland, amygdala, hippocampus, and cerebrum.
- The four lobes of the cerebrum are the frontal, parietal, occipital, and temporal lobes. They are covered by the cerebral cortex.
- Interference with development during sensitive periods can compromise further development.
- The body deals with stress through the process of allostasis, but when stress is chronic, the result is allostatic load. Allostatic load has been associated with various health problems, as well as academic and behavior problems in children.

## Children's Well-Being in Society

**[ KEY QUESTION ] 5. How does health- care policy affect children's well-being?**

- Indicators of children's well-being include family and social environment, economic circumstances, health and health care, physical environment and safety, and education.
- Many children have been uninsured in the past. The State Child Health Insurance Program makes health insurance available to uninsured children through government subsidies to insurance companies. The Patient Protection and Affordable Care Act, signed into law in 2010, will, when it takes full effect in 2014, provide health care to an estimated 32 million uninsured Americans.
- Children may experience disparities in health care. A disparity exists when a racial, ethnic or socioeconomic group receives care that is lower in quantity or quality than would be expected based on accepted standards.

## KEY TERMS

Alleles 51
Allostatic load 73
Central nervous system 66
Cerebral cortex 70
Chromosome 48
Deoxyribonucleic acid (DNA) 46
Dizygotic twins 63
Executive function 72
Frontal cortex 72
Gametes 45
Gene 48
Genome 46
Genotype 52
Glia 67
Heterozygous 52
Homozygous 52
Lateralization 71
Mitosis 48
Monozygotic twins 63
Myelination 67
Neurogenesis 67
Neurons 67
Neurotransmitters 69
Occipital cortex 72
Parietal cortex 72
Peripheral nervous system 66
Phenotype 52
Ribonucleic acid (RNA) 46
Somatic cells 45
Synapse 69
Temporal cortex 71

## CRITICAL THINKING QUESTIONS

1. **The Biology of Life.** What does it mean to say that "human development is shaped by a dynamic and continuous interaction between biology and experience"? Give some examples.
2. **Genes and Heredity.** Compare and contrast the differences between autosomal and sex-linked chromosomal patterns of heredity. How are chromosomal abnormalities different?
3. **Gene-Environment Interactions.** We presented several explanations for how genes and environment work together to shape human development. Which of these explanations do you favor most and least? Why?
4. **The Physiology of Thinking and Feeling.** Describe the structures of the central nervous system and how they support thinking and feeling.
5. **Children's Well-Being in Society.** Analyze the connections among the biology of life, child development, child health, and social policy.
6. **Cultural Perspectives.** We noted that "genetically, there is only one race among the people of the Earth—the human race. Culture, ethnicity, and what we call 'race' are not based on biology, but are social constructions based on patterns of human behavior and beliefs about similarities within groups and differences between them. These constructions come from individual experiences and from the collective experiences of families and social groups passed to us over time." Explain what this means. Can you give some examples of how cultural differences develop?

## REAL Development

### Biological Foundations of Child Development

In the accompanying Real Development activity, you help Adeline Gray predict the likelihood that her new baby sister will have blonde hair like her mom, Julianne. After watching the video and using the genetic diagram provided, you will determine the possible alleles for hair color. Assume that Matt, who has brown hair, carries the recessive gene for blonde hair (Bb) and that Julianne carries two recessive genes for blonde hair (bb).

**WileyPLUS** Go to WileyPLUS to complete the *Real Development* activity.

# Chapter 3

Rubberball/Getty Images

# Prenatal Development

## CHAPTER OUTLINE



MAKING A

**difference**

## Advocating for Care of Pregnant Women

At the beginning of the 20th century in the United States, 6 to 9 women out of 1,000 died of pregnancy-related complications, and approximately 100 infants per 1,000 died before their first birthday (Centers for Disease Control, 1999). A century later, the infant mortality rate had declined to 6.6 per 1,000 live births in 2008 (Mathews & MacDorman, 2012), and the maternal mortality rate to 14.5 per 100,000 in 2003 (Berg, Callaghan, Syverson, & Henderson, 2010). What has made the difference? Access to professional health care for mothers and babies before, during, and after birth. While many people and institutions played roles, two names are worth remembering as the trailblazers of this effort: Julia Lathrop and Jeannette Rankin.

After graduating from Vassar College, Julia Lathrop (1858–1932) studied law and then moved to Chicago to work for reformer and social worker Jane Addams, at Hull House, a settlement house for the poor. Over the next few years, she catalogued the deplorable living conditions of thousands of impoverished families in Illinois, with special attention to the welfare of children. In 1912, President William Howard Taft appointed her chief of the Children's Bureau, a new agency within the Department of Commerce and Labor, where she focused on infant mortality, poor nutrition, and juvenile delinquency. She was the first woman to head a federal bureau (Vassar College, 2005).

Meanwhile, Jeannette Rankin (1880–1973), a graduate of the University of Montana, was shocked by the urban slums that she saw on a trip to Boston. She was especially troubled by the high rate of maternal and infant mortality: Childbirth was the second-leading cause of death for women, and 20% of infants died in their first year. In 1916, Rankin was elected to the U.S. House of Representatives from Montana, becoming the first woman elected to Congress (Women in Congress, 2009). In 1919, she introduced legislation, drafted by Bureau Chief Julia Lathrop, that would fund health clinics to provide care and education to pregnant women, mothers, and children. The bill was not passed in 1919 but was revived in 1921 and passed as the Sheppard–Towner Act, the first federal legislation to provide federal funds for health care.

## [KEY QUESTIONS] *for* READING CHAPTER 3

1. How does life begin?
2. What happens in the womb before birth?
3. How do a pregnant woman's health habits and environment affect the developing embryo and fetus?
4. What is considered a healthy pregnancy?
5. What is the role of social institutions in supporting pregnancy and parenting?

**IN THIS CHAPTER,** we begin by describing conception. Next, we describe normal fetal development in the womb, and then we discuss the agents outside of the womb that can affect a child's development for a lifetime. Finally, we begin discussions on health, parenting, and culture that we will continue throughout this book. As part of this discussion, we address the science and policy of fertility, infertility, and reproductive assistance.

# Conception

**[ KEY QUESTION ] 1.** How does life begin?

You are lucky to be here. The odds of your particular DNA configuration existing in this time and place are amazingly small. Your biological mother was born with about 2 million ova (egg cells); 400,000 survived until she reached puberty, 400 of those ripened during menstrual cycles over the course of her natural reproductive life, and one of them became you. Your biological father released up to 300 million sperm during sexual intercourse; only about 200 reached an available egg, and the one that fertilized it became you. More than 50% of fertilized eggs fail to implant on the wall of the uterus, and another 20% fail to survive to 7 weeks of gestation. In other words, only about 3 in 10 fertilized eggs develop to maturity; one of them became you (Cunningham et al., 2005). Let's take a closer look at how fertilization occurs.

## Gametes and Meiosis

In order to understand fertilization, we need to remember from Chapter 2 that we have two types of cells. Somatic cells, such as bone cells, contain 46 chromosomes arranged in 23 *pairs*. When a somatic cell divides through mitosis, it produces cells identical to itself. In contrast, you may remember from a biology class that gametes—that is, egg and sperm cells—divide by **meiosis,** as shown in Figure 3.1. Meiosis results in four new cells, each containing 23 *single* chromosomes. Each of these new cells is different from the parent cell, and all are different from one another.

Gametes originate from specialized somatic cells in the ovaries in females and the testes in males. In the first phase of meiosis, the 23 pairs of chromosomes in the somatic cells cross over and separate into 23 *new* pairs of chromosomes in *different* combinations. During the second phase, the 23 new pairs of chromosomes split down the middle, and the cell divides in half. Now, each cell has *two* sets of 23 *single* chromosomes. These two cells divide again, each sorting its two sets of chromosomes into two new cells. The result is four cells, each with 23 single chromosomes. The four cells have four different combinations of genetic material, accounting for the incredible genetic variability among humans.

As we mentioned in Chapter 2, the 23 chromosomes in each cell include 22 autosomes and one sex chromosomes—either X (female) or Y (male). Female ova carry only the X chromosome, whereas male sperm can carry either the X or Y chromosome. Thus, males determine the gender of their offspring.

**meiosis** The process of cell division in which gametes are formed; it results in four new cells, each containing 23 single chromosomes, each different from the parent cell, and all different from one another.

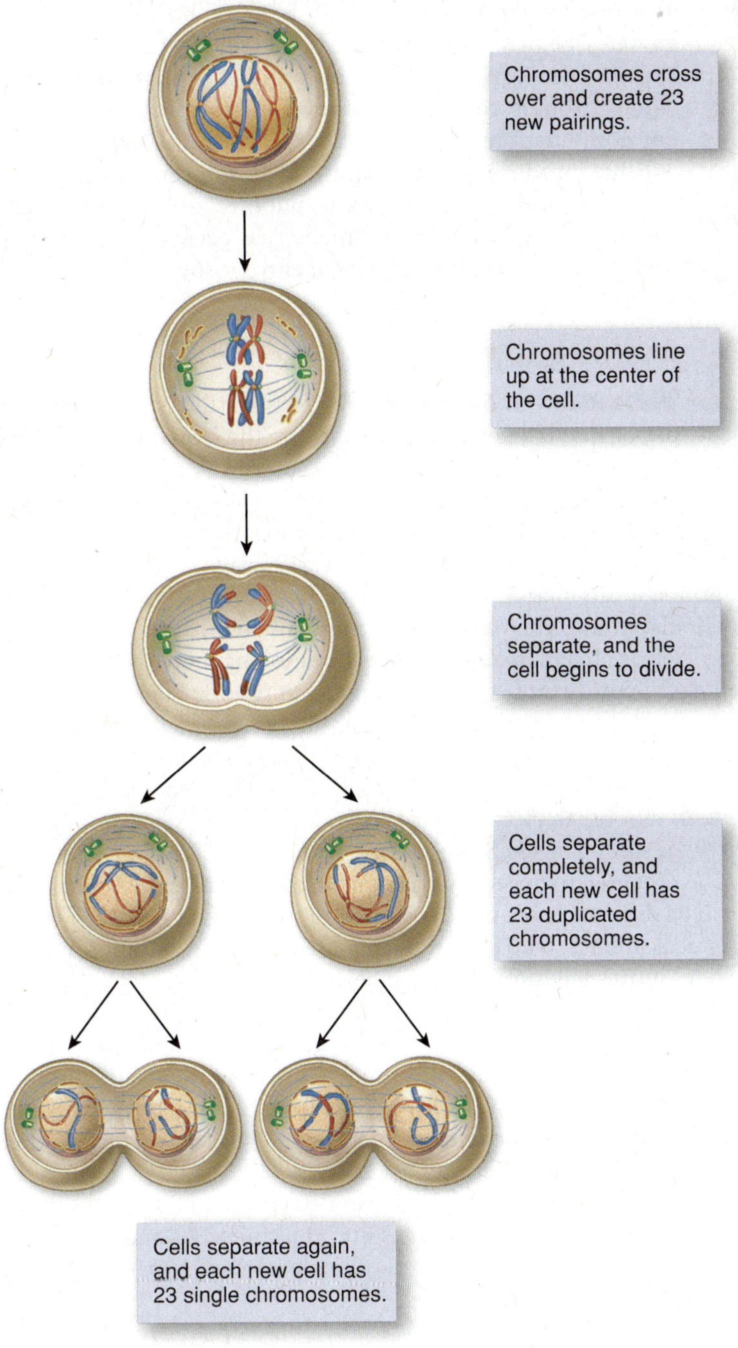


**FIGURE 3.1 Meiosis** Gametes divide by meiosis, resulting in four new cells, each containing 23 single chromosomes. The four cells are different from one another and from the original gamete cell.

Adapted with permission of John Wiley & Sons, Inc., from Freudenrich, C. C., & Tortora, G. J. (2011). *Visualizing Anatomy and Physiology*. Hoboken, NJ: Wiley, p. 70, Figure 3.21.

*Everyday stories*

HEREDITY AND HISTORY For most of human history, people assumed that the mother determined the gender of her child. Thus, women were often blamed for failure to produce a male heir. The consequences of this thinking have changed history. King Henry VIII of England divorced his first wife and executed his second, both of whom had borne daughters. In order to divorce, he had to break from the Roman Catholic Church and found the Church of England. Finally, his third wife produced a son, Edward. Edward succeeded Henry as king but died young. Ultimately, it was Henry's daughter Elizabeth who ascended the throne, and became one of the longest–lived and most powerful monarchs in British history.

Gamete production varies in males and females. In males, gametes arise from meiosis in the testes beginning at the time of puberty. Males continue to produce new sperm throughout their lives. In females, however, the production of gametes begins while the female is still a fetus. The special somatic cells in her ovaries undergo only the first phase of meiosis, which is when chromosomes cross over and separate into 23 new pairs in different combinations. The resulting cells are the eggs, or ova. A female will not produce any new ova during the remainder of her life. The second meiotic phase begins in puberty and is repeated monthly on roughly day 14 of a 28-day menstrual cycle. The resulting four cells each contain one set of 23 single chromosomes.

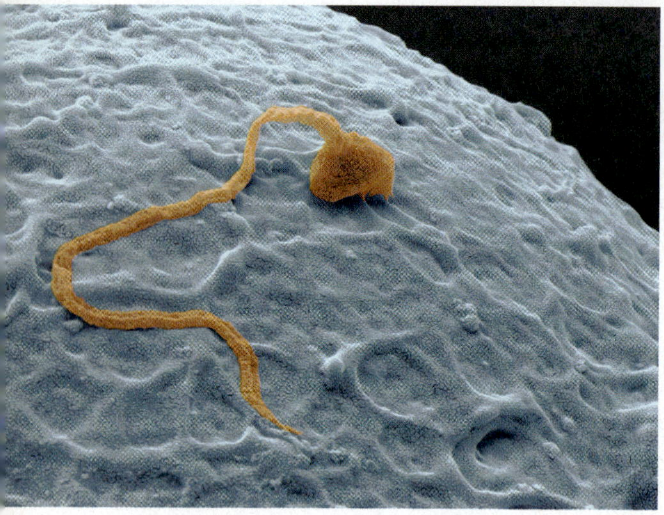

*Thierry Berrod, Mona Lisa Production/Science Source*

A sperm cell fertilizing an egg cell. Once the sperm cell gets through the egg cell's surface, rapid chemical changes will make the outer layer of the egg cell thicken, preventing any other sperm cells from entering.

## Fertilization

The window of opportunity for fertilization is relatively narrow. After the egg cell, or ovum, is released by the ovary, it is swept into the fallopian tubes and travels into the uterus. A mature ovum is fertile for about 24 hours; but as fertilization usually occurs in the fallopian tubes and not the uterus, the optimal time period for fertilization to occur is a few hours, and not more than a day, after ovulation. Sperm can survive in the female reproductive tract for 72 hours; it can take 200 of them up to four hours to reach the fallopian tubes after being ejaculated into the vagina (Cunningham et al., 2005).

Only one sperm can fertilize an ovum; fertilization by more than one causes death of the fertilized egg. Sperm compete for the opportunity to fertilize an ovum, and it may well be that the ovum is not a passive bystander but is choosy about which sperm to take in (Perry, Wilson, Hockenberry, & Lowdermilk, 2005; Primakoff & Myles, 2002). As the sperm enters the ovum, a membrane covering the ovum hardens, and its sperm receptors are destroyed, so that other sperm cannot enter. The 23 single chromosomes in the two gametes pair up, resulting in 46 chromosomes, arranged in 23 pairs—a genetically unique cell that has the potential to develop into a human individual, either female (XX) or male (XY), who will be different from either parent and from everyone else. The exception, of course, is identical siblings, who have the same DNA in their chromosomes.

Worldwide, more males (XY) are conceived than females (XX), in a ratio of 160 males for every 105 females. Among newborns, the ratio is 105 males to 100 females; it is 1 to 1 by age 18. The reason for the lopsided ratio is that male embryos and fetuses are less likely to survive, and boys are more vulnerable to health problems during childhood. Why this is the case is unclear, but may be because boys, unlike girls, do not have a second healthy X chromosome to offset any disorders carried on their single X chromosome (Kraemer, 2000; Perry et al., 2005).

After fertilization, the fertilized egg, a single cell called a **zygote,** travels through the fallopian tubes to the uterus. It cleaves into multiple cells and attaches itself to the uterine wall. We describe the three stages of its development in the next section.

### what if...?

Remember that in Chapter 2 we discussed chromosomal abnormalities that are not due to genetic inheritance but to a random mistake that occurs during meiosis or fertilization for no apparent reason. What if such a mistake occurs? What are examples of the consequences?

### CHECK YOUR PROGRESS

1. Discuss why meiosis results in genetic variety.
2. Describe the differences in meiosis for males and females.
3. Describe how fertilization occurs.

**zygote** A single-cell organism that results from the fertilization of an egg cell by a sperm; the fertilized egg.

# Prenatal Growth and Development

[ KEY QUESTION ] 2. What happens in the womb before birth?

We turn now to the fertilized egg and its development through the 40 weeks (approximately 9 months) of gestation. Let's begin with a biological definition of the human **embryo**: a "discrete entity that has arisen from . . . the first mitotic division when fertilization of a human oocyte by a human sperm is complete . . . and has not yet reached 8 weeks of development" (Findlay et al., 2007, p. 905)—that is, from fertilization until 8 weeks. Those first 8 weeks occur in two phases: the germinal period (0 to 2 weeks) and the embryonic period (3 to 8 weeks). Starting at about 9 weeks and continuing until birth, the developing human organism is called a **fetus**. Note that pregnancy is frequently discussed in terms of 3 roughly equal periods of about 3 months each, called *trimesters*. Thus, the phases of prenatal development do not necessarily correspond to the trimesters of pregnancy.

**embryo** The term given to a developing human organism between the first cleavage of the single-cell zygote into multiple cells and 8 weeks postfertilization.

**fetus** The human organism from about week 9 until birth.

**blastocyst** The term given to the embryo at about day 5 or 6 postfertilization. It consists of three cell masses: the embryoblast, a hollow cavity that becomes the amniotic sac, and the trophoblast.

**embryoblast** The inner cell mass of the blastocyst, which is the developing human organism.

**amniotic sac** A thin membrane arising from a cell mass within the blastocyst that completely surrounds the embryo/fetus and contains a protective fluid in which the embryo/fetus is immersed.

**trophoblast** A cell mass within the blastocyst that becomes the placenta.

**placenta** A structure formed when the trophoblast burrows into the lining of the uterus, joining the uterine mucous membrane with the membranes of the fetus. Substances ingested by the mother cross the placenta via the umbilical cord to the developing fetus, providing nourishment for its development.

## The Germinal Period: 0 to 2 Weeks

As noted earlier, the egg is generally fertilized in the fallopian tube. The fertilized egg, or zygote, divides several times as it moves toward the uterus. (For a video showing these early cell divisions, go to http://stemcells.nih.gov/info/cellmovie.htm.) In days 2 to 3, the embryo is at the cleavage stage, when it consists of fewer than 16 cells. At this point, it may spontaneously split into two separate but genetically identical zygotes, resulting in identical twins, or monozygotic twins. As we noted in Chapter 2, fraternal twins, or dizygotic twins, arise from two different fertilized eggs; they are siblings who just happen to be born at the same time.

### Implantation

During days 5 to 6, the embryo is at what is called the **blastocyst** stage. The blastocyst is already much more complex than the fertilized egg and consists of three structures: an inner cell mass called the **embryoblast,** which is the developing embryo itself; a hollow cavity filling with fluid that becomes the **amniotic sac** in which the embryoblast develops; and the **trophoblast**, a layer of cells that becomes the **placenta**. By day 6 or 7, the blastocyst consists of 100 to 250 cells and has attached to the wall of the uterus. The trophoblast burrows deeper into the uterus to form the placenta, which will exchange nutrients, oxygen, and wastes between the mother and the developing organism and prevent the exchange of blood between the two (see Figures 3.2 and 3.3).

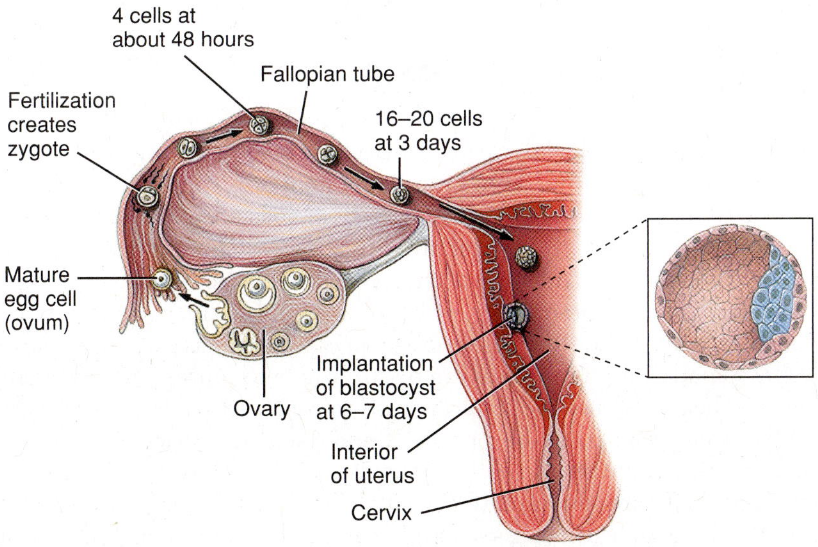


FIGURE 3.2 **The Embryo's Journey from Fertilization to Implantation** The egg cell leaves the ovary and moves into the fallopian tube, where it is fertilized by a sperm cell. It immediately begins to divide as it moves into the uterus. At about day 6 or 7, it implants in the uterine wall. At that point, it is a blastocyst made up of the embryoblast, which develops into the fetus; the trophoblast, which becomes the placenta; and the amniotic sac.

Adapted with permission of John Wiley & Sons, Inc., from Comer, R., & Gould, E. (2013). *Psychology Around Us* (2nd ed.). Hoboken, NJ: Wiley, p. 72, Figure 3.4.

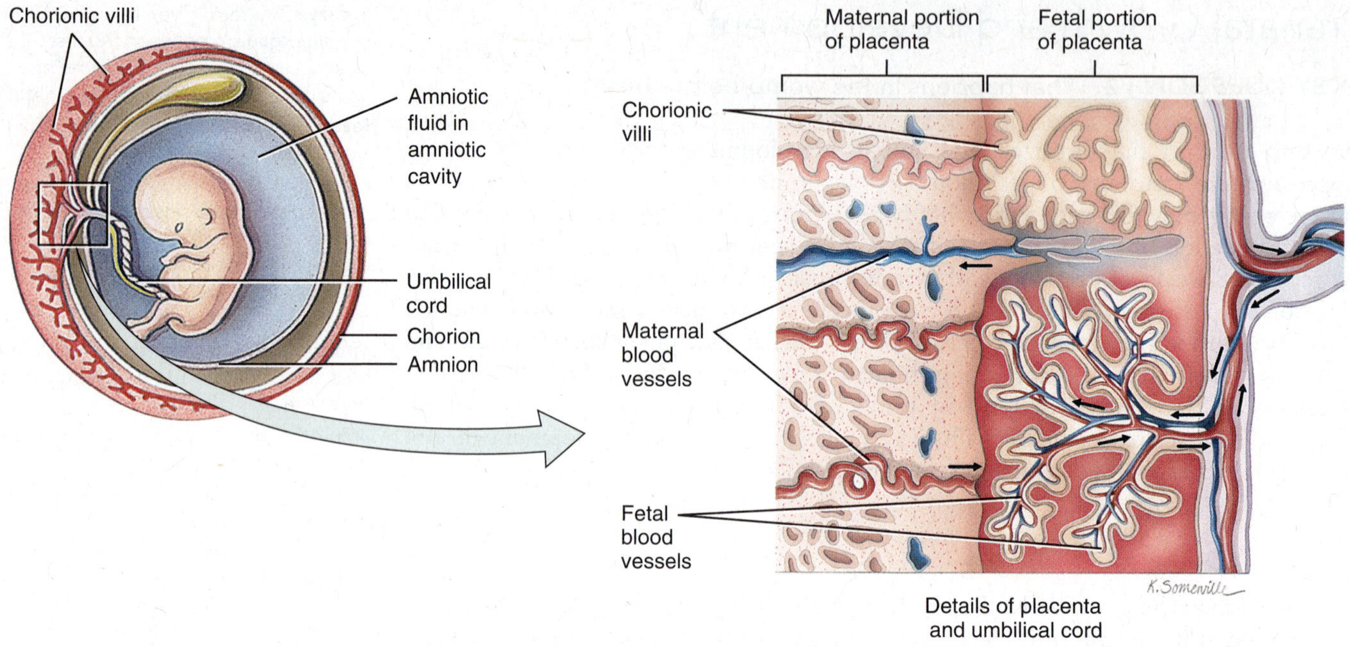


**FIGURE 3.3 The Placenta and Umbilical Cord** The placenta is formed from the *endometrium*, the lining of the uterus, and the *chorion*, the outermost membrane of the fetus. Tiny vessels called *chorionic villi* project into the uterine lining and exchange nutrients and wastes between the blood of the fetus and that of the mother.

Adapted with permission of John Wiley & Sons, Inc., from Freudenrich, C. C., & Tortora, G. J. (2011). *Visualizing Anatomy and Physiology*. Hoboken, NJ: Wiley, p. 491, Figure 16.13b.

## Differentiation of the Embryonic Germ Layers

The first two weeks are called the **germinal period** because this is when the cells in the embryoblast separate and differentiate into three distinct embryonic germ layers, which will develop into all of the major organs of the body. The outer germ layer–the **ectoderm**—develops into the nervous system (including the brain and spine), skin, nails, and hair, as well as the salivary, pituitary, and mammary glands. The innermost layer—the **endoderm**—becomes the thyroid gland, bladder, lungs, and digestive system. The **mesoderm**, which emerges between the ectoderm and endoderm, becomes the heart, circulatory and lymph systems, connective tissue, muscle, and bones. By the third week after fertilization, the embryonic period of organ development begins, at just about the time a woman would be expecting her next menstrual period (Cunningham et al., 2005; Moore & Persaud, 2003; Perry et al., 2005).

### The Politics of Stem Cell Research Policy

There are two types of human stem cells: **embryonic stem cells** and **adult stem cells** (National Institutes of Health, 2009). Embryonic stem cells come from the three germ layers that develop from the blastocyst. These stem cells are extracted from embryos that have been fertilized *in vitro*—literally, "in glass," as in a test tube—but not yet implanted into the uterus. Embryonic stem cells have not yet differentiated into specific somatic cells, such as brain, lung, or heart cells, and so retain the ability to do so. The promise of embryonic stem cells is this *pluripotence*, the ability to transform into virtually any somatic cell. If scientists can discover how to reprogram embryonic stem cells, they may be able to use the resulting cells to treat certain diseases. For example, new healthy nerve cells could be produced and used to replace cells damaged by Parkinson's disease, a disease of the nervous system.

Adult stem cells are also undifferentiated human cells, but they are found in specific mature tissues and organs, such as the brain, bone, and skin. The body can use

**germinal period** The first two weeks of prenatal development from fertilization of the egg to the separation of the three germ layers of somatic cells, and including implantation of the blastocyst of the embryo into the uterine wall.

**ectoderm** The outer germ layer of the blastocyst that develops into the nervous system (including the brain and spine), skin, nails, and hair, as well as the salivary, pituitary, and mammary glands.

**endoderm** The innermost germ layer of the blastocyst that becomes the thyroid gland, bladder, lungs, and digestive system.

**mesoderm** The germ layer between the ectoderm and endoderm that becomes the heart, circulatory and lymph systems, connective tissue, muscle, and bones.

**embryonic stem cells** Cells that result when, under the right conditions in a laboratory, the germ cells within the blastocyst can multiply without becoming differentiated into the three distinct germ layers. These cells are pluripotent; that is, they maintain the ability to become any somatic cell.

**adult stem cells** These cells are undifferentiated cells that are found in mature tissues and organs, such as the brain, bone, and skin. The body can use these stem cells to renew and repair the specific tissues and organs in which the stem cells are located.

these stem cells to renew and repair the tissues or organs in question; that is, they differentiate into these specific cell types. For example, researchers recently used the adult stem cells of patients to treat their heart disease (Bolli et al., 2011).

Human stem cell research holds some promise for advances in treating various illnesses. However, embryonic stem cell research is highly controversial. The embryo from which the embryonic stem cells are extracted stops developing. It cannot be implanted into the uterus and develop into a fetus. That is why people who consider the embryo a live human being are opposed to this research. Controversy over when life begins has prevented the U.S. government from developing a consistent policy toward embryonic stem cell research.

In 1996, Public Law 104–99 prohibited the use of federal money for "research in which a human embryo or embryos are destroyed" (Balanced Budget Downpayment Act). Research on existing embryonic stem cells–that is, stem cells that had been removed from an embryo before the law was implemented—was allowed. In 2001, then President George W. Bush issued an executive order restricting federal funding for research on these existing stem cells. In 2009, President Obama issued an executive order to remove those restrictions, an order later upheld by the courts (National Institutes of Health, 2011). Nevertheless, the language in Public Law 104–99 remains in effect: That is, no new stem cells can be removed from embryos. The controversy is far from over.

what if...?

What if you were a member of Congress? A bill that would permit federal funds for embryonic stem cell research is up for debate. How would you vote? Do you think the federal government should fund embryonic stem cell research, or should this be done by private companies and not with taxpayer money? Should embryonic stem cells be used in research at all? What trade–offs are involved in such decisions?

## The Period of the Embryo: 3 to 8 Weeks

Once the germ layers—the ectoderm, endoderm, and mesoderm—have separated, the business of major organ development, called **organogenesis,** begins. This process is 95% completed by week 8. In organogenesis, we can begin to see a difference, one that will be an important topic of discussion throughout this text: the distinction between growth and development. *Growth* refers to an increase in size, whereas *development* refers to changes in functional ability—in this case, resulting from the organization and reorganization of cells into new forms. Following are some of the key events of the period of the embryo.

- *Third week.* An indentation of cells, called the neural plate, forms in the ectoderm, giving rise to the brain and neural tube (spinal cord). Neurogenesis, the production of neurons that are responsible for transmitting information throughout the nervous system, begins immediately, at a rate of more than 250,000 per minute (Nelson, Thomas & De Haan, 2006). The chambers of the heart and blood vessels develop from the mesoderm.
- *Fourth week.* The heart begins to beat, although is not audible outside the womb. The buds of the arms and legs are visible. Eyes, ears, nerves, and muscular, skeletal, and digestive systems begin to form. Vertebrae in the spine are present; major veins and arteries are completed. The neural tube closes; failure to close results in spina bifida ("split spine"), which can adversely affect the function of the nerves and muscles of the lower body. The embryo is about 0.2 in. (0.5 cm) long and weighs 0.14 oz (0.4 g).
- *Fifth week.* The brain has developed into five components. Nose and lips begin to form.
- *Sixth week.* Although gender is determined at fertilization, differentiation of external genitalia and internal reproductive organs begin now. The head and brain are most

**organogenesis** Development of major organ systems during the embryonic period, weeks 3 to 8 of prenatal development. By the end of week 8, 95% of major organs are complete.

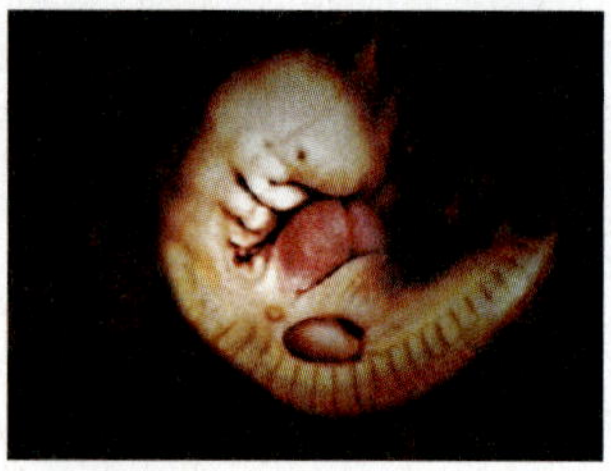
Anatomical Travelogue/Science Source

The embryo at 5 weeks.

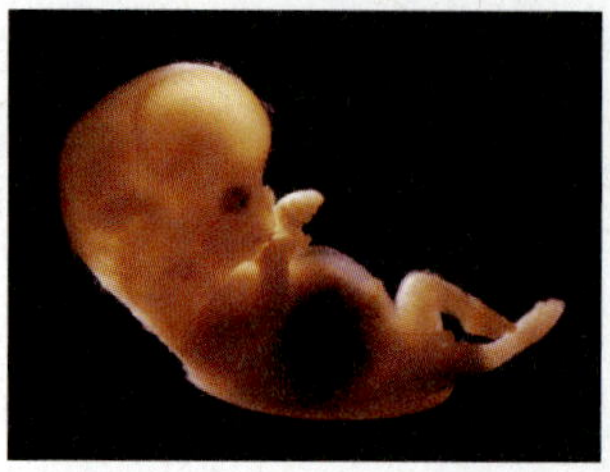
Last Refuge, Ltd./Phototake

The fetus at 10 to 11 weeks.

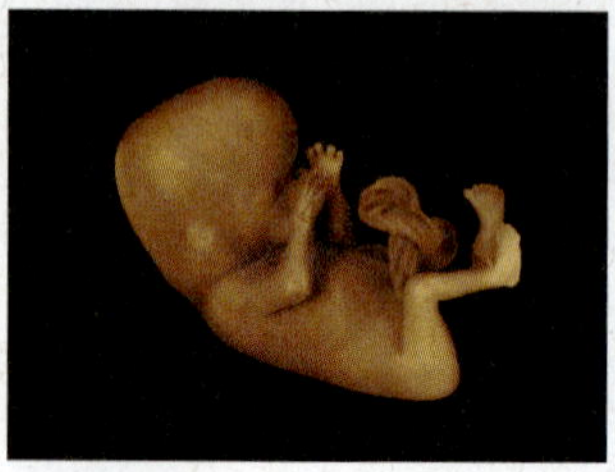
Omikron/Science Source

The fetus at 13 weeks.

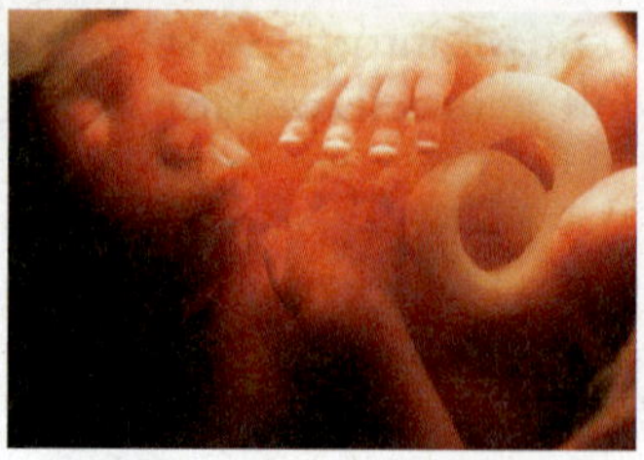
Neil Bromball/Science Source

The fetus at 5 months (about 20 weeks).

prominent; the lower jaw fuses, and the parts of the upper jaw are present. The arms and legs have grown longer; hands and feet have fingers and toes. The lungs begin to develop.

- *Seventh week.* The face, eyelids, and neck begin to form. The stomach and other internal organs are in position. Muscles are forming throughout the body; the arms and legs are apparent; and neurons continue to develop at the rate of thousands per minute. The embryo can move, especially in response to touch.
- *Eighth week.* The head is elevated so that the neck and ears are distinct, making the embryo appear more human. The inner and middle ear develop. The embryo is about the size of a grape, 0.8 to 1.2 in. (2 to 3 cm) long and weighing 0.7 oz (2 g). The mother is probably now aware that she is pregnant, although she cannot feel any movement from the embryo at this time.

## The Period of the Fetus: 9 Weeks to Birth

By the end of the eighth week, all essential organs are in place. They can now grow and develop further, and begin to work. This marks the end of the **embryonic period** and beginning of the **period of the fetus.** The following list describes some of the major developments of the fetal period. The timing presented is fairly general, and there may be individual differences in fetal development, just as in the development of infants and children. For example, a development we refer to as taking place between 9 and 12 weeks may begin at week 10 and be completed by week 13.

### Fetal Development from Week 9 to Week 12

- *9 to 12 weeks.* The intestines are in position, the spinal cord is visible, the eyes take final form, and the eyelids can close; red blood cells form in the liver. Sex organs are now apparent. Toothbuds appear. The heartbeat is audible with the right equipment. The fetus is 2.4 to 3 in. long (6 to 8 cm) and weighs 0.7 oz (19 g).
- *13 to 16 weeks.* The skin is almost transparent. The fetus's bones and joints are distinct; the two halves of the brain are visible. **Lanugo** (fine hair) and **vernix caseosa** (oil) begin to appear on the skin. The fetus is 4.7 in. long (12 cm) and weighs 3.5 oz (100 g).

  At this point, the mother's pelvis can no longer contain the expanding uterus, and she can feel its hard edge below her navel as it begins to move up and out. As early as 14 weeks, the mother may feel the fetus's movement, initially a butterfly effect called "quickening." Some of this early movement results from reflexes in response to stimuli, such as noise (the fetus can hear quite well in the uterus) and maternal movement.
- *17 to 20 weeks.* Dental enamel forms. Nerve fibers throughout the body begin to develop myelin sheaths, along which the electrical impulses that move our bodies and direct our organs are conducted; this process, called myelination, will not be completed for several years. The fetus actively kicks and moves about, which is readily felt by the mother. The heartbeat is easily heard with a regular stethoscope. The intestines and kidneys work. The fetus has been swallowing amniotic fluid, and

**embryonic period** The period of prenatal development starting at the beginning of week 3 and continuing through week 8; organogenesis takes place during the embryonic period.

**period of the fetus** The period of prenatal development that begins after organogenesis is 95% complete, at about week 9, and continues until birth.

**lanugo** Fine downy hair that covers the fetus in the womb beginning at around 16 weeks. It insulates the fetus—which lacks body fat—and helps with body temperature regulation. It usually disappears by birth.

**vernix caseosa** An oily substance with dead skin cells that covers the fetus in the womb; thought to provide insulation and maintain body temperature. It usually disappears by birth.

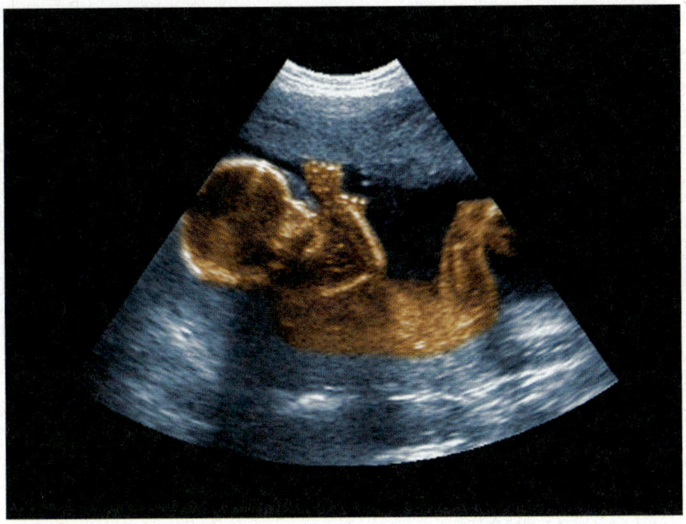

Getty Images/Photo Researchers

Ultrasound offers a safe way to look at the unborn fetus. Women often have an ultrasound at about 20 weeks to determine that the placenta and fetus are developing as expected.

excretes urine, which remains in the amniotic sac and is expelled at birth. The fetus is 6 to 7 in. (16 to 18 cm) long and weighs 10.5 oz (300 g).

Women typically have an **ultrasound** at around 20 weeks to determine whether the placenta and fetus are developing as expected. An ultrasound uses sound waves, not radiation, to produce an image. The ultrasound picture is often the first one that parents have of their baby, and typically it is proudly shared with family, friends, and prospective grandparents.

*Everyday stories*

DETECTING ANOMALIES WITH ULTRASOUND Sometimes an ultrasound will detect a *congenital anomaly*, which is an abnormality in the physical development of the fetus that is apparent at or shortly after birth. Anomalies can be caused by substances or diseases to which the mother has been exposed during pregnancy. (We discuss these later in the chapter.) But sometimes, anomalies result from random mistakes in cell development; they occur for no apparent reason during meiosis of the gamete, organogenesis, or any other point in fetal development. Heart defects are the most common congenital anomalies. Fortunately, they can usually be repaired.

- *By 24 weeks.* Fat begins to accumulate under the skin. The fetus may become less active, because further development of the brain causes purely reflexive movement to diminish. The bone marrow begins to produce red blood cells. The eyes are fully formed. The fetus is 9 in. long (23 cm) and weighs 21.6 oz (600 g).

## Fetal Development from Week 25 to Week 40

The issue of viability emerges at the threshold of the third trimester, about week 24 to 25. **Viability** is the ability of the fetus to survive outside the womb, and depends in part on whether the lungs are producing *surfactant*, a substance that coats the inside of the lungs and allows the baby to breathe. Today, with the aid of modern medicine and technology, the age of viability has decreased to between 22 and 26 weeks. However, infants born this early have only about a 50% chance of survival, and even then may survive with significant impairments (Pignotti & Donzelli, 2008; Vanhaesebrouck, et al., 2004). The closer to 40 weeks the infant is born, the better the chances it has for a healthy survival. As development continues through the third trimester, the fetus becomes larger and stronger, with more mature organ systems.

- *By 28 weeks.* As the brain continues to develop, fetal activity increases, and now it is more purposeful, as the fetus changes position. Fat forms beneath the skin. Fingernails appear. The eyes open, close, and blink in response to loud sounds and

**ultrasound** A noninvasive procedure in which part of the body is exposed to high-frequency sound waves from a machine, which produces real-time pictures of the inside of the body and helps physicians to diagnose problems.

**viability** The ability of the fetus to survive outside the womb.

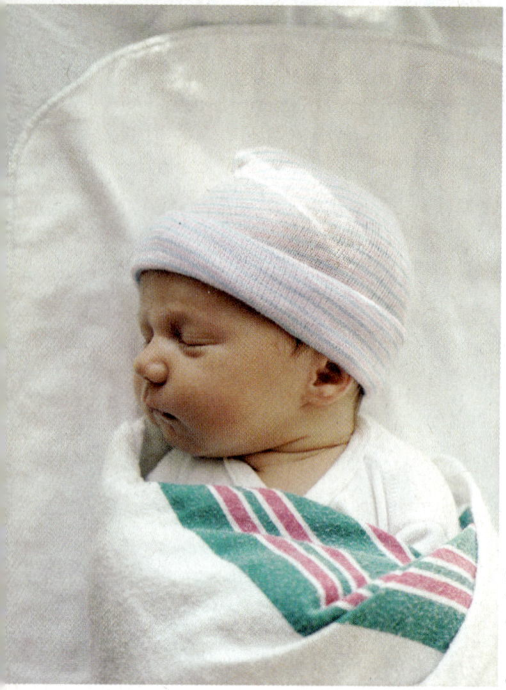

A full-term infant is born after about 40 weeks of development in the womb.

bright light. There is sufficient surfactant to support breathing outside of the womb. The fetus is 10.6 in. long (27 cm) and weighs 38 oz/2.4 lb (1,100 g).

- *By 32 weeks.* The fetus responds to external sounds and may push back in response to external pressure. In males, testes descend into the scrotum. The fetus looks smooth and chubby. The brain has reached 25% of its adult weight. The fetus is 12.2 in. long (31 cm) and weighs 63.5 to 74 oz/4 to 4.6 lb (1,800 to 2,100 g).
- *By 36 weeks.* The lanugo hair begins to disappear. Physical growth slows while the brain develops further, becoming more convoluted. The fetus has discernible wake-sleep cycles and is awake about 11% of the time, increasing to 16% by birth.
- *By 40 weeks.* The fetus adds 50% of its birth weight in the last month of prenatal development. It has smooth skin, moderate to profuse hair on its head, and lanugo hair on the shoulders only. Myelination of the brain begins in earnest. The fetus is the size of the average newborn: 17.57 to 19.7 in. in length (45 to 50 cm) and weighs about 7 lb, or 3.2 kg (3,200 g).

THE DEVELOPING BRAIN

## A Closer Look

Throughout this book, we give special emphasis to the role of the brain in development and behavior. So let's take a moment here to look more closely at the processes by which the brain and nervous system develop during gestation from a thin layer of cells in the germinal period into the complex system we described in Chapter 2 (Monk, Webb, & Nelson, 2001):

1. **Neural proliferation and migration.** Brain cells are developed (*neurogenesis*) and then migrate into specific areas of the developing brain.
2. **Neural differentiation and myelination.** The migrating brain cells differentiate into specific types of cells in the various parts of the brain and nervous system, and myelin sheaths develop around their axons.
3. **Synaptogenesis and pruning.** As the differentiated cells mature, synapses develop between them so that the cells become connected, forming a complex, integrated network of activity. At first, a surplus of cells develops; later, these cells will be "pruned"—their numbers will be reduced—for greater efficiency.

These processes overlap, because the fetal brain develops from the inside out—from the hindbrain and midbrain deep inside to the cerebral cortex, which is closer to the surface. That means the cerebral cortex—the part of the brain involved in higher-order functions such as learning, memory, attention, language, and thought—develops later than parts of the brain needed for life-essential functions, such as breathing and sensing. You can see this progression in Figure 3.4. Thus, the cells bound for the cerebral cortex must pass through earlier-arriving brain cells in interior areas (Ayala, Shu, & Tsai, 2007; Kolb & Fantie, 2008). One effect of this pattern of development is that environmental influences—for example, alcohol drinking by the mother, exposure to radiation, or a serious illness—could affect all areas of the developing brain through which migrating cells pass, but in different ways. (We examine environmental influences on development in the next section.)

Between about 25 and 40 weeks gestation, the brain is the organ with the most dramatic development, raising the interesting issue of prenatal learning, as discussed in the accompanying Research Insights feature. As the brain develops during this period, the cerebral cortex becomes more convoluted and complex. Nevertheless, since the fetal brain cannot grow any larger than the birth canal will allow, newborn infants are neurologically immature. This accounts for some of their primitive behaviors, such as reflexes, as we shall see in Chapter 4.

In recent years, prenatal learning has been a hot topic in the popular press. Most of the information we find in media sources is scientifically unfounded, however. For example, a study suggested that college students' spatial reasoning scores on IQ tests could improve after they listened to Mozart, which became known as the Mozart

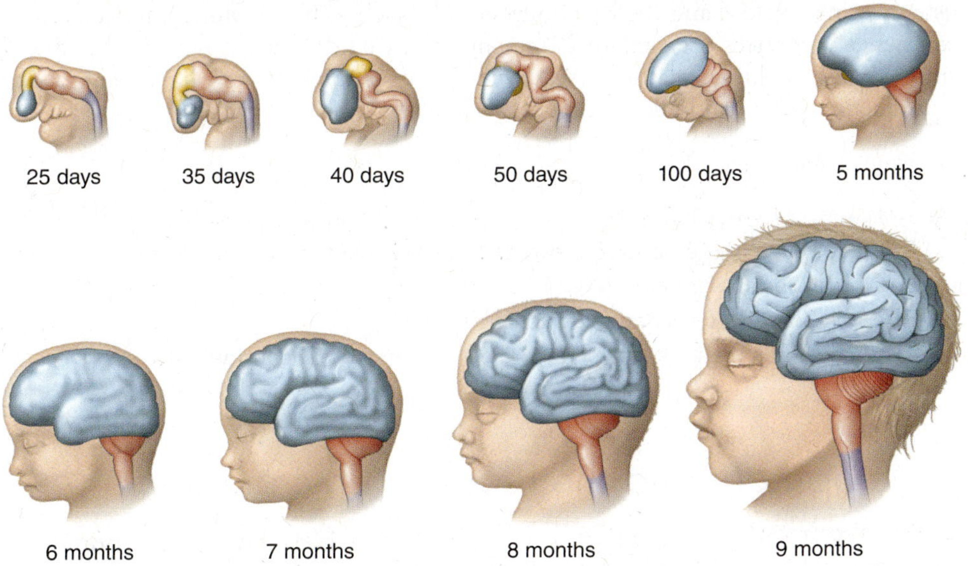


**FIGURE 3.4 Prenatal Development of the Brain** In this conceptual rendering of prenatal brain development, note that the brain becomes more complex and convoluted as it develops, as we discussed in Chapter 2. Note also that the brainstem area is more prominent during the early phases of development. The brainstem is the so-called primitive part of the brain that automatically regulates essential body systems.

Reprinted with permission of the author's estate, from Cowan, W. M. (1979). The development of the brain. *Scientific American*. 241: 112–133.

effect. Believing that the Mozart effect could raise the IQ in an unborn fetus, expectant parents began placing headphones on the mother's abdomen so that the fetus could listen to Mozart. Although there has been much research on the brain and music, the so-called Mozart effect has not been scientifically demonstrated. It's simply a popular legend (Bangerter & Heath, 2004; Jenkins, 2001).

The fact that the fetus recognizes the mother's voice in the womb, as described in the Research Insights feature, reminds us that the relationship between individual and environment begins before birth. Fetuses experience life in the womb through touch,

## Research Insights: Learning Before Birth?

In 1986, Anthony DeCasper and Melanie Spence published a landmark paper about learning before birth (DeCasper & Spence, 1986). In a study conducted by the researchers, each day during the last six weeks of pregnancy, mothers read aloud the Dr. Seuss book *The Cat in the Hat*. Previous research had indicated that a fetus was able to hear its mother's voice, but the question remained, would it remember that voice after birth? The answer was yes. The researchers used the newborn's ability to control its sucking behavior as an indication of its preferences. An artificial nipple like one on a baby bottle was wired to a recorder that had a tape of the mother's voice, so that when the baby sucked on the nipple, the recorder would turn on and the mother's voice could be heard. Babies not only sucked harder to hear their mothers' voices than the voices of others, but they also sucked hardest to hear their mothers read *The Cat in the Hat*. This suggested that they had learned that a particular result—hearing their mother's voice—was contingent on an action of their own—sucking. (This phenomenon will be discussed further in Chapter 4.)

Further studies in the last few weeks of gestation have used fetal heart rate as an indicator of attention. Results suggest that fetuses can distinguish between male and female voices, between their own mother's voice and that of an unknown woman, and between familiar and unfamiliar melodies (DeCasper, Lecanuet, Busnel, Granier–Deferre, & Maugeais, 1994; Kisilevsky, Pang, & Hains, 2000; Lecanuet, 1996). The ability of the fetus to sustain attention to music appears to mature at about 33 weeks (Kisilevsky, Hains, Jacquet, Granier–Deferre, & Lecanuet, 2004). Furthermore, between 35 and 37 weeks, the fetus will habituate to familiar sounds (Morokuma et al., 2008). Habituation means the fetus gets used to certain sounds and so pays less attention to them than to novel ones. This natural tendency to habituate to the familiar but attend to the novel is often taken advantage of to study attention in babies, as you will see in later chapters.

taste, hearing, seeing, and their own physiology, such as heart rate and movement. If experience influences prenatal development, then we hope that it is optimal and well timed. Sadly, we know that adverse environmental influences can have long-lasting consequences for a child's development. We address this issue in the next section.

### ✓CHECK YOUR PROGRESS

1. What are the three periods of prenatal development?
2. When does implantation occur?
3. When is a fetus considered viable, and why?
4. What does it mean that the fetal brain develops from the inside out?

## Development and the Prenatal Environment

**[ KEY QUESTION ] 3. How do a woman's health habits and the environment affect the developing embryo and fetus?**

There was a time when people assumed that the placenta was like a cocoon, providing an impermeable barrier that separated the developing organism from both its mother and the outside world. We now know this is not true; a broad range of environmental agents *can* damage the developing organism in the womb. Broadly speaking, any agent that can cause damage to the embryo or fetus is called a **teratogen** (from *teras* for "monster" and *genesis* for "origin"). The nature of the abnormalities produced by teratogens depends on three things:

- *The timing of prenatal exposure to the teratogen.* During certain *sensitive periods* in prenatal development, the developing organism is particularly vulnerable to environmental influences. Figure 3.5 identifies sensitive periods in prenatal development and the possible consequences of exposure to teratogens during those times. Note that the central nervous system, which includes the brain, is vulnerable throughout gestation.
- *The dosage of the teratogen—that is, the level of exposure.* The relationship between the dosage and the result of exposure is called the **dose-response effect**. A related concept is the **threshold effect,** the point of exposure below which no effect can be identified.
- *Individual differences in sensitivity to a particular teratogen.* Fetuses may have different levels of sensitivity to the dosage of teratogens, with some being affected at a lower or higher threshold than what is typical, or having a response that is more or less pronounced.

In this section, we review the effects of several different types of teratogens: chemical substances, diseases, illness, stress, and environmental hazards. It is worth noting that abnormalities caused by these teratogens result from assaults on an otherwise normally developing fetus. Although the effects of teratogens are often irreversible, they are also preventable.

**teratogen** From *teras* for "monster" and *genesis* for "origin," any agent that can cause permanent damage to the embryo or fetus.

**dose-response effect** The relationship between the dosage of a substance, such as alcohol or radiation, and the result of exposure; usually, higher doses are associated with greater effects.

**threshold effect** Related to the dose-response effect; the point of exposure below which no effect can be identified.

### Chemical Substances

Some of the chemical substances that have been identified as teratogens include alcohol, tobacco, and illegal drugs, such as cocaine. Certain medications that may be prescribed by a woman's physician also have the potential to harm the developing organism.

#### Alcohol

Human beings have been drinking alcohol in various forms ever since they happened upon the pleasing effects of fermentation in fruit and grain. It is part of the cultural, religious, and economic fabric of virtually all societies. But alcohol is a central nervous system depressant, and the brain is the organ most sensitive to its effects—which partly explains its appeal. It is rapidly absorbed into the bloodstream and carried throughout the body, so that all parts of the body quickly contain approximately the same concentration of alcohol. Thus, it slows cell functioning throughout the body.

Alcohol is one of the most common causes of birth abnormalities, as it easily crosses the placenta, interfering with cell division and growth in the developing organism. Fortunately, it is also one of the most preventable causes of birth abnormalities. The extent and nature of the effects of exposure depend on how much the mother drank during pregnancy, and when she drank, as well as individual differences in sensitivity to alcohol in both the mother and the fetus (Sampson, Streissguth, Bookstein, & Barr, 2000). Lifestyle factors often associated with heavy use of alcohol, such as poor diet and cigarette smoking, compound the risks.

**Fetal Alcohol Spectrum Disorders (FASDs).** The term *fetal alcohol spectrum disorders (FASDs)* refers to a continuum of alcohol-related deficits. Prevalence can be difficult to determine because deficits can be mild to severe. Symptoms may be identified at birth or may not become apparent until later, when a child develops behavior or academic problems. Estimates are that FASDs occur in approximately 1% of the U.S. population in general (Sampson et al., 1997; Sokol, Delaney-Black, & Nordstrom, 2003), although recent studies have found rates as high as 2 to 5% (May et al., 2009).

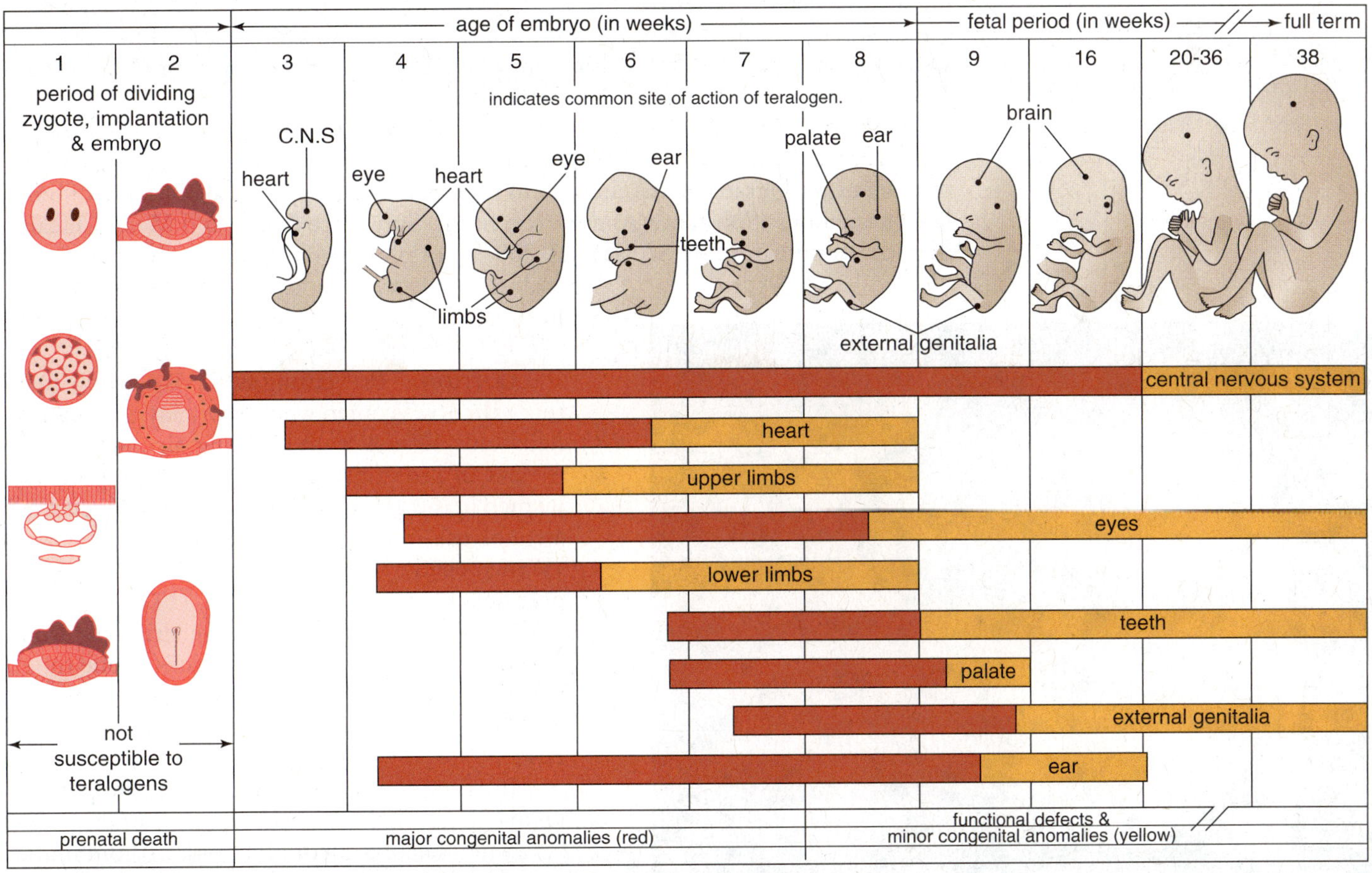


*Note*: Red indicates highly sensitive periods when teratogens may induce major anomalies.

**FIGURE 3.5 Sensitive Periods in Prenatal Development** During certain sensitive periods in prenatal development, the developing organism is particularly vulnerable to the effects of teratogens. Sensitivity is greatest during the embryonic period, when all organs form. Each organ is more vulnerable to different teratogens at certain periods.

Reprinted with permission of John Wiley & Sons, Inc., from Harwood, R., Miller, S. A., & Vasta, R. (2008). *Child Psychology: Development in a Changing Society* (5th ed.). Hoboken, NJ: Wiley, p. 119.

Fetal alcohol syndrome (FAS), the most serious of the FASDs, may occur in 0.2 to 1.5 of every 1,000 live births in certain areas of the United States (Centers for Disease Control [CDC], 2012). FAS is characterized by distinctive facial features, intellectual disabilities (defined as an IQ score of less than 70) (Sampson et al., 2000), and physical growth that is below the 10th percentile in height or weight for age and race (Wattendorf & Muenke, 2005). Infants born to mothers who drink heavily will also likely experience withdrawal from alcohol at birth (Hannigan & Randall, 2000).

The dose-response effect of alcohol is critical to the outcomes for the child, but the relationship is not well understood. Although it is clear that chronic high levels of maternal alcohol use will lead to FAS, a direct correlation of dose to effects at low to moderate use is not as clear. We cannot, in other words, say that "this much alcohol will always cause this particular deficit" (Sampson et al., 2000). Even so, a dose-response effect has been found at exposure as low as one drink per week (Sood et al., 2001). There also may be a threshold for alcohol exposure: Exposure above the threshold may result in FAS, while a lower level of exposure may result in more subtle disorders (Sampson et al., 2000; Sood et al., 2001).

Because the timing and dosage of prenatal alcohol exposure varies, the characteristics of children with FAS can vary as well (Jacobson & Jacobson, 2002; Sampson et al., 2000). For example, some children with FAS may have low to normal IQ scores, whereas others may have normal IQs (Jacobson & Jacobson, 2002; Streissguth, Bookstein, & Barr, 1996). Some studies have identified deficits in mathematics skills (Howell, Lynch, Platzman, Smith, & Coles, 2006), while other studies have not (Streissguth et al., 1996). Children with FAS may be misdiagnosed with attention deficit hyperactivity disorder (ADHD), when closer examination reveals difficulties not with attention but rather with concentration, visual/spatial skills, comprehension, and flexibility in problem solving (Coles et al., 1997; Jacobson & Jacobson, 2002; Larkby & Day, 1997; Sampson et al., 2000). These difficulties contribute to poor social skills, which in turn may lead to social withdrawal and even antisocial behavior (Streissguth, 1993). Early identification and early intervention programs that help both mother and child may help avoid some of these later difficulties (Substance Abuse Prevention, Substance Abuse and Mental Health Services Administration [SAMHSA], 2007). For more about Fetal Alcohol Syndrome and its discovery, see the *Focus On* feature on the next page.

Fetal alcohol syndrome is characterized in a child by distinctive facial features, including small eye openings, a thin upper lip, and a smooth philtrum (the area between the nose and upper lip). It may also cause intellectual disabilities and compromise physical growth.

**Prevention.** Preventing FASD is a simple matter in theory: Women who are or may be pregnant need only refrain from drinking alcohol. Nevertheless, in a recent survey, about 7.6% of pregnant women in the United States aged 18 to 44 reported alcohol use in the month preceding the survey. Women aged 35 to 44 years reported the highest prevalence of any alcohol use (14.3%). About 1.4% of women reported binge drinking while pregnant (having five or more drinks at one time). Drinking during pregnancy was highest among white, college-educated women (Marchetta, et al., 2012).

In recent years, some reports in the popular media suggested that pregnant women could have an occasional alcoholic drink without undue concern. These reports were immediately discredited. Given the complexity of the dose–response effect, the United States Surgeon General (CDC, 2005) and the American College of Obstetricians and Gynecologists (ACOG) (2008) have stated unequivocally that women who are pregnant or planning to become pregnant should abstain completely from alcohol. *There is no known minimum amount of alcohol that can be safely consumed during pregnancy.*

### WHEN SYSTEMS CONNECT

**Alcohol and Pregnancy.** Let's look at how systems connect when it comes to use of alcohol during pregnancy. On their way to the cerebral cortex, new neurons in the fetal brain migrate through areas of the brain already damaged by alcohol and become damaged as well. The mother may not know that alcohol can damage the fetus, or she may be so dependent on alcohol that she cannot quit drinking, even during pregnancy. She may not receive prenatal health care, either because she cannot afford it, because it is unavailable in her area, or because she is too impaired to seek help.

Should her child be born with FAS, the child will require more services than average: medical, educational, and so on. Perhaps the child will have to be placed in foster care or will need to live in a residential center for children with developmental disabilities. The costs to the social system for FAS have been estimated at from $250 million in 1987 to over $5 billion dollars in 2003. This wide range depends on how FAS is defined and counted, and which services are needed, and for how long (to age 21 or to age 65). A diagnosis of FAS can carry lifetime health-care costs of $860,000 for a single individual. When all the services required and the income lost because of health problems are combined, the costs for an individual may reach $5 million (Lupton, Burd, & Harwood, 2004).

## Tobacco

For over 50 years, researchers have known that smoking cigarettes during pregnancy can have adverse consequences (Simpson, 1957), yet some 10 to 13% of pregnant women smoke (Tong, Jones, Dietz, D'Angelo, & Bombard, 2009). Carbon monoxide in cigarette smoke reduces the amount of oxygen in the maternal bloodstream, thus reducing oxygen to the embryo or fetus as well. Nitric oxide constricts arteries, including those to and within the placenta, further decreasing blood flow. In addition, nitric

### Focus On: Ann Streissguth and Fetal Alcohol Syndrome

Ann Streissguth pursued a career in psychology hoping that she could make a difference in society. And did she! In the early 1970s, Dr. Streissguth, a clinical psychologist, was asked by some pediatricians to evaluate a group of children born to alcoholic mothers. She was stunned by the damage exhibited in these children—damage different from what she had seen related to poverty and physical disabilities. After finding no literature on the effects of prenatal exposure to alcohol on subsequent child development, she pursued further study. In 1973, she was one of the authors of the first publication that identified fetal alcohol syndrome. Since then, her research into the effects of prenatal alcohol exposure on cognitive development, along with the resulting implications for behavioral and social functioning, has been widely published; and she is recognized internationally as an expert in the field.

Dr. Streissguth is an advocate for these children and families and continues to promote education about the risks of drinking alcohol during pregnancy. She founded the Fetal Alcohol and Drug Unit in the Department of Psychiatry and Behavioral Science at the University of Washington School of Medicine, where she is now Professor Emeritus.

University of Washington/Mary Levin

**placenta previa** A condition in which the placenta attaches low on the wall of the uterus, with the potential to cause bleeding late in pregnancy.

**placenta abruptio** A life-threatening emergency condition in which the placenta peels away from the wall of the uterus, causing massive bleeding.

oxide interferes with maternal absorption of calcium, vitamins, and other nutrients vital to fetal growth.

Women who smoke during pregnancy are about twice as likely to experience two specific complications: placenta previa and placenta abruptio. In **placenta previa,** the placenta attaches low on the wall of the uterus, with the potential to cause bleeding late in pregnancy. **Placenta abruptio** is a life-threatening emergency in which the placenta peels away from the wall of the uterus. Smoking also places women at higher risk for premature delivery (Tong et al., 2009). Even in infants not born prematurely, maternal cigarette smoking is often associated with lower birth weight (weight of less than 5.5 lb, or 2,500 g). Research indicates a reduction of almost 5% in the infant's relative weight per pack of 20 cigarettes smoked by the mother per day (Kramer et al., 1990). These infants are also more likely to have shorter length and smaller head circumference (CDC, 2007a; Cornelius & Day, 2000; Weitzman, Byrd, Aligne, & Moss, 2002).

Nicotine in cigarettes also crosses the placenta, causing disruptions in the autonomic nervous system in the fetus, such as heart rhythm (Zeskind & Gingras, 2006). Prenatal tobacco exposure has been linked to other autonomic irregularities in the newborn as well, evidenced by tremors, difficulty orienting to the source of a sound nearby, and being easily startled (Cornelius & Day, 2000).

Consequences continue through time for infants and children whose mothers smoked during pregnancy. Controlled studies have reported effects from disruptive behavior and academic difficulties (Weitzman et al., 2002) to problems with breathing, such as coughing and wheezing, throughout childhood (Jedrychowski et al., 2007).

## Drugs and Medications

Among other chemical substances that can act as teratogens are illegal drugs and some prescription drugs. We discuss some of the more common and better-known risks here.

**Cocaine.** Cocaine is a powerful stimulant that directly affects the brain. Within seconds of entering the body, cocaine constricts blood vessels, increases blood pressure, causes irregular and increased heart rate, and raises body temperature. In a pregnant woman, cocaine affects the heart rate and blood pressure of both mother and fetus. Constricted maternal blood vessels can result in placenta previa and cause uterine contractions; it also increases the risk for miscarriage, premature birth, and death. For the newborn, exposure to cocaine in the womb may result in reduced size at birth, smaller head circumference, and increased risk for ventricular hemorrhage (bleeding into the brain), and perhaps abnormalities of the urinary tract (Bateman & Chiriboga, 2000; National Institute on Drug Abuse, 2010; Organization of Teratology Information Specialists, 2010).

During the 1980s, the increased use of "crack" cocaine, a form of the drug that is smoked, resulted in a widely publicized epidemic of "crack babies," infants who were "born addicted" because of their mothers' drug use during pregnancy (Chavkin, 2001). Newborns exhibited such behaviors as tremors, irritability, and disturbed wake–sleep cycles. They also were difficult to soothe (Bauer et al., 2005). Initial predictions were that prenatal cocaine exposure would have permanent and severe effects on these children, especially on their cognitive development.

After 25 years of follow-up studies, the dire predictions of far-reaching consequences have not been realized. By age 6 months, most babies who were exposed to cocaine in the womb catch up in growth, and their jitteriness subsides (Lumeng, Cabral, Gannon, Heeren, & Frank, 2007). No one disputes that cocaine is bad for prenatal development, and the long-term effects of prenatal exposure on children's brain development and behavior *are* statistically significant. Nevertheless, these effects are relatively small compared with the devastating effects of alcohol (Frank, Augustyn, Knight, Pell & Zuckerman, 2001; Lester, LaGasse, & Seifer, 1998; Shankaran et al., 2007).

Most children who were exposed to cocaine before birth have normal intelligence. Indeed, one study found no effects on memory and language in adolescents who had been exposed to cocaine in the womb (Betancourt et al., 2009). That said, subtle learning problems may be associated with exposure, including some language delays, attention problems, and difficulties with executive function (Cone–Wesson, 2005; Frank et al., 2001; Linares et al., 2006; Singer et al., 2004). Boys in particular may exhibit behavioral problems (Lester et al., 1998). Of course, any learning and behavioral problems that do exist cannot necessarily be attributed to cocaine exposure alone, as women who used cocaine during pregnancy may also have used tobacco, marijuana, or alcohol, and may also provide a less than optimal postnatal environment for their children (Frank et al., 2001; Lester et al., 1998; Shankaran et al., 2007).

Leonard McCombe/Life Magazine/Time & Life Pictures/Getty Images

Thalidomide, which was once prescribed for severe morning sickness, caused severe birth defects, such as missing or malformed limbs and fingers. Thousands of children were affected before thalidomide was removed from markets worldwide in 1962.

**Opiates.** Women who are dependent on heroin and other opiates are 6 times more likely to experience complications during pregnancy, and their babies are more likely to weigh less than average. During pregnancy, the fetus may go through repeated withdrawal from heroin, as the mother's use may vary; and the baby will withdraw again after birth. Women who seek treatment for drug addiction during pregnancy are usually placed on methadone or buprenorphine, both synthetic forms of heroin. The steady blood level of the opiate during pregnancy may still lead to withdrawal in the infant after birth, although it prevents the repeated withdrawal that causes fetal distress (Ludlow, Evans, & Hulse, 2004; Minozzi, Amato, Vecchi, & Davoli, 2008).

**Medications.** The dangers of ingesting prescribed medications during pregnancy made headlines around the world during the 1960s, when thalidomide was prescribed to women in England, Canada, and other countries for relief of severe morning sickness. Unfortunately, thalidomide was later found to cause severe birth defects, such as missing or malformed limbs and fingers. It is estimated that some 10,000 children were affected before thalidomide was removed from markets worldwide in 1962 (Rägo & Santoso, 2008). The drug was never approved for use in the United States for use in pregnant women; it is used for some immune disorders, however.

Today, a physician's decision to prescribe medication(s) to a pregnant woman comes down to one question: *Does the benefit outweigh the risk*? For example, it is usually better for both the mother and the embryo or fetus to treat the mother for an infectious disease than to risk the effects of the disease on the infant. The U.S. Food and Drug Administration [FDA] has a classification system for drugs to guide physicians' decisions about prescribing them for pregnant women (USFDA, 2007). Table 3.1 describes the system's five categories, which go from A (the safest) to X (the most dangerous). If a woman must take one of the higher–risk drugs for her own health, it is imperative that she be carefully monitored by a physician familiar with the risks (Andrade et al., 2004; Briggs, Freeman, & Yaffe, 2011; Buhimschi & Weiner, 2009; Cunningham et al., 2005; Howland, 2009; Lattimore et al., 2005; Nielsen, Sorensen, Larsen, & Pedersen, 2001; Organization of Teratology Information Specialists, 2003).

**Herbal Medicines and Supplements.** Herbal medicines and supplements are basically chemical compounds created by nature rather than in a lab. Indeed, some human-made medications are based on herbs or vitamins. For example, Accutane, listed in Table 3.1 as a Class X drug, is a form of vitamin A. Unfortunately, there are almost no studies on the effects of herbal remedies and nutritional supplements on pregnant women and their unborn offspring. Furthermore, the use of these substances is largely unregulated, so the dosage may vary from one manufacturer to another. Women who are pregnant should discuss the use of any supplements or herbal remedies, as well as other over-the-counter medications, with a professional health-care provider (Cunningham et al., 2005; Hepner et al., 2002).

## Maternal Disease, Illness, and Stress

So far, we've focused on substances that women ingest during pregnancy, such as alcohol, and their effect on the developing embryo or fetus. Disease, illness, and stress in the mother can also have an effect on their babies.

**Table 3.1** FDA Classification System for Drug Use During Pregnancy

| Class | Studies | Examples of Medications |
|---|---|---|
| A | In human studies, pregnant women used the medicine and their babies did not have any problems related to that use. | Folic acid<br>Prenatal vitamins<br>Thyroid medication for women with thyroid disorders |
| B | There are no good studies in humans, but in animal studies, pregnant animals received the medicine, and their babies did not show any problems related to the drug.<br>Or:<br>In animal studies, pregnant animals received the medicine and some babies had problems. But in human studies, pregnant women used the medicine and their babies did not have any problems related to that use. | Some antibiotics, like amoxicillin<br>Zofran (ondansetron), for nausea<br>Glucophage (metformin), for diabetes<br>Some insulins used to treat diabetes, such as regular and NPH insulin<br>Tylenol (acetaminophen), Advil, Motrin (ibuprofen), but only before the third trimester. Pregnant women should not take ibuprofen during the last three months of pregnancy due to increased risk of heart malformation in fetus. |
| C | There are no good studies in humans, but in animals, pregnant animals treated with the medicine had some babies with problems. However, the medicine may sometimes help the human mothers and babies more than it might harm them.<br>Or:<br>No animal studies have been done, and there are no good studies in pregnant women. | Diflucan (fluconazole), for yeast infections<br>Ventolin (albuterol), for asthma<br>Zoloft (sertraline) and Prozac (fluoxetine), for depression |
| D | Studies in humans and other reports show that when pregnant women use the medicine, some babies are born with problems related to it. However, in some serious situations, the medicine may help the mother and the baby more than it might harm. | Paxil (paroxetine), for depression<br>Lithium, for bipolar disorder<br>Dilantin (phenytoin), for epileptic seizures<br>Some cancer chemotherapy<br>Valium (diazepam) for anxiety |
| X | Studies or reports in humans or animals show that mothers using the medicine during pregnancy may have babies with problems related to it. There are no situations where the medicine can help the mother or baby enough to make the risk of problems worth it. These medicines should never be used by pregnant women. | Accutane (isotretinoin), for cystic acne<br>Coumadin (warfarin), a blood thinner<br>Methotrexate |

*Source:* FDA Drug Labeling, 2012; U.S. Department of Health and Human Services, Office on Women's Health. (2010); Organization of Teratology Information Specialists, 2003; Buhimschi & Weiner, 2009.

## Communicable Diseases

Communicable diseases, which may be caused by viruses, bacteria, or parasites, represent another potential danger to the developing organism. Communicable diseases can pass from the pregnant woman to her offspring by crossing the placenta or be transmitted during a vaginal birth when the mother's blood and other bodily fluids come in contact with the newborn infant's eyes, nose, and mouth. Some of these diseases can result in serious birth defects, depending on the extent of exposure, the timing of exposure, and whether or not the mother was treated for the disease during pregnancy.

A number of communicable diseases known to adversely affect the fetus are described in Table 3.2. In developed countries, some of these diseases have decreased in incidence thanks to improvements in treatment and prevention. For example, early syphilis is readily treated with the antibiotic penicillin, and widespread vaccination against rubella has been effective in decreasing its incidence. However, these diseases continue to ravage developing countries—and their children.

In the United States, cytomegalovirus (CMV) is the most common viral infection in newborns (1% of births); it can result in deafness, retardation, and blindness.

**Table 3.2** Characteristics and Effects of Some Communicable Diseases During Pregnancy

| Disease Characteristics | Incidence Among Pregnant Women or Live Births per Year | Effects |
|---|---|---|
| Syphilis: Bacterial infection transmitted through sexual contact | Between 2003 and 2004, overall rate decreased 17.8%, from 10.7 to 8.8 cases per 100,000 live births | 40% of untreated early syphilis results in death of the fetus or newborn; infants who survive may be intellectually disabled, blind, deaf, or all three. |
| Toxoplasmosis: Parasitic infection transmitted to humans from animals, especially cat feces and raw meat | 1–10 per 10,000 live births | Risk of miscarriage, premature birth, low birth weight, and intellectual disabilities. |
| Rubella (German measles): Viral infection transmitted through coughing, sneezing, and the like | Fewer than 1 per 1,000 live births | Infection during first trimester causes deafness, heart defects, and cataracts in child. |
| Cytomegalovirus (CMV): Viral infection of the herpes simplex group; transmitted through contact with infected body fluids, such as saliva, mucus, urine, and blood | 1% percent of all neonates; 1 in 150 live births | 10–23% of infected babies develop hearing loss, vision loss, or learning problems. |
| Gonorrhea: Bacterial infection transmitted through sexual contact | 13,200 pregnant women infected in 2007 | Miscarriage, premature birth; eye infection or blindness in newborn |
| HIV/AIDS: Virus transmitted through contact with bodily fluids, such as through sexual contact or sharing contaminated needles | 6,400 pregnant women infected in 2007; 2% rate of transmission to fetus if woman is being treated | Risk of death to child; infants who survive may be slow to reach milestones and may have neurological and learning problems |

*Source:* CDC, 2004; CDC, 2007b; CDC, 2010; Lopez, Dietz, Wilson, Navin & Jones, 2000; Nigro et al., 2005; U.S. Department of Health and Human Services Center for the Evaluation of Risks to Human Reproduction, 2003.

Of children who develop these conditions, about 10% have signs of infection, such as fever, at birth; but another 8 to 13% have none (CDC, 2010; Nigro, Adler, La Torre, & Best, 2005). Yet only 22% of women in the United States have heard of CMV, compared with 98% who have heard of HIV/AIDS (Jeon et al., 2006).

## HIV and AIDS

Over the past 25 years, the implications for pregnant women and their infants of contracting maternal human immunodeficiency virus (HIV) and acquired immune deficiency syndrome (AIDS) have captured considerable attention. HIV attacks the immune system, leaving persons with the virus vulnerable to infections. AIDS is the final stage of the HIV infection, when the damaged immune system, aided by powerful antibiotics, can no longer guard against opportunistic infections, such as pneumonia, eventually resulting in death. The progression of HIV infection to its final stage can be slowed through treatment, but HIV is not curable.

Women can transmit the virus to their offspring during pregnancy, during a vaginal birth, and during breast-feeding, as the virus can be found in breast milk (CDC, 2007c). In the United States, HIV infection by these paths has dramatically decreased in recent years. The transmission rate is now less than 2% for pregnant women whose health care follows these guidelines: prenatal HIV counseling and testing, taking medications before and during pregnancy to slow the progress of HIV infection, having cesarean delivery to avoid vaginal birth, and not breastfeeding. By comparison, the transmission rate is 25 to 30% for women who do not follow these guidelines (Mofenson et al., 2006; Perinatal HIV Guidelines Working Group, 2009).

There are two patterns of HIV infection among infants and children. About 20% of infected infants progress to the late stage of the disease, AIDS, in the first year of life; most of them die by age 4. The remaining 80% infected with HIV at birth have a slower progression of the disease, and may not develop symptoms until school age or later. Symptoms of disease progression include being slow to reach physical milestones, such as crawling; neurological problems, such as seizures; and difficulty learning in school. Because of the effect of HIV/AIDS on the immune system, infected children are especially vulnerable to bacterial and viral infections (National Institute of Allergy and Infectious Diseases [NIAID, 2004]).

what if...?

What if a woman who has HIV refuses to follow the recommended guidelines during her pregnancy? Or refuses to have a cesarean delivery? When her baby is born with HIV, what might be the consequences?

### Diabetes Mellitus

Diabetes is not a communicable disease, but it affects more women than HIV/AIDS and all sexually transmitted diseases combined. About 10% of American women of childbearing age have either type 1 or type 2 diabetes before becoming pregnant—about 12 million women, plus another estimated several million with undiagnosed type 2 diabetes, which is associated with obesity. Because of the prevalence of this disease, we take a look at its effects during pregnancy next.

Diabetes is a chronic condition characterized by abnormally high glucose (sugar) levels in the blood. Glucose is the body's main source of energy. In the case of type 1 diabetes, the pancreas does not make enough insulin. In type 2 diabetes, the body cells are not sensitive to the action of insulin (CDC, 2007d). Diabetes affects pregnancy when high blood glucose levels are not controlled. Abnormally high maternal blood glucose levels during the third to sixth weeks of prenatal development may result in heart defects, hydrocephalus (excess fluid on the brain), and other problems in the developing organism. Later in pregnancy, high levels of blood glucose cross the placenta from mother to fetus, and the fetus begins to experience high levels of blood glucose as well. As a result, the fetus's pancreas produces more insulin. However, the fetus may then become resistant to insulin, and the excess blood glucose is stored in fat cells.

Infants of diabetic mothers are heavier than average at birth. In addition, they may have difficulty managing glucose levels on their own. This difficulty predisposes them to an acute drop in glucose after birth and to obesity and insulin resistance in childhood. Diabetes also places pregnant women at increased risk for preterm delivery and eclampsia, an emergency condition involving high blood pressure and seizures (Cunningham et al., 2005; Feig & Palda, 2002; Reece, 2008; Sheffield, Butler–Koster, Casey, McIntire, & Leveno, 2002).

A different form of diabetes is *gestational diabetes*, which usually occurs in mid to late pregnancy in women with no previous history of diabetes. Gestational diabetes generally goes away after the baby is born. Nevertheless, the risks associated with gestational diabetes are the same as the risks mentioned for types I and II diabetes. Furthermore, although the mothers' blood sugar levels usually return to normal after delivery, they are at greater risk for developing diabetes later (Cunningham et al., 2005; London, Ladewig, Ball, & Bindler, 2003; Sheffield et al., 2002).

### Maternal Stress

The normal stressors of everyday life continue during pregnancy, and very stressful events, such as the death of a loved one or the loss of a job, can occur at any time. For some women, pregnancy itself is a cause of stress. Physiological changes, coupled with social and emotional difficulties, can take their toll. Some studies suggest that pregnant women with very high levels of stress and anxiety are at increased risk for miscarriage and premature labor, and that the growth of their offspring in the womb has been compromised (Mulder et al., 2002). Other studies, though, show no such effects (Nelson et al., 2003).

Part of the difficulty in researching this topic is the definition of stress. While life events appear to be an objective measure of stress, extensive research also indicates that the subjective meaning of an event is key to understanding a person's response to it (Lazarus & Folkman, 1984)—one person's stressor is another person's inconvenience.

Also, as you learned in Chapter 2, stress increases heart rate, blood pressure, glucose levels, and, especially, the stress hormone cortisol. Studies have focused on the effect on the developing fetal brain of cortisol and other hormones from this source (Lupien, McEwen, Gunnar, & Heim, 2009). Too much cortisol is linked to permanent changes in the brain and endocrine systems in infants (Kapoor, Dunn, Kostaki, Andrews, & Matthews, 2006). However, the dose-response effect and its timing during prenatal development are not clear (O'Donnell, O'Connor, & Glover, 2009). In addition, individual mothers and offspring differ in their responses to stress (Owen, Andrews, & Matthews, 2005).

Most women across cultures believe that their own stress and negative moods will adversely affect their pregnancies and offspring (Schaffir, 2007). This belief by itself can be stressful! Nevertheless, while no one can avoid stress for nine months, it is prudent for a woman to moderate her response to stressful events during pregnancy, if possible.

## Environmental Pollutants and Hazards

Finally, we look at two examples of substances in the external environment that may affect pregnant women: radiation and environmental chemicals.

### Radiation

Science encountered the effects of radiation on fetal development in 1945 after the atomic bombing of Hiroshima and Nagasaki, Japan, and again in 1986 after the meltdown of a nuclear power plant in Chernobyl, Ukraine, which was then part of the Soviet Union. In both cases, it was difficult to correlate the amount of exposure to adverse effects, because it was impossible to determine the amount of exposure by any one person. That said, the children of Chernobyl have demonstrated a much higher incidence of thyroid and other cancers than usual, which has been attributed to their exposure to radiation (Boice, 2006). We also know that anomalies in major organs, including limb deformities, can occur when a fetus is exposed to high doses of radiation before the eighth week of prenatal development. Between 8 and 15 weeks of prenatal development, there is a clear dose-response effect of increased risk of microcephaly—a small brain—and severe intellectual disabilities. Higher doses are needed to have the same effect after 16 weeks (Baverstock & Dillwyn, 2006; Boice, 2006; Brent, 1999; Cunningham et al., 2005; Greskovich & Macklis, 2000).

*Everyday stories*

NUCLEAR DISASTER IN JAPAN In March 2011, an earthquake and tsunami damaged a nuclear power plant in Fukushima, Japan. Explosions at the plant exposed populations living nearby to radiation. Significantly less radiation was released in this incident than had been released at Chernobyl. Nevertheless, given the previous histories of radiation exposure in Ukraine and Japan, and improved technologies for tracking exposure, Japanese children exposed to this more recent release of radiation will no doubt be followed closely.

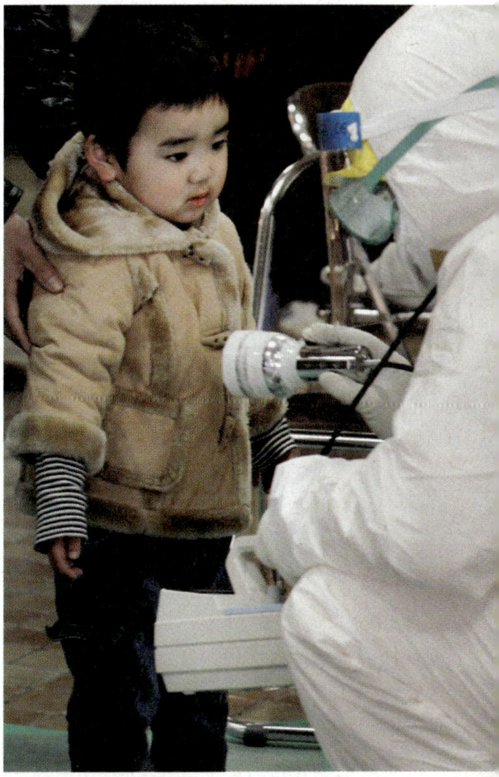

*Tayama TATSUYUKI/Gamma-Rapho via Getty Images*

In March 2011, a massive earthquake and tsunami severely damaged a Japanese nuclear power plant, exposing people who lived nearby to radiation. Here, a little boy from the area is tested for radiation exposure.

### Environmental Chemicals

In 1959, after four years of investigation, an epidemic of neurological disorders in a fishing village in Minamata Bay, Japan, was attributed to mercury poisoning from a nearby industrial plant. In December 1984, methyl isocyanate gas leaked from a tank at a Union Carbide plant in Bhopal, India, killing 3,800 people and exposing as many as 500,000 to the toxic gas. The effects of these disasters on embryos and fetuses, newborns, and young children were devastating: severe developmental delay and cerebral palsy (Japan) (Cordero, 1993); four times the normal rate of miscarriage (Bhopal) (Cordero, 1993); and diseases of the eyes and lungs, increased chromosomal abnormalities, impaired motor function, and cognitive problems (Bhopal) (Broughton, 2005).

The United States is not immune to such tragedy. Across the country, residential communities have been built—sometimes knowingly, sometimes not—on or near disposal dumps where hazardous chemicals known to cause birth defects and other illnesses are buried in large barrels. These chemicals may percolate to the surface or enter drinking water; but it has not been easy to identify a causal relationship between the chemicals and subsequent physical and behavioral disorders (Carpenter, Shen, Nguyen, Le, Lininger, 2001). As a result, funding for cleanup from the federal government or from lawsuits is delayed, while the practice of chemical dumping continues in other areas.

✓ CHECK YOUR PROGRESS

1. What are the dose-response and threshold effects?
2. Why is alcohol especially damaging to the developing human organism?
3. How does a woman know which medications are safe during pregnancy?
4. How do communicable diseases affect the fetus?
5. Discuss historical events involving environmental hazards to prenatal development.

## Health During Pregnancy

**[ KEY QUESTION ] 4.** What is considered a healthy pregnancy?

A healthy pregnancy increases the likelihood of a healthy baby and mother. As the accompanying feature, Culture and Pregnancy, points out, producing healthy mothers and babies is an important value across time and cultures. In this section, we discuss health during pregnancy: the normal changes that accompany pregnancy; recommendations for a healthy pregnancy; some common complications among pregnant women; some special cases, such as high-risk pregnancies and adolescent pregnancy; and access to health care, and its implications.

### Physiology of Pregnancy

Even though pregnancy is a natural phenomenon, it puts significant physiological stress on the female body. For example, during pregnancy, the uterus grows to 20 times its former size. A pregnant woman breathes 30 to 40% more air each minute, amounting to a 15 to 20% increase in oxygen. The pregnant woman's heart enlarges by 12%, since the cardiovascular system needs to pump 30 to 50% more blood, primarily to the uterus, kidneys, and lungs. And because red blood cells use iron to carry oxygen from the lungs, pregnant women need sufficient iron in their diets and/or iron supplements. There is also an increase in plasma, which is mostly water, in the bloodstream (Cunningham et al., 2005; London et al., 2003). The discomfort caused by these normal physiological changes may vary considerably between individual women and even between pregnancies in the same woman.

# Culture and Pregnancy

Birth and death are the bookends of life, shared by all human beings since the beginning of time. Uncertainty among our ancestors about what comes before birth and after death generated rituals and beliefs about the life cycle that are still part of human society. Even as we have come to better understand science and adjust some of our practices accordingly, these powerfully emotional events continue to fill us with awe, fear, sorrow, and joy.

Most cultural beliefs about pregnancy address the mother's behavior and emotional state, the food she eats, and the effects of all this on the unborn child. Some of these beliefs are surprisingly similar among cultures, suggesting that millennia of experience with pregnancy and birth brought our ancestors to similar conclusions about what to do and what not to do to help ensure the survival of mother and child.

For example, many cultures warn a pregnant woman against reaching over her head lest in doing so the umbilical cord become wrapped around the baby's neck. Some cultures prohibit the mother from wearing necklaces for the same reason. In other cultures, pregnant women are advised to avoid becoming upset, attending funerals, or viewing a dead body or a terrible accident. Doing so will, it is thought, invite evil into her presence and thus adversely affect her child.

*Tim Graham/Getty Images*

A woman's food cravings must be indulged, certain cultures believe, or else the baby will be "marked," literally—that is, have a birthmark. Birthmarks, others believe, may also be caused by eating strawberries. The type of foods women eat, some think, may affect the color or smoothness of the baby's skin. While some cultures advise pregnant women to avoid iron-rich foods like red meat during pregnancy, others insist on it. Although some of these beliefs may appear to be pure superstition to those unfamiliar with their cultural origins, their persistence is remarkable, and they remain meaningful to millions of people (Purnell, 2009; Spector, 2009).

*Everyday stories*

MORNING SICKNESS DURING PREGNANCY Morning sickness is a familiar example of discomfort associated with pregnancy. In fact, the nausea of morning sickness, which results from hormonal changes, can be one of the first signs of pregnancy. The symptoms usually begin around the 6th week of pregnancy and stop around the 12th week, although they may continue longer. Fatigue is another fairly common problem experienced by pregnant women, as is swelling in the legs and ankles. The swelling comes from an increase in plasma, which is mostly water, in the bloodstream. And as the fetus grows larger, it puts greater pressure on the mother's internal organs, causing some women to experience heartburn, gastrointestinal distress, and urinary frequency as time goes by. Others experience shortness of breath when lying on their backs from the pressure of the fetus against the diaphragm, the muscle involved in breathing that separates the lungs from the abdomen.

Given the profound physical changes that accompany a normal pregnancy, it is easy to appreciate the fact that a woman who is not in optimal health before becoming pregnant will be at increased risk for complications when she does. Furthermore, as noted earlier, pregnancies involving more than one fetus are always considered to be high risk for both mother and babies. Let's look at some recommendations for a healthy pregnancy.

2A Images/Gallo Images ROOTS Collection/Getty Images

Good nutrition is important for a healthy pregnancy.

## Recommendations for a Healthy Pregnancy

*Prenatal care* refers to health care during pregnancy. The purpose is to monitor the health of mother and baby; to provide education and counseling about pregnancy, birth, and newborns to women and their partners; to manage any regular health problems that pregnant women may have; and to prevent complications of pregnancy or to intervene early when they arise. Ideally, a woman who is planning to become pregnant will seek care before she conceives, so that she is healthy when she becomes pregnant. For example, if she has not already been immunized for rubella or chickenpox, which can cause birth defects, she should be immunized *before* pregnancy, never during pregnancy. Table 3.3 lists recommendations for health during pregnancy.

## Complications of Pregnancy and High-Risk Pregnancies

Common complications of pregnancy include high blood pressure, problems during labor, and premature birth. Most can be medically managed, although they increase the risk for surgical delivery, better known as caesarean section. While complications can occur for any pregnant woman, some women are at higher risk: older women having their first child; women with chronic illnesses, such as diabetes and

**Table 3.3** Recommendations for a Healthy Pregnancy

| | |
|---|---|
| Frequency of prenatal care appointments | A pregnant woman should see her health–care provider every 4 weeks until the 28th week of pregnancy, every 2–3 weeks between the 28th and 36th weeks, and weekly between the 36th and 40th weeks. |
| Folic acid | Folic acid is the synthetic form of folate, or vitamin B-12. In one form or other, folic acid is found in leafy green vegetables, fruits, dried beans and peas, vitamins, and fortified foods such as breakfast cereals. Pregnant women should get at least 400 mcg of folic acid each day. Folic acid is important in the growth of new cells and helps to prevent certain birth defects. Low levels are associated with spina bifida and with cleft lip and cleft palate. |
| Vitamin supplements | Prenatal vitamin supplements contain the recommended amounts of folic acid and other compounds, such as iron, zinc, calcium, and vitamin A. The supplements should contain no more than 5,000 international units of vitamin A, as it can cause birth defects in larger amounts. |
| Nutrition | Pregnancy is not an excuse to overeat. Increase daily intake by about 300 kcal per day using these choices:<br>Increase milk products from 2 to 3–4 cups per day.<br>Increase protein intake from 2–3 to 3–4 servings per day (about 60 g).<br>Increase fruits and vegetables from 3–5 to 5–7 servings per day.<br>Increase breads, cereals, pasta, and rice from 6–11 to 8–13 servings per day. |
| Weight gain | For healthy women of normal weight: 25–35 lb<br>For overweight women: 15–25 lb<br>For underweight women: 28–40 lb<br>Obese women should lose weight before becoming pregnant. |
| Exercise | Mild to moderate exercise is safe in uncomplicated pregnancies.<br>Activities with a risk for abdominal trauma should be avoided.<br>The pregnant athlete should guard against becoming dehydrated. |
| Sexual activity | Women with normal pregnancy may continue to have sexual intercourse. Sexual desire may or may not change. |

*Source:* Badovinac, Werler, Williams, Kelsey, & Hayes, 2007; DeWals, et al., 2007; Institute for Clinical Systems Improvement (ICSI), 2008; Institute of Medicine, 1998; Mattson & Smith, 2010; Mayo Clinic, 2012.

high blood pressure; women with previous history of difficulties during pregnancy; and any pregnancy involving multiple fetuses (Cunningham et al., 2005; London et al., 2003; Luke & Brown 2007).

Obesity, which affects more than 30% of adults, has also become a prevalent risk factor. The bodies of obese women are already experiencing physiological stress, especially on the cardiovascular system. In addition, obesity is often associated with undiagnosed diabetes. Obese women have three times the risk for miscarriage and four times the risk for eclampsia, a serious complication, discussed in the next section (Yu, Teoh, & Robinson, 2006).

**preeclampsia** A treatable medical condition that begins to develop after the 20th week of pregnancy, characterized by high blood pressure, protein in the urine, and sometimes swelling.

**eclampsia** A medical emergency in which untreated symptoms of preeclampsia lead to maternal seizures and/or coma and even death of mother and baby. It may require immediate surgical delivery of the fetus.

**ectopic pregnancy** A condition in which the blastocyst phase of the embryo implants outside of the uterus, usually in the fallopian tube, where it cannot continue to develop. It quickly outgrows the space, resulting in pain and possible rupture of the fallopian tube.

## Preeclampsia and Eclampsia

**Preeclampsia** is the most common complication during pregnancy, occurring in about 5 to 8% of pregnant women. It occurs more commonly in women with diabetes and those carrying multiple fetuses. Preeclampsia is characterized by high blood pressure, protein in the urine, and sometimes swelling. The condition usually begins to develop after the 20th week of gestation. By 30 weeks, small spasms and constrictions of the mother's blood vessels decrease blood flow to the fetus, which can result in either premature birth or a baby that is smaller than expected at birth. When detected during routine care in pregnancy, preeclampsia can be managed medically (Cunningham et al., 2005; London et al., 2003; March of Dimes, 2009b). When untreated, however, it may develop into **eclampsia**, a serious medical emergency that is often accompanied by seizures in the mother. Eclampsia can even cause coma and death of the mother and baby. Thus, it may require immediate surgical delivery of the fetus.

## Ectopic Pregnancy

In an **ectopic pregnancy,** the embryo implants outside of the uterus, usually in the fallopian tube. This situation occurs in 1 to 2% of all pregnancies and is associated with fallopian tubes having been damaged as a consequence of sexually transmitted diseases, scarring from previous surgery, or a naturally occurring variant in the

Women whose pregnancies involve no complications can safely engage in mild to moderate exercise.

Ty Downing/Getty Images

**Rh incompatibility** A complication of pregnancy in which a mother who is Rh negative carries an Rh-positive fetus; under certain conditions, antibodies in the mother's blood can attack the fetus's red blood cells.

mother. An ectopic pregnancy is not sustainable. Within a few days, the developing embryo outgrows its confined space and dies, causing bleeding and sharp pain in the mother. If the condition is not detected quickly and treated, the fallopian tube may rupture and become permanently damaged; or it may have to be removed altogether (Cunningham et al., 2005; London et al., 2003).

### Rh Incompatibility

If you have ever given or received blood, you probably know what your blood type is: A, B, AB, or O. The vast majority of people also have an antigen on their red blood cells called the D antigen; these people have *Rh-positive blood type*—for example, A-positive. Blood without the D antigen is referred to as *Rh-negative blood type*—for example, A-negative.

Problems can arise when an Rh-negative mother is carrying an Rh-positive fetus, a situation known as **Rh incompatibility**. The red blood cells from the fetus can get into the mother's bloodstream. The mother's immune system treats the Rh-positive fetal cells as if they were a foreign substance and makes antibodies to attack them. A woman's first pregnancy is often not affected because it takes time for the mother to develop these antibodies. However, if the woman becomes pregnant again with an Rh-positive offspring, the antibodies will attack that fetus's blood cells, causing damage and, potentially, death to the fetus. Fortunately, women who are Rh-negative can receive a vaccine, Rh immune globulin (RhoGAM), to prevent sensitization to the D antigen (London et al., 2003).

## A Special High-Risk Case: The Pregnant Adolescent

Adolescent pregnancy—defined as pregnancy in women aged 19 and under—is a complex issue, touching every system of human development. The birth rate for pregnant 15- to 19-year-olds has declined by more than 50% since 1970, from 68.3 to 31.3 per 1,000 in 2011, as shown in Figure 3.6. The 2011 rate represents a historic low for teenagers of all racial and ethnic backgrounds: Hispanic, non-Hispanic white, non-Hispanic black, and Asian or Pacific Islander teenagers. However, there were differences among these groups. The overall rate was highest for Hispanic teenagers (49.4),

Thomas Barwick/Getty Images

For many reasons, pregnancy poses greater risks for teenagers—especially girls aged 14 and under—than for adult women.

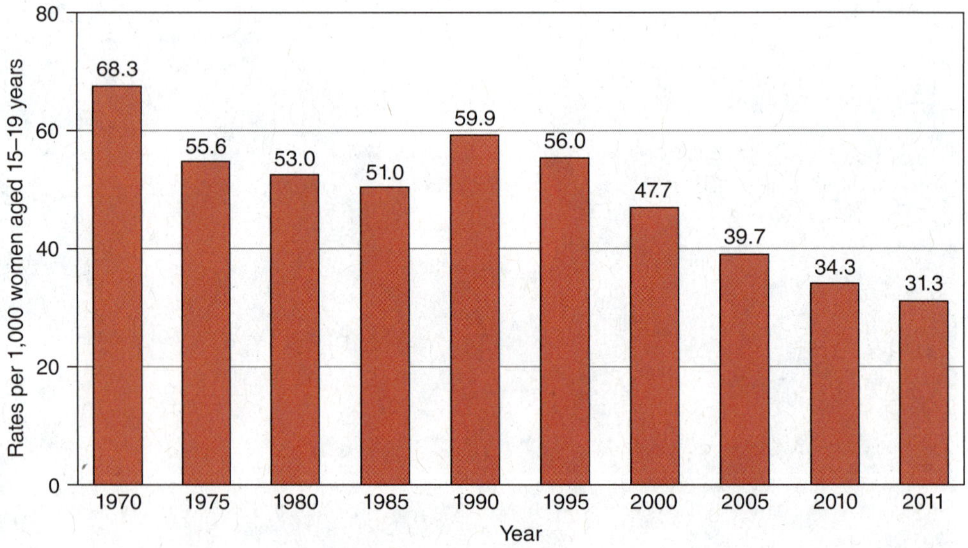


SOURCE: CDC/NCHS, National Vital Statistics System. www.cdc.gov/nchs/data/nvsr/nvsr60/nvsr60_02.pdf

**FIGURE 3.6 Births to U.S. Teenage Mothers** The birth rate for 15- to 19-year-olds has declined fairly steadily since 1970.

Adapted from Martin, J. A., Hamilton, B. E., Ventura, S. J., Osterman, M. J. K., Wilson, E. C. & Mathews, T. J. (2012). Births: Final data 2010. *National Vital Statistics Report 61*(1). http://www.cdc.gov/nchs/data/nvsr/nvsr61/nvsr61_01.pdf Hamilton, B. E., Martin, J. A., & Ventura, S. J. (2012). Births: Preliminary data 2011. *National Vital Statistics Report 61*, (5). http://www.cdc.gov/nchs/data/nvsr/nvsr61/nvsr61_05.pdf.

followed by non-Hispanic black teens (47.4), Native American and Alaskan indigenous teens (36.2), non-Hispanic white teens (21.8), and Asian or Pacific Islander teens (10.2) (Hamilton, Martin, & Ventura, 2012; Martin, Hamilton, Ventura, Osterman, Wilson, & Mathews, 2012).

Physiologically, most adolescent women are not in optimal health to carry a pregnancy (Forrest, 1993). Many are still growing physically, and their pelvic bones are not fully mature. Their health behaviors also play a role; they may have poor eating habits, their wake-sleep cycles and menstrual cycles are often irregular, and the possibility of alcohol and drug use is always a concern (we discuss this issue further in Chapter 14). To make matters worse, the vast majority of teen pregnancies are unplanned, and pregnant teens often delay telling anyone about their pregnancies, delaying prenatal care (Chandra, Martinez, Mosher, Abma, & Jones, 2005; Guttmacher Institute, 2012). As a result of all these factors, teenagers are at greater risk for anemia, infection, and preeclampsia during pregnancy. Their babies are more likely to be premature, two times as likely to have low birth weight, and three times more likely to die within a month of birth. In general, risk is greatest for younger adolescents aged 14 and under (Jolly, Sebire, Harris, Robinson, & Regan, 2000; Klein & Committee on Adolescence of the American Academy of Pediatrics, 2005; Satin et al., 1994).

Pregnancy alters the development of both adolescent women and their children, which in turn affects society in general. Teenage mothers are more likely to drop out of school and to be single parents, which compromises their socioeconomic status. Between 22% and 30% under age 18 who have a baby will have a second one within two years after their first. And because adolescent women generally are not economically prepared for parenthood either, there is a resulting cost to society: $9 to $11 billion each year in welfare payments and other government assistance programs, such as health care, food stamps, and job training (Hoffman & Maynard, 2008; Klein & Committee on Adolescence of the American Academy of Pediatrics, 2005; National Campaign to Prevent Teen Pregnancy, 2011). In addition, teenage mothers often are not emotionally prepared to parent a dependent infant; they tend to be self-centered, given they are also working through their own developmental tasks related to identity.

Clearly, pregnant adolescents require a great deal of support in order to have healthy babies. The relationship between the pregnant mother, her family, and the baby's father plays a significant role in the support available to her. Often, however, girls who become pregnant as teenagers have had a history of poor or unstable family relationships, making support during pregnancy less likely (Hillis et al., 2004). Factors that contribute to a good outcome include parents with higher education levels, a mother who is employed outside of the home, and smaller family size (Klein & Committee on Adolescence of the American Academy of Pediatrics, 2005).

## what if...?

What if a teenage girl is pregnant? How might that affect her relationship with her family and the father of her baby? What if she decides to raise her baby? What support would she need to complete her education? To prepare for parenthood? What if she decides that the baby would be best cared for through adoption? What support would she need? What is the father's role? Who should make these decisions?

## CHECK YOUR PROGRESS

1. What are some of the normal physiological changes that occur during pregnancy?
2. What are some of the recommendations for a healthy pregnancy? Why do these matter?
3. What are common complications of pregnancy?
4. Why are pregnant adolescents considered to be at high risk?

## Pregnancy and Society

**[ KEY QUESTION ] 5.** What is the role of social institutions in supporting pregnancy and parenting?

Parents have children for many reasons: because they want to share their love, to find meaning in their lives beyond self-interest, to establish a family that will carry on after their deaths (Cowan & Cowan, 2000). Sometimes, too, a pregnancy is unplanned. Nevertheless, the desire to bear children is deeply rooted in our biological, social, and cultural makeup. In this section, we touch on social and cultural values as they affect family composition, access to health care, and infertility. We cover the important matter of the transition to parenthood in Chapter 4.

### Birth-Rate Trends

Between 1800 and 2003 in the United States, the average number of children a woman could expect to bear in her lifetime dropped from 7.0 to 2.0, with lower rates in the Northeast and higher rates in the Southwest (CDC, 2003). Between 1970 and 2005, the mean age of all women at first birth rose from 21.4 in 1970 to 25.2 in 2005 (Mathews & Hamilton, 2009), with the lowest mean age (22.6 years) in Mississippi, and the highest in Massachusetts (27.7 years). These changes can be attributed to the widespread use of contraceptives and changing attitudes about women, education, and work. Thus, women are able to plan their pregnancies so that they are able to complete schooling and/or achieve some financial footing before starting a family.

Another change in birth-rate trends involves births to unmarried women. The yearly birth rate for unmarried women ages 15 to 44 increased from 26.4 per 1,000 women in 1980 to 51.8 in 2007, then declined to 46.1 in 2011. Thus, the percentage of all births accounted for by unmarried women more than doubled, from 18.4% in 1980 to 41% in 2011, with women aged 25 to 39, accounting for the largest proportion of the increase (Child Trends, 2012; Hamilton et al., 2012; Martin et al., 2009).

Educational levels play a major role in both trends. Research strongly supports a positive relationship between marital status, mother's level of education, and child well-being. Mothers with higher levels of education are more likely to be married, to work, and to have fewer children than mothers who have a high school education or less. They also tend to have their first child at a later age (Martin et al., 2009). In turn, married couples, especially those with higher education levels, have more financial resources and more time available to spend with children. Their children are also healthier. By comparison, single parents typically have less education and fewer financial and parental resources (Chandra et al., 2005).

These two trends, considered together, represent a fundamental change in our culture that cannot be underestimated. As the cost and complexity of raising a child in our society has increased, the resources to do so have decreased for an ever-larger number of parents—that is, for a growing number of unmarried mothers with few resources. The disparities between children with and without sufficient financial and parental resources have widened, straining the education and health-care systems. Furthermore, when these children have families of their own, their children are likely to face a similar situation.

### Access to Health Care

Unfortunately, nearly 1 million pregnant women in the United States deliver babies every year without having received adequate health care, putting their babies at three times the risk for premature birth and five times the risk for death (U.S. Department of Health and Human Services, 2013). In 1970, 68% of women of all ethnic and racial backgrounds in the United States received care beginning in the first trimester of pregnancy; by 2003, it was 84.1%. However, by 2010 that number had fallen to 73%. Furthermore, it had fallen across all ethnic and racial groups (National Center for Health Statistics, Health United States, 2006; U.S. Department of Health and Human Services, Health Resources and Services Administration, Maternal and Child Health

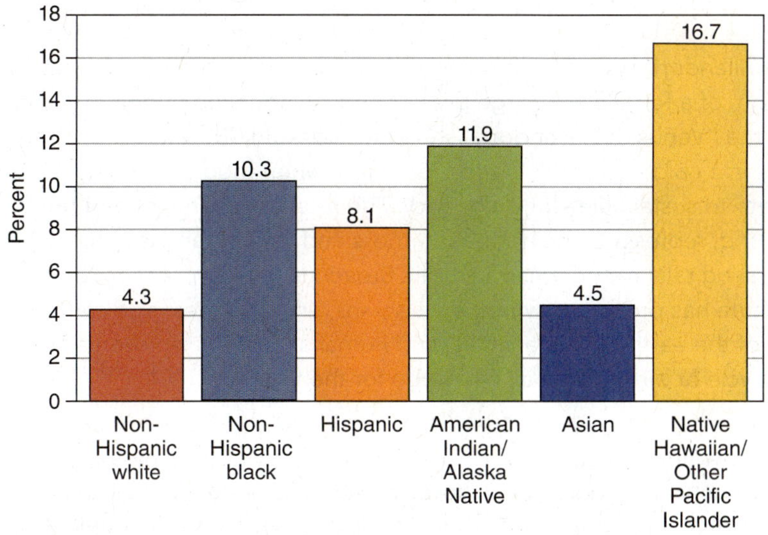


**FIGURE 3.7 Percentage of Mothers Receiving Late or No Prenatal Care, by Race and Hispanic Origin, 2010** Late prenatal care is care that does not begin until the third trimester. Babies whose mothers do not receive adequate prenatal care are at much greater risk for premature birth and even for death.

Adapted from http://mchb.hrsa.gov/chusa12/hsfu/pages/pc.html. U.S. Department of Health and Human Services, Health Resources and Services Administration, Maternal and Child Health Bureau. (2013). *Child Health USA 2012*. Rockville, Maryland: U.S. Department of Health and Human Services.

Bureau, 2013). Figure 3.7 shows the percentage of women in various groups who received no prenatal care or late prenatal care as of 2010.

As of 2010, 78.3% of whites, 62.5% of African Americans, and 67.6% of Hispanic Americans received health care beginning in the first trimester. Receiving care was highest among women of Asian background (78.6%) (U.S. Department of Health and Human Services, Health Resources and Services Administration, Maternal and Child Health Bureau, 2013). In 2008, these women also had the lowest infant mortality rate, at 4.5 per 1,000 live births. African Americans had the highest infant mortality rate, at 12.67 per 1,000 live births (MacDorman & Mathews, 2012). Let's put the rate of 12.67 for African-Americans in a global context. Of 31 industrialized countries this rate would rank 29th, better than only Mexico and Turkey (about 15 per 1,000 each) (National Center for Health Statistics, 2012).

Why does the United States, and why do African Americans in particular, rank so poorly compared with other industrialized nations? A major reason is lack of access to quality affordable health care, before and during pregnancy, increasing the risk for a variety of health problems that can complicate pregnancy. Most industrialized countries have government-funded health care for all citizens. The United States does not, although the 2010 Patient Protection and Affordable Care Act, mentioned in Chapter 2, is expected to provide health care to an estimated 32 million uninsured Americans. In addition, some women are unable to understand and follow through with recommendations for healthy pregnancy due to language barriers, lower levels of education, or lack of resources. For example, they may fail to appreciate the effect of alcohol, or they may not have access to healthful food, such as fresh fruits and vegetables. Distrust of the health-care system among some groups is another cause of disparities in health care in the United States (Betancourt et al., 2009).

## Infertility

We mentioned at the beginning of this section that the desire to bear children is deeply rooted in our biological, social, and cultural makeup. Cultures around the world and across time have placed high value on childbearing and on fertility—the ability to bear children.

FERTILITY: A CULTURAL VALUE In 1908, an archaeologist working near the town of Willendorf, Austria, came upon a small limestone figurine, about 4½ in. high, of a female with large breasts and pronounced abdominal girth. Dubbed the "Venus of Willendorf," she dates back 25,000 years to hunter-gatherers in a cold and bleak Europe, at a time when food sources were often inadequate to sustain life—or pregnancy. The rotund figurine, one of the oldest found, represents the hope for fatness and fertility, and is considered a childbearing talisman, or charm (Public Broadcasting Corporation, 2009). Every culture has produced symbols, talismans, and figurines representing fertility—of the earth, crops, animals, and humans. Fertility represents life itself—a cycle of birth, renewal, and hope for the future.

*Everyday stories*

It is no wonder, then, that for couples who expect to have biological children, the inability to conceive comes as a shock. Sometimes, a couple who had no difficulty conceiving their first child are unable to conceive again. Or a couple who had conceived with previous partners may not be able to conceive together. About 10 to 15% of American couples are infertile, defined as the inability to conceive after one year of trying with regular unprotected intercourse for couples in which the female is under 35, and 6 months of trying for couples in which the female is over 35 (Centers for Disease Control, 2013; Kuohung & Hornstein, 2012).

## Causes of Infertility

In the past, it was often assumed that infertility was a female problem. Although in 40 to 50% of cases that may be true, the cause involves only the male partner in about 20% of cases. In about 30 to 40% of cases, infertility is due to causes involving both the male and female, or the causes are not clearly identified (Kuohung & Hornstein, 2012; Mayo Clinic, 2009). Given the complexity of the reproductive tracts in both men and women, and the precision with which fertilization and implantation occur, any abnormality in either anatomical structures or hormonal balance can interfere with fertility.

**Female Infertility.** The optimal physiological age for a woman to become pregnant is about 19 to 26 years of age. About 8% of women under age 26 have difficulty becoming pregnant. By ages 27 to 34, 13 to 14% of women experience infertility, increasing to 18 to 22% for women aged 35 to 39 years. After age 40, the rate can increase to almost 1 in 3 women. The increase in infertility with maternal age is attributed to decreases in the number and quality of eggs in older women (American Society for Reproductive Medicine, 2003; Coccia & Rizzello, 2008; Dunson, Baird, & Colombo, 2004). In general, about 12% (7.3 million) of women between 15 and 44 are unable to conceive or carry a pregnancy to term (Chandra et al., 2005). There are many possible causes of female infertility, as indicated in Table 3.4.

© Barbara Gindl/epa/Corbis

Throughout their history, humans have placed a high value on fertility. The Venus of Willendorf, which dates back some 25,000 years, is thought to be a fertility charm, or talisman.

**Male Infertility.** Normally, men release from 1.5 to 5.0 ml of semen with each ejaculation, and each milliliter contains about 20 to 150 million sperm. A count below 20 million sperm per milliliter is often associated with infertility and is frequently a symptom of underlying problems (see Table 3.5). Age can be a factor for infertility in men as well. As men age, their testes get smaller, motility of sperm decline, and sperm heads may become misshapen. Other health problems can also be factors (American Society for Reproductive Medicine, 2003; Dunson et al., 2004). By ages 35 to 40 years, 18 to 28% of men experience infertility.

## Treatments for Infertility

Of course, there is no treatment that can turn back the biological clock, in men or women. Nevertheless, some causes of infertility can be treated so that couples can

**Table 3.4** Causes of Female Infertility

| | |
|---|---|
| **Problems with How Ova Are Produced** | |
| Polycystic ovary syndrome | A hormonal imbalance causes the ovary to form multiple small cysts, which interferes with ovulation. |
| High levels of insulin | In obese women with type 2 diabetes, high blood levels of insulin interfere with ovulation. |
| Hormonal disorders | A disruption in how the pituitary gland produces certain hormones interferes with ovulation. Hormonal and ovulation disorders account for almost 25% of infertility in women. |
| **Problems with How Ova Are Transported from the Ovaries Through the Fallopian Tubes** | |
| Blocked fallopian tubes | Scarring from surgery or from pelvic inflammatory disease blocks the tubes, and sperm cannot travel into them. Endometriosis, a condition in which endometrial tissue (uterine tissue) grows outside the uterus can also block the tubes. |
| **Problems with the Wall of the Uterus or the Cervix** | |
| Luteal phase defect | The ovary does not produce enough of the hormone progesterone to prepare the lining of the uterus for implantation of the fertilized egg. |
| Fibroids | Fibroids (benign tumors in the uterus) block the fallopian tubes or disrupt implantation. |
| Intrauterine contraceptive devices (IUDs) | Intrauterine devices can cause scarring and infection that later interfere with implantation. (IUDs are no longer widely used.) |
| Cervix | If the cervical mucus is too thick or contains antibodies that attack the sperm, then fertilization is impossible. |
| Age and lifestyle | After age 32, the quantity and the quality of a woman's eggs begin to decline. |
| | Also, being either overweight or underweight, smoking, and heavy alcohol use can result in hormonal disorders that cause infertility. |

conceive naturally. The first step is a thorough medical evaluation. Hormonal imbalances can be treated with hormones—for example, to stimulate the ovaries to produce more eggs. Some fallopian tube blockages can be reversed, though scar tissue from infection is difficult to remove. Obesity can be treated with diet, some medications, and surgery.

Treatment should also address the psychological distress associated with infertility. Anxiety and depression are common, especially in the infertile partner, and stress is the major reason couples stop seeking treatment. Sadly, family and friends may attribute infertility to stress, although infertility may in fact be the cause rather than the effect of stress (Chen, Chang, Tsai, & Juang, 2004; Domar, 2009; Eugster & Vingerhoets, 1999; Schmidt, 2009).

**Artificial insemination** has been a solution for male infertility for quite some time. Sperm is introduced directly into a woman's cervical canal or uterus. The sperm may come from the woman's partner or may be donor sperm taken from a sperm bank. Donor sperm may be used when the male partner's sperm count is low, when he is sterile, or when he has a family background of genetic disorders or disease.

## Assisted Reproductive Technology

If treating underlying physical and emotional health problems is not effective, or if artificial insemination is not an option, couples may turn to **assisted reproductive technology (ART)**. ART includes any procedure in which both the male and female gametes—the egg and sperm—are handled outside of the human body. ART does not

**artificial insemination** A medical procedure in which sperm is introduced directly into a woman's cervical canal or uterus; the sperm may be from her partner or from a donor.

**assisted reproductive technology (ART)** Any procedure in which both the male and female gametes—that is, the egg and sperm—are handled outside of the human body. ART does not refer to treatment that includes only the use of hormones that spur egg or sperm production.

**Table 3.5** Causes of Male Infertility

| | |
|---|---|
| **Problems with How Sperm Are Produced** | |
| Varicoceles | A varicocele (a swollen vein in the scrotum) may prevent normal cooling of the testicle. Because testicles are sensitive to heat, this can lead to reduced sperm count and motility. |
| Undescended testicles | Undescended testicles occur when one or both testicles fail to descend from the abdomen into the scrotum during fetal development. Undescended testicles are exposed to internal body temperatures, which are higher than the temperature in the scrotum, potentially affecting sperm production. |
| Hormonal disorders | Infertility can result from disorders of the testicles or an abnormality affecting the glands in the brain that produce hormones involved in sperm production. |
| **Problems with How Sperm Travel from the Testes Out to the Penis** | |
| Infections | Infections such as chlamydia, mumps, and gonorrhea can cause scarring and inflammation of the testes. |
| Blockage of epididymis or vas deferens | Some men are born with blockage of the part of the testicle that stores sperm (epididymis) or have a blockage of the tube that carries sperm (vas deferens) from the testicle to the penis. |
| Sexual issues | Difficulties with erection of the penis (erectile dysfunction), premature ejaculation, painful intercourse (dyspareunia), or psychological or relationship problems can contribute to infertility. |
| **Problems with How Sperm Function** | |
| Motility | Sperm do not move easily through the cervix into the uterus and fallopian tubes. |
| Morphology | Sperm are misshapen or lack the substances needed to bind to the egg or penetrate the outer membrane of the egg. |
| **Other Issues** | |
| Environmental exposure | Overexposure to toxins and chemicals, such as pesticides, can reduce sperm production or function, as can radiation. Overuse of saunas and wearing tight-fitting garments can interfere with production of healthy sperm. |
| Substances | Heavy alcohol use, use of anabolic steroids, smoking, and some cancer medications may cause infertility. |
| Others | Infertility may be related to age (over 35), being overweight, a previous vasectomy, or some treatments for cancer. |

refer to treatment that includes only the use of hormones that spur egg or sperm production. In ART, the egg and sperm can be introduced into the female body separately, usually into the uterus. Or egg and sperm are brought together in a culture dish outside of the female body, resulting in either a fertilized egg or embryo, which can then be introduced into the uterus.

About 12% of women in the United States have sought the services of a clinic offering assistive reproductive services. Demand for these services has increased as more women delay childbirth, since older women are more likely to need and use assisted techniques.

The most commonly used assisted reproductive technology is **in vitro fertilization (IVF)**. IVF involves transfer of an embryo into the uterus, whereas other types of ART use a fertilized egg. In 1978 in England, Louise Brown became the first person born as a result of IVF. After years of struggling with infertility, her parents consented to what

**in vitro fertilization (IVF)** The most commonly used assisted reproductive technology, in which sperm and egg cell are united in a petri culture dish.

was then a very experimental technique: fertilization "in vitro," which means "in glass." Consequently, many people referred to Louise Brown as a "test tube baby," although in fact fertilization took place in a flat petri dish in a laboratory—and still does.

In IVF, a woman is treated with hormones to stimulate maturation of eggs in the ovary, and she is monitored to determine the timing of ovulation. The mature eggs are harvested using a laparoscope, a thin tube that is inserted through a small opening in the abdomen. The tube has a tiny lens attached, enabling the physician to see the ovary and retrieve the eggs. Individual eggs are placed into specialized petri culture dishes. Sperm are treated separately and then added to the petri dish with the ovum, and fertilization occurs. The process results in multiple embryos; those that are not transferred into the mother within a matter of days can be frozen for later use. The cost of IVF is quite high. The price for one ovulatory cycle can be $10,000 to $20,000, regardless of the number of embryos transferred, and insurance often does not cover the treatment (Little, 2006).

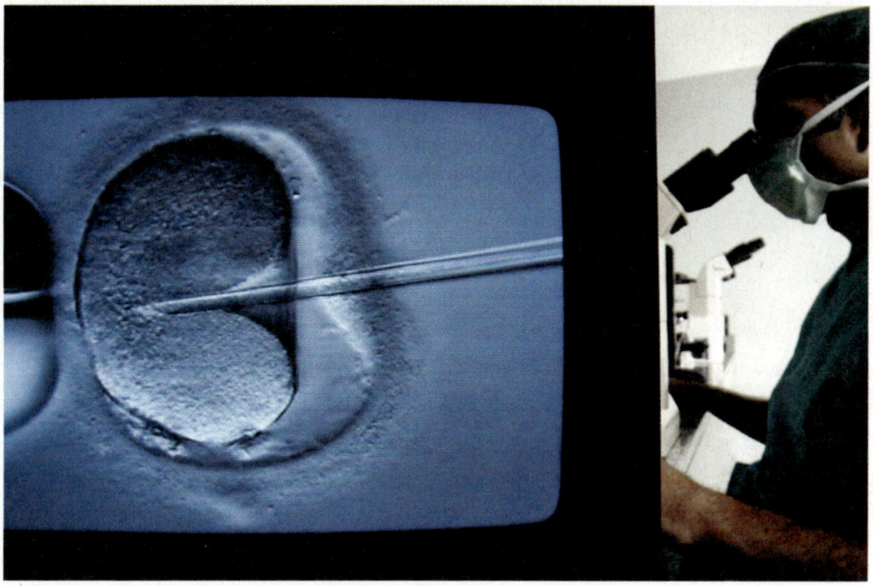

*Mauro Fermariello/Photo Researchers*

This fertility doctor is injecting a human sperm cell into an egg cell, part of the in vitro fertilization process. Later, the resulting zygote will be placed in the mother's uterus to develop.

In 99% of IVF procedures, the embryo is the biological offspring of the couple seeking reproductive assistance, and is implanted in the biological mother (Sunderam et al., 2009). In the remaining 1%, either the egg or sperm or both may come from donors. Donor traits are carefully recorded, however, since most couples want to match the donor's characteristics as closely as possible to those of the parent whose eggs or sperm are being replaced. In yet another option, an embryo that is not biologically related to either the woman seeking to become pregnant or her partner can be implanted in her uterus. Rarely, the embryo is implanted in a surrogate, a woman who is biologically unrelated to the child she carries to term and who has agreed to surrender that child upon birth to the couple seeking her services (Sunderam et al., 2009). State laws govern surrogacy arrangements, and some states forbid them.

## what if...?

Do you know anyone who has had experience with in vitro fertilization? If so, what was that person's experience like? What if you found that you and your partner were unable to conceive a child naturally? Do you think that you might turn to assistive reproductive technology? What factors would you consider in reaching this decision?

Telling the Children

## Parenting and ART

What do parents who have used ART tell their children about how they were conceived, or what their biological heritage might be? It depends to some extent on the techniques used. Among biological parents who used IVF with their own sperm and eggs, the vast majority tell the child when he or she is able to understand, especially when child-friendly materials are available to facilitate the conversation (Peters, Kantaris, Barnes, & Sutcliffe, 2005). In contrast, a veil of secrecy has surrounded the use of donated sperm for many years: Most parents prefer to not disclose that the father is not biologically related to the child (Cook, Golombok, Bish, & Murray, 1995; Golombok, Murray, Brinsden, & Abdalla, 1999; Nachtigall, Becker, Quiroga, & Tschann 1998; Rowland, 1985). Similarly, egg and embryo donation tend to be kept secret (Golombok et al., 1999; Greenfeld, 2008). Bioethicists argue that such secrecy is unethical and that privacy concerns of the parents are outweighed by the potential harm of keeping secrets, especially medical background information, from the child (McGee, Brakman, & Gurmankin, 2001).

Does conception through the use of ART affect the relationship between parent and child? Not really. While some IVF parents may continue to experience negative feelings about their infertility even after a baby is born, the stress of their transition to parenthood is no different from that of parents who have conceived naturally (Hjelmstedt, Widström, Wramsby, & Collins, 2004). Also, there are no real differences in the quality of parenting and the children's psychosocial development between parents who used ART and those who did not (Colpin & Bossaert, 2008; Golombok et al., 1999; Hjelmstedt et al., 2004).

### Multiple Births **P**ractice

Between 1980 and 2004, the rate of twin births in the United States increased by 70%. The rate of higher-order multiple births—that is, three, four, or more babies—quadrupled between 1980 and 1998, then declined to 21% by 2006. One reason for the dramatic increase in multiple births is that more women are delaying childbirth until their late 30s and early 40s, when changes in ovulation increase the chance that multiple eggs will be released and then fertilized. The main reason for the increase, however, is the increased availability and success of IVF; and the main reason for recent declines in higher-order multiple births involves changes in IVF practices (Martin et al., 2009).

When IVF was first practiced, it was not uncommon for more than one embryo to be introduced into the mother to increase the likelihood that at least one would successfully implant on the uterine wall. In fact, many prospective parents undergoing such procedures consider a multiple birth an ideal outcome after their long struggle with infertility (Child, Henderson, & Tan, 2004). However, any pregnancy involving multiple fetuses is considered a high-risk pregnancy. The mother is at greater risk for medical complications, and the babies are more likely to be premature. IVF babies are especially likely to be premature, although why is unclear.

During the same time that the number of multiple births associated with IVF increased, there were dramatic improvements in the care of premature infants, so that younger and smaller babies were more likely to survive. Nevertheless, they remain at greater risk for cerebral palsy, brain injury, and respiratory disorders, which can require a lifetime of special medical and educational services. IVF success came at a high price (Blickstein, 2006; Helmerhorst, Perquin, Donker, & Keirse, 2004; McDonald, Murphy, Beyene, & Ohlsson, 2005).

In 2006, in response the growing alarm about the downside of IVF and multiple births, the American Society for Reproductive Medicine (ASRM) and the Society for Assisted Reproductive Technology (SART) issued guidelines about the number of embryos that should be transferred to the prospective mother. Recognizing that the chances for success decrease with maternal age, ASRM and SART recommend one to two embryos for women under the age of 35, two to three for women between ages 35 and 40, and three to four embryos for women over age 40 (ASRM & SART, 2006). The number depends on the stage of development of the embryo. As blastocyst-stage embryos are more ready to implant into the uterus, fewer need be transferred.

## Health, Family, and Culture **P**arenting

Pregnancy is a time of rapid psychological adjustment for men and women. Pregnant women worry about their own health and that of their babies. Hormonal fluctuations and fatigue, especially early in pregnancy, coupled with the realization of impending parenthood, result in mood swings. Even when a pregnancy is planned and wanted, when a woman feels well physically, feelings of joy often alternate with feelings of anxiety. This is normal.

Pregnancy requires both the woman and her partner to reevaluate their sense of self and their beliefs, values, and priorities, as well as their behavior patterns and relationships with others (Stern, 1995). For the mother, it requires a shift in identity. "Will I be a good mother? Will I be like my own mother? How will my partner feel about me sexually when 'mother' is added to my identity? How will having a baby change my priorities and relationships? How will I go back to work?" (Messias & DeJoseph, 2007). This shift is not simply giving up the old identity. It involves a psychological reorganization—a new understanding of herself as an independent adult *and* a mother, a wife/partner *and* a mother.

© Edward Bock/Corbis

Across cultures, family and friends provide vital support to pregnant women, as well as to their partners.

The father has a similar shift in identity, a psychological reorganization, from partner to partner *and* father, requiring him to support the mother emotionally while sharing her body, her attentions, and her attachments with the new arrival (Birss, 2007). Expectant fathers typically worry about their adequacy during childbirth, and as a father and provider for their families (Finnbogadóttir, Svalenius, & Persson, 2003).

Across all cultures, family and social networks play important roles in providing support to the pregnant woman and her partner, such as assurance about normal aspects of the pregnancy experience, helping them to plan for the baby's arrival, and promoting habits that ensure a healthy pregnancy and baby. Expectant parents who have such support are more likely to fare better physically and emotionally during the pregnancy and after the baby is born than those who do not (Boyce, Condon, Barton, & Corkindale, 2007; Harley & Eskenazi, 2006; Mayberry, Affonso, Shibuya, & Clemmens, 1999).

Cultural beliefs about pregnancy and the unborn child also influence the experience of pregnancy. For example, Mexican, Indian, and Iranian women may follow the hot-cold system of foods, in which a healthy diet consists of a balance of these foods: Fresh vegetables are cold, animal foods such as eggs are hot (Ahlqvist & Wirfalt, 2000; Bonder, Martin, & Miracle, 2002; Nag, 1994). Other practices draw the expectant mother into the social circle of family generations of women and mothers. Baby showers are given in cultures in which the outcome of a healthy birth can be expected, whereas in other cultures there may be no or little acknowledgment of the pregnancy until the baby is safely born. In many cultures, older women attempt to guess the gender of the unborn child based on the mother's silhouette, food cravings, or how she carries the pregnancy on her physical frame.

Sharing personal stories about childbirth and new babies is an important tradition of oral history in most cultures as well. Social support, cultural beliefs, and practices such as these strengthen the bonds between pregnant women, their partners, and their families and communities, laying the foundation for parenting when the new baby arrives.

### ✓ CHECK YOUR PROGRESS

1. What are some recent trends in birth rates and family composition?
2. How does access to health care affect the outcome of pregnancy?
3. What is the most common method of assistive reproductive technology, and what does it involve?
4. What roles do family and culture play in the preparation for parenthood?

# CHAPTER SUMMARY

## Conception

**[ KEY QUESTION ] 1.** How does life begin?

- Male and female gametes divide through the process known as meiosis, resulting in cells with 23 individual chromosomes.
- Fertilization of the egg by the sperm usually occurs in the fallopian tubes when a single sperm enters the ovum, causing a membrane covering the ovum to harden and destroying its sperm receptors so that no other sperm can enter.

## Prenatal Growth and Development

**[ KEY QUESTION ] 2.** What happens in the womb before birth?

- The zygote is the fertilized egg, a single cell that has not begun to divide. The embryo is a "discrete entity," arising from the first cleavage of the fertilized egg that has not yet reached 8 weeks of development. The blastocyst, the name given to an embryo that has reached 5 to 6 days of development, consists of three structures: the embryoblast, the trophoblast, and a hollow cavity filling with fluid that becomes the amniotic sac.
- During the germinal period (0 to 2 weeks), the blastocyst stage of the embryo implants into the uterine wall, and the embryoblast within it separates and differentiates into three distinct embryonic germ layers—the ectoderm, endoderm, and mesoderm—which will develop into all of the major organs of the body.
- Organogenesis occurs during the period of the embryo (3 to 8 weeks), so that 95% of major organs are developed by week 8.
- During the period of the fetus (9 weeks to birth), the fetus grows and develops from an embryo that is barely an inch in length and weighs about half ounce to a full-term infant, who weighs about 7 lb and is 17 to 19 in. long.
- The development of the brain occurs through these processes: neurogenesis and migration, differentiation of the cells according to type of nerve cell, maturation, and integration.

## Development and the Prenatal Environment

**[ KEY QUESTION ] 3.** How do a pregnant woman's health habits and environment affect the developing embryo and fetus?

- The damaging effects of teratogens depend on timing of prenatal exposure to the teratogen (the sensitive period), dosage of the teratogen (dose-response effect and threshold effect), and individual differences in maternal or fetal sensitivity to a particular teratogen.
- Fetal alcohol syndrome refers to the irreversible and profound damage to the developing embryo and fetus caused by the mother's heavy use of alcohol during pregnancy.
- Babies born to mothers who abuse alcohol and opiates go through withdrawal after birth.
- The Food and Drug Administration developed the Classification System for Drug Use During Pregnancy to identify the effects of medications prescribed by a physician for maternal illness on the developing embryo and fetus.
- The safety of herbal medicines and supplements during pregnancy has not been established.
- Women can transmit the HIV virus to their offspring during pregnancy, during a vaginal birth, and while breast-feeding (the virus can be found in breast milk), although the transmission rate is now less than 2% for women who follow guidelines for treatment of HIV during pregnancy.
- Maternal diabetes can affect the developing embryo and fetus when high blood glucose levels from the mother cross the placenta to the fetus. Pregnant women with diabetes are at increased risk for preterm delivery and eclampsia.
- Environmental disasters involving radiation or chemicals can cause miscarriages, birth defects in fetuses, and cancer in children.

## Health During Pregnancy

**[ KEY QUESTION ] 4.** What is considered a healthy pregnancy?

- Even though pregnancy is a natural phenomenon, it puts significant physiological stress on the female body.
- Regular health care and good health practices before and during pregnancy play a major role in ensuring the health of the mother and fetus, as well as preventing complications such as premature birth and birth defects.
- Common complications of pregnancy and high-risk pregnancies include high blood pressure, preeclampsia, problems during labor, and premature birth.
- The pregnant adolescent is considered to be at high risk because her pelvic bones are not fully mature, she tends to have poor eating habits, her hormonal cycles are irregular, and alcohol and drug use is always a possibility. Most pregnant teens also delay receiving prenatal care.

## Pregnancy and Society

**[ KEY QUESTION ] 5.** What is the role of social institutions in supporting pregnancy and parenting?

- In the United States, the average number of children a woman can expect to bear in her lifetime has dropped, and the mean age at first birth has risen.
- Almost 40% of births in the United States are to unmarried women, who have less education and fewer financial resources than married, better-educated women.
- Each year, nearly 1 million pregnant women in the United States deliver babies without having received adequate health care, putting their babies at three times the risk for premature birth and five times the risk for death.
- Infertility in both males and females can be attributed to a number of factors: hormonal imbalances; scarring or blockage caused by infections; and lifestyle issues, such as excessive alcohol use.
- Assisted reproductive technologies (ART) include any procedure in which both the egg and the sperm are handled outside of the human body. The most commonly used assisted reproductive technology is in vitro fertilization (IVF), which involves transfer of an embryo into the uterus.
- Pregnancy requires both the woman and her partner to reevaluate their sense of self and their beliefs, values, and priorities, as well as their relationships with family, friends, and community.

## KEY TERMS

adult stem cells *86*
amniotic sac *85*
artificial insemination *111*
assisted reproductive technology (ART) *111*
blastocyst *85*
dose-response effect *92*
eclampsia *105*
ectoderm *86*
ectopic pregnancy *105*
embryo *85*
embryoblast *85*
embryonic period *88*
embryonic stem cells *86*
endoderm *86*
fetus *85*
germinal period *86*
in vitro fertilization (IVF) *112*
lanugo *88*
meiosis *82*
mesoderm *86*
organogenesis *87*
period of the fetus *88*
placenta *85*
placenta abruptio *96*
placenta previa *96*
preeclampsia *105*
Rh incompatibility *106*
teratogen *92*
threshold effect *92*
trophoblast *85*
ultrasound *89*
vernix caseosa *88*
viability *89*
zygote *84*

## CRITICAL THINKING QUESTIONS

1. **Conception.** Describe how fertilization occurs.
2. **Prenatal Growth and Development.** Compare and contrast the germinal, embryological, and fetal periods of prenatal development.
3. **Development and the Prenatal Environment.** The nature of the abnormalities produced by teratogens depends on three factors. What are they? What predictions about a child's postnatal development can you make based on these factors and prenatal exposure to alcohol?
4. **Health During Pregnancy.** Taking a developmental systems perspective, why is an adolescent pregnancy considered high risk, and what would mitigate that risk?
5. **Pregnancy and Society.** Two trends in birth rates, considered together, represent a basic change in our culture that cannot be underestimated. What are those trends? Evaluate the effect they will have for future generations of children.
6. **Cultural Perspectives.** Find examples of cultural beliefs and practices regarding pregnancy. How did these beliefs develop? Where does the father fit in these beliefs?

## REAL Development

### Prenatal Development

In the accompanying Real Development activities, you will be observing two expectant mothers, Julianne and Erica. In the first activity, you will observe them engaging in routine, everyday activities. You will be helping them decide whether or not it is safe to participate in each activity, given the status of their pregnancies. In the second activity, you will sit in with Julianne and Erica as they visit their physicians. You will take on the role of a medical provider who must record relevant information in their medical charts and, based on their responses and what you have learned in this chapter, identify risk factors the expectant mothers may be facing.

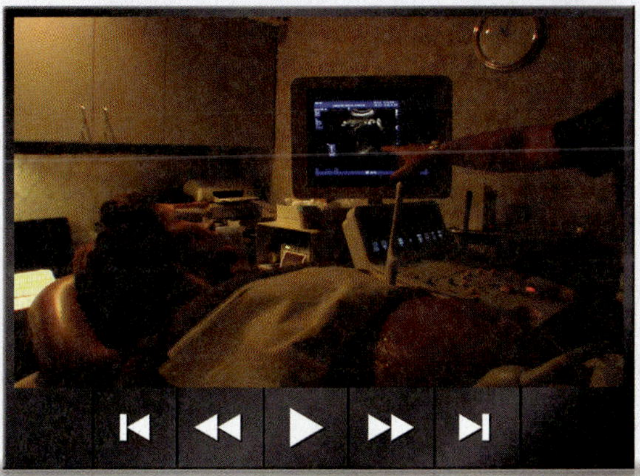

© *John Wiley & Sons, Inc.*

**WileyPLUS** Go to WileyPLUS to complete the *Real Development* activity.

03.01

# Chapter 4

# Birth and the Newborn

MAKING A **difference**

## An Unexpected Birth Experience

First-time parents Lena and Sami wanted to do everything right to prepare for their baby's safe arrival. They attended birth-preparation classes and worked with Tanya, a doula, to draw up a birth plan. Both prospective parents came to rely on Tanya's training and experience. Tanya would also be there during labor and childbirth and afterward to give Lena support—including information about what to do, physical help, and emotional comfort.

Above all, Lena and Sami wanted an unmedicated "natural" birth. But when Lena began to have contractions and Sami took her to the hospital to deliver the baby, they were told that the baby was "breech." "That means that he'll come out buttocks or feet first," the doctor explained. "There's a chance that that the head could get stuck, and there could be problems with the umbilical cord. Although you could deliver vaginally, it's generally safer to deliver breech babies surgically by cesarean section."

Lena and Sami were terribly disappointed, but they knew they had little time to make a decision. Fortunately, Tanya was there to help them stay calm while thinking it through. She explained that Lena would be able to remain conscious during the birth and that Sami could still be with her. It was hard for Lena and Sami to give up their dream of a natural birth, but they decided that a cesarean section would be less risky for their baby. Tanya proceeded to devote her attention and energy to giving Lena all the support she needed to prepare for the delivery. Encouraged, and with more information about what would actually be taking place, Lena began to feel that everything would turn out right after all.

Lena was given an epidural anesthetic, which numbed only the area below her waist, and soon was wheeled into the operating room. Within a short time, Adam—a healthy 8-pound baby boy—was born. There were no complications. As Lena and Sami held Adam and looked into his eyes, they were overwhelmed with love. He was perfect! It may not have been the "natural" birth they dreamed of, but that didn't affect the happiness of the moment. They knew, too, that without the supportive wisdom of Tanya, their birth doula, the experience could have been far different.

## CHAPTER OUTLINE

## [KEY QUESTIONS] *for* READING CHAPTER 4

1. What happens during labor and delivery, and how do the different approaches to childbirth affect these processes?
2. What are the long-term effects of preterm birth on the infant and on the infant's family, and what kinds of interventions can promote the development of preterm infants?
3. What can newborns actually do?
4. What are the developmental challenges facing the newborn?

THE NEWBORN, or **neonatal**, period is a very short phase compared with the whole life span. It is brief even compared with the whole of infancy. This period, after all, lasts only from birth through the first month of life. For the child and for the family, though, the newborn period may well be one of the most crucial phases in life. This chapter is guided by the assumption that the birth of a child is a pivotal, life-changing transition, not only in the life of the child but also in the life of the family. To illustrate this, we first examine the experience of childbirth for parents. Next, we discuss the effects of birth complications, such as prematurity and low birth weight, on the child's future development. We also ask why—despite advances in technology—so many newborn babies die and what we can do to prevent infant mortality in our own communities and across the world. We then go on to examine the remarkable capacities of the newborn infant and his or her ability to engage caregivers from the very beginning. Finally, we discuss the emergence of the parent-infant bond and the developmental challenges facing the infant as the newborn period comes to an end.

# Birth

**[ KEY QUESTION ] 1. What happens during labor and delivery, and how do the different approaches to childbirth affect these processes?**

We noted in Chapter 3 that the desire to create new life is a powerful force motivating humans across time and place. Not surprisingly, then, in cultures around the world, the birth of a child is celebrated as an occasion of great joy in ceremonies and rituals that are associated with hope, promise, and new life. These birth rituals may occur immediately after birth, as in many communities in the United States, or may be delayed until the survival and safety of the baby are ensured, as among the Mayan-speaking people of the Yucatan Peninsula in Mexico (Jordan, 1993).

*Everyday stories*

BIRTH RITUALS AROUND THE WORLD In a village in Rajasthan, India, the neighbors and kin gather shortly after a birth at a "cradling ceremony" to sing songs and sew clothes for the new baby (Hrdy, 1999). Among the Kipsigis in western Kenya, the mother's relatives and women from the community bring gifts of maize, water, and firewood to the mother in her hut (Super & Harkness, 2009). The !Kung mother gives birth alone in the bush. Only when she returns with the baby will the formal recognition and acceptance of the new baby by the community take place (Shostak, 1981). In Japan, a special naming ceremony is conducted on the seventh day after the baby's birth. At 1 month, the baby is taken to a Shinto shrine for a blessing. In every culture, ceremonies to formally welcome a new baby into the community serve as a public testament to the readiness of the family and the community to embrace the new baby. They offer the promise that the baby will receive all the love and support needed to grow and develop as part of that community.

**neonatal** Relating to the period from birth to 1 month.

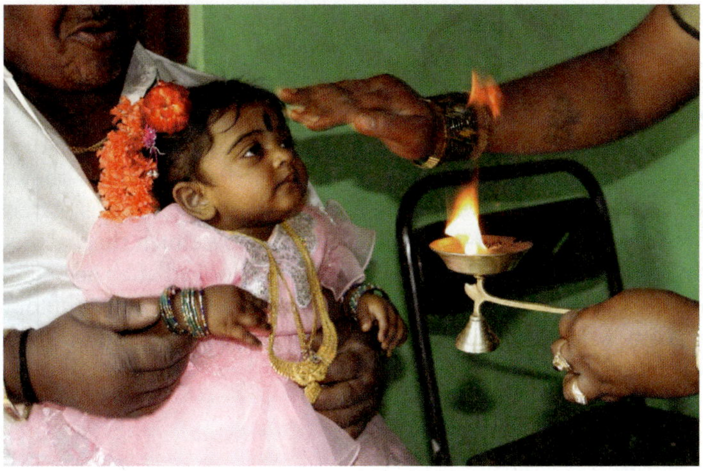

Louise Batalla Duran/Alamy

In India, a mother blesses her baby daughter during the baby's naming ceremony. This traditional Hindu ritual enables friends and family to welcome the baby into their community.

For the new baby's mother and father, the childbirth experience—the birth story—is so profound that it seems to etch itself into long-term memory. Many mothers can still feel the pain of labor and experience the joy of childbirth 10, 20, even 30 years later (Simkin, 1991, 1992). One five-year follow-up study of 1,383 Swedish women (Waldenstrom & Schytt, 2008) found that a woman's long-term memory of pain is associated with her satisfaction with childbirth overall. The more positive the experience, the more successfully women forget how painful labor was. A mother's lasting memories of the birth of her child may be due in part to the fact that the event changes her life irrevocably, as it does the lives of all the members of the family (Garbarino, 1992; Minuchin, 1985). These changes may involve practical matters such as preparing a new room for the baby and shifting work schedules. But it is the emotional and psychological life of the family that will be most tested during this time, as the family moves into a new developmental phase. In this section, we discuss preparations for childbirth and various aspects of the birth process itself. We begin by posing a question: What do you know about childbirth?

## What Do You Know About Childbirth?

Have you ever witnessed a baby being born? Have you ever looked after a newborn baby? Studies of young men and women who are not parents suggest that many young adults know very little about childbirth or even about babies. Young adult women may be excited about the prospect of childbirth and may see it simply as a "miraculous event" (Cleeton, 2001, p. 194). They know little, however, about the specifics of labor and delivery or about practices that might support positive birth outcomes (Wallach & Matlin, 1992). In a large convenience sample of low-risk women expecting their first birth ($n$ = 1,318), regardless of the type of care provider they attended, many women reported knowing very little about the benefits and risks of common procedures used at childbirth (Klein et al., 2011). In a study of college men and women, Lampman and Phelps (1997) found no differences between women and men in knowledge about childbirth. They also reported that young adults did not seem to have much interest in learning about childbirth until they had to face it. Yet because it is a major life transition, it is important for all who will become parents to be well prepared for childbirth. This includes being aware of birth options and the significance of the birth experience for the mother's health and well-being, as well as that of the baby.

## Preparing for the Birth of the Baby

In Chapter 3, we noted that pregnancy is a time of psychological adjustment for parents as they prepare for the birth of their baby (Birss, 2007; Cowan & Cowan, 2000; Klaus, Kennell, & Klaus, 1995; Leckman & Mayes, 1999; McMahon et al.,

2011). During pregnancy most expectant mothers and fathers experience a cascade of changing emotions. As the birth date comes closer, new preoccupations emerge. Mothers tend to become more anxious about the health of the baby. Increasingly, they tend to worry about bringing the baby successfully to term (Bruschweiler-Stern, 2009; McMahon et al., 2011; Slade, 2002; Stern, 1995). They may begin to think more about the uncertainties associated with the birth of their baby. Perhaps they are even concerned whether they will survive the birth and delivery themselves. After all, no matter how well prepared the mother-to-be is, no matter how much this baby is welcomed by her and her partner, and no matter how well she has looked after herself, no one can say whether her labor will be long or short, easy or difficult, or what the outcome will be. That is why many women today choose to attend birth preparation classes, to help them get ready for the birth of their child.

## Birth Preparation Classes

There are many kinds of birth preparation courses available, each with its own approach toward labor and delivery and pain management. The Lamaze approach, for example, stipulates that "birth is normal, natural, and healthy" and that "women have a right to give birth free from routine medical interventions" (www.lamaze.com). When interventions are needed, or pain relief medication is desired, however, Lamaze recommends that women be given the information they need to make an informed choice. Another popular birth preparation course, the Bradley Method, also embraces the idea that childbirth is a natural process and that, with the right preparation, most women can avoid pain medication during labor and birth (www.bradleybirth.com).

Courses such as these teach women a range of coping strategies, including breathing techniques. Some recommend practicing meditation or yoga during pregnancy and childbirth. They may even incorporate self-hypnosis techniques for use during labor. The typical course includes eight or more weekly sessions consisting of lectures, discussion, and exercises, often led by childbirth instructors who are certified by the International Childbirth Education Association (ICEA).

While the approaches to childbirth education may differ, the goal of most of these classes is to increase women's confidence in their ability to give birth. How helpful are the classes? Most studies have reported benefits. One study, for example, found that women who had attended classes required significantly less pain medication and were more likely to have spontaneous deliveries (deliveries not requiring assistance) than a matched group of women who had not attended classes (Hetherington, 1990). Another study found that mothers who attended classes coped better with labor and had healthier babies than those who had less knowledge (Rautava, Erkkola, & Sillanpaa, 1991). A study in Australia found that fathers also found the classes helpful. A large majority (89%) of fathers agreed that the classes helped them feel more confident during labor and in their role as a support person (Fletcher, Silberberg, & Galloway, 2004). Childbirth preparation classes may not benefit everyone in the same way, however. Some studies found no differences between women who attended classes and those who did not, in terms of birth events, satisfaction with care received, or emotional well-being after birth (Bergström, Kieler, & Waldenström, 2009).

## Writing a Birth Plan Parenting

The written **birth plan** provides a way for prospective parents to become more involved in the birth process, and ensure a safe and satisfying childbirth experience for the family. The plan outlines the parents' wishes for labor and birth and can be used to help health-care providers know what parents want and expect, while leaving room for the unexpected. Although parents must realize that nothing can be guaranteed, the birth plan at least enables them to take an active part in planning labor and delivery. Figure 4.1 shows a sampling of the items that may be included. An actual birth plan may be shorter or much longer and more detailed.

**birth plan** A written outline of parents' wishes for labor and birth, intended to help health-care providers know what parents want and expect.

**The Birthing Environment**

I would like the following to be present during labor and/or birth:

- o Partner
- o Parents/relatives
- o Doula[a]

I would also like:

- o To bring music
- o To wear my own clothes during labor and delivery
- o Hospital staff limited to my own doctor and nurses (no students, other hospital personnel, etc.)

**Labor**

I would like:

- o The option of returning home if I am not in active labor
- o My partner to be allowed to stay with me at all times
- o Freedom to walk and move around as I choose
- o To have intermittent rather than continuous electronic fetal monitoring
- o For labor to be allowed to progress without strict time limitations, as long as the baby and I are doing well

**Pain Relief**

I'd like to try the following pain-management techniques:

- o Breathing techniques
- o Massage
- o Please don't offer me pain medication. I'll request it if I need it.

If I decide I want medicinal pain relief, I'd prefer:[b]

- o An epidural anesthetic
- o Other (please specify)

**Vaginal Birth**

I'd like:

- o Episiotomy[c]
- o No episiotomy

After birth, I'd like:

- o To hold my baby right away, putting off any procedures that aren't urgent
- o To breast-feed as soon as possible

**Cesarean Section**

If I have a cesarean section, I'd like:

- o My partner present at all times during the operation
- o To breast-feed my baby in the recovery room

**After Delivery**

After delivery, I'd like:

- o All newborn procedures to take place in my presence
- o My partner to stay with the baby at all times if I can't be there

I plan to:

- o Breast-feed exclusively
- o Combine breast-feeding and formula feeding
- o Formula-feed exclusively

I'd like:

- o 24-hour rooming-in with my baby
- o My baby to room-in with me only when I'm awake
- o My baby brought to me for feedings only
- o To make my decision later, depending on how I'm feeling

*Notes:*

[a] A doula is a nonmedical professional who provides women with assistance before, during, or after childbirth. We discuss the role of the doula later in this chapter.

[b] We discuss the use of medications in childbirth later in this chapter.

[c] An episiotomy is a surgical cut to the vaginal area to make the birth of the baby easier.

FIGURE 4.1 **Sample Items for a Birth Plan Worksheet** A written birth plan gives prospective parents a way to become more involved in the birth process. The figure shows only a small sampling of the many items that may be included in a birth plan.

## Stages of Labor

At some point, generally after about 40 weeks of pregnancy, the expectant mother's waiting comes to an end, and labor begins. Labor is the climax of pregnancy. During labor, the uterus contracts, the cervix (the opening to the uterus) thins and opens, and the baby rotates and moves down the birth canal. The entire process may take from several hours to a day or more. Labor is divided into three stages according to the physiological changes that take place:

1. The first stage, *dilation*, begins with the start of regular contractions and ends when the cervix is completely open. This stage generally lasts the longest—about 6 to 12 hours on average, although for women having their first baby it can continue from 12 to 16 hours. For women having second or subsequent children, dilation can last from 6 to 7 hours. It is marked by regular contractions that increase in length, strength, and frequency over time. During the last part of this stage, called *transition*, contractions are at their strongest and most frequent. Since transition is the most painful phase of labor, it is fortunate that it is also fairly brief, lasting from about 30 minutes to an hour or two.
2. The second stage, *descent and birth*, begins when the cervix is completely dilated and ends when the baby is born. During this period, contractions continue, and the mother feels a natural urge to push with her abdominal muscles. This pushing helps the baby to descend through the birth canal. This stage can extend from 10 minutes to several hours.

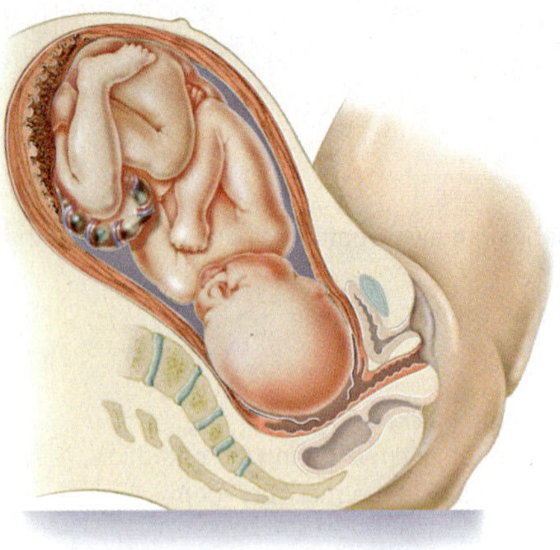

Stage 1. Dilation

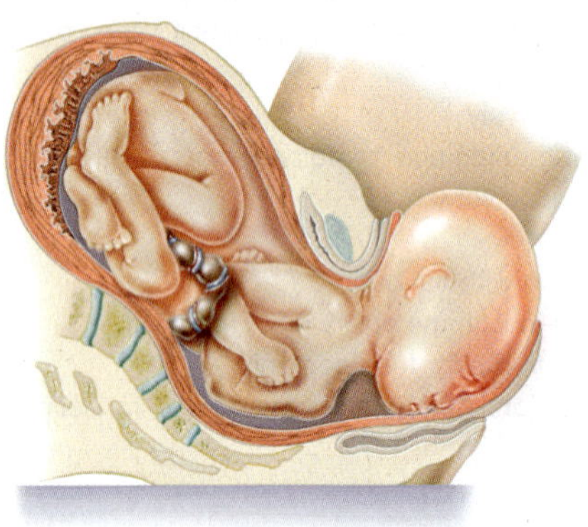

Stage 2. Descent and birth

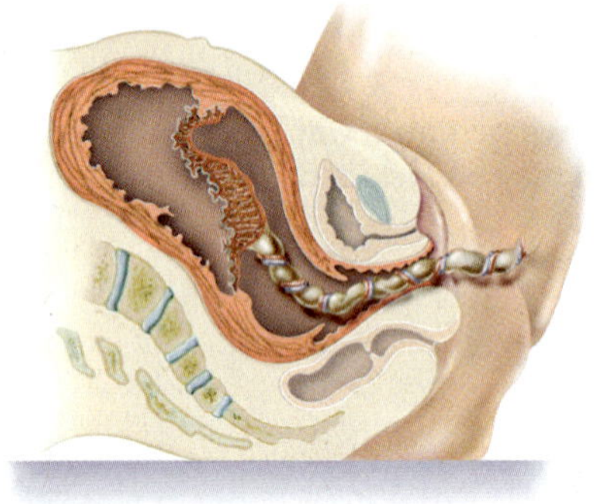

Stage 3. Delivery of placenta

**FIGURE 4.2 The Stages of Labor** Labor is divided into three stages. The first stage, dilation, starts when regular contractions begin, and ends when the cervix is completely open. The second stage, descent and birth, ends when the baby is born. In the third stage, the placenta is delivered.

Adapted with permission of John Wiley & Sons, Inc., from Freudenrich, C. C., & Tortora, G. J. (2011). *Visualizing Anatomy and Physiology*. Hoboken, NJ: Wiley, p. 499, Figure 16.17b.

3. The third stage, *delivery of the placenta*, is very brief. Only a few contractions are necessary to expel the placenta, so this stage lasts only 5 to 30 minutes. (The three stages are shown in Figure 4.2.)

The onset of labor seems to be under the joint control of the endocrine systems of both mother and baby. With the onset of pregnancy, a woman's body begins to secrete high levels of the hormones estrogen and progesterone, which work to sustain the pregnancy. Another hormone, **oxytocin**, which is released from the pituitary gland in the brain, increases significantly in the third trimester. Oxytocin is helpful in reducing the mother's pain both during and after labor by raising her pain threshold and stimulating the uterus to contract during labor. As the baby's head presses against the cervix, estrogen stimulates the pituitary gland to release oxytocin. This in turn stimulates the muscles in the uterus to contract, forcing the head into the cervix and continuing the cycle of contractions.

Most babies are delivered vaginally—that is, through the vagina, as described above—with varying degrees of assistance from medical professionals. However, between 20% and 30% of births in the United States are accomplished through **cesarean delivery**. In this type of delivery, the baby is surgically removed from the uterus through an incision in the mother's abdomen. We look more closely at this and other medical interventions later. First, though, we examine two central issues in childbirth: how pain can be managed, and where the birth should take place.

## Childbirth and Pain

In every culture, the experience of labor and delivery is described as one of the most painful events in a woman's life. There are, however, individual and cultural differences in how women respond to this pain and how they are expected to cope with it (Davidhizar & Giger, 2004). For most women, labor pain is a manageable life experience. A Swedish study revealed that roughly 60% of the women studied reported positive childbirth experiences, and less than 10% reported negative experiences (Waldenstrom & Schytt, 2008). One method of coping with the pain of childbirth, of course, is through use of pain medications.

### Cultural Differences in Dealing with Pain During Labor

For some cultural groups, childbirth pain is an expected and normal part of life, and using pharmacological pain relief is considered inappropriate. A Japanese mother may choose natural childbirth because she wants to "taste" (*ajiwau*) the pain of delivery. She believes that this pain will increase her love for her child (Lebra, 1984). One recent study compared Vietnamese and Australian mothers giving birth in Australia. The Vietnamese women used less pain relief and seemed to strive for self-control during labor, so that they did not express their pain (McLachlan & Waldenstrom, 2005). This may be because childbirth in Vietnam is generally accepted by mothers as a painful experience, and pain, is, according to Buddhist beliefs, an expected part of life and something that gives life meaning (Tran, 1999).

### Pain Medications

Many cultures accept the use of medications to manage labor pain. Several kinds of medications are typically used. **Analgesics** relieve pain and help mothers relax during labor. **Anesthetics** are stronger pain relievers that block sensation. General anesthetics, which result in the total loss of both sensation and consciousness, are rarely used for childbirth. Instead, local anesthetics that block sensation in only part of the body are used. The most common means of pain relief during childbirth is *epidural anesthesia*, which is administered through a catheter (tube) placed in the space around the lower spine. Probably, this method is preferred because the amount of medication can be adjusted over the course of labor, and the mother remains conscious so that she can push during the second stage of labor.

Do these medications affect the baby? The newborn's immature liver and kidneys may be unable to rapidly metabolize or excrete medications, so the effects of some drugs may last longer in the baby than in the mother, although it is not clear for how long. There is some evidence to suggest that the medications may cross the placenta, adversely affect the newborn's behavioral responsiveness, and interfere with the early parent-infant relationship (Sepkoski, Lester, Ostheimer, & Brazelton, 1992). Epidurals have also been shown to cause maternal fever during childbirth (Lieberman et al., 1997). The potential negative effects of medication taken during labor are likely to depend on the type of medication, the time during labor at which it was given, and the dosage level (Golub, 1996).

The choice whether to use pain medication is not an easy one to make for parents. Since two people are involved—the mother and the baby—it is important that mothers take both of them into account when considering anesthesia choices. The benefits are relaxation and relief from pain; the drawbacks are possible effects on the baby's behavior and on the mother's susceptibility to fever. Most physicians today discourage heavy and unlimited use of pain medication, because, as just noted, it is still not known how long these drugs remain in the newborn's system. Childbirth educators typically advise parents to learn about pain medication before labor so that they can evaluate all the advantages and disadvantages of various choices.

**oxytocin** A hormone secreted by the pituitary gland that stimulates the uterus to contract during and after labor, and controls the production of milk in the mammary glands.

**cesarean delivery** A delivery in which the baby is surgically removed from the uterus through an incision in the mother's abdomen.

**analgesics** Drugs used to relieve pain and promote relaxation.

**anesthetics** Drugs that block sensation.

**natural childbirth** Childbirth that takes place without the use of anesthetics or other interventions.

what if...?

Suppose that you are completing, or helping to complete, a birth plan such as the one in Figure 4.1. When you come to the items about medications, you aren't sure what to say. You really don't know much about the medications available and their effects. Where might you go to find out more information? What will you take into consideration in making up your mind about medications?

### Natural Childbirth and the Role of the Doula

In recent times, the development of noninvasive relaxation techniques to ease the pain of labor has received a great deal of attention. The goal of these techniques is to help birthing mothers cope with the pain of labor and, indeed, to make labor less painful by providing human support. The mothers can then give birth without anesthetics or other medical interventions. This practice is called **natural childbirth**. Some of the great pioneers in the natural childbirth movement—Fernand Lamaze, Frederick LeBoyer, Sheila Kitzinger, Marshall Klaus, and John Kennell—are profiled in the accompanying Focus On feature.

A natural-childbirth technique growing in popularity in the United States is *water birth*, in which the mother sits in a tub of warm water to give birth. Being immersed in water is thought to result in a less painful, more relaxed birthing experience for both mother and baby. Some research has supported the benefit of water birth for mothers and babies (Geissbuehler, Stein, & Eberhard, 2004). However, medical experts point out that water birth is not appropriate in every pregnancy and that it should take place under the supervision of health professionals. Other techniques used in natural-childbirth situations include massage and acupuncture, to relieve pain without drugs.

## The Place of Childbirth: Home or Hospital?

For most of human history and in many developing countries today, babies are born at home, with relatives and, usually, a midwife in attendance. In contrast today, almost all of the 4 million babies born in the United States every year are born in a hospital

## Focus On: Pioneers in the Natural Childbirth Movement

Fernand Lamaze, a French obstetrician, was one of the pioneers of "natural childbirth." The Lamaze approach, which originated in the 1960s, is based on the assumption that by controlling breathing during labor, and by focusing on something other than the pain, the mother can control her pain. The LeBoyer method, introduced by French obstetrician Frederick LeBoyer in the 1970s, suggests that the optimal setting for the birth is a quiet environment, amid dim lights and soft voices. Immediately after the birth, the baby is given a warm bath and placed on the mother's abdomen. Smacking the baby on the bottom after delivery to elicit a cry is not encouraged!

Fueled by the growing interest in women's rights, social anthropologist Sheila Kitzinger set out in the 1970s to "humanize" the childbirth experience for women. She sought to take the birth experience out of the control of the medical establishment and return it to the mothers themselves (Kitzinger, 1978). And it was the pioneering research of pediatricians Marshall Klaus and John Kennell that led to the implementation of practices such as "rooming in" in hospitals throughout the world (Kennell, 2009; Klaus et al., 1995; Klaus & Kennell, 1981). Rooming in allows mothers and babies to be together at all times so that they can enjoy skin-to-skin contact and so that the babies can breast-feed on demand. Klaus and Kennell's approach emphasizes providing human support to women during labor to help them cope with the pain of labor. It has also endeavored to shift the focus away from pain and to transform childbirth into a fulfilling experience for mothers and fathers and a less stressful experience for babies.

In addition, Klaus and Kennell and their colleagues stress the value of having a **doula** provide continuous physical and emotional support to the nonmedicated woman during labor (Stein, Kennell, & Fulcher, 2004). The term *doula* comes from the Greek word for the most important female servant in an ancient Greek household. Today, a doula is a nonmedical professional who provides mothers with physical and emotional assistance before, during, or after childbirth (Kennell, 2009). Almost 40 years of research have shown that when mothers have continuous emotional support from a doula during labor, and when they have early and extended contact and interaction with their babies, birth outcomes and maternal satisfaction can improve significantly (Kennell, 2009; Sosa, Kennell, Klaus, Robertson, & Urrutia, 1980).

with a physician, nurse, or certified nurse-midwife in attendance. (*Certified nurse-midwives* are primary health-care providers who specialize in caring for women during labor and birth.)

Andersen Ross/Brand X/Getty Images

Doulas like this one provide physical and emotional support to women during labor and birth. Research shows that women benefit considerably from the support of doulas.

Not everyone agrees that hospitals are the best place for childbirth. Some women question the benefits, safety, and risk of hospital births for healthy childbearing women. There is evidence that hospital births are associated with an increase over time in cesarean-section deliveries, along with other medical interventions (discussed later in the chapter). Moreover, higher cesarean-section rates have been associated with an increase in maternal and fetal mortality rates and a higher rate of admission to neonatal intensive care units (Elvedi–Gasparovic, Klepac–Pulanic, & Peter, 2006; Villar et al., 2006). As a result of growing reservations about the value of "technological" approaches to childbirth, many women are looking for alternatives to the usual physician-provided care. These women may choose to give birth at home or in homelike birth centers.

### Home Births and Birth Centers

Some women choose to deliver in their own homes with the support of a midwife. Often, these women wish to have other family members present. They may also feel they can participate more fully in decision making in their home environments (Janssen, Carty, & Reime, 2006). But what are the risks of home births? In one study, researchers surveyed 5,412 births conducted by certified midwives in North America (Johnson & Daviss, 2005). They found that outcomes for home births were similar to those for low-risk births attended by physicians in hospitals. Furthermore, they reported that medical intervention rates were substantially lower than for low-risk women having hospital births. For example, among the home-birth women, 3.7%

ended up having cesarean sections, compared with 19% among women of a similar risk profiles in the United States as a whole.

While some women choose home births, **birth centers** may be preferred by women who do not wish to or cannot have a home birth but who still want to avoid medical intervention. Birth centers are typically in or near conventional hospitals. They specialize in the care of pregnant women who require little or no medical intervention during labor and birth. While birth centers vary in how they deliver care, consistently their philosophies and guidelines value minimal intervention in labor. The physical environment (furniture, lighting, and so forth) is homelike. Still, in many centers, medical equipment is readily available, concealed behind closets, curtains, or partitions (Fannin, 2003). The core staff of birth centers is usually made up of midwives or nurse-midwives. Research suggests that homelike birth centers offer some benefits over hospitals, including decreased medical intervention and increased maternal satisfaction. They may, however, also increase the risk of delivery in the case of an emergency (Hodnett et al., 2008).

*AP Photo/The Journal-Star, Kristin Streff*

Birth centers, which feature homelike environments, specialize in the care of women who require little or no medical intervention during labor and birth.

## Medical Interventions

As we mentioned earlier, most babies are delivered vaginally. Sometimes, though, spontaneous vaginal delivery does not progress as it should. In such cases, instruments are used to help during the second stage of labor. Sometimes, too, labor is induced, or the baby is delivered by cesarean section.

**Assisted Vaginal Delivery.** A delivery with the help of instruments is often referred to as an **assisted vaginal delivery**. The most commonly used instruments are forceps and vacuum extractors. *Forceps* are tonglike instruments designed to cradle the baby's head as the handles are pulled to draw the baby through the birth canal. A more recently developed alternative is the vacuum extractor. In a vacuum-assisted vaginal birth, a suction device is placed on the baby's head to help its body move through the birth canal.

No type of assisted delivery is entirely free of risk for either the mother or the infant. Forceps-assisted delivery may cause tissue damage to the mother. For the baby, it may result in bruising of the face or, in some cases, severe trauma to the head (Towner & Ciotti, 2007). Vacuum-assisted delivery may also result in tissue damage to the mother, though it is less likely to do so than forceps-assisted delivery. The baby may have a raised bruise at the top of the head where the vacuum was attached. Nevertheless, assisted vaginal delivery appears to be a safer alternative than cesarean section. Furthermore, studies evaluating both its general safety and long-term neurological effects reported no important differences in outcome between children delivered spontaneously and those delivered by either vacuum extraction or forceps (Simonson et al., 2007; Wen et al., 2001).

**Induced Labor.** In certain situations, a doctor may *induce* labor—that is, start it artificially—using various methods, including physical stimulation and drugs. This procedure is generally done when risks to the mother or the baby make it necessary for the mother to deliver as soon as possible rather than waiting for labor to begin naturally. Increasingly, however, in the United States, doctors—and mothers—have been using induction simply to have more control over when birth will take place—a practice called *elective induction*. As a result, the rate of induced-labor births has risen sharply in this country, from 9.6% in 1990 to 23.1% in 2008 (U.S. National Center for Health Statistics, 2010).

**doula** A nonmedical professional who provides women with physical and emotional assistance before, during, or after childbirth.

**birth centers** Facilities typically established in or near conventional labor wards for the care of pregnant women who require little or no medical intervention during labor and birth.

**assisted vaginal delivery** Delivery done when spontaneous vaginal delivery is not possible. Forceps and vacuum extraction are the most common forms. Also called *instrumental delivery*.

As you will see later in this chapter, the rate of premature births in the United States has also risen during this period. Some researchers have proposed that these statistics are linked (Zhang & Kramer, 2012). The reason is that labor increasingly is induced in women who have not reached full term. While the rate of induced-labor births among women who had reached full term increased from 14.9% to 27.3% from 1990 to 2008, for example, the rate for women at 37 to 39 weeks increased from 7.9% to 22.1% (U.S. National Center for Health Statistics, 2010).

The American College of Obstetricians and Gynecologists has stated that while a number of health conditions may warrant inducing labor, elective induction for reasons of convenience generally isn't appropriate. Unnecessary intervention of this kind poses unnecessary risks (American College of Obstetricians and Gynecologists, 2009). For example, in some cases, induction fails to start labor, but the birth must go forward, and so a cesarean delivery is necessary.

**Cesarean Delivery.** We noted earlier that between 20% and 30% of births in the United States are accomplished through cesarean delivery. Like the rate of induced labor, the rate of cesarean births has been increasing, as shown in Figure 4.3. Over the last several decades, the increased use of cesarean delivery has contributed to lowering infant mortality, particularly among small and premature babies. Nevertheless, the rising rate of cesarean delivery has been debated widely.

In a cesarean birth, as mentioned, a surgical procedure is used to deliver the baby through incisions in the abdomen and uterus. It is preferred to a vaginal delivery if labor or vaginal birth is deemed too difficult or dangerous for either the baby or the mother. Sometimes, events near or during childbirth make an emergency cesarean delivery necessary. Examples include cases of placenta abruptio or placenta previa (which were defined in Chapter 3), cases where the baby's position in the uterus would make normal delivery difficult, and cases where the baby's head is too large to fit through the mother's pelvis. Some cesarean deliveries are planned in advance. If a pregnant woman has a problem, such as heart disease, which could be made worse by the stress of labor, a cesarean delivery may be scheduled. The same is true if the mother has an infection that could be passed on to the baby during a vaginal delivery, as in the case of a mother who is HIV positive.

Women who have had a cesarean delivery are more likely to have cesarean deliveries for subsequent children. Sometimes, though, a woman who has had a cesarean delivery may be offered the option of a *vaginal birth after cesarean (VBAC)* if she has had a healthy pregnancy and goes into labor on her own at term. VBAC has both risks and benefits, which differ for the woman and her fetus. According to the National Institutes of Health (NIH), more evidence about the risks and benefits of VBAC is needed (National Institutes of Health Consensus Development Conference Statement, 2010).

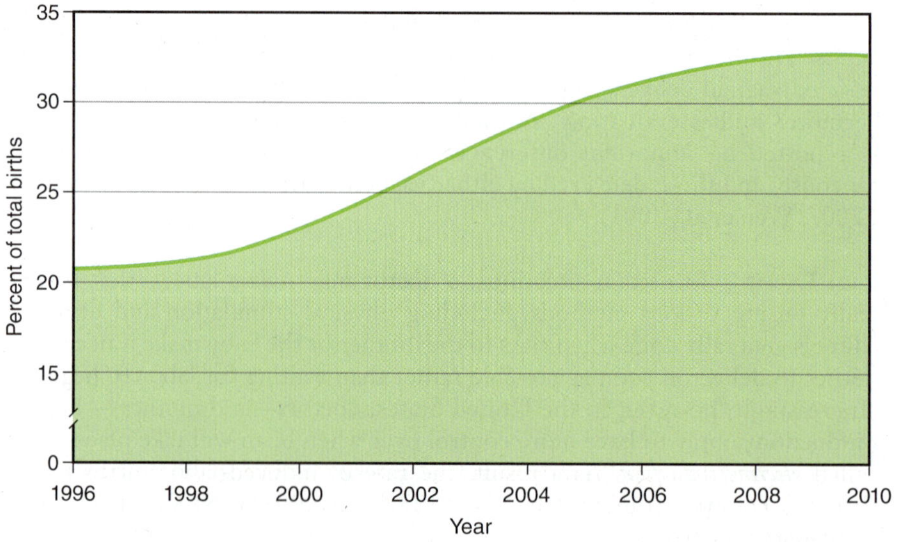


SOURCE: CDC/NCHS, National Vital Statistics System. www.cdc.gov/nchs/data/nvsr/nvsr60/nvsr60_02.pdf

**FIGURE 4.3 U.S. Cesarean Births, 1996–2010** The rate of cesarean births in the United States has been increasing. Today, 20 to 30% of U.S. babies are delivered by cesarean section.

Adapted from Centers for Disease Control and Prevention/National Center for Health Statistics, National Vital Statistics System.

## Research Insights: Risks in Planned Cesarean Delivery

As we noted in the text, cesarean delivery is a very safe procedure today. Nevertheless, there is evidence to suggest that cesarean deliveries place mothers and infants at risk for a number of negative outcomes. One group of researchers compared neonatal outcomes among women with planned cesarean versus planned vaginal deliveries in Norway (Kolas, Saugstad, Daltveit, Nilsen, & Oian, 2006). This survey involved 18,653 singleton deliveries (that is, deliveries of single infants rather than multiple births) representing 24 maternity units during a 6-month period. Results showed that planned cesarean delivery doubled both the rate of transfer of infants to the neonatal intensive care unit and the risk for pulmonary disorders in infants. Based on these results, the researchers emphasized the importance of limiting planned cesarean deliveries to cases with proven benefits for the mother or child.

A Canadian study compared nearly 47,000 Canadian women who had had scheduled cesarean deliveries with nearly 2.3 million who had planned to deliver vaginally (Liu et al., 2007). The cesarean group had higher rates of cardiac arrest, blood clots, infection, and hysterectomy, although the difference in death rates between the two groups was not statistically significant. A similar study in the United States found that women who had planned cesarean deliveries were more than twice as likely to be hospitalized in the first month after birth than women who had planned vaginal deliveries (Declercq, Menacker, & MacDorman, 2006). In addition, the average initial hospital cost of a planned cesarean for a first-time mother was 76% higher than that for a planned vaginal birth.

In some cases, mothers request a cesarean delivery even when there is no medical reason for doing so. These are sometimes referred to as "elective" cesarean deliveries. The NIH estimates that in 2004, the most recent year for which data are available, 4 to 18% of cesarean deliveries were performed not for medical reasons but because the mothers requested them. Mothers may feel that cesarean delivery is the safest option. Alternatively, they may wish to have more control over when they are going to give birth in the midst of a busy work schedule.

Although a cesarean delivery is a very safe procedure today, the risk of complications is still higher for cesarean delivery than for vaginal delivery. In fact, as the rate for cesarean deliveries has risen, so has the rate of pregnancy-associated deaths. The pregnancy-related death rate for the eight-year period from 1998 through 2005 was 14.5 per 100,000 live births. By comparison, the rate in 1986 was 7.4 per 100,000 live births (Berg, Callaghan, Syverson, & Henderson, 2010). Activists opposed to the growing use of cesarean delivery, as well as some doctors, argue that this increase probably can be attributed at least in part to the larger number of surgical deliveries. Others, however, argue that the increase is due mainly to better reporting of these deaths.

Those who are attempting to bring down the number of cesareans include academics, groups interested in improving health-care quality, business groups, hospital associations, and state lawmakers (Blanchette, 2011). Cost is an important issue for many of these groups. In 2009, the average cost of a cesarean section ranged from $13,000 to $20,000, compared with $11,400 for a vaginal birth.

So what are we to conclude about cesarean delivery? In some cases, it is necessary to protect the life and well-being of mother and baby. At other times, though, it is a matter of choice. In these cases, pregnant women and physicians should be aware of the potential risks of cesarean delivery. Their decisions should be based on the risks and benefits for mother and infant alike. The accompanying Research Insights feature discusses some risks that emerged in studies of planned cesarean deliveries versus vaginal deliveries.

### ✓ CHECK YOUR PROGRESS

1. Describe the stages of labor.
2. What is natural childbirth, and what do doulas do?
3. Compare the advantages and disadvantages of giving birth in a hospital, at home, and in a homelike birth center.
4. Why are cesarean deliveries performed, and what risks may they involve?

**premature infant** or **preterm infant** An infant born before 37 weeks' gestational age.

**gestational age** Age as measured in weeks from the first day of the mother's last menstrual cycle.

**low birth weight (LBW)** Birth weight below 5 lb 8 oz (2,500 g).

**very low birth weight (VLBW)** Birth weight below 3 lb 5 oz (1,500 g)

**extremely low birth weight (ELBW)** Birth weight below 2 lb 3 oz (1,000 g)

**neonatal intensive care unit (NICU)** Hospital unit that specializes in the treatment of at-risk newborns.

# At-Risk Infants: A Different Beginning

**[ KEY QUESTION ] 2. What are the long-term effects of preterm birth on the infant and on the infant's family, and what kinds of intervention can promote the development of preterm infants?**

Most newborns are healthy. Some babies, though, are born at risk for complications. There are a number of reasons for at-risk births. As we pointed out in Chapter 3, certain conditions in the mother—and certain behaviors, such as alcohol use—place the developing fetus at risk. So do certain genetic conditions. Sometimes problems during labor and birth generate complications. But the single most common cause of risk to newborns is prematurity, the focus of this section. We conclude the section with a discussion of infant mortality.

## Prematurity and Birth Weight

A **premature infant**, or **preterm infant**, is defined as a baby born before completing at least 37 weeks of gestation. In other words, the baby is born before reaching the **gestational age** of 37 weeks (recall that the normal gestation period is 40 weeks). More than 500,000 premature infants are born in the United States every year. These infants tend to experience major complications due to their low birth weight and the immaturity of their body systems (March of Dimes, 2008). The lungs, digestive systems, and nervous systems of premature babies are particularly vulnerable to complications. In addition, their body temperature, blood pressure, and heart rate may be difficult to regulate.

We should note that although we focus on premature babies here, they are not the only newborns who may have low birth weight. A baby who does not weigh as much as it should *for its age* is described as *small for gestational age*. These small-for-date or small-for-gestational-age (SGA) infants are more at risk for negative outcomes than infants who are simply born prematurely. Several terms are used to describe degrees of underweight for both premature and SGA infants:

- **Low birth weight (LBW):** weight below 5 lb, 8 oz (2,500 g).
- **Very low birth weight (VLBW):** weight below 3 lb, 5 oz (1,500 g).
- **Extremely low birth weight (ELBW):** weight under 2 lb, 3 oz (1,000 g).

The immediate treatment for preterm infants depends on the types of complications that are present. Care is usually provided in a hospital's **neonatal intensive care unit (NICU)**, which specializes in the treatment of at-risk newborns. The NICU may also be called a Special Care Baby Unit or an Intensive Care Nursery. Babies who need to go to the NICU are often admitted within the first 24 hours after birth.

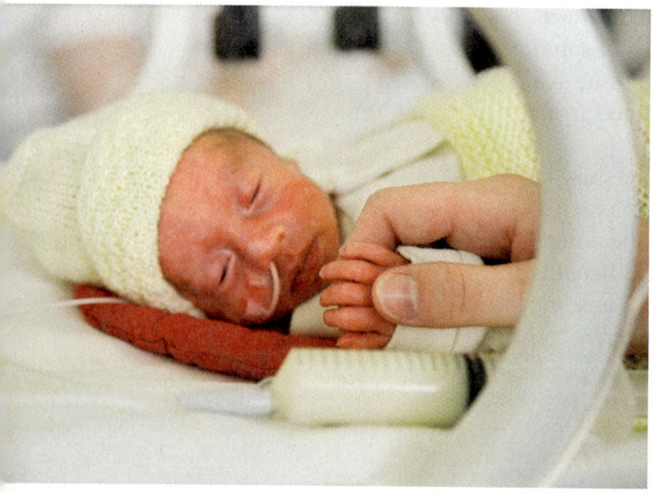

Samuel Ashfield/Science Source

Premature infants are generally placed in incubators to maintain their body temperature. Oxygen, fluids, nutrients, and perhaps medications may be administered as well.

Most premature infants need to be placed in a heat-controlled unit (an *incubator*) to maintain their body temperature. Infants who are having trouble breathing on their own may need oxygen, either pumped into the incubator or administered through small tubes. These infants also may require fluids and nutrients to be administered through an intravenous line, in which a small needle is inserted into a vein. If the baby needs drugs or medications, these may also be administered through the intravenous line. If heart rate is irregular, the baby may have heart monitor leads taped to his or her chest.

Babies in the NICU are cared for by a team of specialists. The team includes nurses who have been especially trained to work with premature babies, respiratory therapists, physical and occupational therapists, social workers, and doctors who specialize in the care of very young and sick infants. Infants remain in the NICU until they are stabilized. At that point, they can be moved into more general nurseries or released to go home. Many premature infants require time and support until they mature enough to breathe and eat unassisted.

Advances in medical technology have made it possible for infants born after only 23 weeks of gestation to survive. (These preterm babies are so small they could fit into the palm of your hand.) However, extremely premature infants are at higher risk for death or serious complications. Today, most babies born after 26 weeks gestation survive (about 80%). Some may, however, face an extended stay in the newborn intensive care unit (National Center for Health Statistics, 2008). About 98% of babies born at 32 to 33 weeks gestation survive.

Of the 500,000 babies born prematurely each year in the United States, 75 percent are *late-preterm* infants, born between 34 weeks and 36 weeks, 6 days (www.nationalperinatal.org/lptguidelines.php). Late-preterm infants look like smaller versions of healthy term babies, and for a long time they were treated as though they were developmentally mature and at low risk. Research has now revealed that these babies remain at higher risk than full-term babies for newborn health problems, including issues with breathing and feeding, difficulties regulating body temperature, and jaundice (Engle, Tomashek, Wallman, & American Academy of Pediatrics, Committee on Fetus and Newborn, 2007). Moreover, compared with healthy term infants, healthy late-preterm infants face a greater risk for developmental delay, school-related problems, and socioemotional issues up through the first 5 or 6 years of life (Morse, Zheng, Tang, Roth, 2009; Talge, Holzman, Wang, Lucia, Gardiner, & Breslau, 2010).

## Causes and Treatments of Prematurity

What causes prematurity? Several factors may play a role. As mentioned in Chapter 3, preeclampsia or placenta previa may result in premature birth. If the amniotic sac tears, causing the amniotic fluid to leak out, or if the cervix opens too soon, premature birth may occur. While one of these conditions is often the immediate reason for a premature birth, the underlying causes of prematurity are still unknown.

We can identify some conditions associated with premature births. Prematurity is much more common in multiple-birth pregnancies, for mothers who have a history of miscarriages, and for mothers who have given birth to a premature infant in the past. Other possible risk factors in the mother include high blood pressure, diabetes, clotting disorders, obesity, and infections during pregnancy, as well as cigarette smoking, alcohol use, or illicit drug use during pregnancy. There are also ethnic differences in rates of prematurity. Compared with white women, African American women have a 60% higher risk for premature delivery in general and 3 times the risk for extreme prematurity (fewer than 28 weeks gestation). Furthermore, African American women experience high rates of prematurity regardless of their socioeconomic status. This unexplained gap has led to speculation that genetic factors contribute to the incidence rate of premature births (Fiscella, 2005).

## Prematurity and Developmental Outcomes

We noted earlier that 96% of babies born after 28 weeks of gestation survive. Nevertheless, prematurity remains the leading cause of death in newborns. Babies who died of preterm-related causes accounted for 36.5% of infant deaths in 2005, up from 34.6% in 2000, according to the National Vital Statistics Report on Infant Mortality (Hamilton, Martin, & Sutton, 2004). Even for infants born just a few weeks early, mortality rates are 3 times the rates for full-term infants.

In addition, those who survive face the risk of lifelong health consequences. Premature infants are much more likely than normal-weight, full-term term infants to experience significant medical complications, chronic illness, developmental delays, attention-deficit disorder, and physical and behavioral problems that persist well into the school-age, adolescent, and early adult years (Bhutta, Cleves, Casey, Cradock, & Anand, 2002; Casey, Whiteside–Mansell, Barrett, Bradley, & Gagus, 2006; Davis et al., 2011; Hack et al., 1991, 2004; Hack, Klein, & Taylor, 1995; McCormick, 1993; Saigal, Hoult, Streiner, Stoskopf, & Rosenbaum, 2000).

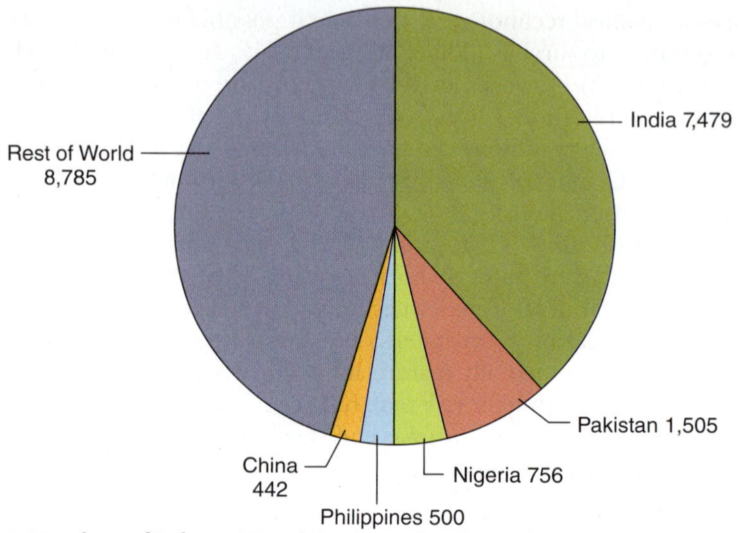

**FIGURE 4.4 Number of Infants Weighing Less than 2,500 Grams at Birth, in Thousands, 2007–2012** Mothers in the developing world are much more likely to give birth to low birth weight infants than mothers in developed countries. These infants face a variety of risks.

*Source:* UNICEF global databases 2012, from Multiple Indicator Cluster Surveys (MICS), Demographic and Health Surveys (DHS) and other national surveys, as found on www.childinfo.org/low_birthweight_status_trends.html, last updated January 2012.

The risks of serious long-term complications depend on many factors. These factors include how premature the infant was, how much the infant weighed at birth, whether the infant had breathing difficulties, and whether the infant suffered intracranial hemorrhage—that is, bleeding within the skull. In general, children's brain development benefits from a longer gestation. Extremely premature infants and infants whose birth weight is extremely low are more prone to exhibit conditions, such as intracranial hemorrhage, that affect brain development (Davis et al., 2011). We describe some research on these long-term effects in the accompanying Research Insights feature.

## Low Birth Weight in the Developing World

Globally, an estimated 15% of infants, or more than 1 in 7, weigh less than 2,500 grams at birth—over 20 million newborns annually. More than half of low-birthweight infants are born in South Asia, the region with the highest incidence of low birthweight and where more than 1 in 4 infants are born low birthweight. As you can see in Figure 4.4, more than half of newborns weighing less than 2,500 grams globally are from just 5 countries. India, one of the countries with the highest incidence of low birthweight, has nearly 7.5 million low-birthweight babies annually—the highest of any country.

That said, data from 60 developing countries reveal that the incidence of low birth weight decreased between 1997 and 2007 for many (United Nations Standing Committee on Nutrition, 2010). Decreases occurred, for example, in 5 of 10 countries in Asia, 7 of 15 in South America, and 13 of 28 in sub-Saharan Africa. Critical interventions to prevent low birth weight include improving food intake and nutrition, preventing and treating diseases such as malaria and HIV/AIDS, educating girls and expectant mothers, and preventing teenage pregnancies (UNICEF, 2009).

## A Different Beginning for Parents, Too

Premature birth, followed by the intensity of the experience of the neonatal intensive care unit, is highly stressful and sometimes traumatic, not only for the baby but also for the parents and the whole family (Browne & Talmi, 2005; Fox, Levitt, & Nelson, 2010; Nugent, Blanchard, & Stewart, 2008). The stress on parents of meeting a premature infant's daily needs, the isolation they may feel in caring for

## Research Insights: The Long-Term Risks of Prematurity

A study of 206 extremely low birth weight (ELBW) infants who were born in Finland followed the children's progress over time. At the age of 5, one fifth of these children had major and minor disabilities that affected their everyday lives (Mikkola et al., 2005), including cognitive impairment (9%), cerebral palsy (14%), and coordination difficulties (50%). The mean IQs of the tested children, despite being within normal limits, were significantly lower than normal population means. And the slow growth pattern that had started in the womb for these children continued during the follow-up period of 5 years.

Does low birth weight also affect mental health later in life? The results of a study of the mental health and development of young adults who had been very low birth weight (VLBW) infants indicated that it may (Hack et al., 2004). In adulthood, VLBW women reported more emotional and mood disturbances than control subjects, with significantly higher rates of emotional problems. Parents tended to agree with the symptoms reported by their VLBW daughters. They noted significantly more anxious, depressed, and withdrawn behavior, as well as more attention problems, than parents of control subjects.

Results were more promising in a Canadian study that compared former ELBW infants at ages 22 to 25 with peers who had been born at term. These two groups of young adults were similar in high school graduation rates, employment status, and rates of marriage and parenthood (Saigal et al., 2000). A higher proportion of the former ELBW infants were neither employed nor in school. Still, a significant majority of them had overcome their earlier difficulties to become functional young adults. Such studies suggest that while some very low birth weight babies have lasting problems, early intervention—along with home, school, and societal advantages—can combine to moderate these effects.

their at-risk infant, the associated financial costs, and the strain of preserving marital and family relationships can place a family at risk of dysfunction. These factors can also affect the quality of parental care for the preterm infant. The quality of care in turn affects the infant's development (Als et al., 1994, 2003, 2004; Fox et al., 2010; Minde, 2000; Verkerk et al., 2012). Parents of preterm infants, who are themselves "premature parents" (Birss, 2007), frequently develop misperceptions of their infants and have difficulty interacting with them in a developmentally sensitive manner.

*Everyday stories*

PREMATURE PARENTS Throughout the pregnancy, John and Julissa dreamed of a healthy, full-term baby with big bright eyes, soft skin, and chubby legs—a baby who was ready to nestle into their arms from the very beginning. But baby Jason was born six weeks before he was due and had to be admitted to the NICU before John and Julissa could even hold him. When they first saw the feeding tube, the catheters inserted into his tiny arms, and the ever-blinking monitors measuring his heart rate and breathing, they were shocked and frightened. Then, when they saw their little baby's strained face through all the tubes, chest heaving as he struggled to breathe, they were overwhelmed with sadness. For the next three weeks, they watched anxiously until Jason was able to breathe on his own and gained enough weight so that he could be discharged. They were relieved and overjoyed to go home. But when they got home, although they tried to interact with him, Jason was not very responsive, and he cried a great deal. How could they get him to settle and respond to them? They felt anxious, alone, and vulnerable.

How can parents best support their preterm baby's development? How can they overcome the tendency to respond inappropriately to their preterm infants? How can they help their babies develop while gaining confidence in their own abilities to parent? Various intervention programs have been set up to help (Als et al., 2004; Browne & Talmi, 2005; Nugent et al., 2008). We discuss some of these interventions next.

WHEN SYSTEMS CONNECT

## Early Intervention for At-Risk Newborns

Early intervention programs that provide developmental information and strong emotional support to parents can make important contributions to successful outcomes for children and parents (Fox et al., 2010; Rutter, 1990; Verkerk et al., 2012). Clinical interventions are best when they begin early, in the neonatal intensive care unit. It is best, too, for interventions to emphasize providing parents with information on their infant's behavior and development, along with guidelines on how to respond sensitively to the infant's communication cues (Browne & Talmi, 2005; McManus & Nugent, 2012; Melnyk, Feinstein, & Fairbanks, 2002). Ideally, these early interventions should be followed up after the infant is released from the hospital. Unfortunately, some studies indicate that many children do not receive adequate follow-up (Needelman, Jackson, McMorris, & Roberts, 2008).

**Individualized Developmental Care.** Many intervention approaches have been used for premature infants in hospitals. Often, in the past, interventions focused on special medical care and the use of new technologies to ensure the infants' survival. Today, the focus is shifting to the long-term development of these infants.

One recent approach uses *individualized developmental care*, care that is sensitive to the particular status and needs of each infant. This approach aims to reduce the differences

### Focus On: Heidelise Als

Before she came to the United States from Germany in the late 1970s, Dr. Heidelise Als had been working as a grade school teacher. Even then, she was intrigued by individual differences in children's learning styles and by the difficulties experienced by children with learning disabilities. Studying psychology at the University of Pennsylvania, she decided to search for the origins of learning disabilities by focusing on newborn infants. Later, she joined T. Berry Brazelton at the Children's Hospital in Boston, where she was drawn to the study of prematurely born infants.

From the outset, she was deeply impressed by the efforts of these infants as they struggled to face the challenges of life outside the womb. "Preterm infants are fetuses who find themselves too early and unexpectedly in a hospital environment instead of the . . . mother's womb," she observes. She began to try to see and feel the world through the eyes, ears, and fragile skin of premature babies, and has dedicated herself to improving the prospects for preterm babies by developing better assessment techniques and intervention strategies.

Als and her colleagues developed the Assessment of Premature Infant Behavior (APIB) (Als, Lester, Tronick, & Brazelton, 1982), which is recognized as the most sensitive measure of premature infant behavior available. Later, they developed the Newborn Individualized Developmental Care and Assessment Program (NIDCAP), aimed at providing a more appropriate environment in the neonatal intensive care unit (NICU). With its strong emphasis on parent-infant interactions, the program has revolutionized care across the world.

Evan Richman/The Boston Globe via Getty Images

Als would like the NICU to mimic the womb as much as possible. In an interview with *The New York Times*, Als said that she would like to eliminate the incubator altogether from the NICU (Raeburn, 2005). "My dream is a womb room for each baby and each family. Each family would be given a room of its own, with controlled temperature, humidity and oxygen. The mother . . . and the rest of the family would live in the womb room until the baby was ready to go home. . . . For many people, it's a big, big step even to envision this. I don't think it's unrealistic," she says. That dream may be a while off, but Heidelise Als remains passionate about her roles as researcher, teacher, and advocate for premature children.

between the womb and the intensive care unit. Sound levels are kept at a minimum, and lighting is kept soft. The rooms may be darkened at night to help the baby develop a regular sleep-wake cycle. Changing diapers, checking vital signs, and feeding are done on the baby's schedule. If the baby is sleeping, the nurse or doctor comes back later. Mothers and fathers are encouraged to hold their babies during difficult and stressful procedures. Babies can enjoy skin-to-skin contact even when on a respirator. A number of studies have supported the benefits of individualized developmental care (Browne & Talmi, 2005; Buehler, Als, Duffy, McAnulty, & Liederman, 1995; Kleberg, Westrup, & Stjernqvist, 2000; McAnulty et al., 2013). An example of such care is the Newborn Individualized Developmental Care and Assessment Program (NIDCAP), which we discuss in the accompanying Focus On feature.

**kangaroo care** An intervention often used with preterm newborns in which the newborn is placed in skin-to-skin contact on the mother's breast to promote thermal regulation, breast-feeding, and bonding.

**infant mortality rate** The death rate among babies in the first year of life.

**neonatal mortality rate** The death rate among newborns in the first 28 days of life.

KANGAROO CARE. Another form of intervention is **kangaroo care**. Here, the premature newborn is carried on the mother's breast in skin-to-skin contact, usually for several hours a day over several months. This contact with the mother helps to promote temperature regulation, breast-feeding, and bonding. In the kangaroo position, the baby also receives stimulation through a combination of senses: hearing the mother's voice, for example, feeling and smelling her skin, and seeing her face. Kangaroo care has been shown to enhance mother-infant interactions and to create a climate in which parents become progressively more aware of their child and more prone to sensitive caring (Als & McAnulty, 2011; Ohgi et al., 2002; Tessier et al., 2003). Kangaroo care can therefore be used to support the goals of neonatal care mentioned earlier—the goals of optimizing the infant's long-term development and enhancing the competence of the parents.

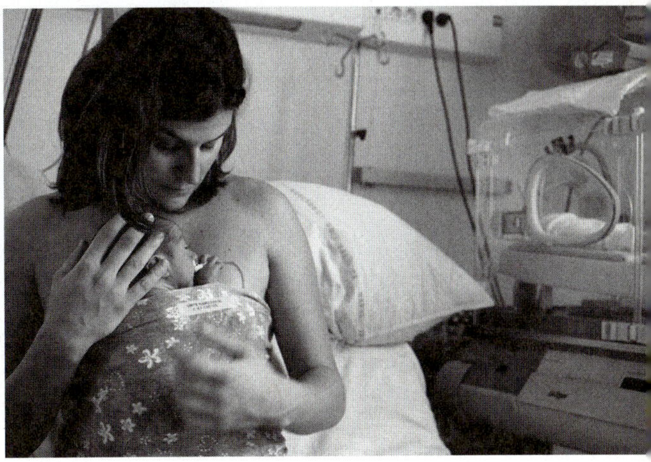
*Daniel Herard/REA/Redux*

Kangaroo care provides premature newborns with skin-to-skin contact with their mothers, helping to promote temperature regulation, breast-feeding, and bonding.

## Neonatal Mortality

We have been discussing babies born at risk. Many of these babies survive and prosper. However, of the more than 130 million babies born every year across the world, almost 8 million die before their first birthday. The overall death rate among babies during their first year is called the **infant mortality rate**. The death rate among newborns is called the **neonatal mortality rate**. Neonatal deaths account for a large proportion of child deaths. In fact, the neonatal mortality rate is often used as an indicator of general maternal and newborn health. Thus, we pay particular attention here to deaths in the neonatal period.

There are a variety of causes for neonatal deaths. Many are related to lack of adequate care during pregnancy, childbirth, and the neonatal period. Neonatal deaths may stem from poor maternal health, inadequate care during pregnancy, inappropriate management of complications during pregnancy and delivery, poor hygiene during delivery and the first hours after birth, or lack of newborn care. Babies also may die soon after birth because they are severely malformed, are born very prematurely, suffer from complications before or during birth, or undergo harmful practices after birth that lead to infections. After the first week of life, infections are the main cause of neonatal death in many countries.

### Incidence of Infant Mortality

Ninety-eight percent of infant deaths take place in the developing world (see Figure 4.5). Furthermore, in developing countries, the risk of death in the neonatal period is 6 times greater than in developed countries. In the least developed countries, it is over 8 times higher. The neonatal death rate in Africa is 41 per 1,000 live births, with even higher rates in the sub-Saharan regions of the continent. The rate in south central Asia is 43 per 1,000 live births. Because of this high rate and the very dense population in the area, over 40% of global neonatal deaths take place here.

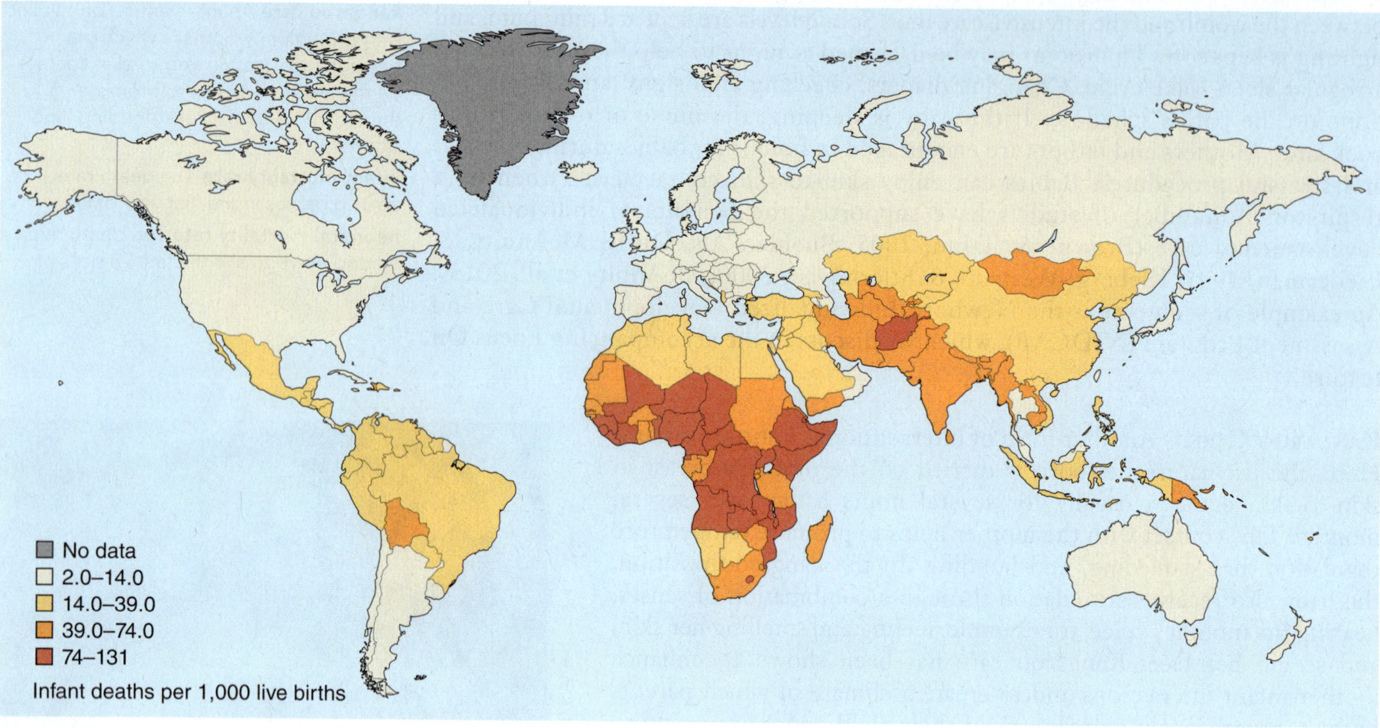


**FIGURE 4.5 Infant Mortality Rates Around the World** Worldwide, 98% of infant deaths take place in developing countries. Rates in the United States are low compared with those of developing regions but are relatively high compared with those of most other developed countries.

Reprinted with permission from Haub, C. (2008). *2008 World Population Data Sheet.* Washington, DC: Population Reference Bureau.

In the United States, the infant mortality rate in 2004 was 6.87 per 1,000 live births, and the neonatal mortality rate was 4.54 (Health Resources and Services Administration, U.S. Department of Health and Human Services, Child Health USA, 2007). These rates are certainly low compared with those for the developing regions mentioned earlier. But they are high compared with those of most other developed nations. In fact, the United States has been steadily losing ground in the area of infant mortality, falling to 29th in the world in 2004, an all-time low (U.S. Centers for Disease Control and Prevention, 2008). The infant mortality rate showed a slight decline to 6.7 per 1000 in 2009, but the United States still has a higher infant mortality rate than most of Europe (Murray & Frenk, 2010).

What might account for this disturbing trend in this country? For one thing, as we mentioned earlier, prematurity is the leading cause of death in newborns. In the United States, the rate of premature births rose steadily for over a decade. Though it has recently begun to decline, the 2010 rate was still above the rate for 2000, as shown in Figure 4.6.

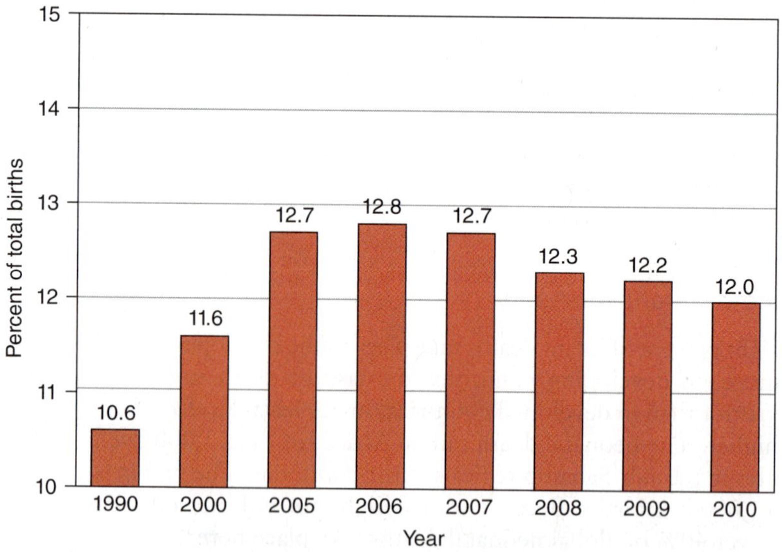


**FIGURE 4.6 Premature Births in the United States** Prematurity is the leading cause of death in newborns. In the United States, the rate of premature births rose steadily for over a decade, but has recently begun to decline.

Based on Hamilton, B. E., Martin, J. A., & Ventura, S. J. (2011). Births: Preliminary data for 2010. *CDC National Vital Statistics Reports 60*(2).

Prematurity may help to explain another alarming statistic: the difference in infant mortality for blacks and whites. In 2005, for instance, the infant mortality rate for non-Hispanic black women was 13.63, compared with 5.76 for non-Hispanic white women (U.S. Centers for Disease Control and Prevention, 2008). In part, this risk may be explained by inadequate health care. Lack of prenatal care is associated with a 40% increase in the risk of neonatal death, and African American women are more than 3 times as likely as white women not to receive prenatal care (Rosenberg, 2002). Furthermore, as we mentioned earlier, African American women have a higher risk for premature delivery regardless of socioeconomic status.

### The Fourth Millennium Development Goals **Policy**

How can we meet the formidable challenges posed by infant mortality around the world? The Fourth Millennium Development Goals provide us with guidelines for action. These goals, listed in Table 4.1, are the result of a historic commitment made by 189 world leaders at the United Nations Millennium Summit in 2000. As you can see in Table 4.1, the fourth goal is to reduce child mortality by two-thirds by 2015, and the fifth is to reduce deaths of women during childbirth by three-fourths by 2015. Investments in education, nutrition, and health care are among the means to be used to achieve these goals.

Unfortunately, we are unlikely to meet the 2015 target date for achieving the Millennium Development Goals. Overall, the child mortality rate has fallen (Kattwinkel, 2013). Some nations, though—especially in sub-Saharan Africa—have made little or no progress in reducing deaths of children (United Nations, Millennium Development Goals Report, 2008). Furthermore, the number of women who die due to complications in pregnancy and childbirth is not declining fast enough to achieve the global target by 2015 (Winch et al., 2005). For example, the odds that a sub-Saharan African woman will die from complications of pregnancy and childbirth during her life are 1 in 16, compared with 1 in 3,800 in the developed world. According to the United Nations, maternal health remains a regional and global scandal.

**Table 4.1** The United Nations Millennium Development Goals

1. **Eradicate extreme poverty and hunger.** Reduce by half the proportion of people living on less than a dollar a day. Reduce by half the proportion of people who suffer from hunger.
2. **Achieve universal primary education.** Ensure that all boys and girls complete a full course of primary schooling.
3. **Promote gender equality and empower women.** Eliminate gender disparity in primary and secondary education, preferably by 2005, and at all levels by 2015.
4. **Reduce child mortality.** Reduce by two-thirds the mortality rate among children under 5.
5. **Improve maternal health.** Reduce by three-fourths the maternal mortality rate.
6. **Combat HIV/AIDS, malaria, and other diseases.** Halt and begin to reverse the spread of HIV/AIDS. Halt and begin to reverse the incidence of malaria and other major diseases.
7. **Ensure environmental sustainability.** Integrate the principles of sustainable development into country policies and programs; reverse loss of environmental resources. Reduce by half the proportion of people without sustainable access to safe drinking water and basic sanitation. Achieve significant improvement in the lives of at least 100 million slum dwellers, by 2020.
8. **Develop a global partnership for development.** Develop further an open, rule-based, predictable, nondiscriminatory trading and financial system. Deal comprehensively with developing countries' debt. In cooperation with developing countries, develop and implement strategies for decent and productive work for youth. In cooperation with pharmaceutical companies, provide access to affordable essential drugs in developing countries. In cooperation with the private sector, make available the benefits of new technologies, especially information and communications technologies.

## what if...?

The Millennium Development Goals represent a global commitment in which rich and poor countries agree to work together to end poverty, its root causes, and its many effects. What if you would like to help move these goals forward? You could be part of a global movement of people who are asking their governments to honor their commitments to achieve the Millennium Development Goals by 2015. If you are interested in finding out more about this movement, go to www.endpoverty2015.org.

### ✓CHECK YOUR PROGRESS

1. What is the relationship between preterm birth and birth weight?
2. What are some long-term effects of preterm birth?
3. What are the goals of modern interventions to help preterm newborns?
4. What are some causes of infant mortality?
5. What are the United Nations Fourth Millennium Development Goals?

# The Newborn

**[ KEY QUESTION ] 3.** What can newborns actually do?

So far, we have discussed childbirth and have taken some time to examine problems that may arise for preterm and other at-risk newborns. Now, we turn to the newborn. The truly remarkable capacities of newborn babies have only come to light relatively recently. For much of the last century, the dominant view among students of infant development was that newborns could neither see nor hear and that they could respond to their environments only with inborn, programmed reflexes. Beginning in the 1960s, however, researchers began to discover that newborns' senses were much better developed than had once been thought. They discovered, too, that newborns were capable of certain organized behaviors.

In this section, we look more closely at newborn behaviors and abilities. As you will see, the newborn emerges as an already competent and complex individual.

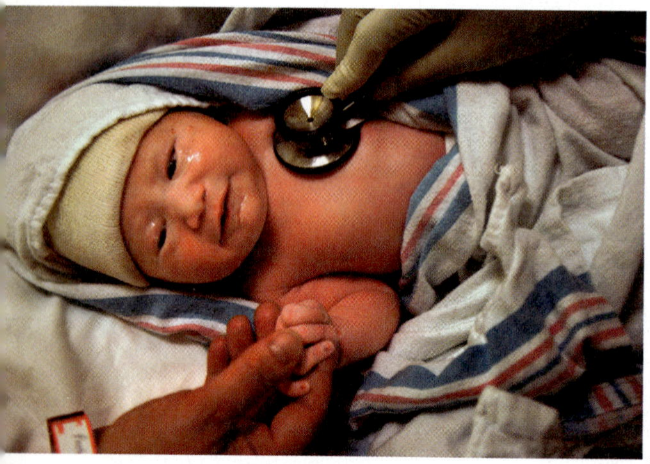

*Jay L. Clendenin/Aurora Creative/Getty Images*

Newborns like this baby girl have just made a dramatic transition into a new and challenging environment.

## A Dramatic Transition

For newborn infants, the moment of birth marks a dramatic transition. At that moment, they move from the relative quiet and security of the intrauterine world into a new, dynamic, and ever-changing environment. Suddenly, they must face a whole new set of challenges. As soon as the umbilical cord has been cut, they must breathe on their own for the first time. A new danger presents itself if a baby has difficulty breathing and experiences **anoxia**—lack of oxygen. This may happen if the umbilical cord has been pinched during labor or has been wrapped around the baby. A baby who has been deprived of oxygen for a short time will quickly recover. If, on the other hand, the anoxia is severe, lasting for a few minutes, the baby is at risk for brain damage, because brain cells need a continuous oxygen supply.

### The Apgar Score and Screening Tests

To determine whether a newborn is healthy, care providers in modern industrialized societies conduct a series of assessments in the moments after birth. The most widely used screening assessment across the world is the **Apgar score**, introduced in 1953 by the anesthesiologist Virginia Apgar. The Apgar score was designed to standardize the way caregivers evaluated the baby's physical well-being at birth. The scale includes five

**anoxia** Lack of oxygen.

**Apgar score** Assesses the condition of newborn infants; it measures respiratory effort, heart rate, muscle tone, reflex irritability, and color.

**Table 4.2** The Apgar Score

| | 0 | 1 | 2 |
|---|---|---|---|
| Heart rate | Absent | Below 100 beats/min | Over 100 beats/min |
| Respirations | Absent | Weak cry | Strong cry |
| Muscle tone | Limp | Some bending | Active motion |
| Reflex irritablility | No response | Grimace | Cry |
| Color | Blue or pale | Body pink, arms and legs blue | Completely pink |

*Source:* Information from Virginia Apgar, "A Proposal for a New Method of Evaluation of the Newborn Infant," *Current Researches in Anesthesia and Analgesia*, July–August, 1953, p. 260.

criteria: heart rate, respiration, muscle tone, reflex irritability, and color, as shown in Table 4.2. Newborns are observed at one minute after birth and again at five minutes after birth. Each time, they receive a score of 0, 1, or 2 on each of the five dimensions, with 10 a perfect score. A score lower than 8 indicates that the infant needs assistance, and a score below 5 indicates that the infant needs immediate assistance. That said, a child who has a low score at 1 minute and a normal score at 5 minutes should not have any long-term problems.

While the Apgar score is a useful measure, the American Academy of Pediatrics (2006) warns that it has limitations. One retrospective analysis, for example, concluded that the Apgar score is a valid predictor of neonatal mortality but that it should not be used to predict long-term outcomes (Casey, McIntire, & Leveno, 2001).

*Getty Images/Fuse*

Care providers conduct a series of assessments to make sure newborns are healthy.

Most states now screen newborns for more than 30 disorders. Many of these **screening tests** are designed to identify certain harmful or potentially fatal disorders that are not otherwise apparent at birth. For example, there are screening tests to determine whether newborns have phenylketonuria (PKU) or sickle cell disease, both of which we discussed in Chapter 2. There is a test for congenital hypothyroidism, a disorder that affects babies who do not have enough thyroid hormone. This condition may result in delayed growth and brain development. Another test identifies cystic fibrosis, a genetic disorder that particularly affects the lungs and digestive system and makes children more vulnerable to repeated lung infections. In addition, because congenital hearing loss affects about 1 in every 1,000 newborns, Universal Newborn Hearing Screening (UNHS) has been implemented in most states (Hyde, 2005; Wrightson, 2007). UNHS is a way to identify hearing-impaired newborns so that they can be referred for additional testing and intervention services (Durieux–Smith, Fitzpatrick, & Whittingham, 2008; Lim & Fortaleza, 2000).

**THE DEVELOPING BRAIN**

## Newborn Reflexes and Behavioral States

After delivery, newborn infants appear helpless, almost totally dependent on their caregivers for their very survival. Yet newborns have a set of remarkable reflexes, some of which are clearly designed to enable them to survive outside the womb. **Reflexes** can be described as unlearned involuntary movements or actions that are controlled by brain structures below the level of the cerebral cortex. Table 4.3 describes some of the normal reflexes seen in newborn babies. The presence or absence of these reflexes, as well as their strength, is an indicator of the integrity of the newborn's central nervous system. All these reflexes disappear at some point over the first year of life, to be replaced by more highly developed functions.

**screening tests** Tests designed to identify certain harmful or potentially fatal disorders that are not otherwise apparent at birth.

**reflexes** Unlearned involuntary movements or actions that are controlled by neural structures below the level of the cerebral cortex.

## Table 4.3 Newborn Reflexes

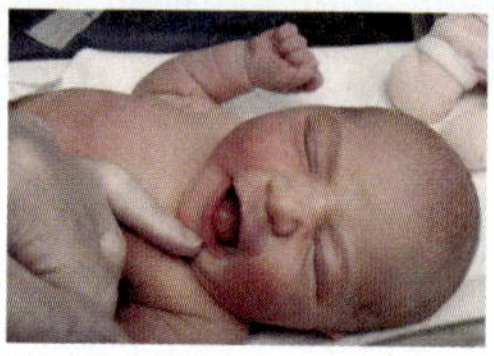

Matthew J. Lee

**Rooting reflex**
The head turns toward gentle stimulation of the skin at the corner of the mouth. The rooting reflex facilitates the newborn's search for the mother's breast.

**Sucking reflex**
When a finger is placed in the infant's mouth with the pad toward the palate, the baby sucks rhythmically.

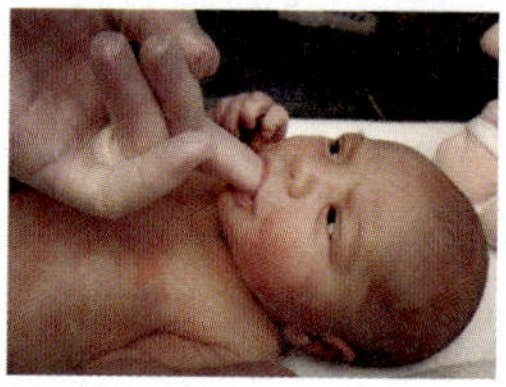

Matthew J. Lee

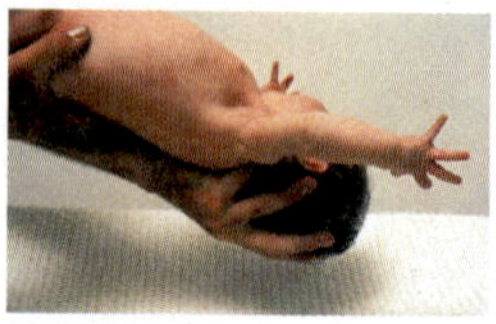

Petit Format/Science Source

**Moro reflex**
The Moro reflex is often called a startle reflex because it usually occurs when a baby is startled by a loud sound or movement. In response, the baby arches his back, flings his arms outward, and stretches his legs outward; he then closes his arms back in toward his body.

**Hand grasp**
This reflex can be elicited by placing the thumb on the baby's palm. The baby's fingers flex around the thumb or finger in a grasp-like movement.

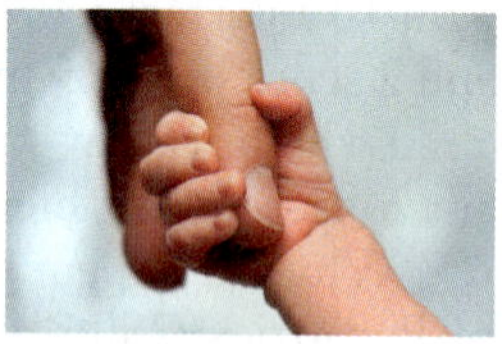

Anthony Bradshaw/Getty Images

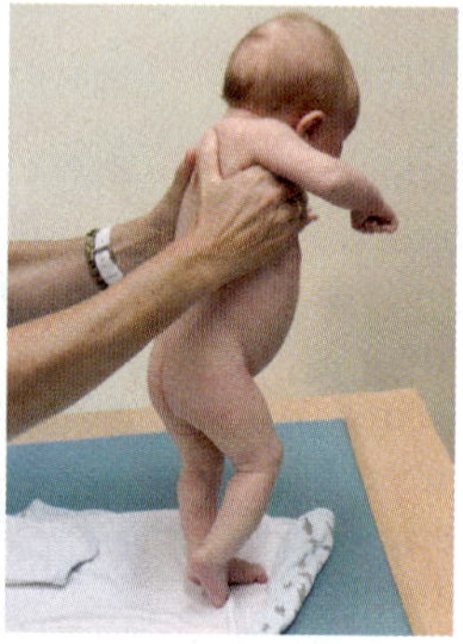

Picture Partners/Science Source

**Stepping reflex**
When the baby is held under the arms in a standing position on a flat surface, she is able to support her weight and take a few steps forward. Hence, this reflex is also called the walking reflex.

**Crawling reflex**
When the infant is placed on her stomach, her legs and arms move in a crawling motion.

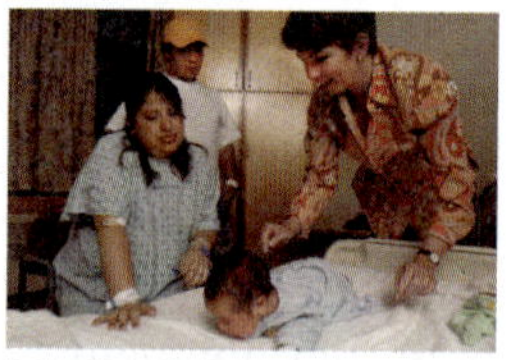

Matthew J. Lee

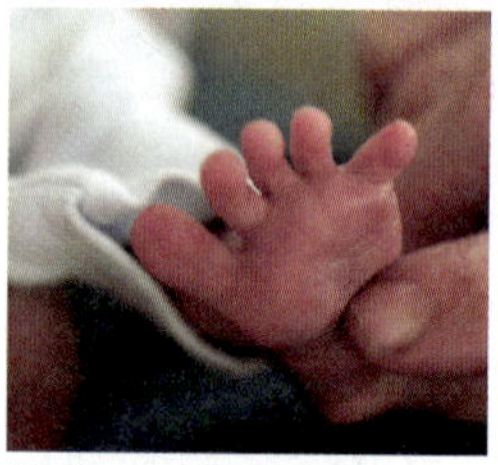

Mathew Spolin/Flickr RF/Getty Images

**Babinski reflex**
When the sole of the baby's foot is stroked from the toe toward the heel, the toes fan out and curl, and the foot twists inward.

As compelling as the newborn reflexes are, they do not even begin to tell us just how competent the newborn really is. Beginning around 1960, Peter Wolff's groundbreaking work on **newborn behavioral states** led to a greater appreciation of the newborn's capacity for organized behavior (Wolff, 1959, 1987). Spending hours observing and recording newborn behavior, Wolff discovered that this behavior is not as random as it first appears. He found that certain behavioral patterns tend to recur and can be reliably recognized in newborns. Wolff identified six behavioral states: deep sleep, light sleep, drowsiness, quiet alert, active alert, and crying. Each state is described in Table 4.4.

**newborn behavioral states** Behavioral patterns that recur and can be reliably recognized in newborns; the six states are deep sleep, light sleep, drowsiness, alertness, active alert, and crying.

Next, we take a moment to look at the most widely used newborn assessment tool that takes behavioral states, as well as many other factors, into account.

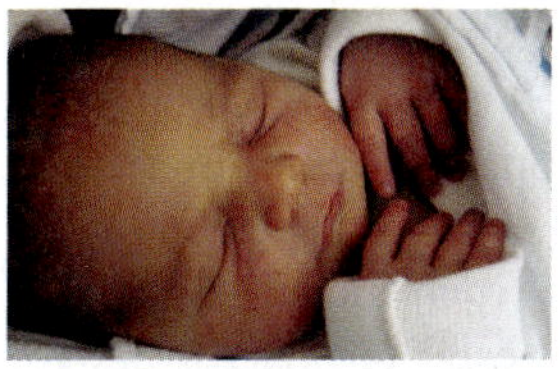
Matthew J. Lee

Kidstock/Blend Images/Getty Images

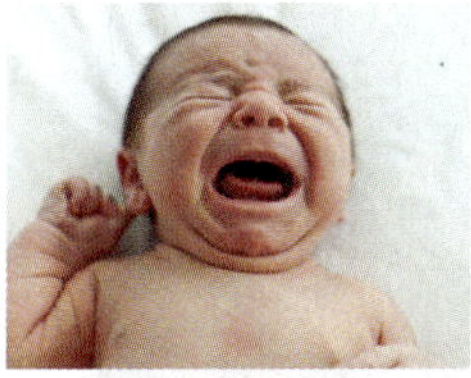
Siri Stafford/Getty Images

**Table 4.4** Newborn Behavioral States

| | |
|---|---|
| Deep sleep | Sleep with regular breathing; eyes closed; no spontaneous movement (except possible startles, occasionally); no rapid eye movement |
| Light sleep | Sleep with eyes closed, irregular respiration, some motor activity (Because of the presence of rapid eye movements, this sleep is often called REM sleep.) |
| Drowsiness | Drowsy or semialert; eyes may be open or closed; activity levels variable. |
| Quiet alert | Alert with bright look; minimal motor activity. |
| Active alert | Eyes open; considerable motor activity; sometimes fussing. |
| Crying | Intense crying; high motor activity. |

*Source:* Information from Brazelton and Nugent (2011), The Neonatal Behavioral Assessment Scale.

## The Neonatal Behavioral Assessment Scale

The **Neonatal Behavioral Assessment Scale (NBAS),** developed by T. Berry Brazelton and his colleagues, added to the notion that newborn infants have organized states, by showing that each newborn is a unique individual, with his or her own style of responding to the world from the very beginning. The NBAS is a neurobehavioral scale designed to examine the newborn's responses to his or her new environment outside the womb (Brazelton, 1973, 1984; Brazelton & Nugent, 1995, 2011). The NBAS is unique in that it assesses the infant's social competencies and describes his or her behavior in a way that is highly individualized.

The NBAS describes the infant's functioning in seven key areas—habituation, orientation, motor activity, range of state, regulation of state, autonomic functioning, and reflexes—as described in Table 4.5. Extensive research has shown that the NBAS is sensitive to a wide range of variables, such as the effects of growth retardation in the womb; the mother's use of cocaine, alcohol, caffeine, or tobacco; and the effects of prematurity. This means that the NBAS can be used to assess the effects of these diverse prenatal influences on the baby's behavior. In addition, the use of the NBAS in

**Table 4.5** The Neonatal Behavioral Assessment Scale: Areas of Newborn Functioning

| | |
|---|---|
| Habituation | The ability to respond to and inhibit distinct, separate stimuli while asleep |
| Orientation | Includes the ability to attend to visual and auditory stimuli, and the quality of overall alertness |
| Motor | Measures motor performance and the quality of movement and tone |
| Range of state | Measures infant arousal and lability of state change |
| Regulation of state | Measures the infant's ability to regulate his or her state in the face of increasing levels of stimulation |
| Autonomic stability | Records signs of stress related to adjustments of the central nervous system |
| Reflexes | Records the number of abnormal reflexes |

**Neonatal Behavioral Assessment Scale (NBAS)** A neurobehavioral assessment scale that describes an infant's functioning in seven key areas: habituation, orientation, motor activity, range of state, regulation of state, autonomic functioning, and reflexes.

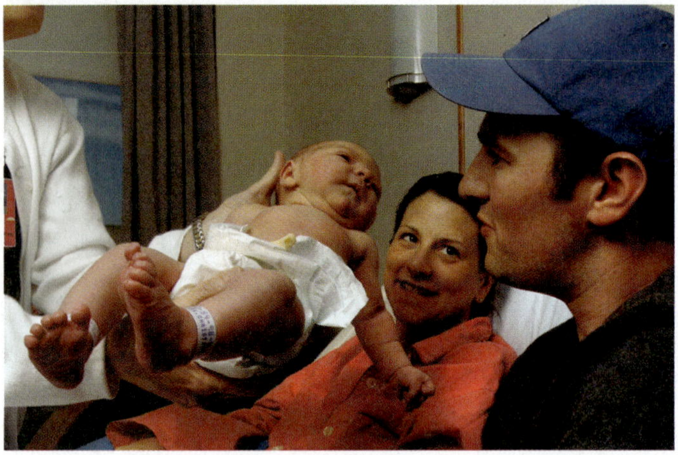

Matthew J. Lee

These new parents are learning more about their baby's individual characteristics by participating in the Newborn Behavioral Observations (NBO) system. Here the two-day-old baby turns to the sound of his father's voice.

various cultural settings has highlighted the fact that even cultural differences can be observed in newborn behavior. Thus, whereas the basic organizational processes in infancy may be universal, the range and form of these adaptations are shaped by the demands of each individual culture (Brazelton & Nugent, 1995, 2011; Lester & Sparrow, 2010; Nugent, Lester, & Brazelton, 1989, 1991; Nugent, Petrauskas, & Brazelton, 2009).

Research generated by the NBAS can be said to have played a major role in expanding our understanding of the remarkable capacities of the newborn. It established the fact that babies are different from one another and that each newborn is an individual with his or her own sensibilities and capabilities. Furthermore, the use of the NBAS as an educational tool for parents (Nugent, 1985; Nugent & Brazelton, 2000) led to the development of the more clinically oriented **Newborn Behavioral Observations (NBO)** system. The NBO is being used more and more in hospital, clinic and home settings around the world to help parents learn more about their baby's unique characteristics and overall adaptation during the first months of life. While the NBAS is typically used by researchers, the NBO is used by nurses, doctors, and other health-care and early intervention professionals to help parents become more aware of their baby's capacities and temperament, and promote the bond between parents and their infant (McManus & Nugent, 2011, 2012; Nugent & Alhaffer, 2006; Nugent, Keefer, Minear, Johnson, & Blanchard, 2007; Sanders & Buckner, 2006).

*Everyday stories*

CULTURAL DIFFERENCES IN NEWBORN BEHAVIOR Intrigued by the question of when and how individual differences emerge and develop, T. Berry Brazelton went to southern Mexico, where he used the Neonatal Behavioral Assessment Scale to study newborn infants among the Zinacanteco Indians in the highlands of Chiapas. He discovered that compared with their Caucasian counterparts in North America, these babies had very different behavioral competencies, even at birth. Their motor behavior, for example, was characterized by organized, smooth, fluid movements of the arms and legs: "At birth, they were very quiet, gently and gracefully moving with all extremities" (Brazelton, 2009, p. 280). Moreover, in contrast to the North American babies in this study, these babies did not cry very much. And these Mexican newborns were so alert and responsive that they could "pay attention to auditory and visual signals for 30 minutes without a break" (Brazelton, 2009, p. 281). Brazelton concluded that such differences are based on the infant's biological and cultural heritage, and that they enable the infant to engage in the kind of caregiving interactions and practices that ensure the baby's survival and successful adaptation to that culture.

The NBAS has inspired a number of other assessments and techniques, three of which are summarized in Table 4.6.

## Sensory Capacities and the Social Newborn

As we mentioned earlier, scientists' ideas about the sensory capacities of newborns changed considerably in the relatively recent past. Up to the early 1960s, it was generally assumed—at least in research and medical settings—that newborns could see only light and shadow. It's true that vision is the least developed sense at birth, compared with smell and taste, touch, and hearing. Still, newborns can see more than was once thought.

**Newborn Behavioral Observations (NBO) system** Based on the NBAS, a clinical tool used to sensitize parents to their newborn's capacities and individuality, and to promote a positive relationship between parent and infant.

**Table 4.6** Newborn Assessments and Techniques Inspired by the NBAS

| Instrument | Description |
|---|---|
| Assessment of Premature Infant Behavior (APIB) | The most widely used and detailed assessment of the behavior of preterm infants (Als, Lester, Tronick, & Brazelton, 1982) |
| Neonatal Intensive Care Unit Network Neurobehavioral Assessment Scale (NNNS) | A scale developed to assess the behavior of drug-exposed infants (Lester & Tronick, 2004) |
| Newborn Behavioral Observations (NBO) system | Developed primarily as a relationship-building tool to sensitize parents to their newborn's capacities and individuality, with the goal of promoting a positive relationship between parent and infant and between clinician and family (Nugent et al., 2007). |

## What Can Newborns See?

Infants can see at birth, and they depend on vision to explore the world around them. But how well can they see? The **visual acuity** of newborns—that is, the clarity with which they can see detail—is not nearly as good as that of adults. Indeed, it is not even as good as it will be at 3 months. The reason newborns' vision is limited is that their eyes and the visual structures in their brains are not yet fully developed. Newborns have a very narrow visual range, but they can focus on objects—and especially faces—that are between 10 and 12 inches away. Newborns can also visually track objects, moving their eyes or heads to follow visual stimuli (Dannemiller & Freedland, 1991; Laplante, Orr, Neville, Vorkapich, & Sasso, 1996; Slater, Morison, Town, & Rose, 1985). They seem to prefer to look at curves over straight edges, and attend most to points of highest contrast—which explains why a checkerboard pattern interests them more than a nonpatterned object (Fantz & Miranda, 1975).

Newborns pay particular attention to faces.

**The Importance of Faces.** Newborns seem to pay special attention to faces (Johnson, Posner, & Rothbart, 1991; Macchi Cassia, Turati, & Simion, 2004; Mondloch & Lewis, 1999; Morton & Johnson, 1991). They respond differently to faces than to nonfacelike objects (Kleiner, 1993). Furthermore, they can learn to identify a face in eight-tenths of a second (Walton, Armstrong, & Bower, 1998). They seem particularly interested in the faces of their mothers. One study found that newborns could recognize their mothers after spending four continuous hours with them, and tended to look longer at their mothers than at female strangers (Field, Cohen, Garcia, & Greenberg, 1984). In another study, newborns were able to control whether a videotaped image of their mother or of a female stranger was presented by varying the rate at which they sucked on a pacifier. Newborns sucked significantly more intently to see an image of their mother's face than an image of a stranger's face (Walton, Bower, & Bower, 1992).

The newborn's preference for the human face suggests that nature has programmed humans to be ready very early for contact with the social world. Because the mother is generally the infant's primary caregiver, hers is the most important and most likely face the newborn will recognize. We should note here that there is little research on whether infants recognize their fathers' faces early on. Some studies have suggested that this recognition develops only later (Walton et al., 1992; Ward, Phillips, & Cooper, 1998). We can easily see why early recognition of the primary caregiver is adaptive. Each time the newborn recognizes his or her mother and responds to her, the emotional bond between the two grows stronger.

**Neonatal Imitation and Mirror Neurons.** Another sort of visual interaction with social implications involves the ability of newborns to imitate. In 1977, Andrew Meltzoff

**visual acuity** The ability to see detail clearly.

**FIGURE 4.7 Imitation in Newborns** Around 30 years ago, Andrew Meltzoff and M. Keith Moore created a sensation by reporting that newborns could imitate facial expressions they observed in adults. Later, other researchers proposed that mirror neurons may underlie this surprising ability.

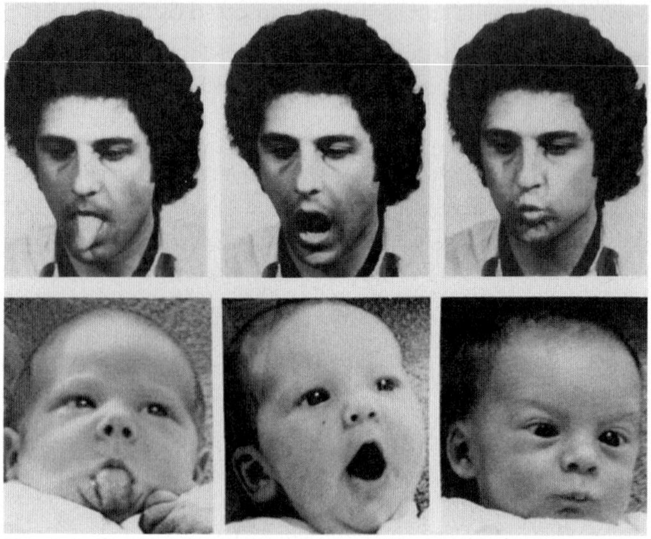

*From Imitation of Facial and Manual Gestures by Human Neonates, Andrew N. Melzoff and M. Keith Moore, Science, New Series, Volume 198, Issue 4312 (October 7, 1977), 75–78. Reprinted with permission from AAAS.*

and M. Keith Moore created a sensation by reporting that human infants just 12 to 21 days old imitated facial expressions they observed in adults, as shown in Figure 4.7 (Meltzoff & Moore, 1977). A second demonstration showed such imitation in infants as young as 42 minutes (Meltzoff & Moore, 1983).

For years, these reports were met with some skepticism. Such imitation was thought to be far too sophisticated an accomplishment for a newborn, because it would seem to involve high-level matching across different sensory systems. Consider that a baby girl can feel but not see her own mouth and tongue movements, and can see but not feel the mouth and tongue movements of others. Thus, to imitate an adult man sticking out his tongue, the newborn would have to make a connection between what she could see the man doing and what she could feel herself doing. Although these results have been confirmed in many studies (for example, Nagy & Molnar, 1994, 2004), the question remains: How could a newborn accomplish such a feat?

The discovery of mirror neurons (Rizzolatti & Craighero, 2004) has provided a mechanism that could underlie newborns' ability to imitate facial expressions. **Mirror neurons** fire when an individual performs an action or when an individual observes someone else performing that action. It has been demonstrated that newborn chimpanzees (Myowa–Yamakoshi, Tomonaga, Tanaka, & Matsuzawa, 2004) and rhesus monkeys (Ferrari et al., 2006) also imitate the facial expressions of adult humans. This finding implies that several species share the neural framework of mirror neurons.

## What Do Newborns Hear?

While vision plays a central role in establishing a bond between parent and baby, hearing may permit the fullest level of communication during the newborn period. Young infants can hear people talk to them, and prefer their mothers' voices over the voices of others. You may recall from Chapter 3 that this preference appears to develop in the womb.

At birth, newborns can turn to and locate a sound. They are more responsive to voices than to pure tones (DeCasper & Fifer, 1980; DeCasper & Spence, 1991; Moon, Cooper, & Fifer, 1993; Muir & Field, 1979; Spence & Freeman, 1996). Indeed, they can detect the overall patterns of rhythm and pitch that differentiate one person's voice from another (Nazzi, Floccia, & Bertoncini, 1998). A baby can identify his or her mother's voice, and, as noted, seems to prefer it. It is also possible that even newborns can map auditory with visual information very quickly (Macchi Cassia et al., 2004).

Mothers, and other adults as well, intuitively tend to use a particular style when speaking to their infants (Stern, 1974). This style is variously referred to as **child-directed speech,** *motherese*, or *parentese*. Child-directed speech has several distinctive

**mirror neurons** Neurons that fire when an individual performs an action, or when an individual observes someone else performing that action.

**child-directed speech** A style of speech typically used with infants, characterized by a higher-than-normal pitch, exaggerated intonation and rhythm, and simplified structure; also called *motherese* or *parentese*.

features, including high-pitched tones, exaggerated intonation and rhythm, and simplified structure. Infants show a preference for this style of speaking. An adult holding an infant at about 7 to 15 inches and talking softly in this style is perhaps an ideal stimulus for the young newborn.

Can infants understand language? Over 30 years ago, Peter Eimas and his colleagues (1975) showed that newborn infants 1 month old can discriminate the sound "ba" from the sound "pa." On the basis of these findings, the researchers argued that the ability to distinguish speech contrasts such as these is inborn. Newborns seem to be able to detect the sounds of any language and can make fine-grained distinctions between many speech sounds (Aldridge, Stillman, & Bower, 2001). Newborns can even perceive phonetic distinctions that do not occur in their own native language but only in another language. By about 4 or 5 months, infants can tell their own language from another within the same general language group (for example, English and Dutch). How infants acquire language will be discussed in greater detail in Chapter 6.

### The Importance of Touch for Newborns

Touch is the first sense to develop in the fetus. Touch is, in fact, crucial for newborn development. We have already seen how skin-to-skin contact can help develop the relationship between parents and their premature babies. Touch also plays a powerful role for infants in counteracting stress. Massaging newborns, for example, lowers their stress levels and helps them gain weight (Field et al., 2004, 2009). The improved weight gain from neonatal massage has been replicated cross-culturally. It is not that these infants sleep or eat more; rather, stimulating their bodies through massage triggers the release of hormones that help them to absorb their food—a good example of how systems connect! Human infants who receive little touching grow more slowly, release less growth hormone, and are less responsive to growth hormones that are administered externally (Frasier & Rallison, 1972). Throughout life, they show stronger reactions to stress, are more prone to depression, and are more vulnerable to deficits in cognitive functions commonly seen in depression or during stress (Lupien, King, Meaney, & McEwen, 2000).

It follows that if newborns are sensitive to touch, they can also feel pain, especially pain resulting from contact with the skin. Neural pathways for pain are present by about 26 weeks from conception. Pain in infants has been measured by changes in expression and by physiological measures such as heart rate. Touch can alleviate pain in newborns. So can the sounds of the mother's heartbeat, a sucrose solution to suck (Blass & Shah, 1995), and odors such as milk and lavender (Kawakami et al., 1997).

### Newborn Smell and Taste

Humans do not have as good a sense of smell as dogs or cats—at least in terms of locating the source of a smell. Newborn humans do, though, have at least as good a sense of smell as adults. Newborns can locate a smell, and prefer some smells to others. For example, fruit odors elicit positive facial expressions in newborns, while rotten-egg odors elicit expressions of disgust (Steiner, 1979).

The adaptive value of having a keen sense of smell is illustrated by a study showing that newborn babies prefer the smell of their mother's breast pad to that of an unfamiliar nursing mother. This preference helps to ensure the infant's survival by promoting feeding and the mother-infant bond. Close physical contact, such as breast-feeding, in the hours after birth allows a mother and infant to recognize each other through smell, as well as touch (Porter & Winberg, 1999). This recognition is a precursor to any enduring attachment.

Babies also have a well-developed sense of taste at birth. This may be in part because they have had significant experience with taste in the womb. From about 9 or 10 weeks from conception, the fetus inhales and exhales amniotic fluid, which contains a range of tastes that reflect what the mother has been eating and drinking. Newborns can also discriminate between stimuli using their mouths. In one study, for example, newborn infants could tell the difference between smooth and "nubbly" textured nipples (Hernandez–Reif, Field, & Diego, 2004). In several studies, infants responded with

Newborns have a well-developed sense of smell. Close physical contact in the hours after birth enables them to recognize their mothers through smell, as well as touch.

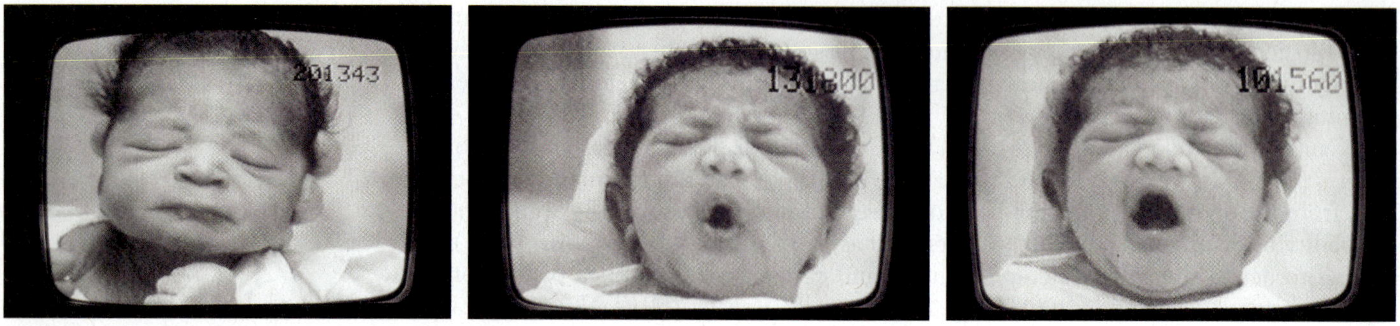

Diana Rosenstein

**FIGURE 4.8 Newborns' Responses to Taste** Infants respond to the tastes of sweet, sour, and bitter solutions with different facial expressions. They smile in response to the sweet solution. The sour solution evokes a pucker, and the bitter solution a disgusted expression.

different facial expressions to the tastes of sweet, sour, and bitter solutions (Rosenstein & Oster, 1997). They seem to prefer the sweet solution, indicated by smiling in response to it. The sour solution, in contrast, evoked a pucker; and the bitter solution a disgusted expression, as shown in Figure 4.8.

## what if...?

Joseph, your good friend from high school, has just become a new dad. He is happy and excited, but he is not very involved with Jon, his 2-week-old baby. He leaves all the care to the baby's mother. "I *am* crazy about him," he emphasizes, "but he can't do much yet. He sleeps a lot, wakes up and cries, and then needs to be fed and changed. That's about it. He really can't see or hear much. Even if he could hear, he's too little to understand anything. I can't wait until he can walk and talk. Then I can really have a relationship with him."

What would you say to your friend? What evidence might you offer that he could, and should, begin to develop a relationship with his baby right now?

### The Beguiling Newborn

Studies on the sensory capacities of the newborn, together with research on imitation, reveal the newborn infant as a socially competent organism, beautifully designed to elicit from the caregiving environment all he or she needs for survival and adaptation (Nugent et al., 2009; Nugent & Brazelton, 2000). "It is fortunate for their survival that babies are so designed by nature that they beguile and enslave mothers," wrote John Bowlby, a theorist who studied infant attachment (1958, p. 367). Indeed, infants' ability to communicate with their mothers and other caregivers is essential for survival, just as communication is essential for the survival of all other animals living in social groups. Some of these animals, such as bees and ants, communicate through intricate but relatively inflexible behaviors that change little over their lifespan. In contrast, human infants must learn to convey information about their needs through vocal, facial, and motor behaviors, and must also learn to monitor the behavior of others in order to read their intentions and make sense of their actions. As we have seen, even in the first months of life, infants are communicating through such means as facial and vocal expressions as they build toward the ability to communicate through language.

### ✓CHECK YOUR PROGRESS

1. Name and describe several infant reflexes.
2. What are the six newborn behavioral states?
3. What is the difference between the Apgar scale and the Neonatal Behavioral Assessment Scale?
4. Describe the visual and auditory competencies of the newborn infant.
5. What are mirror neurons? How do they explain how newborns can imitate?

## The Developmental Tasks of the Newborn Period

**[ KEY QUESTION ] 4.** What are the developmental challenges facing the newborn?

**bonding theory** A theory suggesting that the period immediately after delivery is a sensitive one in the development of a close emotional bond between mother and child.

**colostrum** A precursor to mature breast milk that consists primarily of enzymes, anti-infective agents, hormones, and growth factors.

The newborn period is one of developmental challenges for infants, as they shift from the world inside the womb to the external world. We have seen that newborns come into this world with a rich behavioral repertoire. Still, they clearly must depend on support from caregivers to continue to survive and develop (Buss & Plomin, 1984; Damon & Lerner, 2008; Lester, Tronick, & Brazelton, 2004; Nugent et al., 2007; Sameroff, 2010). The success of this transition depends on the quality and appropriateness of the caregiving environment and the degree to which the infant's needs are met. In this section, we discuss some issues relating to the infant-parent bond and examine more closely the challenges faced by the newborn.

### The Parent-Infant Bond

The first moments, hours, and days after delivery are a time of great emotional intensity for new parents. Pediatricians Marshall Klaus and John Kennell were so impressed by the power of the emotional exchanges between newborns and their mothers that they proposed that the period immediately after delivery may be crucial to the development of a close emotional bond between mother and child. Their theory came to be known as **bonding theory**. According to this theory, the mother-child bond may not form as it should if certain important experiences—such as prolonged skin-to-skin contact between mother and child during the first few hours or days after birth—fail to occur (Klaus et al., 1972, 1995; Klaus & Kennell, 1981). Critics of bonding theory, however, note that slight variations in early contact—as in the case of a baby born prematurely or an adopted baby—do not appear to produce lasting differences in the mother-infant relationship (Eyer, 1992, 1994; Goldberg, 1983; Harmon, 1981; Lamb, 1983; Maestripieri, 2001; Myers, 1984). Klaus and Kennell later revised their theory, acknowledging that the bonding process is much more flexible than they had first believed.

As with any relationship, then, the development of the bond between parents and their child takes time. Nevertheless, during these early days and months of life, the comfort and nurturance parents provide is already making it possible for infants to learn to regulate their arousal and to focus on and explore the world around them (Als et al., 2004; Lester & Sparrow, 2010; Nugent et al., 2007). In addition, a large body of evidence shows us that the mother's sensitivity in responding to her baby's needs is a key determinant in the development of the baby's sense of security and the growth of his or her sense of attachment to the caregiver (Als et al., 2004; Zeanah & Boris, 2000). In Chapter 7, we will examine how this relationship changes and develops over the course of infancy—what can go right and what can go wrong. The newborn period is simply the first step in this process. But it is a vital one.

Camille Tokerud/Getty Images

Starting breast-feeding soon after birth offers benefits for both babies and mothers.

### Breast-Feeding: A Developmental Issue

Another consideration at the forefront in the neonatal period is nutrition, which is vital for the infant's growth and development. Breast milk generally offers the best nutrition for babies. It is rich in nutrients that promote brain growth and nervous system development. It contains the right balance of fats, carbohydrates, and proteins for the newborn, along with the right mix of vitamins. Thus, starting breast-feeding in the first hours after birth, and continuing it longer term, can have important consequences for the baby's health and development. The effects of breast-feeding beyond the newborn period will be discussed in the next chapter.

#### Breast-Feeding in the First Hours After Birth

During the first hours after birth, the mother secretes **colostrum**, a yellowish precursor to mature breast milk (Emmett & Rogers, 1997; Hartmann, Rattigan, Saint, & Supriyana,

1985; Humenick, Mederios, Wreschner, Walton, & Hill, 1994). Colostrum has a higher protein and lower fat content than breast milk produced later. Its protein component consists primarily of enzymes, anti-infective agents, hormones, and growth factors, many of which serve to support neonatal growth and development (Kunz, Rodriguez–Palmero, Koletzko, & Jensen, 1999; Xu, 1996). Beginning breast-feeding while colostrum is still being produced is thought to decrease infant illness—especially in nonindustrialized populations—by reducing the risk of various infections (Carlsson et al., 1976; Cruz et al., 1982; Feachem & Koblinsky, 1984; Popkin et al., 1990; Shortridge, Lawton, & Choi, 1990).

The mother also receives benefits from breast-feeding within hours of giving birth. Breast-feeding initiates the release of oxytocin (Ojeda, 1996). Oxytocin causes uterine contractions and may help to expel the placenta (Carr, 1996) and reduce maternal blood loss (Carr, 1996; Trevathan, 1984). Breast-feeding within an hour or two of delivery is associated with the establishment of longer and more successful breast-feeding and the development of a positive relationship between mother and baby (Hill, 1991; Kurinij & Shiono, 1991; Salariya, Easton, & Cater, 1978; Trevathan, 1984). Based on research supporting the nutritional and psychological value of breast-feeding, the American Academy of Pediatrics (AAP) and other professional groups concerned with the care of newborns, advocate breast-feeding whenever possible. Specifically, the AAP recommends that babies be breast-fed exclusively for about the first 6 months. Studies have related breast-feeding to positive mother-infant interactions (Maestripieri, 2001). Some researchers have even suggested that it may affect intelligence, as discussed in the accompanying Research Insights feature.

If breast-feeding is so beneficial to both the baby and that mother, why do many mothers not breast-feed? There are a number of reasons. Some relate to the baby, some to the mother, and some to the environment. In the case of a baby who is born prematurely and/or has a physically limiting condition, such as cleft lip and palate, breast-feeding can be extremely difficult. In addition, formula feeding may be recommended when the mother has certain conditions—for example, if she is HIV positive or has been using street drugs. But many mothers (and fathers) may opt out of breast-feeding simply because they do not have adequate information on the value of breast-feeding or adequate support from their health-care providers (Simkin, Bolding, & Keppler, 2010).

*Everyday stories*

OPTING OUT OF BREAST-FEEDING A number of environmental influences may have the effect of discouraging women from breast-feeding. For example, the commercial promotion of infant formula by the companies that make it may sometimes play a role. Hospital discharge gift packs often include formula, along with baby toys. Some new mothers, especially those who have had trouble initiating breast-feeding, may be tempted to begin using the formula and then end up using it all the time. Other women may be tempted to give up breast-feeding because their work sites generally do not support the needs of lactating employees.

To promote breast-feeding, the American Public Health Association has called on the media to portray breast-feeding as normal, desirable, and achievable for women of all cultures and socioeconomic levels (American Public Health Association, 2007).

## The UNICEF/WHO Baby-Friendly Hospital Initiative

**Practice**

The *Baby-Friendly Hospital Initiative (BFHI)* is a global program sponsored by the World Health Organization (WHO) and the United Nations Children's Fund (UNICEF) to encourage and recognize hospitals and birthing centers that offer an optimal level of care for breast-feeding. It is based on the assumption that providing infants with human milk gives them the most complete nutrition possible and provides the optimal mix of nutrients and antibodies necessary for them to thrive.

The BFHI helps hospitals in giving breast-feeding mothers the information, confidence, and skills they need to successfully begin, and continue, breast-feeding their babies. BFHI-recognized hospitals promote and support breast-feeding as the normal mode of feeding babies. They recommend that breast-feeding take place within one hour after delivery, that no bottles be offered, and that rooming-in be observed for all mothers and babies. In the United States, the BFHI "envisions a culture that values the enduring benefits of breast-feeding and human milk for mothers, babies, and society." (See www.babyfriendlyusa.org for more information.)

what if…?

What if you and your partner were going to have a baby and were interested in learning more about hospitals designated as "Baby Friendly"? Would you be able to find one in your area? If it were available, would you choose such a hospital? Why or why not? Most U.S. hospitals have not received the BFHI designation. Why do you think more hospitals have not done so?

## Developmental Tasks Facing the Newborn

We conclude this chapter by discussing the developmental agenda of the newborn period—what the newborn must become able to do to continue on a healthy developmental course. The developmental tasks facing the newborn center on the process of self-regulation. It has been hypothesized that, over the first few months of life, newborns face a series of challenges, or tasks, in self-regulation that are in some ways similar to stages (Als et al., 1982; Nugent et al., 2007). These include infants' capacity to regulate their autonomic systems, their motor behavior, their state behavior, and their interactive behavior. Although there may be some variation, and some overlap, development is generally thought to progress in a hierarchical pattern from one to the next. The challenges, or tasks, are summarized with the acronym AMOR, for autonomic, motor, organization of state, and social responsiveness, as shown in Figure 4.9 and summarized below (Nugent et al., 2007):

1. The first developmental task for newborns is to organize *autonomic behavior*. Recall from Chapter 2 that the autonomic system is the part of the nervous system that is responsible for controlling involuntary functions, such as heart rate and breathing. This task thus involves stabilizing breathing and maintaining temperature control, among others.

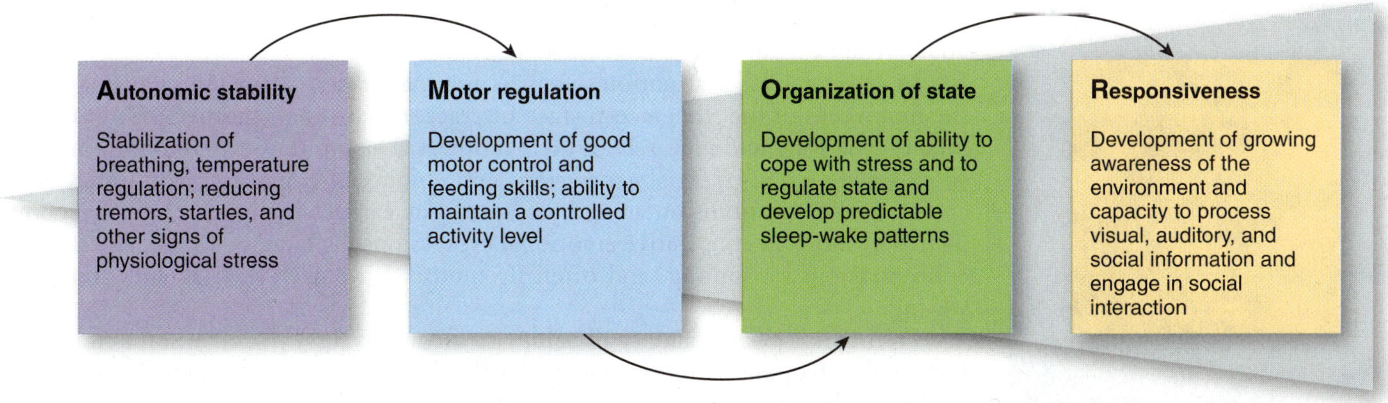


**FIGURE 4.9 Developmental Challenges Facing the Newborn: The AMOR Hierarchy of Newborn Behavioral Organization** Over the first few months of life, infants develop in their ability to regulate themselves. In general, self-regulation progresses from the autonomic system, to motor behavior, to state behavior, and to interactive behavior.

Based on Nugent, J. K., Keefer, C. H., Minear, S., Johnson, L., & Blanchard, Y. (2007). *Understanding Newborn Behavior and Early Relationships: The Newborn Behavioral Observations (NBO) System Handbook*. Baltimore: Brookes Publishing, p. 173.

## Research Insights: Effects of Breast-Feeding on Intelligence

Can breast-feeding make a child smarter? A longitudinal study in Denmark found that the duration of breast-feeding was associated with significantly higher scores on the verbal, performance, and full-scale Weschler Scales of Intelligence at age 27 (Mortensen, Michaelsen, Sanders, & Reinisch, 2002). Adults who as infants were breast-fed for less than 1 month had an average IQ of 99.4; those who were breast-fed from 2 to 3 months, 101.7; those who were breast-fed from 4 to 6 months, 102.3; and those who were breast-fed from 7 to 9 months, 106.0.

How can these findings be explained? Using statistical methods, the researchers ruled out the effects of the mother's education and social status, along with cigarette smoking during pregnancy, birth weight, and birth complications, among other variables. The researchers did not control for the mothers' IQ scores, however, and acknowledged that this variable might be a factor. They proposed, though, that breast milk contains nutrients that stimulate brain development during the early months of life—a period of rapid brain development. Another explanation offered was that the extra physical contact between mother and baby associated with breast-feeding may be an index of the quality of the child's caregiving environment, which may in turn play a key role in promoting the child's intellectual development. Whatever the explanation, this study suggests that breast-feeding a child over the first 9 months of life may influence intellectual development into adulthood.

2. When the first adjustment has been achieved, the newborn can move on to the second task: regulating *motor behavior*. This means gaining control over random motor movements, developing good muscle tone and control, and reducing excessive motor activity.
3. The third task is *state regulation*. State regulation includes the ability to develop strong and predictable sleep and wake states. It also involves what could be called *sleep protection*, the ability to screen out disturbances, such as noise, while asleep. State control means, too, that the infant is able to deal with stress, either by crying to gain the caregiver's help or engaging in such self-comforting behaviors as placing a hand in the mouth.
4. The final developmental task for the newborn is the regulation of *attentional-interactive*, or *social*, *behavior*. This involves the capacity to maintain prolonged alert periods, to attend to visual and auditory stimuli, and to seek out and engage in social interaction with caregivers.

© Matt Hess/Golden Pixels LLC/Corbis

Rocking, walking, and cuddling are three of the many ways to soothe a fussy baby.

The process of self-regulation proceeds over the first weeks and months of life. As infants become better able to regulate their behavior, they can prolong their periods of alertness and social availability. In other words, they grow more ready and able to interact socially with their caregivers. This is a special period of developmental change and reorganization in the patterns of infant attention and emotion (Lavelli & Fogel, 2005; Tronick, 2007).

In general, simple attention seems to dominate face-to-face interactions during the first weeks of life. In a face-to-face interaction with their mothers, for example, infants look long and intensely at their mothers. During the second month, infants show a wide range of facial expressions and emotional responses, from interest to concentration to astonishment and pleasure. The earlier simple gaze is now accompanied by more active positive emotional expressions, by demonstrations of effortful concentration, by smiling, and often by motor excitement such as animated arm waving.

During this period, almost all babies go through a fussy period at some time during the day. Coping with excessive or inconsolable crying can be a challenging task for both baby and parent (Kaley, Reid, & Flynn, 2011). Crying that lasts for longer than about 3 hours a day, and is not caused by a medical problem, is referred to as *colic*. The timing varies, but colic usually affects babies beginning at about 3 weeks of age and peaks somewhere between 4 and 6 weeks of age. Most infants who cry excessively are free of symptoms by the third month (Clifford, Campbell, Speechley, & Gorodzinsky, 2002). Although it is stressful to deal with, colic or excessive crying is normal and has no relation to later adjustment, according to cry researcher Ronald Barr and his

## Culture and Crying

Babies everywhere cry, especially during the first 3 months. Even baby chimpanzees follow this pattern (Tomonaga et al., 2004). But while the crying curve over the first 3 months applies to babies all over the world, persistent, inconsolable crying is not found in every culture.

Consider, as an example, the !Kung San of Africa (Barr, Konner, Bakeman & Adamson, 1991; Konner, 2005). Among these modern-day hunter-gatherers, lengthy, inconsolable bouts of infant crying—or *colic*—are rare (Fouts, Lamb, & Hewlett, 2004). Crying bouts are also shorter than those observed in babies in Western societies, which means that they spend about half as much total time crying (Small, 1998).

Eric LAFFORGUE/Gamma-Rapho via Getty Images

Lengthy bouts of crying are rare among babies of the !Kung San tribe. Constant physical contact with caregivers may help to explain this phenomenon. For the first year, !Kung San babies are carried virtually all the time.

Why might this be? We don't know for certain, but it may be due in part to different feeding patterns. Hunter-gatherer babies are fed on demand, and very frequently—sometimes as often as 4 times an hour. The meals are small, which may protect babies from digestive difficulties associated with less frequent and larger meals at an early age (Konner, 2005).

Differences in physical contact offer another possible explanation. Throughout the first year of life, the !Kung infant is carried constantly by a parent or a caring other, either in arms or in a sling (Hrdy, 2009). Western parents spend significantly less time in physical proximity to their infants, placing them in cribs to sleep, usually in a separate room, and often in strollers, bouncy seats, and high chairs when they are awake.

Finally, social support may play a role. Among hunter-gatherers, parents are virtually never alone with their infants. Western parents—especially mothers—may spend long hours alone with their babies. This could sometimes contribute to maternal anxiety and depression, which in turn could aggravate colic. It is, of course, impractical to suggest that parents in North America abandon their Western lifestyle and adopt the practices of the !Kung San. They can, however, apply these principles where and when appropriate when dealing with colic.

colleagues (Barr & Fujiwara, 2011; Barr, Paterson, MacMartin, Lehtonen, & Young, 1995). The accompanying Culture and Crying feature discusses cultural aspects of colicky crying.

By the third month, babies are crying much less, and their smiles are becoming more open, and are accompanied by playful cooing. This more active pattern of attention is accompanied by excitement during face-to-face interactions. Now the stage is set for the infant to become truly engaged with another person (Adamson, 1996; Brazelton, Kozlowski, & Main, 1974; Stern, 1995; Trevarthen, 2003; Tronick, 2003). This development constitutes the major task of the next stage of the infant's life, which we will be examining in detail in the next three chapters.

### ✓ CHECK YOUR PROGRESS

1. What is the basic assumption of bonding theory?
2. What are the benefits of breast-feeding?
3. What are the four developmental challenges infants face during the newborn period?

# CHAPTER SUMMARY

## Birth

**[ KEY QUESTION ] 1.** What happens during labor and delivery, and how do the different approaches to childbirth affect these processes?

- Pregnancy is a period of rapid psychological adjustment for new parents. Preparations for the birth of a baby may include attending birth preparation classes and writing a birth plan.
- The end of pregnancy is labor, which includes four stages: dilation, descent and birth, delivery, and recovery.
- Labor is painful, and there are various approaches to dealing with this pain. Medications represent one approach. In recent times, natural childbirth has gained favor as an alternative.
- In more developed countries, hospitals have become the setting for most births. Some women, however, prefer to give birth at home or in homelike birth centers.
- Most babies are delivered vaginally, sometimes with medical interventions. About 20 to 30% of births in the United States are accomplished using cesarean delivery, however, and this figure is increasing annually.

## At-Risk Infants: A Different Beginning

**[ KEY QUESTION ] 2.** What are the long-term effects of preterm birth on the infant and on the infant's family, and what kinds of intervention can promote the development of preterm infants?

- More than 500,000 premature infants are born in the United States every year, and these infants often experience major complications due to their low birth weight and the immaturity of their body systems.
- The underlying causes of prematurity are unknown, but there are several known risk factors, including pregnancies involving multiple fetuses.
- Prematurity is the leading cause of death in newborns, and those who survive face the risk of lifelong health consequences, including physical, behavioral, and cognitive problems.
- Prematurity affects the parents as well as the infant, causing stress and potentially affecting the quality of care the parents are able to provide.
- Early intervention programs can make important contributions to successful outcomes for preterm infants and their parents. Current trends in intervention focus on individualized care and long-term development.
- Infant mortality is a very serious problem, especially in the developing world. More than 130 million babies are born every year across the world, and almost 8 million of them die before their first birthday. The Fourth Millennium Development Goals represent one attempt to reduce infant mortality.

## The Newborn

**[ KEY QUESTION ] 3.** What can newborns actually do?

- To determine whether a newborn is healthy, care providers in modern industrialized societies use the Apgar scale and a number of other screening assessments.
- Babies are born with a number of reflexes clearly designed to enable them to survive outside the womb.
- Newborns exhibit organized behavior in the form of six well-defined behavioral states, which go from deep sleep to alert activity and crying.
- The Neonatal Behavioral Assessment Scale added to the idea that newborns have organized states by showing that each newborn is a unique individual with his or her own style of responding.
- Newborns cannot see details clearly, but they can focus on and visually track objects, and they pay special attention to faces—especially their mothers'. They can even imitate facial expressions, perhaps because of the actions of mirror neurons.
- Newborns can hear voices, and show a preference for their mothers'. They are more responsive to voices than pure tones and can discriminate among language sounds as early as 1 month of age.
- Touch is the first sense to develop in the fetus, and remains very important during the neonatal period in counteracting stress and promoting development.
- Newborns have well-developed senses of smell and taste, as well as preferences for some smells and tastes over others.

## The Developmental Tasks of the Newborn Period

**[ KEY QUESTION ] 4.** What are the developmental challenges facing the newborn?

- Bonding theory proposes that the parent-child bond may not form as it should if certain important experiences fail to occur, such as prolonged skin-to-skin contact during the first few hours or days after birth. The consensus today, however, is that while early contact is important, the parent-child bond continues to develop over time.
- Good nutrition is vital to growth and development, and breast milk offers the best nutrition for babies, as well as promoting positive mother-baby interactions.
- The developmental challenges facing the newborn center on the process of self-regulation. In a stagelike progression, the newborn must become able to regulate autonomic, or physiological, behavior; motor behavior; state; and attentional-interactive, or social, behavior.

# KEY TERMS

analgesics *125*
anesthetics *125*
anoxia *138*
Apgar score *138*
assisted vaginal delivery *127*
birth centers *127*
birth plan *122*
bonding theory *147*
cesarean delivery *125*
child-directed speech *144*
colostrum *147*
doula *127*
extremely low birth weight (ELBW) *130*
gestational age *130*
infant mortality rate *135*
kangaroo care *135*
low birth weight (LBW) *130*
mirror neurons *144*
natural childbirth *125*
neonatal *120*
Neonatal Behavioral Assessment Scale (NBAS) *141*

## CRITICAL THINKING QUESTIONS

1. **Birth.** Many first-time parents today want to experience childbirth as natural, without anesthetics or other medical interventions, and are looking for alternatives to physician-assisted hospital care. Based on your understanding of the needs of mothers and babies, explain what you think is in the best interests of parent and child.
2. **At-Risk Infants: A Different Beginning.** Premature infants are much more likely than normal-weight, full-term infants to experience significant medical complications, developmental delays, and physical and behavioral problems that persist well into the school-age and adolescent years. How can we improve outcomes for these babies?
3. **The Newborn.** What are the major challenges newborn infants face over the first months of life, and what kind of support do they need from their caregivers to grow and thrive?
4. **The Developmental Tasks of the Newborn Period.** If breast-feeding is so beneficial to the health and development of newborns, why do many mothers not breast-feed? What can be done to promote breast-feeding?
5. **Cultural Perspectives.** In every culture, babies cry, especially during the first 3 months after birth. But while the crying curve over the first 3 months of life applies to babies all over the world, colic—persistent inconsolable crying—is not found in every culture. Why might this be?

## REAL Development

### Birth and the Newborn

In the accompanying Real Development activities, you will be learning about birth plan options and the APGAR scale used for newborns. In the first activity, you will observe Julianne meeting with a doula to learn about possible options for labor and delivery. In the second activity, you will observe and respond as the health, behavioral states, and reflexes of baby Olivia are measured using the APGAR scale.

© *John Wiley & Sons, Inc.*

**WileyPLUS** Go to WileyPLUS to complete the *Real Development* activity.

# Chapter 5

*Jose Luis Pelaez Inc/Blend Images/Getty Images*

# Physical Development and Health in Infancy and Toddlerhood

## MAKING A difference

### Beating the Odds

When she was born, Katelyn could have fit in the palm of her father's hand. She was born after only 25 weeks and weighed less than 1 lb at birth. Her parents were told that Katelyn had a 1 out of 20 chance of surviving. She could not breathe on her own, so she had to be placed in an incubator. She battled many infections, underwent heart surgery, and suffered from bleeding in the brain. But her parents, family, and the nurses and doctors never left her side, and Katelyn survived against overwhelming odds. After 5 months in the Neonatal Intensive Care Unit, her parents were able to take their little daughter home.

When she got home, Katelyn was still on supplementary oxygen and had to take 10 medications every day. Because of her premature birth, she was late in meeting the motor milestones of infancy. She began walking and talking late for her age. Without the support of the early intervention team that came to the house each week for her speech and physical therapy, Katelyn's parents did not know how they could have coped. It was the ongoing encouragement of the team, their understanding of Katelyn's developmental needs, and their commitment to her development that enabled them to stay hopeful throughout. (You'll read more about early intervention teams later in this chapter.)

Today, Katelyn is 5 years old. She has slight cerebral palsy, which affects the left side of her body, and she still needs support from speech, occupational, and physical therapists. Despite these motor disabilities, Katelyn acts like a typical 5-year-old. She leads a full life. She loves to run and play outside with her dog, Sequoia. She is the joy of her parents' lives (March of Dimes, 2009).

## CHAPTER OUTLINE

## [KEY QUESTIONS] *for* READING CHAPTER 5

1. What are the key elements of the Harvard Center on the Developing Child framework for children's health and physical development?
2. In what ways are the first years of life a period of rapid physical, motor, and perceptual development?
3. What role does the brain play in the rapid physical, motor, and perceptual development of the first years of life?
4. What are some important nutrition concerns regarding infants and toddlers?
5. How do the physical, caregiving, and cultural environments affect development in infants and toddlers?
6. What are some effects of neuromuscular disabilities on development, and how can early intervention help?

TODAY, more than ever before, we understand how health shapes children's development. In keeping with this understanding, the Center on the Developing Child at Harvard University has developed a framework that underscores the complex relationship between health and development. We introduce this framework here and refer to it in our other chapters dealing with physical development and health—Chapters 8, 11, and 14.

In this chapter, we also examine children's early physical, motor, and perceptual development. We explain why these first years of life are so critical for health and brain development—indeed, for every aspect of psychological development. You will see that, in terms of both the nature and the rate of change, the infant's physical and motor development involves one of the most amazing developmental transformations across the life span. You will also learn what happens when physical and motor abilities are compromised. As you will see, early intervention is vital in preventing motor dysfunction in the first place and ensuring that those who are born with disabilities enjoy the best possible quality of life.

# A Framework for Children's Health and Physical Development

**[ KEY QUESTION ] 1. What are the key elements of the Harvard Center on the Developing Child framework for children's health and physical development?**

As we have noted throughout this book, children's development is the result of dynamic interactions among the physical, cognitive, and psychosocial domains. Recently, the Center for the Developing Child at Harvard University proposed a framework to help us appreciate the importance of health in children's development. The framework emphasizes the role of caregivers, communities, and policymakers in supporting a healthy childhood.

*Everyday stories*

CHILDREN'S HEALTH IS A NATION'S WEALTH In the words of the Harvard framework's developers, the foundations of lifelong health are built in early childhood:

> Health is more than merely the absence of disease—it is an evolving human resource that helps children and adults adapt to the challenges of everyday life, resist infections, cope with adversity, feel a sense of personal well-being, and interact with their surroundings in ways that promote successful development. Nations with the most positive indicators of population health, such as longer life expectancy and lower infant mortality, typically have higher levels of wealth and lower levels of income inequality. In short, children's health is a nation's wealth, as a sound body and mind enhance the capacity of children to develop a wide range of competencies that are necessary to become contributing members of a successful society (Center on the Developing Child, 2010, p. 4).

As just noted, we use the Harvard Center on the Developing Child framework to organize our chapters about physical development. The Harvard framework borrows from Urie Bronfenbrenner's bioecological model, discussed in Chapter 1. Both approaches emphasize how individuals interact with a broad range of surrounding environmental systems. Both also recognize how family, community, and culture influence the child's health and physical development, and how the child, in turn, influences these systems. As shown in Figure 5.1, the Harvard framework's levels include the following elements that influence a child's health and development:

1. Biology of health—the child's physical makeup
2. Foundations of health—involving the child's relationships with others, the immediate environment, and nutrition
3. Caregiver and community capacities—including the time, commitment, resources, and knowledge available from caregivers and communities
4. Policy and program—including public health, education, and other policy- and program-level elements in the community

The Harvard framework is especially helpful in our examination of physical development in infancy. There is sound evidence to show that health in the earliest years of a child's life—a sound body—lays the groundwork for a lifetime of good health. An extensive body of scientific research now shows that many of the most common chronic diseases in adults—such as hypertension, diabetes, cardiovascular disease, and stroke—are linked to processes and experiences occurring in the first years of life (Shonkoff, Boyce, & McEwen, 2009).

Research shows, for instance, that inadequate nutrition and recurrent exposure to infectious diseases in infancy are associated with increased rates of chronic cardiovascular, respiratory, and psychiatric diseases in adulthood (Nomura et al., 2007). Inadequate levels of iron and of vitamins A and D are significant health concerns for many infants and toddlers, who need increased levels of these nutrients to support the rapid growth of blood cells, bones, and other tissues. These types of deficiencies early in life can affect a wide range of cognitive, motor, and psychosocial development. They may

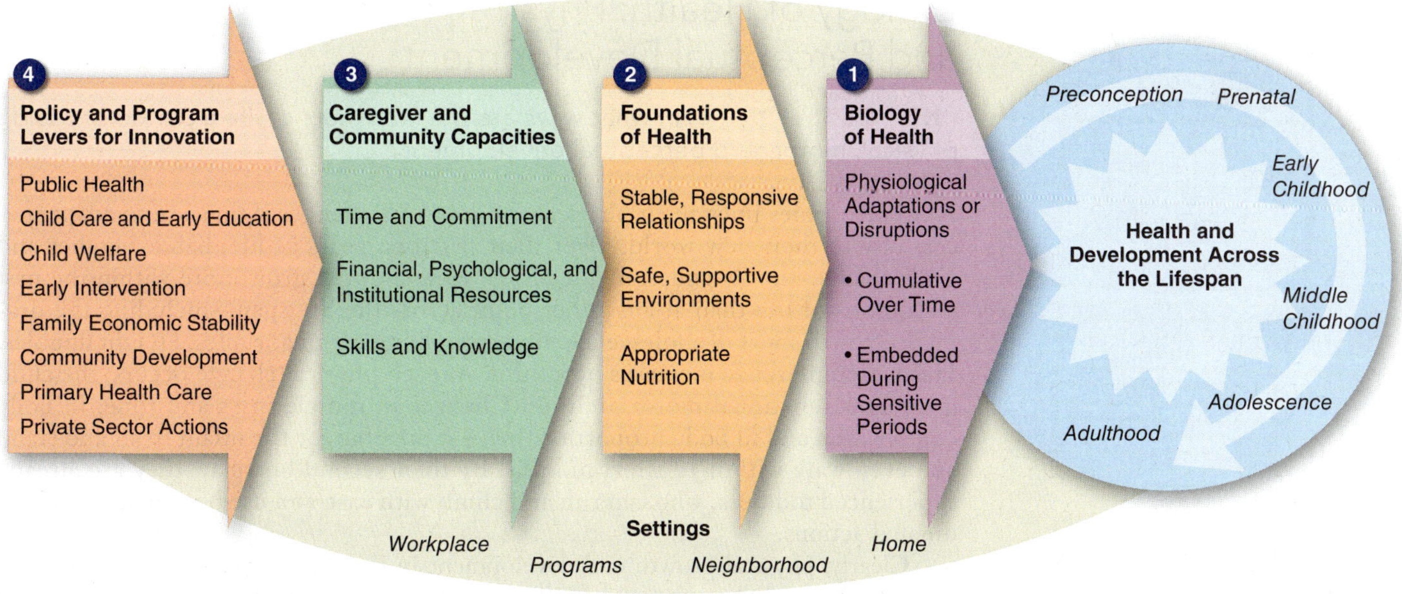


**FIGURE 5.1 A Framework for Child Health and Development** The Harvard Center on the Developing Child has proposed a framework for understanding children's health and development. The framework emphasizes how individuals interact with a broad range of environmental systems, including family, community, and culture.

*Source:* Center on the Developing Child at Harvard University (2010). *The Foundations of Lifelong Health Are Built in Early Childhood* (p. 3). Graphic courtesy of the Center for the Developing Child at Harvard University.

also lead to chronic medical conditions, such as osteoporosis, asthma, and diabetes, later in life (Lozoff & Georgieff, 2006).

what if...? Joanna takes her 18-month-old daughter, Cheryl, to a child-care center before going to her full-time job each morning. One day, Cheryl's teacher tells Joanna that Cheryl is less active than the other 18-month-olds in the group. Often, she seems uninterested in her surroundings. Sometimes, she is fussy. Because Cheryl is often out sick, the teacher asks Joanna if she has spoken to her daughter's pediatrician. As they talk, Joanna confides that she is often so rushed in the morning that they don't have time for breakfast. Cheryl's teacher thinks that this nutritional shortcoming may be affecting Cheryl's behavior and development. Of course, one way to fix the situation would be for Joanna to take extra time in the morning to prepare a nutritious breakfast. But, with the Harvard Framework in mind, what other solutions can you think of for problems like this one?

In short, we need to pay special attention to physical development in infancy. When developing biological systems are strengthened by positive early experiences, children are more likely to thrive and grow up to be healthy adults. Conversely, adverse conditions in these early years can have lifelong consequences for both physical and mental well-being.

CHECK YOUR PROGRESS

1. What does it mean when we say that the foundations of lifelong health are built in the early years of life?
2. In what ways is the Harvard framework similar to Bronfenbrenner's bioecological model of development?

## Biology of Health: Physical, Motor, and Perceptual Development

**[ KEY QUESTION ] 2.** In what ways are the first years of life a period of rapid physical, motor, and perceptual development?

Newborn babies must meet physical and motor challenges if they are to adapt successfully to their new world. Over their first two years of life, babies' bodies and skills change rapidly and dramatically. In fact, children grow more within the first 24 months of life than at any other point across the life span—including the dramatic growth spurt of adolescence. Body weight nearly quadruples. Height doubles. Head circumference increases by a third. As each physical change occurs, the child gains new functional motor abilities. Changes in muscle mass and tone, in body composition and in body proportion, make it possible for the infant to sit and stand and even walk within 12 short months. By their second birthday, they are already experienced toddlers, who can run and climb with ease and use both hands in coordinated actions.

Clearly, physical growth and development in these early years is dramatic, even amazing. Nevertheless, researchers have tended to focus more on the cognitive and psychosocial development of this period. Perhaps this is so because the most striking thing about physical, motor, and perceptual development in infancy is that it seems to unfold in a fairly predictable sequence, with few surprises. It seems that nothing—well, almost nothing—will stop the typical healthy child from moving through the physical and motor milestones of infancy. Sitting with support, sitting unaided, crawling, standing, walking, and climbing all almost always occur in that order, for example. True, children in some cultural groups acquire certain abilities more quickly and others more slowly. But virtually every baby, from virtually every culture, sits and reaches around the middle of the first year and walks near the end of that same year. So what is there to learn, you might ask? Before we discuss the details of physical, motor, and perceptual development in infancy, let's take a closer look at that question, focusing in particular on motor development.

## New Directions in Infant Motor Research

If you think that learning to walk is not as interesting or engaging a topic as forming attachments with caregivers or developing language skills, you are not alone. Up until now, at least, scholars and researchers have not devoted a great deal of time to the study of children's motor development (Adolph & Berger, 2006; Adolf & Robinson, 2013; Goodman, 2002). As suggested earlier, this may be because, traditionally, researchers tended to think of motor development as occurring automatically, with maturation. But does this development really happen automatically? Is it genetically preprogrammed?

The application of new techniques, such as neuroimaging, to study children's brain development is revealing much about how the human brain shapes, and is shaped, by early motor experiences (Adolph & Berger, 2006). A new body of cross-cultural research also illustrates the extraordinary range of diversity in normal motor skill acquisition (Adolph, Karasik, & Tamis-LeMonda, 2010; Karasik, Adolph, Tamis-LeMonda, & Bornstein, 2010). As a result of this new research, we are learning more about the complex challenges faced by children as they learn to negotiate the physical world of infancy. (For more about how the brain works to control walking, see the accompanying feature What Happens in the Brain: Beginning to Walk.)

Let's look at new research on learning to walk. After all, learning to walk is one of the great challenges and achievements of childhood—if not of the entire life span. It is the single event that propels children from being almost wholly dependent on adult caregivers to becoming independent. With the ability to walk comes the opportunity for toddlers to explore the ever-expanding world on their own. But infants need resourcefulness, determination, and an uncanny ability to solve problems and overcome obstacles before they can successfully take their first steps. How do they gain all these skills?

Using microanalytic techniques, Karen Adolph and her colleagues have revealed that the infant's everyday experiences with walking occur "in truly massive doses reminiscent of the amount of daily practice that promote performance in world-class musicians" (Adolph, Vereijken, & Shrout, 2003, p. 494). Walking infants practice for a total of more than 6 hours per day. Each hour, 14-month-old infants take more than 2,000 walking steps, travel an accumulated distance equal to 7 football fields, and take 15 (usually minor) falls (Adolph, Robinson, Young, & Gill-Alvarez, 2008). By the end of each day, these infants will have traveled the length of 29 football fields (Adolph et al., 2003; Adolph & Eppler, 2002).

Learning to walk requires not just practice but also a great deal of complex problem solving (Adolph, 2002a, 2002b, 2005; Adolph & Berger, 2006; Adolf & Robinson, 2013). Variability and novelty are the rule, not the exception (Gibson & Schmuckler, 1989; Thelen, 1995). And yet, after only a few months of experience, walking infants can virtually race across the floor.

Learning to walk has dramatic effects on the infant's cognitive, emotional, and social life. The ability to walk transforms the child's sense of competence and sense of self, giving the infant a growing awareness of him- or herself as independent and autonomous. Have you ever seen the pride in a small child's face—the "I did it!" look—when he or she has taken that first step? If so, you have seen evidence of how physical development affects other realms of development.

We next examine physical, motor, and perceptual development in the first two years of life. Although we examine these areas separately, keep in mind that these

Learning to walk is a life-changing achievement that gives toddlers the ability to explore the world on their own.

# What Happens in the Brain

## Beginning to Walk

Have you ever watched a baby beginning to walk? You have to be impressed by the excitement and persistence the baby brings to this challenging milestone. Babies, on average, walk on their own at around 11 months of age. But that first step depends on many other developments. For one thing, babies' legs must grow strong enough to support their body weight. In addition, independent walking depends on maturation in several key brain areas, as well as increased interconnections among these areas. We can see babies developing in these ways as they achieve prewalking milestones like pulling themselves up to a standing position and walking with some support—cruising around the living-room furniture, for example.

Now imagine a baby about to take an unsupported voluntary step. Here's a highly simplified sketch of what happens:

- A command is initiated in the prefrontal cortex to prepare the plans for this movement, based in part on information from the senses.
- The primary motor cortex, the main brain area controlling voluntary movement, receives messages from the prefrontal cortex and dispatches messages to the leg muscles.

Vanessa Davies/Dorling Kindersley/Getty Images

- The basal ganglia, located deep within the brain, act as a filter, controlling which motor actions are carried out and which are suppressed.
- The cerebellum plays a key role in coordinating all these commands. Located at the back of the brain, behind the cortex, the cerebellum is important in motor and spatial coordination and timing.
- The spinal cord carries information from the brain to the muscles via the peripheral nervous system.

This elaborate network enables the baby to do all the things necessary to take a step: adjust posture, control the trunk of the body, maintain balance on one leg, and swing the other leg forward to take a step. The baby's first steps are small, jerky, and uneven. But with growing maturation of body and brain and a great deal of practice, walking patterns strengthen and stabilize. The first awkward steps are soon replaced by smooth, graceful strides that propel the child into a new world of discovery and a new sense of confidence and independence.

Liz Banfield/Jupiter Images/Getty Images

## Initiating Movement

Using visual, auditory, and other sensory information, the **prefrontal cortex** determines the body's position in space, preparing the body for movement. The **primary motor cortex** then generates nerve impulses that will pass down the spinal cord, telling the leg muscles when to contract and how to adjust for future movement.

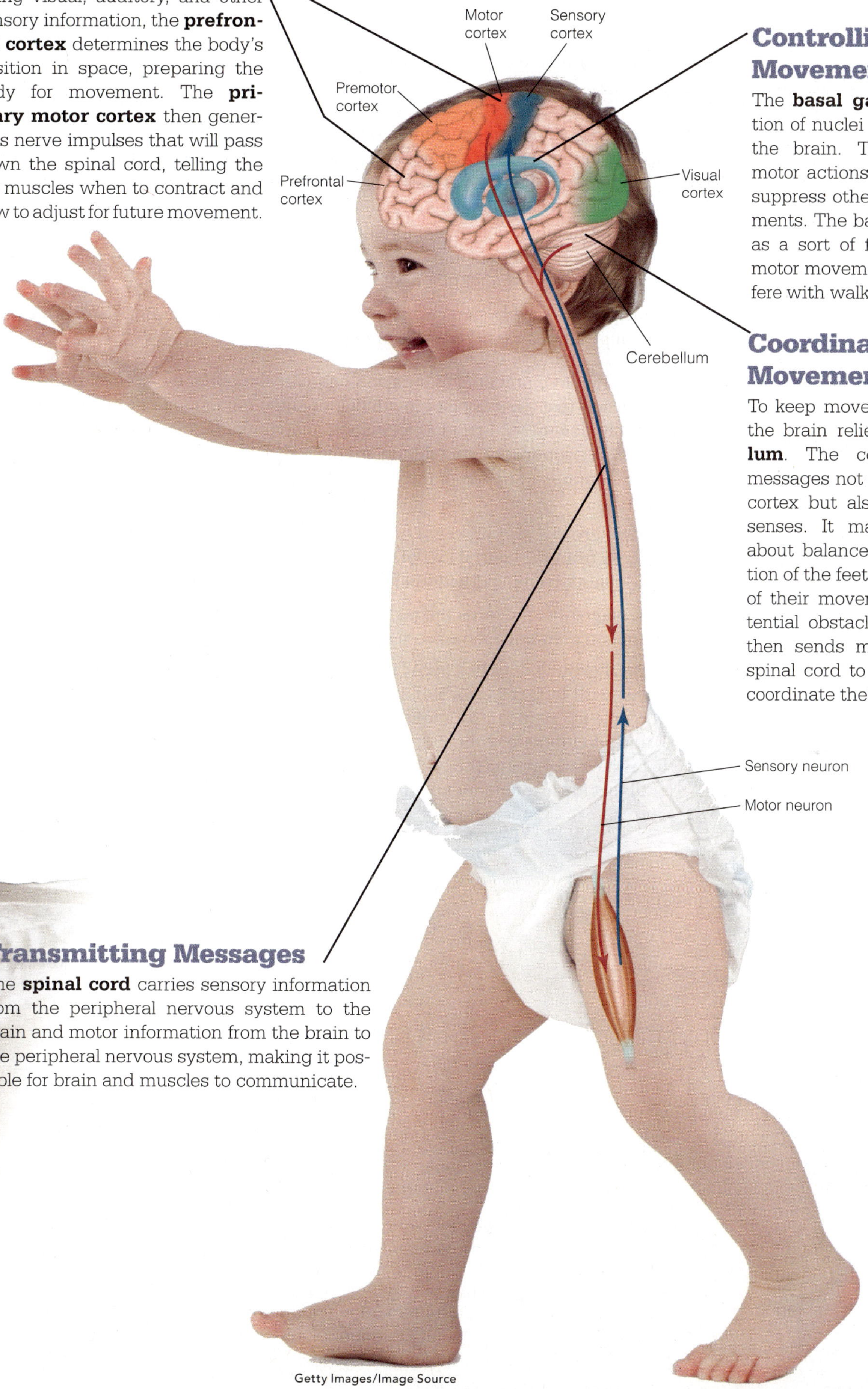


## Controlling Movement

The **basal ganglia** are a collection of nuclei located deep within the brain. They control which motor actions are carried out and suppress other, involuntary movements. The basal ganglia thus act as a sort of filter, blocking other motor movement that would interfere with walking.

## Coordinating Movement

To keep movements coordinated, the brain relies on the **cerebellum**. The cerebellum receives messages not only from the motor cortex but also from the various senses. It manages information about balance, posture, the position of the feet and legs, the speed of their movements, and the potential obstacles in their path. It then sends messages down the spinal cord to the leg muscles to coordinate their actions.

## Transmitting Messages

The **spinal cord** carries sensory information from the peripheral nervous system to the brain and motor information from the brain to the peripheral nervous system, making it possible for brain and muscles to communicate.

Getty Images/Image Source

**cephalocaudal** The direction of physical growth as it proceeds "from head to tail," with the greatest growth beginning at the top of the body and moving gradually downward.

**proximodistal** The direction of physical growth as it proceeds "from near to far," from the central axis of the body outward to the periphery.

**differentiation** The process whereby physical structures become more specialized over time.

different aspects of development are working in a dynamic relationship with each other, each transforming and changing the others.

## Physical Development: How Babies Grow into Toddlers

Usually, physical development is measured in terms of height and weight. But it also refers to changes in areas such as growth, head circumference, and fat-to-muscle ratio. We look more closely at some of these changes after introducing some general patterns that characterize them.

### Principles of Physical Development

Four principles govern physical change in infancy. As you will see later, these principles also have implications for other areas of development.

1. Physical growth proceeds in a **cephalocaudal** direction, or "from head to tail." This means that the greatest growth begins at the top of the body and then moves gradually downward—head before arms and trunk, and arms and trunk before legs. Body proportions also change in this way. As you can see in Figure 5.2, half of the 2-month-old fetus is the head. This proportion shrinks to one-eighth by maturity.
2. Physical growth also proceeds outward, in a **proximodistal** direction; that is, it proceeds from the central axis of the body outward to the periphery, or from near to far—head, trunk, and arms before hands and fingers.
3. Physical growth proceeds through a process of **differentiation**. This means that physical structures become more specialized over time.
4. Physical growth does not occur in steady increments over time. Infants grow in spurts, with longer periods of no growth in between. In fact, infants can grow in height by as much as about 0.3 to 0.6 in. (0.8 to 1.65 cm) in a single day (Lampl, Veldhuis & Johnson, 1992)! Thus, we say that growth is *asynchronous*; that is, not all parts of the body grow at the same rate at the same time. You may recall that in Chapter 2 we noted that the parts of the brain also develop at different rates.

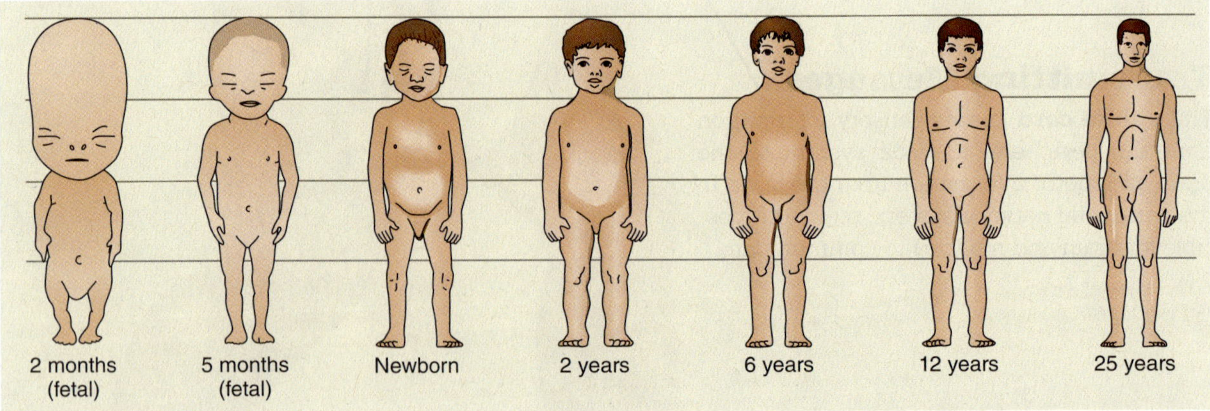


**FIGURE 5.2 Changes in Body Proportions** Body proportions change as children mature. A newborn's head is one-fourth his total length, while an adult's head is one-eighth his or her height.

Adapted with permission from Robbins, W. J., Brady, S., Hogan, A. G., Jackson, C. J., & Greene, C. W., Eds. (1928). *Growth*. New Haven, CT: Yale University Press, p. 118. © Yale University Press.

### Physical Growth Over the First Two Years

**motor development** Advances in functional motor ability and changes in the quality of motor skills.

As noted earlier, children grow more within the first 24 months of life than at any other point across the life span. The average birth weight for a term infant is 7½ lb (3.2 kg). Newborns normally lose 5 to 7% of their birth weight during the first few days of life. They regain this weight by the end of the first 2 weeks as they start to eat more. After this, steady weight gain generally results in a doubling of birth weight by age 5 months and a tripling by 1 year. The average length of a newborn is 20 in. (50 cm). Length increases about 30% by age 5 months, and by more than 50% by 1 year. By age 2, toddlers will stand about 34 in. (86 cm) tall and weigh about 27 to 28 lb (12.25 to 12.7 kg), on average. The average head circumference is 14 in. (35 cm) at birth and increases rapidly to 18.5 in. (47 cm) by age 1 year. The rate of growth then slows, reaching an average of 21.7 in. (55 cm) by age 6 years.

During the first years of life, physical growth and development are typically measured through the use of growth charts (see Figure 5.3). At each visit to the doctor or nurse practitioner, the infant's weight and length are reviewed to make sure that growth is proceeding at a steady rate. Weight gain in the early months of life especially is the most reliable index of the baby's health and development. In contrast, weight loss is a worrisome sign that the child may not be getting adequate nutrition (Rudolf & Logan, 2005). Growth charts are not intended to be used as the only diagnostic instrument, however. For a baby who appears to be healthy and eating well, growth in itself is less likely to be considered important in its own right (Lucas et al., 2007). It is interesting to note, though, that in studies of parents' perspectives, mothers and fathers stated that they viewed physical growth as an indicator of the quality of care they were providing their infant (Lucas et al., 2007).

**what if...?**

Jenna is sitting on the park bench in the playground watching her son, Jalen, play in the sandbox. Jalen is focused and engaged as he busily loads sand into his dump truck. Another mother comes along with her small child. "What a cute little boy," she says to Jenna, as her own little girl moves toward the slide. "How old is he?"

"Fifteen months," answers Jenna, "and how old is yours?"

"She'll have her first birthday in a week. Isn't it hard to believe how much they change in a year?" she says as she follows her child toward the slide.

"It is," replies Jenna. Then, to herself she says, "This little girl is 3 months younger than Jalen, and she can walk and even climb. I wonder why Jalen isn't walking yet."

What if Jenna asked you this question? What would you tell her?

## Motor Development: From Sitting to Jumping

While physical development refers to increases in size and changes in body structure, **motor development** refers to increases in functional motor ability and changes in the quality of motor skills, such as reaching, sitting, and walking. We have seen that the infant's body changes rapidly. Changes in motor skills are equally dramatic. Changes in the central nervous system, which we discuss later, go hand in hand with dramatic development in muscle mass, muscle fiber characteristics, muscle tone, body composition, and body proportion. All these characteristics are vital contributors to the infant's ability to achieve various motor milestones.

### Continuing Motor Development from Birth

In Chapter 4, we emphasized that the newborn is not a "blank slate" at birth. Rather, newborns have a rich repertoire of motor competencies that are elegantly

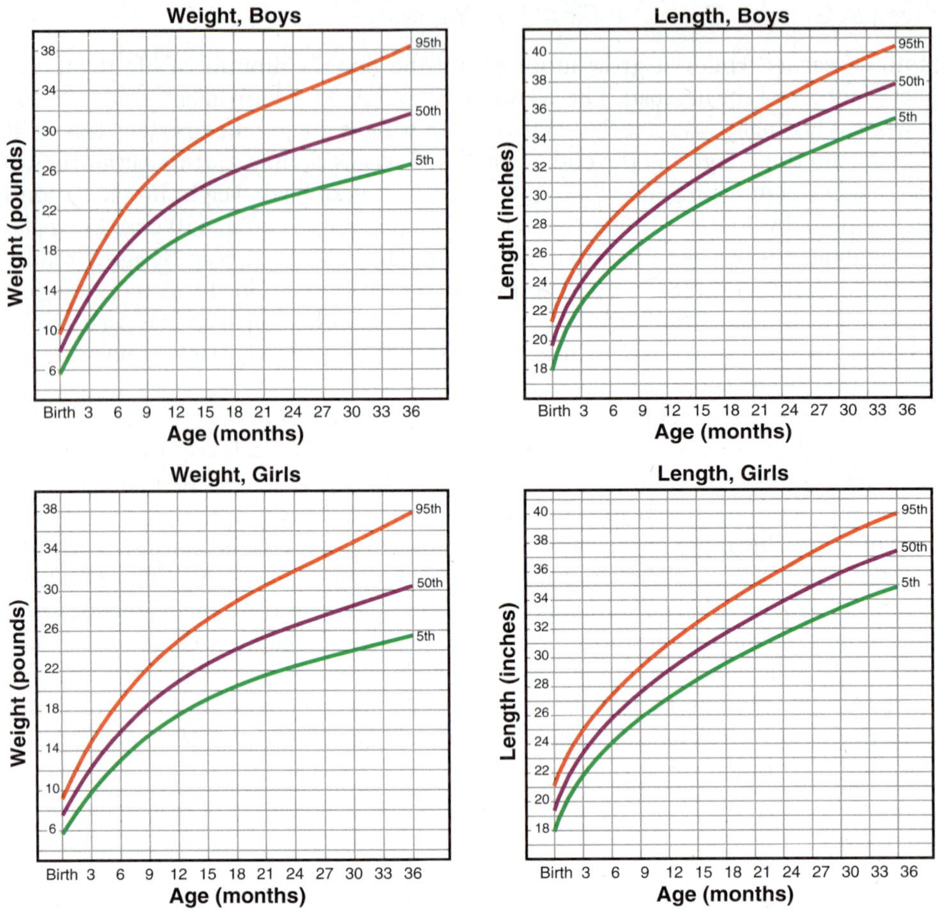


**FIGURE 5.3 Growth Charts, Infants and Toddlers** These charts show weight-for-age and height-for-age data for boys and girls up to age 2. We include the average weight and height (the 50th percentile) as well as weights and heights near the higher and lower ends (the 95th and 5th percentiles).

Adapted from U.S. Centers for Disease Control and Prevention, www.cdc.gov/growthcharts.

designed to enable them to adapt to life outside the womb. We noted that newborns are capable of self-directed, self-initiated, and organized behaviors (Brazelton & Nugent, 1995, 2011). As we learned in the last chapter, many of the so-called motor reflexes, such as hand-grasp and sucking, are neither automatic nor primitive, as their name implies. On the contrary, many of them are purposeful, goal-directed actions.

Although newborns are not a blank slate, they have a long way to go. They still need to be able to support their weight and gain control over their muscles before they can begin to move by themselves and act on their environment. Babies younger than 6 months depend mainly on caregivers for their daily experiences. As their ability to control their movements grows, though, everything seems to draw their interest. Rapid changes in motor skills follow. Babies engage the physical world—are affected by it and affect it—through their bodies. As each physical change occurs, children gain new functional motor abilities.

Newborns move from being dependent and immobile to being able to sit up and stand without support in a matter of months. By the end of the first year, they can take their first steps. By their second birthday, they are experienced toddlers who can run, climb stairs with ease, and use both hands in coordinated actions. Research into stair climbing is described later in the Research Insights feature. Next, we look at some features of motor development during this period of dramatic growth. We also consider two important theories of motor development.

## Gross and Fine Motor Skills

Changes in motor skills fall into two main areas: gross, or large, motor skills, and fine motor skills. **Gross motor skills** involve the use of the large muscles of the legs, arms, back, and shoulders. These are the muscles required in sitting, walking, running, jumping, and climbing. (See the accompanying Research Insights feature for more about climbing.) The development of gross motor skills requires postural control—basically, control over body position and balance. Such skills as sitting without support and walking depend on postural control (Thelen & Smith, 2006).

As babies continue to gain more control over their posture, their ability to move from place to place improves. Pulling to stand is followed quickly by cruising sideways along furniture. Improvements are rapid. After only a few months of experience in crawling and walking, infants can race across the floor upright (Adolph, Vereijken, & Denny, 1998; Adolph, Vereijken, & Shrout, 2003; Bril & Ledebt, 1998).

**Fine motor skills** involve use of the small muscles of the fingers and hands for activities such as grasping objects, holding, cutting, drawing, buttoning, and writing. Here again, skill building is progressive. The prereaching movement of the newborn period, for example, is transformed into a smooth, coordinated reach

**gross motor skills** Motor skills that involve use of the large muscles of the legs, arms, back, and shoulders, which are used in sitting, walking, running, jumping, and climbing.

**fine motor skills** Motor skills that involve use of the small muscles of the fingers and hands, for activities such as grasping objects, holding, cutting, drawing, buttoning, and writing.

### Research Insights: Climbing Stairs

Stair climbing has been considered a major milestone in motor development for decades (Kretch & Adolph, 2013). Still, little research has addressed the circumstances surrounding how infants learn to climb stairs. Clearly, going up or down stairs is more difficult than walking on flat ground. Going up stairs requires walkers to use extra energy, because the muscles must pull up the body against gravity (Andriacchi, Andersson, Fermier, Stern, & Galante, 1980; McFadyen & Winter, 1988). Going down stairs requires walkers to support their weight on a bent leg, maintain their balance on one leg at a time, and control forward momentum (Andriacchi et al., 1980; McFadyen & Winter, 1988).

In a study of stair climbing, 732 parents reported on when and how their infants learned to climb stairs (Berger, Theuring & Adolph, 2007). They reported their children typically mastered going up stairs several months after they began crawling and several weeks before they mastered going down stairs (the mean age for ascent was 10.97 months, compared with 12.53 months for descent). Most infants (94%) crawled up the stairs the first time they ascended by themselves, and a high percentage of infants (76%) turned around and backed down the first time they descended. Other descent strategies included walking, scooting down while sitting, and sliding down face first.

Children with stairs in their homes were more likely to learn to ascend stairs at a younger age, to use backing as a descent strategy, and to be explicitly taught to descend by their parents. Parents' teaching strategies and infants' access to stairs worked together to affect the acquisition of stair-climbing milestones.

Stair climbing vividly illustrates how multiple, interacting factors affect the acquisition of developmental milestones. Stair climbing does require physical ability. But being in a specific environment (one with stairs) and having environmental and social supports (such as helpful parents) also play roles.

© Heide Benser/Corbis

Climbing stairs calls for more effort than walking on flat ground. Both physical ability and environment—having steps available to climb—play roles in developing this ability.

As babies become better able to use the small muscles of their fingers and hands, they grow more adept at reaching and grasping. Grasping a toy with the whole hand, for example, requires less fine-motor skill than picking up a blueberry with two fingers.

motion by 4 months of age. By the end of the first year, babies can use their hands independently and manipulate tools in play. Soon they will be able to use tools such as cups, spoons, and crayons. These emerging fine motor abilities will lead to the development of children's art. The ability to draw will evolve from simple scribbles to representations of people and scenes, as children move into the preschool years.

We can see the three principles of physical development mentioned earlier at work in the development of gross and fine motor skills. For example, recall that physical development occurs in a cephalocaudal direction, from head to foot. Accordingly, babies can hold their heads erect before they can push up with their arms, and can push up with their arms before they can stand up on their legs. We can see examples of both the proximodistal principle and differentiation in infant reaching. Reaching progresses from batting motions in the first months of life to more refined reaching and grasping motions by 12 months of age. By the end of the second year, reaching is approaching that of the typical adult profile (Berthier & Keen, 2006).

### Motor Milestones and Milestone Tables

**Motor milestones** can be defined as motor behaviors that emerge over time, forming the building blocks for growth and continued learning. These milestones are identified according to the average age at which children demonstrate certain skills, abilities, and physical attributes. Table 5.1 presents an example of some major motor milestones. As you look at these developmental milestones, remember that children develop at their own speed and pace. Thus, there is a wide age range of individual and ethnic variability in the achievement of milestones. Milestones merely help organize and summarize this information easily and clearly.

Milestone tables are often used to identify developmental delay (Kelly, Sacker, Schoon, & Nazroo, 2006). Early identification is important so that interventions can begin as soon as possible. Delay is said to occur when a child does not reach developmental milestones at the expected age. However, as mentioned, milestones should be viewed with some caution. The timing for reaching specific milestones varies widely among typically developing children. Thus, children who have not achieved milestones at the average age may simply be experiencing individual variations. Furthermore, some children progress faster in some areas of development than in others, so that progress in one area does not necessarily predict progress in another area.

**motor milestones** Motor behaviors that emerge over time and are identified according to the average age at which children develop and demonstrate certain skills or physical attributes.

## Theories of Motor Development

When we look at the motor milestones over the first two years, we can see that they emerge in a regular sequence. Sitting with support, sitting unaided, standing, walking,

**Table 5.1** Examples of Motor Milestones

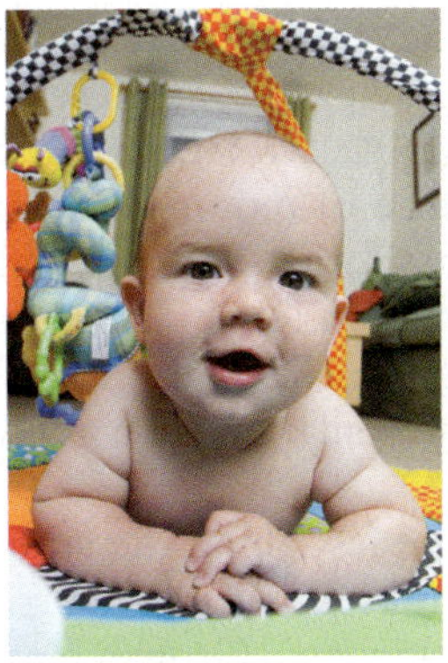

Alex Bramwell/Flickr RF/Getty Images

Victoria Blackie/Getty Images

Mel Yates/Getty Images

Leanne Temme/Getty Images

| Skill | Average Age of Attainment | Age Range in Which 90% of Infants Achieve This Skill |
|---|---|---|
| Holds head erect and steady in upright position. | 6 weeks | 3 weeks–4 months |
| Pushes self up with arms when lying on stomach. | 2 months | 3 weeks–4 months |
| Grasps cube. | 3 months, 3 weeks | 2–7 months |
| Rolls over from back to side. | 4.5 months | 2–7 months |
| Sits unsupported. | 7 months | 5–9 months |
| Crawls. | 7 months | 5–11 months |
| Pulls self to standing position. | 8 months | 5–12 months |
| Walks unassisted. | 11 months, 3 weeks | 9–17 months |
| Builds tower with two cubes. | 13 months, 3 weeks | 10–19 months |
| Walks up stairs with help. | 16 months | 12–23 months |
| Jumps. | 23 months, 2 weeks | 17–30 months |

Adapted with permission of John Wiley & Sons, Inc., from Harwood, R., Miller, S. A., & Vasta, R. (2008.) *Child Psychology: Development in a Changing Society* (5th ed.). Hoboken, NJ: Wiley, p. 158, Table 5.3; based on information from Bayley, N. (1969). *Manual for the Bayley Scales of Infant Development.* New York: Psychological Corporation; and Bayley, N. (1993). *Bayley Scales of Infant Development* (2nd ed.). New York: Psychological Corporation.

and climbing almost always occur in that order, for instance. At the same time, as noted, there is a considerable age range within which individual infants achieve these skills. Some infants crawl at 5 months, for example, while others do not crawl until around 11 months. These two aspects of development form the basis of two major theories of motor development in infancy: maturational theory and dynamic systems theory.

**maturational theory** A theory of motor development proposing that motor behaviors develop in a relatively uniform sequence as the muscles and the brain mature. This approach assumes that motor behaviors are genetically predetermined and develop independently of experience.

## Maturational Theory

**Maturational theory**, which dates from the first part of the 20th century, has been the most widely accepted theory of motor development (Bayley, 1935; Gesell, 1928; McGraw, 1932). Researchers such as Arnold Gesell, Myrtle McGraw, and Nancy Bayley used longitudinal studies to document the sequence of motor behaviors displayed by infants. They found the sequence generally uniform and universal. As a result, they attributed this early motor development to maturational factors. In their view, development occurs relatively automatically as the muscles and brain mature. This approach assumes that motor behaviors are genetically predetermined and develop independently of experience.

Maturational theory is supported by longitudinal data describing the attainment of six gross motor milestones by children aged 4 to 24 months in several countries (see Figure 5.4). The data, collected as part of the WHO Multicentre Growth Reference Study (2006), show normal variations in ages of milestone achievement among healthy children. About 90% of the children in the sample achieved the milestones in the same sequence.

Critics point out, however, that the maturational legacy paid too little attention to the roles that learning, environmental influences, and children themselves play in shaping motor behavior (Adolph et al., 2008). Recent work suggests that motor development does not really unfold automatically (for example, Adolph & Berger, 2006; Thelen & Smith, 2006). Instead, it involves a great deal of problem solving on the part of the infant. We saw this in the earlier discussion of learning to walk. Evidence also indicates that motor development in infancy is influenced by cultural and environmental factors. Poverty and poor nutrition can affect the progress of infant growth and development, for example. So can child-rearing practices, parents' expectations, and even the season of birth (Benson, 1993).

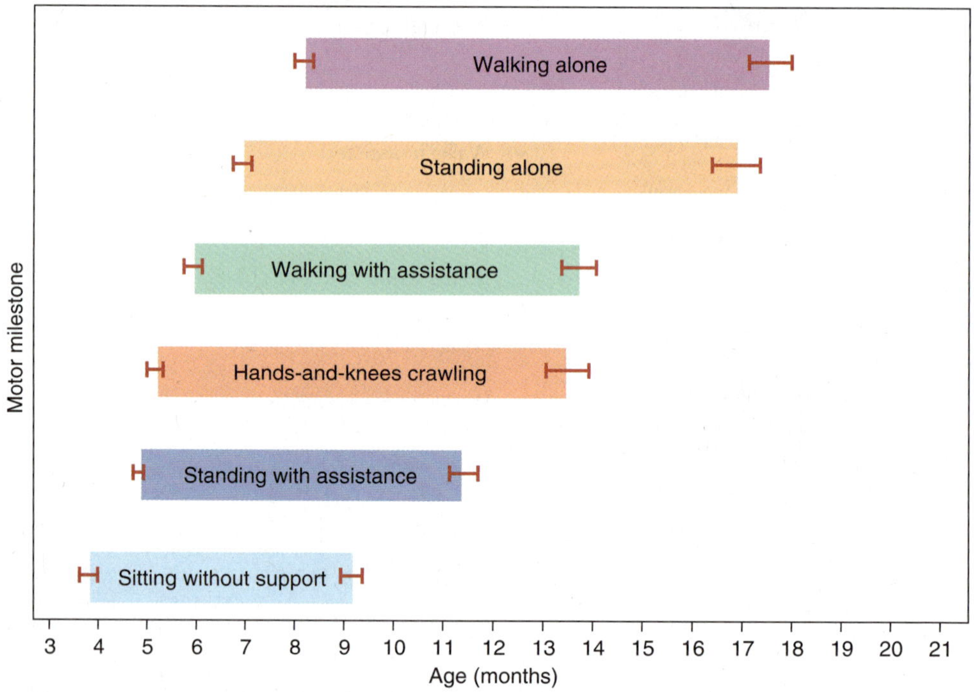


**FIGURE 5.4 Motor Milestones for a Sample of Infants from Various Countries** The chart shows the ages at which a sample of children aged 4 to 24 months in Ghana, India, Norway, Oman, and the United States reached several motor milestones. You can see that the children varied in the age at which they reached each milestone. About 90% of the children achieved the milestones in the same sequence, though, supporting the idea that maturation plays a role in early motor development.

Adapted with permission from Heywood, A. H., Marshall, T., & Heywood, P. F. (1991). Motor Development and Nutritional Status of Young Children in Madang, Papua New Guinea. *Papua New Guinea Medical Journal 34*, 109–116.

WHEN SYSTEMS CONNECT

## Dynamic Systems Theory

While acknowledging the contribution of maturational theory, contemporary motor researchers have proposed a more dynamic approach (Adolph et al., 2008; Einspieler, Prechtl, Bos, Ferrari, & Coini, 2005; Ferrari, 2011; Thelen & Smith, 2006). These researchers, who include Esther Thelen, Karen Adolph, and Heinz Prechtl, have applied systems theory to the study of motor development in infancy.

**Dynamic systems theory** is a developmental theory that views infants' motor development in terms of a complex system of interacting components (Thelen & Smith, 2006; Thelen & Spencer, 1998). These components include brain organization, muscle strength, joint structures and range of motion, motivational and arousal levels, the support surface, and the task itself. Furthermore, in this view, reaching a particular motor milestone is not an isolated event. Rather, it affects all other aspects of development (Adolf & Robinson, 2013).

This shift in emphasis has led some researchers to conclude that early motor experiences are an essential agent for developmental change. Every reach, every step, and every social encounter sets the stage for the next. The acquisition of any single developmental skill, such as reaching or stepping, brings about changes in person-environment interactions that set the stage for future development (Campos, et al., 2000). As a result, much infant motor development research today crosses traditionally separate domains—motor, perceptual, cognitive, and psychosocial.

*LWA/Dann Tardif/Getty Images*

According to dynamic systems theory, reaching a motor milestone affects all other aspects of development. Now that this toddler can walk, for example, he will interact differently with his environment and those in it, setting the stage for future development.

# Sensory and Perceptual Development: Taking in the World

Even if their motor interactions with the environment are limited in the beginning, infants come into the world able to experience it through their senses—through looking, hearing, and touching, and taste and smell (Kellmann & Arterberry, 2006; Spelke, 1991; Spelke & Newport, 1998). **Sensation** involves detecting and discriminating information from the senses, such as distinguishing different sounds or colors. **Perception** involves recognizing and interpreting objects and people through one or more of the senses. We look next at three critical areas of sensory and perceptual development: touch, hearing, and vision. We then review a theory that emphasizes the importance of experience in perceptual development.

## The Sense of Touch

We have already seen how important the sense of touch is to the newborn's development. Over the first years of life, touch and the ability to integrate visual information with touch play an increasingly important role in perceptual development. Infants are at first limited in what actions they can take, largely because they lack control of their heads and trunks. But even young infants can see and touch objects, bring them to their mouths, and manipulate them.

The ability to perceive the size, texture, and hardness of objects through touch develops over the first 6 to 9 months of life. This development parallels changes in how infants use their hands to explore objects (Galloway & Thelen, 2004). With experience in visually guiding their reaching, infants can increasingly coordinate moving their arms toward an object and actually grasping the object.

As the sense of touch continues to develop, infants learn more and more about the physical properties of objects, and they use this newly acquired knowledge to plan future actions. For example, infants rely on what they touch, see, and feel when crawling or walking over different surfaces to continuously update their actions. They can then adjust their actions to fit the ever-changing demands of, say, walking on smooth indoor surfaces, grassy yards, and graveled drives. Perception and action, in other words, are closely related (Gibson, 2003).

**dynamic systems theory** A theory that describes motor development as a complex system of mutually interacting components in continuous interaction with each other.

**sensation** The detection and discrimination of sensory information.

**perception** The process of recognizing and interpreting objects and people through one or more of the senses.

## Hearing

As we have already noted, most babies are born with fully functional auditory systems. As infants experience sound, the brain's auditory cortex explodes with new connections and growth. Especially during the first year, the auditory system of infants is shaped dramatically by experience with sound.

Perhaps most important is exposure to speech (Kuhl, 2004; Pinker, 1994). Infants exposed to speech quickly learn, for example, to identify discrete units of speech sound. Spoken language grows out of this experience. Infants cannot produce recognizable words until they are about a year old. Nevertheless, younger infants have remarkable abilities to distinguish among speech sounds, to recognize names of familiar objects, and to interpret voice tone (Imada et al., 2006). By 12 or 13 months, we can see a dramatic upswing in the infant's understanding of specific word sounds. (We discuss language acquisition in more detail in the next chapter.)

What happens if an infant has a hearing loss? Each year, as many as 3 out of every 1,000 babies born in the United States are born with hearing loss.

*Everyday stories*

"OUR BABY CAN'T HEAR!" Carmen's second child, Yolanda, was born with no apparent health problems. However, a newborn hearing screening revealed that Yolanda was profoundly deaf. Carmen and her family were stunned. The pregnancy was normal, and both Carmen and her husband, Joe, had normal hearing, as did their older daughter. They knew of no hearing issues in either of their families. But according to the American Academy of Audiology, most babies born with hearing loss are born healthy with no family history of hearing problems (American Academy of Audiology Clinical Practice Guidelines: Diagnosis, Treatment and Management of Children and Adults with Central Auditory Processing Disorder, 2010). Carmen and Joe were reassured after their meeting with an early intervention team. The team's teacher of the deaf and hard of hearing (TOD) told them that deaf and hard of hearing children generally grow up to be productive, well-adjusted adults who work, drive, go to college, marry, have children, and, in fact, are not much different from the adults that hearing children become.

A consequence of hearing loss in young children involves language and literacy development (Lederberg, Schick, & Spencer, 2013). For infants and toddlers with hearing loss, auditory input is limited or distorted. Consequently, they are at risk for delays in speech and language development. Early identification is thus extremely important for children with any type of hearing loss. When infants with hearing loss are identified prior to 6 months and receive appropriate early intervention services, their language development can proceed similarly to that of peers (Yoshinaga-Itano, 1999).

Jose M. Osorio/ZUMA Press/Newscom

Even for a child with a cochlear implant, sign language and spoken language can still play an important role.

Increasingly, children who are born deaf are receiving cochlear implants in order to improve their ability to hear, understand and, eventually, speak. The surgery consists of placing a small electronic device into the ear that bypasses the inner ear's damaged nerve cells and transmits sound signals to the brain. A growing body of research has demonstrated that children who receive cochlear implants when they are very young make greater gains in acquiring age-appropriate language skills than children implanted when they are older (Houston, Beer, Bergeson, Chin, Pisoni & Miyamoto, 2012).

## Vision

Although newborns can see more than was previously thought, as we mentioned in Chapter 4, their vision is rather limited (Braddick & Atkinson, 2011). These limitations result from the immaturity of their eyes and the visual structures in their brains. Newborns can, however, focus on objects between 10 and 12 in. (about 25 and 30 cm) away (Brazelton & Nugent, 2011). This means they can easily see many of the things most important to them: their caregivers' faces and their own hands and fingers, for example. Studies show that within a few days after birth, infants prefer looking at an image of their mother's face to that of a stranger. They seem to attend most to points of highest contrast. Thus, they may depend on large, high-contrast stimuli, like the boundary of the mother's hairline, to recognize her face (Atkinson, 2000; Kellmann & Arterberry, 2006; Mercuri, Baranello, Domenico, Cesarini, & Ricci, 2007).

*Visual acuity*, or the ability to distinguish detail, improves from about 20/400 at birth to 20/30 at around 8 months. This change is due largely to an explosion of synapse formation in visual areas of the cerebral cortex. Over the next several years, acuity improves gradually, to adult levels of 20/20. The most dramatic change, though, occurs over that first 8 months!

What about color vision? When can a child see all the colors of the rainbow? By about 2 to 3 months of age, infants' color vision is very similar to that of adults, and they can discriminate many colors (Brown, 1990; Kellmann & Arterberry, 2006). So within the first few months of life, infants appear to become sensitive to the same spectrum of color as adults (Franklin & Davies, 2004).

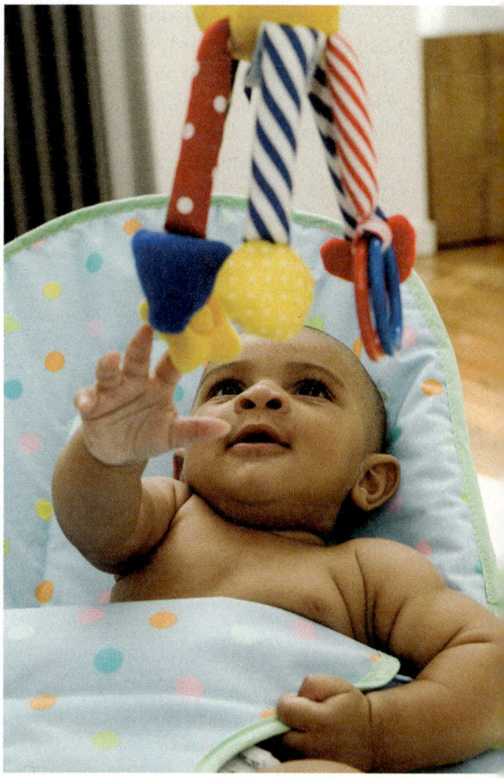
*Vanessa Davies/Dorling Kindersley/Getty Images*

Visually, young babies are most attentive to areas of highest contrast.

## Perceptual Development

While sensory development involves distinguishing different sounds, sights, and other sensations, perceptual development involves giving meaning to these sensations. During the first years of life, infants and toddlers are learning to discriminate among the different faces, shapes, and sounds in their environment. In the process, they are learning to interpret and attach meaning to these objects and events. They learn to "take in" information from the environment that is significant to them, whether it is the expression on a caregiver's face, the sound of an oncoming car, or the tastes and textures of different objects in their environment.

In the early months of life, babies' perceptual abilities are linked to the maturity of their sensory systems. But these abilities are also influenced by the experiences the babies encounter. The **ecological theory of perceptual development**, proposed by Eleanor Gibson and James Gibson, especially emphasizes the importance of the environment and infants' abilities to take in important information from it (Gibson, 1979; Gibson, 2003; Gibson & Schmuckler, 1989). As infants act on the world, they learn to differentiate information in their environment and discover **affordances**—opportunities for exploration. Different objects in the infant's environment provide different kinds of affordances. A soft teddy bear provides opportunities for touching and cuddling, more than mouthing or exploration, for example. A toy with a handle affords opportunities for grasping and manipulation, more than holding and cuddling.

Another example of how experience affects perception is Eleanor Gibson and Richard Walk's (1960) classic work on infants' perception of depth, known as the "visual cliff" experiment. Babies typically learn to crawl during the second half of their first year. To examine the effects of crawling on the development of depth perception, the researchers placed infants who could crawl on one side of a Plexiglas surface that created the illusion of a drop-off. Even though the babies could see their mothers at the other side of the "deep end" of the surface the babies would not cross it. The infants

**ecological theory of perceptual development** Theory that emphasizes the importance of the environment and the infants' abilities to get information from and act on the environment. The concept of affordance is central to this idea; the child acts on what the environment affords, as it is appropriate.

**affordances** Opportunities for exploration of an environment.

**FIGURE 5.5 The Visual Cliff** In a visual cliff experiment, researchers place infants on one side of a Plexiglas surface that creates the illusion of a drop-off. Infants of crawling age will not cross the glass, an indication that they have developed depth perception.

could tell the surface was solid by patting it. Still, they did not cross. (See Figure 5.5.) Gibson and Walk saw this as evidence that infants of crawling age had gained enough experience with depth to know that it could mean danger. Thus, with the ability to move around, infants gain an appreciation of depth.

Over the first two years of life, children's ability to interact with the world expands, and their perceptual world becomes increasingly organized. The development of perceptual capacities enables children to learn about the world of people, to begin to classify information, to make sense of the world of objects and space, and to comprehend speech. All these abilities combine to provide the foundation for the child's cognitive understanding of the world of objects and people.

✓CHECK YOUR PROGRESS

1. What do the studies on learning to walk discussed in this section tell us about the nature of infant development?
2. How do physical and motor development differ?
3. What is the evidence for the maturational approach to infant motor development? What are the limitations of this approach?
4. What does dynamic systems theory tell us about the relationship between motor development and cognitive and emotional development?
5. How does experience influence perceptual development in infancy?

## The Developing Brain: Biology of Health

**[ KEY QUESTION ] 3. What role does the brain play in the rapid physical, motor, and perceptual development of the first years of life?**

The dramatic developments of sensory and motor skills in infants are made possible by equally dramatic changes in the brain. During the first three years of life, the brain changes rapidly in size and structure (Kagan, 2006; Nelson, 2004; Nelson et al., 2008; Shonkoff & Phillips, 2000). We focus here on how the brain controls body movements during the first years of life. We begin with a brief review of a vital structural change in the brains of babies.

## An Exuberant Burst of Synapse Formation

The brain triples in weight from birth to about the age of 3. But it is what is happening to the *structure* of the brain during this period that is especially significant for the baby's growth and development. At birth, the neurons in the baby's brain are not well connected. The dramatic changes in the structure of the brain during this period are due largely to the enormous growth of new dendrites and synapses, which enable neurons to connect. Forming and reinforcing these connections are the key tasks of early brain development.

After birth, the cerebral cortex produces most of its synaptic connections in a massive burst of synapse formation known as "the exuberant period." This period varies in different parts of the cerebral cortex. It begins earlier in primary sensory regions, like

### Focus On: Santiago Ramon y Cajal and Wilder Penfield, Pioneers in Brain Research

The great Spanish neuroanatomist and Nobel Prize winner Santiago Ramon y Cajal laid the foundation for the modern study of the brain around the turn of the 20th century. He had originally intended to be a painter, and studied anatomy with his father, a surgeon, to learn more about the human body. Fascination with the human skeleton led him to study the anatomy of the human brain. Cajal was the first to discover that nerve cells, or neurons, were the fundamental building blocks of the brain. He then proposed that all nerve cells in the brain contain a nucleus, a single axon, and many dendrites, and that each nerve cell forms synapses and disseminates information in a single direction across the brain in very predictable patterns.

As scientists began to learn more about the anatomy of the cortex, they also began to discover which regions of the brain governed each of the senses. Building on the work of Cajal, neurosurgeon Dr. Wilder Penfield, in Montreal, attempted to compose a detailed map of the brain. He used brain operations to confirm the location of the different senses, including the primary motor cortex. Because the brain contains no pain receptors, surgery could be carried out with a local anesthetic, meaning that Dr. Penfield's patients could remain fully conscious during surgery and, therefore, were able to report their experiences. He explored much of the surface of the cerebral cortex in more than a thousand subjects. The experiments in stimulating the cortex enabled Penfield to develop a complete map of the motor cortex, known as the *motor homunculus*, as shown in Figure 5.6.

The most striking aspect of this map is that the areas assigned to various body parts on the cortex are proportional *not* to their size, but rather to the complexity of the movements that they can perform. Hence, the areas for the hands and face are especially large compared with those for the rest of the body. This should not surprise us, because the speed and dexterity of human hand and mouth movements are precisely what give us two of our most distinctly human faculties: the ability to use tools and the ability to speak. Penfield's pioneering work on the localization of brain function has been extended by many scientists, such as the Nobel Prize-winning neuroscientist Eric Kandel, whose groundbreaking work is featured in Chapter 12.

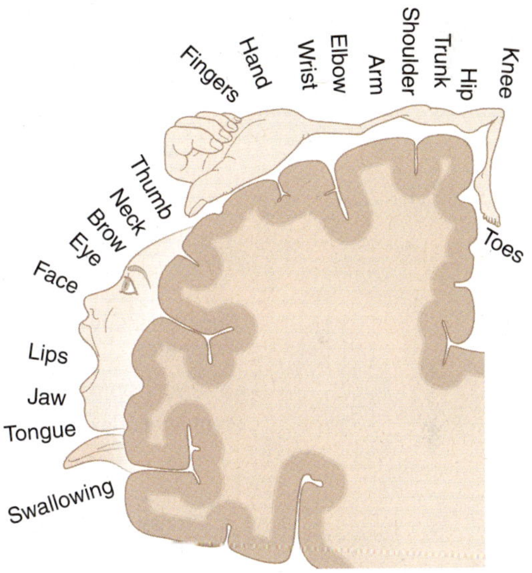


**FIGURE 5.6 The Motor Homunculus** The motor homunculus is a map of the motor cortex. The areas assigned to various body parts are proportional not to the size of their respective body parts but to the complexity of the movements they can perform.

Adapted with permission of John Wiley & Sons, Inc., from Comer, R., & Gould, E. (2013). *Psychology Around Us* (2nd ed.). Hoboken, NJ: Wiley, p. 158, Figure 4.12; based on Penfield, W., & Rasmussen, T. (1950). *The Cerebral Cortex of Man*. New York: Macmillan.

the visual cortex and the primary touch area of the cortex. It develops somewhat later in the temporal and frontal lobes—brain areas involved in higher cognitive and emotional functions. The process of synapse formation continues through much of the first year and well into the second year of life (Monk, Webb, & Nelson, 2001; Thomas & Johnson, 2008).

## The Brain and Motor Functions

Now let's examine specifically how the brain influences the development of the infant's motor system. As we have seen, all of the body's voluntary movements are controlled by the brain. So many different structures in the brain are involved in motor functions that practically the entire brain contributes. One of the brain areas most involved in controlling voluntary movements is the motor cortex, located in the rear portion of the frontal lobe (see Figure 5.7). This area includes three parts: the primary motor cortex, the supplementary motor areas, and the premotor cortex. The primary motor cortex directs all voluntary movements. The other two areas work at a higher level, "planning and executing more complex sequences of movements" (Eliot, 1999, p. 264).

Let's take a look at how the motor cortex functions. Imagine an infant reaching to pick up a toy. Electrical activity increases in the frontal region of the infant's cortex. The neurons in the frontal cortex then send impulses to activate the motor cortex itself. Using information supplied by the visual cortex, the motor cortex plans the path the baby's hand will follow in reaching for the toy. The motor cortex then calls on other parts of the brain, such as the cerebellum, to help activate the necessary muscles involved in the action. The axons of the neurons of the primary motor cortex descend all the way into the spinal cord, where they relay information to the motor neurons of the spinal cord. These neurons are connected directly to

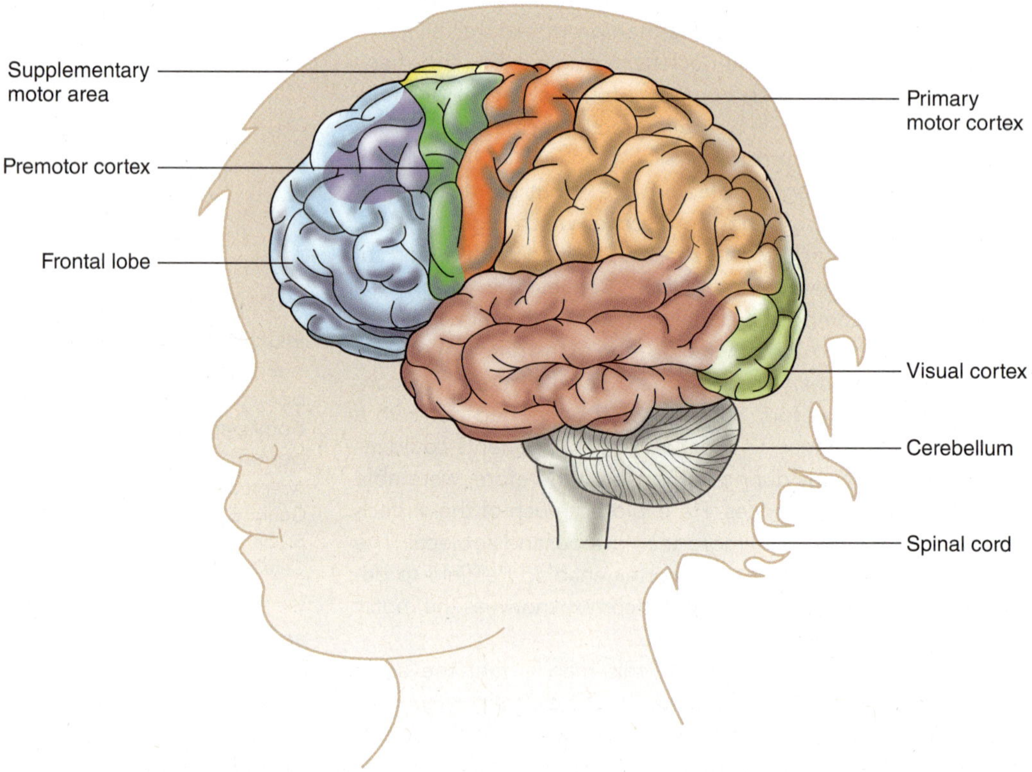


**FIGURE 5.7 The Motor Cortex** The motor cortex includes three parts. The primary motor cortex directs all voluntary movements. The supplementary motor area and the premotor cortex are involved in planning and executing more complex sequences of movements.

## Research Insights: Mirror Neurons

In the early 1990s, Italian researchers made an astonishing, and quite unexpected, discovery (Iacaboni, 2008). They had implanted electrodes in the brains of several macaque monkeys to study the animals' brain activity during different motor actions, including the clutching of food. One day, as a researcher reached for his own food, he noticed neurons begin to fire in the monkeys' premotor cortex—the same area that showed activity when the animals made a similar hand movement. How could this be happening when the monkeys were sitting still and merely watching him?

The answer, as you may recall from Chapter 4, involves *mirror neurons*. This special class of brain cells fire not only when an individual performs an action but also when the individual observes someone else perform that action. These neurons are activated not only when the infant is engaged in a task—reaching for a toy, for instance—but when the infant watches another person reaching for the toy. Thus, they can help explain how observational learning occurs. Of course, even the simplest motor abilities result from complex interactions among many different kinds of neurons. Nevertheless, research into mirror neurons can help us to reinterpret the neurological underpinning of infant motor development and explain one way by which even very young infants learn complex motor actions.

the muscles and cause them to contract. In contracting, the muscles pull on the bones of the arm and hand. This produces the movement that enables the infant to pick up the toy. To ensure that all these movements are fast, precise, and coordinated, the nervous system constantly receives sensory information from the outside world and uses it to adjust the hand's path. These adjustments depend chiefly on the cerebellum, which receives information about the body's position in space from the sensory receptors. To learn more about mirror neurons, see the Research Insight feature above.

Complex interactions in the brain make it possible for this baby to pick up and manipulate blocks.

pruning The elimination of unused neural circuits, which streamlines neural processing and makes the remaining circuits work more quickly and efficiently.

## Pruning: Refining the Brain Through Experience

Brain development is activity dependent. This means that the electrical activity in every circuit, or pathway, of neurons—sensory, motor, emotional, cognitive—shapes the way that circuit is put together. Every experience in infancy—whether it is reaching out for a toy or learning to walk—excites certain neural connections while leaving others inactive. Those that are consistently turned on over time will be strengthened. Those that are rarely excited may be dropped away. As neuroscientists sometimes say, "Cells that fire together, wire together" (Shonkoff & Phillips, 2000).

Recall that we began this section by saying that the first few years of life are a period of rapid synapse formation. It is synapses that enable neural circuits to be formed. During this time, the brain actually overproduces synaptic connections—some 50 percent more than will be preserved in adulthood. At the same time, other synapses are being eliminated.

The elimination of synapses is referred to as **pruning**. Pruning streamlines neural processing, making the remaining circuits work more quickly and efficiently. Pruning takes place throughout life but is far more common in infancy. (Pruning also characterizes adolescent brain development, as you will see in Chapter 14.) During this period, a child's experiences—sensory, motor, emotional, and intellectual—determine through pruning which connections will be strengthened and which will not.

### what if...?

Today, many babies spend much of the day in devices that restrict or prevent movement. They are carried in backpacks, left in car seats, placed in playpens, put in walkers, wheeled in strollers, and otherwise confined to a range of restrictive devices. Given what we have seen about experience-dependent brain development, what are the implications of this practice for the development of their motor skills?

A child's brain is built over a succession of sensitive periods. As noted in Chapter 2, a sensitive period is a time during which the child is extremely sensitive to a particular kind of environmental input. If the environmental input does not occur at that time, development will be compromised. Strong development through sensitive periods in the early years increases the probability of positive outcomes. Weak development increases the odds of later difficulties.

### Everyday stories

CROSSED EYES *Binocular vision*, the ability to see with both eyes together, typically emerges in the fourth or fifth month of life. By then, babies' brains have learned how to fuse the pictures coming in from both their right and left eyes into a single image. Because this is a sensitive period for vision development, anything that interferes with the infant's vision may compromise the infant's visual abilities. Babies who have crossed eyes, for example, will fail to develop binocular vision if the problem persists beyond 6 to 8 months of age. Thus, early detection and treatment of crossed eyes is essential.

### CHECK YOUR PROGRESS

1. What are some of the parts of the brain involved in motor activity?
2. What role does pruning play in brain development in infancy?

# Foundations of Health: Nutrition and Health

**[ KEY QUESTION ] 4.** What are some important nutrition concerns regarding infants and toddlers?

We turn next to promoting good health in infants and toddlers. The period from birth to 2 years of age is a critical window for the promotion of growth and health. Optimal growth and health, in turn, require optimal nutrition.

We begin this section by summarizing some guidelines about nutrition for infants and toddlers. We then discuss several issues related to poor nutrition.

## Nutrition for Infants and Toddlers

We've seen that the first year is when humans grow fastest. To support that growth good nutrition during infancy and the toddler years is essential. But nutrition is about more than getting plenty of nutrients. During the first two years of life, infants graduate from breast milk or formula to table foods. They learn about taste and texture. They also learn about feeling full and feeling hungry, as well as about how to signal their needs and likes and dislikes to caregivers. And, importantly, they learn to feed themselves.

Therefore, the goal during the first two years is to ensure that infants and toddlers learn to regulate their own food intake. That way, they will learn to eat the right foods in the right amounts for healthy growth and development. Helping infants and toddlers reach this goal can have a lifetime effect on their health and weight.

### Birth to 6 Months: Breast Milk and Formula

Babies get all the nutrients they need from breast milk or formula for the first 6 months. As we noted in Chapter 4, the American Academy of Pediatrics recommends that babies be breast-fed exclusively for about the first 6 months. Human milk is ideally composed for optimal infant growth and development (Penn, Altshuler, Small, Taylor, Dobkins, & Schmid-Schönbein, 2012). It is naturally high in cholesterol and fat, both of which are needed during the first year of life to support brain development (Sacchetti et al., 2009).

Several studies have identified other potential benefits of breast-feeding. In a nationally representative sample of U.S. children, for example, researchers found an association between breast-feeding and language and motor skill development (Dee, Li, Lee, & Grummer-Strawn, 2007). There is evidence, too, suggesting that breast-feeding may also help to prevent obesity. A meta-analysis of studies investigating the association between infant feeding and obesity later in life found that breast-feeding was associated with a reduced risk of obesity, compared with formula feeding. That said, other genetic and environmental determinants, such as socioeconomic status, parental obesity, smoking, birth weight, and rapid weight gain in infancy, may also be important risk factors for childhood obesity. (We discuss childhood obesity later in this chapter and again in Chapters 8 and 11.)

Between 4 and 6 months, some babies are ready to try a few spoonsful of fortified baby cereal liberally mixed with breast milk or formula. At first, the consistency must be thin. As babies learn to work their mouths, it can be made thicker. Cereal should not be a primary source of nutrition, however, and it should never be offered in a bottle. In order to take in even semisolid foods of this type, infants must be able to sit up with some support and have good control of their heads and necks (Kliegman, Behrman, Jenson, & Stanton, 2007).

### Six to 12 Months: Solid Foods

Breast milk and formula continue to be a major source of nutrition up to age 12 months. Babies are ready for solid food when their birth weight has doubled, when they can indicate fullness by turning their heads away or not opening their mouths, and when they show interest in food when others are eating. Of course, babies' first "solid" foods are pureed. It is best to introduce one new food at a time, and wait a few days in between to check for any allergic reaction or indigestion. Parents typically start with cereals and fruit and then introduce vegetables. Strained meats are added to the diet at about 8 months (Kliegman et al., 2007).

Even very young babies can demonstrate clear food likes and dislikes; and many prefer the sweeter taste of fruits to the somewhat acidic taste of vegetables. As we will discuss in Chapter 8, there is no point in getting into a conflict with children about food. Instead, it is best to continue to offer a variety of healthy foods and let them learn to regulate their appetite along the way.

Babies' first teeth begin to emerge at around 6 months of age, accompanied by drooling and mouthing of any object they can get their hands around. Soft toast, crackers, and teething biscuits help soothe the discomfort associated with teething; they also serve to introduce babies to chewing. By 8 months, they can handle finger foods, such as noodles and small pieces of cooked fruit and vegetables (Kliegman et al., 2007). More often than not, finger foods are more tools of exploration than nutrition, as babies squeeze, mash, wipe, and throw food about. This messiness is normal, and often a source of amusement for family members, especially siblings.

*Image Source/Getty Images*

Messiness is an inevitable result when babies begin to feed themselves.

*Everyday stories*

"I CAN FEED MYSELF!" By 8 months, a baby girl is ready to use her new fine-motor skills to pick up and eat food. But before she puts the food in her mouth, she enjoys playing with it—fingering it, squeezing it, smearing it, throwing it. The baby is not trying to test her parents when she throws her food on the floor. She cannot yet speak, but if you watch her face, you will see that she is enthralled. This is not just about eating; it is also about the refinement of fine motor skills and the development of a sense of mastery. After being fed for all those months, the growing girl now experiences the sensation of managing her food on her own. She is becoming independent.

### Twelve to 36 Months: More Self-Feeding

Growth slows during the toddler years. Children of this age should be getting most of their nutrition from meats and other protein sources, fruits and vegetables, breads and grains, and dairy products. Breast-fed babies typically wean themselves as they become more active, but the breast or bottle can still be a source of comfort. Busy toddlers are less interested in eating, and even less interested in sitting at the dinner table. They also want more control over feeding themselves. It takes time to master the fine motor skills needed to use utensils and cups. By about 18 months of age, though, toddlers can handle a cup fairly well, and by 24 months of age, they can feed themselves neatly with a spoon.

## Nutritional Problems

We've sketched the basics of good nutrition for infants and toddlers. But what happens when young children do not get the nutritional care they need? Next, we discuss some nutritional problems that relate to nutrition in these early years: malnutrition, iron deficiency and anemia, failure to thrive, and obesity.

### Malnutrition

**malnutrition** The cellular imbalance between the supply of nutrients and energy and the body's demand for them to ensure growth, maintenance, and specific functions.

Basic malnutrition involves inadequate intake of calories (which provide energy) and protein (which is necessary to keep the body healthy and build muscle), as well as other associated nutrients. The World Health Organization (WHO) defines **malnutrition** as the cellular imbalance between the supply of nutrients and energy and the body's demand for them to ensure growth, maintenance, and specific functions (Stevens,

Mascarenhas, & Mathers, 2009). Malnutrition contributes to more than half of deaths in children worldwide (Torpy, Lynm, & Glass, 2004). In the developing world, one child in four under the age of 5 is underweight due to malnutrition—a total of 143 million children, according to a UNICEF report (2007).

Poverty, low levels of education, and poor access to health services are all major contributors to childhood malnutrition. In addition, regional conflicts and natural disasters have worsened the situation in many nations. In some countries in Africa, the devastating effects of the HIV/AIDS epidemic, especially in recent years, have reversed earlier gains (Heird, 2007). But most of the factors that lead to malnutrition relate to poor diet or severe and repeated infections. Inadequate diet and disease, in turn, are closely linked to the general standard of living, environmental conditions, and the population's ability, or inability, to meet basic needs, such as food, housing, and health care.

Basic protein-energy malnutrition includes several related disorders. **Kwashiorkor**, which is the most common type of malnutrition, can be seen in children under 12 months of age, if breast-feeding is discontinued. The term is taken from the language of Ghana, Ga, and means "the sickness of the weaning." This type of malnutrition can be life threatening. Without protein in the diet, muscles such as the heart and respiratory system weaken.

A more acute form of malnutrition is **marasmus**, which is due to food deprivation. Marasmus involves inadequate intake of both protein and calories, and is characterized by emaciation. It eventually leads to death.

Malnutrition commonly affects all groups in a community. Infants and young children are the most vulnerable, though, because of their high nutritional requirements for growth and development. And malnutrition has cascading effects. A malnourished mother is likely to give birth to a low birth weight baby, susceptible to disease and premature death. This further undermines the economic development of the family and society and continues the cycle of poverty and malnutrition (Stevens et al., 2009).

Because the first year of life is important for brain development, children who become undernourished during this time may fall permanently behind their peers, even if their physical growth later improves (Branca & Ferrari, 2002). Poor nutrition in the early years also can affect the development of the baby's brain. Extreme malnutrition can have irreversible effects on cognitive development (Martorell, Rivera, Kaplowitz, & Pollitt, 1992; Mendez & Adair, 1999; Pollitt, Gorman, Engle, Martorell, & Rivera, 1993). Malnutrition also impacts the acquisition of motor skills (Heywood, Marshall, & Heywood, 1991).

**kwashiorkor** The most common form of malnutrition; occurs when protein consumption does not meet the body's needs.

**marasmus** The most severe form of malnutrition during early infancy; is characterized by emaciation and eventually leads to death.

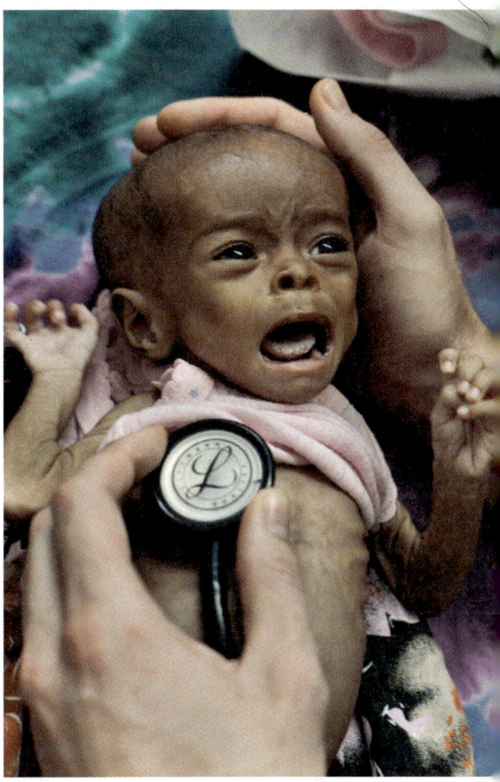

*Juergen Escher/laif/Redux*

Malnutrition plays a part in more than half of deaths in children worldwide. In Somalia, civil unrest and drought contributed to malnutrition in this infant.

### The Special Supplemental Nutrition Program for Women, Infants, and Children (WIC)

**Policy**

Poverty and malnutrition exist in the United States, too, despite the fact that it is one of the richest countries in the world. As you can see in Figure 5.8, a substantial number of U.S. children live in either poverty or extreme poverty. In fact, the American Human Development Report 2008–2009 Measure of America, published by the United Nations Development Programme (UNDP), states that the United States has a higher percentage of children living in poverty than any other of the world's richest countries (Burd-Sharps, Lewis, & Borges Martins, 2008). Comparisons among different groups of Americans show that African American babies are 2½ times more likely to die before age 1 than their Caucasian counterparts. And a baby born in Washington, DC is almost 2½ times more likely to die before age 1 than a baby born in Vermont.

**what if...?**

Many readers may find it difficult to believe that childhood hunger is widespread in the United States. But pediatricians, nurses, and public health professionals see the tragic effects of this unnecessary condition every day in their offices and clinics. What effect might widespread childhood hunger have on our health-care system? On our schools? What are some options for addressing this problem?

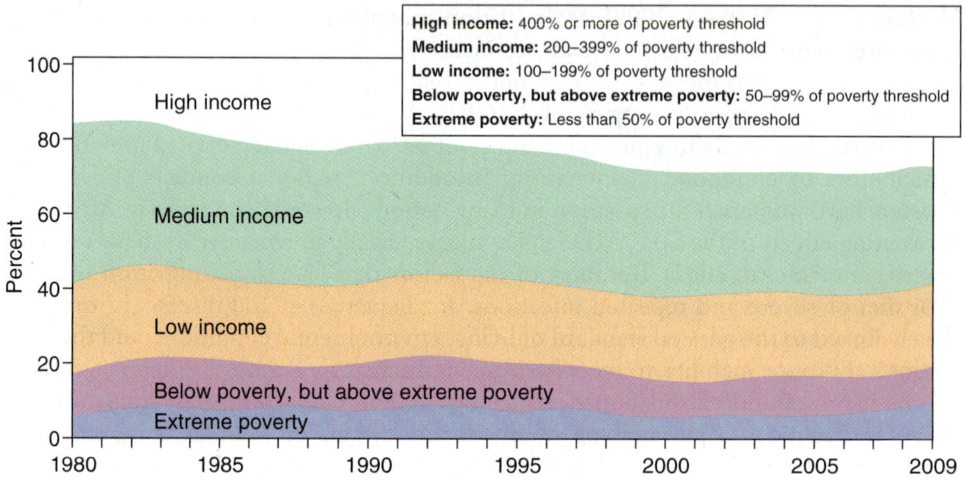


**FIGURE 5.8 Children Living in Poverty in the United States, 1980–2009** The chart includes children 17 and under living with their families or other relatives. The income classes are derived from the ratio of the family's income to the family's poverty threshold. The poverty threshold is an income level set by the U.S. government and adjusted annually. For example, in 2009, the poverty threshold for a family of four was $21,756.
Reprinted from U.S. Census Bureau, *Current Population Survey*, annual social and economic supplements.

To help address the nutritional needs of U.S. children living in poverty, Congress created the Special Supplemental Nutrition Program for Women, Infants, and Children (WIC), which provides nutritious foods, nutrition education, and referrals to health and other social services to participants, at no charge. WIC, which is administered by the Food and Nutrition Service of the U.S. Department of Agriculture, serves low-income pregnant women and new mothers, as well as infants and children up to age 5 who are at risk for poor nutrition. To be eligible for WIC, families must have income at or below a certain level (www.fns.usda.gov/wic). They may need to meet a standard set by the agency in their state that manages the program, or they may be automatically income-eligible based on participation in certain programs, such as Medicaid. Many older children today might not have survived without support from WIC. (See Figure 5.8.)

## Iron Deficiency and Anemia

Iron deficiency is the most common form of nutritional deficiency in the world. Infants are at particular risk due to their rapid growth and potentially limited dietary sources of iron (Lozoff & Georgieff, 2006; Pollitt, 2000). Poverty is a contributing factor to iron deficiency because families living at or below the poverty level may not be getting enough iron-rich foods, which include leafy green vegetables, beans, and red meats. Iron is a necessary mineral for body function and good health. It is involved in many central nervous system processes that could affect infant behavior and development. In addition, every red blood cell in the body contains iron in its hemoglobin, the pigment that carries oxygen to the tissues from the lungs. A lack of iron in the blood can lead to **iron-deficiency anemia**. Iron-deficiency anemia is often first noticed during a routine physical examination, based on symptoms such as fatigue and decreased appetite.

Controlled studies generally find that infants with iron-deficiency anemia have lower mental and motor test scores than comparison groups (Grantham-McGregor & Ani, 2001; Lozoff & Georgieff, 2006; Pollitt, 2000). Another characteristic of infants with iron-deficiency anemia is a lower energy level, characterized by wariness, hesitance, and absence of positive emotional expression. This behavior can affect the infants' interactions with caregivers. If an iron-deficient infant is unable to interact warmly with a caregiver, he or she may have fewer enriching experiences that foster development.

**iron-deficiency anemia** A condition caused by lack of iron in the blood; causes symptoms such as fatigue and decreased appetite.

Preventing iron deficiency requires an adequate diet, including iron-rich foods. Treatment of iron deficiency may involve increasing iron intake through fortified foods and iron supplements. A number of studies suggest that healthy full-term infants may benefit from iron supplementation in the first year of life (Idjradinata & Pollitt, 1993; Lozoff, et al., 2003).

**failure to thrive** A diagnosis given to children who are consistently underweight or who fail to gain weight as expected.

**body mass index (BMI)** A simple ratio of weight to height that is commonly used in classifying overweight and obesity.

**overweight** In children, having a body mass index (BMI) at or about the 85th percentile for age.

**obesity** Extreme overweight; in children, having a body mass index (BMI) above the 95th percentile.

## Failure to Thrive

**Failure to thrive** is a diagnosis given to children who are consistently underweight or who fail to gain weight. Children who fail to thrive either do not receive or are unable to take in, retain, or use the calories needed to gain weight and grow as expected. Diagnoses of failure to thrive are made in infants and toddlers in the first few years of life—which, as we know, is a crucial period of physical and mental development. Effects may include delays in physical and motor development.

Failure to thrive can be classified as organic, nonorganic, or a combination of both. Organic failure to thrive is caused by an underlying medical condition or disease, such as Gastroesophageal Reflux Disease or having a cleft palate. Nonorganic failure to thrive usually results from environmental and psychosocial factors that interact to keep the child from getting the needed nutrition. Families characterized by less adaptive relationships, higher levels of family conflict, and less emotional support for the mother, for example, have an increased percentage of children with this condition. Evidence indicates that failure to thrive in infancy is associated with persistent limitations in physical size and adverse intellectual outcomes (Corbett & Drewett, 2004).

Treatment of this disorder depends on the cause. If a medical cause is found, it is treated. In general, treatment aims to provide sufficient resources to promote satisfactory growth. Providing adequate nutrition may require changes to the diet, feeding schedule, or feeding environment. Psychosocial stressors contributing to undernutrition also must be addressed. Severe failure to thrive is treated in the hospital, where social workers, nutritionists, feeding specialists, psychiatrists, and other specialists work together to determine the most likely causes of the condition and the best approach to addressing them.

## Early Nutrition and the Risk of Obesity

Childhood overweight and obesity have increased substantially in the United States in the past two decades (Li, Dai, Jackson, & Zhang, 2008). Both overweight and obesity are measured using the **body mass index (BMI)**. The BMI is a simple index of weight to height. To calculate it, we divide weight in pounds by height in inches or squared, and multiply by a conversion factor. Childhood **overweight** is defined as having a BMI at or about the 85th percentile for age, while childhood **obesity** is defined as having a BMI above the 95th percentile.

Recent data suggest that early life is a sensitive period for the development of obesity (Günther, Remer, Kroke, & Buyken, 2007; Oddy, 2012). While genes may predispose people to be become overweight or obese, the environment must be conducive to overeating to realize this potential. For babies and toddlers, the environment is controlled almost completely by caregivers, especially mothers.

The weight of parents may also be a factor in the development of obesity in their children. It is well documented that overweight children are more likely to have overweight parents, an association that reflects both genetic and environmental influences. Parental obesity more than doubles the risk that both obese and nonobese children under 10 years of age will become obese as adults (Whitaker, Wright, Pepe, Seidel, & Dietz, 1997). We return to the subject of childhood obesity in Chapter 8.

### ✓ CHECK YOUR PROGRESS

1. In what sequence are foods added to infants' diets?
2. What are the effects of malnutrition on infants' growth and development?
3. What are the causes of failure to thrive, and how can it be treated?
4. Can obesity be prevented in infancy? Why or why not?

## Capacities for Health: Caregivers, Environment, and Community

**[ KEY QUESTION ] 5.** How do the physical, caregiving, and cultural environments affect development in infants and toddlers?

We turn now to the question of which environmental factors shape physical development in the earliest years. We have already seen that all normally developing babies arrive at the same motor milestones despite the diversity of their surroundings—whether born to mothers in the Kalahari, or reared by the Navajo in the southwestern United States; Norwegian babies born in the Arctic Circle; Pakistani and Bangladeshi babies born in northern England; babies born in the Goto Islands off the coast of Japan; and babies born and raised in Beijing, Dublin, Rio de Janeiro, or Boston. Yet we have also seen that children vary in the speed at which they achieve these milestones. One reason for this variability involves the kind of environment in which the children live—not only in regard to its physical features but also to the caregivers who inhabit it.

### The Physical Environment

What kind of environment do children need in order to thrive in their early years? We are accustomed to thinking in terms of the social supports and services that are so important to them—the love and protection of their families, the health services provided within their communities, and so forth (Bartlett, 2003). But children also need supportive physical environments to contribute to their physical and motor development.

One important consideration is children's need for the security, stability, and protection provided by adequate housing. Secure housing is fundamental to a secure family life and can provide a foothold for tackling other problems of poverty (Evans, Lepore, Shejwal, & Palsane, 1998). Along with a healthy, safe environment, children need access to play and the many supports for development that are provided by diverse, stimulating, accessible neighborhoods. To promote motor development, infants and toddlers also need an environment that encourages exploration and physical activity. They need plenty of space for rolling, scooting, and eventually crawling and walking. They need the opportunity to grasp and manipulate objects. They need to look at and

ADEK BERRY/AFP/Getty Images

A refugee camp is home, at least temporarily, to Indonesian women and children who survived an earthquake. Such camps often cannot meet the special environmental needs of babies and young children.

Babies who sleep on their backs (supine), as opposed to their stomachs (prone), are less likely to die of sudden infant death syndrome. When babies spend many waking hours on their backs, however, they may experience delays in motor development, because motor skills like rolling over and sitting up are more easily achieved from a prone position.

reach for moving objects, such as mobiles, and to have plenty of human conversation to listen to.

When these basic requirements are not met, children can be affected in every area of their development. For poor urban children in particular, the physical environment can present major problems, undermining their well-being and their prospects for the future. Even the most committed parents can be limited in their capacity to provide appropriate living conditions for their children when poverty prevents them from doing so.

## The Caregiving Environment

Adults play an active role in their children's motor development by providing access to the space, the conditions, and the kinds of materials that help children to develop their gross and fine motor skills (Bartlett, 2003; Bartlett, Hart, Satterthwaite, de la Barra, & Missair, 1999; Pomerleau et al., 2005). Parents tend to spontaneously offer such opportunities to their infants, from giving them engaging toys to taking them outdoors to explore different environments (Fogel, Hsu, Shapiro, Nelson-Goens, & Secrist, 2006). To examine this issue further, let's investigate what has been called the "back to sleep" and "prone to play" debate.

### The "Back to Sleep" and "Prone to Play" Debate

In 1992, the American Academy of Pediatrics (AAP) released a statement urging that all healthy infants born full term be placed on their backs (or *supine*) to sleep (American Academy of Pediatrics, 1992). The AAP has confirmed its recommendation many times since then (American Academy of Pediatrics, 2011). This advice was based on many research reports concerning **sudden infant death syndrome (SIDS)**. In developed countries, SIDS is the most common cause of death in infants after the newborn period. Deaths from SIDS commonly occur during sleep, while babies are lying on their stomachs (*prone*), although the actual cause of death remains unknown (Machaalani & Waters, 2008). Placing infants in the supine position to sleep has been associated with a dramatic decline in the incidence of sudden infant death syndrome.

Recently, however, studies suggest that the supine sleep position may be associated with delays in reaching gross motor milestones (Majnemer & Barr, 2006). The idea is that infants who sleep on their backs also spend more awake time on their backs. This may interfere with the development of motor skills such as rolling over and sitting up. These skills are more easily achieved from a prone position.

A review of 19 studies examined the effects of sleep and play positions, as well as the use of infant equipment, such as baby walkers, on motor development (Pin, Eldridge, & Galea, 2007). These studies provide the first empirical evidence that "back-to-sleep" positioning may slow infants' gross motor development. The studies

**sudden infant death syndrome (SIDS)** The most common cause of postneonatal deaths in developed countries; commonly occurs during sleep while the babies are lying on their stomachs, although the actual mechanism of death is still unknown.

# Culture and Sleeping Arrangements

© a.collectionRF/amanaimages/Corbis

Babies in Western cultures generally sleep alone, in their own beds and their own bedrooms. This is not the case in most other countries around the world, where babies sleep with their mothers. In much of southern Europe, Asia, Africa, and Central and South America, this so-called co-sleeping is the norm until children are weaned, and sometimes long after weaning (LeVine et al., 1994). In Japan, for example, a child sleeps with the mother until the next child is born. Then the older child relocates to sleep with the father or a grandparent (Kawasaki, Nugent, Miyashita, Miyahara, & Brazelton, 1994; Nugent, 1994).

Mother–infant co-sleeping takes different forms (Hrdy, 1999). In some cultures, such as those of Vietnam and the Philippines, babies sleep in separate baskets or hammocks beside where the mother sleeps. Generally, though, the most common arrangement is for mothers and infants to sleep side by side in the same bed (or other sleep surface) (Morelli, Rogoff, Oppenheim, & Goldsmith, 1992; Young & Fleming, 1998). The underlying belief is that this form of co-sleeping makes breast-feeding more available to the baby, and that the physical closeness deepens the bond between mother and child (McKenna & McDade, 2005).

In Western countries, there is some research to show that bed sharing increases the risk that the baby will die from sudden infant death syndrome (SIDS) or suffocation (Scheers, Rutherford, & Kemp, 2003). Findings such as these have prompted the American Academy of Pediatrics to issue a recommendation against bed sharing in the first year of an infant's life. Interestingly, in most cultures where co-sleeping is common, instances of SIDS are rare (McKenna & McDade, 2005). Thus, it appears that bed sharing does not lead inevitably to a higher infant death rate.

showed a temporary delay in motor development for healthy fullterm and low-risk preterm infants who were not exposed to the prone position. However, in most of these studies, infants walked unaided within a normal time frame. (For a discussion of the cultural aspects of babies' sleeping arrangements, see the accompanying feature.)

### Safety Issues in Infancy: New Skills and New Dangers

During infancy, challenges and achievements are an integral part of the developmental experience. But learning new skills also bring danger to infants. New hazards develop as the baby grows and learns to walk, climb, and open doors and cabinets. Hundreds of infants and children are seriously injured or die each year as a result of household accidents. In fact, such accidents are the leading cause of injury and death in children between 1 and 4 years of age (Hoyert, Heron, Murphy, & Kung, 2006).

As children become more physically active, it can be difficult for caregivers to draw the line between taking sensible safety precautions and being overprotective. The goal is to maintain a high level of safety while allowing children to experiment with mild risks that build competence and confidence as they are met and mastered.

Parents are certainly aware of the need to teach their young children to avoid risky situations. Mothers report, for example, that many of their verbal prohibitions are intended to keep infants safe (Gralinski & Kopp, 1993). Parents also ensure safety by limiting infants to activities within their abilities and using such safety devices as electrical outlet covers, gates, barriers, and locks. At the same time, parents want to challenge their children to engage in tasks beyond their ability, which involve a certain amount of risk, in an effort to promote motor skill development. For example, mothers may encourage infants to walk up and down stairs, instead of carrying them (Gralinski & Kopp, 1993).

A recent study sheds some light on the choices parents make in this regard. Researchers asked parents of 11-month-olds to adjust a ramp in three ways: to the steepest slopes they thought their infants *could safely* crawl down, the steepest slopes they thought the infants *would attempt* to crawl down, and the steepest slopes *they would allow* the infants to crawl down by themselves (Ishak, Tamis-LeMonda, & Adolph, 2007). Although most parents expected their infants to attempt slopes that were beyond their ability, 70% of the parents made safety-oriented choices. Specifically, they said they would allow their infants to crawl by themselves down only those slopes they believed the infants could crawl down safely. Choices such as these strike a balance between reducing the likelihood of accidents (safety) and promoting infants' motor development (challenge).

In light of the safety strategy taken by a high percentage of parents in the study just cited, what accounts for the reported high rates of injury to young infants generally? For one possible answer, let's discuss the study further. We noted that most parents made safety-oriented choices; but there were differences. Individual parents were sometimes inconsistent—making safety-oriented choices on some occasions and challenge-oriented choices on others. Furthermore, mothers and fathers were sometimes inconsistent with one another. Mothers overall were more likely to make safety-oriented choices, and fathers challenge-oriented choices. Thus, infants may receive dramatically different levels of parental supervision, depending on variations in individual parental responses from one occasion to another, and on which parent is caring for them.

## Products for Infants **Parenting**

Each year in the United States, parents spend millions of dollars on products to make their infants safer and more comfortable, and to promote their development. Many of these products offer valuable benefits for both parents and infants. Unfortunately, not all of them perform as advertised, and some can actually present dangers for babies.

Consider as an example baby walkers—wheeled seats that allow babies to propel themselves around by pushing against the floor with their feet. It has been reported that in the United States 70 to 90 % of 1-year-olds use baby walkers. Yet in 1994, a report from the U.S. Consumer Product Safety Commission cited baby walkers as being responsible for more injuries to children than any other product designed for them! Walkers do give children who cannot walk the ability to move around on their own. However, researchers in the United States and Ireland found that use of baby walkers was not associated with earlier achievement of motor milestones, such as sitting, standing, and walking. Instead, they revealed strong associations between the amount of baby-walker use and the extent of developmental delay. The researchers concluded that the use of walkers should be discouraged (Garrett, McElroy, & Staines, 2002; Siegel & Burton, 1999).

In contrast, the infant-restraint seat for motor vehicles is an essential product. Motor vehicle crashes are the leading cause of death for children aged 1 year or older (Committee on Injury, Violence and Poison Prevention, 2011). Nearly half of children under age 5 killed in motor vehicle crashes were riding unrestrained. One in four of these deaths involved a driver who had consumed alcohol. Between 1997 and 2002,

© Hello Lovely/Corbis

All 50 states require car seats for infants and young children. The American Academy of Pediatrics recommends that children ride facing the rear until they have reached the greatest height and weight allowed by the manufacturer—or, at a minimum, until they are 1 year old and weigh at least 20 lb.

68% of U.S. children killed in alcohol-related automobile accidents were riding in the same vehicle as the drinking driver (www-nrd.nhtsa.dot.gov/Pubs/809762.pdf). These children were less likely to be properly restrained than children who died in crashes that did not involve alcohol.

By law, all 50 states require infants and younger children to be restrained in a crash-tested child restraint seat while riding in a motor vehicle. But using child safety restraints is not important just because it is the law. Such restraints are also the best way available to prevent child injury and death in motor vehicle accidents. Child safety seats lower the risk of death by about 70% for infants and by about 55% for toddlers aged 1 to 4. (To learn more about motor vehicle injuries in the United States, visit www.cdc.gov/injury.)

Two types of child restraint seats are available: infant only and convertible. Convertible seats can be used facing the rear or the front. The American Academy of Pediatrics (AAP) recommends that children ride facing the rear of the car until they have reached the maximum height and weight allowed by the manufacturer—or, at a minimum, until they are 1 year old and weigh at least 20 lb. The AAP offers advice on buying and installing seats at www.aap.org/family/Carseatguide.htm.

## Infant and Toddler Child-Care Settings **Practice**

Increasing numbers of U.S. infants and toddlers spend hours each day in child-care arrangements, because their parents work or attend school. Child care in infancy is characterized by diverse and complex settings. Infants can be found in varying physical settings, on varying schedules, among varying numbers of other infants and alternating child-care providers (Clarke-Stewart & Allhusen, 2002; Hegland & Rix, 1990; Lamb, 1998). What features of child-care settings can promote physical and motor development?

To promote development, the setting should be designed in accordance with developmentally appropriate practice. In such a setting, the curriculum and other features take each child's developmental level into account, including children with special needs (Gestwicki, 2011). The setting should provide sufficient time, indoor and outdoor space, equipment, materials, and adult guidance for active play and movement, to support the development of gross and fine motor skills.

"Messy" experiences are separated from "neat" ones, quiet activities from noisy ones, and fine motor experiences from large motor ones. Leaving an open area in the center of the room, for example, allows toddlers to engage in vigorous walking or crawling, and creates a space for gross motor equipment, such as a tunnel. The equipment in this area may be altered to meet the changing needs of the group or individuals.

Areas of learning may include fine muscle manipulation (for example, stacking, sorting, nesting, dumping, and filling), dramatic play, reading, and sensory and large motor experiences, as well as art and music. Learning is enhanced when the room has cozy spaces where infants and toddlers can regulate intense emotions of excitement, sadness, or anger. Spaces should be designed to enhance learning for individuals as well as for the group as a whole. It is equally vital to establish designated areas for daily routines such as eating, sleeping, and diapering.

### what if...?

Yoko and Ren are searching for a child-care setting for their 1-year-old, Kyoko. They have listed safety, health, and aesthetics as critical to their decision. They want an environment where their daughter can move about freely and explore without being in danger. The tables and chairs should be small and low, with rounded corners, and the shelves and pictures should be at child height. The equipment should be made of nontoxic materials. Health is also a fundamental issue. All the areas must be clean, and diapering and toileting areas should be separate from food preparation and feeding areas. Finally, the environment should be calm and aesthetically pleasing. What if you were in this same position? What would be on your list?

How do parents know if their baby's child-care center is safe? Babies and toddlers have immature immune systems and may engage in behaviors and activities that make them particularly vulnerable to illness. Alarmingly, a health report conducted in Massachusetts found that 70% of observed child-care centers failed to meet minimal standards for personal care routines in the areas of feeding, napping, and diapering (Glantz, 2009). Family child-care homes were also found to be below minimal standards for health (69%) and safety (65%) (Marshall et al., 2003).

Training specific to the health and safety needs of young children can be effective in addressing this problem, particularly when paired with follow-up, supports, and monitoring (Porter, Paulsell, Del Grosso, Avellar, Hass & Vuong, 2010). Simple training and ongoing monitoring of diapering and hand-washing practices have been shown to reduce the incidence of illness in young children (Carabin et al., 1999). The American Academy of Pediatrics, American Public Health Association, and National Resource Center for Health and Safety in Child Care and Early Education recommend that providers be prepared to work with infants and toddlers. They should be knowledgeable and competent in the areas of diapering, bathing, feeding, holding, comforting, SIDS prevention, developing responsive and continuous relationships with young children, and creating opportunities for child-initiated activities (American Academy of Pediatrics, American Public Health Association, & National Resource Center for Health and Safety in Child Care and Early Education, 2002).

Susan Woog-Wagner/Science Source

A well-designed child-care setting should provide separate spaces for many different activities.

### Well-Child Visits

An important element of caregiving in the early years is to establish a schedule of well-child visits with a health-care provider (Haflon, Stevens, Larson, & Olson, 2011). The more we understand about early childhood development, and especially development of the brain, the more we recognize how important these visits are. It is often recommended that infants and toddlers see a health-care provider at 3 to 5 days of age, then at 1 month, and thereafter at 2, 4, 6, 9, 12, 15, 18, 24, 30, and 36 months (American Academy of Pediatrics. http://www.aap.org/en-us/Pages/Default.aspx).

The emphasis during these visits is on promoting good health and screening for conditions that can be addressed early. Examples include problems with vision and hearing, delays in meeting motor milestones, and language development. Vaccines, which we discuss in more detail in Chapter 8, are also administered. If needed, lifetime management of a chronic condition such as cystic fibrosis can begin.

Four types of activities are incorporated into well-child visits (Halfon et al., 2004; Regalado & Halfon, 1998):

- *Assessment.* Includes evaluating information from parents about the child and the caregiving environment, monitoring the child's growth and attainment of developmental milestones, screening for developmental problems, observing parent-child interactions, and assessing child behavior.
- *Education and health promotion.* Involves counseling and guidance for parents about child behavior, family relationships, and child-rearing challenges, such as a child's sleep and eating habits and appropriate disciplinary practices. Also includes administering immunizations.
- *Intervention.* Covers treatment of acute health problems, such as ear infections, fever, and abdominal pain.
- *Care coordination.* Focuses on making referrals for diagnostic assessments or to other specialists for care.

## Motor Development in Different Cultural Environments

Do cultural practices influence motor development in infants? We know that children in some ethnic groups acquire certain motor abilities more quickly, compared with children in other groups who acquire them more slowly. Traditionally reared infants in Africa, for example, tend to reach many motor milestones earlier than they typically do in the United States (Super & Harkness, 2009). Explanations for these observed differences have ranged from those based on biological distinctions to those emphasizing the influence of parental expectations and child-rearing practices (Adolph et al. 2010; Freedman & DeBoer, 1979; Huang, O'Brien Caughy, Genevro, & Miller, 2005; Kolobe, 2004; Miller, 1988; Nugent, Petrauskas & Brazelton, 2009; Pachter & Dworkin, 1997; Werner, 1972).

*Everyday stories*

LEARNING TO WALK IN DIFFERENT CULTURES One well-known example of the influence of child-rearing practices involves the Kipsigis people of rural Kenya. Kipsigis mothers promote walking from birth. According to Charles Super and Sara Harkness, "From the first days of life, the stepping reflex is exercised on the outstretched legs of the mother or grandmother sitting on the floor of the hut or, after a week, outside in the sun on a cool day, or in a shade when the sunshine is too bright and hot" (2009, p. 93). Kipsigis babies develop motor skills (for example, sit and walk) earlier than infants in American and European societies, although only in the areas in which they are specifically taught or encouraged. In contrast, among the Zinacanteco Indians in Mexico, rapid motor development is discouraged (Brazelton, 1977; Greenfield, 1991). The Zinacanteco infants show relatively slow motor development (walking, in particular). This may be due, in part, to mothers discouraging independent activity of infants on cold floors (Solomons & Solomons, 1975).

One review examined studies of motor development in children of Asian and European ethnic backgrounds (Mayson, Harris, & Bachman, 2007). These studies suggest that children from many countries in Asia attain gross motor skills significantly later than their European and American peers. The researchers hypothesized that sociocultural and environmental factors may partially explain these differences. However, they cautioned that because most of the studies did not include representative samples, and used Western measurement tools, that they may not be appropriate for application to other settings.

In general, researchers have reported finding wide variations across ethnic groups in terms of what parents consider "normal" infant development (Hopkins & Westra, 1989; Huang et al., 2005; Kolobe, 2004; Pachter & Dworkin, 1997). Parental beliefs and expectations clearly influence child-rearing practices. Thus, for example, parents who expect children to sit or walk early may, in essence, train them to do just that.

This body of research demonstrates that children's motor development does vary across cultures, and that caregiving practices undoubtedly influence the motor behavior of infants (Mayson et al., 2007). Nevertheless, while these practices may reflect differences in family life and cultural tradition, all seem to promote the same basic motor abilities (Kelly et al., 2006).

### ✓CHECK YOUR PROGRESS

1. What kind of physical environment do children need in order to thrive in infancy?
2. What is the "back to sleep" and "prone to play" debate about?
3. In light of the overall concerns of most parents for their children's safety, what might account for the reported high rates of injury to young infants?
4. How do you explain cultural differences in infant motor development?

# Disruptions in Health: Neuromotor Disabilities

**[ KEY QUESTION ] 6. What are some effects of neuromuscular disabilities on development, and how can early intervention help?**

**cerebral palsy (CP)** A group of permanent disorders in the development of movement and posture that are attributed to nonprogressive disturbances in the developing fetal or infant brain.

Most of us take our motor skills for granted, since we can use them easily and effectively without the need for conscious control. In fact, though, all our movements require fast and complex control by the central nervous system. It is only when skills are impaired or delayed that we realize how much they affect every aspect of our lives. When a disability interferes with what an infant is able to see and hear, or when it impairs the infant's overall motor functioning, then the infant will not follow the normal developmental sequence. In this section, we focus on three neuromotor disorders that affect infant motor development: cerebral palsy, muscular dystrophy, and Down syndrome.

## Cerebral Palsy

**Cerebral palsy (CP)** is the most common cause of long-term motor function impairment, with a frequency of about 1 in 500 births (see Table 5.2). "Cerebral" refers to the brain, while "palsy" is a traditional name for conditions involving uncontrollable body tremors. Cerebral palsy affects muscle tone, movement, and motor skills. It can be described as a group of permanent disorders in the development of movement and posture that are attributed to nonprogressive disturbances in the developing fetal or infant brain. Many different types of injury to the brain can cause cerebral palsy. Often, more than one cause is involved. Birth injuries and poor oxygen supply to the brain before, during, and immediately after birth cause 15 to 20% of cases. Prenatal infections, such as rubella, also sometimes result in cerebral palsy.

Premature infants are particularly vulnerable, possibly in part because the blood vessels of the brain are poorly developed and bleed easily. Indeed, despite advances in the technical aspects of neonatal intensive care, the two major areas of disability found in preterm children remain developmental impairment and motor problems (Hack & Fanaroff, 2000). During the first years of life, severe illness, such as inflammation of the tissues covering the brain (meningitis), sepsis (a condition resulting from infection), trauma, and severe dehydration, can cause brain injury and result in cerebral palsy. Cerebral palsy can also lead to other health issues, including vision, hearing, and speech problems, as well as learning disabilities. There is no cure for CP; however, treatment, therapy, special equipment, and, in some cases, surgery, can improve the quality of life of the child who is living with the condition (Roebroeck, Jahnsen, Carona, Kent, & Chamberlain, 2009).

It is important to remember that cerebral palsy is not a disease. Rather, it is a group of symptoms that results from damage to the parts of the brain that control

**Table 5.2** Cerebral Palsy Statistics

| |
|---|
| Cerebral palsy is one of the most common congenital (existing before birth or at birth) disorders of childhood. |
| About 500,000 children and adults of all ages in the United States have the condition. An additional 4,500 infants and children are diagnosed yearly. Some of these cases may be preventable. |
| About 2 to 3 children per 1,000 have cerebral palsy (March of Dimes, 2007). |
| In 2003 dollars, the average lifetime cost of cerebral palsy is an estimated $921,000. This does not include hospital visits, emergency room visits, residential care, and other out-of-pocket expenses (National Institute of Neurological Disorders and Strokes, 2006). |
| Two-thirds of children with cerebral palsy will be mentally impaired. |

*Source:* Adapted from National Institute of Neurological Disorders and Stroke. (July 2006). *Cerebral Palsy: Hope Through Research.* NIH publication No. 06–159.

**muscular dystrophy (MD)** A broad term for a group of inherited diseases that cause muscle to degenerate and weaken.

**Down syndrome** A condition that results from having an extra copy of chromosome 21; associated with mild to moderate intellectual disabilities, motor impairment, heart defects, early onset of Alzheimer's disease, and childhood leukemia.

muscle movements. Once the brain damage has occurred, it does not get worse, even though the symptoms may change as the child grows and matures. Many children with cerebral palsy grow normally and attend regular schools. Others require extensive physical therapy, need special education, and are severely limited in activities of daily living. Even severely affected children can benefit from education and training.

## Muscular Dystrophy

Many people in the United States probably know about **muscular dystrophy (MD)** mainly from the annual television fundraiser dedicated to raising money to find a cure for it. But to the estimated 55,000 Americans and their families who live with this disability, MD is a daily challenge. Muscular dystrophy is a broad term for a group of more than 30 diseases that cause muscles to degenerate and weaken. All types of MD are inherited, as you may recall from Chapter 2. They are caused by a defect in one of the thousands of genes that help the body make proteins crucial for muscle control. Symptoms can appear at any age, can affect any muscles, and can advance at any pace. The most severe forms of the disease result in premature death. Although medications and therapy can sometimes slow MD's course, so far, there is no cure. Existing treatments include physical and speech therapy, orthopedic devices, surgery, and medications. New gene-based therapies are also being developed (Trollet, Athanasopoulos, Popplewell, Malerba, & Dickson, 2009)

Duchenne muscular dystrophy, which occurs primarily in boys, is the most common fatal genetic disorder diagnosed in childhood. The condition affects about 1 in every 3,500 live male births (about 20,000 new cases each year) (http://www.genome.gov/19518854). Duchenne affects mainly boys because the gene responsible for it is found on the X chromosome, as we discussed in Chapter 2. Girls can be carriers of Duchenne but usually exhibit no symptoms. Duchenne is caused by a mutation in the gene that encodes for a protein that helps keep muscle cells intact. Because the protein is absent, the muscle cells are easily damaged. Boys with the disorder experience progressive loss of strength, which leads to serious medical problems, particularly issues relating to the heart and lungs. Young men with the disorder typically live only into their late 20s.

## Down Syndrome

**Down syndrome** is the most frequent genetic cause of mild to moderate intellectual disabilities and associated medical problems. The condition is named after John Langdon Down, the first physician to describe its common features. Physical characteristics of infants born with Down syndrome include epicanthic folds around the eyes (folds of skin on the upper eyelids that partially cover the inner corners of the eyes); a broad and flat nasal bridge; a round, flat face; eyes that slant upward; small ears, a short neck, and a downward-turned mouth.

Down syndrome, as you may recall from Chapter 2, is the result of having an extra copy of chromosome 21. It is associated with mild to moderate intellectual disabilities, motor impairment, heart defects, early onset of Alzheimer's disease, and childhood leukemia. In general, some areas of the development of children with Down syndrome are more delayed than others, leading many researchers to describe a typical profile of strengths and weaknesses. Nevertheless, children with Down syndrome differ greatly. Any group of 100 infants with Down syndrome will vary as widely in their abilities, behavior, personality characteristics, size, and appearance as any group of 100 typically developing infants. Their development is influenced not only by their biology but also by their social and learning opportunities, as with all other children.

Research indicates that the pattern of motor skill development for individuals with Down syndrome is largely one of delay rather than difference (Sacks & Buckley, 2003). The most effective way to improve motor skills for any individual is with practice. Thus, individuals with Down syndrome need more practice than typically developing individuals to improve their performance. Most teenagers and adults can continue to develop their motor skills, and many will achieve high levels of skill if given the opportunity and support.

As a group, children with Down syndrome are progressing faster and achieving more than they did 25 years ago. This progress is due in no small part to the availability of more information on children with Down syndrome, and to the effects of early intervention programs on their development (Hauser-Cram et al., 1999; Hauser-Cram, Krauss, & Kersh, 2009).

**early intervention programs** Statewide integrated developmental services available to families with children up to 3 years of age whose healthy development is compromised.

## Early Intervention — Policy

**Early intervention programs** are statewide, integrated developmental services that are available to families of children between birth and 3 years of age. These programs were mandated by Congress in 1986 under the Individuals with Disabilities Education Act (IDEA). The mission of the programs is to identify and evaluate as early as possible those infants and toddlers whose healthy development is compromised, and to provide for appropriate intervention to improve child and family development. To be eligible for services, children must be under 3 years of age and have a confirmed disability or an established developmental delay in physical, cognitive, communication, psychosocial, or adaptive development.

- Early intervention can be remedial or preventive in nature. That is, it can aim to treat existing developmental problems or to prevent the occurrence of problems.
- Services range from identification to diagnostic and direct-intervention programs, and they may begin at any time between birth and school-age. These services may include physical therapy to help a child develop motor skills, or speech therapy to help with language development.
- Early intervention may focus on the child alone or on the child and the family together.
- Programs may be center-based, home-based, hospital-based, or a combination—although most early intervention services take place in the home.

*Everyday stories*

HOME VISITING AND EARLY INTERVENTION Early intervention home-visiting practices have begun to shift from a teaching model to a family-centered consultation model. In other words, more home visitors focus on joining and supporting parents in their interactions with their child, rather than trying to teach the parents. Instead of using the home visitor's favorite books, songs, or games in interventions with a child, for example, the home visitor can ask the parents to suggest books, songs, or games that are a part of the family's culture. Intervention strategies can then be integrated into the family's routine activities and customs. The idea is that home visits will be most effective when they are culturally sensitive and support the confidence and competence of caregivers in their own use of the intervention strategies.

Nearly 50 years of research gives us evidence—both quantitative (data-based) and qualitative (reports of parents and teachers)—that early intervention increases the developmental and educational gains for children, and improves the functioning of families (Hauser-Cram & Steele, 2001; Powell, 2006; Ramey & Ramey, 2004). It also provides long-term benefits for society. For example, infants and toddlers who have benefitted from early intervention services have less need for special education and related services once they reach school age, thus reducing the educational cost to the state. Access to early services also reduces the need to institutionalize people with disabilities, while maximizing their potential for independent living.

Robin Sachs/Photo Edit

This speech therapist is working with a deaf toddler. Research has confirmed that early interventions like this offer many benefits for children, their families, and society.

It is unlikely that early intervention will prevent the development of such conditions as cerebral palsy and muscular dystrophy. But it can help to lessen the effects of many conditions, as well as prevent secondary problems from developing. At the same time, it can enhance the child's quality of life and support the parents in their own efforts to meet the unique needs of their infant or toddler. In the case of infants who may be at risk for developmental delays due to prematurity or poor nutrition, detecting the risk as early as possible enables interventions to be started long before the delays become severe.

Remember the story of Katelyn, whom we introduced at the beginning of this chapter. From the time she left the hospital, Katelyn needed weekly physical and occupational therapy to support her motor development; and she still requires physical and speech therapy. Yet today, despite having mild cerebral palsy and some speech difficulties, Katelyn is a happy, vivacious 5-year-old who enjoys playing with her friends. Her family attributes her successful development to the support they received from the early intervention team in the first years of her life. If you were to meet Katelyn, you would see a determined, energetic, smart, thoughtful, and generous-spirited young girl. She is a child who has disabilities, but she is not a disabled child.

## what if...?

It is often difficult for a person who has not come face to face with a small child who has a disability to understand the challenges facing such children and their families. What if you had an opportunity to become involved in the lives of such families? Would you consider volunteering at an early intervention center in your community, for example? Or, as you look to the future, can you envision yourself as part of an early intervention team, perhaps working as an infancy developmental specialist, a nurse, a physical therapist, or a speech pathologist, and conducting home visits with infants and their families? Or can you imagine a future career in research, so that you can join in the search for causes and treatments for infants with disabilities? These are surely some of the most challenging professions anyone could imagine, but they are also some of the most fulfilling.

✓CHECK YOUR PROGRESS

1. What is the cause of muscular dystrophy?
2. What do we mean when we say that the pattern of motor skill development for individuals with Down syndrome is largely one of delay rather than difference?
3. What are some of the chief benefits of early intervention programs?

# CHAPTER SUMMARY

## A Framework for Children's Health and Physical Development

**[ KEY QUESTION ] 1. What are the key elements of the Harvard Center on the Developing Child framework for children's health and physical development?**

- Similar to Bronfenbrenner's bioecological model, the Harvard framework recognizes multiple systems of influence on the developing child, including the biology of health, foundations of health, caregiver and community capacities, and policy and programs.

## Biology of Health: Physical, Motor, and Perceptual Development

**[ KEY QUESTION ] 2. In what ways are the first years of life a period of rapid physical, motor, and perceptual development?**

- Physical growth is characterized by four general principles: It proceeds in a cephalocaudal direction, in a proximodistal direction, and through a process of differentiation, and it is asynchronous.
- Children grow more within the first 24 months of life than at any other point across the life span. Body weight nearly quadruples in the first two years, height doubles, and head circumference increases by a third.
- Physical development refers to increases in size and changes in body structure. Motor development refers to increases in functional motor ability and changes in the quality of motor skills, including both gross and fine motor skills. Motor milestone tables are used to identify whether children's motor skills are developing typically.
- The maturational theory of motor development holds that motor development simply occurs as physical development proceeds, with little or no influence from the environment. In contrast, dynamic systems theory views the infant's motor development in terms of a complex system of mutually interacting components.
- In the areas of sensation and perception, infants develop as their brains continue to mature and as they continue to have new experiences.

## The Developing Brain: Biology of Health

**[ KEY QUESTION ] 3. What role does the brain play in the rapid physical, motor, and perceptual development of the first years of life?**

- The rapid physical, motor, and perceptual development experienced in infancy is made possible by the equally dramatic changes taking place in the size and structure of the infant's brain.
- Forming and reinforcing the connections between synapses are the key tasks of early brain development.
- Many different brain structures are involved in motor functions, but the motor cortex is especially important in controlling voluntary movements.
- Through the process of pruning, neuron circuits that are consistently used will be strengthened, while those that are rarely used may be dropped away. Through this process, early experiences create a foundation for lifelong learning and behavior.

## Foundations of Health: Nutrition and Health

**[ KEY QUESTION ] 4. What are some important nutrition concerns regarding infants and toddlers?**

- The period from birth to 2 years of age is a critical window for the promotion of growth and health, and optimal growth and health require optimal nutrition.
- Infants get most of their nutrition from breast milk or formula for the first 6 months; cereal is added next, followed by pureed solid foods, then finger foods. Toddlers should get most of their nutrition from meats, fruits and vegetables, breads and grains, and dairy products.
- Problems related to nutrition include malnutrition, which contributes to more than half of deaths in children worldwide; iron deficiency and anemia, which results from inadequate iron intake; failure to thrive, in which children are consistently underweight; and overweight and obesity, a growing problem in the United States that may begin in infancy.

## Capacities for Health: Caregivers, Environment, and Community

**[ KEY QUESTION ] 5. How do the physical, caregiving, and cultural environments affect development in infants and toddlers?**

- Children need safe and supportive physical environments to contribute to their physical and motor development. These environments should encourage exploration and physical activity.
- Parents play a central role in their infants' motor skill acquisition by encouraging and guiding motor skill development. New hazards develop as the infant grows and learns to walk, climb, and open doors and cabinets. As children become more physically active, it can be difficult for caregivers to draw the line between taking sensible safety precautions and being overprotective.
- Child-care settings designed in accordance with developmentally appropriate practice can support children's physical, motor, and perceptual development, as well as their health. Also important is a regular schedule of well-child visits to a health-care provider.
- Children's motor development varies across cultures, and caregiving practices undoubtedly influence the motor behavior of infants.

## Disruptions in Health: Neuromotor Disabilities

**[ KEY QUESTION ] 6.** What are some effects of neuromuscular disabilities on development, and how can early intervention help?

- Cerebral palsy is a group of permanent disorders in the development of movement and posture. There is no cure for CP, but various means are used to help children living with the condition.
- Muscular dystrophy causes muscle to degenerate and weaken. All forms of MD are inherited. Duchenne muscular dystrophy, which occurs primarily in boys, is the most common fatal genetic disorder diagnosed in childhood.
- Down syndrome, which results from having an extra copy of chromosome 21, is associated with mild to moderate intellectual delay, motor impairment, heart defects, early onset of Alzheimer's disease, and childhood leukemia. Children with Down syndrome vary greatly in their abilities.
- Early intervention programs are available to families of children up to 3 years of age who meet certain criteria. Such programs aim to provide developmental and educational gains for children, improve the functioning of families, and offer long-term benefits for society.

# KEY TERMS

affordance *171*
body mass index (BMI) *181*
cephalocaudal *162*
cerebral palsy (CP) *189*
differentiation *162*
Down syndrome *190*
dynamic systems theory *169*
early intervention programs *191*
ecological theory of perceptual development *171*
failure to thrive *181*
fine motor skills *165*
gross motor skills *165*
iron-deficiency anemia *180*
kwashiorkor *179*
malnutrition *178*
marasmus *179*
maturational theory *168*
motor development *163*
motor milestones *166*
muscular dystrophy (MD) *190*
obesity *181*
overweight *181*
perception *169*
proximodistal *162*
pruning *176*
sensation *169*
sudden infant death syndrome (SIDS) *183*

# CRITICAL THINKING QUESTIONS

1. **A Framework for Children's Health and Physical Development.** The Harvard Center on the Developing Child framework maintains that the early foundations of lifelong health are being built during the first years of life. Do you agree or disagree? Why?
2. **Biology of Health: Physical, Motor, and Perceptual Development.** There is a widely held belief that physical and motor development in the first years of a child's life emerges in a regular predictable sequence, and independently of experience. But does the environment have a role to play? Explain.
3. **The Developing Brain: Biology of Health.** Every experience in infancy—whether it is reaching out for a toy or learning to walk—excites certain neural circuits and leaves others inactive. How does experience influence brain growth?
4. **Foundations of Health: Nutrition and Health.** The period from birth to 2 years of age is a critical window for the promotion of growth and health. Optimal growth and health in these years require optimal nutrition. How does poor nutrition affect children's development?
5. **Capacities for Health: Caregivers, Environment, and Community.** Children vary in the speed at which they achieve motor milestones. What do cross-cultural studies tell us about the kind of child-rearing practices infants and toddlers need to grow and thrive?
6. **Disruptions in Health: Neuromotor Disabilities.** What happens when a child's motor skills are impaired or delayed? What can early intervention do in such cases?
7. **Cultural Perspectives.** Every healthy infant walks. But why do some African infants walk earlier than European and American infants? The phrase "learning to walk" implies that experience plays a key role in when infants begin to walk, but what factors determine the age of onset of walking? How malleable is the development of motor skills in infants and toddlers? What role do child-rearing beliefs and practices play?

# REAL Development

## Physical Development and Health in Infancy and Toddlerhood

In the accompanying Real Development activity, you are studying to be a child psychologist. Tia Wagner is considering enrolling her son, Brandon, in a "Mommy and Me" class in her neighborhood. Offered in various locations across the United States, "Mommy and Me" classes provide structured and unstructured play for specific age groups. As you know, children undergo a number of changes during the first two years related to motor development and your task is to discern whether these children appear to be developing at normal rates. In the activity, you will observe the class and report your observations to Tia in order to help her make this decision.

© John Wiley & Sons, Inc.

**WileyPLUS** Go to WileyPLUS to complete the *Real Development* activity.

03.01

# Chapter 6

*Jose Luis Pelaez Inc/Blend Images/Getty Images*

# Cognitive Development in Infancy and Toddlerhood

## MAKING A difference

### Does Infant Stimulation Matter?

Parents today are inundated with commercials, posters, videos, and talk shows promoting programs that promise to make babies smarter, train them to read earlier, and even teach them to play a musical instrument. Parents are very susceptible to these claims. They know that the first years of life are a time of massive brain development, and they desperately want to give their children the best possible start in life. Of course, every parent wants to have a smart baby. But the evidence suggests that advanced learning or reading skills rarely come in a neatly packaged box. Indeed, lengthy drills or the use of flash cards may place the infant's spontaneous interest and pleasure at risk.

After all, forcing children to learn a task before their brains are naturally ready to take on that task does not have any advantage. The line between satisfying stimulation and overstimulation at this age can be thin, more for some children than for others. For many young infants, for example, brightly colored crib toys that spin in perpetual motion, displaying flashing lights and repeating a musical jingle, can overwhelm their sensory system. Many computer and handheld electronic action games can also stress a toddler's sensory capabilities.

So how *can* parents help their small children to learn? Research has shown that to promote early learning in infants and toddlers, parents and other caregivers should provide an environment that offers opportunities for exploration. Babies are naturally curious. No one has to teach a baby to explore. Caregivers also must be sensitive. They need to follow the baby's cues so that they can provide the kind of choices and materials that match the child's abilities while challenging and reinforcing the infant's developing skills.

In the end, human interaction—caregivers responding to infants' interests in a way that is engaging and pleasurable—is superior to every other kind of infant stimulation. Developmentally appropriate cognitive and language stimulation allows infants to proceed at their own rate of development by allowing them freedom to explore their new world and offering them encouragement and support as they do so. Providing this kind of environment—whether it is in the home or a child-care center—is also the key to narrowing the achievement gap between children from different socioeconomic backgrounds and improving the lives of infants and toddlers everywhere.

## CHAPTER OUTLINE

# [KEY QUESTIONS] *for* READING CHAPTER 6

1. How do Piaget, Vygotsky, and information-processing theorists explain how infants and toddlers learn?
2. What research techniques are used to assess cognitive development in infants and toddlers?
3. How does language develop in infants and toddlers?
4. What are the benefits of infant-toddler education?

**AS RECENTLY AS** the first part of the 20th century, many people, including behavioral scientists, assumed that babies could not think. Perhaps because infants cannot share their thoughts using words, it was assumed that very little was happening in their minds. In this view, infants could only react passively to what was happening around them. More recently, researchers have demonstrated that earlier investigators severely underestimated the mental capacities of infants (Tenenbaum, Kemp, Griffiths and Goodman, 2011). As a result, our understanding of infants has changed dramatically. You will soon see that infants and toddlers have the ability to think, to remember, to plan, and even to reason in complex and systematic ways.

In this chapter, we discuss the emergence of the remarkable cognitive abilities of infants and toddlers. We begin by examining the various theories that try to explain how children in the early years of life come to understand the world of people, objects, and events. We review the ingenious research methods and technological advances in neuroscience that have allowed scientists to study infant and toddler behavior in ways that could scarcely have been imagined earlier. We go on to discuss the equally remarkable story of how language emerges and develops in these first years of life. We end the chapter with a review of a range of education programs specifically designed for infants and toddlers. The research we review in this chapter demonstrates that infants can be thought of as serious scientists who spend much of their waking time formulating and testing hypotheses, solving problems, and coming up with novel solutions. The infant is, indeed, a true philosopher (Gopnik 2009)!

## Theories of Cognitive Development

### [ KEY QUESTION ] 1. How do Piaget, Vygotsky, and information-processing theorists explain how infants and toddlers learn?

When we discussed the amazing competencies of newborn infants in Chapter 4, we noted that many of them are evident shortly after birth. For that reason, here, we first ask whether some of these early infant competencies are innate or emerge only through experience in the world. This question is an old one, whose answer is still being argued in debates about infant cognition today (for example, Cohen & Cashon, 2006; Diamond & Amso, D., 2008; Haith, 1998; Hamlin, Ullman, Tenenbaum, Goodman, & Baker, 2013; Kagan, 2006; Nelson, De Haan, & Thomas, 2006; Pinker, 1994; Rogoff, 1990; Rose & Feldman, 1990; Sameroff, 2010; Spelke 1998; Spelke, Breinlinger, Macomber & Jacobson, 1992).

In this section, we first examine the hypotheses of several important theorists who have attempted to answer this question. We begin with the theory of Jean Piaget and then turn to the many insights offered by Lev Vygotsky. We go on from there to discuss systems approaches to early learning before we examine several information-processing approaches. Finally, we discuss the developing brain and explain how changes in brain structure influence emerging mental development in infants and toddlers.

**sensorimotor stage** Piaget's first stage of development, which lasts from birth to about the end of the second year; infants in this stage use senses and motor abilities to understand the world.

**schemas** Organized patterns of thought that are continually being modified through assimilation and accommodation.

**assimilation** A part of adaptation in which children interpret their experiences in terms of existing cognitive structures.

**accommodation** A part of adaptation in which children change existing cognitive structures or create new ones to account for new experiences.

**disequilibrium** Occurs when infants interact with the environment, encounter something new, and experience a discrepancy between their existing way of thinking and their ability to understand this novel experience or situation.

## Piaget's Sensorimotor Stage

| Piaget's Stage Theory |
|---|
| Sensorimotor<br>• Infants understand the world through action. |
| Preoperational |
| Concrete operational |
| Formal operational |

Recall that Piaget refers to the first stage of development as the **sensorimotor stage**. This stage lasts from birth to about the end of the second year. As the term implies, the infant uses senses and motor abilities to understand the world, beginning with reflexes and ending with complex combinations of sensorimotor skills.

After extensive observations of infants and toddlers, especially his own three children, Piaget came to believe that infants and toddlers are intrinsically motivated to explore and experiment with their environment from the very beginning of life. It is for this reason that he described children—even infants and toddlers—as "little scientists." In Piaget's view, children are constantly trying to solve problems and construct their own knowledge in response to their experiences. Furthermore, they learn to do this on their own, without the intervention of older children or adults and without the need for rewards from adults to motivate their learning. This is why Piaget's theory is called *constructivist*. Children, in Piaget's view, construct their cognitive abilities through self-motivated action and through interaction with the environment (Piaget, 1952, 1954).

As noted in Chapter 1, Piaget's theory suggests that child development unfolds in an invariant sequence of cognitive stages. Each stage defines the way the child views the world and processes information at that point in time. Piaget believed that in the first stage of development, sensorimotor experience is essential for the emergence of cognitive abilities. Motor behavior and cognitive behavior are tightly linked, with each influencing the other. Thus, sitting, reaching, grasping, and walking are all important motor milestones in sensorimotor development. And it is through these motor behaviors that infants learn about and adapt to their environment. When infants explore an object, they may be refining their fine motor behavior. Above all, though, they are developing an understanding of the object and expanding their mind.

Piaget (1952, 1954) envisioned a child's knowledge as composed of **schemas**, or organized patterns of thought. The schemas represent things the child has experienced. Schemas are continually being modified through the processes of assimilation and accommodation, as discussed briefly in Chapter 1. **Assimilation** occurs when children fit something they learn into a mental structure they have already formed. **Accommodation** occurs when a new experience doesn't fit into an existing structure, and the structure must be changed.

Learning involves an ongoing attempt to achieve a balance, or equilibrium, between the assimilation and accommodation processes. For example, 18-month-old Roberto goes to the zoo and sees a zebra for the first time. He thinks it is a horse. He assimilates this information into his schema for horses because he is familiar with horses. But then he begins to see how the stripes make zebras different from horses. At this point, he can he begin to accommodate this new information into a new schema for zebras.

This example shows that as infants and toddlers interact with the environment and encounter something new, they experience a discrepancy between their existing way of thinking and their ability to understand this novel experience or situation. Their view of the world is thus challenged, and they are cast into a state of **disequilibrium**. This is what motivates problem solving and learning. It is the resolution of disequilibrium that leads to learning and the formation of new cognitive schemas.

During the sensorimotor period, according to Piaget, infants go through six substages. We summarize the substages in Table 6.1 and discuss them in more detail below.

### Substage 1: Reflexes (Birth to 1 Month)

In the first month of life, infants' behaviors reflect innate reflexes—automatic responses to particular stimuli. For instance, if you place something in the palm of a newborn girl's hand, her fingers will automatically close around it. Many of these inborn reflexes are designed to ensure the infant's survival. But, as we will see, the infant soon begins to modify these reflexes to better accommodate the environment. For instance, a 4-month-old baby girl, having gained control of the automatic grasp, is now able to reach out and grasp the mobile that is hanging from her crib.

*JGI/Jamie Grill/Getty Images*

Each time a baby explores an object, she is learning about and adapting to her environment.

**Table 6.1** Substages of the Sensorimotor Period

| Substage and Age | Characteristics |
|---|---|
| Reflex stage: birth–1 month | Associated primarily with the development of reflexes |
| Primary circular reaction phase: 1–4 months | Associated with the development of habits |
| Secondary circular reaction phase: 4–8 months | Associated primarily with the development of eye-hand coordination |
| Coordination of secondary circular reaction stage: 8–12 months | Ability to construct mental representations of objects |
| Tertiary circular reaction phase: 12–18 months | Active experimentation and creativity—the actions of the "little scientist" |
| Beginnings of symbolic representation: 18–24 months | Ability to use mental combinations to achieve a goal without resorting to trial-and-error experiments |

### Substage 2: Primary Circular Reactions (1 to 4 Months)

In the first few months of life, infants' behaviors are focused almost exclusively on their own bodies (in Piaget's terminology, the behaviors are *primary*). The behaviors are also repeated over and over again (that is, they are *circular*). Infants also begin to refine their reflexes and combine them into more complex actions, which they may repeat if the actions are pleasurable. Through a trial-and-error process, infants eventually repeat such actions until they become habits and can be performed voluntarily. An infant may discover that having his thumb in his mouth is soothing, for example. He begins to repeat this over and over again, especially when he is stressed (Brazelton & Nugent, 2011). While infants may discover something like this by chance, they repeat the action because they enjoy it.

After he discovers that sucking his thumb is soothing, a baby may develop this habit, especially when he is stressed.

### Substage 3: Secondary Circular Reactions (4 to 8 Months)

Sometime around 4 months, infants become more aware of and more responsive to the outside world (their behaviors become *secondary*). They also begin to notice that their behaviors can have interesting effects on the objects around them. They begin to act upon the world. For instance, an infant may pick up and then drop a rattle and listen to the sound as it crashes on the hard floor. Each time his caregiver gives the rattle back to him, he may drop it again. Infants in this substage seem fascinated by the effects of their actions. At this point, however, they are not necessarily making a conscious connection between the things they do and the resulting consequences.

Two new abilities emerge at this stage. First, we see *intentional grasping*, in which infants intentionally reach for or point in the direction of a desired object. Second, we see the first evidence of *means-end behavior*. This kind of behavior involves taking a deliberate and planned step to achieve a goal when there is an obstacle, such as recovering a toy from under a cover.

Toward the later part of this substage, infants begin to have a sense of **object permanence**, the understanding that objects continue to exist even when they cannot be seen, heard, or touched. As you will see, Piaget did not consider this sense to be reliably in place until later. In the third substage, infants still make what is referred to as the *A-not-B error*. The error is made by infants who have successfully uncovered a toy at location A and continue to reach to that location for the toy even after watching it being moved to a nearby location B, as shown in Figure 6.1. It is as if they do not

**object permanence** Understanding that objects continue to exist even when they cannot be seen, heard, or touched.

realize that the toy is now under the new cover. Babies only gradually learn how to make predictions about how objects appear and disappear once they vanish from sight.

### Substage 4: Coordination of Secondary Circular Reactions (8 to 12 Months)

The fourth substage is an extremely important period of development. Here, the infant displays what Piaget refers to as the first proper intelligence. For one thing, the period marks the beginning of goal orientation—the deliberate planning of steps to meet an objective. In engaging in goal-directed behavior, infants behave in ways that they *know* will bring about desired results. For example, suppose an infant sees the string of a pull-toy near her. In an earlier stage, she might have crawled over to the toy itself to play with it. Now, she grabs the string and purposely pulls the toy to her. New discoveries are no longer accidental but intentional.

Infants in this stage also begin to combine behaviors in new ways to accomplish their goals. An infant at this stage, for example, may see a bowl of cereal behind his cup, push aside the cup, and reach for the cereal. By combining the pushing and reaching schemas, he is able to reach his goal of getting the bowl of cereal.

But the major accomplishment at this substage is object permanence, one of the main developmental tasks of the infant-toddler period. As we noted earlier, object permanence can be defined as the realization that physical objects continue to exist even when they are removed from view. The infant at this stage is no longer susceptible to the A-not-B error. Thus, when a caregiver hides an attractive toy beneath a blanket, the infant knows that the toy still exists, knows where it is, and attempts to retrieve it. The acquisition of object permanence means that the infant has some ability to use symbolic thought, because the infant can now construct mental representations of objects.

### Substage 5: Tertiary Circular Reactions (12 to 18 Months)

Beginning sometime around their first birthday, infants show increasing flexibility and creativity in their behaviors. Their experimentation with objects often leads to new outcomes (the term *tertiary* reflects this new versatility). Piaget illustrated tertiary circular reactions with a description of his daughter Jacqueline, then 14 months old:

> Jacqueline holds in her hands an object which is new to her; a round, flat box which she turns all over, shakes, rubs against the bassinet, etc. She lets it go and tries to pick it up. But she only succeeds in touching it with her index finger, without grasping it. She nevertheless makes an attempt and presses on the edge. The box then tilts up and falls again. Jacqueline, very much interested in this fortuitous result, immediately applies herself to studying it. . . . Jacqueline immediately rests the box on the ground and pushes it as far as possible (it is noteworthy that care is taken to push the box far away in order to reproduce the same conditions as the first attempt, as though this were a necessary condition for obtaining the result). Afterward Jacqueline puts her finger on the box and presses it. But as she places her finger on the center of the box she simply displaces it and makes it slide instead of tilting it up. She amuses herself with this game and keeps it up (resumes it after intervals, etc.) for several minutes. Then, changing the point of contact, she finally again places her finger on the edge of the box, which tilts it up. She repeats this many times, varying the conditions, but keeping track of her discovery: now she only presses on the edge! (Piaget, 1952, p. 272)

**FIGURE 6.1 The A-not-B Task** In the A-not-B task, a researcher hides a toy in one position (position A), and the baby retrieves it. After several repetitions, the researcher takes the toy from the baby and places it in a different position (position B) as the baby watches. But the baby once again searches for the toy in position A. This behavior is taken as evidence that the baby cannot predict what happens to an object when it disappears.

As we see from this example, this stage is associated primarily with the discovery of new means to meet goals. It is at this point that Piaget describes the child as a "young scientist," conducting experiments to discover new methods of meeting challenges.

© Yukmin/Asia Images/Corbis

The emergence of symbolic thought makes it possible for toddlers to engage in make-believe play.

### Substage 6: Mental Representation (18 to 24 Months)

Piaget proposed that in the latter half of the second year, young children develop symbolic thought. That is, they think about objects and events in terms of internal, mental entities, or *symbols*. They may "experiment" with objects in their minds, first predicting what will happen if they do something to an object, then transforming their plans into action. To some degree, mental prediction and planning replace overt trial-and-error, as growing toddlers experiment and attempt to solve problems. For example, suppose a toddler's ball rolls under the bed. He will now move around the bed and anticipate where the ball will come out, rather than follow the ball directly. He can imagine the whereabouts of an invisible object. The child now fully understands object permanence and no longer makes the A-not-B error. The child can now reason about where the object may be when invisible displacement occurs.

Symbolic or make-believe play now becomes possible. Toddlers can recall and copy another person's behaviors hours or days after observing the behaviors. This ability, called *deferred imitation*, is another aspect of mental representation. Because toddlers can recall and imitate other people in their absence, they can engage in make-believe and pretend play—for instance, by "talking" on a toy telephone or "driving" using the toy steering wheel attached to their car seats. The capacity for symbol use and representational thought marks the young child's passage into the preoperational stage, which we discuss in Chapter 9.

**what if...?**

Suppose you play a hiding game with a 6- or 7-month-old baby. You need a cloth and a toy or something that really interests the baby. Show the baby the toy, watch her reaction, and then hide the toy under a cloth within her reach. Now watch what she does. She may freeze, with a look of puzzlement on her face. She will not search for the toy. But if you pull the cloth off the toy, she will become excited again. It is clearly "out of sight, out of mind," as far as the baby is concerned. Try the same trick with a 12-month-old. You will see that she easily finds the toy under the cloth. What has happened to make this development possible in the older child?

## Challenges to Piaget's Theory: Alternative Explanations

Research confirms Piaget's contention that the infant is an active learner. It generally supports his belief that exploration and interaction with the environment promote cognitive growth. Indeed, research in psychobiology and the neurosciences demonstrates that stimulation from the external environment can have profound effects on the pattern of connectivity in the developing nervous system (Fields, Yu, & Nelson, 1991; Nelson & Luciana, 2008; Tenenbaum, 2011). These effects can be detected in changes in the functional properties of the nervous system, as well as structural changes in branching and synapse formation in the baby's brain (Als et al., 2004; Diamond & Amso, 2008; Diamond & Goldman-Rakic, 1989; Greenough & Black, 1992).

However, Piaget's accounts of infant development have been challenged on several grounds (Cohen & Cashon, 2006). First, as Piaget himself acknowledged, development does not always progress as smoothly as his theory seems to predict. Gaps occur in the developmental progression, suggesting that the stage model is at best a useful approximation—a general guide to cognitive development.

Second, many modern infancy researchers disagree with Piaget's findings about when and how object permanence develops. A burgeoning body of research shows that infants seem to understand much earlier than Piaget believed that objects continue to exist after they are hidden. One group of researchers, for example, found that

4-month-olds remembered the location of a hidden object from 2 to 8 seconds after it was put out of sight (Ruffman, Slade, & Redman, 2005). Researchers have also shown that even at 3 to 4 months, infants expect objects to be substantial (in the sense that other objects cannot move through them) and permanent (in the sense that they continue to exist when they are out of sight) (Aguiar & Baillargeon, 2002; Baillargeon, 1987, 2004; Baillargeon, Kotovsky, & Needham, 1995; Luo & Baillargeon, 2005). How did these researchers know what the infants were expecting? We discuss their methods later in this chapter.

Third, many theorists have demonstrated that Piaget's conclusions tend to underestimate infants' knowledge and reasoning abilities. As mentioned in Chapter 5, the newborn is capable of much more complex behavior than the simple reflexive behavior Piaget described. According to modern researchers, infants' perceptual abilities also are more highly developed earlier than Piaget believed. In addition, some information-processing principles may be hardwired into the brain. We discuss information-processing theories later in this section.

*Elizabeth Crews Photography*

By the end of the first year, infants have mastered object permanence. They know that a hidden object still exists, and they can uncover it, as this little girl has done. Recent research suggests that information processing principles may be hardwired into the brain.

## Vygotsky's Sociocultural Perspective

Like Piaget, Lev Vygotsky saw children as actively engaged in their own learning from the beginning of their lives. Vygotsky did not, however, subscribe to Piaget's hypothesis that cognitive development unfolds in an invariant sequence of cognitive stages. Vygotsky's theory also differs from Piaget's in the fundamental role that it assigns to social interaction (Gauvain, 2001; Hatano, 1993; Vygotsky, 1978, 1986, 1987). He argued that cognitive development results from a process whereby a child learns by sharing problem-solving experiences with someone else, often a parent or teacher but sometimes a sibling or peer. Cognitive activity and development occur in social situations. Thus, children—even infants—engage in problem-solving activities in collaboration with others (DeVries, 2000; Moll, 1990). The human infant cannot, even theoretically, learn in isolation.

### The Zone of Proximal Development and Scaffolding

A core aspect of Vygotsky's sociocultural theory is the zone of proximal development, which we first mentioned in Chapter 1. Vygotsky described the **zone of proximal development (ZPD)** as the distance between a person's actual developmental level, as determined by independent problem solving, and the higher level of development that could be achieved under the guidance of an adult or a more capable peer (Vygotsky, 1978, p. 86).

Closely tied to the concept of the zone of proximal development is the concept of scaffolding. **Scaffolding** can be described as the support that enables a child to solve a problem, carry out a task, or achieve a goal that would be beyond his or her unassisted efforts (Bruner, 1985). The person providing scaffolding may be a parent, a teacher, an older sibling, or a more experienced peer. Scaffolding can take various forms, such as prompts, modeling, explicit verbal direction, and encouragement. Whatever the precise nature of the scaffolding, it enables a child to accomplish increasingly challenging goals—whether learning to use a spoon, to talk, or to kick a ball (Bruner & Sherwood, 1975). As children experience success in solving increasingly difficult problems, they internalize the skills required to solve the problems independently and are no longer reliant on the support of others (Rogoff, Mistry, Goncu, & Mosier, 1993).

Studies have confirmed the value of scaffolding for infants and toddlers. Participants in one study, for example, were toddlers who had been born preterm or low birth weight (Dilworth-Bart, Poehlmann, Hilgendorf, Miller, & Lambert, 2010). The toddlers whose mothers provided scaffolding as they performed tasks—using verbal, nonverbal, or physical efforts to help the children and maintain their attention, for example—scored higher on standardized tests of verbal working memory. This finding is consistent with those of previous studies linking parental scaffolding to preterm infants' developmental capacities (for example, Als et al., 2004; Landry, Miller-Loncar, Smith, & Swank, 2002). In another study, researchers found that scaffolding provided by child caregivers enhanced infants' social competence with peers (Williams, Mastergeorge, & Ontai, 2010). And a study of scaffolding during mother-infant play

**zone of proximal development (ZPD)** Vygotsky's term for the distance between a person's actual developmental level, as determined by independent problem solving, and the higher level of development that could be achieved under the guidance of an adult or a more capable peer.

**scaffolding** Support that enables a child or novice to solve a problem, carry out a task, or achieve a goal that would be beyond his or her unassisted efforts.

**guided participation** Rogoff's term describing the process by which children actively acquire new skills and problem-solving capabilities through their participation in meaningful activities alongside parents, adults, or other more experienced companions.

found that scaffolding provided at 9 and 15 months was related to improved scores on standardized tests (Stevens, Blake, Vitale, & MacDonald, 1998). Mothers' efforts to scaffold their 2-year-olds' attention have also been positively associated with their children's social and cognitive development as they enter school (Landry et al., 2002; Landry, Smith, Swank, & Miller-Loncar, 2000). As we will see later in the chapter, mothers also tend to scaffold their infants' language learning by naturally modifying their own speech and behavior (Kuhl & Damasio, 2012).

### Challenges to Vygotsky's Approach: Guided Participation

Critics of Vygotsky's approach maintain that by emphasizing the social context of learning, his theory seems to neglect the contribution of the child, and to give too much prominence to the role of direct teaching (DeVries, 2000). Barbara Rogoff's construct of guided participation, while grounded in Vygotsky's theory, corrects this apparent imbalance. Rogoff stresses the active role of children in their own cognitive growth and the complementary role of parents and other caring adults in supporting, assisting, and guiding children's intellectual development (Rogoff, 1990).

**Guided participation** is a process by which children actively acquire new skills and problem-solving capabilities through participation in meaningful activities alongside parents, adults, or other more experienced companions. In this view, "the child is not merely a learner, or a naïve actor who follows the instructions or prompts of the more experienced partner. Rather, the child is a full participant, albeit a participant of a specific type characterized by individual and developmentally related skills, interests, and resources" (Gauvain, 2001, p. 38).

Some of the most compelling illustrations of guided participation are evident in parents' interactions with infants and toddlers. Parents may support the learning of infants and toddlers by giving them explicit verbal and nonverbal guidance, such as labeling or modeling. They also provide more subtle direction by arranging and organizing their children's interactions with the environment. The basic processes of guided participation can be found in all cultural settings, although it may take different forms, reflecting different cultural practices (Rathunde & Csikszentmihalyi, 2006). The accompanying feature, Culture and Fatherhood, discusses one such cultural variation.

Comparisons of parent-toddler interaction from four cultural settings—Utah, Mexico (Mayan culture), Turkey, and India—demonstrate striking similarities, as well as distinctive differences, in guided participation practices (Rogoff et al., 1993). In one study, the authors compared U.S. mother-child pairs with Mexican Mayan mother-child pairs.

By arranging her daughter's play and offering support and guidance, this mother is encouraging her little girl to learn new skills.

## Culture and Fatherhood

Much research has shown that having an involved father is related to enhanced cognitive development and school achievement in children (Cabrera & Garcia-Coll, 2004; Shannon, Tamis-LeMonda, & Cabrera, 2006; Wilkinson, Magora, Garcia, & Khurana, 2009). Even in infancy, various aspects of father involvement, such as engaging in cognitively stimulating activities and providing physical care and warmth, are associated with cognitive gains (Nugent, 1991) and with a lower likelihood of cognitive delay (Bronte-Tinkew, Carrano, Horowitz, & Kinukawa, 2008).

Worldwide, fathers contribute much less than mothers to caring for infants and toddlers. Still, there is tremendous variation across countries and among men (Bruce, Lloyd, & Leonard, 1995; Population Council, 2001). Until recently, Latino fathers have been among those considered minimally involved in the care of their young children. They have often been depicted as authoritarian, "macho" figures who maintained respect by instilling fear in their children (Barker & Verani, 2008; Coltrane, Parke, & Adams, 2004; Falceto, Fernandes, Baratojo, & Giuglianai, 2008; Robbers, 2011). Now, however, an emerging body of research on Latino fathers calls this idea into question (Prado, Piovanotti, & Vieira, 2007).

According to this new research, while there are differences across settings, Latino fathers are warm and affectionate with their children (Benetti & Roopnarine, 2006; Cabrera & Garcia-Coll, 2004; Coltrane, 2001). One group of researchers, for example, studied a national sample of 9-month-old Latino infants born in the United States and living with both biological parents. The researchers found that, with some exceptions, the fathers had moderate to high levels of engagement with their infants (Cabrera, West, Shannon, & Brookes-Gunn, 2006). We cannot generalize these and other findings to all Latino men, of course. Nevertheless, the results suggest that Latino fathers are much more involved with their young children than older research indicated.

© Jeremy Woodhouse/Blend Images/Corbis

All mothers and their 20-month-old infants were observed in their homes as they interacted with selected materials, such as a baby doll and nesting dolls (a set of wooden dolls that fit one inside the other). Toddlers in both communities were similarly engaged in their tasks. In addition, all demonstrated a skillful approach to playing with the nesting dolls, and included a counting routine as they interacted with their mothers.

Even in these similar situations, however, there were differences. The Mayan caregivers did not direct the toddlers' activities by providing lessons or insisting that an activity be done in a certain way. The Mayan toddlers were responsible for observing, and even initiating, the activity. Their caregivers oriented the children to the activity, made suggestions, monitored the activities, and provided sensitive assistance when the toddlers needed help. In contrast, in the U.S. community, caregivers often took charge of problem solving and directed the toddlers' activities. These studies show that there are many different ways in which adults can effectively structure experiences for infants and toddlers.

### Other Theories

Two additional theories of particular interest for infancy and toddlerhood are dynamic systems theory and core knowledge theory. We discuss them briefly, next.

## Dynamic Systems Theory

As we pointed out in Chapter 1, systems theories emphasize the interactions between the child and the environment and how these interactions influence development. In the area of infant learning and development, many researchers have adopted concepts, methods, and tools from dynamic systems theory, introduced in Chapter 5 (Fischer & Bidell, 2006; Rose & Fisher, 2009; Thelen & Smith, 1994). From this perspective, an infant actively puts together a skill to achieve a goal within the limits set by the infant's body and environment.

For example, the development of the ability to grasp requires a good deal of object exploration. This capacity does not emerge until after the baby is able to maintain a stable posture and coordinate eye and hand movements (at about 3 months of age). These events depend on physical maturation. As parents observe their baby's emerging ability to stabilize his head and shoulders and refine his reach, they begin to present many daily opportunities for him to interact with objects—presenting him with toys to explore, for example (Fogel, Messinger, Dickson, & Hsu, 1999; Lobo & Galloway, 2008). With this kind of support, the baby develops a whole new reaching and exploring repertoire, which in turn elicits new responses from his caregivers. Thus, learning comes from more than just the child and the context: It is always about the child-in-context (Rose & Fisher, 2009). Learning *emerges* through continuous interactions between person and context.

## Core Knowledge Theory

*Nativist* perspectives contrast with systems theories in their emphasis on abilities that are essentially hardwired into the brain at birth. Theorists who hold a nativist view assume that infants are born with a certain amount of innate knowledge, called *core knowledge*. They propose that infants come into the world with innate organizing concepts that enable them to structure their experiences and learn about their physical world with little explicit instruction (for example, see Baillargeon, 2004; Baillargeon, Kotovsky & Needham, 1995; Carey, 1993, 1999, 2009; Clifton, Perris, & McCall, 1999; Spelke, 1998; Spelke & Kinzler, 2007).

© KidStock/Blend Images/Corbis

Even at 5 or 6 months of age, a baby expects that water will react differently from a solid surface.

In support of this view, research has demonstrated that, by 6 months of age, infants already have expectations about physical events. For example, infants as young as 5 months of age notice the difference between liquids and solids, and have different expectations for both (Hespos, Ferry, & Rips, 2009). By about 7 months of age, infants know that a solid object cannot pass through another solid object (Spelke et al., 1992). You will read more about studies in this area later in the chapter.

# Information-Processing Approaches

We turn next to theoretical approaches that explain specific aspects of infant cognitive development. Broadly speaking, these approaches take an information-processing perspective. As we pointed out in Chapter 1, this perspective focuses on explaining what's going on in the human mind as it seeks to acquire, process, retain, and comprehend information. Information-processing theories aim to show how information is organized and stored in memory and how processing changes with age and experience. Although they may not qualify as formal theories, these approaches share certain assumptions and predictions about infant cognition. They also use specific research techniques to investigate those predictions.

One strength of the information-processing approach is that it breaks down cognitive processes into their component steps. The focus is on specific aspects of development rather than on a whole stage of development. Contrast this with Piaget's theory, which proposes that cognitive maturation occurs at the same time across different domains of knowledge. We call this a "domain-general" approach. Information-processing theorists argue that infant competencies are too complex to be learned through a domain-general process. For that reason, they take a "domain-specific" approach; that is, they tend to confine their research to specific aspects of infant cognitive development, such as memory, imitation, categorization, or understanding of objects and people. We next focus on their ideas about two developmental areas: memory and **categorization**.

**categorization** The process of forming groups of similar objects; enables infants to effectively reduce the amount of information they must process, learn, and remember.

**explicit memory** Conscious memory; permits recall and recognition of names, places, and events. Also called declarative memory.

**implicit memory** Automatic and unconscious memory. Also called *procedural* or *nondeclarative memory.*

## Memory

Memory is fundamental to learning. We depend on memory to remember the past, to predict the future, and to build up knowledge of the world. Memory can be divided into short-term and long-term elements. Information is initially stored in short-term (also called working) memory, where it is either passed to long-term memory or lost. Long-term memory holds the information we have previously gathered. There it remains available for use—at a moment's notice—for some future task or challenge. We will discuss memory in more detail in later chapters.

For now, we discuss just how much infants can remember. Can you remember anything from the time you were an infant or toddler? Adults tend to have few (if any) memories from the first two years of life. Until recently, this "amnesia of childhood" was widely attributed to immaturity in areas of the brain related to memory. However, changing perspectives on the nature of the infant mind (Mandler, 2004) and brain (Csibra, Kushnerenko, & Grossmann, 2008; Nelson et al., 2006; Squire & Knowlton, 1995), coupled with methodological advances, have changed our appreciation of how much infants remember (Bauer, 2002, 2004, 2005, 2006, 2007; Bauer, San Souci, & Pathman, 2010; Collie & Hayne, 1999; Usher & Neisser, 1993).

In order to understand what babies remember and how much they can store in their memories, we need to examine the development of explicit and implicit memory. **Explicit memory**, also called declarative memory, is conscious. It is the part of memory that permits us to recognize and consciously recall names, places, and events. It is the kind of memory that enables us to tell a story that makes sense of something that happened. **Implicit memory**, also called procedural or nondeclarative memory, in contrast, is automatic and unconscious. The skill of bike riding is an example of implicit memory in adults. You can probably ride a bike effortlessly today, though you have no conscious recall of the process of learning to ride.

Infants do not recall information using explicit memory in the same way adults do. There is evidence, however, of implicit memory systems in infants, even very young ones. They appear to progressively store their experiences, even if they cannot recall them during infancy. Infants may not consciously remember their repeated interactions with their caregivers, for example, but these interactions may still create implicit memories that are critical for their future development (Siegel, 2001).

Explicit memory is assumed to develop as a function of neurological and cognitive development (Nelson, 1986; Nelson, 1995; Nelson & Fivush, 2000; Nelson & Luciuana, 2008; Schacter, 1992). But when does this development occur in infants? Piagetian theory suggests that for the first 18 to 24 months of their lives, infants lack the ability to mentally represent objects and events. Although Piaget did not use the term, this seems to imply that he assumed that infants of this age lack explicit memory. However, in one of the first experimental studies of early memory, researchers found that children as young as 3 years of age could provide brief but well-organized reports about common activities such as going to a fast food restaurant, grocery shopping, and making cookies (Nelson & Gruendel, 1981,1986). Studies such as these opened the door for investigations of memory in children younger than 3 years. After all, if 3-year-olds already have well-organized representations of past events, then the capacity to construct them must have developed earlier.

Studies of infant memory show that the full neurological network that supports explicit memory reaches functional (though not full) maturity late in the first year (Bauer, 2004, 2006, 2007; Bauer and Lukowski, 2010; McCandliss, Sandak, Beck, &

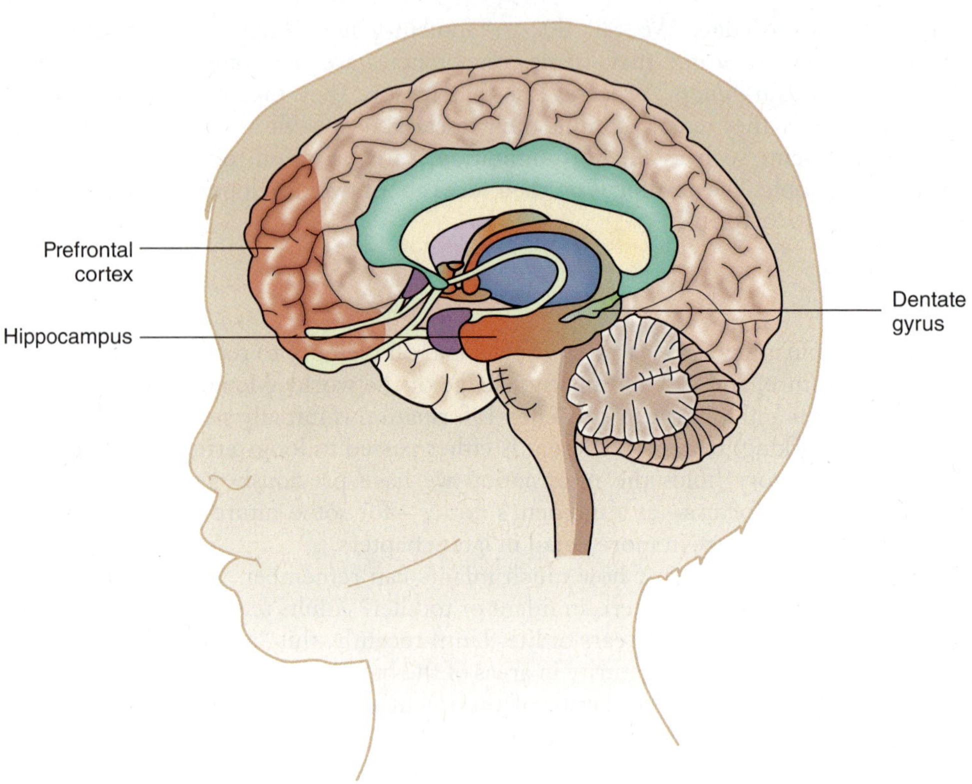


**FIGURE 6.2 Memory Regions in the Brain** Memory regions in the brain include the hippocampus and the prefrontal cortex. The dentate gyrus region of the hippocampus matures later than the rest of the structure, at around 12 to 15 months. The density of synapses in the prefrontal cortex increases dramatically at 8 months and peaks between 15 and 24 months. Both these developments lead to improvements in memory.

Perfetti, 2003). Which brain areas support the development of explicit memory? The *hippocampus* plays a key role (see Figure 6.2). The cells that make up most of this structure are formed by the end of the prenatal period. However, the cells in one part of the hippocampus, called the *dentate gyrus*, do not appear adultlike until 12 to 15 months of age. This area links the rest of the hippocampus with the cortex—the outer part of the brain. Another area involved in memory function in infants is the *prefrontal cortex*. The density of synapses in this area increases dramatically at 8 months and peaks between 15 and 24 months. The growing density of synapses increases the efficiency and speed of memory. Not surprisingly, near the end of the first year, infants show great strides in their ability to recall. Thus, the timing of improvements in performance of memory tasks corresponds to the timing of changes in the developing brain.

Researchers have used *elicited imitation* to assess explicit memory in infants (Bauer, 2006, 2007). In these experiments, infants are given objects and shown how to use them to make something interesting happen. For example, they are given two nesting cups and a block, and the experimenter shows them that by putting the block into one cup, covering it with the other cup, and shaking the cups, they can make a rattle sound. This task is used to see how well infants encode new experiences into memory and later retrieve them. (*Encoding* involves first paying attention to information and then forming an internal representation of it. We discuss it further in Chapter 9.) Researchers test encoding by measuring immediate imitation—how well the child makes the rattle sound right after seeing the adult do it. They test retrieval by measuring delayed imitation—how well the child makes the rattle sound weeks or months later.

Such research reveals that two dimensions of memory improvement are especially noticeable: the length of time infants remember and the robustness of their memories. *Robustness* refers to the strength of memories and is evidenced by the number of repetitions infants require in order to remember an experience. Table 6.2 describes some of these changes.

## Categorization

The ability to categorize contributes to human survival. Humans must frequently decide, for example, whether one species of animal is likely to be harmless or dangerous,

**Table 6.2** Changes in Explicit Memory in Infants 6 to 20 Months of Age

| Duration of Memory | |
|---|---|
| **Age** | **Research Findings** |
| 6 months | Able to remember for 24 hours some of the actions of a 3-step sequence involving a puppet (Barr, Dowden, & Hayne, 1996). |
| 9 months | Exhibit memory for individual actions after delays of up to 5 weeks (Carver & Bauer, 1999, 2001). |
| 10–11 months | Exhibit memory after delays as long as 3 months (Carver & Bauer, 2001; Mandler & McDonough, 1995). |
| 14–16 months | Exhibit memory after 6 months (Bauer, Wenner, Dropik, & Wewerka, 2000). |
| 20 months | Exhibit memory after as long as 12 months (Bauer, 2006; Bauer et al., 2000). |

| Robustness of Memory | |
|---|---|
| **Age** | **Research Findings** |
| 6 months | Actions modeled 6 times are remembered 24 hours later (Barr et al., 1996). If the actions are modeled only 3 times, there is no evidence of memory. |
| 9 months | Actions modeled 3 times are remembered over 24 hours (Meltzoff, 1988). In one study, 9-month-olds who saw actions modeled as few as 2 times within a single exposure session remembered them a week later (Bauer, Wiebe, Waters, & Bangston, 2001). |
| 14 months | A single exposure session is all that is necessary to support recall of multiple actions over 4 months (Meltzoff, 1995). |

whether one type of food is a fruit or a vegetable, or whether an object is a knife or a spoon. Along with memory, the ability to categorize is especially important for learning in infancy, when many new objects, events, and people are encountered every day. Without the ability to categorize, infants would have to respond anew to each novel thing they experienced (Bornstein, 1984, 1985; Ferry, Hespos, & Waxman, 2010; Rakison & Oakes, 2003; Welder & Graham, 2006). By forming groups of similar objects, infants can effectively reduce the amount of information they must process, learn, and remember (Mervis & Rosch, 1981; Younger & Fearing, 2000).

*Everyday stories*

TODDLERS—COLLECTORS IN THE MAKING Are you a collector? What do you collect? Why do you collect? People generally collect things because they find collecting fun. And part of the fun is deciding what belongs in your collection and what does not. This is exactly what toddlers are beginning to learn. If your give your 18-month-old cousin a set of nesting objects or stacking cones, you are likely to make him very happy. Most toddlers take great pleasure in trying to arrange the rings of stacking cones or fit and nest objects inside each other. Because they are now concerned with similarities and size, they try to line things up and put objects in piles of the same color, size, or shape. They are also beginning to learn that they don't need to look through big piles or boxes every time they want to find a special toy. Putting all of the Legos together and all the play dishes together, for example, makes life simpler—for the toddlers themselves, as well as for their parents.

Stephan Zabel/Getty Images

Like this little boy, most toddlers enjoy arranging objects in piles of the same size, color, or shape.

Forming categories requires that infants attend to, perceive, and compare the features of multiple items (Mandler, 2004; Quinn, 2010; Quinn & Bhatt, 2012). When can infants do that? The answer is, in the first year of life. By about 7 to 9 months of age, infants are able to form conceptual categories. In one study of 7- to 11-month-olds, for example, infants correctly classified birds as animals and airplanes as vehicles, even though the objects were perceptually similar (Mandler & McDonough, 1993). Jean Mandler's research has demonstrated that infants' first categories tend to be broad, such as "animal." Gradually, over the first two years, these broad concepts become more finely differentiated into concepts such as "land animal," then "dog" (Mandler, 2006, p. 4). You may wonder how researchers study categorization in infants. Generally, they use *visual preference procedures*, which we discuss in the next section.

Some investigators believe that infants' categorization is based only on specific surface features (Oakes & Madole, 2003; Quinn, 2011; Quinn & Eimas, 1996, 1998), such as facial information or external shape. Quinn and Eimas (1996) found that the early categorization of dogs and cats is primarily based on differences in their facial features, rather than overall appearance. We look more closely at the development of infants' ability to categorize faces in Chapter 7.

Recent research, then, has demonstrated infants' ability to categorize. The specifics of various theories of categorization may differ (Cohen, 2009; Younger & Fearing, 2000). What they have in common, though, is the idea that specialized, innate processes enable infants to categorize. Over time, they become sensitive to increasingly sophisticated and detailed levels of perceptual information. By the end of infancy, the ability to form categories is enhanced by language—as we will soon see. But what changes in the brain make all this possible?

THE DEVELOPING BRAIN

## The Basis for Cognitive Gains

As noted in Chapter 5, the brain changes rapidly in size and structure during the first years of life (Bell & Fox, 1992; Kagan, 2006; Nelson et al., 2006; Nelson, Furtado, Fox, & Zeanah, 2009; Nelson & Luciana, 2008; Shonkoff & Phillips, 2000). Although scientists still have much to learn about brain development in the early years, it is clear that different parts of the brain develop at different rates. As you can see in Figure 6.3, development begins earlier in primary sensory regions like the auditory and visual cortex and later in the temporal and frontal lobes, which are involved in higher cognitive functions. Notice in the figure how steeply the developmental curves rise and fall

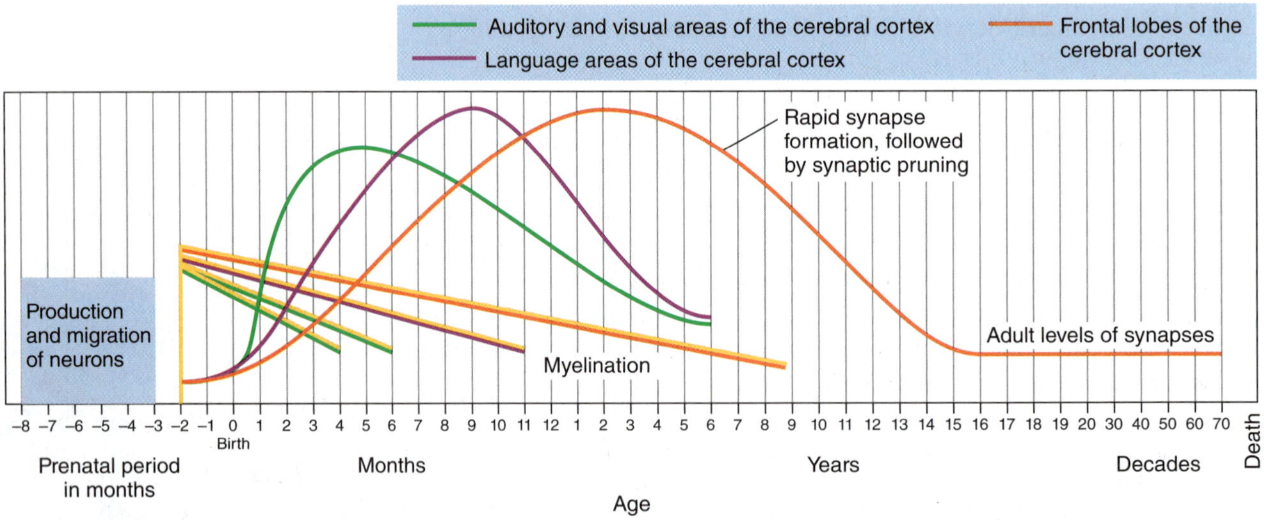


**FIGURE 6.3 Rapid Brain Development in the First Years** The brain develops rapidly during the first years of life, but the various parts of the brain develop at different rates. Development begins earlier in primary sensory regions like the auditory and visual cortex, and later in the temporal and frontal lobes, which are involved in higher cognitive functions. Myelination, synapse formation, and pruning are all part of the developmental process.

Reprinted from Thompson, R. A., & Nelson, C. A. (2001). Developmental science and the media: early brain development. *American Psychologist* 56(1):5 -15; reprinted with permission from Charles Nelson III, PhD, Professor of Pediatrics and Neuroscience, Harvard Medical School, and the American Psychological Association.

during the first months and years of life. This pattern shows just how massive and rapid the structural changes in the brain are during this period.

As we continue to look at how cognitive development proceeds in infancy, we need to keep in mind that thinking is not localized to any specific region of the brain. Rather, it can be seen as a global attribute of the brain. Nevertheless, the prefrontal area plays a particularly important role in cognition. This is because it participates in the important mental activities of attention, categorization, memory, and language. Recall from Chapter 2 that the prefrontal area is the region of the frontal lobe closest to the forehead. This area, and specifically the prefrontal cortex on the area's surface, is associated with *executive function*, the ability to regulate thinking and behavior. (You can see the position of the prefrontal cortex by looking back at Figure 6.2.)

The prefrontal cortex is one of the last areas to develop during the early years of life, and its immaturity places limits on the infant's capacity for remembering and planning. At around 8 months, however, there is evidence to show that the prefrontal cortex is beginning to play a greater role. There is a striking parallel, for example, between activity in the prefrontal cortex and the infant's ability to solve the classic A-not-B problem. As we mentioned earlier, to solve this problem, infants must realize that physical objects continue to exist even when they are removed from view (Baird et al., 2002; Marcovitch & Zelazo, 1999; Shinskey & Munakata, 2003; Wang, Baillargeon, & Brueckner, 2004). The ability to plan, remember, and categorize are all functions that are emerging at this time. As the infant grows over the next 12 months, brain maturation makes prolonged attention, concentration, and more complex problem solving possible.

### ✓ CHECK YOUR PROGRESS

1. Describe the substages in Piaget's sensorimotor stage.
2. How does Vygotsky's theory of learning differ from Piaget's theory?
3. What is Rogoff's "guided participation" approach?
4. How does memory develop in infants?
5. Why is the ability to categorize so important in infancy?
6. What is the importance of the prefrontal cortex in cognitive development in infancy?

## Research Methods

**[ KEY QUESTION ] 2.** What research techniques are used to assess cognitive development in infants and toddlers?

We have already seen that Piaget thought of small children as "little scientists." But how did he reach this conclusion? After all, while physical growth and change are easily observed and measured in infants and toddlers, cognitive change and development are harder to evaluate. Since babies have no language, we cannot ask them what they are thinking. Piaget, as well as Vygotsky and others, realized that the only way to unlock babies' minds was to observe their nonverbal behavior carefully and systematically. Using pen and paper, Piaget recorded in minute, crystallized detail the patterns of behavior of young infants in natural settings in daily diaries. His observations were the building blocks of his theory.

Systematic observation remains the essential method for infancy researchers today. In recent times, though, the use of videotape and digital technology has enabled them to objectively measure what babies do by looking at these recordings slowly, over and over again. In addition, modern scientists have devised many ingenious ways to look into the infant's mind and study how it works. Over the last two decades or so, researchers have developed various indirect research methods to help them understand what infants and toddlers perceive, learn, remember, and understand. We review some of those methods here.

**visual preference procedures** Indirect research methods that use visual attention as a way of assessing the thought processes of babies and very young children.

**habituation techniques** Indirect research techniques based on the tendency of babies to become bored with a familiar stimulus and look away from it and toward something less familiar.

**violation-of-expectation method** A visual preference research method that assesses infants' ability to distinguish between an expected and an unexpected event.

*Everyday stories*

A LITTLE SCIENTIST What is going on in a baby's mind as she looks at you? As she looks at a patch of shimmering sunshine on the wall beside her crib? Does she like what she sees? To find out, we need to know what babies like to look at. One way researchers have investigated this question takes advantage of babies' sucking abilities. Babies suck in short bursts, pause for a moment, and then begin another burst. They can control the length of the bursts and pauses. How can sucking tell us what babies like to look at? Researchers place a nipple into a baby's mouth. The nipple is connected electronically to a monitor so that the baby can see the monitor screen. A baby of 3 or 4 months quickly learns that when she wants to change pictures, she needs to suck. When she wants to look longer at a picture, she pauses. The baby will turn over the pictures at the rate that reflects her interest in each picture.

## Visual Preference Procedures

The most popular indirect methods for the study of infant learning are **visual preference procedures**. These procedures measure visual attention. A researcher may, for example, show an infant colorful photographs of common objects, or movies of animated shapes that move around a computer screen. Then the researcher simply records how long the infant looks at each object or shape. Special eye-tracking equipment (basically, a special camera embedded in a computer monitor) may enable the researcher to determine exactly where the infant is looking. Visual preference procedures are based on the assumption that infants prefer to look at something novel, rather than something familiar, and so will look longer at the novel object (Cohen & Cashon, 2006). The habituation techniques discussed next rely on inferences based on infants' visual preferences.

Helen Maris

Visual preference procedures tell researchers what a baby is choosing to look at, and how long that item will hold the baby's attention.

### Habituation Techniques

Many contemporary researchers use **habituation techniques** in studying infant cognition (Turk-Browne, Scholl, & Chun, 2008). Habituation occurs when we become familiar with something because of repeated exposure to it. When this technique is used with infants, researchers familiarize them with particular stimuli and then compare their reactions to the familiar stimuli with their reactions to new, and perhaps inconsistent, stimuli.

In well-known experiments, for example, Spelke and colleagues (1992) wanted to find out whether 3- to 4-month-old infants could tell that an object that falls from view follows a continuous path and cannot pass through solid surfaces (see Figure 6.4). To investigate this question, they first habituated the infants to a display in which they dropped a ball behind a screen. They then lifted the screen to show the infants the ball resting on the floor of the display. For the test trials, they introduced a horizontal surface above the floor. In the "consistent," or "possible," test condition, infants saw the ball resting on the top of the surface after falling. In the second test condition, the ball rested under the surface—a condition that is "inconsistent," or "impossible," because falling balls cannot pass through solid surfaces. The infants looked longer at the impossible condition. This result suggested to the researchers that the infants "inferred that the ball would move on a connected, unobstructed path" (p. 613).

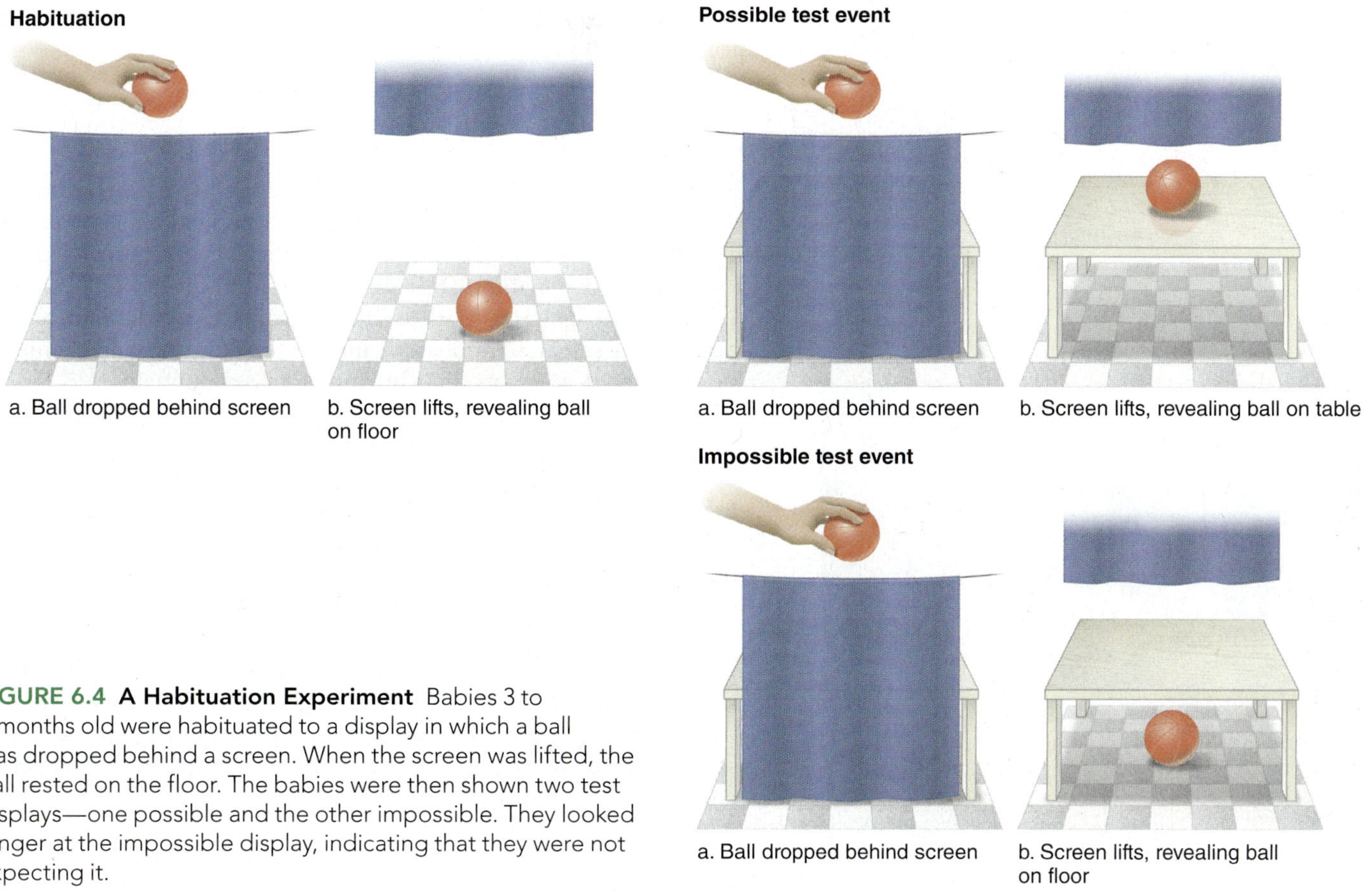


**FIGURE 6.4 A Habituation Experiment** Babies 3 to 4 months old were habituated to a display in which a ball was dropped behind a screen. When the screen was lifted, the ball rested on the floor. The babies were then shown two test displays—one possible and the other impossible. They looked longer at the impossible display, indicating that they were not expecting it.

## The Violation-of-Expectation Method

Another variation on the visual preference paradigm is the **violation-of-expectation method**. If infants look reliably longer at the unexpected than the expected event, experimenters take this as evidence of what is going on in the infants' minds. Infants see two test events: an expected event, which is consistent with the expectation examined in the experiment, and an unexpected event, which violates this expectation. They infer that the infants (1) possess the expectation under investigation, (2) detect the violation in the unexpected event, and (3) are "surprised" by this violation. The term *surprised* denotes a state of heightened interest or attention.

In one violation-of-expectation experiment, researchers investigated expectations concerning object permanence (Wang, Baillargeon, & Paterson, 2005). Infants aged 2½ to 3 months first saw a toy duck resting on the left end of a platform. When they became familiar with these props, an experimenter's hand lowered a cover over the duck (see Figure 6.5). The hand slid the cover to the right end of the platform and then lifted the cover to reveal no duck. This cleverly designed study implies that babies as

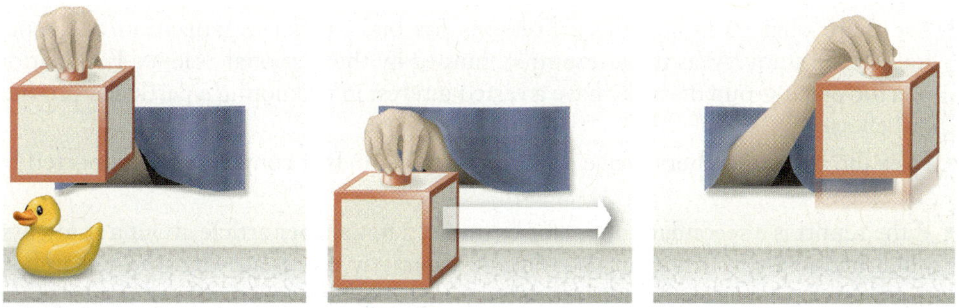

**FIGURE 6.5 A Violation-of-Expectation Experiment** In this violation-of-expectation experiment, infants 2½ to 3 months old saw two violations, each involving a duck that seemed to disappear while hidden behind a screen. The infants were surprised by the violations, suggesting to the researchers that the infants believed the duck continued to exist after it was hidden.

**object exploration approach** An approach in which researchers observe infants' exploration and manipulation of objects to assess their learning and development.

young as 3 months may know that objects exist continuously in space—even when they cannot see the objects.

## Object Exploration Approaches

The studies just described illustrate how investigators have used visual preferences to make inferences about infants' cognitive abilities. Some researchers believe that early cognitive processing can be better assessed by observing infants performing tasks, such as active exploration, that involve manipulation and interaction (for example, Lobo & Galloway, 2008; Mandler, 2004; Oakes & Madole, 2003). Using this **object exploration approach**, researchers observe infants' exploration and manipulation of objects to assess their learning and development.

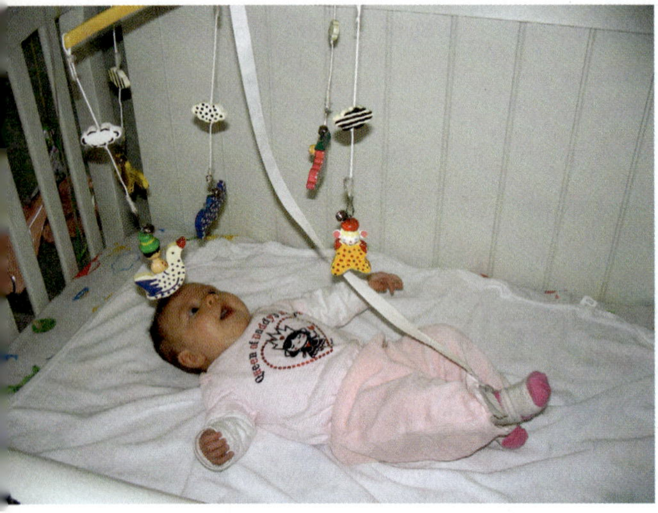

Courtesy of Carolyn Rovee-Collier

Carolyn Rovee-Collier and her colleagues discovered that even young infants could quickly learn to entertain themselves by kicking to make a mobile move.

One of the best examples of this kind of study of infant exploration is a classic experiment devised by Carolyn Rovee-Collier and her colleagues in the 1960s (Rovee & Rovee, 1969). The experiment examined the responses of 8- and 10-week-old infants at home in their cribs as they looked up at a mobile containing highly detailed, painted wooden figures. The researchers wanted to see if infants could learn to make the mobile move by kicking their feet. After measuring an infant's baseline level of kicking, the researchers used a cord to connect the infant's foot to the mobile. When the infant kicked, the mobile moved. And if he kicked hard enough, the wooden figures would bump into each other and make a pleasant knocking sound. The study revealed that even infants as young as 8 weeks old could learn the association between kicking and mobile movement. The use of this kind of active exploration procedure has enabled researchers to learn more about the memories and cognitive capacities of very young infants.

## Making Sense of Media Reports — Practice

The headline declared, "Babies can perform addition." The report that followed suggested—at first glance, at least—that 5-month-old infants could add and subtract. What could this mean? Should parents buy flash cards and teach their babies about math?

The media regularly feature stories about childhood development with a view to informing the public about new research and what it might mean for parents. Unfortunately, such reports do not always accurately reflect reality. How, then, should we judge their accuracy? How do we know which ones to trust? Whether you are a teacher, a parent or other caregiver, or a student, you need to get answers to a series of probing questions to determine which media reports on child development are to be trusted:

- Was the research conducted at a reputable research institution and by bona-fide, qualified scientists?
- Was it initially reported in a peer-reviewed research journal? If so, a committee of scholars assessed the merits of the study before it was published and judged its conclusions reliable and trustworthy.
- Are there obvious indications of reasons for bias? What organization or agency funded the study? Was it, for example, funded by the National Science Foundation or a for-profit group that may have a vested interest in promoting a particular product or behavior?
- How did the researchers arrive at their conclusion? Is it convincingly supported by the facts?
- If the report is a secondary one—for example, a newspaper article about a study first published in a scientific journal—does it accurately represent what the researchers discovered? Or has a reporter translated (and probably simplified) the results of the research in order to catch the attention of the reader or viewer?

In the case of the study just mentioned, about babies able to add and subtract, the research was conducted by Karen Wynn, Paul Bloom, and Chi Chiang, from Yale University, and was reported in the prestigious peer-reviewed journal *Cognition* (Wynn, Bloom, & Chiang, 2002). The study was funded by a grant from NICHD (first author) and the Spencer Foundation (second author). The authors used a series of visual-preference tests to see whether 4- to 5-month-old infants are in some sense counting when they look at objects, or are simply responding to color, size, and other variables. The results showed that infants looked longer at incorrect mathematical outcomes than at correct ones. These results were interpreted as demonstration of the fact that babies are sensitive to small changes in quantity. Thus, they may have a basic sense of the number of objects, which allows them to detect changes in that number. But this does not mean that babies can count, or add and subtract, in the conventional sense. Thus, media reports suggesting that "Babies can perform addition" were potentially misleading to readers who did not get all the facts behind the headline.

**deferred imitation** The ability to imitate after a delay; used to assess infants' memory and understanding.

**electroencephalogram (EEG)** A test that measures and records spontaneous electrical activity produced by the firing of neurons within the brain.

## Studies of Infant Imitation

Another body of research conducts studies of infant imitation to assess level of cognition in babies. This is based on the assumption that even young infants can learn new behaviors from watching others—an idea already mentioned in Chapters 4 and 5. Researchers who use this method argue that copying another person's behaviors is a more active response than simply watching (Anisfeld et al., 2001; Melzoff & Moore, 1977; Over and Carpenter, 2013). Melzoff and Moore (1994) refer to this copying behavior as *intermodal matching*, because it involves not only visual recognition but also the ability to reproduce the observed behavior.

**Deferred imitation**—imitation after a delay—is another method used to assess infant understanding (Melzoff, 1988, 1990). To imitate after a delay, the infant must recall a past event and attempt to reproduce it—a measure of memory, as well as the ability to imitate an observed action. Infants as young as 9 months of age, for example, can remember a sequence of two or three complex events (Bauer, Wiebe, Carver, Waters, & Nelson, 2003).

## Neuroimaging Techniques

Many neuroimaging techniques have emerged with the growth of developmental neuroscience over recent years. Developmental neuroscientists use these techniques in an attempt to understand the links between brain development and the development of behaviors associated with cognition. We discuss several of these techniques here; but keep in mind that new techniques continue to emerge.

The 100 billion or so neurons in the human brain communicate by generating small electrochemical signals. This ongoing electrical activity can be measured with an **electroencephalogram**, or **EEG**. In a typical EEG session, a number of recording

E. Dygas/Getty Images

At around 6 months of age, babies not only can imitate what they *see* people doing but also what they *remember* seeing people doing.

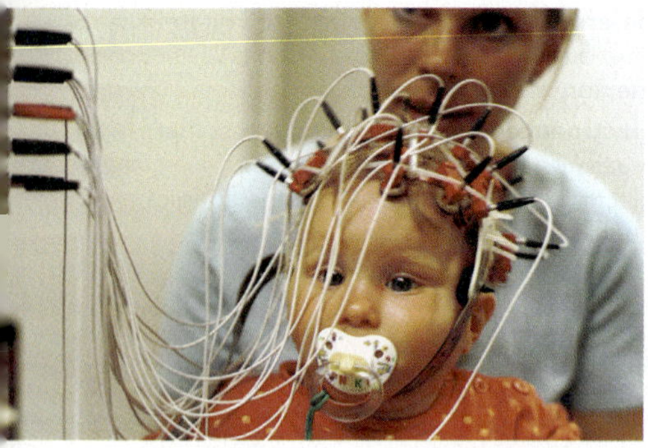

Heidorn/laif/Redux

Electroencephalograms, or EEGs, measure electrical activity in the brain. Neuroscientists use information from EEGs to study the connection between brain development and the development of specific behaviors.

electrodes are placed on the subject's head—usually by means of a special cap or net. The electrodes are plugged into a machine that displays the activity as a set of lines on a moving sheet of paper or on a computer screen.

A variation on the EEG is the **event-related potential (ERP)**, which records more specific processing events than the EEG. The ERP is the most widely used technique for measuring brain activity in infants today. For this technique, too, small caps or nets with sewn-in electrodes are used to gather measurements that enable researchers to learn about changes in electrical activity in the brain. The difference is that, with ERPs, researchers measure brain activity associated with responses to specific stimuli—for example, brain activity that accompanies an infant's viewing a face or hearing a sound. The use of ERPs has led to exciting discoveries about human brain functioning and cognition, including auditory and visual attention (Ceponiene, Alku, Westerfield, Torki & Townsend, 2005; Kushnerenko et al., 2002; Nelson et al., 2006; Nelson & McCleery, 2008), memory (Bauer, 2007; Bauer & Lukowski, 2010), and perception (Scott, 2011; Scott & Monesson, 2010; Scott & Nelson, 2006 ).

Functional imaging—specifically, **functional magnetic resonance imaging (fMRI)**—can also be used to identify the regions of the brain used to perform a particular task. This method works by detecting the increased blood flow that accompanies increased activity in particular brain regions (for example, Als et al., 2004; Turke-Browne, Scholl, & Chun, 2008). Studies using functional magnetic resonance imaging have shown, for example, activity in the left prefrontal cortex of young children during memory retrieval tasks (Schacter & Scarry, 2000).

## what if...?

Suppose you are a researcher investigating infant cognition. What would you be interested in studying? Which of the approaches discussed in this section might be the best one to use in your study? What techniques can you imagine might be developed over the next decade to help us learn more about how babies think?

## Standardized Tests of Infant Cognitive Development

Many researchers and clinicians use standardized tests to measure infants' cognitive abilities. This is referred to as the *psychometric approach*, because it seeks to understand cognitive development by focusing on measurement, particularly the measurement of individual differences in cognition. There are many infant development tests. They include the Bayley Scales (Bayley, 1969, 1993, 2005), the Mullen Scales (Mullen, 1995), Ages and Stages Questionnaire (ASQ) (Bricker, Squires, & Twombly, 2003; Squires et al., 2002), the Fagan Test of Infant Intelligence (Fagan & Detterman, 1992; Fagan, Holland, & Wheeler, 2007), and the Gesell Developmental Schedules for Very Young Children (Gesell Institute of Child Development, 2010).

The **Bayley Scales of Infant Development (BSID)** (Bayley, 1969, 1993, 2005) are probably the best known and most widely used of the infant development tests. The BSID is a standard series of measurements used primarily to assess the motor, language, and cognitive development of infants and toddlers up to 3 years of age. These tests are particularly useful in providing a picture of an infant's current mental and motor development. They also may identify possible developmental delay.

Standardized tests of this kind can be very useful as an indication of a child's current level of functioning. In certain cases, they can, as just noted, also be used as a means of identifying possible developmental delay. But do measures of mental development in infancy predict school success or other aspects of development later in life? Results from a number of longitudinal studies have led to the conclusion that, in general, these tests tell us little about the infant's future mental development. Specifically, studies

**event-related potentials (ERPs)** Measurements derived from electroencephalographs (EEGs) that make it possible to relate the information from EEGs to the cognitive processes in which the brain is engaged.

**functional magnetic resonance imaging (fMRI)** A form of magnetic resonance imaging (MRI) that registers blood flow to functioning areas of the brain; enables researchers to identify the regions of the brain used to perform a particular task.

**Bayley Scales of Infant Development (BSID–III)** A widely used standardized test conducted to measure infant cognitive abilities, such as intelligence.

show very low correlations between scores on standardized infant tests and later intelligence scores (Colombo, 1993; Colombo & Frick, 1999; DiLalla et al., 1990; Hack et al., 2005; Kavsek, 2004; Kopp & McCall, 1982; McCall, 1981; McCall, Appelbaum, & Hogarty, 1973; Rose & Feldman, 1990; Rose, Feldman, & Jankowski, 2005; Slater, 1995).

**CHECK YOUR PROGRESS**

1. Why are visual preference techniques valuable in assessing infant cognition?
2. What is the violation-of-expectation method?
3. Why do some researchers prefer to use object exploration approaches to understand the quality of infant thinking?
4. What do studies on imitation add to the understanding of infants' thinking capacities?
5. How are neuroimaging techniques used to assess infant learning and thinking?

# The Beginnings of Language

**[ KEY QUESTION ] 3.** How does language develop in infants and toddlers?

The development of language is one of the child's most natural—and impressive—accomplishments. Is there anything more exciting for parents than hearing their baby's first word? As single words grow into sentences, and sentences grow into conversation, parents are witnessing the miracle of language development.

Language—whether spoken, signed, or written—is a system of symbols used to communicate. Evidence indicates that the most intensive period of language development for humans is the first three years of life, a period when the brain is developing and maturing rapidly. It is at this time that the brain is most attuned to learning the rhythms and rules of a language. For that reason, researchers have sometimes referred to this period as the "critical period" for language development. As we explained in Chapter 1, however, the term *sensitive period* is more appropriately used. After this period, language can still be learned, but with greater difficulty and less efficiency.

There are, of course, many languages in the world. Each has its own set of rules for phonology (phonemes, or speech sounds; or, in the case of signed language, hand shapes), morphology (word formation), syntax (sentence formation), semantics (word and sentence meaning), prosody (intonation and rhythm of speech), and pragmatics (effective use of language). Amazingly, most children, given the amount of stimulation common in everyday environments, will acquire and use basic language during the first years of life (Acredolo, Goodwyn, Horobin & Emmons, 1999; Shonkoff & Phillips, 2000). Most young children learn their mother tongue rapidly and effortlessly, following similar developmental paths, regardless of culture.

We start our discussion of early language development by describing the main language areas of the brain. Next, we discuss some important theories about how children acquire language. We go on to review some general features of language acquisition. Finally, we discuss the role that experience plays in acquiring language.

## The Language Areas of the Brain

For more than 95% of us, the left hemisphere of the brain is the dominant location for language. As noted in Chapter 2, two areas of the brain play important roles in language. These areas are shown in Figure 6.6. **Broca's area**, located at the front of the left hemisphere, is important in speech production (putting together sentences and using proper syntax, among other things) and is critical to language and reading. **Wernicke's area** is involved in language processing (untangling the sentences of others and analyzing them for syntax, inflection, and the like). Infants comprehend more than they can express, and this capability is reflected in the maturation of these two areas of the brain. Wernicke's area develops before Broca's area.

**Broca's area** An area in the front of the left hemisphere of the brain thought to be partially responsible for speech production.

**Wernicke's area** An area in the brain thought to be partially responsible for language processing.

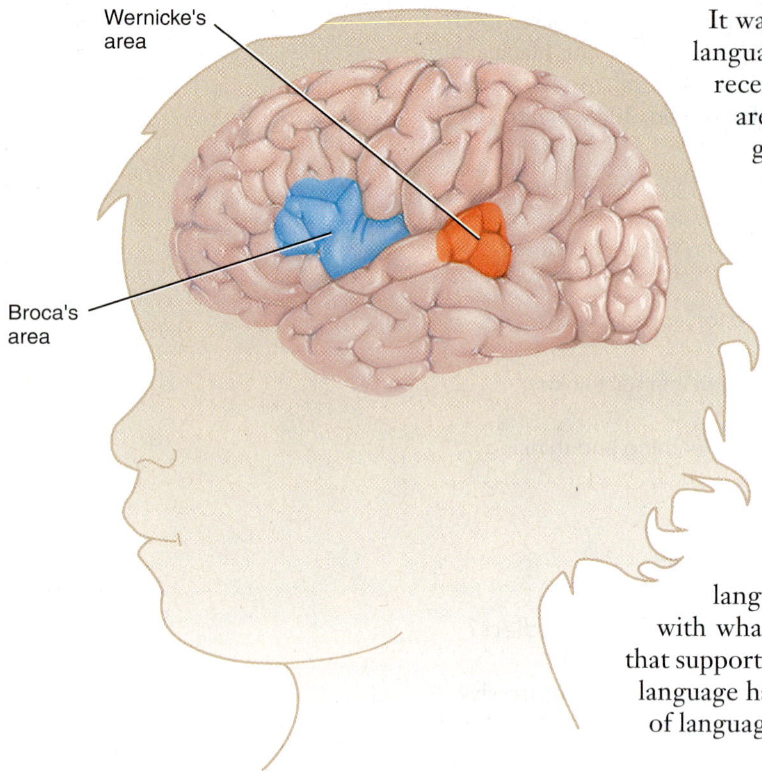


**FIGURE 6.6 Two Important Language Areas of the Brain** Broca's area, located in the frontal lobe, is important in producing spoken language. Wernicke's area, located in the temporal lobe, is important for understanding language. Infants comprehend more than they can say, and this capability is reflected in the fact that Wernicke's area develops before Broca's area.

Adapted with permission of John Wiley & Sons, Inc., from Comer, R., & Gould, E. (2013). *Psychology Around Us* (2nd ed.). Hoboken, NJ: Wiley, p. 131, Figure 4.11.

It was initially believed that Broca's area was responsible for language output, and Wernicke's for language input. More recent research does not confirm such a simple split. Other areas in the brain have been found to be involved in language in addition to these two regions. In the last decade, brain and behavioral studies have identified a very complex set of interacting brain systems involved in the initial acquisition of language (Aslin, 2012; Aslin & Schlaggar, 2006; Dehaene-Lambertz, Hertz-Pannier & Dubois, 2006; Kuhl, 2011; Kuhl & Damasio, 2012; Leroy et. al., 2011). Functional neuroimaging studies, for example, have uncovered strong evidence that the frontal lobes and certain structures deep in the brain become active during many language tasks. As the frontal lobes in the left hemisphere continue to mature, the infant's ability to comprehend complex sentences expands.

Overall, the changes we can observe in cognitive and language behavior across the first years of life is consistent with what we know about developments in the brain structures that support these capacities. Nevertheless, exactly how infants learn language has become the focus of debate on the nature and origins of language.

## Theories of Language Development

Three major theories have emerged to explain how children learn language: (1) the behaviorist, or learning theory, approach; (2) the nativist approach; and (3) the interactionist approach.

### The Behaviorist Approach

B. F. Skinner, whom we first discussed in Chapter 1, proposed that children acquire spoken language as a result of behavioral conditioning. That is, they acquire spoken language through the principles of reinforcement. Skinner believed that infants begin by imitating the language of their caregivers. Caregivers pay attention and express pleasure when the infant reproduces "correct" utterances. In response to these expressions of approval, the child remembers those utterances and forgets "incorrect" ones that do not gain approval. Simply stated, then, successful utterances are reinforced and remembered, while unsuccessful ones are forgotten. By trial and error, the infant learns to use the language of his or her family.

### The Nativist Approach

The *nativist approach*, proposed by Noam Chomsky, argues that there is much more to language learning than imitation and reinforcement. The rapidity and ease with which children learn to understand and produce speech during the first years of life led Chomsky and his colleagues to propose that human beings come biologically equipped to learn a language (Chomsky, 1965; Gleitman & Wanner, 1988; Pinker, 1984). A hypothetical brain mechanism Chomsky calls the **language acquisition device (LAD)** makes it possible for children to acquire the syntactic structure of language. The LAD consists of brain structures and neural wiring unique to human beings. To support his argument, Chomsky pointed out that since any language has a virtually infinite number of sentences, it would be impossible for a child to learn all the possible grammatical combinations through imitation and reinforcement. He also noted that

**language acquisition device (LAD)** A hypothetical brain mechanism proposed to explain human acquisition of the syntactic structure of language.

children acquire language quickly, effortlessly, and at identical stages across cultures, suggesting that an innate mechanism is at work in this process.

Chomsky proposed that all human beings are born with the same linguistic competence, in the form of a *universal grammar* that is part of the LAD. The principles embodied in the universal grammar are common to all languages. Children need only learn how these principles play out in their own language. Environmental influences—including parents' input—merely act as "switches" that set these universal principles in motion.

WHEN SYSTEMS CONNECT

### The Interactionist Approach

In recent years, the *interactionist approach* to language development, sometimes called *cognitive functional linguistics*, has begun to dominate. This approach includes several theoretical perspectives. All of them assume that language structures emerge from language use in social settings (Fitch, Hauser, & Chomsky, 2005; Kuhl 2004; Newport & Aslin 2004; Pinker, 1994; Pinker & Jackendoff, 2005; Tomasello, 2006). Interactionists argue that language development is both biological and social (Bates & Elman, 2000; Mandler, 2000, 2004, 2006; Tomasello, 2003). That is, while there may be a biological basis for language, children learn linguistic structures through language usage, specifically through their interactions with others (Tomasello, 2006). Children are motivated to learn language by their desire to communicate with others in social contexts.

## Acquiring Language: From Speech Perception to First Words

What are the features that characterize language in the early years? It is important to note that acquiring language requires infants to *comprehend* speech and to *produce* speech. To comprehend speech, infants must learn to distinguish one sound from another, to discriminate intonations of language, and to learn to associate sounds and gestures with objects and people. To produce speech, they must learn to vocalize, to move from coos and babbling to the use of "speech" sounds to the use of words. This is an impressive set of achievements.

Learning how to communicate depends crucially on the infant's ability to select meaningful signals from the environment. For human infants, this requires being able to selectively attend to those auditory (or visual) units that are meant to communicate. This challenge is made all the more complex by the sheer variability and richness of the infant's world. Fortunately, as noted in Chapter 4, infants come well prepared for this demanding task. Newborn infants can discriminate and categorize many aspects of human language (Cooper & Aslin, 1990; Fernald & Simon, 1984; Fernald, Taeschner, Dunn, & Papoušek, 1989; Werker & McLeod, 1989). Thus, infants perceive a variety of characteristics of the human voice and patterns of speech in the first months of life.

Infants and toddlers, as we've mentioned, comprehend more than they can say. By 12 or 13 months, there is a dramatic upswing in the infant's understanding of specific word sounds. Although some 12-month-old infants understand as few as three words, others may understand up to a hundred (Hoff, 2006). By 2 years of age, comprehension involves much more than learning new words (Ganea & Harris, 2010). Words have begun to become ideas that enable the child to think about and interact with the world in a whole new way (Conboy, Sommerville, & Kuhl, 2008).

Turning to speech production, we can see that even in the first few months of life infants engage in nonverbal forms of communication, such as crying and smiling. At about 2 months of age, they begin to produce one-syllable vowel sounds, called *cooing*. By about 6 months, they can *babble*, or produce repetitive syllables such as "ba, ba, ba" and "da, da, da." Babbling soon turns into a type of nonsense speech that may have the tone and cadence of human speech but does not contain real words.

By the end of their first year, most children can say a few simple words. By 18 months of age, word production increases by 5 or 6 new words a week, so that by 20 months, many children can use up to 100 words and by 24 months, the average child has about 200 words. Most children are putting words together in short combinations, such as "more milk," by the time they are 2 years old. Of course, there is a good deal of variability among children. Some normally developing children develop language faster, others more slowly. Table 6.3 summarizes language achievements over the first two years.

**Table 6.3** Common Language Achievements Over the First Two Years

| Age | Common Achievements |
|---|---|
| Between birth and 3 months | Cry to express needs.<br>Turn and locate a sound source.<br>Recognize familiar voices, such as the mother's voice.<br>Watch and respond to a face when spoken to.<br>Make cooing and gurgling sounds in face-to-face play. |
| Between 3 and 6 months | Focus on the caregiver's eyes during face-to-face interaction.<br>Respond to changes in the tone of caregiver's voice.<br>Pay more attention to music and, perhaps, coo along with the music.<br>Imitate familiar sounds and actions.<br>Begin to babble with repetitive syllables, starting with vowel sounds ("oh" and "ah") and moving on to new sounds and combinations with "p," "m," "b," and "d" in them. |
| Between 6 to 9 months | Try to communicate using actions or gestures.<br>Listen intently when spoken to.<br>Notice that some toys make sounds.<br>Use their voices to express pleasure and displeasure.<br>Babble repetitive syllables, such as "ba, ba, ba" and "ma, ma, ma." |
| Between 9 and 12 months | Follow simple instructions, especially if vocal or physical cues are given, such as "drink your milk," and simple commands, such as "no."<br>Recognize their name when called.<br>Understand the names of familiar objects or people.<br>Try to mimic familiar sounds, such as car and animal noises.<br>Focus on the speaker's mouth and try to imitate words and practice inflection.<br>Say a few two-syllable words, such as "dada," "mama," and "uh-oh." |
| Between 12 and 18 months | Point to an object or picture when it is named.<br>Enjoy songs, music, and being read to.<br>Recognize names of familiar people, objects, and body parts.<br>Answer simple questions nonverbally.<br>Follow simple directions accompanied by gestures; possibly use both gestures and vocalizations together.<br>Use several words (8 to 10 or even 20) meaningfully. |
| Between 18 and 24 months | Understand simple sentences, such as "There's your shoe."<br>Respond to such commands as "Show me your eyes [nose, mouth]."<br>Listen to stories, label pictures, and sing simple songs, such as "Twinkle, twinkle, little star."<br>Use simple phrases, such as "more milk" (or "más leche") and "milk all gone."<br>Begin to use pronouns, such as "mine."<br>Refer to self by name.<br>By 2 years, speak 50 to 100 words and understand more. Some 2-year-olds have a vocabulary of 150–300 words. |

## The Role of Experience in Language Development

**infant-directed speech** A special way of speaking that caretakers use to address infants; characterized by careful pronunciation, slow pacing, exaggerated intonation, and short sentences featuring much repetition.

Recall that an important issue in theories of language acquisition involves the relative roles of innate language mechanisms and learning. Consistent with nativist theories, studies have demonstrated that at birth infants exhibit a universal capacity to detect differences between phonetic contrasts used in the world's languages (Eimas, Sigueland, Jusczyk, & Vigorito, 1971). However, this capacity is dramatically altered by language experience (Kuhl, 2007; Kuhl & Damasio, 2012).

One group of researchers studied infants and children from birth to 5 years of age in Japan, U.S., Russia, Sweden, Finland, and France (Kuhl et al., 1997). This research showed that that by the age of 6 months, infants respond differently to the sound units used in their own language than to sound units not used in their language. By 6 months, infants raised in Sweden respond in a special way to the vowel sounds of Swedish, for example. They do not respond in that way to the vowel sounds of English. American infants do the opposite: They respond to the vowel sounds of English rather than those of Swedish. Early in development, then, the infant brain appears to be mapping the patterns of language: by 6 months, individual vowels and consonants; and by 9 months, the patterns of words. By the end of the first year, the infant brain is no longer universally prepared for all languages. Instead, it is primed to acquire the language (or languages) to which the infant has been exposed.

*Everyday stories*

INFANTS ARE CITIZENS OF THE WORLD! In English, we make a sharp distinction between the *r* and *l* sounds. Adult Japanese speakers do not. Even Japanese linguists have difficulty distinguishing these two sounds. They hear no difference between the words *lake* and *rake,* for example. But 7-month-old Japanese babies do. Like 7-month-olds in Mexico, Belarus, or the United States, they can distinguish the sound of *r* from the sound of *l*. By the time they reach 10 months, however, the Japanese babies can no longer hear this distinction. Their speech categories have begun to resemble those of the adults in their culture. And by the time they are 1 year old, their brains are "committed" to their native language. They babble in a way that sounds Japanese, and they are quickly learning the specific properties of their own language.

### Social Interactions and Language

Social interaction is essential for language learning (Kuhl, 2007). Consider that infants exposed to a foreign language at 9 months learn rapidly—but only when experiencing the new language during social interchanges with other humans (Meltzoff, Kuhl, Movellan, & Sejnowski, 2009). For example, American infants exposed in a laboratory to Mandarin Chinese rapidly learned sounds and words in the language when they were exposed to it during naturalistic play with a live human being. Infants exposed to the same input via television or audiotape showed no learning (Kuhl, 2011).

Thus, the people in an infant's life play a critical role in facilitating the infant's language growth (Pinker, 1994). Caretakers, as if in response to their role as language teachers, tend to use a special way of speaking when they address infants. This special kind of speech, called **infant-directed speech**, is an important way to facilitate language learning. Infant-directed speech is characterized by careful pronunciation, slow pacing, exaggerated intonation, and short sentences featuring much repetition (Fernald & Cummings, 2003; Thiessen & Saffran, 2003). Infants show a preference for this style of speech.

*JGI/Jamie Grill/Blend Images/Getty Images*

Mothers—as well as other caregivers—tend to use infant-directed speech when they talk to their babies. This slow, deliberate speech style helps babies to learn language.

The importance of social interaction during this period is confirmed by studies of language acquisition in congenitally deaf children. Whereas most babies begin babbling at about 6 months, congenitally deaf infants show obvious deficits in their early vocalizations. If they are not provided with an alternative form of expression (such as sign language), they fail to develop language. If, however, caregivers and others introduce these babies to sign language at an early age (from approximately 6 months onward), they begin to "babble" with their hands, just as a hearing infant does audibly. Although it is extremely difficult for deaf children with profound hearing losses to acquire spoken language, deaf children who are exposed to sign language learn it "as naturally and as effortlessly as hearing children learn spoken language" (Goldin-Meadow, 2006, p. 346).

There is a growing consensus that language skills develop best in an environment that is rich with sounds, sights, and consistent exposure to the speech and language of others (Kuhl, 2007). Research has found a wide range of variability in young children's vocabulary skills as early as 2 years of age (Hart & Risley, 1995). This variability was highly correlated with the number of words spoken by their parents. The amount of talk parents directed at their children was strongly related to the children's vocabulary growth. Socioeconomically disadvantaged toddlers were generally exposed to substantially fewer words per day than toddlers from more advantaged families. As a result, their vocabularies were substantially smaller. It is clear from such research that environmental variations can lead to striking differences in language development.

what if...?

**Parents and Baby Signs**

Infants find ways to communicate using gestures, referred to as "baby signs," well before they learn to speak. Have you noticed how easily babies learn to wave bye-bye and shake their heads no? To help them communicate, some parents teach their babies this kind of sign language, often starting with signs to describe routine activities and objects in the child's life—for example, drink, dog, eat, sleep, and hug. Teaching and practicing baby sign language is clearly fun, and gives parent and child an opportunity to interact. But based on what we've seen about providing a language-rich environment, what might be a disadvantage of teaching a baby sign language? Would you encourage parents to teach their hearing infants sign language? Or do you think it is more important for parents to learn to read and understand their baby's own communication cues?

Roger Charity/Getty Images

On average, infants and toddlers spend two hours each day watching television or other screen media.

## Screen Media and Language Learning

One element of the environment important to consider today in the developed world is the early and frequent exposure infants have to screen media, such as television and computers (Calvert, Rideout, Woolard, Barr, & Strouse, 2005; McCarthy, 2013; Wartella, Richert, & Robb, 2010). The American Academy of Pediatrics (1999) has recommended that children younger than 24 months of age not be exposed to screen media like televisions, computers, and video games. Recent data indicate that these recommendations have gone unheeded, however. One phone survey of over 1,000 parents of children aged 6 months to 6 years in the United States found that almost all the respondents' homes had at least one television (99%), and most had two or more (84%) (Rideout & Hamel, 2006). The same survey found that 19% of children under 2 had a television in their bedrooms. By 3 months of age, about 40% of children are exposed to television or videos. By age 2, this rises to 90% of children (Zimmerman, Christakis, & Meltzoff, 2007). The average age at which infants begin watching programming designed for their age group is 5 months (Richert, Robb, Fender, & Wartella, 2010; Rideout, Vandewater, & Wartella, 2003). Finally, even when infants are not watching it, television is typically on somewhere in the house about 6 hours per day (Anderson & Pempek, 2005). A nationally representative study of U.S. parents/caregivers with 1 child between the ages of 8 months and 8 years, reported that the average U.S. child was exposed to 232.2 minutes of background television on a typical day. Leaving the television on while no one is viewing and children's bedroom television ownership were associated with increased background television exposure (Lapierre, Taylor Piotrowski & Linebarger, 2012).

What impact does all this media exposure have on infants' language learning? One group of researchers reported that with each additional hour spent in front of a screen, babies at 8 to 16 months learned 6 to 8 fewer vocabulary words than infants who did not spend time in front of screens (Christakis, Zimmerman, DiGiuseppe, & McCarty,

2004). Another study showed that average daily TV viewing by infants between birth and 2 years of age was not associated with improved language at age 3 (Schmidt, Rich, Rifas-Schiman, Oken, & Taveras, 2009). Even though infants do not actively view adult-directed television, they are exposed to it. A growing body of evidence shows that such "passive" exposure may be detrimental to play, language development, and executive functioning (Barr, Lauricella, Zack, & Calvert, 2010). A recent cross-sectional survey found a 17-point drop in standardized test scores for each hour that infants between the ages of 8 and 16 months viewed DVDs, even though these programs were designed for their age group (Zimmerman et al., 2007). Similarly, a study of the effects of watching educational DVDs on vocabulary acquisition found no evidence that children learned the words specifically highlighted in the DVDs (Richert et al., 2010). Watching these DVDs was also unrelated to measures of general language learning, the study showed.

There is research, however, that suggests that screen media specifically designed for young children may have some beneficial effects, at least in comparison with other media (Linebarger & Walker, 2005). Wright and his colleagues (2001) found that 2-year-olds who were exposed to child-directed educational television programming, such as *Sesame Street*, had higher levels of school readiness than those who were primarily exposed to adult-directed programs. In general, though, the impact of infant-directed media on cognitive development remains largely untested. As discussed in the accompanying Research Insights feature, there may be real limitations on the ability of infants and toddlers to learn from screen media.

### Wireless Parents **Parenting**

As we have just seen, even infants are spending an increasing amount of time exposed to electronic devices, leading to growing concerns about the possible negative effects of media on infants' cognitive development. But what about parents' constant use of electronic media—smart phones, laptops, e-mail, and social media such as Twitter? Does the digital environment affect parents' relationships with their children and, ultimately, their children's development?

Smart phones and laptops certainly have made it possible for working parents to spend more time at home with their young children. But the new communications technologies may be a double-edged sword for parents. Research shows that

## **Research Insights:** The Video Deficit

Educational programming is created on the assumption that infants and toddlers learn from television viewing. But it is not at all clear how much they actually do learn from it. What might stand in the way of such learning? Obviously, content is a key factor, along with the child's cognitive capacity. But there is also a possibility that infants learn little from television because of what Anderson and Pempek (2005, p. 511) refer to as a "video deficit." These researchers suggest that infants and toddlers take away very little knowledge from TV and videos because they cannot transfer what they learn from videos to real-life situations as well as they can from face-to-face interactions.

In one series of studies, for example, one group of 2-year-olds watched a live video monitor showing a person in the next room hiding a toy. A second group watched the same activity directly, through a window between the rooms. The children in both groups were then asked to retrieve the toy. Although the only difference between the conditions was the source of the information regarding the location of the toy, this turned out to be crucial. Children who had viewed the hiding event directly almost always found the toy. Those who had viewed it on video usually did not (Troseth, 2003; Troseth & DeLoache, 1998). Thus, the second group of children had found it difficult to transfer information they had learned from videos to solve a real-world problem.

The video deficit effect is not apparent at 6 months of age. It peaks at around 15 months and persists until at least 36 months, depending on the task complexity (Barr, 2010; Barr & Hayne, 1999; Barr, Muentener & Garcia, 2007; Flynn & Whiten, 2008; Hayne, Herbert, & Simcock, 2003; Hudson & Sheffield, 1999; Nielsen, Simcock, & Jenkins, 2008; Schmitt & Anderson, 2002; Sheffield & Hudson, 2006; Simcock & DeLoache, 2006; Simcock & Dooley, 2007).

Josh Rinebults/iStockphoto

Today's communication technologies offer constant distractions. Parents may sometimes be tempted to pay more attention to their smartphones than to their children.

communications devices can also become constant distractions from family life (Anderson & Pembek, 2005; Kirkorian, Pempek, Murphy, Schmidt, & Anderson, 2009). Supporting these research studies are anecdotal reports of, for example: dads who read and send texts at the dinner table; moms who browse the Internet while their young children watch TV; dads on their mobile phones in the park, oblivious to their toddlers' antics; and moms who cut short bedtime reading to check their e-mail.

Sherry Turkle, director of the Massachusetts Institute of Technology Initiative on Technology and Self, points out that this type of technology involvement is compulsive and solitary, and that children immediately sense a barrier when their parents are using it. Of course, parents have always had to divide their attention, and combine working and caring for their growing children. But today, interactions with computers, smart phones, and the like are so engrossing that they seem to cause people to shut out the world (Turkle, 2011). There is, still, little research on how parents' constant use of communications technology affects their children. But there is research showing that engaged parenting—which includes talking with and explaining things to children and responding to their questions—enriches early learning. For example, in the context of language development, parents who are regularly engaged with their children, and who supply a language-rich environment, help them develop a broader vocabulary. This, in turn, contributes to their ability to read (Hart & Risley, 2003). More research is needed to find out whether communications technology is interfering with parent-child relationships and reducing opportunities for improving language and other cognitive development in children. Nevertheless, these preliminary observations should give parents food for thought.

## Raising a Bilingual Child

Many people living in the United States think that learning to speak one language is the most natural or typical way for children to learn language. In fact, speaking a single language is the exception in many parts of the world. In India and Singapore, for example, most families speak two or three languages interchangeably in their homes, and expect their children to do likewise (Zurer Pearson, 2008). As we have seen, children learn their first language naturally, and without instruction, as they interact with their caregivers. But how do infants learn two or more languages? And how does this affect their language and cognitive development?

For much of the 20th century, the prevailing view was that bilingualism and second-language acquisition early in life confused children and interfered with their ability to develop normal cognitive functions and succeed in school (Macnamara, 1966). Bilingualism does appear to have some costs. Bilingual children tend to have a smaller vocabulary in each language they learn than children who speak only one language, for example (Oller & Eilers, 2002). But recent research has shown that, in general, children who speak two languages perform better on a wide range of intelligence tests and aspects of school achievement than children who speak only one language (Bialystok, Majumder, & Martin, 2003; Bialystok, McBride-Chang, & Luk, 2005). Furthermore, children learning to read in two languages that share a writing system (for example, English and French) show faster progress in learning to read. Children whose two languages do not share a writing system (for example, English and Chinese) show no special reading advantage. At the same time, neither do they demonstrate any deficit relative to single-language speakers (Bialystok et al., 2005). Evidence for the benefits of bilingualism, together with evidence that learning two languages causes no cognitive deficits, indicates that exposing infants and toddlers to more than one language may be a positive practice.

### ✓ CHECK YOUR PROGRESS

1. What are the key language areas of the brain?
2. What are three major theories of language acquisition, and how do they differ?
3. What role does experience play in language acquisition?
4. How do the various forms of screen media affect language learning?

# Infant and Toddler Education

**[ KEY QUESTION ] 4.** What are the benefits of infant-toddler education?

We know today that during the first few years, children develop many of the basic learning patterns and abilities that they will build on for the rest of their lives. We also know that how they do this depends on the interplay between nature (the child's genetic endowment) and nurture (including nutrition, surroundings, care, and stimulation). This knowledge has changed the landscape of early childhood education in the United States and in other parts of the world (Scott-Little, Kagan & Frelow, 2006; Wittmer & Peterson, 2006; Zigler & Syfco, 2004). There is growing interest in the quality of educational settings for infants and toddlers (Bredekamp & Copple, 1997; Roopnarine & Johnson, 2005; Schumacher, Hamm, Goldstein, & Lombardi, 2006; Shannon et al., 2006). Along with this increased appreciation of the importance of infant-toddler education comes a growing concern about the achievement disparities that children from at-risk backgrounds show during the first 3 years of life (Brooks-Gunn, Rouse, & McLanahan, 2007; Brooks-Gunn, Smith, Klebanov, Duncan, & Lee, 2003; Children's Defense Fund, 2005; Cochran, 2007; Halle et al., 2009). For more about economic disparities, see the Focus On feature below about James J. Heckman. We next take a look at what these disparities are and consider some attempts to remedy them.

## Disparities in Cognitive Development in the First Years of Life

**Policy**

A number of studies have noted that children from low-income families, on average, perform worse on indicators of academic achievement than their more advantaged peers (Chernoff et al., 2007; Rouse, Brooks-Gunn, & McLanahan, 2005). These disparities are already identifiable in the first years of life—long before school begins. Data from a recent nationally representative study in the United States show

### Focus On: James J. Heckman, Nobel Prize Winner in Economics

James J. Heckman was awarded the Nobel Prize in Economics in 2000 for his work on the economics of human development. Heckman's work has been devoted to examining the origins of economic disparities in society, and developing a scientific basis for economic policy. His interest in the relationship between economics and opportunity probably can be traced to his own experiences. As a youth in the late 1950s, Heckman spent time in several southern states. It was the Jim Crow era, when there were separate water fountains, bathrooms, and restaurants for whites and blacks. This injustice shocked him and motivated his lifelong study of the sources of disparities in educational opportunity in the United States.

Heckman's economic perspective focuses on intervention in the first years of life. This approach differs from the more common emphasis on elementary, adolescent, and young-adult remediation programs, such as reduced pupil-teacher ratios, public job training, convict rehabilitation programs, and tuition subsidies. Heckman has analyzed investments in early childhood programs and determined that the greatest gains can be made at early ages, because the social and cognitive skills learned by the very young set a pattern for acquiring important skills later in life. He believes that early interventions result in much higher economic returns than later interventions. Research on the effects of educational programs for infants and toddlers show that investment in high-quality early childhood development for disadvantaged children yields an 8 to 10% annual rate of return through better education, health, and social outcomes.

Investing in early education generates economic development for communities in the form of jobs and the purchase of goods and services, and makes for a more efficient workforce. Above all, children who receive quality early education arrive at school ready to learn. As a result, they do better in school and need fewer costly special education classes. They also are more likely to graduate and to hold jobs and less likely to be on welfare. In contrast, neglecting early education serves to perpetuate an underclass, which may be growing in the United States, Heckman argues. Heckman's message, that high-quality early intervention can narrow the economic divide, is particularly relevant today as policymakers face difficult decisions about using funds wisely.

that disparities in child outcomes—including cognitive, social, behavioral, and health outcomes—are evident at 9 months and expand by 24 months of age (Halle et al., 2009). The most consistent and prominent risk factors were found to be low income and low maternal education. The more risk factors a child has, the wider the disparities. These results are confirmed by findings from a longitudinal study of over 1,000 infants born in Norway. The study showed that "double risk"—signified by a combination of biological and social/demographic risk factors at 7 months of age—correlated highly with developmental problems at age 4 (Rostad, Nyberg, & Sivberg, 2008).

What can be done to prevent these early disparities from negatively affecting children's cognitive and academic development in the future? The implications for learning opportunities and educational practices in the first years of life are substantial (Galinsky, 2006). Until recently, much of the research and policy on early education have focused on the preschool years (ages 3 to 5), leading directly into the transition to kindergarten (Andreassen & Fletcher, 2007). Education during the first three years of life and preschool and elementary education—each with its own funding sources, infrastructure, values, and traditions—have remained largely separate. In fact, the educational establishment has not typically thought of schooling during the first three years of life as a full-fledged part of the American public education system. In general, infant-toddler education is neither publicly funded nor mandatory (Takanishi & Kauerz, 2008).

SHAWN POYNTER/The New York Times/Redux

High-quality services for infants and toddlers, such as those supplied by this Head Start classroom, have a long-lasting, positive impact on children's development.

In recent years, however, the educational potential of quality infant-toddler programs has increasingly been recognized. (See the accompanying Focus On feature for an economic view of this potential.) This recognition has contributed to a blurring of the boundary between the first years and the preschool-elementary period (Clarke-Stewart & Althusen, 2005). Educational professionals in the two spheres now have important reasons to strive for greater collaboration.

We have noted on many occasions that changing young children's experiences can markedly affect their development and learning. This is especially true when intervention starts early in life and includes a broad set of strategies (Ayoub et al., 2009; Klein & Knitzer, 2006). The success of programs such as Early Head Start, which we describe below, illustrates that high-quality services for infants and toddlers can have a long-lasting and positive impact on children's development, learning abilities, and capacity to regulate their emotions (Brookes-Gunn et al., 2003; Epstein, Schweinhart & McAdoo, 1996; Galinsky, 2006; Zigler & Syfco, 2004). Unfortunately, such programs are still relatively rare in the United States.

what if...?

We mentioned earlier in this chapter that socioeconomically disadvantaged toddlers are generally exposed to substantially fewer words per day than toddlers from higher-status families. As a result, their vocabularies are notably smaller. Now suppose that these disadvantaged children, when they reach age 3, begin to attend preschools that provide lots of books, schedule field trips, support free play activities, and focus on vocabulary-building conversations. Do you predict that the vocabulary gap will shrink? Why or why not?

## High-Quality Programs for Infants and Toddlers

An emerging body of research demonstrates the potential of both home-based and center-based interventions to address gaps in educational achievement of low-income infants and toddlers before they reach school-age (Wittmer & Peterson, 2006). The following examples highlight several high-quality, effective approaches.

- As an example of a home-based approach, the Nurse-Family Partnership model (Olds et al., 1997) provides first-time teen mothers with home visits from a public health nurse who provides information on prenatal care, child development, and family planning. Experimental evaluations of this model indicate positive outcomes in the form of wider spacing between births, less child abuse, better child health, and better academic and social outcomes for both parent and child (Eckenrode et al., 2010).

- Models that combine home-based and center-based approaches show particular potential. One example is the Infant Health and Development Program (IHDP), which began as a clinical trial of an early intervention program for premature, low birth weight infants. IHDP provides home visits and service referrals, enrollment at a child development center, and developmental assessments. An experimental evaluation showed that IHDP had a positive impact on the cognitive and motor skills in child participants. It was particularly effective with those from the most at-risk families and those who had been born on the "heavier" side of the low birth weight range (Brookes-Gunn et al., 2003).
- Early Head Start is a federally funded community-based program for low-income families with infants and toddlers. The program supports families through center-based services, home-based visits, and a combination of the two. Recent evaluations of Early Head Start suggest that offering these center-based and home-based services can result in improved outcomes for infants and toddlers (Ayoub et al., 2009; Vallotton, Harewood, Ayoub, Pan, Mastergeorge, & Brophy-Herb, 2012; Zigler & Syfco, 2004). Moreover, these improved outcomes do not diminish over time. Children who participated in Early Head Start and went on to formal child care programs after age 3 had improved early literacy skills. Furthermore, they did not show the increase in aggressive behaviors found in some studies to be associated with time spent in formal programs.

MAGNUM/Richard Kalvar

Shortly after World War II, the citizens of Reggio Emilia, Italy, established a school that today is recognized worldwide for its innovative approach to infant-toddler education. A key element is the strong community support the school enjoys.

*Everyday stories*

REGGIO EMILIA: A COMMUNITY APPROACH The city of Reggio Emilia in Italy is recognized worldwide for its innovative approach to infant-toddler education. One of the most distinguishing features of the Reggio model is its tradition of community support. In fact, it was the citizens of Reggio Emilia who established the first of the schools right after World War II. Today, infants and toddlers are still seen as is a vital part of the community, as reflected in the high level of financial support from the community for infant-toddler education. Parents are viewed as partners, collaborators, and advocates for their children. They are expected to take part in discussions about school policy, curriculum planning, and evaluation. The result is an atmosphere of community and collaboration that is developmentally appropriate for adults and children alike (Edwards, Gandini & Forman, 1993; Malaguzzi, 1993; New, 2000; Vakil, Freeman, & Swim, 2003).

More research is needed to examine how quality early care and education for children from low-income households could help narrow the achievement gap. Still, it seems clear that high-quality interventions can produce sustained gains if provided continuously throughout early childhood, from birth through age 5. Much remains to be done to make programs of this type available, and affordable, in our communities.

**CHECK YOUR PROGRESS**

1. What are some disparities in early learning and development in the first years of life?
2. What are some examples of high-quality infant-toddler programs?

# CHAPTER SUMMARY

## Theories of Cognitive Development

**[ KEY QUESTION ] 1. How do Piaget, Vygotsky, and information-processing theorists explain how infants and toddlers learn?**

- Piaget refers to the first stage of development, which lasts from birth to about the end of the second year, as the sensorimotor stage because the infant uses senses and motor abilities to understand the world. Piaget subdivided this stage into six substages (see Table 6.1).
- Object permanence, one of the main developmental tasks of the infant-toddler period, can be defined as the realization that physical objects continue to exist even when they are removed from sight. In Piaget's view, object permanence is a feature of the fourth substage.
- The major theme that distinguishes Vygotsky's theory from Piaget's is the fundamental role of social interaction in the

development of cognition. Vygotsky believed that with help from others, called scaffolding, children can solve problems, carry out tasks, and achieve goals that would otherwise be beyond their unassisted efforts. The zone of proximal development describes the difference between what children can achieve with and without assistance.

- Piaget's conclusions have been challenged because they tend to underestimate infants' abilities. Vygotsky's approach has been criticized because, by emphasizing the social context of learning, he may have neglected the contribution of children to their own learning.
- Systems theories recognize that continuous reciprocal interactions between person and environment shape learning. Core knowledge theorists assume that infants are born with a certain amount of innate knowledge.
- Information-processing approaches focus on specific aspects of cognitive development, such as memory and categorization, and describe how infants process the information in their environment.
- Memory is fundamental to cognition. Children under 6 months of age seem to have fragile memories that last only a limited period of time, but by 24 months of age, they show robust memory even after long delays.
- The ability to categorize is especially important for learning in infancy, because infants must organize their experiences of the many new objects, events, and people they encounter. The ability to form conceptual categories is present by about 7 to 9 months of age and progresses steadily over the months that follow.
- The brain undergoes rapid changes in size and structure during the first year, largely due to the massive growth of new dendrites and synapses, which enable neurons to be connected.
- Brain development begins earlier in primary sensory regions like the auditory and visual cortex, and somewhat later in the temporal and frontal lobes.
- The prefrontal cortex plays an important role in significant role cognitive development and in memory development.

## Research Methods

**[ KEY QUESTION ] 2.** What research techniques are used to assess cognitive development in infants and toddlers?

- The most popular indirect methods for the study of infant learning are visual preference procedures, which assess visual attention. Habituation techniques exploit the tendency of infants to look at interesting displays until they become bored and look away, while the violation-of-expectation method assumes that infants look longer at an unexpected than an expected event.
- Researchers using object exploration techniques observe infants exploring and manipulating objects to assess their learning and development.
- Researchers also assess infant cognition by examining infants' ability to copy another person's behaviors.
- Neuroimaging techniques are used to examine links between brain development and behavior. These techniques include: electroencephalogram (EEG), event-related potentials (ERPs), and functional magnetic resonance imaging (fMRI).
- Many researchers and clinicians use standardized tests to measure infant cognitive abilities, such as intelligence. This is referred to as the psychometric approach.

## The Beginnings of Language

**[ KEY QUESTION ] 3.** How does language develop in infants and toddlers?

- Language is, to some degree, localized in a section in the left hemisphere in which Broca's area and Wernicke's area are located. Other brain structures are also involved in language, however.
- The behaviorist approach proposes that infants learn language through a process of reinforcement.
- The nativist approach assumes that all human beings are born with the same linguistic competence, which is built into the brain.
- Interactionists argue that language development is both biological and social, and that language learning is influenced by the desire of children to communicate with others.
- To comprehend speech, infants must learn to distinguish one sound from another, to discriminate intonations of language, and to learn to associate sounds and gestures with objects and people. To produce speech, they must learn to vocalize—to move from coos and babbling to the use of "speech" sounds to the use of words.
- Caretakers tend to use a special way of speaking when they address infants, called infant-directed speech, which is one of the primary ways language learning is facilitated.
- While more research needs to be done on the effects of screen media on language learning, recent evidence suggests that infants and toddlers learn very little from watching TV and videos.
- Research suggests that bilingualism is a positive force that enhances children's cognitive and linguistic development.
- Language skills appear to develop best in a world that is rich with sounds, sights, and consistent exposure to the speech and language of others.

## Infant and Toddler Education

**[ KEY QUESTION ] 4.** What are the benefits of infant-toddler education?

- In recent years, the educational potential of quality infant-toddler programs has been increasingly recognized.
- Children from at-risk backgrounds on average perform worse on indicators of academic achievement than their more advantaged peers. These disparities are already identifiable in the first years of life—long before school begins.
- Changing young children's experiences can substantially affect their development and learning, especially when intervention starts early in life and includes a broad set of strategies.
- Research demonstrates the potential of various interventions to address the gaps in educational achievement of low-income infants and toddlers before they reach school age.

# KEY TERMS

accommodation 198
assimilation 198
Bayley Scales of Infant Development (BSID) 216
Broca's area 217
categorization 207
deferred imitation 215
disequilibrium 198
electroencephalogram (EEG) 215
event-related potential (ERP) 216
explicit memory 207
functional magnetic resonance imaging (fMRI) 216

guided participation *204*
habituation techniques *212*
implicit memory *207*
infant-directed speech *221*
language acquisition device (LAD) *218*
object exploration approach *214*
object permanence *200*
scaffolding *203*
schemas *198*
sensorimotor stage *198*
violation-of-expectation method *212*
visual preference procedures *212*
Wernicke's area *217*
zone of proximal development (ZPD) *203*

## CRITICAL THINKING QUESTIONS

1. **Theories of Cognitive Development.** Most researchers today agree with Piaget that infants and toddlers are natural learners, but there is still a great deal of disagreement about *how* infants and toddlers learn. Distinguish between the approaches of Piaget, Vygotsky, and information-processing theorists. Which approach do you consider the most compelling?
2. **Research Methods.** What do neuroimaging techniques such as EEG or fMRI add to the traditional behavioral approaches, such as habituation, in efforts to learn more about how infants and toddlers think and learn?
3. **The Beginnings of Language.** Many researchers refer to this period as a "critical" or "sensitive" period in language development, but what role does the environment play? What is a "language-rich environment" for infants and toddlers, and what is its effect?
4. **Infant and Toddler Education.** There is a growing concern about the quality of educational settings for infants and toddlers. What characteristics of infant-toddler education programs have been shown to promote better outcomes for children from at-risk backgrounds? Explain how these programs might produce their effects.
5. **Cultural Perspectives.** Although there is tremendous variation across cultures, fathers contribute much less than mothers to infant and toddler caregiving. Despite the fact that families are not as rigidly structured along age and gender lines as before, mothers are still the principal caregivers of infants and toddlers. If father involvement is related to enhanced cognitive development and school achievement, why are many fathers still relatively uninvolved in their children's development? What role do cultural factors play in this?

## REAL Development

### Cognitive Development in Infancy and Toddlerhood

In this module, you are studying to be a child psychologist. As part of your field experience as a psychology major, you have been asked to visit Julianne and baby Olivia, who is now 4½ months old. You will observe baby Olivia and then assess her cognitive development.

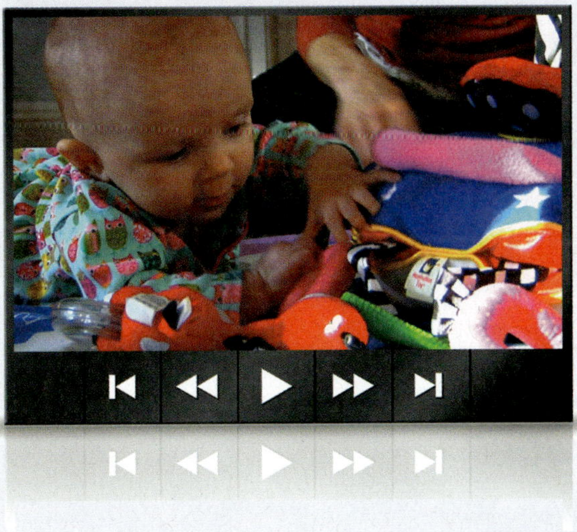

© John Wiley & Sons, Inc.

**WileyPLUS** Go to WileyPLUS to complete the *Real Development* activity.

03.01

# Chapter 7

# Psychosocial Development in Infancy and Toddlerhood

MAKING A **difference**

## The Infant Mental Health Professional

Some people have the mistaken impression that infants and toddlers cannot develop mental health problems. They may believe that children so young are immune to the effects of early adversity because they are inherently resilient. They may believe, too, that young children will simply "grow out of" behavioral problems and emotional difficulties as they grow older (Osofsky & Lieberman, 2011).

The field of infant mental health—one of the most rapidly developing fields in the area of child health and development—takes a different view. This relatively new field is based on the assumption that what happens in the early years affects the course of development across the life span. Accordingly, infant mental health professionals work with babies, parents, and families to ensure that infants and toddlers get the best possible start. Their goal is not just to treat existing problems, but to prevent problems from developing in the first place (Brandt, Perry, Seligman & Tronick, 2013; Lillas & Turnbull, 2009; Paul & Thomson-Salo, 2013).

Infant mental health as a field got its start with the work of psychoanalyst and social worker Selma Fraiberg. Deborah Weatherston (2000, p. 3) describes it this way:

> Under Fraiberg's careful direction, social workers, psychologists, nurses, and psychiatrists—seasoned practitioners and student interns—worked together at the Child Development Project in Ann Arbor, Michigan, to translate new knowledge into practice through the infant mental health approach. Parent and infant were seen together, most frequently in their own homes, for early identification of risk and treatment, to reduce the likelihood of serious developmental failure and relationship disturbance. Each practitioner returned to "the source," the home where an infant and parent lived, to observe, firsthand, the infant or toddler within the context of the emerging parent-child relationship. Sitting beside the parent and infant at the kitchen table, or on the floor, or on a sofa, the infant mental health practitioner watched and listened carefully in an effort to understand the capacities of the child and family, the risks they faced, and the ways in which the practitioner might be helpful to the infant or toddler and family.... Services included concrete assistance, emotional support, developmental guidance, early relationship assessment and support, infant-parent psychotherapy, and advocacy.

CHAPTER OUTLINE

Early infant mental health professionals came from many different backgrounds, and that continues to be true today. These include nursing, early childhood education, occupational therapy, physical therapy, psychology, social work, pediatrics, and psychiatry. Is there a place for you in this emerging, dynamic field, a place where you can make a difference in the lives of young children and their families?

## [KEY QUESTIONS] *for* READING CHAPTER 7

1. What do the theories of psychosocial development say about the emotional needs of infants and toddlers?
2. How important is the parent-child attachment relationship?
3. How do emotions develop, and how do changes in the brain influence this development?
4. How do infants and toddlers develop a sense of self and the social skills necessary to interact with others?
5. What role do caregivers and the child's own temperament play in the child's psychosocial development?

**RECALL FROM CHAPTER 1** that psychosocial development relates to patterns of change in children's personalities and their social and emotional skills. This chapter describes psychosocial development in the infant and toddler years. We begin by examining how the major theories of psychosocial development explain the changes that occur over these early years. We then discuss the lifelong importance of infants' attachment relationships with caregivers. We go on to cover specific aspects of emotional development. You will see that emotional development is governed in part by changes in the brain. You will see, too, that emotional and social growth are interwoven. It is through the countless social interactions between caregivers and infants that young children become aware of their own feelings and learn the social skills they need to interact with others. An important part of psychosocial development involves developing a sense of self, so we discuss that topic next. Finally, we explain how parents and other caregivers, on the one hand, and the child's own temperament, on the other, play vital roles in psychosocial development during the first two years of life.

# Theories of Psychosocial Development

**[ KEY QUESTION ] 1. What do the theories of psychosocial development say about the emotional needs of infants and toddlers?**

Several of the theorists introduced in Chapter 1 were particularly interested in children's psychosocial development. Here, we discuss some of the key theories in this field: Freud's psychoanalytic theory, Erikson's psychosocial theory, and Bowlby's attachment theory. We also introduce more current models that focus on the interactive nature of the relationships between infants and toddlers and their caregivers.

## Freud's Psychoanalytic Theory

Freud, with his psychoanalytic theory, was one of the first to suggest that very early experiences, especially with parents, shape emotions and personality much later in life. Freud believed that, as children, we pass through five psychosexual stages, as discussed in Chapter 1. Each stage has a major function, which is based on a pleasure center. This pleasure center must be stimulated appropriately (not too much, not too little). If it is not, the person becomes fixated (remains at that stage) and is unable to move successfully to the next stage (Kahn, 2002).

During infancy and toddlerhood, children are first in the oral stage and then in the anal stage. In the first year and a half of life, the focus is on the oral zone. In this stage, the infant seeks gratification through stimulation of the mouth, primarily through sucking. During the second and third years, the anal zone is the focus of energy. Gratification derives from exercise and control of the anal musculature. The degree to which infants' oral and anal needs are gratified in the first years of life determines their future development and personality. When these needs are not met in a satisfactory way, the result can be adjustment problems in adulthood, such as difficulty in maintaining relationships with other adults.

Freud's enduring legacy is based on his insight into the singular importance of the infant's first relationship in terms of later development. Freud saw the mother (not the father or other caregiver) as the primary agent in infants' ongoing development. He maintained that infants' feelings toward their mothers are unique and without parallel. Freud reasoned that a human's first encounter with intimate behavior is with his or her mother during breast-feeding. Thus, the mother-child relationship serves as the prototype for all love relationships that develop later in life (Freud, 1940, 1964).

Freud, however, never studied infants, and many of his ideas have never been empirically validated. Nevertheless, his emphasis on infants' basic needs still guides many clinicians working in infant mental health settings. It has also influenced many of the theorists we discuss next.

## Erikson's Psychosocial Theory

Like Freud, Erik Erikson proposed a stage theory of development. But Erikson emphasized the influence of environment and culture on psychosocial development. His psychosocial theory includes eight stages that cover the life span, as described in Chapter 1 (Erikson, 1950, 1959). In each stage, individuals experience a crisis that challenges their emotional equilibrium. How they resolve these crises determines their continuing healthy psychological development.

The first psychosocial stage extends over about the first year of life. In this stage, infants face the developmental task of achieving a sense of "basic trust versus basic mistrust." Because infants are utterly dependent, such trust is based on the nurturance and warmth they receive in their caregiving environment. Erikson described basic trust as a capacity "to receive and accept what is given" (Erikson, 1950, p. 58). Infants who receive the warmth and consistent support they need form a basic sense of trust in themselves and in the world in general. They begin to develop a strong sense of self, the basis of what Erikson refers to as a *strong ego identity*. But for infants whose needs for a warm, supportive environment are not met, trust will not develop. The sense of self will be fragile, and the child will feel inadequate.

In the second stage, the developmental task involves achieving "autonomy versus shame and doubt." This task emerges when toddlers begin to have control over their bodies between the ages of 1 and 3. At this time, children are capable of making choices—holding on to or letting go of objects and bodily functions. Toilet training, which we discuss later in the chapter, is one of the many challenges facing infants and toddlers during this stage as they attempt to achieve a sense of autonomy, or independence. How can parents help children meet these challenges? They can allow their toddlers to act independently, when it is appropriate for them to do so. They can also refrain from criticizing and shaming their children when they make mistakes.

| **Erikson's Psychosocial Stage Theory** |
|---|
| Trust vs. mistrust<br>• Infants develop a basic trust in others. If their needs are not met by their caregivers, mistrust develops. |
| Autonomy vs. shame, doubt<br>• Children exercise their new motor and mental skills. If caregivers are encouraging, children develop a sense of autonomy versus shame and doubt. |
| Initiative vs. guilt |
| Industry vs. inferiority |
| Identity vs. identity confusion |
| Intimacy vs. isolation |
| Generativity vs. stagnation |
| Integrity vs. despair |

## Bowlby's Attachment Theory

Attachment theory began with the joint work of John Bowlby and Mary Ainsworth, in the 1960s and 1970s (Ainsworth, Blehar, Waters, & Wall, 1978; Bowlby, 1951, 1969). Along the way, many other researchers contributed to its growth (Bretherton, 2000; Cassidy & Shaver, 1999; Sroufe, Egeland, Carlson, & Collins, 2005; Sroufe & Waters, 1977). Bowlby shared the psychoanalytic view that early experiences in childhood, in particular the relations between the child and the primary caregiver, have an important influence on development and behavior later in life.

Warmth and nurturance will help this young baby to develop a sense of security, which is a precursor of secure attachment relationships and subsequent emotional competence.

Bowlby worked with children who had been evacuated and placed with strangers after World War II. He developed an enduring interest in how separation from parents affected children's development. Drawing on concepts from psychoanalysis, ethology, and developmental psychology, he formulated the basic tenets of attachment theory in his landmark trilogy, *Attachment and Loss* (Bowlby, 1969, 1973, 1980).

A core principle underlying attachment theory is that sensitive, responsive maternal care is the single most important precursor of secure attachment relationships and subsequent social and emotional competence. The emotional bond formed between children and the mother or other caregivers provides children with a sense of security and allows them to explore their environment, returning to the adult during periods of distress. In this view, the attachment relationship between mother and child has the evolutionary function of protecting the infant from danger.

Attachment theory is perhaps the most influential and well-researched theory of psychosocial development in infants and toddlers, so we consider it in some detail later in the chapter.

WHEN SYSTEMS CONNECT

## The Transactional Model

The idea that children are in a dynamic relationship with their caregiving environment is a basic tenet of the theories we have just described. Nevertheless, these theories still assume that the direction of influence in parent-infant interaction travels from parent to infant. This assumption places the primary responsibility for quality of interaction on the parent. The transactional model, in contrast, emphasizes the interdependent effects of child and environment (Adolf & Robinson, 2013; Sameroff, 2010; Sameroff & Chandler, 1975; Sameroff & Fiese, 2000). An example of the transactional nature of development can be seen in the case of postpartum depression.

*Everyday stories*

DEPRESSED MOTHERS AND THEIR BABIES Depression during pregnancy and the postpartum period is a widespread, serious health problem. Many new mothers experience the so-called baby blues after childbirth, marked by mood swings and crying spells. For most, these symptoms usually fade away quickly. Some new mothers, unfortunately, experience a more severe, long-lasting form of depression known as *postpartum depression*. These mothers feel sad and socially withdrawn, and also unconnected to their babies. They do not respond to their babies' cries and cues, and they engage in less face-to-face interaction with them. Their babies, meanwhile, are actively seeking their mothers' response and attention. Eventually, in the absence of such response and attention, they begin to give up. They show less positive expressions of emotion and higher irritability. They have difficulties engaging with others and regulating their emotional states. These babies have become depressed, too, and their mothers, as a result, may feel even worse than before. Infants of depressed mothers may be at increased risk of developing various problems in childhood and adolescence, including cognitive and emotional difficulties. Fortunately, treatment of both mother and baby can end the cycle of depression.

The transactional model shares many of the assumptions of Bronfenbrenner's bioecological model, which also was described in Chapter 1. This model describes an active, ever-changing environment and an active developing child, each adapting to and influencing the other over time. Such approaches highlight the importance of stable and nurturing relationships in promoting development. They also emphasize that children—through their temperament and personality—play an active role in their own development (Bornstein, 2002, 2003; Lewis, 2000; Sameroff, 2010).

**what if...?**

In his popular—nonscientific—book *Outliers: The Story of Success*, Malcolm Gladwell describes the life course of a number of individuals who have succeeded in various fields (Gladwell, 2008). Mozart, Bill Gates, and the Beatles are among his case studies. Gladwell argues that neither rock stars, nor software billionaires, nor great composers make it on individual effort and talent alone. Birth circumstances, family background, culture, luck, privilege, and circumstances of various sorts together determine success.

How would you describe Gladwell's ideas in terms of Bronfenbrenner's model and transactional theory?

**✓CHECK YOUR PROGRESS**

1. What are the major challenges infants and toddlers face during the oral and anal periods, according to psychoanalytic theory?
2. How does Erikson characterize the main tasks of infancy and toddlerhood?
3. What are the main features of Bowlby's attachment theory?
4. What is the major contribution of the transactional model to our understanding of infant psychosocial development?

## The Importance of Attachment

**[ KEY QUESTION ] 2. How important is the parent-child attachment relationship?**

We introduced Bowlby's attachment theory in the preceding section. A core principle of this theory is that enduring early relationships are critical for developing a sense of self, of others, and of trust (Bowlby, 1951; Fonagy, 2001). If the relationship between caregiver and child is a healthy one, the child will feel loved and accepted, will develop a healthy and strong sense of self, and will begin to learn the values of love and empathy. These results, in turn, will promote healthy development in other areas. Bowlby placed particular emphasis on the role of the mother. He summarized the ideally sensitive mother as "being readily available, sensitive to her child's signals, and lovingly responsive when he or she seeks protection and/or comfort and/or assistance" (Bowlby, 1988, p. 4).

### How Does Attachment Develop?

**Attachment** can be defined as lasting psychological connectedness between human beings. According to attachment theory, attachment is governed by three important principles:

1. Alarm of some kind, stemming from an internal source (such as physical pain) or an external source (such as a loss of contact with a caregiver), activates "the attachment behavioral system."
2. Once this system is activated, the infant is motivated to seek out soothing physical contact with the "attachment figure." In seeking contact, the infant looks for an attachment figure that is near, available, and responsive (typically, the mother).
3. If the infant's attempt to find protection succeeds, the attachment system deactivates, anxiety is reduced, the infant is soothed, and play and exploration can resume. But if no attachment figure is found, the infant experiences extreme arousal and anxiety.

These principles imply that having an early trusting relationship with an attachment figure gives children a *secure base* from which to explore, learn, and develop. Indeed, both Bowlby and Ainsworth "placed the secure-base phenomenon at the

**attachment** Lasting psychological connectedness between human beings.

**Strange Situation procedure** A laboratory procedure designed by Mary Ainsworth to capture individual differences in attachment; it involves separating infants and toddlers from their caregivers for brief periods and observing their responses when the caregivers return.

**secure attachment** Attachment that characterizes children who use caregivers as a secure base from which to explore.

**insecure-avoidant attachment** Attachment that characterizes children who appear to avoid their caregivers.

**insecure-resistant attachment** Attachment that characterizes children who seek closeness to their caregivers but resist this closeness at the same time.

**disorganized attachment** Attachment that characterizes children who display confused and disorganized reactions to caregivers.

**Attachment Q-Sort (AQS)** A measure of attachment behavior that can be used in clinic or home settings; it consists of a series of 75, 90, or 100 cards, each describing a specific behavioral characteristic of children between 12 and 48 months.

center of their analysis and defined an attachment figure as a person whom the child uses as a secure base across time and situations" (Posada et al., 1995, p. 27). Bowlby (1973) believed that secure attachment relationships were the foundation for the growth of self-reliance. Thus, infants who were effectively able to use their caregivers as a secure base for exploration would later be more independent. Those who had ineffective or anxious attachment relationships, in contrast, would later be more dependent and less self-reliant.

According to Bowlby (1969), attachment develops through a series of phases. The *preattachment* phase begins at birth, as infants begin to connect with various caregivers. Over the first two years, during the *attachment-in-the making* and *clear-cut attachment* phases, preattachment matures into attachment to the primary caregiver. Finally, at about age 2, child and caregiver develop a "partnership" of mutual appreciation and influence; this is the *goal-directed partnership* phase. These four phases are described in more detail in Table 7.1.

## Measuring Attachment

We mentioned earlier that Mary Ainsworth's ideas helped expand attachment theory. Above all, Ainsworth wanted to test some of Bowlby's ideas empirically. Perhaps her greatest contribution was the development of the Strange Situation procedure, an innovative way to measure the quality of a child's attachment (Ainsworth, Blehar, Waters & Wall, 1978). While various methods are used to measure attachment, the two most widely used measures are Ainsworth's Strange Situation procedure and the Attachment Q-Sort (AQS) developed by Waters (1987).

### The Strange Situation Procedure

The **Strange Situation procedure** was designed by Ainsworth to capture individual differences in attachment (Ainsworth et al., 1978; Johnson et al., 2010; Main & Solomon, 1990). This 30-minute experimental procedure involves a series of separations and reunions between a caregiver, a child, and a stranger. Parent and

**Table 7.1** Bowlby's Four Phases of Attachment Development

| | |
|---|---|
| Preattachment phase: *0–6 weeks* | Infants' behaviors, such as crying, sucking, rooting, and eye-gaze, are beautifully designed to promote proximity and contact with a protective, caregiving adult. However, babies are not yet attached to any one caregiver. They respond indiscriminately to caregivers other than the mother or primary caregiver. |
| Attachment-in-the-making phase: *6 weeks to 6–8 months* | Infants begin to focus on preferred caretakers, typically their mothers. They begin to react differently and more quickly to primary caregivers than to strangers. They are building up trust that these caregivers will meet their needs. However, they are still not distressed at being separated from particular caregivers. |
| Clear-cut attachment phase: *6–8 months to 18–24 months* | Babies become solidly attached to their caregivers, and separation anxiety emerges. They also exhibit stranger anxiety in the presence of unfamiliar people. They can now crawl and walk, so they are able to actively seek proximity to chosen caregivers. They use caregivers as a secure base from which to explore their environment. |
| Goal-corrected partnership phase: *24 months onward* | Toddlers can now see their caregivers as independent persons. They modify and align their personal goals with the goals of the attachment figures. Child and caregiver develop a "partnership" of mutual appreciation and influence. |

*Source:* Based on Bowlby, 1969.

**FIGURE 7.1 The Strange Situation Procedure** The Strange Situation consists of eight brief episodes: (1) Parent and infant are introduced to the experimental room. (2) Parent and infant are alone in the room. (3) A stranger joins them. (4) The parent leaves the infant alone with the stranger. (5) The parent returns and the stranger leaves (reunion). (6) The parent leaves, and the infant is completely alone. (7) The stranger returns. (8) The parent returns, and the stranger leaves (reunion). The researchers observing the procedure are interested in how the infant responds to these comings and goings.

After mother and baby have been introduced to the experimental room and spent some time together, a stranger enters.

The mother then leaves the baby alone with the stranger.

The mother returns, and the stranger leaves.

The mother leaves, and the baby is alone until the stranger returns.

Once again, the mother returns, and the stranger leaves.

infant are introduced to a laboratory playroom. Later, they are joined by an unfamiliar woman. While the stranger plays with the baby, the parent leaves briefly and then returns. A second separation ensues during which the baby is completely alone. Finally, the stranger and then the parent return (see Figure 7.1). Observers are interested in the infant's behavior during the separations and the reunions, especially the reunions.

Observations of infant behavior in the Strange Situation allow researchers to classify infant behavior patterns as secure, insecure-avoidant, insecure-resistant, or disorganized.

- **Secure attachment.** Securely attached infants are moderately distressed when their caregivers leave the room, and they are happy and easily comforted when the caregivers return. They tend to use caregivers as a secure base from which they can explore.
- **Insecure-avoidant attachment.** Infants with insecure-avoidant attachment are unresponsive to caregivers and are not distressed when they leave the room. They focus on the environment at the moment of reunion, ignoring or even turning away from the caregivers.
- **Insecure-resistant attachment.** Infants with insecure-resistant attachment stay close to caregivers and are distressed when they leave the room. When the caregivers return, the infants make anxious contact with them, clinging but at the same time resisting contact. These interactions may have an angry quality.
- **Disorganized attachment.** Infants with disorganized attachment show confused and contradictory behavior when reunited with caregivers. For example, they may simultaneously display distress and avoidance (Main & Solomon, 1990). They may appear dazed or depressed and may cry out unexpectedly.

Hundreds of studies support the classifications described in Ainsworth's original descriptions and the distinct parenting behaviors associated with each (Carlson & Harwood, 2003; Cassidy & Shaver, 2008; van IJzendoorn & Sagi-Swartz, 2008). These studies also show that in a range of cultural settings, from Africa to China, Israel, Japan, Western Europe, and America, most children—about two-thirds of them—are securely attached to their caregivers (van IJzendoorn & Sagi, 1999).

## The Attachment Q-Sort (AQS)

The laboratory setting in which the Strange Situation procedure is administered can be stressful for small children because it involves separating the children from their caregivers. For that reason, Everett Waters (1987) developed another method for assessing attachment, called the **Attachment Q-Sort (AQS).** The AQS uses a series of 75, 90, or 100 cards, each describing a specific behavioral characteristic of children. The items on the cards include behaviors such as "Child readily shares with mother" or "Child is happy or affectionate when he returns to mother between or after play times." An observer watches a child for several hours and then sorts the cards from "most descriptive of the child" to "least descriptive of the child." By comparing the resulting description with behavioral profiles of the various kinds of attachment, the observer can compute a score for attachment security.

As mentioned, the AQS avoids the stress of separation for children. It has several other advantages as well. It can be used in clinic or home settings (van IJzendoorn, Vereijken, Bakermans-Kranenburg & Riksen-Walraven, 2004; Vaughn & Waters, 1990). It can also be applied in cultures in which parent-infant separations are uncommon, such as in Japan (Kazui, Endo, Tanaka, Sakagami, & Suganuma, 2000). The AQS thus provides an economical methodology for the examination of individual differences in attachment security in a wide range of contexts (Vaughn & Waters, 1990).

## what if...?

Joanne made a vow that if she ever had children, she would not spoil them. She watched in horror as her friends jumped up every time their babies burped or fussed. Giving babies everything they want, she was sure, could not be good for them. Then she had her own baby boy and she found herself doing all the same things her friends had done. But each time she ran to pick up her fussing infant, she shuddered at the thought of raising a spoiled, self-centered child. How could her baby develop a sense of self-reliance and independence if she took care of all his needs? Many child development experts who are influenced by attachment theory, such as T. Berry Brazelton (1992), maintain that during the first six months at least, it's actually impossible to spoil a child. What do you think? Will Joanne's baby end up being spoiled and self-centered? Would you be afraid of spoiling your baby? Why or why not?

## Cultural Differences in Attachment

Recall that attachment theory is based, in part, on ethology. As discussed in Chapter 1, ethological theory emphasizes underlying biological forces in development. We would expect, then, that attachment is a universal phenomenon found in every culture across the globe. Research from around the world does seem to support the claim that all infants develop attachment relationships, secure or insecure, with their primary caregivers. Some form of attachment behavior can be seen in every culture that has been studied (Bakermans-Kranenburg, van IJzendoorn, & Kroonenberg, 2004; LeVine, & Norman, 2001; Posada et al., 1995; van IJzendoorn & Sagi, 1999; van IJzendoorn & Sagi-Schwartz, 2008; Wieczorek-Deering, Greene, Nugent, & Graham, 1991).

There are differences, however, in how attachment behavior is expressed. Sensitive parenting and attachment behavior in non-Western settings may contrast with what attachment theorists have typically described as sensitive responding and attachment behavior in Western settings. Studies of attachment in Japan, for example, show that secure attachments in Japanese families are characterized by a great deal of physical closeness. In Northern American and many European countries, this is not necessarily

© Studio Tec/amanaimages/Corbis

Physical closeness characterizes secure attachments in Japanese families. As a result, Japanese children are more likely than American children to be upset when physically separated from caregivers during the Strange Situation procedure.

the case. As a result, Japanese infants are more likely than American infants to become very upset during separations from their caregivers during the Strange Situation procedure, and are less likely to explore the environment (Behrens, Main, & Hesse, 2007; Takahashi 1986). Some researchers have argued that these results do not mean that Japanese infants are less emotionally secure than their American counterparts. Rather, both the Strange Situation procedure and the underlying assumptions of what constitute attachment behavior are embedded in Western thinking and so cannot be considered universally applicable (Rothbaum, Weisz, Pott, Miyake, & Morelli, 2000).

*Everyday stories*

DIFFERENT CULTURES, DIFFERENT VALUES In Western cultures (which refers here to the United States, Canada, and Western European countries), secure attachment is associated with infant characteristics such as independence, emotional openness, and sociability. But these characteristics may be less valued in other cultures. For example, wanting to be on mother's lap, and crying or clinging to her when she leaves, are inconsistent with the Western-Anglo emphasis on promoting confidence and independence. On the other hand, these same behaviors are consistent with the Latino emphasis on appropriate relatedness and interdependence (Carlson & Harwood, 2003). As another example, being "clingy" may be seen as a negative attribute for toddlers in one culture, but appreciated as an affirmation of closeness in another. Similarly, parents who exercise persistent physical control and set strong limits on infant behavior might be seen as interfering with the infant's development of autonomy in a North American Anglo setting. In contrast, in a Latino setting, the same behavior may be seen as positive evidence of efforts to raise a well-behaved, respectful child (Harwood, Miller, & Irizarry, 1995).

One of the greatest contributions to date of cross-cultural studies on attachment is the understanding that not all cultures expect the mother to be the sole caregiver (Bornstein et al., 1992). In both Western and non-Western cultures, children may have relationships with several attachment figures, rather than just one. Many cultures involve other family members or even community members in significant parenting roles. African cultures such as the Dogon, Efe, and Gusii, for example, rely on multiple caregivers, even if the babies' primary relationship remains with their mothers (LeVine, 2010; LeVine et al., 1994; Morelli, Rogoff, Oppenheim, & Goldsmith, 1992; True, Pisani, & Oumar, 2001).

Partly as a result of cross-cultural research, most attachment researchers now agree that caregiver sensitivity is only one important contributor to attachment security. In all cultures, other factors can influence the development of attachment. These factors include the physical setting itself, the stimulation caregivers provide, and the availability of other caregivers, as well as the children's own characteristics, such as temperament. For that reason, how we define attachment behavior and parental sensitivity must take into account variation across cultures (Harwood et al., 1995; LeVine, 2010; LeVine et al., 1994; van IJzendoorn & Sagi-Schwartz, 2008).

## Long-Term Effects of Early Attachment

Although Bowlby focused on the development of attachment during infancy and childhood, he viewed the system as enduring over the life course (Bowlby, 1969). But is there evidence that early experience affects development later on in life, as attachment theory proposes? A number of longitudinal studies have demonstrated that attachment patterns observed in infancy do continue into adulthood.

Several studies have linked attachment styles in infancy to relationship satisfaction in adulthood. People with secure attachment styles usually express greater satisfaction with their relationships than people who have other attachment styles (Brennan & Shaver, 1995; Collins & Freeney, 2004; Hazan & Shaver, 1987; Pietromonaco, Feldman Barrett, & Powers, 2006). The absence of secure attachment, in contrast, may cause considerable distress, resulting in vulnerability to a variety of physical, emotional, social, and moral problems in adulthood (Castle et al., 1999; Kreppner et al., 2010).

Longitudinal studies have also suggested that attachment status can change in either direction (from secure to insecure or from insecure to secure). Results of a 20-year study indicated that individual differences in attachment can be stable across much of the life span and yet remain open to change in the light of experience (Waters, Weinfield, & Hamilton, 2000). In this study, around 70 to 80% of people experienced no significant changes in attachment styles over time. But around 20 to 30% of people did experience such changes. The term *earned secure* has been used to describe individuals who moved from an insecure status to a secure status. Nevertheless, for most of us, the way we learned to regulate attachment early in life will continue.

Attachment, then, seems to be an organizational core in development that is always integrated with later experience and never lost. Infant attachment in particular is important because of its connection with so many critical developmental functions—social competence, emotional regulation, the sense of self, and moral behavior, to name just a few. To be sure, it is not appropriate to think of attachment as directly causing certain outcomes. Nor can we look at attachment as the only important factor in development. Nevertheless, nothing we can examine about infancy is more important, because attachment experiences remain, even in this complex view, and are vital to the formation of the adult person (De Wolff & van IJzendoorn, 1997; Grossmann, Grossmann, & Waters, 2006; Sroufe, 2005; Thompson, 1997, 2000a).

## How Maternal Employment During the First Year Affects Attachment

Policy

Is there a possibility that maternal employment interferes with the establishment of a secure attachment relationship and the child's overall psychosocial development? Most contemporary American mothers work at jobs outside the home, even when their children are quite small. The overwhelming majority of mothers (80%) work in the first year of their baby's life. Of these, 75% work full-time. Almost all of these women are working by the time their infants are 6 months old, and many by the time they are 3 months old (Brooks-Gunn, Han, & Waldogel, 2010). Given the role that parents play in their infants' lives, it is not surprising, then, that questions have arisen about how this pattern affects subsequent child development. In particular, concerns have been raised about maternal employment during the baby's first year of life.

jacky chapman/Alamy

Some 80% of American mothers work in the first year of their babies' lives. Most are working by the time their children are 6 months old.

Do mothers who work provide lower-quality parenting and a less stimulating home environment for their babies? Not all studies have found that maternal employment has negative effects (for example, Clarke-Stewart, 1989). But according to a number of studies, problem behaviors are associated with maternal employment in the first two years, with the amount of nonmaternal care received, or with a combination of both (Bates et al., 1994; Baydar & Brooks-Gunn, 1991; Belsky, 1986, 1990; Belsky & Eggebeen, 1991; Haskins, 1985; Vandell & Corasaniti, 1990). Furthermore, these effects may persist over time (Vandell & Corasaniti, 1990). Recent findings from the Study of Early Child Care, a longitudinal study sponsored by the National Institute of Child Health and Human Development, seem to support the earlier findings (Brooks-Gunn et al., 2010). Families where mothers worked full-time by 3 months had poorer scores on the Home Observation for Measurement of the Environment **(HOME)** scales, which measure the quality of the child's home learning environment. The children in those families also had more caregiver- and teacher-reported behavioral problems, such as disobedience and aggression, at age 4½ years and in first grade.

Other studies indicate that when mothers are home longer in the first year, their children are more likely to be breast-fed, fully immunized, and up to date on their well-baby visits (Berger, Hill, & Waldfogel, 2005). Finally, infants, and especially toddlers, who attend full-day, center-based child care have higher levels of cortisol during the days when they are at child-care than during the days when they are at home (Watamura, Donzella, Alwin, & Gunnar, 2003). Recall from Chapter 2 that cortisol is a stress-related hormone and that chronic stress can negatively affect children's development.

Among advanced industrialized countries, the United States is exceptional in not requiring employers to provide a period of paid maternity leave (Brooks-Gunn et al., 2010; Tanaka, 2005; Waldfogel, 2006). Under the federal Family and Medical Leave Act (FMLA) of 1993, about half of new mothers in the United States are eligible for a period of job-protected leave. The law makes no provision for paid leave, however. In addition, the period of leave—12 weeks—is very short (see Figure 7.2). It is difficult to say how many new mothers would stay home longer if an extended period of leave were offered, or if paid leave were available. Evidence from other countries, however, strongly suggests that when leave benefits are extended, women and men do take advantage of them (Duvander & Andersson, 2006; Gaertner, Spinrad, Eisenberg, & Greving, 2007; Gregg, Gutierrez-Domenech, & Waldfogel, 2007). More limited evidence from the United States, based on changes after the FMLA came into effect, as well as differences in state leave laws, also suggests that women take longer leave when provisions are more generous (Han, Ruhm, & Waldfogel, 2009; Han & Waldfogel, 2003).

## The Effects of Early Adverse Experiences

What are the effects of unfavorable early experiences on infant attachment and later development? What happens if there is no consistent, nurturing care in the infant's life, or if the infant is neglected or even abused? Child neglect and abuse are major problems in the United States, as well as elsewhere. About a million cases of child abuse and neglect are substantiated in the United States every year (U.S. Department

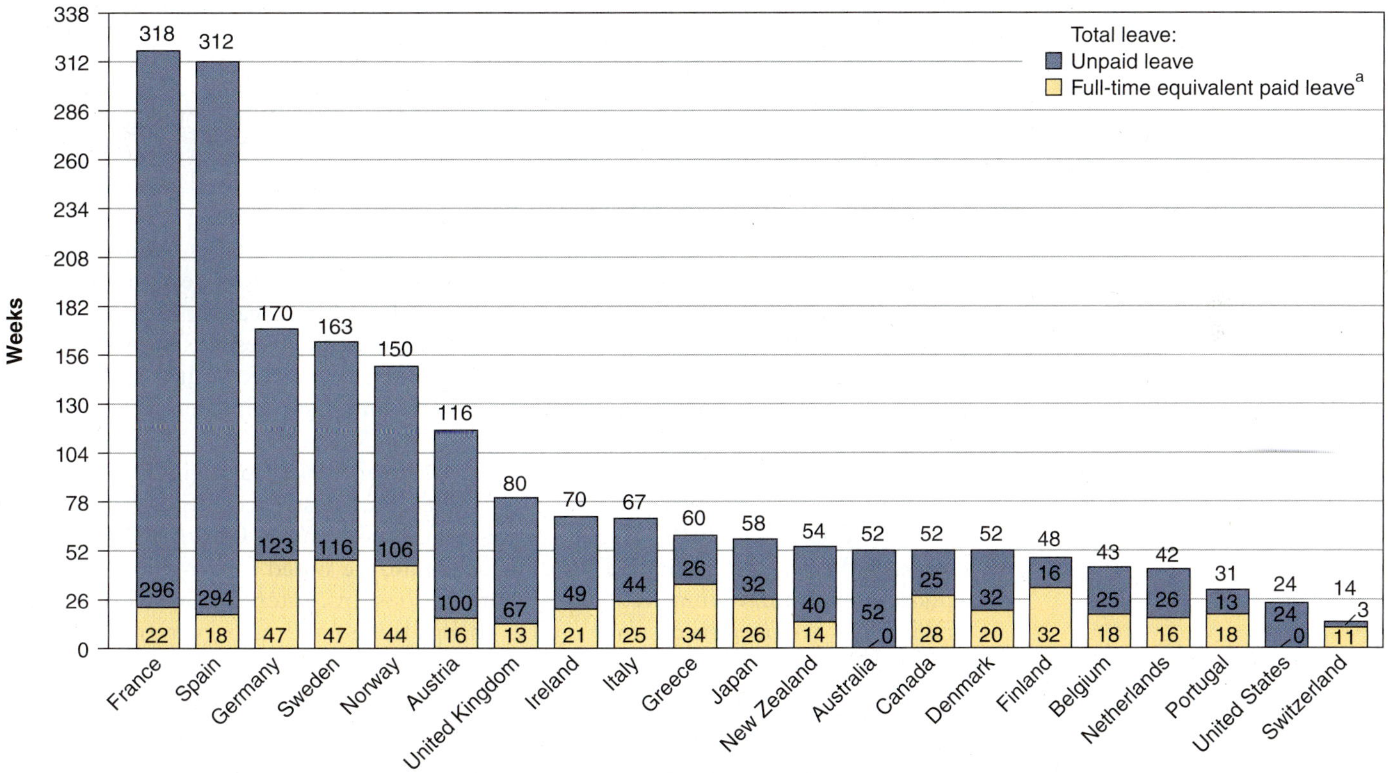


a. *Full-time equivalent paid leave* is a calculation that allows comparisons among countries with different types of paid leave—such as fully paid or partially paid leave.

**FIGURE 7.2 Parental Leave for Two-Parent Families in Selected Countries** Among developed nations, the United States is near the bottom in terms of granting both total leave and paid leave for new parents. Many U.S. mothers and fathers thus are forced to return to work much earlier than they would like.

Reprinted with permission from Ray, R., Gornick, J. C., & Schmitt, J. (2008, rev. 2009). *Parental leave policies in 21 countries.* Washington, DC: Center for Economic and Policy Research, p. 6, Figure 1.

**FIGURE 7.3 Potential Lifelong Effects of Early Adverse Experiences** Early adversity can form the base for lifelong problems. However, children differ in how they respond to adversity, so its effects are far from universal.

Reprinted from U.S. Centers for Disease Control and Prevention. Adverse Childhood Experiences (ACE) Study. Accessible at www.cdc.gov/ace/pyramid.htm.

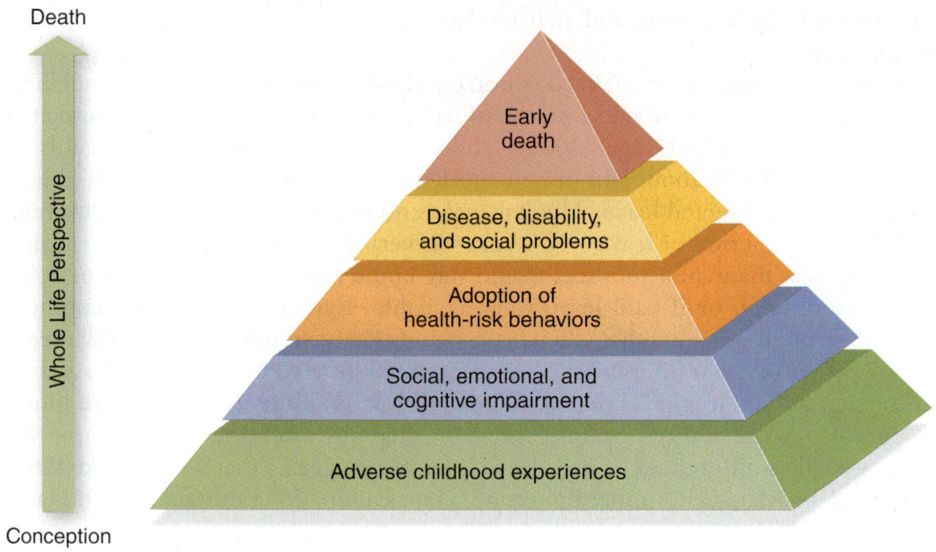


of Health and Human Services, 2010), and it is likely that the actual number is higher. Each year, thousands of children under the age of 3 enter the U.S. child welfare system because they have been neglected or abused by their caregivers (State of Child Welfare in America, 2011).

Maltreated children do have impaired attachment relationships. Furthermore, research suggests that abuse and neglect early in life can lead to lasting changes in neurotransmitter systems implicated in emotional regulation and responses to stress (Anda et al., 2006). Infants who experience such changes are more vulnerable to developing stress-related psychiatric disorders, such as major depression, in adulthood (Caspi et al., 2002; Felitti et al., 1998; Heim & Nemeroff, 2001; Kaufman, Plotsky, Nemeroff, & Charney, 2000; Kumsta, Kreppner, Rutter, Beckett, Castle, Stevens & Sonuga-Barke, 2010; Rutter, 2006; Rutter et al., 2007). In addition, developmental delays are 4 to 5 times greater for abused than nonabused children (Dore, 2005; Leslie et al., 2005; Mills et al., 2006). The possible lifelong effects of early adversity are shown in Figure 7.3. That said, these effects are far from universal. Research has shown that children vary a great deal in the way they respond to adversity (Collishaw et al., 2007; Kochanska, 2001; McLaughlin, Zeanah, Fox, & Nelson, 2012; Rutter, 2006; Rutter & English and Romanian Adoptees (ERA) Study Team, 1998; Rutter, & O'Connor, 2004; Sroufe et al., 2005; Werner & Smith, 1992). Some children are less adversely affected than others, and these children are often described as *resilient*.

Can the effects of early neglect or abuse be reversed? Encouragingly, preventive interventions can produce a variety of positive outcomes (Cicchetti & Toth, 2010; Osofsky & Osofsky, 2010; Smyke, Zeanah, Fox, Nelson, & Guthrie, 2010; Toth, Rogosch, Manly, & Cicchetti, 2006). For example, we noted earlier that maltreated children tend to have impaired attachment relationships. Interventions with mothers and infants have been successfully used to change these attachment patterns (Cicchetti & Toth, 2010).

### ✓ CHECK YOUR PROGRESS

1. How does attachment develop?
2. How can attachment be measured?
3. How does culture affect the attachment process?
4. What are some long-term effects of early attachment relationships?
5. How do early adverse experiences affect attachment?

## Emotional Development

**[ KEY QUESTION ] 3. How do emotions develop, and how do changes in the brain influence this development?**

**limbic system** The brain system that governs emotion.

Before we delve into the world of emotions in infancy and toddlerhood, let's reflect for a moment on our own emotions. We experience many emotions every day, some positive and some negative. We may be happy or excited at one moment and sad or angry at another. Our emotions may energize and motivate us, or they may sap our energy and spirits. They may draw us toward certain situations and people and prompt us to avoid others, so they also guide our social exchanges. And connecting with another person's emotions marks the beginning of our understanding of that person as an individual.

There are big differences between adult and infant emotions, of course, because emotions are tied to cognitive and physical development and general life experiences. Babies haven't yet gained the experience that adults have, so they do not experience emotions in quite the same way. Nevertheless, for every emotion we experience as adults, the seeds of that emotion can be seen even in very young infants.

In this section about emotional development, we begin by discussing the brain structures that govern emotion. We go on to describe how infants and toddlers express their emotions, how they learn to regulate them, and how their emotions are tied to their social competence. We also discuss autism spectrum disorder, which affects social interaction, among other things.

THE DEVELOPING BRAIN

### The Limbic System

Recall that the first years of life are a time of rapid and dramatic brain development. Recall, too, that this development depends not only on children's genetic structure but also on their experiences. Indeed, their brains are literally waiting for experiences to determine how connections are to be made (Als et al., 2004; Fox, Levitt, & Nelson, 2010; Huttenlocher, 2002; Johnson, 2005; Rutter, Moffit, & Caspi, 2006).

The emotional development of infants and toddlers is governed by the **limbic system.** As noted in Chapter 2, the limbic system is a network of connections among the thalamus, hypothalamus, amygdala, and hippocampus—although definitions vary somewhat, and other structures are often included as well. Table 7.2 and Figure 7.4 show structures generally included in the limbic system.

The interconnected structures within this complex, multilayered system rest in different places in the brain (Benes, 1994; Eliot, 1999; Fox & Bell, 1990; LeDoux, 1996, 2009; Schore, 1996, 2000). The hippocampus, orbitofrontal gyrus, and cingulate gyrus are part of the cerebral cortex, which is the gray matter covering the brain. The hypothalamus, amygdala, and thalamus lie below the cerebral cortex, and so are called *subcortical* structures.

**Table 7.2** Structures of the Limbic System

| Subcortical Structures | | Structures in the Cerebral Cortex | |
|---|---|---|---|
| Thalamus | Relays sensory information. All of our senses, except smell, have pathways through the thalamus. | Hippocampus | Important for certain types of learning and memory. |
| Hypothalamus | Involved in functions including emotion, thirst, hunger, and control of the autonomic nervous system. | Orbitofrontal gyrus | Involved in reward evaluation, social reasoning, and "reading" other people's emotions. |
| Amygdala | Processes information about emotions, particularly fear, and is especially sensitive to facial expressions. | Cingulate gyrus | Involved in coordination of sensory input with emotions, emotional responses to pain, and regulation of aggressive behavior. |

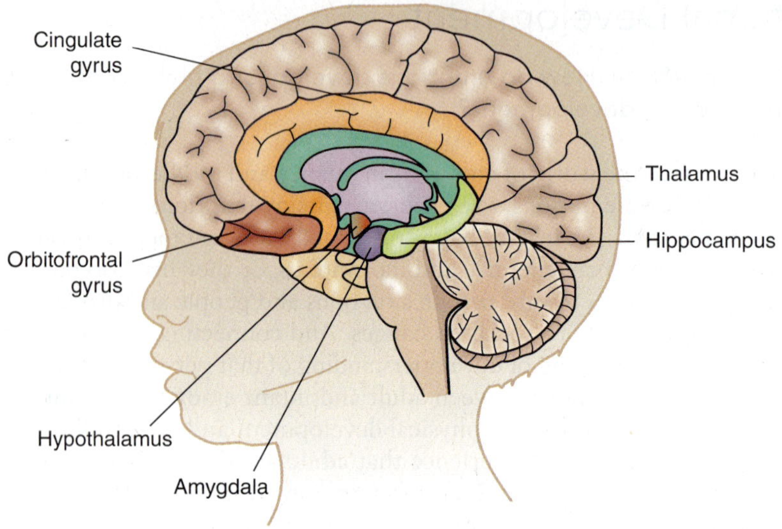


**FIGURE 7.4 The Limbic System** The hippocampus, orbitofrontal gyrus, and cingulate gyrus are parts of the cerebral cortex. The hypothalamus, amygdala, and thalamus are referred to as subcortical structures because they lie below the cerebral cortex.

The subcortical structures in the limbic system produce spontaneous expressions of emotion that are instinctive and therefore universal. These are the *primary emotions*, which include joy, sadness, and fear. We discuss the primary emotions later in this section. For example, when a young baby hears a very loud crashing noise, the subcortical limbic structures may interact to produce a fearful response. The sound is processed through the thalamus and the amygdala, which activates the hypothalamus. The hypothalamus in turn may trigger a cascade of physiological changes, such as a faster heart rate, dilation of the eyes, and rapid breathing (Everitt, Cardinal, Parkinson, & Robbins, 2003).

While the subcortical limbic system is responsible for generating emotions, the limbic cortex is where awareness of, and control over, feelings occur (Damasio, 2001; Halgren, 1992; Johnson, 2007; Joseph, 1992, 1999). This system is devoted to *conscious* emotional experience—that is, the *self-conscious emotions*. We discuss these emotions later in this section as well. Consequently, this part of the limbic system may not play much of a role during the first 6 months (Braun, 2011; Schore, 2000). Beginning at around 6 months, however, the emotional life of infants takes a giant leap, as the cortex begins to influence other parts of the brain. Massive increases in dendrites and synapses in this region now make it possible for babies to become more finely tuned to their social environments and to their own feelings.

The cortical regions that are involved in emotional experience include the orbitofrontal gyrus, the cingulate gyrus, and the hippocampus (Devinsky, Morrell, & Vogt, 1995). It is through the orbitofrontal gyrus and the cingulate gyrus that the amygdala informs the conscious mind about the emotional state generated in the subcortical region. Beginning at around 6 months, these structures allow babies to become more aware of their feelings and to assume some degree of control over them (Minagawa-Kawai et al., 2009). They also enable them to become aware of the emotions of others (Posner, Rothbart, Sheese, & Tang, 2007). The limbic system plays a role in memory, as well, through the hippocampus. The hippocampus appears to be especially important in forming episodic memories—memories about events. We discuss episodic memory in more detail in Chapter 12.

As we consider the role of the limbic system, it is important to remind ourselves once again that emotional development, particularly early in life, unfolds in response to the caregiving environment (Diamond, 2011; Johnson, 2005). The limbic system generates emotion, but like every other part of the brain, it is shaped by both nature and nurture (Barrett & Satpute, 2013; Carver & Vaccaro, 2007; Damasio, 2005; Izard,

Woodburn, & Finlon, 2010; LeDoux, 2009; Nelson, Furtado, Fox, & Zeanah, 2009). Having a stable, secure relationship with caregivers is essential to normal brain development and, in particular, to the development of a healthy limbic system. It should not surprise us, then, that depressed brain activity has been found in children who grow up in deprived environments (Nelson et al., 2007; Nelson et al., 2009). In contrast, infants whose caregivers expose them to a variety of stimulation—talking, touching, playing—are most likely to develop to their full potential. This means that children who receive sensitive, responsive care from their parents and other caregivers enjoy an important head start in their emotional development.

## Emotion: The Language of Babies

We have just seen that the needs of infants and toddlers must be met if their development is to proceed as it should. One of the most fundamental tasks for infants and toddlers, then, is to make sure that their needs *are* met. Infants communicate their needs and their feelings through a rich vocabulary of emotional expressions, from cries to babbling to chortling belly laughs. If, for example, the adults in a baby boy's life respond predictably to his cries by comforting him, if they return his smiles and provide for his needs, he will be more likely to be content. He can then focus his attention on exploring and learning about his new, ever-expanding world. Suppose, however, that this child's needs are met only occasionally, and that his pleas for comfort are ignored or met with dismissive or harsh words. As time goes on, he will likely have more and more difficulty interacting with the people and objects in his environment. Moreover, his brain will shut out the stimulation it needs to develop healthy cognitive and social skills (Lieberman & Zeanah, 1995; Shonkoff & Phillips, 2000).

In short, the experiences of these early years establish the emotional foundation on which all learning and development is based.

## Expressing Emotion

Now, let's think about how we can tell which emotions babies are feeling; that is, how do babies express their emotions? Of course, once children develop the ability to use words, they become better able to explain and describe their own (and others') emotions, as you will see in Chapter 10. Until then, infants and toddlers must use other ways to express their emotions.

### Primary Emotions

One body of researchers believes that we are born with a group of core emotions whose expression and recognition is fundamentally the same for all individuals in all cultures. This approach, referred to as **discrete emotions theory**, is traditionally traced back to Darwin (Darwin, 1872). It is based on the assumption that each emotion has distinctive features—for example, a smile signifies a happy feeling, and a cry-face indicates a sign of distress. From this theoretical perspective, one way to understand emotions and their development is by investigating facial expressions.

Even young infants exhibit a wide range of emotions (Izard, 1971, 2009, 2011). The emotions present in newborns are called the **basic** or **primary emotions**. Because they can be seen from the beginning of infancy, these emotions are assumed to be innate, consistent with discrete emotions theory (Barrett, 2006, 2009; Ekman, 1984; Izard, 1971; Izard et al., 1995, 2010; Lewis, 2000; Tomkins, 1962, 1984; Trevarthen & Aitken, 2001). Although there is some disagreement about the exact number, many scholars identify eight primary emotions: joy, sadness, fear, anger, disgust, interest, surprise, and excitement. Each has its own distinctive pattern of arousal and characteristic facial and vocal expressions. Take a look at Figure 7.5, and see if you can identify the emotions these infants are expressing.

**discrete emotions theory** A theory holding that people are born with a group of core emotions whose expression and recognition is fundamentally the same for all individuals in all cultures. These emotions are distinct from one another from a very young age, and each has its own neural, physiological, behavioral, and expressive features.

**primary, or basic, emotions** Emotions that can be seen from the beginning of infancy and that are assumed to be innate. They are often believed to include joy, sadness, fear, anger, disgust, interest, surprise, and excitement.

Gallo Images—Emielke van Wyk/Getty Images

Ruth Jenkinson/Dorling Kindersley/Getty Images

Vladimir Godnik/beyond fotomedia/Getty Images

Emielke van Wyk/Getty Images

Aping Vision/STS/Getty Images

Mats Persson/iStockphoto

**FIGURE 7.5 Emotional Expression in Infants** Each baby is showing one of these emotions: interest, fear, disgust, anger, sadness, and joy. Can you tell which baby is expressing which emotion?

Cross-cultural studies have demonstrated that people all over the world produce and recognize these expressions (Ekman, 1994, 2003; Izard, 1994; Izard et al., 2010; Ruhm, 2000). While there are subtle cultural variations, there is remarkable consistency in the facial expressions and physiological sensations associated with certain feelings, like fear, sadness, and happiness. From Detroit to Nagasaki to Dar es Salaam, smiles can be reliably recognized as discrete expressions of joy or pleasure in infants. The cheeks are raised and the mouth tends to be open, with the lip corners upturned. Similarly, cries can be easily identified as signs of negative emotion, conveying distress. The cry-face is characterized by lowered brows, with the lip corners pulled to the side. Likewise, expressions of anger are recognized by people anywhere.

## Secondary Emotions

While the primary emotions appear to be universal, other emotions—**secondary emotions**—reflect, to some extent, the unique life experiences of each child. The secondary emotions include shame, embarrassment, guilt, envy, and pride. They are sometimes called *self-conscious emotions*, because experiencing them requires a certain level of self-awareness (Lewis, 2000). They may also be called *cognitive-dependent emotions*, because they begin to appear during the second year of life, along with growing cognitive abilities (Izard, 2011). Remember from our earlier discussions that emotion and cognition cannot be separated; they are two sides of the same coin. Thus, the significant cognitive developments children exhibit in the second year are bound to produce emotional changes as well (Fischer & Bidell, 2006; Raver, 2002; Rochat, 2003). The secondary emotions require greater self-awareness and a better defined sense of self. If you think about it, it's easy to understand that a child could not feel shame, guilt, or pride unless he or she had some self-awareness.

**secondary emotions** Emotions that are not innate but that depend to some extent on cognitive development and self-awareness. They appear during the second year of life and include shame, embarrassment, guilt, envy, and pride.

## Transitions in Emotional Development in the First Years

A number of researchers have pointed out that key transitions mark children's emotional development over the first years of life (Brazelton, 1992; Emde, 1998; Heimann, 2010; Stern, 1995; Tronick, 2009; Winnicott, 1960). T. Berry Brazelton describes these transitions in emotional development as *touchpoints.* Touchpoints are predictable periods of disorganization in a child's development that precede periods of developmental growth (Brazelton, 1992; Singer & Hornstein, 2010; Stadtler & Hornstein, 2009).

The following five transitions occur over the first two years. As you read these descriptions, remember that ages are approximate. In addition, individual variations in the timing of transitions become greater as children get older.

- *Birth: The transition from life inside the womb to life outside the womb.* Typically, developing babies express what, according to some, is their first emotion as they emerge from the womb: a cry (Winberg, 2005). Crying is how babies communicate hunger, pain, fear, a need for sleep, or a need to be touched and soothed. The emotional expressions of interest, disgust, surprise, pleasure, and attentiveness can also be observed at this time, as noted in Chapter 4. All these behaviors, as we pointed out earlier, are beautifully designed to engage the caregiver and to elicit the support and care infants need to ensure their survival (Bowlby, 1969; Brazelton & Nugent, 2011; Stern, 1995).
- *The 2- to 3-month transition: The awakening of sociability.* The 2- to 3-month emotional transition is marked by the onset and flowering of the social smile, sometimes referred to as "an awakening of sociability" (Emde, 1985, 1998). Clear expressions of joy can be seen in babies at 2½ months as they interact socially with their mothers or fathers. Expressions of sadness can also be seen in infants at this age when their mothers are unresponsive in face-to-face social interactions (Izard et al., 1995; Tronick, 1989, 2009; Tronick, Als, & Brazelton, 1980). This transition comes along with enhanced wakefulness and greater capacity for eye-to-eye social contact. These changes in turn provide new opportunities for engagement and learning.

Howard Shooter/Dorling Kindersley/Getty Images

At 2 or 3 months of age, babies begin to display "social smiles," especially when interacting with caregivers.

Christina Kennedy/PhotoEdit

Babies become more wary when they reach 5 or 6 months of age, often showing "stranger anxiety" in the presence of unfamiliar adults.

© I Love Images/Corbis

Walking, typically achieved at around 10 to 13 months, brings elation—a sense of "I can do it!"

- *The 5- to 6-month transition: Stranger anxiety.* The transition that occurs at about 5 to 6 months is characterized by focused attachment. Infants are now more "tuned in" both to their primary caregiver and to other people in their environment. Consequently, as we mentioned earlier, they are more wary and less positive in unfamiliar situations and in the presence of unfamiliar adults (Waters, Matas, & Sroufe, 1975).
- *The 10- to 13-month transition: Walking and the growing sense of self.* The next transition is marked by the effects of walking and the drive toward independence. Children at this age often appear elated. They begin to express emotions that communicate a sense of pride—an "I can do it" expression (Adolph, 2008; Mahler, Pine, & Bergman, 1975; Stipek, Recchia, & McClintic, 1992). At the same time, though, they also may experience more distress. As they become more autonomous, they are more likely to receive caregiver prohibitions and negative emotional signals—for example, a stern no and a frown from a parent (Brazelton, 1992; Heimann, 2010).
- *The 18- to 24-month transition: The transition into early childhood.* The last part of the second year brings other momentous changes. Indeed, this period has sometimes been called the "transition from infancy to early childhood" because of the major psychosocial changes that occur. With their growing self-awareness and developing language, toddlers are now aware of external standards and expectations. They can begin to feel and express shame, embarrassment, guilt, envy, and pride—the secondary emotions that we discussed earlier.

## Emotional Regulation

Despite the dramatic transitions just discussed, the lives of infants and toddlers can still appear to be an emotional roller-coaster ride. An infant may be smiling contentedly one minute and crying uncontrollably the next, while a toddler may move from happy engagement to defiant tantrums in the blink of an eye. It is clear that young children can easily be overwhelmed by emotion because they do not yet have the ability to adjust or calm themselves. They find it difficult to control their anger, to deal with frustration, to overcome sadness, and to maintain a positive emotional state. Learning to control, or *regulate*, emotion is undoubtedly the greatest psychosocial challenge facing infants and toddlers.

**Emotional regulation** is a term used to describe various processes that serve to control emotional experience. It includes internal and external processes responsible for identifying, supervising, evaluating, and altering emotional reactions (Thompson, 1994, 2000b, 2006, 2011; Waters et al., 2010). Emotional regulation, particularly early in life, is a developmental process that unfolds over time. Because of changes in their brains, as they move into the second year of life, infants slowly begin to develop the capacity to regulate their emotions and to channel them into more socially acceptable forms (Gunnar & Donzella, 2002; Perlman & Pelphrey, 2010). Still, without the assistance and monitoring of a caregiver, they can easily become overwhelmed by their emotional states, including those of fear, excitement, and sadness (Kogan & Carter, 1996). An important milestone in the development of emotional regulation occurs when toddlers gradually make the transition from heavy dependence on caregivers for comfort and soothing (external regulation of emotion) to the ability to self-soothe and use more effortful, purposeful internal emotion regulation strategies (Kopp, 1989, 1992; Vaughn, Kopp, & Krakow, 1984).

Tim Winter/Alamy limited

With their growing self-awareness, toddlers of 18 to 24 months begin to feel and express shame, embarrassment, guilt, envy, and pride.

Parents and other primary caregivers, then, provide the support for the emotional regulation that develops in the early years. Among the factors that promote effective emotional regulation, one of the most crucial is emotional availability (Aviezer, Sagi, Joels, & Ziv, 1999; Biringen & Robinson, 1991; Bretherton, 2000; Emde, 1980; Emde & Easterbrooks, 1985; Nicolson, Judd, Thomson-Salo, & Mitchell, 2013). More effective emotional regulation has been linked with social and academic competence, whereas relatively poor emotional regulation has been associated with externalizing and internalizing types of difficulties (Spinrad et al., 2006). Emotional regulation has also been implicated in other important aspects of development, such as executive functioning (Ursache, Blair, Stifter, & Voegtline, 2013) and language and moral development (Eisenberg & Spinrad, 2004).

**Emotional availability** refers to the access parents and children have to each other and to their ability to read and respond appropriately to their respective communications (Biringen, 2000; Biringen & Robinson, 1991; Tronick, 2009). Studies of emotional availability suggest that children who receive sensitive, responsive care in the first years of life enjoy an important head start in their social and emotional development (Bernier, Carlson, & Whipple, 2010; Easterbrooks & Biringen, 2000, 2005; Ispa et al., 2004; McLoyd & Smith, 2002; Pressman, Pipp-Siegel, Yoshinaga-Itano, & Deas, 1999). Daniel Stern (1995) has called the emotional "attunement" of the caregiver to the infant the key to the development of emotional self-regulation. Infants and toddlers need caregivers in their lives to help them adjust so that they are not overcome by intense emotional experiences and are able to manage their emotions and learn from these experiences (Halberstadt, Denham, & Dunsmore, 2001).

**emotional regulation** The process of adjusting internal feeling states in order to achieve goals.

**emotional availability** The quality of emotional exchanges between two people, focusing on their accessibility to each other and their ability to read and respond appropriately to one another's communications.

## what if...?

It is 1-year-old Ellen's second week coming to the child-care center. She seemed to enjoy her first week. Today, though, she is acting as if she does not want to return. She cries and protests as her father places her in the car seat. By the time they arrive the center, she is crying inconsolably. She flails as her father opens the car-seat straps and clings to him when they arrive at the door. A teacher at the center greets Ellen and tries to coax her away from her father, but Ellen continues to sob.

What could Ellen's father and teacher do to help Ellen control her emotions? What should they avoid doing, and why?

**social competence** The skills necessary for interacting with others.

**social referencing** The use of emotional cues from other people, such as facial expression and tone of voice, to regulate one's own emotional reactions.

## Social Competence

Infants and toddlers develop in a world filled with other people, including parents, siblings, other family members, friends, and strangers. The ability to relate socially to these people is therefore essential for infants' healthy emotional development. Through countless social interactions with caregivers, infants and toddlers learn the social skills they need to interact with others. Such skills, collectively termed **social competence**, develop significantly during the infant-toddler years (Halberstadt, Denham, & Dunsmore, 2001; Keller, 2003, 2007; Schneider, Attili, Nadel, & Weissberg, 1989). In addition, researchers have found important links between secure attachment and general measures of social competence, age by age, from early childhood to adulthood (Sroufe, Egeland, Carlson, & Collins, 2005).

To become socially competent, young children need to be able to read and interpret the emotions of others (Bornstein et al., 2008; Dunn, 2003). Two important steps in learning to do this involve decoding facial behavior and social referencing, which we discuss next, in turn.

### Decoding Facial Behavior

Facial expressions are an important way to communicate emotions in social interactions (Izard, 1991; Schupp et al., 2004, Soken & Pick, 1999). Thus, one major task for the infant is to learn to recognize and interpret—*decode*—other people's facial behavior. Newborns, as we mentioned in Chapter 4, appear to have some ability to read and respond to other people's emotions (Bakti, Baron-Cohen, Wheelwright, Connellan, & Ahluwalia, 2000; Brazelton & Nugent, 2011; Farroni et al., 2005; Johnson, Dziurawiec, Ellis, & Morton, 1991; Meltzoff, Kuhl, Movellan, & Sejnowski, 2009; Nagy, 2006; Nagy et al., 2010; Nugent, Keefer, Minear, Johnson, & Blanchard, 2007). In fact, as we've seen, newborns can imitate the facial expressions of others. They can also initiate previously imitated gestures and participate in overlapping imitation-initiation communication cycles (Nagy, 2006).

Newborns are especially attracted to eyes. Indeed, eye gaze plays a fundamental role in nonverbal social communication from the beginning (Charlesworth & Kreutzer, 1973; Emery, 2000; Grossman, Johnson, Farroni, & Csibra, 2007; Kobayashi & Kohshima, 1997, 2001; Tomasello, 2006). Infants use *gaze cues*, or cues from eye expressions, to discriminate expressions of happiness, fear, and anger (Hoehl et al., 2009; Hoehl & Striano, 2008; Hoehl, Wiese, & Striano, 2008; Kestenbaum & Nelson, 1990; Kobiella, Grossman, Reid, & Striano, 2008; Nelson, Morse, & Leavitt, 1979; Striano, Kopp, Grossmann, & Reid, 2006). *Mutual gaze*, or eye contact, also helps establish a communicative link between two people.

*Ariel Skelley/Blend Images/Getty Images*

Eye gaze plays a fundamental role in communication between infants and caregivers.

From around 3 months, infants seem to be sensitive to even subtle changes in emotional expression (Frith, 2007; Tronick, 2009). By 7 months, infants' brains react differently to happy and fearful facial expressions (Nelson & de Haan, 1996). By the end of the first year, infants can respond reliably to an even wider variety of emotions in others and can distinguish between happy, sad, surprised, fearful, and interested expressions (Soken & Pick, 1999). They now become capable of *social referencing*.

### Social Referencing

As they move through the second half of the first year, infants become more reliable in their ability to interpret the emotional signals of others. One example of this can be seen in **social referencing**, in which they use others' emotional reactions to a situation to construct their own interpretation of that situation (Campos, 1983; Campos & Sternberg, 1981; Feinman, 1982; Sorce, Emde, Campos, & Klinnert, 1985; Walden, 1991).

DANGER AVERTED! THE INFANT'S ABILITY TO PICK UP CAREGIVER'S CUES One-year-old Theo has discovered the red tassels dangling from the edge of the tablecloth. He cannot see that there is a vase of flowers on top of the table. If he pulls on one of the tassels, the vase of flowers will come tumbling down. Across the room, his mother looks up with fear and surprise as she realizes she is too far away to stop him in time. As Theo begins to reach for a tassel, he glances back at his mother. The look on her face tells him what he needs to know, and he hesitates long enough for her to rescue him. His mother, with a sigh of relief, quickly removes the enticing tablecloth. Theo has used social referencing to decide what to do. He "read" his mother's face, recognized her fearful expression, and realized it might not be safe to pull the tassel.

*Everyday stories*

Social referencing studies confirm that infants guide their behavior based on the emotional cues people offer them (Camras & Sachs, 1991; Camras & Shutter, 2010; Klinnert, Emde, Butterfield, & Campos, 1986). By 10 to 12 months of age, social referencing is well established. Infants at this age look to their caregivers or friendly adults for cues when they encounter novel situations, such as an ambiguous toy (Hornik, Risenhoover, & Gunnar, 1987; Walden & Baxter, 1989) or a live animal (Hornik & Gunnar, 1988). Recent research suggests that this capacity may be present earlier than 10 to 12 months (Hoehl et al., 2008).

A good example of social referencing involves a version of the visual cliff experiment that we first described in Chapter 5. Recall that the visual cliff involves an apparent, but not actual, drop from one surface to another (refer back to Figure 5.5). Researchers used the visual cliff to study social referencing in 1-year-olds. Infants and their mothers were placed at the opposite ends of the visual cliff construction, with the mothers on the "deep end." The mothers were instructed to show different emotional expressions as their babies approached the cliff. As the babies crawled toward their mothers, they had to decide whether to cross over the visual cliff. At this point, they looked at their mothers, and the researchers noted what the babies did. When the mothers showed a fearful expression, the babies did not venture across the deep side. But when the mothers exhibited a positive expression, the babies crossed to the deep end. These babies recognized their mothers' expressions and decided what to do, based on what they read on their mother's faces (Kim et al., 2010; Vaish & Striano, 2004).

Mark Richards/Photo Edit

Researchers have found that 1-year-olds will use their mothers' facial expressions to help them decide whether or not to cross the "visual cliff."

Eventually, infants can even modify their actions and reactions in response to an emotional communication that does not directly involve them—what some researchers have called "emotional eavesdropping" (Repacholi & Meltzoff, 2007). By 18 months of age, infants do not have to wait for emotional information to be communicated to them directly. Rather, they can use information available from the emotional exchanges of others to guide their own actions. Moreover, infants are apparently selective in how they use this information. Rather than responding to every emotional expression they see or hear, infants have some capacity to determine whether the information is relevant to them. Thus, by 18 months of age, infants are becoming discriminating users of emotional information (Repacholi & Meltzoff, 2007).

Over the course of the first years, infants and toddlers slowly refine their ability to reliably read, interpret, and respond to the emotional expressions of others. But what happens when this process is disrupted, as in the case of autism spectrum disorder? Children with this disorder have specific impairments in the processing of social and emotional information (Baron-Cohen, 1995; Baron-Cohen, Tager-Flusberg, & Cohen, 1993; Davies, Bishop, Manstead, & Tantam, 1994; Dawson, Meltzoff, Osterling, Rinaldi, & Brown, 1998; Hutman et al., 2010; Rutter, 2000; Sigman, Mundy, Sherman, & Ungerer, 1986; Smith & Bryson, 1994; Teunisse & de Gelder, 1994).

**autism spectrum disorder** A group of developmental disorders that may be marked by deficits in social interaction, communication, and imagination, as well as repetitive and restricted patterns of interests and behaviors.

## Autism Spectrum Disorder

**Autism spectrum disorder** is actually a group of developmental disorders marked by a range of difficulties, most notably including deficits in social interaction and communication and, sometimes, in imagination, as well as repetitive and restricted patterns of interests and behaviors (American Psychiatric Association, 2000, 2013; DSM–IV–TR, 2000; DSM–5–TR, 2013; Merin, Young, Ozonoff, & Rogers, 2007; Tager-Flusberg, 2012; Teunisse & de Gelder, 1994; Volkmar, Lord, Bailey, Schultz, & Klin, 2004, Yirmiya et al., 2006). Until recently, the overall category included autistic disorder (also called classic autism), Asperger's syndrome, and pervasive developmental disorder not otherwise specified (PDD–NOS, or atypical autism). In the fifth edition of the *Diagnostic and Statistical Manual of Mental Disorders*, published in 2013, the separate diagnostic labels of autistic disorder, Asperger's syndrome, and PDD–NOS were replaced by the umbrella term *autism spectrum disorder*. The nature of the impairments that characterize autism spectrum disorder suggests that it is related to dysfunction of brain regions specialized for the processing of social information, including areas of the prefrontal cortex and the amygdala, as well as other areas (Baron-Cohen et al., 2000; Boersma et al., 2013; Charman et al., 1997; Chawarska, Klin, & Volkmar, 2003; Dapretto et al., 2006; Hoehl et al., 2009; Klin & Jones, 2008; Oberman et al., 2005; Sweeten, Posey, Shekhar, & McDougle, 2002; Wolff et al., 2012). However, many risk factors act together to produce these complex disorders (Levy, Mandell, & Schultz, 2009).

### Early Identification of Autism Spectrum Disorder

Autism spectrum disorder is difficult to diagnose before 24 months, although symptoms may surface between 12 and 24 months (Centers for Disease Control and Prevention [CDC], 2012; Chakrabarti & Fombonne, 2001). A growing body of research suggests that risk factors can be identified in some cases in the first two years of life and a number of early screening techniques for risk factors have recently been developed for children under two (Hazlett et al., 2012; Klin et al., 2004; Pierce et al., 2011; Tierney, Gabard-Durnham, Vogel-Farley, Tager-Flushing, & Nelson, 2012; Wolff et al., 2012; Zwaigenbaum et al., 2005). These tools measure behaviors such as visual tracking and response to faces, visual engagement and disengagement, perceptual sensitivity to sensory stimuli and atypical movement patterns. Still, investigators are becoming aware that early identification of risk for ASD will require not one, but a battery of multiple tests including observational parent and/or clinician behavioral measures administered along with some other combination of biomarkers (e.g., eye tracking, brain imaging, event related potentials [ERPs]) and genetic testing (Al-Qabandi, Gorter & Rosenbaum, 2011). Having a biological sibling with autism spectrum disorder is the strongest indicator of risk in infants (Bailey et al., 1995; Ozonoff et al., 2011; Steffenburg et al., 1989). In families with one or more children on the autism spectrum, the chances that a baby sibling will develop autism are around 1 in 5. Recent research shows that 18.7% of infants with at least one older sibling with autism spectrum disorder developed the disorder (Ozonoff et al., 2011).

Early identification of autism spectrum disorder is very important, given the current consensus that the sooner intervention programs begin, the more effective they are likely to be (CDC 2012; National Research Council Committee on Educational Interventions for Children with Autism, 2001). The ability to identify signs of autism spectrum disorder during the first year would support efforts to screen for it and to begin treatment earlier than has previously been possible.

### Red Flags for Autism Spectrum Disorder

Parenting

According to the National Institute of Mental Health, several early behaviors are possible indicators of autism spectrum disorders. Following are some of these warning signals:

- Does not babble, point, or make meaningful gestures by 1 year of age.
- Does not speak any words by 16 months.

- Does not combine two words by 2 years.
- Does not respond to name.
- Loses language or social skills.
- Makes poor eye contact.
- Does not seem to know how to play with toys.
- Excessively lines up toys or other objects.
- Is attached to one particular toy or object.
- Doesn't smile.
- At times seems to be hearing impaired.

It is very important to note that there are many possible explanations for most of the behaviors listed above. A child's attachment to a particular toy, or difficulty with language skills, is not, in itself, a sign of autism. It is also important to note that a child with excellent language skills may still be diagnosable on the autism spectrum. In fact, some children who are diagnosed with Asperger's syndrome have extraordinary language and reading skills.

✓ CHECK YOUR PROGRESS

1. Which brain structures play a role in infant-toddler emotional development?
2. Distinguish between the primary and secondary emotions.
3. Describe the key transitions in emotional development in the first years.
4. What is emotional availability, and how does it affect the development of emotional regulation in infants and toddlers?
5. How do infants and toddlers develop social competence?

# The Emerging Sense of Self

**[ KEY QUESTION ] 4. How do infants and toddlers develop a sense of self and the social skills necessary to interact with others?**

As we have seen, over the first two years, children grow in their emotional expressiveness, their ability to manage and control their emotions, and their ability to identify the emotions of others. These capacities set the stage for the emergence of self-awareness, which becomes more evident in the latter part of the second year. When toddlers begin to label their internal emotions with evaluative phrases such as "me good," it is interpreted as evidence that they see themselves as separate individuals, with their own set of feelings and emotional states (Emde, 1983; Stipek et al., 1992; Thompson, 2006; Thompson, 2011).

The **sense of self**—the idea of "me" and "mine"—is often described as the accumulation of knowledge about the self. Such knowledge includes beliefs about personality traits, physical characteristics, abilities, values, goals, and roles (Harter, 1998, 2012). It would seem that a person who has this kind of knowledge has an awareness of self that is constant and coherent. Many theorists have paid special attention to the development of the sense of self in the first years. Here, we focus on two of them: Erik Erikson and Daniel Stern.

## Erikson, Stern, and the Sense of Self

To Erik Erikson, whose work we discussed earlier in this chapter, the development of a sense of self is the core challenge of the toddler years. Recall that during the first year, infants whose needs for a warm, supportive environment are met will develop a sense of trust—the basis for a strong sense of self. The conflict, or developmental

**sense of self** The accumulation of knowledge about the self, such as beliefs regarding personality traits, physical characteristics, abilities, values, goals, and roles.

challenge, of Erikson's second stage, between the ages of 1 and 3, involves a struggle between the development of a sense of autonomy on the one hand and a sense of shame or doubt on the other.

Toddlers begin to assert their independence by moving away from their caregivers, as noted earlier. These struggles are often played out around toilet training, as toddlers attempt to assert their control over their own bodies. If children in this stage are encouraged and supported in their efforts to become independent, they become more confident and secure in their own ability to survive in the world. If they are criticized, overly controlled, or not given the opportunity to assert themselves, they begin to feel inadequate in their ability to survive. They may become overly dependent on others, lack self-esteem, and feel a sense of shame or doubt in their own abilities.

*Everyday stories*

TOILET TRAINING AND THE STRUGGLE FOR INDEPENDENCE Erikson believed that learning to control one's body functions—including toileting functions—leads to a feeling of control and independence. In many cultures, including North America, mastering the toilet is seen as one of childhood's earliest rites of passage. Toilet training begins in the early months of life in many parts of the non-Western world (DeVries & DeVries, 1977). In the United States and other Western societies, though, most children do not begin training until 18 to 24 months. This process can often result in an unhappy battle of wills between parents and their child. What is the best way for parents to toilet train their toddler while supporting his or her sense of autonomy? There is little reliable research on this topic. The American Academy of Pediatrics (2010), however, advocates a child-centered approach. That is, children should not be forced to start toilet training until they are behaviorally, emotionally, and developmentally ready.

Daniel Stern is primarily concerned with the development of the infant's subjective experience of self (Stern, 1985, 1995). Stern presents evidence to show that infants can distinguish between themselves and others right after they are born. Thus, the infant has an *emergent sense of self* from the very beginning. Through thousands of daily interactions with caregivers, the infant's sense of self develops, along with the capacity to deal with his or her emotions. From 9 months to around 18 months, the *subjective self* emerges. During this time, the sense of self involves attention, intention, and emotion, which are shared between caregiver and child. By the second birthday, the *verbal self* has become apparent. Here, words are shared between self and other. The toddler begins to use "I," "me," and "mine," as well as his or her own name. The child also starts to assert his or her own wishes. What Stern emphasizes is that the infant's sense of self emerges in the context of interactive emotional exchanges with caregivers.

## Self-Recognition and Self-Concept

Let's review some of the empirical evidence for the ideas just outlined. Contemporary research shows that certain aspects of self-development occur in the first year of life, as Stern argues. However, children do not show clear evidence of *reflective self-awareness*—that is, the ability to represent or reflect on themselves as independent, objective entities—until the latter part of the second year (Brownell, Nichols, Svetlova, Zerwas & Ramani, 2010; Kagan, 1981, 2010; Kärtner, Keller, & Chaudhary, 2010; Keller et al., 2004; Lewis, 2000; Rochat, 2003).

Toddlers, of course, have limited language, so how can researchers tell how self-aware they are? Some researchers have used visual self-recognition as a measure of self-awareness. Michael Lewis developed a mirror-recognition method to study this development (Lewis, 2000; Lewis & Brooks-Gunn, 1979). Babies who have had a spot of rouge surreptitiously applied to their noses are placed in front of a mirror. How will they react? Children under 18 months do not seem to recognize themselves in the mirror and are unlikely to try to touch the rouge on their noses. Children between 18 and 24 months, however, recognize themselves in the mirror and try to touch the red dot.

Using the same mirror-recognition test, researchers have found that self-recognition is associated with specific brain regions (Lewis & Carmody, 2008). The researchers used MRIs to obtain structural brain images of 15- to 30-month-old children taking part in the mirror-recognition procedure. They concluded that the emergence of self-recognition (as well as self-representation, discussed next) is associated with brain maturation.

Over these early years, the self-concept evolves from self-recognition to self-representation. That is, toddlers develop a realization that the self possesses certain characteristics that can be represented verbally. They begin to refer to themselves using their names or personal pronouns like "I" and "me." They also apply descriptive and evaluative terms to themselves—for example, "me little," "me big," "good girl" (Stipek et al., 1992). This level of self-understanding is referred to as the *objective self*. It is also called the *categorical self*, because it enables children to place themselves into a whole series of categories (Kagan, 1981; Thompson, 2006, 2011). As children develop a conscious sense of self, they are better able to notice and respond to the needs of others.

This toddler seems to enjoy looking at herself in a mirror. Children develop the ability to recognize themselves in mirrors at around 18 to 24 months of age.

## Empathy

**Empathy** can be defined as "an affective state that stems from the apprehension or comprehension of another's emotional state or condition" (Eisenberg, 2002, p. 135). As we have just suggested, the desire to help others without expecting anything in return would seem to require a conscious sense of self (Lewis, 2000). It also would seem to call for the ability not only to read another person's emotional cues but also to put oneself in that person's place.

Remarkably, even in the newborn period, infants appear to show empathic responses to the distress of others (Sagi & Hoffmann, 1976). Babies often cry when they hear another baby crying, for example, suggesting that they may be aware of that baby's pain. More specifically, studies have documented the ability of 1-year-olds to comfort others in distress, participate in household tasks, and help adults by bringing or pointing to out-of-reach objects (Liszkowski, Carpenter, Striano, & Tomasello, 2006; Rheingold, 1982; Warneken & Tomasello, 2006, 2007; Zahn-Waxler et al., 1992). Toddlers who are barely able to use language already show signs that they offer such help without expecting anything in return. By the end of the second year, behaviors and expressions of empathic concern occur with increasing frequency, whether the infant caused or merely witnessed distress in others (Brownwell, 2013; Dunfield & Kuhlmeier, 2010; Eisenberg & Fabes, 1998; Thompson & Newton, 2013; Warneken & Tomasello, 2006, 2007, 2009; Zahn-Waxler et al., 1992).

An example comes from studies by psychologists Felix Warneken and Michael Tomasello (2006, 2009). These researchers placed 18-month-old toddlers in different situations in which an adult was struggling to get something done. A man might, for example, be trying to open a cabinet door with his hands full, or get to an object out of reach. For each of the tasks, there were control conditions to rule out the possibility that the toddlers would perform helping behavior (opening the door or attempting to grasp the out-of-reach object) for reasons other than the adult's need for help—for example, because they liked to hand things to adults or open cabinet doors. The researchers found that the children displayed spontaneous, unrewarded helping behaviors. Moreover, helping was observed in diverse situations. In all the scenarios, the toddlers helped without being explicitly asked to do so and without being rewarded or praised for their effort.

**empathy** An affective state that stems from the apprehension or comprehension of another's emotional state or condition.

what if...?

Asia, a teacher in a toddler classroom, takes out two baskets of blocks and brings them to the middle of the room. The children love to build. Within seconds, eight toddlers surround Asia and the blocks—all shoulder-to-shoulder and toe-to-toe. Before long, one child grabs another's blocks. While the teacher encourages this pair to "be kind," a similar battle breaks out between two other children. Adding to the ensuing chaos, a toddler who has been racing around the classroom suddenly crashes into the tower another child has built while deeply involved in play. How might Asia resolve this situation?

**moral behavior** A disposition to do something on behalf of another person, or to behave in accord with a moral norm or standard bearing on human welfare or justice.

## Are Babies Capable of Moral Acts?

It is easy to see how empathy might motivate **moral behavior**. William Damon, a leading scholar in human development, describes empathy as "one of morality's primary emotional supports" (Damon, 1990, p. 14). Moral behavior can be said to flow from an interest in and concern for other people. It requires an understanding of what is right and wrong and what is ethical, fair, and just. It also features a sense of responsibility for acting on one's concerns for others (Eisenberg & Valiente, 2002; Hoffmann, 1991). Are very young children really capable of that kind of moral behavior?

Charles Darwin proposed that babies might actually enter the world equipped with moral principles—with some inborn readiness to tell right from wrong. Darwin tells the story of how his first son, William, was deceived by his nursemaid into

### Research Insights: The Beginnings of Moral Development

In a series of studies, researchers had 6- and 10-month-old infants watch a puppet show in which a toy puppy dog, watched by two kittens, was attempting to open up a box to get a toy (Hamlin, Wynn, & Bloom, 2007). The dog could only open the box part way. One kitten then helped the puppy get the toy. The other kitten prevented the puppy from getting the toy (see Figure 7.6). Once the infant had seen both puppets and the experimenter, the puppets were moved within reach of the infant. The researchers watched to see which kitten the infant chose to play with. The babies preferred the kitten that had helped the dog open the box, suggesting that they approved of this kitten's helping behavior.

In another experiment by the same researchers, 6- and 10-month-old infants watched a puppet show in which a character tried, but repeatedly failed, to reach the top of a steep hill (Hamlin et al., 2007). In subsequent attempts, the climber was either helped up the hill by a second puppet or pushed down the hill by a third puppet. Offered a choice between the helping and hindering characters, most of the infants again chose the helper.

Results such as these have led some researchers to claim that the human tendency toward cooperation is present from very early in life so that some sense of right and wrong may be "bred in the bone" (Bloom, 2010).

The puppy wants to play with the toy but can't get the box open.

"Helping Kitty" opens the box for the puppy.

"Hindering Kitty" slams it shut.

**FIGURE 7.6 An Experiment on Moral Development** Infants 6 and 10 months old watched a puppet show in which one kitten helped a puppy to get a toy, and a different kitten prevented the puppy from getting the toy. Later, the infants had the opportunity to play with the kitten puppets, and they tended to choose the kitten that had helped the puppy.

Based on Bloom, P. (2011). Moral nativism and moral psychology. In Milkulincer, M., & Shaver, P. R., eds. *The social psychology of morality: exploring the causes of good and evil*. Washington, DC: American Psychological Association.

expressing sympathy at a very young age. "When a few days over 6 months old, [she] pretended to cry, and I saw that his face instantly assumed a melancholy expression, with the corners of his mouth strongly depressed" (Darwin, 1872/1955, p. 358). Today, a growing body of evidence suggests that infants do have an elementary moral sense. Thus, the ability to tell the difference between good and bad may be hardwired into the brain at birth. With the help of well-designed experiments, such as those described in the accompanying Research Insights feature, we can see glimmers of moral thought, moral judgment, and moral feeling even in the first 2 years of life.

It is important to note here that although we may see glimmers of moral behavior in very young infants, it is only preliminary. Most researchers believe that true moral behavior can be seen only when the necessary changes take place in the brain, and children's cognitive capacities are sufficiently developed, in the second year of life (Dunfield & Kuhlmeier, 2010; Dunn, 1987; Emde, Johnson, & Easterbrooks, 1987; Kagan, 1998; Thompson, 2006).

### ✓ CHECK YOUR PROGRESS

1. How do Erikson and Stern describe the development of the sense of self?
2. How do infants and toddlers demonstrate a sense of self?
3. How do infants and toddlers show that they are capable of empathy?
4. What evidence indicates that babies have a moral sense?

# Environment, Temperament, and Psychosocial Development

**[ KEY QUESTION ] 5. What role do caregivers and the child's own temperament play in the child's psychosocial development?**

Although they may use different terms and frames of reference, all the researchers and theorists we have discussed in this chapter agree on one thing: the importance of healthy, satisfying relationships between children and their primary caregivers. Positive relationships enable children to develop self-confidence, sound mental health, the motivation to learn and to achieve, an understanding of the difference between right and wrong, the capacity to develop and sustain relationships, and, ultimately, the ability to be successful parents themselves (Biringen & Robinson, 1991; Bretherton, 2000; Brinker, Seifer, & Sameroff, 1994; Emde & Easterbrooks, 1985; National Council on the Developing Child, 2004; Parke, 1996; Sameroff, 2010; Sroufe, 2005). In contrast, children who are deprived of positive relationships with caregivers in infancy may suffer impaired development that lasts into their adult lives. Thus, there is strong theoretical support for the notion that enjoying a secure relationship with caregivers is essential to infants' social and emotional development.

In this final section, we discuss the role of caregiving practices in psychosocial development. (To read about one activist's work to improve children's caregiving environments, see the accompanying Focus On feature.) We first discuss how caregiving strategies vary across cultural contexts. We then examine the role of fathers, siblings, peers, and grandparents in early psychosocial development. Finally, we take a close look at the role of the child's own temperament in social and emotional development.

## Cultural Differences in Parenting Practices During Infancy

As we pointed out in our earlier discussion of attachment, parents in different cultures may use different child-rearing strategies to foster their children's sense of security. The strategies they use embody values that have come down through generations within their own cultures. Thus, what constitutes sensitive, responsive caregiving can

## Focus On: Marian Wright Edelman and the Children's Defense Fund

Jesse Grant/WireImage/Getty Images

The Children's Defense Fund (CDF) is a private nonprofit organization that is committed to the social welfare of children, especially those who are poor, who are members of a minority group, or who have disabilities. Founded in 1973, the CDF grew out of the civil rights movement, under the leadership of Marian Wright Edelman. Edelman, the first black woman admitted to the Mississippi bar, worked with Dr. Martin Luther King, Jr., as counsel for his Poor People's Campaign.

Under Edelman's leadership, CDF became a strong voice for children and families. The CDF has focused much of its energy on initiatives involving the earliest years of life, including child-care and health-care funding, prenatal care, among other areas. Today, the CDF focuses on four priorities for children:

1. Securing comprehensive health and mental health coverage for every child and pregnant woman.
2. Preventing young people from starting on life paths that often lead to prison.
3. Developing youth leaders who will become the next generation of child advocates.
4. Ending child poverty and stabilizing families.

Edelman has challenged young people today to become involved in the lives of disadvantaged children in their own neighborhoods: "When I fight about what is going on in the neighborhood, or when I fight about what is happening to other people's children, I'm doing that because I want to leave a community and a world that is better than the one I found....." (Retrieved from http://www.childrensdefense.org/newsroom/child-watch-columns/child-watch-documents/americas-broken-hearts.html).

Wendy Kaveney/Jaynes Gallery/DanitaDelimont.com

Western parents tend to emphasize the development of independence, whereas non-Western parents may favor interdependent, cooperative values. Nevertheless, parenting strategies overlap a great deal in Western and non-Western settings.

differ from one culture to the next (Deater-Deckard, Dodge, Bates, & Pettit, 1996; Halgunseth, Ispa, & Rudy, 2006; Morelli et al., 1992; Richman et al., 1988; Rogoff, 2003; Whiting & Whiting, 1975).

Generally speaking, there is a great deal of overlap between parenting strategies in Western and non-Western cultural settings. However, there are differences, as shown in Table 7.3. Western parents tend to emphasize the development of independence, assertiveness, competitiveness, self-assuredness, efficiency, and self-sufficiency in their young children (Baumrind, 1971; Markus & Kitayama, 1991). In contrast, in many non-Western cultural communities, parents want to promote interdependent, cooperative values. Parents in these cultures value a child who is fundamentally connected with others and who subordinates his or her individual interests to the interests of the group. They want their children to be respectful, dependent, empathic, dutiful, self-sacrificing, conforming, and cooperative. Mothers in these cultures tend to keep their babies in close physical contact with them and to rely on empathy and nonverbal means to communicate with them.

What is viewed in one culture as normal and appropriate may be regarded in another culture as strange or deficient (Greenfield, Keller, Fuligni, & Maynard, 2003; Keller, 2003, 2007; LeVine, 2010). But while Western and non-Western practices might sometimes seem to be pitted against each other, we should not define these practices as good or bad, better or worse. They simply highlight the different ways that people around the world practice parenting. They demonstrate, too, how parents in different cultures have varying goals and expectations for their children. The accompanying feature, Culture and School Readiness, presents additional examples.

**Table 7.3** Differences in Western and Non-Western Parenting Values

| Western Parenting Values | Non-Western Parenting Values |
|---|---|
| Independence | Cooperativeness |
| Assertiveness | Self-sacrifice |
| Competitiveness | Duty/respect |
| Self-assuredness | Self-effacing |
| Self-sufficiency | Conformity |
| Efficiency | Empathy |

# Culture and School Readiness

Michael Newman/Photo Edit

Parents everywhere want their children to be able to "fit in well" to the wider world outside the home, such as in school. For preschool-age children, one aspect of fitting in well is school readiness—having the social skills as well as the academic skills that make learning in kindergarten possible (Blair, 2002; Edwards, Gandini, & Biovaninni, 1996; García Coll et al., 1996; La Paro & Pianta, 2000). Parents help their children develop such skills from very early in life—indeed, from the beginning.

Developing appropriate social and academic skills is a particular concern for low-income, Mexican-heritage children, one of the fastest-growing minority populations in the United States. Many of these children speak Spanish in their homes and then attend English-speaking schools. They now have to master both a new language and academic skills when they start school. In addition, there has been some concern that the behavior parents of these children expect early in life does not match the behavior that will be expected of them later, in school (Farver, Xu, Eppe, & Lonigan, 2006; Reese, Garnier, Gallimore, & Goldenberg, 2002).

But what does research tell us about these parents' expectations? At least one study has shown that Mexican-heritage children are indeed ready for school in terms of teacher expectations (Zucker & Howes, 2009). The study, which included Mexican immigrant children and U.S.-born children of Mexican-heritage mothers, found a general pattern of respectful relationships between these mothers and their children, along with teacher perceptions that the children were socially ready to go to school.

We may be able to explain this finding by looking at certain values expressed by immigrant Mexican mothers. When asked what kind of children they want to have, these mothers often speak in terms of *educado* (Reese, et. al., 2002; Richman, Miller, & Levine, 1992). *Educado* is a term used to describe children who are attuned to social relationships and respectfully attentive to the teaching, directions, and advice of elders. Mexican mothers' goals of producing children who are *educado*, and teachers' expectations of how children should behave in school, appear to be consistent.

## Fathers and Their Infants

Much of the research on early psychosocial development focuses on the critical role of mothers, and we discussed such research in earlier parts of this chapter. There is considerable evidence to show that fathers also play a critical role, beginning in infancy (Corwyn & Bradley, 1999; Cox, Owen, Henderson, & Margand, 1992; Lamb, 1987, 1997, 2004; Mezulis, Hyde, & Clark, 2004; Roopnarine, Fouts, Lamb, & Lewis-Elligan, 2005; Ryan, Martin, & Brooks-Gunn, 2006; Tamis-LeMonda, Shannon, Cabrera, & Lamb, 2004; Yeung, Sandberg, Davis-Kean, & Hofferth, 2001). Nevertheless, in general, fathers are not as involved as mothers in caregiving during this period.

### Why Caregiving by Fathers Is Important

Fathers who participate more in caregiving activities experience many benefits, as do their families.

Miho Aikawa/Taxi Japan/Getty Images

Fathers, as well as mothers, play an important role in their babies' development.

- These fathers are more sensitive with their infants (Aldous, Mulligan, & Bjarnason, 1998; Feldman, 2000; Roggman, Boyce, Cook, & Cook, 2002).
- They are more likely to report secure attachment relationships with their infants (Bronte-Tinkew, Carrano, Horowitz, & Kinukawa, 2008; Caldera, 2004).
- These fathers experience better psychosocial health and self-development (Palkovitz, 2002).
- Both these fathers and their spouses report greater marital satisfaction (Bradford & Hawkins, 2006; Levy-Shiff, 1994; Mezulis et al., 2004).
- The fathers' involvement produces improvements in the mother-child relationship (Feldman, Greenbaum, Mayes, & Erlich, 1997).
- Their infants experience enhanced cognitive development (Nugent, 1991; Sarkadi, Kristiansson, Oberklaid, & Bremberg, 2008).

Fathers' participation in child care during infancy may be especially important given the amount of direct care required at this age. Direct interaction may be a particularly vital influence on the developing father-child relationship and, consequently, on the child's emotional outcomes (Amato & Gilbreth, 1999; Gaetner, Spinrad, Eisenberg, & Greving, 2007).

There is plenty of evidence to show that infants develop attachments to both their fathers and mothers (Dulude, Wright, & Belanger, 2000; Lamb, 1997, 2004; Yeung et al., 2001). Studies of infant-mother and infant-father attachment reveal that 7-, 8-, 12-, and 13-month-old infants show no systematic preference for either parent over the other on attachment behavior measures (Parke, 2002). But is the father's role as important as the mother's in the early years of life? The evidence clearly suggests that fathers are not inferior to mothers as caregivers and that both play important roles in their baby's development.

Fathers and mothers do, however, tend to interact with their infants in different ways (Cabrera, Tamis-LeMonda, Bradley, Hofferth, & Lamb, 2000; Feldman, 2000; Feldman & Masalha, 2010; Kaczynski, Lindahl, Malik, & Laurenceau, 2006; Lovas, 2005; Pelchat, Lefebvre, & Perreault, 2003; Roopnarine et al., 2005; Ryan et al., 2006; Volling, Blandon, & Gorvine, 2006). For example, fathers are just as good at reading a baby's emotional cues as mothers; but they respond differently. More specifically, fathers tend to engage their young children in more physical and stimulating interaction during play (Lamb, Pleck, Charnov, & Levine, 1987; Palkovitz, 1997; Parke & Buriel, 2006).

### Obstacles to Fathers' Caregiving

Recent decades have seen significant increases in fathers' involvement with their young children. Still, even today, fathers on average spend considerably less time in parenting activities than do mothers (Bonney, Kelley, & Levant, 1999; Davis, Davis, Freed, & Clark, 2011; Pleck & Masciadrelli, 2004; Yeung et al., 2001). Why is this so? Is it that mothers are more competent, and that fathers know it? Or could it be that highly protective mothers are more likely to take charge of child care and family work, restricting their spouses' opportunities to do so (Allen & Hawkins, 1999; Beitel & Parke, 1998; Gaertner et al., 2007)? There is some research to suggest that some mothers engage in "gatekeeping" behaviors to restrict fathers' involvement with their children (Allen & Hawkins, 1999).

Gatekeeping mothers are certainly not responsible for most of the situations in which fathers fail to participate actively in child care. Sometimes, fathers just are not around. And even if they are, they leave caregiving to mothers. Paternal depression during the first year of the child's life can also be a factor (Institute of Medicine, 2009, Wilson and Durbin, 2010). In a representative U.S. sample, 7% of fathers living with 1-year-old children reported a major depressive episode within the previous year. These fathers were only half as likely as nondepressed fathers to read to their children, but were 4 times more likely to spank them (Davis et al., 2011; Garfield & Fletcher, 2011). Finally, in books, in movies, and on television, fathers are frequently portrayed as neglectful, uninterested, abusive, "deadbeat," and/or lazy (Parke & Brott, 1999). These "TV dads" may be serving as very poor role models for young men today.

## The Role of Siblings and Peers

We may tend to think of parents and adult caregivers as being the primary influences on infants' psychosocial development. In fact, very young children with siblings spend more time interacting with their brothers and sisters than with any other persons, including their parents (Abramovitch, Corter, & Lando, 1979; Barr & Hayne, 2003; Dunn & Dale, 1984; Hinde & Stephenson-Hinde, 1987; McHale & Crouter, 1996; Rubin, Bukowski, & Parker, 1998). We know that infants acquire social skills by observing and emulating the people around them. They may be more attracted to imitate models, such as siblings, who seem more like themselves than do adults (Dunn, 2004; Mosier & Rogoff, 1994). Older siblings provide more advanced models for younger siblings. They also help create a stimulating, enriched environment that seems to enhance younger siblings' psychosocial development (Barr & Hayne, 2003; Woollett, 1986).

Peers—other infants and toddlers—may also play a role in young children's development. This is especially true for children who spend time in child-care settings with other children of about the same age. As with siblings, young children respond differently to peers than to parents. Even infants have a surprising capacity for group interaction (Bradley, 2010; Selby and Bradley, 2003; Fogel, 1979). Infants at 15 months of age can imitate their peers and learn from them (Bellagamba, Camaioni, & Colonnesi, 2006).

*Everyday stories*

SOCIABLE BABIES Ben Bradley studied babies between 7 and 9 months of age in groups of three in his laboratory in Bathurst, Australia (Bradley, 2010; Selby & Bradley, 2003) . The babies were placed together in strollers arranged in an equilateral triangle with each baby in touching distance of the others. The sessions lasted between 5 and 25 minutes, with an average length of 12 minutes. The babies showed a number of communicative "systems" during these sessions. For example, they touched with feet and hands, vocalized, and gazed at one another with various facial expressions. The babies often interacted with more than one other baby at a time. For example, they sometimes reached out with both feet, making contact with the feet of both the other babies in the trio. The group actions of the babies appeared to have distinctive meanings. Specifically, they sometimes acted playful, sometimes imitative, sometimes anxious. They tended to act concerned when another baby appeared upset, and seemed to like some babies more than others. The conclusion was clear: Even babies at this age are capable of group interaction and seem to enjoy communicating with their peers.

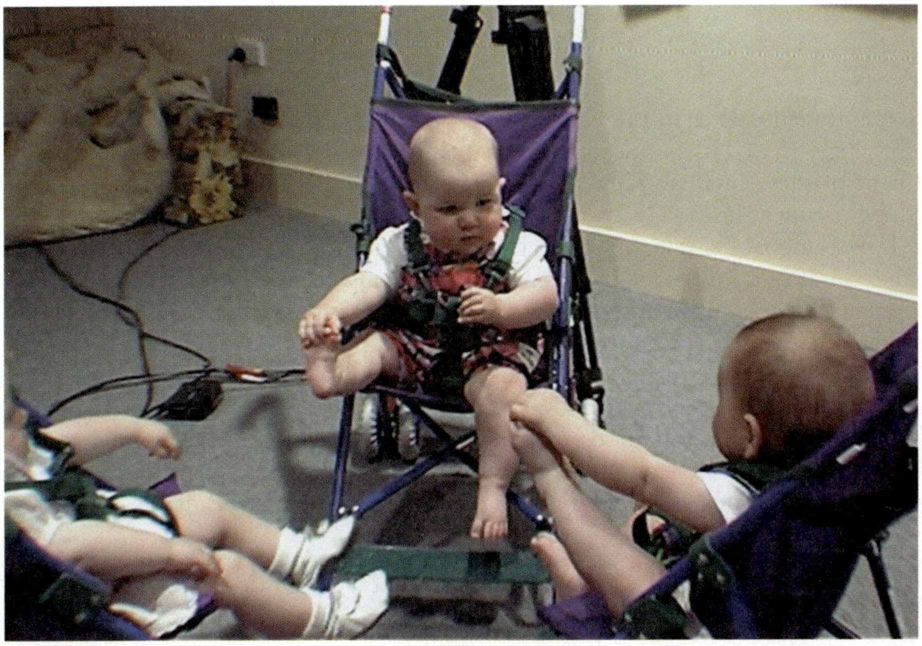



Babies between 7 and 9 months of age interact with and learn from each other. This is reassuring news for parents whose children spend long hours in child care.

R. Michael Stuckey/Comstock Images/Getty Images

Grandparents are becoming more important than ever in children's lives. In fact, 1 child in 10 in the United States lives with a grandparent.

## The Changing Role of Grandparents

The involvement of grandparents in childrearing is an integral part of family life in many, if not most, cultures across the world (Dunifon, 2013; Fergusson, Maughan, & Golding, 2008; Goodfellow & Laverty, 2003; Grundy, Murphy, & Shelton, 1999). It also characterizes many cultural communities in North America and Europe. But for many families in predominantly Anglo cultures (such as the United States, the United Kingdom, and Australia), grandparents have not typically been deeply involved in the care of their young grandchildren (Australian Institute of Family Studies, 2005; Chichester & Cairns, 2001; Dench, Ogg, & Thomson, 1999). This may be changing, however. For one thing, life expectancy is increasing. For another, fertility is decreasing. Women are choosing to have fewer children than in the past and to start their families later. Over time, smaller family size reduces the numbers of aunts, uncles, siblings, and cousins available to help, and places greater emphasis on the role of grandparents. High rates of divorce and remarriage also have an impact on the availability of family members to care for infants and toddlers.

According to a 2009 Pew Research Center analysis of U.S. Census Bureau data, 1 child in 10 in the United States lives with a grandparent—a significant increase since 2000 (Livingston & Parker, 2010). Grandparents who serve as primary caregivers for their grandchildren are disproportionately black and Hispanic (Burton, 1992). In a study of multigenerational African American households, mothers were the primary caregivers, followed by grandmothers and then fathers (Pearson, Hunter, Ensminger, & Kellam, 1990). In Hispanic families, not only grandparents but also siblings, aunts, uncles, cousins, close friends, and godparents (*padrinos*) tend to be involved in the caregiving.

Despite the fact that grandmothers and grandfathers are very often important attachment figures, there is still little research on the effects of grandparents on infant and toddler development. Research does show one important effect, however: A grandchild's sense of emotional closeness to a grandparent, frequency of contact with the grandparent, and view of the grandparent as a source of social support can buffer the effects of maternal depression on the child (Silverstein & Ruiz, 2006).

## The Enduring Effects of Early Child Care **Practice**

We mentioned earlier in the chapter that 80% of mothers work in the first year of their babies' lives. How important is the quality of child-care to the long-term development of these infants? How does child-care provided outside the home compare with parenting at home?

The National Institute of Child Health and Human Development (NICHD) began a study in 1991 to discover the immediate and long-term effects of early child-care experiences on cognitive and psychosocial development. Starting with 1,364 children and their families, the researchers studied the participants throughout infancy and childhood. They investigated the nature, quantity, and quality of child-care arrangements. They also assessed the children's cognitive, language, psychosocial, and physical health outcomes. The methods used included interviews and questionnaires, along with observation in the laboratory, at home, and in child-care settings. As the children entered and progressed through school, teacher reports and academic achievement were added.

The most recent report associated with this important study extends the findings to children in fifth and sixth grades (Belsky et al., 2007). What did the study find?

Susan Woog-Wagner/Photo Researchers/Getty Images

Not surprisingly, the long-term effects of child care depend in part on the quality of the care.

1. As we would expect, the quality of child care proved important. This is true whether the participating children were cared for at a child-care center, at a family day-care home, or in some other setting.
2. Parenting quality had a far stronger influence on these children's cognitive and psychosocial development than did the child-care experience. This is true no matter how much time the children spent in child-care settings. Children whose mothers were more sensitive, supportive, and responsive had higher scores on reading, math, and vocabulary achievement in fifth grade. In sixth grade, teachers rated them higher as well on work habits and social skills, and lower on problem behavior in the classroom.
3. Children who had more experience in child-care centers were rated by their teachers in sixth grade as showing somewhat more disruptive behavior, such as being argumentative or uncooperative. Note that these behaviors were only slightly elevated—although still within the normal range—for children with *center-based* early experience. They were not elevated for children in other types of care.

What are the implications of these findings? First and foremost, that parents are the most important influence on their children's development. Nevertheless, when children spend extensive time in care with large groups of other children, attention to the quality of care and to classroom and playground dynamics is important for ensuring positive development (American Academy of Pediatrics, 2011). The findings concerning disruptive behavior suggest that greater attention to early social and emotional skills in preschool classrooms, including teacher training focused on these issues, is important in helping children get along with others and benefit from learning opportunities.

## what if...?

Janet's employer has promised her a three-month maternity leave, adding, however, that she must return to work at the end of that period if she wants to keep her job. What will she do about child care after that, she wonders. Janet herself was raised in part by her maternal grandmother, who cared for her while her mother worked during the day. But neither Janet nor her husband, Wayne, has family in the area where they now live. Janet "feels uncomfortable" with what she has heard about center-based day care. Besides, the only center that takes in infants is in the next town.

Wayne and Janet want the best for their new baby. What are their options? How do you think they should proceed? What would you do if you were in their place?

**temperament** A set of inherited personality traits that are observable from the beginning of life and reflected in individual differences in reactivity and self-regulation in the domains of affect, activity, and attention.

## The Role of Temperament

Throughout this chapter, we have seen that the emotional availability of parents is the most important influence on their children's psychosocial development. But we now need to ask what role the child's own personality plays in all of this. We noted earlier that the transactional model emphasizes that children play an active role in how their caregivers respond to them. Some researchers have found, for example, that highly irritable infants tend to receive less sensitive care from their caregivers (Crockenberg, 1981; van den Boom, 1994, 1997). This places them at greater risk for developing insecure relationships. Toddlers who had been both highly irritable and insecurely attached, in turn, explored less and were less sociable than other toddlers (Stupica, Sherman, & Cassidy, 2011). These individual characteristics and patterns of behavior are what developmental psychologists call *temperament*. The quality of parent-infant relationships may affect temperament, and vice versa.

Marilyn Conway/Getty Images

It's easy to see how a newborn's temperament can affect how caregivers react to him or her.

### What Is Temperament?

There is no universally accepted definition of **temperament**. In general, though, temperament refers to a set of inherited personality traits that are observable from the beginning of life. It is reflected in individual differences in reactivity and self-regulation in the domains of affect (the expression of emotion), activity, and attention (Bates, 1987; Kagan & Snidman, 2004; Kagan, Snidman & Arcus, 1998; Majdandzic & van den Boom, 2007; Rothbart & Bates, 2006; Strelau, 1998). Stella Chess and Alexander Thomas (1989, 1996) define temperament as a general term referring to the *how*, or style, of behavior. It differs from ability, which is concerned with the *what* and *how well* of behaving. It also differs from motivation, which accounts for the "why" of behaving. A child's temperament, then, is his or her typical, consistent style of interacting with the environment—describing, for example, whether the child generally reacts quickly or slowly, intensely or mildly. Temperament seems to comprise the core of each child's personality, and undoubtedly influences the direction of the child's development from early in life (Fox, 1998; Goldsmith, 1989; Goldsmith, Lemery, Aksan, & Buss, 2000; Goldsmith, Lemery, Buss, & Campos, 1999; Hubert, Wachs, Peters-Martin & Gandour, 1982; Kagan & Snidman, 2004; Lemery, Goldsmith, Klinnert, & Mrazek, 1999; Plomin, & Saudino, 1994).

Almost all definitions of temperament suggest that it has a strong genetic basis, and that differences in temperament are based on specific neurobiological and behavioral processes (Buss & Plomin, 1975, 1984; Rothbart & Bates, 2006). Most current temperament researchers would agree with the notion that the early appearance of certain characteristics, moderate stability, and distinctive biological manifestations are key ingredients of a definition of temperament (Berdan, Keane, & Calkins, 2008; Pedlow, Sanson, Prior, & Oberklaid, 1993; Zentner & Bates, 2008).

Thus, many theorists believe that individual differences in temperament should be stable over time and across contexts (Kagan, Snidman, Kahn, & Towsley, 2007; Strelau, 1998; Thomas, Chess, Birch, Hertzig, & Korn, 1963). There are data to support this view. Beginning when the infants were 2 to 3 months of age, the New York Longitudinal Study followed 138 middle-class white children into adolescence and adulthood and rated them on several dimensions of temperament (Chess & Thomas, 1996). About 70% of the infants rated as "difficult" went on to develop behavior problems in later childhood. Only 18% of the "easy" infants did.

In another longitudinal study, 4-month-old infants were classified as either high or low in reactivity, based on their motor and crying behavior in reaction to selected stimuli (Kagan, Snidman, & Arcus, 1998). *Reactivity* refers to the quickness and intensity of reactions. A "high reactive" infant would cry and thrash when confronted with unfamiliar stimuli, while a "low reactive" infant would not. When these children were in their teen years, 20% of the "high reactive" group preserved their apparent dislike for the new and strange, manifested now by shyness. The researchers speculated that inhibited, shy children have a lower threshold of reactivity in limbic structures in the brain, including the amygdala, that control fear. Another study reported similar stability in temperamental reactivity and proneness to distress from 4 months to 4 years of age (Fox & Calkins, 2003).

Finally, researchers compared temperament differences in monozygotic (identical) twins, who share 100% of their genes, and dizygotic (fraternal) twins, who share only 50%, on average. Correlations between the identical twins ranged from .50 to .80, while correlations between the fraternal twins were .50 or less (Goldsmith et al., 2000). Based on these findings, the researchers concluded that individual differences in temperament may be heritable.

## Dimensions of Temperament

Given the findings just described, it should not be surprising that even newborns show differences in temperament. Some babies are easily startled and upset, are highly sensitive to noises, and have irregular eating and sleeping patterns. Others are calm and placid and quickly adapt to regular eating and sleeping routines. Similarly, many 2-year-olds are energetic, intense, and quick to respond, whether they are eating or playing with friends. Others have a deliberate tempo, and take time to adjust to new situations, new foods, and new people. Parents who have several children are well aware that one son may be outgoing and enthusiastic, while his brother is shy and "low-key."

Thomas and Chess (1977) identified nine dimensions of temperament. These dimensions provide a framework for describing individual differences in temperament. The dimensions—which include activity level, sensory threshold, intensity, rhythmicity, adaptability, mood, approach/withdrawal, persistence, and distractibility—are described in Table 7.4.

In addition, Thomas and Chess described three patterns of temperament that influence parent-child relationships and family life. They found that about 60% of children fall into one of three groups: easy, difficult, and slow to warm up.

- *Easy children* are typically adaptable, mild or moderate in activity and intensity, positive in mood, and interested in new experiences.
- *Difficult children* tend to be intense, low in adaptability, and negative in mood.

**Table 7.4** Thomas and Chess's Nine Temperament Dimensions

| | |
|---|---|
| Activity level | A child's general level of motor activity when awake and asleep. |
| Sensory threshold | The level of stimulation necessary to evoke a response. |
| Intensity | The reactive energy of response, whether happy, sad, or angry. It describes how expressive a child is. |
| Rhythmicity | The predictability of bodily functions such as appetite, sleep/wake cycle, and elimination patterns. |
| Adaptability | The ease with which a child adjusts to changes and transitions. |
| Mood | Disposition. A child's mood may be more positive (a happy or cheerful child) or more negative (a cranky or serious child). |
| Approach/ withdrawal | The initial response to novelty—new places, situations, or things. |
| Persistence | The ability to continue an activity when it is difficult or presents obstacles—"stick-to-it-iveness." |
| Distractibility | The ease with which a child's attention is affected by extraneous stimulation. Conversely, the child's level of concentration or focus. |

*Source:* Based on Thomas & Chess, 1977.

Lawren/Flickr Open/Getty Images

This mother and child seem to match each other in temperament and behavioral style. Goodness of fit refers to the match or mismatch between a child and other family members.

**goodness of fit** The match or mismatch in temperament and behavioral style between a child and caregivers.

- *Slow-to-warm-up children* are upset by change, are characteristically reluctant and withdrawn in new situations, and are shy with new people—although given time, they adapt well (Keogh, 2003).

### Goodness of Fit  Parenting

Temperament may be based in biology, but there is an emerging consensus today that it is not fixed nor unaffected by experience. Rather, it reflects interactions between inborn characteristics and life events (Kagan, 2010; Rothbart & Bates, 2006). According to Chess and Thomas, temperament difficulties in infancy do not necessarily lead to maladjustment. Instead, developmental outcomes are best understood in terms of the "goodness of fit" between specific temperament profiles and the characteristics of the caregiving environment.

The idea of goodness of fit was developed by Thomas and Chess to help parents think about how temperament and parenting can interact to influence their children's adjustment. In the context of the family, **goodness of fit** refers simply to the match or mismatch between a child and other family members. For example, a high-activity, intense child may upset and irritate a quiet, slow-paced, reflective parent. An active, quick-responding parent may be impatient with a slow-to-warm-up child. When both parent and child are intense and quick to respond, conflicts may arise. Understanding a child's temperament can help parents reframe how they interpret a child's behavior and how they explain this behavior to themselves. They can then guide their child in ways that respect the child's individual differences.

#### CHECK YOUR PROGRESS

1. How do different socialization practices influence psychosocial development?
2. What impact do fathers, grandparents, siblings, and peers have on the psychosocial development of young children?
3. What are some enduring effects of early child care?
4. What is temperament, and how does it interact with the caregiving environment?

# CHAPTER SUMMARY

## Theories of Psychosocial Development

**[ KEY QUESTION ] 1.** What do the theories of psychosocial development say about the emotional needs of infants and toddlers?

- Freud's psychoanalytic theory focuses on the child seeking gratification through a series of "pleasure centers." In the first year and a half of life, the focus is on the oral zone, as the infant seeks gratification through stimulation of the mouth. During the second and third years, the anal zone is the focus of energy. Gratification derives from exercise and control of the anal musculature.
- According to Erik Erikson's stage theory, in the first stage infants face the developmental task of achieving a sense of "basic trust versus basic mistrust." In the second stage, the developmental task involves achieving a sense of "autonomy versus shame and doubt."
- Attachment theory maintains that the secure relationships infants develop with the important adults in their lives lay the foundation for their social and emotional development, and helps protect them from the many stresses they may face as they grow.
- The transactional model focuses on how an ever-changing environment and a developing child interact and affect each other.

## The Importance of Attachment

**[ KEY QUESTION ] 2.** How important is the parent-child attachment relationship?

- Attachment theory maintains that nurturing and stable relationships with caring adults are essential to the development of a sense of self, of others, and of trust.
- The two most widely used measures of attachment are Ainsworth's Strange Situation procedure and the Attachment Q-Sort (AQS).
- Although one of the core assumptions of attachment theory is that infant-caregiver attachment is a universal phenomenon, there is wide variation in how attachment behavior is expressed and fostered in cultures around the world.
- Longitudinal studies have demonstrated that attachment patterns observed in infancy tend to continue into adulthood, although sometimes these patterns can change through experience.
- Maternal employment during the first year of a child's life has been associated with problem behaviors and other negative outcomes in the child.
- Adverse experiences, such as abuse and neglect, early in life are often associated with behavioral and mental health problems later in life.

## Emotional Development

**[ KEY QUESTION ] 3.** How do emotions develop, and how do changes in the brain influence this development?

- Emotions have both physical and mental components and serve to direct and energize behavior.
- Emotional development in infants and toddlers is governed by the limbic system, which consists of several interconnected structures. Some of these structures are located in the cerebral cortex; they include the orbitofrontal gyrus, the cingulate gyrus, and the hippocampus. Others are subcortical structures, including the thalamus, hypothalamus, and amygdala.
- The subcortical structures of the limbic system produce spontaneous expressions of emotion that are instinctive and, therefore, universal. The limbic cortex is where awareness of and control over feelings occur.
- Discrete emotions theory holds that babies are born with a group of core emotions that are distinct from one another from a very young age. Some researchers identify eight primary, or basic, emotions in infants: joy, sadness, fear, anger, disgust, interest, surprise, and excitement.
- Secondary, or self-conscious, emotions appear during the second year of life; they include shame, embarrassment, guilt, envy, and pride.
- Children pass through five key social transitions during the first two years of life. During this period, emotional expressions become more organized, to convey a broader and richer range of emotion.
- Emotional regulation includes various processes that allow children to control their emotional experiences. Emotional availability of caregivers is a crucial factor in the development of emotional regulation in children.
- As infants and toddlers become aware of their own feelings, they begin to develop social competence, the social skills they need to interact with others.
- One major task for infants is to learn to recognize and interpret other people's facial expressions.
- Through the second half of the first year, infants become more reliable in their ability to construct their own interpretations of a situation, a phenomenon called social referencing.
- Autism spectrum disorder is a developmental disorder marked by deficits in social interaction and communication, as well as other characteristics.

## The Emerging Sense of Self

**[ KEY QUESTION ] 4.** How do infants and toddlers develop a sense of self and the social skills necessary to interact with others?

- The sense of self comprises the accumulation of knowledge about the self, such as beliefs regarding personality traits, physical characteristics, abilities, values, goals, and roles.
- Erikson describes the development of the self as resulting from the resolution of the autonomy-versus-shame conflict. Stern emphasizes the importance of early parent-child interactions in this process.
- Self-recognition seems to emerge at around 18 months. Self-representation arises somewhat later.
- Infants show empathic responses even in the newborn period. However, the development of true empathy would seem to require a sense of self.
- A growing body of evidence suggests that an elementary moral sense may be hardwired into the brain at birth. Most researchers believe, however, that true moral behavior appears only when

the necessary changes take place in the brain and after children's cognitive capacities are sufficiently developed, in the second year of life.

## Environment, Temperament, and Psychosocial Development

**[ KEY QUESTION ] 5. What role do caregivers and the child's own temperament play in the child's psychosocial development?**

- What constitutes sensitive, responsive caregiving can differ from one society to the next. Practices that are viewed in one culture as normal may be seen in another culture as strange or deficient.
- Sensitive and responsive relationships between infants and toddlers and their mothers, fathers, siblings, peers, grandparents, and other adult caregivers are associated with enhanced social competence.
- Parenting quality has a far stronger influence on children's cognitive and psychosocial development than does their experience in child-care settings outside the home. Nevertheless, especially for children who spend extensive time in child-care settings with large groups of other children, attention to the quality of care is important for ensuring positive development.
- Temperament generally refers to a set of inherited personality traits that are observable from the beginning of life. All definitions of temperament suggest that it has a strong genetic basis, while acknowledging that it can be affected by environmental experiences.
- Thomas and Chess identified nine dimensions of temperament. They also identified three patterns of temperament: easy, difficult, or slow to warm up.
- The idea of "goodness of fit" was developed by Thomas and Chess to help parents think about how temperament and parenting may interact to influence their children's adjustment. Goodness of fit refers to the match or mismatch in behavioral styles between a child and other family members.

# KEY TERMS

attachment *235*
Attachment Q-Sort (AQS) *236*
autism spectrum disorder *252*
discrete emotions theory *245*
disorganized attachment *236*
emotional availability *249*
emotional regulation *249*
empathy *255*
goodness of fit *266*
insecure-avoidant attachment *236*
insecure-resistant attachment *236*
limbic system *243*
moral behavior *256*
primary, or basic, emotions *245*
secure attachment *236*
secondary emotions *246*
sense of self *253*
social competence *250*
social referencing *250*
Strange Situation procedure *236*
temperament *264*

# CRITICAL THINKING QUESTIONS

1. **Theories of Psychosocial Development.** What does the transactional model of development add to the contributions of Freud, Erikson, and Bowlby in helping us understand how infants' psychosocial needs are met?
2. **The Importance of Attachment.** How may early adverse experiences have long-term effects on the child's development? What are the implications of these findings?
3. **Emotional Development.** Learning to regulate emotion is undoubtedly the greatest psychosocial challenge facing infants and toddlers. What do infants and toddlers need to learn to regulate their emotions?
4. **The Emerging Sense of Self.** As children develop a conscious sense of self, they become better able to notice and respond to the needs of others. Do you think infants and toddlers are capable of empathy? Can they tell right from wrong? What research supports your point of view?
5. **Environment, Temperament, and Psychosocial Development.** How does child care provided outside the home compare with parenting at home? Discuss how to determine what is in the best interests of the child and the family in choosing child care.
6. **Cultural Perspectives.** In many communities, children are socialized to interdependence rather than to the individuality stressed in the European-American middle class. In these communities, where people are constantly present, infants seldom sit alone and play with objects or engage in one-to-one interaction. They spend most of their time oriented to the group and observing what is happening around them. Although they are in close physical contact with a caregiver, either held or carried on the back or hips, they do not face the caregiver but instead face outward, ready to engage with the group. Are these child-rearing practices better or worse for children's psychosocial development than western child-rearing practices, or are both equally appropriate within their cultural settings? Discuss your answer fully.

# REAL Development

## Psychosocial Development in Infancy and Toddlerhood

In this module, Tia Wagner is considering enrolling her son Brandon in a "Mommy and Me" class in her neighborhood. Offered in various locations across the United States, classes provide structured and unstructured play for specific age groups. As you know, children's social skills change in various ways during the first two years. Your task is to observe the class and decide whether the children appear to be developing normally. You will then report your observations to Tia to help her make her decision.

**WileyPLUS** Go to WileyPLUS to complete the *Real Development* activity.

# Milestones in Infancy and Toddlerhood

## Birth to one month

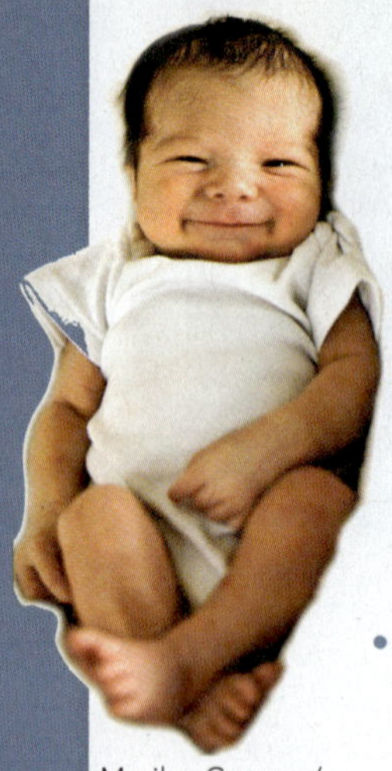

Marilyn Conway/ Getty Images

### Physical

- On average, a full-term infant weighs around 6–9 pounds and is around 19–21 inches long
- Reflexes include rooting, sucking, hand grasp, stepping, crawling
- Sleeps for up to 16–18 hours a day

### Cognitive

- Responds to high-pitched sounds
- Can see faces or bright objects within 10 to 12 inches
- Can imitate facial expressions
- Has well-developed senses of touch, taste, and smell

### Psychosocial

- Cries to communicate needs
- Recognizes mother's voice
- Prefers to look at the human face
- Can self-soothe by sucking on fingers or fist

## 1–3 months

### Physical

- Maintains head in midline while being held
- Holds up head when lying on tummy

Ariel Skelley/Blend Images/Getty Images

- Can open hand to grasp a small toy briefly
- Thrusts out arms in play

### Cognitive

- Alert for longer periods
- Can discriminate many colors
- Smiles and coos
- Can distinguish a "da-da" sound from a "pa-pa" sound

### Psychosocial

- Social smile emerges
- Enjoys face-to-face play with adults
- Can tell a smile from a frown
- May have to cope with colic

## 3–6 months

### Physical

- Rolls over
- Can reach out for an object
- Can grasp a small object using whole hand
- Can transfer a toy from hand to hand
- Has 20/20 vision with depth perception

### Cognitive

- Learns by touching, holding, mouthing, banging objects
- Can tell the difference between liquids and solids
- Can remember actions in a three-step sequence for up to 24 hours

### Psychosocial

- Directs social smile to familiar people
- Can become wary in unfamiliar settings and with strangers
- Brain reacts differently to happy and fearful expressions

Ben Gunsberger/WorkbookStock/Getty Images

## 6–12 months

### Physical

- By 12 months, height is about 28–32 inches, and weight around 19–27 pounds
- The two bottom front teeth appear
- Sits alone unsupported

- Picks up small objects with thumb and first or second finger
- Crawls, pulls to standing position, and eventually stands alone

## Cognitive

- Knows that a toy still exists even if it cannot be seen
- Enjoys simple puzzles
- Babbles and begins to produce word-like sounds
- Can imitate and remember actions after a delay of 5 weeks (deferred imitation)

## Psychosocial

- Shows intense positive and negative emotions in response to specific people
- Enjoys rhymes, songs, and interactive games like peek-a-boo and pat-a-cake
- Looks at others' faces for cues in ambiguous situations
- Seeks comfort from caregiver and uses caregiver as secure base for exploration

© KidStock/Blend Images/Corbis

# 12–18 months

## Physical

- Takes first step and soon can walk alone
- Reaches, grasps, and releases with either hand
- Can build a tower with two cubes
- Climbs and walks up and down stairs while holding rail

## Cognitive

- Can solve the A not B problem
- Can sort objects into a single category
- Dramatic spurt in understanding word sounds
- Imitates and remembers everyday actions

© Roberto Westbrook/Blend Images/Corbis

## Psychosocial

- Engages in pretend play and includes parents in play
- Growing awareness of other's emotional states
- Uses words to define own emotional states ("sad," "happy")
- Shows growing autonomy and sense of self, in part as a result of walking

# 18–24 months

## Physical

- By 2 years of age, height is around 32–36 inches, and weight around 23–33 pounds
- Can bring food to mouth, turn pages of a book, scribble with a crayon
- Can zip up zippers and unbutton large buttons
- Can walk, run, jump, kick a ball, squat, and climb

## Cognitive

- Begins to combine words into sentences ("milk all gone")
- Uses words to label self and possessions ("me," "mine")
- Can remember an action for up to six months
- Uses new, inventive strategies to solve problems

## Psychosocial

- Has more physical and verbal exchanges with peers
- Can cooperate with peers
- Has more conflict with parents ("No mean no") as the emerging sense of self evolves
- Refers to self by name, gender, and family role

Susan Woog-Wagner/Photo Researchers/Getty Images

# Chapter 8

*Susanna Price/Dorling Kindersley/Getty Images*

# Physical Development and Health in Early Childhood

MAKING A

**difference**

## Soap

Derreck Kayongo, a native of Uganda and an American citizen, traveled to Philadelphia in the early 1990s. While staying at a hotel, he noticed that he was provided a new packaged bar of soap each day. Thinking that he was being charged for each new bar, he tried to return them, only to learn that the hotel threw away the partially used soaps every day and replaced them with new ones. He was shocked. Then he learned that each year, hundreds of millions of soap bars are discarded in North America. In his native country, many children and adults do not have soap with which to wash their hands. When the average wage is $1.00 a day, spending 25 cents on soap is a luxury.

Why does soap matter? The United Nations Children's Fund (UNICEF, 2009) estimates that 1.5 million children, most under the age of 5, die every year from diarrhea caused by infectious diseases that are spread through body fluids. Kayongo knew that hand washing is the number-one way to prevent the spread of infectious diseases, and so a bar of soap can literally save lives. He contacted his father, a former soap maker, and told him the story of the discarded soap. Together, father and son found a way to collect used bars of soaps from hotels and ship them to Atlanta, Georgia, where they are sanitized, heated, chilled, and cut into new bars. After being tested for safety, they are shipped for free to people who need them.

To date, Kayongo's Global Soap Project has provided more than 100,000 bars of soap for communities in nine countries. In 2011, he personally delivered 5000 bars of soap to Kenya Relief's Brittney's Home of Grace orphanage, acknowledging that he had escaped being orphaned himself. "When we were distributing the soap, I could sense that there was a lot of excitement, joy, a lot of happiness," he said. He taught children the simple act of washing their hands, providing them what he called "that sense of decency" that can also save their lives. Kayongo was one of CNN's Top 10 Heroes of 2011. You can learn more about his Global Soap Project at www.globalsoap.org.

## CHAPTER OUTLINE

## [KEY QUESTIONS] *for* READING CHAPTER 8

1. How do changes in growth and development support physical, cognitive, and social skills during early childhood?
2. How can children be provided with a good foundation for lifelong health?
3. How can parents and other caregivers keep children safe?
4. How do common illnesses such as asthma and ear infections affect children's development?

IN CHAPTER 5, we introduced a framework developed by the Center on the Developing Child at Harvard University (2010). That framework uses a developmental systems approach to understand children's health and physical development, and we follow that approach again in this chapter. Health and physical development can easily be taken for granted. Good health does not happen by itself, however. And good health forms the foundation for cognitive and psychosocial development.

We begin the chapter with a discussion of physical growth, brain development, and motor development during early childhood. We then describe various ways of promoting health in young children. Our opening story about soap and hand-washing hygiene underscores an important point: young children's immune systems are immature, making them vulnerable to infection. Immunization is thus one aspect of health promotion, along with nutrition and dental health. After discussing these issues, we review the role of caregivers and community resources in keeping children healthy and safe. We conclude with coverage of asthma and ear infections—two of the most common health disruptions in young children.

# Biology of Health: Physical Growth and Development

**[ KEY QUESTION ] 1. How do changes in growth and development support physical, cognitive, and social skills during early childhood?**

As you have already learned, the biology of human growth depends on a complex interplay between genetic and environmental factors. Accordingly, growth for an individual child depends not only on the child's genetic heritage but also on health and nutrition (Cameron, 2006). In this section, we review changes in body shape and size in early childhood and then discuss changes in the brain and in motor abilities.

*Frances Litman/All Canada Photos/Getty Images, Inc.*

A child of 5 is less rounded than a toddler, with legs that are longer in proportion to his torso.

## Growth and Size

The rate of growth slows between ages 2 and 6 compared with the dramatic changes seen during the first two years. (See Figure 8.1.) Children gain about 5 pounds (2.3 kilograms) per year and add about 2.5 to 3 inches (6.75 to 7.5 centimeters) per year in height, with more growth in height in the legs than in the torso. The transition from a pot-bellied toddler to a longer, leaner, and flatter-bellied preschooler is also accompanied by better agility and a straighter posture (Hockenberry, 2003).

In Chapter 5, we noted that growth is asynchronous—that is, it does not occur steadily over time. Overall, growth in height and weight is most rapid in the infant and toddler years, and then again during puberty in adolescence, with less dramatic growth during the preschool and school years between. In addition, not all parts of the body grow at the same rate at the same time. Figure 8.2 shows growth rates in the brain, lymph system, and genitals compared with overall growth from birth to age 20. Notice that the brain and lymph system, which is part of the body's immune system, develop more quickly and earlier than do the genitalia and body size in general.

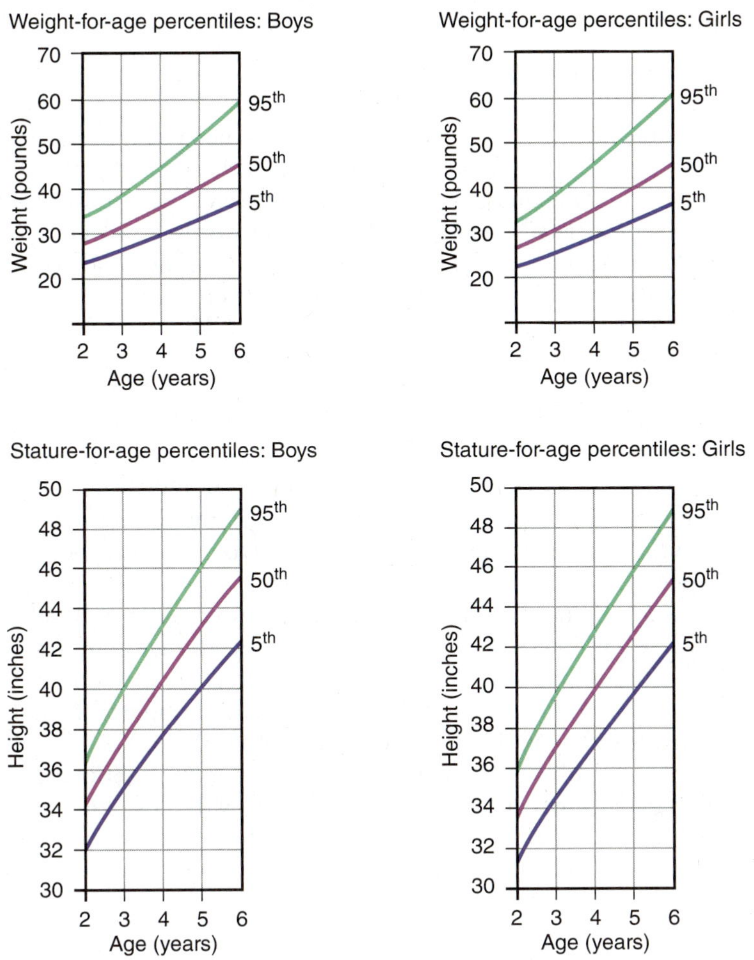


*Source*: Developed by the National Center for Health Statistics in collaboration with the National Center for Chronic Disease Prevention and Health Promotion (2000).

**FIGURE 8.1 Growth Charts, Ages 2 to 6** These charts show weight-for-age and height-for-age data for boys and girls from ages 2 to 6. As in Chapter 5, we include not only the average weight and height (the 50th percentile) but also weights and heights near the higher and lower ends (the 95th and 5th percentiles). As you can see, weight and height can vary considerably among children of the same age.

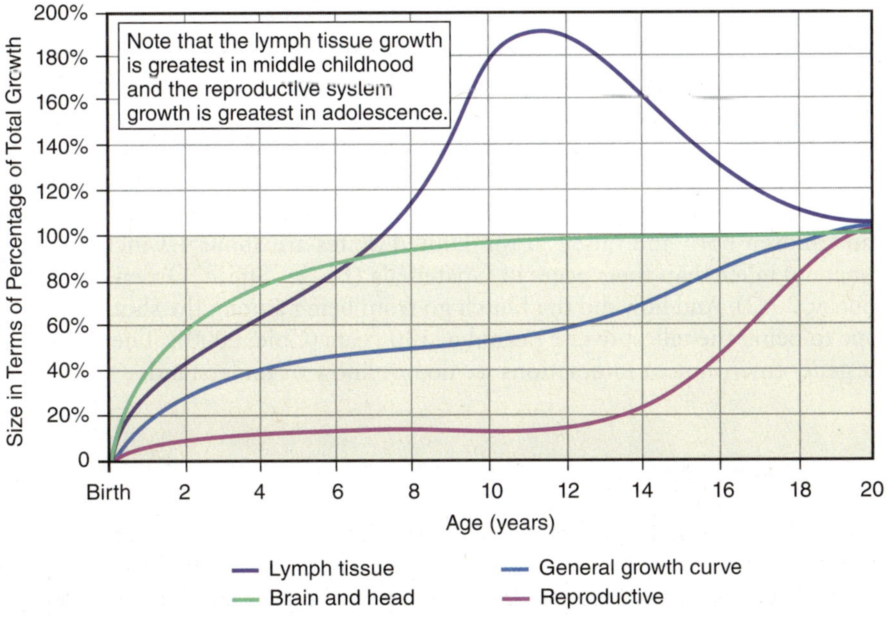


*Source*: Figure 8.2. Adapted by permission of the publisher from FETUS INTO MAN: PHYSICAL GROWTH FROM CONCEPTION TO MATURITY by J. M. Tanner, p. 16. Cambridge, Mass.: Harvard University Press, Copyright © 1978, 1989 by J. M. Tanner. Redrawn from R. E. Scammon, The measurement of the body in childhood. In Harris, J. A, Jackson, C. M., Paterson, D. G., and Scammon, R. E., *The Measurement of Man.* University of Minnesota Press, 1930, Fig. 73, p. 193.

**FIGURE 8.2 Growth Rates of Three Systems Compared with Overall Growth** The graph compares growth rates in the brain, lymph system, and genitals with overall growth from birth to age 20. Notice how rapidly the brain develops during the first six years of life.

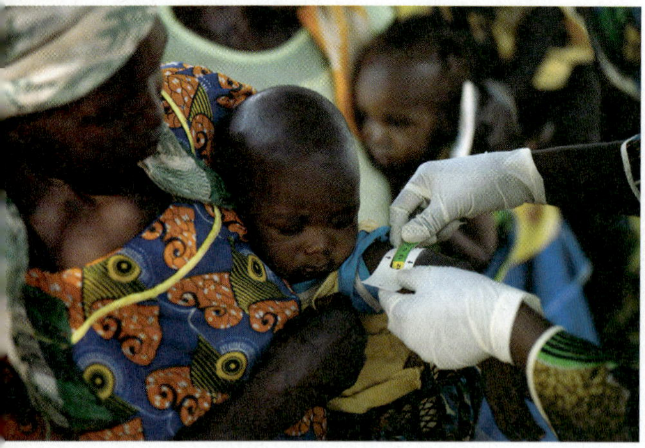


A WHO worker measures the circumference of a child's upper arm, which is a good predictor of malnourishment.

### Growth Norms for Young Children

The growth charts for early childhood in Figure 8.1 were developed by the National Center for Health Statistics and the Centers for Disease Control (CDC, 2000), which track this type of data nationally. Thus, the charts are based on national averages in the United States. Body size in general for an individual child is considered to be a "mirror of the condition of society" (Tanner, 1987). In other words, it reflects environmental factors that affect the entire society in which the child is developing, as well as the child's individual genetic makeup.

Health-care professionals use the CDC growth charts to identify children who rank especially low or high, as a pattern of growth far from the norm may indicate health problems. However, the CDC growth charts are not appropriate for all populations. For example, children with Down syndrome tend to be smaller in general, and so charts have been developed to track an individual child's growth trajectory against all other people with Down syndrome. What may be small on the CDC growth chart may be average on the Down syndrome growth chart (Cronk et al., 1988).

The CDC growth charts are also inappropriate for children in developing countries. Most of these children will not measure up to the average American child, who is much heavier in comparison. When a majority of poor children are below the American average, it is difficult to sort the genetic from the environmental influences on size. Consequently, the World Health Organization (WHO) has developed growth charts for children that are based not on typical height and weight in a population or ethnic group but on what constitutes life-sustaining growth. For example, a good predictor of severe malnourishment is the circumference of a child's upper arm. The new WHO standards for growth have significantly improved identification of infants and children who need immediate treatment for malnourishment (de Onis et al., 2007; WHO, 2009).

### Differences in Growth

Recall that in Chapter 2, we talked about genotype and phenotype. How quickly children grow and what their final adult height and body shape will be is influenced to a great extent by their genetic heritage—that is, their genotype. For example, tall parents tend to have tall children. This genetic blueprint determines what is possible—being tall—but environmental factors often determine the extent to which that possibility is realized. You may be genetically programmed to be 6 feet tall, but poor nutrition and poor health could result in your being shorter.

It is not always easy to sort out the relative effects of genes and environment, however. For example, Mayan people from Guatemala tend to be shorter than the average American—until they move to the United States. Within one generation, Mayan children born and raised in the United States are about 4.3 inches (about 11 centimeters) taller than their peers in Guatemala (Bogin, Smith, Orden, Valera Silva, & Loucky, 2002). And how did the Dutch go from being among the shortest people in Europe to being the tallest over a period of 130 years (Cole, 2000)? There is still a lot about gene–environment interactions we do not know or understand.

## Brain Development

During early childhood, the brain changes both in size and in structure, reaching approximately 90% of its adult volume by age 6 (Lenroot & Giedd, 2006; Stiles & Lernigan, 2010). Structural changes mirror functional capacities (Huttenlocher, 2003). For example, the brain becomes more differentiated as children develop their capacities for speech and language, for attention and memory, and for cognitive and social skills (Bell & Wolfe, 2007; Blakemore, 2008; Gogtay et al., 2004; Shing, Lindenberger,

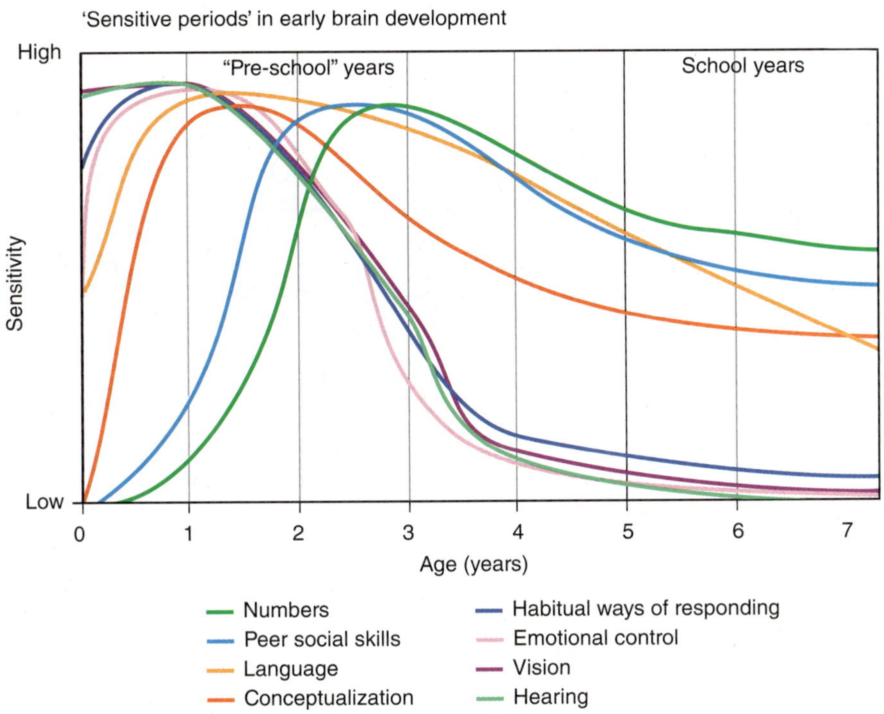


*Source*: Graph developed by Council for Early Child Development; reprinted with permission from Clyde Hertzman, Director, Human Early Learning Partnership, Vancouver, BC, Canada.

**FIGURE 8.3 Sensitive Periods in Early Brain Development** This figure indicates that development of the brain roughly corresponds with emerging functional capacities in the child. Each line represents a different capacity. The peaks in the lines indicate periods of change in the brain, sometimes called sensitive periods, when the environment has an especially strong effect. Note that the peaks occur in the early years of life. For example, in the development of social skills involving peers, the period from about 2 to about 3 is a sensitive period.

Diamond, Li, & Davidson, 2010). Figure 8.3 shows that functional capacities develop over time and not necessarily at the same time. In the figure, sensitive periods are times of peak development when environment has an especially strong effect. Notice how many sensitive periods occur in early childhood.

We have said that areas of the brain become more differentiated during early childhood. That means they become more distinct from one another and more specialized. At the same time, they become more integrated as they build increasingly complex networks across and within areas of the brain. Together, the individual areas of the brain and the networks connecting them are referred to as the brain's *architecture*. As the architecture of the brain takes shape, it provides a critical foundation for a child's cognitive, social, emotional, and physical development, not just during early childhood but also for life (Shonkoff, Boyce, & McEwen, 2009).

Let's look at how that works for two of the most important cognitive, social, and behavioral achievements of early childhood: self-regulation and executive function.

## Self-Regulation and Executive Function

As children develop through early childhood, we expect them to increasingly conform to societal expectations for civilized behavior. We expect them to be able to wait, to quiet down, to take turns, and to pay attention. We expect them not to grab toys or hit other people. These behaviors require a combination of self-regulation and executive function. The development of these capacities is related to significant changes in the brain between ages 2 and 6.

**Self-regulation** is the capacity to alter our behavior so that we can adjust to social and situational demands. As we mentioned in Chapter 6, *executive function* refers to a broad array of processes that regulate and coordinate goal-directed behavior (for example, memory, attention, and shifting focus). It also refers to the ability to inhibit an impulse to do or say something in the moment without thinking it through. This is something young children find very difficult (Diamond, 2006; Garon, Bryson, & Smith, 2008). We will discuss these very important areas of development further in the next two chapters. Here, we look at their neural underpinnings.

**self-regulation** A person's capacity to alter his or her behavior to adjust to social and situational demands.

FIGURE 8.4 **Brain Areas That Support Self-Regulation and Executive Function** Development in the prefrontal cortex, the orbitofrontal cortex, and the anterior cingulate cortex leads to improvements in self-regulation and executive function. As these areas of the brain differentiate, mature, and become more integrated, children are better able to regulate their thoughts and behavior.

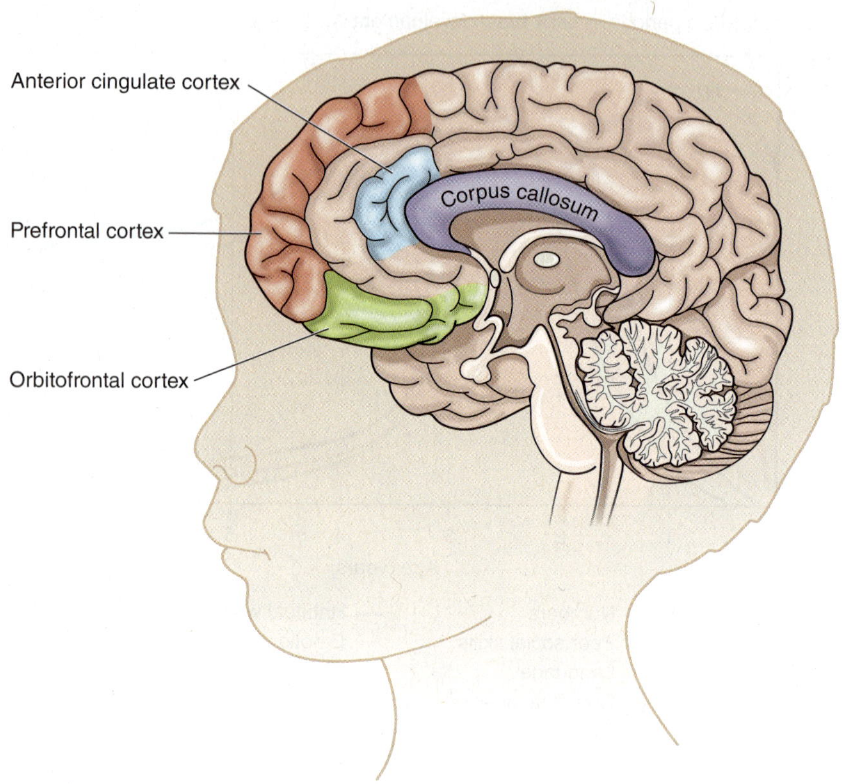


Several areas of the brain must work together to support effective self-regulation and executive function. These areas are identified in Figure 8.4. The *prefrontal cortex*, just behind the forehead, is involved in executive functioning—paying attention and organizing thoughts and actions, such as following rules, reasoning, and inhibiting impulses. The *orbitofrontal cortex*, located just behind the eyes, is involved in making decisions, especially decisions related to reward. The *anterior cingulate cortex* is a separate structure. It wraps around the *corpus callosum*, which connects the left and right hemispheres of the brain. The anterior cingulate cortex integrates motor, cognitive, and emotional processes and helps to balance logical thought and emotional impulse (Posner, Rothbart, Sheese, & Tang, 2007; Tarullo, Obradović, & Gunnar, 2009; Zelazo, Carlson, & Kesek, 2008).

As these areas of the brain differentiate, mature, and become more integrated, children are better able to regulate thoughts and behavior. For example, given a choice between having a small piece of candy now and waiting for a bigger piece later, 3-year-olds will generally find waiting too difficult and will instead take the smaller piece now. Brain wave studies indicate that young children use a broader area of the brain while trying to resist impulses to act immediately than do older children and adults (Rueda, Posner, Rothbart, & Davis-Stober, 2004). The anterior cingulate cortex becomes more active between ages 3 and 6, and the prefrontal cortex becomes better differentiated and more efficient. Thus, by age 6, our young candy lovers are able to wait for the bigger payoff (Rueda, Posner, & Rothbart, 2005).

It is important to understand that these changes in the brain do not happen automatically. As we have noted in other chapters, our genes make it possible for the brain to mature, but experience is needed to build circuitry (Shonkoff & Bales, 2011). Sensitive responses from caregivers support the development of self-regulation and executive control by challenging the brain to develop and refine the required architecture (Bernier, Carlson, & Whipple, 2010; Tarullo et al., 2009).

## Self-Regulation: Sleep and Toileting

Two forms of self-regulation of great importance to many parents are getting their young children to go to sleep—and stay asleep—and toilet-training. Both involve neurological and physiological maturation. They are related to the extent that children with irregular sleep habits have more difficulty managing their own behavior during the day (Bates, Viken, Alexander, Beyers, & Stockton, 2002), and that nighttime bedwetting occurs during sleep (Neveus et al., 2010). Furthermore, parental behaviors are major contributors to children's sleep and toileting habits (Kiddoo et al., 2006; Mindell, Sadeh, Kohyama, & Hwei Howd, 2010).

Studies indicate that children between ages 2 and 5 years spend a total of 10–12 hours each day sleeping at night, napping during the day, and being awake at night (Acebo et al., 2005). Napping decreases from about 2 hours to 30 minutes, although being awake at night seems to peak at about age 3 at 1–2 hours per night on average, during which time a child might be quiet or fussy. Bedtime resistance, trouble falling asleep, awakening during the night, demanding attention, and nightmares are fairly common. As young children benefit from routine habits, the American Academy of Pediatrics advises parents to set a consistent bedtime, limit television and other media, and develop bedtime routines such as washing up and reading books in bed. Reassure children who awake from nightmares, and return children to their beds when they do get up. It takes time, and consistency is key (Shelov & Altmann, 2009).

Between 18 and 24 months, children demonstrate physiological and behavioral readiness for toilet-training. They have longer periods of dryness during the day, have sufficient muscle tone to control urinary and anal sphincters, can pull up their pants, are able to understand instructions, name or point to body parts, and are motivated to become more independent. How parents proceed from there varies. Two common approaches are (1) a child-oriented approach, in which parents cue children about toileting, and (2) structured behavioral training, in which parents place the child on the toilet at regular intervals and reward performance. Girls are usually easier to train than are boys, and most children are fully trained at about age 3 (Kiddoo et al., 2006).

While many children may occasionally wet their beds during the night, about 20% of children aged 4–5 years struggle with nocturnal enuresis. Some children, especially boys, simply require more time to develop control over the sensations from the nervous and muscle systems of the bladder that need to be suppressed during sleep. Children may also wet their beds during times of emotional stress and anxiety. Persistent problems require professional attention, as they may indicate a problem with bladder muscles or kidneys, infections, a sleep disorder, or more serious emotional problems or abuse. Bedwetting is embarrassing for children. Parents should approach the problem calmly, without blaming or shaming the child. Limiting fluids before bedtime, awakening the child to use the toilet, mattress alarms that signal wetness and some medications can be helpful (Neveus et al., 2010; Shelov & Altmann, 2009).

## STRESS AND THE DEVELOPING BRAIN

Unfortunately, not all caregiving environments support the development of young brains as well as they could. Remember that in Chapter 2 we talked about the stress response and allostatic load, which occurs when the stress response fails to shut off after a period of time. Extensive research tells us that childhood stress can be classified as positive, tolerable, or toxic, and each type of stress affects the brain differently (National Scientific Council on the Developing Child, 2005).

*Positive stress* is short-lived and may be caused by, for example, frustration, disappointment, or physical discomfort. Positive stress has no lasting effects on the brain. Indeed, learning to deal with such stress strengthens children's ability to understand and cope with life.

*Tolerable stress*, such as death of a parent, divorce of parents, or serious illness, is more serious and may affect brain structure. Supportive relationships help children deal with such stressful situations, however, allowing the brain to recover and even enabling children to grow emotionally as a result (Shonkoff et al., 2009).

*Toxic stress* is a prolonged stress response—that is, allostatic load. It can develop as a result of persistent abuse, neglect, poverty, and interpersonal conflict. This is especially likely when children have no supportive relationships to protect them. Children's brains continue to develop through toxic stress. They do not wait for the optimal environment. Thus, toxic stress can have enduring adverse effects on the brain (National Scientific Council on the Developing Child, 2005). Areas affected include the prefrontal cortex and anterior cingulate cortex, discussed above, and the

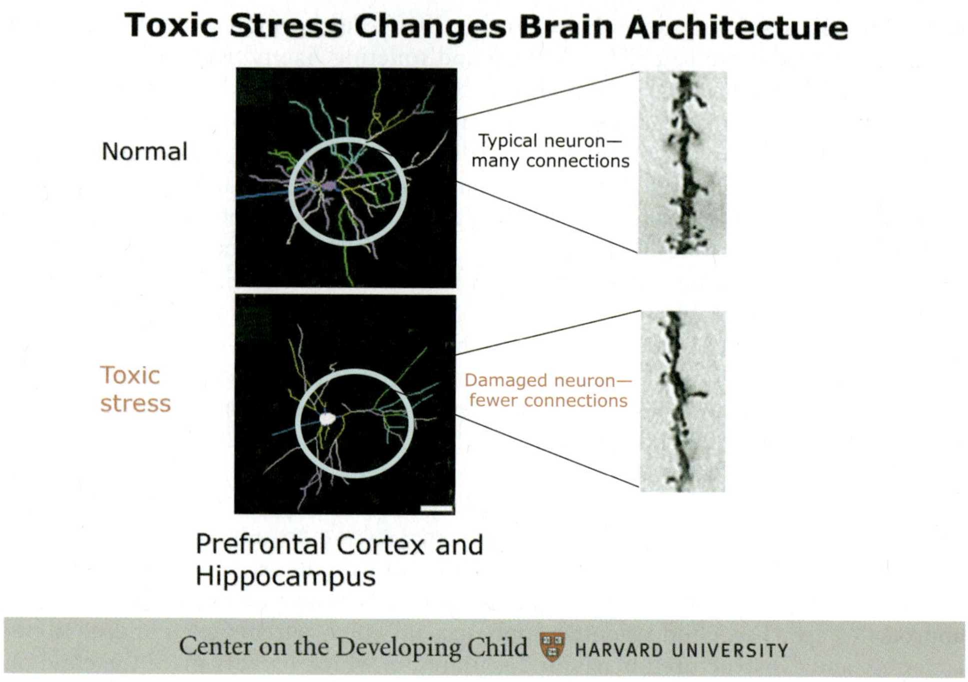


**FIGURE 8.5 Toxic Stress and Brain Architecture** Persistent stress can result in changes in neuron structure. As you can see in the figure, neurons in the prefrontal cortex and hippocampus that develop under normal conditions have many more connections than those that develop under conditions of toxic stress. By weakening such connections, toxic stress affects every aspect of development.

From: Radley, J. J., Sisti, H. M., Hao, J., Rocher, A. B., McCall, T., Hof, P. R., et al. (2004). Chronic behavioral stress induces apical dendritic reorganization in pyramidal neurons of the medial prefrontal cortex. *Neuroscience*, *125*(1), 1–6. Courtesy of Bruce McEwen. From: Boch, J., Gruss, M., Beckers, S., and Braun, S., Experience-induced Changes of Dendritic Spine Densities in the Prefrontal and Sensory Cortex: Correlation with Developmental Time Windows. *Cerebral cortex*, (June 2005) *15*(6): 802–808. Graphic courtesy of the Center on the Developing Child at Harvard University.

hippocampus, which affects memory (Lupien, McEwen, Gunnar, & Heim, 2009; Shonkoff et al., 2009). As Figure 8.5 indicates, toxic stress can even damage the brain's circuitry at the cellular level, weakening the architecture that is the foundation for cognitive, psychosocial, and physical development.

Consequently, children growing up in toxic stressful circumstances without supportive relationships to protect them are not prepared as well as they could be to meet the demands for self-regulation and cognitive executive functioning that are part of this developmental period (National Scientific Council on the Developing Child, 2005). As their better-prepared peers continue to the next level of developmental challenges, children exposed to toxic stress may be at increased risk for behavior and learning problems (National Institute of Child Health and Human Development [NICHD] Early Child Care Research Network, 2005).

### WHEN SYSTEMS CONNECT

## National Well-Being and Young Brains

Our developmental systems framework reminds us that brain development takes place within the ecosystems of individual health, the caregiving environment, and the larger community and society. Researchers and policymakers have begun to consider that developing healthy brains (and healthy children) is essential for our nation's economic viability and security. Poverty and other circumstances that can create enduring stress have the potential to alter the developmental path of the brain, undermining children's educational and social development and affecting their path to a productive adulthood.

We have noted that the brain has some plasticity. That is, some neural circuitry can recover to some degree under certain circumstances. But the more we know about the brain in early childhood, the more we realize that it is better to "get it right the first time" than to fix problems when children are older and have already fallen behind. According to many experts, reducing the impact of poverty, neglect, and abuse on early cognitive development and health is a better investment than attempts at remediation later on (Center on the Developing Child at Harvard University, 2007; Heckman &

Masterov, 2007). A leading proponent of this view has been Dr. Jack P. Shonkoff, the subject of the accompanying Focus On feature.

**what if...?** What if a child grows up under circumstances associated with toxic stress? What factors do you think will place this child at greater risk than other children in the same circumstances? What factors do you think could help protect the child from the effects of toxic stress? As you think about this, try to use a developmental framework, starting with a child's individual biology and extending through family, community, and social and health policies.

## Motor Development

As we noted in Chapter 5, motor development is best understood as an integrated system involving many aspects of development (Adolph & Berger, 2006; Thelen & Smith, 1994). How the physical environment supports or constrains an activity, and the demands of the activity itself, are also considerations (Newell, 1986). For example, catching a football is different from catching a baseball because the sizes and shapes are different. In this section, we describe the typical sequence of development of gross and fine motor skills in American children, while noting variations around the world. Table 8.1 identifies some milestones in motor development. Note, though, that there is a good deal of individual difference in when children achieve these milestones.

### Focus On: Jack P. Shonkoff, MD, and the Center on the Developing Child at Harvard University

We frequently refer to works by Jack Shonkoff in this book. Further introductions would seem in order. Dr. Shonkoff, a developmental and behavioral pediatrician, is professor of child health and development at the Harvard School of Public Health and the Harvard Graduate School of Education and professor of pediatrics at the Harvard Medical School. He is also the founding director of the Center on the Developing Child at Harvard University, to which we often refer in this text.

Dr. Shonkoff's career has been dedicated to improving the lives of children by translating into health and education policy the research that furthers our understanding of the relationships between biology and experience. Under the auspices of the National Academy of Sciences, Dr. Shonkoff served as chair of the Board on Children, Youth, and Families and as chair of a blue-ribbon committee that produced the landmark report *From Neurons to Neighborhoods: The Science of Early Childhood Development* (Shonkoff & Phillips, 2000), to which we first referred in Chapter 2. He has served in numerous professional organizations, including the MacArthur Research Network on Early Experience and Brain Development, has received multiple honors, and has been a visiting professor at major universities around the world.

The Center on the Developing Child, founded in 2006, seeks to build a unified science to explain children's health, learning, and behavior. The center describes its mission by stating that it was founded on "the belief that the vitality and sustainability of any society depend on the extent to which it provides opportunities early in life for all children to achieve their full potential and engage in responsible and productive citizenship. We view healthy child development as the foundation of economic prosperity, strong communities, and a just society and our mission is to advance that vision by leveraging science to enhance child well-being through innovations in policy and practice."

*Jack Shonkoff*

The center has partnered with many government and private organizations across the United States, and around the world, to advance its mission and spread research findings to policymakers, educators, and health-care professionals through scientific papers, videos, and other media. It has a wealth of information that you, as a student of child development, could find very interesting, including information about leaders in this field who make a difference in children's lives through scholarship, policy, and practice. Remember, normal child development depends on good health, and good health doesn't happen by itself. Find out more about the center at http://developingchild.harvard.edu.

**Table 8.1** Gross and Fine Motor Development Milestones

| Age | Gross Motor Skills | Fine Motor Skills |
|---|---|---|
| 2–3 years | Runs for pleasure without falling but bumps into things<br>Climbs easily onto chairs, out of cribs, and up ladders<br>Walks upstairs two feet at a time<br>Pushes riding toy | Preference for right or left hand more obvious<br>Holds crayon with thumb and all fingers<br>Takes off shoes and socks<br>Pulls up pants<br>Unzips pants or jacket<br>Scribbles<br>Feeds self with spoon<br>Washes hands with help<br>Rolls clay or Play-Doh® |
| 3–4 years | Walks upstairs alternating feet<br>Runs easily<br>Kicks and throws a ball<br>Jumps with two feet<br>Hops on one foot<br>Pedals riding toys<br>Throws and catches inefficiently | Can fasten simple snaps, large buttons, and zippers<br>Strings large beads<br>Builds block towers<br>Puts on clothing<br>Brushes teeth with help<br>Uses safety scissors<br>Copies line and circle<br>Draws "tadpole" images of people |
| 4–5 years | Walks downstairs alternating feet<br>Gallops and hops to music<br>Jumps over things<br>Throws by rotating torso<br>Pedals a tricycle with speed; steers well | Uses fork<br>Gets dressed/undressed independently<br>Cuts with scissors on a line<br>Copies triangle, cross, some letters and numbers<br>Makes drawings of people that have more detail, may have bodies<br>Drinks from a cup with one hand<br>Strings small beads |
| 5–6 years | Throws a ball<br>Skips<br>Runs faster and more gracefully<br>Can catch a ball with hands<br>Rides bicycle with training wheels | Ties shoelaces<br>Uses a knife to spread food items and cut soft foods<br>Copies words<br>Makes more complicated drawings<br>Builds a five block "bridge" |

## Gross Motor Development: Walking, Running, Throwing, Catching

Professional athletes spend years honing the complex skills of running, throwing, and catching. For young children, the development of gross motor skills also requires effort and practice. They spend a lot of time in motion: running, climbing, jumping, and throwing. Some activities depend on cultural and family expectations. For example, some children might be expected to learn to skate on ice, while others might be encouraged to learn to ride a horse. Considering how often they suffer bumps and bruises, it is to their developmental advantage that children find great joy being in motion!

Young children spend a lot of time in motion, and they clearly enjoy it. All this practice helps in their development of gross motor skills.

*Getty Images/Altrendo RR/Getty Images, Inc.*

FIGURE 8.6 **A Beginning Walker** The toddler's flat-footed stride, wide stance, and raised arms are designed for balance. As she develops physically, her walking will become better coordinated.

*Source:* Adapted with permission from Mary Ann Roberton. From Haywood, K. & Getchell, N. (2009). *Lifespan motor development*. Champaign, IL: Human Kinetics, p. 114, Figure 7.2. Tracings from film originally collected by the Motor Development and Child Study Laboratory, University of Wisconsin-Madison, and now housed in the Motor Development Film Collections, Kinesiology Division, Bowling Green State University. (c) Mary Ann Roberton.

**Walking and Running.** Recall our discussion in Chapter 5 about the principle of proximodistal development in motor skills. That is, children develop muscle control from the torso outward to the arms and legs, which require more coordinated movement. Recall also our discussion of differentiation, by which physical structures become more specialized over time. Both principles can be seen in the development of walking and running.

The toddler's torso is longer than the legs, so walking at this age is designed for balance rather than efficiency—a short flat-footed stride, wide stance, and raised arms that do not swing, as shown in Figure 8.6. By age 2, longer legs and a lower center of gravity improve balance and support a coordinated stride. By age 3, children straighten and flex the legs at the knee, plant their heels first, and roll forward onto their toes. Their arms swing rhythmically in opposition to the legs—that is, the right arm and left leg move forward together (Adolph, Vereijken, & Shrout, 2003; Haywood & Getchell, 2009; Bjornson et al., 2011).

Running is not fast walking. It involves flight—propelling the body into the air with one leg and landing upright with the other. It is difficult for toddlers to run, as they must balance the torso at the expense of forward motion. They stumble, but get up and try again! Two-year-olds run without falling but lack grace. They bump into things. By age 5, movements of the torso, legs, and arms are designed for flight, speed, and efficiency (Haywood & Getchell, 2009). (See Figure 8.7.)

**Throwing and Catching.** The principles of proximodistal development and differentiation in motor skills apply to throwing and catching as well. Children under the age of 3 throw mostly by raising an arm to push the ball forward while standing still. By age 6, children step forward, rotate the torso and upper arm, extend the arm to release the ball, and follow through, thus maximizing thrust (Haywood & Getchell, 2009). (See Figure 8.8.)

FIGURE 8.7 **A Beginning Runner** Beginning runners have a shorter stride and limited range of motion in their arms.

*Source:* Adapted with permission from Mary Ann Roberton. From Haywood, K. & Getchell, N. (2009). Lifespan motor development. Champaign, IL: Human Kinetics, p. 114, Figure 7.2. Tracings from film originally collected by the Motor Development and Child Study Laboratory, University of Wisconsin-Madison, and now housed in the Motor Development Film Collections, Kinesiology Division, Bowling Green State University. © Mary Ann Roberton.

a. A beginning thrower

b. A relatively advanced thrower

**FIGURE 8.8 Advances in Throwing** Beginning throwers simply push the ball forward using their arms. More advanced throwers step forward, rotate the torso and upper arm, extend the arm to release the ball, and follow through.

*Source:* Adapted with permission from Mary Ann Roberton. From Haywood, K. & Getchell, N. (2009). *Lifespan motor development*. Champaign, IL: Human Kinetics, pp. 145 and 148, Figures 8.2 and 8.4. Tracings from film originally collected by the Motor Development and Child Study Laboratory, University of Wisconsin-Madison, and now housed in the Motor Development Film Collections, Kinesiology Division, Bowling Green State University. © Mary Ann Roberton.

Catching is far more difficult than throwing. To catch a ball, you must track its path over space and time, move to where you think the ball will be, and adjust the position of your body and hands to accommodate the size and shape of the ball. You must also adjust to the ball's forward-moving force, pulling it toward you as you catch it. Young children trying to catch a ball stand still with rigid, outstretched arms, and attempt to trap the ball against their bodies. While children have become better at catching by the time they start school, most are not reasonably proficient until around age 8 (Haywood & Getchell, 2009). (See Figure 8.9.)

a. A beginning catcher

b. A proficient catcher

**FIGURE 8.9 Advances in Catching** The beginning catcher holds his arms out rigidly and traps the ball against his chest. The more advanced catcher uses his hands to catch the ball.

*Source:* Adapted with permission from Mary Ann Roberton. From Haywood, K. & Getchell, N. (2009). *Lifespan motor development*. Champaign, IL: Human Kinetics, p. 178, Figures 9.5 and 9.6. Tracings from film originally collected by the Motor Development and Child Study Laboratory, University of Wisconsin-Madison, and now housed in the Motor Development Film Collections, Kinesiology Division, Bowling Green State University. (c) Mary Ann Roberton.

### Fine Motor Development

In Chapter 5, we noted that a baby's grasp becomes more differentiated and refined during the first year. During the preschool years, fine motor skills, which involve primarily the hands and fingers, continue to become more sophisticated.

Different tasks and tools make very different demands on a child's ability to coordinate the brain, vision, and very small muscles at the same time. Many fine motor skills require two hands to do different things at the same time. Thus, fine motor skills are more difficult for children to master than gross motor skills. They require more concentration, patience, and practice. In addition, like gross motor skills, fine motor skills develop in the context of cultural and family expectations.

*Nicole Hill/Getty Images, Inc.*

Gains in fine motor coordination enable children to master skills like buttoning and zipping.

*Augustus Butera/Workbook Stock/Getty Images, Inc.*

Activities involving the use of tools, such as cutting with scissors, require eye–hand coordination.

**Grooming.** Young children take pride in tending to their own needs. Two-year-olds can take off and put on simple articles of clothing. By age 3, children can manipulate larger zippers, snaps, and buttons, making using the toilet on their own easier. By age 4, they can brush their teeth, wash their face, and try to comb their hair. The hardest skill, tying shoelaces, may not be accomplished until about age 6. Young children like to choose their wardrobe, although their fashion preferences may be unusual. A little girl may insist on wearing her pink tutu, long "pearl" necklace, and new rain boots to the grocery store! Such flights of whimsy are part of the joy of early childhood.

**Using Tools.** Eating utensils are among the first tools children master. Among Western children, the spoon is easiest (age 2), followed by fork (age 4), and knife (age 5 or 6).

*Everyday stories*

EATING UTENSILS—NOT JUST SPOONS AND FORKS Lest you think the progression from spoon, to fork, to knife is natural and universal, look at the accompanying photo. The photo shows an 11-month-old toddler from Zaire (now the Democratic Republic of the Congo) cutting a melon with a machete as a relative watches. Consider, too, that Chinese children begin using short chopsticks as toddlers. By the age of 4 or 5, most Chinese children can use chopsticks reasonably well (Wong, Chan, Wong, & Wong, 2002). Meanwhile, young children in India and Ethiopia use their fingers to eat rice dishes and use skewers to roast meat over an open flame.

*Photograph courtesy of David Wilkie*

An 11-month-old toddler from Zaire (now the Democratic Republic of the Congo) cuts a melon with a machete as a relative watches.

Many activities involving tools require hand–eye coordination, such as cutting with scissors, stringing beads, and doing puzzles. Here again, we can see the effects of social and cultural expectations. While American 5-year-olds are pasting macaroni onto picture frames, Mayan girls are learning to weave on a frame. Western 3-year-olds masterfully move an electronic mouse across a screen to select a favorite program. And while one preschooler rings chimes in time to music, another is playing the violin.

a. Scribbling

b. Amoeba figure

c. More complex amoeba figure

d. Drawing that tells a story

**FIGURE 8.10 Examples of Children's Drawings** Young children's drawing starts with scribbling (a) and progresses to so-called amoeba figures (b and c). Between the ages of 4 and 6, children begin to produce more complex drawings that tell stories. The girl who made the drawing in (d), for example, explained, "This is me eating ice cream."

*Source:* Figures a and b reprinted with permission of Jolley, R. P. (2010). *Children and pictures: drawing and understanding.* Hoboken, NJ: Wiley-Blackwell, pp. 39 and 107.

**Writing, Drawing, and Painting.** One of the most significant accomplishments of early childhood is using pencils, crayons, markers, chalk, and paintbrushes to write, draw, and paint. These tools are more forgiving than are forks and zippers—the child ends up with a final product of his own making regardless of skill. Perhaps this is why young children love these activities. There are significant qualitative changes in children's drawings during the preschool years that mirror both motor and cognitive changes (Golomb, 2004; Jolley, 2010). Some examples are shown in Figure 8.10. The following descriptions will give you a sense of the sequence.

- *18 months to 3 years: Scribbling*. The *scribbling* stage can begin around 18 months of age, when the toddler can hold a fat crayon in her fist. At first, the child is interested only in making marks or watching the color flow onto the paper with no particular purpose in mind. Asked to identify her creation, she may give it any name that strikes her fancy at the time. A scribble of lines, for instance, may become spaghetti.
- *2 to 4 years: Early figures and copying*. Circles become pictures that represent people or animals. The circles are given dots for eyes, and they may have arms or legs that extend from what appears to be a head—sometimes called tadpole or amoeba drawings. By age 4, figures start to have more facial features, as well as hands and feet, but no recognizable bodies. Pictures are often crafted to represent particular people. A drawing of "Mommy" might have more hair. Attention to detail can depend on the child's natural talent, what is noticeable to him—for example, earrings for Mommy—and guidance. Children who draw with adults generate more detailed and recognizable figures (Braswell & Callanan, 2003). Chinese children, who are taught to copy specific images line by line, demonstrate greater representational skill than Western children, who are encouraged to draw as they please (Huntsinger, Jose, Krieg, & Luo, 2011; Winner, 1989).
- *4 to 6 years: Realistic drawings and symbols*. From ages 4 to 6, children begin to produce more realistic drawings that include people and objects that tell a story. Changes in the brain that support perception, memory, and fine motor skills allow children to include perspective and depth in their drawings. Three-dimensional shapes may be attempted, but they are not generally mastered until school age (Toomela, 1999). Writing also develops during this period. Writing requires practice and is accompanied by the emerging recognition that symbols represent language. We discuss emergent writing in more detail in Chapter 9.

**primary prevention** A type of prevention that focuses on health promotion and the prevention of specific diseases and accidental injuries.

**health promotion** Incorporating healthy behaviors into daily life and avoiding known risks.

**secondary prevention** A type of prevention that focuses on detecting, diagnosing, and treating disease in the earliest stages, and on halting the spread of communicable diseases by persons already infected.

**tertiary prevention** A type of prevention that focuses on slowing the progress of a disease and limiting its disabling complications.

## ✓CHECK YOUR PROGRESS

1. How do changes in the brain influence the development of self-regulation and executive function?
2. Describe developmental changes in walking and running.
3. Describe developmental changes in fine motor skills.

Terry Vine/Patrick Lane/Getty Images, Inc.

Wearing a bike helmet to keep injuries from happening is a form of primary prevention.

# Foundations of Health: Health Promotion

**[ KEY QUESTION ] 2.** How can children be provided with a good foundation for lifelong health?

You may recall that at the beginning of Chapter 5, we said that "children's health is a nation's wealth" and that promoting it is a wise investment (National Research Council and Institute of Medicine, 2004). Health is more than the absence of disease. Good physical and emotional health is the foundation for how we adapt to life, a vital resource for personal growth and development as well as for the success of communities and nations (Robert Wood Johnson Foundation Commission to Build a Healthier America, 2009). In this section, we review several health-related topics that are particularly important during early childhood. We begin by presenting the *Healthy People 2020* goals for children, which include well-child visits and developmental screening. We then discuss nutrition, immunizations, and dental health.

Peter Dazeley/Photographer's Choice/Getty Images, Inc.

The goal of secondary prevention is to detect health problems in the earliest stages so that they can be treated more effectively. Screening for vision problems is an example of this type of prevention.

## Health Promotion and Disease Prevention

It is always better to promote health and to prevent injury, illness, and disease than to treat them. In 1979, the U.S. government released *Healthy People: The Surgeon General's Report on Health Promotion and Disease Prevention* (U.S. Department of Health and Human Services [USDHHS], 1979). This report laid the foundation for a national agenda that has set health promotion and disease prevention goals for each decade beginning in 1980. Table 8.2 lists some of the goals of *Healthy People 2020* that apply to children.

### Levels of Prevention

*Healthy People* addresses three levels of prevention: primary, secondary, and tertiary (Commonwealth Fund Commission on Chronic Illness, 1957). While primary prevention is designed to prevent issues from arising in the first place, secondary and tertiary prevention address issues that have already arisen to prevent them from developing further.

- *Primary prevention.* **Primary prevention** falls into two broad categories. The first is **health promotion**, which focuses on incorporating healthy behaviors into daily life and avoiding known risks. For example, *Healthy People 2020* promotes access to health care and good nutrition for children. The second category of primary prevention targets prevention of specific diseases and accidental injuries. Examples include immunization against infectious diseases and use of bike helmets.
- *Secondary prevention.* One purpose of **secondary prevention** is to detect and diagnose a health problem in the earliest stages in order to cure it, slow its progression, and prevent or minimize complications that may result without early treatment. An example from *Healthy People* is screening for vision and hearing problems. The other purpose of secondary prevention is to stop the spread of communicable diseases by persons who are already infected.
- *Tertiary prevention.* When a person has been born with a health problem or has sustained an injury or developed an illness that cannot be reversed, **tertiary prevention** comes into play. The goal of tertiary prevention is to slow the disease's progress or to limit its disabling complications. An example from *Healthy People* is management of asthma. Early intervention programs for children with disabilities and developmental delays also fit into this category.

Guy Cali/© Corbis

Physical therapy is a form of tertiary prevention, which is aimed at slowing an existing disease's progress or limiting its disabling complications.

**Table 8.2** Healthy People 2020

| | |
|---|---|
| Access to health care | Increase the proportion of persons with health insurance.<br>Increase the proportion of children with special health-care needs who have access to a medical home.[a]<br>Increase the proportion of territories and states that have service systems for children with special health-care needs. |
| Routine screening | Increase the proportion of preschool children aged 5 years and under who receive vision screening. |
| Asthma | Reduce hospitalization rates for pediatric asthma, uncontrolled diabetes, and immunization-preventable pneumonia and influenza.<br>Reduce the number of school days missed among children (aged 5 to 17 years) with current asthma. |
| Immunizations | Increase the proportion of young children and adolescents who receive all vaccines that have been recommended for universal administration. |
| Health promotion | Increase the proportion of local health departments that have established culturally appropriate and linguistically competent community health promotion and disease prevention programs.<br>Increase the proportion of elementary, middle, and senior high schools that provide comprehensive school health education. |
| Dental health | Increase the proportion of children who have received dental sealants on their molar teeth. |
| Nutrition | Reduce growth retardation among low-income children under age 5.<br>Increase the proportion of persons aged 2 and older who consume:<br>• at least two daily servings of fruit<br>• at least three daily servings of vegetables<br>• no more than 30% of calories from fat |
| Developmental readiness | Increase the proportion of children who are ready for school in all five domains of healthy development:<br>• physical well-being and motor development<br>• social emotional development<br>• approaches to learning<br>• language development<br>• cognition |

You can see more at www.healthypeople.gov/hp2020

[a]A medical home is housed in the offices of primary care providers, such as a pediatrician or family practitioner. It coordinates care for children with special health-care needs who see multiple providers in different specialties.

## Well-Child Visits and Developmental Screening Practice

As we noted in Chapter 5, well-child visits should be scheduled at frequent intervals during the first three years of life, and regular visits should continue through the years of early childhood. These visits typically include four broad categories of activities, as described in Chapter 5: physical examination and screening for health problems, education and health promotion, intervention, and care coordination. The emphasis is on primary and secondary prevention—that is, promoting good health and screening for conditions that can be addressed early through in-depth assessment. When appropriate, tertiary prevention, such as lifetime management of a chronic health condition, can begin early. The more we understand about development in early childhood, and especially development of the brain, the more important these visits are.

**Denver Developmental Screening Test** An instrument used to assess the development of children between birth and 6 years of age.

One aspect of well-child visits is *developmental screening*, the process of identifying children who are not meeting developmental milestones and who may need to be further assessed by specialists. This screening is particularly important in identifying special health-care needs early in life so that they can be treated. *Children with special health-care needs* are defined by the U.S. Maternal and Child Health Bureau as "those who have or are at increased risk for a chronic physical, developmental, behavioral, or emotional condition and who also require health and related services of a type or amount beyond that required by children generally" (McPherson et al., 1998). In Chapter 11, you will learn that between 12% and 26% of children under age 18 have a chronic condition, depending on what conditions are included.

Some special needs are apparent at birth or shortly thereafter, such as Down syndrome and cerebral palsy. Others may not become apparent until early childhood, such as delays in speech and language as well as certain learning disabilities. Early intervention programs can help children with special needs, but only if the needs are diagnosed. This is the purpose of developmental screening.

Health-care professionals use many tools to screen children for health and learning issues that can benefit from early intervention. The **Denver Developmental Screening Test**, for example, is suitable for children from birth to age 6 (Frankenburg & Bresnick, 1998). It assesses language skills (such as understanding oral directions and naming pictures), fine motor and gross motor activities (such as building a block tower or standing on one foot), and personal-social behaviors (such as dressing, eating, and helping out).

The National Health Survey indicates that about 93% of all children between birth and age 6 have had at least one well-child visit in the previous year (National Center for Health Statistics, 2009). In general, African American children and children whose parents have a college education are most likely to make such a visit (90.8% and 91.8%, respectively) (Child Trends DataBank, 2010). Health insurance matters, too. Children with some form of insurance—private, Medicaid, or States Children's Health Insurance Program (SCHIP)—are more likely to have well-child visits (94.4%) than those with no insurance (80%) (National Center for Health Statistics, 2009). However, not all insurance plans cover the cost and time of developmental screening.

## Nutrition, Food Allergies, and Malnutrition

We turn next to another health promotion issue: nutrition. You read in Chapter 5 that both good nutrition and good eating habits have lifelong implications. Here, we first discuss the nutritional needs and eating habits of the preschool group and then go on to examine two additional issues: food allergies and poor nutrition.

### Nutritional Needs

Between ages 2 and 3, children require about 1000 to 1400 calories per day. Between ages 4 and 8, the moderately active child needs 1400 to 1600 calories per day. Calories do not tell the whole story, however. Children need a variety of foods, including daily helpings of grains, fruits and vegetables, dairy products, and meat or other protein sources. A variety of fresh fruits and vegetables is especially important because they provide essential vitamins and micronutrients required for development in general and for development of the brain and bones in particular. And there are foods young children should *not* eat or eat in limited quantities. For example, sweets (such as cookies and candy) and high-sodium foods (such as potato chips and most fast foods) should be a special treat only. In addition, the American Dietetic Association (2011) recommends that after the age of 2, children drink low-fat milk rather than whole milk.

Jose Luis Pelaez Inc./Blend Images/Getty Images, Inc.

When conflict disrupts the dinner table, no one wins. Parents should work to keep mealtimes pleasant.

## Eating Habits

Many preschoolers develop strong opinions about what foods they like and dislike. They are often wary of new foods, so new foods need to be introduced gradually. The taste, texture, or appearance of a food can form a lasting negative impression. Young children may become picky eaters, go through "food jags" when they want to eat one particular food all the time, or eat almost nothing at all. All of this is normal behavior, but it can lead to conflict at the dinner table. Parents and other caregivers may worry that the child is not getting sufficient nutrition or may feel that the child is disrupting mealtime with "unreasonable" demands and behavior.

Sharing food and eating together is a powerful socializing experience in most cultures. Therefore, getting into a power struggle with young children over food isn't a good idea: nobody wins. Parents' handling of these normal developmental challenges can affect children's relationship with food and with parents for a long time. Here are some recommendations for keeping mealtimes pleasant (American Dietetic Association, 2011; Patrick & Nicklas, 2005):

- Young children like routines, and they like to be helpful. Having meals at about the same time each day and including children in preparation—for example, asking them to help set the table—promote positive feelings about eating and being together.
- Be clear about responsibilities. Parents are responsible for providing nutritious foods that children will eat at mealtimes and for snacks. Children are responsible for eating them. As long as the food is child-friendly, whether children eat, how much they eat, and what they eat should be up to them. Most young children tend to eat well enough over the course of several days or a week to be well nourished. Beware of cooking special meals to suit one child's demands.
- Be clear about expectations. Mealtime is social time. No TV, no phone calls, no electronic devices in use. Most children cannot sit for a long meal, so be clear about when a child can be excused. Even a child who is not hungry can be expected to join everyone at the table for a short time. Children are more likely to eat and be open to new foods when everyone surrounding them is relaxed about eating and engaged socially. Rather than putting a new food on the child's plate, signaling an expectation that it be eaten, tell her she has to try just a taste of yours.
- Don't use food, and especially sweets, as a reward or for comfort during a stressful time. Don't withhold food as punishment.

## Food Allergies

It seems that we can't visit an early child-care center or school today without encountering a child with a food allergy. Two in 25 children may have a food allergy (Gupta et al., 2011), and one-third of parents report some sort of food sensitivity in their young children. However, most people who think they have food allergies have food intolerance. Confusion about these two different types of sensitivity muddies diagnostic, preventive, and management efforts (Chafen et al., 2010; Lieberman & Sicherer, 2010). Let's look next at how they differ.

**food intolerance** Sensitivity to a particular food that does not result from an allergic reaction but occurs when a person's digestive system lacks the enzymes or microorganisms needed to digest the food.

**Food Intolerance and Food Allergies.** **Food intolerance** occurs when a person's digestive system lacks the enzymes or microorganisms needed to digest certain foods. Common examples include milk, gluten, and sulfites (Chafen et al., 2010; National Institute of Allergy and Infectious Diseases [NIAID], 2010a). For example, a person with milk intolerance may experience bloating, gas, vomiting, diarrhea, and similar symptoms after drinking milk. Other symptoms of food intolerance may include flushing or headache.

A **food allergy** is an immune response. That is, when a child is allergic to a particular food and ingests some of that food, his body produces a specific protein called an antibody to attack the food now present in his system. The antibody can be detected in the bloodstream. The resulting allergy symptoms may be digestive but may also involve rash or hives, trouble breathing, or swelling and tingling around the mouth. A severe allergic response, which can occur within seconds of exposure, is **anaphylaxis**. This condition is life-threatening and requires emergency treatment (NAIAD, 2010a, 2010b).

Eight types of food account for over 90% of food allergies: cow's milk, hen's eggs, peanuts, tree nuts, fish, shellfish, soy, and wheat. Across the globe, cow's milk and hen's eggs are the most common food allergies among young children. Children tend to outgrow some food allergies. How this happens is not clear. Allergies to peanuts and tree nuts, however, are lifelong (Lack, 2008; Sampson, 2004; Wood, 2011).

**Prevalence and Prevention of Food Allergies.** From 1997 to 2007, the prevalence of reported food allergies among school-aged children seems to have increased by 18%, affecting 3.9% of children (Branum & Lukacs, 2008). However, it is uncertain whether this reflects a true increase in allergies, better reporting, or confusion between allergy and intolerance. Several theories about this apparent increase in food allergies, especially peanut allergies, have been proposed, but there are no clear conclusions (Lack, 2008; Wood, 2011).

It was once thought that women could prevent food allergies in their children by avoiding problem foods during pregnancy and breast-feeding as well as avoiding giving these foods to infants. Research has not supported this belief, however (Greer, et al., 2008; Koplin et al., 2010). In fact, it is possible that eating these foods may actually increase tolerance of them (Lack, 2008). For example, peanut allergy is fairly rare in places where peanuts are consumed throughout pregnancy and early childhood, such as parts of Africa, Asia, and Israel (Hill et al., 1997; Lack, 2007, 2008; Levy, Broides, Segal, & Danon, 2003; Sampson & Ho, 1997). Of course, women who have an established food allergy should continue to avoid allergen-producing foods during pregnancy and breast-feeding (Lack, 2008; NIAID, 2010b; Sicherer & Sampson, 2010).

Some recent efforts to desensitize children with peanut allergies by introducing them to microscopic doses under controlled clinical conditions have met with some success (Edwin et al., 2011; Jones et al., 2009). However, until a cure can be found, the only available treatment for children who have established food allergies is to avoid the foods that cause the allergic response and to treat an allergic response immediately—a coordinated effort that involves everyone who interacts with that child (Houle, Leo, & Clark, 2010). Parents should *never* try to desensitize children by including the foods in their diet at home.

## Malnutrition

Malnutrition is an imbalance between what a person eats and what the body needs for growth, maintenance, and specific functions. The World Health Organization identifies two types of malnutrition (Stevens, Mascarenhas, & Mathers, 2009): undernutrition and overnutrition. We discuss both issues here.

**Undernutrition.** As defined by the United Nations Children's Fund (UNICEF), **undernutrition** is the result of insufficient food intake *and* repeated infectious diseases. Undernourished children are underweight for age, short for age (stunted), dangerously thin for height (wasted), and deficient in micronutrients. **Micronutrients** are substances required by the body in very small amounts, such as vitamins and minerals. Undernutrition accounts for more than half of the 8.8 million deaths of children under age 5 each year worldwide; half of those are in sub-Saharan Africa (Bhaskaram, 2002; Torpy, Lynm, & Glass, 2004; UNICEF, 2010). In addition, more than 200 million children under 5 years of age in developing countries do not reach their developmental potential because of undernutrition (Black et al., 2008).

**food allergy** An immune response to a particular food.

**anaphylaxis** A life-threatening allergic response requiring emergency treatment.

**undernutrition** A type of malnutrition that results from insufficient food intake and repeated infectious diseases.

**micronutrients** Substances required by the body in very small amounts, such as vitamins and minerals.

Young children who are undernourished are especially vulnerable to infectious diseases, such as malaria, that cause chronic diarrhea. Chronic diarrhea, in turn, results in dangerous imbalances in electrolytes, such as potassium and sodium, and rids the gastrointestinal track of beneficial microorganisms that support the immune system, rendering children vulnerable to yet another cycle of disease. Chronic diarrhea is the leading cause of death for children around the world (Caufield, de Onis, Blössner, & Black, 2004).

Across the globe, deficiencies in micronutrients, especially vitamin A, zinc, iron, calcium, and iodine, are major nutritional problems (American Dietetic Association, 2011) that contribute to cognitive and behavioral difficulties (Black et al., 2008; Thomas, Grant, & Aubuchon-Endsley, 2009). Micronutrients are essential to the physical and cognitive development of children under age 5. These biochemical elements affect many functions of children's bodies and brains. Calcium, for example, is important to cellular metabolism. In fact, it is so important that the body will break down bones and teeth to get calcium if it is not supplied in children's diet. Deficiencies in calcium can keep bones from growing and affect dental health, among other things. Iodine and zinc are essential for brain development (Prasad, 1998), so deficiencies can affect brain functioning. Iron-deficiency anemia can lead to lowered energy levels and deficits in motor and mental development (Grantham-McGregor & Ani, 2001). UNICEF has estimated that 750 million children suffer from iron-deficiency anemia (UNICEF, 2003, 2010).

*Everyday stories*

TREATING MALNUTRITION You might think that giving a severely malnourished child more food would reverse her malnourished state. However, the small bodies of severely malnourished children lack the protein-based enzymes needed to digest food, and regular food may do much more harm than good. So how do we treat malnutrition? UNICEF provides us one example. In 2011, drought had delayed the harvest of corn, peanuts, cabbage, potatoes, and other vegetables in eastern Ethiopia, leaving many people starving. Zara Ahmed's youngest child, Nayle, had lost so much weight that Zara brought the girl to a local health center for help. Nayle was enrolled in an outpatient therapeutic feeding program, through which she was fed ready-to-use therapeutic food (RUTF)—a peanut-butter-based paste full of essential micronutrients, protein, vitamins, lipids, and carbohydrates. Over a few weeks, Nayle gained weight and grew healthy enough that she could begin to eat small amounts of real food in addition to the RUTF.

**Overnutrition: Obesity as Malnutrition.** When we think about malnutrition, we usually think of starving children in developing countries. Let's challenge that thinking. The 1967 International Conference on Obesity acknowledged that obesity is also malnutrition (Taubes, 2011). UNICEF calls this *overnutrition*—that is, more calories are consumed than are needed (UNICEF, 2010). It makes sense that this condition is more likely found in developed countries.

Overweight is defined as having a body mass index (BMI) for age and gender above the 85th percentile, whereas obesity is having a BMI above the 95th percentile. Over the last 30 years, the prevalence of overweight in the United States among all age groups has tripled. Among children from 2 to 5 years old, one in five (22%) is overweight (Wang & Beydoun, 2007) and 10% to 14% are obese (Ogden & Carroll, 2010). Overweight and obesity in early life sets the stage for lifelong weight problems. Obesity in young children thus is not "baby-fat" that they will outgrow. Overweight preschoolers become overweight school-aged children, who become overweight adolescents and adults. We discuss the significant long-term health risks in more detail in Chapter 11.

For now, let's consider one important similarity between undernourished and overweight children: children in both these groups may not have access to sufficient healthy foods. As a result, less than optimal nutrition becomes the norm. We might understand how that can happen in poor countries, but it can happen in the United States as well. It is called *food insecurity*, and we discuss it next.

**food insecurity** A condition that results from not having enough food for one's next meal, or from not having enough food of sufficient nutritional quality.

**food desert** A geographic area, rural or urban, where residents have limited access to large supermarkets that sell a variety of foods.

### Food Insecurity and Food Deserts Policy

People have food security when they have access at all times to enough healthy food for an active, healthy life. They have **food insecurity** when they don't have enough food for their next meal, resulting in hunger, or when their food, while sufficient to avoid hunger, is of poor nutritional quality. According to the U.S. Department of Agriculture, food insecurity of one type or another exists in about 14.6% of American households (Nord, Coleman-Jensen, Andrews, & Carlson, 2010). The cost of food is one factor that contributes to food insecurity. The processed foods in the center aisles of large supermarkets are usually less expensive than fresh fruits and vegetables. Unfortunately, they are also higher in sodium, corn syrup, and empty carbohydrates, which lack nutritional value but often supply lots of calories. Eating large amounts of cheap processed food contributes to obesity (Monteiro, Levy, Claro, de Castro, & Cannon, 2010; Pollan, 2008).

**Food deserts** can also contribute to food insecurity. A food desert is a geographic area, rural or urban, where residents have limited access to supermarkets that sell a variety of fresh foods (U.S. Department of Agriculture, 2009). In urban areas, people typically shop on foot and do not buy in bulk or load up the trunk of a car. The cost of operating a supermarket in urban areas can be high, discouraging larger retailers (Bitler & Haider, 2009). In addition, urban food deserts are generally characterized by higher levels of racial segregation and income inequality (Nord et al., 2010). In small-town and rural areas, lack of transportation is an issue (Nord et al., 2010). Families that rely on higher-priced local convenience stores or nearby fast-food restaurants are more likely to be poorly nourished and overweight (Powell, Chaloupka, & Bao, 2007; Powell, Slater, Mirtcheva, Bao, & Chaloupka, 2007).

The existence of food deserts shows us how multiple systems connect to influence what children eat. While family eating habits certainly contribute to poor nutrition and obesity, it is also important to look at the social, economic, and political environment beyond the control of an individual family. In recent years, city, state, and federal governments have increased their efforts to provide incentives for large

David Howells/©Corbis

Consumers who live in urban food deserts may have to rely mostly on fast food restaurants and convenience stores, making it difficult for them to choose healthy foods.

**acquired immunity** The immune system's response to specific pathogens that it has learned to identify.

**vaccine** A substance used to stimulate the production of antibodies and provide immunity against one or several diseases.

**herd immunity/community immunity** Group immunity that exists when 80% to 95% of the people in a community have been immunized against a disease.

food retailers to locate in city neighborhoods and to help smaller grocers purchase fresh foods at lower prices. The motive is economic as well as health-related because supermarkets create jobs, and when they move into an area, other retail businesses open nearby.

When children enter school, they encounter another larger-scale influence on what they eat: the school lunch program. We discuss school lunch programs in Chapter 11.

## Immunizations and Vaccines

Immunization against infectious diseases has improved the health of children worldwide more than any other single public health effort. Immunization has virtually eradicated smallpox, which killed more than 300 million people in the first seven decades of the 20th century (Burton, 2002). Vaccines have eliminated measles and polio in some parts of the world and substantially reduced childhood deaths from diphtheria, tetanus, and pertussis (whooping cough) (CDC, 2006). The World Health Organization (WHO) estimates that 2 million childhood deaths were prevented by vaccinations in 2003. A million children died in 2002 from diseases that could have been prevented by vaccinations (CDC, 2006; WHO, 2005).

### About Immunity and Vaccines

Our natural environment can be hostile to humans: disease-causing organisms—called *pathogens*—abound, including bacteria, viruses, and other microorganisms. Our immune systems represent our responses to these organisms. Our first level of response relies on our skin and mucous membranes, such as those in the nose and mouth, which provide a generalized response to the routine bacteria and viruses we encounter on a daily basis. Our second level of response rests more with the body's immune system, which confers **acquired immunity**. Acquired immunity arises when the immune system learns to identify a particular organism or substance and to begin producing *antibodies* to attack and destroy it before it can cause serious illness.

The purpose of **vaccines** is to stimulate the immune system to recognize and respond to specific pathogens and thus produce antibodies against the diseases they cause. A vaccine contains a harmless version of a particular pathogen. When it is introduced into the body, the immune system responds by producing antibodies that remember the pathogen. If the person is exposed to that disease again, the immune system can quickly recognize and attack pathogens when they appear, thereby providing immunity against the disease.

The purpose of administering vaccines is twofold. The first is to protect the individual child from life-threatening communicable diseases—that is, infectious diseases that easily spread from one person to another. The second is to protect the general public. Public health professionals call this **herd immunity** or **community immunity**. Depending on the disease, herd immunity requires that 80% to 95% of people in a community be immune. Thus, there are fewer people who can infect others, which reduces the incidence of disease for everyone.

If you look at the vaccination schedule in Table 8.3, you will see that many vaccinations are delivered during the first two years of life. You may wonder why there is a need to vaccinate children at such a young age—why not wait until they are older? The answer is related to their developing immune systems. We noted in Figure 8.2 that the lymph system, which is part of the immune system, develops quickly in early childhood. Until about age 2, the response of the immune system to some specific pathogens is less than in older children and adults, making young children more vulnerable to certain diseases (Offit et al., 2002). Vaccines provide protection. Prior to the development of vaccines, many young children routinely died of these infectious diseases before their 5th birthday; in some places, many still do (CDC, 2006).

Not all American children are vaccinated according to CDC standards. Some parents do not make regular well-child visits. Thus, doses are missed, individual immunity is not completely conferred, and herd immunity is compromised. The *Healthy*

**Table 8.3** Recommended age range for vaccine schedule for the 4:3:1:3:3:1:4 series*

<table>
<tr><th></th><th>Birth</th><th>1 mos</th><th>2 mos</th><th>4 mos</th><th>6 mos</th><th>12 mos</th><th>15 mos</th><th>18 mos</th><th>24 mos</th><th>4–6 yrs</th></tr>
<tr><td>Diphtheria, pertussis, tetanus (DPT)</td><td></td><td></td><td>DPT #1</td><td>DPT #2</td><td>DPT #3</td><td></td><td colspan="2">DPT #4</td><td></td><td></td></tr>
<tr><td>Inactivated polio vaccine</td><td></td><td></td><td>IPV #1</td><td>IPV #2</td><td colspan="4">IPV #3</td><td></td><td>IPV #4</td></tr>
<tr><td>Measles, mumps, rubella (MMR)</td><td></td><td></td><td></td><td></td><td></td><td colspan="2">MMR #1</td><td></td><td></td><td></td></tr>
<tr><td>Haemophilus influenza type b (H flu)</td><td></td><td></td><td>Hflu #1</td><td>Hflu #2</td><td>Hflu #3</td><td></td><td></td><td></td><td></td><td></td></tr>
<tr><td>Hepatitis B</td><td>HepB #1</td><td colspan="2">HepB #2</td><td></td><td colspan="4">HepB #3</td><td></td><td></td></tr>
<tr><td>Varicella (chicken pox)</td><td></td><td></td><td></td><td></td><td></td><td colspan="3">Var #1</td><td></td><td></td></tr>
<tr><td>Pneumococcal vaccine (protects against pneumonia)</td><td></td><td></td><td>PCV #1</td><td>PCV #2</td><td>PCV #3</td><td colspan="2">PCV #4</td><td></td><td></td><td></td></tr>
</table>

*4:3:1:3:3:1:4 series means: 4 doses of DPT vaccine; 3 doses of poliovirus vaccine; 1 dose of MMR vaccine; 3 doses of haemophilus influenza type b vaccine (depending on the type of vaccine used, the third dose may not be needed); 3 doses of hepatitis B vaccine; 1 dose of varicella (chicken pox) vaccine (if there is no history of having had the disease); and 4 doses of pneumococcal vaccine.

*Source:* Centers for Disease Control, 2012. http://www.cdc.gov/vaccines/recs/schedules/default.htm.

*People 2010* objective for childhood immunization was to achieve 90% coverage for each of the universally recommended vaccines in the 4:3:1:3:3:1:4 series described in Table 8.3. However, in 2008, only 68% of children 19–35 months of age received the full series. As we have seen with other health disparities, there are differences in coverage among groups. Native Americans and Alaskan natives have the lowest overall rate of coverage (63%), followed by non-Hispanic blacks (66%) (CDC, 2008).

what if...?

What if the percent of people in the population immunized against a certain disease, such as pertussis (whooping cough), were to fall below the level needed to achieve community immunity? What do you think would happen? Should preschool and early child-care settings require that children be immunized? If there were a pertussis outbreak at your child's care center, how do you think you would react?

## Immunizations and Autism

Recently, some parents have questioned the wisdom of vaccines. They worry about vaccine safety. While many studies have concluded that vaccines are safe, there is one issue that has generated enough controversy to warrant special attention: the proposed link between vaccines and autism.

We briefly described autism spectrum disorders in Chapter 7. Over the past two decades, the rates of these disorders have essentially doubled. This increase has been attributed in part to better diagnosis and reporting (Fombonne, 2009; Matson & Kozlowski, 2010). However, some people have noted that the time at which certain vaccines (specifically, the MMR vaccine) are given—namely, sometime in a child's second year—coincides with the onset of signs of autism. They have gone on to propose that the vaccines somehow cause autism. Despite the fact that there is no conclusive evidence to support this claim (Price et al., 2010), it has created considerable controversy. As prospective teachers, nurses, child-care workers, and parents, it is important for you to understand the research in this area and the science involved.

**The Original Study.** In 1998, the British medical journal *Lancet* published a paper linking the MMR vaccine to intestinal problems and development of autism (Wakefield et al., 1998). The study consisted of 12 children (11 boys and 1 girl), ages 3–10. In the study, 10 of the children were described as having a history of "pervasive developmental disorder," also referred to as "autism" in the study. This history was said to have begun within a certain period of time after they had either received the MMR vaccine or had the measles or another infection. All of the children had gastrointestinal problems that were attributed to an immune response either to the vaccine or to the infection. The immune response was identified by a biological marker. A biological marker is a substance such as a protein or antibody found in the blood or other tissues that are a sign of a disease or change in condition. The authors interpreted evidence of an immune response as a biological marker supporting a link between the vaccine and developmental delay.

**Follow-Up Studies.** The conclusions of the original study have been refuted by a great deal of subsequent research (Drutz, 2010). First, the original authors did not offer a plausible biological mechanism by which the vaccine would *cause* autism. Furthermore, studies seeking biological markers for immune responses in people with autism failed to find them (Baird et al., 2008; Fernell, Fagerberg, & Hellstrom, 2007). Second, well-designed, large-scale epidemiological studies have found no association between the MMR vaccine and autism (Dales, Hammer, & Smith, 2001; Farrington, Miller, & Taylor, 2001; Fombonne & Chakrabarti, 2001; Hornig et al., 2008; Kaye, Melero-Montes, & Jick, 2001; Madsen et al., 2002, 2003; Makela, Nuorti, & Peltola, 2002; Taylor et al., 1999). Systematic reviews of the epidemiologic literature also have failed to find support for an association between the MMR vaccine and autism (Institute of Medicine [IOM], 2004; Stratton, Wilson, & McCormick, 2001).

*Lancet* itself retracted the authors' original interpretation of their findings in February 2010 after evidence mounted that the conclusions were without merit and

## Research Insights: Lessons from the Autism–Vaccine Controversy

The autism–vaccine controversy offers many lessons for researchers (Horton, 2004): from theory testing and research methods, to interpretation and reporting of findings, to ethical conduct. Let's start with theory. It was hypothesized that a causal biological mechanism—MMR vaccine—was responsible for the onset of autism. The favored research method for testing cause-and-effect relationships in the medical sciences has long been the randomized control trial. However, it would be unethical to give one group of children a vaccine and withhold it from another group to see who develops autism, so such a study cannot be done. The alternative would be to rely on other theoretically sound measures as substitutes for the causal relationship. These substitutes could be evidence of biological markers in people with autism that would indicate an immune response or a statistical measure called relative risk. Studies that used these measures later did not confirm the original findings.

The methods of the original 1998 paper raised doubts about the findings as soon as it was published. First, it was a descriptive study of a small group of children. There were no case controls, so conclusions about causal relationships could not be drawn. Second, the study reported that the children were seen in the clinical setting one-by-one over a period of time, a sampling method often used in clinical research. This turned out not to be true, raising the possibility that the children were selected for the study, thus biasing the results. Third, an ethics review board had not approved the study, as had been reported by the authors. Fourth, the *Lancet*'s review process before accepting the original paper for publication was found to lack rigor ("Retraction," 2010).

Misunderstandings about scientific principles have distorted the public discussion about the link between vaccines and autism. In particular, the concept of causality in the biological sciences can be difficult to appreciate. It may be easy to conclude, for example, that if signs of autism begin to appear after MMR vaccine administration, the vaccination must have caused the autism. The statistics of causality refuting this belief may be difficult for many to understand.

Precisely because most people are not scientists, scientific findings have to be trustworthy. Falsifying data is a serious breach of ethical conduct among scientists. But it is also a damaging breach of trust with society at large because it sows the seeds of doubt about the validity of scientific methods. How many people do *you* think will still believe that vaccines cause autism even in light of the later findings that convincingly refute this idea?

had contributed to false beliefs among the public and some professionals ("Retraction," 2010). Then, in January 2011, the *British Medical Journal* declared that the original study was "fraudulent" (Godlee, Smith, & Marcovitch, 2011)—an extraordinary and unprecedented charge by one group of scientists against another.

Ken Seet/© Corbis

Children usually lose their first baby tooth at the age of 5 or 6.

## Promoting Dental Health

Most children have their first set of teeth by the time they are 3 years old. These are sometimes called baby teeth, and there are 20 in all. At age 5 or 6, permanent teeth developing behind the baby teeth push the baby teeth out, one by one. Most children have lost all of their baby teeth and have a full set of 28 permanent teeth by the time they are 12 or 13.

The American Academy of Pediatric Dentistry (2010) advises that children should first visit a dentist before their first birthday. Most, though, do not see a dentist until school age (Milgrom, Zero, & Tanzer, 2009). The result may be dental caries, that is, tooth decay. Toddlers and young children may be more susceptible to tooth decay than older children, adolescents, and adults (Harris, Nicoll, Adair, & Pine, 2004). Serious damage to baby teeth can also damage the developing permanent teeth below.

Risk factors for dental caries include a diet high in sugary and starchy foods as well as infrequent or inadequate tooth brushing. Infants and toddlers who are put to bed with a bottle containing juice or some other sugary or starchy substances, or who grip such a bottle with their teeth throughout the day, can have tooth decay by the age of 3. This condition is sometimes referred to as "baby bottle mouth." Children whose parents are poorly educated, are unemployed, and have poor oral health habits themselves are also at greater risk. Because these parents often do not have dental health insurance, their children are less likely to see a dentist (Edelstein 2002; Harris et al., 2004; Isong et al., 2010; Tinanoff & Palmer, 2000).

### Dental Health as a Foundation for Healthy Development

Why does dental health matter in child development? First, **dental caries** is the single most common disease of childhood—five times more common than asthma, which is second (National Center for Health Statistics, 2009; USDHHS, 2010a). Yet most people would not think of dental caries as a disease. Second, children need their teeth to eat, to talk, and to smile. Dental caries can compromise all three of these activities, with implications for nutritional status, for speech production, and for social interaction. Painful caries can interfere with learning. Finally, dental health is a marker for socioeconomic and nutritional status and for access to health care in general. It is the number-one unmet child health need in the country, and failure to provide it is considered a form of neglect (American Academy of Pediatric Dentistry, 2010; Edelstein, 2002; Mouradian, Wehr, & Crall, 2000).

The prevalence of dental caries has declined since the early 1970s, due in large part to prevention efforts such as fluoride in community water supplies and in toothpastes and rinses. Nevertheless, there are significant disparities based on racial or ethnic minority grouping and socioeconomic status, as is the case with other health indicators. Among children under age 5, the group most affected by untreated dental caries are Hispanic/Mexican children (30%), followed by African American (24%) and white (15%) children (National Center for Health Statistics Health, 2009).

### Dental Health and Fluoride **Policy**

Dental caries is a preventable disease. Prevention includes a healthy diet, avoidance of sugary foods, regular tooth brushing, and flossing. Regular dental checkups can also help to prevent decay. In keeping with our systems approach to child health, we want to emphasize here that prevention also occurs at the level of community and public health policy. One example would be to increase access to dental health care for all children. Another example involves fluoride.

**dental caries** Tooth decay.

Fluoride occurs naturally in water, soil, and plants. It helps to mineralize the enamel on teeth as they are forming and can also aid in remineralizing enamel in the early stages of decay. Fluoride makes teeth stronger and more resistant to decay-causing agents. Dentists often prescribe fluoride supplements to young children whose families use bottled water or well water at home, since both are low in fluoride.

In the 1940s, epidemiological studies found that fluoridated water reduces the incidence of dental caries in young children by as much as 50% to 60%. As a result, communities around the world began to add fluoride to community water supplies (Ripa, 1993), making it the most effective and least expensive method of reducing the occurrence of caries (CDC, 1999, 2001). In 2004, the Surgeon General noted that for every $1 spent on water supply fluoridation, an average $38 or more is saved in treatment costs (Carmona, 2004).

Nevertheless, water fluoridation remains controversial (Freeze & Lehr, 2009). First, while low concentrations are beneficial and cause no harmful side effects, very high concentrations of fluoride may cause discoloration of tooth enamel. Second, concerns have been voiced about safety, even though extensive research has indicated that the fluoridation of the water supply is safe for adults as well as children (National Health and Medical Research Council of the Australian Government, 2007). Third, opposition to fluoridation of community water supplies is political. Opponents argue that by adding fluoride to the water supply, governments impose themselves on their citizens. Some also claim that the governments are not truthful about potential harm.

### ✓CHECK YOUR PROGRESS

1. Give examples of primary, secondary, and tertiary prevention activities that improve children's health.
2. Why are well-child visits important for children's health and development?
3. How can parents support good eating habits in young children?
4. What is the difference between food intolerance and food allergies?
5. Discuss how vaccines work and the controversy regarding their use.
6. Why does dental health matter in child development?

## Capacity for Health: Caregivers, Community, and Child Safety

**[ KEY QUESTION ] 3. How can parents and other caregivers keep children safe?**

In this book, we have emphasized the importance of caregivers and communities in providing children with a healthy start. For most young children, this group includes parents, family members, child-care providers, and preschool teachers. The circle of influence also begins to include peers and often their families as well. Because adults are responsible for the health of children, it is important for those adults to understand what it takes for children to grow, develop, and be healthy as well as to be safe at home and in the community.

### Health Literacy — Parenting

The Institute of Medicine defines **health literacy** as the capacity to obtain, process, and understand basic health information and services needed to make appropriate health-care decisions (Nielsen-Bohlman, Panzer, & Kindig, 2004). Health literacy also requires basic knowledge of how the body works; how infections spread; and how to read labels, insurance forms, and charts. Unfortunately, many people in the United States have poor health literacy. According to some sources, more than 90 million

**health literacy** The capacity to obtain, process, and understand basic health information and services needed to make appropriate health-care decisions.

adults in the United States (Berkman et al., 2004; Rudd, Anderson, Oppenheimer, & Nath, 2007; Wolf et al., 2009), including 29% of parents (Yin et al., 2009), are not health-literate. Some sources report that more than 50% of parents cannot read tables to determine appropriate weight by height and over 46% do not understand how to administer their child's medication (Yin et al., 2009).

*Everyday stories*

A WELL-INTENTIONED MISTAKE A mother takes her young child to the local clinic, where it is determined that the child has an ear infection. The prescribed antibiotics come in liquid form with a dropper cap. The directions indicate the medicine should be given by mouth, but the mother puts drops of the antibiotic into the child's ear. She may not be able to read well, she may not understand the directions, or she may not know how antibiotics work. She may think that putting the antibiotic directly onto the infected area is the most direct way to treat the infection, not realizing that the infection is inside the ear and out of reach of the drops she diligently applies. Needless to say, her approach will not eliminate the infection, and she may have to bring her child back to the clinic.

To add to the challenge, the Internet is filled with health-related sites of dubious merit, which some people take at face value. Not surprisingly, poor adult health literacy is associated with poor health outcomes for children at home, at early child care, and at school (DeWalt & Hink, 2009). Efforts to improve health literacy in adults require a multipronged approach, including improving general reading ability and science literacy as well as challenging false health beliefs (Nutbeam, 2000).

## Kids, Germs, and Early Child Care

If it seems like young children always have a runny nose or cough, it's because they can get three to eight colds a year (Turner, 2009). Furthermore, as we noted earlier, children who attend early child care and preschool have a higher risk for respiratory infections, ear infections, and diarrhea than those who do not regularly spend time in the company of many other children (Coté et al., 2010; Hagerhed-Engman, Bornehag, Sundell, & Aberg, 2006). Before you decide that this is a good reason to keep children home, let's review why young children get sick more frequently than older children and adults and what this means for their health in general.

### The Chain of Infection

The chain of infection is a term commonly used to describe how infectious diseases spread. Think of this chain in terms of the following six links: (1) Germs (*infectious agents*) live in (2) a person (*reservoir host*) who either is sick with an infectious disease or is a carrier for the disease. (3) The germs escape from that person in blood, saliva, nasal or throat secretions, or fecal material (*exit portals*). (4) The germs travel by air (coughing and sneezing), by direct contact (a child wipes a runny nose with his hand and then touches other children), or by indirect contact (a child picks up a toy that another child then handles) (*transmission*). (5) The germs enter a second person through the person's lungs, digestive system, broken skin, urinary tract, or genital tract (*entry portals*) and (6) infect their new *host*.

It is very difficult to break the chain of infection with young children and thus prevent the spread of common infectious agents. Young children regularly touch their bodies, other people, and objects in rapid succession. They often put things into their mouths, and their bathroom habits leave something to be desired. Sink faucets are usually the dirtiest surfaces in early child-care and preschool settings. One sick child can spread germs not only to other children but also to child-care workers and

**Table 8.4** How to Limit the Spread of Infection in Early Child-Care and Preschool Settings

| | |
|---|---|
| Frequent hand washing | • Soap and warm water along with 15 seconds of thorough washing is usually enough to be clean. It takes about 15 seconds to sing the ABCs. Sing along to help children remember.<br>• Put footprints on the floor of the bathroom leading from toilet to sink.<br>• Use individual paper towels to dry hands, not cloths that are shared.<br>• Inspect hands before eating. Make it a game.<br>• Early child-care workers and preschool teachers must wash hands after changing diapers and helping children in the bathroom and before food preparation.<br>• Install automatic faucets or foot-activated ones.<br>• Do not use antibacterial soaps, as children need exposure to routine bacteria to build immunity. If soap and water are not available, substitute alcohol gels. |
| Proper food preparation | • Make sure that counters or tables for food preparation are nonporous and in good condition. Keep counters clean.<br>• Don't let kids share foods, drinks, or utensils.<br>• Food preparation should not be done near diaper-changing areas. |
| Caregiver training | • Make sure caregivers have been properly trained on hygiene practices for limiting the spread of infection.<br>• Understanding how diseases are spread and which ones to look out for can be a huge asset in infection prevention. |
| When to keep a child home | • Children who have a fever, are vomiting, have diarrhea, or have eye discharge (pinkeye) should remain at home. |

*Source:* Adapted from Grossman, L. B. (2003). *Infection control in the child care center and preschool* (6th ed.). New York: Lippincott Williams & Wilkins.

preschool teachers, who then take the illness home with them. Table 8.4 lists some suggestions for stopping the spread of harmful germs.

## Why Some Germs Are Good for Children

Earlier in this chapter, we mentioned that the immune system of young children is still developing, rendering them more vulnerable to infectious agents. Some infectious diseases can overwhelm their immune systems, and immunization against these diseases saves children's lives. However, the common cold virus and most bacteria and viruses that cause common gastrointestinal ailments are not usually life-threatening in otherwise healthy children.

Such viruses and bacteria are everywhere, all the time. While some of them harbor serious disease, most do not. In fact, some bacteria must be ingested into the gastrointestinal system to aid digestion and protect it from more serious pathogens. A young child's immature immune system needs to be exposed to routine microorganisms in order to recognize them as familiar. That way, it can ignore them and focus on foreign pathogens that pose a greater danger. This process of exposure is called "the education of the young immune system" (Yazdanbakhsh, Kremsner, & van Ree, 2002).

The more medical researchers learn about the immune system, the more they appreciate dirt (Ruebush, 2009; Weiss, 2002). According to the **hygiene hypothesis**, the environments of Western children are unnaturally clean, which dramatically decreases their exposure to routine microorganisms. Children today spend far less time than previous generations outdoors walking barefoot through the grass, playing in dirt, climbing trees, and being around outdoor animals. The widespread use of antibacterial soaps and the frequent use of antibiotics have further decreased

**hygiene hypothesis** A hypothesis that suggests the environments of Western children are unnaturally clean, dramatically decreasing their exposure to routine microorganisms.

exposure. As a result, day-to-day germs are not familiar to the immune system, and the immune system responds to them as if they were more threatening than they actually are. Hypersensitive responses to these substances may take the form of allergies or asthma.

The result is a paradox of immunity. On the one hand, vaccines have contributed to a decrease in dangerous childhood infections. But on the other hand, there has been a significant increase in allergies and asthma in the industrialized world but not in developing countries (Strachan, 1989; Weiss, 2002; Yazdanbakhsh et al., 2002). While precautions against bacteria and viruses that cause serious illness should not be ignored, caregivers should not be afraid of the natural environment. That is, all children should eat a little dirt! But they should also wash their hands with regular soap and water frequently, as discussed next.

Henry the Hand reminds children to wash their hands—an important element of good hygiene.

### Promoting Good Hygiene in Young Children

We started this chapter with a story about soap and its importance in disease prevention. It is important to teach young children to use good hygiene, as habits formed early in life are likely to last a lifetime. As you will read in Chapter 9, young children need reminders to follow through on activities, such as washing their hands and brushing their teeth. They respond well to having a routine set for them by adults who also model the activity. Posters of "Henry the Hand," for example, remind children of four important principles:

1. Wash your hands after toileting, after playing outside, and before eating.
2. Don't cough into your hands (cough against your upper arm).
3. Don't sneeze into your hands.
4. Don't put your fingers in your eyes, nose, and mouth. (These are the only entryways into the human body for respiratory and gastrointestinal infection.)

## Safety at Home and in the Community

Young children are busy and curious, exploring their world. They run and climb; put things into their mouths; reach out to grab items of interest; open and close cupboards, windows, gates, and doors; and love to play with mechanical objects.

Sven Hagolani © Corbis

Good hygiene habits formed early in life will likely last a lifetime.

However, they cannot read warning labels, they lack judgment about possible danger, and they may not take "no" for an answer. It is normal for busy young children to have bruises on their legs and arms, but the consequences of their behavior are sometimes more serious. In fact, according to the National Center for Injury Prevention and Control (NCIPC) (2012a), unintentional injuries are the leading cause of death between the ages of 1 and 5 years, accounting for 45% of all deaths (Figures 8.11 and 8.12).

## Unintentional Injuries

Among unintentional fatal injuries, motor vehicle accidents (26%) and drowning (30%) account for a large proportion of deaths of young children. Figure 8.12 shows the data from NCIPC (2012a) for 2010, which is representative of recent years. Unintentional nonfatal injuries in children in this age group also account for 30% of young children's visits to emergency rooms (Ben-Isaac, Schrager, Keffer, & Chen, 2010). Almost half of nonfatal injuries are related to falling from some height, followed by being struck by or against something, animal bites or stings, ingesting or inhaling a foreign object, and serious breaks in the skin, such as cuts. Fortunately, most such injuries do not require hospitalization, but they are certainly upsetting for parent and child alike (NCIPC, 2012b).

It is the responsibility of parents, family members, and other caretakers—such as babysitters, child-care staff, and preschool teachers—to keep young children safe (CDC, 2012). Given the number of injuries and fatalities that occur, it is not an easy job. Children's day-to-day environments abound with hazards: stairs, breakable items, sharp objects, hot appliances, cleaning supplies, and so on. As children develop, it often becomes difficult to balance concerns for safety with respect for children's ability to negotiate these hazards. Precautions necessary for a toddler, such as gates on staircases, are too restrictive for a 6-year-old. At some point, there must be a first time for a child to do something by herself, such as going down a slide on the playground, being left alone in another room, getting something from a cupboard, and using sharp utensils. Table 8.5 lists some suggestions from the CDC for preventing unintentional injuries in young children.

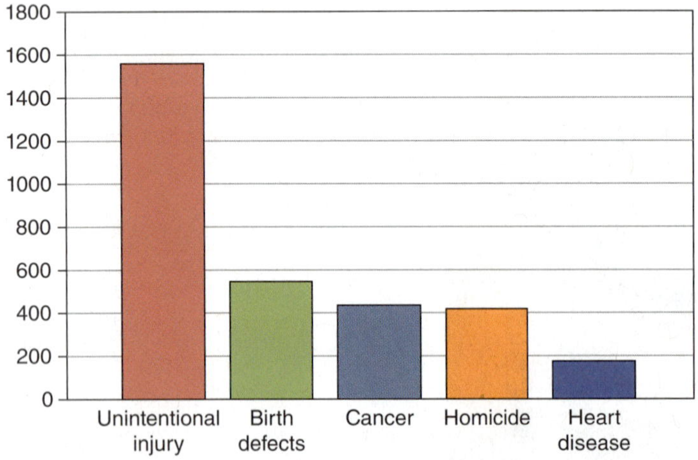


**FIGURE 8.11 Leading causes of death ages 1–5, 2010** Unintentional injury is the leading cause of death in children from 1 to 5 years old, followed by birth defects, cancer, homicide, and heart disease.

*Source:* National Center for Injury Prevention and Control (2012) http://webappa.cdc.gov/sasweb/ncipc/leadcaus10_us.html.

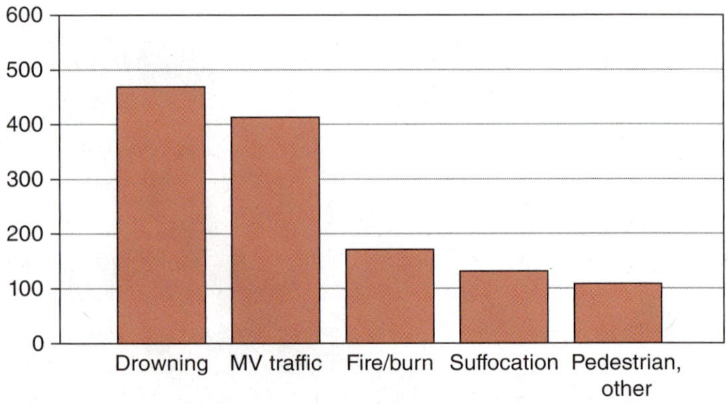


**FIGURE 8.12 Leading Causes of Death from Unintentional Injury, Ages 1–5, 2010** Drowning and motor vehicle accidents account for a large proportion of deaths from unintentional injury in children from 1 to 5 years old, 30% and 26% respectively. Other leading causes are fire or burns, suffocation, and transportation-related pedestrian accidents.

*Source:* National Center for Injury Prevention and Control (2012) http://webappa.cdc.gov/sasweb/ncipc/leadcaus10_us.html.

**Table 8.5** Injury Prevention in Early Childhood

| Type of Injury | Prevention Strategies | |
|---|---|---|
| Motor vehicle accidents | • Make sure children are properly buckled up in a seat belt, booster seat, or car seat, appropriate for age, height, and weight.<br>• All children ages 12 and younger should ride in the back seat.<br>• Child passengers should never be seated in front of an airbag. | • When toddlers move from rear-facing to front-facing car seats, they should use those seats until they are at least 4 years old and weigh 40 pounds.<br>• Once children outgrow a front-facing car seat, they should use a booster seat until they are big enough for the seat belt to fit right. Use booster seats for children until they are at least 8 years of age or 4′9″ tall. |
| Drowning | • Young children can drown in any level of water that covers the nose and mouth, as little as 2 inches. Supervise young children at all times around bathtubs, swimming pools, and bodies of water.<br>• Do not allow young children in hot tubs.<br>• Install a four-sided isolation fence, with self-closing and self-latching gates, around backyard swimming pools. | • Make sure kids wear life jackets in and around bodies of water, even if they know how to swim.<br>• Learn cardiopulmonary resuscitation (CPR).<br>• Adults watching kids near water should avoid distracting activities like playing cards, reading books, or talking on the phone. |
| Burns/fire | • Install and maintain smoke alarms in your home—on every floor and near all rooms family members sleep in.<br>• Have an escape plan. While some children ages 4–6 may remember to leave the house on their own if the family has practiced this, you cannot count on their having the presence of mind to do so. Many tend to hide under beds and in closets. | • Use safe cooking practices, such as never leaving food unattended on the stove. Turn handles on pots and pans away from little hands that reach up and grab. Supervise young children whenever they're near cooking surfaces.<br>• Set your water heater's thermostat to 120 degrees Fahrenheit or lower to avoid burns. |
| Dogs and dog bites | • Do not approach an unfamiliar dog.<br>• Do not run from a dog and scream.<br>• Remain motionless ("be still like a tree") when approached by an unfamiliar dog.<br>• Do not play with a dog unless supervised by an adult. | • Do not disturb a dog who is sleeping, eating, or caring for puppies.<br>• Do not pet a dog without allowing it to see and sniff you first. |
| Falls | • Check to make sure playground equipment is properly designed and maintained and there's a safe, soft landing surface below.<br>• Use home safety devices, such as guards on windows that are above ground level.<br>• Supervise young children at all times around fall hazards, such as stairs and playground equipment. | • Make sure your child wears protective gear such as wrist guards, knee and elbow pads, and a helmet when riding a bicycle or playing a sport in which injury is a known risk, such as skiing. |
| Poisoning | • Keep medicines and toxic products, such as cleaning solutions, in locked or childproof cabinets.<br>• Follow label directions and read all warnings when giving medicines to children.<br>• Safely dispose of unused, unneeded, or expired prescription drugs. Don't just throw them in the trash. Most pharmacies will dispose of old drugs for you. | • Put the nationwide poison control center phone number, 1-800-222-1222, on or near every telephone in your home. Call poison control if you think a child has been poisoned and if the child is awake and alert.<br>• Keep syrup of ipecac in your cupboard in case the poison control center suggests using it to induce vomiting. *Vomiting is not recommended for all ingested poisons, however.*<br>• Call 911 if you have a poison emergency and your child has collapsed or is not breathing. |
| Ingesting or inhaling small objects | • Keep small objects such as coins, buttons, toys, and so on away from small children. Small objects quickly disappear into a child's mouth, nose, or ear.<br>• Swallowing: Contact a health-care provider if you suspect a child has swallowed an object or has placed one in the nose or ear that is not easily retrievable. While many small objects may pass through the gastrointestinal system without harming a child, they can also obstruct narrow areas and sharp edges may cut into the intestinal wall. | • Inhaling: Some foods, such as grapes and hot dogs, are choking risks for young children. Young children also should not run, talk, or laugh with food, candy, or gum in their mouths and should not tilt back their heads to catch food like popcorn or a peanut in their mouths. These activities increase the likelihood of inhaling the food into the trachea and closing off the air supply. This is a medical emergency. Learn to do the Heimlich maneuver on small children. |

*Source:* Adapted from Centers for Disease Control, www.cdc.gov/safechild "Safe Child Home."

**e-waste** Discarded electronic devices that contain mercury, lead, arsenic, and heavy metals.

## Environmental Hazards: Lead and Toxic Waste

In Chapter 3, we discussed environmental hazards that can cause birth defects in a fetus. Children continue to be vulnerable to the adverse effects of chemicals and other toxic substances. Two are especially worth noting: lead and toxic substances from electronic waste.

**Lead.** Lead was banned from use in paints, toys, and furniture in 1978 in the United States. Thus, the major sources of lead exposure for children today are lead-based paint and lead-contaminated dust in older buildings. About 24 million housing units are affected, many of them publicly funded low-income housing. Young children play on dusty floors, handle items that have been contaminated, and put chips of lead paint into their mouths. Contaminated soil and water are also dangers, especially from older construction sites, old plumbing, and wells (CDC, 2009).

Lead is highly toxic to young developing bodies. Depending on the level and duration of exposure, lead poisoning can cause irreversible damage to the nervous system, brain, and kidneys. Lead poisoning causes sluggishness, irritability, seizures, and delays in development—and it can be fatal (Markowitz, 2007). Because early detection and treatment can minimize the long-term effects, the Centers for Disease Control recommend testing blood levels in young children at risk, including children from other countries, where exposure to lead may be more common (CDC, 2009). If lead is detected in the blood, avoiding further exposure is the first step in treatment. This may be sufficient for children with lower blood levels of lead. Higher blood levels require treatment with chemicals that bind the lead in order to remove it from the body (Hurwitz & Dean, 2011; Rusyniak et al., 2010).

**Electronic Waste.** Over the last decade, developed countries have been illegally shipping their electronic waste to third-world countries, especially African port cities. This waste includes discarded electronic devices such as computers and cell phones, called **e-waste**. It is dumped in open areas where children play and scavenge. Children dismantle and sell the components, which contain mercury, lead, arsenic, and heavy metals. These substances get on children's hands and clothing and into their lungs. They also leak into soil and water, where they remain indefinitely, contaminating water supplies, crops, and livestock. Researchers are just beginning to document the rising incidence of death, disability, and serious illness among children that have resulted from e-waste dumping (Kimani, 2007; Srivastava, Kesavachandran, & Kumar, 2011).

*Kate Davison/eyevine/Redux Pictures*

The illegal dumping of electronic waste in developing nations has resulted in death, disability, and illness in children, who often scavenge in the e-waste sites for materials they can sell.

### Intentional Injury: Child Endangerment

In 2010, for children ages 1 to 5, homicide was the fourth leading cause of death, accounting for more than 400 deaths that year (NCIPC, 2012a). Children under age 4 account for 80% of homicides under age 9. Maltreatment is one of the significant means of child endangerment. The leading form of maltreatment is chronic neglect, but maltreatment also includes physical, sexual, and emotional abuse. Higher rates of victimization occur among African American, Native American/Alaskan, and mixed-race children, but white children are more likely to die. Sadly, the perpetrator of maltreatment is most likely a parent or other caregiver, someone a child knows well and should be able to trust (USDHHS, 2010b). We discuss the family dynamics and emotional consequences of maltreatment in a later chapter. For now, it is important to recall that maltreatment may have lasting adverse effects on the developing brains of young children, as we discussed earlier in this chapter.

**what if...?**

What if you were ready to buy a new cell phone or computer? Where would you dispose of your old ones? How would you find out what would happen to your electronic waste? What if they ended up at a landfill in the United States or in an African port city where they posed a threat to young children and the environment? What could you do to prevent this?

**CHECK YOUR PROGRESS**

1. What is health literacy?
2. Why do children in early child care and preschool get more colds than children who do not attend these programs?
3. What are some precautions that adults need to take to keep young children safe from unintentional injuries and environmental hazards?

## Common Disruptions in Health

**[ KEY QUESTION ] 4. How do common illnesses such as asthma and ear infections affect children's development?**

We noted earlier that, after dental caries, asthma is the most common chronic disease of childhood in the United States. We also noted that preschool-aged children have more colds and infections than do older children. This can lead to ear infections, a common health disruption for young children. We discuss both asthma and ear infections here.

### Asthma

More than 10 million children aged 17 and under (14% of children) have been diagnosed with asthma at some point in childhood; 7.1 million children have active cases (10%) (Akinbami, Moorman, Garbe, & Sondik, 2009; CDC, 2010b). Although asthma can occur at any age, the vast majority of children have their first symptoms before age 5. Boys are more affected than girls. For children, asthma is the primary reason for absence from school as well as for emergency room visits and admissions to the hospital (Dean et al., 2009; James & Rosenbaum, 2001; Weiss, Sullivan, & Lytle, 2000).

© Science Photo Library/Alamy Limited

Children with asthma may use inhalers to deliver both long-term and short-term medications.

## About Asthma

**Asthma** is caused by complex interactions among genetic susceptibility, environmental exposures, and the immune response (Schwartz, 2009). You have probably heard the analogy that your lungs are like an upside-down tree, with larger airways branching into smaller and smaller airways. In asthma, the smooth muscles of these airways become inflamed. Inflammation causes swelling, mucus collects, and the airways spasm. Spasms narrow the airways and obstruct air flow. Depending on several factors, including the severity of the spasms, the results range from mild, intermittent symptoms that interfere with physical activity to persistent severe symptoms that are life-threatening: tightness in the chest, wheezing, coughing, shortness of breath, and gasping for air.

Two types of environmental elements can trigger an asthma attack. One is an antigen—that is, some substance to which the child is allergic. The most common allergic triggers are dust mites, cockroach antigen, mouse antigen, animals (or sometimes what they carry in their fur), mold, and pollen. Nonallergic triggers include irritants such as cold air, exercise, and tobacco smoke, as well as some viruses. Polluted air can fall into either category. Children with nonallergic asthma usually develop it earlier in childhood and are more likely to outgrow it than those whose asthma is based on an allergic immune response (Gilliland, 2009; Hockenberry, 2003; Litonjua & Weiss, 2010; Schwartz, 2009).

Of course, the best treatment for asthma is to reduce exposure to antigens and irritants. As that is not always possible, most children are treated with medications. These fall into two general categories: long-acting for maintenance and short-acting for immediate relief (Guilbert et al., 2006; Hockenberry, 2003). Corticosteroids (such as cortisone and prednisone) are the most commonly used long-acting medications for children over the age of 2. They are usually inhaled but can also be taken orally. Short-acting medications called bronchodilators quickly cause the affected airways to relax and open. These so-called "rescue inhalers" should not be used more than three times per day, however. (Not all cultures favor the use of medications for asthma, as we explain in the accompanying feature "Culture and Beliefs about Asthma.")

what if...?

What if you are a preschool teacher or child-care provider, and you have a child with asthma in your classroom? What do you think you need to know in this situation? What do you think it must be like for a young child to have asthma? How much do you think the child is likely to understand about the condition? How do you think having asthma might affect the child's physical and social development?

## Social and Economic Disparities in Asthma Prevalence and Treatment

There are significant disparities in the prevalence of asthma that can be attributed to social and economic factors. Children from racial and ethnic minorities and children who are poor have more severe forms of asthma, more emergency room visits, more hospitalizations, and more deaths due to asthma than the general population (Akinbami, Parker, & Gold, 2010; Gold & Wright, 2005; Williams, Sternthal, & Wright, 2009). Children residing in urban areas are also disproportionately affected (Hulin, Caillaud, & Annesi-Maeano, 2010), whereas children growing up on farms are least affected (Ege et al., 2011).

**asthma** An allergic condition that causes spasms of the airways in the lungs, making it difficult to breath.

## Culture and Medical Beliefs

The hot/cold system is perhaps the most widely known medical belief system in the world, with variations practiced in Asia, the Middle East, and Latin America. Practitioners aim for balance among the four elements—air, water, wind, and fire—as well as combinations of hot, cold, wet, and dry. Foods, illnesses, and health remedies are classified by their inherent attributes. For example, a diet of hot foods, such as fried foods and chili peppers, should be balanced by cold foods, such as melons and green tea.

Asthma, like other respiratory problems, is considered a cold disease. It may be caused by a mother eating too much cold food or being cold during pregnancy. The person with asthma may have been exposed to cold drafts and wind, have weak lungs, or is easily upset. Prevention includes warm clothing, keeping room temperature warm, and avoiding cold air and getting upset. The remedies that balance a cold disease are hot, such as hot tea, cod liver oil, garlic, honey, or lemon. Other remedies include hot compresses applied to the chest, and remaining calm (Bearison, Miniam, & Granowetter, 2002; Leong, 2006; Pachter et al., 2002). These practices are generally harmless, and may even be helpful. You have probably been warned to not venture into cold weather without a coat, and been offered a hot beverage on your return.

*Marc Volk/fstop/Corbis*

Malaysian and Latina mothers believe that taking medicine for asthma weakens the lungs further, as the body gets lazy and comes to depend on the medicine. Inhalers may be perceived as cold dry air, and as such do not balance cold disease. They may not be used to manage asthma but only to treat acute episodes. Steroid medications make children jittery and upset, and so are avoided (Ariff & Beng, 2006; Pachter et al., 2002). Thus a family's approach to asthma is based on health beliefs that align with their culture, but may be at odds with standard medical practice.

*Everyday stories*

INNER CITY ENVIRONMENTS AND ASTHMA The Inner-City Asthma Study, sponsored by the National Institute of Allergy and Infectious Diseases and the National Institute of Environmental Health Sciences, has examined why asthma is more prevalent among inner-city children. For one thing, buildings in close proximity—apartment buildings, schools, businesses—are often home to cockroaches, rodent droppings, mold, and dust mites, which are significant environmental allergens (Gruchalla et al., 2005; Matsui et al., 2006). Indoor and outdoor air pollution play a role as well, including tobacco smoke and exhaust fumes from cars, trucks, and buses (Eggleston, 2007; Gehring et al., 2010). However, violence plays a greater role than polluted air (Wright et al., 2004). Children who move from violent neighborhoods to more stable and less stressful areas within the same city find that their symptoms improve (Williams et al., 2009). This finding does not mean stress *causes* asthma. Remember that stress is a physiological response that involves increased levels of cortisol. In turn, these high cortisol levels interfere with the immune system, which is already affected by asthma. This finding suggests that the immune systems of children with asthma are more vulnerable to the stress of living in a violent neighborhood.

**otitis media** Inflammation of the middle ear.

**WHEN SYSTEMS CONNECT**

### An Ecological Perspective on Asthma Management

Given that the determinants of asthma are not only genetic but also social and economic, a comprehensive approach to asthma management is needed (Clark, Mitchell, & Rand, 2009; Williams et al., 2009). Accordingly, researchers, psychologists, and health-care professionals are turning to an ecological perspective on this important issue, consistent with the framework from the Center on the Developing Child at Harvard University we are using in this book. Figure 8.13 shows the circles of influence for managing asthma, with the child and family at the center, expanding outward to community and national policies on health care, economic development, and pollution (Clark et al., 2009). Again, we see that changes in a biological process—the immune system—can affect families, communities, and ultimately policy.

## Ear Infections: Otitis Media

We noted that young children may have three to eight episodes of the common cold per year (Turner, 2009), with higher rates among children who attend out-of-home early child care and preschool. They also develop other types of *upper respiratory infections*, which include various types of bacterial and viral infections that affect the upper respiratory tract—the nose and throat. Many such infections develop into acute **otitis media**—inflammation of the middle ear, which is the area behind the eardrum. Inflammation causes a buildup of fluid that increases pressure in this small space, and the blockage may cause pain.

Typical signs of acute otitis media in young children include crying and fussiness, pulling on the affected ear, problems swallowing, and poor sleep. The fluid in the ear may or may not become infected. Thus, not all episodes of acute otitis media are true bacterial infections, even though otitis media is commonly referred to as an "ear infection." By age 3, 80% of children have had at least one episode of acute otitis media (Revai et al., 2007; Klein & Pelton, 2010).

Why do young children develop otitis media so easily? One reason is the immaturity of their immune systems, which makes them more susceptible to infections in general. The other reason is that the anatomy of their ears is different from that of older children and adults. The middle ear is connected to the back of the throat by the eustachian tube. In young children, the eustachian tubes are shorter and more horizontal than in older children and adults, so fluid collects more easily and does not drain into the back of the throat. As children grow, the tubes lengthen and develop a more vertical pitch and thus drain more easily.

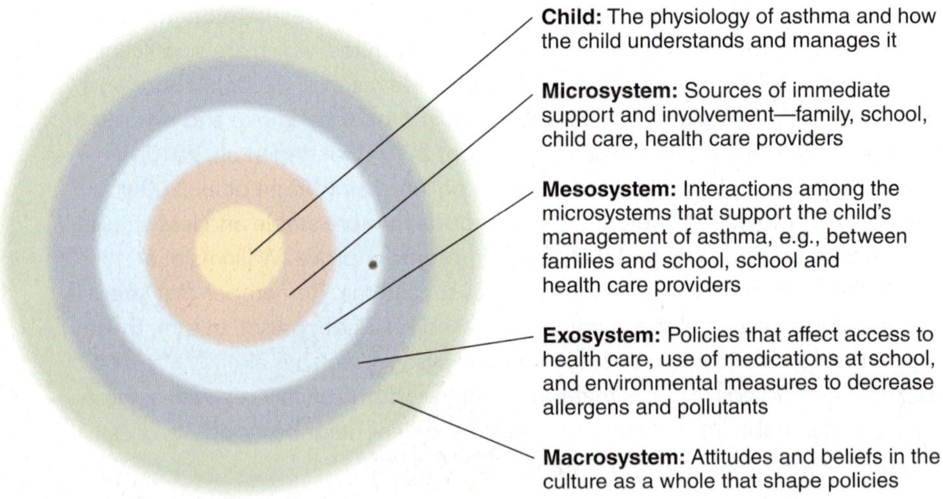


**FIGURE 8.13 Circles of Influence for Management of Childhood Asthma** In the figure, we use Bronfenbrenner's terminology to show the circles of influence for managing asthma, starting with the child and extending through the microsystem, mesosystem, exosystem, and macrosystem. Remember that in Bronfenbrenner's view, each system affects all the others.

*Source:* Based on Clark, N. M., Mitchell, H. E., & Rand, C. S. (2009). Effectiveness of educational and behavioral asthma interventions. *Pediatrics* 123:S186, Figure 1.

### Treatment and Prevention

Most episodes of otitis media clear up on their own. Therefore, treatment guidelines suggest that health-care providers treat the pain but "wait and see" before prescribing antibiotics. For cases clearly involving true bacterial infection, however, antibiotics should be prescribed (American Academy of Pediatrics and American Academy of Family Physicians, 2004). About 7% of children experience recurrent ear infections. Doctors sometimes treat these cases by surgically inserting very small tubes in the children's ears. The tubes are designed to allow air into the middle ear, equalizing the pressure between the middle ear and the atmosphere (Kogan, Overpeck, Hoffman, & Casselbrant, 2000).

The best way to prevent otitis media is to prevent upper respiratory infections by using good hygiene. But as we have noted, this is more easily said than done with young children. Interestingly, fewer tubes have been inserted over the past decade to treat otitis media. One reason is that more young children have received the pneumococcal vaccine since it was added to the vaccination schedule in 2000, lowering the incidence of upper respiratory infections that can lead to otitis media (Isaacson, 2010).

### Ear Infections and Hearing Loss

The potential for permanent hearing loss can be a concern with recurrent ear infections in young children because recurrent *untreated* infections can damage the inner ear (National Institute on Deafness and Other Communication Disorders, 2002; Sanford & Weber, 2010; Smith, Bale, & White, 2005). Permanent hearing loss from ear infections is not common, however, and it is preventable. Therefore, it is important to evaluate children as soon as hearing loss is suspected, especially if they experience recurrent infections (Sanford & Weber, 2010). Untreated hearing loss can result in delays in speech, language, and cognitive development.

**CHECK YOUR PROGRESS**

1. What social and economic disparities are found in the incidence and treatment of asthma?
2. Why do young children develop otitis media so easily?
3. How does otitis media affect hearing?

# CHAPTER SUMMARY

## Biology of Health: Physical Growth and Development

**[ KEY QUESTION ] 1.** How do changes in growth and development support physical, cognitive, and social skills during early childhood?

- The rate of growth slows between ages 2 and 6 compared with the dramatic changes seen during the first two years, with more growth in height in the legs than in the trunk.
- Gene–environment interactions account for some of the individual differences in height and size among children and across populations.
- Structural changes in the prefrontal cortex, the orbitofrontal cortex, and the anterior cingulate cortex support functional capacity for self-regulation and executive function.
- Toxic stress can have enduring adverse effects on the brain that interfere with children's cognitive and behavioral development.
- The development of gross motor skills in early childhood follows the principles of proximodistal development and differentiation. Walking, running, throwing, and catching all improve over the early childhood period.
- Fine motor skills require the ability to coordinate the brain, vision, and very small muscles at the same time. Learning to use tools to write, draw, and paint are significant milestones for young children.

## Foundations of Health: Health Promotion

**[ KEY QUESTION ] 2.** How can children be provided with a good foundation for lifelong health?

- There are three types of health prevention: primary, secondary, and tertiary. Health promotion is a type of primary prevention that emphasizes good nutrition, exercise, and other healthy habits.

- Well-child visits are a critical aspect of health prevention. They include four categories of activities: physical examination and screening, education and health promotion, intervention, and care coordination.
- Young children often develop strong opinions about foods they like and dislike and can become picky eaters. How parents handle their children's eating habits can affect children's relationship with food and with parents for a long time.
- Many parents confuse food intolerance with food allergy, but food intolerance does not involve an allergic reaction, as food allergy does. The most common food allergies are cow's milk and hen's eggs.
- Undernutrition is a form of malnutrition and is one of the leading causes of death among children worldwide. It is caused by both insufficient food intake and repeated infectious diseases, such as malaria.
- Overweight and obesity are also forms of malnutrition.
- Food insecurity and food deserts contribute to poor nutrition in children in developed countries.
- Young children are more vulnerable to certain infectious diseases because their immune systems are immature. The purpose of vaccines is to stimulate the immune system to recognize and respond to specific pathogens before the pathogens cause disease, creating acquired immunity.
- Recent controversy about the relationship between autism and the vaccine for measles, mumps, and rubella has resulted in fewer children being vaccinated, possibly compromising herd immunity. The original study that proposed this relationship has been deemed fraudulent.
- Dental caries is the most common infectious disease in children. Dental caries can compromise speech production, social interaction, and eating.

## Capacity for Health: Caregivers, Community, and Child Safety

**[ KEY QUESTION ] 3.** How can parents and other caregivers keep children safe?

- Health literacy enables parents to better care for their children's health.
- Children in daycare and preschool settings get more colds and certain other infections than children who do not regularly spend time outside their homes. This happens because children's immune systems are immature and because it is difficult to break the chain of infection with young children.
- Some germs are good for children. The hygiene hypothesis asserts that the environments of Western children are too clean—too free of helpful germs. This may account for the rise in allergies and asthma among children.
- Young children respond well to routine, so promoting good hygiene means adults have to organize the environment and daily schedule to encourage good health habits.
- Unintentional injuries are more common in early childhood than later because young children are still mastering motor skills, cannot read warning labels, and lack judgment about possible danger. It is the responsibility of adults to keep young children safe from hazards.
- Lead poisoning remains a health hazard for young children in the United States, particularly for those living in older homes and large public housing projects where lead paint was used before being banned in 1978.
- Homicide was the fourth leading cause of death for children aged 1 to 6 in 2009.

## Common Disruptions in Health

**[ KEY QUESTION ] 4.** How do common illnesses such as asthma and ear infections affect children's development?

- After dental caries, asthma is the most common chronic illness among young children. It is caused by complex interactions among genetic susceptibility, environmental exposures, and the immune response.
- There are significant disparities in the prevalence of asthma that can be attributed to social and economic factors.
- An ecological perspective on asthma management emphasizes the roles of not only the child and family but also the larger community.
- Many upper respiratory infections develop into acute otitis media—that is, inflammation of the middle ear. Young children are more vulnerable to ear infections because the anatomy of their ears is different from that of older children and adults.
- Untreated chronic ear infections can cause hearing loss, which interferes with the development of language and social skills. Early identification and treatment can prevent this outcome.

# KEY TERMS

acquired immunity *294*
anaphylaxis *291*
asthma *306*
dental caries *297*
Denver Developmental Screening Test *289*
e-waste *304*
food allergy *291*
food desert *293*
food insecurity *293*
food intolerance *290*
health literacy *298*
health promotion *286*
herd immunity/community immunity *294*
hygiene hypothesis *300*
micronutrients *291*
otitis media *308*
primary prevention *286*
secondary prevention *286*
self-regulation *277*
tertiary prevention *286*
undernutrition *291*
vaccine *294*

# CRITICAL THINKING QUESTIONS

1. **Biology of Health: Physical Growth and Development.** Explain what it means to say that children's early experiences shape the architecture of their developing brains, laying a foundation for further physical, cognitive, social, and emotional development.
2. **Foundations of Health: Health Promotion.** Provide examples of health promotion and disease prevention in early childhood. What difference do you think these efforts can make in the well-being of children, their families, and communities?

3. **Capacity of Health: Caregivers, Community, and Child Safety.** Explain how poor adult health literacy is associated with poor health outcomes for children at home, in early child-care settings, and at school.
4. **Common Disruptions in Health.** Asthma management in children is presented in the text as an example of how developmental systems connect. Describe those systems and how they should work together. What might the consequences be for children with asthma if these systems are not working well together?
5. **Cultural Perspectives.** There is great variation in health beliefs across cultures. In the developed first world countries, people look for empirical evidence to support decisions about prevention and treatment of illnesses. In other countries, traditional practices take precedence. In many countries, western and folk medicine exist together. What do you think the effect on a child might be when her family's traditional cultural beliefs about health are not compatible with treatments recommended by a local American clinic?

# REAL Development

## Physical Development and Health in Early Childhood

In this module, you will observe preschoolers' physical development, including height, weight, and motor development.

In the first activity, you are the new director of Pleasantville Preschool, where Adeline attends school. One of your first initiatives concerns nutrition. Using the charts provided by the CDC, you will compare the body mass index of children in your school with a nationally representative sample made up of children of all ages and racial groups.

In the second activity, you are an assistant teacher at Pleasantville Preschool. One of your responsibilities is to evaluate your students' readiness to enter kindergarten. As you know, children undergo a number of changes during the preschool years related to motor development. Your task is to determine whether your students are developing at normal rates. You have designed a series of activities to help you identify students' fine and gross motor skills, and you will assess their development based on these activities.

©*John Wiley & Sons, Inc.*

**WileyPLUS** Go to WileyPLUS to complete the *Real Development* activity.

03.01

# Chapter 9

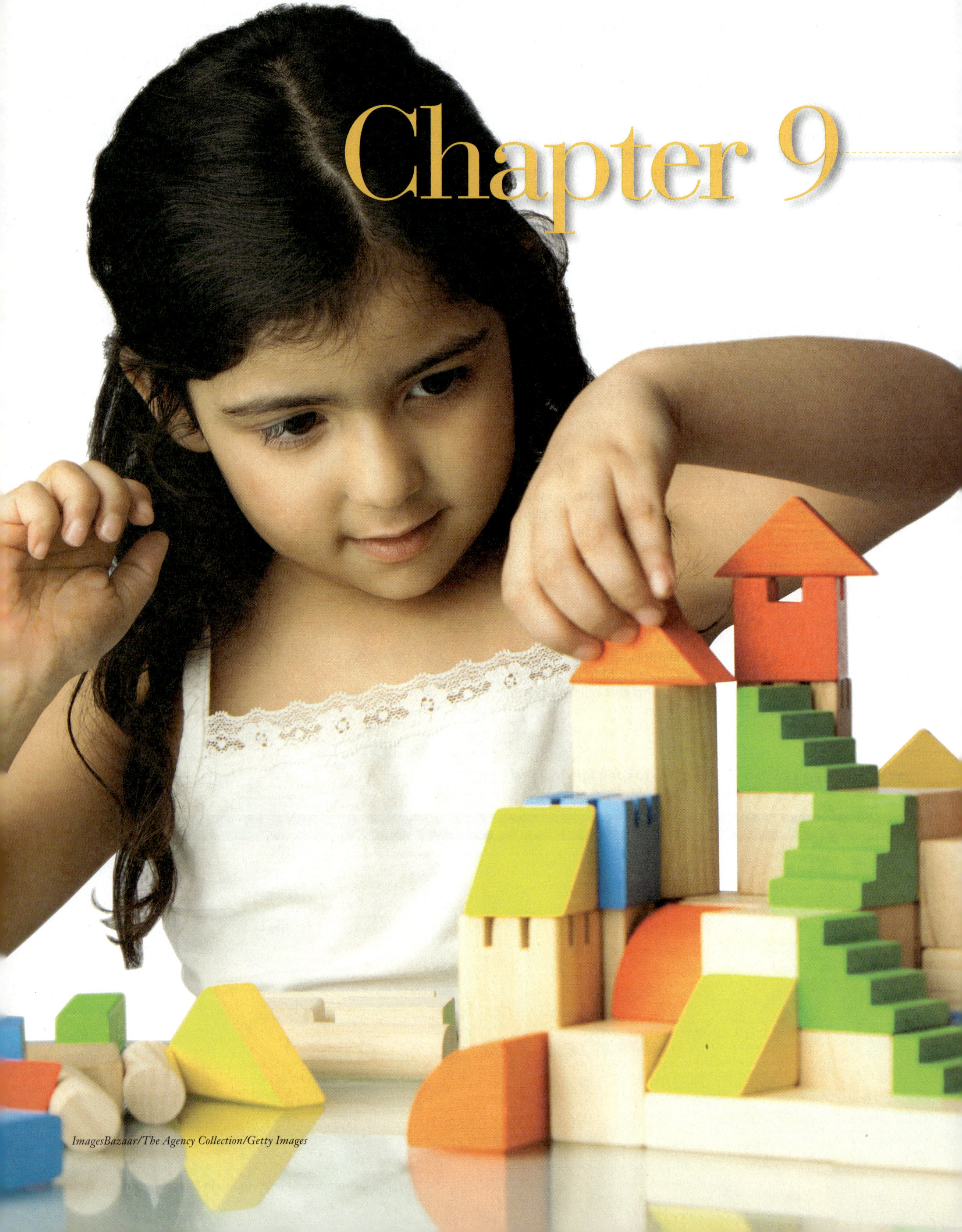

*ImagesBazaar/The Agency Collection/Getty Images*

# Cognitive Development in Early Childhood

## CHAPTER OUTLINE



## MAKING A *difference*

### The Harlem Children's Zone

Geoffrey Canada became an activist for children because of his own experiences growing up in the South Bronx in New York. He knows firsthand the struggles of children and families living in poverty. His father left the family after his mother had given birth to four sons. His mother often had trouble finding work, and she sometimes lacked enough money to feed and clothe Geoffrey and his brothers. But he recalls that despite these struggles, his mother took the time to emphasize the importance of getting an education, encouraging her boys to read and taking them to museums. "My mother was famous for finding out when things were free" (Quoted in Tough, 2008, p. 101). His first-grade teacher introduced him to books that told stories through rhymes, and many years later, at a talk he gave at Syracuse University, Geoffrey emphasized that "poetry saved my life" (Stevens, 2004). As early as age 9, he decided he wanted to help children like himself who live in the inner city.

Now a public advocate, Geoffrey Canada has established the Harlem Children's Zone, a 60-block area that offers a range of educational, social, medical, and support programs to families, wrapping children in a safety net of supportive programs. Those programs include a preschool program, a family support center, classes for new parents, an after-school program, and a charter school. He reflects that his motivation "is all based on a personal understanding of what these kids go through and what the rest of the world doesn't see" (quoted in Tough, 2008, p. 123).

The Harlem Gems, the preschool program in the Harlem Children's Zone, has elements similar to other preschools in its strong support of children's psychosocial development, but it differs in substantial ways as well. It is a full-day program, has a low teacher–child ratio, and operates 11 months of the year. Although the activities are similar to those in any preschool, including imaginative play, music, and block-building, it differs in its emphasis on language. Because studies indicate that children from the lowest socioeconomic group enter school with little knowledge about letter names and letter–sound associations and a limited range of vocabulary, Canada worked with teachers to develop a preschool program that introduces language skills in all activities, essentially making the classroom a verbal "hothouse." In addition, the staff at the Harlem Children's Zone encourages parents to read to their preschool-aged children every night.

Although the Harlem Children's Zone was developed to support all aspects of children's development, Canada is particularly interested in giving children living in poverty the maximal opportunity for being successful students. He explained, "There's no way that in good conscience we can allow poverty to remain the dividing line between success and failure in this country, where if you're born poor in a community like this, you stay poor. We ought to even that out. We ought to give these kids a chance" (quoted in Tough, 2008, p. 18). Geoffrey Canada's work demonstrates that the experiences provided by parents, peers, schools, and communities in children's early years all contribute to this goal.

Harlem Children's Zone

## [KEY QUESTIONS] *for* READING CHAPTER 9

1. What are the characteristics of children's thinking during the preoperational stage, according to Piaget?
2. In what ways do others assist children in learning, according to Vygotsky?
3. What are examples of executive function displayed in early childhood?
4. What changes occur in children's language development during early childhood?
5. What are some important skills that help prepare children for formal schooling?

**IN THIS CHAPTER,** we discuss children's cognitive growth during the early childhood years. We begin with two contrasting views of how young children develop cognitively. First, we examine Jean Piaget's perspective. Then we consider the views of Lev Vygotsky. We also examine developments in cognitive processes, especially those related to executive function, such as paying attention. Next we discuss the central aspects of language development during this period. Language development is one of the most important accomplishments of early childhood. These processes serve as a foundation for school readiness skills. Finally, we look at the role of preschool programs, such as the one established by Geoffrey Canada, in influencing children's cognitive development and school readiness. In particular, we examine the role of quality programs in promoting children's cognitive development.

# Piaget's Theory and Preoperational Thought

**[ KEY QUESTION ] 1. What are the characteristics of children's thinking during the preoperational stage, according to Piaget?**

**constructivism** A view that children construct knowledge through interaction with objects and others.

**preoperational** Piaget's second stage of development, generally occurring during ages 3 to 7 years, in which children begin to use symbols but still are not logical.

**animism** The belief that inanimate objects have life-like qualities such as thought, language, and control of action.

Recall from Chapter 1 that Jean Piaget's theory is based on **constructivism**. According to this perspective, children construct knowledge, rather than memorize facts or have knowledge "poured" into them. They create their own view of the world through their experiences with it and through the type of thinking they apply to these experiences. Piaget considered children's thinking during the early childhood years of 3 to 7 to be **preoperational**. Operational thinking is logical thinking. Preoperational thinking is *pre-logical*—, which means not only that it comes before logical thinking but also that it makes logical thinking possible. Although children in this stage cannot use adult-type logic, they have predictable ways of reasoning. By carefully observing children solving various problems during the preschool years, you can begin to understand their reasoning as well as see the limitations in their thinking. Understanding how a young child thinks, and recognizing that such thinking differs a great deal from that of the older child or adult, is central to Piaget's theory.

| **Piaget's Stage Theory** |
|---|
| Sensorimotor |
| Preoperational<br>• Preschoolers begin to use representation, including words and pictures, rather than actions, to understand the world. |
| Concrete operational |
| Formal operational |

## Advances and Limitations in Preoperational Thought

According to Piaget, children are in the preoperational stage of thinking once they have fully accomplished an understanding of object permanence. Recall from Chapter 6 that this accomplishment occurs in the sensorimotor stage. Now, children can begin to think about objects, events, and people when they are not present. One aspect of this thinking involves the use of symbols. Children's use of the symbol systems of their own culture greatly expands during early childhood. This symbolic representation is a necessary step into the world of literacy and mathematics. Despite advances in the use of symbols, children's thinking during this age period is quite different from the logic used by older children and adults. According to Piaget, young children's thinking is limited by certain characteristics. We next discuss three of these characteristics: animism, egocentrism, and centration.

### Animism

As mentioned in Chapter 1, Piaget is known for his in-depth conversations with children. He was less interested in the specific language used by children than in the concepts expressed during such discussions. In one conversation, Piaget listened to a 4-year-old who talked about whether the moon is alive:

> *The moon moves, it moves because it's alive. . . . The clouds go very slowly because they haven't any paws or legs; they stretch out like worms or caterpillars, that's why they go slowly. (Piaget, 1945/1962, p. 251)*

This child has a notion that movement is an attribute of "being alive," but he lacks a scientific concept of why clouds move. Instead, he relates their movement to something he has witnessed—the movement of caterpillars.

We often find that what young children say is charming because of the life-like qualities they attribute to objects. According to Piaget, **animism**—the belief that inanimate objects have life-like qualities—is one characteristic of preoperational thought. During this phase of development, children often consider objects and even natural forces, such as the wind, to be alive (Beran, Ramirez-Serrano, Kuzyk, Fior, & Nugent, 2011). It may not surprise you, then, that many authors pick up on the theme of animism and use it in books for young children. (Think, for example, about "the little engine that could.") Children's own storytelling can be full of animism as well. For example, here is a story told by a 4-year-old:

> *Once there was a real camera and it took pictures whenever they wanted. One night it went to bed and snored. They [the children] said, "Get to sleep!" . . . They played some records in the morning and the camera danced around. . . ." (quoted in Pitcher & Prelinger, 1963, p. 84)*

*Opus/a.collectionRF/Getty Images, Inc.*

Young children often attribute lifelike qualities to inanimate objects, like clouds. Piaget called this animism and considered it a key characteristic of preoperational thought.

An adult reading a picture book to a group of children will turn the book so that the children can see the pictures. This shows that the adult is not egocentric—she does not believe that what she sees is what others see.

## Egocentrism

If you are reading a book to a group of young children, you probably will turn the book toward the children so they can see the pictures. You do this because you know that just because you can see the pictures does not mean that the children can see them. This kind of thinking indicates that you are not egocentric. **Egocentrism** is the belief that others experience the world the same way you do. This belief is another quality of preoperational thought. To be *egocentric* is not the same as to be *egotistical*, which means thinking only about oneself. Instead, egocentric thinking implies that young children think that what they see is what others see and that what they feel is what others feel. They assume that if they can see the pictures in a book, others can as well.

Piaget had an interesting way of studying egocentric thinking in young children using the "three mountains task." In this task, the young child is shown a model display of three mountains on a table. A doll sits on the opposite side of the display, as shown in Figure 9.1. The child is then shown a series of drawings and is asked to choose the one that shows what she is looking at. Most children have little difficulty doing this. The child is then asked to choose the drawing that illustrates what the doll is looking at. Many children will again choose the drawing that they themselves are looking at. According to Piaget, this shows how young children consider what they see to be what others see (Flavell, Everett, Croft, & Flavell, 1981). We discuss how young children understand the mind of others (that is, what others know and think) in Chapter 10 when we examine children's theory of mind.

Egocentrism is also evident, according to Piaget, in children's **egocentric speech**, which is self-talk that is said aloud. Sometimes children say words like *rhinoceros* aloud simply because they enjoy the sounds produced. Other times, they talk as if they were thinking aloud. For example, if you watch a young child building with a construction toy, you might hear her say, "The green piece goes here, the red one goes here . . . what happens if I put the black one here?" The child is asking only herself, not others, the question. Piaget (1923/1926) claimed that such speech dies out as children develop and as they learn that others have a perspective different from their own. Through using speech in interactions with others, and through engaging in disagreements with their peers, children begin to use less egocentric speech. Instead, they use **socialized speech**, which takes into account the perspective of the listener. This transition from egocentric to socialized speech occurs at the end of the preoperational stage, according to Piaget.

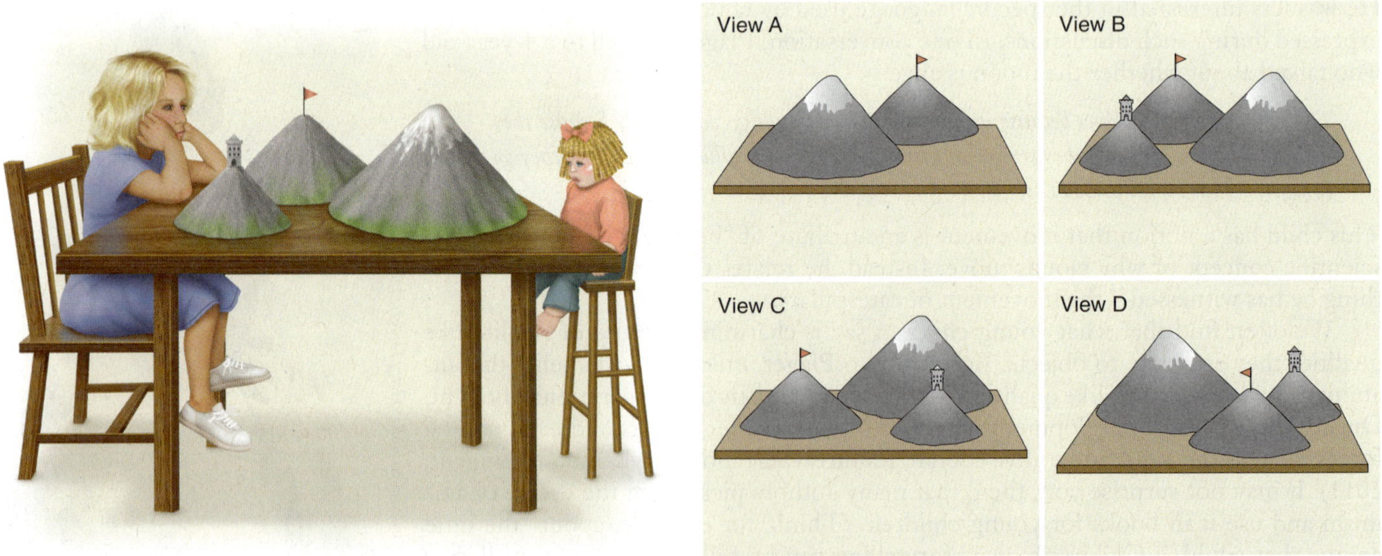


**FIGURE 9.1 The Three Mountains Task** A child and a doll sit on opposite sides of a table. On the table is a model of three mountains. The child is shown four cards, each representing what the mountains look like from a different side of the table, and is asked which view the doll sees. A child in the preoperational stage will choose the view *she* sees (View C), not the view the doll sees (View A). Views B and D are side views.

*Everyday stories*

PRESCHOOLERS AND EGOCENTRIC SPEECH Preschool-aged children often give directions to others in an egocentric way, assuming that others know what they mean. For example, Meiko and Jorge are arguing about which one of them lives closer to their preschool. Meiko explains, "Well, you go out the door and walk by the building where my mother works. Then you cross the street at my favorite place to get ice cream, and my apartment is right there." Jorge retorts, "Well, I live much closer. You just walk out of the school and cross the street, then go through the park where my brother plays basketball, cross the street where my grandmother lives, and then you're at my building." As they develop and become less egocentric, Meiko and Jorge will get better at taking the perspective of the other when giving directions. Eventually, they will learn to give directions in a way others can follow.

**egocentrism** Piaget's term for the inability to distinguish one's own view from the viewpoints of others.

**egocentric speech** Piaget's term for children's tendency to talk to themselves out loud.

**socialized speech** Piaget's term for children's ability to take into account the perspective of the listener.

## Centration

Another way in which young children's thinking differs from that of older children involves their tendency to focus on only one, rather than several, aspects of a task. We refer to this tendency as **centration**. For example, suppose you show a young child a series of pictures of different-colored shapes—say, a circle, a square, and a triangle—and ask him to group the pictures. The child might choose to focus on the shapes or on the colors, but he will not focus on both simultaneously. Furthermore, he is likely to have difficulty if asked to regroup the items in a different way. Such regrouping requires the child to **decenter**. That is, he will be required not to focus on the original attribute (for example, shape or color) alone.

Michael Newman/PhotoEdit

According to Piaget, children in the preoperational stage of development have difficulty reasoning through the transformation that occurs when a liquid is poured into a different shaped jar. This young girl focuses only on her perception that the taller glass has more fluid because the water level appears higher.

Young children's tendency toward centration is quite apparent when they are given a series of tasks about **conservation**. In conservation tasks, children are asked about a core component, such as number or mass, and whether it changes when the appearance of the object is changed through a simple transformation. Tasks used to understand children's thinking about the core components of liquid volume, numerical quantity, length, and mass are shown in Figure 9.2.

In each of these tasks, an adult first determines whether the child views two sets of objects as identical. Then the adult creates a transformation and asks the child if the two groups are still identical in relation to the core component. Let us consider an example. Say a child is shown two identical jars of water. Once he agrees that both jars contain the same amount of water, the experimenter pours the water from one jar into a taller and narrower one. The experimenter then asks the child if the two jars still have the same amount of water or if one jar now has more water in it. You might be surprised to find that young children will generally claim the taller and narrower jar has more water, because the water level appears higher. (Sometimes a child will claim that the wider, fatter jar has more water because the jar is wider.)

What explains this response? According to Piaget, young children have difficulty reasoning through the transformation that occurs when the water is poured into a different jar. Such reasoning would require the child to think something like this: "Nothing has been added or taken away, so although it now looks like there is more water in one jar, there really isn't." But this kind of reasoning would require the child to consider more than one attribute at the same time. A child at the preoperational stage is not able to do that. The child instead uses preoperational thinking, focusing only on his perception of the height of the jar and not taking the width into consideration at the same time.

We should note that young children differ in the age at which they begin to understand conservation (Zhang, Chen, & Fang, 2011). In addition, they do not understand all aspects of conservation at the same time. For example, a child may understand conservation of number before conservation of liquid volume. Piaget developed the construct of **horizontal décalage** to explain that children develop conservation of some aspects of objects sooner than they do others.

Young children's difficulty in decentering appears in other types of tasks as well. One such type is the **class inclusion** task, which requires understanding that a superordinate class of objects contains subordinate classes. For example, you could easily organize your books (a superordinate classification) into fiction and nonfiction books (subordinate

**centration** The focusing of attention on one characteristic of an object or task to the exclusion of others.

**decenter** The ability to focus on several aspects of an object or problem and relate them.

**conservation** A recognition that the core component of a substance remains the same (that is, is conserved) despite transformations in the appearance of the substance.

**horizontal décalage** A term used by Piaget to describe children's tendency to understand certain types of conservation before other types.

**class inclusion** A description of objects or terms in which a smaller set can be conceptually grouped within a larger set.

| | Number | Volume | Length | Mass |
|---|---|---|---|---|
| **Initial equality** | | | | |
| **Transformation** | | | | |
| **Final state** | | | | |
| **Conservation question** | Do the two rows have the same number of chips, or does one row have more chips than the other? | Do the two glasses have the same amount of water, or does one glass have more water than the other? | Are the two sticks just as long as each other, or is one stick longer than the other? | Do the two pieces have the same amount of clay, or does one piece have more than the other? |
| **Typical answer from preoperational child** | The longer row has more chips. | The taller glass has more water. | The stick that was moved to the left is longer. | The flattened piece has more clay. |

SOURCE: Harwood, R., Miller, S.A., & Vasta, R. (2008). *Child psychology: Development in a changing society* (5th ed.). Hoboken, NJ: Wiley, p. 247, Figure 7.5. This material is reproduced with permission of John Wiley & Sons, Inc.

**FIGURE 9.2 Piaget's Conservation Tasks** Piaget used a number of tasks, including the ones shown here, to test children's ability to judge whether certain characteristics of an object, such as its mass, change when the appearance of the object is changed through a simple transformation.

classifications) and then place your textbooks into the nonfiction category. Furthermore, you would have no difficulty in comparing these groupings. Young children can separate objects into categories. They do, however, have difficulty with comparisons that require them to understand that a subordinate class cannot be larger than the superordinate class that contains it (Borst, Poirel, Pineau, Cassotti, & Houde, 2012).

For example, suppose we ask a child to separate her stuffed animals into groups—say, teddy bears and dogs—and suppose she has many more teddy bears than dogs. If we ask this child whether she has more teddy bears or more stuffed animals, she will likely claim that she has more teddy bears (see Figure 9.3). She is unable to see the subordinate group (teddy bears) as a part of the superordinate group (stuffed animals). Instead, she focuses on which of two subordinate groups is larger. This tendency to focus on one attribute (subordinate groups) to the exclusion of another (superordinate class) again illustrates how centration limits the thinking of young children.

## what if...?

Suppose you are visiting some relatives who have two young children, ages 3 and 4. Over lunch, you hear the children begin to argue about who has more milk. You notice that the glasses are different shapes—one is tall and thin, one is short and squat. Miki says his glass has more milk because it is taller than Slater's glass. Slater says his glass has more milk because it is wider than Miki's glass. The argument gets louder. Finally, they turn to you and ask for your opinion about which of them is right. Given your knowledge of Piagetian theory on children's understanding of conservation, what are some ways you could help them resolve their argument?

FIGURE 9.3 **A Class Inclusion Problem** When asked to separate her stuffed animals into two groups, dogs and teddy bears, and then asked if there are more teddy bears or more stuffed animals, a child in the preoperational stage will say "more teddy bears." She is comparing the two subclasses of stuffed animals with each other rather than comparing the subclass of teddy bears with the larger, superordinate class of stuffed animals.

## Criticisms of Piaget's Theory

Many researchers have conducted studies that support Piaget's claims about the limitations of preoperational thinking (Houde et al., 2011). Others, though, have raised questions about the validity of Piaget's theory (Kesselring & Muller, 2011). Many of those questions concern whether children actually go through stages in their thinking (for example, Phillips & Kelly, 1975). Other questions focus on whether Piaget viewed children as learning primarily in isolation, thereby neglecting the role of social interactions in cognitive development (Matusov & Hayes, 2000).

Much critical work suggests that Piaget underestimated young children's thought processes. Some studies have shown that if we change the way that conservation tasks are presented, children can grasp the concept of conservation at a younger age than that proposed by Piaget. This has been illustrated in particular with conservation of number tasks (refer back to Figure 9.2). For example, young children sometimes realize that rows have the same number of objects despite a transformation if the number of objects is small (Gelman, 1972). In addition, if children think a transformation is accidental, rather than intentionally created by an adult, they sometimes reason that the two rows have the same number of objects (McGarrigle & Donaldson, 1974). Finally, Siegler (1995) studied 5-year-olds who were not able to conserve number. He found that if he gave children his reason for selecting the correct response after a transformation, they were then able to reason through the transformation themselves. This study indicates that young children can learn from reasoning supplied by others. Most studies, however, indicate that generally children cannot spontaneously grasp conservation before the age of 5 years (Halford & Andrews, 2006; Houde et al., 2011).

## Implications of Piaget's Theory for Preschool Classrooms

**P**ractice

Piaget's emphasis on children's construction of knowledge has many implications for educational settings. You can see from the following suggestions that this orientation often involves providing young children with opportunities to learn by engaging in activities.

1. Children learn best by being engaged in an activity, not by simply being told information or being asked to memorize information. For example, encourage children to discover what happens when they blend primary colors in their painting rather than telling them that "blue and yellow make green."
2. Children need many opportunities to explore objects and their properties. For example, provide balls of different sizes and made of different materials during play outside so children can see which bounce higher and which can be thrown farther.
3. Children's reasoning is best explored through questions like "I wonder why" or "I wonder what would happen if . . ." rather than statements of fact. For example,

instead of telling children that a square can be cut into two triangles, you could say, "I wonder if there's any way two triangle blocks could make a square."

4. Children can be encouraged to be less egocentric by having the opportunity to state their own viewpoint but also by listening to the views of others. They benefit from challenges that allow a variety of viewpoints to be expressed with no obvious right answer. For example, when reading a book to children you might ask them about what different characters in the story might be thinking.

✓CHECK YOUR PROGRESS

1. According to Piaget, what are three limitations to children's thinking in the preoperational stage?
2. Give an example of how children's egocentrism might affect their communication with other children or adults.
3. Suppose you hear a 3-year-old girl say "It's a rose, it's not a flower." In what way would her thinking be typical of children in the preoperational stage?

# Vygotsky's Sociocultural Theory

**[ KEY QUESTION ] 2.** In what ways do others assist children in learning, according to Vygotsky?

Like Piaget, Vygotsky believed that children *construct* knowledge. Unlike Piaget, however, Vygotsky emphasized the **co-construction** of knowledge. That is, he believed that children construct knowledge with the assistance of others. In this view, children learn first at the social level and then gradually internalize that learning. Because of the social importance of language, Vygotsky focused on how children develop language and how language skills promote children's dialogues with others. Through such interaction, Vygotsky maintained, children advance in their cognitive development. The social emphasis of Vygotsky's view also highlights the sociocultural context in which children are developing. In both of these ways—its focus on language and its concerns with the sociocultural context—Vygotsky's theory differs from that of Piaget.

## Features of Vygotsky's Theory

Let us look more closely at how Vygotsky's theory focuses on language and the sociocultural context. We first consider how children develop inner speech and then explain how children's development is influenced by other people and by their surroundings.

### Children's Inner Speech

Consider how you approach a task like following a set of directions to put together a piece of furniture, like a bookcase. It's quite possible that you talk to yourself about the steps you need to go through. ("Find the piece labeled A, and then put it at right angles to the piece labeled B.") Such self-talk is common among both adults and children. According to Vygotsky, it emerges from children's **inner speech**—internal speech used to guide behavior.

You may recall Piaget's claim that such speech (which Piaget termed *egocentric speech*) dies out in favor of socialized speech. In contrast, Vygotsky believed that it serves as a foundation for self-guidance and self-regulation. Almost all studies in which Piaget's and Vygotsky's views on such speech have been contrasted support Vygotsky's perspective (Berk & Harris, 2003), indicating that inner speech does not die out but instead becomes internal. Young children who use such speech to guide them during challenging activities tend to be more attentive and show better performance than those who do not (Al-Namlah, Fernyhough, & Meins, 2006). In one study, researchers gave children a challenging task in which they had to draw lines between printed letters and numbers

**co-construction** A term used to describe Vygotsky's view that children construct knowledge using the assistance of others.

**inner speech** Vygotsky's term for the self-directed speech used when trying to guide behavior.

on a page (Winsler & Naglieri, 2003). They found that young children who used self-talk while completing this task performed better on academic achievement tests than those who did not use it. In examining whether self-talk differs for different age groups, they found that children in the 5- to 8-year-old age group are more likely than older children to use overt (out-loud) self-talk when trying to solve a challenging task, whereas older children more often report using internalized self-talk.

*Everyday stories*

DRAWING A STAR WITH SELF-TALK Isabella is working on drawing a star for a picture she is making of the night sky. Her friend has shown her a way of making a five-pointed star, and she is trying to remember and follow the directions the friend gave her. As she draws the star, she says out loud, "You start here. Then it goes down to here, then up to here, then over to here, then down, then up. And you're done!" Repeating these directions to herself out loud has helped her remember how to draw the star in the way her friend taught her. Eventually she will be able to make this kind of drawing without saying the directions out loud, but she still may say them to herself silently.

## Scaffolding

Children develop not only through the self-regulation provided by inner speech but also through the assistance of teachers and more advanced children. Vygotsky referred to such support as collaboration and direction, now usually termed scaffolding, and considered it especially important. As we described in Chapter 6, *scaffolding* refers to the guidance or support given to a child by a person who is more skilled and who can adjust the guidance offered according to the child's level of performance. The goal in providing scaffolding is to gradually decrease the amount of assistance provided so that eventually the child can succeed independently.

Scaffolding promotes development when it helps the child move to the next level of understanding or accomplishment. Some individuals refer to this as the "one step ahead strategy" (Heckhausen, 1987). Parents often use it unknowingly as they help children learn to perform tasks like zipping a zipper. Of course, the challenge for the helper is to determine what type of scaffolding might best help the child learn. For example, consider how an adult might scaffold a child learning to ride a two-wheeler, as illustrated in Figure 9.4. The child is first scaffolded by having training wheels on the back of the bike. Once they are removed, an adult will provide the scaffolding by holding on to the back of the bike while the child learns to balance on two wheels. Eventually, the adult lets go of the back of the bike, and the child rides on his own.

**FIGURE 9.4 An Example of Scaffolding** At first, this little boy can ride a two-wheel bicycle only if it has training wheels. But with help—scaffolding—from an adult, he can learn to balance the bicycle without training wheels. Finally, he can ride the two-wheeler on his own. He no longer needs scaffolding to support him as he rides.

Learning through scaffolding will occur only if the assistance offered is not so far above the child's current level that the child cannot understand or benefit from it. According to Vygotsky, teachers, parents, and others must operate within the child's *zone of proximal development* (ZPD) if they are to help the child learn. As you may recall from Chapter 1, Vygotsky (1978) defined the ZPD as "the distance between the actual developmental level as determined by independent problem solving and the level of potential development as determined through problem solving under adult guidance or in collaboration with more capable peers" (p. 86). The ZPD comprises the learning goals that are too difficult for the child to undertake successfully alone but that the child can reach through the scaffolding of another (Chaiklin, 2003).

what if...?

Suppose you are helping out in a kindergarten classroom, and you notice that Jesse has started to put together a complex, 100-piece jigsaw puzzle. You can see Jesse getting more and more frustrated by the puzzle. What are some ways you could help Jesse with the puzzle without doing it for him? Consider how you might find out what parts of the puzzle he could do on his own and what parts are too complex for him to accomplish even with your help.

Larry Kolvoord/The Image Works

Vygotsky emphasized that children learn the cultural tools of their society through interactions with others. This Mayan girl will learn all the steps in the weaving process by watching, and eventually helping, her mother.

### Cultural and Social Contexts of Development

Vygotsky also stressed the importance of the child's cultural and social context (Bottcher & Dammeyer, 2012). He emphasized that children learn the cultural tools of their society through their interactions with others. These tools may vary from one culture to another. In most industrialized nations, the tools involve learning to read, write, and manipulate numbers. Vygotsky himself emphasized the importance of learning school-based skills. These skills were emphasized in the Russian culture in which he lived, just as they are in the United States today. Different tools may be emphasized by different cultural groups, however. For example, Rogoff (2003) examined how Mayan girls in Guatemala learned to become weavers. She described the guidance provided by the girls' mothers and older sisters as they helped the girls learn each step of the weaving process. (For more about Barbara Rogoff, see this chapter's **Focus On** feature.)

Children learn the tools of their culture, whatever these tools may be, through *guided participation* in the everyday activities of their group. As you may recall from Chapter 6, guided participation is a process by which children actively acquire new skills and problem-solving capabilities through their participation in meaningful activities alongside more experienced individuals. Consider how guided participation occurs when Eduardo takes his 5-year-old daughter, Nina, grocery shopping. Nina sees her father take out a shopping list. He reads the list to her, and together they decide which items can be found in which aisles. He may have her check off the items as they put them into the cart. This simple task involves many steps, including planning, reading, organizing, and checking, to make sure all items have been found. Nina is likely to learn a great deal about grocery shopping from this activity, provided that she is included in its various steps. This example shows that even when parents or others are not intending to formally teach children, but rather are including children in their daily tasks, children learn through this participation, especially when guidance is provided.

## Criticisms of Vygotsky's Theory

Developmental psychologists have generally embraced Vygotsky's theory. It provides a broad view of development by considering the importance of the social and cultural context in which a child lives. In addition, unlike Piaget's theory, it emphasizes the role of teachers, other adults, and more skilled children in helping a child learn new skills

## Focus On: Barbara Rogoff

*In referring to cultural processes I want to draw attention to the configurations of routine ways of doing things in any community's approach to living. I focus on people's participation in their communities' cultural practices and traditions, rather than equating culture with the nationality or ethnicity of individuals. (Rogoff, 2003, p. 3)*

Barbara Rogoff contributes to our understanding of child development by recognizing the importance of everyday routines and showing us how children's participation in those activities is shaped by culture. Inspired by the work of Lev Vygtosky, she has studied how children are guided by older children and adults in the communities in which they live. For example, young girls in a Mayan community in Guatemala often learn from mothers and older sisters how to help with the various tasks involved in weaving. In the United States, children might learn from a parent or older sister or brother how to use a computer program. Rogoff emphasizes that children learn both the skills and the value systems of a culture through such participation.

Rose Cartwright

Rogoff's work draws on examples from many cultural groups and shows how we make assumptions about what is "normal" from experiences within our culture. For example, she describes how views of praising a child differ in different cultural groups. We may think that praising a child by saying "good job" or "good for you" is a normal part of good parenting. In some cultures, however, such praise is avoided because it is seen as making children conceited and arousing dangerous envy. As Rogoff says, "Cultural practices surround all of us and often involve subtle, tacit, taken-for-granted events and ways of doing things that require open ears, eyes, and minds to notice and understand" (Rogoff, 2003, p. 11). Barbara Rogoff has helped many psychologists open their minds to such cultural practices.

and processes (Göbel, Shaki, & Fischer, 2011; Gredler, 2010; Scrimsher & Tudge, 2003). Because it is a broad theory, however, it is somewhat vague about how children actually develop concepts.

Despite the importance attributed to instruction from teachers and more skilled peers, for example, the nature of how instruction actually advances children's development has not been fully described (Eun, Knotek, & Heining-Boynton, 2008). In a study on the role of collaboration in problem-solving activity, researchers gave 5-year-old children easy and difficult puzzles to be solved either alone or in pairs (Arterberry, Cain, & Chopko, 2007). Only half of the children were told that their performance would be evaluated. The children who worked in pairs had more success in completing the puzzles than children working alone, but only when the puzzles were easy and when they thought their performance was being evaluated. Clearly, the conditions under which collaborative activity benefits young children's cognitive development need to be further investigated.

Creasource/©Corbis

Grocery shopping involves many steps, including planning, reading, organizing, and checking to make sure all items have been found. Children can learn a great deal about grocery shopping when they are included in all these various steps.

## Implications of Vygotsky's Theory for Preschool Classrooms

**Practice**

Vygotsky emphasized the role of teachers and more-skilled individuals in helping a child learn. In keeping with this co-constructivist view, many implications of Vygotsky's theory for preschool settings focus on the role of the teacher or provider.

1. Consider the child's ZPD in determining the types of support that will lead the child to the next step in learning. What can the child do on her own, and what is just one step beyond her capabilities? For example, if a child is having difficulty counting a set of 10 objects, reduce the number of objects and see how many she can count on her own. Then add one or two more objects at a time to see just how many objects she can count on her own and how many she can count with your help.
2. Provide scaffolding to children as they attempt to master tasks. The type of scaffolding might differ for each child or each small group of children. For example,

if a child is having difficulty writing a letter (like the letter *S*), you might draw dots on the page for him to connect in writing the letter.

3. **Encourage more skilled children to help those who are less skilled.** The more skilled children are likely to need suggestions about how to help their peers rather than complete tasks for them. For example, if you see that a child is having difficulty zippering his jacket, you can ask another child to show him how to first pull the zipper down to the bottom and then put the two sides together.
4. **Encourage children to use inner speech to talk through difficult tasks.** You can model how such self-talk might be helpful. For example, in helping a child with a puzzle, you could say, "This piece goes here" or "If I turn this piece, it might fit."

### CHECK YOUR PROGRESS

1. Why is Vygotsky considered a co-constructivist?
2. What is the role of inner speech according to Vygotsky?
3. How does scaffolding differ from simply giving directions to a child?
4. What is meant by considering a child's zone of proximal development?

## Information Processing Theory

**[ KEY QUESTION ] 3.** What are examples of executive function displayed in early childhood?

As you may recall from Chapter 1, the information processing theory of cognitive development uses the computer as a metaphor for the various functions required in learning. Information moves from being perceived to being stored and eventually to being retrieved. In understanding how these processes operate, we first need to consider how information flows through the processes, as shown in Figure 9.5.

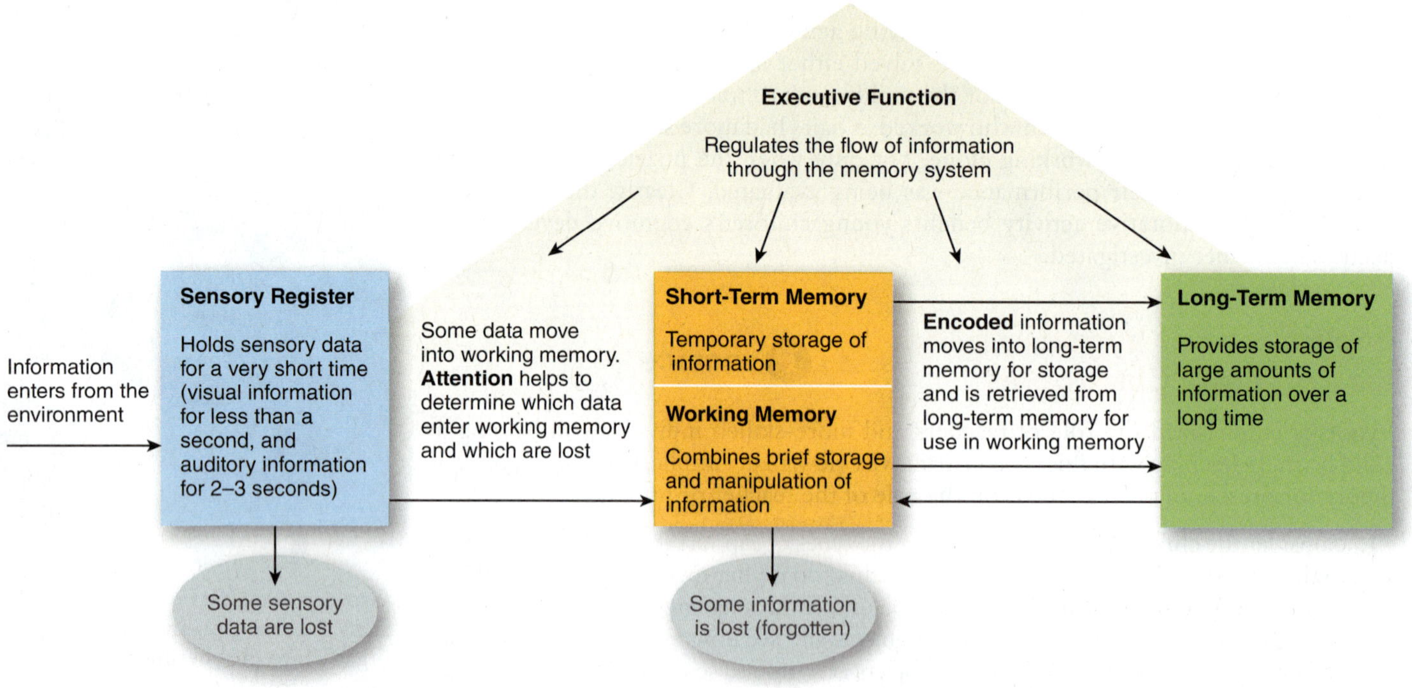


**FIGURE 9.5 The Information Processing Model** Information flows from the sensory register, to short-term and working memory, to long-term memory. The information flow is regulated by the executive function, which plays a supervisory role.

| | | | |
|---|---|---|---|
| K | Z | R | A |
| Q | B | T | P |
| S | G | N | Y |

SOURCE: from Huffman, K. *Psychology in action* (9th ed.). Hoboken, NJ: Wiley, p. 252, Figure 7.3. This material is reproduced with the permission of John Wiley & Sons, Inc.

FIGURE 9.6 **A Test of Visual Memory** Researchers use an array of letters such as this one to test visual memory. When the letters are flashed very briefly, for 1/20 of a second, most people can remember only four or five of the letters.

According to the information processing model, information from the environment enters the *sensory register*, which holds information only briefly. It holds visual information for less than a second and holds auditory information a little longer, for 2 to 3 seconds. Consider an early experiment on visual sensory memory (Sperling, 1960). The experimenter asked participants to look at a screen while he flashed an arrangement of 12 letters, such as the ones in Figure 9.6, for a brief 1/20 second. Most people could recall only four or five of the letters later.

The information that enters the sensory register, such as the letters in the experiment just described, will not stay with you unless you *encode* it. That means first paying attention to the information and then forming an internal representation of it. When you pay attention, you direct your attention toward particular information and then focus on it. For example, suppose you walk into a store selling many flavors of ice cream. You look at the list and choose the flavor you want. Suppose after leaving the store you were asked to name all of the flavors. You could probably remember a few of the flavors, especially the ones you were considering ordering. If you had been told in advance, however, that you would get free ice cream for a year if you remembered all the flavors, you would probably pay attention to the entire list and figure out a way to encode it.

The encoding of information occurs in your *working memory*. This is a part of the short-term memory system that holds information for a short time while you are working on it. As we discuss in a later section, children's working memory is much less efficient than that of adults, but it improves during the early childhood years (Nevo & Breznitz, 2013; Simmering, 2012). Information that is encoded well is stored in *long-term memory*. From there, it can be retrieved and moved back into working memory. Working memory, however, has a limited capacity. Try completing the following problem in your head: 5166 ÷ 63. Were you able to arrive at the correct answer of 82 without writing anything down? You probably learned division tables many years ago and have stored that information in long-term memory. But you need to both retrieve that information and keep in mind the several steps necessary to solve this multistep problem. Because it is difficult to keep all the aspects of the problem in working memory, most people need to write down at least parts of the solution.

Long-term memory can store a wide range of information for a long period of time. The better information is labeled and arranged in long-term memory, the better it can be retrieved. Retrieving information from long-term memory into working memory is an important part of the memory process.

WHEN SYSTEMS CONNECT

## The Role of Executive Function

One of the critical processes in this model of learning involves the supervisory system often referred to as *executive function*. As you saw in Figure 9.5, executive function involves the regulation of the flow of information and forms the critical link to other processes, including attention, working memory, and long-term memory. Because such processes are fundamental to cognitive development according to the information processing theory, we begin with a discussion of executive function.

Susan Woog-Wagner/Photo Researchers

To successfully sort the blocks according to height, this little girl must remember that color doesn't matter.

*Everyday stories*

SORTING—NOT A SIMPLE TASK Three-year-old Ligia is sorting a set of multicolored wooden squares, triangles, and circles by shape. Although to an adult this seems like a simple task, it actually involves many processes. Ligia first has to pay attention to the objects and resist being distracted by other children. In order to make a decision about where each shape will be placed, she needs to keep in mind that shape is the only characteristic that matters. That means she must inhibit, or restrain, other types of sorting categories, such as "large versus small" or "red versus blue." Given the processes involved, you can see why sometimes young children begin by sorting objects one way, such as by shape, and end by sorting them another, such as by color.

Like its business-referencing name, *executive function* refers generally to the idea of management. In child psychology, it refers to the management of cognitive processes such as planning, decision making, and inhibition. As we discussed in Chapter 2, executive function is the capacity to regulate one's thinking and behavior. Such processes are important to children's ability to *self-regulate* their behavior. Generally, executive function is a supervisory system involving goal-directed behaviors that allow a child to override automatic responses when solving novel problems (Garon, Bryson, & Smith, 2008). As you saw in Figure 9.5, executive function relates to several components of the information processing system, including attention, working memory, and long-term memory.

**THE DEVELOPING BRAIN**

## A Growth Spurt in Executive Function

Adele Diamond (2001) proposes that a growth spurt occurs in executive function from ages 3 to 6, making early childhood a critical time for changes in this area of functioning. As mentioned in Chapter 8, much of this growth occurs in the prefrontal cortex, as stronger networks are created between this area of the brain and other regions of the cortex in which language, mathematical, and spatial skills are represented (see Figure 9.7).

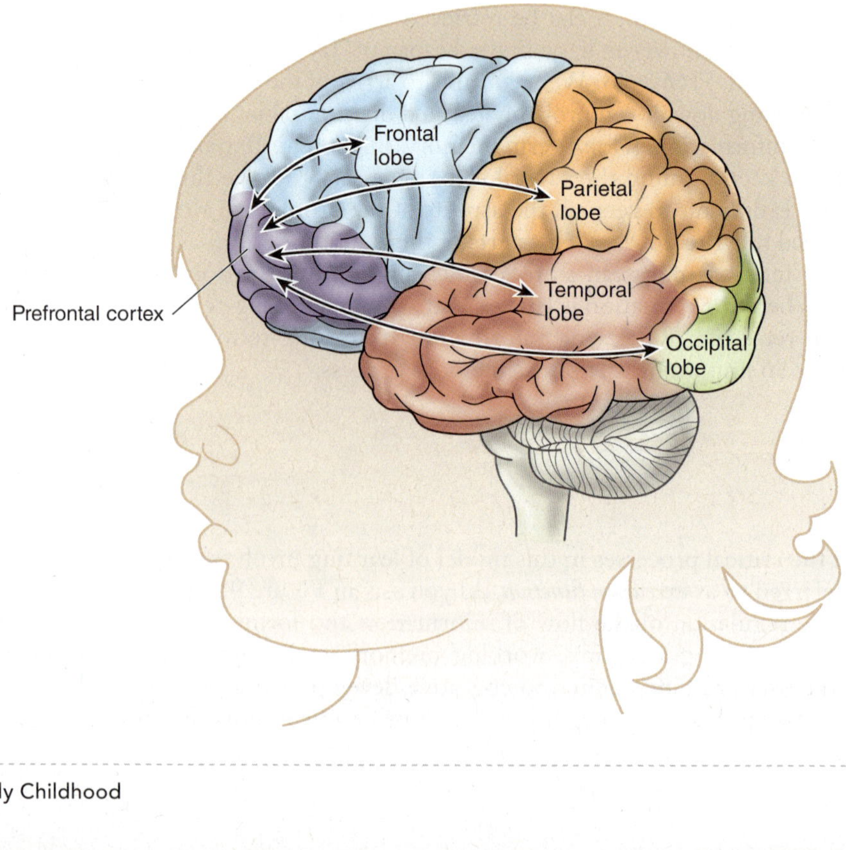


**FIGURE 9.7 The Growing Connections of the Prefrontal Cortex** Networks connect the prefrontal cortex to other brain regions. The growth in connections from the prefrontal cortex (executive function) to the parietal lobe (spatial relations), temporal lobe (audition), and occipital lobe (vision) during early childhood shows us that these pathways are becoming stronger.

Executive function is an umbrella concept that encompasses a complex set of cognitive processes necessary to regulate behavior in novel situations that involve challenge (Cartwright, 2012; Hughes & Graham, 2002). Many researchers divide executive function into two types: "hot" and "cold" (Hongwanishkul, Happaney, Lee, & Zelazo, 2005; Zhang, Liu, & Song, 2010). *"Hot" executive functions* involve self-monitoring and emotion regulation during social and emotional challenges, such as disagreements with peers. These will be discussed in the next chapter. *"Cold" executive functions* involve children's self-monitoring during cognitive challenges, such as trying to complete a jigsaw puzzle or build a bridge out of blocks. Several aspects of "cold" executive functions show important changes during early childhood. Children improve in their ability to focus and shift attention, to purposefully remember, to inhibit responses, and to show cognitive flexibility (Best & Miller, 2010; Miller, Kelly, & Zhou, 2005; Miur et al., 1993; Muller, Kerns, & Konkin, 2012; Wiebe, Sheffield, & Espy, 2012). We next consider each of these aspects of executive function.

## Focusing and Shifting Attention

As discussed in Chapter 6, infants begin to orient their attention during the first year of life. This orientation of attention is critical to the later ability to control the focus of attention, which improves during early childhood. Think of what you need to do to pay attention to this paragraph. You not only have to focus on the text itself, but you also have to ignore competing stimuli, such as incoming text messages. In addition, you need to focus on the core ideas in the paragraph and ignore irrelevant information, such as the position of the paragraph on the page.

During early childhood, children gradually improve in their ability to select their attention (that is, decide what to focus on) and then focus their attention for longer periods of time. One way to test these abilities in young children is with the *continuous performance task*. Children sit in front of a computer screen, and various objects (such as a cat, a dog, a car, and a hat) flash on the screen in random order. The children are asked to press a button only when the target object (for example, the dog) appears on the screen. Because this is a monotonous and repetitive process, it involves a great deal of focused attention. Three-year-olds can only successfully press the button when the target appears about 50% of the time. However, 5-year-olds have success about 80% of the time (Danis, Pêcheux, Lefèvre, Bourdais, & Serres-Ruel, 2008).

*Lisa Passmore*

In a continuous performance task, a child sits in front of a computer screen as various objects (such as a cat, a car, a dog, and a hat) flash past in random order. The child is to press a button only when the target object (for example, the dog) appears on the screen.

Shifting attention is another aspect of attention regulation that improves during early childhood. Being able to shift attention from one task to another becomes increasingly important as children enter preschool settings. For example, a child may become very involved in building a block structure. When it is time for another activity, such as listening to a story, the child needs to stop that activity and shift attention. At around 3 or 4 years of age, focusing attention and shifting attention are often negatively correlated. In other words, children who are good at one are likely to be poor at the other. By the end of the preschool period, though, the two processes are integrated, and children who can focus attention well also can shift attention appropriately (Jones, Rothbart, & Posner, 2003). As you will see in Chapter 12, children's abilities in aspects of attention improve greatly during middle childhood, but the core elements of these processes are laid down during early childhood.

## Working Memory

Recall that **working memory** is the part of the short-term memory system where we keep information that we are currently working on (Baddeley, 2001; Soderqvist et al., 2012). For example, when we solve multidigit math problems, such as 9 × 38, without the use of a calculator, we are using working memory. Simple tasks that require children to repeat numbers or words are often used to test working memory. This testing is meant to determine how much children can hold in working memory and how long they can hold it there. For example, in a *digit recall test*, a researcher might say five numbers to a child and ask the child to repeat them, perhaps after a delay. The

**working memory** The part of the memory system where problems are actively worked on.

researcher might say, "Listen and then I want you to say these numbers in this order: 7, 5, 2, 8, 6." From early childhood through adolescence, children show a steady increase in the number of items they can retain and repeat in such tests. During the early childhood years, however, children have few strategies for helping them to succeed in such tasks. For example, they do not spontaneously rehearse information that is given to them even if they know they will be asked to repeat that information (Gathercole, Pickering, Ambridge, & Wearing, 2004). Children's strategies for remembering information increase during middle childhood, as you will read in Chapter 12.

Another aspect of working memory is the ability to manipulate and update information stored there. One way to assess this ability in young children is through tasks that require them to keep track of what they have selected in order to make a different selection. Consider, for example, the *self-ordered pointing task* (Luciana & Nelson, 1998). In a computer version of this task, children are told that three tokens are hidden on the screen, each behind a different-colored square. The child touches the squares one at a time to open them—that is, to reveal if there is a token behind them. When the child finds a token, she needs to remember the color of the square she chose to avoid making errors by repeatedly choosing the same color. For example, she might say to herself, "I found one token behind the red square, so I shouldn't look behind the red one again." Researchers have found large differences in how 3-year-olds and 5-year-olds perform on this type of task (Luciana & Nelson, 1998), indicating improvements in the ability to update retained information.

## what if...?

You have designed a game to play with preschool-aged children. The game requires them to think of an object beginning first with the letter *A*, then the letter *B*, and so on. Other children are to guess what the object is. When you are playing this game with the children, you notice that several of them keep forgetting what letter was used during the last turn. They will need this information in order to correctly select the next letter. What are various ways you could help them remember where they are in the alphabet when they play this game?

### Response Inhibition

If you have ever watched a 3-year-old receive gifts at a birthday party, you have probably seen how difficult it is for a child that age to wait to open the gifts. Tearing open the gifts right away is the child's natural response, and he has to inhibit that response if asked to wait. **Response inhibition** involves withholding a motor or verbal response that is inappropriate in a given situation (Garon et al., 2008). It takes *effortful control* on the part of the child to inhibit natural responses.

Terry Vine/Blend Images/Getty Images, Inc.

This little girl must be very eager to open her birthday gift, but response inhibition allows her to wait for the appropriate time.

**response inhibition** A process that involves withholding an inappropriate motor or behavioral response.

Researchers have often used *delay of gratification tasks* to assess preschoolers' ability to inhibit responses (Neubauer, Gawrilow, & Hasselhorn, 2012; Steelandt, Thierry, Broihanne, & Dufour, 2012). In one version of this task, children are shown two sets of treats, such as 10 marshmallows and 2 marshmallows. They are then given a choice: they can have all 10 if they wait the full time—say, 8 minutes—or they can have 2 immediately or at any time within the 8-minute period. In one such study, the researchers found that 3-year-olds on average waited only 4½ minutes before deciding to eat the 2 treats. In contrast, most of the 4- and 5-year-olds could wait the full 8 minutes to get the 10 treats (Atance & Jackson, 2009).

The familiar game Simon Says provides a good example of a test of children's ability to both pay attention and inhibit a response. As you may recall, the leader in the game gives directions to children, who are instructed to follow the directions only when they are preceded by the words "Simon says." So, for example, when the leader says "Simon says put your hands on your knees," children are expected to put their hands on their knees. Most preschool-aged children have no difficulty with that part of the game. But suppose the leader says "Put your hands on your ears" and doesn't include "Simon says" with that instruction. Many young children will incorrectly put their hands on their ears and will be ruled "out" of the game. Most of us have made that mistake at some time.

In a more complex task requiring response inhibition, children are asked to say "day" when the examiner shows pictures of the moon in a dark sky and to say "night" when the examiner shows pictures of the sun in a bright sky (Gerstadt, Hong, & Diamond, 1994) (see Figure 9.8). This task involves not only suppressing an automatic response but also keeping a rule in mind each time to make the correct response. Four-year-olds tend to make many errors on this task (Montgomery, Anderson, & Uhl, 2008). By the end of the early childhood period, though, most children can perform the task successfully (Carlson, 2005; Pasalich, Livesey, & Livesey, 2010; Organisation for Economic Co-operation and Development, 2006). Being able to use effortful control to suppress an automatic response and to follow directions are fundamental to children's ability to learn in a classroom setting (Valiente, Swanson, & Lemery-Chalfant, 2012).

Will Hart/PhotoEdit

In the game "Simon Says," players follow the leader's command only when it is preceded by the words "Simon says." The game provides a good test of children's ability to both pay attention and inhibit a response.

## Cognitive Flexibility

One aspect of cognitive flexibility is the ability to *shift sets*. A child needs to shift sets when she is asked first to follow one set of rules and then to follow a different set of rules in the same situation. To follow the second set of rules, she must keep those rules in mind while suppressing the previous rules. The type of task most frequently used to assess children's ability to shift sets is the *dimensional card sort*. In this task a child might be given a deck of cards that have different shapes and colors (a red triangle and a red square, a blue triangle and a blue square, etc.). She is asked to sort the cards based on one dimension, such as color. After completing this sort, she is asked to sort the same deck of cards based on the shape dimension. Most 3-year-olds can sort according to the first set of rules, regardless of whether the first rule is color or shape. But they make many errors when the rules shift. After age 4, most children can successfully sort the cards after the rule shift (Garon et al., 2008).

**FIGURE 9.8 An Illustration of the Day–Night Task** Children are asked to say "day" when they see pictures of the moon and "night" when they see pictures of the sun. Their first response, though, would be to say "day" when they see the sun and "night" when they see the moon. To succeed, children must suppress this automatic response and remember the rule about what to say.

**neo-Piagetian** A term given to developmental psychologists who elaborate on Piaget's theory by giving attention to additional aspects of cognition-like memory.

Very young children have difficulty disengaging from the first rule to follow the second one. They also find it difficult to keep in mind the "if–then" component of having two different rules to follow (Zelazo & Frye, 1998). That is, the need to say to themselves, "If I'm following the first rule, then I have to do this, but if I'm following the second rule, then I have to do that." If you think about some of the skills children need in learning to read, write, and manipulate numbers, you can see why it is important that children be able to accomplish the if–then sequence of thinking. For example, when learning to read or write in English, children need to apply if–then rules such as "If the letter *y* is at the beginning of a word, then it sounds like 'yuh.' If it is at the end of a word, then it sounds like 'ee.'" The ability to shift sets and apply the appropriate rules to each set becomes very important in learning school-related skills.

## Combining Theories: Neo-Piagetian Approaches

Some developmental psychologists, like Robbie Case, have proposed a view of young children's cognitive development that combines information processing and Piagetian approaches (Case, 1991). This view, termed **neo-Piagetian** theory, elaborates on Piaget's theory but also incorporates aspects of information processing theory by focusing on children's attention, memory, and strategy use. Case considered the stage-like quality of children's thinking proposed by Piaget to be valid. He believed, in addition, that children move from one stage to another because of two attributes: brain maturation and increases in efficient use of working memory. For example, consider how experience with counting objects might relate to conservation of number. Children learning to count objects have to remember that the number 3 follows the number 2 and so on. When this task is new to the young child, it takes up a great deal of working memory. With experience, counting eventually becomes automatic, and children do not need to use so much working memory to count a small number of objects. They can then concentrate on other aspects of the task, like paying attention to the total number regardless of the way objects are grouped. Recall that this is important for understanding conservation of number. In this way, the neo-Piagetians blend Piaget's theory about how children's thinking differs at different stages of development with information processing theory about how children's thinking changes as a result of experience and brain development.

## Criticisms of Information Processing Theory

Information processing theory has many advantages. It is useful in understanding how children learn. It is also useful in breaking down cognitive tasks into their components. It is especially valuable in considering how attention, working memory, inhibition, and cognitive flexibility differ between older and younger children or less-skilled and more-skilled learners. Criticisms of information processing theory are based on its core metaphor, which is the computer, and on its emphasis on how children process information rather than on how children make sense of the world (Bruner, 1990). Information processing theory assumes that cognitive development is linear and logical. In doing so, it overlooks the role of other important processes, such as creativity and motivation, in cognitive development.

## Implications of Information Processing Theory for Preschool Classrooms

Practice

Because of its focus on children's learning, information processing theory has many implications for the preschool classroom. As discussed in the accompanying *Research Insights* feature, a series of strategies have been developed to help children learn to plan their activities and develop critical aspects of executive function. Some examples of ways that preschool teachers could use information processing theory to structure children's activities include:

## Research Insights: Can We Teach Executive Function Skills to Young Children?

A preschool curriculum, *Tools of the Mind*, has been developed to teach children executive function skills (Bodrova & Leong, 1996). This curriculum was inspired by Vygotsky's emphasis on children's self-regulation. From an information processing perspective, it has value in helping us to understand how children can improve in their skills in executive function. The curriculum has 40 activities to help children improve their self-regulation. Many of these activities are incorporated into dramatic play. For example, rather than just giving children props and letting them play, teachers work with the children in planning and selecting the play scenarios and considering the next steps in the dramatic play sequence. By planning ahead, children learn cognitive flexibility as they consider various ways in which a scene could be played. Some of the activities are aimed at helping children learn to inhibit their behavior. For example, children are given markers and paper and instructed to draw while music is playing but to stop drawing as soon as the music stops.

Felicia Martinez PhotoEdit

Evaluators of this program have compared groups of children randomly assigned to either the *Tools* curriculum or a traditional early childhood program. Children in the *Tools* program have shown higher levels of executive function skills (Barnett et al., 2008; Diamond, Barnett, Thomas, & Munro, 2007). These research findings demonstrate that it is possible to help young children improve their skills in executive function.

1. Limit distractions so children can attend to various tasks and activities.
2. Reduce the load on working memory by teaching children ways to symbolize information using pictures, letters, and numbers.
3. Strengthen self-regulation by encouraging children to talk about what they are doing as they work on a difficult task.
4. Encourage children's ability to inhibit their first responses to a situation through providing a variety of games, like Simon Says, that give children experience with response inhibition.
5. Provide activities, such as games that involve shifting sets, that stimulate cognitive flexibility.

### CHECK YOUR PROGRESS

1. Describe the various aspects of executive function.
2. How does working memory differ from long-term memory?
3. Explain why response inhibition is important.
4. Give an example of a way children might show cognitive flexibility.
5. In what way does neo-Piagetian theory blend Piaget's theory and information processing theory?

**syntax** The combination of words and phrases into meaningful sentences.

**semantics** The meaning of sentences or phrases within sentences.

**pragmatics** The use of appropriate rules of conversation.

**fast mapping** A process in which children learn a new word rapidly by forming a quick guess about its meaning.

# Language Development

**[ KEY QUESTION ] 4. What changes occur in children's language development during early childhood?**

Words are not objects, ideas, actions, or feelings—they are symbols that represent those things. Because learning language involves learning a symbol system, children's language development is an important aspect of their cognitive development. In Chapter 6, we discussed the development of language during the infant and toddler period. Here, we discuss language development as part of the expanding symbol system of children ages 2 to 7. For a summary of language development in early childhood, see Table 9.1.

Language is defined by a set of rules, especially relating to use of syntax, semantics, and pragmatics.

- **Syntax** refers to the way words are combined to form understandable phrases or sentences (Tager-Flusberg & Zukowski, 2009). For example, in English, adjectives generally precede nouns (such as "black car"). If someone said to you, "See the car black," you might be able to figure out what that person meant, but you also would recognize that the sentence followed a pattern not typically found in English.
- **Semantics** refers to the meaning of sentences or phrases within sentences (Cruse, 2004). Sentences can be syntactically correct but semantically incorrect. For example, the sentence "The phone decided to ring" is correct grammatically but is not correct semantically because a phone cannot make a decision.
- **Pragmatics** refers to the use of appropriate rules of conversation (Cruse, 2004). You use pragmatics when you take turns in speaking to someone in a conversation. For example, you might ask friends, "What are you doing this weekend?" but then wait for them to respond before you say something else.

Although these rules of the language system are not usually explained to young children, they quickly learn them. The growth in language development during the early childhood years is remarkable, as rapid changes occur in vocabulary size, use of grammar, and application of basic rules of conversation.

## Vocabulary Growth

Children's vocabulary expands rapidly during the early childhood years. As we discussed in Chapter 6, most children have a vocabulary of about 150 to 300 words at age 2. Researchers estimate that children learn an average of 10 words a day between ages 2 and 6. By first grade, they know about 14,000 words (Clark, 1993). Vocabulary size tends to be smaller, however, for children from low-income families, at least partially because they are exposed to a smaller range of vocabulary (Pan, Rowe, Singer, & Snow, 2005; Nelson, Welsh, Trup, & Greenberg, 2011). One way that children's vocabulary increases is through having stories read to them (Farrant & Zubrick, 2012). Parents with lower levels of education tend to read stories less frequently to children, as shown in Figure 9.9.

How does growth in vocabulary occur? Researchers have found that children often increase their vocabulary through **fast mapping.** In this process, they learn a

**Table 9.1** Language Development During Early Childhood

| Vocabulary | Grammar | Rules of Conversation |
|---|---|---|
| Increases an average of 10 words a day | Sometimes uses overregularizations for forms that do not follow conventions | Gradually learns to adjust speech to the conversational partner |

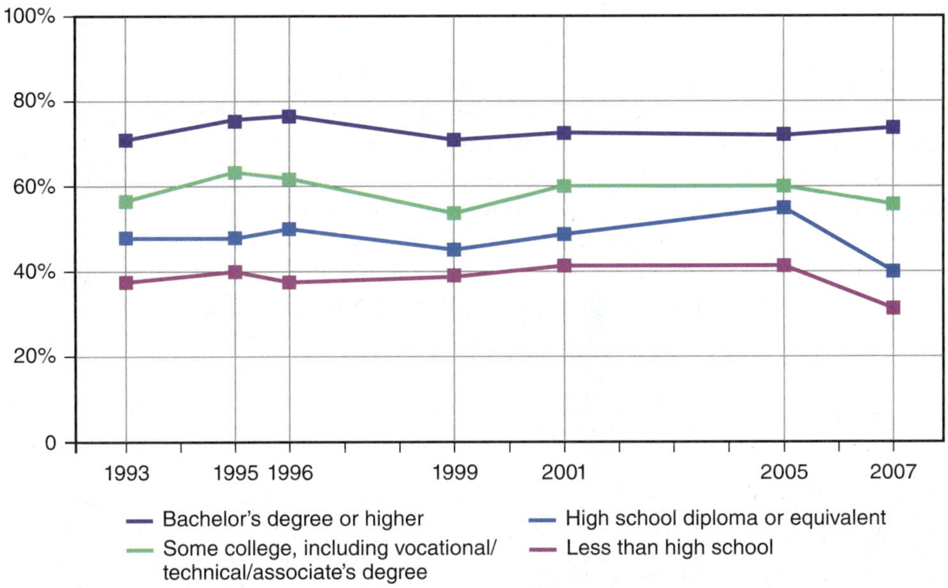


NOTE: Data are available for 1993, 1995, 1996, 1999, 2001, 2005, and 2007. Estimates are based on children ages 3–5 who have yet to enter kindergarten.

SOURCE: U.S. Department of Education, National Center for Education Statistics, *National Household Education Surveys Program*.

**FIGURE 9.9 Reading to Children as a Function of Mother's Education** This figure shows the percentage of children ages 3–5 who were read to by a family member every day over a specified period. The children are separated into four groups according to the mother's level of education. As you can see, the higher the mother's education level, the higher the percentage of children who received the benefits of being read to.

new word rapidly by forming a quick and reasonable guess about what the word means. They often do this by narrowing down the possibilities. For example, suppose a 3-year-old child is familiar with dogs and cats but not guinea pigs. She is shown a series of photographs of various dogs, cats, and guinea pigs and asked to select the photographs with the guinea pigs. She will likely use a strategy that eliminates the animals she knows to determine that the unknown one must be a guinea pig. Young children need only a few exposures to a novel word to add it to their vocabulary. This type of learning often occurs without explicit instruction (Tomasello, 2003). Although mapping of new words onto current vocabulary begins during the toddler years, it accelerates during early childhood. If children are provided with a rich vocabulary by those who interact with them, they become even better at fast mapping.

A study of children ranging in age from 26 to 52 months illustrates fast mapping in action (Wilkinson, Ross, & Diamond, 2003). Children were shown a set of familiar objects, including a toy airplane, a ball, and a cup, along with one of two unknown "junk" objects, which were given the labels "pafe" and "shede." The researchers tested the children's acquisition of the new word by asking them, for example, to "show me the airplane" or "show me the pafe." They found that 70% of children could identify the "junk" object with the nonsense label. When presented with an unknown object and an unknown word, these children quickly paired the two and learned the word. Although the older children learned the novel names more rapidly than the younger ones did, both older and younger children learned the new word in the same way. Of course, children do not necessarily understand this process, even though they engage in it.

As discussed in Chapter 6, toddlers first learn words associated with specific objects. For example, at 18 months, a toddler might say "cup," but he is talking only about the cup he uses every day. By 24 to 30 months, however, children begin to understand that a word represents a category. For example, children begin to realize that "cup" can refer to a range of items people drink from, including mugs and glasses. Some languages, such as Vietnamese, assist children in learning such categories because they add a classifier before the noun. For example, "orange" and "apple" include the classifier "fruit" (Dien, 1998). Sign language also includes such classifiers (Wilbur, 1979), but spoken English does not, so English-speaking children need to learn the classifiers on their own.

Adjectives take a while for English-speaking children to learn, but children's use of adjectives increases greatly from ages 3 to 6 (Bornstein et al., 2004). Children tend to label objects first—that is, they learn nouns first. They add adjectives only gradually.

Parents use nouns more frequently than adjectives when speaking to children, so it is not surprising that children have more difficulty learning adjectives. The first adjectives children learn tend to be those describing size (*big*, *small*) and colors (*red*, *blue*, *green*).

Although 3- to 5-year-olds can differentiate *big* and *small*, they often have difficulty distinguishing other adjectives referring to size, confusing words like *tall* and *big*. You can see why young children might have trouble with adjectives related to size, because these are relative terms. A refrigerator is big relative to a shoebox but small relative to the Empire State Building.

Kelly Sillaste/Flickr/Getty Images, Inc.

By the time they are 36 to 40 months of age, most children know at least 9 of the 11 basic colors—yellow, blue, black, green, white, pink, orange, red, and purple. Experiences like this one surely promote such learning.

Parents and teachers often emphasize color naming when speaking to young children, and by 36 to 40 months of age, most children know at least 9 of the 11 basic colors (yellow, blue, black, green, white, pink, orange, red, and purple). Children do not learn colors in any particular order. Most children, however, learn the colors brown and gray after they learn the other colors (Pitchford & Mullen, 2005).

Children around age 3 or 4 often make up adjectives by adding *y* to nouns, which generally works in English. For example, adding *y* to *snow* results in a *snowy day*. When children begin to do this, it shows that they have developed rules about language, even though they could not necessarily tell you what those rules are. Sometimes English has exceptions to such rules. When young children are first learning, they make many errors by applying the general rules.

*Everyday stories*

AN ADJECTIVE ERROR Three-year-old Jeb is visiting a park with his parents. A house made of stones is in the park, and Jeb is fascinated by it. He has a rock collection and has been busy collecting rocks he has found in the park. He has never seen a stone house before, and when he sees it, he smiles at his parents and excitedly says to them, "Look, a rocky house!"

## Grammar Usage

As mentioned in Chapter 6, Noam Chomsky (1957) proposed that children are born with a *language acquisition device* that gives them an innate knowledge of grammatical rules. Chomsky pointed out that children in all cultures rapidly learn the language of their culture, including the language's often complex grammatical rules, long before they are explicitly taught these rules. He reasoned that children must therefore have an innate system that contains a *universal grammar*. Other linguists disagree. They claim that grammar is acquired as a part of cognitive development in which children begin to see and understand patterns in many phenomena, including language (MacWhinney, 2005).

Children quickly learn to use the word order of the language they most frequently hear. In English-speaking families, children typically hear sentences in which the order is subject–verb–object. A series of studies showed that by 3½–4 years of age children in English-speaking families have developed the ability to apply this basic structure to verbs they have just learned (Tomasello, 2006). In one study (Akhtar, 1999) adults said sentences to children ages 2 to 4 years in grammatically correct and incorrect orders using novel words to represent actions. For example, they used the nonsense word "dacking" to illustrate a puppet knocking a toy down a chute. Once they established that children understood the meaning of the nonsense word, they showed each child a puppet named Ernie and used either correct word order ("Ernie's dacking the cow") or incorrect word order (for example, "Ernie the cow dacking") to describe what the puppet was doing. They then gave the puppet to the children and asked them to describe what the puppet was going to do. They found that the descriptions provided by the younger children tended to match the word order the adults had used, whether it was grammatically correct or not. In contrast, those of the older children tended to incorporate the correct order, using the typical subject–verb–object order of English. By age 4, then, most children use the word order typical of their home language even when doing so means changing the order in which they first heard a new word.

**overregularization** A process by which children apply general rules of grammar even in cases where exceptions apply.

In addition to rules about word order, each language has rules for such matters as forming plurals and conjugating verbs. English is a more complex language than some because of its inconsistencies in these areas. For example, we usually make a noun plural by adding *s*—but not always. The plural of *house* is *houses*, for example, but the plural of *mouse* is not *mouses* but *mice*. Similarly, we generally form the past tense of a verb by adding *ed*. So to place the sentence "I walk to the store" in the past, you would say "I walked to the store." However, replace *walk* with *go* in this example, and you can see why you often hear young children say "I *goed* to the store." Such errors, based on inconsistencies in English, are examples of **overregularization**, which occurs when young children apply general rules even in cases where exceptions apply (Maratsos, 2000; McDonald & Roussel, 2010).

Should parents and teachers correct children's overregularizations? Adults will often correct children's misunderstanding of an event or object. For example, if a child says, "Look at that sheep," but it's really a goat, an adult will often correct the child, saying, "That's a goat." Adults are less likely to correct overregularizations directly. Instead, they will model correct speech back to the child. Nevertheless, as the following illustration shows, children often fail to incorporate the model into their speech:

CHILD: *My teacher holded the baby rabbits and we patted them.*
ADULT: *Did you say your teacher held the baby rabbits?*
CHILD: *Yes*
ADULT: *What did you say she did?*
CHILD: *She holded the baby rabbits and we patted them.*
ADULT: *Did you say she held them tightly?*
CHILD: *No, she holded them loosely.*

*(O'Grady, 2005, pp. 168–169)*

There are two hypotheses about how children progress past the use of overregularization. One, called the *blocking hypothesis*, indicates that once a child learns the correct form, the overregularized form is seldom used (Marcus et al., 1992). The other, termed the *competition hypothesis*, proposes that individual children tend to produce both the correct and the overregularized form of a word in the same speech sample and only gradually give up the overregularized form (Maratsos, 2000). Although there are no definitive findings indicating which hypothesis is valid, samples of children's speech studied in detail over time tend to support the competition hypothesis (Maratsos, 2000). Generally, in any case, children make few overregularization errors by age 7 unless they have language impairment or brain injury (Marchman, Saccuman, & Wulfeck, 2004).

## what if...?

You are taking care of 3-year-old Julia, who really enjoys telling stories. One day she tells you about her two goldfish. "I buyed them at the fish store. When I bringed them home, I gived them some fish food. They eated it, but when they were done with all the food, they fighted with each other." Her older brother overhears her story and starts making fun of her, saying that she doesn't know how to talk. How might you help him understand the kinds of errors that Julia is making and why they actually show that she is applying the rules of grammar?

## Rules of Conversation

Next time you have a conversation with someone, consider the unspoken rules you follow. Such rules include taking turns, staying on topic, and following certain cultural conventions, such as those that govern how much eye contact is appropriate (Levinson, 1983). Understanding and using these rules enables individuals to express their intentions, interests, and desires, as well as to understand those of others. The study of the social rules of language is known as *pragmatics.*

Young children gain in their pragmatic skills as they engage in conversations with others and begin to understand how to express themselves in ways that others can understand. Even by age 3, most preschoolers can engage in a simple conversation that involves taking turns and adjusting to the remarks made by another (Pan & Snow, 1999). By the end of the early childhood years, children begin to adjust their conversations to the person with whom they are speaking. Thus, for example, they speak differently to a toddler than to a child their own age (Shatz & Gelman, 1973). This adjustment may be partially due to children's imitation of the way adults speak to toddlers, but it also relates to young children's growing ability to take the perspective of others. Recall that in Piaget's view, this ability is associated with a decrease in egocentrism, which occurs as children move to the next stage of cognitive development.

MacGregor & Gordon/Getty Images, Inc.

The older girl is not speaking to the younger one in the same way that she would speak to a girl her own age. Her pragmatic skills have improved enough that she has begun to make adjustments to accommodate her conversational partners.

Another aspect of pragmatics involves the ability to interpret what others are saying. Through the early childhood years of 3 to 7, children become increasingly able to use the context in which a statement is made to interpret the meaning of the statement (Ryder & Leinonen, 2003). For example, consider the following exchange between a parent and child:

JAMAIL: *Can I have some cookies?*
JAMAIL'S FATHER: *Your lunch is almost ready.*

In this example Jamail needs to interpret his father's response as "no," even though his father does not actually answer Jamail's question. Jamail understands his father's response because of the context (in this case, lunchtime). Young children also often use others' gestures and facial expressions as cues to what the others are intending to communicate. For example, people often point to an object they are trying to draw attention to. Pointing provides a cue letting the young child know what is being talked about even if the vocabulary is beyond her knowledge bank.

## Speaking Two Languages

Many children in the United States come from families that speak languages other than English or that speak multiple languages including English. Indeed, more than 20% of children in the United States live in homes in which English is not the primary language (ChildStats, 2009). Some of these children are bilingual, with equal skills in two or more languages. Many, however, are stronger in a language other than English. These children are referred to as *English language learners or dual language learners.*

As we discussed in Chapter 6, each language has a unique set of sounds, and by their first birthday, babies can distinguish the sounds of the primary language they hear. But what if infants and young children are spoken to in more than one language? Recent research (Conboy & Mills, 2006; Petitto et al., 2012) indicates that the brains of children simultaneously exposed to two languages show different patterns of neural activity than do those of children exposed only to one language.

Is bilingualism helpful or detrimental for children? Most of the research indicates that bilingualism is helpful because it assists children in understanding aspects of language that children who speak only one language tend to ignore (Lee, 1996). For example, in one study (Siegal, Iozzi, & Surian, 2009), 3- to 6-year-old children played a computer game in which two figures have a conversation. The first asks the second a question, such as "What game do you know?" The second gives a response that is either expected, such as "I like football," or that violates expectations, such as "I know your name." Children had to indicate whether the responses were expected or were violations. Bilingual children outperformed monolingual children by finding more of the language violations. This result indicates that they had a better understanding of how a language functions in communication with others.

KidStock/Blend Images/Getty Images, Inc.

Children in bilingual families may have some advantages over monolingual children, because they understand aspects of language that children who speak only one language tend to ignore.

Other researchers have found cognitive advantages for children who are bilingual and who constantly use two languages (Bialystok, 2007). Furthermore, these advantages persist over the lifespan (Bialystok, Craik, & Ryan, 2006). For one thing, children who are bilingual show greater skill in controlling their attention while performing tasks (Martin-Rhee & Bialystok, 2008). This may occur because constant exposure to and use of two languages has required them to learn attention control. Recent work also indicates that children as young as 3 years of age who are bilingual show better inhibitory skills—that is, they can inhibit their first reaction to produce a more accurate outcome. Again, the need to monitor two languages may have enhanced development in this area (Kovács, 2009).

Children who are bilingual tend to have smaller vocabularies in either language than monolingual children, especially during the preschool and kindergarten years (Uccelli & Páez, 2007; Umbel, Pearson, Fernández, & Oller, 1992). Some researchers have proposed that children who are dual language learners may develop knowledge of concepts in one language or the other based on the context in which the concepts are most often used. Hence, these children develop vocabularies in two different settings, with little transfer between the settings. For example, bilingual children may develop a vocabulary in English related to school-specific events (*story time*, *cubbies*, *recess*) and a vocabulary in the home language related to concepts encountered only at home, such as home appliances (*vacuum cleaner*, *coffee pot*, *can opener*). Across both languages, however, children who are bilingual tend to develop the same number of concepts as monolingual children (Menyuk & Brisk, 2005). Also, bilingual and monolingual children meet the basic language milestones at a similar time (King & Fogle, 2006). Nevertheless, some researchers have expressed concern that children who are bilingual do not have the same depth of word knowledge as children who are monolingual (Nagy & Scott, 2000). For example, they may not have as great a supply of synonyms for a particular term as monolingual children do.

Children who are bilingual, as well as dual language learners, develop the skill of **code switching**, a form of language alternation (Cantone, 2007). Code switching involves learning which language to speak to whom and in which setting. Children sometimes alternate languages within a single sentence, either because they know a specific term is better known in one language or because they prefer one language for a specific topic. One pair of researchers describe a child who generally spoke English with her mother, who was a native Spanish-speaker (Menyuk & Brisk, 2005). The child switched to Spanish when she was trying to persuade her mother, however, realizing that her mother might be better persuaded in Spanish than in English. Children who are bilingual begin to develop this skill during the early childhood years and do not generally need to be taught how to code-switch. Children who are dual language learners generally learn to code-switch through peer interaction in school.

**code switching** A form of language alternation based on the context, usually referring to bilingual language use.

Should parents whose English skills are weaker than their native language skills speak English at home to encourage English language learning in their children? Research indicates that in most cases, that is not a good idea because it will model weak language skills for the children. Instead, parents should speak to their children in the language in which the parents are strongest. That will enable the parents to provide a language-rich environment, which in turn will help their children learn the range of skills they need in language acquisition (Menyuk & Brisk, 2005).

WHEN SYSTEMS CONNECT

### Language Delays

Some children are quite delayed in their language development. Children with forms of genetically based intellectual disabilities like Down syndrome or Williams syndrome are delayed in many aspects of language development (Abbeduto, Warren, & Conners, 2007; Landry, Russo, Dawkins, Zelazo, & Burack, 2012; Mervis, 2009). Other children have language delays for unknown reasons. Still others have delays due to exposure to *teratogens*, like cocaine, before birth. These substances are likely to affect the brain and the development of language. As we discussed in Chapter 3, teratogens are agents that can cause permanent damage to an embryo or fetus.

Several studies indicate that preschool-aged children who were exposed to cocaine prenatally have language delays (Bandstra et al., 2002; Lester & Lagasse, 2010; Lewis et al., 2004). The higher the levels of exposure, the greater the delays (Nulman et al., 1994). Researchers hypothesize that cocaine exposure disrupts children's attentional systems and results in poor memory and poor processing of information. This, in turn, affects their language abilities. The interaction between children's biological predispositions and the environment in which they are cared for is evident here, however. In one study of children exposed to cocaine prenatally (Lewis et al., 2004), researchers found that some of the children had remained with their biological families whereas others had been adopted or raised by foster parents. In general, the children who had greater levels of prenatal exposure to cocaine were raised in adoptive or foster homes. By age 4, the children in adopted or foster homes had language skills similar to nonexposed children and much better than children who had been exposed but remained in less nurturing environments. These results indicate that *both* the prenatal and the postnatal environment affect children's language learning.

CHECK YOUR PROGRESS

1. How do young children acquire new vocabulary?
2. What is an example of children's tendency to use overregularization?
3. What are some of the advantages of bilingual language development?

## School Readiness

**[ KEY QUESTION ] 5.** What are some important skills that help prepare children for formal schooling?

Parents in the United States typically think ahead almost from their children's birth about how well the children will do in school. The *school readiness skills* involved in eventually learning to read, write, and manipulate numbers are important to children's later academic success (Duncan et al., 2007), and we discuss the acquisition of these skills in this section. School readiness skills are considered to be *experience-dependent* aspects of development. In other words, acquiring them depends on being exposed to specific learning experiences. Fortunately, most young children are highly motivated to learn these skills. Furthermore, they are generally aided in doing so by their experiences at home, in child care settings and preschool classrooms, and in the community. Because so many young children attend preschool programs, we end this section with a discussion about quality in preschool programs.

## Emergent Reading

Many experiences help the young child prepare to become a reader. Knowledge of the alphabet, an important skill, is usually encouraged by parents and preschool teachers. Often, children first learn the letters in their own names. Knowing the names of letters in kindergarten predicts a child's reading ability in first grade. Children who have not learned this basic skill have difficulty with reading instruction (Scanlon & Vellutino, 1996). Knowing letter names, however, is not the only part of learning to read. As you will notice in the *What Happens in the Brain* section, learning to read is very complex and involves brain networks.

**phonological awareness** The awareness that words are made up of sequences of sounds.

### Phonological Awareness

Knowing the name of each letter and knowing the sound (or sounds) associated with it are two different tasks. Children usually learn the names of letters before they learn letter–sound associations (Paris & Paris, 2006). Kindergartners who know the various letter–sound combinations tend to be better readers in the first few grades of school (Byrne & Fielding-Barnsley, 1995).

Learning letter–sound associations in English is not necessarily an easy task. Consider the letter *e*, for example. Sometimes the sound represented by this letter is the same as the letter's name—"ee"—but sometimes the sound is "eh." Understanding letter–sound associations is part of **phonological awareness**—the awareness that words are sequences of sounds. Four broad areas of phonological awareness are often assessed in kindergarten-aged children: rhyme, beginning and ending sounds of words, segmenting words into parts, and putting sounds together with letters (Torgesen & Mathes, 2000). Table 9.2 gives some examples of how each of these is assessed.

Children who develop good phonological awareness learn to read more easily (Adams, 1990; Adams, Trieman, & Pressley, 1998). Do some groups of children have better phonological awareness than others? Some researchers have found that children who are bilingual tend to have better phonological awareness skills than children who are monolingual (Oller, Cobo-Lewis, & Eilers, 1998), especially when the two languages share similar sounds and features (Snow & Kang, 2006). Bilingual children often need to pay attention to language differences, which can improve their phonological awareness. Whether bilingual or monolingual, young children can improve their phonological awareness by playing games related to language. Listening, rhyming, and games involving segmenting words all lead to better phonological awareness (Bus & van IJzendoorn, 1999). Such games can be incorporated easily into classrooms or everyday conversation between adults and children. In fact, children often develop rhyming games themselves.

*Everyday stories*

A RHYMING GAME Nadia and Justin are playing a game of bingo. They are both very competitive and only one call away from winning the game. In anticipation of winning, Justin calls out "bing, bing, bing." Nadia returns his call with "sing, sing, sing." Justin responds with "ring, ring, ring," to which Nadia retorts "king, king, king." They go back and forth until they run out of rhymes. By then, both are laughing and are no longer concerned about being the winner. Rhyming itself is often fun for children during the early childhood years.

**Table 9.2** Ways to Assess Phonological Awareness

| Type | Example |
|---|---|
| Rhyme | What word rhymes with *red*? |
| Beginning/ending sounds | What sound do *pig* and *penny* start with? |
| Segmenting words | Say *popcorn*.... Now say *popcorn* without the *corn*. |
| Putting sounds together with letters | Write *at*. Now put different letter sounds in front of *at*, like *c*, *b*, *h*. |

*Source:* Torgesen & Mathes, 2000.

# What Happens in the Brain?

## Beginning to Read

Think about learning to read. It is different from learning to talk, as it requires explicit instruction as well as much practice. Thus, studying children as they learn to read provides a unique opportunity for researchers to learn more about the influence of experience on the developing brain.

When we learn to read, at the most elementary level—the level of the beginning reader—we translate a set of written letters into a meaningful word. This may seem like a simple task, but it's actually very complex. Moving from looking at a series of symbols to understanding a word requires transmitting nerve impulses over a specific brain pathway.

Here's a simplified sketch of some key things that must happen for a young child to look at, for example, the letters C-A-T and end up thinking of a furry little animal with whiskers and a long tail.

- First, the child perceives the written letters as light rays entering her eyes. The rays are changed to electrical nerve impulses, which travel to the visual cortex. The visual cortex is in the occipital lobe and recognizes previously learned simple visual patterns like lines.
- The impulses travel from the visual cortex to the Visual Word Form area located in the left occipital-temporal cortex in the middle region called the fusiform gyrus. This region is involved in translating the simplistic pattern of the written word into recognizable previously learned words.
- Then the impulses travel to the angular gyrus, which matches the visual word with the sounds of the word.
- Next, the impulses move to Wernicke's area, responsible for language comprehension. This area processes the word as if it has been heard.
- If the word C-A-T were part of a sentence, like "The cat sat," then the impulses would also travel to Broca's area, which is involved in processing syntax, such as word order and grammar.

In beginning readers, this pathway becomes stronger with practice, and the pathway becomes more focused in the left hemisphere of the brain. As reading becomes more complex—for example, as young readers must remember the words they've already read and decode unknown words—many other areas of the brain also come into play.

Alex Mares-Manton/Asia Images/Getty Images, Inc.

## Recognizing Visual Patterns

Nerve impulses representing visual patterns travel from the primary visual cortex to the visual word form area of the fusiform gyrus. If this area hasn't learned the visual patterns of our alphabet, it won't recognize them. Children generally need explicit training to learn letter patterns—which explains why we see so many letter shapes and activities in preschools.

warrengoldswain/Age Fotostock America, Inc.

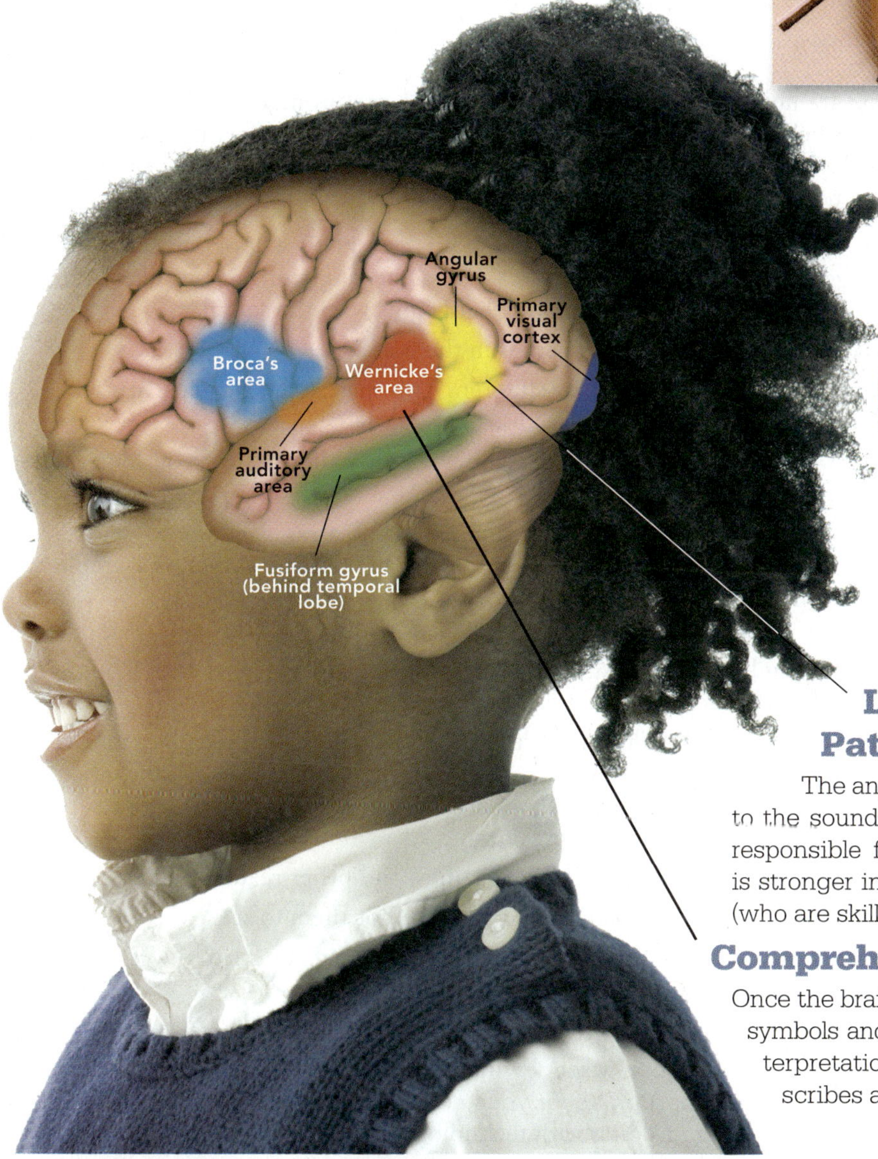


Jose Luis Pelaez Inc./Blend Images/Getty Images, Inc.

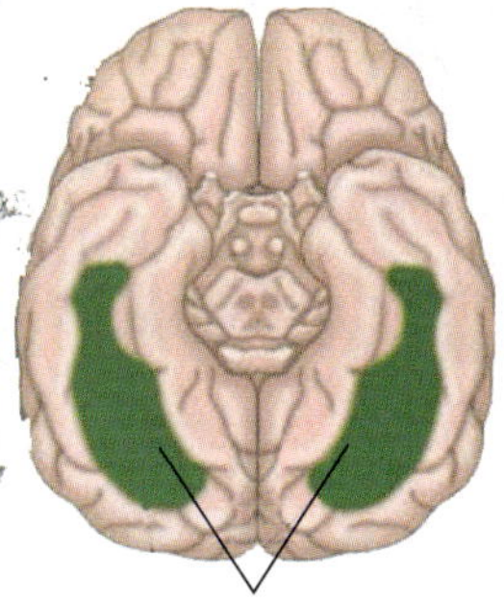

Fusiform gyrus (as seen from the bottom of the brain)

This fMRI image shows increased activity (yellow areas) in the fusiform gyrus in kindergarten children after several sessions of instruction in associating sounds with letters.

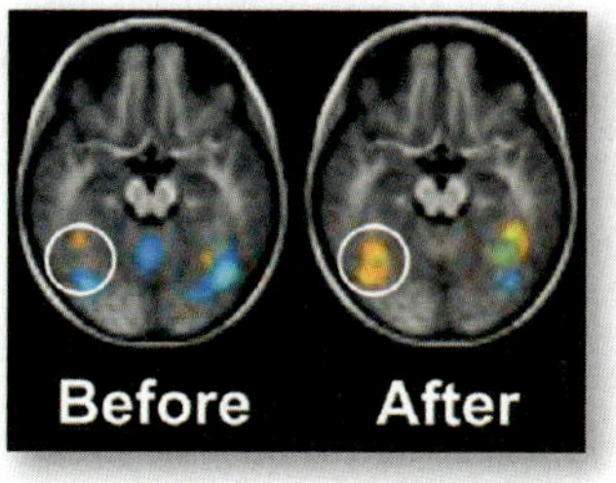


Bruce D. McCandliss, "Educational Neuroscience: The Early Years" PNAS, Vol. 107, no. 18, pages 8049–8050.

## Linking Visual Patterns with Sound Patterns

The angular gyrus translates the visual pattern of the word to the sounds of the word when spoken. The angular gyrus is responsible for phonological processing. Activity in this area is stronger in children (who are learning to read) than in adults (who are skilled readers).

## Comprehending Meaning

Once the brain has made the connection between the alphabetic symbols and the word sounds, Wernicke's area provides an interpretation of the sound pattern—the familiar word that describes a furry little animal.

## C-A-T

- Light rays entering the eyes are changed to electrical nerve impulses.
- The visual cortex recognizes the visual patterns these impulses represent.
- The fusiform gyrus translates a simple visual pattern into a known word.
- The angular gyrus translates the word to the sounds of the word.
- Wernicke's area is involved in comprehension of the word.
- Broca's area processes syntax.

iStockphoto

Tim Hale/Photographer's Choice/Getty Images, Inc.

Young children need to develop print awareness to become good readers. This includes, for example, learning not to hold a book upside-down.

### Print Awareness

Print awareness is another factor that helps young children become good readers. But even print awareness is not a simple concept (Rathvon, 2004). Children need to be aware of book orientation—that is, which way to hold a book. They also need to learn about the direction of print (left to right in English), the boundaries between letters and words, voice–word matching, and eventually the meaning of punctuation marks. Children who are exposed to many literacy-related experiences develop print awareness more rapidly than children who lack these experiences (Lonigan, Burgess, & Anthony, 2000). Such experiences include being read to frequently and being encouraged to dictate stories to an adult or older child (see the next section on emergent writing).

### Helping Preschool Children Become Readers — Parenting

Even if parents are not strong readers themselves, they can promote preliteracy skills in their preschool children. Parents can integrate many of these tasks into their daily routines with their children. Epstein (2002) lists 12 ways in which parents can help young children become readers:

1. Have daily conversations with children. This can involve looking at family pictures together and discussing them, as well as playing word games like, "I'm thinking of something in the refrigerator that begins with the sound '*m*'.
2. Keep lots of printed and written materials in the home.
3. Set up a reading and writing space for children. This space can have pens, markers, and paper that are only for the child to use.
4. Let children observe you writing and reading. Show children how you look up information, such as recipes.
5. Read with children every day. When parents set aside a regular time to read to children and discuss stories, children learn to associate reading with a pleasurable time with parents.
6. Call children's attention to reading and writing in everyday activities. Show children shopping lists, maps, lists of phone numbers, and other types of reading and writing for daily use.
7. Make a message board for children to "read" every day. It can include plans for the family, such as simple messages about the sequence of events for the day, including pictures of those events. In this way, children can learn to predict an order of events, such as brushing teeth after breakfast.
8. Encourage children to look at books, magazines, and other reading material.
9. Display children's writing and mount it at eye level for them to see.
10. Make a word bank to give each child a growing file of favorite written words and corresponding pictures.
11. Take children to the library.
12. Use television and technology wisely by limiting their use and choosing specific programs and websites appropriate for young children. Have conversations about what children are seeing or doing with technology.

SOURCE: Adapted with permission from Epstein, A. S. (2002). Helping preschool children become readers: Tips for parents. *High/Scope ReSource 21*(1): 4–6.

## Emergent Writing

Children gradually realize that writing is a form of communication—that they can make certain marks on paper to convey a message. *Emergent*, or developing, writing includes many forms of writing, from scribbled marks, to letters, to words and sentences.

Children around age 3 do not distinguish scribbling from drawing. By age 5, many children can write several letters of the alphabet, usually the letters that are in their own name (Tolchinsky, 2006). Writing generally advances from randomly placed scribbles, to left-to-right scribbles, to letter-like forms, to letters that have some association with the sound of the word being communicated. You can see some examples in Figure 9.10.

**FIGURE 9.10 Emergent Writing** Children usually begin to write by drawing left-to-right scribbles in imitation of writing. Eventually, they begin to make shapes that resemble letters, although these shapes occur in no particular order.

## Invented Spelling

As they begin to understand that certain letters are associated with certain sounds, children gradually begin to write combinations of letters to represent words. These combinations are often not exactly the way the words are spelled but instead use **invented spelling** (sometimes called *transitional spelling*). Such spelling usually includes some of the main consonants heard in a word. For example, a 4-year-old might write "pakas" for *pancakes*, as in Figure 9.11. In general, invented spelling progresses from using only initial consonants, to using initial and end consonants, to adding vowels (Treiman, 1993). Kindergarten-aged children often use a mixture of actual spelling for words they have learned and invented spelling for other words. Children's use of invented spelling shows that they have a degree of phonological awareness.

Invented spelling is a precursor to early word reading. Children often learn conventional spelling through a process of memorization. When they use their own invented spelling, however, they analyze the sounds they hear in words. Several studies indicate that young children who are encouraged to use invented spelling develop better phonological and orthographic awareness than other children the same age (Martins & Silva, 2006; Ouellette & Sénéchal, 2008). **Orthographic awareness** involves awareness of the visual representation of words—how they are spelled. In general, researchers have found that children who use invented spelling before receiving formal instruction in writing and reading are more likely to become good spellers and readers in elementary school (Dixon & Kaminska, 2007).

**FIGURE 9.11 An Example of Invented Spelling** The 4-year-old who drew and then wrote about this event came very close to saying exactly what she meant: "Then it was morning. We had breakfast and we had pancakes."

## A Text-Rich Environment

One way that children learn writing skills is by being exposed to a text-rich environment. Classrooms with labels on items and areas of the room (for example, "blocks," "markers," "bathroom") at children's eye level encourage children to learn that written words have specific meanings. Children become more proficient at writing when they are encouraged to copy such labels or to make their own labels—for instance, a sign that says "fortress" and rests on their block construction (Clay, 2001; Schickendanz, 1999). Additional writing tasks include making a grocery list with a parent and sending a card or an e-mail to a relative (Mayer, 2009).

Parents and teachers can also write down stories or sentences that children tell them and help children put these into a book (Tunks & Giles, 2009). When taking dictation from children, one expert recommends that the adult do the following (Morrow, 2005):

(1) *Write legibly and use standard spelling.*
(2) *Sit so that the child can watch the words being written.*
(3) *Read the dictation back to the child, pointing to each word as it is said aloud.*
(4) *Encourage the child to "read" by retelling the story to others.*

Another way that children can be encouraged to write is through activities with other children. By writing with a peer, children learn about the choices necessary to construct a story. For example, suppose two first-grade girls, Vanessa and Denise, are

**invented spelling** An unconventional type of spelling that develops from paying attention to the sounds of words.

**orthographic awareness** The awareness of the visual representation of words and their conventional spelling.

trying to write a scary story together. Vanessa asks Denise for help with spelling some of the words, and together they try to find a good title for the story:

VANESSA: *What's the title going to be?*
DENISE: *"One Boy and Two Girls."*
VANESSA: *That's not good.*
DENISE: *What should it be then? "The Man and Two Women."*
VANESSA: *That's not good either.*
*After several more suggestions, Denise continues.*
DENISE: *I know what it should be called: "The Vampire."*
VANESSA: *Ah, whatever you want. . . . Wait it should be, "Be Careful What You Wish For."*
DENISE: *And a girl could say, "I wish I was a vampire." And she could turn into a vampire.*

*(Mayer, 2009, pp. 113–114)*

By the end of early childhood, emergent writing skills have advanced significantly. Children can spell many words, know how to ask for assistance with conventional spelling, and begin to write simple stories with a theme. Their writing skills have come a long way from the simple scribbles they made only a few years earlier.

## Emergent Number Concepts

There is some debate about the extent to which children are born with an innate or intuitive sense of number (Baroody & Li, 2009; Geary, 1996; Van de Walle, Carey, & Prevor, 2000). There is agreement, however, that understanding of number advances significantly through the preschool years and has important consequences. In a longitudinal study of children's development, researchers assessed children's understanding of mathematical concepts, such as number sequence and order, at the time they entered school (at age 5 or 6). They found it to be an even stronger predictor of later school achievement than literacy skills (Duncan et al., 2007).

What are the core concepts that young children need to learn about number? Researchers (National Research Council, 2009) have identified four main concepts that most children learn during the preschool years. These include (1) cardinality (how many numbers are in a set), (2) number word list (the order in which numbers occur), (3) one-to-one correspondence in counting (so an object is paired with one number word), and (4) written number symbols.

As described in Chapter 6, even infants and toddlers can recognize differences in small number sets. For example, they can differentiate two objects from three objects (Lipton & Spelke, 2003; Strauss & Curtis, 1984) before they know the words for "two" and "three." Young children often develop informal ideas about mathematical concepts, such as number and shape, from playing with objects and interacting with adults, peers, and siblings (Ginsburg, Lee, & Boyd, 2008). For example, when you watch young children playing with blocks, you will see that they often spontaneously want to determine which tower is higher and which shapes are alike (Seo & Ginsburg, 2004). This tendency shows that they are interested in concepts that are critical to mathematics. Over the early childhood years, children move from counting objects to solving simple problems in arithmetic using objects. This understanding is an important foundation for learning the type of mathematical skills taught in school.

### Counting Objects

It is interesting to note that reciting numbers by rote memory and counting objects are quite different skills. Just because a child can count out loud from 1 to 10 does not mean that he can count 10 objects. To be sure, learning to count by rote memory helps

# Culture and Learning Numbers

Many studies have found that children in East Asian countries tend to outperform children in North America on assessments of mathematics skills (Göbel, Shaki, & Fischer, 2011; Organisation for Economic Co-operation and Development, 2006). Although there are many reasons for this difference, one involves the way that math ideas are represented by language. For example, in Chinese the term for a triangle is "sao jiao xing" which means "three corner shape." Although in English the word "triangle" describes the meaning of the shape, which has three angles, to a young child this is a complex term because the child needs to understand that "tri" means "three" and needs to know what an angle is. Numbers are also represented differently in English and East Asian languages. Think for a minute about counting in English. As children learn to count from one to twenty, they also have to learn that the number "eleven" looks like two numeral ones (1-1) but is not said to be "one-one" and that number "twelve" looks like the numerals 1-2 but is not said to be "one-two." This makes counting in English complex. The pattern of counting in English is irregular and not as straightforward as it is in Japanese, Korean, or Chinese (Miura, Okamato, Kim, Steere, & Fayol, 1993). In the following chart you can see how the pattern in counting beyond the number 10 is consistent in those languages.

| *Language* | *Number 1* | *Number 10* | *Number 11* |
|---|---|---|---|
| Japanese | ichi | juu | juu-ichi |
| Korean | ii | ship | ship ii |
| Chinese | yi | shi | shi-yi |

Best View Stock/Getty Images, Inc.

Researchers studying how young children count have found that by kindergarten children in East Asian cultures like China are faster and more accurate in their counting skills than children in North America (Göbel, Shaki, & Fischer, 2011). This is often attributed to the easier pattern that children can follow in counting in Chinese. In addition, children in East Asian cultures also better understand place value because of the structure of their number words, as the base 10 is obvious in the way the words are said (Miller, Kelly, & Zhou, 2005). To some extent, then, skill differences in mathematics among cultures begin at an early age and relate to the way language is used to represent basic mathematics ideas.

the child learn to count objects. After all, counting requires knowledge of the sequence of the numbers. As you can see in the *Culture and Learning Numbers* feature, learning to count is easier in some languages than in others. Counting objects, however, requires the child not only to know the number sequence but also to recognize that each object needs to be counted once and that no object can be counted more than once. The child also has to realize that the last number counted in a sequence represents the total number of objects that are in the set. For example, suppose a child is asked how many dinosaurs are in a group of eight put on a table in front of him. He begins to count. He says "1, 2, 3, 4, 5, 6, 7" as he points to each dinosaur. When he gets to 8, he needs to stop counting and realize that the last number he said represents the total of eight dinosaurs. Around age 3, most children are beginning to associate number words like *three* and *four* with specific quantities, but learning to map numbers onto quantities beyond four seems especially difficult at this age. Thus, looking at a group of five objects and realizing it is a group of five without counting is difficult for the typical 3- or 4-year-old. Children usually accomplish this around kindergarten age (Geary, 2006).

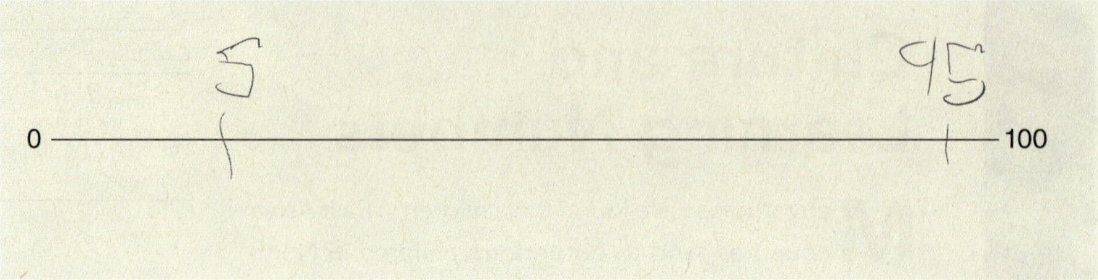


**FIGURE 9.12 Illustration of a Number Line and Examples of Children's Placements on It** As in this example from a 4-year-old, preschool children tend to show the difference between low numbers (such as 0 and 5) as greater than the difference between same-spaced numbers at the high end of the line (such as 95 to 100). Not until they are around 7 or 8 can children place numbers accurately along a number line.

## The Linear Number Line

In Western cultures, children develop an internal sense of a *linear number line*—that is, the sense that numbers proceed in order and that the difference between 0 and 3 is the same as the difference between 50 and 53—but this concept takes several years to develop. Robert Siegler and his colleagues (Booth & Siegler, 2008; Laski & Siegler, 2007; Siegler & Booth, 2004) tested kindergarten-aged children's number-line concepts by asking them to place various numbers, like 5, 26, and 83, on a line with the endpoints of 0 and 100 (see Figure 9.12). They found that 5-year-olds tended to show the difference between low numbers (such as 0 and 5) as greater than the differences between same-spaced numbers at the middle of the number line (such as 45 and 50) or at the high end of the line (such as 95 and 100). Not until they are around 7 or 8 can children place numbers accurately along a number line.

## Manipulating Numbers

© Yossan/© Corbis

There's more to counting objects than simply reciting numbers in the correct order. Counting objects does require the child to know the number sequence, but it also requires him to recognize that each object needs to be counted once and that no object can be counted more than once.

Counting objects helps children learn both the order of numbers and the relationships between them. You can see why an understanding of the conservation of number (discussed earlier in this chapter) is important to the development of more complex skills using numbers. Not until a child understands that a row of seven objects contains the same number of objects whether it is spread out or condensed will she be able to accurately manipulate numbers, such as by adding or subtracting an object from the row.

In early childhood, children use simple strategies to add numbers together—usually simple counting. Suppose you give Ethan, a 4-year-old, a group of five cars and ask him to count them, which he does. You then give him three more cars and ask, "How many cars are there all together?" He will probably count all eight cars one by one to come up with the answer. Of course, he will need to count each car once and only once, indicating that he understands the one-to-one correspondence between number and object.

Researchers have found that kindergartners tend to use two different approaches to solve the addition problem above. The simple counting that Ethan did is called the "counting up" procedure. By age 5 or so, some children have figured out a different way to approach this problem. Let us say you give 5-year-old Emma five cars and have her count them. Then you present three more cars and ask her how many she has now. She starts with the number 5 and continues counting from there, "6, 7, 8." This procedure, called "counting on," is a more advanced and efficient way of counting two groups of numbers than the "counting up" approach (Fuson, 1988; Groen & Parkman, 1972). The approaches are illustrated in Figure 9.13.

During the early childhood years, children slowly make the transition to storing some "number facts," such as "2 plus 3 equals 5" (Siegler & Shrager, 1984). Children in some cultures, especially China, are encouraged to memorize such facts earlier than children in the United States (Geary, Bow-Thomas, Liu, & Siegler, 1996). Regardless of how much adults emphasize memorization, however, providing children with a range of experiences in counting and manipulating objects during early childhood is important to their later ability to apply mathematical reasoning. Children of this age learn to work with numbers best through hands-on manipulation of objects (Clemens & Sarama, 2007). The accompanying *Research Insights* feature describes a board game that helps children improve their number skills.

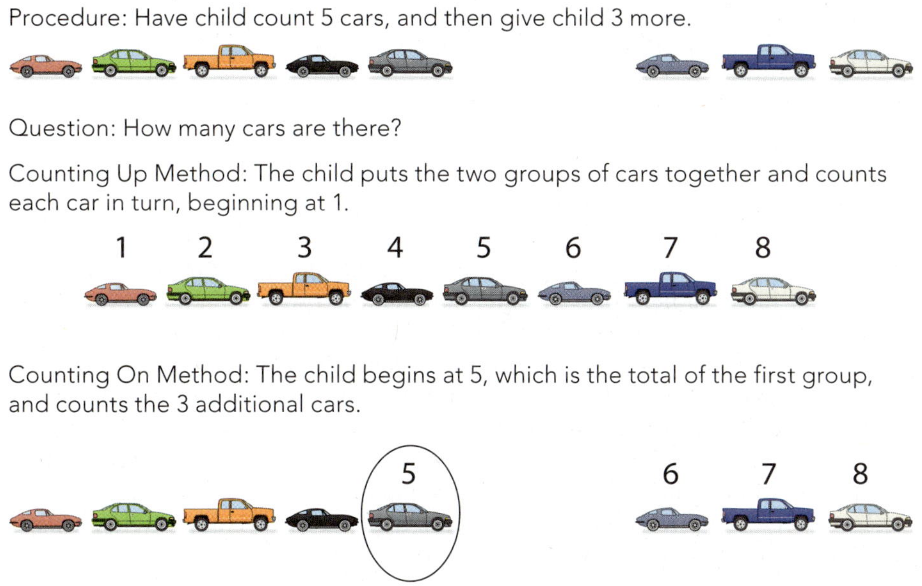


**FIGURE 9.13 Two Solutions to an Addition Problem** When grouping two sets of objects, the "counting up" method involves simply counting all the objects, starting with 1. The "counting on" method involves beginning with the total number of the largest group and counting from that number.

## Preschool Education

The United States has no general federal policy supporting child care and preschool for typically developing preschool-aged children. Nevertheless, more young children in the United States are in such programs than ever before. This is partially due to parents' interest in the role of preschool programs in improving children's readiness for school, but it is also due to federal reforms related to the employment of low-income women. We briefly describe these reforms next. Then we discuss issues related to the quality of preschool programs.

### Research Insights: Young Children and Board Games

Can a board game help children learn to "count on" and improve their number skills? Ramani and Siegler (2008) set out to examine that question in a study involving 136 children (ages 4 to 5½ years) from 10 urban preschools. The children were randomly assigned to play a number board game or the same game using colors instead of numbers. The game was played with two game pieces and a spinner on a game board with squares arranged in a line from "Start" at the left to "End" at the right. In the number game, each square was imprinted with a number, from 1 to 10. In the color game, the squares were different colors. The number spinner had the numerals 1 and 2 on it, whereas the color spinner had the range of colors on the board. Play involved spinning the spinner, moving the game piece accordingly, and reciting aloud the names of the squares the game piece moved across. For example, if a child's game piece was on numeral 3 and she spun a 2, she would say "4, 5" as she moved her token, whereas if she played the color game she might say "yellow, red." Children completed four game sessions over a 2-week period, each lasting about 15 to 20 minutes. After the 2-week period, the researchers found that children who had played the number game had better counting and number identification skills than those who had played the color game. These advantages still existed 9 weeks after the end of the game-playing sessions.

**Table 9.3** Child Care Arrangements of Preschoolers Under Age 5 Living with Employed Mothers

| Relatives | Child Care Center/Preschool/ Head Start | No Regular Arrangement | Other |
|---|---|---|---|
| 33.8% | 25.1% | 34.4% | 6.7% |

*Source:* U.S. Census Bureau, Housing and Household Economic Statistics Division, Fertility & Family Statistics Branch, Who's Minding the Kids? Summer 2006.

### P.L. 104-193: The Personal Responsibility and Work Opportunity Reconciliation Act

**Policy**

The Personal Responsibility and Work Opportunity Reconciliation Act (PRWORA) of 1996 (P.L. 104-193) (reauthorized in 2005) requires that low-income women with children 3 months of age or older work within 2 years of asking for government assistance in the form of financial help with income, housing, food stamps, and health care. This requirement means that their young children need to have some form of nonparental care. As a result, demand for such care has skyrocketed (Cabrera, Hutchens, & Peters, 2006).

Funds are provided by the federal government to the states to help support the child care needs of families whose incomes fall below 85% of the state median income when the parents are working or looking for work. States also are required to provide some of their own funds to support child care needs. Despite the federal and state funding, the actual decisions about child care subsidies are usually made at the community level. Parents therefore must choose care for their child based on what is available in their community.

Communities vary substantially in the type and quantity of child care options available. Generally, such options include a range of settings, such as at-home care, family day care, and center-based day care. As Table 9.3 indicates, about one-quarter of children under age 5 with employed mothers are in center-based child care. You can also see from the table that many children have no regular arrangement for care, making their care unstable.

The child care system in the United States varies widely, with about 10% of care provided by public agencies, 60% by nonprofit private agencies, and 30% by for-profit private agencies (Cryer & Clifford, 2003). In contrast, the child care systems in some countries receive much more public support. In France and Belgium, for example, 100% of child care for 3-year-olds is publicly funded (Lamb & Ahnert, 2006). Because of the inconsistencies in the U.S. system, it is hard to determine the experience a child might have in child care, but researchers have focused on issues of quality regardless of setting. We turn next to the question of quality in preschool programs.

### Quality in Preschool Programs

Consider the contrasting preschool experiences for two 4-year-old girls, Juanita and Maria. Juanita spends her days in a child care setting where the television set is on continually, where she has no opportunity to play outside, and where the adults seldom speak to her. Maria is cared for at a place where books are read to her frequently, where she can play on safe equipment designed for children, and where adults converse with her about the activities in which she is engaged. Are these children likely to differ in their readiness skills for school? Much research indicates that they will. What do we know about the effects of preschool settings on young children's school readiness skills?

*Juan Silva/Photodisc/Getty Images, Inc.*

High-quality preschool programs offer diverse, developmentally appropriate stimulation to their young students.

Several organizations, including the National Association for the Education of Young Children (NAEYC) and the American Academy of Pediatrics, have developed recommended standards for preschool quality. The standards tend to fall into three categories. The first category relates to health and physical safety. The second concerns the structural elements of the preschool, such as class size, teacher–child ratio, and teacher training. The third relates to the processes that occur in the preschool setting. These processes include the interactions between children and adults and the types of activities adults provide to children. There is general agreement about the core elements of quality, which include the following (Cryer & Clifford, 2003, p. 33):

1. Safety in the setting, equipment, toys, and furnishings, as well as supervision by adults.
2. Healthful care in terms of sanitation, cleanliness of the environment, good nutrition, and a blend of active and rest time, and an emphasis on self-help skills relating to cleanliness.
3. Developmentally appropriate stimulation, including learning through play with activities that involve language and preliteracy development, math learning, nature and science activities, motor activities, and creativity through art, music, and dramatic play.
4. Positive interactions with adults who can be trusted.
5. Encouragement of emotional growth in becoming independent and competent.
6. Positive relationships with peers, guided by adults when necessary.

Some early childhood educators point out that other features should be included in this list. First, they add the need to assist children of color with racial coping and to advance all children's racial socialization and respect for the range of cultural traditions represented by the children and families participating in the setting (Johnson et al., 2003). Second, they add the need to consider including children with disabilities along with those who are developing typically. Children with disabilities need the following: access to the various activities available in the setting, ways to participate with others, and the supports they require to learn, such as additional services from speech and language therapists or physical therapists (National Association for the Education of Young Children, 2009).

what if...?

A friend of yours has asked that you give some advice about choosing a preschool for his 4-year-old, Jeremiah. He has been thinking that choosing a location near his home and one with hours that correspond to his work hours would be important. He is wondering if there are other features that might be worthwhile to consider in selecting a preschool. He knows you've been studying child development and might have some ideas about the features of quality programs. What would you tell him?

## The Effects of Preschool Quality

Several studies have focused on the relationship of preschool quality to children's development (Anders et al., 2012; Li, Farkas, Duncan, Burchinal, & Vandell, 2012; Pinto, Pessanha, & Aguiar, 2013). These studies consistently find that children learn more in higher-quality settings and that children's cognitive development in particular is enhanced by quality (National Institute of Child Health and Development [NICHD] Early Child Care Research Network & Duncan, 2003). Certain features of program quality appear to be especially important in this regard. In particular, providers' interactions with children are critical in affecting children's learning. Positive provider–child interactions occur more frequently in settings with smaller group sizes, lower child–teacher ratios, and better-trained providers (Hauser-Cram & Mitchell, 2013; NICHD Child Care Research Network, 2000, 2002).

Not all children in the United States receive high-quality care, however. In some countries, like Sweden, child care is highly regulated (Hwang & Broberg, 1992), so that quality does not vary greatly from one location to another. In the United States, though, we can see large differences in how child care is provided. For one thing, child care regulations differ from one state to another. In fact, not all states even require care providers to be licensed (Lamb & Ahnert, 2006). In addition, the quality of care differs based on family demographics. Not surprisingly, children from advantaged backgrounds tend to receive the highest quality of care (Lamb & Ahnert, 2006). Children from low-income families often have less access to center-based care (Capizzano & Adams, 2004; Ertas & Shields, 2012), sometimes because their parents work nonstandard hours when center-based care is unavailable (Cabrera et al., 2006). Children of color, in particular, are more likely to receive poorer care (Kontos, Howes, Shinn, &

Galinsky, 1997; NICHD Early Child Care Research Network, 1997). These variations in quality work against the needs of children who would likely benefit most from high-quality preschool settings, especially those from low-income families.

## Preschool Programs for Children from Low-Income Families

Because children from low-income families often enter school with lower levels of school readiness skills than other children, psychologists have long been interested in developing preschool programs that will help improve those skills (Ansari & Winsler, 2012; Bell, Greenfield, & Bulotsky-Shearer, 2013; McWayne, Cheung, Wright, & Hahs-Vaughn, 2012). Several well-known programs have been found to be effective. One of the earliest was the High/Scope Perry Preschool Project, begun in Michigan in 1962 (Schweinhart, Barnes, & Weikart, 1993; Schweinhart et al., 2005). This model program involved children of African American backgrounds who were from low-income families. Children entered at age 3 and attended highly staffed center-based preschools based largely on Piaget's theory. Teachers also made home visits to families. These children were compared with children in a randomly assigned group who did not attend the program and were followed well into adulthood. Those who had attended the Perry Preschool Program showed both cognitive benefits at school entry and later life benefits, such as higher levels of educational attainment and higher incomes. Several other similar model programs also have shown that quality preschool programs can have long-term benefits to children living in low-income neighborhoods. These programs include the Abecedarian Project (Campbell, Ramey, Pungello, Sparling, & Miller-Johnson, 2002), the Brookline Early Education Project (Palfrey et al., 2005), and the Chicago Child–Parent Centers (Reynolds, Ou, & Topitzes, 2004).

Currently, two types of preschool programs stand out because of their focus on children from low-income families living in many different communities in the United States. The first of these is Head Start, which is available primarily to children from low-income families. The second includes state-supported preschools, which focus on low-income families but do not serve them exclusively. Head Start has a long history, whereas state-supported preschools are a more recent and growing phenomenon. We describe each program briefly below.

**HEAD START.** Head Start, which began in 1965, is a federally funded program for 3- and 4-year-old children whose families live at or below the poverty line (Zigler & Muenchow, 1992). In 2012, the poverty threshold for a family of four was $23,497, which means that a family earning that amount or less was considered to be living in poverty (Health and

© AP/Wide World Photos

Head Start is a federally funded preschool program for 3- and 4-year-olds whose families live at or below the poverty line. Research has generally shown that Head Start makes valuable differences in children's school readiness, especially in the area of literacy.

Human Services, 2012). The goals of the program are broad-based, addressing children's health and nutritional needs along with their educational and learning needs. There are over 2000 Head Start programs in the United States, and each is required to meet defined standards of quality. What do we know about the effectiveness of these programs?

Numerous studies on Head Start have been conducted, and the findings have generally shown positive advantages for children who attended Head Start, although the advantages are sometimes small. In one recent study, the Family and Child Experiences Survey (FACES), for example, children's early literacy skills were tested before and after attending Head Start, and their scores were compared with national norms. (National norms indicate how children across the general population perform on certain tests.) The results indicated that children in Head Start showed gains in early writing skills, vocabulary, letter recognition, and word knowledge—but still lagged behind national norms (Zill et al., 2003).

A second study, the Head Start Impact Study (Puma, Bell, Cook, Heid, & Lopez, 2005), used a randomized design, which is the best approach to use to make causal inferences. A total of 5000 children who were eligible for Head Start, but who lived in locations where more children were eligible than could be served, were randomly assigned to receive Head Start services or to be in a control group that did not receive those services. Members of the control group could receive other community services, however. The 3- and 4-year-olds in Head Start had more positive outcomes than the controls in cognitive skills such as pre-reading, pre-writing, vocabulary, and literacy. No differences were found for early math skills. These studies indicate that Head Start programs have made valuable differences for young children's readiness skills, especially in areas related to literacy.

**State-Supported Pre-Kindergarten Programs.** Over the last few years, more and more states have established their own pre-kindergarten (pre-K) programs. Most of these programs are targeted toward children from low-income families. Some (those in Florida, Georgia, Massachusetts, New York, and Oklahoma) are termed "universal"—that is, available to all children—but funding shortfalls have often made it difficult for these programs to be truly universal (Morrissey, Lekies, & Cochran, 2007). Even with budgetary constraints, though, the number of 4-year-olds enrolled in state-supported programs now exceeds the number enrolled in Head Start (Gormley, Gayer, Phillips, & Dawson, 2005).

State pre-K programs differ in terms of the length of the school day and exact ages of children served. They are similar, however, in maintaining relatively low class sizes (from 15 to 20 students) and high standards for teacher qualifications, including licensing and certification in early childhood education. More-qualified teachers would be expected to have higher-quality interactions with children. In turn, high-quality interactions with adults predict the growth that children show in academic and social skills (Curby et al., 2009). Have the standards used in state pre-K programs had the expected effect on children's skills?

Although the long-term effects of state pre-K programs have not yet been studied, the early studies indicate that such programs are generally effective. In fact, some researchers have found that state pre-K programs produce greater cognitive gains than Head Start programs (Gormley et al., 2005). In a study of five states (Michigan, New Jersey, Oklahoma, South Carolina, and West Virginia), researchers compared children who had attended the pre-K programs with other similar children (Barnett, Lamy, & Jung, 2005). They found that the children who had attended the programs had better skills in vocabulary and math and better print awareness. In general, studies of state-supported pre-K programs indicate that children from low-income families can benefit cognitively from high-quality preschool programs and make important gains in their school readiness skills.

## ✓ CHECK YOUR PROGRESS

1. Why is rhyming a good example of phonological awareness?
2. What are the four main concepts children need to learn about number?
3. What are the three indicators of quality in preschool settings?
4. What have been the primary benefits of preschool programs for children from low-income families?

# CHAPTER SUMMARY

## Piaget's Theory and Preoperational Thought

**[ KEY QUESTION ] 1. What are the characteristics of children's thinking during the preoperational stage, according to Piaget?**

- Piaget emphasized that during early childhood, children are preoperational (that is, prelogical) and are not yet able to reason with logical mental operations. As a result, they tend to provide human qualities to inanimate objects (animism), have difficulty considering perspectives other than their own (egocentrism), and concentrate on one, rather than multiple, attributes of objects (centration).
- Piaget described children's speech at this stage as egocentric—that is, focused more on themselves than on helping others understand what they are saying. This speech eventually dies out in favor of more socialized speech.

## Vygotsky's Sociocultural Theory

**[ KEY QUESTION ] 2. In what ways do others assist children in learning, according to Vygotsky?**

- Vygotsky emphasized that children learn through interactions with others, especially with more experienced peers or adults.
- In contrast to Piaget, Vygotsky considered children's inner speech to be useful for helping children with self-regulation. He considered that this speech does not die out but becomes internalized.
- Children learn best when adults or more advanced peers scaffold their learning by helping them move to the next level of understanding. Children's learning occurs within the zone of proximal development.

## Information Processing Theory

**[ KEY QUESTION ] 3. What are examples of executive function displayed in early childhood?**

- The information processing theory of children's cognitive development uses the computer as a metaphor for describing the way children learn. Information flows through the sensory register to short-term memory and is encoded into long-term memory. It can then be retrieved into working memory.
- Executive function, which involves the regulation of cognitive processes, is a fundamental aspect of information processing. Children improve in their executive functioning during early childhood, especially in their ability to focus and shift attention, to purposefully remember, to inhibit responses, and to show cognitive flexibility.

## Language Development

**[ KEY QUESTION ] 4. What changes occur in children's language development during early childhood?**

- Children's vocabulary growth increases rapidly through a process called fast mapping.
- Children at this stage tend to make language errors that show they can apply the rules of grammar but are not yet aware of the many exceptions to those rules.
- Children's pragmatic skills increase during this period as they use cultural conventions in speaking to others and gradually improve their conversational skills. By the end of this period, children can adjust their speech to the people with whom they are speaking so that others can better understand their intentions.

## School Readiness

**[ KEY QUESTION ] 5. What are some important skills that help prepare children for formal schooling?**

- Children who acquire good phonological awareness in early childhood are aware of the sounds in words and become better readers and spellers in school.
- As children begin to understand letter–sound associations, they can more effectively practice writing skills, often using invented spelling to express their ideas.
- Early number concepts develop from rote counting, to simple counting of objects, to using simple counting strategies to add two groups of objects together. Young children do not have an accurate concept of a number line, as they seem to consider the space between low numbers to be greater than the same space between high numbers.
- There are three types of indicators of the quality of preschool programs: health and safety standards; structural elements of the classroom, such as class size and teacher training; and process features, such as characteristics of adult–child interactions.
- Children who attend higher-quality preschool programs display better academic skills in their later schooling.

# KEY TERMS

animism *315*
centration *317*
class inclusion *317*
co-construction *320*
code switching *337*
conservation *317*
constructivism *315*
decenter *317*
egocentric speech *317*
egocentrism *317*
fast mapping *332*
horizontal décalage *317*
inner speech *320*
invented spelling *343*
neo-Piagetian *330*
orthographic awareness *343*
overregularization *335*
phonological awareness *339*
pragmatics *332*
preoperational *315*
response inhibition *328*
semantics *332*
socialized speech *317*
syntax *332*
working memory *327*

## CRITICAL THINKING QUESTIONS

1. **Piaget's Theory.** What do you consider to be the most important criticism of Piaget's theory and why?
2. **Vygotsky's Sociocultural Theory.** Do you think it is possible for classroom teachers to instruct all children in a classroom based on knowledge of each child's ZPD? Why or why not?
3. **Information Processing Theory.** What are some predictions you would make about the different behaviors you might see in children on a playground based on whether they had strong or weak response inhibition skills?
4. **Language Development.** Do you think that all children should learn to speak more than one language? Discuss your response, using research.
5. **School Readiness.** Why do you think that learning to say the alphabet is a necessary but not sufficient aspect of learning to read?
6. **Cultural Perspectives.** Vygotsky proposed that culture affects the tools children learn to become full participants in society. Consider how the tools necessary to learn in American society today might differ from those of a different cultural group, such as a nomadic society. How might the process of learning those tools be in some ways similar, and in other ways different in these different cultural groups?

**REAL Development**

### Cognitive Development in Early Childhood

In this module, you are again an assistant preschool teacher in Adeline's school, the Pleasantville Preschool. As you know, children undergo a number of changes during the preschool years related to cognitive development. Your task is to determine whether your students are developing normally. You will help the teacher, Mrs. Smith, evaluate students' thinking and reasoning skills as they engage in various in-class activities.

© *John Wiley & Sons, Inc.*

**WileyPLUS** Go to WileyPLUS to complete the *Real Development* activity.

03.01

# Chapter 10

# Psychosocial Development in Early Childhood

MAKING A

difference

## Being a Voice for a Child

It doesn't take a hero to change the life of a child, but it does take a great deal of persistence and care. Many children who have experienced abuse or neglect are removed from their homes and must participate in the court system. Imagine how confusing that must be for a young child. The child might wonder, "What have I done wrong?" when being removed from an abusive home. The child might also fear losing contact with siblings and other family members, neighbors, and friends. How can a young child make his or her voice heard?

A national program, Court Appointed Special Advocates (CASA), has been created to help children have a voice. In some states, a CASA volunteer is called a "guardian *ad litem*," which means that the volunteer is appointed by a judge to represent the child in court. What do CASA volunteers do? Frankye Hull describes her role as a CASA volunteer. "Being a guardian *ad litem* volunteer is a lot like being a detective. You have to be nosey. To help a child find a safe home, you've got to really want to know what's going on." CASA volunteers are trained to make sure a child's needs and desires are considered in any court decision, such as going to live with a foster family, being adopted, and being reunited with a parent. They create a relationship with the child and maintain that relationship until the child is in a safe and caring family.

Pamela Butler, now a college student, praises her CASA volunteer for the support she received. She describes her experiences before being removed from her mother's care: "We would move a lot. We weren't in school a lot." She moved from homeless shelters to run-down hotels. "There was a bed with no blankets, a closet overflowing with trash, and a dresser against the wall. The carpet was littered with cigarette ashes, and the entire apartment reeked of smoke, waste, and mildew. . . . I lay down on the mattress and cried." A CASA volunteer helped Pamela express her wishes in court for a foster family that would support her desire to stay in school and eventually get a college education.

You might consider ways you can help. Agencies like CASA exist in all states, and volunteers are of various ages and from many walks of life. Children are learning a great deal about themselves at this age, and relationships with peers and adults are critical to this learning process. As Pamela tells us in her story, a caring person can make an important difference in a child's life.

(*Source:* Information about CASA from www.casaforchildren.org)

## CHAPTER OUTLINE

## [KEY QUESTIONS] *for* READING CHAPTER 10

1. What are some processes young children develop to regulate their emotions?
2. How do young children view themselves?
3. Why do some young children have good peer relationships while others have poor ones?
4. During the early childhood years, how do children change in the way they view right and wrong and what is fair and unfair?
5. What parenting practices support positive psychosocial development in young children?

**IN THIS CHAPTER,** we begin with a discussion of Erik Erikson's view of the important psychosocial tasks of early childhood. Children develop in positive ways when they are able to experience success with challenges posed by such tasks. Because successful pathways through this phase of development require children to increasingly be able to regulate their emotions, we discuss aspects of emotional development. Next, we consider how young children gradually acquire a sense of self. Since play is the most important activity of this developmental period, we examine the different types of play children engage in and describe how play becomes more elaborate over time. As young children play together, they develop friendships and use both positive and negative ways of engaging others. We then explore how children begin to make moral judgments about what is right and wrong and what is fair and unfair. Finally, we emphasize how young children benefit from parenting that provides warmth, nurturance, guidance, and responsive, reasoned discipline.

# Emotional Development

**[ KEY QUESTION ] 1.** What are some processes young children develop to regulate their emotions?

As children begin to develop a sense of themselves, engage in relationships with their peers, and experience limits placed on them by parents, teachers, and other adults, they face new challenges. One of these challenges involves the ability to regulate their emotions, especially in situations that are stressful or that are positive but highly charged, such as attending a birthday party. Positive psychosocial development requires children to be able to both recognize and regulate their emotions appropriately, but such tasks are not always easy for a young child.

| Erikson's Psychosocial Stage Theory |
|---|
| Trust vs. mistrust |
| Autonomy vs. shame, doubt |
| Initiative vs. guilt<br>• Children enjoy initiating activities and mastering new tasks. Supportive caregivers promote feelings of power and self-confidence versus guilt. |
| Industry vs. inferiority |
| Identity vs. identity confusion |
| Intimacy vs. isolation |
| Generativity vs. stagnation |
| Integrity vs. despair |

## Psychosocial Theory

As you may recall from Chapter 1, Erik Erikson (1950) described early childhood as a time when children, secure in their attachment to their parents, are busily engaged in a range of activities and thus show much *initiative*. By this he meant that children begin to try new activities, many of them in imitation of the life around them, and start to develop friendships with peers. In keeping with his theory of psychosocial development, Erikson also maintained that children who are criticized or threatened for initiating such activities struggle with feelings of *guilt*. Erikson thus described this time as a struggle between children's sense of **initiative versus guilt**. Children's initiatives may produce many positive emotions, such as a sense of pride in learning to zip a jacket or happiness in developing a new friendship. But they can also lead children to feel negative emotions, such as anger or guilt, when things go wrong. According to Erikson, children emerge from early childhood with a sense of self that is largely either positive, based on feelings of satisfaction, or negative, based on feelings of guilt.

## Recognizing Emotions

Learning to recognize emotions is an important part of psychosocial development in early childhood. Do young children realize when they are happy or sad? Can they recognize these emotions in others? If you listen to young children talk, you will often hear them refer to their emotions, using terms like *sad*, *happy*, *mad*, and *afraid*. If asked, they will usually say that their emotions are directed at someone or something (for example, "I'm mad at Sam") rather than on what caused their emotion (such as Sam's unwillingness to share a toy) (Harris, 1995).

Young children recognize some emotional expressions and experiences better than others (Broerena, Murisa, Bouwmeestera, Field, & Voerman, 2011; Durbin, 2010; Szekely et al., 2011). In one study (Widen & Russell, 2003), children were shown photographs of faces displaying different emotional expressions. The researchers found that around age 3, most children placed emotional expressions into one of two categories: (1) *happy* and (2) *sad* or *angry*. As children approached age 5, they could also identify *surprised*, *scared*, and, eventually, *disgusted*. The researchers pointed out, however, that cultural differences exist in recognizing and labeling emotions. For example, in English many synonyms exist for *anger*, whereas in Chinese many synonyms exist for *shame*. Therefore, children from different cultural groups may become more skilled at recognizing certain emotions than others. We discuss cultural differences in children's expression of other emotions, such as pride and shame, in the accompanying *Culture and Showing Pride and Shame* box. Young children who have poor relationships with their peers have certain difficulties in recognizing the emotions of others. These children are more likely to interpret a peer's face as angry even when that peer is not angry (Barth & Bastiani, 1997). Children who misinterpret the expressions of others and tend to see them as angry or hostile are likely to react inappropriately.

Digital Vision/Getty Images, Inc.

What emotional expression would you say this child is showing? Most of us would agree that her expression is neutral. But children who have been abused are likely to interpret a neutral expression as anger.

what if...?

You are at a birthday party for a 5-year-old boy, the son of your cousin. The children are playing a game, and you notice that one of the boys seems confused and on the verge of tears. You go over to him to help out when another boy yells at him, saying, "Why are you so angry?" How might you help the boys understand each other?

## Emotional Regulation

Developing the ability to regulate emotion is another important task of early childhood. As we discussed in Chapter 8, the brain network that supports children's self-regulation is beginning to become more integrated during the early childhood years. The self-regulation skills most necessary to children's psychosocial development are considered the "hot" executive function skills that promote emotional regulation (Hongwanishkul, Happaney, Lee, & Zelazo, 2005). These skills usually come into play when a child reacts to events or feelings. In contrast, the "cold" executive function skills (discussed in Chapter 9) are used in controlling self-regulation during cognitive tasks, such as completing a puzzle. Some researchers postulate that the hot system is an emotional "go" system, whereas the cold system is a cognitive "know" system (Metcalfe & Mischel, 1999).

*Emotional regulation*, as we noted in Chapter 7, describes various processes that serve to control emotional experience. It has been said to involve the ability "to inhibit, enhance, maintain and modulate emotional arousal to accomplish one's goals" (Eisenberg et al., 1997, p. 642). The ability to use specific skills and strategies to inhibit inappropriate behaviors when frustrated or otherwise emotionally aroused is also a part of emotional regulation. Researchers have found that children who can exert such regulation tend to be more socially competent and show more prosocial behaviors (Dedham et al., 2012; Garner & Waajid, 2012; Spritz, Sandberg, Maher, & Zajdel, 2010). Those who cannot tend to show more antisocial behaviors and have more behavior problems (Chang, Shelleby, Cheong, & Shaw, 2012; Eisenberg & Fabes, 1992; Onchwari & Keengwe, 2011).

**initiative versus guilt** In Erikson's theory, the psychosocial conflict of the early childhood period; the child emerges with a sense of self that is largely either positive, based on feelings of satisfaction from successful initiations, or negative, based on feelings of guilt from perceived failures.

Patricia Marroquin/iStock

## Culture and Showing Pride and Shame

Pride and shame are emotions related to self-evaluation. A child learning to pump a swing may enthusiastically shout, "Look at me" to her nearby parent as she goes higher and higher. She shows pride in her achievement. Another child may show shame when she can't shoot a basketball through a hoop. She may look downcast and walk away from the challenge, especially if other, more successful children are watching.

The first signs of pride and shame appear during the toddler years. Over the course of this period, children first begin to understand that there are standards for behavior and then learn to evaluate their own behavior in relation to those standards. By age 3, most children show pride and shame related to success and failure (Lewis & Ramsey, 2002; Stipek, Recchia, & McClintic, 1992). But do children in different cultures show these emotions in the same way? Research indicates

JGI/Jamie Grill/Getty Images

that they do not. In one study of preschool children, for example, Japanese children showed less pride and more embarrassment after they had succeeded at

**effortful control** The voluntary restraining of a dominant response in order to use a more adaptive response.

Young children often need assistance from others to help them control their behavior in stressful situations. *Extrinsic emotional regulation* refers to the processes used by others to help children become less aroused and control their behavior. *Intrinsic emotional regulation* refers to the processes children have developed to control their own responses (Fox & Calkins, 2003). During the early childhood years, children often need extrinsic emotional regulation, but they increasingly develop intrinsic emotional regulation processes. Intrinsic processes are usually voluntary and involve children's **effortful control**. Children show effortful control when they voluntarily refrain from using a dominant response and use a more adaptive response instead. Children may exert effortful control by shifting attention during moments of distress or by using language such as self-talk to guide themselves (Todd & Lewis, 2008).

*Everyday stories*

EFFORTFUL CONTROL Su-mai really enjoys the swings in the playground. Every day when she is in preschool, she looks forward to swinging and is especially happy when her good friend Lea is able to get on the swing next to her. Su-mai's teacher usually arranges for the children to go out to the playground in groups so that they all do not emerge from the classroom at the same time. Today her teacher calls the groups according to colors, saying "those who have red on may go out now." Su-mai looks carefully at the clothes she has on and notices that neither she nor Lea is wearing red. She is immensely disappointed that she will not be part of the first group to go to the playground. She looks out the window and sees that others have settled into the swings, leaving no places for her or Lea. Su-mai starts to cry and stomp her feet but then distracts herself by looking at the sandbox instead of the swings. When she sees some interesting sand molds there, she decides that she and Lea could enjoy playing with those instead.

a challenging task than either African American or European American children (Lewis, Takai-Kawakami, Kawakami, & Sullivan, 2010).

To understand such differences, we need to consider how parents in East Asian and American cultures differ in their beliefs about expressing pride in individual accomplishment (Ng, Pomerantz, & Lam, 2007). In one ethnographic study, American mothers said that they emphasize pride in success. They encourage their children to show pride because they believe it will enhance the children's self-esteem. This, in turn, will help the children to persist in future challenges (Miller, Wang, Sandel, & Cho, 2002). Mothers of Taiwanese children, in contrast, consider an emphasis on pride in accomplishment undesirable. They believe such pride may make their children less receptive to being corrected in the future. Through these studies, we can see how children's differences in expressing emotions may be embedded in cultural belief systems and patterns of parenting.

Derek E. Rothchild/Getty Images, Inc.

Emotional regulation is affected by temperament (Dennis, Hong, & Solomon, 2010; Yagmurlu & Altan, 2010). The ability to regulate emotions might also impact other types of well-being; one study found links between emotional regulation in toddlerhood and obesity in childhood (Graziano, Calkins, & Keane, 2010). As we discussed in Chapter 7, children have different temperaments. Some children are highly reactive. These children's biological responses, such as their heart rates, are unusually sensitive to stressful situations (Fox, Henderson, Rubin, Calkins, & Schmidt, 2001). If these highly reactive children do not develop intrinsic regulatory processes, they are likely to have problems with aggression, anxiety, and depression later in childhood and adolescence (Posner & Rothbart, 2000). Most children, however, show increasing ability to control impulsive behavior between the ages of 3 and 6.

In a study of effortful control, one group of researchers showed 4- to-6-year-old children angry and happy faces on a screen (Todd & Lewis, 2008). A colored frame appeared around each face, and children were taught to press a button to make the face disappear—but only when the frame was a certain color. The researchers found that children showed more frontal lobe activity when they were required to withhold the response to press the button (and make the face go away) when the face was angry. This suggests that the children had to use effortful control to inhibit their automatic response, which was to push the button to make the angry face disappear. Of course, it may be more difficult for children to show such inhibition when they are in high-conflict situations with a group of peers.

## ✓CHECK YOUR PROGRESS

1. What is the psychosocial focus of the early childhood years according to Erikson?
2. What emotions do young children recognize?
3. Describe some ways young children exert effortful control.

**self-concept** An individual's view of himself or herself in terms of traits, personality, and values.

**self-representations** Children's descriptions of themselves to themselves.

**self-esteem** Judgments about one's own worth.

# The Development of a Sense of Self

**[ KEY QUESTION ] 2.** How do young children view themselves?

You may recall that we first discussed the development of a sense of self in Chapter 7. Here, we look more closely at two important aspects of sense of self that are especially important in early childhood: self-concept and gender identity.

## Self-Concept

How would you describe yourself to someone who has never met you? You would probably have a long list of descriptors, some of which might have to do with your appearance (for example, short with brown eyes), others with your interests (for example, sports, reading, video games), and yet others with aspects of your personality (for example, outgoing, caring, diligent). **Self-concept** relates to an individual's view of himself or herself in terms of traits, personality, and values. When you were 3 years old, however, your self-concept was probably much more narrow. Young children begin to develop a sense of who they are and how they differ from others slowly, based on their interactions with objects, activities, and others. In this section, we discuss this development of self.

What do we know about children's **self-representations**? That is, how do children describe themselves to others? When asked to describe themselves, most 3- and 4-year-old children will in fact provide concrete examples of what they look like ("I have brown eyes"), what they can do ("I can run fast"), or the friendships they have made ("I'm Juan's friend") (Damon & Hart, 1988; Harter, 1990). They usually see themselves in very positive ways, indicating that they have high **self-esteem**, or judgments about their own worth. This may lead them to make claims about their skills that go beyond the actual evidence ("I can jump as high as that tree") (Harter & Pike, 1984). One reason why young children have such inflated self-esteem is that they cannot yet compare themselves to others. In middle childhood, a boy might say to himself, "Maybe I'm not so good at running because I see that Keisha and Ernesto are much better at it than I am." At 3 or 4 years of age, though, children lack the ability to make these social comparisons and tend to overestimate their abilities (Frey & Ruble, 1990). At around ages 5 to 7, children begin to make comparisons to their own past performance ("I can climb so much higher this year than last") (Ruble & Frey, 1991). Such comparisons to their own previous behavior in fact promote even more positive self-esteem.

Young children usually consider themselves good at many skills. Preschool children may say that they run better than they did last year. Children are not likely to compare their running skill to that of other children until they reach middle childhood, however.

Mark Bowden/Getty Images

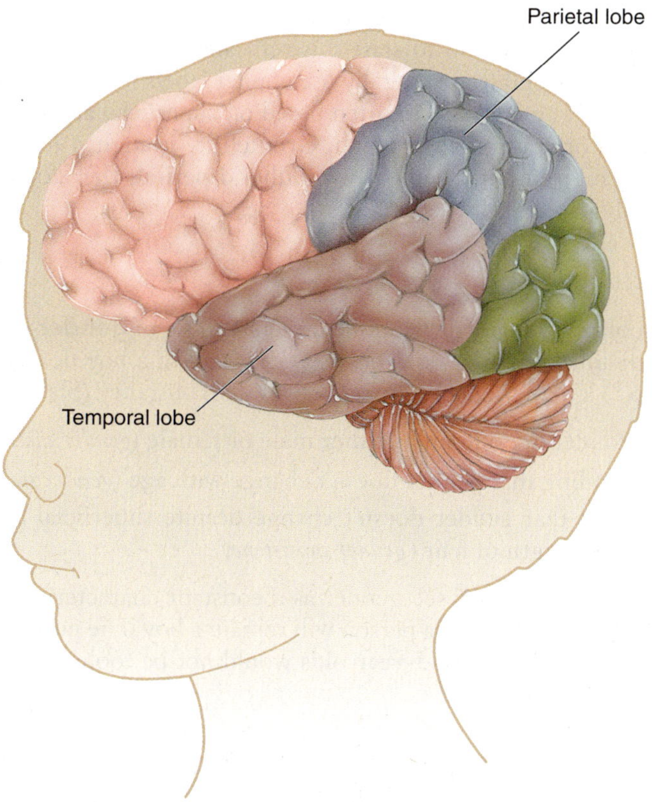


**FIGURE 10.1 Temporal and Parietal Areas of the Cerebral Cortex** The degree of brain maturation in the area where the temporal and parietal lobes meet is related to the development of children's self-representation—how they describe themselves to others.

Adapted with permission of John Wiley & Sons, Inc., from Comer, R., & Gould, E. (2013). *Psychology around us* (2nd ed.). Hoboken, NJ: Wiley, p. 129, Figure 4.9.

THE DEVELOPING BRAIN

## Self-Representation and the Brain

Recent studies indicate that specific brain regions are implicated in tasks involving self-representation such as mirror self-recognition, personal pronoun use, and pretend play (Lewis & Carmody, 2008). The degree of brain maturation in the area where the temporal and parietal lobes meet (see Figure 10.1) is related to the emergence of children's self-representation. Especially in right-handed children, these findings are strongest for the left hemisphere. However, both hemispheres are thought to be related to tasks involving self-understanding, but in different ways. The left hemisphere is most active in tasks involving self-representation, whereas the right hemisphere is more active in tasks involving comparisons of the self to others (Lewis & Carmody, 2008). Thus, the maturation of the brain is important in children's development of a sense of self, although experience also plays a role.

## Gender-Role Development

One critical way in which young children begin to define themselves is in regard to their sex. How early do children define themselves as boys or girls? How does children's sense of what it means to be a boy or girl develop?

Researchers distinguish **sex differences**, which are biological differences, and **gender differences**, which are social or cultural differences in the acceptable behaviors for each sex. The concept of gender is central to the way we organize activities and friendships in our culture. Therefore, it is not surprising that one of the first questions people ask of new parents is whether their newborn is a boy or girl.

**sex differences** Biologically based differences.

**gender differences** Differences in behavior based on concepts of female and male.

**gender schemas** The categories children develop to determine differences between males and females.

### Gender Schema

Probably because of our society's emphasis on gender, young children themselves are quick to pick up on the idea of **gender schemas**—that is, the behaviors associated with being a particular sex. Children are not born with gender schemas. A few months

**gender constancy** The understanding that sex remains the same regardless of dress or actions.

before they turn 2 years of age, however, they begin to label themselves as boys or girls (Zosuls et al., 2009). Girls tend to start this self-labeling a few months earlier than boys. By the age of 2½, children generally use gender labels (boy, girl) appropriately in reference to others. These labels are often based on superficial aspects of appearance, such as hair length or voice pitch (Etaugh, Grinnell, & Etaugh, 1989; Fagot & Leinbach, 1989). As children enter the early childhood period, therefore, most identify themselves readily in terms of their sex.

### Gender Constancy

Young children only gradually develop the understanding of **gender constancy**—the idea that an individual's gender does not change. ("If I'm a boy now, I will be a man when I grow up.") There are three aspects of gender constancy (Slaby & Frey, 1975):

1. The ability to identify oneself as either male or female (*gender identity*)
2. The understanding that gender doesn't change with age (*gender stability*)
3. The knowledge that gender doesn't change despite superficial changes such as type of dress or length of hair (*gender consistency*)

Three-year-olds do not always see gender as a constant characteristic. For example, 3-year-olds are not always sure if a person will remain a boy if he puts on a long-haired wig or a dress. In contrast, most 5-year-olds would not be fooled by such superficial changes (Ruble et al., 2007).

D. Hurst/Alamy Limited

Very young children are not always sure if a boy remains a boy when he puts on a wig. Children develop a sense of gender constancy during the preschool years.

### Gender Stereotypes

Think of the last time you bought a toy for a young girl. Would you have purchased the same toy for a young boy? The types of clothing, toys, and activities that children associate with each gender are socially based and vary from culture to culture. For example, men in some Middle Eastern cultures wear long robes. Such dress may be associated with females by young children in the United States, who have not had much exposure to individuals from Middle Eastern cultures. In some cultures, men and women have very distinct and defined roles. In other cultures, like the United States, men and women can have similar occupations and pursue similar forms of entertainment. Nevertheless, important gender-related differences exist in the United States, and children internalize those differences in early childhood.

If you watch children in preschool, you will see that even at as young an age as 3, girls and boys differ in their choice of playmates (usually choosing children of the same

© Celia Peterson/arabianEye/Corbis Images

© Neha Nath/India Picture/Corbis Images

commerceandculturestock/Getty Images, Inc.

Walter Bibikow/Photolibrary/Getty Images, Inc.

Cultures vary in their view of what is appropriate dress and behavior for men and women. The roles of men and women differ more in some cultures than in others.

sex) and in play activities (Goble, Martin, Hanish, & Fabes, 2012; Martin et al., 2012). By age 3, children have often formed **gender stereotypes**. That is, they have constructed a mental model of the behaviors and activities of each sex based on socially sanctioned attitudes about what is appropriate for individuals of that sex. These stereotypes are most pronounced and rigid at ages 4 and 5.

**gender stereotypes** The rigid determination of appropriate dress and actions based only on sex.

For example, children associate certain colors with being male (usually primary colors) or female (usually pastel colors) (Cherney & Dempsey, 2010; Picariello, Greenberg, & Pillemer, 1990), as well as certain shapes (angular versus curved) and textures (rough versus soft) (Blakemore, 2003). Children even begin to associate certain musical instruments with each gender (Marshall & Shibazaki, 2012). In one study (Harrison & O'Neill, 2003), researchers found that children considered the piano, violin, and flute to be feminine instruments, while they considered the trumpet, the guitar, and drums to be masculine instruments. Some girls said they wanted to play the masculine instruments, but few young boys said they would choose to play the feminine instruments.

## what if...?

Suppose you see two 4-year-olds, a boy and a girl, arguing in the dramatic play center in a preschool classroom. The boy insists that "girls can't wear fire hats." The girl responds that "boys can't pretend to be nurses." What does the dispute tell us about how these children view gender? Do you think you could help them resolve their dispute?

© Gaetano/Corbis Images

Despite young children's gender stereotypes about appropriate toys and activities for boys and girls, they sometimes violate these stereotypes in their own choices during play.

Although stereotypes tend to decrease somewhat after age 5, they continue to be present during the entire early childhood period (Ruble et al., 2007). Consider, for example, this dialogue between a mother and her 6-year-old son:

MOTHER: *Does Cynthia ever play with trucks?*
CHILD: *Sometimes.*
CHILD: *Girl trucks.*
MOTHER: *What are girl trucks?*
CHILD: *Pink ones.*
MOTHER: *Does Cynthia have pink trucks?*
CHILD: *Yeah.*
MOTHER: *Really?*
CHILD: *[nods "yes"]*
CHILD: *Well, she has pink cars but not pink trucks.*
MOTHER: *So she drives the cars while you and Brian drive the trucks?*
CHILD: *Yup.*

*(Gelman, Taylor, & Nguyen, 2004, p. 105)*

The 6-year-old boy in this dialogue first assumes that if Cynthia plays with trucks, they must be pink—a female color. Then, as he considers cars and trucks, he decides that she must play with cars, not trucks, since cars are smaller than trucks and hence more feminine. This boy has acquired a view of the differences between objects suited for girls and those suited for boys, even though in both cases the objects are vehicles.

## Theories on the Development of Gender Roles

How does gender-role development occur? There are four primary theories to explain why children tend to develop behaviors typical of their sex: biological theory, psychoanalytic theory, social learning theory, and cognitive-developmental theory. Each offers a very different explanation of how such development occurs.

**BIOLOGICAL THEORY.** According to the biological view, boys and girls develop differently because their brains are wired differently. This difference results at least in part from variations in prenatal hormones. Greater levels of androgens, a predominately male hormone, are released in males before birth, resulting in different brain organization and neural circuits (that is, wiring) for males and females.

As an example of the importance of androgen, researchers point to a rare genetic disorder (termed *congenital adrenal hyperplasia*) that results in increased levels of androgen in female fetuses. When girls with this disorder are given a choice of items to play with, they select more stereotypically male toys (such as vehicles and balls) and fewer stereotypically female toys (such as tea sets) than girls without the disorder (Servin, Nördenstrom, Larsson, & Bohlin, 2003). They are also rated by day-care providers and teachers as choosing more stereotypically masculine activities in their play, such as playing games involving cars rather than activities involving household objects.

From the biological perspective, then, children's early brain wiring predisposes them to choose certain activities. These activities are then associated with gender differences in behavior (Cohen-Bendahan, van de Beek, & Berenbaum, 2005). Typical boys and girls tend to find certain types of toys and activities to be more attractive than others and will select the toys and activities associated with their sex over those associated with the opposite sex when given the choice.

**Oedipus complex** In psychoanalytic theory, a young boy's romantic love for his mother and his corresponding hostility toward and fear of his father.

**Electra complex** In psychoanalytic theory, a young girl's romantic love for her father and her corresponding feelings of competitiveness with her mother.

**PSYCHOANALYTIC THEORY.** Psychoanalytic theorists proposed a quite different view of how gender schemas develop. Based largely on the work of Sigmund Freud and his followers (discussed in Chapter 1), psychoanalytic theory holds that young children experience a series of events that result in identification with the same-sex parent. Freud claimed that males and females develop gender identity in distinct ways (Freud, 1949).

In Freud's theory of psychosocial development, boys aged 3 to 6 are in the phallic stage. The name of this stage was based on Freud's belief that pleasure for the young boy comes primarily from the *phallus* (a Greek term for penis). The task for a young boy in this stage is to break away from his romantic love for his mother and instead identify with his father. This is a complicated task for the boy, one that involves what Freud termed the **Oedipus complex**. (In Greek mythology, Oedipus was the son of a king who was abandoned at birth and raised in a different kingdom. Through a complex series of events, he later ended up killing his father and marrying his mother.) According to Freud, the boy is afraid that because of his feelings of love for his mother, his father will castrate him. The fear of castration is sufficient for the boy to identify with the strength of the father. Only then has the boy achieved sex-role identity with his father.

The experience for a girl is quite different, according to Freud. She suffers from the "feminine Oedipus attitude," later termed the **Electra complex**. (Electra, another figure in Greek mythology, wanted her brother to avenge the death of their father by killing their mother.) Freud describes the young girl as first blaming her mother and eventually trying to put herself in her mother's place by trying to be attractive to her father. As with the Oedipus complex, the situation is resolved when the girl eventually identifies with her mother.

Although much evidence exists that children identify with their same-sex parent, Freud's perspective on how this occurs has been criticized for lacking a scientific basis (Popper, 1962) and therefore is not in keeping with current views. The two approaches discussed next, in contrast, assume that children readily identify with those of the same sex. These approaches concentrate more on children's observations and understanding of the different roles taken on by males and females in a society.

© Monalyn Gracia/Corbis Images

Young children often imitate the roles they see males and females playing in their own lives. In doing so, they often imitate the gender-stereotyped roles.

**Social Learning Theory.** Like psychoanalytic theory, social learning theory focuses on parents. At the same time, though, it widens the focus to include other children and adults in the child's social network as well as other societal forces, such as the media. We discussed Bandura's (1986) work on the importance of observation and imitation as a form of learning in Chapter 1, and this work is central to his view on gender development.

According to social learning theory, children learn behavior that is considered appropriate for their gender through first observing and then imitating children and adults of the same sex. Such observations can be direct, as in situations where a girl imitates her mother by putting on jewelry and carrying a purse or a boy imitates his father by wearing a hard hat and carrying a flashlight. Observations also can be indirect, through the media. Researchers have found that even cartoon characters with male and female voices appear to differ in stereotypical ways. One set of researchers (Thompson & Zerbinos, 1995) analyzed 175 children's cartoon shows. They found that the male characters, in comparison with the female characters, were more likely to show leadership and ingenuity, express anger and opinions, issue threats, and use aggression. The female characters, in contrast, were more likely to show affection and ask for protection.

Young children have access not only to television programming but also to video and online games. In a study of 47 popular games, Beasley and Standley (2002) found some interesting features. For one thing, female characters were less frequently portrayed than males (only 13% of the characters were female). For another, they were less clothed than their male counterparts. According to social learning theory, children are more likely to imitate the portrayals of their own sex, and the portrayals in the media are important influences on children's development of gender schema.

© Nicole S. Young/iStockphoto

**Cognitive-Developmental Theory.** The role of children's concept development in their understanding of gender roles is of primary importance to cognitive-developmental theory. From this perspective, children become primary actors in their own construction of concepts of gender. They begin to see patterns associated with gender, and from these patterns they develop the basic categories (or schemas) of "male" and "female" behavior, activities, and interests. Children then use these categories to explain and even predict behavior, sometimes distorting information so it fits with their concept of that category.

Researchers have found that young children actively develop rules about gender based on very little information (Ruble, Martin, & Berenbaum, 2006). A young child who sees her father drink coffee and her mother drink tea, for example, might decide that coffee is a "male" drink, whereas tea is a "female" one. Especially between the ages of 3 and 5, children work on developing such rules and as a result often exaggerate gender differences and become rigid in their thinking about them, making claims like "Boys don't wear pink." Children's rigidity around gender differences is short-lived, however, and lessens in middle childhood (Trautner et al., 2005).

*Everyday stories*

NOT A JOB FOR MOMMIES Four-year-old Julian's mother drove him to his day-care center every morning on her way to work. At least once a week, she would need to stop to buy gas for her car. He would watch her fill the gas tank. One day, out of the blue, he said to her, "Mommies can't put gas in cars. That's a job for daddies." Even though he had seen his mother put gas in her car many times, he was beginning to try to figure out how gender roles differ for women and men.

**Relationship of the Theories.** As you reflect on these theories, remember that each offers a different perspective on children's gender-role development. Depending on the theory you are considering, you will regard different aspects of a child's world as important: the child's hormones and brain (biological theory), the child's identification with the same-sex parent (psychoanalytic theory), the child's observation of the behavior of others (social learning theory), and the child's construction of categories (cognitive-developmental theory).

Despite these important differences, these theories share some common elements. They assume that children differentiate people according to sex and that they begin to identify with those of the same sex in early childhood, developing a gender schema associated with being either male or female. Children quickly become attuned to their society's view of what is appropriate and inappropriate behavior for males and females.

✓ CHECK YOUR PROGRESS

1. What is gender constancy?
2. Which theory would predict that 4-year-old Sophia might claim she is going to marry her father when she grows up?
3. Five-year-old Zander enjoys playing soccer. How would the biological and the social learning perspective differ in their claims about why he enjoys soccer?
4. Margarita recently told her kindergarten classmates that "purple is a girl color." According to the cognitive-developmental perspective, what might be the reason for her claim?

## Relationships with Peers

**[ KEY QUESTION ] 3.** Why do some young children have good peer relationships while others have poor ones?

**parallel play** A form of play in which children engage side by side in the same activity but do not interact.

**associative play** A form of play in which children engage in different activities but interact.

**cooperative play** A form of play in which children interact while engaging in a common activity and with a common goal.

Do you remember your first friendship? It may have formed during your early childhood. These years are an expansive time for young children as they engage with peers in a variety of ways and often develop their first friendships. Most of their interactions with peers occur through play. Indeed, play is the primary activity for young children in Western cultures during the early childhood years. Although play may seem like a simple construct, it actually involves many elements.

In this section, we discuss various types of play and explain why play is important to children's development. We then focus on children's friendships and their acceptance by peers. We consider the importance of children's ability to regulate their emotions as they interact with peers and the prosocial and antisocial behaviors they exhibit. We look closely at one form of antisocial behavior, aggression, and examine various reasons why some children are more aggressive than others. Finally, we consider the changes young children undergo in their understanding of the mental states of others.

Susan Woog-Wagner/Photo Researchers/Getty Images, Inc.

Children who are playing side by side but not interacting are engaged in parallel play.

### Play

Many adults think of children's play as being merely a form of entertainment. Those who study play, however, consider it to be a serious activity, especially in regard to its role in promoting learning from others and developing friendships (Lifter, Foster-Sanda, Arzamarski, Briesch, & McClure, 2011; Mathieson & Banerjee, 2010). Play is generally identified as an activity that is exploratory rather than goal-focused; is intrinsically motivated; is freely chosen; and occurs when the child feels psychologically safe and secure (Stegelin, 2005).

#### Types of Play

Many years ago, Mildred Parten (1932) observed young children playing and developed a typology of play that can easily be applied to the way children play today. Some children, she noted, are more likely to observe the play of others than to participate. She considered that type of play to be *nonsocial activity*. With respect to *social activity* in play, she proposed that children develop through a three-step sequence:

Allen Donikowski/Flickr/Getty Images, Inc.

These children are exchanging crayons, but each is creating a drawing individually—an example of associative play.

1. In **parallel play**, a child plays near another child who is engaged in the same type of activity (for example, both children might be pouring sand into buckets in a sand table). Despite the similarity in the activity, children engaged in parallel play do not try to influence each other.
2. **Associative play** is a more social activity in which children exchange toys and comment on each other's activities while engaged in different pursuits. For example, two children might be exchanging markers, but one child might be drawing a picture while the other is making signs to hang in the classroom.
3. The highest level of play is **cooperative play**, in which children work together toward a common goal. This often occurs in role play, where children are acting out a scene (such as pretending to eat breakfast and leave for work). It also occurs when children are working together to make a common product, such as constructing a building out of blocks.

Andersen Ross/Digital Vision/Getty Images

Children working together on a common goal are engaged in cooperative play.

**symbolic play** A type of play in which a child uses one object to substitute for another.

**sociodramatic play** A type of symbolic play in which children enact social roles.

Cooperative play increases during the early childhood years, so 5-year-olds are more likely to engage in such play than younger children (Pan, 1994). The amount of cooperative play that children engage in, however, differs according to the culture in which they live and the extent to which the belief systems of that culture emphasize the importance of harmony. For example, researchers have found differences based on family ethnicity within a middle-income sample in the United States. The researchers observed children's responses when other children invited them to play or offered them objects to play with. The Korean American children in this sample were more cooperative, tending to accept invitations and offers more often than their European American peers (Farver, Kim, & Lee, 1995).

Regardless of ethnicity, preschool children not only advance in their tendency to engage in cooperative play but also show developmental differences in their use of **symbolic play**. In symbolic play, children use an object to stand for another object. For example, a child may pretend a block is a car and push it along the ground. As we pointed out in Chapter 9, the ability to use one object to symbolize another is a critical component of cognition, as it involves the use of substitutions in thinking. Children must be able to make such substitutions in order to learn to read, perform mathematical calculations, and engage in higher-level thinking. Thus, the simple use of symbols, such as using one object to substitute for another, illustrates how systems (in this example, the cognitive and social systems) come together to advance children's development.

**Sociodramatic play** is an elaborate form of symbolic play in which children act out familiar adult roles. These adult roles, of course, differ among cultures. For example, children who live in a Mayan agricultural community in Guatemala or a foraging community in the Democratic Republic of Congo (formerly Zaire) are quite different in their sociodramatic play from children living in middle-income communities in the United States (Morelli, Rogoff, & Angelillo, 2003). Young children in the Guatemalan or Congolese communities participate more in the work lives of adults than do children in the United States. Thus, they are more likely to emulate the work they see adults doing in their play, such as by making pretend tortillas out of dirt or pretending to shoot animals. In contrast, most children in American and European cultures are segregated from the work life of parents and other adults. Instead of acting out work roles, these children often imitate superheroes or the adult life they see in the media (Rogoff, 2003).

You may recall that according to Vygotsky (1962), as discussed in several earlier chapters, children learn first in the social realm and then internalize what they have learned. Sociodramatic play offers a good example of how play advances children's cognitive development through learning in the social realm (Vygotsky, 1978). Think, for example of children playing "house." Each child needs to have a designated role (father, mother, baby, cat), and each needs to stick to that role because the play demands it. For example, the cat could not suddenly pretend to drive the car, nor could the father start meowing. To succeed, children need to inhibit their natural behaviors, such as telling others what to do, and regulate each other's compliance with what they consider to be the "rules" of a family scene.

This little girl, in pretending to be a doctor, is likely to ask the kinds of questions she thinks that doctors ask of patients. She is beginning to understand how to carry out a role.

*blue jean images/Getty Images, Inc.*

Sociodramatic play is thought to serve three important functions in children's development during the preschool years (Gioia & Tobin, 2010; Howes, 1992).

1. It creates a context in which children can learn to share a common but complex goal, such as enacting a scene. In this way, children participate in "shared meaning," which is necessary for productive communication with others.
2. It gives children the opportunity to learn to pay attention to the ideas of others and to adapt and compromise based on the common task of pretending and enacting a scene (Bodrova & Leong, 2003).
3. It provides a safe context for children to try out new ideas and roles, such as figuring out what is involved in being an astronaut or a television chef.

### Caregivers' Roles in Children's Play

Some educational theories and research findings suggest that teachers and other caregivers advance children's skills by getting involved in their dramatic play rather than just letting it unfold (Trawick-Smith & Dziurgot, 2011). Teachers clearly influence children's play by the types of materials they make available in the classroom. But teachers can also help children plan the elements of a sociodramatic scene in advance. The teacher can ask the children what they will need to enact the scene, can encourage them to use one object to symbolize another (for example, a cone-shaped block for a baby bottle), and can suggest that they consider which role each will play (Diamond, Barnett, Thomas, & Munro, 2007). By helping children learn to "think out loud" as they plan, create rules, develop symbols, and solve problems, caregivers encourage children to use these thought processes in a public way. This type of thinking will later become the "inner speech" that children will use silently to help themselves through a problem, as discussed by Vygotsky (1962). In this way play is not only entertaining but also serves as a strong promoter of children's learning (Bishop-Josef & Zigler, 2011; Garaigordobil & Berrueco, 2011).

## How Can Preschool Teachers Support Play? Practice

Here are four principles to help preschool teachers and caregivers support children's play to optimize its benefits and advance children's development (Van Hoorn, Scales, Nourot, Scales, & Alward, 2010):

1. *Take the child's view.* Consider their level of development in providing objects for children to play with in the classroom. For example, younger children need replicas of real objects (like fire chief hats), but older children can use nondescript objects (like blocks and pieces of material) in a variety of ways to symbolize other objects.
2. *Be a keen observer of children's behavior.* When children are playing, do not ignore what they are doing. Watch how children play during times when they can make choices. Use these observations to see the level of play children are engaging in (for example, parallel, associative, or cooperative; incorporating objects in a symbolic way; thinking out loud) and how they interact with others. These observations help us understand each child's level of development.
3. *See how children construct meaning through their play.* Encourage children to talk about what they did when they were playing, what they tried to do, what worked, and what did not work. Use this conversation to encourage children to consider what they might do differently in the future.
4. *Become the stage manager.* Consider the physical environment and how it stimulates or discourages play. Change the types of items available in the classroom for sociodramatic play.

## Friendships

Play advances children's social development in many ways. Through play, children learn to negotiate their relationships with their peers and develop friendships (Bulotsky-Shearer et al., 2012; Newton & Jenvey, 2011). By age 3, most children start to express preferences for some peers over others, and by age 5, about 75% of children have a "best friend" (Dunn, 1993). Children usually choose as friends other children who are similar to them in age, sex, interests, and behavior (Rubin, Bukowski, Parker, & Bowker, 2008; van den Oord, Rispens, Goudena, & Vermande, 2000; Walden, Lemerise, & Smith, 1999). Inevitably, though, some children have more friends than others. In this section, we consider aspects of peer acceptance, including peer acceptance of children with disabilities. Because children's behaviors are related to their skills in developing friendships, we also focus on young children's prosocial and antisocial behaviors. Finally, we look at the research on children's theory of mind, which includes the understanding of their own minds as well as those of others.

**popular children** Children who are selected by many other children as potential playmates.

**rejected children** Children who are selected by many other children as those they do not want to play with.

**neglected children** Children who are ignored when other children choose playmates.

**Table 10.1** Types of Peer Nominations

| Type | Description |
|---|---|
| Popular | Many children say that they want to play with this child. |
| Rejected | Children say that they do not want to play with this child. |
| Neglected | Few children say that they either want to play or do not want to play with this child. |

## Peer Acceptance

Children differ a great deal in their social skills. Even as young as preschool age, some children clearly get along well with others and are sought after as friends and playmates, whereas other children are avoided or left out (Tarullo, Mliner, & Gunnar, 2011; Wilson, Petaja, & Mancil, 2011). What do we know about why these differences occur?

Preschool teachers can readily tell us which children in a class are popular. Children themselves can also tell us. When children are asked about which children in the class they like or dislike, three categories of children emerge (see Table 10.1) (Dodge, Schlundt, Schocken, & Delugach, 1983). Children who are **popular** are placed in the "like" category by many other children in the class. Children who are **rejected** are nominated by many other children as being disliked as a playmate. Finally, children who are **neglected** are not nominated by others in either the "like" or "dislike" categories.

If you look carefully at the behavior of the children in each of these three categories, you will notice some important differences, especially in the preschool classroom. One of the most complicated dynamics for young children in a group setting is entering an already formed group of children (Putallaz & Gottman, 1981). Although children use many approaches in trying to enter such a group, some approaches are more likely to succeed than others. Table 10.2 summarizes these strategies, which

**Table 10.2** Ways in Which Children Enter Groups of Peers

| Risk Category and Entry Codes | Definitions |
|---|---|
| **Low risk** | |
| Wait/watch | Stops own activity and watches others play for at least 30 seconds |
| Make eye contact | Attempts to make direct eye contact |
| Smile/laugh | Smiles or laughs appropriately at others' activity |
| **Moderate/low risk** | |
| Approach | Moves closer to others' play |
| Join in | Joins others' play without verbal marker |
| Imitate | Copies play of others |
| Agree | Makes statement of agreement |
| Share | Offers object or helps without being prompted |
| **Moderate/high risk** | |
| Information | Gives general information to others |
| Request information | Requests information from others |
| Direct request | Asks to play |
| "Me" statement | Talks about self |
| Feeling statement | States own feeling or need |
| **High risk** | |
| Disagree | Disagrees with statement or behavior of others |
| Demand | Demands that others do something |
| Takes object/toy | Takes or tries to take toy or object from others |
| Aggression | Physically aggressive toward toys or others |

*Source:* Wilson, B. J. (2006). The entry behavior of aggressive/rejected children: The contributions of status and temperament. *Social Development* 15(3):468, Table 1. This material is reproduced with permission of John Wiley & Sons, Inc.

range from low to high risk. The low-risk strategies are more likely to result in acceptance by the group, whereas the high-risk strategies are more likely to result in rejection.

As you can see in the table, some children stay on the outside of the group and watch, others gradually enter into the group's activity, and still others leap in and disrupt it. Popular children enter groups by slowly integrating themselves into the activity. For example, if a group of children are making roads in the sand, the popular child will tend to watch for a short time and then find a way to contribute to the roads other children are constructing. A rejected child might disrupt the road construction, kicking the sand and destroying what the other children have created. A child who is neglected by others might watch the road making but never enter into it. Clearly, even simple sand play can show us that social situations can be very complex for the young child.

## what if...?

As his preschool teacher, you have noticed that Damian is quite shy. He spends a great deal of time watching other children play. One day you see him building a block structure by himself, but while he is doing that, he frequently glances at a group of children nearby who are building an elaborate series of block structures. You ask Damian if he would like to join the other children and he nods, indicating that he would. What suggestions would you give him to help him join successfully with the others?

Derek E. Rothchild/The Image Bank/Getty Images

A girl watches two other girls before she tries to join them. By observing them, she is more likely to find a positive way to join in what they are doing.

**developmental disabilities** Conditions that cause children's development to be delayed or different from that of other children their age; these conditions may be genetically based (such as Down syndrome) or may result from trauma or other causes.

**inclusive** With respect to a classroom or similar setting, including both children with disabilities and children without disabilities.

## Peer Relationships among Children with and without Disabilities

Children with **developmental disabilities**, like Down syndrome, have some condition that causes their development to be delayed or different from that of other children their age. These children are often not at the same cognitive or social level of development as their peers, and this may affect not only their style of learning but also their relationships with other children. Children with disabilities are entitled to receive preschool services and generally do so in settings with typically developing children. Next, we describe the policy that establishes this right to preschool services for children with disabilities. Then we consider research on peer relationships of children with and without disabilities.

### The Individuals with Disabilities Education Act (IDEA) Policy

In 1975, federal legislation was enacted to ensure that the more than 6 million children with disabilities in the United States would receive the education they needed from birth to early adulthood. The law, now known as the Individuals with Disabilities Education Act (IDEA), has been revised several times since it was first enacted in 1975 as Public Law 94-142. The law currently has three major provisions, which apply to individuals from ages 3 to 21:

1. *Children with disabilities are entitled to receive a free and appropriate public education.* The interpretation of what "appropriate" means is usually made at the district and state level.
2. *Education should be provided in the least restrictive environment.* This provision is usually interpreted to mean that a child should be in a classroom setting as much as possible like the one provided to other children.
3. *Preschool children are to receive services under IDEA.* Even though free public education is not provided for all 3- and 4-year-olds in the United States, it is provided to children of that age with disabilities under Part B of the act.

Under current educational policy in the United States, beginning at age 3, the majority of children with disabilities are educated in inclusive settings. Settings are considered to be **inclusive** when they include both typically developing children and those with disabilities, unlike settings (such as special schools) developed exclusively for children with disabilities. What do we know about how both children with disabilities and typically developing children fare in inclusive classrooms?

Researchers have found that children with developmental disabilities in inclusive classrooms spend more time engaged in social interaction with their peers than those in classrooms serving primarily children with disabilities (Hauser-Cram, Bronson, & Upshur, 1993; Odom et al., 2004). Therefore, inclusive settings appear to offer important social opportunities for children with disabilities. Such opportunities, however, do not guarantee that children with disabilities will be well accepted by their peers. One study indicated that about 28% of children with disabilities in inclusive classrooms were rejected by their peers, compared with approximately 15% of typically developing children (Odom et al., 2006).

Even though most children with disabilities are not rejected by their peers, they tend to have fewer reciprocal friendships than children without disabilities (Guralnick, 2010; Guralnick, Neville, Hammond, & Connor, 2007)—that is, friendships in which both children name the other as a friend. One set of researchers found that children with developmental disabilities spent less time in cooperative play and more time in solitary play than their peers (Hestenes & Carroll, 2000). As a result of these different play patterns, children with disabilities had fewer opportunities to engage with peers. These same researchers, however, found that children with and without disabilities interacted more frequently when a teacher was nearby. Preschool teachers thus have an important role in helping young children with disabilities develop friendships with others in the classroom (Diamond & Hong, 2010).

Do typically developing children gain anything from their interactions with peers with disabilities? It appears that they do. One group of researchers interviewed young children who attended preschool classes that were either inclusive or included only typically developing children. They found that children in the inclusive classes had a greater knowledge of the implications of disabilities and a greater acceptance of those with disabilities (Diamond, Hestenes, Carpenter, & Innes, 1997). In a related study, a researcher interviewed 45 typically developing children who attended an inclusive preschool (Diamond, 2001). She found that those who had made social contact with children with disabilities in the classroom scored higher on measures of social understanding and acceptance of individuals with disabilities than children who had not made such contact. Other researchers have found that typically developing children in inclusive preschools have improved social skills and display less disruptive behavior than their peers enrolled in preschools that do not include children with disabilities (Strain & Cordisco, 1994).

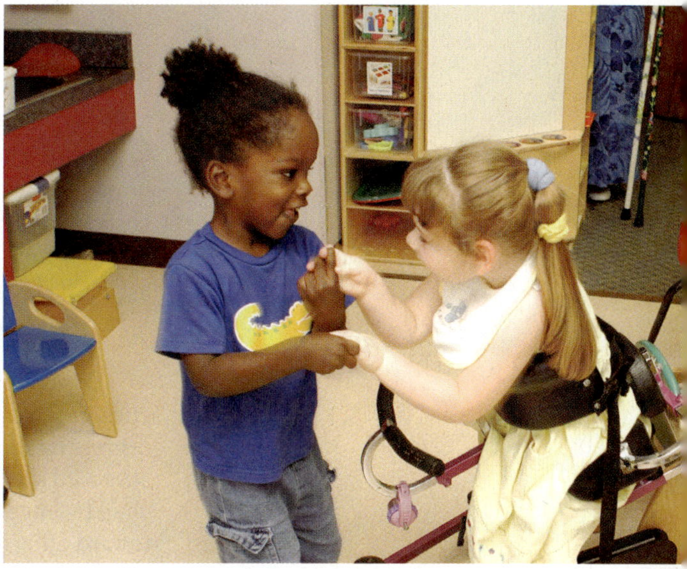

*Realistic Reflections/Getty Images, Inc.*

Children with disabilities and typically developing children both benefit from the friendships and social interactions they share in classrooms like this one.

Children learn a great deal from their interactions with their peers. If their classrooms include children with disabilities, as many classrooms do, typically developing children gain a greater acceptance and understanding of children with disabilities. This enhanced understanding and acceptance may produce psychosocial skills valued in our society.

## Prosocial and Antisocial Behaviors

Young children display a range of behaviors that affect their relationships with others. Some of these behaviors are prosocial, and others are antisocial. Children engage in **prosocial behaviors** when they help others without obvious benefits for themselves (Eisenberg & Murphy, 1995). They engage in **antisocial behaviors** when they act in ways that enable them to get what they want without concern about others. Although most children show both types of behaviors during the early childhood years, some children are more likely to show one type than the other.

### Prosocial Behaviors

Two important prosocial behaviors that have been studied in young children are empathy and sympathy. Recall from Chapter 7 that empathy is "an affective state that stems from the apprehension or comprehension of another's emotional state or condition" (Eisenberg & Fabes, 1998, p. 702). Empathy requires three components: (1) an emotional response to another person, (2) a cognitive ability to take the perspective of another, and (3) emotional regulation (Decety & Jackson, 2006).

Empathy often results in an emotional state in the observer that is identical or similar to the emotional state of the person being observed (Eisenberg, Fabes, & Spinrad, 2006). Indeed, recent neuroimaging studies indicate the same neural circuits are activated in an individual who is showing emotion and a person who is feeling empathetic toward that individual (Decety & Jackson, 2006). Children may show empathetic overarousal, however, when they respond to the emotional state of a person who is obviously distressed by getting distressed themselves. They may also show sympathy, which is a desire to improve the emotional state of the other (Eisenberg & Fabes, 1990). Because sympathy is a form of empathy that attempts to help others, it is considered a prosocial skill.

**prosocial behavior** Actions that benefit another person or a relationship.

**antisocial behavior** Actions that harm another person or a relationship.

*Everyday stories*

A SYMPATHETIC RESPONSE Several children are going down a long slide in their school's playground. The slide is very slippery, and going down it in good form can be a challenge. The teachers have arranged for the children to wait for their turns in a line behind the slide, so only one child is on the slide at a time. The children begin to cheer on the child going down the slide. When Li slides down, however, she falls on her side and tumbles off the end of the slide. Several children see her fall, but only Mya runs up to her and hugs her, asking if she is okay. Mya is showing sympathy toward Li.

Preschool teachers often note the "contagion effect," which occurs when one child cries and then several others start crying as well. In this situation, children are recognizing distress by showing distress. Some children, though, will show the more developmentally advanced skill of sympathy when they see a child in distress. They may try to comfort the child by hugging, distracting, or offering kind words. Children who show more sympathy toward others also tend to have a greater understanding of emotions (Eggum et al., 2011). They can recognize emotions in others and interpret them accurately.

Why do some young children show more sympathy than others? Researchers have found that children with better emotional regulation are able to show more sympathy toward others (Valiente et al., 2004), perhaps because they do not become overaroused by others' distress. In one study, researchers measured children's effortful control to see if it was related to their ability to show sympathy to others. The children were asked to work on a puzzle without peeking at hidden pieces behind a cover. They found that children who could resist the temptation to peek also showed more sympathy toward their peers in situations of social distress. This result suggests that both effortful control and sympathy involve self-regulation. Children who are indifferent to the distress of others, as well as those who become overaroused by others' distress, may have difficulty showing sympathy because they are struggling with their own self-regulation.

Children may also show differences in sympathy because of their cultural backgrounds. Cultures vary in the extent to which they emphasize prosocial skills (Kartner, Keller, & Chaudhary, 2010). For example, infants in West Africa are encouraged to hand back objects that are handed to them (Nsamenang, 1992). Such basic routines may encourage sharing—a practice that frequently causes conflict among children in the United States. Another example comes from a study of families in Japan. Lewis (1995) found that Japanese parents reported that they send their children to preschool in order to learn empathy and related prosocial skills, such as functioning as part of a group. In contrast, parents in the United States placed greater emphasis on academic goals for their preschool children.

© Heide Benser/Corbis Images

Some young children show sympathy to others and try to help them feel better when they are upset.

## Antisocial Behaviors

During the preschool years, aggression is the most frequently observed antisocial behavior. Aggression occurs when children are not able to regulate their emotions sufficiently to find other solutions to a problem (like disengaging, taking turns, or talking about a solution). Although aggression is sometimes appropriate, such as when fending off an aggressor, such situations are rare, and most aggressive actions are inappropriate reactions to a conflict or problem.

Psychologists have identified several different types of aggression. In the preschool years, **instrumental aggression** occurs most frequently. Children engage in this type of aggression when they want to obtain an object, privilege, or space but do not intend to harm others. A child might grab a toy another child is playing with, for example, to get the toy—not to hurt the other child. When aggressive actions are coupled with the intention to harm others, they are considered **hostile aggression**. Hostile aggression can either be **overt aggression**, which involves harming others through physical injury or threats of physical injury, or **relational aggression**, which involves attempts to damage a relationship with another (for example, whispering mean things about a peer behind the peer's back). After the toddler years, boys are more likely to show overt aggression and girls more likely to engage in relational aggression (Brown, Arnold, Dobbs, & Doctoroff, 2007; Ostrov & Crick, 2007).

**instrumental aggression** Attempts to gain an object, privilege, or space without the intent of harming another.

**hostile aggression** Actions that have the intent of harming another.

**overt aggression** Actions that harm another through physical injury or threats of physical injury.

**relational aggression** Actions that harm another by damaging a relationship.

One group of researchers followed children from birth through third grade to study patterns of physical aggression, one component of overt aggression (NICHD Early Child Care Research Network, 2004). They found that physical aggression generally decreases over the preschool years. At ages 2 to 3, about 70% of children engage in hitting others. That figure declines rapidly to about 20% at ages 4 to 5 and to about 12% by middle childhood.

Why does aggression occur more often in some young children than in others? Psychologists have looked at this question from two different perspectives. The first perspective relies heavily on a biological explanation. Biological differences can be inborn, but they can also be a result of environmental effects.

In considering inborn differences, many psychologists have maintained that children are born with different temperaments (as discussed in Chapter 7). Therefore, some children are more biologically primed to be highly reactive and aggressive than others (Yaman, Mesman, van IJzendoorn, & Bakermans-Kranenburg, 2010). Some children are slower at developing the emotional regulation required in high-conflict or frustrating situations. As discussed earlier in this chapter, the ability to self-regulate is related to changes in the brain, especially to the maturity of areas in the frontal cortex (Diamond, Prevor, Callender, & Druin, 1997; Rueda, Checa, & Combita, 2012). Although this area of the brain is not considered to be fully mature until early adulthood, maturation of this region begins early and continues through early childhood. The rate of maturation differs across individuals, and some children may therefore lack the ability to self-regulate because their brains have not reached the necessary level of maturation (Hum & Lewis, 2013).

Events during children's early years can also affect biological aspects of self-regulation. As we discussed in Chapter 8, toxic stress alters brain development. Brain alterations are likely to occur in children raised in very stressful circumstances, especially if they have been neglected or abused, as we discuss later in this chapter. Unfortunately, because of their early experiences, some children may have great difficulty regulating their emotions and will show high levels of behavior problems.

We have seen that one explanation for why some children are aggressive is related to their biology, either through inborn temperament or through alterations caused by early stressful environments. Social learning theorists provide yet another explanation. These theorists emphasize children's ability to imitate the actions they observe in those around them. We discuss one central theorist, Albert Bandura, in the accompanying Focus On feature.

In a classic study, Albert Bandura and his colleagues (Bandura, Ross, & Ross, 1961) conducted an experiment to see if children who observed an adult being aggressive would show more aggression themselves. The researchers studied 3- to-5-year-old

## Focus On: Albert Bandura

*Jon Brenneis/Time & Life Pictures/Getty Images, Inc.*

Albert Bandura first became well known because of his Bobo doll experiments. In later work, Bandura demonstrated that when children are exposed to television violence, they became more aggressive. He showed that exposure to television violence produces four effects: (1) it teaches aggressive styles of action, (2) it weakens restraints against aggression by glamorizing violence, (3) it desensitizes the viewer to violence, and (4) it shapes the viewer's images of reality. Bandura was often called to Washington to testify about the effects of television violence on children. His testimony helped shape some of the Federal Communications Commission's guidelines about children's television programming.

In recent years, Bandura has been primarily interested in self-efficacy. Do you believe that your hard work will get you the result you hope for? That is the type of question Bandura is now exploring as he emphasizes the importance of perceived self-efficacy (Bandura, 2006; Bandura, Caprara, Barbaranelli, Gerbino, & Pastorelli, 2003). He is interested in understanding why people choose certain actions in their attempts to complete goals. He emphasizes that the most effective way to build self-efficacy is through mastering challenges that require a person to overcome obstacles and to persevere (Bandura, 2008). Although it may seem that his work on perceived efficacy has moved him away from studies of imitation and modeling, Bandura says that "the Bobo doll continues to follow me wherever I go" (Kester, 2001). Furthermore, he has brought together his work on modeling and his work on self-efficacy by noting that observing others succeed through perseverance increases our own sense of efficacy and hope of succeeding (Kester, 2001).

children in a preschool. Half of the children saw aggressive "models," and half did not. In addition, half of the children of each sex observed an aggressive model of the same sex.

Children in the study were invited into a playroom by an experimenter. The experimenter then brought the model into the playroom and had that person sit at a table with a construction toy, a mallet, and a 5-foot "Bobo" doll (an inflated punching bag). The model was either aggressive or nonaggressive. Both types of models began by playing with the construction toys. The aggressive model, however, quickly turned to the Bobo doll. The model hit the doll on the head with the mallet and tossed it into the air, making comments like "Sock him in the nose," "Hit him down," "Throw him in the air," and "Kick him."

The experimenter then took the children to another playroom stocked with a range of toys, including a Bobo doll, dart guns, a tether ball, a tea set, baby dolls, a ball, and art materials. The researchers recorded the children's behaviors during a 20-minute session in this playroom. As you can see from Figure 10.2, the children who had seen the aggressive model engaged in more aggressive acts in the playroom than the children who had seen the nonaggressive model. Although both boys

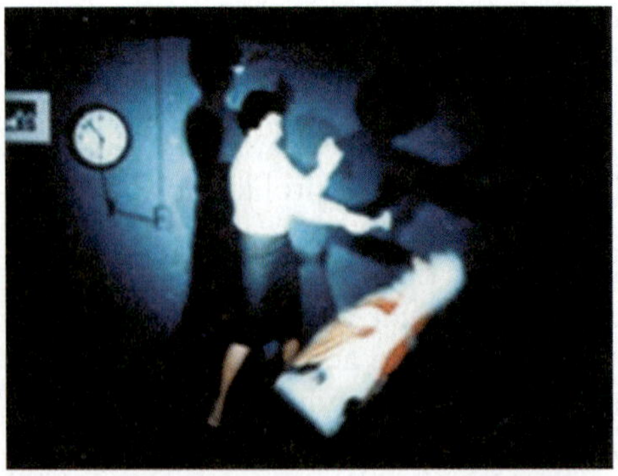

*Courtesy Albert Bandura*

In his famous study using Bobo, an inflatable clown, Bandura found that children learned to imitate aggression by observing an adult hitting Bobo.

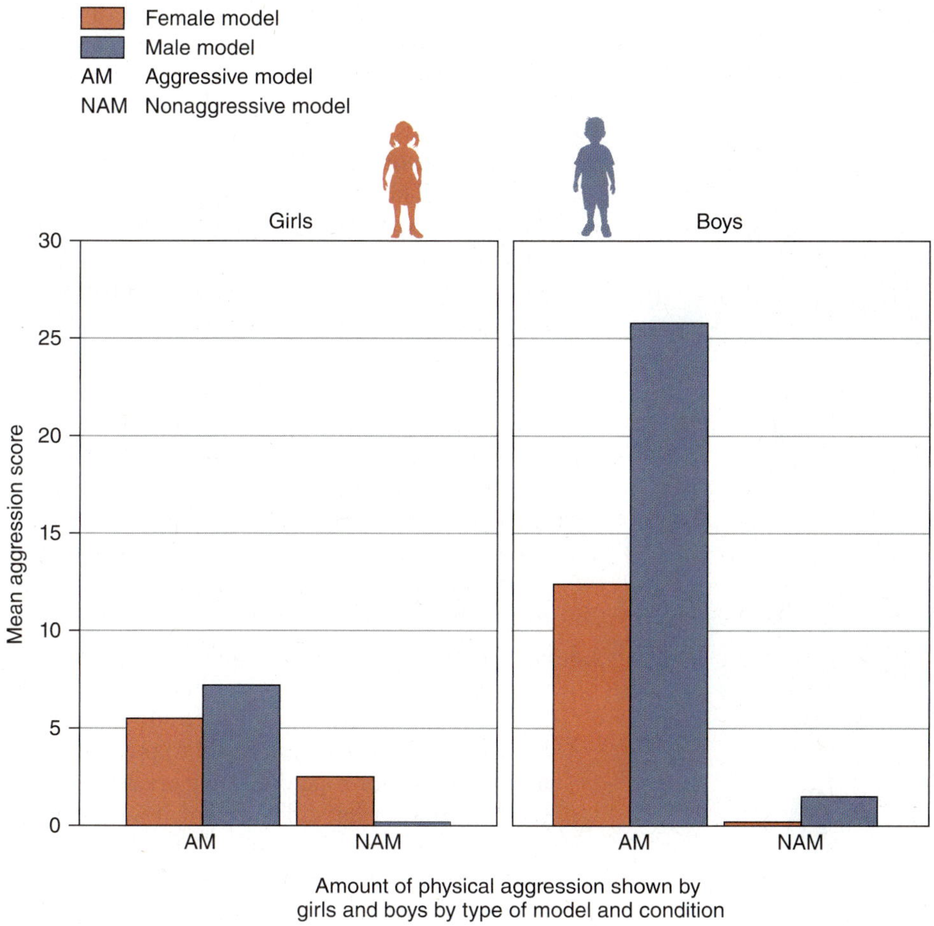


**FIGURE 10.2 Physical Aggression by Sex, Type of Model, and Condition** Children watched models who were either male or female and either aggressive or nonaggressive. Children who watched an aggressive model engaged in more aggressive acts afterward than children who watched a nonaggressive model. The effect was especially pronounced in boys who witnessed male aggressive models.

*Source:* Bandura, A., Ross, D., & Ross, S. A. (1961). Transmission of aggression through imitation of aggressive models. *The Journal of Abnormal and Social Psychology*, *63*(3), 575–582. Adapted with permission from the American Psychological Association.

and girls tended to imitate aggression when they had seen it, boys who witnessed male aggressive models were more aggressive than other children. This study is frequently used to illustrate the view that mere observation of aggression can lead to the imitation of it.

This study, and many that have followed it (Bandura, 1973, 1977), indicate that observation is a powerful learning tool. Children have many opportunities to observe aggression, including at home, in their communities, and in the media. According to social learning theory, children who witness high levels of aggression are more likely to display aggression toward their peers.

WHEN SYSTEMS CONNECT

## Developing a Theory of Mind

Communicating well with others requires children to understand that others may think differently than they do and have a different perception of a situation. This type of thinking requires a "theory of mind." **Theory of mind** is a term used to refer to children's understanding of the mental states (that is, the "minds") of themselves and of others (Tager-Flusberg, 1999). Theory of mind is an aspect of social cognition, because it involves using cognitive skills to understand social dimensions of life. Children are considered to have a mature theory of mind if they recognize that the perspective, desires, and beliefs of others are different from their own. You can probably imagine that understanding these differences requires the cognitive and psychosocial systems of development to work together. Children begin to acquire basic aspects of theory of mind during the preschool years.

**theory of mind** Children's understanding of the mental states (that is, "the minds") of themselves and others.

A range of tasks have been developed to test both simple and more advanced notions of children's theory of mind. The three following tasks are often used:

1. *Perspective tasks.* A child is shown a card with a picture of a cat on one side and an ice cream cone on the other. The child views both sides of the card. Then the experimenter holds up the card so the child sees only one side. The child is told, "In this game I am looking at a picture. See if you can tell me what picture I'm looking at." (Flavell, Botkin, Fry, Wright, & Jarvis, 1968)
2. *False-belief tasks.* Children are told a story about Sally and Anne, illustrated in Figure 10.3: "Sally has a basket and Anne has a box. Sally has a ball and puts it in her basket while Anne looks on. Sally then goes for a walk. While Sally is on the walk, Anne takes the ball out of Sally's basket and puts it in her box. When Sally returns, where will she look for the ball?" (Frith, 1989)
3. *Appearance–reality tasks.* Children are shown a sponge that looks like a rock. They are asked to look at it for 30 seconds, then they are allowed to hold it for 1 minute, then they are told to put it down and look at it but not touch it. They are asked, "When you first saw it, what did you think it was, before you touched or squeezed it? Did you think it was a rock or did you think it was a sponge? What does it look like now? What is it really? Is it really a rock or really a sponge?" (Flavell, Flavell, & Green, 1983)

Most children have success with these tasks at around 4 years of age (Tager-Flusberg, 1999). They begin to understand that another person can have different information than they have. Therefore, they can understand an event or object differently. A more complex understanding of the perspectives of others develops during middle childhood and adolescence, but the essential elements are established in early childhood.

In Chapter 7, we mentioned that children with autism spectrum disorders have deficits in social interaction and communication skills (Hutman, Chela, Gillespie-Lynch, & Sigman, 2012; Lerna, Esposito, Conson, Russo, & Massagli, 2012). Children with this disorder tend to have more difficulties with theory-of-mind tasks than do other children their age, and this lack of understanding likely affects their often inappropriate interactions with others (Lind & Bowler, 2010; Losh, Martin, Klusek, Hogan-Brown, & Sideris, 2012). (See the Research Insights feature for more on this subject.)

**FIGURE 10.3 The Sally and Anne False-Belief Task** Sally has a basket and Anne has a box. Sally puts a ball in her basket while Anne looks on. Sally then goes for a walk. While Sally is away, Anne takes the ball out of the basket and puts it in her box. When Sally returns, where will she look for the ball? Figuring out the answer depends on being able to see the situation from Sally's point of view.

## Research Insights: Do Children with Autism Lack a Theory of Mind?

As we noted in Chapter 7, autism spectrum disorders are developmental disorders marked by severe deficits in social interaction, communication, and imagination, as well as repetitive and restricted patterns of interests and behaviors (DSM-5, 2013; Volkmar, Lord, Baily, Schultz, & Klin, 2004). Children with autism fail to orient to social stimuli when they are young and have difficulties with social reciprocity and communication skills (Tager-Flusberg, 2010). Current estimates from the Centers for Disease Control and Prevention (2012) indicate that approximately 1 in 88 children in the United States have been diagnosed with the disorder. This is an estimated 350% increase in the last 10 years, and the reasons for that increase are not yet known (Hauser-Cram, Cannarella, Tillinger, & Woodman, 2013).

The theory-of-mind deficits in children with autism have been replicated many times. Although most typically developing children have success with theory-of-mind tasks at around ages 4 and 5, children with autism often still struggle with these tasks at ages 9 and 10, and they have particular difficulties with false-belief tasks (Peterson, Wellman, & Liu, 2005). Researchers conclude that children with autism most likely process these types of tasks in a different way than do typically developing children and that such differences also lead to the social aloofness seen in children with autism (Peterson et al., 2005).

One type of current neuropsychological research is focusing on specific neurons, called *mirror neurons* because they react when an individual observes an action as well as produces one. (You may recall that we discussed mirror neurons in Chapter 4.) Some studies have found that the mirror neurons in specific brain regions (e.g., the medial prefrontal cortex and the superior temporal sulcus) show abnormal activity when individuals with autism attempt to process theory-of-mind tasks (Marsh & Hamilton, 2011; Oberman & Ramachandran, 2007). This has led to a debate about whether the deficits in social processing seen in children with autism spectrum disorders are related to flaws in the mirror neuron system (Gallese, Rochat, & Berchio, 2013; Williams, 2008).

### ✓CHECK YOUR PROGRESS

1. Describe the types of play you are likely to see in a preschool classroom, and give an example of each.
2. How might children who are accepted, rejected, and neglected act when they want to play with a group of children already engaged in an activity like building a castle out of blocks?
3. Provide two explanations for why a child might be aggressive.
4. How do researchers study theory of mind in young children?

# Moral Development

**[ KEY QUESTION ] 4. During the early childhood years, how do children change in the way they view right and wrong and what is fair and unfair?**

Children's moral perspectives often involve their views of how they should treat others as well as how they like to be treated. Indeed, moral development evolves in interaction with others. **Moral development** describes how children acquire the standards of behavior that are considered right and wrong in their society. These standards include an understanding of what is considered to be ethical, fair, and just.

Moral development requires abstract thought about issues of right and wrong (Shweder, Much, Mahapatra, & Park, 1997). During the early childhood years, children are not capable of abstract reasoning, but they do show the beginnings of moral thought (Kenward & Dahl, 2011). As you think about the daily lives of young children at home and in preschool or day-care settings, you realize they are surrounded by rules, standards, and expectations that help them develop a sense of right and wrong. These external guides are not enough, however, to ensure that children will develop an internal sense of what is right and wrong and what is fair and just. How do children internalize this sense of morality?

**moral development** Children's acquisition of society's standards regarding what is right and wrong and what is just and unjust.

**moral transgressions** Actions that aim to cause harm to another person.

**conventional transgressions** Actions that violate social norms but do not harm others.

## Right and Wrong

Preschoolers can differentiate between **moral transgressions**, which cause harm to other people, and **conventional transgressions**, which violate a notion of politeness or appropriate behavior (Smetana & Braeges, 1990). Thus, a 5-year-old might burp on purpose to get a reaction from peers, realizing that although such behavior may not be considered appropriate, it is not morally wrong. In contrast, that same 5-year-old would likely realize that secretly taking another child's toy and hiding it is not "right."

### Cognitive-Developmental Theory: Piaget and Kohlberg

Much writing about children's moral development has evolved from cognitive-developmental theory. Piaget (1965), as you may recall from Chapter 1, studied children's reasoning and proposed that children evolve in their ability to incorporate different aspects of a moral dilemma. In particular, he focused on children's ability to consider the intentions, or motives, of others. Piaget gave a good illustration of young children's inability to incorporate intentions in their reasoning when he provided children with a story about two boys, John and Henry. Both boys broke cups, but the situations were different, as you can see in Figure 10.4.

> JOHN: *A little boy who is called John is in his room. He is called to dinner. He goes into the dining room. But behind the door there was a chair, and on the chair there was a tray with fifteen cups on it. John couldn't have known that there was all this behind the door. He goes in the door, knocks against the tray, bang go the fifteen cups, and they all get broken!*
>
> HENRY: *Once there was a little boy whose name was Henry. One day when his mother was out he tried to get some jam out of the cupboard. [He knew he wasn't allowed to get the jam.] He climbed up on a chair and stretched out his arm. But the jam was too high up and he couldn't reach it and have any. The cup fell down and broke.*

**FIGURE 10.4 John, Henry, and the Broken Cups** In judging John's and Henry's behavior, younger children tend to say that John deserves more punishment because he broke more cups. Piaget believed that young children have difficulty considering motive and outcome at the same time and so focus only on outcome.

John accidentally breaks 15 cups when he goes into the dining room after being called to dinner. He didn't know the cups were behind the door.

Henry accidentally breaks one cup while trying to get jam out of the cupboard—which he knows he isn't supposed to do.

Piaget asked preschool-aged children which boy, John or Henry, should be punished more for his actions. Younger children tended to say that John deserved the greater punishment because he had broken more cups. In Piaget's view, these children had difficulty considering *both* motive (accidental breakage in the case of John and breakage while being disobedient in the case of Henry) and outcome (the number of cups broken) simultaneously. Instead, they tended to focus on the outcome. Piaget claimed that young children are unable to determine that motive could be more important than the end result. By the end of the early childhood period (at around age 7), children have begun to understand that it is important to take motives as well as outcomes into account when determining what is ethical behavior.

## what if...?

You see two 5-year-olds arguing on the playground. Eric cries out, "You hit me with that tube you were carrying." Sara acts surprised and says, "I didn't mean to hurt you. I didn't see you when I was carrying the tube across the playground." Eric replies, "You're wrong because you hurt me." Sara argues, "No, you're wrong because I didn't mean to hurt you." How would you analyze this argument? How might you help the children settle the argument?

Piaget also stressed that when children are quite young (around ages 3 and 4), they consider society's rules to be ready-made. He termed this view a **heteronomous orientation**. By the end of the early childhood period (at around age 7), children have moved to an understanding that individuals participate in establishing the rules of society, termed an **autonomous orientation**. By *autonomous*, Piaget did not mean that children make decisions on their own. Rather, he meant that they understand that people participate in decision making about ethical behavior in a society.

One of Piaget's students, Lawrence Kohlberg, also studied children's moral development. In his studies, he provided individuals with hypothetical situations and asked them to describe what would be the "right" thing to do in that situation. Based on their answers, Kohlberg proposed three general stages of moral reasoning (Kohlberg, 1976).

During early childhood, most children exhibit **preconventional morality**, the earliest stage. This stage includes two substages. In the first substage, children tend to obey rules to get rewards or avoid punishment. In the second, children act so as to exchange favors with another person—"I'll help you if you'll help me." In both of these substages, thinking remains preconventional in that it is focused on the needs of the self, not on the needs of others or of society as a whole. The next two stages of moral development typically occur after early childhood and will be discussed in more detail in later chapters. Table 10.3 summarizes Piaget's and Kohlberg's stages.

**Table 10.3** Moral Reasoning during Early Childhood

| Theorist | Stage | Reasoning |
|---|---|---|
| Piaget | Heteronomous | Rules are ready-made |
| | Autonomous | Rules are made by individuals |
| Kohlberg | Preconventional: | |
| | Substage 1 | Obey rules to get rewards and avoid punishments |
| | Substage 2 | Act to exchange favors with others |

**heteronomous orientation** In Piaget's theory, the young child's view that moral rules are ready-made.

**autonomous orientation** In Piaget's theory, children's understanding that moral rules are established by humans and can change over time.

**preconventional morality** Kohlberg's first stage of moral reasoning, in which children focus on obeying in order to gain rewards or avoid punishments.

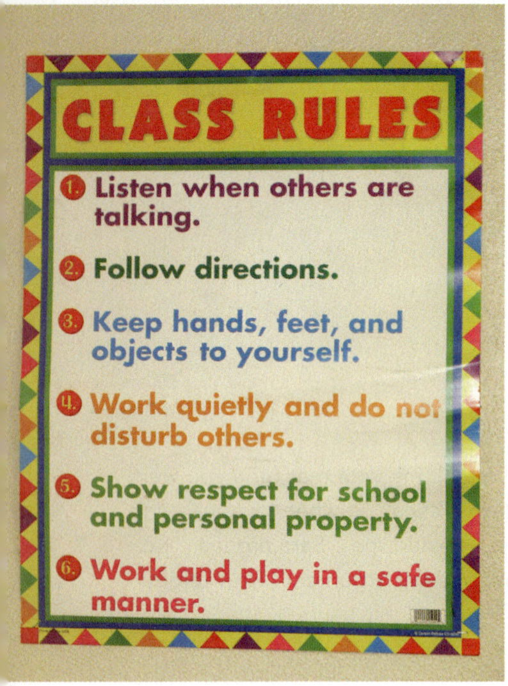


© Richard Mittleman/Alamy Limited

Sets of rules are posted in many classrooms. Although young children often follow the rules, they also need to develop an internal sense of what is right and wrong.

### Recent Research on Ideas of Right and Wrong

More recent work on children's moral development has considered how children reason through actual situations, rather than how they think about hypothetical moral dilemmas posed by researchers. Investigators have found that even young children consider it wrong to hurt others because they are concerned for others' welfare rather than just because they fear punishment (Helwig & Turiel, 2002; Smetana, 2006). One study found that between the ages of 2½ and 4, children developed their ability to independently evaluate moral dilemmas, without relying on rules imposed by authority figures (Smetana, Rote, Jambon, Tasopoulos-Chan, Villalobos, & Comer, 2012). These findings suggest that previous work might have overestimated children's reliance on rules and underestimated their concern for other people.

Although young children can show concern for others, this concern only goes so far. One creative study helps us understand the distinctions that children make in reasoning about their own wrongdoing and that of others (Wainryb, Brehl, & Matwin, 2005). In the study, researchers interviewed children about their experiences of being hurt (being a victim) and of hurting others (being a perpetrator). Most children have experience with both of these situations.

The preschool children in the study tended to provide largely narrative descriptions of getting hurt, usually physically hurt, by another child. In contrast, children's descriptions of hurting another child tended to incorporate additional elements, usually justifications for what they had done. Here are some examples:

> *"It wasn't wrong that I didn't let her play [tag] because I wanted to be* it.*"*
>
> *"It was okay that we told him he couldn't be on our team, because we didn't want to be on a bad team." (Wainryb* et al.*, 2005, p. 65)*

When these young children had caused harm to others, they often realized they had done so, but they considered their actions to be justified because of their own personal goals. Thus, even though young children can show concern about others, they are usually more involved in their own perspective, especially when they think they have been wronged or when they want to justify their actions in harming someone else. The young child of 3 or 4 is quite **egocentric**. As you may recall from Chapter 9, this is a term Piaget (1952, 1965) used to mean that the child considers mainly, and often only, his or her own point of view.

Parents often become concerned with an aspect of children's behavior that emerges in the preschool period and has implications for their moral development: telling lies. If young children lie, do they have a sense that such behavior is not morally acceptable? In an innovative study, researchers studied lying behavior in young children ages 3 to 8 (Talwar & Lee, 2008). A researcher took children into a room, asked them to turn their backs while he played a sound from a toy, and then told them not to peek at the toy when he left the room. When the researcher returned, the children were asked if they had peeked at the toy and what they thought the toy was. The children were instructed to tell the truth. In fact, no child could have correctly guessed what the toy was by having heard the sound because the researcher had played a sound from a greeting card, not from the toy.

The researchers found that 82% of the children actually peeked at the toy. Only 36% of those who had peeked confessed to doing so, however. Many of the children who had peeked and not confessed actually blurted out the name of the toy, thus implicating themselves, often without realizing it. The older children were able to produce more plausible lies, indicating that there is a cognitive component to this type of behavior. In order to lie successfully, a child needs to anticipate what is plausible in the mind of the person listening to the lie, a task that requires a decrease in egocentricity and a mature sense of theory of mind.

**egocentric** Piaget's term for children's tendency to consider only their own perspective.

**distributive justice** Justice involving the way in which objects, rewards, and penalties can be distributed fairly.

## Distributive Justice

Parents and teachers often hear children exclaiming, "It's not fair!" Some psychologists have studied children's notions of **distributive justice**—that is, how objects or actions such as praise or punishment can be distributed fairly. As we would expect, these notions change over time.

Many parents have found that the best way to have 3-year-olds share a cookie is to have one child break the cookie in half and the other child select the half he or she wants. This is because very young children's views of distributive justice are based on their own desires ("It's fair because I want it" or "It's not fair because I didn't get what I wanted"). When 4- or 5-year-olds are asked to give rewards to others after participation in a mixed-age group activity, they often give a larger reward to the person who is the oldest. By the age of 6 or 7, children's idea of distributive justice is often based on equality for all, regardless of need or merit. One study found that 6- to 8-year-old children were likely to throw away resources if these resources could not be equitably distributed (Shaw & Olson, 2012). Not until middle childhood (around age 10 or 11) do children usually reason that other aspects of a situation, such as hard work or need, should be considered in determining what is a fair distribution (Damon, 1980; Damon & Hart, 1988; Thomson & Jones, 2005).

*Everyday stories*

WHAT'S FAIR? Three boys—Marcelo, Jim, and Darrell—are arguing about who deserves the most praise for putting together a tent to be used on their school playground. Marcelo thinks that Darrell should get the most praise because he is the oldest of the three. Jim says he worked the hardest, so he should get the most praise. Darrell thinks they each should get the same amount of praise. Each of the boys has taken a different view about fairness.

We have seen that children's moral development changes throughout early childhood. The very young child is concerned mainly with her own wants and needs, even though she may know that hurting others is not "right." Her sense of fairness tends to be based on her own needs and desires. As she develops, she begins to incorporate the intentions of others as well as a sense of fairness based on equity. Not until middle childhood, though, do most children begin to weigh several factors simultaneously, such as need and effort, in making decisions about fairness.

**CHECK YOUR PROGRESS**

1. What is the difference between moral transgressions and conventional transgressions?
2. According to Piaget, young children reason about society's rules using a heteronomous orientation. How does that differ from the autonomous orientation children acquire at the end of the early childhood years?
3. Kohlberg proposed that during early childhood children reason about moral situations using preconventional morality. How are the two substages of preconventional morality similar? How do they differ?
4. How would you describe the typical 4-year-old's sense of fairness?

## Parenting Practices

**[ KEY QUESTION ] 5. What parenting practices support positive psychosocial development in young children?**

As we noted in Chapter 7, parents play a very important role in advancing children's psychosocial development. Investigations of parenting practices have found that different types of parenting produce different behavior patterns in children (Roisman & Fraley, 2012; Wahl & Metzner, 2012; Wilson, Havighurst, & Harley, 2012). In this section, we consider the effects of different parenting styles and practices. We

**authoritarian parenting** A type of parenting that attempts to control children through coercive demands and punishment accompanied by little warmth.

**permissive parenting** A type of parenting that places few demands or limits on children and that often includes warmth.

**uninvolved parenting** A type of parenting that places few demands on children and that provides them with little warmth.

**authoritative parenting** A type of parenting that places demands on children through reasoning coupled with warmth.

then turn to the issues of child abuse and neglect and the effects of such treatment on the psychosocial development of the young child.

## Parenting Styles

By *parenting styles,* we mean parenting practices and behaviors that remain consistent across many situations. One of the best known studies of parenting styles was conducted by Diana Baumrind (1967, 1971, 1989). We discuss her work next and then describe some cultural differences in parenting styles.

Baumrind began by studying children in middle-class families. She first observed 100 children in preschool and rated their self-control and self-confidence, among other characteristics. Because she wondered if the mothers of the children rated differently on those dimensions differed in their parenting styles, she then interviewed the mothers and observed them interacting with their children. She found that mothers differed on four important dimensions:

1. How much warmth and affection the mother showed toward the child
2. Whether the mother used persuasion, explanation, or harsh discipline in attempting to control the child's behavior
3. How well the mother communicated with the child
4. Whether the mother expected the child to display self-control and other mature characteristics

Based on these dimensions, Baumrind developed a typology of four parenting styles that fit the majority of mothers (Maccoby & Martin, 1983) (see Figure 10.5):

1. **Authoritarian parenting** makes coercive demands and imposes punishments on children in attempts to control their behavior. It provides little warmth or emotional support.
2. **Permissive parenting** places few demands on children and exerts little control over them. It emphasizes learning through experience rather than through punishment, and it provides warmth and emotional support.
3. **Uninvolved parenting** places few demands on children and also provides them with little warmth.
4. **Authoritative parenting** places demands on children but provides explanations for those demands. It prefers reasoning over punishment, and it offers warmth and emotional support.

Much research has indicated that these basic styles are prevalent among middle-class mothers in the United States. Furthermore, children tend to differ in predictable ways based on which style their parents use, as shown in Table 10.4 (Baumrind, 1989; Chao, 2001). Children of authoritarian mothers tend to focus on what others think of them, to have low levels of social competence with their peers, and to lack curiosity.

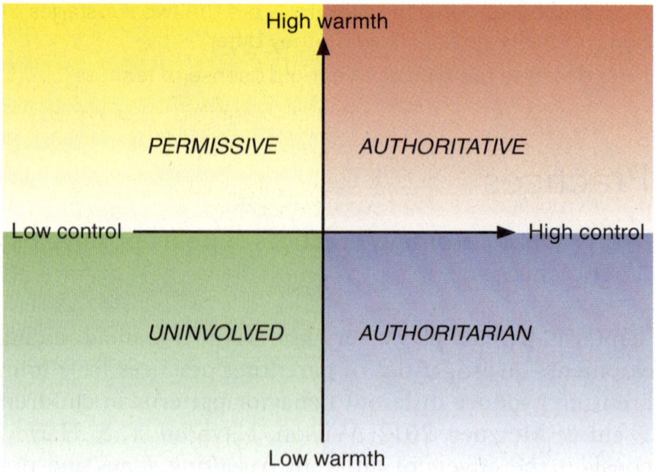


**FIGURE 10.5 Parenting Styles** The dimensions of warmth and control combine to produce four parenting styles: authoritarian, permissive, uninvolved, and authoritative.

**Table 10.4** Parenting Styles and Child Outcomes

| Parenting Style | Child Outcomes |
|---|---|
| Authoritarian | Has poor relationships with peers<br>Lacks curiosity |
| Permissive | Is disrespectful of others<br>Has poor self-regulation |
| Uninvolved | Has poor self-regulation<br>Has low sense of self-esteem<br>Has difficulty with independence |
| Authoritative | Has good self-regulation<br>Is self-reliant<br>Is curious |

Children whose mothers are permissive tend to become overly dependent on others and show poor self-regulation, such as impulse control. Children whose mothers are uninvolved typically show poor self-regulation, have a low sense of self-esteem, and have difficulty in situations requiring independence. Finally, children whose mothers use authoritative styles tend to be self-reliant, self-controlled, and curious.

*Everyday stories*

AN AUTHORITATIVE PARENTING STYLE Yoshi's mother is reading a book to him while he sits in her lap. Yoshi points to some of the humorous pictures in the book, and they both laugh. After a few minutes, Yoshi gets tired of the story. He takes the book from his mother and holds it overhead as if he is starting to throw it. She says to him, "Yoshi, the book may be hurt if you throw it, and then we can't read it another day. Give me the book and we can put it away." Yoshi calmly gives his mother the book. Yoshi's mother displays a good example of authoritative parenting.

© Jose Luis Pelaez, Inc./Blend Images/Corbis Images

A father talks with his son about why his son should not have taken another child's toy. The father is showing authoritative parenting by displaying warmth and providing reasoning his son can understand.

Most research on parenting styles has focused on mothers. One of the few studies of fathers' parenting style (Winsler, Madigan, & Aquilino, 2005) found that fathers and mothers often differ. In that study, fathers frequently saw mothers as having a parenting style different from their own. The fathers perceived their spouses to be less authoritarian than themselves. Other research provides additional evidence that fathers in the United States use authoritative approaches less than mothers (Porter et al., 2005). We don't know what the effects on children may be of having parents with different parenting styles. These differences may complement each other, or they may be a source of conflict in the family.

## Cultural Differences in Parenting Style

Some researchers have questioned whether Baumrind's parenting styles have the same effects on children in different cultures. In one comparative study of parenting style in the United States and China, researchers found that Chinese mothers and fathers were more authoritarian than U.S. mothers and fathers (Porter et al., 2005). The optimal parent in China is involved closely with the child, is willing to make sacrifices for the child, and serves as an agent of control (Chao & Sue, 1996). That type of control may be seen in the United States as an indicator of authoritarian parenting, which can lead to maladaptive child behaviors. In China, though, it may be seen as a support and as an indicator of positive parenting that leads to adaptive child behaviors. These differences may relate to parents' **ethnotheories** about good parenting (Harkness & Super, 1996). As we discussed in Chapter 1, ethnotheories involve parents' cultural beliefs about which parenting practices lead to positive child behaviors.

One way in which cultures vary is in the extent to which they promote individualistic or collectivist values. In **individualistic cultures**, like the United States and

**ethnotheories** Parents' cultural beliefs about parenting practices that lead to positive child behaviors.

**individualistic cultures** Cultures in which the goals of the individual are considered more important than group goals.

**collectivist cultures** Cultures in which the goals of the group are considered more important than the goals of individuals.

Canada, individuals are expected to assert themselves and actively pursue their own wishes and needs. In **collectivist cultures**, like China and Japan, individuals are expected to adjust their own needs and wishes to those of the group (Markus & Kitayama, 1991). When analyzing parenting styles, you can see how they might have different meanings in individualistic cultures that aim for children to assert themselves and in collectivist cultures that aim for children to be part of a group (Sorkhabi, 2005).

### Responding to a Child's Distress

Parents' responsiveness to children's distress is another important dimension of parenting style (Luebbe, Kiel, & Buss, 2011; Suchodoletz, Trommsdorff, & Heikamp, 2011). How do parents react when their child is upset? Responses vary from negative (hostile, dismissing, or teasing) to positive (comforting and helping). When parents deal with a child's distress in positive and effective ways, the child learns that distress can be relieved and may begin to perceive emotionally arousing events as less threatening (Gottman, Katz, & Hooven, 1996). This type of parenting helps children increase in their emotional regulation and prosocial behaviors toward others. A study of children aged 6 to 8 found that when mothers and fathers react in a supportive way to their children's distress, the children show more empathy toward others (Davidov & Grusec, 2006). In contrast, when parents respond to their children's distress in a dismissive or hostile way, the children are likely to show more negative emotions and poorer regulation of their emotions when upset in the future (Eisenberg et al., 1999; Kochanska, Aksan, Prisco, & Adams, 2008).

© Jose Luis Pelaez, Inc./Blend Images/Getty Images, Inc.

A child who is comforted when he is distressed learns that his feelings of distress can be relieved.

Very few studies have considered this dimension of parenting in relation to children with developmental disabilities, but it appears that a parent's responsiveness to distress is also important in furthering the development of these children. One group of researchers studied children with biologically based disabilities, such as cerebral palsy, who were born preterm (Young & Hauser-Cram, 2006). The researchers observed interactions between mothers and children while the mothers were teaching the children a task that was slightly challenging. When children became distressed, the mothers' responses to that distress were recorded. Researchers were interested in positive actions, including physical support (such as hugging), emotional support (such as soothing words of empathy), and strategies to help the child change focus and regain emotional regulation (such as distraction). Children whose mothers engaged in more of these positive actions later showed more persistence in problem-solving tasks (such as sliding a lever to get a toy to appear). The researchers speculated that the self-regulation of these preschool children was enhanced by their mothers' early patterns of positive responses to distress.

In summary, we can point to several aspects of parenting that have positive effects on children's development. One dimension is emotional. It includes warmth and support. This dimension becomes especially important during times when the young child is distressed. Another dimension involves setting limits. Limit setting should be firm but not coercive or punitive and should be responsive to the child's needs and level of understanding. These aspects of parenting guide children as they begin to explore their expanding social worlds.

## Spanking as a Form of Discipline Parenting

When confronted with children's misbehavior, how do parents react? One possible reaction is spanking, which has received a lot of attention from both psychologists and policy makers. Many countries (for example, Austria, Germany, Italy, Norway, and Sweden) have policies or laws that prohibit parents from using spanking and other forms of corporal punishment. Studies indicate, however, that over 90% of parents in the United States report having spanked their children by the time their children were 3 or 4 years old (Gershoff, 2002; Straus & Stewart, 1999).

Parents in the United States vary in how much they use spanking and other forms of corporal punishment (Gershoff, Lansford, Sexton, Davis-Kean, & Sameroff, 2012). Parents who use this form of discipline more frequently are from lower socioeconomic groups and also tend to be under higher levels of stress (Mackenzie, Nicklas,

Waldfogel, & Brooks-Gunn, 2012; Pinderhughes, Dodge, Bates, Pettit, & Zelli, 2000). Such parents are also likely to hold strong beliefs about the value of harsh discipline, to view their child as having hostile intentions, and to be concerned about their child's future if the child is not immediately compliant (Pinderhughes et al., 2000). There are also cultural differences in beliefs about the value, necessity, and disadvantages of this form of discipline (Lansford & Deater-Deckard, 2012). Children from some cultural groups see spanking as normal, while others do not (Gershoff et al., 2010).

Since spanking is so widely used, it might seem to be a necessary way to discipline children. Furthermore, spanking appears to be effective in that it often results in immediate compliance (Gershoff, 2002). But is there any harm in spanking children? One group of researchers (Strassberg, Dodge, Pettit, & Bates, 1994) studied 273 preschool children (ages 4 to 6 years) and their parents to see if there was any relation between punishment at home and aggression in preschool. The researchers found that children who had been spanked were almost three times more likely than children who had not been spanked to be aggressive with their peers when provoked. Even children who were spanked infrequently showed more aggression than children who were never spanked. The researchers speculated that children who had been spanked had learned a specific response pattern when they were provoked, which was to react quickly and physically.

Some psychologists consider any form of corporal punishment to be harmful to children (Straus, 2001). Most psychologists agree that spanking is harmful when it is harsh (like slapping a child in the face or hitting the child with an object) (Benjet & Kazdin, 2003). Furthermore, although spanking may produce immediate compliance, its long-term effects may work in the opposite direction. Many studies have found that children are more compliant with parents' wishes when they experience positive moods and emotions (Lay, Waters, & Park, 1989; Parpal & Maccoby, 1985). In contrast, negative emotions can lead children to resist and to focus on themselves rather than on the event (Lazarus, 1991). Therefore, the pain, fear, and anger a child experiences when physically punished may trigger less compliance with adults in the future.

## Maltreatment of Children

Unfortunately, as we noted in Chapter 8, not all parents use positive parenting practices. Instead, they maltreat their children or allow others to do so. Maltreatment of children is a critical concern in the United States. As you can see in Figure 10.6,

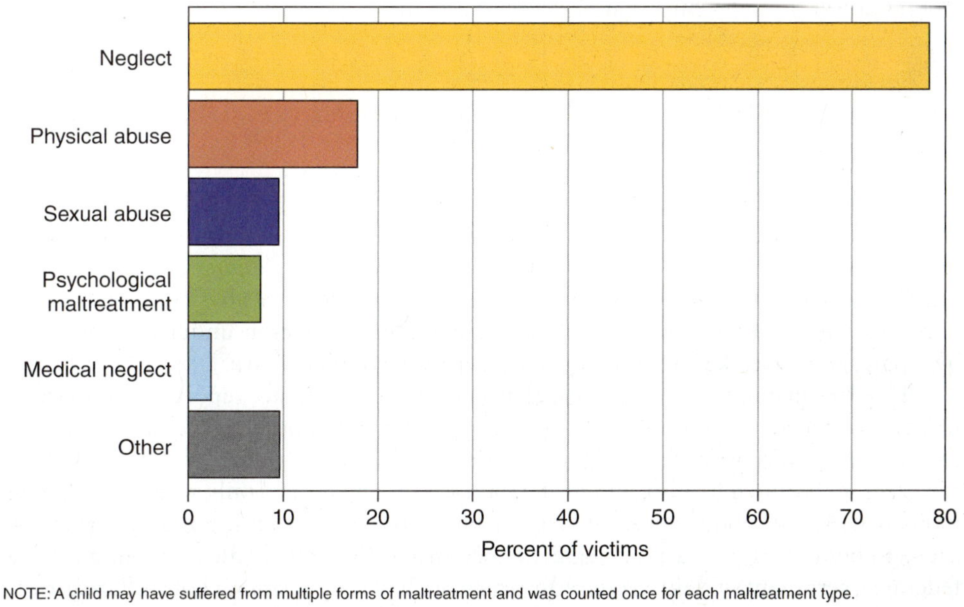


**FIGURE 10.6 Abuse and Neglect among U.S. Children under Age 18, 2009** Neglect is by far the most common type of maltreatment of children in the United States. Children may be neglected physically, educationally, medically, or emotionally.

*Source:* Reprinted from U.S. Department of Health and Human Services, Administration for Children and Families, Administration on Children, Youth and Families, Children's Bureau (2010). Child Maltreatment 2009. Available at http://www.acf.hhs.gov/programs/cb/pubs/cm09/index.htm.

**FIGURE 10.7 Perpetrators of Maltreatment by Relationship to Victims, 2009** Most often it is a parent who neglects or abuses a child. As you can see, more than 80% of the perpetrators of maltreatment are parents.

*Source:* Adapted from U.S. Department of Health and Human Services, Administration for Children and Families, Administration on Children, Youth and Families, Children's Bureau (2010). Child Maltreatment 2009. Available at http://www.acf.hhs.gov/programs/cb/pubs/cm09/index.htm.

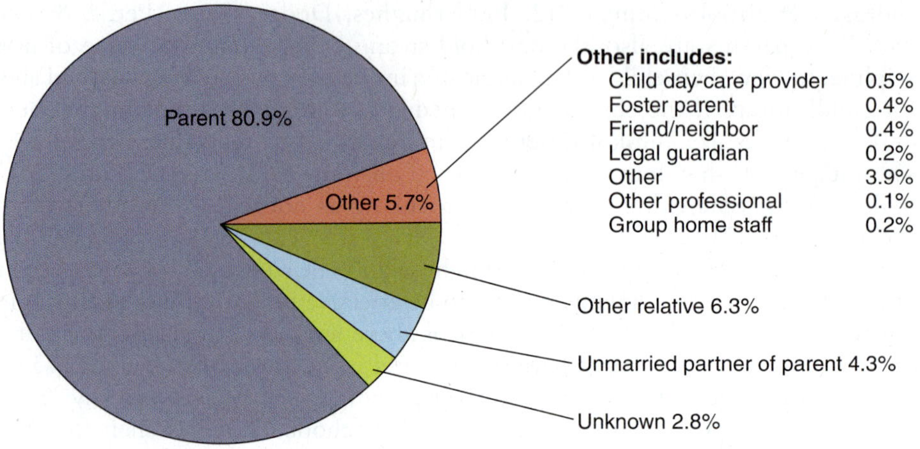


neglect is the most common type of maltreatment, followed by physical abuse. More than 80% of the perpetrators of abuse and neglect are children's parents, as shown in Figure 10.7.

There are various kinds of abuse and neglect. Abuse may take the following forms:

- Physical abuse (such as hitting or slapping)
- Sexual abuse (such as touching a child's genitals for purposes other than daily care)
- Psychological abuse (such as taunting, mimicking, or degrading)

Neglect can occur in any of the following areas:

- Physical neglect (failure to provide sufficient nutrition, shelter, clothing, hygiene)
- Medical neglect (failure to provide health and medical treatment)
- Educational neglect (failure to make sure the child receives education and related services)
- Emotional neglect (failure to provide appropriate affection and emotional response to the child)

Because of the seriousness of child maltreatment, a federal law has been enacted to prevent it from occurring and to require that it be reported when it does occur. The law requires certain professionals to report any incidents of abuse or neglect as well as *suspicions* of abuse or neglect. Each state has a process for such reporting, but the federal policy provides important general guidelines.

## The Federal Child Abuse Prevention and Treatment Act (CAPTA)

Policy

The Child Abuse Prevention and Treatment Act (CAPTA) was passed in an attempt to prevent child maltreatment. It was originally enacted in 1974 and has been amended several times since then. The act defines abuse or neglect as "any act or failure to act that results in imminent risk of serious harm, death, serious physical or emotional harm, sexual abuse, or exploitation of a child (usually a person under the age of 18) by a parent or caretaker who is responsible for the child's welfare."

The law mandates, or requires, that certain professionals report child abuse or neglect. For teachers, nurses, doctors, social workers, psychologists, child-care workers, and others who work with children professionally, failure to report abuse or neglect can result in criminal liability and civil liability. This applies not only when one of these individuals knows about abuse or neglect but also when he or she has a "reasonable cause to believe" that abuse or neglect is occurring. (For more information, go to the federal government's Child Welfare Information Gateway at www.childwelfare.gov.)

Clearly, it is important that individuals who work with children know the signs of abuse and neglect. They also need to know how these suspicions of abuse and neglect should be reported. Failure to report abuse and neglect can have critical consequences for professionals—and certainly has grave consequences for abused or neglected children.

what if...?

Suppose you are a day-care provider at a neighborhood center. You notice that Ben, who is usually upbeat, seems quite gloomy and distracted today, and then you see that he has a burn on his arm. When you ask him about the burn, he covers it up by pulling his shirt sleeve down, and then he runs away from you. You are concerned about him but don't want to make him uncomfortable in the classroom. What would you do?

## The Effects of Maltreatment on Children

Because children rely so much on those who care for them, they suffer terribly when those individuals either turn on them or fail to provide for their basic needs. Research shows that maltreatment has negative effects on children, extending even to a very basic biological level (Cicchetti & Rogosch, 2011; Spratt et al., 2012).

One biological effect of maltreatment involves levels of a hormone, cortisol (Cicchetti, Rogosch, Gunnar, & Toth, 2010). As we discussed in Chapter 2, levels of cortisol in the human body generally increase in response to stress. Such stress can be caused by persistent poverty and unrelenting interpersonal conflict. Levels of cortisol generally vary throughout the day, with the highest levels occurring in the morning, followed by decreases throughout the afternoon and evening. In one study, children who had been both sexually and physically abused had higher-than-normal levels of cortisol in their saliva in both the morning and the afternoon (Cicchetti & Rogosch, 2001). These abnormal levels may indicate a form of physiological dysregulation, which can also be seen in the children's poor coping skills and inappropriate behaviors.

**The Effects of Abuse.** Much research indicates that children who have been maltreated have difficulties in their relationships with peers (Alink, Cicchetti, Kim, & Rogosch, 2012; Kim & Cicchetti, 2010). The types of difficulties the children experience differ, however, depending on whether they have been abused or neglected. We look first at findings concerning abused children.

One study found that children who have been abused are just as accurate as other children in labeling facial expressions (such as happy or angry). However, their brains showed different responses at the neurological level (Pollak, Cicchetti, Klorman, & Brumaghim, 1997). Children who have not experienced maltreatment showed similar brain patterns in response to happy and angry faces, whereas children who had been abused showed a stronger response to the angry faces. The researchers reasoned that children who have experienced abuse are uniquely sensitive to the angry and negative expressions of others.

Several researchers have found that children who have been abused are more likely to respond in a hostile way to angry or aggressive cues from others (Dodge, Pettit, Bates, & Valente, 1995; Pollak et al., 1997; Rieder & Cicchetti, 1989). As noted earlier, children who have been abused tend to detect even minor facial expressions of anger—expressions that their peers either do not see or choose to ignore (Pollak & Sinha, 2002). Furthermore, they are likely to experience a strong reaction to these expressions. Such hostile responses make it difficult for children to have positive interactions with their peers, and the lack of positive interactions further limits their psychosocial development.

One study of children who had been abused focused on their responses to the distress of their peers (Klimes-Dougan & Kistner, 1990). The researchers observed young children during supervised playground activity in day-care centers. Observers recorded each child's reaction when a peer fell down near the child. The observers did not know which children had been abused when they were recording the responses. Later, though, it turned out that the children who had been abused had made more inappropriate responses. These responses consisted of teasing the distressed peer, using verbal or physical aggression, or moving away from (rather than comforting) the peer. This finding suggests that children who have been abused may become dysregulated when they see a peer in distress. As a result, they may behave in a hostile or aggressive way.

**The Effects of Neglect.** Children who have been neglected also suffer emotionally and show unusual responses to their peers. These children often have more difficulty than other children in discriminating among emotional expressions (Pollak, Cicchetti, Hornung, & Reed, 2000). Even identifying the simple emotions of happy, sad, angry, and scared in line drawings of facial expressions appears to be much more difficult for neglected children than for other children (Pears & Fisher, 2005). One explanation is that neglected children have a limited emotional environment in their homes because their parents are less expressive and less engaged with them than are other parents (Bousha & Twentyman, 1984). Therefore, these children simply have less experience in discriminating emotional expressions.

Neglected children also tend to be at risk for having poor relationships with their peers because they lack the important skills necessary to respond appropriately to a peer's emotional signals. They have fewer social interactions with other children and tend to be more socially isolated than others (Camras & Rappaport, 1993). Neglected children also tend to have a less developed sense of humor, and they often show unusual behaviors, such as tics, stealing, toileting accidents, dependency, and clinginess (Hildyard & Wolfe, 2002).

Children who have been neglected do poorly on tasks involving theory of mind (Cicchetti, Rogosch, Maughan, Toth, & Bruce, 2003; Pears & Fisher, 2005). It is likely that no adults have helped these children to become aware that people have different points of view. This neglect has led to the children's impoverished understanding of their own emotions as well as of the emotions of others. Without such an understanding, children may have difficulty creating meaningful relationships.

Extreme neglect leads to a range of problems for children. Such stressful experiences alter brain development (Shonkoff & Phillips, 2000), as discussed in the accompanying Research Insights feature. Because of extreme emotional neglect, some children have difficulty regulating their emotions and show many behavioral problems.

**Interventions.** Research on the effects of maltreatment clearly indicates serious consequences for children's development. Children who have been abused tend to be more aggressive with their peers. Children who have been neglected tend to be more withdrawn from their peers. Both of these reactions limit children's abilities to have positive interactions with others. These limitations can have broad consequences, since peer relationships are a critical way for children to learn psychosocial skills as well as to experience enjoyment. Early identification of children who have been maltreated is a national concern. Nevertheless, many children remain unidentified and are therefore prevented from having the positive psychosocial development that they deserve.

Hope exists for these children in the form of intervention programs for parents. Many types of programs exist. Some programs help parents understand child development. Others help parents learn skills for coping with their own frustration. Still others encourage the use of community supports. These programs operate from the view that providing help to parents who become stressed in their caregiving duties will result in more positive psychosocial development in their children.

The Task Force on Community Preventive Services at the Centers for Disease Control gathered research on programs designed to prevent child maltreatment. In 21 studies, the task force found evidence of the effectiveness of home-visiting

## Research Insights: The Effects of Extreme Emotional Neglect

At one time, Romanian orphanages were very poor in quality, and children were neglected in a variety of ways. The children were provided with food and clothing but had few toys to play with and few adults who could comfort and play with them. Many of the children were adopted into homes in the United States, Canada, or Europe once news of their horrific living conditions became public. Several researchers later studied children who had spent their first few months or years in Romanian orphanages. What happened to these children as a result of such early deprivation?

One study of preschool children who had been adopted from Romania found an unusually high rate of difficulties among the children. Of the 65 children in the study, 55 had medical, developmental, or behavioral problems (Johnson et al., 1992). Another study of 130 adoptees from Romania found that although some problems decreased over time, many children continued to have medical problems, sleep difficulties, and behavior problems, especially tantrums (Marcovitch, Cesaroni, Roberts, & Swanson, 1995). And a study of children from Romanian orphanages adopted into homes in the United Kingdom found a higher rate of emotional disturbance by age 11 in these children than in children adopted from less deprived circumstances (Rutter et al., 2007). It seems that early deprivation, especially the lack of contact with a loving caregiver, affects children's ability to regulate their emotions (Nelson, Bos, Gunnar, & Sonuga-Barke, 2011).

© Daily Mail/Rex/Alamy Limited

Children in some orphanages have received only basic care and little comfort from adults or stimulation from the environment. The lack of comfort and stimulation affects development.

Recent studies of children who lived in Romanian orphanages and were later adopted have used neuroimaging techniques. Researchers have found both brain differences and behavioral differences between these children and children who had never been institutionalized (Mehta et al., 2009). One set of researchers (Tottenham et al., 2010) focused on the limbic system, an area of the brain important in emotional processing. The researchers used magnetic resonance imaging to measure the volume of the amygdala, which is part of the limbic system. Recall from Chapter 2 that the amygdala plays a significant role in emotional processing. They found that children who had been institutionalized at birth and adopted after the age of 15 months had greater amygdala volume and less adequate emotional regulation than children who had been adopted before the age of 15 months and children who had not been institutionalized. This research suggests that some of the behavioral differences seen in these children may be the result of lasting damage to their brains from early deprivation.

programs. The programs generally employ professionals, such as nurses, social workers, or mental health workers, to visit a parent and child on a regular basis. They provide parents with information about child health and development, offer emotional support, and suggest community resources. They also often model positive parenting practices, such as using time-out methods effectively so a child can cool down during an emotionally charged event. In general, these programs have been found to be effective in preventing child maltreatment, especially among teenage parents, single mothers, families of low socioeconomic status, and parents previously investigated for maltreatment. (For more information on these findings, go to the CDC website at www.cdc.gov/ViolencePrevention/childmaltreatment/index.html.)

### ✓ CHECK YOUR PROGRESS

1. How do authoritarian, permissive, and authoritative parenting styles differ?
2. What are the negative effects of spanking?
3. In what ways does child abuse affect children's behaviors?
4. Explain how child neglect could limit young children's positive peer relationships.

# CHAPTER SUMMARY

## Emotional Development

**[ KEY QUESTION ] 1. What are some processes young children develop to regulate their emotions?**

- According to Erikson, young children struggle with a sense of initiative versus guilt in the challenges they face in trying new activities and interacting with others.
- Young children recognize some emotions—especially happy, sad, and angry—more readily than others. They are gradually able to identify more complex emotions, such as surprised, scared, and disgusted.
- Emotional regulation involves a process of effortful control. Children learn to control their emotions during times of distress by shifting their attention and by using self-talk.

## The Development of a Sense of Self

**[ KEY QUESTION ] 2. How do young children view themselves?**

- Children gradually develop a sense of self during early childhood. Their sex, male or female, is one of the most salient characteristics they focus on in developing a sense of self.
- Sex differences become associated with different behaviors and preferences through gender-role development.
- There are four major explanations of children's gender-role development. Biological theory stresses the role of prenatal hormones in children's behavior and selection of activities. Psychoanalytic theory emphasizes identification with the same-sex parent, although this process differs for males and females. Social learning theory focuses on children's imitation of the behaviors they see in others and in the media. Cognitive-developmental theory stresses the importance of the concepts that children develop about male and female behaviors and actions.

## Relationships with Peers

**[ KEY QUESTION ] 3. Why do some young children have good peer relationships while others have poor ones?**

- Children learn to negotiate friendships through play. To do this, they need to employ emotional regulation in situations of conflict.
- Through play with peers, children acquire prosocial skills like cooperation and compromise; such skills are important to friendship development.
- Children develop the beginnings of a theory of mind during early childhood. They begin to have success with understanding that both they and others have mental states, perspectives, and beliefs. They realize that others can have different beliefs from their own because others may have different information.

## Moral Development

**[ KEY QUESTION ] 4. During the early childhood years, how do children change in the way they view what is right and wrong and what is fair and unfair?**

- According to Piaget, in the first part of the early childhood period children tend to see societal rules as predetermined, whereas later in early childhood they recognize that individuals are involved in making rules and laws.
- At the beginning of early childhood, children tend to focus on the outcome of an event in determining whether behavior was ethical; by the end of early childhood, they can incorporate both motive and outcome in such determinations.
- During the first part of early childhood, children consider an action to be just, or fair, if it is biased toward them, which is a reflection of their egocentricity. At the end of this period, they tend to view an action as just if it involves equality for all those involved. Only later in childhood do they consider issues like effort and need in their sense of justice.

## Parenting Practices

**[ KEY QUESTION ] 5. What parenting practices support positive psychosocial development in young children?**

- Four major parenting styles have been found in the United States: the authoritarian, permissive, uninvolved, and authoritative styles. The authoritative parenting style appears to result in children who are self-reliant, are curious, and have good self-regulation. This style includes elements of warmth and affection, especially in times of distress; makes use of explanation as an aspect of discipline; and involves high but appropriate expectations for the child.
- Child maltreatment, either abuse or neglect, results in poor outcomes for children, especially in relation to emotional regulation and social interaction with peers. Children who have been abused tend to misinterpret the nonverbal cues of other children. Those who have been neglected tend to have difficulty discriminating the emotional expressions of their peers.

# KEY TERMS

associative play *367*
authoritarian parenting *384*
authoritative parenting *384*
autonomous orientation *381*
collectivist cultures *386*
conventional transgressions *380*
cooperative play *367*
developmental disabilities *372*
distributive justice *382*
effortful control *358*
egocentric *382*
Electra complex *365*
ethnotheories *385*
gender constancy *362*
gender differences *361*
gender schemas *361*
gender stereotypes *363*
heteronomous orientation *381*
hostile aggression *375*
inclusive *372*
individualistic cultures *385*
initiative versus guilt *356*
instrumental aggression *375*
moral development *379*
moral transgressions *380*
neglected children *370*
Oedipus complex *365*
overt aggression *375*
parallel play *367*

permissive parenting 384
popular children 370
preconventional morality 381
prosocial behavior 373
rejected children 370
relational aggression 375
self-concept 360
self-representations 360
sex differences 361
sociodramatic play 368
symbolic play 368
theory of mind 377
uninvolved parenting 384

## CRITICAL THINKING QUESTIONS

1. **Emotional Development.** Why do you think some young children have great difficulty with emotional regulation while others do not?
2. **The Development of a Sense of Self.** Gender-role development is one important aspect of self-concept. What do you see as the strengths and drawbacks of each of the theories of gender-role development discussed in the chapter: biological theory, psychoanalytic theory, social learning theory, and cognitive-developmental theory?
3. **Relationships with Peers.** Suppose you are visiting a day-care center and see a young child who is quite aggressive with the other children. Provide several explanations for why that child might be so aggressive.
4. **Moral Development.** What are some ways that parents can encourage children's moral development?
5. **Parenting Practices.** Why do you think that parenting styles differ by culture? Provide examples of ways in which ethnotheories about parenting differ among cultural groups.
6. **Cultural Perspectives.** Culture not only affects what children learn but also how they express their emotions. Why do you think that cultures place different values on showing certain emotions such as pride and shame?

## REAL Development

### Psychosocial Development in Early Childhood

In the accompanying Real Development activity, you are interested in learning more about the development of peer interactions. A developmental psychologist at your university, Dr. Jones, has researched extensively on different types of play. You will read about different types of play described below and then use these descriptions to help Dr. Jones identify different forms of play in Adeline's pre-school classroom.

© *John Wiley & Sons, Inc.*

**WileyPLUS** Go to WileyPLUS to complete the *Real Development* activity.

03.01

# Milestones in Early Childhood

## 2 years

### Physical

- Climbs easily onto chairs, out of cribs, up ladders
- Walks upstairs two feet at a time
- Takes off shoes and socks, pulls up pants
- Holds crayon with thumb and all fingers, scribbles
- Uses spoon to feed self

Imagemore Co., Ltd./©Corbis

### Psychosocial

- Labels self according to gender
- Shows interest in activities of peers
- Engages in parallel play

© Rubberball/Rubberball/Corbis

### Cognitive

- Often attributes animate qualities to inanimate objects
- Tends to focus attention on one characteristic of an object or task while neglecting to focus on others
- Can sort objects into categories
- Uses overregularizations when talking
- Uses speech to guide problem solving, usually by talking out loud
- Uses invented spelling
- Associates small numbers (like 3 and 4) with specific quantities

Dorling Kindersley/Getty Images, I

### Cognitive

- Begins to understand that a word represents a category
- Has a vocabulary of 150 to 300 words. Vocabulary expands at rate of approximately 10 words a day
- Has beginning signs of print awareness
- Recognizes differences in very small number sets

iStockphoto

## 3–4 years

### Physical

- Walks upstairs alternating feet
- Kicks, throws, and catches ball, but inefficiently
- Pedals riding toys
- Uses safety scissors and fork
- Can fasten simple snaps, large buttons, and zippers
- Builds block towers
- Copies line and circle, draws "tadpole" people

Fuse/Getty Images, Inc.

### Psychosocial

- Uses concrete details when describing self
- Identifies emotions as "happy" or "sad"
- Has strong sense of gender stereotypes
- Uses theory of mind to understand "false beliefs" of another person
- Engages in sociodramatic play
- Sense of fairness is based on own needs or desires
- Engages in associative play

## 5–6 years

### Physical

- Walks downstairs alternating feet
- Throws by rotating torso
- Catches ball with hands, but still inefficiently
- Skips and gallops; runs gracefully
- Ties shoelaces; gets dressed and undressed
- Uses knife to spread and cut soft food
- Copies triangles, letters, numbers, and words
- Drawings of people have more detail
- Builds a five block bridge

*Jose Luis Pelaez, Inc./Blend Images/Getty Images, Inc.*

### Cognitive

- Begins to take into account the visual perspective of the listener
- Increasingly uses adjectives with nouns
- Produces grammatically correct statements even if model is incorrect
- Improves in selectively attending to tasks

*Ocean//©Corbis*

- Shifts attention in tasks involving a rule change
- Begins to be able to update retained information
- Rhymes words and shows other signs of phonological awareness
- Begins to use "counting on" strategy when counting two or more groups of objects

### Psychosocial

- Makes comparison to own past performance
- Identifies a range of emotions, including scared, surprised, and disgusted
- Understands gender constancy
- Shows increasing ability to control impulsive behavior
- Can show empathy and sympathy to peers
- Engages in cooperative play
- Uses one object to substitute for another in play (symbolic play)
- Differentiates moral and conventional transgressions
- Obeys rules to get rewards and avoid punishments

*Symphonie Ltd./Cultura/Getty Images, Inc.*

# Chapter 11

# Physical Development and Health in Middle Childhood

## MAKING A difference

### School Health

It's a few minutes before lunchtime, and first-grader Abby makes her way to the school nurse's office to check her blood glucose level. She was diagnosed with diabetes when she was 5 years old. Now, she is learning to manage it during a full day of school. When she arrives at the nurse's office, several other children are waiting as well. One has a stomachache, another has an ice pack on her arm after falling on the playground, and a third seems to be having problems with his asthma. The school nurse is on the phone with the state public health department about flu immunizations, even as she anxiously glances at the clock. She is supposed to be at another school across town in half an hour, but she realizes she'll have to be late so that she can attend to the children in her office at this location.

School nurses first appeared on the scene more than a hundred years ago. During the late 19th century, the major health problems children faced were the communicable diseases we discussed in Chapter 8. At that time, the prevailing policy in school districts in the United States and Europe was to dismiss sick children from school, leaving them to spread their diseases in their neighborhoods. School absenteeism was so widespread that it raised concerns not just about children's health but also about the effectiveness of public education.

In 1902, nurse Lillian Wald negotiated with the City of New York to hire, on a trial basis, the first public health nurse to work in a school—Lina Rogers Struthers, R.N. Earlier, in 1893, Wald had founded the Henry Street Settlement in New York to meet the health-care needs of poor European immigrants. Wald believed that having nurses in schools would reduce the spread of contagious diseases among school-aged children, and she was right. In her first month, Struthers treated 893 students, made 137 home visits, and helped 25 children who had received no previous medical attention to recover and return to school. As a result, the Board of Education hired her permanently, along with many additional nurses. In one year, these nurses decreased the rate of absenteeism by almost 90% (Wald, 1915).

Today, more than 70,000 registered nurses work as school nurses in public schools in the United States (U.S. Department of Health and Human Services Health Resources and Services Administration, 2010). They continue to be responsible for reporting contagious diseases and immunization rates to public health officials. Over time, their role has expanded to include screening for potential health problems,

## CHAPTER OUTLINE

health education, treatment of injuries, management of chronic illness with individual children, and participation in disaster planning. Every day, they make a difference in the lives of children and their communities.

## [KEY QUESTIONS] *for* READING CHAPTER 11

1. How do qualitative and quantitative changes in growth and development support physical, cognitive, and social skills during middle childhood?
2. What can we do to promote health and prevent disease in middle childhood?
3. How can caregivers and communities keep children safe during middle childhood?
4. How can disruptions in health affect children's learning and behavior?

IN THE PAST, middle childhood was often seen as a busy but untroubled time during which children prepared for the onslaught of adolescence. Children played in the backyard, on playgrounds, and in sports arenas. They took dance and music lessons, made friends, and joined youth organizations, such as the Boy and Girl Scouts. They just grew up. The use of the term "tweens" to describe the latter part of middle childhood reinforces the idea that children of this age group are simply between stages, no longer small children but not yet teenagers. However, this view largely ignores significant changes in the brain, physical growth, and motor skills that occur during this period. Middle childhood is, in fact, a unique period, and so deserves more specific attention.

In this chapter, we begin by reviewing the physical changes of middle childhood and addressing the implications of these changes on school readiness, physical fitness, and participation in sports. As we examine growth changes during these years, we also note the problems that can arise for many children: poor nutrition, obesity, illness, and the unrelenting pressure to succeed, which can lead to emotional stress and physical injuries. We go on to discuss the role of school health services in improving and maintaining children's health. We end the chapter with a review of the potential effects of disease and treatment on learning and behavior.

# Biology of Health: Physical Growth and Development

**[ KEY QUESTION ] 1. How do qualitative and quantitative changes in growth and development support physical, cognitive, and social skills during middle childhood?**

During middle childhood, changes in physical growth and in the brain support increasingly more sophisticated cognitive and physical development, which in turn supports social development. In this section, we review those changes, discuss the roles of genes and environment in how children grow, and illustrate emerging abilities in motor development during middle childhood.

## Growth and Size

Between ages 6 and 11, height increases about 2 or 3 in. (5–7 cm) per year, and weight gains of about 5 or 6 lbs (2.2–2.7 kg) per year are common, as shown in Figure 11.1. By 11 years of age, the average child is still slightly under 5 ft (152 cm) in height and weighs less than 80 lbs (36 kg). During these years, girls begin to grow at a more rapid rate, and by age 12 are taller and heavier than boys.

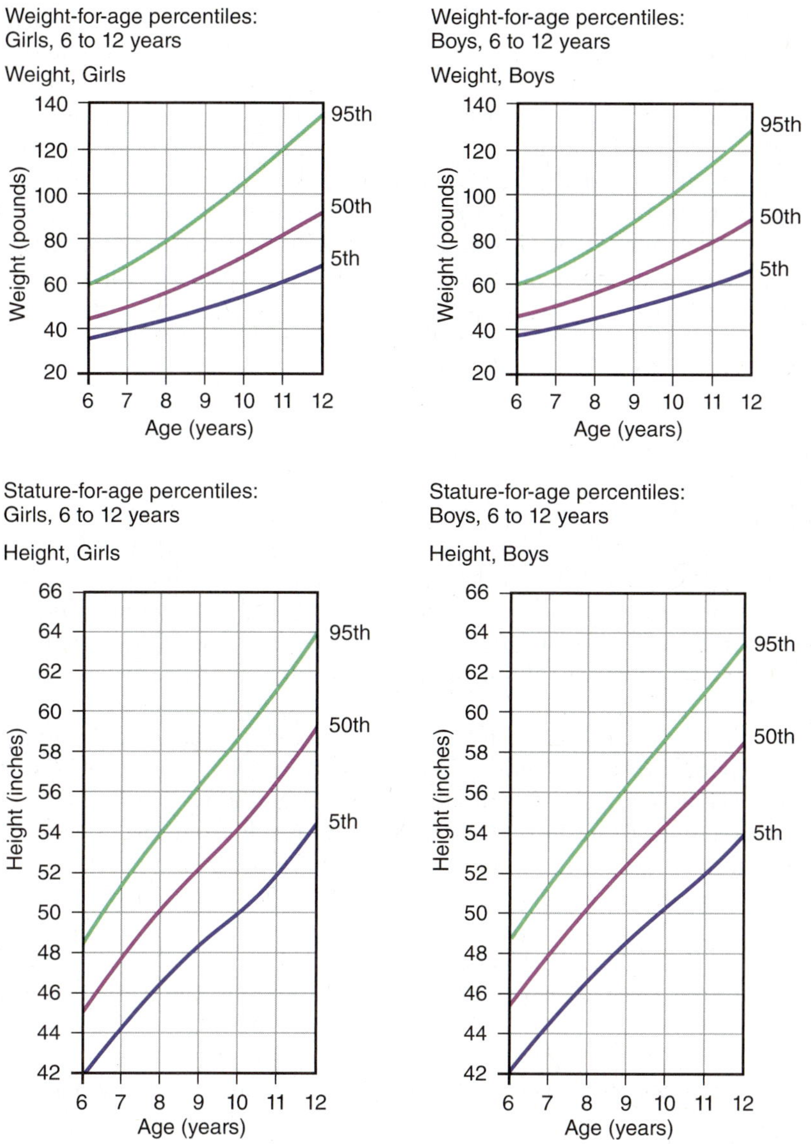


SOURCE: Developed by the National Center for Health Statistics in collaboration with the National Center for Chronic Disease Prevention and Health Promotion (2000).

**FIGURE 11.1 Growth Charts for U.S. Children Ages 6 to 12** These charts show weight-for-age and height-for-age data for adolescent boys and girls ages 6 to 12. They include the average weight and height (the 50th percentile) and weights and heights near the higher and lower ends (the 95th and 5th percentiles, respectively).

Body proportion also changes. For example, a preschooler's head size is about one-fourth of total body size, while an adult's is roughly one-seventh. The sharp difference between the two gradually decreases during the middle childhood years. Baby teeth are lost, and the emergence of permanent teeth changes the shape of the lower jaw. By age 11 or 12, with changes in height, weight, and proportion, the middle-childhood youngster's body looks more like that of an adult. Many factors combine to determine how and when children grow during middle childhood. Let's look at those factors.

## Genetic Constancy in Physical Growth

Remember that most of our genes are designed for constancy—that is, children are genetically programmed to grow along a certain path. As children grow, they should

**midgrowth spurt** An increase in the rate of growth between ages 5 and 8.

gain height and weight in a pattern that keeps their growth path close to what would be expected based on their length and weight at full-term birth (Cameron, 2007; Karkach, 2006). These are the paths we see in Figure 11.1.

The general path of human growth includes three periods of acceleration: infancy, middle childhood, and adolescence. As noted in previous chapters, the rate of growth is rapid during infancy and slows during the preschool years. The growth rate increases again between ages 5 and 8. This increase is called the **midgrowth spurt**, or juvenile spurt (Tanner & Cameron, 1980). As you will see in Chapter 14, the adolescent growth spurt begins at around age 10 to 12 and continues into young adulthood.

## Individual Differences in Physical Growth

We can also see from Figure 11.1 that physical growth varies considerably among individual children during middle childhood. For example, some of the lightest 11-year-old children have body weights similar to the heaviest 6-year-olds, and some 10-year-olds may be no taller than the tallest 8-year-olds (Finkelstein, 2000). We can attribute part of this difference to genotype, inherited traits that set the parameters for children's size, shape, and body composition. To fully understand differences in development among children of the same age, however, we need to recall our discussions from previous chapters about the complex interactions between heredity and environment.

Phenotype—how children ultimately turn out—depends not only on genotype but also on environmental conditions. As we have noted, developmental systems theory helps to account for phenotypic differences in children's physical development and health by emphasizing how these differences result from interactions between the child and the context in which the child develops, including genetic, neural, behavioral, and environmental systems (Gottlieb, 1997, 2002; Gottlieb, Wahlsten, & Lickliter, 2006; Shonkoff & Phillips, 2000). Just a few of the environmental conditions that can affect physical development are diet, serious illness or disease, and psychological and social stressors (Rutter, 2002; Tanner, 1991; Tanner, Healy, & Cameron, 2001).

Researchers often study growth paths over time to determine whether individual children are experiencing deviations. Such studies of children indicate that deviations

*Christopher Futcher/Getty Images*

Physical growth varies considerably among individual children during middle childhood. Both heredity and environment play a role in this variation.

within the three phases of growth noted earlier—infancy, middle childhood, and adolescence—may indicate poor health and adverse environments during childhood. What is a deviation? Statistically speaking, it means a child's growth path deviates, or departs, from the path that would be expected based on birth size.

For example, let's look at three 9-year-olds who are in the 50th percentile for weight (see Figure 11.1). Mary's birth weight placed her in the 85th percentile, but she grew more slowly during infancy than would be expected and continued to drop through percentiles during early and middle childhood. Beth's birth weight was at the 35th percentile, but she showed unusually rapid growth during infancy and early childhood, rising through percentiles. Kate has been at about the 50th percentile since birth. We worry that Mary is not getting enough nourishment or is otherwise living in adverse circumstances. We wonder about Beth, too. Has she grown rapidly to catch up from a birth weight that was low because of stunted prenatal growth and poor maternal health? All three girls weigh about the same, and all three may appear healthy, but two of them show deviations in growth patterns that deserve further attention.

Individual differences in growth also highlight the reciprocal interactions between physical development and social experiences. Children who are shorter and lighter in weight than average are frequently perceived as younger than they are, whereas those who are taller and heavier than average are perceived as older. Adults and peers may treat children based on their perceived age rather than their actual age. Taller and heavier children may also make friends who are older than they are and who introduce them to more mature behavior and activities (Bogin, 1999; Cameron, 2007; Finkelstein, 2000).

Despite individual differences, children in middle childhood are alike in one important area of growth: Their brains have the innate potential to grow and develop during this period. But how their brains mature depends on the interaction between the brain and experience. As we have seen, enriched environments challenge the brain to build complex and robust networks of connections.

**positron emission tomography (PET)** A test that uses a special camera and a radioactive chemical called a tracer to look at organs inside the body. The tracer is injected into a vein in the arm. As it moves through the body, it gives off tiny positively charged particles (positrons). A camera records the positrons and shows the results as pictures on a computer.

THE DEVELOPING BRAIN

## Middle Childhood

Let's briefly retrace brain development from the prenatal months to the middle-childhood years. Recall that the brain has an oversupply of neurons at birth, and that infancy is a period of exuberant growth of synaptic connections. **Positron emission tomography (PET)** scans, in which "busy" parts of the brain are highlighted in three dimensions, indicate that the parts of the brain absolutely essential for survival—the brainstem, thalamus, and cerebellum—are active in newborns (Chugani, Muller, & Chugani, 1996). At the same time, the brain cells in the temporal and occipital lobes are busy processing sensory stimuli, eagerly seeking information from the outside world through the eyes, ears, nose, and hands (Corbit & Carpenter, 2006). In fact, some of this processing likely began before birth (Pascalis & Kelly, 2009).

As babies engage with their environments, brain connections are stimulated. In other words, connections among different parts of the brain build and strengthen in response to the infant's experience. At about 2 to 3 years of age, a child's brain is more active than that of an adult, because it is laying down its essential architecture of neural networks (Corbit & Carpenter, 2006). However, the toddler's brain is also less efficient than the adult brain. The great task of middle childhood is to build on the brain architecture developed during early childhood.

### Brain Growth and Organization in Middle Childhood

The human brain reaches about 90 to 95% of its adult weight during middle childhood (Gogtay et al., 2004; Lenroot & Giedd, 2006), but size does not account for the

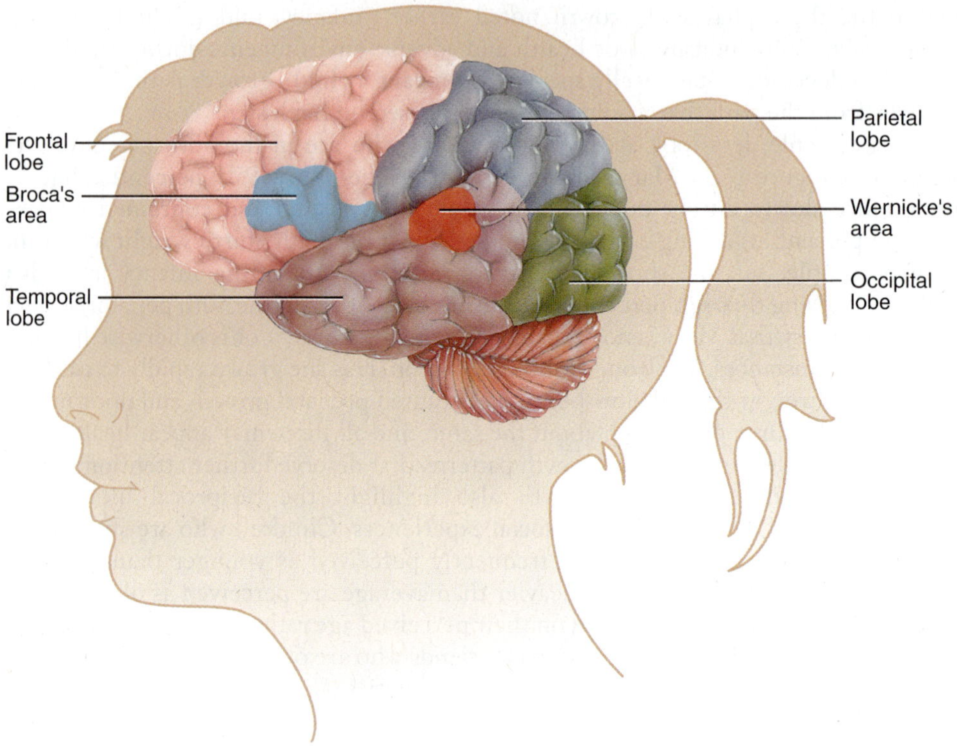


**FIGURE 11.2 Brain Areas Showing Complex Development in Middle Childhood** Areas of the brain associated with increased cognitive abilities demonstrate more complex patterns of growth and development during middle childhood. These areas include regions in the frontal lobe, the parietal lobe, the occipital lobe, and the temporal lobe, as well as Broca's area (located in the frontal lobe) and Wernicke's area (located in the temporal lobe).

changes we see in functional abilities. The networks of neural connections developed in infancy and early childhood continue to evolve in size and complexity (Stevens-Smith, 2006). Synaptogenesis begins to slow as undeveloped connections are pruned and new connections are made. Connections between synapses travel increasingly longer distances across the brain, forging a greater network of connections. Myelination—which, as noted in Chapter 5, increases the efficiency of transmission along these networks—continues through adolescence.

Researchers have found that areas of the brain associated with increased cognitive abilities demonstrate complex patterns of growth and development during middle childhood. These areas, highlighted in Figure 11.2, include the frontal lobe (reasoning, executive functioning), the parietal lobe (spatial information), and the occipital and temporal lobes (visual perception and recognition), as well as areas associated with language (Broca's area and Wernicke's area) (Gogtay et al., 2004; Shaw et al., 2008; Sowell et al., 2004).

These developments in the brain support the increasingly mature cognitive processing that is the hallmark of middle childhood. Processing is faster, and memory retention and retrieval improve, so that children literally think more quickly. They are able to make and revise plans as circumstances change. Children transition from Piaget's preoperational period to the period of concrete operations. This means they appreciate cause and effect, can reason logically, and gain a greater understanding of people, situations, and events within their environments (Bergen & Coscia, 2001). (We discuss cognitive development in middle childhood in detail in Chapter 12, including the role of brain development in improvements in attention and memory.)

THINKING ON HER FEET An example of the evolving abilities during middle childhood can be found on a soccer field. Ask a 10-year-old girl, an experienced player, what she was thinking about as she raced down the field and you might get this explanation:

> I'd pass if I had to go through the defense; Lauren would pass back and I'd score. Or she would shoot and I'd be there for the rebound if she missed. But if there were no defense, I'd take the shot. If our goalie made a good save and a good drop-kick out to me, I'd kick to get by the defense and shoot. But if someone got behind the defense, I'd pass.

Our soccer player's brain is making split-second decisions in real time based on her knowledge of the game, memory of previous games and practice sessions, and experience with problem-solving strategies in those games. A 5-year-old cannot think this way, regardless of experience and training. But this 10-year-old can, while controlling her emotional excitement and focusing on her task. This behavior represents increasingly complex interactions among various parts of the brain: the hippocampus (memory), areas of the cerebral cortex including the frontal cortex (problem solving), and the amygdala (emotion). At the same time, it rests on this soccer player's confidence in her motor coordination. She is no longer a novice. She does not have to think about how to kick and pass the ball. She just does it.

*Everyday stories*

## Gender Differences

You may be wondering if there are differences between boys and girls in brain development. To answer this question, here again researchers examine developmental paths over time, because differences among children at a given age are not always meaningful. Generally speaking, the development of the lobes and gray matter of girls' brains is 1 to 2 years ahead of boys, but with peaks occurring in different lobes at different times. (Remember from Chapter 2 that neuron cell bodies are gray matter, and that myelin sheaths around axons are white matter.)

For example, in the frontal lobe, gray matter volume peaks at age 9½ for females and 10½ for males; in the parietal lobe, at age 7½ in females and 9 in males; and in the temporal lobe, at age 10 for females and 11 for males. However, the *rate* of change throughout childhood and adolescence is higher in boys, and boys' brains are 8 to 10% larger than girls' (Lenroot et al., 2007).

What does this mean? It's hard to draw definitive conclusions. As you will learn in Chapter 14, girls begin puberty earlier than do boys, which might lead us to think that reproductive hormonal changes are involved. However, these hormones do not account for the differences in brain development in middle childhood, although they may play a small role in some aspects of brain development during adolescence (Blakemore, Burnett, & Dahl, 2010). We also need to remember that gender plays a profound role in shaping a child's social experiences, and those experiences help to shape the brain.

In the past, gender differences in the brain, and the implications for learning and behavior, have been studied more in adult men and women than in children. Today, gender differences in brain development during middle childhood are of increasing interest to educators. For example, girls tend to develop verbal and reading skills earlier than do boys, a difference attributed to brain development. This and other differences have led some educators to propose that same-sex classrooms would benefit both boys and girls (Sax, 2005).

## what if...?

What if gender differences in the brain suggest that boys and girls learn differently? Should they attend same-sex schools? Should boys be held back in school a year so that their brain development is more similar to that of the girls in their class? What about the role of individual differences in development over time? How would such differences affect these decisions?

### Environmental Influences

As in early childhood, the brain does not develop its potential in middle childhood without being challenged to do so. For example, the brain needs to be trained through experience to make the visual and phonological connections required to read and write. Because the brain is constantly being shaped by experience, its development is tightly bound to all aspects of a child's life (Hilgetag & Barbasthis, 2009) and to every decision parents and others make about that child's experience (Eliot, 1999).

We noted in earlier chapters that children's environments can be enriched and supportive or impoverished and stressful. Appropriate choices during pregnancy, sensitive caretaking in infancy, and good nutrition in early childhood, among many other factors, have long-term consequences. Brain development during middle childhood continues to be affected by parental choices, including disciplinary measures, diet, the value placed on learning at home, exposure to television and video games, and social activities involving friends.

## Motor Development in Middle Childhood

We have already seen in earlier chapters that motor development is best understood as an integrated system involving many aspects of growth and development (Adolph & Berger, 2006; Thelen & Smith, 1994). We have seen, too, that the physical environment and the demands of an activity itself have effects (Newell, 1986). As a result, children's development is dynamic, creating differences both among children and in an individual child over time.

Let's compare a 12-year-old boy with his 5-year-old self. He is taller and heavier at 12, of course. He also has greater respiratory efficiency, muscle strength, and the like. He can jump higher and run faster with more grace. He is still growing and developing, though; he is not a miniature adult. This is a fact often overlooked when 11- or 12-year-old children begin to demonstrate the skilled movements at the core of athletic performance (Rowland, 2005). For example, a young tennis player, no matter how talented, must constantly adjust his or her serve to account for changes in body proportions.

We start this section by looking at physical activity during middle childhood. We review models that explain some characteristics of movement, after which we revisit the gross motor skills discussed in connection with early childhood, to see how school-aged children are faring.

*Koji Aoki/Score/Getty Images*

Young athletes like this tennis player must constantly adjust their skills to accommodate their changing body proportions.

### Physical Activities During Middle Childhood

During the middle-childhood years, children gradually acquire physical skills that benefit their health and encourage their exuberance and energy. They continue to refine important and complex motor skills. The purpose behind activities also changes, moving more toward competitive goals, although at all ages physical activity is often designed more for fun than for competition (Patrick, Spear, Holt, & Sofka, 2001).

Children at ages 5 and 6 are still developing fundamental physical skills, such as jumping, kicking, and throwing. Most of their activities do not require complex motor and cognitive skills, such as those illustrated earlier by our 10-year-old soccer player. Instead, they often repeat simple activities, such as running around, that call for little instruction and are not restricted by rules. For example, in the excitement of the game, all of the 6-year-old players on a soccer team, including the goalie, may run down the field after the ball.

Between ages 7 and 9, children continue to master fundamental skills but are moving toward more coordinated efforts, such as throwing a ball for distance and accuracy at the same time. They understand that participating in a sport involves rules, and are learning to organize their behavior to follow those rules. (You will learn more about understanding rules in Chapter 12.) By ages 10 and 11, we see increased proficiency in coordinating physical skills with strategy and teamwork—consider again, our soccer player described earlier. Older school-aged children also take instruction better than do younger ones, and are better able to develop the self-discipline to practice complex skills.

### Constraints in Physical Activity: Interactions Among Person, Task, and Environment

Clearly, skilled movements call for complex coordination between brain and body. Our appreciation of the complexity of this interaction is fairly recent, as we explain in the accompanying Research Insights feature. The researchers discussed in the feature focused on factors within the individual. K. M. Newell (1986) extended this thinking to include additional factors.

## **Research Insights:** Degrees of Freedom

In 1967, Soviet neurophysiologist Nikolai Bernstein proposed that a key element in understanding motor coordination was the concept of *degrees of freedom*. Bernstein borrowed this term from the field of statistics, where it refers generally to the number of values in a set that are free to vary without affecting the final solution. In Bernstein's scheme, these "values" correspond to all the various components of movement (nervous system, bones, muscles, joints, and so forth). The "solution" is the desired movement. The key idea is variability. That is, most of us can run, but we accomplish this in countless different ways, depending on such things as our age, physical characteristics, and experience.

Bernstein realized that it is not possible to individually regulate the interactions of the components of movement—the degrees of freedom. Control of the components depends on coordination among them as whole. But how do our nervous systems choose which components to use for a particular movement? And how do we learn to make the right choices so that the movement becomes better coordinated? These are key questions in mastering skilled movements.

Later researchers proposed three stages of learning to control the degrees of freedom involved in acquiring a particular skill (Steenbergen, Marteniuk, & Kalbfleisch, 1995). As you read these stages, think about how you have learned a new motor skill yourself.

1. *Freezing* occurs early in the process of acquiring a motor skill. The learner awkwardly puts together the individual components required for the skill. In learning to serve a tennis ball, for example, a young girl must focus in turn on placing her feet in the right position, placing her fingers on the grip of the racquet, throwing the ball into the air, hitting it on its way down, following through, and so on. As a beginner, she demonstrates considerable variation in how she performs each component each time she hits the ball.
2. *Freeing* occurs as learning progresses. The learner may add, eliminate, or change movements to improve performance. Our tennis player is better coordinated now, and her movements more efficient and purposeful. She has eliminated unnecessary variation in how she holds the racquet, tosses the ball into the air, and places her feet. She can work on adjusting the arc and power of her swing for greater accuracy, speed, and spin on the ball.
3. *Exploiting* occurs with greater mastery. The learner begins to experiment with new techniques. Our tennis player has mastered how to serve the ball as a single consolidated skill, rather than multiple components, and she can now try new ways of doing it so as to outwit her opponent.

**constraints model of motor development** Newell's idea that physical movements arise from the interactions of the individual body, the task prompting the need for movement, and the environment.

Specifically, Newell suggested that physical movements arise from the interactions of the individual body, the task prompting the need for movement, and the environment, as diagramed in Figure 11.3. This is the **constraints model of motor development**. For example, a baseball bat may be too long or too heavy for one child on the team but the right fit for another of the same age (person-task interaction). If no other bats are available (person-environment interaction), the first child will not be able to perform as well as the second. The child might even be injured. This is true even if the first child could have performed as well as the second, given the right baseball bat.

**FIGURE 11.3 Newell's Constraints Model** According to K. M. Newell, physical movements arise from the interactions of the individual body, the task prompting the need for movement, and the environment. Constraints involving any of these elements will affect how the task is carried out.

Of course, experience with particular movement matters, as well (person-task interaction). For example, ballet dancing *en pointe*—that is, in toe shoes—depends not just on the physical maturation of a young dancer's body but also on her mastery of ballet technique, acquired through years of practice. For example, she must be proficient at performing multiple pirouettes, which require coordinated head, leg, and arm turns, on the balls of her feet before pirouetting on her toes. While some girls are ready at about age 12 years, others may need to wait until adolescence to dance *en pointe*.

With Newell's model in mind, let's think about the gross motor skills we discussed in Chapter 8. Over the course of the middle-childhood years, children's skills continue to develop. They progress from such fundamental activities as running, jumping, throwing, and catching to more demanding tasks such as throwing for distance, running for speed, and kicking for accuracy. In the final years of the period, children demonstrate more complex abilities (Thomas & Thomas, 2008). They can better coordinate physical skills with strategy and teamwork. Examine Figures 11.4, 11.5, and 11.6 and note the complexity of the movements involved, movements that are crucial in such sports as basketball and soccer.

These figures illustrate the accomplished performance that characterizes some children by the end of middle childhood. By ages 11 to 12, children usually are comfortable with, and proficient at, a wide variety of physical activities. At the same time, however, many physical activities, especially sports, require strength, endurance, and coordination beyond the capability of children—even when adjusted for the children's age, experience, and ability.

Knowledge of Newell's model can aid parents, teachers, and coaches in improving children's motor performance while avoiding potentially damaging instruction (Gagen & Getchell, 2006). Adults need to make sure there is a good fit between children's bodies and abilities, the motor tasks they are to perform, and the support provided by the environment, including equipment, adults, and expectations. Children should not engage in a motor task that they are not ready to take on based on their physical and

© *ImageState/Alamy*

Both physical maturation and mastery of technique, gained through years of practice, affect a young dancer's readiness to go *en pointe*.

**FIGURE 11.4 Advanced Running** Unlike the beginning runner shown in Figure 8.7, the advanced runner here exhibits a full range of leg motion.

*Source: Life Span Motor Development, 4th edition;* by Kathleen M. Haywood, Nancy Getchell, Ph.D. © Mary Ann Roberton; January 2005.

**FIGURE 11.5 Advanced Jumping** Starting in a crouch, and reaching a peak with arm extended in the air, this young jumper engages in a complex series of movements that enable her to reach high.

*Source: Life Span Motor Development, 4th edition;* by Kathleen M. Haywood, Nancy Getchell, Ph.D. © Mary Ann Roberton; January 2005.

**FIGURE 11.6 Advanced Kicking** As he gets ready to kick a soccer ball, this advanced kicker rotates his trunk and moves his arms back and away from his body. In kicking, he extends his leg and foot more fully than a younger and less experienced kicker would be able to do.

*Source: Life Span Motor Development, 4th edition;* by Kathleen M. Haywood, Nancy Getchell, Ph.D. © Mary Ann Roberton; January 2005.

cognitive development, or that the environment can support. Unfortunately, children tend to overestimate their own abilities and will lobby for opportunities that may not be in their best interests. Consequently, adults need to understand what is at stake and monitor children's efforts (Shepard & Trudeau, 2008).

**CHECK YOUR PROGRESS**

1. How would you explain individual differences in physical growth and development during the middle-childhood years?
2. How does the example of the 10-year-old soccer player exemplify changes in both brain and physical development?
3. Why do environmental influences matter in brain development during middle childhood?
4. Using as a guide our example of playing tennis, apply Bernstein's concept of degrees of freedom to swinging a baseball bat.
5. What are the lessons of Newell's constraint model for adults who supervise children's physical activities?

# Foundations of Health: Health Promotion

**[ KEY QUESTION ] 2. What can we do to promote health and prevent disease in middle childhood?**

As we pointed out in Chapter 8, primary prevention is designed to prevent health issues from arising in the first place. It includes health promotion, which focuses on incorporating healthy behaviors into daily life and avoiding known risks. It also targets prevention of disease and injuries—for example, through immunizations and use of seat belts.

The Bright Futures program is a comprehensive set of guidelines for health promotion and disease and injury prevention specifically for children from birth through adolescence. Introduced in the 1990s by the Maternal Child Health Bureau of the federal Department of Health and Human Services, today it is also sponsored by the American Academy of Pediatrics. Its materials are used by health-care providers, schools, and parents throughout the country (Hagan, Shaw, & Duncan, 2008).

In this section, we follow the Bright Futures guidelines as we review health topics relevant to middle childhood. We begin by discussing several activities important in promoting health and preventing disease. We go on to examine nutrition in the middle-childhood years, including the important issues of overweight and obesity.

## Health Promotion and Disease Prevention

Well-child visits, immunization, and dental health continue to be important in the middle childhood years, and we review those practices next. We will discuss another important topic, sports injury prevention, later in the chapter.

### Well-Child Visits

During middle childhood, children should continue to see a health-care provider for a routine yearly checkup. As noted in earlier chapters, these well-child visits focus on assessment, education and health promotion, intervention, and coordination among specialists, as needed. The purpose is more than just to evaluate a child's physical growth and development; it is also to assess for behavioral, learning, and other developmental differences so that they can be addressed promptly. Questions about school performance, peer relationships, nutritional habits, and family dynamics can yield insight into the child's developmental path and sense of self.

**anticipatory guidance** Guidelines explaining what to expect and what to pay attention to during middle childhood; part of well-child visits.

**5-2-1-0 Program** A health promotion effort recommending 5 servings of fruit and vegetables daily, no more than 2 hours of television, 1 hour of physical activity, and 0 consumption of sugar-sweetened beverages.

Well-child visits also give parents and children an opportunity to talk confidentially with health-care professionals about topics that may be sensitive. Bright Futures refers to this as **anticipatory guidance**. The idea is to help parents and children know what to expect and what to pay attention to during middle childhood so that the children will be better prepared to navigate adolescence. As you will learn in the following chapters, children are forming their attitudes and values about a wide range of topics and behaviors during their school years. Middle childhood is thus a good time to begin having conversations about personal safety, violence, sex, substance use, and responsible use of media—conversations that will continue during the teen years.

The American Academy of Pediatrics encourages health-care professionals to include information about the **5-2-1-0 Program** in routine visits. The program is a health promotion effort to provide parents and children with an-easy-to-remember guide for wellness during middle childhood. It addresses four key factors: nutrition, television, physical activity, and soft drinks, as shown in Figure 11.7. The program also has been successful in school settings. Students, teachers, and parents have noted that it helped children to change their habits in school and at home (Rogers & Motyka, 2009).

*Everyday stories*

TALKING ABOUT HEALTH WITH KIDS One way for a health-care provider to discuss healthy habits with children and their parents is to ask specific questions. Don't ask a child questions like, "Are you eating enough fruits and vegetables?" or "How much television do you watch?" You are likely to get vague and defensive answers. Instead, ask, "What fruits and vegetables did you eat yesterday? How about the day before?" "What TV shows did you watch this week? What video games did you play?" For some topics, however, an indirect approach may work better. By asking a school-aged child what he or she knows about drugs and alcohol, you can start an open-ended conversation, taking your cues from the child's answers.

Unfortunately, the percentage of children receiving well-child visits declines with age. In 2009, 88.7% of children aged 4 years and younger had preventive health care, compared with 78.5% of children 5 to 9 years of age and 71.6% of children 10 to 14 years of age. Non-Hispanic black children were significantly more likely to have had a well-child visit in the past year (83.6%) than non-Hispanic white and Hispanic children (77.6 % and 74.9 %, respectively). Non-Hispanic American Indian/Alaskan native children had the lowest reported rate of preventive care (72.1 %) (U.S. Department of Health and Human Services [USDHHS], 2011).

As we have seen in previous chapters, health insurance matters. Among children living at or below federal poverty guidelines, only half without insurance see a provider, compared to 87% with insurance (National Center for Health Statistics, 2010). As a result, health-care needs among many poor children go unmet. Furthermore, they and their parents do not benefit from anticipatory guidance, widening the gap between these children and others.

## Immunizations

Children who did not receive immunizations according to the suggested schedule during early childhood can catch up in middle childhood. Most states require immunization against diphtheria, pertussis, tetanus, polio, measles, mumps, rubella varicella (chicken pox), and hepatitis B for school entry. Fortunately, more than 90% of children comply with these requirements by the end of their first year in school (Centers for Disease Control [CDC], 2011). This information is usually shared with local public health departments for tracking purposes.

**FIGURE 11.7 The 5-2-1-0 Program** The 5-2-1-0 Program provides parents, teachers, and children with an-easy-to-remember guide for wellness during middle childhood. It includes guidelines on nutrition, television watching, physical activity, and soft drinks.

**meningococcus** Bacterial meningitis, an acute infection of the brain and spinal fluid that spreads through casual contact with other persons.

**hepatitis A** A bacterial infection spread through feces.

**human papillomavirus** A virus, spread through sexual activity, that causes genital warts, which can cause cervical cancer in women later in life.

**Table 11.1** Immunizations During Middle Childhood

| Vaccine | Ages 7–10 | 11–12 |
|---|---|---|
| Diptheria, pertussis, tetanus (DPT)[a] | | DPT |
| Inactivated polio vaccine (IPV) | IPV series catch-up period | |
| Measles, mumps, rubella (MMR) | MMR series catch-up period | |
| Haemophilus influenza type B (flu) | Yearly during flu season | |
| Hepatitis B (hep B) | Hep B series catch-up period | |
| Varicella (chicken pox)[b] | Varicella series catch-up period | |
| Pneumococcal vaccine | Recommended for high-risk groups | |
| Hepatitis A[c] | Recommended for high-risk groups | |
| Meningococcus vaccine (MCV)[d] | Recommended for high-risk groups | MCV |
| Human papillomavirus (HPV)[e] | | HPV series |

a. A single booster dose for those who completed the series in early childhood.
b. One dose if there is no history of having had the disease.
c. Can be administered anytime after age 1; two doses six months apart.
d. Single dose.
e. Single dose.

Several new vaccines are recommended for this age group to prevent meningococcus, hepatitis A, and the human papillomavirus (see Table 11.1). **Meningococcus** is bacterial meningitis, an acute infection of the brain and spinal fluid. The disease spreads through casual contact with other persons, such as food sharing and kissing. Although relatively rare, it can cause death within 12 hours of onset and spreads rapidly among a young victim's friends and classmates. **Hepatitis A** is transmitted through feces—for example, when water is contaminated or people do not wash their hands after using the toilet. Unlike hepatitis B, hepatitis A does not cause chronic liver disease, but it can cause serious illness among children with other chronic diseases. The **human papillomavirus** causes genital warts, which are usually spread through sexual activity. These warts, in turn, can cause cancer in women years after exposure. Fortunately, the vaccine is given at age 11 to 12 years, before the vast majority of girls become sexually active. We discuss this vaccine further in Chapter 14.

Monkey Business Images/Getty Images

By about age 12, children's "baby teeth" have been replaced by adult teeth. Often, children need to have braces applied between ages 9 and 12, to straighten their teeth or improve their bite.

## Dental Health

Most children begin losing their primary, or "baby," teeth at around age 6, with the front teeth the first to go and the first to be replaced by permanent teeth about a year later. By about age 12, all 20 primary teeth will have been replaced by 28 adult teeth. Four additional molars, called wisdom teeth, generally emerge between ages 17 and 21.

Children should see a dentist or hygienist at least twice a year to have their teeth cleaned and sealants applied as needed. These visits should be supplemented by brushing at least twice a day and flossing at least once a day. Fluoride supplementation, which we discussed in Chapter 8, should continue as needed. Unfortunately, 23% of all young people ages 6 to 19 years, have not seen a dentist in the previous year (National Center for Health Statistics, 2010).

About 40% of children have dental caries (Edelstein & Chinn, 2009), but many do not receive treatment. Disparities in children's dental health, as in their physical health, are often associated with low family income, particular race/ethnicity characteristics, and poor health literacy among caregivers. One third of children living at or below the federal poverty level, and 30% of children of Hispanic origin, have untreated dental caries (National Center for Health Statistics, 2010), which can lead to premature loss of permanent teeth, pain, gum disease, and bad appearance.

Dental braces used to be the scourge of the teenage years. Today, treatment begins much earlier, when permanent teeth are emerging and the mouth is growing in size to accommodate them. Bright Futures endorses the recommendation of the American Academy of Orthodontists (2004) that children be assessed for malocclusion, poor

**Table 11.2** Caloric Needs in Middle Childhood

| Girls | | Boys | |
|---|---|---|---|
| Ages 4–8 | Ages 9–13 | Ages 4–8 | Ages 9–13 |
| 1,200–1,800 calories, depending on activity level | 1,400–2,200 calories, depending on activity level | 1,200–2,000 calories, depending on activity level | 1,600–2,600 calories, depending on activity level |

*Source:* United States Department of Agriculture, 2011. *Dietary Guidelines for Americans, 2010.*

**MyPlate** A guide to healthy eating from the United States Department of Agriculture.

alignment of their teeth, by age 7. Orthodontic appliances, including braces, rubber bands, and various types of headgear, are usually applied between ages 9 and 12. Not surprisingly, parents tend to be more motivated than their children in seeking such treatment. However, the success of treatment relies on the child's own level of compliance: adhering to the required oral hygiene, wearing the appliances, and avoiding food and activities that can damage them (Daniels, Seacat, & Inglehart, 2009).

## Nutrition

As we've already seen, children experience a midgrowth spurt in middle childhood. Between ages 6 and 12, children's height increases by about 12 in. (30.4 cm), and they gain about 30 lbs (13.6 kg). In addition, as their gross motor skills mature, the demands on their heart, lungs, muscles, and bones increase significantly. The need for proper nutrition, then, is obvious. Children do not, however, always make good choices about what they eat, and busy family schedules make it too easy for everyone to "eat on the go." In this section, we address normal nutritional needs and school lunch programs. We also look at why obesity is on the rise, why it is unhealthy, and what to do about it.

### Nutritional Needs

During middle childhood, as at other times, caloric needs must be balanced against caloric expenditure. In other words, very active children need more calories than those who are less or not at all active. Table 11.2 gives an idea of the wide range of caloric needs during middle childhood, based on gender and activity level.

Not all calories are created equal. So-called empty calories—for example, from refined sugar—provide fuel but little or no nutritional value. They do not help build brains, bones, and muscle. What, then, are the best foods for growing children? One set of dietary recommendations comes from the U.S. Department of Agriculture. The plan, called **MyPlate**, was introduced in 2011 as an easy-to-use guide to healthy eating (see Figure 11.8) (USDA, 2011). It includes the following recommendations:

- Make half your plate fresh fruits and vegetables.
- Drink only skim or 1% milk.
- Make at least half your grains whole grains, such as whole wheat bread.
- Vary your protein food choices: poultry, seafood, lean red meat, beans, eggs.
- Keep food safe to eat—for example, by eating and storing food at the right temperature, washing fresh fruits and vegetables before eating them, and washing your hands after handling certain foods, such as raw chicken.

Unfortunately, what children should eat and what they actually eat are two different things, as you will see in our later discussion of the school lunch program. The MyPlate guidelines suggest, for example, that children fill half their plate with fresh fruits and vegetables. But while both girls and boys eat fruit when it is offered, boys are less likely to eat vegetables than girls (Caine-Bish & Scheule, 2009; Hare-Bruun et al., 2011).

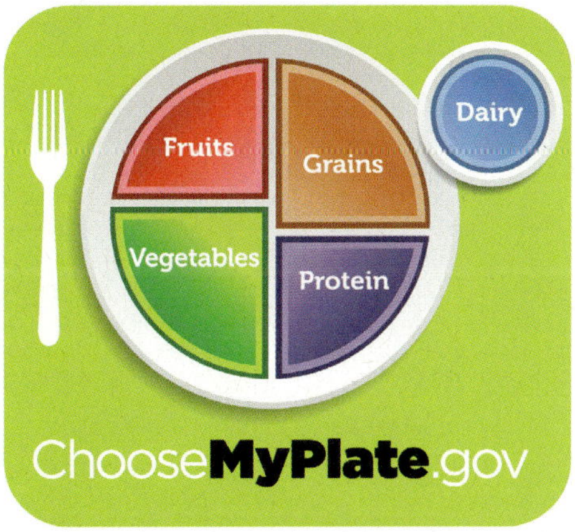


**FIGURE 11.8 MyPlate for Kids** The U.S. Department of Agriculture introduced MyPlate in 2011 as an easy-to-use guide to healthy eating. As you can see, the guidelines recommend that children get half of their daily food calories from fruits and vegetables, and the other half from grains and protein sources.
*Source:* U.S. Department of Agriculture, http://www.choosemyplate.gov.

### The School Lunch Program

In 1906, the book *The Bitter Cry of the Children* highlighted the plight of hungry American schoolchildren. The author, John Spargo, lamented that "children are in very many

© Bob Daemmrich/Alamy

School lunches supply about half the calories children consume each day.

cases incapable of successful mental effort, and much of our national expenditure for education is in consequence an absolute waste"' (1906, p. 117). As heightened awareness of the issue spread, school lunch programs for needy children became established in major cities throughout the United States, supported by a mix of public schools, local charities, and parent organizations (Gunderson, 1971). In 1936, during the Great Depression, Congress voted to support school meal programs by purchasing surplus agricultural products (Nestle, 2007).

After World War II, President Harry Truman learned that many young men had been rejected from military service because of medical conditions caused by childhood malnutrition. Citing concerns for national security, he signed the national school lunch program into law in 1946. About 7.1 million children participated in the school lunch program that first year, at a cost of $70 million. More than 60 years later, during the 2008–2009 school year, $9.8 billion was spent providing nutritionally balanced lunches to more than 31 million children each school day (U.S. Department of Agriculture [USDA], 2010). Government-sponsored school lunch programs are now offered in most countries around the world.

It's important to note that *any* child can purchase lunch through the program. And children whose families meet certain income qualifications can get meals free or at a reduced rate. The federal government reimburses schools at a higher rate for free and lower-cost meals, and at a lower rate for children who pay full price (USDA, 2010).

### What's on the Menu?

Children eat half of their daily calories at school. To see what they're eating, take a look online or in the newspaper at the lunch menu available for your school district. Pizza, fajitas, hot dogs, hamburgers, chicken nuggets, French fries, macaroni and cheese, and barbecued beef sandwiches probably appear frequently. These are children's favorite foods. Unfortunately, many of these foods are high in fat, sugar, and starches.

Schools have argued that serving healthier foods is more expensive, not only because such foods cost more but also because more is wasted when children don't eat the meals. Given concerns about the troubling rise in the incidence of child obesity, however, the United States Department of Agriculture announced new guidelines for school lunches in 2012—the first new guidelines in 15 years (USDA, 2012). The guidelines are based on an Institute of Medicine (2008) report on improving school lunches: reduce saturated fat, sugar, and sodium; increase whole grains; and serve both fruits and vegetables daily. And, for the first time, the guidelines list maximum calorie counts in addition to minimum ones.

### Malnutrition: Obesity and Overweight

Our discussion of children's eating habits leads us to an important topic: obesity. There was a time when we worried whether children had enough to eat—and in many parts of the world, that is still true today. But more often now we worry about what children eat and whether they consume too many calories, especially too many empty calories. This is a global concern, especially among developed nations, although famine and obesity increasingly exist side by side in developing countries (Swinburn et al., 2011; World Health Organization [WHO], 2000, 2003). (For a different perspective, see the Culture and Body Weight feature.)

We mentioned the alarming statistics in Chapter 8: The prevalence of childhood overweight has more than tripled in the past three decades. Among children ages 6 to 11, 35.5% of are either overweight or obese (Ogden, Carroll, Curtin, Lamb, & Flegal, 2010). Recall that overweight is defined as having a body mass index (BMI) above the

# Culture and Body Weight

Leemage/Universal Images Group/Getty Images

Cultural attitudes about body weight are social constructs—that is, they are created by society. As such, body weight can mean different things in different cultures at different times. A culture develops and changes its attitudes and values about various social phenomena—such as gender, body weight, and sexuality—over time, influenced by religious, economic, and social forces (Watkins, Farrell, & Hugmeyer, 2012).

In many cultures, for example, being stout has long been associated with good health, affluence, sensuality, and fertility. In such a culture, a layer of body fat and rounded facial features indicate that a family can afford plenty of food, a marker for economic success and higher social status. As a result, heavyset men and women are considered attractive as possible mates. Thinness, in contrast, is associated with poor health, poverty, and lower social status. In this view, a thin person is regarded as sickly and unattractive. The preference for a fuller-figured body shape is most prominent in the South Pacific and in some African countries. To name two, the Tahitian practice of *ha'apori* and the practice of *gavage* in Mauritania are designed to make girls fatter and thus more attractive. Girls are overfed, sometimes against their wills, and also remain inactive.

Full-figured women were also the ideal in much of Europe and the United States before the 20th century. Then, around the turn of the 20th century, standards among more affluent Caucasian Americans, in particular, began to change. By mid to late century, being overweight implied a lack of self-control, a moral failing, and was seen as a symptom of downward mobility. Today, being slender has come to mean not just good health but self-discipline, both of which are associated with the upwardly mobile (Farrell, 2011).

We've already discussed the widespread alarm about the rise of obesity and overweight in the United States. This concern is being countered by those who believe that it has more to do with the American cultural obsession with weight over health (Campos, 2004; Farrell, 2011). They argue that thinness is a false standard, one that promotes stigma and shame among heavier people. *Fat culture*, a challenge to the "anti-fat" campaign, seeks to reconstruct cultural values about body weight and size. Its message is that people can be healthy at every size, and that being overweight is not a personal failure (Watkins et al., 2012).

85th percentile, whereas obesity is having a BMI above the 95th percentile. As you can see in Figure 11.9, the percentage of children ages 2 to 19 who are obese more than tripled from 1971 to 2008, from 5% to almost 17%, essentially redefining the statistical meaning of the 95th percentile. Obesity is higher among Hispanic and African American populations than among white youth.

Why should we be concerned about childhood obesity? We noted in Chapter 8 that obesity is a form of malnutrition, because of the serious health consequences associated with it. Being overweight or obese increases the likelihood of developing type 2 diabetes, heart disease, high blood pressure, and other chronic illnesses (Freedman, Mei, Srinivasan, Berenson, & Dietz, 2007). Let's now consider why that is the case.

**FIGURE 11.9 Prevalence of Obesity in U.S. Children Ages 2 to 19, 1971–2008** The data shown in the figure were obtained from thousands of children who participated in the National Health and Nutrition Examination Surveys (NHANES) conducted by the National Center for Health Statistics. For the group taken as a whole, obesity increased from 5% to 16.9% between 1971 and 2008. For the middle childhood group, it increased even more, from 4% to 19.6%.

*Source:* Ogden, C. & Carroll, M. (2010). Prevalence of obesity among children and adolescents: United States, Trends 1963–1965 through 2007–2008. National Center for Health Statistics. www.cdc.gov/nchs/data/hestat/obesity_child_07_08/obesity_child_07_08.pdf.

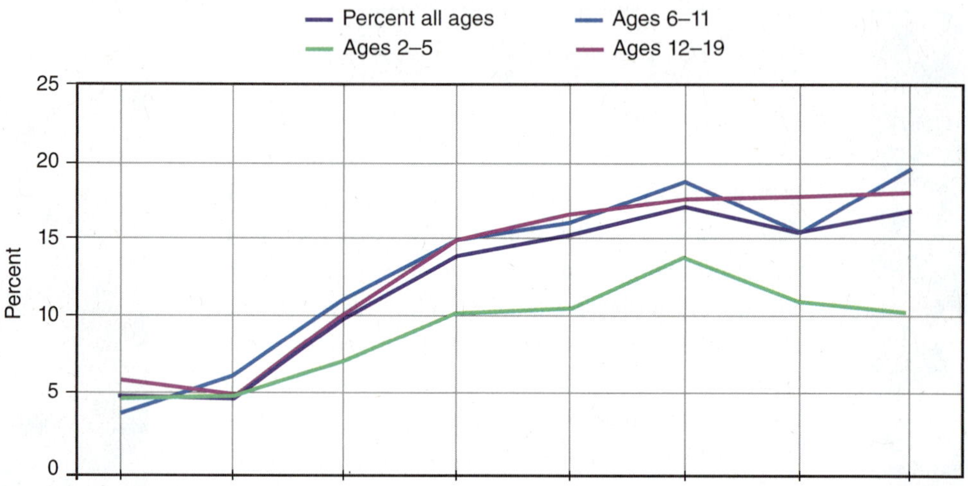


| 1971–1974 | 1976–1980 | 1988–1994 | 1999–2000 | 2001–2002 | 2003–2004 | 2005–2006 | 2007–2008 |
|---|---|---|---|---|---|---|---|
| 5 | 5 | 10 | 13.9 | 15.4 | 17.1 | 15.5 | 16.9 |
| 5 | 5 | 7.2 | 10.3 | 10.6 | 13.9 | 11 | 10.4 |
| 4 | 6.5 | 11.3 | 15.1 | 16.3 | 18.8 | 15.1 | 19.6 |
| 6.1 | 5 | 10.5 | 14.8 | 16.7 | 17.4 | 17.8 | 18.1 |

Calories that are not expended as energy are stored as **white adipose tissue**—in other words, white fat. White adipose tissue is not an inert reservoir of fat stored for future energy needs. It is a complex and active endocrine organ. It secretes enzymes, hormones that raise resistance to the body's own insulin, and *adipokines*, which are protein molecules that cause inflammation in vital organs (Fantuzzi, 2005; Maury & Brichard, 2010). White adipose tissue also stores biological contaminants that we ingest with our food, such as bacteria and pesticides (Müllerová & Kopecký, 2007).

In other words, obesity causes more problems than strain on the heart, blood vessels, and lower joints. Excess white adipose tissue significantly changes the metabolism and immune system. The bodies of obese children are suffering damage before they are fully grown in a way usually found in older adults as their bodies decline in vitality. Because the effect is cumulative over time, obesity is considered to be a chronic health condition in children (Van Cleave, Gortmaker, & Perrin, 2010).

**WHEN SYSTEMS CONNECT**

## Why the Incidence of Overweight and Obesity Has Increased

The increase in overweight and obese American children—and adults—is an almost perfect storm of interactions among multiple systems (USDHHS, 2001; WHO, 2000): genes, behavior, and social and economic factors. Experts generally agree that genetic factors can contribute to a child's susceptibility to excess body weight. But genes alone cannot account for the threefold rise of overweight and obesity in three decades (Ogden, Carroll, & Flegal, 2008). After all, those same genetic factors existed 30 years ago, when the prevalence of obesity was much lower.

So what has changed? For one thing, we eat differently than we did 30 years ago, because we also live differently. Children tend to be less physically active than they once were, as you'll see later. In addition, both parents of many children work outside of the home, and school age children may participate in organized after-school activities. All this means less time at home preparing and eating family meals together—and probably more time eating snack foods and fast foods.

We noted earlier that children favor hot dogs, hamburgers, chicken nuggets, and the like on their school lunch menu. In part, that's because those are the foods they are

**white adipose tissue** White fat, in which excess calories are stored in the body. It is a complex and active endocrine organ that secretes enzymes, hormones, and adipokines.

accustomed to eating at home, in the car, and at the fast-food restaurants that they visit at least once a week. Furthermore, when parents believe their children don't like healthy foods, such as fruits and vegetables, Mom and Dad are less likely to buy them, and the children are less likely to have them available to eat (Vann, et al., 2011). For parents, cooking a meal at the end of a long workday often just means more work. Thus, fast food can be both a pleasure and a crutch (Guthman, 2011). It is easy, and it tastes good, because fat, carbohydrates, and sugar usually do. (Remember that even newborns seem to like the taste of a sweet liquid.)

Donna Day/Alamy

Too much snack food coupled with too little physical activity can easily result in overweight children.

The food industry knows that fast food can become habit-forming (Moss, 2013). Indeed, Marion Nestle, a professor of nutrition at New York University, has made the case that—although individual choices and behavior are certainly a factor in the rise in obesity—the food industry has powerful economic interests at stake in our eating habits (Nestle, 2007).

As an example of the influence of the food industry on our eating habits, let's look at fast-food marketing aimed at children. This advertising is very successful. The more advertisements children see on television for fast-food brands, the more they prefer those brands (Boyland et al., 2011). (Table 11.3 lists a number of facts about marketing fast food to children.) In addition, many schools allow vendors to sell foods at school, providing competition for the school cafeteria menu. These vendors include well-known national pizza chains and soft drink companies, which may in return give the school cash through fund-raisers or a percentage of sales (Robert Wood Johnson Foundation [RWJF], 2010).

To sum up, the ready availability of snack foods, fast foods, beverages high in sugar, and the like, mean more empty calories taken in. At the same time, children today spend less time engaging in physical activity and more time watching TV and/or video gaming (we discuss this matter shortly). That means fewer calories expended. Taken together, these two factors add up to overweight and obesity, especially for children with a genetic tendency to be overweight (Ogden, Carroll, & Flegal, 2008).

Finally, obesity and overweight are now considered public health problems, and not just individual ones (USDHHS, 2001). The medical care costs of obesity for people of all ages in the United States are staggering—$147 billion in 2008 dollars. These costs cover the care required for the health-related consequences of obesity, such as type 2 diabetes, high blood pressure, and heart disease; lost time from work is another consequence. These costs are passed on to all Americans in the form of higher

**Table 11.3** Fast-Food Facts in Brief, 2009

| |
|---|
| The fast-food industry spent more than $4.2 billion advertising on TV and in other media. |
| The average preschooler (2–5 years) saw 2.8 TV ads per day for fast food; children ages 6–11 years saw 3.5; and teens (12–17 years) saw 4.7. |
| McDonald's and Burger King created sophisticated websites with "advergames" and virtual worlds to engage children (for example, McWorld.com, HappyMeal.com, and ClubBK.com). |
| McDonald's 13 websites recorded 365,000 unique child visitors and 294,000 unique teen visitors on average each month. |
| African American children and teens saw at least 50% more fast food ads on TV than their white peers. That translated into twice the number of fast-food calories consumed daily. |
| Eighty-four percent of parents reported taking their child to a fast-food restaurant at least once a week. |
| The average restaurant posted 15 signs promoting specific menu items, but just 4% of them promoted healthy menu items. |
| Just 12 of 3,039 kids' meal options at fast-food restaurants met nutrition criteria for preschoolers; 15 met nutrition criteria for older children. |

*Source:* Adapted from the Rudd Center for Food Policy and Obesity at Yale University. http://fastfoodmarketing.org/fast_food_facts_in_brief.aspx.

health insurance premiums and publicly funded programs (Finkelstein, Trogdon, Cohen, & Dietz, 2009). This figure will rise as the next generation of overweight and obese children age into adulthood with serious health problems that prevent them from being fully productive members of their communities (Institute of Medicine, 2005).

### Reducing and Preventing Childhood Obesity **Policy**

Many organizations are working toward reducing and preventing childhood obesity. As the nation's largest philanthropy devoted solely to the public's health, the Robert Wood Johnson Foundation (RWJF) funds many of those efforts through grants. Its priorities include the following:

- *Ensure that all foods and beverages served and sold in schools meet or exceed the most recent Dietary Guidelines for Americans.* This includes eliminating from schools vending machines that serve sugary soft drinks and fund-raisers associated with food corporations.
- *Increase access to high-quality, affordable foods through new or improved grocery stores and healthier corner stores and bodegas.* As part of this effort, many communities are building new farmers' markets, bringing supermarkets back to lower-income areas, and getting more healthy foods to rural areas.
- *Increase the intensity and duration of physical activity during the school day and in out-of-school programs.* RWJF supports efforts at schools and local organizations, such as the YMCA, to increase children's physical activity.
- *Increase physical activity by improving the built environment in communities.* The "built environment" includes sidewalks, bike paths, parks, and playgrounds.
- *Use pricing strategies—both incentives and disincentives—to promote the purchase of healthier foods.* Food prices influence consumers' purchasing decisions. Healthy food needs to be more affordable, and taxing unhealthy food and beverages can help that to happen.
- *Reduce young people's exposure to the marketing of unhealthy foods through regulation, policy, and effective industry self-regulation.* RWJF favors restrictions on marketing to children.

**what if...?** What do you think would change if every child ate a healthy diet every day? What role, if any, should government play in regulating processed foods and food marketing aimed at children? Why?

### Family Mealtime **Parenting**

Family mealtime is one of the most powerful opportunities to shape children's development. The food on the table, the conversation around the table, and the chores associated with preparing the meal and cleaning up afterward contribute to the comfort of routine and belonging. Family meals, while only about 20 minutes in length, contribute to many positive child outcomes, including a healthier diet, improved language development, fewer eating disorders, better sleep, and lower rates of obesity (Fiese & Schwartz, 2008).

How many families take advantage of the opportunities offered by family mealtime? On average, more than 50% of families report eating together from 3 to 5 times per week. For children ages 6 to 11, the numbers are a bit higher: 56% of families have

Mark Bowden/Getty Images

When family mealtimes include healthful food, a relaxed atmosphere, and open communication, they become a powerful positive influence on child development.

a meal together 6 to 7 times per week (Fiese & Schwartz, 2008). These numbers also mean, of course, that children often eat away from home. As we've seen, food eaten away from home is more likely to be fast food, perhaps consumed in the car traveling from one activity to another (Poti & Popkin, 2011).

Furthermore, the positive outcomes of family mealtime depend on several factors: a healthy meal; a relaxed atmosphere; and parents and children who converse about their day, the news, and other events. Sadly, 46% of families watch television while eating at least 1 or 2 times per week, and 31% watch television during most meals (Hare-Bruun et al., 2011).

Here are some tips for making the most out of the family meal:

- Keep it simple. Family meals don't have to be elaborate. Include salads and vegetables in meals.
- Get the family involved. Let kids help prepare meals and set the table.
- Family meals are for nourishment, comfort, and support. Leave the stressful discussions for another time.
- No electronics: no watching television, answering the phone, checking e-mail, or texting.

Another thing parents can do to promote healthier eating habits is to keep healthy snacks on hand. Stock the kitchen with fresh fruits, nuts, and low-fat cheese—items children can snack on after school instead of chips and cookies.

## Physical Activity

Physical activity builds bones and muscles and contributes to motor coordination, heart and lung function, and overall good physical and mental health. Evidence also suggests that being physically active is good for the brain, since physically active children tend to perform better academically (CDC, 2010; Coe, Pivarnik, Womack, Reeves, & Malina, 2006; Taras, 2005). This is especially true for tasks involving executive functions (Tomporowski, Davis, Miller, & Naglieri, 2008).

Kennet Havgaard/Aurora Photos/Getty Images

A generation or so ago, many boys this age would have been outdoors playing with friends. Now, video games and similar pastimes often take the place of physical activity.

**Table 11.4** CDC Physical Activity Guidelines for Children

| Type of Physical Activity | School-Aged Children |
|---|---|
| Moderate-intensity aerobic | Active recreation such as hiking, skateboarding, rollerblading<br>Bicycle riding<br>Walking to school |
| Vigorous-intensity aerobic | Active games involving running and chasing, such as tag<br>Bicycle riding<br>Jumping rope<br>Martial arts, such as karate<br>Running<br>Sports such as ice or field hockey, basketball, swimming, tennis, or gymnastics |
| Muscle-strengthening | Games such as tug-of-war<br>Modified push-ups (with knees on the floor)<br>Resistance exercises using body weight or resistance bands<br>Rope or tree climbing<br>Sit-ups<br>Swinging on playground equipment/bars<br>Gymnastics |
| Bone-strengthening | Games such as hop scotch<br>Hopping, skipping, jumping<br>Jumping rope<br>Running<br>Sports such as gymnastics, basketball, volleyball, tennis |

*Source:* http://www.cdc.gov/physicalactivity/everyone/guidelines/what_counts.html.

As part of the Healthy People 2020 initiative, which we mentioned in Chapter 8, the Physical Activity Guidelines for Americans recommend that children get a total of about 60 minutes of physical activity each day (Strong et al., 2005; USDHHS, 2008). However, as we stated earlier, many American children do not meet this activity goal. Indeed, the Healthy People baseline data indicate that only seven states and 57% of school districts across the country even require recess at school.

Children are less active at home, as well. Many children stay indoors at home after school until their parents return from work. According to a recent study, which we first mentioned in Chapter 1, today's young people watch television about 4½ hours per day, which includes time spent watching TV content on other platforms, such as laptops, smart phones, and tablets (Rideout, Foehr, & Roberts, 2010). This is time that children used to spend outdoors, playing.

Many communities around the country are working to promote children's physical activity, and not just through organized sports. The Centers for Disease Control (CDC) offers a guide for community action that suggests activities for all age groups. The activities listed in Table 11.4 include suggestions for school-age children. The accompanying Focus On feature describes the efforts of First Lady Michelle Obama to promote both exercise and a healthy diet.

## ✓ CHECK YOUR PROGRESS

1. What are the benefits of well-child visits during middle childhood?
2. What are the MyPlate guidelines for children?
3. What are the new guidelines for the national school lunch program?
4. What factors have caused overweight and obesity to increase over the past 30 years?
5. Why is obesity unhealthy?

## Focus On: Michelle Obama and Let's Move!

First Lady Michelle Obama has made healthy eating and exercise a priority in her family's life, busy though it is. When she learned about the rise in childhood obesity, she decided to make it a focus of her time in the White House. In 2010, she launched Let's Move!, described on its website as a "comprehensive initiative dedicated to solving the challenge of childhood obesity within a generation, so that children born today will grow up healthier and able to pursue their dreams." Working with the White House Task Force on Childhood Obesity, Mrs. Obama has built a network of partnerships with government and private organizations aimed at reducing obesity to 5% by 2030, the percentage before the current rise in overweight and obesity began.

Mrs. Obama has been a visible and vocal proponent of ensuring that families have access to healthy and affordable food, improving school lunches, and educating parents about healthy choices. She has invited schoolchildren to help her plant and tend a much-publicized vegetable garden on the grounds of the White House, and has promoted the value of eating locally grown produce. She has been videotaped while exercising and has challenged celebrities in foot races and other physical activities. The First Lady also has been interviewed on television and in many magazines about the importance of reducing childhood obesity, including one conducted by a child reporter for *Scholastic* magazine for children. Critics have suggested that she is promoting the intrusion of government into food choices that are better made by individuals. She counters that obesity is a problem that affects many Americans and that everyone needs to be part of the solution. For more about Let's Move!, visit the website: http://www.letsmove.gov.

File/AP Photo

## Capacity for Health: Caregivers and Community

**[ KEY QUESTION ] 3. How can caregivers and communities keep children safe during middle childhood?**

During middle childhood, children make more of their own choices and spend less time with parents. At the same time, they continue to benefit from the capacity of their communities to keep them safe and foster good health habits. In this section, we talk about general safety issues, sports and sports injuries, and the role of adults in keeping children safe, both physically and psychologically. We also discuss school health, including the role of the school nurse and school-based clinics.

slobo/iStockphoto

Crossing the street carefully is just one basic safety habit school-aged children need to learn.

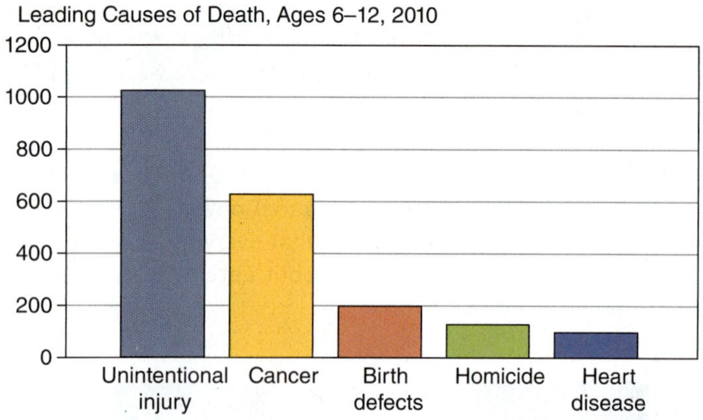


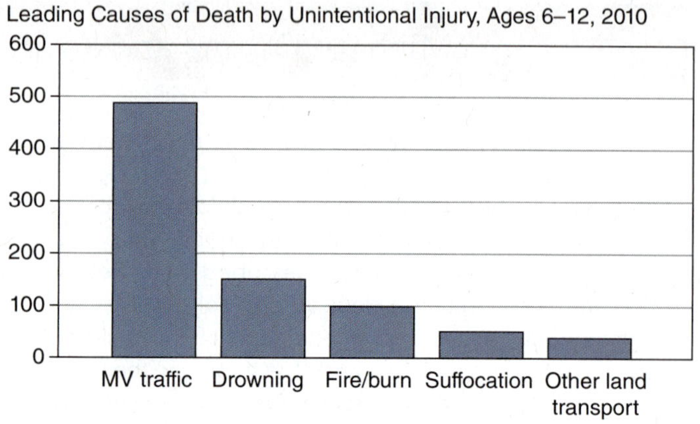


**FIGURE 11.10 Leading Causes of Death in U.S. Children Ages 6 to 12**
**(a) Leading Causes of Death**
**(b) Leading Causes of Death by Unintentional Injury**
Unintentional injuries are the leading cause of death for children between ages 6 and 12. In turn, most unintentional deaths of children between 6 and 12 result from motor vehicle accidents.

*Source:* National Center for Injury Prevention and Control (2012) http://webappa.cdc.gov/sasweb/ncipc/leadcaus10_us.html.

## Safety from Unintentional Injuries

Figure 11.10a shows that unintentional injuries are the leading cause of death of children between ages 6 and 12, accounting for 42% of childhood deaths. Figure 11.10b indicates that motor vehicle accidents are the number-one cause of unintentional deaths of children between ages 6 and 12 (47% of all deaths), followed by drowning; incidents involving fire (burns and smoke inhalation); suffocation; and deaths caused by other land transport vehicles, including bicycles, all-terrain vehicles, snowmobiles, and such. It is disturbing to note that about 90% of motor vehicle accident deaths of children up to age 14 involve a driver under the influence of alcohol, and that 68% of the time the child was a passenger in the drinking driver's vehicle (Shults, 2004).

Most accidental deaths among children can, however, be prevented. Table 11.5 lists some basic safety habits developed by the American Academy of Pediatrics to help keep children safe. As you read the suggestions in the table, remember that children change significantly during middle childhood, both cognitively and socially. (We discuss these changes further in Chapters 12 and 13.) Thus, what is appropriate for a 6-year-old may be too restrictive for a 12-year-old.

Perhaps the greatest challenge for adults is determining how well children understand and can respond to potentially dangerous situations. It can be easy to forget that children's physical and cognitive abilities are not fully mature yet. Their show of self-confidence can be deceiving. Children may know the rules of safety, but may not yet be able to anticipate changes in circumstances or account for the presence of multiple factors that call for more complex problem solving. For example, an 8-year-old who walks the same three blocks from bus stop to home every day with an older sibling may lose his or her way when walking alone if, say, landmarks are altered by a construction zone, piles of snow, or even the new paint color on a house.

Ultimately, of course, children do become more independent from parental supervision in middle childhood. By the time they are 11 or 12, they may spend time at home by themselves. Thus, it becomes increasingly important for them to develop good safety habits, which means that the adults and older adolescents with whom they spend time need to promote and model safety habits themselves.

**Table 11.5** Safety Habits for School-Aged Children

| | |
|---|---|
| Car | Children should use a booster seat in the car until they can wear the lap belt low and flat on the hips, and the shoulder belt across the shoulder, rather than the face or neck—usually at about 4 ft 9 in. tall (144.7 cm) and between 8 and 12 years old. When in the car, the safest place for all children is in the back seat. |
| Bicycle | At all ages, children should wear a properly fitted, approved helmet every time they ride their bikes.*<br>Under the age of 8, children should not ride their bikes in the street. By age 8, they should be taught the "rules of the road." They need to be capable of being in control of the bike and of using good judgment. They should not be allowed to ride in the street as dark approaches.<br>As they get older, children may want to ride their bikes farther away from home; be clear about how far they can go. |
| Fire | Every family should have an escape plan in case of fire at home. Practice fire drills so that children know what to do when the smoke alarm sounds, and how they should exit the dwelling.<br>Most home fires are caused by a cigarette that has not been put out completely, so avoid smoking inside the home entirely.<br>Install smoke alarms on every level of the house, especially in furnace and sleeping areas, and test the alarms every month. It is best to use smoke alarms that use long-life batteries; otherwise, change the batteries once a year.<br>Teach children proper safety habits for the use of matches, fireworks, gas stoves, portable heaters, and campfires. Familiarize children with Stop-Drop-Roll, the national slogan that tells them what to do if their clothes catch fire. |
| Firearms | Children in homes where guns are present are in more danger of being shot, by themselves, friends, or family members, than of being injured by an intruder. Handguns are especially dangerous. It is best to keep guns out of the home. Parents who choose to keep a gun should store it unloaded and in a locked place, with ammunition stored and locked away separately. Parents should ask if people in the homes where their children visit or are cared for have guns, and how the guns are stored.<br>Talk to children about guns in school or on the street. Find out if children's friends carry guns. |
| Water | Children should be supervised by an adult at all times when they are near water (lake, stream, swimming pool, or ocean), even if they know how to swim. The adult should know water safety procedures, and be prepared to recognize and respond when a child needs help. Children need to learn water safety practices, as well. They should learn how to swim and be taught to not dive head first into shallow or unfamiliar water. |
| Street safety | Because children may dart out into traffic without thinking, they should not be allowed to play near the street.<br>When crossing a street, children should be taught to stop at the curb, look to the left and the right, and back to the left again before proceeding. Younger children should not cross the street without a responsible adult at their side. |
| Self-help | Even young children who cannot read should learn to dial 911. Post other emergency numbers near the telephone, as well.<br>School-aged children can also learn basic first aid, and how to prevent injuries. |

*Source:* Based on information from American Academy of Pediatrics at http://www.healthychildren.org.

*The U.S. Consumer Product Safety Commission is the organization most often cited in state laws that mandate approved bike helmets for children.

## Sports

As we've already seen, various national guidelines encourage children to engage in regular physical activity, and that includes sports. Recently, however, many changes have occurred in the sport scene of middle childhood (Saar, 2007). In the past, playgrounds were crowded with children engaged in casual pick-up games, along with a wide variety of other physical activities. Today, adult-organized and competitive sports are much more common.

According to Safe Kids (2008), a national coalition of state organizations, about 30 million children and teens participate in some form of organized sports, involving nearly three-quarters of U.S. households. Playing organized sports can be a wonderful experience for children. It keeps them active, and they make new friends. They learn teamwork, self-control, new physical skills, and that most important lesson: sometimes you win, and sometimes you lose.

This widespread involvement in organized sports activities requires parents, teachers, coaches, and other adults to exercise caution as they supervise children involved in sports. Children can be injured participating in the very activities that promote their physical development (Ramey, Ramey, & Lanzi, 2006). Their bodies are, after all, still immature. Motor coordination comes with practice, and must be constantly adjusted to changes in body size and proportion. In addition, as we noted in the earlier section on constraints in motor development, the demands of a particular activity may not fit the readiness and ability of a particular child. Finally, children should be free of unreasonable pressure to perform. In this section, we discuss how to make sure participation in organized sports is as safe as it is enjoyable and formative.

### Sports-Related Injuries

The national Safe Kids campaign estimates that children under the age of 14 suffer about 3.5 million sports-related injuries each year. The most common types of injuries involve soft tissue, such as muscle and ligaments. These include ankle sprains, muscle strains, and repetitive motion injuries. A child might develop a repetitive motion injury, for example, by pitching in Little League games or serving in tennis (Brenner, 2007). Consider the following statistics from Safe Kids (2011):

- Children ages 5 to 14 years account for nearly two-thirds of all sports-related injuries treated in hospital emergency departments. Most of these injuries occur as a result of falls, being struck by an object, collisions, and overexertion.
- About 50% of injuries are related to overuse of muscles in repetitive specific actions, such as pitching a ball.
- Contact sports involve the highest rates of injury, but individual sports involve more severe injuries.
- About 62% of all organized sports-related injuries occur during practice. Yet 33% of parents do not take the same safety precautions for practices as they would for games.
- The leading cause of death from sports-related injury is brain injury. Thankfully, such deaths are rare. Almost 50% of head injuries to children occur during bicycling, skateboarding, or skating incidents.
- Winter sports are especially high risk for injury. Each year, children sustain approximately 49,000 injuries while skiing, snowboarding, or sledding.

Most sports injuries are minor. Some, however—such as those that involve head injuries, broken bones, and muscle tears—are more serious and can have long-term consequences. Children are not young warriors, and such injuries should not be treated as a badge of courage. In Chapter 14, we address two common injuries, concussions and knee injuries, and discuss the drive to play injured—especially among girls.

### Keeping Children Safe During Sports

Preventing sports injuries to children is a team effort that requires the involvement of parents, coaches, and children themselves. Of course, wearing protective gear is one important safety practice. But remember, too, our earlier discussion of constraints on motor development. Children's bodies are still developing, making them more vulnerable to injury. Thus, to prevent injuries, it is important to accommodate the demands of the sports to each child's body and ability. Table 11.6 lists several recommendations for making such accommodations. And, always, remember to keep the fun in the game.

Alistair Berg/Getty Images

Coaches, along with parents, play an important role in helping to prevent sports injuries in children.

## Performance Pressure

For most children, playing sports is an enjoyable pastime—part of the challenges and successes that make up an integral part of the middle-childhood experience. But more and more youngsters are now experiencing pressures closely linked to adult expectations. The American Academy of Pediatrics warns that "when the demands and expectations of organized sports exceed the maturation and readiness of the participant, the positive aspects of participation can be negated" (2001/2007, p. 1459). Such demands can lead to injuries, as we've just seen, and to psychological stress. They can even alter growth, such as when female gymnasts and

**Table 11.6** Preventing Sports Injuries to Children

| Guidelines for Parents and Coaches |
|---|
| Ideally, group youngsters according to skill level and size, not by chronological age, particularly during contact sports. If this is not practical, modify the sport to accommodate the needs of children with varying skill levels. |
| Match the child to the sport, and don't push the child too hard into an activity that he or she may not like or be physically capable of performing. |
| Do not allow a child to play when injured. No child should ever be allowed or encouraged to "work through the pain." |
| Ensure that coaches know the sport well and, in particular, appreciate the demands it places on a child's body. Coaches should always keep in mind that these athletes are still children. |
| Look for sports programs that include certified athletic trainers. These people are trained to prevent, recognize, and give immediate care for sports injuries. |
| Provide a safe environment for sports. An unkempt playing field, unsafe gym sets, unsecured soccer goals, and the like can be the cause of serious injury to children. |
| Be sure that athletic and protective gear fit each child properly. Ice skates that are too small and cleats that are too big increase risk of injury. Make sure that the equipment used, such as a baseball bat or hockey stick, fits the child's body proportions and skill level. |
| Discourage the consumption of "sports drinks." Caffeine and other stimulant substances contained in such drinks have no place in the diet of children or adolescents, and children should not be pushing their bodies so hard that they lose electrolytes. |
| **Guidelines for Children** |
| Prepare for practice as you would for a game. |
| Follow the rules of the game. Know how to play. |
| Train for the sport. Do not assume that practice sessions and games will develop the skills, muscles, and motor coordination needed to play well and safely. Learn how to land on your feet. |
| Take breaks, and stay well-hydrated. Water is sufficient! |

*Sources: National Institute of Arthritis and Musculoskeletal and Skin Diseases*, 2009; American Academy of Pediatrics, 2001/2007, 2011, 2012.

ballet dancers become excessively thin, delaying the onset of menstruation during adolescence (Bergeron, 2007).

In some sports, children as young as 8 or 9 become part of elite teams, which stand apart from town recreation leagues that provide opportunity for all children. Typically, the members of these teams go on in a few years to dominate varsity sports. Indeed, tryouts for high school teams may occur as early as grade school, with high school coaches scouting these younger top-level players. In addition, the long-term possibility of collegiate athletic scholarships can intensify pressure for top performance, from parents, teachers, and coaches. Such scholarships, of course, are rare, and depend not just on ability but also on marketing and grooming a child for a high level of success. Adults who engage in these activities may in fact be motivated by a sincere desire to help children succeed; but they may also be using children's superior ability to further their own personal interests (Farrey, 2008).

*Everyday stories*

HOW YOUNG IS TOO YOUNG? In 2003, when Kendall Marshall was 12 years old, he was ranked the top sixth-grade basketball prospect in the country by a major recruiting analyst. Marshall, who went on to become a college basketball star at the University of North Carolina at Chapel Hill, was 5 ft 2 in. (157.4 cm) tall and weighed 90 lbs (40.8 kg) at the time (Himmelsbach, 2009). Many young athletes like Marshall have already begun to show their potential for excellence by the time they are 12, arousing the interest of not only high school coaches but also college recruiters. In the past, colleges were not permitted to recruit student athletes until they had begun ninth grade. This was true for Marshall, who made his commitment to the University of North Carolina when he was a junior in high school. But a number of college coaches got around that rule by working off-season in privately run camps and clinics for seventh and eighth graders, where they had early access to young players. In 2009, the National Collegiate Athletic Association (NCAA) officially recognized seventh-grade male basketball players as "prospective athletes," who could be recruited by colleges, giving the NCAA more power over how this recruiting could be done (Sander, 2009). The result is that, now, promising fifth and sixth graders may be under even more pressure to perform like stars.

For children to benefit from organized sports, the adults who set the policies for these activities must also set clear, reasonable, and attainable goals concerning children's acquisition of necessary motor skills, capacity for increased physical activity, and possession of the social abilities they need to perform as a teammate. The American Academy of Pediatrics (2001/2007) recommends the following:

- Organized sports programs for preadolescents should provide time for free play and physical education programs.
- Pediatricians should be consulted to assess children's developmental readiness and medical suitability for the sport.
- Adults in charge of youth programs should be aware of any medical concerns about developmental and safety issues.
- Research should be ongoing to identify safe and effective training strategies.
- Research should be ongoing to identify the proper developmental time for children to participate in organized youth sports.

## School Health

During middle childhood, children spend more time at school than in almost any other setting. School health, then, is a major element in the community's capacity for children's health. It includes strategies, activities, and services designed to promote students' physical, emotional, and social development. Indeed, as our example of school nurses at the beginning of this chapter showed, schools also play an important role in public health. Although the primary mission of schools is to educate the country's students, the positive relationship between academic success and good health is compelling—not just for individual children but for the health of our nation as a whole. In other words, healthy kids make better students, and better students make healthier communities (Association for Supervision and Curriculum Development, 2011; Basch, 2010; CDC, 2010).

For example, hunger, physical and/or emotional abuse, and chronic illness can lead to poor school performance (Dunkle & Nash, 1991). Youngsters who engage in risky behaviors, such as substance use, violence, and physical inactivity, are more likely to do poorly in school and to eventually drop out, a factor associated with poor health in adulthood. Conversely, academic success is an excellent indicator of overall well-being during childhood and adolescence, and is a primary predictor of positive health outcomes in adulthood (Freudenberg & Ruglis, 2007; Harper & Lynch, 2007). In this section, we discuss two approaches to school health.

**coordinated school health program (CSHP)** A comprehensive program with eight interactive components designed to promote optimal health in children and their physical and social environments.

**school-based health center** A health clinic readily accessible to children and families operated as a partnership between the school and a community health organization.

## The Coordinated School Health Program (CSHP) Model

Practice

The Centers for Disease Control (CDC) recommend that schools adopt a **coordinated school health program (CSHP)** model. According to the CDC, school health programs typically have four overlapping goals: increasing health knowledge, attitude, and skills; increasing positive health behavior and outcomes; improving educational outcomes; and improving social outcomes. Schools can best achieve these goals by addressing all of them at the same time.

The CSHP model includes eight interactive components, listed in Table 11.7. We have addressed some of these components—health education and health literacy, physical education, and nutrition—in various parts of this book. Not every school has all eight components in place, and components that are in place are not necessarily well coordinated with each other. Nevertheless, most school districts nationwide have implemented some policies and programs that address health education, physical education, nutrition, and basic physical and mental health services (Kann, Brener, & Wechsler, 2007). Interestingly, the most neglected component of the model is health promotion for school staff.

## School-Based Health Centers

**School-based health centers** often operate as partnerships between the school and a community health organization, such as a community health center, hospital, or local health department. You can think of these centers as clinics that are readily accessible to children and families, in a school building or on school grounds, rather than across town at a hospital. The services vary depending on the needs of the community. Children's health records are kept confidential, just as they would be at any clinic, and so school personnel are not permitted access to them without parental permission.

According to the National Assembly on School-Based Health Care, nearly 2,000 school-based health centers operated nationwide during the 2007–2008 school year (Strozer, Juszczak, & Ammerman, 2010). Several factors contributed to the rise of school-based health centers over the last decade (Lear, 2007): the numbers of children without health insurance and disparities in health-care services; a federal initiative to expand mental and behavioral health services for children (President's New Freedom Commission on Mental Health, 2003); the Institute of Medicine's (2005) call for increased surveillance of obesity; and the No Child Left Behind Act of 2001 (Public Law 107–110), which focused attention on children's health problems as barriers to learning. The premise is the same as a century ago when schools introduced school nurses and lunch programs: Healthy children are the foundation for a healthy community and nation.

As a public health effort, school-based health centers bring services to the children who need them, where those children are—at school. Funding for school-based centers comes from federal, state, and local governments, as well as private organizations. Some services are reimbursed by health insurance. In an extensive analysis of these centers in one state (Ohio), researchers found that they resulted in a net savings to

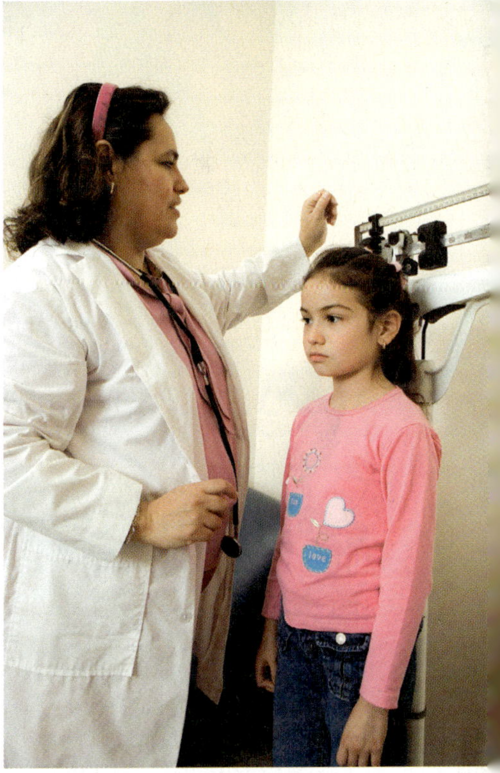
Michael Newman/Photo Edit

School-based health centers provide important services for children at a convenient location—school.

**Table 11.7** The CDC Coordinated School Health Program (CSHP) Model

| Component | Description |
|---|---|
| Health Education | Instruction on how to make health-promoting decisions, achieve health literacy, and adopt health-enhancing behaviors; 14 essential topics include substance use and abuse, nutrition, emotional health, nutrition, safety and injury prevention, sexual health, tobacco use, and violence prevention. |
| Physical Education | Instruction in the skills and knowledge necessary for lifelong participation in physical activity. |
| Health Services | Services intended to prevent and control communicable disease and other health problems; provide emergency care for illness or injury; promote and provide optimum sanitary conditions; provide educational and counseling opportunities for individuals, families, and community health; provide referral to primary health-care services. |
| Nutrition Services | Services intended to provide a variety of nutritious and appealing meals that accommodate the health and nutrition needs of all students. |
| Counseling, Psychological, and Social Services | Services intended to improve students' mental, emotional, and social health; these include individual and group assessments, interventions, and referrals. |
| Healthy and Safe School Environment | Provision of optimal physical conditions, such as temperature, noise, and lighting; provision of physical and social safety for students and staff; and protection from exposure to biological or chemical agents that are detrimental to health. |
| Health Promotion for Staff | Provision of opportunities for school staff members to improve their health status through activities such as health assessments, health education, and health-related fitness activities. |
| Family/Community Involvement | Provision of an integrated school, parent, and community approach that includes school health advisory councils, school health program efforts, parental involvement, and engagement of community resources. |

*Source:* Information from http://www.cdc.gov/healthyyouth/cshp/components.htm.

Medicaid, a federal program that pays for health services for qualified poor children. The centers closed the health-care gap for African American children, in particular (Guo, Wade, Pan, & Keller, 2010).

## what if...?

Which approach do you think would result in the greatest improvement in children's health: the coordinated school health program model or the school-based health center approach? Why? What role—if any at all—should schools play in children's health? Should schools take responsibility for children's health, or should that be up to parents?

## ✓ CHECK YOUR PROGRESS

1. What are some common causes of unintentional injury?
2. What are some of the safety habits that children, parents, and other adults need to develop to prevent unintentional injury?
3. How can adults help to prevent sports-related injuries?
4. What are the dangers of putting pressure on young children to excel at sports?
5. Explain how children's health and education are related.

# Common Disruptions in Health

**[ KEY QUESTION ] 4.** How can disruptions in health affect children's learning and behavior?

We have already discussed the most common disruption in health during middle childhood: unintentional injury. As we noted, exercising good safety habits can prevent most injuries. In Chapter 8, we focused on asthma and ear infections because they are common and are related to the immature immune response during early childhood. In this section, we examine the rise in chronic health conditions in children and describe the challenges of managing them at school and at home. We also address how these conditions and their treatments can affect children's learning and behavior.

## Chronic Conditions in Childhood

A chronic health condition is generally defined as one that lasts or can be expected to last 12 months or more, thus requiring additional health-care services. The population of children with chronic conditions has grown considerably over the last 30 years. There are several reasons for this. First, some chronic conditions, especially asthma, have increased in prevalence. Second, more children survive life-threatening conditions, such as prematurity and cancer, only to later require health care and other services for an extended period of time. Similarly, children with developmental disabilities such as Down syndrome, and illnesses such as cystic fibrosis, are living longer than was once the case. In 1994, about 12 to 15% of children were identified as having a chronic physical condition (Halfon & Newacheck, 2010; Perrin, Bloom & Gortmaker, 2007; Van Cleave et al., 2010).

In 1998, the U.S. Department of Health and Human Services, Maternal and Child Health Bureau, defined "children with special health-care needs" to include "those [children] who have or are at increased risk for a chronic physical, developmental, behavioral, or emotional condition, and who also require health and related services of a type or amount beyond that required by children generally" (McPherson et al., 1998, p. 138). Based on this new definition, the prevalence of chronic health conditions among children and adolescents in the United States in 2006 was 26.6%. Although this is double the 1994 estimate, many believe it is a more accurate reflection of the demand for services (Van Cleave et al., 2010).

Under the new definition, the most prevalent chronic conditions among children fit into two general classifications: physical illnesses and behavioral conditions/learning differences. Table 11.8 lists some of the more common chronic conditions.

**Table 11.8** Common Chronic Conditions in Childhood

| Physical Conditions | Behavioral Conditions and Learning Differences |
|---|---|
| Asthma | Learning disability |
| Respiratory and lung disorder other than asthma | Attention-deficit disorder (ADD) |
| Vision, hearing, and speech impairment | Attention-deficit hyperactivity disorder (ADHD) |
| Allergic condition | Intellectual disability |
| Orthopedic disability (for example, cerebral palsy) | Serious emotional disturbance |
| Heart problems | |
| Blood disorder or immune deficiency | |
| Epilepsy or seizures | |
| Other conditions (for example, diabetes, cystic fibrosis) | |

*Source:* Based on information from Van Cleave et al., 2010.

Increasingly, obesity is also counted as a chronic health condition (Perrin, 2008; Van Cleave et al., 2010). When it is counted, it adds up to the most prevalent chronic health condition in children, ahead of asthma.

### Management of Chronic Conditions in Childhood

Schools and parents often ask when children can self-manage a chronic physical condition, such as asthma. There is no simple answer. Over the last two decades, extensive research has indicated that management of a chronic condition involves a continuing partnership among children, their families, schools, and health-care providers. (Note that this approach is consistent with the Framework for Child Health and Development that we introduced in Chapter 5.) In fact, the management of chronic illness in adults is also considered best handled as a partnership between patient, family, and health-care providers over time; it is not, in short, something to be tackled alone (Bodenheimer, Wagner, & Grumbach, 2002; Wagner 1998; Wagner & the MacColl Institute, 2007).

The course of chronic conditions can be uneven and unpredictable, making their management an ongoing process. And management encompasses more than knowing how to perform hands-on tasks, such as using an inhaler. Individuals also must recognize and manage symptoms, problem-solve, adopt good health habits, address emotions such as anxiety and distress that often accompany a chronic condition, and manage the effect of the condition on their social lives, such as at work and school (Chronic Care Self-Management Guideline Team, Cincinnati Children's Hospital Medical Center, 2007; Von Korff, Gruman, Schaefer, Curry, & Wagner, 1997).

As children develop, the physiological demands of their illness can change. Their ability to understand their illness and adjust treatment needs under a variety of physical, social, and emotional conditions changes as well. Experience with the illness is also factor, as the following example describes (Erickson, Splett, Mullett, Jensen, & Belseth, 2006; Knafl, Breitmayer, Gallo, & Zoeller, 1996; LaGreca & Bearman, 2003).

© B BOISSONNET/BSIP/Age Fotostock

This mother is helping her daughter, who has diabetes, test her blood sugar with a glucometer. Children with this disease need such support as they learn the skills necessary to manage their health in the years to come.

*Everyday stories*

DIFFERENT AGES, DIFFERENT HISTORIES, DIFFERENT NEEDS Shareen, a 12-year-old, was recently diagnosed with type 1 diabetes. Scott, a 9-year-old, was diagnosed at age 3. Scott's experience makes him seem more confident than Shareen in carrying out the routine tasks of diabetes care. For example, he handles the glucometer to test his blood sugar well. But he lacks the ability to problem-solve in situations that are not routine. When his blood sugar levels, and thus his need for insulin, are affected by fatigue, exercise, and sweating, for example, Scott relies on his mother or the school nurse for help. Because Shareen is older, you might assume she would be better able to problem-solve under similar circumstances by herself. However, she is just learning how to manage her illness while dealing with the distress of the diagnosis and the changes it will make in her life. Right now, she not only needs help with routine tasks like using a glucometer, but she also needs help making decisions about how to balance her blood sugar levels, diet, and insulin. Her problem-solving skills in general may be more mature than Scott's, but it will take a while before she is able to apply them to the management of her illness. Thus, both Scott and Shareen need support that is tailored to their individual experiences and needs.

In spite of the importance of the partnership approach, though, schools may not always have enough resources to contribute fully to the health care of children enrolled in them. This fact is important because the vast majority of children with chronic conditions attend school. According to the National Association of School Nurses (NASN) (2006), the three most prevalent chronic conditions—of more than 200!—among school students that require nursing care are asthma, diabetes, and allergies (including life-threatening allergies).

An audit of five school nurses who covered multiple schools in different districts revealed that they administered a total of 154 different medications to children during the school day, including antibiotics, seizure medication, insulin for diabetes, inhalers for asthma, and medications for attention deficit disorders and mental health problems. The audit also noted discrepancies in how the nurses interpreted physician orders not written specifically to the school setting, and how they kept records and stored medications (Canham et al., 2007).

NASN recommends that school districts develop written medication policies and procedures, as well as emergency plans for children with chronic conditions (NASN, 2006, 2011). Federal education laws also mandate that schools provide required health services, including medication administration, to children with special health-care needs (O'Dell, O'Hara, Kiel, & McCullough, 2007). However, only 50% of schools have a full-time school nurse; many states do not require schools to have a nurse at all; and most school nurses cover multiple schools (NASN, 2010). These circumstances can make it difficult for schools to partner with children, their families, and health-care providers in the day-to-day management of chronic health conditions.

**what if...?**

What if you had just been diagnosed with a long-term illness, such as diabetes, asthma, or cancer? Who would come to mind as people you could rely on to help you manage the illness and treatments? What if these people were not available to you? How do you think you would feel if you were 8 years old and in the same circumstances?

### Effects of Diseases and Medications on Learning and Behavior

Children's physical health affects their cognitive and psychosocial development. Disease conditions, medications, and treatments may affect cells in the central nervous system, and thus learning and behavior (Armstrong, 2006). Of course, under certain circumstances, we want an effect, such as when medications are prescribed to children with attention deficit disorder: We want the medications to help them pay attention. But when the effects are unintended, such as the effects of radiation on the brain, it is cause for concern. We look at a few examples of unintended effects on learning and behavior here.

A word of caution is in order before you read further here: Keep in mind that there are many different ways to measure learning and behavior, and that children take medications and receive treatments in different combinations and dosages depending on their individual needs. For these reasons, it can be difficult to compare results from studies (DuPaul, McGoey, & Mautone, 2003).

**Effects of Disease Processes.** In type 1 diabetes, the body fails to make enough insulin to transmit circulating blood glucose into the cell as a source of energy. Thus, children with type 1 diabetes need to inject insulin into their bodies. Because of problems in regulating the balance of insulin and sugar in the bloodstream, the blood sugar levels of children with this disease may be too high or too low. In either case, fluctuating levels of blood glucose can affect cells in the central nervous system, causing both short-term and long-term effects.

**corticosteroids** A class of medications used to treat inflammation of soft tissues in a wide variety of chronic conditions, including asthma and other respiratory conditions, arthritis, and cancer.

The short-term effects of sudden episodes of low blood sugar include impaired attention and memory (Sommerfield, Deary, McAulay, & Frier, 2003). Thus, during such an episode, it may take a child longer to work through problems on, say, a math test (Gonder-Frederick et al., 2009). Long-term effects are usually seen more often in children who were diagnosed before the age of 6, because the fluctuations in blood sugar can permanently affect their developing brains. Such children may have problems with attention, learning, and memory skills (both visual and verbal), affecting reading ability in particular (Gaudieri, Chen, Greer, & Holmes, 2008; Silverstein et al., 2005).

Sickle cell disease (SCD), which we first discussed in Chapter 2, offers another example of how a disease process can affect learning. In this disorder, when oxygen in the bloodstream drops below a critical level, red blood cells collapse into a sickle shape. They clump together, blocking blood vessels that carry oxygen to the brain and causing inflammation and swelling. As a result, many children with SCD experience strokes. The cognitive effects depend on which parts of the brain are affected and how severe the individual child's illness is. Children may have difficulty with verbal skills and verbal working memory. They may process information more slowly than their peers and have difficulty paying attention, making decisions, and regulating their behavior and emotions. As the disease progresses, the consequences of multiple sickling episodes become cumulative and the cognitive difficulties more pronounced. Fortunately, there are new therapies that may help to minimize the cognitive effects of the disease (Puffer, Schatz & Roberts, 2007; Schatz, & McClellan, 2006).

**Effects of Treatments.** Acute lymphoblastic leukemia (ALL) is a cancer that affects white blood cells, causing them to rise to dangerous levels. In the treatment of ALL, chemotherapy medications are administered directly into the brain, because the brain and spinal column have large reservoirs of circulating white blood cells that can be readily targeted. The brain often undergoes radiation therapy as well. Children treated for ALL often also receive high doses of corticosteroids, such as prednisone. (We discuss corticosteroids later.) Together, these treatments are well known to cause certain cognitive difficulties, which may not be evident for two or more years after treatment ends.

Of long-term survivors of ALL who have had brain-administered medications and radiation, about 17% have moderate to severe declines in cognitive function (Horton & Steuber, 2011). These children may have difficulty with nonverbal and verbal short-term memory and performing tasks requiring attention and concentration (Robaey et al., 2000). The younger the child—and the brain—at the time of ALL treatment, the more extensive and long-lasting the effects. Research on these cognitive effects has resulted in the use of less toxic cancer treatments in children.

**Effects of Medications.** **Corticosteroids**, such as prednisone, are drugs used to treat inflammation in a wide variety of chronic conditions, including asthma and other respiratory conditions, arthritis, and cancer. Children who take prednisone may feel jittery and anxious and may have trouble sleeping and paying attention. As a result, they may have difficulty in the classroom. Fortunately, these effects wear off when the medication is stopped. However, some children may need to take corticosteroids for a long period of time. Long-term use increases vulnerability to infection and may also cause depression.

The drug Ritalin® (methylphenidate) is an amphetamine, which means it is a central nervous system stimulant. It is used in the treatment of attention deficit disorder, which we discuss further in Chapter 12 (Subcommittee on Attention-Deficit/Hyperactivity Disorder et al., 2011). It works by blocking the re-uptake of the neurotransmitter dopamine, increasing the amount left in the synapse in the brain, and thus improving a child's ability to focus on a task. At the same time, it quiets neurons not associated with the task and that distract the child's attention. Children typically take Ritalin® 2 to 3 times during the day, as the amount in the bloodstream needs to be replenished every few hours. It is one of the most common medications given out at school.

**Implications.** Our discussion here is intended to help you to appreciate the relationship between children's physical health and their development. If you eventually work with children as a teacher, guidance counselor, social worker, psychologist, or health professional, you will encounter many children who have chronic health conditions. When these children do well in school and with friends, it will be thanks to adults like you who provided support to and understanding for them and their families during this crucial period in their lives.

Often, these chronic conditions are not readily apparent, such as asthma or diabetes, and so it can be easy for people to dismiss the effects of such diseases and their treatments on affected children's day-to-day lives. By realizing that physical health is integral to children's cognitive, social and emotional development, you will be better prepared to help all children under your care thrive.

### CHECK YOUR PROGRESS

1. What is a chronic health condition?
2. Why does management of a chronic health condition require a partnership between the child, parents, school, and health-care provider?
3. Provide examples of how chronic conditions can affect children's learning and behavior.

# CHAPTER SUMMARY

## Biology of Health: Physical Growth and Development

**[ KEY QUESTION ] 1. How do qualitative and quantitative changes in growth and development support physical, cognitive, and social skills during middle childhood?**

- Between ages 6 and 11, height increases of about 2 or 3 in. (5–7 cm) per year and weight gains of about 5 or 6 lbs (2.2–2.7 kg) per year are common. By 11 years of age, the average child is still slightly under 5 ft (150cm) in height and weighs less than 80 lbs (36 kg).
- A child's phenotype depends on both genotype and environmental conditions. It is important to compare a child's current size against his or her own personal growth path to assess physical development.
- Increasingly complex patterns of development in the brain support the cognitive changes that are the hallmark of middle childhood: faster processing time, improved memory retention and retrieval, and logical reasoning. There are some gender differences in brain development during this period.
- The constraint model of motor development holds that physical movements arise from the interactions of the individual body, the task prompting the need for movement, and the environment.
- Over the course of the middle-childhood years, children's skills progress from such activities as running, jumping, throwing, and catching to more demanding ones, such as throwing for distance, running for speed, and kicking for accuracy. In the final years of the period, children demonstrate the more complex abilities needed for strategy and teamwork.

## Foundations of Health: Health Promotion

**[ KEY QUESTION ] 2. What can we do to promote health and prevent disease in middle childhood?**

- During well-child visits, parents and children receive anticipatory guidance about what to expect and what to pay attention to during middle childhood so that children will be better prepared to navigate adolescence. Unfortunately, the number of children who visit a health-care provider regularly is lower in middle childhood than in early childhood.
- More than 90% of children comply with basic immunization requirements by the end of their first year in school. Several new vaccines are recommended for this age group to prevent meningococcus, hepatitis A, and the human papillomavirus.
- Most children begin losing their primary teeth at around age 6. By about age 12, all 20 primary teeth have been replaced by 28 adult teeth. About 40% of children have dental caries.
- Children's caloric needs depend on their level of activity. The MyPlate program provides a guide to healthy eating.
- Children eat half of their daily calories at school. School lunch programs provide meals free or at lower cost to needy children. New school lunch guidelines focus on providing more healthful meals.
- Among children ages 6 to 11, 35.5% are either overweight or obese. Obesity causes more problems than strain on the heart, blood vessels, and lower joints. Excess white adipose tissue significantly changes metabolism and the immune system.
- The ready availability of snack foods, fast foods, and beverages high in sugar, together with the lack of physical activity, mean children take in more empty calories and expend fewer calories.

## Capacity for Health: Caregivers and Community

**[ KEY QUESTION ] 3.** How can caregivers and communities keep children safe during middle childhood?

- Unintentional injuries remain the leading cause of death of children between ages 5 and 14. The top three causes of unintentional injury are motor vehicle accidents, drowning, and fire.
- It is important for children to develop good safety habits, which means adults and older adolescents need to promote and model such habits themselves. The greatest challenge for adults is determining how well children understand and can respond to potentially dangerous situations.
- Children under the age of 14 suffer about 3.5 million sports-related injuries each year. The most common involve soft tissue, such as muscles and ligaments: ankle sprains, muscle strains, and repetitive motion injuries. About 62% of all organized sports-related injuries occur during practice.
- Children's bodies are still developing and changing proportion during middle childhood. To prevent injuries, parents and coaches must accommodate the demands of sports to individual children's bodies and abilities. Parents and coaches must also be aware that performance pressure can be detrimental to children's physical and emotional health.
- During middle childhood, children spend more time at school than in almost any other setting. School health, then, is a major element in the community's capacity for overseeing children's health.
- A coordinated school health program includes health education; physical education; health, nutrition, and counseling services; a healthy safe school environment; health promotion for staff; and family and community involvement.
- A school-based health center is often operated as a partnership between the school and a community health organization, such as a community health center, hospital, or local health department.

## Common Disruptions in Health

**[ KEY QUESTION ] 4.** How can disruptions in health affect children's learning and behavior?

- The prevalence of chronic health conditions among children in the United States increased from 12.8% in 1994 to 26.6% in 2006. The three most prevalent chronic conditions are obesity, asthma, and behavior and learning problems.
- Management of a chronic condition involves a partnership among children, their families, their schools, and health-care providers.
- Only 50% of schools have a full-time school nurse, and many states do not require that schools have nurses.
- Diseases, medications, and other treatments can have both short- and long-term effects on children's learning and behavior.

# KEY TERMS

5-2-1-0 Program *408*
anticipatory guidance *408*
constraints model of motor development *406*
coordinated school health program (CSHP) *425*
corticosteroids *430*
hepatitis A *410*
human papillomavirus *410*
meningococcus *408*
midgrowth spurt *400*
MyPlate *411*
positron emission tomography (PET) *401*
school-based health centers *425*
white adipose tissue *414*

# CRITICAL THINKING QUESTIONS

1. **Biology of Health: Physical Growth and Development.** Let's say you have volunteered to coach a youth baseball or softball team for 10-year-olds. How will you use Newell's constraint model of motor development in your role as coach?
2. **Foundations of Health: Health Promotion.** Explain how the increase in overweight and obesity in American children is an almost perfect storm of the interactions of multiple systems. What changes in those systems need to occur to reverse this trend?
3. **Capacity for Health: Caregivers and Community.** How can schools help children to be healthy?
4. **Common Disruptions in Health.** What are the implications of chronic illness for children's development? What are some efforts that parents, schools, and communities can make to mitigate these effects?
5. **Cultural Perspectives.** We pointed out that attitudes about body weight are social constructs. How do you think American culture changed to favor thinness? How are attitudes about being overweight communicated to children? What would it take to change cultural attitudes about being overweight, especially among children? Do you think that being overweight is a health issue? A cultural issue? Both? Why?

# REAL Development

## Physical Development and Health in Middle Childhood

In this module, you are a nutritional consultant for Washington Middle School. The school has been required to adopt new nutritional standards released by the U.S. Department of Agriculture. Acting as a liaison for the department, you will evaluate the school's current lunch offerings and provide guidance on how the school can meet the new federal guidelines. As you complete the activity, consider what you have learned about nutrition and health in this chapter.

© John Wiley & Sons, Inc.

**WileyPLUS** Go to WileyPLUS to complete the *Real Development* activity.

# Chapter 12

Jena Cumbo/Getty Images

# Cognitive Development in Middle Childhood

## CHAPTER OUTLINE



## MAKING A difference

### Be a Buddy

Nine-year-old Jamel has a new job. He has volunteered to be a buddy to 5-year-old Julio, who is in kindergarten at Jamel's school. Every Friday morning, Jamel goes to the kindergarten classroom and meets with Julio. Together, they choose a book to read. Jamel knows that Julio likes stories about animals, so they often choose a book with animal characters in it. After reading the title of the book to Julio, Jamel asks him some questions about what he thinks the book might be about.

Julio is just learning to associate letters with their sounds, so as Jamel reads to him, he points to certain letters, such as the "b" in bear, and asks him what sound the letter makes. By doing this, Jamel is helping Julio take the first steps of learning to read. At the same time Jamel makes sure Julio enjoys the process of understanding a story. As Julio sits next to Jamel, he puts his head on the older boy's shoulder, and together they look at the book while Jamel reads. As he does, Jamel asks Julio questions about the story, and Julio enjoys pointing to the pictures in the book that illustrate the action. After they have finished the story, Jamel asks Julio to draw a picture about it. Julio likes to draw, and he works hard at making sure he includes important details in his picture that reflect the story.

Many schools are now starting buddy programs. They are helpful to kindergarten children, who are proud to know an older child in the school. But they also benefit the volunteer (Lowery, Sabis-Burns, & Anderson-Brown, 2008). If, say, Jamel is a weak reader himself, he will gain confidence by reading simple books to Julio. In this way, he practices his own knowledge of letter-sound combinations, as well as his understanding of the flow of a storyline. He also discovers that when he reads using different voices for the various characters in the story, Julio will be more engaged in it. Jamel can thus become a better and more fluent reader himself by reading to a younger child.

## [KEY QUESTIONS] *for* READING CHAPTER 12

1. What are the characteristics of children's thinking during the concrete operational stage, according to Piaget?
2. What are some themes in Vygotsky's theory that are especially relevant to the middle-childhood years?
3. What are the main types and functions of attention and memory, and why do they assume such significance in middle childhood?
4. What are some different perspectives on intelligence?
5. What significant advances in language development, literacy, and mathematical understanding occur in the middle-childhood years?

**IN THIS CHAPTER,** we examine how children develop cognitively in the middle childhood years. Teachers, parents, and others who share the responsibility of preparing children for the future can be sure of one fact: The future will demand more and more cognitive competence as the environment becomes ever more intricate. We begin by discussing Piaget's ideas about these developments and then revisit Vygotsky's theory. Next, we turn to information-processing theory, focusing on recent research into attention and memory. We continue by considering the meaning of *intelligence*, the role of IQ tests, and different perspectives on what it means to be intelligent. Finally, we discuss language development, including the need for many children to learn a second language, and the school-related skills of literacy and mathematics acquired during middle childhood.

# Piaget's Theory and Concrete Operational Thought

**[ KEY QUESTION ] 1. What are the characteristics of children's thinking during the concrete operational stage, according to Piaget?**

| Piaget's Stage Theory |
|---|
| Sensorimotor |
| Preoperational |
| Concrete operational<br>• Children develop the ability to reason about concrete objects. |
| Formal operational |

As we've seen in earlier chapters, Jean Piaget believed that children's thinking changes with age and experience in a stage-like manner (Feldman, 2013; Johnson, Munakata, & Gilmore, 2002; Piaget, 1929). At around 7 years of age, according to Piaget, children enter the stage of **concrete operations**. Many, but not all children, move from concrete operations into the next stage, formal operations, around age 11 or 12.

Children in the stage of concrete operations think very differently from children at the preoperational stage (Bjorklund & Rosenblum, 2002), as we discussed in Chapter 9. The critical differences that separate the preoperational from the concrete operational child stem from the concrete operational child's acquisition of a coherent and integrated system of internalized mental actions, referred to as **cognitive operations** (Flavell, 1963; Ginsburg & Opper, 1988). Piaget maintained that during this stage of development children show the beginnings of logic, such as deductive reasoning. Children's logical reasoning during this stage, however, is limited to concrete, not abstract or hypothetical, experiences. That is, children in the concrete operational stage show logical reasoning only if they can actively manipulate concrete objects or symbols, rather than just think about them (Flavell, Miller, & Miller, 2002).

As an example, consider problems of *transitive inference*, which require us to infer a relationship between two objects based on a comparison with a third object. Suppose we have three blocks: A, B, and C, which differ only in height. A is taller than B, and

**concrete operations** Piaget's term to describe the thinking of 7- to 11-year-old children; logical thinking about physical, concrete objects.

**cognitive operations** Internalized mental operations.

B is taller than C. If we *show* concrete operational children blocks A and B, they can easily determine that block A is taller than block B. If we remove block A and then show the children blocks B and C, they will have no trouble telling us that B is taller than C. If we then ask them about the relationship between block A and block C, they can deduce that block A is larger than block C even though they have not actually seen block A and C together. But if we now *tell* them that Liz is taller than Rosita, and Usha is shorter than Rosita, they will have difficulty telling us who is tallest of all, because this problem requires them to think internally about the various heights, rather than actually viewing them.

The ability to perform concrete operations enables children to begin to think logically and make reasonable deductions, as they are no longer only making guesses (Pillow, Pearson, Hecht, & Bremer, 2010). As you will see in Chapter 15, when children become older and enter the next cognitive stage, they gain the ability to use logical operations on abstract ideas.

**conservation** Realization that the essence of something remains the same even though surface characteristics change; characteristic of the cognitive operational stage.

## Accomplishments of the Concrete Operational Period

Let's look at some of the specific accomplishments of the concrete operational period to understand how children of this age differ from younger children. Key accomplishments of the period include the ability to conserve, seriate, and classify quantities and objects. Underlying each of these accomplishments is the ability to use simple forms of logic to solve a concrete problem.

### Conservation

**Conservation** is the realization that the essence of something remains the same even though surface characteristics may change. Think of the water jar problem that we discussed in Chapter 9. Two water jars are filled to the same height, and then the contents of one are poured into a taller and slimmer jar so that the liquid reaches a higher level. Unlike younger children, children at the concrete operational level are not deceived. They know that the contents of both jars are equal.

Remember too from this example that reasoning through the transformation that occurs when the water is poured into a different jar requires a child to think something like this: "One jar is taller but narrower, and the other is shorter but wider so the water level looks different, but the amount of water is the same. Nothing has been added or taken away, so although it now looks like there is more water in one jar, there really isn't." This kind of reasoning requires the child to consider more than one attribute at the same time—and concrete operational children can do that. In other words, they can *decenter* from focusing on only one attribute. This ability allows them to *conserve* the idea of equal amounts of water even when perception indicates that the water levels look different.

During middle childhood, children show abilities to conserve number, volume, length, and mass. The logical arguments they use to explain their reasoning include identity, reversibility, and compensation. Here is an example of each type of reasoning applied to the conservation of liquid.

- *Identity.* Children state that no water has been added to or subtracted from either jar, so the amount of water must be the same.
- *Reversibility.* Children reason that you can pour the water back into the original jar and it will look the same as it did originally. Reversibility is one of the key features of developing cognitive operations. It means that children can retrace their thinking.
- *Compensation.* Children argue that the water in the taller jar is higher, but it's also narrower. They have compensated for the height increase by noting the decrease in circumference.

As we mentioned in Chapter 9, children vary in the age at which they understand conservation. Also, most children understand some types of conservation earlier than other types. For example, conservation of number typically occurs before conservation of weight. Piaget used the term *horizontal décalage* to explain that children develop some types of conservation earlier than others.

Lisa Passmore

A preoperational child would have difficulty arranging this many sticks by length, but the task presents no problem for a child in the concrete operational stage.

## Seriation

**Seriation** refers to children's ability to arrange objects by increasing or decreasing size. For example, we might give children 10 sticks of differing lengths and ask them to order them from tallest to shortest. According to Piaget, children in the preoperational stage can select the tallest and shortest stick but often have difficulty ordering the full set of 10 sticks in a systematic way, and instead order them haphazardly (Inhelder & Piaget, 1964). In contrast, children in the concrete operational stage have little difficulty accomplishing this task, which requires them to understand that each stick (other than the shortest and tallest) has a relationship to both a taller and a shorter one. Thus, success here requires children to *decenter* by considering two relationships simultaneously. They must logically and systematically compare each new stick to the ones already set down and determine where in the series it belongs.

As with conservation, children understand some aspects of seriation before others. Generally, children first develop seriation of length (around 7 to 8 years), then weight (around 9 to 10 years), and finally volume (around 11 to 12 years). The ability to seriate objects becomes increasingly important to solving mathematical problems in which quantities require comparison.

## Classification

Classification involves the ability to put like objects together into the same category or class. A simple classification task might involve showing a child 10 toy cars, each colored red, blue, or green, and asking the child to put the cars that are alike together. This type of task is easily accomplished by a child in the preoperational stage. *Class inclusion* tasks, however, are more complex.

Class inclusion tasks require an understanding of *hierarchical classification*, which involves knowing that small groups, or subclasses, are part of larger groups, or classes. In Chapter 9, we discussed a class inclusion task that involved showing children a large group of teddy bears and a smaller group of stuffed dogs and asking them whether there were more teddy bears or more stuffed animals. Children in the preoperational stage were often puzzled and typically replied, "more teddy bears," because they were focusing only on the larger of the two subclasses. In contrast, concrete operational children have little difficulty with this concept, and they will usually reply, "more stuffed animals." They can consider the class and the subclass simultaneously, especially if they can actually see the objects or pictures of objects being discussed, as opposed to having to consider the problem abstractly. The ability to understand hierarchical classification requires that children *decenter* from focusing only on the subclass. This type of skill is often required in elementary school when children are asked to classify objects in the natural world, such as plants and animals.

© JGI/Jamie Grill/Blend Images/Corbis

Having mastered classification skills, many children in middle childhood enjoy using these skills in their hobbies—for example, coin collecting.

Understanding the concept of class inclusion is also required for many problems in mathematics, especially those involving redundant data (Setti & Caramelli, 2007). Problems with redundant data have more information than is needed to solve the problem. Children need to sort through the information and decide what information is necessary and what information is not. Here's an example: You have arranged for a truck to bring containers of food to sell at a farmers' market. You have 15 containers of vegetables, including 9 containers of beans, and 6 containers of carrots, as well as 7 containers of apples. How many containers will the truck bring to the market? To solve this problem, a child has to resist simply adding all the containers and instead realize that the beans and carrots are subclasses already counted in the class of vegetables. Once children master hierarchical classification, they often enjoy such challenges. During middle childhood many children begin to spontaneously use classification skills in their hobbies, such as coin collecting.

CLASSIFYING BY CLASSES AND SUBCLASSES Robert and Tia have both started coin collections. Robert has organized his coins first by country, then by denomination, so that coins worth more are separated from coins worth less. Tia has decided to collect quarters from the different states in the United States. She has first organized them by region of the country: Southwest, Northeast, and so on. Within that organization, she puts coins in alphabetical order by state. Both Robert and Tia have shown that they can classify by classes and subclasses, a skill that children in the concrete operational stage have mastered.

*Everyday stories*

**seriation** The ability to arrange objects by increasing or decreasing characteristics, such as height or weight; typical of the concrete operational stage.

what if...?

What if you were playing the game 20 Questions with two children, one still in the preoperational stage and one in the concrete operational stage? As you may recall, the game involves guessing the object another person is thinking of by asking a series of up to 20 questions, each of which can only be answered "yes" or "no". How might you expect each of the two children to approach the game based on their cognitive development? How would an understanding of hierarchical classification help the children be more efficient at this game?

## Helping Children Develop Their Cognitive Skills in the Classroom

**Practice**

Although Piaget himself was not focused on children's experiences in the classroom, his work has several implications for classroom teachers. Teachers, as well as other adults, can use concrete materials to help children progress through the concrete operational stage and eventually learn to work with abstractions. Here are a few suggestions:

1. **Provide opportunities for children to learn to classify information using classes and subclasses.** For example, have children figure out how to classify a series of fruits and vegetables by determining what makes the two classes different and what makes the objects within a class similar. Present challenges to their natural classification schemes. In one, children might at first classify a tomato as a vegetable rather than a fruit, but they then correct their classification by noting the characteristics of each class.
2. **Construct problems involving seriation, such as having children place typical classroom objects in a series based on weight.** If a scale is available, children can check the actual weights of the objects. Challenge children further by having them seriate the same objects by height. Since taller objects are not necessarily heavier than shorter objects, the children will see that different rules of seriation can result in different series of the same objects.
3. **Help children to understand conservation by reversing their thinking.** After viewing a transformation, such as liquid being poured from a short, wide glass into a tall, narrow glass, a child can reason that the liquid could be poured back into the short, wide glass with the water level remaining the same as it originally was. Encouraging practice in such reasoning can support children's cognitive development. A way to do this is by asking children to make predictions that require them to reverse their thinking. One exercise to achieve this is to place a series of different-colored balls in an opaque tube and instruct the children to predict the order in which the balls will fall out of the tube when it is turned upside down once. Then ask them to predict the order when the tube is turned upside down 3 and 4 times.

© blickwinkel/Alamy

By sorting leaves into categories, these children learn to classify information using concrete objects.

## Criticisms of Piaget's Theory

Piaget's work has contributed much to our understanding of children's cognitive development. Still, as we've seen in earlier discussions, critics have raised several problems with Piaget's theory. Perhaps especially relevant to middle childhood is that Piaget based his conclusions on the observation of only a small number of Swiss children and then generalized them to all children. Research has not necessarily supported the universality of Piaget's ideas.

Early research on children in non-Western cultures indicated that they do not show certain elements of concrete operations, like conservation of number, at the same ages as European and American youngsters (Dasen, 1972). One reason may be that attending school is helpful in advancing children's logical thought processes, especially those related to classification and class inclusion, during middle childhood (Cahan, Greenbaum, Artman, Deluya, & Gappel-Gilon, 2008).

Researchers have also found that performance on Piagetian tasks varies based on the familiarity of the material, concepts, and activities (Rogoff, 2003). When tasks are presented in more familiar contexts, even children with little formal schooling show concrete operational reasoning. For example, in one study, 6- to 9-year-old street vendors in Brazil displayed high levels of class inclusion skills when asked to reason about the classes and subclasses of the chewing gum they were selling (Ceci & Roazzi, 1994). This research suggests that the basic logic shown by children in concrete operations may be universal if such mental operations are considered within the context of the requirements of children's culture and daily experiences.

Another criticism of Piaget's model is that it operates from a *deficiency perspective* (Roth & Thom, 2009). According to this view, Piaget focused on how children's reasoning differs from that of adults, and identified the differences as deficiencies in children's thinking. Moreover, the type of reasoning that Piaget was most interested in was formal logic as typically used by Western scientists. Thus, the theory neglects other important areas of development that relate to cognition but are not based on logic alone, such as art, poetry, and music (Feldman, 2013; Gardner, Kornhaber, & Wake 1996).

### ✓CHECK YOUR PROGRESS

1. How do the thought processes of children in the stage of concrete operations differ from the thought processes of children in the preoperational stage?
2. What is the importance of reversibility in children's ability to reason logically?
3. What are the three arguments that children use to conserve?
4. What are some of the criticisms of Piaget's theory applied to middle childhood?

# Vygotsky's Sociocultural Theory

**[ KEY QUESTION ] 2. What are some themes in Vygotsky's theory that are especially relevant to the middle-childhood years?**

You know by now that Lev Vygotsky focused on the importance of children's social and cultural worlds to their development. In his view of development through middle childhood, Vygotsky continues to emphasize social interactions, language, and learning in the zone of proximal development. Unlike Piaget, Vygotsky stresses the importance of school instruction as a way to advance children's cognitive development. As a result, his theory has generated much research related to education.

## Development in Middle Childhood

During middle childhood, children's cognitive capabilities continue to develop through social interactions with others, such as skillful adults and more expert peers. Because children have interactions with a variety of people during this period, especially as they progress through school, they are influenced by a larger number of others. According to Vygotsky, the role of teachers in advancing children's cognitive development becomes increasingly important during middle childhood.

As we've noted, Vygotsky stressed the role of instruction in children's cognitive development, especially as it relates to information that children would be unlikely to learn on their own. Vygotsky (1934/1986) distinguished two forms of knowledge and thinking. The first type, called *spontaneous concepts*, is informal and unscientific. Spontaneous concepts are general ideas about the way the world works that are based on experiences outside of formal education. The second type, called *scientific concepts*, is formal and is taught in schools. (Note that by "scientific," Vygotsky meant information that is related to academic learning, not just material related to scientific subjects.)

Let's consider an example of the difference between these two types of knowledge (Vygotsky, 1934/1986). Perhaps you have had the experience of learning a second language in school. When you learned your first language, you did not do so by following a set of rules someone gave you, such as that nouns generally come before verbs. Instead, you learned it through experience. When you learned a second language, in contrast, you needed to be taught the rules of that language, such as about word order. Thus, learning a first language occurred spontaneously, whereas learning a second language occurred through systematic teaching. Interestingly, although you are probably much more fluent in your first language, you may be more aware of the rules of your second language and better able to explain them to others. Also, as a result of the systematic instruction in the rules of your second language, you probably then became more aware of word order and grammar in your first language than you were before.

In Vygtosky's view, as language skills become more sophisticated in middle childhood, children become better at using language—along with other symbols systems, such as numbers—to solve problems. Consider the following simple example: Rashad has 12 blocks, and then Ethan takes 5 of them; how many blocks does Rashad have left? One solution, often chosen by children in the early childhood years, is to count out 12 blocks, take 5 of them away, and arrive at the solution by counting the number of blocks remaining. Of course, a quicker solution involves simple subtraction using numbers. The advantage of using numbers as symbols is apparent as problems become more complex. Children must be taught the rules of using symbol systems, such as numbers, and these rules are usually taught in schools.

During middle childhood, children also increasingly use language to help control their behavior. The use of *inner speech*, or subvocalized thinking, increases during the middle-childhood period and helps children to control their actions and certain aspects of their learning (Winsler, Fernyhough, & Montero, 2009). An interesting feature of inner speech is that it is more abbreviated than speech used to interact with other people (Vygotsky, 1934/1986). It tends to consist of short phrases rather than full sentences.

Because of the central role of schooling in children's lives during middle childhood, Vygotsky's work has particular importance in the field of education. In Piaget's view, development was a prerequisite for learning; in other words, a child must have reached a certain level of development to benefit from instruction. In contrast, Vygotsky believed that learning, especially of academic knowledge, precedes and promotes development. Thus, the role of a teacher is to recognize a child's understanding of a concept and then to challenge it by providing instruction that is slightly more advanced than that understanding. The instruction must occur within the *zone of proximal development*. If the new information is too advanced, the student may get frustrated and give up. If it is too easy, then the student might not move to a higher level of understanding.

© Hero/Corbis

Instruction within the zone of proximal development uses many techniques. Here, students learn about phototropism by observing how plants grow.

*Everyday stories*

A NEW CONCEPT Rosa Archuleta, a fourth-grade teacher, is introducing the term *phototropism* to her class. The term refers to the growth of plants toward light. The children don't seem to understand her explanation, however, because they don't believe that plants can move. Therefore, the teacher first provides a definition of the term and then proceeds to give the class specific examples. She instructs the children to put seedlings in specific places in the classroom so that light from the windows hits them at different angles. Within a few days, the stems of plants that have been placed to the right of the window are starting to bend to the left, while those to the left of the window are bending to the right. In this way, the children come to understand the effects of phototropism on a plant's growth.

## Vygotsky in the Classroom Practice

As we described in Chapter 9, learning within the zone of proximal development depends in part on the use of *scaffolding*, guidance or support adjusted to the child's level of performance. One way to use scaffolding in the classroom involves *reciprocal teaching* (Palinsar & Brown, 1984; Spörer, Brunstein, & Kieschke, 2009), which is used to improve reading comprehension. Students in groups of 3 to 6 read a text and discuss it with a teacher. In providing scaffolding, the teacher employs 4 cognitive strategies: questioning, summarizing, clarifying, and predicting (Berk & Winsler, 1999).

- *Questioning*. First the teacher and students raise questions about the story's content. What is the setting? Is the setting important to the story? Who are the main characters?
- *Summarizing*. Next, the teacher summarizes or asks a student to summarize what he or she thinks is the substance of the story. The teacher and other students discuss actions or ideas that may have been misunderstood.
- *Clarifying*. The group discusses any ideas or terms that may cause confusion. Teachers may ask students about certain terms to make sure they understand their meaning.

© MBI/Alamy

As part of reciprocal teaching, students read a story and, in a group, discuss it with their teacher. The teacher uses several techniques, such as asking students to make predictions about what might occur next in the story, to establish scaffolding.

- *Predicting*. The teacher asks class members to predict what will happen next, based on what has happened so far in the story. In order to make reasonable predictions, students need to understand the details of a story, including the basic plot and the attributes of the different characters. By checking their predictions as they read the next part of the story, the students will be able to evaluate their understanding of the story.

Although initially the teacher explains and models the strategies to the students, eventually they learn the steps and can lead each other in these types of discussion. This approach has been found to be more successful in improving children's reading comprehension than traditional methods of teaching reading, such as whole-group instruction (Spörer et al., 2009).

what if...?

What if you were tutoring children who were having difficulty with reading comprehension? They can read a story aloud with few errors, but they have difficulty understanding the main plot and details of the story. Why might asking them to predict what would happen next help them synthesize what they know and lead them to a better understanding of the plot and the characters?

## Criticisms of Vygotsky's Theory

Vygotsky's theory has many strengths, especially as applied to teaching, but like all theories, it also has limitations (Karpov, 2005). Some have criticized it for being, in some respects, vague. For one, although the concept of the zone of proximal development is useful in a general way, its description is vague, and its application to teaching a classroom of children is ambiguous (Bergen, 2008). The theory leads to the conclusion that the zone differs for each child in each subject area. That raises the question of how a teacher could pay sufficient individual attention to all these various zones for all children in a classroom. Thus, the implications of Vygotsky's theory for instructing an entire classroom of children are not clear. A related criticism is that Vygotsky's

**attention** Selectively focusing on one source of information while ignoring others.

emphasis on the role of instruction underrates the importance of children's independence in learning (Crain, 2000).

✓CHECK YOUR PROGRESS

1. What role does language play in Vygotsky's theory?
2. What is the difference between spontaneous concepts and scientific concepts according to Vygotsky?
3. What are some of the criticisms of Vygotsky's theory as applied to middle childhood?

# Information-Processing Theory

**[ KEY QUESTION ] 3. What are the main types and functions of attention and memory, and why do they assume such significance in middle childhood?**

As we've seen, information-processing theorists are concerned with what happens in the human mind as it seeks to acquire, process, retain, and comprehend information. These theorists differ from Piaget in that they do not view children's development as occurring in stages. And they differ from Vygtosky in that they do not focus explicitly on the importance of social interaction. Instead, they concentrate on the development of cognitive processes such as attention and memory (Morra, Gobbo, Marini, & Sheese, 2008).

We discussed several aspects of the information-processing model in earlier chapters. (You may want to refer back to the information-processing model shown in Figure 9.5.) In this chapter, we focus on two aspects of the model: attention and memory. Controlling attention and memory is important to self-regulation and executive function. Both attention and memory improve in children during middle childhood. They are able to process information more quickly and more accurately, and they develop strategies that enable them to attend to information and remember it more effectively.

## Attention

**Attention** refers to the selective focus on one source of information, while ignoring others. The ability to focus selectively continues to develop steadily through childhood (Bear, Connors, & Paradiso, 2007; Passow et al., 2012; Rueda, 2005). In Chapter 9, we discussed improvements in *executive function* during the early childhood years, including children's expanding ability to both focus and shift attention from one task to another. In middle childhood, the need for selective attention becomes increasingly important to answer the demands made by schoolwork.

### Developments in Attention

In fact, cognitive control of attention does show major developmental changes across the middle-childhood years (Durston & Casey, 2006). During this period, children's attentional abilities improve in several ways. They are better able to selectively attend to information, they inhibit inappropriate responses, and they improve in their abilities to use and describe strategies for increasing selective attention (Brocki & Bohlin, 2004).

Selective attention involves two facets: (1) the ability to focus on significant information, such as what the teacher is saying, and (2) the ability to ignore unimportant and distracting information, such as noises in the hallway or thoughts about lunch (Nelson, Thomas, & de Haan, 2006). It is easy to see why both of these skills are necessary for school-related tasks such as reading and solving mathematical problems (Stevens & Bavelier, 2012). For example, suppose students are asked to respond to a question about a reading assignment. They must mentally sort through the information they have read to determine which of it is relevant to the question. In doing so,

Brad Wilson/Getty Images

Being able to control their attention is increasingly important for children as they advance through school.

they must not be distracted by information that they may have found interesting but that is not relevant to the question asked. Similarly, in a mathematical story problem, children need to disregard irrelevant information while focusing on the information necessary to solve the problem at hand.

Both auditory selective attention and visual selective attention in children improve during middle childhood (Couperus, 2011). Researchers have used various methods to track these improvements. In relation to visual attention, for example, researchers may ask children to locate a particular item, such as a red letter *S*, on a computer screen that also contains distractions that are somewhat similar, such as a red letter *R* and a red number 8. Children around age 5 often respond randomly, whereas 7-year-olds have more systematic approaches and provide more correct responses. Even 7-year-olds, however, are likely to respond with "false alarms" by reacting to the distracting items (Baranov-Krylov, Kuznetsova, & Ratnikova, 2009). By the time they reach age 9 or 10, children show marked improvement in such tasks (Donnelly et al., 2007). The type of distracting material affects children's selective attention skill. When the distracting information is quite similar to the target information, it is even more difficult for children to attend and respond with both speed and accuracy. By about age 10, though, most children's performance on these visual selective attention tasks is close to that of adults (Couperus, 2011).

Another sort of task researchers use in studying visual attention skills is the "go/no-go" task. For example, participants are told to press a button if a certain object (such as a dog) appears on a computer screen but not to press the button if another object (such as a house) appears. The goal is for participants to be both quick and accurate in responding. In addition, the task requires children to inhibit responses when the object is "no-go." In one study, researchers found that young children tend to focus on the "go" items (Davis, Bruce, Snyder, & Nelson, 2003). Therefore, they often make mistakes by pressing "go" in the "no-go" situation. By the end of middle childhood, they have learned that a better way to succeed is to focus on the "no-go" items. This strategy is especially valuable when the comparisons between groups are cognitively complex, such as when categories of items, rather than a single object, must be compared (Maguire, White, & Brier, 2011).

Children's auditory attention skill also improves during middle childhood (Stevens, Lauinger, & Neville, 2009). One way that researchers examine auditory attention is to play recordings of two different stories at the same time, one through a speaker to the child's right and the other through a speaker to the child's left. The child is told to pay attention to only one story. By asking the child questions about the story, the researchers can assess his or her success in attending to the right story. You can imagine how important auditory attention is for children when they are in classrooms. They need to suppress attention to many irrelevant sounds while paying attention to the relevant ones.

## Difficulties with Attention

Attentional control is not easy for some children during the middle-childhood years (Waszak, Li, & Hommel, 2010). Children from low-income families, in particular, appear to have more difficulty with auditory selective attention, especially with suppressing distracting information, than do children from other income groups (Stevens et al., 2009). Although the reasons for these differences are not entirely known, some researchers speculate that children may experience higher levels of stress when they live in low-income households. The resulting stress hormones may affect their brain development, making it more difficult to pay attention (Lupien, King, Meaney, & McEwan, 2000). Researchers emphasize, however, that regardless of the source of these problems, attentional difficulties can be improved through training (Rueda, Rothbart, Saccomanno, & Posner, 2007; Stevens & Bavelier, 2012). Such training can produce positive changes in the neural processing associated with tasks involving selective attention (Stevens et al., 2013).

Another reason that children vary in their selective attention skill levels during middle childhood relates to potential disabilities. For example, children who have *dyslexia*, a biologically based difficulty in learning to read, show distinct patterns of selective attention to letters in words (Vellutino, Fletcher, Snowling, & Scanlon, 2004). Researchers have found that children with dyslexia may focus on letter-sound combinations at the beginning of words but have difficulty focusing on the same letter-sound combinations in other positions in words (McCandliss, Beck, Sandak, & Perfetti, 2003). Children with dyslexia may focus on the *ST* in *stop*, for example, but fail to see the same letter-sound combination in *past*. Clearly, it is important to be able to attend to such letter-sound combinations no matter where they occur in a word.

Studies in neuroscience tell us that children with dyslexia show different patterns of brain activity when they are reading than other children do (Rezaie et al., 2011). The functional connections in their brains also differ from those of typical readers (Koyama et al., 2010). Reading interventions that focus on the development of skills like phonological awareness can result in improvements for many children with dyslexia. Subsequently, these children also come to show brain patterns more like those of typical readers (Simos et al., 2007).

## Attention and Metacognition

During the middle childhood years, children improve in both using and describing strategies for selective attention. These processes involve **metacognition**, children's ability to think about their own thought processes and use that knowledge to reach a goal. Metacognition, which is necessary for regulation of executive function, strengthens during the middle-childhood years (Metcalfe & Finn, 2013). One strategy that improves selective attention is *planning* how to direct attention. During middle childhood, children start to use such planning skills effectively (Collins, Madsen, & Susman-Stillman, 2002; Masur, McIntyre, & Flavell, 1973).

In one selective-attention study, for example, children were shown a panel containing 12 doors in 2 rows, as shown in Figure 12.1. Children were allowed to open a door to see the object behind it. On half of the doors was an image of a cage, indicating that an animal was behind that door. On the other half of the doors was a drawing of a house, indicating that a household object (like a chair or a lamp) was behind the door. Children were told that they would need to remember either the animals or the household objects. By recording which doors the children opened, researchers could

**metacognition** The ability to think about the mental processes involved in thinking.

**FIGURE 12.1 A Test of Selective Attention** The pictures on the doors indicate whether a household item (indicated by a house) or an animal (indicated by a cage) lies behind the door. Children were told to remember either the household objects or the animals. Younger children tended to open all the doors, whereas older children opened only the doors for the type of object they needed to remember.

determine whether they used the most efficient strategy—that is, to open only those doors relevant to the type of object to be remembered. Young children usually opened all the doors, but those in middle childhood often used the more efficient strategy (Miller, 1990). In addition, children's memory of the specific objects improved as they become more efficient in their attention strategy.

What is happening in children's brains as they are improving their attentional skills? By studying attentional networks in children's brains, researchers are learning a great deal about children's ability to pay attention. We consider some results of this research next.

**THE DEVELOPING BRAIN**

## Attention

Thanks in part to neuroimaging studies, scientists today view attention as having its own underlying brain structure (Raichle, 2010). Studies of attention in monkeys show that it acts in the brain by allowing neurons to fire as if only the target object (and no distractions) were present (Mitchell, Sundberg, & Reynolds, 2009). Scientists believe that this same general process occurs in humans. Two major facets of the attention network are developing rapidly in children during the middle-childhood years. One facet is concerned with what a child is focusing on, and the other with filtering distractions. Both facets engage the frontal lobe in the brain (Stevens & Bavelier, 2012).

Neuroscientists (Petersen & Posner, 2012; Posner & Rothbart, 2007) have identified three specific neural networks that help to explain attentional processes:

1. The *alerting network* helps children reach and maintain an alert state. This part of attention is developed during infancy.
2. The *orienting network* helps children sustain attention when working on a task. It includes several facets. One, located near the top of the brain, activates when a child orients to something, such as a flickering light. Another, located in the junction between the temporal and parietal lobes, becomes involved when a reorientation needs to occur, such as when the location of the light changes. These areas become more highly developed and interconnected during middle childhood.
3. The *executive control network* helps children regulate their thoughts and emotions. It controls executive function, which you have read about elsewhere in this book. Executive function involves goal-directed behavior such as planning a task and suppressing inappropriate responses (Wang, Deater-Deckard, Cutting, Thompson, & Petrill, 2012). Current research suggests that the executive control network is made up of two separate control systems. One is centered in the frontal and parietal lobes. It helps us maintain attention when task requirements change. The other is located in the middle part of the frontal lobe and involves the frontal lobe's connections with other areas, such as the angular cingulate gyrus, as well. This part of the network is responsible for maintaining task performance.

For example, suppose researchers ask children to watch a basketball game between a red team and a blue team. The children are instructed to count the number of times the ball bounces when the red team has the ball and to count the number of passes when the blue team has the ball. In this example, the children need to keep track of how the rules change when the ball moves from one team to the other. The first executive control network enables them to do that. The second executive control network is responsible for keeping track of either the bounces or passes depending on which team has the ball.

Much of the neural basis of the executive function network is located in or extensively connected to the brain's *prefrontal cortex*. This part of the frontal area begins to become increasingly interconnected with other brain regions in early childhood. The prefrontal cortex and its interconnections continue to develop during middle childhood, although some areas do not fully develop until early adulthood.

Figure 12.2 shows an example of the brain areas involved in each network during a visual attention task. These networks mature from infancy through childhood and interact with other brain systems affecting perception and action. As the networks continue to develop throughout middle childhood, children's ability to attend improves, as we have already seen. Some children, however, have difficulty in controlling their attention, as discussed in the accompanying Research Insights feature.

Reading calls for visual attention, which involves all the brain networks shown in Figure 12.2.

## Memory

Like attention, memory improves during middle childhood. More and more, children of this age are challenged to remember material they have read or learned about in the classroom. To succeed in school, they need to improve in both what they remember and how they remember. We examine several aspects of this improvement next.

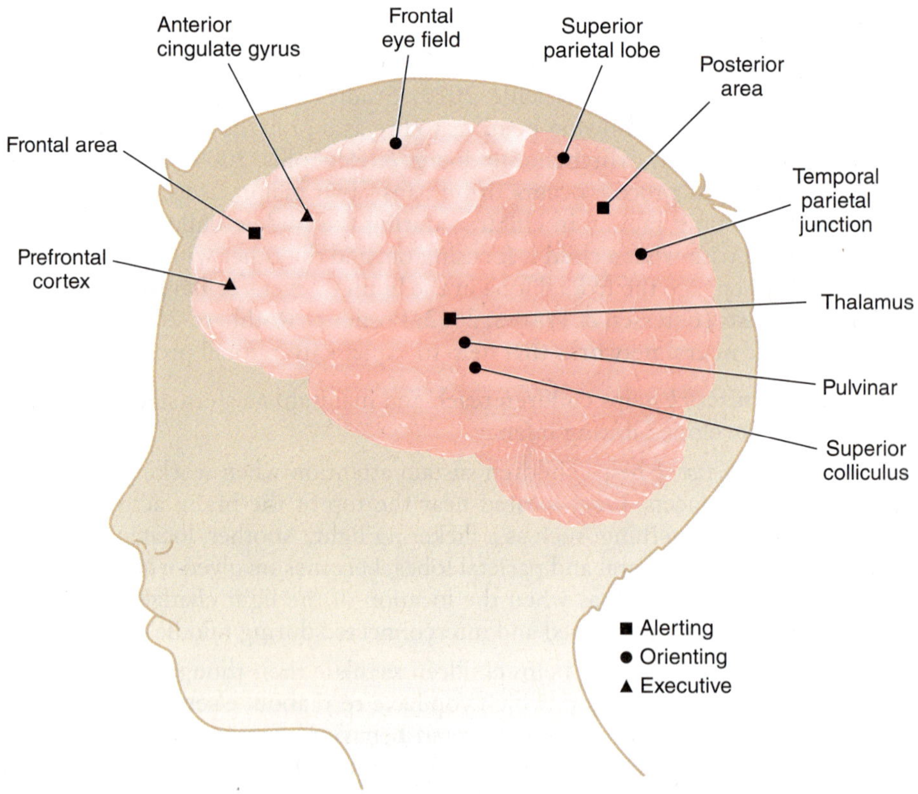


**FIGURE 12.2 The Attentional Networks of the Brain** Children develop the ability to attend due to the brain's attentional networks. The alerting network prompts them to be aware. The brain's orienting network helps them to focus on relevant stimuli; and the brain's executive network aids in controlling these processes.

*Source:* Adapted from Michael Posner and Mary Rothbart (2007). *Educating the human brain.* Washington, DC: American Psychological Association.

## Research Insights: Children with Problems with Attention

We just mentioned that some children have difficulty with aspects of attention. Children with significant attentional problems may be diagnosed with **attention deficit hyperactivity disorder (ADHD)**. ADHD is one of the most common childhood disorders, affecting 3 to 5% of school-age children (Barkley, 2011). Russell Barkley, a well-known researcher who has studied children, adolescents, and adults with ADHD, describes it as "not a disorder of knowing what to do, but of doing what one knows" (p. 249). Although the first signs of ADHD are often seen in early childhood, diagnosis frequently is not made until middle childhood, when children show difficulty attending to school-related tasks, including homework (Mautone, Marshall, Costigan, Clarke, & Power, 2012). The attentional difficulties of ADHD continue for many individuals throughout adolescence and adulthood (Barkley, Fischer, Smallish, & Fletcher, 2006).

Three subtypes of ADHD have been identified:

- *Predominantly hyperactive-impulsive.* Children have trouble sitting still, talk nonstop, appear to be in motion constantly, have difficulty attending to quiet tasks or activities, are impatient, have difficulty waiting, and often interrupt others.
- *Predominantly inattentive.* Children are easily distracted from a task; do not attend to details; have difficulty organizing a task; often lose track of homework, pencils, calculators, and other objects necessary for schoolwork; and often daydream during class.
- *Combined hyperactivity-impulsive and inattentive.* Children have a combination of the other two subtypes; they are both hyperactive and inattentive. This is the most common subtype (http://www.nimh.nih.gov/health/publications/attention-deficit-hyperactivity-disorder).

Research on children with ADHD indicates that they are slower to process visual attention tasks, especially when those tasks require them to respond to a target item and to inhibit their response to distracting stimuli (Alderson, Rapport, Sarver, & Kofler, 2008). Studies also indicate age differences in the types of functioning shown by children with ADHD. Young school-age children with ADHD (around age 6 to 7) have great difficulty with inhibitory control, whereas older school-aged children with ADHD (around age 11 to 13) have greater difficulty with skills involving working memory (Brocki & Bohlin, 2006; Tillman, Eninger, Forssman, & Bohlin, 2011). (We discuss working memory in the next section.)

Although researchers are not certain what causes ADHD, they know that ADHD often runs in families (Greven, Asherson, Rijsdijk, & Plomin, 2011) and that a genetic component is likely to play a role (Rosenberg, Pennington, Willcutt, & Olson, 2012). Other possible causes include cigarette smoking and alcohol use by the mother during pregnancy and children's exposure to high levels of lead (often found in paint or pipes) during the early years of life (Froehlich, et al., 2009; Mick, Biederman, Faraone, Sayer, & Kleinman, 2002).

Children with ADHD are sometimes given stimulant medication under the care of a physician (Prock & Rappaport, 2009). Although it may seem counterintuitive to give stimulants to children who are highly active, this type of medication operates on neurotransmitters in the brain and is quite effective in helping children focus their attention (D'Alli, 2009). The medication has side effects, however, such as poor appetite and difficulty getting to sleep and therefore, it needs to be carefully monitored for the appropriate dosage.

Although medication alone may change children's behavior in the short term, it does not help them learn to control their attention in the long term. The most effective treatment includes medication coupled with interventions by parents and teachers, who model and reward appropriate behavior (Smith, Barkley, & Shapiro, 2006). Some promising interventions focus on teaching children to monitor their behaviors themselves (Reid, Trout, & Schartz, 2005). For example, children may be taught how to set goals, determine behaviors that help them accomplish those goals, use a checklist to help them stay on task, and use methods to provide self-reinforcement, such as giving themselves points or other tokens when they focus well (Gureasko–Moore, DuPaul, & White, 2007).

### Episodic and Autobiographical Memory

Suddenly, a sound, a sight, a feeling triggers a powerful memory, some of which never go away (Westbury & Dennett, 2000). You undoubtedly have vivid memories of momentous events in your life, both pleasant and unpleasant. You can probably also remember more mundane events, such as parking your car earlier today. The ability to remember events is termed *episodic memory* (Tulving, 1972, 2002). Episodic memory is tied to a particular time and place.

One type of episodic memory, *autobiographical memory*, involves memories of personally relevant events in our own lives. You probably have many memories from your childhood.

But how far back can you remember? As we pointed out in Chapter 5, adults tend not to remember anything from the first two years of life. We might or might not

**attention deficit hyperactivity disorder (ADHD)** A disorder, often diagnosed during middle childhood, that involves hyperactivity and impulsivity, inattention, or both.

remember a few events from when we were 3 or 4, but we will almost certainly remember many more events from middle childhood. That is because episodic memory, and especially autobiographical memory, improves from early childhood on, with great change occurring in middle childhood (Sander, Werkle-Bergner, Gerjets, Shing, & Lindenberger, 2012).

In an innovative study designed to compare autobiographical memory with nonautobiographical episodic memory in children and adults, researchers organized two groups of children and one group of adults and had them meet at a museum (Pathman, Samson, Dugas, Cabeza, & Bauer, 2011). The children in one group were 7 to 9 years old, the children in the other group were 9 to 11, and the adults were around age 20. All participants were given cameras and instructed to take 60 photographs of specific exhibits in the museum. Afterward, they individually viewed, on laptop computers, 60 photographs of museum exhibits taken by someone else and were asked to rate the quality of each of the photographs from "bad" to "really good."

One to two days later, the participants returned to look at random orderings of the 60 photographs that they had taken and the 60 photographs that they had rated, plus 30 additional photographs of museum exhibits that they had not seen before. Participants placed each photograph in one of three categories: "remember taking," "viewed on the laptop," or "new." The results were considered in terms of autobiographical memory (based on photographs correctly classified as taken by the participant) and nonautobiographical episodic memory (based on photographs correctly classified as having been seen on the computer). As you can see in Figure 12.3, all age groups were better at autobiographical than nonautobiographical episodic memory. Also, both types of memory improved during middle childhood, with autobiographical memory of children at the end of middle childhood ranking close to that of adults.

An issue related to episodic memory is *suggestibility*—that is, the extent to which memory is easily influenced by suggestion. Although children are less suggestible during the middle-childhood years than they were earlier, they still are susceptible to

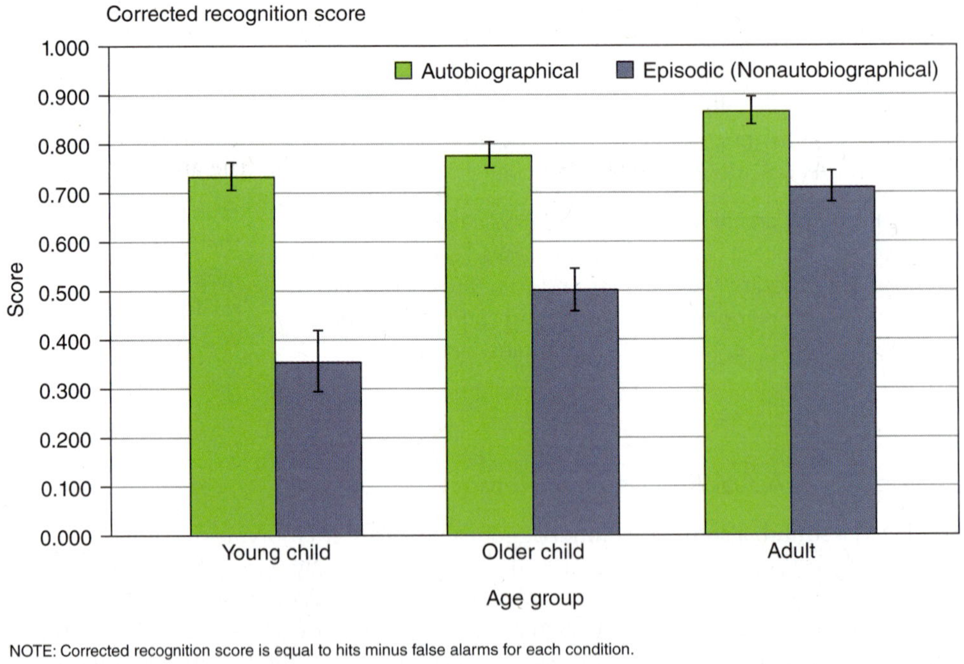


**FIGURE 12.3 Autobiographical and Nonautobiographical Episodic Memory in Three Age Groups** As you can see, memory improves with age. In this study, all age groups performed better with autobiographical memory than with nonautobiographical memory. Young children showed greater differences in the two types of memory than did older children and adults.

*Source:* Pathman, T., Samson, Z., Dugas, K., Cabeza, R., & Bauer, P. J. (2011). A "snapshot" of declarative memory: Differing developmental trajectories in episodic and autobiographical memory. *Memory, 19*(8), p. 831.

**FIGURE 12.4 Testing Suggestibility** Researchers use experiments similar to this one to test suggestibility. Children are told a story about an aviary at a zoo. Later, half of the children are given misinformation by suggesting that the story was about a robin at the aviary, the other half are not. The idea is to assess how much children are influenced by misinformation.

suggestion. This issue is especially important when a child is asked to be an eyewitness. The question here is whether the child's recall of an event is distorted when he or she is provided with misleading information.

In one study, researchers tested the suggestibility of children at ages 4 and 9 (Ceci, Papierno & Kulkofsky, 2007). The children were told stories involving a set of critical items, such as a lemon, an egg sandwich, milk, and a bear. Two days later, half of the children were randomly assigned to a control group and half to a group that was given misinformation about the stories. Children in the misinformation group were provided with false suggestions about what was in the original stories. For example, researchers might mention an orange, a cheese sandwich, soda, and a horse. Children in the other group were provided with true information. Several days later, the children in both groups were shown pictures that represented both the true and false information and were interviewed about which they remembered seeing in the stories. (See Figure 12.4, which sketches a similar procedure.)

Both younger and older children who had been given misinformation tended to provide false information, but they did so in different ways. The younger children tended to group objects into functional or perceptual categories, such as things to drink (substituting soda for milk) or large animals (substituting horse for bear), whereas the older children used more sophisticated categories, such as citrus fruits (substituting orange for lemon) or dairy products (substituting cheese sandwich for egg sandwich). This study suggests that memory is very much tied to categories of thought, with more complex categories developed by older children.

In general, older children have been found to be less susceptible to false information than younger ones (Ceci, Kulkofsky, Klemfuss, Sweeney, & Bruck, 2007). This is the case because older children have developed a better understanding of how to remember events. We turn next to this process of remembering.

## The Process of Remembering

Let's begin by considering what children must do to remember something:

1. **They must encode the information.** If children are to remember, say, the names of the capitals of all the states, they must first place that information in memory, a process known as *encoding*. This process occurs in working memory, which we

consider in more detail later in this section. As we discussed earlier, attention plays a role in the encoding process. The more attentive children are to the important features that need to be remembered, the more long-lasting will be the memory.

2. **They must store the information.** Once information is encoded, it must be transferred from short-term, or working, memory into long-term memory, or it will be lost. The encoding process actually involves the synthesis of proteins in the brain. (The accompanying Focus On feature discusses the scientist who made this discovery.)
3. **They must retrieve the information.** To use stored information, children must recall it from long-term memory and move it into working memory.

We've already seen, in Chapter 11, that the brain grows in both size and complexity during middle childhood, and that development is more complex in areas of the brain associated with increased cognitive abilities. These developments support improvements in cognitive processing. Thus, children in middle childhood get increasingly better and faster at encoding, retaining, and retrieving information. They literally think more quickly and remember better.

### Improvements in Working Memory

Let's focus on just one aspect of how children's memory improves in middle childhood. In Chapter 9, we discussed what the information-processing model has to say about how we learn new information. You may recall that, in that model, working memory serves an important function involving the temporary storage and manipulation of information. Here, we look more closely at working memory, with the help of a well-known model developed by Alan Baddeley (Baddeley, 2012; Baddeley & Hitch, 1974), shown in Figure 12.5.

Baddeley's model of memory has several components. It distinguishes between *fluid systems*, which provide short-term storage of information, and *crystallized systems*, which provide long-term storage (Kay, 2005). The fluid systems comprise working memory. The model includes two limited storage systems for sensory input. The first is the *phonological loop*, which briefly stores and manipulates speech-based information, such as new vocabulary. Information stored here is lost after only a few seconds

## Focus On: Eric Kandel

"Memory has always fascinated me. Think of it. You can recall at will your first day in high school, your first date, your first love. In doing so you are not only recalling the event, you are also experiencing the atmosphere in which it occurred—the sights, sounds, and smells, the social setting, the time of day, the conversations, the emotional tone" (Kandel, 2006, p. 3).

With these words, the neuroscientist Eric Kandel begins an account of his life and the journey that led him to a Nobel Prize, in 2000. He was fascinated by the biological basis of learning and memory. The path to his success began when Kandel decided to study the learning process in a marine snail known as *Aplysia*. His rationale for this choice was that the way to solve a problem in biology is to approach it in its simplest representation, and *Aplysia* has only 20,000 neurons in comparison to the human brain which has 200 billion nerve cells. Kandel studied memory by training these small snails and observing the results.

Spencer Platt/Newsmakers/Getty Images

After many years, he, along with his colleagues, found that learning produces short-term memories by causing changes in the strengths of the connections between the synapses in the neurons of the brain. Those changes are termed *synaptic marking*. Long-term memory involves two processes. One process perpetuates the changes in the strength of these marked synapses, and the other involves the synthesis of new proteins in the brain. In the book he wrote about his life as a scientist, *In Search of Memory: The Emergence of a New Science of Mind*, Kandel quipped, "Thus, if you remember anything of this book, it will be because your brain is slightly different after you have finished reading it" (2006, p. 276). From his research on snails to humans, Kandel's work has stimulated much new knowledge about the neuroscience of memory.

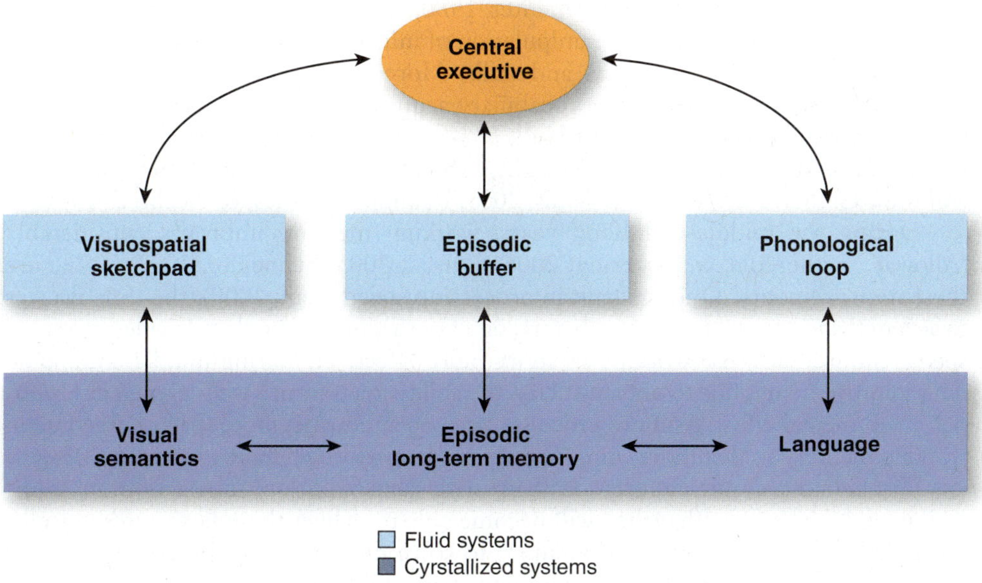


**FIGURE 12.5 Baddeley's Model of Memory** In Baddeley's model, the phonological loop, the visuospatial sketchpad, and the episodic buffer are "fluid systems"—that is, working memory. The central executive controls whether information from working memory becomes part of the "crystallized systems" of long-term memory.

Reprinted by permission from Macmillan Publishers Ltd: *Nature Reviews Neuroscience*, Alan Baddeley, Working memory: Looking back and looking forward. 829–839 (October 2003).

unless it is rehearsed. The second is the *visuospatial sketchpad*, which briefly holds and manipulates visual and spatial information, such as a location on a map or a visual pattern.

A third component of the fluid systems, called the *episodic buffer*, can bring together chunks of information gathered from both the phonological loop and the visuospatial sketchpad (Baddeley, Allen, & Hitch, 2010). This is also a temporary storage unit with a limited capacity, but it is important because it allows information that was coded in one way (for example, spatially) to be considered in another way (for example, verbally).

The crystallized systems, as mentioned, involve long-term storage of information. This storage can take the form of visual semantics (or visual memory), language (or verbal memory), or episodic long-term memory (in which information might be stored both verbally and visually). As you can see in the figure, each form is associated with an element of the fluid systems.

Finally, the *central executive* controls all the parts of the memory system. It is capable of attentional focus, storage, and decision making. It is also involved in the coordination of two or more processes, as when we hold information in mind while working on that information. The central executive can become burdened by the tasks it is asked to perform. For example, it has a light load in simple tasks, like repeating a series of 3 or 4 digits. It has a heavier load in tasks requiring those digits to be repeated backward, and a heavier load still in more complex tasks, like counting backwards by 4 from 362.

Repeating a few digits does not demand that we hold information in memory for a long time. But learning the addition and subtraction facts needed to count backward by, say, 4 requires information to be moved into long-term memory. What does it take for that important transfer into long-term memory, and what do we know about this process during the middle-childhood years?

You can think of working memory as a computer tablet where tasks to be worked on are brought together and placed on the desktop, where

*John Giustina/Getty Images*

School makes many demands on memory. Fortunately, working memory improves considerably in middle childhood.

**automaticity** The ability to perform a well-learned task without much mental effort.

**learning disabilities** Neurological disorders that make it difficult to receive, process, store, and respond to information.

they are managed (Daneman & Carpenter, 1980). Because working memory involves both temporary storage and the manipulation of information, it is critical to children's ability to acquire new knowledge and skills. More specifically, it is related to their abilities in school subjects such as vocabulary acquisition (Daneman & Green, 1986), language comprehension (Cain, Oakhill, & Bryant, 2004), reading skill (Christopher et al., 2012; Gathercole, Pickering, Knight, & Stegmann, 2004), and math performance (Alloway, Gathercole, Adams, & Willis, 2005; Raghubar, Barnes, & Hecht, 2010).

During the middle-childhood years, working memory improves considerably (Alloway, Gathercole, & Pickering, 2006; Cowan, 2005; Schneider, 2002). What are these improvements? One is a gain in processing speed (Kail, 2000), the time it takes to accomplish a mental process such as recognizing a word or number. Besides increased speed, children also use working memory more effectively during middle childhood. This improvement is due to **automaticity**, the ability to perform a well-learned task without much mental effort. As more processes become automatic, more space is freed up in working memory so that more complex tasks can be performed there (Johnson, 2013).

Teachers often quiz children on their math facts (addition, subtraction, multiplication, and division) so that they will become able to deliver these facts automatically. That way, they can use working memory to solve more complex problems in math, such as story and multistep problems. Similarly, children learning to read are often taught "sight words" such as *and*, *the*, and *who*. These words occur frequently in text, so automaticizing them frees up working memory, enabling children to deal with more unusual words or complex sentences.

Children who have **learning disabilities** in math, reading, or both often have difficulty developing automaticity (Shaywitz, 2003; Swanson & Sachse-Lee, 2001). Learning disabilities are neurological disorders that make it difficult to receive, process, store, or respond to information (http://www.ncld.org/ld-basics). Lack of automaticity makes school-related tasks increasingly difficult for these children.

Another improvement in working memory during middle childhood occurs because children become better at using strategies to remember information (Bayliss, Jarrold, Baddeley, Gunn, & Leigh, 2005). We discuss some of those strategies next.

### Memory Strategies

Brain development in middle childhood makes memory improvement possible. In addition, other improvements in how children think enable them to use strategies to help them remember. Children change considerably in their ability to generate and use memory strategies during the middle-childhood years (Murphy, McKone, & Slee, 2003). They use increasing numbers of strategies, and employ them more effectively (Bjorklund & Douglas, 1997). Some children devise their own memory strategies, whereas others need to be taught strategies. In either case, by age 9 or 10, most children are making use of a number of memory strategies, including the following:

- *Imagery*. Children can be encouraged to remember information, such as the events leading up to the Boston Tea Party, by drawing a visual image.
- *Chunking*. Children come to realize that they can remember some things better by chunking individual units into larger groups (Mastropieri & Scruggs, 1998). For example, it's difficult to remember an unbroken string of independent numbers, say, 718217649. But if you group the numbers into threes—like this: 718–217–649—you're memorizing not 9 separate units but 3 units of 3 numbers each, a much easier task.
- *Meaning*. Children assign a unique, usually personal, meaning to a memory task. It would be easier to remember the date when the American colonies declared their independence, for example, if 1776 happened to be part of a child's telephone number.
- *Categorizing*. Children use familiar categories to aid their retention. For example, asked to memorize 20 pictures—of 5 animals, 5 plants, 5 buildings, and 5 fruits—younger children can usually recall only a few of the pictures. Children of middle-childhood age, however, typically recall many more pictures, and do so by categories (Schleepen & Jonkman, 2012). This is termed *semantic organization*. At first, children

may need to be coached to use this method to remember (Pressley & Hilden, 2006). Around age 10, children become better at spontaneously using semantic organization to improve their memory skills (Hasselhorn, 1992).

- *Rehearsal.* Although rehearsal may seem like an obvious way of remembering something, children usually do not spontaneously begin using rehearsal strategies until they are around 7 years old (Gathercole & Pickering, 2000). Even when they use this strategy, younger children (ages 7 to 8) rehearse differently than older children (ages 11 to 12). Younger children tend to rehearse words one at a time, whereas older children use cumulative rehearsal, repeating earlier words as they add new ones to a rehearsed list (Guttentag, Ornstein, & Siemens, 1987). As you can see in Figure 12.6, children tend to make this change in rehearsal strategy between grades 3 and 4 (Lehman & Hasselhorn, 2012).
- *Elaboration.* Children may impose meaning on a list of items or on unrelated pieces of information by creating a sentence or an acronym for them. This is often the most effective strategy for remembering factual information (Mastropieri & Scruggs, 1998; Scruggs & Mastropieri, 2000). For example, you may have learned that one way to remember the order of operations in mathematics is by recalling this sentence: "Please excuse my dear Aunt Sally." The first letter of each word in that sentence refers to an operation: *P* stands for parentheses, *E* for exponent, *M* for multiplication, *D* for division, *A* for addition, and *S*, for subtraction. Instead of the sentence, you may have learned to remember the order of these letters by the acronym PEMDAS.

## Memory and Metacognition

Earlier in this section, we discussed *metacognition*, children's ability to think about their thought processes and use that knowledge to reach a goal. Just as children in middle childhood use metacognition to improve their attentional strategies, they also use this aspect of cognition to think about and employ memory strategies. Psychologists usually discuss three types of metacognition that are relevant to the process of remembering:

- *Declarative metacognition* is knowing what to do when faced with a challenge. This involves explicit and conscious knowledge about what our cognitive skills are and what strategies we have available to use.

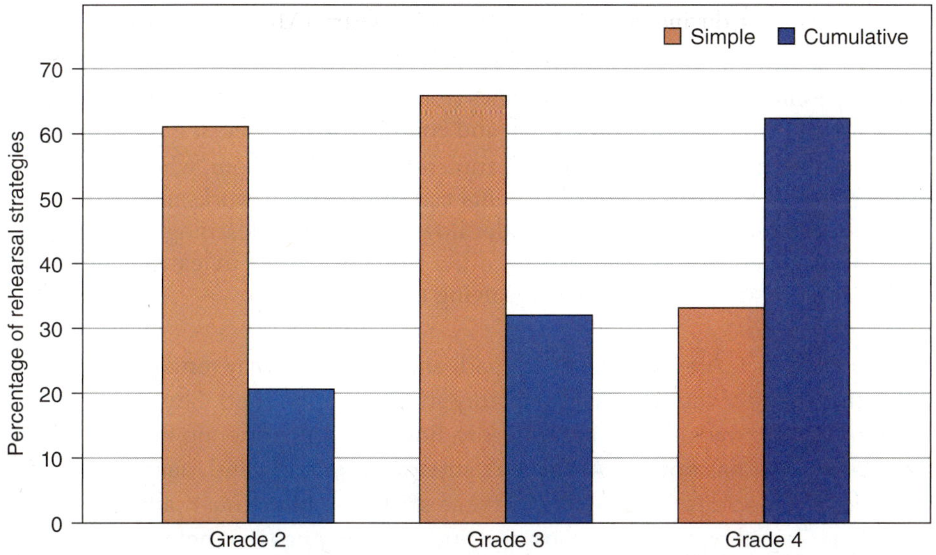


**FIGURE 12.6 Development of Rehearsal Strategies from Grade 2 to Grade 4** When they use the memory strategy of rehearsal, second and third graders more often prefer the simple strategy of rehearsing words one at a time. Fourth graders tend more often to use cumulative rehearsal, repeating earlier words as they add new ones to a rehearsed list.
*Source:* Based on information from Lehmann & Hasselhorn (2012), Table 1, p. 555.

- *Procedural metacognition* is knowing how to apply the available strategies. This aspect of metacognition may not be conscious. In other words, we might apply strategies without fully realizing that we are doing so, as when we slow our reading speed when we encounter a complex passage in a text (Siegler & Alibali, 2004).
- *Conditional metacognition* is knowing when and why to apply certain strategies (Schneider & Lockl, 2002; Schunk, 2012).

All three of these aspects of metacognition improve during the middle-childhood years. Conditional metacognition is more complex, however, and often improves later in middle childhood than the other two types (Coyle & Bjorklund, 1997; Kreutzer, Leonard, & Flavell, 1975).

what if...?

Suppose you are working at an after-school program, helping a group of 8- and 9-year-olds with their homework. One of the boys is frustrated because he has to learn the names of the United States presidents in chronological order. What are some suggestions you might give him for remembering them?

## Teaching Effective Memory Strategies Practice

In studying children's use of strategies, Lynn Meltzer (2010) has found that children with learning disabilities often have poor executive function, which affects their use of memory strategies. Children with learning disabilities may have difficulty with one or more academic areas, like reading and math, and they may have difficulty with social skills, as well. When children have learning difficulties, they may know fewer strategies and may fail to use those they do know (Meltzer & Krishnan, 2007).

Based on her work, Meltzer has proposed ways that teachers can help all children in their use of memory strategies in the classroom. Many of these strategies can be used across different content areas, such as reading, math, social studies, and science. Here are a number of her suggestions for creating a classroom climate that promotes children's use of strategies:

- Teach children to use metacognition—to think about how they learn—by asking them specific questions about how they remembered certain material.
- Grade students on the use of their strategies, not just on their final answers.
- Develop a checklist of memory strategies (for example, use of acronyms and elaboration) for children to use as they study and complete assignments.
- Promote strategy-sharing time for all students in the classroom, when they can discuss strategies with each other. Students can discuss what works and what doesn't work for them individually and consider how strategies for learning certain types of material (such as dates in history) may differ from those used in learning other types of information (such as processes in solving math problems).

Everyday stories

A NEW STRATEGY Alejandra loves to read, and she can usually remember and discuss many of the details from a story she has just finished. She also enjoys making up rhymes. She has difficulty, however, remembering math facts. Her teacher has noticed Alejandra's strength in reading and making up rhymes and decides to help her use these skills to improve her math capabilities. Together, they go online and find some rhymes that help Alejandra, such as "He stood in line and ate a ton, 9 times 9 is 81" (from http://www.mltiplication.com). When Alejandra couldn't find a rhyme she liked, she began to make up her own. The rhyming strategy helped her remember her math facts.

Brian Shumway/Redux

Using memory strategies can help children to learn many different types of material.

## Criticisms of Information-Processing Theory

Information-processing theory has direct application to children's learning processes, such as attention and memory. The theory's detailed description of these processes has helped us to understand many aspects of children's performance in school. The theory has also generated much research into applications for instruction of school-aged children, in particular, children with learning disabilities (Meltzer, 2010).

The theory is sometimes criticized, however, for using the computer as its basic metaphor. After all, people dream, speculate, and create in ways that computers cannot (Kuhn, 1992). Some critics believe that the computer metaphor has limited our view of children's learning and behavior. Furthermore, even though certain aspects of children's psychology, such as children's feelings about school (Hauser-Cram, Durand, & Warfield, 2007), affect their school performance, they are not incorporated in the information-processing model. In short, it is not a holistic theory of children's cognitive development.

### CHECK YOUR PROGRESS

1. How does attention change during middle childhood?
2. What are the different subtypes of ADHD?
3. Describe the process a child needs to go through to remember something.
4. What are the components of working memory, according to Baddeley's model?
5. What are some memory strategies?

# Intelligence and Thinking

**[ KEY QUESTION ] 4.** What are some different perspectives on intelligence?

As we continue our exploration of the cognitive world of middle childhood, we arrive at the topic of intelligence. What, exactly, is intelligence? Think about how you would define the term. However you define it, you would probably agree that a child demonstrates intelligence by acquiring knowledge, thinking about knowledge, and using knowledge. And as children race through the middle-childhood years, they pass many milestones that mark continued growth of intelligent behavior.

Although we might all agree on certain core features of intelligent behavior, researchers and theorists have conceptualized intelligence in several different ways. We discuss a number of those ideas in this section.

## The Search for Intelligence

As just suggested, intelligence is a somewhat mysterious concept. One mystery, touched upon in Chapter 3, concerns individual and group differences in intelligence. We know that both genes and environment account for these differences, but research continues to reveal the complexity of how heredity and environment interact to determine intelligence (Zimmer, 2008).

Here, we're concerned with a different mystery: the fact that we don't know exactly what intelligence is. Although we generally believe we recognize intelligent behavior when we see it, there is no universally accepted definition of the term, and as we discuss in the feature Culture and Views on Intelligence, cultures vary in their view of what comprises intelligent behavior. In their attempts to address this dilemma, Western psychologists have searched for effective ways to measure intelligence, as well as for an understanding of just what it is.

In attempting to reach a definition of intelligence, theorists have proposed a broad range of ideas. Some have argued that intelligence is a general ability; that is, a child who is good on one task will tend to be good on other tasks (Spearman, 1927). Others have argued that intelligence is a set of different factors, so that individuals may have some kinds of intelligence but not others (Thurstone, 1938). In the following subsections, we describe proponents of both views.

## Culture and Views on Intelligence

We often refer to someone as being "bright," but what do we mean by that? As you consider your answer to that question, you might also think about whether your view of what it means to be intelligent could be applied to someone in a culture very different from ours.

In the United States children are usually expected to arrive at their answers to a test independently, whereas in Mayan culture children are expected to collaborate with others to solve test problems.

One predominant view of intelligence in the United States focuses on cognitive competence in the areas of speed, accuracy, accumulated knowledge, and vocabulary (Cattell, 1971). In contrast, rural Kenyans' conception of intelligence includes four parts: *rieko* (knowledge and skills), *luoro* (respect for others), *winjo* (comprehension of how to handle real-life problems), and *paro* (initiative) (Grigorenko et al., 2001). *Rieko* is considered positive only if *luoro* is present. In other words, knowledge and skills without respect for others is not viewed as intelligence.

## Binet, Wechsler, and Intelligence Testing

**intelligence quotient (IQ)** A measure of intelligence based on an intelligence test. It is constructed from a ratio of a child's mental age to chronological age multiplied by 100.

Two important scientists who held the general ability view are Alfred Binet and David Wechsler. Both developed intelligence tests still in wide use today, tests you are probably quite familiar with.

### Binet's Test

In 1904, the Parisian minister of public instruction asked Alfred Binet to devise a method for identifying children whose lack of success in the typical classroom setting suggested the need for special education. In creating this instrument, Binet wanted to focus on basic processes of reasoning rather than on learned skills, like reading, that might rely on the quality of instruction (Gould, 1996). He thus developed a series of short tasks related to problems of everyday life. He assigned an age level to each task to make it possible to identify children who were 9 years of age but could complete only those tasks assumed to be at the 7-year-old level (Roid, 2003). Binet emphasized that the purpose of the test was not to understand or label children's innate abilities (Gould, 1996). Instead, the purpose was to identify children who were behind in completing the tasks for their age group so they could be provided with special education.

Binet developed the test so that a single score representing the "mental age" of a child could be determined. To measure mental age in relation to chronological age, the **intelligence quotient**, or **IQ**, was devised. We calculate IQ by dividing mental age by chronological age and then multiplying the result by 100 (to eliminate the decimal point). If, then, a child's mental age is exactly the same as his chronological age, his IQ will be 100.

EDUARDO VERDUGO/Associated Press

Even within the United States, different cultural groups perceive intelligence differently. Researchers who interviewed Latino, Asian, and Anglo parents living in San Jose, California, for example, found that the Latino parents tended to stress social competence, whereas the Asian and Anglo parents more often emphasized cognitive competence (Okagaki & Sternberg, 1993).

The way children approach taking tests of intelligence also varies by culture. Mayan children, for instance, view taking a test differently than do children in the United States (Greenfield, 1997; Maynard & Greenfield, 2003). The Mayans expect to collaborate when taking a test—indeed, they consider it unnatural not to collaborate. In contrast, children in the United States are expected to arrive at their answers on their own, with no help from others. Such differences relate to how people think of themselves in individualistic versus collectivist cultures (Markus & Kitayama, 1991; Sternberg, 2007a).

The Binet scale proved successful, and its success led an American psychologist, Lewis Terman, to adapt it for use in this country. Terman's revision, called the Stanford-Binet Intelligence Scale, first appeared in 1916, and has been revised on a regular basis to ensure that the questions on it are appropriate to the experiences of children in the current era (Boake, 2002).

### Wechsler's Test

David Wechsler, a clinical psychologist at New York's Bellevue Hospital, also developed tests of general intelligence, which he defined as the *aggregate* or *global capacity* of the individual to act purposefully, to think rationally, and to deal effectively with the environment (Wechsler, 1958). Wechsler criticized earlier versions of the Stanford-Binet scale for relying too heavily on verbal skills. Therefore, he included nonverbal items, called *performance subtests*. These subtests involve solving spatial puzzles, completing mazes, and rearranging sets of pictures to tell a story. You can see examples of items similar to those in both the verbal and performance areas of the most recent version of the scale, the *Wechsler Intelligence Scale for Children* (WISC-IV) in Figure 12.7.

The Wechsler scale, like the Stanford-Binet, yields a general intelligence score, but it also yields scores in two subtest areas: verbal skills and performance (perceptual and spatial) skills. Thus, although two children may have the same overall score, one may score higher in the verbal area of the test, while the other may score higher in the performance area.

### Understanding Test Scores

Tests of intelligence are especially important during the school years. They are often used, for example, to assess the general cognitive capacities of children with disabilities as part of the process of developing plans for placement and instruction. Because of the important implications of intelligence testing for such children, let's take a closer look at its use.

When we compare large numbers of IQ scores, we find that they follow a *normal distribution*, as shown in Figure 12.8, with most scores clustering near the middle. A

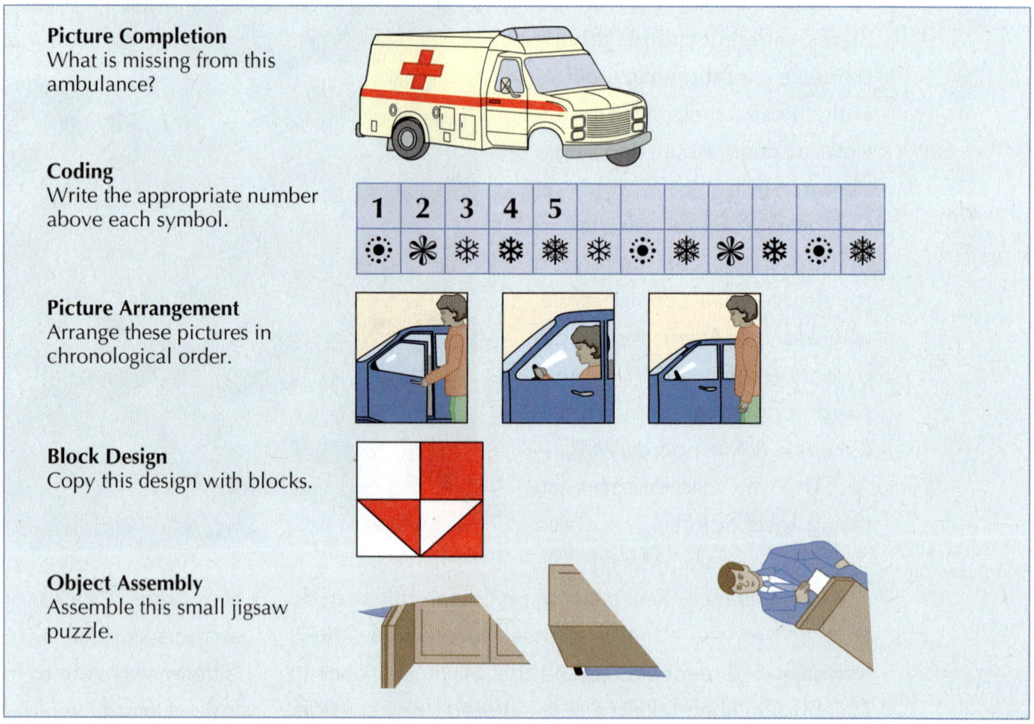


**FIGURE 12.7 Subtests of the WISC–IV** The items here are similar to those used on the actual test.

*Source:* Reprinted with permission of John Wiley & Sons, Inc., from Huffman, K. (2010). *Psychology in Action* (9th ed.). Hoboken, NJ: Wiley, p. 301, Table 8.6.

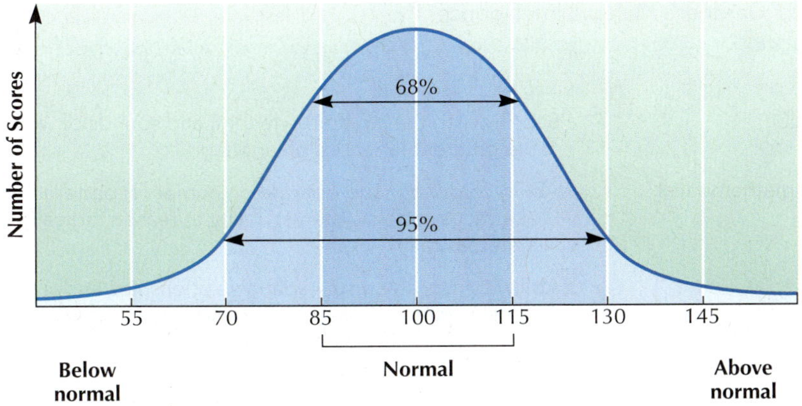


**FIGURE 12.8 Standard Distribution of Scores on the Stanford-Binet Intelligence Test** This bell-shaped curve describes the variability of scores around an average, which is 100 for IQ tests. About 68% of individuals who take an IQ test will score between 85 and 115, and 95% will score between 70 and 130.

*Source:* Reprinted with permission of John Wiley & Sons, Inc., from Huffman, K. (2010). *Psychology in Action* (9th ed.). Hoboken, NJ: Wiley, p. 301, Figure 8.11.

normal distribution is a bell-shaped curve that describes the variability of scores around an average, which is set to be 100 for IQ tests. Half of the population is expected to score above the average and the other half below the average.

About 3% of children score at the highest end of the distribution. These children are sometimes considered to be "gifted." Another 3% score at lowest end of the distribution. These children—if they also have low functional skills in daily living tasks, such as getting dressed, feeding themselves, and basic communication with others—are considered to have an **intellectual disability**, defined as "a disability characterized by significant limitations both in intellectual functioning and in adaptive behavior, which covers many everyday social and practical skills. This disability originates before the age of 18" (American Association of Intellectual and Developmental Disabilities, 2013, retrieved from http://aaidd.org/intellectual-disability/definition#.UeQyGb7D_IU). It is important to keep in mind that intellectual disabilities are not defined by IQ tests alone, but by a combination of low IQ (usually less than 70) and a low level of the skills required for daily functioning.

*Everyday stories*

BEYOND IQ Many people who score low on IQ tests function well in their everyday lives. Consider Brianna, a 10-year-old who has Down syndrome (a chromosomal disorder, discussed in Chapter 2). Brianna has difficulty learning vocabulary and can read only simple words. She has trouble remembering how to solve many arithmetic problems as well. She works hard in school, though, and has many friends. She also has strong functional skills, like communicating with her friends and following the routines of the school day. Brianna is highly motivated to do well academically and socially in school. Her functional skills and motivation help her to have a successful school experience, despite recording low scores on intelligence tests.

## A Theory of Multiple Intelligences

As we mentioned earlier, Binet and Wechsler, along with many of their contemporaries, believed that intelligence is a general characteristic. Thus, a child who is good on one task will tend to be good on others. More recently, psychologists have questioned that assumption. One important theorist who emphasizes distinct abilities in defining intelligence is Howard Gardner.

Gardner, a psychologist at Harvard University, proposed his **theory of multiple intelligences** in his book *Frames of Mind* (1983). To date, Gardner has identified eight

**intellectual disabilities** Significant limitations both in intellectual functioning and adaptive behavior, including the social and practical skills of daily living.

**theory of multiple intelligences** Gardner's theory that people have eight (possibly nine) separate intelligences: linguistic, musical, logical-mathematical, spatial, bodily-kinesthetic, interpersonal, intrapersonal, naturalistic, and (possibly) existential.

**triarchic theory of intelligence** Sternberg's theory that intelligence is made up of three interacting elements: analytic intelligence, practical intelligence, and creative intelligence.

**Table 12.1** Gardner's Multiple Intelligences

| Type of Intelligence | Key Components |
|---|---|
| Linguistic | Sensitivity to the structure, rhythm, and sounds of words and the different functions of language |
| Logical-mathematical | Ability to discern and operate on numerical patterns and abstract symbols systems; ability to reason logically and systematically |
| Spatial | Ability to perceive visual-spatial relationships and to perform transformations based on visual representations |
| Musical | Sensitivity to rhythm, pitch, and timbre; ability to appreciate forms of musical expressions |
| Bodily-kinesthetic | Ability to control body movements skillfully |
| Interpersonal | Ability to detect the moods, temperaments, motives, and desires of other people |
| Intrapersonal | Sensitivity to one's own emotional state, and recognition of one's own strengths and weaknesses |
| Naturalist | Ability to make distinctions in the natural environment and to understand systems of nature |
| Existential (speculative) | Sensitivity to issues related to the meaning of life and death, as well as to other questions about the human condition |

*Source:* Gardner, 1983, 1999.

separate types of intelligence: linguistic, musical, logical-mathematical, spatial, bodily-kinesthetic, interpersonal, intrapersonal, and naturalistic, as described in Table 12.1. (He has also suggested a possible ninth type, existential.) He points out that the first two of these—linguistic and logical-mathematical—are generally the most highly valued in school (Gardner, 1993, 1999).

Gardner claims that the idea of multiple, independent intelligences lends itself to a more meaningful and richer view of the concept. He maintains that each intelligence is based on a "biological potential to process information in certain kinds of ways to solve problems or fashion products valued in one or more cultures" (Gardner & Traub, 2010, pp. 35–36). In addition, each intelligence is linked to a specific area of the brain and follows a distinct developmental path (Shearer, 2004).

Many educators have been particularly interested in possible educational outgrowths of this theory (Waterhouse, 2006). The notion of multiple intelligences has implications for new pathways for teaching and learning. For example, some educators suggest that teachers evaluate the strengths of each student and provide more effective instruction by teaching *to* those strengths (McCoog, 2007).

There have been criticisms of Gardner's approach, however. Some researchers have claimed that the different intelligences he identifies are actually correlated (related to each other) and not separate, as Gardner believes (Visser, Ashton, & Vernon, 2006). Nevertheless, Gardner's approach has generated valuable discussion about the meaning of intelligence.

## The Triarchic Theory of Intelligence

Robert Sternberg has taken an approach to intelligence that differs both from the original concepts of intelligence testing and from Gardner's view. He has proposed a **triarchic theory of intelligence**, which includes the three following elements, described here and shown in Figure 12.9 (Sternberg, 2003, 2009a).

- The *internal* (analytic) component involves the internal processing of information. This component includes many of the processes involved in executive function, such as planning, monitoring, and following directions. It also includes the use of cognitive strategies and metacognition.

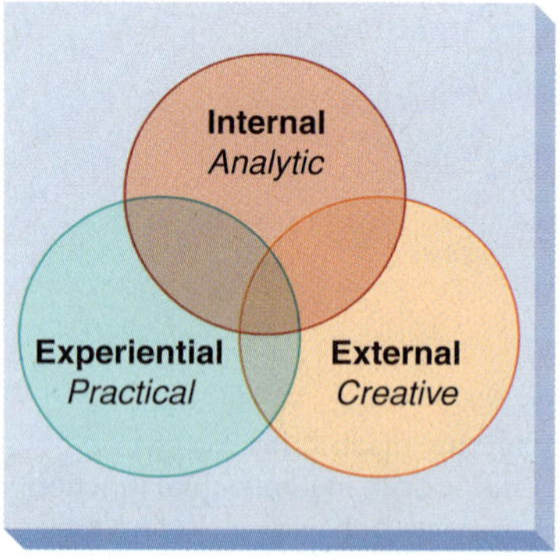


**FIGURE 12.9 Sternberg's Triarchic Theory of Intelligence** According to Robert Sternberg, overall intelligence comes from the successful interaction of three different components: analytical, practical, and creative intelligence.

- The *external* (creative) component involves the ability to deal with novel tasks and situations and to generate unusual solutions to solve problems. It can involve redefining a problem, integrating information in novel ways, and taking new approaches to problem solving.
- The *experiential* (practical) component involves adapting to or changing an environment to better fit a person's needs. It encompasses the twofold ability to figure out what is needed to work well in everyday life situations and then to act on that knowledge.

Sternberg's three elements are not separate and independent, like Gardner's eight intelligences. Rather, they interact. In fact, Sternberg (2007b, 2009b) argues that successful intelligence depends on effective interactions among these three types of intelligence.

what if...?

What if you were asked to recommend the type of intelligence testing to use in your local school district? Consider the various perspectives on the nature of intelligence. Which perspective would you choose, and why? What criticisms would you make of the other perspectives? Do you think that all school districts should choose the perspective you recommend?

CHECK YOUR PROGRESS

1. What were the original purposes of IQ tests?
2. How does Howard Gardner's view of intelligence differ from those of the original test developers?
3. Describe the key components of Robert Sternberg's triarchic theory.

## The Development of Language, Literacy, and Mathematical Skills

**[ KEY QUESTION ] 5. What significant advances in language development, literacy, and mathematical understanding occur in the middle-childhood years?**

So far, we've seen that during the middle-childhood years children come to understand conservation of the properties of objects, such as mass and quantity, despite perceptual transformations, and can begin to use simple logic to solve problems involving concrete objects. We've also seen how cognitive landmarks such as attention and memory improve during this period. In this section, we trace the close tie between cognition and language. We then discuss the special issue of English language learners. Next, we extend our discussion to two important school-related skills: literacy and mathematical understanding. Finally, we focus on the important role of parent involvement in children's school performance.

### Language Development

The cognitive development of children in the middle-childhood years is reflected in their language accomplishments (Ackerman, Izard, Kobak, Brown, & Smith, 2007). Beginning in Chapter 4, we noted the steady increase in vocabulary over the childhood years. By middle childhood, children are learning close to 20 new words a day (Anglin, 1993). Their vocabulary improves through discussions with their peers, information provided by teachers, and through reading (Connor et al., 2009; Pinker, 1994).

Over the course of middle childhood, children expand their language use in many ways. In one study, researchers found that between the ages of 9 and 12, children increased greatly in their use of quantifiers (*several* books), adjectives (the *large, red* book), prepositional phrases (the book *on the table*), and relative clauses (the book *that seemed to go on forever*) (Ravid & Berman, 2010). Children during this period also master the rules that enable them to combine words into complex sentences, negative constructions, questions, compound sentences, and imperatives (Gleason & Ratner, 2009). Use of the passive voice is one example of a complex sentence structure. During middle childhood children not only recognize and understand the difference between the active and passive voice, such as between saying, "Anita drives the car" and the "the car was driven by Anita," but they also use the passive construction with increasing frequency (Tomasello, 2006). Children speaking certain languages, such as Inuktitut (Allen & Crago, 1996), K'iche' Mayan (Pye & Quixtan Poz, 1988) and Zulu (Suzman, 1985), use the passive voice earlier than do children learning English because their languages make frequent use of this construction.

© Tom Koene/age fotostock

This young Inuit boy is learning the symbols of his language. Children of this culture use the passive voice earlier than English-speaking children because the Inuit language makes frequent use of this construction.

Children of this age also develop the ability to comprehend the totality of complex sentences, including those in which one idea is embedded in another (*Luke's bike, which is the color of my father's old car, has very thin tires*). You may not be surprised to learn that children tend to produce more complex sentences when their parents use such constructions (Huttenlocher, Vasilyeva, Cymerman, & Levine, 2002; Nelson, 1977). In addition, experiences at school also have an influence. One group of researchers found that children formed more complex sentence constructions when their teachers used such constructions in speaking to them in the classroom (Huttenlocher et al., 2002). Thus, language development is closely tied to the models provided by adults, as well as to children's increasing ability to pay attention to such models and remember new vocabulary and sentence constructions.

The language improvements just discussed involve syntax and semantics (Hua & Dodd, 2006). Recall from Chapter 9 that *syntax* refers to the way words are combined to form understandable phrases or sentences, and *semantics* refers to the meaning of the phrases and sentences. Children during these years also show great improvement in *pragmatics*, the social rules of language. Pragmatics involves using language to affect others or relay information (Owens, 2011). As children's language use becomes more complex, they become better at communicating to others, because they can be more precise in their meaning (Hurewitz, Brown-Schmidt, Thrope, Gleitman, & Trueswell, 2000). They also become better at clarifying their meaning by changing or adding words when they are misunderstood (Ninio & Snow, 1996). In addition, middle-childhood youngsters are becoming more linguistically sophisticated in their social interactions. This means that they often can detect the undercurrents of meanings as they begin to understand complexities in communication (Filippova & Astington, 2010).

Jokes and riddles become very popular in middle childhood because children are beginning to understand the ambiguous and multiple meanings of words. In one study (Yuill, 2009), 7- to 9-year olds were assigned to either a control group or an intervention group. The children in the intervention group were given riddles—for example, "Why do leopards never escape from the zoo? Because they are always spotted." The children worked in pairs, discussing the ambiguities in the words used in the riddles. After engaging in these discussions, children in the intervention group showed greater improvement in reading comprehension than those in the control group (who were not given the riddles). It appears that encouraging children to analyze the multiple meanings of words helps them think about language in different and productive ways.

Irony is another example of understanding multiple meanings. Irony is quite complex but generally involves a statement or question that has a literal meaning different from its intent. It can include *hyperbole*, which is exaggeration for effect, such as "I ate the biggest hamburger ever made." It can also involve *sarcasm*, which is saying the opposite of what you mean—for instance, saying "Nice move, Jonah" when Jonah

© KidStock/Blend Images/Corbis

Jokes and riddles become very popular in middle childhood as children grow more sophisticated in their understanding of language.

trips on a chair leg. It can include *understatement*, such as "I'm just a little bit upset" when the child is actually very upset. Another feature of language development is the *rhetorical question*, a question that is not meant to be answered, such as "How many times have I told you to hang up your jacket?" Using and understanding irony requires children to understand the intent of the speaker and how it differs from the literal words spoken. During the middle-childhood years, children improve in their ability to both understand and use irony (Recchia, Howe, Ross, & Alexander, 2010).

## English Language Learners Policy

A significant language issue in U.S. schools today concerns children who are *English language learners* (ELLs), those whose first language is not English. The term includes both students who are just beginning to learn English and those who have already developed a level of proficiency. Some educators refer to these children as *dual language learners*, as they are often improving their skills in two languages simultaneously. The experience of these students has been highlighted by educational policy related to children's school achievement.

### The No Child Left Behind Act

The No Child Left Behind (NCLB) Act of 2001 (Public Law 107–110, enacted January 8, 2002) was intended to require schools to focus on traditionally underserved populations, such as low-income students and students with disabilities. ELLs comprise a major subgroup of underserved students.

Current estimates indicate that 21% of school-aged children in the United States speak a language other than English at home, and 24% of these children speak English with difficulty (U.S. Department of Education, National Center for Education Statistics, 2011). Researchers have found that it takes ELLs from 4 to 7 years to move from the lowest level of ability to speak English to the proficient level (Borsato & Padilla, 2008; Working Group on ELL Policy, 2011). The NCLB mandates that schools ensure ELLs master English as quickly as possible (http://www.ncpie.org/nclbaction/english_language_learners.html). The act requires ELL students to take state-mandated tests within three years after entering the school system.

what if...?

Consider the research on the length of time it takes students learning English to become proficient. Now consider the NCLB requirements that students take state-mandated tests within three years of entering the school system. What do you think about those requirements? What recommendations would you make to legislators responsible for these rules?

Ariel Skelley/Blend Images/Getty Images

In bilingual classrooms, two languages are used for instruction.

Most agree that the enactment of NCLB has resulted in greater attention to teaching children who are learning to speak English (Snow & Kang, 2006). There is controversy, however, about this legislation in relation to ELLs. One issue concerns when ELLs should be required to take the state tests mandated by the law. Some educators argue that requiring students to take state-mandated tests within three years of entry to school limits their ability to perform well on the tests (Borsato & Padilla, 2008). A second issue involves how best to serve ELLs: through bilingual education or secondary language learning. The two methods are not identical, as discussed next. Whereas the teaching of English is an essential part of *bilingual programs*, it is only one part. When English is the only subject taught, the program becomes *English as a second language* (ESL).

## Bilingual Education Versus English as a Second Language (ESL)

The National Association for Bilingual Education (NABE) defines **bilingual education** as the use of two languages in school, by teachers or students or both, for a variety of social and pedagogical purposes (Allard, 2008). (Pedagogy refers to the art of teaching.) In other words, bilingual programs are characterized by the use of two languages for instruction. Specific goals identified by the NABE include the following:

- Teaching English.
- Improving the academic achievement of ELLs.
- Helping immigrant children adjust to a new society.
- Aiding children in their efforts to maintain their linguistic and cultural heritage.
- Permitting English speakers to learn a second language.

There are several different types of bilingual education programs. Some focus on helping students learn academic subjects, such as social studies and history, in their home language while learning English. Students may move to English-language classes in these subjects after a year or several years. Two-way bilingual programs (also called dual-language programs) are another type of bilingual education. They target children from two language groups to learn both languages well (Barnett, Yarosz, Thomas, Jung, & Blanco, 2007). To that end, children from both language groups share the same classroom and are often taught by a team of teachers proficient in both languages. One advantage of such programs is that children who only speak English learn to speak another language.

In **English as a second language (ESL)** programs, students receive formal instruction in English from one to several hours per day or week (Brisk, 2006). Instruction in these programs varies from classes that concentrate on grammar, vocabulary, and pronunciation to those that offer assistance in reading. Although the goal of ESL programs is to improve communication skills, an important consideration is to help students acquire language proficiency in English so that they can succeed in academic areas.

Research analyses of the different approaches to teaching ELLs agree on three findings:

1. Bilingual approaches are superior to all-English approaches in terms of students' achievement test scores (Rolstad, Mahoney, & Glass, 2005; Thomas & Collier, 2002).
2. When students receive instruction in their first language along with instruction in English, their scores on tests of English achievement do not suffer (López & Tashakkori, 2006; Lucido, 2000).

**bilingual education** The use of two languages in school for instruction.

**English as a second language (ESL)** A program involving formal instruction in English.

3. Children in schools that offer more services for families of students learning English (such as translators for parents in school meetings and parent-teacher conferences) show greater improvement in their academic skills (Han, 2012).

Many educators argue that there are advantages to helping students maintain skills in their primary language. One is, simply, being able to speak two (or more) languages fluently (Menyuk & Brisk, 2005). Another is that dual language use has positive effects on children's cognitive development (Gibbons & Ng, 2004). As we described in Chapter 9, many of these positive effects involve children's executive functioning, especially their ability to control attention and inhibit incorrect responses. Dual language use, moreover, improves *metalinguistic awareness*, the ability to think about language in relation to its structure and use. In other words, children who are bilingual become more aware of the structure of language (Bialystok & Barac, 2012). As you can see, there are many issues involved in understanding how best to support the education and development of children who are learning English.

**literacy** The ability to read and write; the ability to read and write to relate effectively to a complex environment.

## Literacy Skills

As school-age children move through the early 21st century, they face an array of challenges to their language skills. In a highly technological society, once they have mastered reading and writing skills, they must then learn to implement them in relatively new ways: reading, writing, and working on computers, among them. These are all issues of **literacy**, and they are important in middle childhood because of their importance in school.

Literacy formerly meant, simply, learning how to read and write. Today, in contrast, literacy often refers to using reading and writing in complex ways relating to the increasingly complicated world of work and life outside the school (Tomkins, 2003). Researchers have identified several contemporary literacy skills (Dacey, Travers, & Fiore, 2009; Travers & Travers, 2008; Weis, 2004). Table 12.2 defines a number of these contemporary skills, along with basic literacy skills.

Stockbyte/Getty Images

Working with scientific equipment is helping these students to develop scientific literacy, one of the many types of literacy recognized today.

*Everyday stories*

WHAT'S IN A WORD? Dwayne is frustrated because his teacher has asked him to look up words in a thesaurus. He sees no value in doing this, and demonstrates his resistance by spreading himself lazily in a chair in the classroom. His teacher asks him not to *sprawl*, but he doesn't know what that word means. His teacher tells him to looks it up in the thesaurus. After he does, his eyes light up, and he counters, "I'm not sprawled; I'm draped." He decides maybe there is a good reason to use a thesaurus.

**Table 12.2** Types of Literacy

| Type of Literacy | Description |
|---|---|
| Basic literacy | Reading, writing, listening, and speaking |
| Scientific literacy | Knowledge of science, mathematics, and scientific reasoning |
| Technological literacy | Ability to work with computers, networks, and software |
| Visual literacy | Ability to understand and express ideas using images, charts, graphs, and videos |
| Information literacy | Ability to find, evaluate, and use information effectively |
| Cultural literacy | Knowledge and appreciation of the diversity of peoples and cultures |
| Global literacy | Understanding and recognizing the interrelationships of nations, corporations, and politics around the world. |

**Table 12.3** Chall's Model of Reading Stages

| Stage | Approximate Grade | Description |
|---|---|---|
| 0 | Preschool | Children learn phonological awareness.<br>They develop print awareness. |
| 1 | Grades 1–2 | Children translate letters and letter combinations into sounds.<br>They begin to recognize frequently used words. They can read simple text. |
| 2 | Grades 2–3 | Children begin to be more fluent in their reading (less word-by-word reading).<br>They begin to pay attention to what they read.<br>They make reasonable guesses when figuring out new words, using a combination of simple decoding skills and making sense of the meaning of the content. |
| 3 | Grades 4–8 | Much of the reading process becomes automatic for children, and they become fluent readers.<br>Children read to learn new information. They tend to be limited, however, to learning information from one perspective. |
| 4/5 | Grades 9–12 | Adolescents are competent readers and can access a wide range of material presented from many perspectives. |

*Source:* Based on information in Chall, 1983.

Imagemore/Getty Images

In the middle-childhood years, most children become fluent readers.

Like language development, literacy development begins in early childhood. As we discussed in Chapter 9, children begin to learn prereading skills, such as phonological awareness and print awareness, during early childhood. In middle childhood, these skills advance rapidly. By third grade, children can rapidly recognize many printed words (Howes, 2003). In addition, they begin to read with more emphasis on understanding content, aided by their growing vocabulary.

As we think about children's skill in reading, it is useful to consider Jean Chall's (1983) model of the stages in the reading process, as shown in Table 12.3. You can see that in the middle-childhood years, children advance to fluent reading. By third or fourth grade, they are expected to use reading as a source of learning. In earlier stages, children focus their attention on learning to read. In later stages, they focus on content and, eventually, on content provided from a variety of perspectives. If children are not fluent readers by fourth grade, they often have difficulty with many school subjects (Reed, 2009).

## Mathematical Skills

Schooling does more than advance children's literacy development as it also promotes their understanding and use of mathematics. By age 6, most children have an understanding of numbers, in terms of their order and that they represent a quantity (Geary, 2006). In middle childhood, children's mathematical skills, like their literacy skills, grow rapidly. This improvement occurs in three aspects of mathematical skills (Geary, 2006):

1. Children in the middle-childhood years develop greater conceptual knowledge. They begin to understand certain properties of numbers. They come to recognize, for example, that the order in which a group of numbers are added does not matter, the sum will remain the same. They also begin to understand fractions and simple estimation.

2. Children develop greater skill when performing arithmetical operations, including subtraction, multiplication, and division, and they become quicker and more efficient in using these operations.
3. Children become better at arithmetical problem solving, such as solving word problems. Both their conceptual knowledge and their skills in these operations are important aspects of their improvement in learning to solve problems.

Table 12.4 gives examples of each of these three areas. As you would expect, advances in skills like attention and memory, discussed earlier in this chapter, aid in children's development of mathematical skills, as in other areas.

Paul Bradbury/OJO Images RF/Getty Images

Math skills, such as the ability to work with fractions, develop rapidly during middle childhood.

WHEN SYSTEMS CONNECT

## Mathematical Skills and Executive Functioning

As we've discussed, the mathematical skills of children go through rapid changes during middle childhood. Those changes are at least partly due to developments in brain networks. In one study (Rosenberg-Lee, Barth, & Menon, 2011), researchers examined differences in the brain networks of second and third graders as they

**Table 12.4** Development of Mathematical Skills and Understanding During Middle Childhood

| Type of Knowledge | Specific Knowledge/Skills | Examples |
|---|---|---|
| Conceptual knowledge | Properties of arithmetic | Around second grade, most children understand that the order in which two numbers are added or multiplied doesn't affect the answer. |
| | Base-10 | Most children have difficulty understanding the base-10 structure of multidigit numerals (such as 4325) and benefit by specific instruction in this in elementary school. |
| | Fractions | Most children have a rudimentary understanding of part-whole relationships at the beginning of elementary school. But understanding mixed numbers (whole numbers and fractions, such as 2¾) is difficult for many children and requires instruction during the middle-childhood years. |
| | Estimation | Estimation of arithmetical operations on two-digit numbers can be achieved during middle childhood, but making estimates when larger numbers are involved is often difficult. |
| Arithmetical operations | Addition and subtraction | Although children begin to approach these operations by simple counting or "counting on" procedures, they eventually can rely on memory for arriving at simple solutions. |
| | Multiplication and division | Children generally learn these operations from their knowledge base of addition and subtraction. They learn to decompose problems into simpler components (for example, 3 x 4 is the same as 4 + 4 + 4). Eventually, they learn number facts (such as the times table) and use automated skills, which frees up memory for more complex problems. |
| Problem solving | Problem schema | By first grade, most children can solve simple word problems involving addition. More complex problems in which children have to compare sets of objects can be solved by many children during middle childhood if given instruction and practice. |
| | Problem-solving processes | This involves translating the words of word problems into mathematical information. Complex and multistep problems require executive function skills, which show improvement during middle childhood. However, more abstract problems are too difficult for children this age to solve. |

*Source:* Adapted from Geary, D. C. (2006). Development of mathematical understanding. In D. Kuhn & R. S. Siegler (Eds.), *Handbook of Child Psychology* (Vol. 2. Cognition, perception, and language, pp. 777–810). Hoboken, NJ: Wiley.

© Blue Images/Corbis

By helping his daughter with her homework, this father is showing his involvement with her schooling. Such engagement is associated with better school achievement in children.

completed problems that required mathematical reasoning, including single- and double-digit addition problems. As expected, the third graders solved the problems faster and more accurately than did the second graders.

The researchers also examined fMRIs of the children as they solved the problems and found several differences based on age. One of the important differences was that third graders, in comparison to the second graders, had more *functional connectivity* between a part of the prefrontal cortex and posterior brain regions (particularly the parietal lobe), especially in the left hemisphere.

Consider that to solve double-digit addition problems children need to know basic numerical representation, but they also need to access their knowledge of procedures, such as "carrying" from the ones to the tens place when adding. The integration of networks in the brain suggests how this happens. Brain systems in the prefrontal cortex underlie the cognitive processes involved in executive control of mathematical procedures. Other brain systems, including those in the parietal lobe, are involved in spatial and numerical representation. As these systems develop and work more closely together, children's mathematical skills improve.

## Parental Engagement in Children's Schooling

**Parenting**

Think back to when you were in elementary school. If you went to school in the United States, you may recall that your parents were invited to parent conferences, parents' night meetings, and various plays, science fairs, and fund-raising events. Most elementary schools offer a combination of such activities for parents, all intended to engage parents in their children's school experience. Why is that important?

The answer lies in much research that indicates that parent involvement in their children's schooling is associated with better educational achievement (Barnard, 2004; Jeynes, 2012; Pomerantz, Moorman, & Litwack, 2007). Why does parent engagement in their children's school help them? When parents show that they value their children's learning experience, as well as the role of schools in that experience, children are more motivated to do well in school (Cheung & Pomerantz, 2012; Grolnick, Friendly, & Bellas, 2009). Children also have better relationships with their teachers and more positive feelings about school when their parents are involved (Dearing, Kreider, & Weiss, 2008). Continued parent engagement in children's school experiences through middle childhood sets up a pattern of belief in children about the importance of learning, and that pattern can sustain them throughout their school experiences (Barnard, 2004).

The model in Table 12.5 describes many ways in which parents can be involved in children's schooling (Epstein, 1987, 1988, 2011). As you can see, this model encourages schools to provide parents with a range of opportunities and supports for engagement. Providing such a range of opportunities is necessary to involve as many families as possible. Many parents have complex or inflexible work schedules or inadequate means of transportation. Such limitations can make it difficult for parents to participate in the conventional forms of parent involvement, such as attending parent-teacher organization meetings (Dearing et al., 2008). Therefore, parent engagement in schools is best thought of as a two-way process, with both school outreach and parent response important to its success.

### what if...?

You have been asked to talk to parents in your local school district about ways they could be involved in the schools their children attend. One mother tells you that she can't attend many of the evening school events because of her work schedule, and wonders what else she could do to encourage her son to be engaged in school. What are some suggestions you would give her?

**Table 12.5** Types of Parent Involvement in Schools

| Type of Involvement | What Schools Can Do | What Parents Can Do |
|---|---|---|
| Parenting | Assist parents with parenting skills, including how to provide home conditions that support children's learning. Become familiar with the cultural traditions of families in the school community. | Provide a home environment that values and supports learning. Model reading and learning. Inform school personnel about important family cultural traditions. |
| Communicating | Provide information about school goals and programs, as well as children's progress, in ways (including language) parents can understand. | Describe child's strengths, difficulties, and particular interests. Ask teachers about child's progress in the classroom. |
| Volunteering | Organize volunteer opportunities to support the school and its students. | Propose ways to volunteer that fit with work and family schedules. |
| Learning at home | Ensure that families understand homework expectations; and, when possible, involve family members in some homework activities. | Provide a quiet place for children to do homework. If children are confused by assignments, make sure they know how to ask teachers for help. |
| Decision making | Include families as participants in decision-making groups in the school. | Attend parent organization meetings and volunteer to serve on school-related committees, if possible. |
| Collaboration with the community | Coordinate resources from the community to provide services to children and families. | Provide information to school personnel about community resources and specific neighborhood services. |

*Source:* Based on information in Epstein & Jansorn, 2004.

**CHECK YOUR PROGRESS**

1. What are the major advances in language development during middle childhood?
2. Distinguish several types of literacy and explain how they differ from basic literacy.
3. How do children's reading skills change during middle childhood?
4. What are important skills in mathematics that children develop during middle childhood?
5. What opportunities might schools provide to encourage parental involvement?

# CHAPTER SUMMARY

## Piaget's Theory and Concrete Operational Thought

**[ KEY QUESTION ] 1. What are the characteristics of children's thinking during the concrete operational stage, according to Piaget?**

- At about age 7, according to Piaget, children enter the stage of concrete operations. During this stage, they are able to use simple logic.
- Key accomplishments of the concrete operational period include conservation, seriation, and classification.
- In reasoning about conservation, children use the arguments of identity, reversibility, and compensation.
- Piaget's theory has been criticized because it was constructed based on a small sample of Swiss children and relies heavily on formal logic used by Western scientists.

## Vygotsky's Sociocultural Theory

**[ KEY QUESTION ] 2. What are some themes in Vygotsky's theory that are especially relevant to the middle-childhood years?**

- Vygotsky emphasized that children learn the tools relevant to their culture. In many cultures, schools teach relevant tool use, such as writing, reading, mathematics, and other forms of symbolic activity.
- Vygotsky differentiated spontaneous concepts, which are based on experiences outside of formal teaching, and scientific concepts, which are taught in schools.
- Teachers play a critical role in determining how to provide students with learning that is slightly in advance of their development.
- Children in this period use language to control their behavior and advance their thought processes by learning new concepts.
- Vygotsky's theory is criticized for its relative vagueness and for underrating the importance of children's independence in learning.

## Information-Processing Theory

**[ KEY QUESTION ] 3. What are the main types and functions of attention and memory, and why do they assume such significance in middle childhood?**

- Information-processing theorists are concerned with what happens in the human mind as it seeks to acquire, process, retain, and comprehend information.

- Attention involves selectively focusing on one source of information while ignoring others. The ability to focus selectively shows major improvements during middle childhood.
- The alerting network, the orienting network, and the executive network are brain networks involved in attention.
- Attention deficit hyperactivity disorder (ADHD) is a disorder in attention characterized by hyperactivity, inattentiveness, or (usually) both.
- Children engage in both nonautobiographical and autobiographical episodic memory, with autobiographical memory reaching close to adult performance during the middle-childhood period.
- The memory process involves encoding, storage, and retrieval of information. Brain development in middle childhood makes all these activities stronger.
- The Baddeley model of working memory includes the visuospatial sketchpad, the phonological loop, and the episodic buffer. These fluid components assist in the brief storage of information before it is transferred to the long-term storage components of crystallized systems.
- Children learn to use various memory strategies in middle childhood, including imagery, chunking, meaning, categorizing, rehearsal, and elaboration.
- Children show improved metacognition during middle childhood, which helps direct their attention and memory processes.

## Intelligence and Thinking

**[ KEY QUESTION ] 4. What are some different perspectives on intelligence?**

- Intelligence testing involves assessments of general intelligence. Alfred Binet and David Wechsler developed intelligence tests that are still in use today.
- In his theory of multiple intelligences, Howard Gardner proposed a definition of intelligence that includes eight separate intelligences: linguistic, musical, logical-mathematical, spatial, bodily-kinesthetic, interpersonal, intrapersonal, and naturalistic.
- Robert Sternberg's triarchic theory of intelligence includes three interacting elements: analytic intelligence, practical intelligence, and creative intelligence.

## The Development of Language, Literacy, and Mathematical Skills

**[ KEY QUESTION ] 5. What significant advances in language development, literacy, and mathematical understanding occur in the middle-childhood years?**

- Children's growing cognitive ability is reflected in their language development. They master the rules that allow them to combine words effectively into many kinds of sentences, and they develop the ability to comprehend complex sentences.
- One aspect of language development that improves significantly during middle childhood is pragmatics, the social rules of language.
- A significant issue in U.S. schools today concerns effective teaching for English language learners. Bilingual education focuses on the use of two languages for instruction, while English as a second language focuses on formal instruction in English.
- Today, literacy involves not just learning to read and write but using reading and writing in complex ways attuned to an increasingly complicated environment.
- By the end of middle childhood most children can read fluently and use reading to learn new information.
- Understanding of and skills in mathematics develop considerably during middle childhood in relation to conceptual knowledge, arithmetic operations, and problem solving.
- Parental engagement in children's education can take many forms and is important to their academic success.

# KEY TERMS

attention *444*
attention deficit hyperactivity disorder (ADHD) *449*
automaticity *454*
bilingual education *466*
cognitive operations *436*
concrete operations *436*
conservation *437*
English as a second language (ESL) *466*
intellectual disabilities *461*
intelligence quotient (IQ) *459*
learning disabilities *454*
literacy *467*
metacognition *446*
seriation *439*
theory of multiple intelligences *461*
triarchic theory of intelligence *462*

# CRITICAL THINKING QUESTIONS

1. **Piaget's Theory and Concrete Operational Thought.** In what ways do you think that children's cognitive advances in concrete operations assist them as learners in school?
2. **Vygotsky's Sociocultural Theory.** Vygotsky makes a distinction between spontaneous concepts and scientific concepts. Think of an example of each of these, and analyze why this distinction is important for school-aged children.
3. **Information-Processing Theory.** Explain why children need a range of memory strategies to draw on, and discuss whether schools should explicitly teach various memory strategies to children.
4. **Intelligence and Thinking.** What do you consider to be the strengths and limitations of traditional IQ tests? Analyze whether the triarchic theory of intelligence and the multiple intelligences theory have similar or different strengths and limitations in comparison to those of traditional IQ tests.
5. **The Development of Language, Literacy, and Mathematical Skills.** Provide a rationale for why it is so important that children become proficient readers before they enter fourth grade.
6. **Cultural Perspectives.** Why do you think that different cultures have different views of what is considered to be intelligent behavior?

## REAL Development

### Cognitive Development in Middle Childhood

In this module, you are a student intern in the Washington School District. One of your assignments is to visit classrooms and observe the teaching-learning process. In this activity, you will visit Mr. Timberlake's third-grade science classroom, where his students will be studying crayfish behaviors. Your task is to observe Mr. Timberlake interacting with students, keeping in mind what you have learned in this chapter about cognitive development during middle childhood.

© John Wiley & Sons, Inc.

**WileyPLUS** Go to WileyPLUS to complete the *Real Development* activity.

03.01

# Chapter 13

# Psychosocial Development in Middle Childhood

## MAKING A difference

### Service Learning

In a small New England community, students of all ages come together as members of Connect and Commit. Funded by private donations, this program encourages students to combine their classroom experiences with meaningful community service. For example, an elementary school class visits housing for elderly people and shares a crafts project with the residents. As part of a national project called Empty Bowls, art students design beautiful ceramic bowls, after which other students fill the bowls with ice cream and homemade sauces and sell them to raise money for a local food pantry.

Through programs such as Connect and Commit, students around the country are learning and using skills while deepening their understanding of the challenges faced by their communities. The idea behind these programs is called *service learning*. Service learning is a teaching and learning strategy that integrates meaningful community service with instruction and reflection. It also enriches the learning experience, teaches civic responsibility, and strengthens communities. (For more information on service learning, go to http://www.servicelearning.org.)

Many communities across the country are integrating service projects with classroom learning to encourage students to apply their classroom knowledge to solve real-life problems. As an example of how this integration works, consider students collecting trash from along a lakeshore. If they simply pick up the trash, they are providing a valuable community service. But if they also analyze what they find, identify sources of the problem, and share the results with members of the community, they are engaged in service learning. Not only are they performing a worthwhile service, but they are also learning about water pollution, environmental hazards, and scientific research, as well as improving communication skills by writing and speaking about what they have discovered.

## CHAPTER OUTLINE

Leland Bobbe/Getty Images

## [KEY QUESTIONS] *for* READING CHAPTER 13

1. How do children develop emotionally during middle childhood?
2. How does children's self-awareness during the middle-childhood period change?
3. What contributes to positive relationships with peers and parents during middle childhood?
4. How does the course of moral development change during the middle-childhood years?

**IN THIS CHAPTER,** we examine the meaningful and exciting changes in the psychosocial development of children during middle childhood. Developmental changes, together with daily challenges, help children better understand themselves and their environment. To examine the scope and depth of psychosocial development during middle childhood, we begin this chapter with a discussion of emotional development. As you will see, as they move through middle childhood, children are increasingly aware of their emotions and increasingly able to regulate them. Children's greater understanding of their emotions is related to their sense of themselves, so we next describe the growing complexity of this self-perception during middle childhood. This is also a time when children move away from the close protection of their parents and into a social world of peers and other adults, such as teachers and coaches. We thus go on to discuss the development of friendships and the social cognition necessary to understand the perspective of others, including parents, siblings, and peers. Finally, we consider the realm of moral development and how children of this age think about and reason through moral dilemmas.

# Emotional Development

### [ KEY QUESTION ] 1. How do children develop emotionally during middle childhood?

Tracing children's emotional development from infancy through early childhood and into middle childhood reveals a path marked by crucial milestones. Recall that in Chapter 7 we discussed the meaning of emotion in infants' development, and the importance of attachment for healthy growth. During the early-childhood years, as children continue to expand their relationships, they establish both antisocial and prosocial behaviors while acquiring some techniques of emotional regulation, as described in Chapter 10. What happens next? What are the milestones of emotional development in middle childhood? To examine this question, we begin with a further look at psychosocial theory. We first focus on antisocial behavior, and then consider prosocial behavior and emotional regulation, to see how children are developing in these areas during middle childhood.

**industry versus inferiority** The fourth of Erikson's psychosocial stages, during which children become increasingly involved in activities important to their culture. Those who do not engage successfully in such activities develop a sense of inferiority.

## Erikson's Psychosocial Theory

When you think of the daily activities of children in the middle-childhood period, you probably envision them as being very busy at school, participating in sports activities, and interacting with friends. In fact, according to Erik Erikson (1950), this is a period during which children develop a sense of *industry*. Children who do not become immersed in industrious activity central to their culture develop a sense of *inferiority*. Hence, Erikson identified **industry versus inferiority** as the conflict of middle childhood.

In the United States, as in numerous other countries, many of the activities of middle childhood are related to schooling. In such cultures, children acquire a sense of themselves as learners at this time. They will emerge from middle childhood with a view of themselves as either capable learners or inferior students. Children's sense of industry also encourages them to form productive relationships with others. Such relationships, when accompanied by a growing sense of competence, also help them to avoid feelings of inferiority (Erikson, 1950). Children's antisocial and prosocial behaviors, along with their skills in emotional regulation, make a difference in their ability to foster productive relationships.

| Erikson's Psychosocial Stage Theory |
|---|
| Trust vs. mistrust |
| Autonomy vs. shame, doubt |
| Initiative vs. guilt |
| Industry vs. inferiority<br>• Children become increasingly involved in activities important to their culture, such as schooling and making friends. Those who do not engage successfully in such activities develop a sense of inferiority. |
| Identity vs. identity confusion |
| Intimacy vs. isolation |
| Generativity vs. stagnation |
| Integrity vs. despair |

## Antisocial Behavior

As in the preschool years, aggression is the most commonly seen form of antisocial behavior during middle childhood. Note that aggression differs from assertive behavior. A child behaves assertively when she affirms her legitimate rights, such the right to use a computer available to all children in a classroom. Aggression, in contrast, occurs when children act in ways that enable them to get what they want without concern for others.

### Aggression in Middle Childhood

As you may recall from Chapter 10, there are several different types of aggression. Instrumental aggression is usually aimed at obtaining a particular goal, as when a child pushes a peer out of the way to be first in line. It is not specifically undertaken to harm the other person. The incidence of this type of aggression declines during early childhood and is, therefore, only infrequently displayed during middle childhood. In contrast, hostile aggression involves behaviors *intended* to harm someone else. This type of aggression can be physical, such as hitting someone or destroying property, or relational, such as socially excluding another person from a group. Hostile aggression continues through the middle-childhood years and often into adolescence.

As children mature, most gain more control over their emotions, and hence display lower levels of aggression. Some, however, show increasing levels of hostile aggression, including the relational form (Dodge, Coie, & Lynam, 2006; Tremblay, 2000). Children who do not outgrow temper tantrums and defiant behaviors by around age 8 are likely to display a pattern of aggressive behaviors leading up to their adolescent years (Dodge et al., 2006). Children who show high levels of aggression during middle childhood are often rejected by "good citizen" peer groups, and later affiliate with deviant peer groups, potentially resulting in antisocial behavior and criminal activity (Broidy et al., 2003). Interventions in such cases are warranted to prevent children from eventually engaging in such activities (Coyne, Nelson, & Underwood, 2011).

## Gender and Aggression

Are there gender differences in displays of aggression? Research consistently points to the finding that boys are more physically aggressive than girls (Coyne et al., 2011). Boys tend to be socialized to be more aggressive, whereas adults often discourage physical aggression by girls (Crick, 1997). In addition, boys tend to favor more violent video games than do girls (Gentile, Lynch, Linder, & Walsh, 2004). Playing these games during middle childhood is linked to both current and future levels of physical and verbal aggression in both boys and girls (Anderson, Gentile, & Buckley, 2007). We describe a longitudinal study on the effects of playing violent video games in the Research Insights feature.

In contrast to the research on physical aggression, studies on gender differences in relational aggression among school-age children have produced inconsistent findings. An early study on this topic reported that girls use relational aggression more than boys (Crick & Grotpeter, 1995). More recently, however, a meta-analysis of many studies on relational aggression did not find this difference (Archer, 2004). One way of reconciling these contradictory findings is to consider that although girls may not use relational aggression more than boys, they do tend to use it more than physical aggression, making relational aggression a larger portion of girls' aggressive behavior (Archer & Coyne, 2005).

## Causes of Aggression

Is there a biological basis for aggressive behavior? Some studies suggest that prenatal exposure to nicotine doubles the risk that a child will exhibit aggressive behavior (Fergusson, Woodward, & Horwood, 1998; Weissmann, Warner, Wickramatne, & Kandel, 1999). Children exposed to cocaine prenatally are also more likely to show aggression (Bendersky, Bennett, & Lewis, 2006). Other research suggests that there is a genetic predisposition to aggression (Moffitt & Caspi, 2007). Several genes have been found to be linked to antisocial behavior (Kim-Cohen et al., 2006).

That said, even researchers who have concluded that aggression has a genetic component acknowledge that socialization plays an important role (Moffit & Caspi, 2007). Recall, for example, the phenomenon we first described in Chapter 2 concerning the gene responsible for producing the enzyme MAOA. This enzyme affects brain levels of serotonin, a neurotransmitter associated with emotional regulation (Mitsis, Halperin, & Newcorn, 2000). Certain children, especially boys, have a genetic predisposition to

### Research Insights: Do Violent Video Games Promote Aggression?

Beginning during the middle-childhood years, many children play computer and video games. Violent video games are designed to allow the player to cause virtual harm to an opponent through aggression, such as hitting, punching, shooting, and killing, often in graphic portrayal. Does playing such violent games promote aggression?

Research on this topic has shown mixed results. Many studies have found a relationship between playing violent video games and engaging in aggressive behavior (Saleem, Anderson, & Gentile, 2012; Willoughby, Adachi, & Good, 2012). Others, however, question whether playing such games actually *causes* aggression (Ferguson, Garza, Jerabeck, Ramos, & Galindo, 2013; Gunter, & Daly, 2012).

Although most research in this area has focused on adolescents, several researchers set out to examine this question by conducting a longitudinal study of elementary school children (Anderson et al., 2007). They hypothesized that children who often played violent video games would become more aggressive over the course of a school year. To test their hypothesis, the researchers studied a total of 430 third-, fourth-, and fifth-grade students in five schools in Minnesota. The children were asked to name their three favorite television shows, three favorite movies, and three favorite computer or video games. They were also asked how violent they perceived each one to be and how often they watched or played it. The children were also rated for levels of aggression by peers, teachers, and themselves.

The researchers' prediction proved to be true. Children who played more violent video games increased in aggression, including engagement in physical fighting, over the course of the school year. This increase was greatest in children who indicated that their parents were not involved in restricting their media use or discussing it with them, as you can see in Figure 13.1.

The researchers concluded that although exposure to violent video games affects children's physical aggression, parental involvement can help reduce its negative impact.

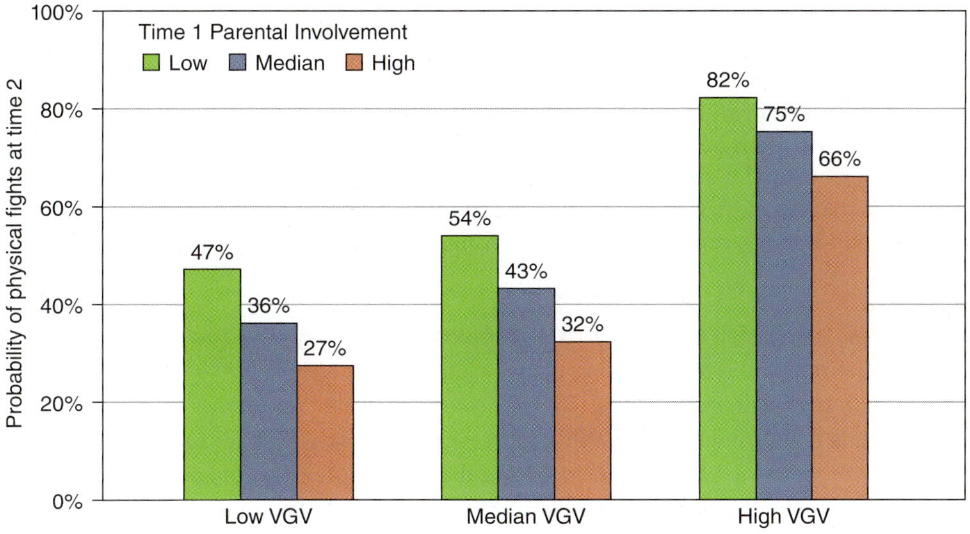


Note: VGV = Video game violence.

**FIGURE 13.1 Video Game Violence and Parental Involvement** Researchers compared children's aggression on two dimensions: exposure to violent video games and parental involvement in children's media use. Aggression and physical fighting in children who played more violent video games increased over the course of a school year. Furthermore, the increase was greatest among children whose parents were not involved in their media use.
*Source:* Anderson, C. A., Gentile D. A., & Buckley, K. A. (2007). *Violent videogame effects on children and adolescents: Theory, research, and public policy.* NY: Oxford University Press.

underproduce MAOA. If boys with this genetic predisposition are also physically abused by their parents or caregivers, they are more likely to show patterns of aggressive behavior than children without the genetic predisposition (Jaffee et al., 2005). The point is, genetic predisposition alone does not result in aggressive behavior. In other words, it is the interaction of genes and environment that can produce aggressive behavior.

In addition to the effects of biology and parenting, children's own reasoning skills make a difference in how aggressively they behave. Much research indicates that children who are unable to see things from the perspective of others, and who do not show high levels of moral reasoning, are more likely to behave aggressively (Dodge et al., 2006: Gregg, Gibbs, & Basinger, 1994).

## Prosocial Behavior

Although it is the antisocial behavior of children that captures most of the headlines (Oh et al., 2008), prosocial behavior quietly and steadily occurs in the lives of children every day. Recall that prosocial behavior, also called altruistic behavior, occurs when children help others without obvious benefits for themselves. Examples of such behaviors include helping, sharing, and sympathizing with others.

What motivates children to act prosocially? Sometimes, in acting this way, children are following an internalized code of conduct that was suggested by their parents or are acting out of empathy or sympathy for others (Farrant, Devine, Mayberry, & Fletcher, 2012). At other times, they are acting prosocially to obtain a reward, to receive parental approval, or to reduce their own guilt feelings (Olthof, 2012). There is also research that identifies a strong link between moral development and the motivation to help others (Malti, Gummerum, Keller, & Buchmann, 2009).

In any case, prosocial behavior increases steadily with age (Eisenberg, Fabes, & Spinrad, 2006). Its development doesn't necessarily

*KidStock/Blend Images/Getty Images*

Children engage in prosocial behavior when they help others with no thought of benefit for themselves.

proceed in a nice, neat path, however. During early childhood, many children start and then stop exhibiting prosocial behaviors (Baillargeon et al., 2011). Then, during middle childhood, children generally proceed from "doing good" to avoid punishment to "doing good" based on an internalized moral code ("I want to help others"), but they may move back and forth between these motives. Their motives for prosocial behavior may also change with the situation, and/or depend on their relationships with others involved in the situation. Generally, though, children advance in their prosocial skills, and show declines in egocentric motives for acting prosocially during middle childhood.

what if...?

Suppose you are shopping in the mall with your two 9-year-old cousins. They have run ahead of you, and as you catch up to them, you see them picking up a wallet with money in it. You hear them discussing what to do with it. Josephine suggests that they return the wallet to the owner "so we won't get in trouble." Julia claims that "someone probably saw us pick this up so we better turn it in to the lost-and-found." They both agree that they should not keep the wallet out of fear of being punished for taking someone else's money. You want to provide other reasons for not taking the wallet, including ideas about the possible needs of the person who lost the wallet. What would you say to them?

Some children tend to be more prosocial than others. Biological differences may affect children's tendencies to be prosocial. Studies of identical twins indicate that they are more alike than fraternal twins in their prosocial behaviors (Zahn-Waxler, Schiro, Robinson, Emde, & Schmitz, 2001). Genetic influences on prosocial behavior are not strong during middle childhood, but become more powerful during adolescence (Knafo & Plomin, 2006). Differences in personality and temperament make a difference during middle childhood, however. Children who are emotionally positive tend to be more prosocial, for example (Eisenberg et al., 2006).

Children identified as prosocial tend to show the following characteristics:

- *Consistency*. Many children display prosocial behaviors across quite different situations (Wojslawowicz Bowker, Rubin, Burgess, Booth-LaForce, & Rose-Krasnor, 2006). Children who show many prosocial behaviors during middle childhood will continue to do so in the future (Grusec, Chaparro, Johnston, & Sherman, 2012).
- *Sociability and adjustment*. Prosocial children tend to be well-adjusted and to cope well with stress. They also have an impressive arsenal of social skills and seem quite comfortable with themselves (McHale, Dariotis, & Kauh, 2003).
- *Cognition*. The relationship between thinking and doing is an important issue. As children engage in increasingly more logical and less egocentric thinking during middle childhood, they tend to become more prosocial, taking into account the needs of others (Eisenberg, 2006).

## Emotional Regulation

Emotional regulation involves a dynamic process in which children need to use their knowledge about appropriate emotional behavior for the situation. For example, the appropriate emotional behavior while cheering for your team at a basketball game is quite different from that required for supporting your friends at a music recital.

During middle childhood, children learn to better understand the different requirements of social situations in regard to emotionally appropriate behavior. One way they do this is by learning appropriate *emotional display rules*, rules that tell them which emotions are appropriate to display under specific circumstances. By the time they are around 8 to 10 years old, children have learned many display rules. The rules may, on occasion, call for expressions that differ from a child's actual emotions. Consider that children learn to smile in certain situations even when they are unhappy or disappointed, such as when they are not selected for a sports team they had hoped to play on, or when they receive a gift they do not like (Saarni, Campos, Camras, & Witherington, 2006; von Salisch, 2008). They are able to do this because they are learning to separate their feelings from their expressions of emotion.

During middle childhood, children also begin to realize that they can have both negative and positive emotions in response to the same situation (Harter, 2006). Thus, a young girl may be happy that she was selected to be in a musical performance but sad that her friend was not. In contrast, during early childhood, children do not believe that they can have opposing emotions; they believe they must feel either happy or sad, for example, but not both. This ability to recognize conflicting emotional reactions adds complexity to the emotional development of children during this age period. Regulating such emotions requires a cognitive understanding of this complex emotional life, as we discuss in the next section.

**coping** A person's active effort to manage stressful situations through the use of psychological resources.

WHEN SYSTEMS CONNECT

## Coping with Stress

During middle childhood, children begin to develop better emotional regulation through the use of coping skills. **Coping** refers to a person's active effort to manage stressful situations through the use of psychological resources (Lazarus & Folkman, 1984). People tend to use two types of coping mechanisms: emotion-focused and problem-focused. *Emotion-focused coping* is directed at regulating emotional responses to the situation, such as denying that a problem exists or walking away from an uncomfortable social situation. *Problem-focused coping* is directed at changing the situation or finding other approaches to a problem that make it less stressful. This type of coping requires, first, a cognitive understanding of the problem and, second, knowledge of possible ways to address it. Thus, when children use problem-focused coping, their cognitive development and emotional development are working together. Generally, problem-focused coping strategies lead to a reduction in stress, whereas emotion-focused ones often result in continued high levels of stress (Compas, Connor-Smith, Saltzman, Thomsen, & Wadsworth, 2001).

As children develop through middle childhood, they become better able to consider causes of stress from different perspectives. They are also able to distinguish uncontrollable stressors (such as a parent's illness) from controllable ones (such as a pileup of homework assignments) (Saarni et al., 2006). In addition, school-aged children can use their improving metacognitive skills to distinguish the types of coping strategies that work well for them in various situations. In one study (Saarni, 1997), children ages 6 to 12 years were presented with vignettes describing typical experiences that result in negative emotional reactions, like feeling hurt, angry, sad, afraid, or embarrassed. In one vignette, a child lent a favorite ball to a friend, and the friend's dog chewed up the ball. The friend refused to replace it. Children were asked to select the best way to deal with the emotions caused by such events. The most frequently selected coping strategies were problem solving and seeking support from others, except in situations involving hurt feelings. In that case, many children chose a strategy involving distancing or avoiding the situation. The children's ability to think about the coping strategies they would use shows that they applied metacognitive skills to emotional situations.

*Everyday stories*

DIFFERENT COPING STRATEGIES Alicia and Alberto are looking at the list of children who have been selected to be in the class play. Alicia becomes very upset when she sees that her name is not on the list, and she reacts by withdrawing from the other children in the class. She remains upset for a long time. Alberto also sees that his name is not on the selection list, and he is upset, too. But his response is to find his friend Jamil, and together they come up with suggestions to give the teacher about what the next class play should be. They make sure the plays they recommend have a wide variety of roles, to ensure that many children will need to be involved. By focusing his attention on a plan he thinks will work, Alberto quickly gets over being upset. In contrast, Alicia continues to focus on how upset she is. She is using emotion-focused coping strategies, whereas Alberto is using problem-focused coping strategies.

**I-self** That part of the self that thinks and makes judgments.

**me-self** That part of the self that is the object of the I-self's thinking and judging.

✓CHECK YOUR PROGRESS

1. What is the psychosocial focus of the middle-childhood years according to Erikson?
2. What are several types of aggression, and how do they differ?
3. What characteristics distinguish children who are more prosocial?
4. How do the two types of coping strategies differ in their effect on reducing stress?

# Relating to One's Self

**[ KEY QUESTION ] 2. How does children's self-awareness change during the middle-childhood period?**

As children's sense of self continues to develop during the middle-childhood years, their ideas about themselves change from the concrete ("I'm tall") to the more abstract ("I'm friendly") (Harter, 2006). Growing physical awareness, increased ability to use logic, and psychosocial maturity all coalesce now to help children formulate a more intricate understanding of *who* and *what* they are.

We discuss several aspects of the developing sense of self in this section, including self-esteem. First, though, we introduce an important idea that will help to explain how the self develops.

## The I-Self and the Me-Self

Imagine for a moment you're looking in a mirror. What do you see? Of course, you see yourself. But do you ever think about the fact that there are two sides to this vision of yourself? The first, called the **I-self**, is the person doing the actual looking. The second, called the **me-self**, is the person being seen. An American psychologist, William James (1842–1910), first described this division of the self into two distinct parts (1890/1981). James thought of the I-self as the knower who thinks, makes judgments, realizes that it is separate from everything it sees, and controls the surrounding world. The me-self is the object of the I-self's thinking, judging, and so on. Children begin to distinguish between these two selves in middle childhood.

If you think of the "me" as your self-concept, it will help you to understand how the "I" develops self-esteem. As a result of the "I" evaluating the "me's" activities, the self is judged good or bad, competent or incompetent, masterful or fumbling. Knowing who both "I" and "me" are shapes children's development, investing them with the poise and assurance to undertake critical challenges. How do children continue to expand their sense of self during the middle-childhood years?

*SW Productions/Getty Images*

The I-self can be described as the observer who looks into a mirror and sees and evaluates the me-self.

## The Developing Sense of Self

Growth through each developmental phase sees a child become a more complex, multidimensional self while also becoming more self-aware (Thompson, 2006).

How do these changes occur? In the current view, physical, cognitive (including language), and psychosocial influences all interact to shape the self, and this interaction is crucial in explaining the growing sophistication of children's ideas about themselves (Harter, 2006; Thompson, 2006). As children move from early childhood into and through middle childhood, they change the way they describe themselves, the way they evaluate themselves, and their understanding of the role of gender in their sense of self. They also develop a more intricate sense of self-esteem.

### Changes in Self-Description

Recall from Chapter 10 that when they are asked to describe themselves, most 3- and 4-year-olds provide concrete examples of what they look like ("I have brown eyes"), what they can do ("I can run fast"), or the friendships they have made ("I'm Juan's friend") (Damon & Hart, 1988). Children in middle childhood have become more sophisticated. Here are the remarks of a 9-year-old girl who describes herself along several dimensions:

*I'm going to be a hippie for Halloween. I'm good at swimming. I like going to the movies and playing basketball. I wear a ponytail. I've got a lot of friends who like me because I'm a good friend.*

Her comments not only mention her appearance, as would be typical of a younger child, but also some of her personality characteristics, such as being a good friend, and her talents, like swimming.

Here are the remarks of an 11-year-old boy:

*I enjoy sports very much. I'm average height. I am smart, although I do not like school. Video games are one of my favorite things to do. I have a lot of friends, and I get along with them very well. Another activity I enjoy is reading. I like mysteries and books that have a lot of action.*

His self-description identifies the activities he enjoys but also includes more abstract concepts, such as intelligence.

The 11-year-old's mention of his height illustrates his ability to compare himself with others his age. **Social comparison**, which involves comparing one's own appearance, traits, abilities, and behaviors with those of others, is a component of self-definition that arises during middle childhood. As you might expect, such comparisons significantly affect children's views of themselves.

© George Shelley/Corbis

Blend Images/Getty Images

In middle childhood, self-descriptions go beyond appearance (for example, "I'm tall") to include other characteristics, such as talents ("I'm good at swimming") and interests ("I enjoy reading").

## Changes in Self-Evaluation

Children's ability to make social comparisons influences not only their self-descriptions but also their self-evaluations. During middle childhood, children steadily incorporate more comparisons with others as their network of social relationships grows and their cognitive ability enables them to express their self-evaluations in more realistic terms (Baumeister, Campbell, Krueger, & Vohs, 2005).

*Everyday stories*

FROM ARTIST TO PHOTOGRAPHER Ten-year-old Liam likes taking photographs and has always considered himself to be a good artist. He attended an art camp during the summer, where he found himself surrounded by other artistic children. Several of the campers were very talented in forms of art that Liam had not tried before, like ceramics and oil painting. He began to see himself differently as he compared his talent with those of others. At the end of camp, he no longer considered himself to be good at art in general, but instead saw himself as good at photography.

Indeed, the relationships and interactions of middle childhood markedly affect children's self-evaluations (Flavell, Miller, & Miller, 2002; Gest, Rulison, Davidson, & Welsh, 2008; Harter, 2006). Interactions with adults, siblings, and peers cause a child's self-evaluation to trend toward either the favorable or the unfavorable, the competent or the incompetent, the popular or the unpopular (Davis-Kean et al., 2008; Thomaes et al., 2010). One powerful influence in the constellation of forces shaping a child's self-evaluation is gender.

**social comparison** The process of comparing one's own appearance, traits, abilities, and behaviors with those of others.

## Gender Development

In Chapter 10, we defined *gender stereotypes* as mental models of the behaviors and activities of each sex based on socially sanctioned attitudes about what is appropriate for individuals of that sex. These stereotypes are rigid and pronounced in children by the time they are 5 years of age. During the middle-childhood years, children's knowledge of stereotypical sexual behavior continues to broaden. By age 7, though, their belief that stereotypes are rigid and inflexible begins to wane. What has happened to produce these changes?

The beginning of middle childhood is the time of the *5- to 7-year shift* (Sameroff & Haith, 1996). Between the ages of 5 and 7, children begin to think in a radically different way. As we described in Chapter 12, according to Piaget, around age 7 children are entering the concrete operational period. Their new abilities enable them to better evaluate information and arrive at logical solutions to concrete problems. Vygotsky (1978) saw these years as the time when internal speech guides children's actions and helps them to evaluate information, including data concerning gender.

Among the developmental changes in children's thinking about gender are the following (Ruble, Martin, & Berenbaum, 2006):

- *Activities and interests*. Entering elementary school, children have considerable, and inflexible, knowledge about which activities are male and which are female. At about 7 years, children begin to realize that there may be individual variations in masculinity and femininity (Ruble et al., 2006). Nevertheless, gender-typical preferences increase with age. Children, especially boys, tend to avoid activities and interests enjoyed by the other sex.
- *Personal and social attributes*. Beliefs about personality, gender-related traits, social behaviors, and abilities gradually become more flexible during middle childhood, as children begin to recognize that even within sex-segregated groups, personality differences are apparent (Trautner et al., 2005).
- *Styles and symbols*. The symbols related to gender—such as hair style, body image, and speech patterns—become increasing complex and valued by children during the middle-childhood period. Children may wear certain styles of clothing and use certain expressions in communicating with friends, and these symbols are often based on group norms (Pasterski, Golombok, & Hines, 2011).
- *Values Regarding Gender*. As children become aware that they are members of a particular sex, they tend to view their own sex more favorably. This awareness arises during early childhood and persists into middle childhood before beginning to decline around adolescence, as children become more sophisticated in their thinking (Ruble et al., 2006).

Lisa Passmore

Girls and boys in the middle-childhood years tend to view members of their own sex more favorably than members of the opposite sex.

## Self-Esteem

Recall from Chapter 10 that *self-esteem* describes a child's personal evaluation of his or her own worth. Many factors affect the continuing development of self-esteem in middle childhood, and we examine several of them in this section.

### Self-Esteem and Competence

**domain-specific attributes** Particular areas of competence. Susan Harter identified five domains that are important in middle childhood: physical appearance, scholastic competence, social acceptance, behavioral conduct, and athletic competence.

In investigating the development of self-esteem, Susan Harter (1999, 2012) identified two different ways in which children can evaluate themselves. First, they can make an overall, or global, evaluation ("I'm a good person"). Second, they can evaluate themselves in terms of **domain-specific attributes**, particular areas of competence. Children begin to focus on these domain-specific attributes in middle childhood. Although, in general, self-esteem declines from early to middle childhood, children with higher levels of self-esteem in middle childhood usually maintain higher levels into adolescence and adulthood (Robins & Trzesniewski, 2005).

Harter and her colleagues identified five domains that are significant for children of the middle-childhood years:

1. Physical appearance
2. Scholastic competence
3. Social competence
4. Behavioral conduct
5. Athletic competence

The Self-Perception Profile for Children (Harter, 1985) is a questionnaire designed for children ages 8 and older that contains questions related to each of the five areas of competence. You can see examples of these questions in Figure 13.2, as well as profiles across the areas for two children. Note that these two children judge themselves differently in the five areas. Indeed, during middle childhood, children begin to view themselves as having a constellation of strengths and weaknesses. That understanding arises to some extent from feedback provided by teachers, coaches, and peers, as well as from the social comparisons children themselves make at this time. The relationship between these self-perceptions and children's actual behaviors becomes stronger during the middle-childhood period (Davis-Kean et al., 2008).

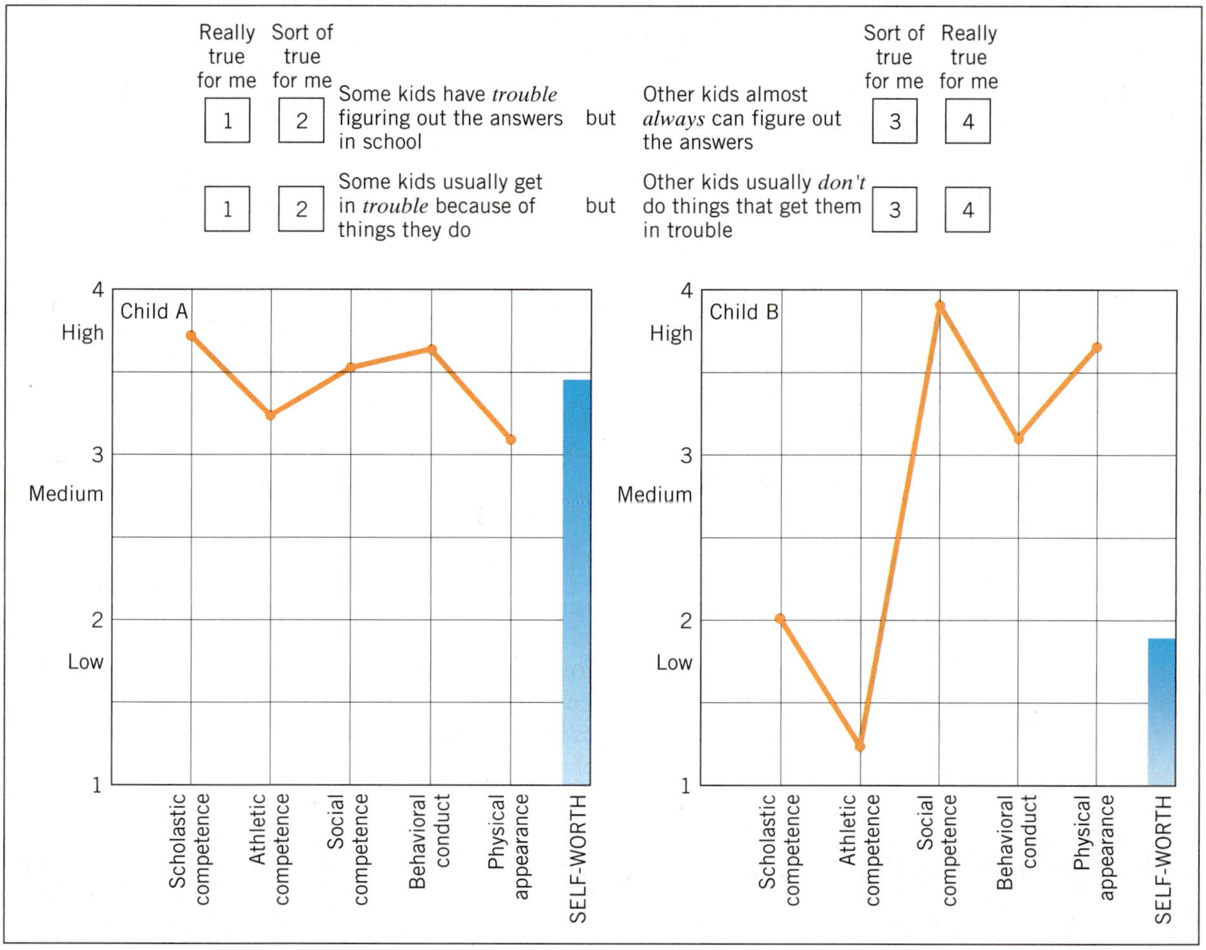


**FIGURE 13.2 Samples from Harter's Self-Perception Profile** These samples show two items from Harter's questionnaire and two profiles of children who completed the questionnaire. As you can see, children's self-perceptions may vary widely across the domains.

*Source:* S.C. Levine, J. Huttenlocher, A. Taylor, and A. Langrock. (1999). Early sex differences in spatial skill. *Developmental Psychology*, 35, 940–949. APA; reprinted with permission.

### Building Self-Esteem Parenting

Parents also affect a child's self-esteem. Parental approval and acceptance often result in a child feeling that he or she is worthy of love (Feiring & Taska, 1996). You may recall our discussion of different parenting styles in Chapter 10. We noted there that the authoritative parenting style produces better results for young children than the authoritarian or permissive style. This is true for children in middle childhood as well. Parents who are more authoritative and democratic during the school-age years tend to raise children who have positive self-esteem (Lamborn, Mounts, Steinberg, & Dornbusch, 1991).

What can adults working with children do to encourage positive self-evaluations? They must walk a careful line between providing the necessary support and encouragement on the one hand, and helping children to keep their accomplishments in perspective on the other. Empty praise can be detrimental to children, as it can make them passive and dependent on the view of others (Dweck, 1999). Furthermore, assigning children easy tasks and then lavishing praise on them when they complete those tasks can make children choose to avoid challenges (Dweck, 1999).

If an adult's reactions comprise an island of praise in a sea of neutral, or even negative, evaluations, children will eventually ignore the praise. Certainly, children should not be exposed to constant criticism, but neither should reactions to their efforts be transparently false, because they will quickly see through contrived praise, especially when it concerns something meaningful to them. Research has indicated that children do not benefit from praise that has no basis in attainment (Damon, 1996). Instead, self-esteem is often heightened when children face a problem realistically and try to solve it (Compas, 2004).

In brief, parents and other adults should recognize and praise children's efforts, and their resulting achievements, honestly (Menon et al., 2007). Honest evaluations, coupled with support and encouragement, go a long way toward helping children to develop self-esteem, as well as positive relationships with others.

### what if...?

Suppose you're a volunteer coach on a soccer team for 8-year-olds. Clearly, some children are better players than others. Some work hard to learn soccer skills, while others seem to want to be on the team merely to socialize. At the end of the season, you need to decide whether you should give a trophy to each child on the team, even those who showed little enthusiasm or expended little effort to improve, or only to those children who worked hard. What would you do, and why?

© Steve Debenport/iStockphoto

Winning a trophy is far more meaningful to a child when it rewards actual achievement.

### Self-Esteem and Shyness

Children who are shy express discomfort in social situations and tend to withdraw when confronted by unfamiliar people or challenging events. Shy children also typically have low levels of self-esteem (Fordham & Stevenson-Hinde, 1999). Cultural differences, however, affect the acceptability of shyness; shyness and social withdrawal from peers is less acceptable in Western European cultures than in some Asian cultures (Chen & French, 2008). Most research on children in Western cultures indicates that children who are shy and socially withdrawn during middle childhood risk being rejected by peers (Rubin, Cheah, & Menzer, 2010). They are also at risk of developing mental health problems during adolescence (Prior, Smart, Sanson, & Oberklaid, 2001; Rubin, Coplan, & Bowker, 2009).

Are shy children helped by having a friend? In general, children who are shy tend to have difficulty forming many friendships, and when they do, are likely to befriend other withdrawn children (Rubin et al., 2009). They often rate the quality of their friendships as poor.

They regard these relationships as involving less fun and help than do other children their age. Because children who are shy have fewer social interactions with peers, they have less opportunity to expand their range of social skills. Therefore, shy children tend to become increasingly anxious and withdrawn as they enter adolescence (Oh et al., 2008). This is especially true for boys, as shyness is less socially acceptable in boys than in girls. Boys who are shy tend to be excluded by peers, more so than girls (Rubin, Copian, Chen, Bowker, & McDonald, 2011).

Several types of interventions have been found to help shy and socially withdrawn children (Schneider, 1992; Smith, Jordan, Flood, & Hansen, 2010). One involves modeling, based on *social learning theory*, in which children view demonstrations of ways to interact with others. A second incorporates coaching: Children are given verbal instructions and feedback about their interactions. A third focuses on social problem solving. Here, children discuss problems they typically encounter and ways to consider these problems that take into account the perspective of others. Each of these approaches offers a way of helping shy children improve their social interactions, which in turn will help them raise their self-esteem.

**CHECK YOUR PROGRESS**

1. What is the difference between the I-self and the me-self?
2. How does children's sense of self change during middle childhood?
3. What are the developmental changes in children's view of gender during this period?
4. What are some ways adults can influence a child's sense of self-esteem?

# Relating to Others

**[ KEY QUESTION ] 3.** What contributes to positive relationships with peers and parents during middle childhood?

As we have noted, during middle childhood, the circle of individuals with whom children interact continues to widen rapidly, and their relationships with others become more and more important. School—with its myriad peers, activities, and expectations—assumes an ever more central role (Stevenson, Hofer, & Randel, 2000). Friendships and other peer relationships are a significant part of the lives of school-age children. Interactions in the family also continue to influence children's development. In this section, we discuss all these types of relationships. We begin by considering changes in the brain that relate to psychosocial development in middle childhood. We go on to discuss how children's understanding of others grows during this period.

**THE DEVELOPING BRAIN**

## The Social Brain

Neuroscientists have become increasingly aware of the role that the brain plays in psychosocial development (Insel, 2010; Olson & Dweck, 2009; Posner & Rothbart, 2007). In fact, some researchers today focus on the neural basis of emotions, personality, and mood in an approach that has been called *affective neuroscience* (Bear, Connors, and Paradiso, 2007). Research in this area is particularly important to gaining an understanding of development during the middle-childhood years, when children's social world expands rapidly, and so we give it special attention here.

Today's neuroscientists view the parts of the brain associated with social processing as a series of systems making up the **social brain** (Purves et al., 2012; Ratey, 2001). The social brain offers a good example of the idea that *brain systems* (combinations of

**social brain** Brain systems that combine to control various aspects of social processing.

brain areas), rather than single brain locations, control behavior. When tasks are complex, the distribution of activity throughout the brain necessary to complete them is wide (Goleman, 2006). As one researcher points out, "There is no single site controlling social interaction anywhere within the brain. Rather, the social brain is a set of distinct but fluid wide-ranging neural networks that synchronize around relating to others. It operates at the system level, where far-flung neural networks are coordinated to serve a unifying purpose" (Goleman, 2006, p. 324).

There is no universally agreed-on map for the social brain, and many brain structures are involved in social skills (Beer & Ochsner, 2006). Several networks, called *nodes*, appear to be involved in different aspects of social interactions (Anderson, 2012; Nelson, Leibenluft, McLure, & Pine, 2005). One is the *detection node*. It involves several brain areas responsive to social signals, such as facial expressions. A second is the *affective node*, which attaches emotional significance to social stimuli. A third is the *cognitive-regulatory mode*, which is involved in cognitive control over emotions, as well as in the evaluation of social situations, including recognizing the knowledge and perspectives of others (Guyer, Choate, Pine, & Nelson, 2012). As you can see in Figure 13.3, these nodes involve different areas of the brain. The three nodes work together.

You should not be surprised to learn that these various brain structures become increasingly efficient during the middle-childhood years (Choudhury, Blakemore, & Charman, 2006; Pelphrey & Carter, 2008). Indeed, much work by neuroscientists on brain changes in social perception and social understanding of others now focuses on middle childhood, because the network of brain regions responsive to social interactions appears to experience extended growth during this period. This is especially true with regard to greater interconnectivity of brain areas and more extensive patterns of axon

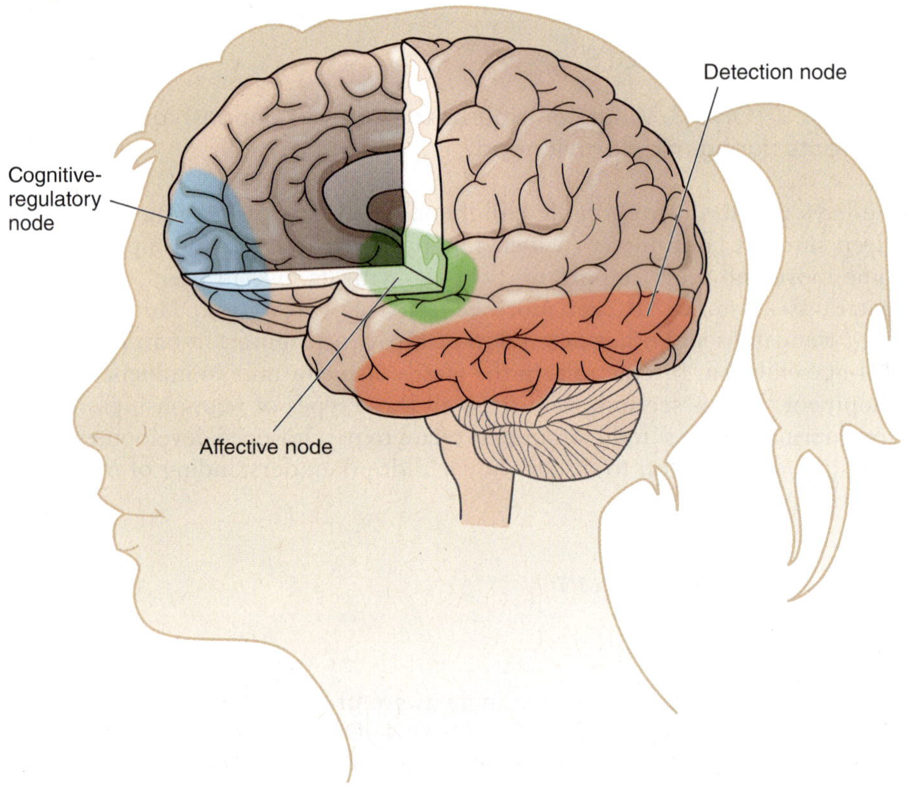


**FIGURE 13.3 The Social Brain** Researchers have proposed that the social brain includes three nodes, which work together in social perception. The detection node, toward the back and rear of the brain, picks up social signals, such as facial expressions. The affective node, deep inside the brain, attaches emotional significance to those signals. The cognitive-regulatory mode, in the prefrontal area, enables children to think about social interactions and control emotions.

## Focus On: Antonio Damasio

Affective neuroscience continues to uncover new data that may someday lead to further breakthroughs in understanding the brain. A leader in this work is Antonio Damasio (1994, 1999, 2003, 2007), director of the Institute for the Study of the Brain and Creativity at the University of Southern California. Damasio has focused his research on the neural basis of language, memory, cognition, and emotions. Contrary to the traditional view that emotion and reason are opposing forces, Damasio argues that feeling is not the enemy of reason, but is, instead, its accomplice. His research and writings have been a major force in promoting the thinking that feelings and reason are strongly connected.

From his work with patients with brain injuries, Damasio came to realize that critical neural networks on which feelings depend include not only traditionally recognized sites, such as the limbic system, but also areas in the frontal cortex. To function successfully in a complex social environment, people require a wide range of knowledge, as well as reasoning strategies. Knowledge and reasoning, in turn, depend on regions located in various parts of the brain.

Damasio (2003) believes that research such as his has powerful practical implications. Understanding the biology of emotions can contribute to the effective treatment of some major causes of human suffering, among them depression, pain, and drug addiction. Such knowledge also opens a broader view of human beings, one that incorporates the social sciences, cognitive science, and biology.

myelination (Gogtay et al., 2004; Hadad, Maurer, & Lewis, 2011; Supekar, Musen, & Menon, 2009). It is important to keep in mind, too, that social experiences, such as those requiring children to interpret someone else's facial expressions and imagine how that person might be feeling in a particular situation, also enhance their brain development (Choudhury et al., 2006). In addition, as we discuss in the accompanying Focus On feature and the following What Happens in the Brain?, emotions and reason often work together in the brain.

## Understanding Others

A number of researchers have investigated how children come to understand social interactions. Here, we discuss two important theories: the social information processing model and social perspective taking. First, however, we revisit an important component of social understanding: children's theory of mind. Recall from Chapter 10 that *theory of mind* refers to children's understanding of their own mental states and those of others. As you would expect, middle-childhood youngsters are much more aware of their own thinking than younger children.

### Theory of Mind in Middle Childhood

As explained in Chapter 10, false belief tasks are often used to assess theory of mind. Young children generally have success with first-order false belief tasks, such as the Sally-Anne task described in Chapter 10, at around 4 years of age. Not until middle childhood do they succeed with second-order false belief tasks. In first-order false belief tasks, children are asked to make inferences about someone else's incorrect belief about a *fact* (such as the location of the ball in the Sally-Anne task). In second-order tasks, children are asked questions about one person's belief about another person's belief. In one of the early studies of such beliefs, children were presented with the following story, which includes several episodes and a question (Perner & Wimmer, 1985, p. 441):

> *This is a story about John and Mary who live in this village. This morning John and Mary are together in the park. In the park there is also an ice cream man in his van.*
>
> **Episode 1.** *Mary would like to buy some ice cream but she has left her money at home. So she is very sad. "Don't be sad," says the ice-cream man, "you can fetch your money and buy some*

# What Happens in the Brain

## Emotional Self-Regulation in Middle Childhood

You might recall a time during your middle-childhood years when you had to regulate your emotional response to an exciting or distressing event. Maybe you "made the team" or failed to, won or lost an election for class office, or received an unexpectedly high or low grade on an important test. Children at this age face more and more situations in which they must regulate their emotions. Fortunately, over the course of middle childhood, they get better and better at it (Thomson, 2011; Woltering & Lewis, 2009).

In Chapter 7, we discussed the limbic system as the brain network responsible for emotion. Researchers sometimes describe this "neural architecture" of emotion in terms of two interconnected systems (Dennis, O'Toole, & DeCicco, 2013):

- The *ventral system* includes several subcortical structures, including the thalamus, the hypothalamus, and the amygdala, that provide rapid processing of emotion. This is often referred to as the "bottom-up" system.
- The *dorsal system* includes cortical structures, such as the cingulate gyrus, the orbitofrontal gyrus, and the hippocampus, that support the deliberate regulation of emotion. This is often referred to as the "top-down" system.

We can think of the basic experience of emotion as a bottom-up activity and the regulation of emotion as a top-down activity. For example, suppose 9-year-old Andrei is losing a chess game he really wants to win. He may experience several basic emotions, such as sadness and anger, through the bottom-up system. But—unlike a 3-year-old—he will work to regulate his feelings through the top-down system. One way to do this is by using positive reappraisal. For example, he might reappraise the importance of the game, saying to himself, "It's just a game—it's not really that important." Or he might consider potential benefits of losing the game, thinking, "I can learn from the mistakes I make this time so next time I play I'll win."

When children work to control their emotions, especially using coping strategies like positive reappraisal, the connections between the ventral and the dorsal systems strengthen and become more effective (Perlman & Pelphrey, 2011). As children get older, this connectivity grows stronger and becomes even more efficient. In this way, cognition and emotion increasingly work together as children progress through middle childhood.

inesbazdar/123F

Sean De Burca/Corbis

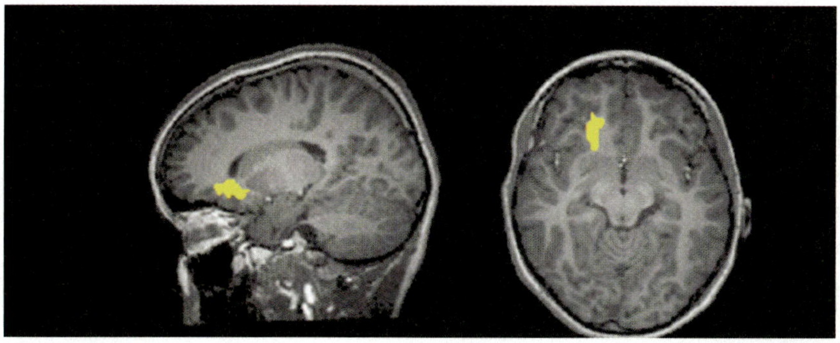

The yellow highlights in these brain scans (side and top views) show the connection between areas in the frontal lobe and the amygdala that become active when children try to regulate their emotions (Perlman & Pelphrey, 2011). This connectivity increases during middle childhood.

Perlman, S. B., & Pelphrey, K. A. (2011). Developing connections for affective regulation: Age-related changes in emotional brain connectivity. Journal of Experimental Child Psychology, 108(3), 607-620. doi:10.1016/j.jecp.2010.08.006

## Regulating Emotions: The Dorsal System

Top-down (dorsal) structures, including the hippocampus, cingulate gyrus, and orbitofrontal gyrus, are involved in a number of higher-level functions, including the deliberate regulation of emotion. When a child losing a game he wants to win tries to control his primary emotional responses by reappraising the situation, he is using top-down structures.

## Experiencing Emotions: The Ventral System

Bottom-up (ventral) structures, including the thalamus, hypothalamus, and amygdala, relay sensory information, primary emotions (such as joy, sadness, and fear), and physiological responses to these emotions. A child losing a game he badly wants to win, for example, may experience the primary emotions of anger and sadness.

Sean De Burca/Corbis

**social information processing model** An information processing model that identifies the steps in perceiving and responding to social information.

*ice cream later. I'll be here in the park all afternoon." "Oh good," says Mary, "I'll be back in the afternoon to buy some ice cream. I'll make sure I won't forget my money then."*

***Episode 2.*** *So Mary goes home.... She lives in this house. She goes inside the house. Now John is on his own in the park. To his surprise he sees the ice-cream man leaving the park in his van. "Where are you going?" asks John. The ice-cream man says, "I'm going to drive my van to the church. There is no one in the park to buy ice cream; so perhaps I can sell some outside the church."*

***Episode 3.*** *The ice cream man drives over to the church. On his way he passes Mary's house. Mary is looking out of the window and spots the van. "Where are you going?" she asks. "I'm going to the church. I'll be able to sell more ice cream there," answers the man. "It's a good thing I saw you," says Mary. Now John doesn't know that Mary talked to the ice cream man. He doesn't know that!*

***Episode 4.*** *Now John has to go home. After lunch he is doing his homework. He can't do one of the tasks. So he goes over to Mary's house to ask for help. Mary's mother answers the door. "Is Mary in?" asks John. "Oh," says Mary's mother, "She just left. She said she was going to get an ice cream.*

*Test question: So John runs to look for Mary. Where does he think she has gone?*



During middle childhood, usually by age 10 or so, children have success using the reasoning required by this type of story. They can reason that based on what John believes about Mary's beliefs, he infers that Mary has gone to the park, even though he knows that the van is at the church. In other words, John thinks that Mary has a false belief about the location of the van (although, in fact, Mary knows where the van really is).

Children who have better use of language about inner states (who use terms like *reflect*, *imagine*, and *believe*) have more success with second-order false belief tasks (Grazzani & Ornaghi, 2012). Children's general ability to hold information in mind also relates to their ability to succeed with this type of task (Olson, 2012). Children's theory of mind thus draws on their cognitive skills, but uses them in a way that promotes social development and understanding of others. During middle childhood, children have a much better idea of what other people are thinking, and of why they are thinking or feeling as they do (Flavell et al., 2002; Weimer, Sallquist, & Bolnick, 2012). Their ability to identify and judge the characteristics of other children becomes critical as they build their network of friends.

## The Social Information-Processing Model

Social interaction is actually a very complex process. The **social information-processing model** (Crick & Dodge, 1994) offers one way to understand this process. The model, like the more general information-processing model discussed in earlier chapters, focuses on *what* information children represent; *how* children represent, store, and retrieve this information; *how* these representations guide their behaviors; and *what* mechanisms lead to changes in these processes across development (Munakata, 2006). All of these aspects of the model show increased efficiency and development during the middle-childhood period. The model, shown in Figure 13.4, includes six steps that children go through as they perceive and respond to social information:

1. Encode social cues. For example: "By the look on his face, I can tell that Kenji is trying to tell me something."
2. Interpret social cues. For example: "Do Kenji's facial expressions show anger or humor?"
3. Clarify the goals of the social interaction. For example: "I don't want to get into a fight with Kenji."

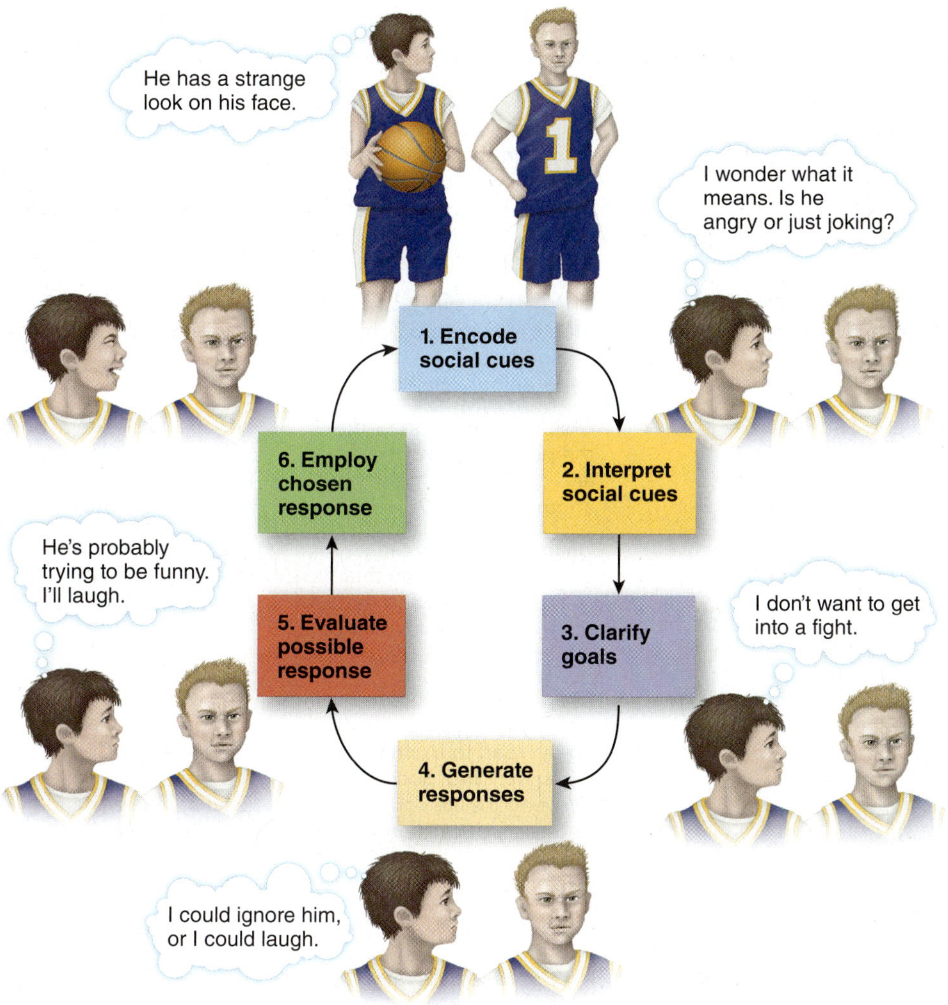


**FIGURE 13.4 The Social Information-Processing Model** According to the social information-processing model, children go through six steps in perceiving and responding to social information. At each step, their response depends in part on their internal store of information and experience.

4. Generate possible responses. For example: "I could ignore him or I could laugh."
5. Evaluate a selected response. For example: "I think I'll laugh, because I believe that Kenji is just trying to be funny."
6. Employ the chosen response. For example, laugh.

The results may be positive (Kenji is amused) or negative (Kenji is angry), and the encoding and interpretation of Kenji's response begins the cycle again. This sequence of steps is then stored in long-term memory to be accessed again in similar situations.

Examining the steps involved in social interaction can be useful in helping children who are having difficulty with their peer relationships. By reviewing the steps, you might see how an adult could guide a child by interpreting another child's behavior, providing examples of possible responses, and helping him or her think about what another child's reactions might be to those responses.

## what if...?

One morning, you are supervising children on a playground. It is a very sunny day, and you notice that Raymond is squinting whenever he faces east, because the sun is very bright from that direction. Geraldo interprets Raymond's squint as making fun of him and so Geraldo tries to trip Raymond as he runs by him, and says, "Stop making faces at me." How could you help the two boys understand each other's behavior by using the social information-processing model?

**Table 13.1** Development of Social Perspective Taking

| Level | Social Perspective | Nature of Friendships |
|---|---|---|
| Level 0: Egocentric viewpoint (Ages 3–6) | Children don't distinguish their own social perspective from those of others. | Friendship depends on physical proximity, such as being in the same preschool, and is often based on having similar behavioral tendencies. |
| Level 1: Social-informational perspective taking (ages 6–8) | Children are aware that others may have different perspectives but tend to focus on only their own. | Friendship depends on enjoying similar activities. |
| Level 2: Self-reflective perspective taking (ages 8–10) | Children can acknowledge the perspectives of others and can put themselves in another's place. | Friendship depends on having desirable interactions and on developing mutual trust. |
| Level 3: Mutual perspective taking (ages 10–12) | Children can view the differences between their own perspective and that of others from the viewpoint of a third-person observer. | Friendship includes mutual interests and sharing of ideas. |
| Level 4: Social and conventional perspective taking (ages 12–15+) | Children realize that mutual perspective taking does not always lead to a common understanding. Social conventions are considered necessary because they are understood by all. | Friendship depends on open and flexible relationships. Close friendships involve a level of intimacy and self-disclosure. |

*Sources:* Selman, R. L. (1976). Social-cognitive understanding: A guide to educational and clinical practice. In T. Lickona (Ed.), *Moral development and behavior: Theory, research, and social issues* (pp. 299–316). New York: Holt, Rinehart, & Winston; Selman, R. L. (1980). *The growth of interpersonal understanding: Developmental and clinical analyses.* New York: Academic Press.

*KidStock/Blend Images/Getty Images*

Over the course of middle childhood, children grow increasingly skilled at understanding the perspectives of others, and their friendships reflect this development.

## Social Perspective Taking

With their deepening comprehension of the thoughts and behaviors of others, children come to realize that other points of view exist. Robert Selman (1980) has described this development in his theory of **social perspective taking**. As you can see from Table 13.1, children advance over time in their social perspective-taking ability. They begin with an egocentric view, assuming others have the same perspective they do. As they advance through different levels of understanding, their friendships take on new characteristics.

During the middle-childhood years, children typically progress through several levels as their ability to recognize the perspectives of others advances. At first, they may be aware that others have different perspectives, but they tend to focus only on their own. Next, they move into a period when they begin to "step into the shoes" of another as they work on understanding that person's perspective. For example, they might say, "I know why you might think I ignored you, but really, I didn't see you." Toward the end of middle childhood, they can often view differences between their own perspective and that of another person from a third position, that of an onlooker. For example, you might hear a child at this stage say, "I can see why Taro thought we were both wrong when we were arguing about which basketball shot showed the most skill."

# Interacting with Peers

As we've seen, children's growing ability to understand others contributes to their ability to form peer relationships. Peer relationships, in turn, contribute to feelings

**social perspective taking** The ability to take into account the perspective of others in a social interaction.

of belonging and security, critical building blocks for typical social development (Berndt, 2004). As children grow and mature during the middle-childhood years, they establish a network of influential peer relationships that becomes a major focus of their lives.

Peer relationships during the middle-childhood years become more intense. Children feel strongly that they must get along with their friends. That, in turn, forces them to think about their relationships—a major step in social development. Furthermore, as we've seen, cognitive development enables children to make more complex judgments about the behavior of others. They become more astute at unmasking meaning in facial expressions and the way something is said.

Developmental psychologists have consistently maintained that experiences with peers are a key element for children. Children differ, however, in how they are regarded by their peers. In Chapter 10, we discussed research in which children are deemed to be *popular*, *rejected*, or *neglected*. In the middle-childhood years, children continue to confront what these statuses mean.

**popularity-by-decency** A type of popularity based on being kind and fun to be with.

**popularity-by-dominance** A type of popularity based on power.

## Popular Children

Popular children rank high in acceptance and low in rejection (Rubin, Bukowski, & Parker, 2006). Children may become popular for different reasons. Some well-liked children are kind and fun to be with. Researchers have described their popularity as **popularity-by-decency** (Rubin & Burgess, 2002). Other children are popular because of their power. They may be attractive, outstanding athletes, or simply larger or tougher than their classmates. Their popularity has been described as **popularity-by-dominance**.

© kali9/iStockphoto

Children are popular for various reasons, but in general, children who are well liked have the ability to establish and maintain positive relationships.

In general, popularity, especially popularity-by-decency, depends on the ability to establish and maintain positive relationships. For example, popular children tend not to be excessively egocentric. They don't talk constantly about themselves, and they typically have good social perspective-taking skills (Hoglund, LaLonde, & Leadbeater, 2008; Leadbeater & Hoglund, 2009). Popular children may be assertive on occasion, but they rarely disrupt the actions and goals of others (Rubin et al., 2006). Finally, during the middle-childhood years, loyalty becomes an important characteristic, and children expect friends to understand them and be loyal in their support of them.

## Rejected Children

Children who are disliked by their peers are classified as rejected. Peer rejection may result in insecurity, difficulty with future interpersonal interaction, and future antisocial behaviors (Asher & McDonald, 2009; Higgins, Piquero, & Piquero, 2011; Ladd, Herald-Brown, & Reiser, 2008).

Using brain imaging, neuroscientists have studied what happens in the brain when school-age children encounter peer rejection (Williams & Jarvis, 2006). In this approach, a child plays a computer game called Cyberball with two virtual players. Each player throws and catches a virtual ball to the other players. The game has two key elements. First, "fair play" involves an equal number of throws to each player, including the child. Second, the "rejection" element involves a period when the two virtual players throw to each other but leave out the child. That element is thought to simulate social rejection.

Brain scans of adults who play this game indicate that during the rejection part of the game, the areas of the brain that respond are the same as those that typically respond to physical pain (Eisenberger & Lieberman, 2004). The results for 8- to 12-year-olds were similar (Crowley, Wu, Molfese, & Mayes, 2010). The children's brains did not respond exactly like the adults' brains, though. Adults showed greater activity in the left hemisphere, in comparison with the right hemisphere. The researchers speculate that adults have a greater capacity to use coping skills during social rejection, producing more activity in the left hemisphere of the frontal lobe. In general, the Cyberball study indicates that children have specific neural responses to social rejection, and that those responses are similar to those experienced during physical pain, but they change with development.

Vicky Kasala/Getty Images

Neglected children tend to be excluded from peer groups and activities. It is not so much that they are disliked but that they are ignored by their peers.

### Neglected Children

Some children are neither liked nor disliked by peers but nevertheless are not included in peer social groups and activities. These children are considered to be neglected. While the status of children who are popular or rejected tends to remain stable over the middle-childhood years, children who are neglected at one point in time may become either popular or rejected at another point in time (Ladd & Burgess, 1999). In the first case, they may develop interests that make them more accepted by their peers. In the second, they may show behaviors that their peers interpret as exceedingly aggressive or demanding, leading to rejection.

*Everyday stories*

FROM NEGLECTED TO POPULAR When Mariella was 8 years old, she was very shy. Few children in her classroom spontaneously chose to include her in their groups on the playground or at lunch. Fortunately, Mariella really enjoyed music, and that same year she began to learn how to play the drums. When she was 11, she finally got up the nerve to play the drums in a school talent show. As a result, several of the children in her class were quite impressed with her talent and asked her to join them in putting together a band. Mariella found that her shyness receded as she began to play music with others, and she became increasingly popular as she entered middle school.

Children who remain neglected or rejected throughout middle childhood are susceptible to mental health issues like depression, both in later childhood and in adolescence (Gooren, van Lier, Stegge, Terwogt, & Koot, 2011; Hoglund et al., 2008). Thus, it is important that adults help them to improve their social skills in the middle-childhood period (Mikami, Lerner, Griggs, McGrath, & Calhoun, 2010). A number of studies have focused on teaching positive social skills to children who are neglected or rejected, and these have met with some success (Asher & Hymel, 1986). A different approach is to study all children in a classroom, not just the neglected or rejected ones. In one such study (Mikami, Boucher, & Humphreys, 2005), children were divided into groups, each with a mix of socially accepted and rejected children. The groups then played a series of cooperative games. To succeed, all the members in each group had to cooperate with one another. For example, in one game, each group had to build a tower out of spaghetti and marshmallows using only one hand. This type of intervention was successful in improving positive peer relationships in the classroom and making children who had been rejected more accepted by their peers.

## Interacting with Parents

As we have emphasized in other chapters, socialization is bidirectional. Parents certainly affect their children's psychosocial development, but children themselves bring their own social and emotional skills to these interactions. Children can provoke or soothe others in their families, and such interactions are dynamic. So as we examine parenting behaviors and, later, sibling relationships, recall that these interactions are not a one-way street (Gruesec et al., 2012). Each member of the family system influences the others (Broderick, 1993).

Although children expand their network of relationships during middle childhood, parents remain central to their well-being. In raising their children during these eventful years, most parents have similar goals: They want their children to understand themselves as individuals, to achieve their full potential, to acquire a sense of self-esteem based on achievement, to relate well to others, and to develop high moral standards. Individual parents may, of course, have different ideas about how to achieve these goals, resulting in a variety of approaches.

**tripartite model** A model that describes three roles that parents can play in their children's development: interactive partner, direct instructor, and provider of opportunities.

## Parenting Roles

One way that parents vary is in their enactment of the three roles they play in relation to their children's psychosocial development. According to the **tripartite model**, shown in Figure 13.5, a parent may act as an interactive partner, a direct instructor, and a provider of opportunities (Parke & Buriel, 2006; Parke, Burks, Carson, Neville, & Boyum, 1994).

- As *interactive partners*, parents participate in their children's daily activities and share in decision making. In this role, parents express mutuality, responsiveness, cooperation, and positive affect, such as laughing with or smiling at their children (Deater-Deckard, Atzaba-Poria, & Pike, 2004).
- As *instructors*, parents may see themselves as coaches, teachers, or supervisors. They may give advice, offer support, and suggest strategies for various social situations, such as forming new relationships and handling conflicts. As stabilizing forces, parents maintain daily routines and rituals, such as family celebrations, that provide consistency in children's daily lives and offer a sense of predictability and stability (Parke & Clarke-Stewart, 2011).
- As *providers of opportunities*, parents present new challenges to children as they progress through the school years. They act as managers of possibilities for widening social contacts and planning new experiences (Dotterer, McHale, & Crouter, 2009).

Playing all of these roles can help parents to establish an environment that encourages children to develop positive relationships with peers and adult contacts (McDowell & Parke, 2009; Parke & Buriel, 2006).

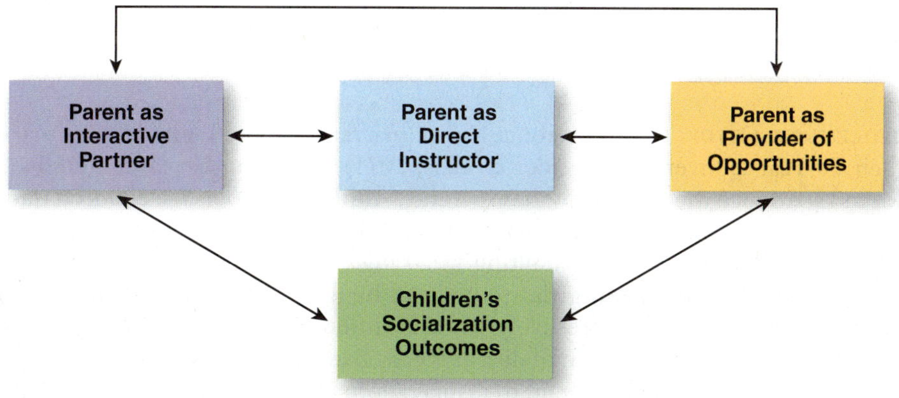


FIGURE 13.5 **The Tripartite Model of Parent-Child Interactions** The three roles that parents may play with their children are designed to lead to positive socialization outcomes.

Adapted from Parke et al., 1994, in Parke, R. D., & Buriel, R. (2006).

## Parenting Styles

We referred earlier to the parenting styles discussed in Chapter 10, pointing out that the authoritative parenting style produced the best results for children's self-esteem during middle childhood. In general during middle childhood, if parents are warm, responsive, fair, and consistent disciplinarians, their children will likely have better relations with peers than children whose parents are harsh and rejecting or overly permissive.

Three dimensions of parenting behavior have been found to be especially important during middle childhood (Kuppens, Grietens, Onghena, & Michiels, 2009):

- *Parental support* involves emotional availability, warmth, and responsiveness. Parents who show high levels of support listen as their child describes difficulties with friends or at school. These parents are also affectionate with their child.
- *Parental behavioral control* involves setting rules and teaching socially and culturally appropriate behaviors for different situations. For example, parents may encourage a child to make eye contact upon meeting a new person and to thank someone for a gift.
- *Parental psychological control* involves attempts to manipulate a child's thoughts, emotions, and feelings (Barber, 1996; Grolnick & Pomerantz, 2009). Parents often do this by pressuring and dominating a child, invalidating a child's feelings (such as by saying, "You shouldn't feel that way"), withholding affection, or withdrawing from the child.

KidStock/Blend Images/Getty Images

Parental support—which includes being available, warm, and responsive—is especially important during the middle-childhood years.

As you might expect, support and behavioral control result in positive child behavior. Psychological control, in contrast, can result in behavior problems, such as aggression or withdrawal; children's peer relationships are negatively affected as well (Barber, 1996; Grolnick & Pomerantz, 2009; Miller, Tserakhava, & Miller, 2011; Rubin & Burgess, 2002).

## Family Structure

Children are raised in many different family structures. In addition to families in which a married mother and father raise children, there are many families in which one parent raises children alone, either by choice or because of divorce or the death of the other parent. Blended families are often created by parents who are divorced and remarried and have children from earlier marriages. Gay and lesbian parents raise children who may be biologically related to one or both parents or who may be adopted. A child may experience several different structures growing up, including living in a single-parent household as the result of divorce, or with a parent's new spouse and step-siblings. What do we know about the effects of these various family structures on the psychosocial development of children during middle childhood?

**Children and Divorce.** Only about half of marriages in the United States make it to their 20-year anniversary (Kreider & Ellis, 2011), meaning that large numbers of children experience the divorce of their parents. Although school-age children understand what divorce means better than younger children, they are, nevertheless, emotionally upset by divorce, often resulting in a range of behavior problems (Weyer & Sandler, 1998). Both boys and girls are affected by divorce (Amato, 2010), although some studies show that they are likely to react differently. Boys tend to show more *externalizing problems*, in the form of disruptive, aggressive, oppositional, and hyperactive behaviors. In contrast, girls tend to display more *internalizing problems*, marked by highly emotionally reactive, anxious, depressed, or withdrawn behaviors (Hakvoort, Bos, Van Balen, & Hermanns, 2011). These reactions occur both because of the parental discord that the children may have witnessed and because of the many changes divorce brings about in the children's lives (Amato, 2010).

Divorce usually affects children's access to both parents, with major declines especially in the father-daughter relationship (Amato, 2010). Even when parents are physically present, they may not be as emotionally available to their children as they were before (Sutherland, Altenhofen, & Biringen, 2012). Further, household income often decreases after divorce, and economic pressures can produce additional negative consequences for children (Hetherington & Kelly, 2002; Sayer, 2006). Divorced parents often need to work more hours, which can result in less time spent with their children (Hetherington, 2006). Nevertheless, many children adjust to these changes within a few years of the divorce. In addition, if the divorce results in less discord between parents, children often have better psychosocial behaviors after the divorce than before or during the divorce (Harvey & Fine, 2010).

Many divorced adults remarry. National statistics indicate that half of all marriages are a remarriage for one or both partners (U.S. Census Bureau, 2000). Remarriage often paves a road out of poverty for divorced women and their children (Hetherington, 2006), and therefore improves the economic circumstances for children. Remarriage can, however, bring its own set of stressors on children. Families are often blended, and children have to learn to live with other children they may not know well, nor like. As a result, some children disengage from family activities and choose to affiliate with an antisocial peer group (Hetherington, 1999). In general, the psychosocial adjustment of children in stepfamilies where all the children are biologically related (such as from a mother's or a father's first marriage) is more positive than that of children in families where unrelated children are brought together (Hetherington, 2006).

**Children in Gay and Lesbian Families.** An increasing number of children in the United States are being raised in gay and lesbian households. The 2000 U.S. census included information on 600,000 same-gender, unmarried-partner couples (U.S. Census Bureau, 2003). In these households, 22% of gay couples and 34% of lesbian couples reported being involved in parenting. This is most likely an underestimate, however, because no information about single gay and lesbian individuals who are raising children was included in the census data, and many of these individuals are also parenting children.

Ruai Von Briel/Photo Edit

Few differences have been found to exist between children raised in gay and lesbian households and those raised by heterosexual parents.

What do we know about the psychosocial effects on children of being raised in a gay or lesbian household? Many studies indicate that few differences exist between these children and those raised in households with heterosexual parents (Goldberg, 2010; Tasker & Patterson, 2007). The psychosocial development of children in gay and lesbian families is similar to that of children in heterosexual families, as well (Goldberg, 2010). In addition, their gender role development is typical (Golombok, 2006; Rivers, Poteat, & Noret, 2008). In relation to parenting, some studies have found that co-mothers are more actively involved in parenting than many fathers in heterosexual families (Bos, van Balen, & van den Boom, 2007; Tasker & Patterson, 2007). In gay and lesbian families, we can predict positive development when parents enjoy playing with their children (Ryan, 2007), set appropriate limits (Bos et al., 2007), and explain rules (Bigner & Jacobsen, 1989). These are the same processes that are important to the psychosocial development of all children, no matter what their family structure.

## Supporting Children's Well-Being After Divorce — Parenting

Divorce sets in motion a cascade of events that can threaten children's well-being. Children may face a physical move that affects both their neighborhood relationships and their school friendships. They may receive less financial support and have less access to either or both parents (Lamb & Malloy, 2013). It is their parents' reactions to the dissolution of the marriage, however, that appear to be most central to children's psychosocial adjustment during this period. What do we know about critical aspects of parenting after divorce?

Divorce requires a period of family reorganization. This reorganization affects the adaptation of all members of the family. Many divorces occur in the midst of hostile conflict between parents. Such conflict often concerns the division of property, financial support, child custody, and child visitation—all issues related to children (Bonach, 2005). If the conflict continues after the divorce, children are likely to adjust poorly (Hakvoort et al., 2011). And if parents involve their children in the conflict, the children often show symptoms of psychopathology (Bing, Nelson, & Wesolowski, 2009; Kelly, 2000). They may feel guilty and develop symptoms of anxiety and depression. In addition, when parents continue to be hostile to one another, the emotional resources they need for parenting are often diminished (Sarrazin, & Cyr, 2007). This can affect children in several ways. Parents may be less sensitive to the needs of their children, and therefore the children may experience their parents as less caring. Parents may also have less time to provide appropriate supervision and guidance to their children, and instead develop inconsistent or ineffective styles of discipline, resulting in behavior problems in the children (Hakvoort et al., 2011).

© Tetra Images/Corbis

When the conflict that generally accompanies a divorce continues even after the papers have been signed, children are likely to adjust poorly.

Studies of children who manage well after experiencing parental divorce indicate that their parents have maintained a warm and caring style of interacting with them (Sandler, Miles, Cookston, & Braver, 2008; Wolchik, Wilcox, Tein, & Sandler, 2000). That style, which includes acceptance, encouragement, and support of the child, also facilitates effective discipline (Sigal, Sandler, Wolchik, & Braver, 2011). Children fare better when their parents use fair, appropriate, and consistent discipline (Wolchik et al., 2000). Finally, as we suggested earlier, children show more positive social and emotional behaviors when their parents do not engage in hostile conflict with each other (Lamb & Malloy, 2013).

Because of the importance of parenting postdivorce, interventions have been developed to assist parents during this period. The number of programs of this type has increased dramatically during the last decade, and now 46 states offer some type of parent education program for adults involved in divorce or separation proceedings (Pollet, 2009; Sigal, Wolchik, Tein, & Sandler, 2012). In fact, some states *require* parents to attend such programs. Successful programs encourage parents to nurture warm and caring relationships with their children, develop skills to provide appropriate and consistent discipline, and understand the importance of low parental conflict to their children's well-being (Sigal et al., 2011).

## Interacting with Siblings

Jack Hollingsworth/Getty Images

Sibling relationships are a powerful force in development.

About 80 to 90% of children have siblings, and these children grow up in a special network of relationships that affects their development in unique ways (Cicirelli, 1995; Pike, Kretschmer, & Dunn, 2009). Sibling relationships are a powerful force in a child's life, since growing up with brothers and sisters is quite different from growing up without them (Kim, McHale, Crouter, & Osgood, 2007). Brothers and sisters probably spend more time with each other than they do with their parents (Volling, 2003). Their relationships last a lifetime—longer often than relationships between a parent and a child. Furthermore, although the relationship between some siblings is marked by tension and hostility, most brothers and sisters get along quite well together (Gass, Jenkins, & Dunn, 2007; Pike, Coldwell, & Dunn, 2005).

## Elements of the Sibling Relationship

If you observe the relationships among several siblings in a large family, you will often note that two of the siblings are closer to one another than to their other siblings. One explanation of this phenomenon is that sibling relationships are influenced by many factors, and that these factors are different for different sets of siblings (Furman & Buhrmester, 1992; Zukow-Goldring, 2002). The factors include age, temperament, sex, friendships outside the family, and school experiences, among others.

Two important dimensions of the sibling relationship are intimacy and power (Emery, 1992). *Intimacy* encompasses emotional components such as warmth, nurturance, and companionship. *Power* involves privileges held by one sibling and not by another. When siblings disagree on how much intimacy they want to share, and when there are power imbalances between them, conflict may result. (Emery, 1992).

*Jupiterimages, Brand X Pictures/Getty Images*

Even siblings who usually help each other and cooperate sometimes come in conflict.

## Help and Conflict in Sibling Relationships

Think of the many things that siblings do for one another. They may exchange clothes and other belongings, borrow money, help with homework, and offer support in life's crises. Younger siblings learn from the experiences of their brothers and sisters—for example, when an older sister tells a younger one what to expect from a teacher that she previously had in the fourth grade. Younger siblings also model the behaviors they see in their older siblings. Observing their behaviors and accepting some while rejecting others helps the younger siblings to develop a healthy sense of identity (Howe, Brody, & Recchia, 2006). Furthermore, siblings may form powerful coalitions, often called the *sibling underworld.* For example, older siblings can warn their younger brothers and sisters about parental moods and prohibitions.

Realistically, though, sibling relationships can also be negative. Indeed, sibling rivalry is a well-known phenomenon (Howe, Fiorentino, & Gariepy, 2003). Even siblings who help each other, share things, and frequently cooperate have conflicts. In fact, sibling conflict is one of the problems that parents most frequently report (Natsuaki, Ge, Reiss, & Neiderhiser, 2009).

Age differences often cause conflict. An older sibling can contribute to feelings of shame, guilt, and inferiority in younger siblings. Imagine the difficulty of a firstborn sibling forced to share parental attention, especially if the spacing between the children is close (less than two years). A firstborn who must also care for younger children can become increasingly resentful. At the same time, younger children often resent the advantages of older siblings. The older children may seem to share in parental power and authority, as well as enjoy such privileges as a later bedtime.

## Sibling Relationships When One Child Has a Disability

What happens when one child in a sibling relationship has a disability? Both older and younger siblings of children with disabilities often take on more helping and caregiving roles than they would with typically developing siblings (Cuskelly & Gunn, 2003). The increased responsibility of helping a brother or sister with a disability sometimes causes resentment and problem behaviors for the typically developing sibling (Hannah & Midlarsky, 1999). Often, however, the sibling who gives help develops greater levels of empathy and tolerance of differences (Dyke, Mulroy, & Leonard, 2009; Hauser-Cram, Cannarella, Tillinger & Woodman, 2013).

*Lauren Shear/Science Source*

Both older and younger siblings of children with disabilities often take on helping and caregiving roles.

Why do some children have a positive relationship with a sibling with a disability while others have a negative one? Some children may be embarrassed by the behaviors of a brother or sister with a disability (Petalas, Hastings, Nash, Dowey, & Reilly, 2009). As with other sibling relationships, family dynamics make a difference in how such embarrassment is handled. Families in which individuals solve problems and communicate with one another in warm and supportive ways provide the context for positive sibling relationships, whether or not one child has a disability (Van Riper, 2000).

INCLUDING TIA Diana has a friendship network that is much larger than that of her older sister, Tia, who has intellectual disabilities. Diana is sometimes embarrassed by Tia's struggles with understanding how to read and learn basic number skills. After discussing the matter with her parents, Diana decides to include Tia in some of the activities she enjoys with her friends, like going to movies. Diana has figured out which activities they can easily share and which ones, like playing card games, are frustrating for Tia. She empathizes with Tia's challenges in wanting to be part of the group.

*Everyday stories*

## Interacting at School

In middle childhood, children are becoming less childlike, less dependent, and less naïve while simultaneously becoming more skilled, more knowledgeable, and more cooperative (Grusec et al., 2013). School provides an important context not only for the development of children's cognitive skills but also for their psychosocial development. Indeed, the school setting requires children to interact with others in a variety of ways, and perhaps more than any other has an influence on changing children's lives.

### Schools as Contexts of Psychosocial Development

Think of the many ways in which school requires social interaction. We have already emphasized how a child's network of relationships expands in school (Perez & Gauvain, 2009). Students—particularly today, with such means of communication as cell phones, texting, and social media—interact with one another almost constantly. School also involves continuous *social comparisons* among children.

During middle childhood, children who have a sense of *belonging* in the school setting have more positive psychosocial development (Juvonen, 2006). Individual teachers make a difference in helping children feel they belong at school, but the social environment of the school plays a role as well (Blumenfeld et al., 2005). Children report feeling proud that they belong to their school when they perceive their classrooms as being low in competition among students, and where there are few conflicts among students or between students and teachers (McMahon, Wernsman, & Rose, 2009). One of the most detrimental conflicts for children involves bullying.

### Bullies at School

Have you ever experienced bullying? Most of us have, either personally or through observation. **Bullying** is a form of violence that may include physical, verbal, and/or psychological aggression, such as teasing, hitting, and manipulating others (DeVoe & Kaffenberger, 2005). Estimates are that between 10 and 30% of children are chronic victims of bullying (Giesbrecht, Leadbeater, & MacDonald, 2011). Not all bullying occurs at schools, but much of it does, and so schools have recognized the need to respond to such behavior. Across the country, many schools have resorted to hiring "recess coaches" to oversee students' free time and try to reduce bullying (Elkind, 2010).

Bullying accounts for a substantial part of the aggression that occurs in peer groups. The dimension that distinguishes bullying from other forms of aggressive behavior is its specificity—bullies direct their behavior toward only certain peers (Rubin et al., 2006). In a recent study (Veenstra, Lindenberg, Munniksma, & Dijkstra, 2010), investigators discovered that bullies themselves are not always socially rejected. Initially, some are well liked by other children because of their social dominance, but over time they often come to be disliked because of their cruelty (Vaillancourt, McDougall, Hymel, & Sunderani, 2010). Researchers also found that bullies chose victims who weren't likely to be defended by others. Victims who do have a friend who supports them often are better adjusted emotionally than those who do not (Hodges, Boivin, Vitaro, & Bukowski, 1999).

**bullying** Acts of verbal or physical aggression that are chronic and directed toward particular victims.

Bullying, as mentioned, may be physical, verbal, or emotional. It may include physical attacks, insulting comments, name-calling, making fun of victims, or refusing to have anything to do with them. It may also come in the form of **racial bullying**, which targets children because of their race or ethnicity. Yet another type is **cyberbullying**, in which bullies use e-mail, social networks, or other forms of technology to attack their victims. The intent of cyberbullies is to harass their victims night and day, seven days a week, via the Internet and other technology pathways (Patchin & Hinduja, 2011).

It is not surprising that bullying has a negative impact on the motivation, self-esteem, mental health, academic achievement, and behavior of children who are victims (Burk et al., 2011). Constant and calculated harassment can result in low self-esteem, poor academic performance, depression, and, in some cases, even suicide (Hinduja & Patchin, 2010; Kim & Leventhal, 2008; Klomek, Sourander, & Gould, 2010). Children who are bullied often enter into a cycle of low self-esteem that, in turn, leads them to view other interactions with peers in a negative way, causing additional problems in peer relationships (Cowie, 2011). Bullies themselves are at risk of continuing to use power abusively rather than finding ways of interacting equitably with others (Cowie, 2011). Those who observe, reinforce, or ignore bullying also play a role in either maintaining or stopping the behavior (Kärnä, Voeten, Poskiparta, & Salmivalli, 2010).

Researchers have analyzed bullying behavior and described it in terms of three categories (Orpinas & Horne, 2006). Table 13.2 describes these three types of bullies, as well as types of victims and bystanders.

Robin Nelson/Photo Edit

Around 32% of students report being bullied at school, leading many schools and parents to look for ways to solve this problem behavior.

**Table 13.2** Types of Bullies, Victims, and Bystanders

**Bullies**

1. *Aggressive bully:* Usually initiates the aggressive action by taking overt physical or verbal actions.
2. *Follower:* Less common than the aggressive bully, this type follows the aggressive bully's lead. Followers often use this behavior to improve their self-esteem.
3. *Relational bully:* Uses less direct forms of aggression, such as isolating or excluding another student.

**Victims**

1. *Passive victim:* Seems to be targeted by bullies for no particular reason. Such children may appear a little different because of their behavior or clothing or because they have few friends. They are typically labeled "victims."
2. *Provocative victim:* Knows the "right buttons to push" to provoke the bully's aggression (teasing, being annoying). Children who are provocative victims may be the most rejected members of a class.
3. *Relational victim:* Victim of more subtle forms of bullying, and may also be the target of rumors.

**Bystanders**

1. Part of the problem
   a. *Instigate:* Encourage bullies in their behavior.
   b. *Watch:* Witness the bullying and do nothing about it.
   c. *Are scared:* Afraid they may be next.
   d. *Feel ashamed or powerless:* Believe they lack the ability to do anything.
2. Part of the Solution
   a. *Ask for help:* Seek help from an adult.
   b. *Help defuse the problem:* Try to reduce tension.

*Source:* Based on data from Orpinas & Horne, 2006, pp. 16–23.

**racial bullying** Bullying in which children are targeted because of their race or ethnicity.

**cyberbullying** Bullying in which the perpetrator uses e-mail, social media, or other forms of technology to attack his or her victims.

### Myths About Bullying

There are many myths about bullying. You may be familiar with some of these:

- You can't do anything about bullying because it has gone on forever.
- Kids are just mean to each other.
- He didn't mean to hurt anyone.
- It was just a bad joke.
- It was a one-time thing.
- Kids will be kids.
- Bullying is wrong, but it isn't a school issue.

The problem with such myths is that when they persist, they allow bullying to occur and persist, and make schools, among other places, unsafe for many children (Cunningham, Cunningham, Ratcliffe, & Vaillancourt, 2010; Kärnä et al., 2010; McGuiness, 2007). If teachers and other adults in schools take the attitude that "kids are just mean to each other," they are, essentially, making a statement that meanness and bullying are a normal and expected part of childhood. In doing so, they accept bullying behavior and fail to protect children who are bullied. Fortunately, today, new policies are emerging to try to prevent bullying in schools.

### Anti-Bullying Legislation Policy

Surveys from the National Center for Education Statistics (NCES) indicate that around 28% of students report being bullied at school (http://nces.ed.gov/whatsnew/commissioner/remarks2011/09_22_2011.asp). As the problem of bullying has become more apparent and common, calls for legislative action to stop this behavior have become more frequent and intense. In response, parents, teachers, and political leaders are now devoting more time and attention to curbing bullying, particularly at school.

That said, to date, no federal law explicitly deals with the issue of bullying. The Safe and Drug-Free Schools and Communities Act, part of the No Child Left Behind Act, promotes school safety but does not specifically address bullying and harassment in schools. In 2005, an act that would have required states, districts, and schools to develop bullying and harassment prevention programs was introduced in Congress but failed to pass.

Antibullying legislation has had greater success at the state level. Almost all states now have enacted some type of anti-bullying law. For example, in Massachusetts, several tragic suicides led legislators to pass a bill that requires all school districts to adopt a policy prohibiting discrimination, harassment, intimidation, bullying, and cyberbullying. The law states that no student is to be subjected to any of these forms of aggression during any educational program or activity while in school, on school property, in school vehicles, at a school event, or through the use of data, telephone, or computer software. Other states have passed similar legislation. (To check whether your state has passed such a law, go to: http://www.olweus.org/public/bullying_laws.page.)

**what if...?**

Think about a time you witnessed or heard about bullying in school. Do you think that having antibullying legislation in place would have reduced or stopped the behavior? What do you think would make such legislation effective? What else could be done to stop bullying?

## ✓ CHECK YOUR PROGRESS

1. What steps does a child go through to understand an interaction with another child, according to the social information-processing model?
2. How do friendships in middle childhood differ from those in early childhood?
3. What roles do parents play in their relationship with their children during middle childhood, according to the tripartite model?
4. Describe two important aspects of the sibling relationship.
5. What are some of the effects of bullying?

# Moral Development

**[ KEY QUESTION ] 4. How does the course of moral development change over the middle-childhood years?**

As children enter middle childhood and move away from close parental supervision, they begin to make more decisions for themselves. Some of those decisions involve determining what is fair and just, while others require children to act ethically and morally. In earlier chapters, we explored several theories of moral development. You may recall that moral development involves an understanding of standards of right and wrong, as well as of what is fair and ethical. We now turn our attention to moral development in the middle-childhood years.

During middle childhood, children develop better skills of emotional regulation. These improved skills enable them to tame many impulsive actions that clash with the rules and regulations of society. Yet increasing demands are made of them as they move through this period. Pressure comes from their own knowledge that they are being compared with others, and from their own desire for peer acceptance. In addition, adults expect more of them, including adherence to moral rules.

Living in an expanding social network of peers and adults, children often face decisions that tax their knowledge and experience, particularly with regard to moral issues. Adults are often not available (or not asked) for advice, however, and so the weight of decision making falls on the children themselves. The decisions they make will be influenced by various factors: what they have learned from their parents, what they know about rules set by others, and the influence of their peers. Let's take a look at this decision-making process. We begin by revisiting two theorists discussed in earlier chapters.

## Cognitive-Developmental Theory: Piaget and Kohlberg

You may recall from Chapter 10 that both Piaget and Kohlberg wrote about children's moral development from the perspective of cognitive-developmental theory. Both emphasized children's reasoning about moral dilemmas.

Piaget claimed that in early childhood, children operate according to a *heteronomous orientation*, assuming that moral rules are ready-made and that justice is determined by adult authority. By middle childhood, however, children begin to take on an *autonomous orientation*, as they come to understand that individuals participate in making the rules of society. Piaget (1966) discussed the differences in these orientations when he wrote about how children play games with rules. When preschool-aged children play games, such as board games or card games, they regard the rules as inflexible. In contrast, during middle childhood, children begin to realize that rules can be modified. When they play games with one another, they often confer to agree on the rules, especially rules that are ambiguous. For example, in playing certain card games, they may agree on which cards are "wild," and how many points will determine the winner. Piaget discussed this as a phase when children begin to understand that rules, including rules about moral behavior, are based on decision making and mutual consent.

*Fuse/Getty Images*

During middle childhood, children often negotiate the rules they will use in playing a game, showing that they now understand how people participate in making society's rules.

**conventional level** Kohlberg's second stage of moral development. Children at this stage conform to social rules in order to maintain social order.

Inspired by Piaget, Kohlberg's theory of moral development also places children in stages. In his theory, too, children in middle childhood have advanced. You may recall that, according to Kohlberg, children are in the *preconventional* stage of moral reasoning in early childhood. That stage has two substages. In the first substage, children obey rules to obtain rewards and avoid punishments. In the second substage, they act to exchange favors with others. In Kohlberg's view, children during middle childhood enter the **conventional level** of moral development. During this phase, children continue to believe that it is important to conform to social rules, but they act less out of self-interest. Instead their concern is on promoting interpersonal cooperation and, eventually, on maintaining social order. They conform to rules to actively support the standards of family and society (Kohlberg, 1976).

The conventional level comprises substages 3 and 4, defined as follows:

- *Substage 3*. Children emphasize interpersonal cooperation. They operate according to a "good boy/good girl" mentality that is guided by such concepts as loyalty and trust. Children in this substage want to behave in ways that will enable them to maintain the affection and approval of people they care about, such as family members, friends, and often teachers or coaches. They aim to have those individuals regard them as "good." For example, a child in this stage might follow the rules of a classroom, such as putting old papers in a recycle bin, because he knows that such behavior is considered appropriate in the classroom.
- *Substage 4*. In this substage, children are interested in maintaining the social order. Children now adopt a law-and-order mentality with regard to the rules of society. They are often concerned with fulfilling duties to maintain the social order. Correct behavior, then, is based on "doing one's duty." For example, a child in this stage might try to convince other children to follow the same classroom rules, such as putting old papers in a recycle bin, by explaining to them that it is their duty to help keep the classroom uncluttered or to support the school's recycling efforts.

| Kohlberg's Stage Theory |
| --- |
| **Preconventional Stage**<br>Substage 1: Obey rules to get rewards and avoid punishments<br>Substage 2: Act to exchange favors with others |
| **Conventional Stage: Conform to Social Rules**<br>Substage 3: Aim for interpersonal cooperation<br>Substage 4: Work to maintain social order |
| **Postconventional Stage** |

*Everyday stories*

DOING THE RIGHT THING Akia and Sami are fourth graders. They have been asked to show Ashanti, a new student, around the school. Both Akia and Sami want to do this, but for different reasons. Akia wants to help Ashanti in order to help her make a smooth transition into the school by explaining the school rules to her and telling her what kind of behavior the teacher and other students will expect. Sami wants to help Ashanti because she thinks others will continue to see her as a "good citizen" if she does so. Each is operating according to the conventional stage of moral development, but Akia is reasoning like someone in substage 4, whereas Sami is showing a thought pattern typical of substage 3.

Both Piaget's and Kohlberg's writings on moral development have been praised for their acknowledgment that moral reasoning changes in systematic ways with age (Snarey & Samuelson, 2008). Their theories also acknowledge the importance of cognitive skills in children's moral reasoning. This approach to moral development, especially Kohlberg's theory, has been criticized, however, for a couple of reasons. First, children reason differently in different situations, so their moral reasoning is not consistent at a particular stage (Rest, 1979). Second, Kohlberg believed that moral action would necessarily follow from moral reasoning. Theorists have disagreed, arguing that after reasoning through a moral dilemma, a person must often then decide whether or not to act according to that reasoning (Blasi, 1983; Lapsley, 2008).

## Telling the Truth

One aspect of moral decision making faced by many children during middle childhood involves telling the truth. Is telling the truth always the best decision? Often, the answer is not clear. Researchers have found cultural differences in how children think about some of the conflicts they face in this area, as you will read about in the accompanying feature, Culture and Children's Evaluations of Truths and Lies.

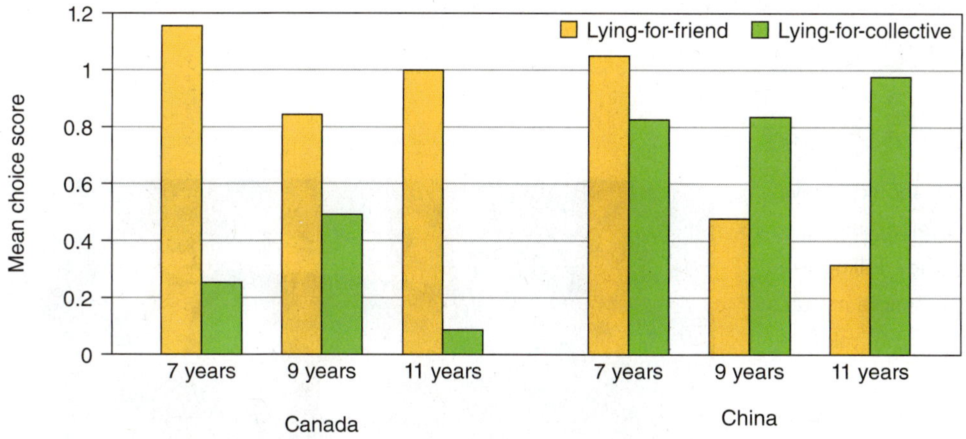


**FIGURE 13.6 Cultural Differences in Children's Evaluations of Lying** In this study, both Canadian and Chinese students viewed lying as not always wrong. That said, Chinese students were more likely to regard lying for the good of the group as less harmful, while Canadian students were more likely to see lying to help an individual as less harmful.
*Source:* Fu, G., Cameron, C. A., Xu, F., Heyman, G., & Lee, K. (2007). Cross-cultural differences in children's choices, categorizations, and evaluations of truths and lies. *Developmental Psychology, 43*(2), 278–293. APA; reprinted with permission.

Consider a common example: telling an untruth to be polite or to protect someone's feelings. A young boy who receives a gift he does not like may wonder whether it is better to be honest about the gift or to be polite and say that he likes it. You may have had a similar experience. How did you approach it? Researchers (Xu, Bao, Fu, Talwar, & Lee, 2010) have studied changes in children's lying for the sake of politeness during the middle-childhood years. In their study, children aged 7 to 11 were given a gift that they had previously said was not attractive to them. When asked about the gift, children varied in their responses according to their age. The older children were more likely than the younger ones to say they liked the gift, even though they didn't (see Figure 13.6).

In addition, the younger children who said they liked the gift did so for different reasons than the older children. When the children who had told a lie were asked why they did so, the 7-year-olds were more likely to say they were afraid of the consequences of telling the truth, such as making the gift-giver angry. The 11-year-olds were more likely to say they didn't want to hurt the gift-giver's feelings. The older children were showing evidence of more advanced perspective taking about the gift-giver's emotions. The younger children were more concerned about their own feelings, an indicator of egocentricity.

what if...?

Suppose you are attending the birthday of a 9-year-old member of your family, Lucas. You watch as he opens many gifts that he clearly enjoys. The last gift he opens is from his 5-year-old cousin who proudly says, "I chose this all by myself." The gift is a coloring book, clearly appropriate for a 5-year-old but not on the top of the desired gift list for a 9-year-old. Lucas says, "Thank you," to his cousin. What are less mature and more mature ways that Lucas may be thinking about this situation?

## Distributive Justice

Children are often very concerned with fairness during the middle-childhood years. Distributive justice, as we noted in Chapter 10, involves how actions or objects can be distributed fairly. At the beginning of middle childhood, children's idea of distributive justice is often based on equality, regardless of need or merit. In other words, fairness means that everyone gets an equal share.

Children's view of fairness takes on more complex dimensions in middle childhood (see Table 13.3). Around age 7, children begin to see fairness as based on *merit*.

## Culture and Children's Evaluations of Truths and Lies

Do children think that they should always tell the truth? When, if ever, do they believe it is acceptable to tell a lie? Telling the truth might at first seem like a simple matter. As children develop through the middle-childhood years, however, they begin to understand the complexities associated with telling the truth and lying. And those complexities may vary based on cultural perspectives.

Jeff Greenberg/Photo Edit

Studies comparing children's evaluations of truth-telling and lying reveal differences between Western and Eastern cultural traditions (Choi, Park, & Oh, 2011; Lee, Xu, Fu, Cameron, & Chen, 2001). In one study 7-, 9-, and 11-year-olds from Canada and from China were told stories about characters who lied or told the truth in a variety of circumstances (Fu, Cameron, Xu, Heyman, & Lee, 2007). In some of the stories, a character lied to benefit a group. For example, a

That is, rewards should be based on how hard someone worked. By around age 8 or 9, children regard fairness as based also on *need*, so that more should be given to those who need more (Damon, 1975, 1990). This indicates that children are showing a more complex understanding of justice. They are coming to realize that it is important to consider various aspects of a situation, such as a person's needs, to make a just decision.

### Making Moral Principles Meaningful **Practice**

How can parents, teachers, and others who work with children make moral principles meaningful? The answer to this question is found in the examples adults use in discussing moral principles and in the level of cognitive reasoning demanded. As you may recall from Chapter 12, children tend to be concrete thinkers at this age; that is, they do best when thinking about a particular scenario rather than about abstract notions of morality. They also learn by listening to the reasoning of others and justifying their own reasoning.

When adults encourage children to discuss moral questions with each other and with adults, the children can benefit from justifying their own thinking while listening and responding to the reasoning of others (Kruger, 1993). Here are three examples of how such discussions might be shaped:

- *Present examples* based on incidents at home, at school, or on the playground. For example, you could describe a situation in which a student sets off an alarm that disrupts the entire school. The teacher threatens to punish the whole class unless the offender confesses. One of the offender's friends knows the boy who did it. When

**Table 13.3** Sequence of Understanding About Distributive Justice

| Approximate Age | Reasoning About Fairness |
|---|---|
| 6 years | Fairness based on equal distribution |
| 7 years | Fairness based on merit |
| 8 years and beyond | Fairness based on need |

*Source:* Based on Damon, 1975.

child told a friend that there were no more spaces in the choir because the friend was a poor singer and would ruin the choir's chance of winning a prize. In other stories, a character lied to help an individual. For example a child told an adult that a friend was a good speller (when he really was not) to help the friend get on the class spelling team.

Both the Canadian and the Chinese students viewed lying as not always wrong, and that view became more prevalent with age. The acceptable reasons for lying, however, differed in the two groups. When a character lied to benefit a group, Chinese students saw that as less harmful than did Canadian students. In contrast, when a character lied to help an individual Canadian students regarded it as less harmful than did Chinese students. Researchers have maintained that such differences are based on cultural views of whether priority should be given to group or individual interests.

*Lawrence Migdale/Photo Researchers, Inc.*

the offender doesn't admit his guilt, what should his friend do: let the entire class be punished or tell on his friend?

- *Apply hypothetical dilemmas to real problems* to give children new perspectives. For example, suppose a girl finds it difficult to remain loyal to a friend when others are making fun of the friend because of the way she dresses. Reading and discussing stories that feature similar themes of discrimination could help this girl to stand by her principles.
- *Discuss real-life issues that a child is facing.* For example, perhaps a boy is finding it difficult to be friends with two classmates who do not like each other. When discussing this dilemma, it is important to check on the child's thinking and to probe for his suggestions of possible solutions. Being sensitive to the child's feelings and providing examples of more advanced reasoning, without overloading him with abstract information could help him find an appropriate solution to this issue.

Research has identified additional ways to discuss morality with children. In one longitudinal study of moral development, researchers observed fifth-grade children talking separately with their mothers about moral issues experienced by children (Walker, Hennig, & Krettenauer, 2000). Consider, for example, a girl who feels conflicted because she knows a friend cheated on a test. Her reasoning about this issue advanced when she and her mother compared each other's opinions and understanding as they talked about it. Children also made gains when mothers probed them by drawing out their reasoning, but not when mothers provided a great deal of information that could be perceived as lecturing.

## ✓CHECK YOUR PROGRESS

1. How do the two substages of Kohlberg's conventional level of moral development differ?
2. How do children change in their view of distributive justice from early childhood through middle childhood?
3. What are some ways that adults can help children think about and understand moral issues?

# CHAPTER SUMMARY

## Emotional Development

**[ KEY QUESTION ] 1.** How do children develop emotionally during middle childhood?

- According to psychosocial theory, children in middle childhood develop a sense of either industry or inferiority. Children who are engaged in activities important to their culture, such as schooling and friendships, during middle childhood develop in a positive direction. If they lack such engagement, they will feel inferior.
- Children express hostile aggression more than instrumental aggression during the middle-childhood period. Biology, parenting, and children's own reasoning affect levels of aggression.
- During middle childhood, most children show increasing levels of prosocial behavior.
- Children who show more prosocial behavior in this period tend to be more consistent in their reactions, to have an array of social skills, to have better logical skills, and be less egocentric.
- One way children improve in their emotional regulation is by learning effective coping strategies to deal with stress. Children gradually learn to distinguish controllable and uncontrollable stressors. Children's development in metacognitive skills allows them to consider a range of coping strategies.

## Relating to One's Self

**[ KEY QUESTION ] 2.** How does children's self-awareness change during the middle-childhood period?

- William James distinguished the I-self as the "knower or thinker" and the me-self as the "object of judgment." Children begin to distinguish between these two selves during middle childhood.
- Children begin to view themselves in more complex ways during this period. Their ability to make social comparisons with others influences both their self-descriptions and their self-evaluations.
- In middle childhood, children develop more flexible ideas about stereotypical sexual behavior. Still, they tend to select activities and friendships based on gender, and to value members of their own sex more highly.
- Children may evaluate themselves globally or in terms of domain-specific attributes. One group of researchers has identified five domains important in middle childhood: physical appearance, scholastic competence, social acceptance, behavioral conduct, and athletic competence.
- False praise does not benefit children's self-esteem, whereas honest praise about actual, earned achievements does.

## Relating to Others

**[ KEY QUESTION ] 3.** What contributes to positive relationships with peers and parents during middle childhood?

- Affective neuroscience focuses on the neural basis of emotions, personality, and mood.
- The social brain is a good example of the idea that brain systems, rather than single brain locations, control behavior. There is no agreed-on map for the social brain, but some researchers include the detection node, the affective node, and the cognitive-regulatory node.
- Children advance in social information processing during middle childhood. The social information process model describes six steps a child goes through in responding to social interactions.
- Children improve in social perspective taking during middle childhood, and their friendships become more reciprocal.
- Popular, rejected, and neglected children differ in their ability to maintain positive peer relationships. Although popular and rejected children tend to maintain the same status throughout childhood, neglected children often move into one of the other two groups, depending on their interests and behaviors.
- Parents remain central to children's well-being during middle childhood. The tripartite model of parent-child interaction illustrates the several roles that parents play in their relationship with their children during this period. As in earlier periods, the authoritative style of parenting produces the most positive development in children.
- Children are raised within many different family structures. Divorce is common in the United States, as are remarriages, resulting in blended families. More children are being raised in gay and lesbian families, as well. In either case, psychosocial development depends on the same factors as in any other family situation.
- Siblings, because of their unique relationship with each other, create a strong and influential family environment that can remain intact for a lifetime. Sibling relationships are determined in part by the issues of intimacy and power. Conflict between siblings is common.
- Schools provide an important context for psychosocial development. Children who have a sense of belonging in their school environment experience better psychosocial development.
- Many children experience or witness different types of bullying, at school or elsewhere. Both children who bully and those who are bullied are at risk of poor psychosocial development.

## Moral Development

**[ KEY QUESTION ] 4.** How does the course of moral development change over the middle-childhood years?

- The moral development of children progresses as they move away from parental supervision and begin to make decisions for themselves.
- Piaget believed that during middle childhood, children move from the heteronomous orientation of early childhood to an autonomous orientation, in which they understand that individuals participate in making the rules of society.
- According to Kohlberg, children during middle childhood enter the conventional level of moral development, and come to believe that it is important to conform to social rules in the interest of maintaining social order.
- During middle childhood, children become more flexible in their views of when it is acceptable to tell a lie. Older children are more likely to believe it is acceptable to lie to protect the feelings of others.
- Children's thinking about distributive justice also changes during this time. They move from defining fairness simply as equality to defining it based on merit and need.
- Adults can assist children in their moral development by discussing with them the actual moral dilemmas that they encounter, using concrete examples, and drawing out children's own interpretations.

## KEY TERMS

bullying *502*
conventional level *506*
coping *481*
cyberbullying *503*
domain-specific attributes *484*
I-self *482*
industry versus inferiority *477*
me-self *482*
popularity-by-decency *495*
popularity-by-dominance *495*
racial bullying *503*
social brain *487*
social comparison *483*
social information processing model *492*
social perspective taking *494*
tripartite model *497*

## CRITICAL THINKING QUESTIONS

1. **Emotional Development.** Analyze Erikson's view of this life stage as one in which children engage in industry or feel inferior. Provide examples to support your analysis.
2. **Relating to One's Self.** Provide a rationale to explain why bolstering children's self-esteem requires providing them with challenging activities, rather than just praising them.
3. **Relating to Others.** Assess the social information processing model, and suggest various ways in which children with social difficulties could be helped at different steps in the model.
4. **Moral Development.** Contrast the two substages of Kohlberg's conventional level of moral development. Why do you think some children are more advanced than others in their moral reasoning?
5. **Cultural Perspectives.** Consider different reasons why a school-aged child might not tell the truth. Analyze possible reasons why cultural differences exist in the evaluation of how harmful a lie might be.

## REAL Development

### Psychological Development in Middle Childhood

In this module, you are a student intern at Washington Middle School. You are asked to help the school counselor select an appropriate brochure on bullying. The brochure will be distributed to students and their parents. As part of your research on students' existing perceptions, knowledge, and experiences of popularity and bullying, you gather a group of students to serve as a focus group. Your task is to select which brochure you will recommend to the school counselor, taking the students' input into account.

© *John Wiley & Sons, Inc.*

**WileyPLUS** Go to WileyPLUS to complete the *Real Development* activity.

# Milestones in Middle Childhood

## Ages 6–8

### Physical

- During the midgrowth spurt, height increases about 2 to 3 inches a year, and weight increases about 5 to 6 pounds a year
- Baby teeth begin to fall out by age 6, beginning with front teeth, and are replaced by permanent teeth
- Muscle strength and respiratory function increase
- Continues to master fundamental motor skills, such as jumping and throwing, but is moving toward more coordinated efforts, such as throwing a ball for distance and accuracy at the same time
- Builds on the brain architecture developed during early childhood

© JGI/Jamie Grill/Blend Images/Corbis

### Cognitive

- Shows beginning of logic when reasoning about concrete objects
- Can focus on more than one attribute of an object or task at one time
- Begins to use symbol systems to aid in thinking
- Applies more systematic approaches when asked to selectively attend to visual or auditory stimuli
- Begins to use planning as a strategy when undertaking tasks
- Vocabulary shows increases of 20 new words a day
- Reading process moves from decoding individual words to paying attention to what is read
- In mathematics, moves from simple counting to use of basic operations like addition, subtraction, multiplication, and division
- Begins to remember basic math facts

### Psychosocial

- Understands a sense of self as both a "knower" and an "object of judgment"
- Begins to compare self with others
- Evaluates self in terms of five domains: appearance, scholastic competence, social acceptance, behavioral conduct, and athletic competence
- Understands that a person can simultaneously have different emotional reactions to the same event or situation
- Recognizes individual differences in masculinity and femininity
- Is aware that others may have a different perspective but tends to focus on own view
- Friendships are based on enjoyment of similar activities
- Tends to segregate friendships and activities based on sex
- Understands that society's rules are made by individuals
- Conforms to social rules based on desire to be viewed as a "good" person

Koji Aoki/Score/Getty Images

KidStock/Blend Images/Getty Images

# Ages 9 –11

## Physical

Alistair Berg/Getty Images

- Individual variations in size due to genetic and environmental factors become more apparent
- By 11 years of age, the average child is slightly under 5 feet tall and weighs less than 80 pounds
- Girls begin to grow at a more rapid rate and by age 12 are taller and heavier than boys
- Thrusts out arms in play
- The adolescent growth spurt begins at around age 10 to 12
- By age 12, all 20 primary teeth have been replaced by 20 adult teeths
- The brain reaches about 90% to 95% of its adult weight, and brain areas associated with increased cognitive abilities show complex patterns of growth and development
- Begins to demonstrate the skilled movements at the core of athletic performance, though many physical activities require strength, endurance, and coordination beyond the capability of children at this age
- Able to coordinate physical skills with cognitive strategies and teamwork

Fuse/Getty Images

## Cognitive

- Selective attention is close to the adult level
- Memory is less distorted by the suggestions of others
- Can use a range of strategies for remembering information
- Language use expands, including use of quantifiers, adjectives, prepositions, and relative clauses
- Understands ambiguous and multiple meanings of words
- Reading process is more fluid, begins to be automatic
- In mathematics, moves to more complex operations like estimation, fractions, and multistep word problems

## Psychosocial

- Has an increased understanding of own strengths and weaknesses
- Self-identity consists of more abstract concepts
- Uses metacognitive skills to select effective coping skills when emotionally distressed
- Uses appropriate display rules in emotionally charged situations
- Shows more flexibility about gender-related behaviors and activities
- Can acknowledge the perspective of others and can put self in another's place
- Can tell a smile from a frown
- Friendships are based on positive interactions and mutual trust
- Can successfully predict one person's beliefs about another's beliefs
- Conforms to social rules based on desire to fulfill duties to maintain the social order
- Notions of fairness include both merit and need

© kali9/iStockphoto

# Chapter 14

# Physical Development and Health in Adolescence

## MAKING A difference

### Youth Advocating for Youth

We start this chapter by hearing how one adolescent with diabetes is making a difference. Meet Abigail Lore of New Hampshire, age 17, and a delegate to the 2011 Juvenile Diabetes Research Foundation's Children's Congress in Washington, DC. (Note: Today, juvenile diabetes is called type 1 diabetes.) Here is Abby's story:

> I was diagnosed with type 1 diabetes when I was 5 years old, right before I started kindergarten. It was a day that changed my life and that of my whole family forever. That day was the beginning of a 24 hours a day, 7 days a week, 365 days a year job to stay healthy. Diabetes is a constant balancing act, of finger sticks to check my blood glucose, of counting the carbohydrates I eat, and the continuous trial and error of determining how much insulin I need.
>
> My involvement with the Juvenile Diabetes Research Foundation [JDRF] started when I left the hospital at age 5 with a "Bag of Hope" equipped with a teddy bear and picture book. Since then, our family has done annual walks and volunteered at annual galas to raise money. One of the proudest moments of my life was when I had the honor to make the Fund-a-Cure speech. It felt good that the public was putting a face to diabetes by looking at me.
>
> The best thing that happened to me was being made a delegate to the JDRF Children's Congress. It was an amazing experience. Children and adolescents from all around the country went to Washington, DC, to meet with Congress to advocate for a cure and to explain what life with type 1 diabetes is like. It felt so good to help other children with diabetes by sharing my story and making my voice be heard. The most inspirational meeting was with Supreme Court Justice Sonia Sotomayor, who also has type 1 diabetes. When I talked with her, I knew that diabetes would never hold me back.
>
> I think of everything that I have gained by having this disease, such as the responsibility for managing my health, and the public speaking and advocacy opportunities that I have had. It's because of diabetes that I know I want to study politics in college, to keep making a difference. I have gained so much by dealing and being strong with this illness. I'm turning a setback into opportunities, and that makes it all worth it.

## CHAPTER OUTLINE

## [KEY QUESTIONS] *for* READING CHAPTER 14

1. How do the body and brain change during adolescence?
2. What are some health-related choices that adolescents make?
3. How can parents and the community help adolescents to stay healthy and safe?
4. What about adolescence makes it the most difficult time of life to have a chronic illness?

**ADOLESCENCE** is the most profound transformation in the human lifespan. It has been described as "that awkward period between sexual maturation and the attainment of adult roles and responsibilities" (Dahl, 2004, p. 9). In this chapter, we examine the paradox of adolescent health. Adolescence is a time when we celebrate the robust promise of youth, yet the leading causes of adolescent death and injury are consequences of behavior—accidents, homicide, and suicide. We will look at the anatomy and physiology of puberty and brain development, adolescent health behaviors, and how the relationships between teens, their families and friends, and school and society shape the trajectory of adolescent health. Abby's story is an example of how these developmental systems have shaped her own passage through adolescence.

# Biology of Health: Physical Growth and Development

**[ KEY QUESTION ] 1.** How do the body and brain change during adolescence?

"Youth are heated by Nature as drunken men by wine," wrote Aristotle. Clearly, the notion that adolescents are victims of their nature has been popular for some time. In 1904, G. Stanley Hall (profiled in our Focus On feature) deemed it normal for adolescents to experience physical, emotional, and behavioral upheaval, which he referred as "storm and stress" (Hall, 1904). By the mid-20th century, adolescence had come to represent not just a transitional period in life but also a unique subculture, with its own language, music, and social customs. At the same time, people began to use the phrase "raging hormones" as a dark metaphor for the hazards of adolescent sexuality (Schalet, 2004).

### Focus On: G. Stanley Hall

Granville Stanley Hall (1844–1924) is often referred to as "the father of adolescence." His book *The Contents of Children's Minds Entering School* (1883) was based on scientific study of what children know, and when they learn it, and thus gave impetus to the "child study" movement, which changed the nature of education in the United States. Hall became the first president of Clark University in Worcester, Massachusetts (1888–1920). In 1904, he published the first of two volumes focusing on adolescence—*Adolescence: Its Psychology, and Its Relations to Physiology, Anthropology, Sociology, Sex, Crime, Religion, and Education*—establishing for the first time adolescence as a distinct stage in development.

Focusing specifically on boys, Hall believed that preparation for adulthood included character-building experiences overseen by adults. He emphasized the importance of peers, physical activity, and bodily changes in youth development, and cautioned against unstructured leisure time. His writing has not always found favor among contemporary psychologists, and must be understood in the context of his time. Nevertheless, his work laid the foundation for the study of adolescence for the next 100 years.

CEFutcher/istock

© TommL/iStockPhoto

The physical changes of puberty are dramatic, as you can see by comparing the appearance of the young people in these two groups—first at the beginning of this period and then nearer the end of it.

Are adolescents victims of raging hormones? In this section, we review the basic biology of puberty and its accompanying physical changes. We also examine the relationship between hormones and behavior and consider the adolescent brain. As we have throughout the book, we take a developmental systems perspective (Susman & Rogol, 2004) and view **adolescence** as a period of reorganization of the biological, psychological, social, and cognitive processes required for children to transform into young adults.

**adolescence** A period of reorganization of the biological, psychological, social, and cognitive processes required for children to transform into young adults.

**puberty** The set of physical changes that signal the onset of reproductive maturation.

**menarche** The beginning of menstruation in adolescent females.

**adolescent growth spurt** A period of rapid increase in height, weight, and muscle mass; girls' growth spurt occurs between 12 and 14 years, and boys' between 14 and 16 years.

**primary sexual characteristics** Maturation of reproductive organs: ovaries, uterus, penis, and testes.

**secondary sexual characteristics** External signs of sexual maturation, such as hair in the armpits, around the genitalia, and, in males, on the face and chest; growth and development of the penis in males, and breasts and labia in females.

## Puberty

**Puberty** refers to the set of physical changes that signal the onset of reproductive maturation. In girls, puberty is typically associated with the beginning of menstruation, known as **menarche**. The average age for observable puberty in the United States is about 12 years for girls and 14 years for boys. However, the beginning and ending of puberty are ambiguous for both sexes. Biological changes begin about two years before and extend at least two years beyond the onset of observable changes, as bones, muscles, and the reproductive organs fully mature. Thus, pubertal changes can range from ages 8 to 16 for girls and ages 10 to 17 for boys. These changes affect all parts of the body and are dramatic. Height, weight, and muscle and bone growth increase rapidly—a phenomenon often called the **adolescent growth spurt**. Sexual characteristics also appear. **Primary sexual characteristics** include the maturation of the reproductive organs—ovaries, uterus, penis, and testes. **Secondary sexual characteristics** are more apparent, such as the appearance of pubic hair, changes in voice (in boys), and breasts (in girls). Table 14.1 summarizes the stages of puberty for boys and girls as first described by James Tanner (1978).

**Table 14.1** Stages of Puberty

| Stage | Boys | Girls |
|---|---|---|
| 1 | Prepubertal—no outside signs of sexual development | Prepubertal—no outside signs of sexual development |
| 2 | Testes and scrotum begin to enlarge; little pubic hair | Beginning of breast growth, or "breast budding"; first appearance of pubic hair; height spurt begins |
| 3 | Penis grows longer; testes continue to grow; pubic hair grows fuller and changes in texture | Breasts enlarge; pubic hair grows fuller and changes in texture; vaginal discharge may occur |
| 4 | Penis expands in width; testes and scrotum continue to grow; ejaculations may occur; height spurt peaks | Breasts continue to grow; menstruation typically begins |
| 5 | Mature adult | Mature adult |

**adrenarche** Maturation of the adrenal glands, which begins between the ages of 5 and 9; associated with the production and release of an adrenal hormone called dehydroepiandrosterone (DHEA), an androgen.

**androgens** A group of hormones produced by the adrenal gland. The hormone testosterone is responsible for the development of secondary male sexual characteristics, for example. Androgens also support bone growth in both sexes.

**gonadarche** Development of primary sexual characteristics.

Here are some points to keep in mind as you consider the physical changes of adolescence:

- *Hormones play a major role in the changes of adolescence.* Recall that a hormone is any chemical released by one set of cells that affects other cells in the body. Hormones are involved in reproduction, growth of bones and organ systems; temperature regulation; appetite; sexual behavior; emotion; and the freeze-fight-flight stress response.
- *Growth occurs along different axes. Axes* are intricate feedback loops involving the biochemical relationships between different hormones, glands, and other organs.
- *Despite involving different axes, puberty is a highly synchronized suite of biological changes that occur in a cascade.* That is, once they begin, they unfold in a predictable and interlaced sequence (Susman & Rogol, 2004).

With these facts in mind, we look more closely at several axes of change in puberty.

### Adrenarche

**Adrenarche**, which begins between the ages of 5 and 9, is associated with the release of an adrenal hormone, DHEA, from the adrenal glands, which sit atop the kidneys. DHEA is part of a large group of hormones known as **androgens**. Adrenarche is characterized by the acceleration of bone development and growth in height. It occurs independently from puberty, and it is unclear whether adrenarche is caused by DHEA, or how the adrenal glands are stimulated to produce it (Auchus & Rainey, 2004; Susman & Rogol, 2004; Veldhuis, Roemmich, & Rogol, 2000).

### Gonadarche

**Gonadarche**, which starts a few years after adrenarche, is the maturation of the gonads—ovaries in females and testes in males—via the hypothalamic-pituitary-gonadal (HPG) axis. In middle childhood, the hypothalamus begins to secrete the gonadotropin-releasing hormone (GnRH) (Delemarre-van de Waal, 2002; Seminara et al., 2004) in intermittent small pulses, often peaking during sleep (Buchanan, Eccles, & Becker, 1992). GnRH is transported through the bloodstream to the pituitary gland, which then releases the luteinizing hormone (LH), stimulating the production of sex hormones by the gonads and other endocrine glands in both males and females.

Male sex hormones are produced in the testes, and the principal male sex hormone is testosterone, which is an androgen. At puberty, testosterone stimulates overall growth, including muscular development, thickening of the vocal cords (causing the voice to deepen), growth of body hair, and maturation of the reproductive system. As the reproductive system matures, the male begins to experience erection of the penis and ejaculation of semen, which carries sperm (Gardner & Shoback, 2011).

In females, the gonadotropin-releasing hormone (GnRH) also stimulates the release of the follicle-stimulating hormone (FSH) from the pituitary gland. Together, FSH and the luteinizing hormone (LH) are responsible for the production of female sex hormones, estrogen and progesterone, from the ovaries. During fetal development, the ovaries of a female attain their full complement of about 2 million egg cells, or ova. That is, baby girls are born with all of their ova in place, whereas boys do not begin to produce sperm until puberty. Puberty in girls is marked by the menstrual cycle, during which an ovum matures and is released into the uterus. However, for the initial 12 to 18 months after menarche, an ovum may not be released on a regular basis (Gardner & Shoback, 2011).

### Growth

Another axis involved in growth and development during puberty is the growth hormone/insulinlike growth hormone (GH/IGF–1) axis. The hypothalamus stimulates the pituitary gland to secrete the growth hormone (GH), which like GnRH, occurs in intermittent small pulses, peaking during sleep. GH stimulates the liver and other tissues to secrete insulinlike growth hormone 1 (IGF–1). Together, GH and IFG–1 control bone and muscle growth, promote protein synthesis, and metabolize protein, fat, and carbohydrates (Mauras, Rogol, Haymond, & Veldhuis, 1996), all critical to development. Low body weight can lower the presence of both GH and IFG–1, delaying or even stunting growth and puberty (Golden & Shenker, 1992).

The final 20 to 25% of human growth in height occurs during puberty. The rate of growth reaches its peak at about age 12 in girls, and at about age 14 in boys. The feet and long bones in the legs grow first, followed by the trunk and then the shoulders and chest, giving young adolescents a lanky and gawky appearance, so that their clothes never seem to fit right. This unevenness in growth rate also contributes to adolescents' increased risk for sports injuries, which we discuss later in this chapter (Hockenberry, 2003; Malina, Bouchard, & Bar-Or, 2004).

Growth of the long bones of the legs, arms, fingers, and toes occurs at one end of the bone, in a region called the **epiphyseal plate**, or growth plate, which is a layer of cartilage, shown in Figure 14.1. As adult height is reached, bones are longer and thicker, the growth plate closes, and the epiphyses become calcified—harder and thinner. Girls stop growing about two years after the onset of menarche, whereas boys may continue to grow in height until age 18 or 20.

Weight also increases quickly, with about 50% of adult body weight added during puberty (Hockenberry, 2003; Malina et al., 2004). For boys, the spurt in height and weight gain tends to happen at about the same time, whereas girls more often experience the spurt in height growth about six months before the spurt in weight gain. Figure 14.2 shows growth charts for adolescent boys and girls.

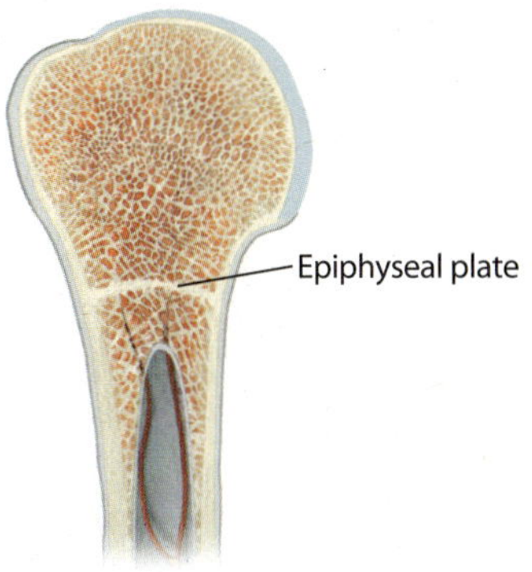


**FIGURE 14.1 Epiphyseal Plates** Epiphyseal plates, or growth plates, are layers of cartilage at the ends of long bones in children and adolescents. Bone growth occurs in these areas.

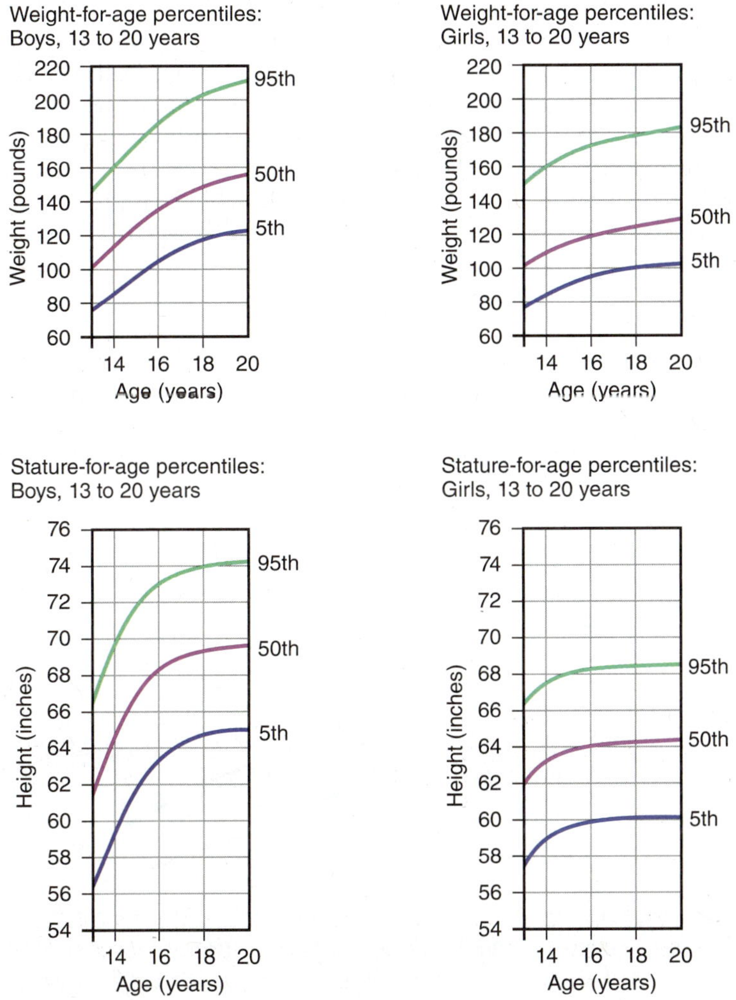


**FIGURE 14.2 Growth Charts, Ages 13 to 20** These charts show weight-for-age and height-for-age data for adolescent boys and girls ages 13 to 20. As in growth charts in earlier chapters, we include the average weight and height (the 50th percentile) and weights and heights near the higher and lower ends (the 95th and 5th percentiles).

*Source:* Developed by the National Center for Health Statistics in collaboration with the National Center for Chronic Disease Prevention and Health Promotion (2000).

**epiphyseal plate** The area at the end of long bones in the arms and legs where new bone develops during the growth spurt in height; also called the growth plate.

## The Timing of Puberty

As you may recall from Chapter 2, genes provide a blueprint for development (genotype), but many other factors contribute to how that blueprint comes to life for each individual (phenotype). Accordingly, the timing for the onset of puberty is very complex, involving multiple factors, such as individual and family genetics, nutrition, and family dynamics. For girls in particular, the relationship between menarche and social and family environments has been the subject of considerable research. Let's look at some of these factors.

### Puberty and Nutrition

Before 1900, the average age of menarche for girls in the United States was over 14, and boys reached puberty at around age 16. By 1970, boys experienced puberty at about 14 years, while the average age of menarche was 12.75 years. Today 80% of all American girls reach menarche between ages 11 and 13.75, with a mean age of 12.5 years (Chumlea et al., 2003). By comparison, the mean age of menarche worldwide is 13.5 years, ranging from 12.5 to 14.5 years, with even later menarche found among malnourished girls in underdeveloped countries (Thomas, Renaud, Benefice, De Meeüs, & Guegan, 2001). The average age of menarche has declined in other nations as well, as shown in Figure 14.3. Read more about how young girls in different cultures prepare for this change in the following box Culture and Menarche.

While a relationship between better diet, more body fat, and earlier puberty has been well established, it is not completely understood. On the one hand, we know that poor nutrition in general, and lack of fresh vegetables in particular, is associated with later menarche. Poor nutrition results not only in low body weight but also, usually, in insufficient fat tissue for the production and storage of sex hormones (Frisch & McArthur, 1974; MacMahon, 1973; Tanner, 1978; Wyshak & Frisch, 1982). On the other hand, the lowering in the age of menarche among American girls mirrors an increase in the percentage who are overweight (Anderson, Dallal, & Must, 2003; Centers for Disease and Control [CDC], 2003). Overweight girls reach puberty earlier than girls of average weight (Garn & Haskell, 1959; Kaplowitz, Slora, Wasserman, Pedlow, & Hermann-Giddens, 2001; Thomas et al., 2001), although a direct cause-and-effect relationship has been difficult to establish (Anderson et al., 2003; Kaplowitz et al., 2001).

### Variability in the Timing of Menarche

Girls reach menarche at about the same time as their biological mothers, suggesting a genetic influence. Racial/ethnic differences are found fairly consistently, even when researchers account for other factors such as height, weight, or diet (Anderson et al., 2003; Chumlea et al., 2003), again suggesting a genetic influence. For example, in the United

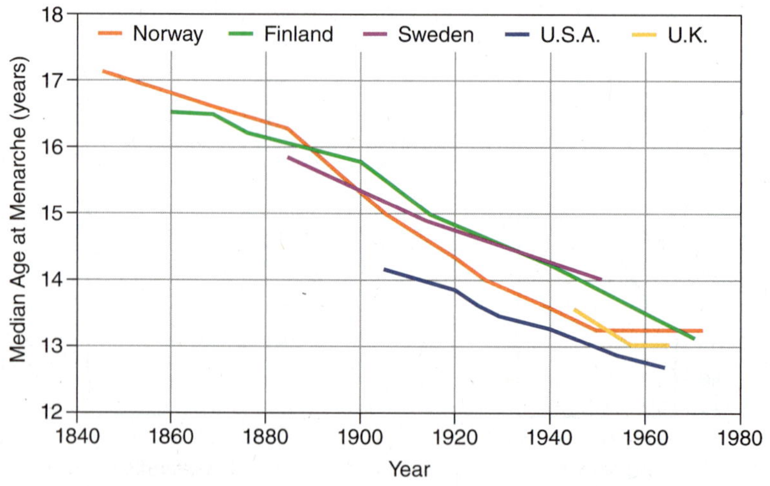


**FIGURE 14.3 Decline in the Average Age of Menarche in Five Western Industrial Nations** The figure shows dramatic declines in the average age of menarche in Finland, Great Britain, Norway, Sweden, and the United States between 1845 and 1969. The change is attributed at least in part to better nutrition, but is not completely understood.

*Source:* Monographs of the Society for Research in Child Development, from A. F. Roche, *Secular Trends in Stature, Weight and Maturation.* Blackwell Publishing. Reprinted with permission of John Wiley & Sons, Inc.

States, Caucasian girls tend to reach menarche between 3 to 5.5 months later than African American and Hispanic girls. However, there is a great deal of variability, based on genetic heritage, weight, and diet. An overweight Caucasian girl may reach menarche earlier than her average-weight biological sister, earlier than a slender African American girl, and at the same time as a Hispanic girl of average weight.

**thought-mediated behavior** Behavior that is the result of thinking before acting in response to a situation.

### Family Environment

Researchers have found that the chronic stress of adverse family environments is associated with earlier onset of puberty (Ellis, 2004). Why? Evolutionary theory offers a possible explanation. The goal of most living beings, in this view, is to grow to maturity and reproduce. If the adults in a given environment do not adequately provide their young with sufficient resources for growth and maturation, the young will have good reason to mature early and strike out on their own. Accordingly, in humans, lack of parental investment in the child, and especially absence of a father, is associated with earlier age of menarche in girls (Belsky et al., 2007; Belsky, Steinberg, & Draper, 1991; Ellis & Essex, 2007; Romans, Martin, Gendell, & Herbison, 2003).

### Social Implications

Anyone who has attended an eighth-grade graduation has probably been struck by the differences among the students: The class is made up of young women, a few young men, and boys. By age 14, most girls are well on their way to womanhood, whereas most boys are just beginning puberty. Consequently, girls and boys of the same age can be at very different stages of puberty. Adolescents for whom puberty arrives at the typical time find these changes challenging under normal conditions. What about boys and girls whose maturation timetables are very different from those of their peers?

Girls who mature much earlier than their peers are more likely to be dissatisfied with their body image, to spend time with an older peer group, to become sexually active earlier, and to give birth earlier. They tend to have less education and less stable partnerships (Brooks-Gunn, Peterson, & Eichorn, 1985; Stattin & Magnusson, 1990). They also experience more emotional distress (Graber, Lewinsohn, Seeley, & Brooks-Gunn, 1997).

Boys, unlike girls, may benefit from maturing earlier than their peers, as this would place them closer to the average time for girls, around age 12 to 13. Classic research indicates that they are described as more mature and more popular and are regarded as leaders—especially in sports, where their physical maturity gives them an advantage. They are also happier with their body image, whereas late-maturing boys are less satisfied (Jones, 1965; Siegel, Yancy, Aneshensel, & Schuler, 1999; Susman & Rogol, 2004). Early-maturing boys, like early-maturing girls, also tend to engage in adult behavior, such as tobacco and alcohol use, earlier than their peers (Ge, Conger, & Elder, 2001; Susman & Rogol, 2004).

*Jeff Greenberg/Photo Edit*

By age 14, most girls are well into the stages of puberty, whereas most boys are just beginning.

## Hormones, Emotions, and Behavior

Let's return to those raging hormones we mentioned earlier. While research indicates that adolescents experience more mood swings and greater emotional intensity, how much of this can be attributed to sex hormones is unclear (Buchanan et al., 1992; Dahl, 2004). Moods and emotions are complex biosocial phenomena involving thinking, feeling, and social expectations and experience. Several parts of the brain are involved in the regulation of moods and emotions.

The frontal lobes of the brain ascribe meaning to events and enable us to think about a situation before we act. This is called **thought-mediated behavior**, more

## Culture and Menarche

Menstruation is a unique sociocultural phenomenon, rife with mythic symbols: blood, the color red, pain, lunar synchrony, fertility, power, sexuality, cleanliness, and secrecy. For example, in many premodern societies, menstruating women lived together in separate quarters, although the rationale for this practice varied among cultures: Menstruation was deemed either unclean or the source of a woman's power (Knight, 1995; Olesen & Woods, 1986; Strassman, 1992).

KidStock/Blend Images/Getty Images

Given the socially constructed meaning ascribed to menarche, how are young girls in different cultures prepared for this change? One universal finding points to the importance of a mother's attitude (Uskul, 2004). Girls often receive mixed messages from their mothers, other female relatives, and friends: It's normal; you're a woman now, but let's not talk about it—especially with males (Britton, 1996; Marvan, Vacio, Garcia-Yanez & Espinosa-Hernandez, 2007; Stubbs, 2008; Uskul, 2004).

In modern societies in particular, menstruation has become medicalized. That is, education about puberty is limited to biology and hygiene. Nevertheless, while education contributes to a more positive menarche—in that girls feel prepared—many girls are surprisingly not very knowledgeable about menstruation (Stubbs, 2008; Yeung, Tang & Lee, 2005), and even less so about sexuality (Britton, 1996; Hill, Gray, Carter, & Schulkin, 2005; Smith, Schmidt, & Rubinow, 2003; Stubbs, 2008). In-depth interviews with American teenaged girls of different racial and socioeconomic backgrounds suggest that the "sex talks" they are given at school, at home, and from physicians generally do not include any information about sexuality—an omission that leaves them confused. When important people in their lives, especially their mothers, acknowledge their sexual feelings as normal, girls have more confidence and are better able to resist sexual peer pressure (Tolman, 2002).

Tony Freeman/Photo Edit

When one adolescent male directly challenges the social dominance of another, both are likely to have the biological urge to take physical action—be "hot headed."

commonly referred to as "keeping a cool head." In contrast, the response of the limbic system and the release of the adrenal hormones cortisol and adrenaline are more reactive. Blood pressure and heart rate go up, the face flushes, muscles tense, and breathing quickens. These reactions explain why we might say that someone is a "hot head" (Lazarus & Folkman, 1984; Lazarus & Lazarus, 1994; McEwen & Lasley, 2002). Keeping the complexity of these matters in mind, let's look at one hormone and one hormonal issue as each relates to behavior and emotion: testosterone and premenstrual syndrome.

### Testosterone, Dominance, and Aggression

Testosterone is secreted by the testes in males at almost 60 times the amount produced in the ovaries in females. It is involved in physical growth and implicated in social dominance and aggression. Let's clarify the difference. Aggression, as we've described in earlier chapters, is behavior intended to inflict harm. **Social dominance**, in contrast, is behavior intended to elevate or maintain social status (Walsh & Barrett, 2005). Social dominance and social status are clearly associated with testosterone in men, but it is not clear which is cause and which is effect. For example, testosterone levels are higher among winners in sports (Nyborg, 2004) and in adolescent boys who are perceived by peers as leaders (Schaal, Tremblay, Soussignan, & Sussman, 1996).

When one young male's social dominance is directly challenged by a second young man, the freeze-fight-flight response may be triggered (Archer, 2006; Mazur & Booth,

1998), potentially giving both males the biological "hot-headed" urge to physical action (van Honk, Schutter, Hermans, & Putnam, 2004). Whether physical aggression erupts or not depends on the young men's expectations about how to resolve differences; it also depends on the size of the aggressor, regardless of which male has the higher testosterone levels (Mazur & Booth, 1998; Rowe, Maughan, Worthman, Costello & Angold, 2004; Tremblay et al., 1998).

**social dominance** Behavior intended to elevate or maintain social status.

*Everyday stories*

A POTENTIAL FIGHT Let's look at a potential fight in the school cafeteria. Henry is accusing Jacob of deliberately fouling him during basketball practice. Jacob denies this and says Henry is just clumsy. Henry, who is big in both size and reputation, is not about to let Jacob win an argument in front of their classmates. If hot-headedness prevails, and if physical fights are common in Henry and Jacob's social environment, physical aggression will likely ensue. But if fighting is rare or to be avoided, it is easier for one of them to override the biological urge to fight and keep a cool head, resolving the situation without physical blows. This is not easy for male adolescents to do. Ideally, an older, well-respected male peer will step in, providing both Henry and Jacob with an opportunity and an excuse to back off.

what if...?

What if there is no older male to step in to prevent the potential fight described in the Everyday Story? What if a female were to try to break up the potential fight? What if neither Henry nor Jacob has any respect for the person who attempts to step in? What roles do you think age, gender, and reputation might have in defusing this kind of situation?

## Premenstrual Syndrome

From 50 to 80% of menstruating girls and women report having some degree of *premenstrual syndrome*, or PMS, which includes alterations in mood and physical symptoms, such as bloating, before the onset of menses (Johnson, 1987). The causes of PMS are unclear. There may be individual differences in how fluctuations in levels of sex hormones, such as estrogen, alter neurotransmitters in the brain. For example, low levels of the neurotransmitter serotonin have been identified in women with PMS (American College of Obstetricians and Gynecologists, 2000). Low levels of serotonin are associated with depressed mood, irritability, anger, aggression, poor impulse control, and increased craving for carbohydrates (Meltzer, 1989), all symptoms of PMS.

Remember, however, our earlier discussion about how culture and a girl's mother play roles in the girl's response to menarche. They also play a powerful role in her experience of PMS. Psychologists argue that while PMS is biologically based, its meaning is socially constructed, with implications about the status of women and their ability to control their emotions. For example, in the United States, PMS is a topic of discussion, and laughter, on television comedies, as well as an alleged factor in some murder trials (Chrisler & Caplan, 2002; Figert, 2005).

## Emotions, Behavior, and Experience: A Developmental Perspective

The changes that constitute puberty present adolescents with many new physical, social, and emotional experiences. These changes are challenging and stressful, in part because of their very newness (Susman & Rogol, 2004). Adolescents often lack sufficient experience to interpret and deal with the numerous physical and psychological changes that bombard them during puberty, leading to emotional turmoil and difficult behaviors. Furthermore, expectations about how adolescents should interpret and deal with this major life transition are shaped by family and culture. When we attribute adolescents' emotions to their hormones, we imply that these emotions are out of their control, and in so doing diminish the importance of the events associated with them.

Instead of talking about raging hormones, we might use this metaphor: Puberty is like starting the engine without a skilled driver at the wheel (Dahl, 2004). We need to help adolescents learn to drive—that is, to understand themselves and to develop thought-mediated behavior. The earlier onset of puberty means that, today, adolescents have sexually mature bodies, but the neural systems necessary for self-control and emotional regulation have not yet fully matured. We look at the neural systems next.

**THE DEVELOPING BRAIN**

## Brain Maturation

Given that puberty occurs earlier than it used to, does the brain develop earlier, too? In other words, do the brain and the body mature at the same time? The answer appears to be, not really. Brain development is clearly associated with age and experience (Dahl, 2004), although puberty appears to play a role in certain aspects of brain development (Blakemore, Burnett, & Dahl, 2010). Furthermore, different parts of the brain mature at different rates (Gogtay et al., 2004). Here, we first discuss the timeline for maturation of various parts of the brain. We then explore the relationship between brain development and behavior, and address why adolescence is a sensitive period in brain development.

### How the Adolescent Brain Matures

To discuss brain maturation, we need to look at the brain's gray matter. Recall from Chapter 2 that gray matter consists of nerve cell bodies and dendrites, and that it makes up the cerebral cortex, the outer layer of the cerebrum. Maturation involves a peaking in the volume of this gray matter. Neuroimaging techniques have revealed that maturation of the different lobes of the cerebrum occurs between the age of 11 and the early 20s, in a somewhat patchwork fashion. The lobes do not mature together at the same rate and time, or in a stepwise sequence one after the other. This irregular, uneven pattern of development is referred to as *dissynchrony*. Figure 14.4 shows the timelines for different lobes based on MRI studies of people aged 2 to 22. The arrows indicate peaks in volume of the gray matter that makes up the cerebral cortex.

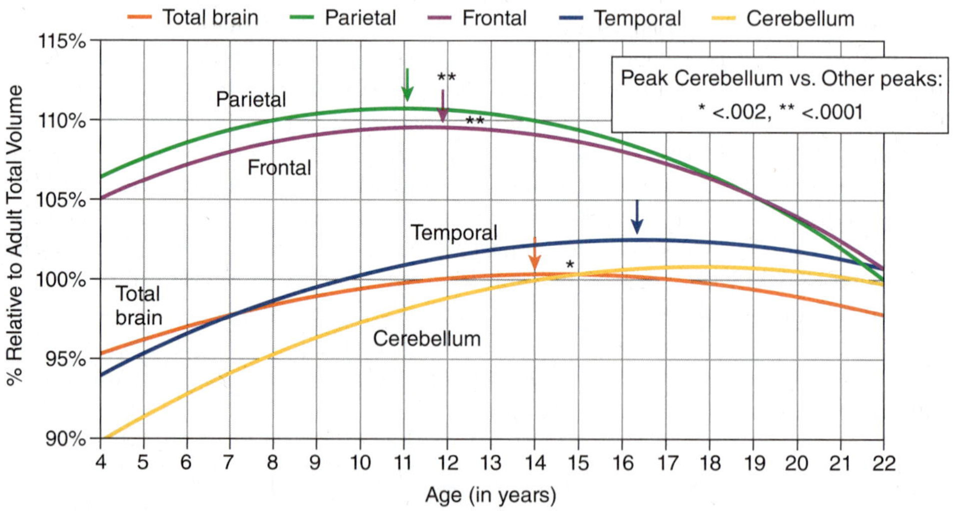


**FIGURE 14.4 Timeline for Maturation of Brain Lobes** The lobes of the cerebrum do not mature together at the same rate and time, nor do they mature in a regular sequence one after the other. This is referred to as *dissynchrony*. The gray matter of the prefrontal cortex, which is one of the last parts of the brain to mature, is associated with abstract reasoning, planning, and decision making, among other capabilities.

*Source:* Reprinted by permission from Macmillan Publishers Ltd: Giedd, J. N., Blumenthal, J., Jeffries, N. O., Castellanos, F. X., Liu, H., Zijdenbos, A., Paus, T., Evans, A., & Rapoport, J. (1999). Brain development during childhood and adolescence: A longitudinal MRI study. *Nature and Neuroscience* 2, 861–863.

Brain development occurs earliest in the primary sensory and motor areas, followed by the secondary and association areas of the brain. By about age 11, the volume of gray matter in the parietal lobes—which are involved in processing spatial relationships and other sensory information—has peaked, as you can see in the figure. The temporal lobes reach maximum gray matter volume at about age 16 or 17. They are involved in memory and in the processing of visual and auditory information (Giedd et al., 1999; Luna et al., 2001). The cerebellum, which also peaks at about age 16 to 17, is involved in the coordination of voluntary motor movement, balance and equilibrium, and muscle tone. Of particular interest in adolescents is the gray matter making up the prefrontal cortex, which is among the last parts of the brain to mature. It is widely accepted that abstract reasoning, planning and decision making, thought-mediated behavior, working memory, and even voluntary motor behavior are related to the development of the prefrontal cortex during adolescence (Casey et al., 2010; Luna et al., 2001).

**Reorganization of the Brain.** Notice in Figure 14.4 that for the brain as a whole and for each lobe, after the volume of gray matter peaks, it begins to decline. Why would this be so? Are adolescents literally losing brain cells? Yes! Extra synapses, as well as synapses that are weak or not well developed, are selectively eliminated, or "pruned," during this period, even while new ones are being formed. At the same time, the myelination of the axons increases, optimizing electrical and chemical signals between nerve cells. These changes support a widespread network of connections that become more highly integrated, occur faster, and are more specialized as development proceeds (Giedd et al., 1999; Luna et al., 2001; Luna, Garver, Urban, Lazar, & Sweeney, 2004).

What is happening is a dramatic reorganization of the brain, moving from relatively local connections to more distant connections between brain regions (Fair et al., 2008). The broader network of connections means that more parts of the brain can be recruited and coordinated more quickly to deal with the complexities of adult life. However, the fact that they *can* be recruited does not mean they *will* be recruited, as we discuss next.

**The Role of Experience in Brain Maturation.** Throughout this book, we have talked about development occurring as a result of the relationship between the individual and the environment. We can see this relationship in the development of the brain in adolescence—specifically, in how development of the frontal lobes is related to the ability to reason abstractly and to control impulses. For example, if adolescents are not exposed to the experiences needed to develop abstract thinking—doing algebra and chemistry, writing a term paper, strategizing in sports, rebuilding a car engine, and so on—the neuronal network of connections that support their development will wither, and abstract thinking will not fully develop. In other words, you need to exercise the brain in order for it to develop fully (Dahl, 2004; Diamond, 2012; Luna et al., 2001).

While experiences that support cognition are positive influences on the adolescent brain, stress is a negative influence. Chronic stress can undermine development of the brain, including the frontal lobes, as we first explained in Chapter 8. The dendrites in the hippocampus that support working memory begin to decline, as do those in the prefrontal cortex that support the ability to pay attention. However, dendrites in parts of the limbic system proliferate as the brain becomes more vigilant to potential threat (Romeo & McEwen, 2006). As a result, chronic stress may make the adolescent guarded and anxious, and can interfere with cognitive processes needed for learning, problem solving, and thought-mediated behavior.

*Mark Langridge/OJO Images/Getty Images*

Experiences such as conducting chemistry experiments help adolescent brains develop abstract thinking.

## The Adolescent Brain and Risky Behavior

As you will read later in this chapter, adolescence is a time of increased risk taking. The relationship between adolescent risk taking and brain development has been a topic of much interest. Three aspects of development in the prefrontal cortex appear to be implicated in increased risk taking between ages 14 and 17. We have mentioned two of these: (1) a change in the ratio of gray to white matter, and (2) an increase in connections with other parts of the brain.

The third is an increase in the neurotransmitter dopamine in the connections between the prefrontal cortex and other parts of the brain, especially the limbic system (which governs emotion), during adolescent development. In addition, dopamine levels have been found to be higher during reward-seeking behavior (Steinberg, 2010; Wahlstrom, White, & Luciana, 2010). What does reward seeking have to do with risk taking? Reward-seeking behavior is often associated with a positive emotional state, and sometimes, the best way to achieve intense positive emotions is to take risks and succeed, or survive, against the odds.

We should note that risk taking can be healthy and even necessary to make the transition from child to adult (Casey, Duhoux, & Cohen, 2010), as when a shy adolescent auditions for a school play or travels away from home. Why adolescents ages 14 to 17 are more likely than older and younger adolescents to engage in potentially harmful risky behavior is unclear. Some researchers suggest that 14- to 17-year-old brains may be more sensitive to the neural mechanisms that motivate reward-seeking behavior, but at the same time have underdeveloped cognitive control to process the consequences of such behavior (Galvan et al., 2006; Somerville & Casey, 2010; Van Leijenhorst et al., 2010). It is clear that the adolescent brain is different from the brains of younger children and adults. To be clear, different, as it is used here, does not mean deficient; adolescents do not have a diminished capacity for decision making (Steinberg, 2010).

**WHEN SYSTEMS CONNECT**

### Adolescent Brain Development

The reorganization of the adolescent brain constitutes a sensitive period in brain development. The adolescent brain's openness to experience makes this a period of both opportunities and vulnerabilities (Dahl, 2004; Steinberg, 2010). In a cognitively enriched and emotionally supportive environment, the brain develops a broad and highly integrated network of connections and specialized functions. Given manageable doses of novelty, challenge, and stress, the adolescent gets to practice how to suppress reacting in favor of thinking, and how to balance irresponsible risk with growth-promoting risk—essential to adult cognition and emotional maturity (Casey et al., 2010). The flip side of being open to opportunity is being vulnerable to events and decisions that can derail healthy development. In the next section, we discuss some of these vulnerabilities.

**✓ CHECK YOUR PROGRESS**

1. What is the difference between adrenarche and gonadarche?
2. What are some factors that have contributed to a decline in the average age of menarche?
3. What are the risks and advantages of early versus late maturation for boys? For girls?
4. How does the prefrontal cortex help a person to "keep a cool head"?
5. In what way is adolescence a sensitive period for brain development?

## Foundations of Health: Health Promotion and Disease Prevention

**[ KEY QUESTION ] 2.** **What are some health-related choices that adolescents make?**

Adolescents are freer to make their own choices than are younger children. Teens who have grown up with good health habits are more likely to continue them, which is one reason why we focused on those habits in earlier chapters. In this section, we address the nutritional needs of rapidly growing adolescent bodies. We also discuss important

## Research Insights: Survey Data

Choosing which data source to use is sometimes challenging. Survey methods vary and may include face-to-face interviews, self-report forms that are returned to the researchers, and online surveys. How participants are chosen also varies among surveys, and the same results may be broken down into different ethnic, racial, socioeconomic, and age categories. Studies may or may not differentiate between white and black teens by Hispanic origin. And there may be a time lag of one, two, or more years between when data are collected and when they are reported.

In this book, we often rely on data collected and reported by federal agencies, such as the Centers for Disease Control (CDC). Because these agencies tend to use the same well-established survey methods over time, we can compare their findings over time and see trends. We cite the most recent available data as this book goes to press, and provide the source websites so that you can access updated data yourself.

For many of the health behaviors we discuss here, we use the CDC's Youth Risk Behavior Surveillance System (YRBS). The YRBS was developed in 1990 to monitor health behaviors among youth and adults in the United States, including tobacco use, eating habits, physical activity, alcohol and other drug use, sexual behavior, and behaviors that contribute to unintentional injuries and/or violence. The YRBS also monitors general health status and the prevalence of obesity and asthma.

YRBS data are derived from various surveys of representative samples of ninth- through twelfth-grade students, further broken down by gender and three racial/ethnic categories: white, black, and Hispanic. These surveys are conducted every two years, usually during the spring semester. A national survey provides data representative of ninth- through twelfth-grade students in public and private schools in the United States. State, territorial, tribal, and local surveys are conducted by individual departments of health and education. Because these surveys and the national survey are conducted separately, the national sample is not an aggregation of state and local surveys.

As you read the data, be aware that using an absolute difference in percentage to describe variations in prevalence can be misleading. It is also necessary to account for the magnitude of the prevalence. For example, the percentage of adolescents who had ever had intercourse decreased between 1991 and 1995 from 54.1 to 53.1%, an absolute decrease of 1% but a 1.9% decrease in prevalence (computed as $[1 \div 53.1] \times 100$). To determine whether such changes are statistically significant, or represent a trend over time, the CDC uses several sophisticated statistical analyses.

For more information on the YRBS, go to http://www.cdc.gov/healthyyouth/yrbs.

health behaviors, such as sleep, sexual activity, and use of tobacco, alcohol, and drugs. In Chapter 16, we address adolescent body image, sexual identity, and relationships; the roles of parents, peers, and popular culture in adolescent behavior; and depression and eating disorders. In the discussion that follows, we refer at times to data from the Youth Risk Behavior Surveillance System (YRBS) conducted by the Centers for Disease Control (CDC). You can read more about this survey data in the accompanying Research Insights feature.

## Nutrition and Physical Activity

The adolescent body needs a certain amount of calories to support its rapid growth and to lay a healthy foundation for adulthood. Table 14.2 indicates caloric needs for girls and boys ages 14 to 18. Boys have higher caloric needs than girls because boys

**Table 14.2** Caloric Needs of Adolescents, Ages 14 to 18, by Sex and Activity Level

| Girls | Boys |
|---|---|
| Sedentary: 1,800 calories per day | Sedentary: 2,000–2,400 calories per day |
| Moderately active: 2,000 calories per day | Moderately active: 2,400–2,800 calories per day |
| Active: 2,400 calories per day | Active: 2,800–3,200 calories per day |

*Note: Sedentary* means a lifestyle that includes only the light physical activity associated with typical day-to-day life. *Moderately active* refers to physical activity that is equivalent to walking about 1.5 to 3 m (2.4–4.8 km) per day. *Active* refers to activity that is equivalent to walking more than 3 m (4.8 km) per day.

*Source:* United States Department of Agriculture, 2011. *Dietary Guidelines for Americans,* 2010.

TINROOF/Getty Images

Teenagers often ignore recommended dietary guidelines, such as eating enough fruits and vegetables to make up half of their daily calorie intake, in favor of consuming fast foods and soft drinks.

have a greater proportion of lean body mass, which uses more calories. A rapidly growing, very active 15-year-old boy may need as many as 3,200 calories or more a day just to maintain his weight. In contrast, an active 15-year-old girl, whose growth is almost completed, may need 2,000–2,400 calories.

Moreover, the need for iron, zinc, protein, and calcium can almost double during adolescence, compared with middle childhood. For example, half of adult bone structure is deposited during adolescence, requiring 1,200 milligrams of calcium a day.

As we have seen in previous chapters, it is important that calories be distributed among food groups. The proportions from each of these food groups for adolescents are the same as listed in the MyPlate graphic that we showed in Chapter 11 (Figure 11.8): Half of daily calories should come from fruits and vegetables, with the remainder from protein (preferably lean meat), grains (preferably whole grains), and dairy (preferably skim or low fat). In addition, fat intake should not exceed 30% of calories, and those fat calories should be from unsaturated fats.

How well do teenagers follow these recommendations? Not very. For example, the 2011 YRBS survey found that only 34% of adolescents ate fruit or drank 100% fruit juice 2 or more times each day, and that only 15% ate vegetables 3 or more times each day. These numbers have not changed significantly since 1999, when YRBS first collected data on nutrition.

### Portion Distortion

One of the challenges of maintaining a healthy distribution of foods is to know how to interpret serving sizes. For today's teens, "supersized" has become the norm. Figure 14.5 puts portion size into perspective, while Table 14.3 compares a fast-food lunch with a meal of more healthy choices. The lunch with a homemade turkey sandwich, for example, has 1,000 fewer calories than the fast-food lunch, and is less expensive as well.

*Everyday stories*

PORTION DISTORTION—IT'S EVERYWHERE! Twenty years ago, a bottle of soft drink contained one serving of 6.5 oz (192 ml), for about 85 calories. Today, that bottle contains 20 oz (591 ml). Because a bottle of soda is typically consumed in one sitting, it is easy to get the impression that it is one serving. Indeed, the label says the drink has 85 calories per serving, but the smaller print notes that there are three servings in the bottle. That adds up to a total of 255 calories. This is called "portion distortion." It means that what we perceive as a single portion is sometimes 2, 3, or more times larger than a single portion.

### Fat, Sugar, Sodium, and Caffeine

Of course, total calories do not tell the whole story. Fat, sugar, and sodium intake can quickly exceed recommended amounts. Let's look at two slices of large, thin-crust pepperoni and cheese pizza (560 calories), plus a 20 oz (591 ml) cola soft drink (255 calories) as an example. At 815 calories, this meal (or snack) is 40% of a 2,000-calorie-per-day diet. Furthermore, the pizza has 22 g of fat, which exceeds the recommended 20 g per day, and 1,560 mg of sodium, two thirds of the recommended 2,300 mg per day (U.S. Department of Agriculture and U.S. Department of Health and Human Services, 2011).

Now let's look at the beverage in our example. Adolescents are the number-one consumers of sugary beverages in the United States, averaging 300 calories per day. These beverages include soft drinks, fruit juices, sports drinks, energy drinks, iced teas, and others (Robert Wood Johnson Foundation, 2009). One level teaspoon of

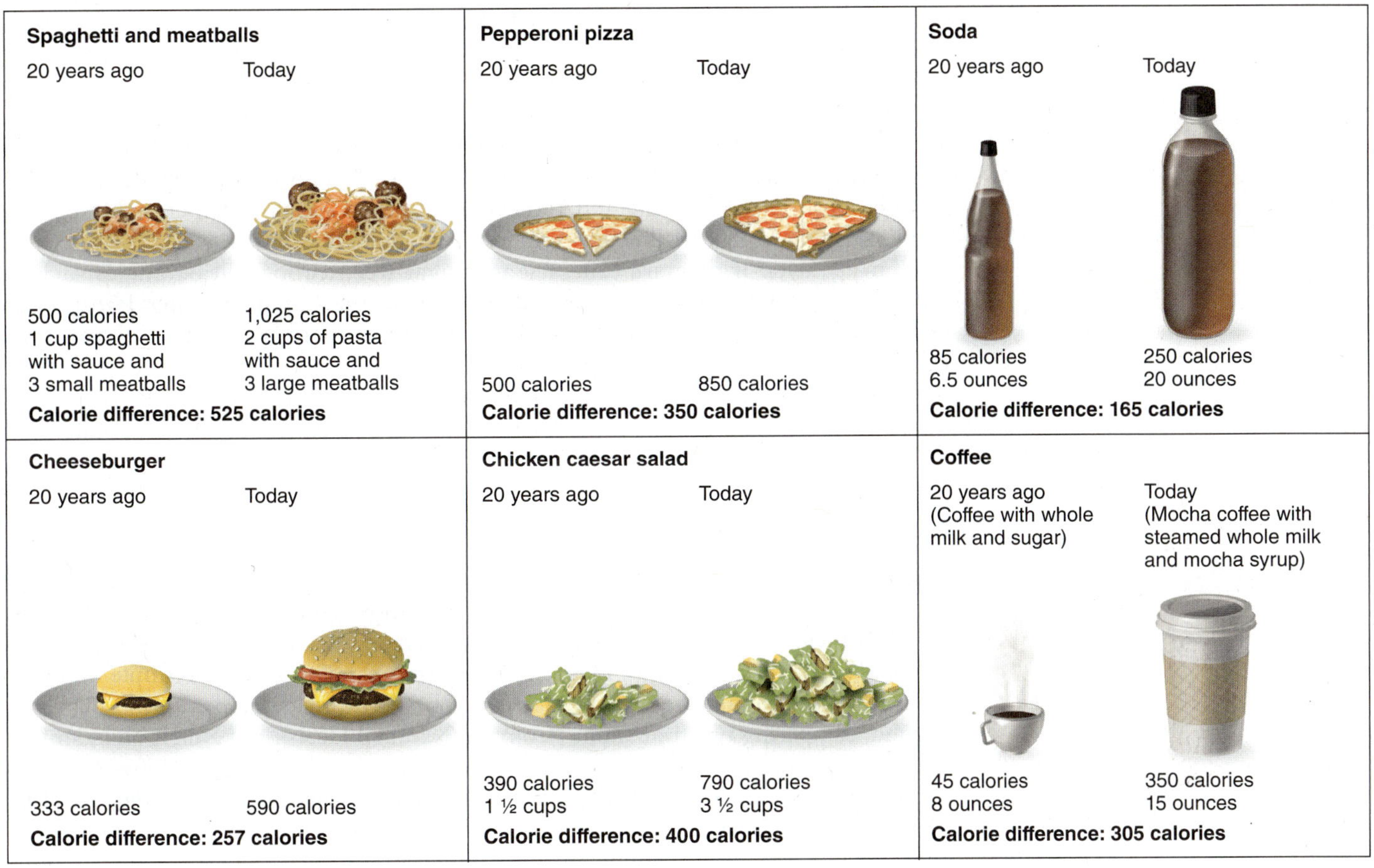


**FIGURE 14.5 Portion Distortion** Serving sizes—along with calories—have shifted upward over the past 20 years. What we think of as a typical bottle of soda, for example, has increased from 6.5 oz (192 ml) 20 years ago to 20 oz (591 ml) today, representing an increase of 165 calories.

sugar equals 4 g and 16 calories. A 20 oz (591 ml) bottle of soda contains 79 g (16 tsp) of sugar, which at 65 g (13 tsp) exceeds the recommended daily limit of 40 g. Many of these drinks also contain caffeine.

A cup of brewed coffee contains 80 to 135 mg of caffeine. Consuming more than 100 mg of caffeine per day has been associated with high blood pressure—not later in

**Table 14.3** A Fast-Food Lunch Compared with a Snack of Healthier Choices

| Fast-Food Lunch | Calories | Brown-Bag Lunch | Calories |
|---|---|---|---|
| Quarter-pound cheeseburger | 510 | Turkey sandwich on whole wheat bread with mustard, lettuce, and tomato | 200 |
| Large fries | 380 | Water | 0 |
| Medium soda (32 oz; X ml) | 210 | Medium apple | 70 |
| 1 chocolate chip cookie | 160 | 1 large graham cracker square | 59 |
| **Total:** | **1,260** | | **329** |
| **Typical Snack** | **Calories** | **Healthier Snack** | **Calories** |
| Snack-size bag of chips (3 oz; X g) | 465 | 1 low-fat yogurt (6 oz; X g) | 140 |
| Regular soda (20 oz; X ml) | 250 | Glass of water | 0 |
| **Total:** | **715** | **Total:** | **140** |

*Source:* U.S. Department of Health and Human Services, 2012.

life, but during adolescence (Savoca, Evans, Wilson, Harshfield & Ludwig, 2004). Energy drinks can have 50 to 550 mg per can or bottle, along with 30 g (7 tsp) of sugar. About 30 to 50% of adolescents report consuming energy drinks, with such serious consequences as a rise in caffeine dependence and caffeine intoxication (Reissig, Strain & Griffiths, 2009; Seifert, Schaechter, Hershorin, & Lipshultz, 2011). The American Academy of Pediatrics (AAP) (2011), and the AAP Committee on Nutrition and the Council on Sports Medicine and Fitness (2011) have issued statements that energy drinks should not be consumed by children and adolescents at all.

Finally, even if they are caffeine- and sugar-free, carbonated beverages such as colas have as much as 500 mg of phosphorus in one 8 oz (236 ml) serving. Phosphorus and calcium are in careful balance in the body. When there is more phosphorus than calcium in the system, the body will draw down the calcium stored in bones and teeth. As 50% of adult bone mass is laid down in adolescence, the lack of a balanced diet compromises bone development, which has lifelong implications for both males and females, in the form of brittle bones (osteoporosis).

### Malnutrition: Obesity

The Centers for Disease Control report that for 2009–2010, 18% of adolescents ages 12 to 19 were obese. Specifically, their body mass index (BMI) was above the 95th percentile for age and sex. The same report notes that 35.7% of adults were obese for this period (Ogden, Carroll, Kit & Flegal, 2012a), setting an unfortunate example for many teens. Figure 14.6 indicates the prevalence of obesity by gender and ethnic/racial background, comparing two time frames from the National Health and Nutrition Examination Survey (NHANES). As you can see, the prevalence of obesity in 2009–2010 was about twice that in 1988–1994 for each group (Ogden, Carroll, Kit & Flegal, 2012b).

We discussed obesity in Chapter 11, noting that one third of children and adolescents are overweight or obese, triple the number in the 1970s, and that genetics alone cannot account for this dramatic increase. The lifestyle factors that contribute to overweight in adolescence are essentially the same as in middle childhood: larger food portion sizes, heavy consumption of high-carbohydrate processed foods, more meals eaten away from home, and a more sedentary lifestyle. Also a factor is that teens have less supervision and so are freer to make poor choices based on the eating habits they developed during early and middle childhood.

A recent study documented the consequences of unhealthy eating during adolescence (May, Kuklina & Yoon, 2012). Of young people ages 12 to 19, 14% need treatment for hypertension and 22% for high cholesterol. Most troubling, the prevalence of type 2 diabetes associated with overweight and obesity increased from 9 to 23% from

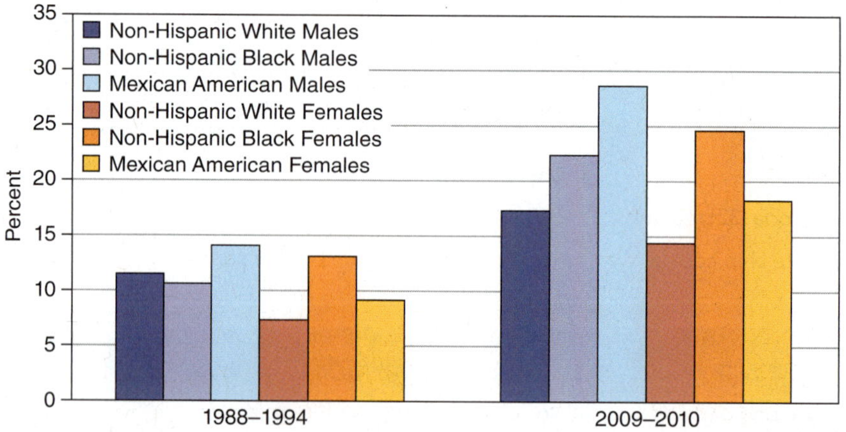


**FIGURE 14.6 Obesity in Adolescents Ages 12 to 19 by Gender and Race/Ethnicity**
Obesity is a significant problem in adolescents (as well as other age groups). As shown in the figure, across genders and racial/ethnic groups, the prevalence of obesity among teens in 2009–2010 was about twice that in 1988–1994.
*Source:* Ogden & Carroll, 2010; Ogden, Carroll, Kit, & Flegal, 2012b.

1999 to 2008. The researchers concluded that American adolescents carry a substantial burden of cardiovascular disease risk factors before they reach adulthood.

As is the case with younger children, overweight and obese adolescents experience more teasing and victimization than their average-weight peers, and they internalize the associated stigma of being overweight. Adolescent girls in particular may respond to this internalized stigma by developing disordered eating habits, such as binge eating, bulimia, anorexia, and the use of diet pills or laxatives (Puhl & Heuer, 2010; Puhl & Latner, 2007). Disordered eating during adolescence is not just a health behavior. It is associated with body image and the developing sense of self, especially sexual self. For that reason, we cover disordered eating in Chapter 16.

*Philippe Garo/Science Source*

About one third of adolescents are overweight or obese, leading to causes of such health problems as hypertension, high cholesterol, and type 2 diabetes.

### Physical Activity

According to 2011 data from the Youth Risk Behavior Surveillance System (CDC, 2012a, 2012b), 49.5% of high school students meet currently recommended levels of physical activity: 60 minutes per day, 5 or more days per week of activity that increases heart rate and breathing. Overall, girls are less active than boys, at 38.5% and 60%, respectively. White males are the most active (62%), and black females the least active (32%). Adolescents become less active as they get older, so that by twelfth grade, 45% report being physically active every day compared with 53% of ninth graders. YRBS data also indicate that daily participation in school-based physical education among adolescents dropped from 42% in 1991 to 31.5% in 2011.

Adolescents spend from 7 to 8 hours each day in sedentary activities (Matthews et al., 2008). Two to 3 of those hours are spent using media—TV, DVDs, computers, and computer games—with older adolescents, males, and teens from lower- and middle-income families spending more time than younger adolescents, females, and teens from higher-income families (Sisson et al., 2009). Such sedentary activities are usually accompanied by excessive snacking on high-calorie foods that are poor in nutrients (Lowry, Wechsler, Galuska, Fulton, & Kann, 2002).

## Sleep and Stress

Anyone who has ever attempted to rouse a sleeping adolescent for school can identify with this quote from the English poet Geoffrey Chaucer: "It is not good a sleeping hound to wake." Teens often stay up too late at night, are drowsy in morning classes, and sleep until noon on weekends—and battle with their parents about it.

Adolescents need 8½ to 9½ hours of sleep per night. Getting as little as 4 to 6 hours of sleep at night over a two-week period—not uncommon among adolescents with busy after-school schedules and lots of homework—is the equivalent of not sleeping at all for three days, in terms of daily performance expectations. Sleep-deprived adolescents are at greater risk for motor vehicle accidents, poor grades, and depression. They also increase their caffeine consumption, which further interferes with sleep, as does alcohol use (Emsellem & Whiteley, 2006; Wolfson & Carskadon, 1998).

Sleep patterns in adolescents relate to brain development, as we discussed earlier. As the brains of young people reorganize, they develop a circadian rhythm different from that of younger children and of adults. (A circadian rhythm is the roughly 24-hour cycle that occurs in the biophysiological processes of the body.) For example, in adolescents, the pineal gland in the brain begins to secrete melatonin, a brain hormone that helps cause drowsiness, at around midnight, almost three hours later in the evening than in children. Then, after 8 or 9 hours' sleep, adolescents start to wake up between 8:00 A.M. and 9:00 A.M., a schedule completely at odds with most of modern life (Emsellem & Whiteley, 2006).

*Peter Byron/Photo Edit*

Sleep patterns change when children reach adolescence, causing them to fall asleep later—and wake up later—than younger children.

Poor sleep causes physiological stress, which leads to more poor sleep. So let's talk again about stress. In Chapters 2 and 8, we discussed allostasis and the allostatic load. Recall that the freeze-fight-flight response is designed to deal with short-term stressors. It raises your heart rate and blood pressure and gives you a jolt of glucose and cortisol to meet immediate demands—and then shuts off. But when stress becomes chronic, the stress response does not shut off. The result is allostatic load, which arises when the same hormones—especially cortisol—that are helpful in responding to short-term stressors become unhealthy. Chronic stress is associated with high blood pressure, loss of protein, compromised immunity, and insulin resistance (McEwen & Lasley, 2002).

Now recall from our earlier discussion of the adolescent brain that chronic stress can also make the adolescent guarded and anxious, as a result of changes in the limbic system. Let's put the brain, nutrition, and sleep together: Adolescents who don't sleep enough, are under a lot of stress, and take in too much sugar and caffeine will likely gain weight, catch every virus going around, and become anxious and even aggressive. It is a vicious, unhealthy cycle.

## Adolescent Health Behaviors: Injury, Sexual Activity, and Substance Use

"I would that there were no age between ten and twenty-three, or that youth would sleep out the rest; for there is nothing in between but getting wenches with child, wronging the ancientry, stealing, fighting." These words are spoken in Shakespeare's play *The Winter's Tale* by a shepherd blaming the loss of two sheep on the reckless behavior of certain youths. Given what we now know about puberty and brain maturation, the bard's choice of "ten and twenty-three" as the time span for adolescence—and objectionable behavior—is quite astute. But thinking about adolescent behavior as an accident waiting to happen is not fair to the adolescents themselves. As we review trends in mortality and injury, sexual behavior, and use of alcohol, tobacco, and illegal drugs, you will find that today's teens are more careful than were their predecessors.

### Causes of Death and Injury

The National Center for Injury Prevention and Control (2011) reports that for many years, the top four causes of death among male and female adolescents have been: unintentional injury, homicide, suicide, and cancer (see Figure 14.7). Motor vehicle accidents account for 47% of all unintentional injury deaths in adolescents, though there are significant gender differences: 60% of unintended deaths in males occur in motor vehicles accidents, compared with 73% for females, who are more likely to be

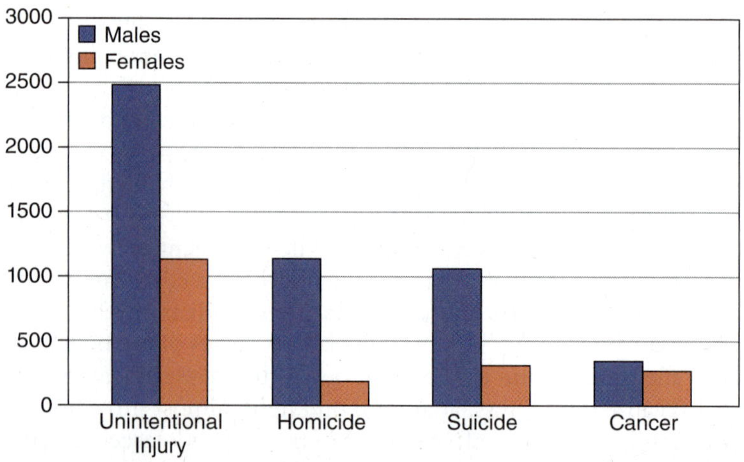


**FIGURE 14.7 Major Causes of Death for Males and Females Ages 13 to 18, 2010**
For many years, the top causes of death among male and female adolescents have been unintentional injury, homicide, suicide, and cancer. In the unintentional injury category, automobile accidents are the chief cause of death.
*Source:* National Center for Injury Prevention and Control, 2011.

in the passenger seat. Other causes of unintended death in adolescents include poisoning, drowning, and other land transport, with male deaths being higher in all categories. In general, males are more likely to die violently than are females.

Nonfatal injuries in this age group involved falls, being struck by or against something, and unintended overexertion—causes that have not changed much over time. Being the passenger in a motor vehicle accident is a cause of injury for older adolescents more so than for younger adolescents.

## General Trends in Health Behavior

The very good news is that today's adolescents are less likely to engage in potentially harmful behaviors than their predecessors of 20 years ago. Figure 14.8 compares data from the 1991 and 2011 Youth Risk Behavior Survey (CDC, 2012a). More specifically, today's teens are more likely to wear a seatbelt while riding in a car and to use a condom during intercourse. (Likely contributing to the latter is that the majority of teens [87%] have been educated about HIV and AIDS.) They are also less likely to smoke cigarettes, drink alcohol, ride with a driver who has been drinking alcohol, or carry a weapon. Teen pregnancy, birth, and abortion rates, too, are at all-time lows, as we will discuss later in this chapter. One worrisome statistic, however, is that about one third of teens admitted to texting or e-mailing while driving.

The positive trends follow substantial investments in health promotion and prevention activities at national, state, and local levels by government and private agencies, as well as heightened vigilance on the part of parents. Nevertheless, a new group of children reach adolescence every year, and efforts to keep them safe will always be in order.

## Adolescent Sexual Health and Activity

Perhaps no aspect of adolescence has been more worried about, talked about, written about, even sung about than sex. The fact is, young people have sex because they can, even if societal conventions, and especially parents, would prefer they not engage in intercourse. Their bodies are sexually mature, and their emotions are strong. Furthermore, in industrialized countries, there is a decade or more between the onset of puberty and marriage, and between the end of childhood and the beginning of adulthood, resulting in a mismatch between adolescent sexual desire, brain development, and emotional, social, and economic maturity.

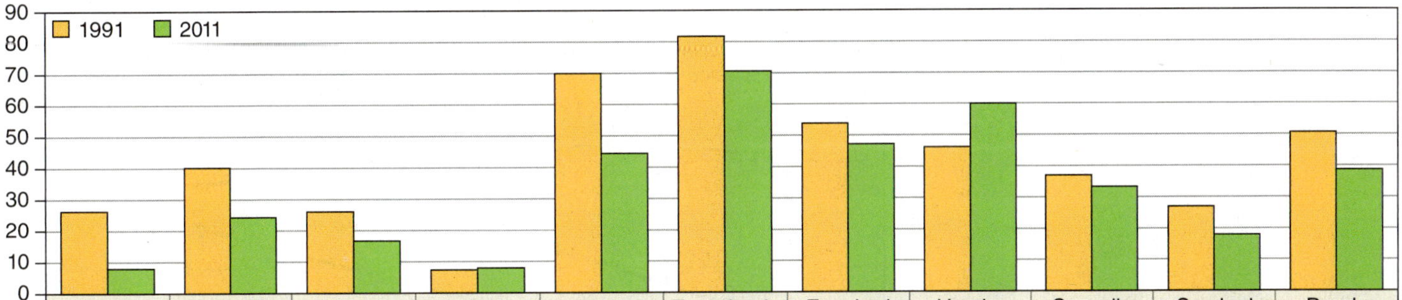


| | Rarely/never wore a seatbelt | Rode with driver who had been drinking | Carried a weapon | Attempted suicide | Ever smoked cigarettes | Ever drank alcohol | Ever had sexual intercourse | Used a condom during last sexual intercourse | Sexually active | Smoked cigarette on at least one day in the 30 days prior to survey | Drank alcohol on at least one day in the 30 days prior to survey |
|---|---|---|---|---|---|---|---|---|---|---|---|
| 1991 | 25.9 | 39.9 | 26.1 | 7.3 | 70.1 | 81.6 | 54.1 | 46.2 | 37.5 | 27.5 | 50.8 |
| 2011 | 7.7 | 24.1 | 16.6 | 7.8 | 44.7 | 70.8 | 47.4 | 60.2 | 33.7 | 18.1 | 38.7 |

**FIGURE 14.8 Adolescent Risk Behavior, 1991 and 2011** Over a range of areas, adolescents in 2011 engaged in less risky behavior than did adolescents in 1991.
*Source:* Youth Risk Behavior Surveillance Systems, 2010, 2012.

Healthy sexual development features four developmental challenges: (1) body image—the adolescent's comfort in his or her sexually maturing body; (2) managing sexual arousal; (3) negotiating sexual behavior; and (4) practicing safe sex (Brooks-Gunn & Paikoff, 1993). In Chapter 16, we talk more about the normal and healthy challenges faced by adolescents in terms of their sexual development. Here, we review a number of trends in sexual activity in adolescents. Before we do, however, we must first note that researchers find it somewhat difficult to investigate adolescent sexuality. Adolescents tend to censor themselves in interviews (especially girls) but exaggerate on surveys (especially boys), and they can be unclear about the timing of sexually related events, such as first intercourse (Savin-Williams & Diamond, 2004; Upchurch, Lillard, Aneshensel, & Li, 2002).

Figure 14.9 shows trends in sexual activity by grade, as reported by the YRBS (CDC, 2012a). Not surprisingly, the figure indicates that adolescents become more sexually active as they get older. On average, young people have sexual intercourse for the first time at about age 17 (Chandra, Martinez, Mosher, Abma, & Jones, 2005; Martinez, Chandra, Abma, Jones & Mosher, 2006). About 70% of females and 56% of males report that their first sexual experience was with a steady partner (Martinez, Copen, & Abma, 2011). Most also report using a contraceptive during their first sexual intercourse (Martinez et al., 2011; Mosher & Jones, 2010). However, the figure also suggests that older teens are less likely to use condoms than are younger teens, and that older females are more likely to use hormonal forms of birth control.

Sexual activity also differs according to gender, race, and ethnicity. The YRBS 2011 data (CDC, 2012a) indicate that about one third of both males and females report being sexually active, with black males most likely to be sexually active (46%) and Hispanic females least likely to be sexually active (31.6%). Black males (75%) are more likely to use condoms than are white (66%) and Hispanic males (64%). Despite the increase in condom use since 1991, many adolescents continue to have unprotected sex, with Hispanic and black females most at risk for pregnancy and disease. In fact, the highest pregnancy rate and highest prevalence of sexually transmitted diseases is among black adolescent females. A sexually active female adolescent who does not use a contraceptive has a 90% chance of becoming pregnant within a year (Harlap, Kost, & Forrest, 1991).

The YRBS does not address all sexual behavior. Studies of same-sex behavior in adolescence depend on self-identification, which occurs in fewer than 2% of adolescents; nevertheless, 6% of girls and 8% of boys report experiencing same-sex attractions or

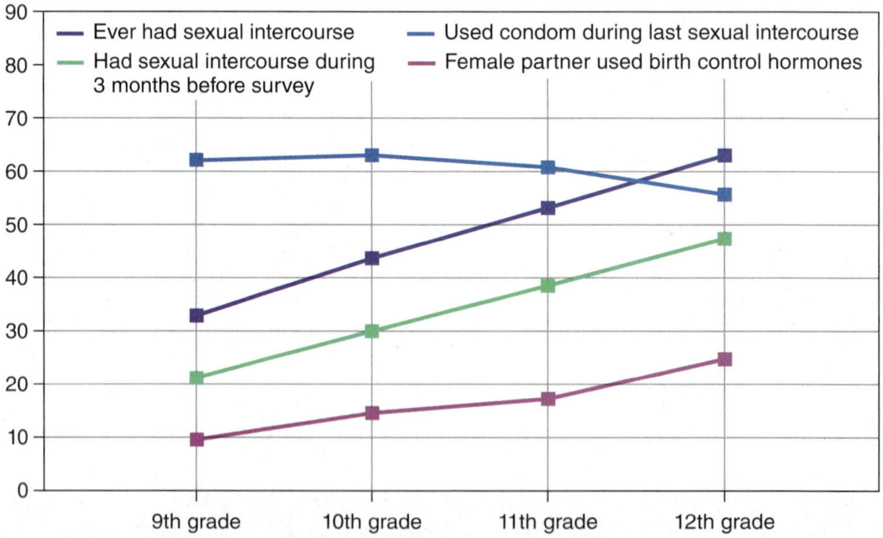


**FIGURE 14.9 Sexual Activity by Grade, 2011** As we would expect, adolescents become more sexually active as they get older. Perhaps more surprising is the finding that older teens are somewhat less likely to use condoms than younger teens.
*Source:* Centers for Disease Control and Prevention, 2012a.

relationships (Russell & Joyner, 2001). Data about oral sex from 2002 indicate that 55% of males and 54% of females aged 15 to 19 had engaged in oral sex with someone of the opposite sex, with many mistakenly believing that oral sex is safer than genital sex (Mosher, Chandra, Jones, 2005).

### Teenage Pregnancy and Birth Rates

As shown in Figure 14.10, the rates of pregnancy, live birth, and abortion among American teenagers aged 15 to 19 have declined markedly across all racial and ethnic groups since 1991, reaching historic lows in 2011 (CDC, 2012c; Hamilton, Martin, & Ventura, 2011, 2012; Martin, et al., 2011; Ventura, Curtin, & Abma, 2012). Nevertheless, pregnancy rates in the United States remain much higher than in most other developed countries. For example, the American rate is double those of Canada and Sweden (McKay, 2006), even though the frequency of adolescent sexual activity is comparable in all three countries (CDC, 2006; Santelli, Sandfort, & Orr, 2008). One reason for this disparity is that European adolescents are more likely to have access to and use contraceptives than their American peers (Santelli et al., 2008).

Figure 14.10 also shows that the rates of induced abortions for girls aged 15 to 19 dropped by half from 1991 through 2008 (Klein & the Committee on Adolescence, 2005; Martin et al., 2011; Ventura et al., 2012). Of girls under 18 who had an abortion, 60% did so with at least one parent's knowledge—which means that 40% did not. Teenaged girls who abort a pregnancy report that they do so because pregnancy is a life-altering event and they feel too young to parent a child (Guttmacher Institute, 2006).

While pregnancy and birth rates have fallen for all groups over the past 20 years or so, there are variations by race and ethnicity (Hamilton et al., 2012). Non-Hispanic black and Hispanic adolescents continue to be more than twice as likely as non-Hispanic white adolescents to become pregnant and give birth. In 2011, Hispanic adolescents had the highest birth rate, at 49 per 1,000. The lowest birth rate in 2011 was among Asian/Pacific Islanders, at 10 per 1,000 adolescents. Birth rates for Native American Indians and Alaskan Natives were similar to those for black teens (Hamilton, Martin, & Ventura, 2010; Martin et al., 2011).

Regardless of race or ethnicity, pregnancy rates are highest among socioeconomically disadvantaged teenaged girls (CDC, 2011a). We noted in Chapter 3 that adolescence is not the optimal time in life to become pregnant, give birth, and raise a child. Physically, teenagers are at greater risk for anemia, infection, and preeclampsia during pregnancy; and their babies are more likely to be born premature. Teen mothers are

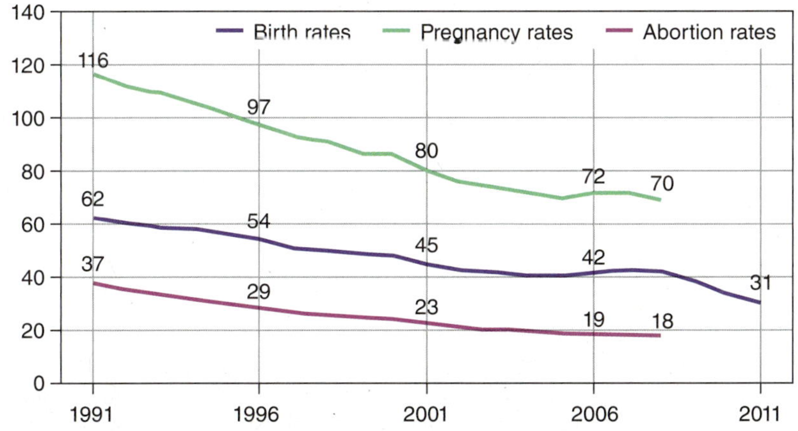


NOTE: Pregnancy and abortion rates (from Ventura et al., 2012) available only through 2008.

**FIGURE 14.10 Pregnancy, Birth, and Abortion Rates per 1,000 Women Aged 15 to 19, 1991–2011** The rates of pregnancy, live birth, and abortion among American teenagers have declined significantly across all racial and ethnic groups since 1991. Still, pregnancy rates in the United States remain much higher than in most other developed countries.

*Source:* Hamilton, Martin, & Ventura, 2011; Hamilton, Martin, & Ventura, 2012; Ventura, Curtin, & Abma, 2012.

**sexually transmitted disease (STD)** One of a group of diseases caused by bacteria or viruses and transmitted between individuals during unprotected oral, genital, or anal sexual contact.

more likely to drop out of school, and they lack the emotional maturity to care for a dependent infant. Thus, pregnancy alters the development of both adolescent women and their children.

## Sexually Transmitted Diseases

Sexual activity brings with it the risk of **sexually transmitted disease (STD)**. Even though young people aged 15 to 24 years represent only 25% of the sexually experienced population, they account for nearly half of the more than 1.6 million newly reported cases of STDs each year in the United States. Young people are more likely to have brief, sequential sexual partnerships, to fail to use protection consistently and correctly, and to experience obstacles in getting health care when symptoms of illness do appear (Forhan et al., 2009).

Some STDs are caused by bacteria and others by viruses. Bacterial infections can be treated and sometimes eliminated with antibiotics, especially in the early stages of infection. Viral infections are more difficult to treat. Medications may manage symptoms, but the virus remains in the body, causing flare-ups. Note, too, that many STDs have mild or no symptoms yet can cause widespread disease in areas of the body beyond the original site of infection. In Chapter 3, we pointed out that these diseases can damage a developing fetus, as well. Table 14.4 offers a brief description of the more common sexually transmitted diseases.

Today, perhaps the most widely known STD is acquired immune deficiency syndrome (AIDS), caused by the human immunodeficiency virus (HIV). In 2009, 60% of

**Table 14.4** Sexually Transmitted Diseases in Adolescents Ages 15 to 19

| Disease | Males Ages 15–19[a] | Females Ages 15–19[a] | Cause | Symptoms and Consequences | Treatment |
|---|---|---|---|---|---|
| Chlamydia | 774 per 100,000 | 3,378 per 100,000 | Bacteria | Discharge from the vagina or penis, burning on urination, low back pain. Untreated, can lead to pelvic inflammatory disease (PID) in females, causing infertility. | Oral antibiotics |
| Human papillomavirus (HPV) | 1% prevalence | 35% prevalence | Virus | Visible genital warts on the penis, vagina, vulva, and around and in the anus. Associated with vaginal cancer later in life. | No cure. Ointments may get rid of warts but not the virus. |
| Gonorrhea | 253 per 100,000 | 571 per 100,000 | Bacteria | Discharge from the vagina or penis, burning on urination, low back pain. Can cause permanent blindness in newborns infected during birth. Untreated, can be life threatening. | Antibiotics can successfully cure gonorrhea in adolescents and adults. |
| Syphilis | 5.6 per 100,000 | 3.0 per 100,000 | Bacteria | Often no symptoms for years. Primary stage: single sore appears and resolves. Secondary stage: rashes and flulike symptoms. Late stage: irreversible damage to all body systems; death. | Penicillin can cure syphilis in the primary stage. |
| Herpes simplex virus (HSV) | 16% prevalence | 16% prevalence | Virus | Genital herpes sores, flulike symptoms, including fever and swollen glands. Most people do not get sores and so are unaware they are infected. | No cure. Antiviral medications can shorten and prevent outbreaks but do not get rid of the virus. |

[a] *Rate* indicates number of cases of a disease per 100,000 members of a given population. *Prevalence* is the percentage of a given population that has the disease.

*Sources:* CDC, 2011b, 2012d, 2012e.

the more than 14,000 newly diagnosed patients infected with HIV were under age 25. Most of the young adults ages 20 to 24 were likely infected as adolescents. African Americans aged 13 to 19 accounted for 73% of the newly diagnosed cases in their age group yet represent only 17% of that group (CDC, 2011b).

The most common infectious diseases transmitted through sexual activity are chlamydia, gonorrhea, human papillomavirus (HPV), and herpes simplex virus. Among both genders and all age groups, adolescent women aged 15 to 19 have the second-highest rate of chlamydia (just after women ages 20 to 24). These adolescent women also have the highest rate of gonorrhea, twice that of male adolescents (CDC, 2011b).

Syphilis among males 20 to 24 has increased significantly, from 5 cases per 100,000 in 2001 to 21.9 in 2010, making this the highest rate among all males for a disease once associated with men ages 35–39. Young men ages 20–24 may have been infected as adolescents (CDC, 2011b). The incidence of syphilis has historically been higher among men having sex with men. It has long been considered among the most dangerous communicable diseases.

Adolescent girls bear a disproportionate burden of STDs: 26% are infected with at least one disease that they acquired through sexual contact (CDC, 2011b). Females are more vulnerable to infection for anatomical reasons. Also, it is likely that most STDs are transmitted from males to females. Males tend to have more sexual partners than females, and may pass on to female partners an infection acquired through male-to-male sexual activity.

Unfortunately, African American adolescent females bear the greatest burden of all of their age mates (CDC, 2011b). The prevalence of chlamydia among these young women is 1.7 times higher than white females and 3 times higher than Hispanic females. African American adolescent girls are also 4 times more likely than young white women, and 8 times more likely than Hispanic girls, to have gonorrhea. Girls who are Asian and Native American have very low rates of sexually transmitted infections.

### Cervical Cancer, Human Papillomavirus, and a Vaccine **Policy**

About 12,000 American women are diagnosed with cervical cancer each year, most often in midlife, years after being infected with human papillomavirus (HPV). In 2006 and 2009, two vaccines against HPV were introduced: Gardasil and Ceravix. The vaccine is given in three doses over an 8-month period and can cost up to $400, which may or may not be covered by insurance. In 2006, the CDC added the vaccine to the routine vaccination schedule for girls between ages 11 to 12, and, in 2011, for boys in the same age group. It can be given as early as age 9, and catch-up vaccinations can be administered up to age 26.

The HPV vaccination requirement has, however, been controversial for many reasons. For one, it protects only the person receiving the vaccine; it does not achieve community immunity, as discussed in Chapter 8. Therefore, some question whether it can or should be mandated by law (Charo, 2007; Lippman, Melnychuk, Shimmin, & Boscoe, 2007). In addition, by focusing on preventing HPV in adolescent girls, more attention is being paid to sexual activity in adolescent females than in adolescent males.

The National Cancer Institute (2012) maintains that prevention practices directed against cervical cancer should include not only immunization but also education about using barrier protection during sex, risk factors such as sexual activity at an early age with multiple partners, and early detection through yearly gynecological examinations. The problem with this approach is that parents and health professionals may be ambivalent about talking with girls as young as 9 about any of these issues (Charo, 2007; Waller, Marlow, & Wardle, 2006).

In 2010, about 32% of girls aged 13 to 17 had completed all three doses of the HPV vaccine, up from 25% in 2008; only 1.4% of males had done so (CDC, 2011c). Unfortunately, the majority of girls being vaccinated mistakenly believe that the vaccine protects them against all sexually transmitted infections (Mullins et al., 2012).

## Adolescent Substance Use

Unlike sexual reproduction, which is required to propagate the human race, the use of substances to alter consciousness is definitely elective. And for thousands of years, human beings have elected to indulge in such substances, resulting in many explicit and implicit religious, social, and legal rules intended to restrict the use of a variety of these substances.

Teens are more vulnerable to the effects of alcohol and illegal drugs, for a number of reasons. Their brains are reorganizing, they lack experience to deal with temptation, and they don't think about the consequences of their actions far into the future. To address this issue, let's start by reviewing data from the Youth Risk Behavior Surveillance System (CDC, 2012a). Figure 14.11 shows that the use of alcohol and cigarettes has declined since 1991. In contrast, marijuana use peaked in 1999 yet remains above 1991 levels. As is the case with other risky health behaviors, the prevalence of substance use among teenagers tends to increase as they get older. With the exception of alcohol, males use restricted substances more often than females, and black females are the least likely to use these substances, as compared with other groups.

**Alcohol.** Because alcohol is the preferred adolescent substance of choice, we examine it first. Although adolescent alcohol use has declined somewhat since 1991, as just stated, its popularity remains widespread among this age group. By twelfth grade, 80% of teens have had at least one alcoholic beverage, and slightly over half had a drink within a month before completing the YRBS survey. According to the YRBS, the use of alcohol by girls and boys is similar, although the National Institute on Alcohol Abuse and Alcoholism (NIAAA) (2006) suggests there is a higher prevalence of serious drinking problems among adolescent males as they get older. Taken together, the YRBS and NIAAA data indicate that drinking and alcohol-related problems are highest among white and Native American or Alaska Native adolescents, followed by Hispanic, African Americans, and Asian youth. *Binge drinking*—that is, having five or more drinks in a row within a few hours—occurs twice as often among white and Hispanic youth than their black peers.

Alcohol is the source of many hazards for adolescents. It can alter neural networks required for information processing, impair working memory, and interfere with the rational decision-making capacity of the prefrontal lobes (Tapert, Caldwell, & Burke, 2004/2005). It is often associated with three leading causes of death among youths: unintended injuries from accidents, homicide, and suicide. Excessive use of alcohol and other drugs is also associated with poor school performance, diminished motivation, and risk taking—behaviors that can have permanent consequences (NIAAA, 2009). And, as one risky behavior is often accompanied by others, drinking—and especially

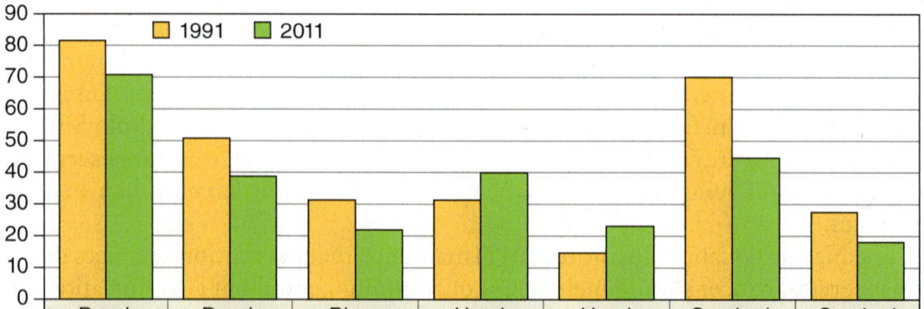


| | Drank alcohol at least once | Drank alcohol recently | Binge drinking recently | Used marijuana at least once | Used marijuana recently | Smoked cigarette at least once | Smoked cigarettes recently |
|---|---|---|---|---|---|---|---|
| 1991 | 81.6 | 50.8 | 31.3 | 31.3 | 14.7 | 70.1 | 27.5 |
| 2011 | 70.8 | 38.7 | 21.9 | 39.9 | 23.1 | 44.7 | 18.1 |

**FIGURE 14.11 Adolescent Substance Use, 1991 and 2011** Teenagers in 2011 used alcohol and cigarettes less frequently than did teenagers in 1991. Marijuana use peaked in 1999, but remains above 1991 levels.
*Source:* Youth Risk Behavior Surveillance Systems, 2010, 2012.

binge drinking—is associated with unprotected sex, violence, drunk driving, unintentional injuries (such as falls, burns, and broken bones), and increased risk taking in general (CDC, 2008; Miller, Naimi, Brewer, & Jones, 2007).

**OTHER SUBSTANCES.** As you can see in Figure 14.11, smoking cigarettes has declined since 1991, while marijuana use has increased slightly. Males are more likely to use tobacco products and marijuana than are girls. Males are also more likely to use anabolic steroids, to stimulate bone and muscle development to enhance athletic performance, appearance, or both. Anabolic steroids can cause the bones to grow too fast, however, and then close the growth plates prematurely. In 2009, 4.3% of adolescent males reported having used this substance illegally. Many of these young men may not appreciate its potential negative effects: Abuse may lead to aggression, mood swings, paranoia, and impaired judgment (Pope & Katz, 1998; Pope, Kouri, & Hudson, 2000), as well as shrinking of the testicles, reduced sperm count, and infertility (National Institute on Drug Abuse, 2008).

Of growing concern is the more widespread abuse of prescription and over-the-counter (OTC) medications by adolescents and adults alike, especially stimulants and pain medications (Johnston, O'Malley, Bachman & Schulenberg, 2008; Setlik, Bond, & Ho, 2009). For example, methylphenidate (Ritalin™) and many diet pills contain amphetamines, stimulants that speed heart rate, raise blood pressure, and decrease appetite. Methylphenidate is a controlled substance commonly prescribed for attention deficit hyperactive disorder (ADHD), but some adolescents taking the drug legally share it with their non-ADHD friends. Prescription painkillers, which are also narcotics, such as Vicodin™ and OxyContin™, are readily available in the medicine cabinet at home and are easy to sell on the street. Teens mistakenly think these drugs are safe because they are legal. Unfortunately, that is not the case.

Male adolescents are more likely than females to use tobacco products, like cigarettes.

## Health Education and Prevention: Focus on Sex and Alcohol

Many educational programs aimed at teaching adolescents about having sex and using alcohol traditionally focused on avoiding the potential consequences of these behaviors. Over time, researchers recognized this as a "crime" mentality—focusing on preventing bad things from happening—and that teaching teens to say no to sex or alcohol was not enough. Scare tactics may capture their attention in the short run, but such tactics alone don't typically lead to permanent changes in behavior.

More recently, youth programs have adopted an "investment" mentality, geared to fostering healthy development (Bales, 2005). These programs aim to encourage teens to avoid being sexually active and using alcohol during adolescence while also preparing them for a not-so-distant young adulthood that will likely include both (Bales, 2005; Catalano, Berglund, Ryan, Lonczak & Hawkins, 2004; Nation et al., 2003; Terrion, 2006).

### Sex Education Programs

Does sex education work? Yes, actually, it does. Hundreds of studies indicate that well-designed programs that combine education, skill development, and a message of personal responsibility can delay first sexual intercourse by as much as a year, increase condom use, lower the rate of STDs and unwanted pregnancy, increase knowledge of HIV and other STDs, and improve social skills that prevent risky sexual behavior (Boyer, Shafer, & Tschann, 1997; Kohler, Manhart, & Lafferty, 2008; Robin et al., 2004; St. Lawrence et al., 1995; Underhill, Montgomery, & Operario, 2008). Many of the programs studied are referred to as "abstinence-plus" or "comprehensive sex education" programs. These programs explain that the best course of action is to abstain from sexual intercourse and that oral sex is not risk-free. They also prepare adolescents by giving them the knowledge and social skills they need to negotiate the challenges of normal sexuality, such as what to say and do when teens find themselves in situations that may lead to sexual behaviors that they want to avoid.

Jeff Greenberg/Photo Edit

Engaging discussions about sex education, like the one taking place here, give adolescents the knowledge and skills they need to deal with questions of human sexuality.

What about abstinence-only programs, which focus exclusively on avoidance of sexual behavior, and may require taking a "virginity pledge? These programs don't work as well as more comprehensive programs. According to studies, the sexual behavior of adolescents who take virginity pledges does not differ from that of peers who do not take these pledges—except that pledgers are less likely to protect themselves from pregnancy and disease. Furthermore, once those who pledge do become sexually active, they may deny having made the pledge in the first place; and those who pledge *after* having sexual experience may deny having had sexual intercourse (Rosenbaum, 2006, 2009; Underhill et al., 2008).

Virginity pledges may, however, be effective when associated with a cohesive group whose members volunteer to pledge and choose to affiliate with one another exclusively. An example is a small group of religious students in a larger secular high school. But in a large group, when almost everyone pledges, the odds are that some students eventually will break their pledge, undermining its long-term value (Bearman & Brückner, 2001; Martino, Elliot, Colling, Kanuse, & Berry, 2008).

## what if...?

What if you were in a position to counsel adolescents about protecting themselves against sexually transmitted infections and diseases? Knowing that girls, and especially African American girls, bear the burden of these diseases, what would you say to them? What would you say to their male peers? Did you listen when concerned adults cautioned you about these risks? Why or why not?

### The Role of Parents in Adolescent Sexual Behavior

Parenting

School-based sex education classes may cover basic information about the anatomy and physiology of puberty, as well as prevention of pregnancy and sexually transmitted diseases, but adolescents do not walk away from them with a full understanding of these topics, nor do they learn how to make decisions about sexual behavior. That is where parents come in.

In general, adolescents whose parents talk with them about sex, and who are open to ongoing discussion on this sensitive subject, have their first intercourse almost one year later than other teens. Moreover, when these adolescents do become sexually active, they have fewer partners and are more likely to use condoms (Blake, Simkin, Ledsky, Perkins, & Calabrese, 2001; Guttmacher Institute, 2006; Miller, 2002).

Across racial and economic groups, mothers are more likely than fathers to have these conversations with both daughters and sons. Although fathers may also talk with their sons about sex, they rarely do so with their daughters (Miller, et al., 1998). In general, family relationships marked by warmth and cohesion foster open and mutually respectful dialogues between parent and adolescent, so that parents, rather than peers or pop culture, become the primary source of information regarding sexual activity. At the same time, a more directive style, such as explicitly warning at-risk teens about the consequences of sexual activity, may be more effective (Blake et al., 2001; Donenberg et al., 2005; Whitaker, Miller, & Clark, 2000).

In talking to teens about sex, parents must keep in mind that sexuality for teens is normal, but also a new experience for them, full of allure, as well as uncertainty and anxiety. Some specific suggestions for parents to help them approach this topic with their teens include (Mayo Clinic, 2011):

Eric Audras/Onoky/Getty Images

Open and ongoing discussions about sex between parents and their teens encourage young people to make better decisions about sexual activity.

- Seize the moment, such as when news, entertainment, or advertising media openly raise sexual issues. Opportune times to talk are during everyday activities, such as riding in the car.
- Be honest. If you're uncomfortable, say so, then keep talking.
- Present the risks, consequences, and responsibilities objectively.
- Understand the pressures, challenges, and concerns of teens. Talk about how to deal with pressure to have sex; explain what constitutes date rape; and identify the risks posed by alcohol and drugs. Talk through specific scenarios and suggest things to say and to do to defuse a tense or difficult situation.
- Teens' concerns about their sexual orientation are common, and they may be confused by their own feelings, and perhaps the behavior of others. Be open to discussion of such issues.
- Talk about feelings, the emotional consequences of sexual activity, values, and, if appropriate, religious beliefs.
- If your teenager becomes sexually active, remember that it is more important than ever to keep the conversation on this subject going.

## Alcohol and Drug Prevention Programs

In addition to prevention programs focusing on adolescent sexual activity, there are programs aimed at preventing teens from using alcohol and drugs. Do alcohol and drug prevention programs work? The results are mixed. Programs that target teens in large groups in a single session, such as a school assembly, don't permanently change behavior. School and community-based programs featuring smaller, interactive sessions have a greater likelihood of long-term success. Such programs may help adolescents to recognize how mass media can glorify alcohol and drugs, or even mislead audiences, about their effects. And as with comprehensive sex education programs, the sessions often focus on developing social skills for negotiating common situations.

*Everyday stories*

HANDLING DIFFICULT SITUATIONS Most adolescents will eventually find themselves at a party or in another circumstance where alcohol is being served. In smaller group sessions of alcohol and drug prevention programs, teens can role-play how to leave a gathering without being noticed, how to refuse a drink in an open cup if they did not see the drink being poured, or how to drink without really drinking. They also can practice how to be the designated driver, how to remove a drunk friend from a party, and how to get help when they need it. Practicing these behaviors beforehand makes it easier for teenagers to know what to do in a real-life situation.

For younger adolescents in particular, family-focused interventions work well. Parents are best qualified to set expectations about responsible behavior earlier in adolescence than later (Grimshaw & Stanton, 2006; Lantz et al., 2000; Spoth, Greenberg, & Turrisi, 2008; Thomas & Perera, 2006; Tobler et al., 2000).

Why are adolescents attracted to alcohol in the first place? Cultural expectations play a major role. Adolescents drink because other people do. The commonly held belief that teenagers in countries with more liberal drinking laws are less likely to abuse alcohol is not true. The evidence suggests that raising the legal age, and placing restrictions on the availability of alcohol, and how media portray alcohol, can lower adolescent alcohol use (Doran, Hall, Shakeshaft, Vos, & Cobiac, 2010; Farhat et al., 2012; Hassan, Csemy, Rappo, & Knight, 2009; Kuntsche, et al., 2011; NIAAA, 2006).

✓ CHECK YOUR PROGRESS

1. What are the nutritional needs of adolescents?
2. What factors contribute to overweight in adolescents?
3. What are the normal challenges of adolescent sexuality?
4. What do the trends in alcohol use tell you? Drug use?
5. What kinds of prevention programs work best?

## Capacity for Health: Caregivers, Community, and Safety

**[ KEY QUESTION ] 3. How can parents and the community help adolescents to stay healthy and safe?**

Let's return to the paradox of adolescent health, which we first mentioned at the beginning of the chapter. It's true that 80.5% of adolescents ages 12 to 17 report being in excellent or very good health (Bloom, Cohen, & Freeman, 2011). Remember, though, that 26% of adolescent women are infected with at least one disease acquired through sexual contact, that two thirds of adolescents are overweight or obese, and that thousands of teens are injured or killed in accidents.

In the previous section, we noted that thinking about adolescent behavior as a problem waiting to happen is not fair to adolescents. In many ways, adolescents live in a world more complex and challenging than that of previous generations. It is often said that they must learn to take individual responsibility for their behavior. This is very important, but not sufficient. In keeping with our developmental systems perspective, we must also consider the adult community's capacity to promote the health and safety of adolescents. As examples of how to do that, we look at motor vehicle safety, access to health care, and sports safety.

### Motor Vehicle Safety

Earlier, we noted that motor vehicle accidents are the leading cause of unintentional injury and death among adolescents, more so than for any other age group. In fact, drivers ages 16 to 19 are 4 times more likely than older drivers to be in a car accident, especially during their first year behind the wheel (Insurance Institute for Highway Safety, 2009; National Highway Traffic Safety Administration, 2010). Several factors contribute to these statistics.

Adolescents underestimate dangerous situations, have less experience responding quickly to unpredictable situations, are more likely to speed (especially males), and are less likely to use seatbelts than adults (American Academy of Pediatrics Committee on Injury, Violence and Poison Prevention and Committee on Adolescence, 2006; CDC, 2010a). Furthermore, driving conditions have changed. The average highway speed limit is faster than the 55 miles per hour of a generation ago, and there are more cars on the road. The risk of accident also increases with the number of peers in the car with the young driver. Talking on a cell phone or texting also raises the risk of accidents, as explained in What Happens in the Brain? Having a Conversation While Driving a Car. Finally, as we noted earlier, driving under the influence of alcohol increases the risk of serious injury and death considerably.

One way that lawmakers in some states have responded to the challenges of teen driving is to introduce a *graduated driver's license* (GDL). Specific restrictions vary, but there are typically three stages to obtaining a GDL. In stage one, a young driver gets a learner's permit, after which he or she must always have an adult aged 21 or older in the car when driving. Stage two begins six months later, when the young driver gets a provisional license, with limits on nighttime driving and the number of peer passengers allowed in the car while he or she is behind the wheel. Stage three is full licensure.

At each stage, there are other requirements: The driver must attend classes and take driving tests; use a seatbelt; not use electronic gadgets or alcohol while driving; not be involved in accidents or receive traffic tickets. And in some states, teens must take a safety pledge, signed by their parents (American Academy of Pediatrics et al., 2006; National Highway Traffic Safety Administration, 2008).

GDL programs work. Multiple studies indicate they have reduced the crash risk by roughly 15% among new drivers, and the overall injury rate by 21% (Russell, Vandermeer, & Hartling, 2011; Shope, 2007). Furthermore, the more restrictions in the GDL program, the greater the reduction in fatalities (Russell, et al., 2011).

## Access to Health Care for Adolescents

Between 1984 and 2005, the proportion of adolescents who had private health insurance through their parents' policies declined from 74% to 65%, largely due to the decline in coverage offered by the parents' employers. During the same period, adolescents covered by public programs, such as the State Child Health Insurance Programs, more than doubled, from 10 to 23% (National Research Council and Institute of Medicine, 2007). By 2010, the percentage of adolescents without any coverage for health care had dropped to 9.8%, with Hispanic and black adolescents disproportionately represented in this group (Bloom, et al., 2011).

Having health-care coverage does not, however, guarantee that adolescents will get the care they need. For over 15 years, clinical guidelines for adolescent health have recommended an annual well-child visit, which includes: a physical examination; screening for blood pressure, cholesterol, vision, and hearing; catch-up with recommended immunizations, if necessary; and guidance for health-related behaviors, such as alcohol use and sexual activity. Girls should have their first pelvic exam by age 18, earlier if they are sexually active; and males should learn how to self-examine their testicles (Hagan, Shaw, & Duncan, 2008). Unfortunately, only 38% of adolescents actually had a routine preventive visit in the previous year, and only 10% of them receive health-related guidance beyond nutrition (Irwin, Adams, Park, & Newacheck, 2009).

This statistic represents a notable lost opportunity. Many adolescents are reluctant to talk with their parents about their health-care concerns, especially related to sexual health. Visits with a health-care provider could give them the opportunity to speak privately with a professional about these subjects. Unfortunately, even when young people do visit a health-care provider, many are too embarrassed to ask questions (National Research Council and Institute of Medicine, 2007). In an attempt to address this issue, the Society for Adolescent Medicine (2004) maintains that confidentiality without judgment be an essential component of health care for adolescents. Moreover, health-care providers need to raise issues such as sexual activity, depression, eating disorders, substance use, physical abuse, family and school issues, and violence of any kind. By doing so, they signal to adolescents that these topics are routine health-care concerns that are discussed with all patients, thereby putting them at ease.

Adolescents also need to be able to make the transition to adult health care (Park, Adams, & Irwin, 2011). In the past, older adolescents and young adults had greater difficulty accessing health care than any other age group (Irwin, 2009). Until recently, adolescents who were not full-time students "aged out" of their parents' insurance coverage and publicly funded programs at 18 or 19. In 2009, nearly 15 million young adults over 18 were uninsured, causing many of them to delay getting needed health care (English & Park, 2012). Since the initial implementation of the Patient Protection and Affordable Care Act, or ACA, in 2010, 2.5 million more young adults ages 19 to 25 have health insurance than would have been covered without the act. Many received coverage under their parents' insurance, which was extended to cover children up to age 26. Beginning in 2014, when all of the ACA's provisions have taken effect, more than 12 million of the nearly 15 million uninsured adults ages 19 to 29 will be eligible to obtain subsidized coverage under public or private insurance programs (Collins, Garber, & Robertson, 2011; English & Park, 2012).

# What Happens in the Brain?

## Having a Conversation while Driving a Car

Driving a car integrates many activities: prepared actions (pulling into traffic, making a turn, stopping), unprepared actions (swerving to avoid hazards), action planning (anticipating moving into the correct lane for exiting a roadway), anticipating and monitoring traffic (watching how others are driving and where they are relative to your vehicle), and thinking about road traffic rules and conditions (speed limits, rain) (Spiers & Maguire, 2007). Thus, driving involves many parts of the brain, including these:

- The cerebellum (motor and spatial coordination).
- The parietal cortex and occipital cortex (sensation and visual information).
- The motor cortex (voluntary motor movement).
- The prefrontal cortex (executive functions such as planning, decision making, focusing and shifting attention, and using working memory, as well as regulating emotional reactions (Jeong, et al., 2006; Spiers & Maguire, 2007).

Although driving engages multiple parts of the brain, the brain does not in fact multitask. Rather, it switches rapidly among tasks. And it seems there's a limit on how much the brain can do this—especially when a driver is also listening to conversation. Spatial, motor, visual, and executive brain functions all decrease when the driver's temporal lobe engages in language-related activities (Just, Keller & Cynkar, 2008).

The fMRI images on the facing page show the brains of adults who are experienced drivers when they are focused only on driving and when they are conversing while driving. If conversation diminishes driving ability in experienced adult drivers, what does that mean for the novice adolescent driver? Remember that the adolescent brain is not fully mature. It is less adept at switching between and integrating tasks, so the young driver is more easily distracted. Conversing with peers only adds to the problem. And that's true whether the peers are passengers in the car, on hand-held cell phones, or on hands-free cell phones (McCartt, Hellinga, & Braitman, 2006; National Safety Council, 2010).

© Cheryl Maeder/CORBIS

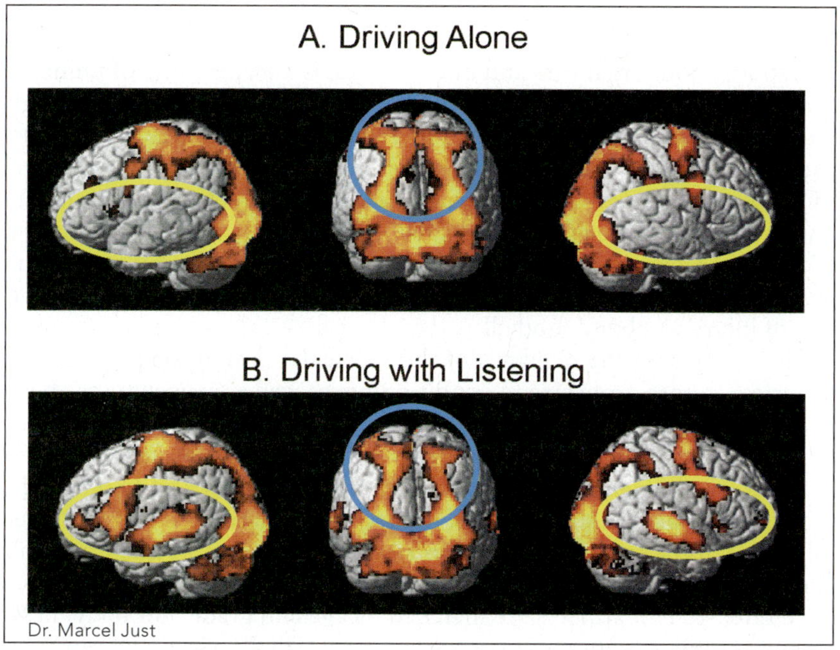

Dr. Marcel Just

## PAYING ATTENTION ONLY TO DRIVING

When we drive without the distraction of conversation, large areas of the parietal and occipital cortex, motor cortex, and cerebellum are engaged, as shown in the middle fMRI above. The temporal lobes, which process spoken language, are not engaged, as shown by the yellow ovals.

## DRIVING WHILE LISTENING TO CONVERSATION

Processing spoken language draws attentional resources away from the task of driving, engaging the temporal lobes (circled in yellow) while decreasing coordinated activity across the parietal, occipital, and frontal areas.

David Papazian/Brand X/Getty Images

**concussion** A brain injury caused by a blow to the head or jaw, causing the soft tissue of the brain to bounce back and forth against the hard bone of the skull, causing bruising, tearing, or twisting of structures and blood vessels deep within the brain tissue.

## Safety: Sports and Injury

Participating in sports, both organized and unorganized, is a major cause of unintentional injuries among adolescents. During the 2010–2011 school year, 7.4 million high school students participated in school sports. The High School Sports Related Injury Surveillance Study, which was funded by the Centers for Disease Control and Prevention, surveyed 168 American high schools during the 2010–2011 school year to determine the number and rate of injuries during practice and competition for 20 sports (Comstock, Collins & McIlvain, 2012). Table 14.5 shows a partial listing of the survey's findings. As shown in the table, the sport with the highest number of injuries and the highest rate of injury was boys' football.

Types of injury vary with the demands of the sport, the skill of the players, and a number of physical factors, from size to conditioning, as well as expectations about winning (Emery, 2003). Contact sports, along with activities in which an athlete can fall against a hard surface, such as snow skiing, have higher rates of impact injury. Injuries from repetitive movements are more common in tennis and baseball. In football and boys' ice hockey, size matters: Injury rates increase as athletes get older—and bigger. Larger size obviously contributes to greater momentum and force in collisions. In addition, even though individual boys do not develop physically at the same rate, student athletes are matched by age and grade, not body mass. The result is considerable variation among players, especially boys, which can contribute to injuries.

Let's look in greater detail at two common injuries: concussions and injuries to the anterior cruciate ligament (ACL) of the knee.

### Concussions

Concussions have garnered a great deal of attention in the media recently following the impairment and deaths of a number of high-profile professional athletes. But the concern is not new. In 1928, the *Journal of the American Medical Association* reported that a blow to the head or jaw causes the soft tissue of the brain to bounce back and forth against the hard bone of the skull (Martland, 1928). (You can see an animated video of what happens in the brain when someone receives a blow to the head at http://www.cdc.gov/concussion.) Such impact causes bruising, tearing, or twisting of structures and blood vessels deep within the brain tissue, resulting in the brain injury called a **concussion** (Blum, 2010). Concussions are categorized from mild to severe, depending on the symptoms, which range from changes in or loss of consciousness to dizziness, vomiting, forgetfulness, and irritability.

**Table 14.5** Number of Injuries and Injury Rate in High School Athletics, 2010–2011

| Boys' Sports | | | Girls' Sports | | |
|---|---|---|---|---|---|
| Sport | Total Reported Injuries | Injury Rate During Competition | Sport | Total Reported Injuries | Injury Rate During Competition |
| Football | 2,346 | 12.22 | | | |
| Wrestling | 493 | 3.77 | | | |
| Soccer | 469 | 3.52 | Soccer | 466 | 2.11 |
| Basketball | 443 | 2.33 | Basketball | 454 | 1.81 |
| Ice hockey | 163 | 5.63 | Field hockey | 164 | 2.9 |
| Track | 135 | 1.09 | Track | 164 | 1.35 |

*Notes: Injury* is an event that required attention from a medical provider or an athletic trainer, *and* restricted participation in the sport; it also includes any fracture, dental, or head injury, regardless of need to restrict participation. *Injury rate* is the number of reported injuries per number of athlete exposures. *Athlete exposure* refers to one athlete participating in one practice or competition in which the athlete is exposed to possible injury.

*Source:* Comstock, Collins, & McIlvain, 2012.

© Dennis MacDonald/Age Fotostock

Playing a contact sport, such as football, puts adolescents at risk for concussions, which have a number of serious, and sometimes long-term, negative effects.

In the past, mild concussions were often treated as relatively benign injuries—an accepted consequence of playing a sport. Emerging evidence suggests, however, that even a single mild concussion can result in serious symptoms and cognitive impairments, which may last longer than previously believed. Recovery from even mild concussions can be slow, and consequences of reinjury—called *second impact syndrome*—can be serious. Long-term problems related to serious or multiple concussive injuries include changes in personality and cognitive abilities, as well as problems with balance and motor coordination (Evans, 2012; Institute of Medicine, 2002; Reddy, Collins, & Gioia, 2008; Wilde et al., 2008).

In 2009, the National Football League conceded to the United States Congress that many of its athletes with a history of concussions suffer the long-term problems noted above (Blum, 2010). The heightened awareness about the seriousness of concussions in young people has prompted several states to institute laws requiring preventive measures, such as education and more effective protective sports equipment (Schwarz, 2010).

### Treating Concussions in Adolescents **Practice**

The Centers for Disease Control (2010b) and the American Academy of Neurology (1997) have issued guidelines for coaches and health-care providers regarding concussions in children and adolescents. Common signs and symptoms are listed in Table 14.6. Note, in particular, that a mild concussion may involve no signs or symptoms (Lovell, Collins, Iverson, Johnston, & Bradley, 2004).

Major concussions, causing severe bleeding in the brain, require immediate medical intervention. In most cases, however, the primary treatment for concussion is time off from sports and rest, to let the brain heal. In 2008, the International Conference on Concussion in Sport issued a consensus statement from multiple disciplines recommending a stepwise six-day return to sports (McCrory et al., 2009). Each day the athlete increases his or her activity level, is evaluated for symptoms, and progresses to the next level the following day if all is well.

### Anterior Cruciate Ligament (ACL) Injuries

The anterior cruciate ligament (ACL) is like a rubber band in the front of the knee, attached to bones in the upper leg (the femur) and the lower leg (the tibia). It restrains

**Table 14.6** Common Signs and Symptoms of Concussion

| Signs Observed by Others | Symptoms Reported by Athletes |
|---|---|
| Appears dazed or stunned | Headache |
| Is confused about assignment | Nausea |
| Forgets plays | Balance problems or dizziness |
| Is unsure of game, score, or opponent | Double or fuzzy vision |
| Moves clumsily | Sensitivity to light or noise |
| Answers questions slowly | Feeling sluggish |
| Loses consciousness | Feeling foggy or groggy |
| Shows behavior or personality changes | Concentration or memory problems |
| Can't recall events prior to hit | Confusion |
| Can't recall events after hit | |

*Source:* Centers for Disease Control and Prevention, 2010b.

forward motion of the tibia, so that the lower leg doesn't bend forward at the knee. The ACL can be injured when more force is applied to the ligament than it can withstand. This can happen through direct impact, such as when a football player is tackled. It can also happen when an athlete pivots on landing, as in soccer or skiing, twisting the knee and tibia into unnatural alignment. The extent of the injury determines the treatment, which may range from avoiding certain activities to surgery. A torn ACL requires reconstructive surgery and rehabilitation, and it can take six to nine months before the athlete can return to competition.

© Hero/Corbis

Female athletes, especially soccer players, are much more likely to suffer from an ACL injury than their male counterparts.

Female athletes, especially soccer players, have 4 to 8 times more ACL injuries than do male athletes (Giugliano & Solomon, 2007). Females have looser knee joints than males, as well as a wider pelvis. The combination of these two features means that a female player's knees are less stable, especially when she lands on her foot while changing direction as she runs. Both males and females with ACL injuries are at increased risk for reinjury, and for developing osteoarthritis within 10 to 15 years of the initial injury. However, female players on average sustain their ACL injuries at a younger age (19 years) than males (23 years). The result is higher prevalence of osteoarthritis among female athletes, which has prompted a call for better means of prevention on the playing field (Lohmander, Östenberg, Englund, & Roos, 2004).

## what if...?

What if adolescent athletes were never allowed to play their sport again after having had surgery for an injury or experiencing a concussion? What if football were banned all together? When does the risk of injury outweigh the benefit of participating in a sport? Is there too much pressure on young people to play sports, given that the vast majority of high school and college athletes never play professionally?

### WHEN SYSTEMS CONNECT

## An Uneven Playing Field

Let's talk more about the metaphorical playing field. In 1972, Title IX of the Education Amendment Act prohibited federally funded schools, colleges, and universities from discriminating on the basis of gender. One result was a substantial increase in schools' funding for women's athletic programs. The numbers of young female athletes since then has soared, although not among nonwhite adolescents (Suggs, 2001). Many girls benefit from their sports experience. Girls who participate in sports feel more empowered and are less likely to become pregnant at an early age (Solomon, 2002). At the same time, their higher rate of specific injuries, such as ACL tears, compared with their male counterparts, has raised several concerns.

Most training programs had been developed with the male body—and male behavior—as the baseline model. But female bodies are not just smaller than male bodies, they are anatomically and physiologically different. Females also have a different distribution of muscle and fat, wider pelvises, looser knee joints, less lung capacity, and weaker neck muscles. But they can be just as aggressive on the playing field, and perhaps have greater endurance and pain tolerance. These factors may lead young female athletes, encouraged by their coaches and parents, to play with injuries, creating a "warrior-girl ethos" (Sokolove, 2008).

We can see that many systems work together to increase the risk of injuries to female athletes: public policies such as Title IX, coaches' expectations about training male versus female athletes, physiological differences between females and males, and parental and societal expectations about competition. As the field of sports medicine continues to mature, and with greater awareness of the need for better training and prevention programs, hopefully, the gender gap in sports-related injuries will close.

*Everyday stories*

A WARRIOR GIRL In a widely read article in *The New York Times* titled "An Uneven Playing Field," Michael Sokolove (2008) used the story of one high school athlete, Janelle, to represent many of her peers. A soccer player since the age of 5, she embodies the warrior-girl ethos: years of membership on traveling teams, club teams, and school teams, year-round, at a pace more demanding than in professional soccer leagues.

Janelle tore the ACLs in both knees in high school. She was not alone: Of the 18 girls on her high school team, 8 suffered ACL tears. Janelle's first injury occurred during a kicking practice drill. The second injury occurred during a game, as she ran down the field. She lay on the ground screaming, more from anger than from pain, as she realized she would have to sit on the bench during most of her senior year, when college scouts were attending games and her teammates went to the state championship without her.

CHECK YOUR PROGRESS

1. What are some reasons that teenage drivers are more likely than older drivers to be in a car accident?
2. How many adolescents have access to health care?
3. What factors contribute to sports-related injuries in adolescence? Why may girls be at greater risk?

## Common Disruptions in Health: Managing Chronic Illness

**[ KEY QUESTION ] 4. What about adolescence makes it the most difficult time of life to have a chronic illness?**

Recall from Chapter 11 that as many as 15 to 25% of children and adolescents have a chronic health condition that requires continued professional care (van Cleave, Gortmaker, & Perrin, 2010). Adolescence is probably the most challenging time in life to have a chronic illness or disability. Adolescents' bodies are changing rapidly, requiring ongoing adjustments in medications, special diets, treatments, and assistive devices such as artificial limbs. At the same time, they are often expected to be more independent in managing their medical regimens, yet their judgment is not fully mature. Like other adolescents, those with chronic conditions are concerned about their appearance and about being like their friends. Finally, their relationships with their parents are changing. Parents who have been managing their child's health problems are understandably anxious about transferring that responsibility. Managing type 1 diabetes is an excellent example of these challenges, thus its management during adolescence is the subject of considerable research.

As we mentioned in Chapter 2, type 1 and type 2 diabetes differ from one another. Type 2 diabetes develops over time, as the pancreas stops producing insulin, usually due to obesity. The onset of type 1 diabetes, in contrast, is sudden, prompted when the immune system begins to mistakenly destroy the cells in the pancreas that produce insulin. While type 2 diabetes usually can be corrected by diet and weight loss, type 1 diabetes has no cure, and mismanagement of fluctuating levels of blood glucose can be life threatening. As noted in the opening of this chapter with the story of Abigail Lore, who was diagnosed with type 1 diabetes at age 5, the disease changed her life, and the lives of her family, forever. Let's hear more of her story:

Abigail Lore

Abigail Lore, the New Hampshire delegate to the Juvenile Diabetes Research Foundation 2011 children's conference.

> *Diabetes is not visible. All of the work, planning, and maintaining my health is something only my diabetes team, my family, and I know about. Not only do I have to worry about school, sports, and my social life, but I have to be my own pancreas, too. There is the constant worry of my blood glucose being out of control, and the long-term severe complications of blindness, kidney failure, or even amputation.*
>
> *For example, a sports team practice to another girl is just another practice. She just shows up. But I have to start planning hours before practice, to eat the right amount of protein and carbs, and alter my insulin pump settings to maintain a healthy blood glucose level throughout the practice so that I can perform at my finest. Even with the best planning, things don't always go well and I have to sit out. It's frustrating, because these times seem to outshine the times when I am spot-on with my management.*
>
> *There are a lot of things I need to think about or do that make me feel alone and different from my friends. For example, my mother and I have to meet with friends' parents before a play date or sleepover, and with teachers or coaches to explain to them that I have diabetes and what that means. Sometimes I wake up in the middle of the night to test my blood glucose, or do finger sticks, or change my infusion pump settings when friends are around. I don't feel well and worry when my blood glucose is too high or too low, but it's hard for others to understand why. Any person living with a chronic disease goes through ups and downs. I honestly couldn't do this without my family. In our family it's not, "I have diabetes," it's "We have diabetes." That gives me the motivation to keep me going.*

As Abby points out, a day in the life of an adolescent with diabetes may be highly regimented on the one hand—set times to test blood glucose, give themselves insulin, and eat a prescribed diet—on the other hand, life can be somewhat unpredictable. The body's need for glucose and insulin can change in response to exercise, sweating, fatigue, and hormonal fluctuations. Consuming alcohol, common among adolescents, can cause blood glucose to skyrocket. If glucose levels in the blood become too high or too low, the adolescent may become shaky, nauseated, or confused, and may even lapse into coma (American Diabetes Association, 2008).

For adolescents with diabetes, self-management is a process in which goals are set and decisions made in collaboration with parents, family, school personnel, and health-care providers. Management of the disease changes as the adolescent matures, but families play a key role in his or her physical and emotional health (American Diabetes Association, 2008; Keough, Sullivan-Bolyai, Crawford, Schilling, & Dixon, 2011; Palladino, & Helgeson, 2012; Schilling, Knafl, & Grey, 2006; Wang, Brown, & Horner, 2010).

Parenting an adolescent with type 1 diabetes is stressful. It is especially difficult for single parents and for parents in lower socioeconomic circumstances, who may lack the resources and self-confidence to manage their child's illness (Streisand, Swift, Wickmark,

Chen, & Holmes, 2005). In general, mothers more than fathers assume responsibility for managing their children's diabetes. A mother will transfer responsibility to her child based on her assessment of the child's competence, her desire to promote competence and maturity in her child, and her own preference for minimizing the hassles and conflict that characterize the parent-child relationship during this time (Palmer et al., 2004).

We can see that type 1 diabetes is a complicated disease. Abby's story demonstrates that managing it successfully requires careful coordination across systems: individual physiology; cognitive, social, and emotional maturity; and family, peers, school, health-care providers, and policymakers. We can also see that for Abby, diabetes is not something that she *has*; it is part of who she is. That fact makes Abby's story an excellent example to conclude our chapters on physical development and health from birth to adolescence. Physical development and health are not separate from cognitive and psychosocial development. They are essential parts of who children are and who they have the potential to be.

**what if...?**

What if you were an adolescent with a chronic health condition? How do you think it would change your life? What if you had an adolescent friend with a chronic condition? What role could you play in helping your friend be as healthy as possible?

**CHECK YOUR PROGRESS**

1. How do type I and type II diabetes differ?
2. What is the role of parenting in managing an adolescent's chronic illness?

# CHAPTER SUMMARY

## Biology of Health: Physical Growth and Development

**[ KEY QUESTION ] 1. How do the body and brain change during adolescence?**

- Adolescence is a period of reorganization of the biological, psychological, social, and cognitive processes required for children to transform into young adults.
- Growth occurs along different axes, feedback loops involving the biochemical relationships between different hormones, glands, and other organs.
- Puberty involves the development of secondary and primary sexual characteristics, measured using Tanner's stages. Puberty is a highly synchronized suite of biological changes that occur in a cascade, unfolding in a predictable and interlaced sequence.
- Many factors influence the timing of puberty, including genes, nutrition, and cultural and family dynamics. In turn, the timing of puberty has its own social implications, with early-maturing boys at an advantage and early-maturing girls at a disadvantage.
- Moods and emotions are complex phenomena without a single cause. That said, increased levels of testosterone in adolescence have been associated with social dominance and aggression in boys, and it is thought that fluctuating levels of sex hormones during the menstrual cycle may play a role in premenstrual syndrome in girls.
- The lobes that make up the cerebrum do not all mature at the same time, leading to dyssynchrony in development. The prefrontal cortex, responsible for such abilities as abstract reasoning, planning, and decision making, is among the last parts of the brain to mature.
- The reorganization, myelination, and pruning of the adolescent brain constitute a sensitive period in brain development during which the environment and experience play significant roles, creating both opportunities and vulnerabilities for adolescents.

## Foundations of Health: Health Promotion and Disease Prevention

**[ KEY QUESTION ] 2. What are some health-related choices that adolescents make?**

- Adolescents often make poor food choices, failing to eat enough healthful food while consuming too many high-fat, high-sugar foods. One result may be overweight or even obesity; about one third of U.S. children and adolescents are overweight.
- Unintentional injury, especially in motor vehicle accidents, is the leading cause of death among adolescents.
- Today's adolescents are less likely to engage in potentially harmful behaviors than 20 years ago, specifically: decreased use of tobacco, alcohol, and drugs; increased use of seatbelts; less likely to ride with a driver who has been drinking alcohol; more likely to use condoms.
- By twelfth grade, 80% of teens have had at least one alcoholic beverage. Alcohol use is a leading factor in motor vehicle accidents and other unintentional injuries. Alcohol-related problems are highest among white and American Indian or Alaska Native adolescents, especially males.

- Healthy sexual development includes four developmental challenges: (1) body image—the adolescent's comfort in his or her sexually maturing body, (2) managing sexual arousal, (3) negotiating sexual behavior, and (4) practicing safe sex. Adolescents whose parents talk with them about sex have fewer partners and are more likely to use condoms.
- The rates of pregnancy, live birth, and abortion among American teenagers aged 15 to 19 have declined significantly across all racial and ethnic groups since 1991, reaching historic lows in 2009. Non-Hispanic black adolescents are more than twice as likely as non-Hispanic white adolescents to become pregnant and give birth. Pregnancy rates are highest among socioeconomically disadvantaged teenaged girls.
- The most common infectious diseases transmitted through sexual activity are chlamydia, gonorrhea, human papillomavirus (HPV), and herpes simplex virus. Adolescent girls bear a disproportionate burden of sexually transmitted diseases: 26% are infected with at least one disease that they acquired through sexual contact.
- Well-designed abstinence-plus or comprehensive sex education programs can delay first sexual intercourse by as much as a year; increase condom use and decrease STDs and unwanted pregnancy; increase knowledge of HIV and other STDs; and improve social skills that prevent risky sexual behavior. Abstinence-only programs and virginity pledges are not as effective.

## Capacity for Health: Caregivers, Community, and Safety

**[ KEY QUESTION ] 3. How can parents and the community help adolescents to stay healthy and safe?**

- Graduated driver's license programs are based on research indicating that adolescent brains are not fully mature. These programs have reduced the crash risk by roughly 15% among new drivers, aged 16, and reduced overall injury by 21%.
- Only 38% of adolescents have a routine annual visit with a health-care provider, and only 10% of them receive health-related guidance beyond nutrition. This represents a major lost opportunity for health education and prevention.
- Sports-related injury, involving both organized and unorganized athletics, is the leading cause of unintentional nonfatal injuries among adolescents. The sport with the highest number of injuries and the highest rate of injury was boys' football, followed by wrestling (boys) and soccer, basketball and hockey (ice and field) for both genders.
- Concussions and knee injuries are common, serious, injuries, with girls more vulnerable to knee injuries.

## Common Disruptions in Health: Managing Chronic Illness

**[ KEY QUESTION ] 4. What about adolescence makes it the most difficult time of life to have a chronic illness?**

- Adolescence is probably the most challenging time in life to have a chronic illness or disability. Adolescent bodies are changing rapidly, requiring ongoing adjustments in medications, special diets, treatments, and assistive devices (such as artificial limbs). Adolescents are often expected to be more independent in managing their medical regimens, yet their judgment is not fully mature.
- Self-management of a chronic illness is a process in which goals are set and decisions made in collaboration with parents, family, school personnel, and health-care providers.

# KEY TERMS

adolescence *517*
adolescent growth spurt *517*
adrenarche *518*
androgens *518*
concussion *546*
epiphyseal plate *519*
gonadarche *518*
menarche *517*
primary sexual characteristics *517*
puberty *517*
secondary sexual characteristics *517*
sexually transmitted disease (STD) *536*
social dominance *523*
thought-mediated behavior *521*

# CRITICAL THINKING QUESTIONS

1. **Biology of Health: Physical Growth and Development.** We've seen that puberty is a highly synchronized suite of biological changes that occur in a cascade, unfolding in a predictable and interlaced sequence. In contrast, brain development is dissynchronous. Explain how these two developmental pathways are different, and why that may be important.
2. **Foundations of Health: Health Promotion and Disease Prevention.** Why might older adolescents be more likely to have sexual intercourse but less likely to use condoms? In general, what do you think could encourage adolescents to choose healthier behaviors regarding eating, alcohol, and sex?
3. **Capacity for Health: Caregivers, Community, and Safety.** What would reduce sports injuries among adolescents? Do you agree that girls are playing on an "uneven playing field?" If not, why not? If so, what could be done about it?
4. **Common Disruptions in Health: Managing Chronic Illness.** What cognitive and social factors might contribute to how well an adolescent manages his or her own chronic health condition?
5. **Cultural Perspective.** The rates of sexually transmitted diseases and pregnancy vary by race and ethnicity, with African American adolescent girls having the highest rates. What might be some reasons for these differences?

# REAL Development

## Physical Development and Health in Adolescence

In this module, you have been asked to interview professionals who can provide insight into aspects of adolescent sexuality so that you can start to develop a sex education awareness initiative. The nurse and counselor at Jenna's school have agreed to answer your questions on sex education.

**WileyPLUS** Go to WileyPLUS to complete the *Real Development* activity.

03.01

# Chapter 15

# Cognitive Development in Adolescence

## MAKING A difference

### Teen-to-Teen Tutors

Halfway through her first year of high school, Mayda found herself struggling with algebra. Her teacher suggested that she contact a program at her high school in which students tutored other students. When Mayda did so, she was paired with Ashley, a student one year ahead of her. The year before, Ashley had been on the other side of the tutoring program. She had struggled with algebra and asked for help from a peer tutor. Ashley understood the types of problems Mayda was having. She knew, too, what had helped her grapple with those problems. "I know how it feels to not 'get' what you are supposed to learn in class. It's so frustrating," commented Ashley. "I really like the opportunity to help others 'get it.'"

Along with the insight that came from her own experiences, Ashley received training in how to work with other students. "We are taught that we should not do the problems for them, but we need to walk with them through the steps until they get it. Don't give an answer, give an example" (Reese, 2002, p. 15).

Peer tutoring has many advantages. Students who have struggled with certain material, as Ashley did with algebra, can empathize with others who are likewise struggling. They can also reflect on their own successes by considering which strategies helped them learn. Tutoring others helps students consolidate their own learning, as well. For example, tutors learn how to break down a problem into the steps needed to help others solve it. Peer tutors need to have a pocketful of strategies they can teach to others. Part of successful tutoring involves helping other students discover which strategies work best for particular types of learning. Through peer tutoring both students *learn to learn*, a key component of adolescent cognitive development. Researchers studying peer tutoring have found that it can be effective, as you will see later in this chapter.

## CHAPTER OUTLINE

## [KEY QUESTIONS] *for* READING CHAPTER 15

1. What are the major contributions of Piaget's theory of cognitive development relevant to the adolescent period?
2. How does Vygotsky's theory explain cognitive growth during adolescence?
3. What cognitive changes occur during adolescence, according to information processing theory?
4. What are some major changes that occur in the adolescent brain?
5. What factors promote or diminish adolescents' success in school?

| **Piaget's Stage Theory** |
|---|
| Sensorimotor |
| Preoperational |
| Concrete operational |
| Formal operational<br>• Adolescents begin to use abstract thinking and reasoning with more complex symbols. |

**IN THIS CHAPTER,** we examine adolescents' thought processes. Do they differ from those of middle childhood or are they just more efficient? Interest in this question has grown in recent years, corresponding with new information about brain changes during adolescence. We know that adolescents vary more in their cognitive development than do younger children (Kuhn, 2008). In part, this variability is due to the fact that adolescents have more choices. They are freer to choose the experiences they are exposed to, for example, and the demands they place on themselves.

We begin with a discussion of Piaget's theory related to this developmental period. We then turn to more recent perspectives on adolescent reasoning, provided by the information processing theorists. We consider as well the sociocultural perspective of Vygotsky. Next, we examine changes in the adolescent brain that relate to cognitive development. Finally, because cognitive development during adolescence is closely related to educational experiences, we consider the role of schooling during the adolescent years.

Getty Images/Purestock

Using new logic skills that develop in the formal operations stage, adolescents are capable of completing complex mathematical problems.

# Piaget and Formal Operations

**[ KEY QUESTION ] 1.** What are the major contributions of Piaget's theory of cognitive development relevant to the adolescent period?

As you read in earlier chapters, Piaget believed that children acquire cognitive abilities in an ordered and invariant manner (Overton, 1998; Piaget 1952/1936). According to Piaget, each stage of cognitive development precedes, and is necessary for, the next. Before adolescence, the child's thinking is concrete operational. As we explained in Chapter 12, that means the child reasons best when using concrete objects. The next stage, which occurs for some children at around age 12, is **formal operations**. This is a time when thinking becomes less tightly tied to the manipulation of concrete objects or examples. Instead, it is more often driven by logic. The hallmark of formal operations is the ability to think abstractly and systematically.

## Cognitive Changes in the Formal Operational Period

According to Piaget, three significant changes in reasoning occur during formal operations. These changes involve improvements in using logical necessity in reasoning, hypothetical-deductive reasoning, and conditional reasoning. All are related to abstract thought.

### Logical Necessity

By the term *logical necessity*, Piaget meant the ability to reason through a series of premises to reach a conclusion using logic even when a premise is known to be false. According to Piaget, children cannot reason in this way until the formal operational period (Gruber & Vonèche, 1977).

**formal operations** The fourth stage of Piaget's theory of cognitive development; involves the ability to use abstract reasoning.

Consider the following series of statements.

All dogs are animals. (*premise*)
Rufus is a dog. (*premise*)
Therefore, Rufus is an animal. (*conclusion*)

If the two premises are true, then by *logical necessity*, the conclusion must be true.

But what if we know very well that a premise is not true? Consider another example.

Cars are bigger than houses. (*premise*)
Houses are bigger than skyscrapers. (*premise*)
Therefore, cars are bigger than skyscrapers. (*conclusion*)

We can see that neither of these premises is true. Still, we can easily apply logical reasoning and arrive at the conclusion. Children in the concrete operational period, however, often consider the reasoning to be false. They cannot overcome the fact that the premises violate their experience (Pillow, 2002). They know, after all, that cars are not bigger than houses and that houses are not bigger than skyscrapers. The children cannot suspend their disbelief in the premises. Thus, they fail to understand the logical necessity of the conclusion. Adolescents who have reached the stage of formal operations, however, are able to suspend such disbelief in order to reach a logical (even if unrealistic) conclusion.

**hypothetical-deductive reasoning**
A form of abstract thinking typical of formal operations that involves the development of hypotheses and the use of logic to draw conclusions based on a systematic test of the hypotheses.

## Hypothetical-Deductive Reasoning

**Hypothetical-deductive reasoning** is often termed *top-down reasoning*. It begins with a set of abstract ideas, often in the form of *hypotheses*, or best guesses. It then uses logic to draw conclusions based on those hypotheses (Keating, 2004). An important aspect of this kind of reasoning is testing each hypothesis. Contrast hypothetical-deductive reasoning with inductive reasoning, often termed *bottom-up reasoning*. Inductive reasoning begins with experience and facts, which are then used to draw more general conclusions. Inductive reasoning predominates during middle childhood, whereas many adolescents also begin to use deductive reasoning (Foltz, Overton, & Ricco, 1995; Overton, 1990).

As an example, consider a task often given to children between the ages of 10 and 18 to assess their use of hypothetical-deductive reasoning. It involves a balance scale. As shown in Figure 15.1, equal-sized weights are placed on pegs at different distances from the scale's center, or *fulcrum* (Inhelder & Piaget, 1958). Children are asked

**FIGURE 15.1 Piaget's Balance Scale Task** In Piaget's balance scale task, participants must decide whether a scale will balance based on the number and distribution of weights. The principle involved concerns weight times distance. The scale will balance when weight times distance from the fulcrum is equal on both sides.

whether the scale will balance when supports holding it in place are removed. Later, they are given the opportunity to work with the scale to make the two sides balance.

To solve the problem, children need to consider three variables:

1. The number of weights on each side of the balance, given that all the weights are the same size.
2. The distance of each weight from the fulcrum.
3. Whether the weights are on a single peg or are distributed across pegs.

The principle involved concerns weight times distance. The scale will balance when weight times distance from the fulcrum is equal on both sides.

When faced with the balance-scale task, children in the concrete operational stage tend to succeed only when the two sides of the scale have the same number of weights at the same distance from the fulcrum. When this is not the case, they use trial and error to balance the scale. In contrast, individuals capable of formal operational thought develop hypotheses about the relation between the number of weights and the distance from the fulcrum. They can then test their hypotheses systematically by trying different combinations of weights and distance. For example, they might test the idea that 4 weights on peg number 2 on one side are equal to 2 weights on peg number 4 on the other side.

*Everyday stories*

A HYPOTHETICAL-DEDUCTIVE REASONING PROBLEM You might want to test your skill at hypothetical-deductive reasoning by trying to solve the following problem (Wason, 1968). Suppose you are shown four cards and told that each card has a letter on one side and a number on the other. You can see only one side of each card. Card one has an *E* on it, card two has a *K* on it, card three has a 4 on it, and card four has a 7 on it. You must determine whether the following hypothesis is true or false:

If there is a vowel on one side, then there is an even number on the other side. What is the minimum number of cards you must examine to test this hypothesis? The correct answer requires you to select two cards. You first choose the vowel card, *E*, to test whether there is an even number on the other side. If there is, then the statement is verified. But you must also test whether the statement may sometimes be false. Choosing the odd-numbered card, 7, will allow you to do that. If the 7 card has a vowel on the back, then obviously not all vowel cards have even numbers on the other side. Testing whether a hypothesis is false is a hallmark of formal operational thinking.

Hypothetical-deductive reasoning allows adolescents to become increasingly skilled at debating and arguing using logic. Such activities have two goals. The first is to present one's own position. The second is to understand the opponent's position well enough to expose weaknesses in it (Kuhn, 2008). Both require the use of logic and deductive reasoning.

In general, hypothetical-deductive reasoning opens up new ways of thinking that are not necessarily limited to experience. For example, you might think about the various effects of a possible educational policy (such as providing tuition-free college courses to all citizens) without having had any experience with such a policy. In discussing the value of hypothetical reasoning, Piaget wrote:

> The individual who becomes capable of hypothetical reasoning, by this very fact will interest himself in problems that go beyond his immediate field of experience. Hence, the adolescent's

Michelle D. Bridwell/Photo Edit

Hypothetical-deductive reasoning enables adolescents to become increasingly skilled at debating.

capacity to understand and even construct theories and to participate in society and the ideologies of adults; that is often, of course, accompanied by a desire to change society and even, if necessary, destroy it (in his imagination) in order to elaborate a better one (Piaget, 1972/2008, p. 42).

Hypothetical-deductive reasoning depends in part on the ability to use symbols. This ability is key to solving complex problems and reasoning beyond personal experience. Adolescents are often called on in school to do these things. Solving problems using algebra or geometry, for example, is a highly symbolic activity. Activities such as comparing and contrasting theories on the causes of World War I require students to analyze situations in which they were not personally involved. Such tasks require abstract cognitive reasoning, and they also advance such reasoning through practice and exposure to problems of increasing complexity (Artman, Cahan, & Avni-Babad, 2006).

Jose Pelaez/© Corbis

This student is solving mathematical problems using abstract reasoning.

## Conditional Reasoning

"Are there more roses or more flowers?" According to Piaget, only when children reach the concrete operational period can they answer such a question. As we saw in Chapter 9, preoperational children cannot consider both a subclass (such as roses) and a class (such as flowers) at the same time. Adolescents make another leap in logical abilities as they reach the formal operations stage. They can begin to analyze the various components of relationships and use such analyses to answer more complex questions.

This ability contributes to the development of **conditional reasoning**. We use this form of logical reasoning to evaluate information based on a stated relationship between two things. Conditional reasoning involves making inferences based on the premise that if one event occurs, then another event will occur. It is thus often called "if-then" reasoning. For example, Piaget presented the following rule to children and adolescents: "All watches that were made in September were broken" (Piaget, 1955/1977). The children and adolescents were then asked to answer the following questions:

This is a watch made in September. Is this watch broken?
Correct answer: The watch must be broken.
This is a watch that was not made in September. Is this watch broken?
Correct answer: Cannot tell, as watches made in months other than September might also be broken.
This watch is broken. Was it made in September?
Correct answer: Cannot tell, as broken watches might be made in other months, in addition to September.
This watch is not broken. Was this watch made in September?
Correct answer: No, it could not have been made in September.

Concrete operational children make errors on the second and third questions because they incorrectly assume that watches not made in September are not broken. To solve those problems by correctly answering "cannot tell," we need to understand that the superordinate class "broken watches" may include not only watches made in September but also watches made in other months. By the same token, we must realize that watches made in months other than September may be broken or not broken. Not until the formal operational period can individuals reach this understanding, through abstract and systematic reasoning.

Many of Piaget's tasks came from scientific fields, such as chemistry and physics. These tasks may not seem relevant to the daily lives of many adolescents. To show that formal operational thinking is required in many fields, current researchers operating

**conditional reasoning** A form of logical thinking that involves evaluating information based on the relationship between two things and the premise that if one event occurs, then another event will occur. It is often called "if-then" reasoning.

**Table 15.1** Classroom Changes and Reading Performance Scores

| Type of Classroom | Average Reading Performance |
|---|---|
| Regular classrooms | Poor |
| Classrooms with new curriculum and teacher aide | Greatly improved |
| Classrooms with new curriculum and reduced class size | Improved |
| Classrooms with teacher aide and reduced class size | Improved |
| Classrooms with new curriculum, teacher aide, and reduced class size | Greatly improved |
| Classrooms with aide | Improved |

*Source:* Kuhn, D., Katz, J. B., & Dean, D. (2004). Developing reason. Thinking & Reasoning, *10*(2), 197–219. Reprinted by permission of the publisher (Taylor & Francis Ltd, http://www.tandf.co.uk/journals).

**imaginary audience** Adolescents' belief that they are the center of others' attention; an aspect of adolescent egocentricity.

from Piaget's perspective have devised broader examples. Their work shows that formal operational thinking relates to a wide range of problem-solving situations. Consider the following problem, which requires the ability to isolate variables (Kuhn, Katz, & Dean, 2004):

> *A school district is experimenting with new methods of improving beginning reading instruction. In different classrooms across the district, they are trying various combinations of the following changes: initiating a new reading curriculum, introducing teacher aides, and reducing class size. Some preliminary results are shown in Table 15.1.*

Based on the information in Table 15.1, which factors affect reading performance?

Examining the table, you can see that only the new curriculum and the teacher aide are required for the status of "greatly improved." Nevertheless, the researchers found that even many college students (almost 40%) made errors in evaluating this information. This and other current research appears to support Piaget's assertion that not all adolescents (and not all adults) reach the stage of formal operations.

Piaget suggested two reasons why not all individuals reach the formal operational level. The first has to do with innate talent (and possibly biological differences). The second concerns environmental factors. Adolescents benefit from opportunities, such as schooling, that require them to apply logical necessity to problems, use hypothetical-deductive thinking, and employ conditional reasoning (Inhelder & Piaget, 1955/1958).

Grant Faint/Getty Images

Adolescents often play-act for an imaginary audience by showing off.

## Adolescent Egocentrism

Another aspect of Piaget's theory relates to egocentrism. Recall that egocentrism is the inability to distinguish between one's own perspective and that of another person. Piaget maintained that a new form of egocentrism emerges in adolescence (Inhelder & Piaget, 1955/1958). David Elkind (1967) interpreted and built on Piaget's writing about egocentrism by describing how this aspect of development operates in adolescence. In Elkind's view, adolescent egocentrism involves two facets. One is the imaginary audience, and the other is the personal fable (Alberts, Elkind, & Ginsberg, 2007).

You are probably familiar with the heightened self-consciousness of adolescents. If you watch groups of adolescents, you may notice that they often behave as if everyone around them considers them as important as they consider themselves. When they behave in this rather self-important way, they are acting for an **imaginary audience**.

Adolescents also view themselves as both unique and invincible. These qualities make up the **personal fable**. We can see this, for example, when an adolescent says to her parents, "You'll never know how I feel." The adolescent believes herself to be unique, that only she has experienced such feelings. We can see feelings of invincibility when an adolescent chooses to engage in dangerous activities, confident that an accident will never happen to him (Alberts et al., 2007). We discuss risky decision making by adolescents later in this chapter. For now, note that it may occur because adolescents have not reached the formal operational level, or because they do not use formal operational thinking in certain emotion-laden situations.

**personal fable** Adolescents' belief about their own importance and uniqueness; an aspect of adolescent egocentricity.

what if...?

Your 17-year-old cousin likes to text his friends while driving a car. You have argued with him that this is dangerous, because it distracts him from keeping his eyes on the road. He retorts that he hasn't had an accident yet, so it is fine for him to do this. What could you say to him?

## Contributions and Criticisms of Piaget's Theory

As you know by now, Piaget's theory—in spite of its strengths—has its limitations. The stage theory that is central to his views does not sufficiently account for variability within an individual person (Flavell, 1982; Miller, 2002). Some individuals apply formal operational thinking to certain types of tasks, for example, but not to others (Kuhn, 2008). Thus, a high school student might succeed with the balance-scale problem discussed earlier but have difficulty isolating variables when reading an essay (Keating, 2004). This evidence challenges Piaget's claim that stages represent unitary structures of thought (Fischer & Bidell, 2006).

Another criticism of Piaget's theory is that, as noted in Chapter 12, it cannot be applied consistently across cultures. This is perhaps particularly true with formal operations, which is not a universal stage of development even within Western cultures. Why? Because formal operational thinking often relies on formal schooling (Artman et al., 2006). Secondary schooling (that is, schooling beyond the elementary level) provides adolescents with practice in solving the types of problems that are the hallmarks of formal operational thought. Children who grow up in cultures where few receive advanced schooling are less likely to succeed with Piagetian-type tasks that demand formal operations. They are quite adept, however, at performing the tasks required in their daily lives. Many such tasks are quite complex and may involve abstract reasoning (Segall, Dasen, Berry, & Poortinga, 1999). Critics maintain that Piaget did not give enough attention to the role of culture and education in advancing this form of thinking (Cole, 1999).

Nicholas DeVore/Getty Images

Children who grow up in cultures where few of them receive advanced schooling nevertheless often develop abstract reasoning skills through carrying out daily tasks assigned to them.

Despite criticisms of Piaget's theory, most developmental psychologists agree with his general perspective that children and adolescents actively construct knowledge and thus advance their own thought processes (Lerner, 2002). His careful observations of children, and his description of how we can understand children's thought processes through the errors in their thinking, have advanced our understanding of development considerably. Finally, he provided an elegant theory that has allowed for much empirical testing. Through such research, we have gained a better understanding of cognitive development in adolescence.

**academic language** The language of a particular discipline; involves both terms and concepts important in that discipline.

**CHECK YOUR PROGRESS**

1. What are some major changes that differentiate the formal operational stage from the concrete operational stage?
2. How does the egocentrism of adolescence differ from that displayed in early childhood?
3. Evaluate the major criticisms of Piaget's theory in relation to the formal operational stage.

# Vygotsky's Sociocultural Theory and the Adolescent Mind

**[ KEY QUESTION ] 2.** How does Vygotsky's theory explain cognitive growth in adolescence?

As you know by now, Vygotsky emphasized sociocultural influences on cognitive development. In his view, cognitive development occurs first through interactions with others. Development is then internalized through inner speech. This internalization process, which occurs during every developmental phase, is central to Vygotsky's theory. For adolescents, as for younger children, help from others who are more skilled is important to making cognitive advances. And again, the more skilled individuals must operate within the adolescents' zone of proximal development. What an individual can perform with the assistance of another today, she can perform alone in the future.

Vygotsky's theory, then, emphasizes that children develop from middle childhood to adolescence through experiences with others. Many of those experiences occur in school. Indeed, some have claimed that Vygotsky's conception of development is really a theory of education (Bruner, 1962). Vygotsky regarded schooling as central to cognitive development, especially in the industrialized society in which he lived. The tools of industrialized society are taught through schooling. Moreover, the role of teachers and more skilled peers is important in this process. One of the tools of industrialized society is academic language (loosely referred to as the *language of schooling*). In this section, we first discuss how adolescents acquire academic language. Next, we consider the role of peers as expert helpers.

## Acquiring Academic Language

**Academic language** is the language of a particular discipline. Physics has its own language, for instance, as does psychology. Academic language is concise and precise, and it differs from the informal language of everyday conversation. How do academic language and informal language differ? Suppose you want to discuss a child's memory problems. Before studying child development, you might have said that the child has trouble remembering things. Now that you have studied memory processes, you can discuss the child's working memory, long-term memory, and memory strategies, and consider his strengths and weaknesses in each. You can see that use of these terms provides a more precise description and understanding of the child's skills.

Academic language is not confined to vocabulary. It extends as well to the concepts key to a discipline, which represent abstract ideas. This factor becomes increasingly important during the adolescent years. Such language is often heard in classrooms. Teachers and students use it to discuss cause-and-effect relationships, make comparisons, create persuasive arguments,

© Nicole Hill/Age Fotostock

The study of academic language extends to the key concepts in a discipline, as shown in the science fair posters here.

support a point with examples, and interpret information (Zwiers, 2007). Textbooks also often contain academic language (Fang, Schleppegrell, & Cox, 2006). As you might expect, the use of academic language differs considerably for high- and low-achieving students (Zwiers, 2008). Current research focuses on how to help adolescents, especially low achievers, acquire skills in the use of academic language.

**intersubjectivity** A term used by Vygotksy for a process by which two individuals reach a shared understanding of a task or activity.

*Everyday stories*

LANGUAGE AND CONCEPTS *Diffusion* is the movement of particles from a region of high concentration to a region of lower concentration. Many students learn about this concept in science class. Before Sophia learned the term, she knew that, say, peeling an orange emitted a scent that could fill a room. She didn't know exactly how that happened or what to call it, however. Now she can describe how odor particles diffuse throughout a room. Knowing the academic term *diffusion* gives Sophia a more efficient way of communicating. It will also enable her to understand related concepts, such as *osmosis*, in the future.

Many studies on how adolescents learn academic language are based on Vygotsky's perspective on the role of language in the learning process. Think about how you learned academic language in science courses in high school, for example. Researchers in one high school biology class used a Vygotskian perspective to help students learn how to "talk science" with the assistance of an expert (a teacher) (Duran, Dugan, & Weffer, 1998). Although the students at first viewed learning science as simply memorizing facts, they eventually developed a more abstract understanding of core concepts. That change evolved through three steps.

1. First, the students gained a *receptive understanding* of biological systems. During this phase, they copied the terms and diagrams introduced by teachers (for example, parts of the respiratory system).
2. Next, students developed a *conceptual understanding* by developing their own diagrams and schematic representations. At this step, teachers initially helped students and then gradually withdrew. Students used their diagrams as shared tools to teach other students.
3. Finally, students gained an *interpretive understanding*. In this stage, they called on each other to clarify, justify, and elaborate on biological concepts applied to real-world situations (for example, what happens to a respiratory cell when exposed to smoke during a house fire).

By working through these steps, students became active constructors of knowledge. As they developed greater understanding, the teacher's role changed. At first, the teacher, acting as expert, selected and defined the activity. Gradually, he moved from leader to guide. Eventually, he acted as a resource as students carried out the activity in collaboration with each other.

## Peer Tutoring Practice

Remember Mayda and Ashley from the opener to this chapter? Mayda was struggling with algebra, and Ashley became her peer tutor. Peer tutoring is a form of collaboration that has been studied a great deal and found effective under certain conditions (Roscoe & Chi, 2007). Much work on peer tutoring comes from a Vygotskian perspective. From this perspective, **intersubjectivity** is central to successful tutoring. Intersubjectivity exists when the tutor and the tutee share the same goals and definition of the problem (Wertsch, 1984). You have probably experienced intersubjectivity, or the lack of it. Perhaps you have asked a teacher a question and received an answer that seemed to

© Ocean/Corbis

Intersubjectivity is a central component of successful tutoring.

**Table 15.2** Tutoring Questions for Guided Inquiry

| Type of Question | Example |
|---|---|
| Review questions | "Describe _____ in your own words." |
| Thinking questions | "What is the difference between _____and _____?" |
| Probing questions | "What do you think would happen if _____?" |
| Hint questions | "Have you thought about _____?" |
| Metacognitive questions | "How did you figure that out?" |

have little to do with the question. In that case, you and the teacher had poor intersubjectivity. In other words, the two of you understood the question in very different ways. In the context of tutoring, intersubjectivity requires that the tutor understand the nature of the difficulty the tutee is having. Why? Think back to the importance of scaffolding to learning in Vygotsky's theory: Appropriate scaffolding requires intersubjectivity (Vygotsky, 1978).

In their review of the tutoring process, Rod Roscoe and Michelene Chi (2007) focused on the development of two types of knowledge.

1. *Knowledge telling* involves memorizing and summarizing information. Learning concrete facts is an example of knowledge telling.
2. *Reflective knowledge building* calls for the development of higher-level learning. Constructing and elaborating on new knowledge and problem solving are examples of reflective knowledge building.

When peer tutoring is unstructured, it helps students only with knowledge telling (Topping, 2005). Tutoring to help with higher-level learning is more complex and requires a structured approach (Roscoe & Chi, 2008; Spörer & Brunstein, 2009; Topping, 2006). In one well-researched model (King, 1998), the tutor guides the tutee using five types of questions. You can see the types of questions and examples of each in Table 15.2. Together, the question types form a hierarchy of understanding, from simple description to analysis of the process of learning itself.

Training tutors to help other students benefits the tutors as well as the tutees. You may have found at some time that by helping a friend learn some material, you came to understand the material better yourself. A review of peer tutoring programs (Roscoe & Chi, 2007) showed that when tutors were trained in strategies to advance abstract thinking skills (such as those described in Table 15.2), the tutors benefited. For example, tutors who had to think about what probing questions to ask also had to think more deeply about the material they were discussing. The potential to benefit both the tutee and the tutor makes peer tutoring a form of peer-mediated learning.

## what if...?

You have signed up to tutor high school students who are having trouble with U.S. history. One of your tutees is Francisca. Meeting with her for the first time, you find out that she is studying for a history test. "How are you studying?" you ask. She responds that she is working hard to memorize the dates of major events for the period. You ask her to show you some of the past tests she has taken for the course. You see that a few questions do require identifying dates. Most of the test questions, though, are focused on understanding the social, political, and economic issues of the time. What are some ways you could help Francisca learn the necessary material for the course?

## Contributions of Vygotsky's Theory

Vygotsky's theory emphasizes the importance of social interaction. Because of this emphasis, the theory has important implications for education. Vygotsky believed that the types of higher cognitive processes developed during the adolescent years are constructed through interaction with others, especially with those who are more advanced in their thought processes. His explanation of the role of intersubjectivity and learning in the zone of proximal development provides a valuable framework for those who aim to promote adolescent development through teaching or tutoring. We return to these topics later in the chapter.

### ✓ CHECK YOUR PROGRESS

1. In what way (or ways) does Vygotsky regard schooling as important to adolescent cognitive development?
2. What is an example of the way in which learning academic language could advance cognitive growth?
3. What core concepts of Vygotsky's theory have implications for successful peer tutoring?

# Information Processing in the Adolescent Years

**[ KEY QUESTION ] 3. What cognitive changes occur during adolescence according to information processing theorists?**

As noted in earlier chapters, the information processing approach to cognitive development is not a stage theory. Instead, information processing theorists focus on cognitive processes and executive functions that improve gradually during childhood and adolescence. In Chapter 12, we discussed attention and memory, two processes that have particular importance during middle childhood. Here, we first examine three components of information processing that advance during adolescence. We then discuss advances in metacognition. We also consider whether processing improvements help adolescents to make good decisions. Finally, we summarize the contributions of information processing theory to our understanding of adolescent cognitive development.

## Cognitive Changes in Processing

Information processing research, as noted, focuses on changes in cognitive processes. Researchers have found that processing improves a great deal during adolescence. Here, we look, in turn, at changes in three aspects of processing: processing speed, working memory, and inhibitory control.

### Processing Speed

Perhaps at some point in your schooling you were presented with 100 multiplication problems and asked to complete as many as possible within a fixed period of time, say 3 minutes. You probably noticed that some students completed many more problems than others in that short period. Why might there be such a difference? One reason is that students differ in their *processing speed.*

Researchers assess processing speed in a variety of ways. Generally, they measure the time it takes for someone to solve a task that involves quick and automatic responding. The task may be simple, such as looking at targets on a computer screen. For this task, researchers measure the time it takes a subject's eyes to move from an initial position (like the center of the screen) to a target position (like the side of the screen). This skill improves through early adolescence, and is mature in most adolescents by around age 15 (Luna, Garver, Urban, Lazar, & Sweeney, 2004). Processing speed in somewhat more complex tasks also improves rapidly by midadolescence. For example, in one group of studies, children and adolescents were shown 60 rows of 6 digits, with a set of identical digits in each succeeding row (Kail & Ferrer, 2007). Participants were asked to circle the identical digits in each row as quickly as possible in a 3-minute time period. Processing speed was measured by the number of rows

zorani/Getty Images

Differences in individual processing speeds and working memory means that some students can complete more math problems than others in a fixed period of time.

completed correctly. Seven-year-old children had a success rate of about 25% on this task. In contrast, 15-year-olds averaged a 50% rate of correct responses, which indicates that their processing speed was much faster.

### Working Memory

Let's return to the earlier example of the number of multiplication problems students can complete in 3 minutes. Another reason why some students may complete more problems than others in the allotted period has to do with *working memory*. As you may recall from Chapter 12, working memory is that part of short-term memory where we keep information that we are currently working on. It is a sort of mental "sketch pad" that allows us to retain or retrieve information (Luna, Padmanabhan, & O'Hearn, 2010). Here's a typical test of working memory: Researchers provide subjects with two sets of random digits, beginning with a set of 2 digits and increasing to a set of 8 digits. The subjects must repeat one set forward and the other set backward. If you try to repeat a set of 8 random digits backward, you can appreciate how you must hold and encode information in working memory to repeat the sequence successfully. The ability to do this improves throughout early adolescence, and tends to reach adult levels by around age 16 (Jolles, Kleibeuker, Rombouts, & Crone, 2011; Steinberg, Cauffman, Woolard, Graham, & Banich, 2009).

Repeating digits is a fairly simple test of working memory. Learning more intricate material, such as the reasons for the Great Depression, involves a more complex test of working memory. First we must learn and store the material. Then we must be able to readily retrieve it—for example, during a history exam. Some researchers have found that using analogies is a helpful way to make connections and remember ideas about processes. For example, suppose biology students are learning about temperature regulation in warm-blooded animals. Using an analogy, they might describe it as similar to the way a thermostat operates in a modern building (Bulgren, Deshler, Schumaker, & Lenz, 2000). Or they might compare the way a thermostat and the body's nervous and endocrine systems send signals when the temperature varies from a set number. Such approaches help in the storage of information, and also in its retrieval.

### Inhibitory Control

We *inhibit* responses when we hold them back. In Chapter 9, we discussed the difficulty that young children have in inhibiting their responses. The difficulty is greater when they need to wait before making a response that they tend to make automatically or find especially compelling. Children can succeed with some aspects of *response inhibition* by middle childhood. Researchers have found, for example, that children can suppress a response when the task involves only one trial. When multiple trials are presented, they have more difficulty. We may see this, for instance, in a study involving many trials or tasks that involve a quick response—say, naming the color of objects when some of them are displayed in unexpected colors, such as a blue banana (Prevor & Diamond, 2005). Adolescents have greater success than younger children with tasks involving multiple trials (Kail, 2002). In general, impulse control continues to improve during the adolescent period, but adolescents, in comparison to adults, are less consistent in regulating their impulsivity (Luna, Paulsen, Padmanabhan, & Geier, 2013).

According to information-processing theorists, inhibition actually requires two processes (Neumann, McCloskey, & Felio, 1999). An *excitatory process* focuses on the target information. An *inhibitory process* suppresses distracting information. Research indicates that although both these processes improve during adolescence (Davidson, Amso, Anderson, & Diamond, 2006), inhibitory processes are not as flexible or efficient as those exhibited by adults (Luna et al., 2013).

### Bidirectional Relationships

It is not surprising that the three aspects of information processing just described—processing speed, working memory, and response inhibition—work together to advance cognitive development. All three show great advances during adolescence, especially during early adolescence (ages 12 to 16). For many individuals, processing speed and working memory in particular reach adult levels by around age 16. Furthermore, the effects of improvement in these functions are bidirectional. For example, processing speed affects working memory. Working memory then affects reasoning skills (such as the hypothetical-deductive reasoning discussed earlier in this chapter). In turn, advances in reasoning skills enhance processing speed and working memory (Keating, 2004). Therefore, in contrast to Piaget's stagelike process, information processing theorists emphasize a process whereby improvements in various parts of the system build on one another.

## Changes in Metacognition

As we have seen, many aspects of cognitive processing improve during adolescence. These improvements contribute to the developing ability of adolescents to think about their own thought processes. Recall that this aspect of cognition is termed *metacognition* (Flavell, 1982; Kuhn, 2008). Even younger children have some awareness of their mental activities, as noted in Chapter 12. However, young people's ability to systematically analyze *how* they think generally improves a great deal from middle childhood to adolescence (Kuhn, 2008).

Deanne Kuhn (2001) has proposed a general model of knowing that involves two *metalevels*—that is, two types of metacognition—as shown in Figure 15.2 and described here.

1. The *procedural metalevel* involves understanding the procedures to use while working productively on a problem or task. These include understanding what is gained by applying certain strategies (such as those you might use to memorize a list of items) and when, where, and why to use them.
2. The *declarative metalevel* involves drawing correct inferences and inhibiting incorrect ones when faced with a cognitive problem (such as the reading performance problem described in the first section). It involves knowing the facts, opinions, and claims related to a topic, as well as the theory on which evidence is based.

Both of these processes relate to executive functioning. Recall that executive function is the ability to manage one's own behavior and regulate one's thinking and emotions. In solving complex problems, executive functions involve planning and self-monitoring, as well as selecting and using appropriate cognitive strategies.

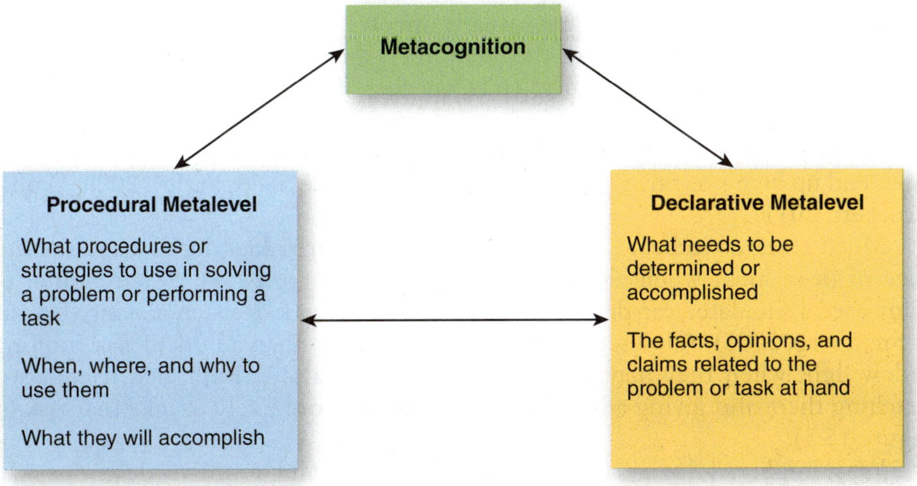


**FIGURE 15.2 Two Types of Metacognition** In Deanne Kuhn's model of metacognition, the procedural metalevel involves understanding the procedures to use while working productively on a problem. The declarative metalevel involves drawing correct inferences and inhibiting incorrect ones to solve the problem.

Based on a figure in Kuhn, D. (2001). How do people know? *Psychological Science*, *12*(1), 1–8.

In Chapter 12, we discussed various memory strategies. Adolescents, compared with younger children, have greater control over the strategies they use. In addition, they are more likely to call upon multiple strategies. Their ability to select from a range of strategies and apply the most appropriate to a particular task, revising the strategy as the task requires, is an indicator of metacognitive skill. Recent evidence suggests that schooling advances metacognitive skills (Van de Vijver & Brouwers, 2009).

*Everyday stories*

USING METACOGNITIVE STRATEGIES Mateo is preparing for an important test in biology. He has read the textbook several times but can't seem to remember how the different body systems (such as the circulatory system and the digestive system) work or how they relate to each other. He decides to talk to the teacher. She tells him that reading the text is only the first step. She then shows him some ways to organize the material so he can see the connections between various systems. Mateo knows that he remembers best when he creates a graphic image, so he tries drawing pictures to represent the various systems. Mateo has shown good metacognition by realizing that his old way of studying was not useful and by incorporating his teacher's suggestions along with his knowledge of his own memory processes to create a more effective way of studying.

## Decision Making

We have reviewed many cognitive advances of the adolescent period. Given those advances, we might expect adolescents to be skilled decision makers. Indeed, research has shown that many adolescents are capable of rational and logical decision making (Byrnes, 2005). Rational decision making improves during adolescence in part because of improvements in memory skills and processing speed (Smith, Xiao, & Bechara, 2012). We pointed out in Chapter 14 that such decision making requires thought-mediated behavior, or keeping a "cool head." Yet we also pointed out that adolescents are sometimes "hot-headed." Often, they take risks that seem counter to their cognitive abilities to analyze risk. Let's look more closely at this tendency.

First, we need to distinguish between two kinds of decision making: *deliberative decision making* and *reactive decision making*. The kinds of problems presented to adolescents in laboratory settings usually involve deliberation (Halpern-Felsher, 2009). In the ideal conditions of the laboratory, they can take the time to carefully evaluate various options and their consequences. In contrast, the decisions many adolescents must make under typical situations require an immediate response, involve emotional arousal, and often occur in unfamiliar situations. These decisions often end up being reactive rather than deliberative (Reyna & Farley, 2006; Wolff & Crockett, 2011).

Much research indicates that adolescents make far riskier decisions in the presence of peers than when alone (Gardner & Steinberg, 2005). For example, one study used a simulated car-driving game to test adolescent decision making (Gardner & Steinberg, 2005). Adolescents were not more likely than adults to risk running a yellow light when they played the simulated game alone. But when friends were watching them and giving advice, they were much more likely to take that risk (see Figure 15.3).

Why might adolescents make more impulsive and intuitive decisions when peers are present? There are several reasons. Some researchers have found that although adolescents can weigh perceived benefits against perceived risks, they tend to see the benefits as outweighing the risks—especially when those benefits relate to goals such as peer acceptance (Ben-Zur & Reshef-Kfir, 2003; Parsons, Siegel, & Cousins, 1997). Other researchers have emphasized that rational decision making is

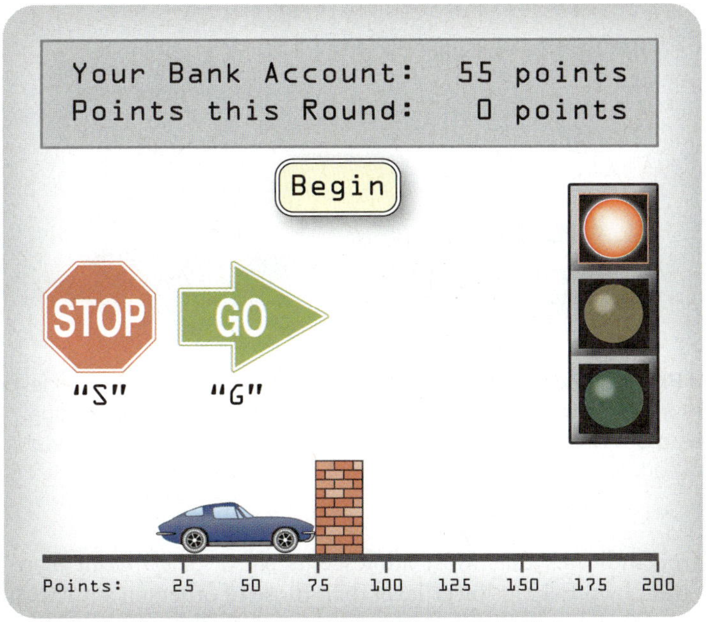


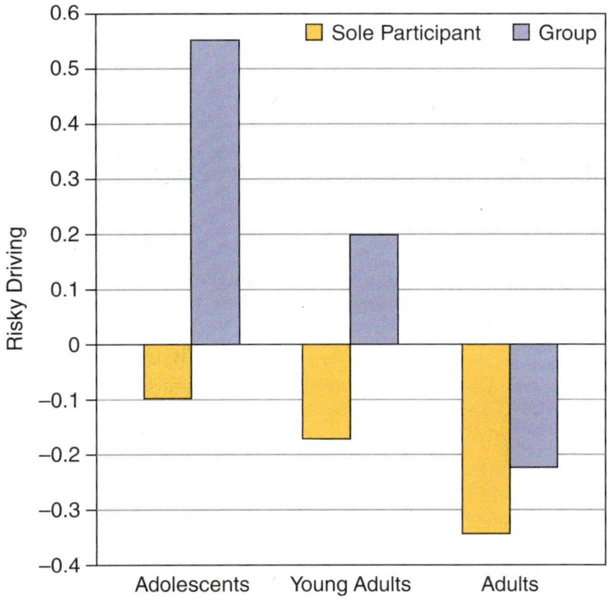


**FIGURE 15.3 Differences in Risk Taking** Researchers used a simulated car-driving task to test decision making in three groups: adolescents (defined in this study as aged 13 to 16), youths (aged 18 to 22), and adults (24 and older). In this image from the task, the traffic light has just turned red. Since the car was still moving when the light turned red, a brick wall appeared, resulting in a crash. Adolescents and youths took more risks than adults when they played the game in the presence of peers.

*Source:* Gardner, M., & Steinberg, L. (2005). Peer influence on risk taking, risk preference, and risky decision making in adolescence and adulthood: An experimental study. *Developmental Psychology*, *41*(4), 625–635. APA; reprinted with permission.

suppressed under conditions of emotional arousal (Reyna & Farley, 2006). Situations involving peers often give rise to such conditions. Emotional arousal overwhelms the deliberative process, especially when an individual has to make a complex decision quickly (Rivers, Reyna, & Mills, 2008). Fortunately, the ability to regulate emotional arousal improves throughout the adolescent period, allowing deliberative processes to gradually increase in frequency (Loewenstein, Weber, Hsee, & Welch, 2001).

sturti/Getty Images

Underage adolescents may feel pressure from friends to drink alcohol, and so fail to analyze the risks of doing so.

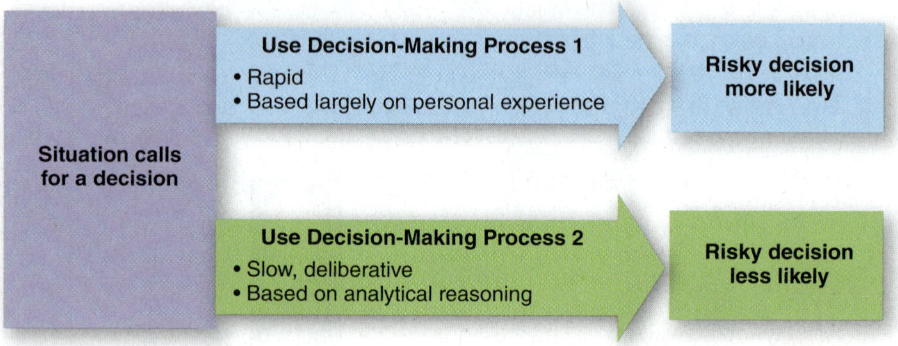


**FIGURE 15.4 The Dual-Process Model of Decision Making** The dual-process model of decision-making systems includes two parts: a rapid process based largely on personal experience, and a slower, more deliberative process. Only gradually through adolescence do the systems come to work together to support optimal decision making.

Additionally, research indicates that most adolescents show an *optimistic bias*. In other words, they view their own risks as lower level than those of others in similar situations. For example, one researcher studied the risk estimates of adolescents who smoked cigarettes (Arnett, 2000). Only 18% of the respondents denied that lifelong smokers would die of smoking-related illnesses. In contrast, 29% denied that they would experience this outcome themselves. These adolescents recognized that smoking involves greater risks than not smoking, yet they perceived their own risks optimistically.

**dual-process model** A description of decision making that involves two processes, one rapid and based on prior experience, the other slow and deliberative, using abstract reasoning.

Researchers have proposed that adolescent decision making is best understood as a **dual-process model,** as shown in Figure 15.4 (Evans, 2003; Kahneman, 2011). One process involves making rapid responses based largely on personal experience. For example, suppose an adolescent has to respond quickly to friends who are pressuring her to drink alcohol. Suppose, too, that she has been around underage drinkers who suffered no obvious consequences from drinking. In this circumstance, then, she might make a quick decision to drink with her friends. The other process involves deliberation, which carefully analyzes the risks and benefits of a decision. Deliberation tends to be slow, to follow a sequence of steps, and to involve abstract thinking. The same adolescent using this process might consider various risks of underage drinking. She might, for example, think about the possibility of getting in a car accident, engaging in unprotected sex, suffering from alcohol poisoning, or being punished by her parents. She might then decide that even if she hasn't experienced any of these risks, they are still too great. These two thinking processes are related to activation of different parts of the brain (Reyna & Farley, 2006). Only gradually through adolescence (and into young adulthood) do the systems come to work together to support optimal decision making.

what if...?

Consider a time when you or a friend made a decision that you now consider to have been risky. Can you think of anything that would have encouraged you to make a less risky decision? How might this information help you if you were mentoring an adolescent who made many risky choices?

## Contributions of the Information Processing Approach

Information processing theory is a dominant force in cognitive psychology. It has generated much research and heightened our understanding of various cognitive processes. In particular, it has advanced our knowledge about how thoughts are organized, remembered, and manipulated. It has also furthered our understanding of how individuals at various life stages develop and use problem-solving skills. Some critics have claimed that the information processing perspective is limited because it focuses mainly on cognition without taking sufficient account of the role of psychosocial processes (Mayer, 2003). However, as we have seen, cognitive psychologists operating from an information processing perspective are increasingly considering the importance of the psychosocial context in which learning and decision making occur (Wolff & Crockett, 2011).

**CHECK YOUR PROGRESS**

1. What types of processing changes occur during adolescence?
2. What are the differences between the two levels of metacognition?
3. Why does decision making sometimes fail to reflect an adolescent's cognitive skills?

**THE DEVELOPING BRAIN**

# The Brain and Adolescent Cognition

**[ KEY QUESTION ] 4. What are some major changes that occur in the adolescent brain?**

So far in this chapter, we have reviewed three major theories of adolescent cognitive development. Before moving on to a consideration of adolescent schooling, let's take a moment to examine a few aspects of brain development in adolescence that are important in cognitive development.

Not too long ago, it was believed that most changes in the brain occurred before adolescence. But as we discussed in Chapter 14, an explosion in neuroscience research has revealed that the adolescent brain undergoes structural refinement and reorganization (Ramsden et al., 2011; Silveri, Tzilos, Yurgelun-Todd, 2008). In this section, we briefly revisit three critical changes in the adolescent brain as they relate to our knowledge of adolescent cognitive development: changes in the prefrontal cortex, synaptic pruning, and increased myelination.

## Changes in the Prefrontal Cortex

As we pointed out in Chapter 14, the *prefrontal cortex* is among the last parts of the brain to mature. It is thought to continue developing until the mid-20s in most individuals (Sowell, Thompson, & Toga, 2007). Adolescent development in the prefrontal cortex is widely held to be responsible for many of the cognitive improvements we have discussed in this chapter. Advances in abstract reasoning, higher-order information processing, metacognitive thinking, deliberative decision making, working memory, and response inhibition all depend at least in part on this development (Spear, 2007).

Neuroimaging studies have indicated that various parts of the prefrontal cortex are active in adolescents while solving analytical problems (Keating, 2004). Interestingly, the adolescent brain shows more prefrontal activity than the brains of either younger children or adults. Since we know this area of the brain is less developed at earlier ages, we might expect differences between adolescents and younger children (Ciesielski, Lesnik, Savoy, Grant, & Ahlfors, 2006). However, adolescents also activate more areas of the brain when solving analytical problems than do adults (Luna et al., 2010). This is so even when the adolescents' performance in solving the problems is similar to that of adults. These results suggest that the adolescent brain may be less efficient than the adult brain. Why might this be so?

The way that various parts of the brain activate together in the performance of a task is called *functional connectivity* (see Figure 15.5). It seems that functional connectivity in the adolescent brain differs from that in the adult brain. Generally, it shows

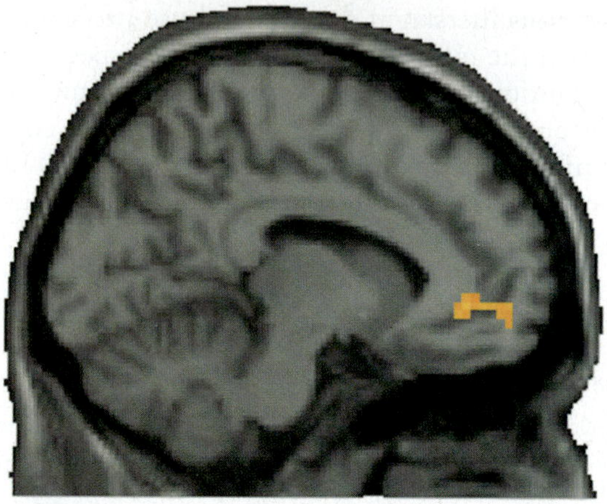

**FIGURE 15.5 Functional Connectivity in the Adolescent Brain** In a study using fMRIs, researchers compared the brains of children and adolescents as they attempted a simple learning task. The connectivity between the prefrontal cortex and the striatum, an interior area of the brain, increased with age. This increased connectivity, highlighted in orange on the fMRI, is typical of the adolescent brain.

*Source:* van, d. B., Cohen, M. X., Kahnt, T., & Crone, E. A. (2012). Striatum-medial prefrontal cortex connectivity predicts developmental changes in reinforcement learning. *Cerebral Cortex, 22*(6), 1247–1255. doi:10.1093/cercor/bhr198 by permission of Oxford University Press.

more widespread but less efficient activation. That means adolescents must put more effort into cognitive processing and executive function than do adults (Luna et al., 2010). This increasing functional connectivity of areas of the brain is one of the hallmarks of the adolescent period (Paus, 2009).

## Synaptic Pruning and Increased Myelination

Studies indicate that a dramatic reorganization of the brain occurs during adolescence (Petanjek et al., 2011). This reorganization supports the ability of most adolescents to advance their cognitive skills. Let's look more closely at structural refinement and reorganization in the adolescent brain. These changes are due at least in part to synaptic pruning and higher levels of myelination. Both have major effects on—but are also affected by—learning processes.

Recall that synapses form most rapidly in infancy and continue to form throughout childhood and adolescence. During adolescence, however, *synaptic pruning* becomes more important. Pruning selectively eliminates extra synapses and synapses that are weak or poorly developed. Gray matter in the frontal lobe, in particular, is reduced during adolescence (Gogtay et al., 2006), suggesting the impact of pruning in this area (Huttenlocher, 2002). Synaptic pruning creates a more precise network of connections across the brain. As a result, processing becomes faster and more complex.

At the same time, increased myelination speeds processing by making transmission more efficient (Lebel & Beaulieu, 2011). As myelination increases, transmission improves, not only within particular locations in the brain but also across brain networks that are farther apart (Paus, 2010). Improved transmission enables different brain networks to interact more efficiently. For example, suppose you need to solve a problem involving spatial relations, such as completing a three-dimensional puzzle. You'll need to use both executive functioning skills (such as planning how to start the puzzle and monitoring whether pieces are placed accurately) and spatial skills (such as turning a piece so it fits). In other words, different parts of your brain need to work together. Neuroimaging studies show that networks become better integrated during adolescence. We see this especially in areas of the brain that are active while engaging in tasks that involve working memory and inhibitory control (Luna et al., 2010).

*Everyday stories*

PUZZLES AND THE BRAIN Aaron, a 15-year-old, is putting together a three-dimensional puzzle. He first sorts the pieces according to the side on which they belong. He then plans the steps he will take to determine what he should do next. He uses the puzzle shapes, as well as other cues, like colors, to decide on his moves. Daisha, a 4-year-old, has been watching Aaron. Now she wants to try to put together the puzzle as well. Rather than planning ahead like Aaron, she jumps in by selecting two pieces that she thinks will fit together. Her 8-year-old brother, Amadi, says, "No, you must think about which side you want to start with." He begins to put together the pieces to form one side, but gets frustrated. Soon, he too is randomly choosing pieces that he thinks might fit on other sides.

Each is showing age-typical approaches. Aaron is able to both plan and be systematic in carrying out his plan. Daisha acts impulsively without a plan beyond finding two pieces that fit together. Amadi begins with a plan but has difficulty carrying it out systematically.

WHEN SYSTEMS CONNECT

## The Effects of Experience

One of the most important findings from neuroscience research has been that biology is not destiny. Experience, too, affects the brain. Specifically, it affects which genes are turned on and off, and when (Diamond & Amso, 2008). It also affects the paths by which neurons interconnect. Several studies have confirmed that repeated use of certain neural circuits in the brain leads to changes in brain structure. For example, certain studies have reported changes in the brains of adolescents as they learned a second language (Osterhout et al., 2008; Richardson, Thomas, Filippi, Harth, & Price, 2010; Stein et al., 2012; van Heuven & Dijkstra, 2010). As a result of these changes, second-language learners are likely to pay attention to types of information they may not have focused on before, such as a particular feature of the second language that is not meaningful in their first language. In other words, learning causes changes in the brain, and those changes can result in sensitivity to different types of environmental input (Karmiloff-Smith, 2009; Westermann, Thomas, & Karmiloff-Smith, 2011).

As we've seen, adolescents' ability to think more abstractly and efficiently corresponds with their brain development. At the same time, engaging in such thinking changes the structure of their brains (Ramsden et al., 2011). Many of the challenges adolescents face in school advance their cognitive and brain development. In the next section, we address the important question of the role of schooling during the adolescent period.

what if...?

Suppose you and a friend are discussing brain development. Your friend claims that brains develop based on their genetic makeup. As long as someone is not involved in a serious accident that damages the brain, that person's brain development will occur as dictated by genes. You have a different idea about what, in addition to genes, affects brain growth. What would you say to convince your friend?

✓ CHECK YOUR PROGRESS

1. How does the adolescent brain differ from that of younger children and adults?
2. What are the major effects of synaptic pruning and myelination on adolescents' ability to perform tasks?
3. Does learning affect changes in the brain?

## Learning and Schooling

**[ KEY QUESTION ] 5.** What factors promote or diminish adolescents' success in school?

Secondary education (that is, schooling beyond a level equivalent to elementary grade 6) advances cognitive skills, as we've seen. It is also important preparation for entering the labor market (Fasih, 2008). In many parts of the world, adolescents do not attend secondary school, although the number who do is growing. Still, percentages vary considerably by region. We find the highest enrollment is in central Asia (95%) and the lowest in sub-Saharan Africa (23%) (UNESCO Institute for Statistics, 2010). But even in countries with high levels of secondary school enrollment, like the United States, not all adolescents remain in school long enough to complete their high school degrees.

In the United States, from ages 11 to 18, adolescents spend about 7,000 hours in school. School, of course, often becomes a focus of adolescent social life, as well as cognitive development. In addition, school performance begins to dictate many consequences in the lives of adolescents. Success in school puts them on a path toward future education and career development. Failure limits their future learning and employment opportunities.

In middle school and beyond, students begin to be evaluated more rigorously (Elmore, 2009). Often, they are sorted into groups according to achievement. By high school, many students are placed in higher- and lower-achieving groups. Such placement affects not only the nature of their academic work but also their social network of friends. In this section, we discuss some of the challenges U.S. adolescents face as they advance through secondary school. In turn, we consider sex differences in mathematical and verbal skills, the role of academic motivation, the effect of school transitions, the issue of completing school versus dropping out, and the interactions of schooling and paid employment.

### Sex Differences in Math and Verbal Skills

Do you believe that your mathematical skills are better than your verbal skills? Or perhaps vice versa? If you consider yourself better at one or other of these skill sets, do you suspect the reason relates to your sex? Research on this topic has been hotly debated. Males and females do not differ in general intelligence, as measured by IQ tests. Nevertheless, current research tells us that they do differ in some aspects of intelligence, especially mathematical and verbal skills, during the high school years (Halpern et al., 2007).

First, let's consider mathematics. Girls receive higher grades than boys in high school mathematics courses. Yet they record lower scores on the mathematics section of the Scholastic Aptitude Test (SAT) (Halpern et al., 2007). In examining responses to the mathematics questions on the SAT, some researchers have found a difference related to types of problems—spatial versus verbal (Gallagher, Levin, & Cahalan, 2002). Males performed better than females on problems that required a spatially based solution, such as mentally rotating a block with a pattern on it. But they did not perform better on verbal problems, such as those embedded in a story. The advantage for males appears to be related to their *visuospatial abilities*, such as the ability to read a map or solve a maze. Although the sex differences in such abilities are sometimes found to be small, they consistently favor males (Casey, Pezaris, & Bassi, 2012; Halpern et al., 2007; Voyer, Voyer, & Bryden, 1995).

In general, researchers have found that male-female differences in mathematical skills are most evident among the students whose scores fall among the highest 5%. One study compared male and female differences in mathematical reasoning over a 30-year period (Wai, Cacchio, Putallaz, & Makel, 2010). The researchers found that a higher proportion of males than females consistently performed at the top of the distribution. The male-to-female ratio changed over the period, however. Thirty years ago, the ratio of males to females in the top-performing group was 13 males to 1 female. Now the ratio is 4 males to 1 female.

In contrast to tests of mathematical skills, tests of verbal reasoning and writing favor females (Halpern et al., 2007). Verbal abilities generally include skills such as the following:

- Selecting words with similar meanings.
- Completing analogies (for example, "Sun is to moon as day is to ____").
- Responding to questions about a complex reading passage.
- Writing in response to specific prompts (such as, " If I could choose an animal most like myself, it would be _____").

Sam Bloomberg-Rissman/Blend Images/Getty Images

On tests of reading skills, females often perform better than their male counterparts.

In tests of reading skills of 15-year-olds in 25 countries, including the United States, females consistently scored higher than males (Mullis, Martin, Gonzalez, & Kennedy, 2003). One reason is that females tend to use more strategies when they read than do males (Cantrell & Carter, 2009). These include three basic types of reading strategies. *Global strategies* involve achieving a general analysis of the text by skimming material and searching for contextual cues. *Problem-solving strategies* are processes used when the text becomes difficult, such as pausing to reflect on material, rereading, making inferences, and using mental imagery. *Support reading strategies* include underlining text and taking notes.

In addition to a reading advantage, females also have a writing advantage. Major differences in writing skills have been found in many reviews of research (Hedges & Nowell, 1995; U.S. Department of Education, 2008). In a national report published by the U.S. Department of Education, the writing scores of eighth-grade females were reported comparable to those of eleventh-grade males (Bae, Choy, Geddes, Sable, & Snyder, 2000). Studies of students with high levels of performance on verbal skills (the top 5%) have found that females outnumber males—especially in writing skills, where twice as many females as males score in the top 5%. In addition, these sex differences appear to be widening (Wai et al., 2010).

What accounts for such differences between males and females? One explanation is based on distinctions in brain structure. Studies have shown substantial variations in how gray matter is distributed in male versus female brains. Compared with males, females have a more equal distribution of gray matter over both brain hemispheres (Halpern et al., 2007). Such anatomical sex differences only *correlate* with differences in skills, however. We do not know whether there is a causal relationship. Researchers are currently working on this area of inquiry.

Another explanation for the sex differences in mathematical and verbal reasoning is based on **expectancy-value theory** (Eccles, 2011). This model describes factors that affect adolescents' decisions about which specific courses to take in high school, such as advanced classes in math or literature. In making this decision, adolescents tend to consider two factors: *expectations for success* and *task value*. Expectations for success relate to their perceptions of their own abilities. Task value encompasses their intrinsic enjoyment of the task or their belief that it might lead to a better outcome in the future, such as a higher salary. Both factors are affected by sociocultural influences. Parental and peer attitudes, gender role socialization, and the norms and values of a school community all play a role. Thus, many elements affect the academic skills adolescents choose to pursue. In turn, those choices may put them on pathways that promote or limit achievement in math or verbal skills.

**expectancy-value theory** A model describing the factors involved in an adolescent's selection of academic courses related to expectation for success and perception of task value.

ACADEMIC CHOICES Brooke enjoys the challenges of math. Now, at the end of tenth grade, she must make a decision about the next math course to take. This year, she has been in an advanced math class. Although her grades have been strong, it seems to her that she is not as quick as some of the other students at completing geometry problems. She is beginning to think that she should not take the next-level math class, because she is afraid she may not be as successful as she'd like. She also tells herself that high-level math may not really be necessary for her occupation of choice, that of veterinarian. Right now, Brooke's decision making is focusing on her expectations for success. At another time, however, she might consider how much she enjoys mathematical reasoning—her intrinsic enjoyment of math. Additional factors might also arise to influence her decision. Her parents, teachers, or friends might encourage her to pursue the higher-level math class, for example, or she might learn that it would help forward her goal to become a veterinarian.

*Everyday stories*

## Academic Motivation

What is motivation? The Latin root of the word means "to move." Accordingly, motivation generally refers to actions taken toward a particular goal. **Academic motivation** involves the effort to achieve educational goals. It also includes the overall value placed on school and commitments to educational pursuits (Eccles & Wigfield, 2002). Students who are academically motivated are likelier to bring cognitive processes to bear in school settings (Ginsburg & Bronstein, 1993).

Motivation may be intrinsic or extrinsic. **Intrinsic motivation** comes from interest or enjoyment of the activity itself, while **extrinsic motivation** derives from external rewards or consequences. You can probably recognize both types of motivation within yourself. Think of the last time you wanted to learn something, perhaps a sport or an artistic skill. Since it was your choice to learn that activity, you were probably intrinsically motivated. In contrast, you may not be intrinsically motivated to engage in an assigned task, such as writing a paper. However, extrinsic motivation can sometimes result in intrinsic motivation to succeed at the task. This can happen through a series of steps (Ryan & Deci, 2000a, 2000b):

1. External regulation: "I have to write this paper to meet the deadline."
2. Internal regulation based on feelings about the behavior: "I'll feel good if I meet the deadline."
3. A sense that the behavior has some value: "If I meet the deadline, I'll succeed in this course."
4. Integrated regulation, which blends the feelings and the value associated with the behavior: "Success in school is important to me."

Academic motivation depends in part on the desire to do well. This desire is, in turn, based on an intrinsic need to be competent (White, 1959). By seeking out and persisting in challenging activities, we become increasingly competent. You may recall our discussions of Bandura's social cognitive model from previous chapters. In this model, Bandura (1997) emphasized the importance of **self-efficacy**, or confidence in one's ability to organize and follow a course of action to solve a problem or accomplish a task. He discussed two types of beliefs related to self-efficacy. One relates to expectations about how to achieve a desired outcome (for example, "If I practice hard, I'll become a good soccer player"). The second has to do with expectations about the ability to perform the skills necessary to reach that outcome (for example, "I can learn the foot movements I need to play soccer"). Beliefs of this second type are called *efficacy expectations*. According to Bandura, they play a major role in how willing a person is to persist in a challenging task or activity. Much research has shown that when we believe we can succeed at certain tasks or activities, we are more likely to engage in those activities, persist even when we confront challenges, and eventually do well (Bandura, 1997; Graham & Williams, 2009; Schunk & Pajares, 2009).

**academic motivation** The effort taken to achieve academic goals; incorporates the overall value placed on school and commitments to educational pursuits.

**intrinsic motivation** Behaviors that are motivated by interest or enjoyment of the activity itself.

**extrinsic motivation** Behaviors that are motivated by external rewards or consequences.

**self-efficacy** Confidence in one's ability to organize and follow a course of action to solve a problem or accomplish a task.

Why do some adolescents think they will do well at a task whereas others think they will fail? Answering this question tells us something about why academic motivation differs among adolescents. Explanations for such differences include the types of goals students choose to pursue, their views of intelligence, and the possibility of stereotype threat.

## Types of Goals

One difference among students' attitude toward success and failure involves the types of goals they choose to pursue (Duchesne & Ratelle, 2010; Wigfield & Cambria, 2010). Researchers have identified three categories of goals:

- *Mastery goals* involve the desire to master tasks, advance skills, and enjoy the intrinsic rewards of such activities.
- *Performance-approach goals* focus on the desire to outperform peers or competitors and thus gain extrinsic rewards through the admiration of others.
- *Performance-avoidance goals* involve the desire not to appear incompetent.

Students who select mastery goals feel more self-efficacious and show advanced academic achievement compared with other students. Those who choose performance-approach goals also record good school achievement, but only when those goals are combined with mastery goals (Pintrich, 2000). Finally, adolescents who set performance-avoidance goals often show anxiety related to performance, and as a result tend do poorly in school (Maehr & Zusho, 2009). These students may fear failure. Fear of failure in turn can prevent them from even attempting a challenging task or activity. (See Table 15.3 for an example of each type of goal.)

Some adolescents are not convinced of the value of setting goals related to academic achievement. They may question why education is important for their own life purposes. Some may point out that certain celebrities—people they admire—have little formal education. Can low-achieving adolescents be motivated to elevate the value they place on education? As you can see in the accompanying Research Insights feature, by providing adolescents with relevant data, we can increase their academic motivation. In doing so, we can also improve their school performance.

Students who set mastery goals for themselves, such as learning to play the keyboard, advance further academically as compared with students who don't.

## Views of Intelligence

Another reason why students' differ in their beliefs about their ability to succeed at challenging academic tasks relates to their beliefs about intelligence. As we discussed in Chapter 12, psychologists have various views on intelligence, based on their theoretical perspectives. Children and adolescents, too, have theories about the nature of intelligence. For example, some may consider biology more important, while others may think environment plays the greater role. An important belief about intelligence concerns whether it is *fixed* or *malleable*—that is, changeable (Dweck, 1999). Consider for a moment your views of your own intelligence. Do you believe your intelligence has changed since you were in elementary school? Or do you see your intelligence as fixed at birth and not under your control? If you think intelligence is fixed, you hold an *entity perspective*. If you believe that intelligence can be changed, you hold an *incremental perspective*.

**Table 15.3** Examples of Types of Goals

| Goal Type | Example |
|---|---|
| Mastery goal | "I want to learn how to play the keyboard because I really enjoy learning to play musical instruments." |
| Performance-approach goal | "I want to learn how to play the keyboard so that others will admire me." |
| Performance-avoidance goal | "I'm terrible at music. I don't want to embarrass myself by trying to learn to play the keyboard." |

## Research Insights: Can Knowledge About Income Differences Motivate Students?

Mesmin Destin and Daphna Oyserman (2010) conducted two studies involving African American middle school students living in low-income neighborhoods. In the first study, they asked students about their educational expectations and about the type of jobs they expected to have in the future. Almost all the students (89%) reported that they expected to attend at least a two-year college. Only half of those students said they expected to take a job that required postsecondary education. Those who did anticipate working in a job requiring higher education put more effort into their schoolwork and had higher grades.

The researchers reasoned that these students did not fully understand how employment and earnings were related to educational level. They further hypothesized that students might be motivated to work harder in school if they knew how much more money they would likely earn by completing a postsecondary education, rather than attaining only a high school degree or less. The researchers randomly assigned the students to two groups. To test their hypotheses, the researchers gave one group a list of salaries reported by top earners among actors, athletes, and musicians. (Note that these careers are not linked to education levels. Many adolescents aspire to such careers, though few can attain them.) They gave the second group information on earnings in the state based on education level. Both groups then completed a survey on the effort they put into schoolwork. In addition, they were given the option of completing an extra-credit assignment for a science class. The students in the second group, which had received information on the level of education in relation to earnings, reported putting more effort into their schoolwork and were 8 times as likely to complete the extra-credit assignment.

What does this research tell us? It indicates that when students understand how educational attainment can affect their future earnings, they will be more highly motivated to do well in school. Even this small intervention shows that adolescent academic motivation can change.

Students with an incremental perspective focus more on mastery goals than on performance-type goals and believe in the positive effects of effort (Hong, Chiu-yue, Dweck, Lin, & Wan, 1999). If these students fail at a task, they often attribute that failure to lack of effort. In comparison, students who have an entity perspective often attribute their failures to lack of ability. These two perspectives have important consequences for success in school, even at the college level (Henderson & Dweck, 1990). As described in the accompanying Research Insights feature (Blackwell, Trzesniewski & Dweck, 2007), adolescents can be taught that intelligence is malleable. Those who change from an entity to an incremental perspective show greater motivation in the classroom.

### Stereotype Threat

There is a third reason why motivation to succeed in school differs among students. Certain students may fear performing poorly because of a stereotype held by others. Claude Steele (Steele, 1997; Steele & Aronson, 1995; Steele, Spencer, & Aronson, 2002) employed the term **stereotype threat** to describe this phenomenon. The idea is that a person who faces a negative stereotype fears that he or she will perform poorly, thereby confirming the stereotype. Steele posits that the apprehension and anxiety associated with the expectation of poor performance creates stress. That stress undermines good performance. Stereotype threat may also lead to less efficient information processing, which in turn influences the quality of a student's performance (Ryan & Ryan, 2005). This type of threat has been associated with poor performance on achievement tests for students of color and on math tests for females (Kellow & Jones, 2008; Ryan & Ryan, 2005). For more on Claude Steele, see the following Focus On box.

Students do not necessarily need to believe a stereotype is true to be affected by stereotype threat. In fact, they often are hoping to counter the stereotype. Regardless of their belief in the stereotype's validity, however, when stereotype threat is activated, they can become anxious. How is such a threat activated? As an example, consider a classic study (Steele & Aronson, 1995). Researchers found that black participants performed more poorly than white participants on a test measuring verbal achievement—but only when they were told that the test measured innate ability rather than acquired

**stereotype threat** Fear that one's performance will conform to a stereotype.

## Research Insights: Can You Grow Your Intelligence?

Adolescents who see intelligence as unchangeable are unlikely to improve their grades. After all, they attribute poor grades to lack of ability rather than lack of effort, implying that they could not improve even if they tried. To test whether adolescents could change their view of intelligence, Lisa S. Blackwell, Kali H. Trzesniewski, and Carol Sorich Dweck (2007) decided to develop an intervention. Seventh-grade students were randomly assigned to one of two groups. Both groups received eight 25-minute periods of instruction about the brain, including basic neuroanatomy, and study skills. The two groups differed in only one respect: Members of the experimental group engaged in activities showing them how to improve intelligence, and watched demonstrations of how learning creates changes in neuronal networks in the brain. In contrast, activities for the control group were related to learning about memory and mnemonic skills.

The results revealed that students in the experimental group developed a more incremental view of intelligence, compared with those in the control group. Their teachers also rated them as showing greater positive change in motivation. Here is a typical comment from a teacher:

> L, who never puts in any extra effort and doesn't turn in homework, actually stayed up late working for hours to finish an assignment early so I could review it and give him a chance to revise it (p. 256).

It seems that students can indeed change their view of intelligence. And by doing so, they can actually "grow their intelligence" through greater motivation to learn.

*Fuse/Getty Images*

Students who are taught to view intelligence as having incremental, not fixed, qualities, are more motivated to learn.

knowledge. Wanting to disprove the stereotype about ability differences between the races, black students became anxious. Their anxiety thus made their cognitive processing less efficient (Ryan & Ryan, 2005). In another study, females performed worse than males on a math test when they were told that in the past the test had revealed sex differences. In contrast, when they were told that the test was "gender fair," females performed similarly to males (Spencer, Steele, & Quinn, 1999).

Stereotype threat seems to affect the types of cognitive strategies students call on to solve problems. For example, in one study, female students were required to solve math problems (Quinn & Spencer, 2001). They used fewer strategies under heightened stereotype threat than under low stereotype threat. When asked to think aloud about how they solved a problem, students in the high-stereotype-threat condition described conventional approaches—a formula or an algorithm—whereas students in the low-stereotype-threat condition used less conventional (but often successful) strategies involving estimation and logic. In a sample of black adolescents, even normally high-achieving students performed more poorly when stereotype-threat conditions were high than when they were low (Arbuthnot, 2009). Some researchers have found that the effects of stereotype threat on school achievement can be lowered by encouraging students to focus on self-affirmation. For example, some interventions have involved students writing

*Spencer Grant/Photo Researchers, Inc.*

When students face a high level of stereotype threat, they are shown to perform poorly on tests.

## Focus On: Claude Steele

Steve Castillo/Stanford Graduate School of Education

Claude Steele, professor of psychology at Columbia University, is a leader in the field of social psychology. In his early days as a psychologist, he became interested in trying to understand the nature of race, and how race might affect academic performance. One set of explanations involved the *stereotype threat*. In Dr. Steele's words:

> If you're a member of a group whose intellectual abilities are negatively stereotyped, this threat might occur. That negative stereotype might be applicable to you right in the middle of an important standardized test. And our general reasoning was that this threat, this prospect of confirming a stereotype or being seen that way would be distracting enough, upsetting enough, to undermine a person's performance right there in the middle of a test.

Dr. Steele is interested not only in what conditions produce stereotype threat but also in how to change learning situations so that this threat is not evoked. He calls these low-threat learning situations "wise schooling." Along with many psychologists inspired by him, he has worked on developing ways to teach and assess students without letting the threat of being judged according to stereotyped views get in the way of optimal performance (Chandler & Steele, 1999).

about their core values and sense of self-integrity. Such activities supported students' sense of self-affirmation which, in turn, insulated them from the effects of stereotype threat (Sherman et al., 2013).

## Promoting School Achievement Parenting

As we have just seen, adolescents' motivation to achieve in school can vary for a number of reasons. Differing levels of motivation, in turn, result in differing levels of achievement. Adolescent achievement also varies according to how parents react to their adolescent's growing maturity. Three aspects of parenting during the adolescent period are critical to students' achievement (Laursen & Collins, 2009; Steinberg & Silk, 2002).

1. *Parental warmth* is characterized by responsiveness and involvement, along with expression of positive feelings toward the adolescent (Fulton & Turner, 2008; Gauvain, Perez, & Beebe, 2013).
2. *Parental supervision* involves monitoring and limit setting, as well as knowing about the adolescent's activities and friendships. Monitoring is most successful when adolescents are willing to communicate openly with their parents and do not view them as intrusive or psychologically controlling. Parents exercise psychological control by such means as withdrawing love or inducing guilt. Control of this nature has negative effects on adolescent achievement (D'Angelo & Omar, 2003).
3. *Parental autonomy granting* requires noncoercive and democratic discipline that allows adolescents to express their individuality, and respects their point of view (Silk, Morris, Kanaya, & Steinberg, 2003; Supple, Ghazarian, Peterson, & Bush, 2009).

The combination of these three aspects of parenting affects an adolescent's sense of self-determination and control. These factors, in turn, relate to success in school, as shown in Figure 15.6.

Tetra images/Getty Images

Positive parenting during the adolescent period is critical to their children's academic achievement.

## School Transitions

One of the most important events in secondary schooling occurs in the transition from elementary school to middle school, junior high school, or high school. School districts

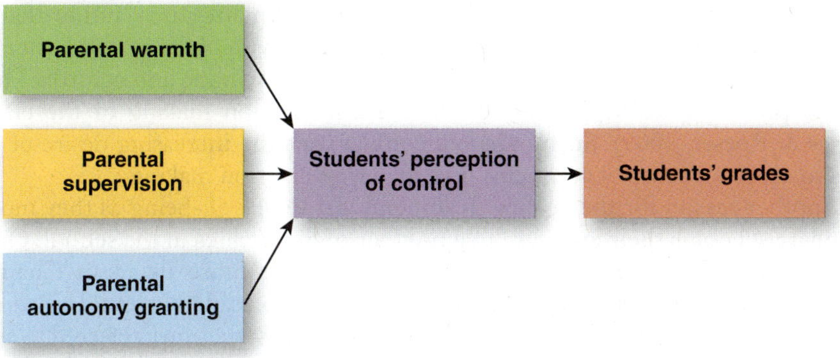


**FIGURE 15.6 How Parenting Affects Students' Grades** Parental warmth, supervision, and autonomy granting affect adolescents' sense of self-determination and control, which in turn relate to their success in school.

*Source:* Fulton, E., & Turner, L. A. (2008). Students' academic motivation: Relations with parental warmth, autonomy granting, and supervision. *Educational Psychology, 28*(5), 521–534. Reprinted by permission of Taylor & Francis Ltd., http://www.tandf.co.uk/journals.

vary in when this transition takes place. Middle schools and junior high schools may span grades 5 through 8, 6 through 8, or 7 through 9, for example. In some smaller districts, elementary school continues through grade 8. Especially when the transition occurs during early adolescence, the move from elementary to secondary school (whether middle school, junior high school, or high school) often leads to declines in motivation and achievement (Eccles & Roeser, 2009). Why do these declines occur?

## How Is Secondary School Different?

What makes secondary school so different from elementary school? For one thing, the transition out of elementary school often coincides with the onset of puberty. As we discussed in Chapter 14, during puberty adolescents are experiencing a wide range of hormonal and physical changes. These changes can be emotionally unsettling. They can also impose distinctions among students based on when they occur—the timing of puberty. In addition, adolescents go through shifts in their natural sleep cycles, with deeper sleep occurring early in the morning (Carskadon & Taylor, 1997). Unfortunately, secondary schools often begin earlier in the morning than do elementary schools. These early start times can disrupt adolescent sleep cycles. And inadequate sleep can affect students' ability to pay attention and make optimal use of their cognitive abilities (Kirby, Maggi, & D'Angiulli, 2011).

A second reason for the decline in motivation and achievement relates to the structure of secondary schools. Jacquelynne Eccles and her colleagues (Eccles et al., 1993; Eccles & Roeser, 2009) have studied the experiences of students making the transition from elementary to secondary school. In the elementary grades, students are generally in self-contained classrooms with a single teacher, who knows them well. Often, the students have known each other throughout the early years of school. Secondary school presents a very different structure.

One important difference involves the student-teacher relationship. As they move from elementary to secondary school, students report declines in the emotional support they receive from their teachers (Hagenauer & Hascher, 2010; Roeser, Peck, & Nasir, 2006). Several factors may contribute to this perception. One is that the student-teacher relationships in

© Image Source/Age Fotostock

The structure of some high schools—in particular, those with early start times, limited opportunities for development of student-teacher relationships, and academic as well as social hierarchies—present many challenges to adolescents.

**stage-environment fit** The relation between a person's developmental needs and the opportunities provided or constraints imposed by the person's environment.

secondary schools are confined to a particular subject-matter area, rather than being broad-based, as in elementary school. Also, compared with elementary teachers, those in secondary schools tend to be more concerned with discipline and control. They also tend to provide fewer opportunities for student decision making in the classroom (Eccles & Roeser, 2009). Such practices conflict with the increasing desire of adolescents to express a sense of autonomy and agency in decision making.

Another reason for the decline in students' sense of well-being as they move into secondary school is their exposure to a number of hierarchies in the school. One such hierarchy involves peer groups, which we discuss in more detail in Chapter 16. Another involves the school's assignment of students to academic levels based on perceived differences in their abilities. These assignments (sometimes referred to as tracking or leveling) often are made first in math but eventually in other subjects as well (Elmore, 2009). Students assigned to the highest academic levels usually show growth in achievement. In contrast, those assigned to the lower levels experience little growth (Hallinan & Kubitschek, 1999; Newton, 2010). Students in the lower levels may fail to achieve because they see themselves as less competent. As a result, they experience a weaker sense of belonging in school (Roeser, Eccles, & Sameroff, 1998). Teacher quality and the quality of assignments also vary by level. Students in the lower academic levels are more likely to have teachers with fewer qualifications. These students also follow a less challenging curriculum (De Luca, Takano, Hinshaw, & Raisch, 2009).

### Stage-Environment Fit

We have seen that students face many changes as they move from elementary to secondary school. These changes can impose demands that undermine students' self-confidence and motivation to learn. In discussing this situation, Eccles and her colleagues (1993) refer to **stage-environment fit**. A good stage-environment fit exists when a particular environment meets the developmental needs of individuals in a particular stage (or phase) of development. We can think about this concept in terms of developmental systems theory (Lerner, 2002, 2006), discussed in Chapter 1. In this view, development results from interactions between an individual and the many contexts in which that individual engages. School is one of the primary contexts of adolescents. So how good is the stage-environment fit between students and secondary schools? Unfortunately, according to Eccles, not good at all.

What can be done about this problem? Some middle and junior high schools have attempted to improve the stage-environment fit by having teachers plan and teach as a team, and by linking teachers to student advisory groups. These changes have met with positive results, especially in improving the self-concepts of early adolescents (Parker, 2009). In one study, students were able to add their voices to the discussion of how to improve school settings (Schmakel, 2008). Seventh-graders in urban schools were asked this question: "If you were a teacher, how would you get your students to improve their school learning and their school achievement?" The students drew up a list of several ways by which teachers could increase motivation for learning. Their suggestions included providing more hands-on and experiential learning, offering suggestions for specific learning strategies, and creating more opportunities for students to make choices about assignments.

## School Completion

Every school day in the United States, 7,000 students leave high school and never return (Alliance for Excellent Education, 2010). Adolescents who drop out of high school face many problems. They are more likely to be incarcerated, experience long stretches of unemployment, and earn lower wages than those who complete high school (Neild, 2009). High school graduation rates in the United States, and the corresponding dropout rates, vary by state, ethnicity, and family socioeconomic status. Although 78% of white students graduate from high school, only 52% of Hispanic and 55% of African American students graduate (Monrad, 2007). In addition, students from low-income families are 6 times more likely to drop out than students from higher-income families (Bloom, 2010; Orfield, 2004). Only about half of those who drop out later receive a high school credential, such as the graduate equivalent degree (GED) (Monrad, 2007).

### The No Child Left Behind Act and High School Completion  Policy

The No Child Left Behind Act (NCLB) was passed in 2001 as a reauthorization of the Elementary and Secondary Education Act. As mentioned in Chapter 12, this act has many provisions. Its main thrust, though, is to hold schools accountable for the academic progress of their students. Schools are required to raise the achievement levels of all students, but especially those of color, from low-income families, with disabilities, and English language learners (Darling-Hammond, 2006). Schools are required also to report graduation rates, defined as "the percentage of students who graduate from secondary school with a regular diploma in the standard number of years" (NCLB, 2001).

A key goal of the NCLB is to close the achievement gap between students of color and other students. A corresponding concern is narrowing the graduation gap among students of different ethnic groups. Under the act, schools are working to close both the achievement gap and the graduation gap. How is your state doing? To find out, visit the NCLB website at http://www2.ed.gov/nclb/accountability/results/progress/index.html and click on your state.

**WHEN SYSTEMS CONNECT**

### School Completion

In Chapter 1, we discussed Bronfenbrenner's *bioecological model* (Bronfenbrenner, 1977; Bronfenbrenner & Morris, 2006). This model provides a rich description of the many systems affecting a child's development. We can use it to take a developmental systems approach to analyzing the factors that either promote high school completion or lead to school dropout. Of course, many factors could be involved. Here, we consider a selection of these factors, as diagramed in Figure 15.7.

- Certain characteristics of the individual
- The microsystem of the school
- The mesosystem of the school and family
- The exosystem, which creates policies related to grade retention
- The macrosystem, which incorporates the values and ideologies of the culture
- The chronosystem, which represents changes over time

When an adolescent experiences difficulties in one part of the system, other parts of the system can converge to assist that child. Or they can fail to connect, possibly leading to school dropout.

Let's start by considering individual factors. Adolescents with disabilities and those who exhibit problem behaviors, such as truancy and other violations of school rules, are most likely to drop out (Stearns & Glennie, 2006). Students who have poor academic skills and low academic motivation also have high dropout rates (Hickman, Bartholomew, Mathwig, & Heinrich, 2008). These disabilities and difficulties may be biologically based, learned, or a combination of both (Bronfenbrenner & Morris, 2006). Students with such difficulties often lack the self-regulation necessary to learn new academic material and meet the behavioral demands of the school setting.

The *microsystem* is the individual's immediate setting. It involves all the activities, roles, and relationships in that setting. In the microsystem of the school, several factors can be important to an adolescent's decision to drop out or to stay. Students are less likely to drop out of schools that offer a large selection of academically rigorous courses, are smaller in size, and promote positive student-teacher relationships (Lee & Burkam, 2003). Rigorous academic classes set expectations that promote cognitive engagement. That is, they encourage students to be involved with what they are learning. In smaller

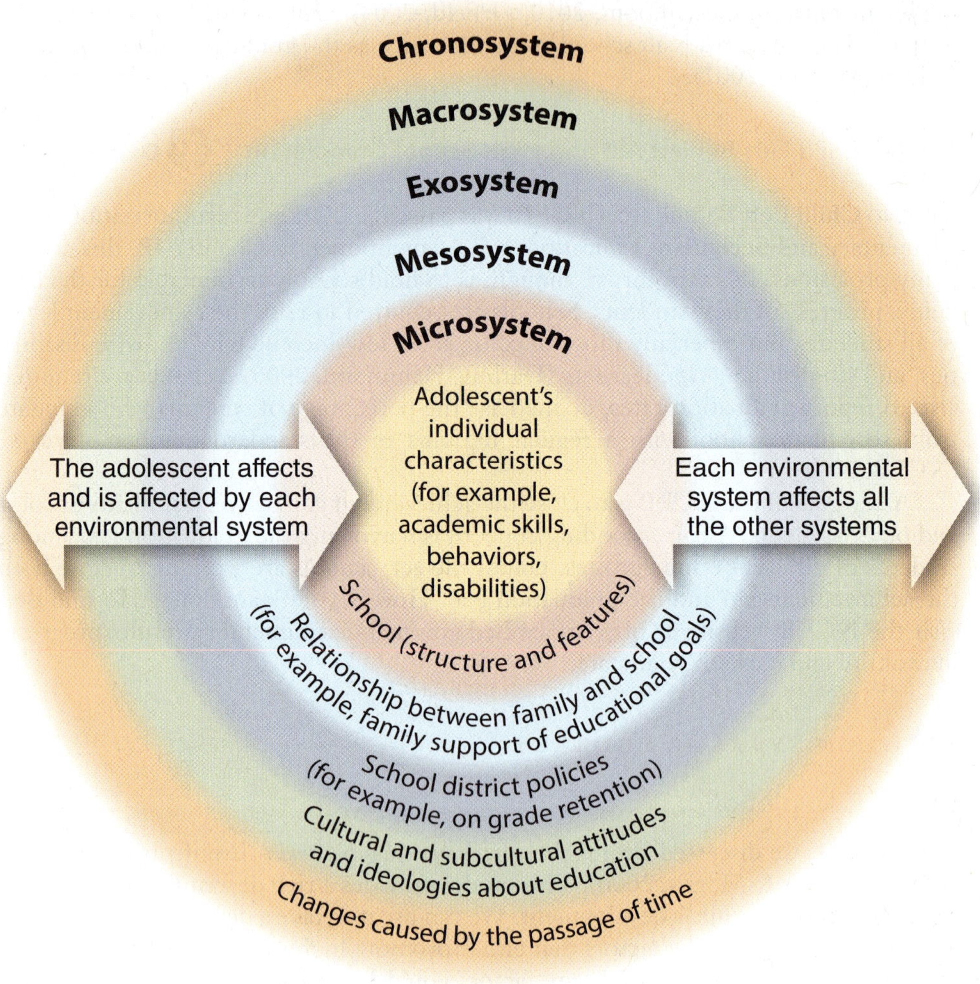


**FIGURE 15.7 The Bioecological Model Applied to School Completion** Various characteristics of the individual, the microsystem, the mesosystem, the exosystem, the macrosystem, and the chronosystem interact to affect whether an adolescent will complete high school or drop out.

schools, teachers get to know students better. The resulting relationships are central to a student's sense of belonging in school. Relationships are especially positive when teachers support students' interests, and when trust develops between students and teachers (Neild, 2009; Strom & Boster, 2007).

The *mesosystem* refers to the relationships among microsystems—the links among settings. Here, we consider the family-school mesosystem. Its effects can be positive or negative. On the one hand, family responsibilities can keep an adolescent from attending school. Females, in particular, are more likely to drop out because of pregnancy or other family needs (Stearns & Glennie, 2006). In addition, frequent family moves can cause problems. Changing from one high school to another often disrupts an adolescent's social ties and sense of belonging to a school community (Ream, 2003). High family mobility rates are especially common among some immigrant groups. On the other hand, the family-school relationship can also promote school attendance. A meta-analysis of 13 broad-based studies found that the messages parents give to adolescents about the importance of school affect school completion rates (Strom & Boster, 2007). When parents express high expectations and educational goals related to education, their children are more likely to stay in school. Even if an adolescent has negative feelings about school, support from parents can prevent dropout.

The adolescent has no direct involvement in the *exosystem*. Nevertheless, this setting can influence what goes on in the microsystem. For example, students play no role in the committee that establishes a school district's policy on grade retention. The committee's decisions, will however, have important effects on students. Schools vary in their policies and practices about retaining students "in grade"—that is, having them repeat a grade. More students are being retained in the ninth grade than ever before, possibly because of state-mandated testing. Of the students who are retained in ninth grade, 70 to 80% fail to complete high school (Abrams & Haney, 2004). Research consistently shows that even though students retained in a grade sometimes show short-term benefits, students who have been retained at any grade are more likely to leave school (Jimerson, 1999).

The *macrosystem* consists of the overarching beliefs and ideologies of a culture or subculture. Different cultural groups hold different ideas about learning, as described in the Culture and Learning Models feature. And even within a particular culture, ideas vary among its subcultures. One subculture may promote educational attainment, for example. Another may believe that identifying with school requires a loss of ethnic identity (Ogbu, 1994). This latter belief has been found most often in schools where family income varies widely (Tyson, Darity, & Castellino, 2005). Such beliefs, of course, do not promote school completion. Moreover, adolescents who live in communities where schooling is not clearly linked with better jobs are more likely to drop out (Stearns & Glennie, 2006).

Finally, the *chronosystem* represents changes over time. Many researchers who have studied dropping out of high school indicate that it is a process (Jimerson, Anderson, & Whipple, 2002). Academic failure is cumulative, and failure at one point in time often results in more failure later (Elmore, 2009). Thus, a series of transactions

## Culture and Learning Models

Cultural learning models are culturally based, shared views of learning (Li, 2011). Though not all individuals in a culture share these views, they serve as a general framework for thinking about what is important in learning. For example, much of the Chinese view of learning has roots in Confucian teaching, which stresses that knowledge comes before inquiry or discovery (Li, 2011). From this perspective, it is important to master material before engaging in inquiry or asking challenging questions about it. In this view, students who are poor learners are so because they either lack desire or are arrogant. Therefore, the model of learning in China (and many other East Asian cultures) stresses diligence, self-exertion, endurance, perseverance, and concentration (Li & Fischer, 2004).

*PARK YEONG-CHEOL/AFP/Getty Images*

The model of learning in East Asian cultures stresses the importance of diligence, self-exertion, endurance, perseverance, and concentration.

In contrast, the European American model is based largely on Greek philosophy, which emphasizes active engagement in learning, personal curiosity, thinking, inquiry, and verbal communication (Li & Fischer, 2004). From this perspective, learning and mastery occur through inquiry and asking challenging questions. Students who are poor learners are so because they are indifferent to challenges or are led by extrinsic (rather than intrinsic) motivation to learn. As you consider these two models, you can imagine how schools in each culture would focus on different dimensions of learning.

between the adolescent and the school leads to dropping out. These transactions may involve low or failing grades, disciplinary actions, and grade retention at different points during an individual's years in school. Conversely, a series of favorable events can promote school completion.

### Preventing School Dropout

Many programs have been developed to prevent school dropout. Most target changes at the individual student level, the classroom or school level, or the level of interaction between school and family. Although the emphasis of these programs varies, most contain the following features (Bloom, 2010; Lehr, Hansen, Sinclair, & Christenson, 2003; Prevatt & Kelly, 2003; Weiss, Kreider, Lopez, & Chatman, 2005):

- *Improving personal skills* through counseling, either individually or in small groups, and instruction on improving self-regulation. For example, instruction might cover conflict resolution and anger management.
- *Improving academic and metacognitive skills* through tutoring, classes on study skills, and remedial programs in specific subjects.
- *Mentoring* by peer buddies, school advisors, and volunteer adults who are paired directly with individual students.
- *Family outreach*, using various strategies to strengthen the home-school relationship, such as encouraging parents to attend school meetings and having teachers make home visits.
- *Changing school or classroom structure* by, for example, adjusting course schedules or reducing class size.
- *Emphasizing vocational or work-related skills* by focusing on vocational exploration and training related to future employment options.

**what if...?**

Suppose you are a high school counselor. A student confides in you that she wants to drop out of school. You know that she feels lonely at school and finds schoolwork challenging, but you also know that her parents want her to complete high school. What would you do?

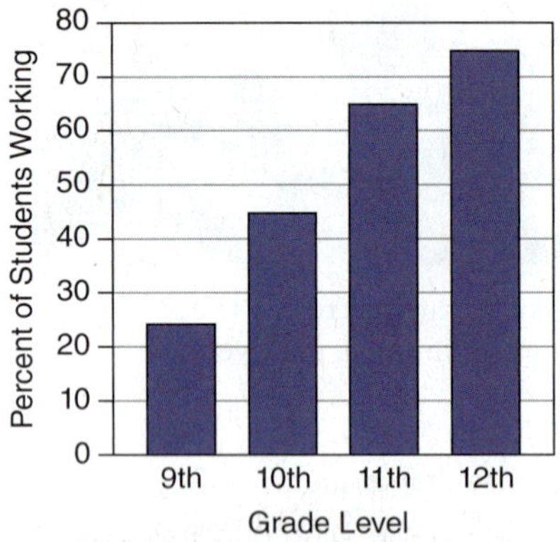


**FIGURE 15.8 Percentage of Students Working, by Grade Level** Employment of adolescents increases steadily by grade level, with 24% of ninth graders reporting formal employment, rising to 75% of twelfth graders. The data shown here are from 1997–2003.

## School and Work

Do you remember your first job? Were you a teenager when you got it? For many people, adolescence is a critical period of development in relation to the world of work. Adolescents often begin to think about their future in terms of employment and career options. They also often get their first "real job," meaning a job with responsibilities and a paycheck. State and federal laws set various requirements for minors who work. In most states, adolescents must be at least 14 to work at most types of jobs. Laws may also regulate the type of work minors can do, and the hours and times they can work.

As you can see in Figure 15.8, employment rates increase steadily through the high school years. By eleventh grade, the majority of high school students are employed, and most work more than 16 hours a week (Staff, Messersmith, & Schulenberg, 2009). The type of work varies, depending on age. Researchers have found that eighth-graders are more frequently employed in babysitting and yard work, whereas by twelfth grade, a large proportion of students are working in retail industries (Staff et al., 2009). Given the large numbers of adolescents in the paid workforce, we might well ask whether paid work is harmful or beneficial to adolescent development.

One view is that employment disrupts academic performance, interferes with school achievement, and causes adolescents to become less connected to school

(Greenberger & Steinberg, 1986; Marsh & Kleitman, 2005). Adolescents who work may have less time to do homework and to take part in school activities. And, importantly, students are earning money. They can, in turn, spend their money on activities that increase the likelihood of delinquency and substance abuse (Osgood, Wilson, O'Malley, & Bachman, 1996). Much research indicates, however, that the harmful effects of adolescent employment are more likely to occur for those who work more than 20 hours a week (McMorris & Uggen, 2000; Monahan, Lee, & Steinberg, 2011). Thus, it seems that *intensive involvement* in paid work, defined as more than 20 hours a week, can have negative effects on adolescents.

A second view stresses the benefits of youth employment. One model of the psychology of work describes it as having three purposes: survival, social connection, and self-determination (Blustein, Kenna, Gill, & DeVoy, 2008). Most adolescents in the United States do not work to survive. By working, however, they do make social connections, often with adults, and advance their own sense of self-determination or agency. Proponents of the benefits of work for adolescents point out that their work experiences can help them make better occupational choices and more easily navigate the school-to-work transition (Rosenbaum, 2001). Such experiences can also foster critical employment-related attributes, such as dependability and responsibility (Ruhm, 1997; Staff et al., 2009). In addition, employment may limit the time adolescents have to engage in passive activities such as watching television (Bachman, Safron, Sy, & Schulenberg, 2003). Finally, adolescents who work can gain the skill to balance paid jobs, schoolwork, and extracurricular activities (Shanahan & Flaherty, 2001). Researchers have confirmed many of these benefits, primarily for adolescents who work 20 hours or less per week. Thus, it appears that *moderate levels* of employment, defined as 20 hours or less a week, can foster many positive skills for adolescents.

© Ariel Skelley/Corbis

Having a job can be beneficial to adolescents, but not when they work more than 20 hours a week, which often leads to diminished engagement in schoolwork.

### ✓CHECK YOUR PROGRESS

1. Give an example of how extrinsic motivation can become intrinsic motivation.
2. What are some reasons why a student might not be motivated to achieve in secondary school?
3. School dropout can be explained by many factors. Which do you consider to be most important, and why?
4. What does research tell us about adolescents and paid work?

# CHAPTER SUMMARY

## Piaget and Formal Operations

**[ KEY QUESTION ] 1. What are the major contributions of Piaget's theory of cognitive development relevant to the adolescent period?**

- Piaget described abstract thinking as the hallmark of formal operations, which many (but not all) individuals reach during adolescence. He highlighted three types of reasoning that occur during formal operations: hypothetical-deductive reasoning, conditional reasoning, and propositional thinking.
- Piaget described adolescent egocentricity as a form of egocentricity that emerges during adolescence and consists of two facets: the imaginary audience and the personal fable.

## Vygotsky's Sociocultural Theory and the Adolescent Mind

**[ KEY QUESTION ] 2. How does Vygotsky's theory explain cognitive growth in adolescence?**

- Vygotsky emphasized the importance of schooling for learning the tools of industrialized cultures. Learning academic language is one of the tools adolescents acquire through schooling.
- The role of collaboration is central to Vygotsky's theory. Peer tutoring is an example of collaboration. Such collaboration is most successful when intersubjectivity exists between the tutor and tutee, and when the tutor focuses on reflective knowledge building.

## Information Processing in the Adolescent Years

**[ KEY QUESTION ] 3. What cognitive changes occur during adolescence according to information processing theorists?**

- Adolescents show improvements in three components of cognitive processing: processing speed, working memory, and response inhibition.
- Adolescents often show performance similar to that of adults on cognitive tasks. At the same time, adolescents have difficulty applying rational thought to making decisions when emotionally aroused, such as when they are among their peers.

## The Developing Brain: The Brain and Adolescent Cognition

**[ KEY QUESTION ] 4.** What are some major changes that occur in the adolescent brain?

- During adolescence, the brain undergoes a great deal of refinement and reorganization. This involves increases in myelination, which aids in accelerating processing speed, and synaptic pruning, which assists in the integration of brain networks.
- Engagement in abstract thinking changes the structure of the brain.

## Learning and Schooling

**[ KEY QUESTION ] 5.** What factors promote or diminish adolescents' success in school?

- Sex differences in math and verbal skills have been found during the adolescent years. In general, males have better math skills, and females have better verbal skills, but such differences tend to be small. These skill differences may be based in part on differences in the brain. Expectancy-value theory also suggests that a student's expectation of success and the value placed on a task make a difference in the types of courses students choose. Such expectations may influence students' decision making about taking advanced classes, such as higher-level math.
- Student motivation is critical to success in school. Adolescents tend to be more highly motivated to achieve in school when they have a strong sense of self-efficacy, have adopted mastery goals rather than performance-type goals, and see intelligence as malleable. Adolescent learning may be diminished under conditions of stereotype threat.
- Adolescents whose parents show warmth as well as provide supervision and grant autonomy tend to have more positive academic achievement.
- School transitions may present problems for adolescents, especially if they result in a poor stage-environment fit.
- High school completion is a challenge for many adolescents. We can use Bronfenbrenner's bioecological model to identify many elements that promote or diminish an adolescent's likelihood of completing high school.
- Adolescent employment can benefit or disrupt school performance. Generally, more negative results occur when adolescents are employed more than 20 hours a week.

# KEY TERMS

academic language *562*
academic motivation *576*
conditional reasoning *559*
dual-process model *570*
expectancy-value theory *575*
extrinsic motivation *576*
formal operations *556*
hypothetical-deductive reasoning *557*
imaginary audience *560*
intersubjectivity *563*
intrinsic motivation *576*
personal fable *561*
self-efficacy *576*
stage-environment fit *582*
stereotype threat *578*

# CRITICAL THINKING QUESTIONS

1. **Piaget and Formal Operations.** Analyze the ways in which formal operational thinking can help adolescents as they debate ideas with others.
2. **Vygotsky's Sociocultural Theory and the Adolescent Mind.** Differentiate receptive, conceptual, and interpretive understanding of course material, and defend the view that conceptual understanding precedes interpretive understanding.
3. **Information Processing in the Adolescent Years.** Describe a time when metacognition helped you to solve a problem during your high school experience.
4. **The Developing Brain: The Brain and Adolescent Cognition.** How does our knowledge of changes in the adolescent brain challenge the view that either nature or nurture exerts the greater influence on development? Provide a rationale for your response.
5. **Learning and Schooling.** Construct examples of how schools could help reduce the difficulties that adolescents may have when making a transition from elementary school to middle school or high school.
6. **Cultural Perspectives.** Contrast the two cultural views of learning discussed in this chapter. Provide examples of the type of student learning that teachers with each perspective would value.

# REAL Development

## Cognitive Development in Adolescence

In this module, you are studying to be a child psychologist. In the accompanying activity, you have been asked to observe a history lesson. As you complete the activity, consider what you have learned about students' cognitive development during adolescence based on the Piagetian, Vygotskian, and information processing models of cognitive development.

**WileyPLUS** Go to WileyPLUS to complete the *Real Development* activity.

03.01

# Chapter 16

# Psychosocial Development in Adolescence

## CHAPTER OUTLINE



## MAKING A difference

### Peer Court

Imagine a courtroom without defendants in handcuffs, judges in robes pounding gavels, or attorneys arguing for their clients. Just such courts, often called peer courts or teen courts, have been developed as an alternative to juvenile courts. In peer courts, administered by the U.S. Department of Justice, first-time adolescent offenders with minor delinquent offenses come before a panel consisting of their peers, community leaders, school personnel, and other participants. The panel reviews each case and hands down judgment.

Across the country, thousands of adolescents volunteer to serve on peer court panels. Some came before the court themselves earlier in their lives, like the young man who describes his experiences here:

> When I was 14, I was caught out past curfew with possession of a cigarette and I had two options: one was to go in front of the judge and have a record, or go to teen court and have this mistake wiped from my record. . . .
>
> That long-dreaded day arrived when I had to go to teen court. . . . When I sat down at the table with my mom, I was scared. The group of five people asked me what happened. I answered the questions to the best of my ability. Then I was sent out in the hall, and the group deliberated. The sanctions as I can remember [included doing community service, writing an apology letter, and attending a smoking-cessation class].
>
> I wrote an apology letter. Then it came time to do my community service. I can remember going to the Cranberry Fest and to the very cold Klondike Days, picking up disgusting garbage. I never knew how messy some people are until I had to clean up their mess. . . .
>
> Then I had to go to smoking class, which . . . cost $20 at the door, and at my age I didn't have a job yet. So I had to do chores and different things to pay my mother back. . . . They told me about the effects of cigarettes. Did you know that things they use for rat poison are in cigarettes?
>
> Now I [am a trained panel member on] teen court to help others get on the right track, like those special people did for me. . . . Being on teen court after being in front of a teen court has really changed my life (National Youth Court Center, 2010).

## [KEY QUESTIONS] *for* READING CHAPTER 16

1. How do adolescents develop a sense of identity?
2. What are important features of adolescents' relationships with their parents and their peers?
3. How does moral development change during the adolescent period?
4. What are some important risk factors and resilient processes that influence adolescent well-being?

**IN THIS CHAPTER,** we focus on psychosocial development in adolescence, a period of great change. It is a time to engage in new and sometimes risky experiences, to develop new and sometimes intimate friendships, and to face new and sometimes moral challenges. All these require psychosocial skills. In this chapter, we consider the major psychosocial changes that occur during the adolescent years. We begin with the central question of identity development. We then turn to ways in which adolescents relate to others who are important in their lives, including parents and peers. Because adolescents often face situations that require making moral decisions, we next discuss this important aspect of adolescents' lives. In the final section, we consider one important risk of the adolescent period: The risk of developing mental health difficulties. Specifically, we discuss major depressive disorder and eating disorders. We also examine the process of resilience, which enables many adolescents to adapt in the presence of risk.

# The Development of the Self: Identity

[ KEY QUESTION ] 1. How do adolescents develop a sense of identity?

"Who am I?" How would you answer that question? How you respond relates to your concept of identity. **Identity** refers to an organized sense of self, which includes the way we maintain our sense of personal beliefs, goals, values, and commitments (Côté, 2009). The development of this complex sense of self is one of the major tasks of adolescence. We begin this section with a review Erikson's and Marcia's ideas about identity formation in adolescence. We move on from there to consider the important issues of racial, ethnic, and sexual identity.

| Erikson's Psychosocial Stage Theory |
|---|
| Trust vs. mistrust |
| Autonomy vs. shame, doubt |
| Initiative vs. guilt |
| Industry vs. inferiority |
| Identity vs. identity confusion<br>• Adolescents seek to develop a satisfying identity and a sense of their role in society. Failure may lead to a lack of stable identity and confusion about their adult roles. |
| Intimacy vs. isolation |
| Generativity vs. stagnation |
| Integrity vs. despair |

**identity** An organized sense of self, which includes personal beliefs, goals, values, and commitments.

**identity crisis** Erikson's term for the intense exploration of potential identities that characterizes adolescence.

## Erikson's Theory

Erikson (1968) was the first to identify the achievement of identity as the major psychosocial task of adolescence. You have probably heard of adolescence as a time of **identity crisis**, a term used by Erikson. What did he mean by it? Erikson used the word *crisis* to refer to both the dangers and the opportunities involved in creating an organized sense of self with continuity from childhood to adulthood. As with all of Erikson's stages, a potential clash exists between the two extremes. In this fifth stage, those extremes are *identity achievement* and *identity confusion*. And the clash between them results in a crisis or, put more mildly, a challenge.

Erikson saw the identity crisis as typical of all adolescents. That said, he did not maintain that all adolescents face a severe form of this crisis, marked by extreme identity confusion and unstable behavior. He did consider, however, that when adolescents enter this phase they tend to experiment with various roles as they search for goals, values, and beliefs that provide a personal fit. Note, too, that identity does not involve only the self. Identity development is relational. It involves distinguishing ourselves from others while at the same time developing connections to others (Kroger, 2004; Phinney & Baldelomar, 2011). Links to others may well extend beyond the immediate family, community, and peer group. They may, for example, include religious or political affiliations.

All societies, according to Erikson, give adolescents guidance through this life stage. The type of guidance varies widely, however. In postindustrial societies like the

United States, we consider it important to give adolescents time to experiment with a range of roles. Hence, adolescents in these societies often do not carry the burden of major social responsibilities, such as financial independence. In contrast, more traditional societies encourage adolescents to follow a parent's occupation or trade and to help support the family financially (Phinney & Baldelomar, 2011). In spite of differences, though, each culture provides adolescents with experiences and relationships that lead to identity formation.

kristian sekulic/Getty Images

Adolescents seek to develop their personal sense of identity and connection to others.

## Marcia's Patterns of Identity Status

James Marcia expanded on Erikson's ideas about identity achievement. In studying identity development, Marcia (1980) proposed that it involves two dimensions: exploration and commitment. He classified adolescents as being in one of four patterns of coping with the task of identity achievement. These patterns, shown in Figure 16.1, are based on the answers to two questions:

- Has the adolescent actively explored choices about his or her own goals, values, beliefs, and roles in life?
- Has the adolescent made a commitment to those choices?

**Identity achievement**, the most mature pattern, involves both exploration and commitment. **Identity diffusion**, the least mature pattern, involves neither (Côté, 2009). Adolescents in **identity foreclosure** make commitments without exploration. We can see this pattern in adolescents who adopt their parents' views without considering whether they agree with those views themselves. This pattern can interfere with the exploration needed for identity achievement. Adolescents in **identity moratorium** have not yet made personal commitments. When asked about their values and commitments, they might say they are not sure. They are, however, exploring different views. This exploration can be a step toward identity achievement.

Marcia's four patterns do not form a stage theory, for the simple reason that adolescents do not necessarily move through all four. Still, most young people living in

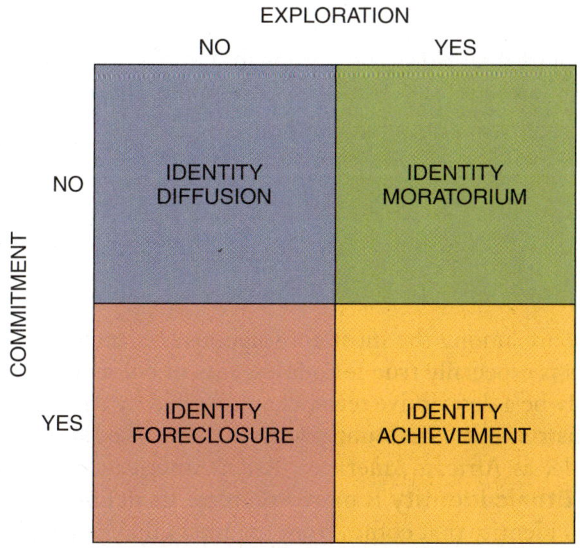


**FIGURE 16.1 Marcia's Four Patterns of Identity Status** Marcia's patterns of identity status are based on two dimensions: exploration and commitment. Adolescents reach identity achievement when they have both explored and then made a commitment to a set of goals, beliefs, and values.

**identity achievement** According to Marcia, the status of an individual who has explored goals, values, and beliefs, and made commitments to them.

**identity diffusion** According to Marcia, the status of an individual who has neither explored goals, values, and beliefs, nor made commitments to them.

**identity foreclosure** According to Marcia, the status of an individual who has made commitments without exploring goals, values, and beliefs.

**identity moratorium** According to Marcia, the status of an individual who is in the process of exploring goals, values, and beliefs but has not yet made commitments to them.

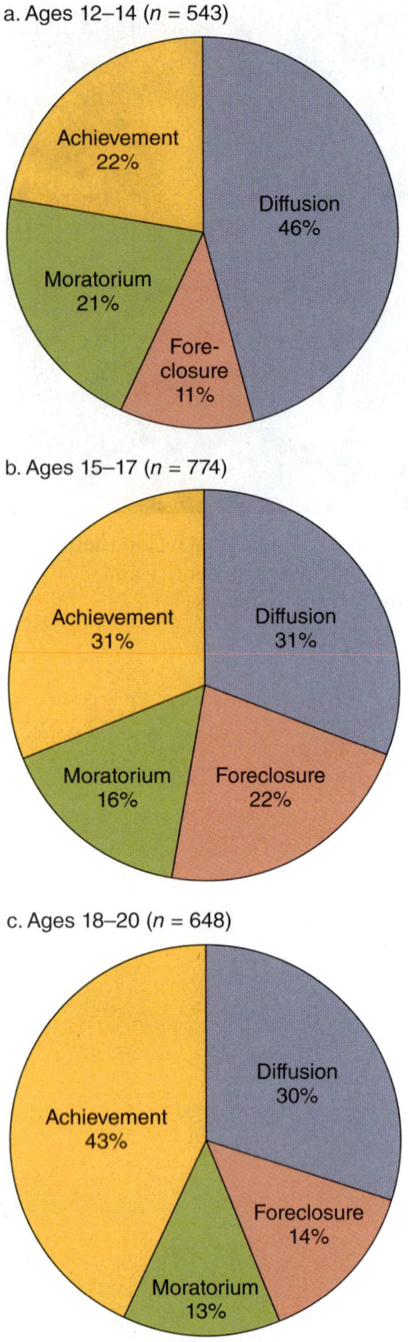


**FIGURE 16.2 Identity Patterns in Adolescents of Different Ages** Over the course of adolescence, the proportion of individuals who have reached identity achievement increases, while the proportion of individuals still showing the diffusion pattern decreases.
*Source:* Information from Meeus, 2003.

Western societies can be placed in one of the patterns at any single point in time. As you can see in Figure 16.2, the percentage of adolescents showing a particular pattern varies from early to late adolescence. As you can also see, many young people reach identity achievement by their early 20s (Meeus, 2003). Young people with an achieved identity have other positive characteristics as well. They show positive psychological adjustment, perform well in school, and live in families where warmth characterizes the interactions between parents and adolescents (Meeus, 2011).

WHEN SYSTEMS CONNECT

## Identity Achievement and Cognitive Skills

Think about the four patterns just described. How might they relate to the cognitive changes we discussed in Chapter 15? Let's take a closer look at that question.

To begin, consider that as adolescents become more analytical in their thinking, they can think in a more multidimensional way (Keating, 2004). They can question the ideology of others, for example, while keeping a variety of perspectives in mind. They also are developing more strategies for such questioning. And they are gaining greater metacognitive skills, which involve thinking about their own thought processes. For example, suppose an adolescent is exploring religious beliefs. She may consider the individual perspectives of her family members, her peers, and the members of the religious group to which she belongs. She may plan to attend religious services of various religious groups. In doing this, she may ask questions of others, as well as of herself, to find the ideas that best fit her own belief system. (You may have noticed that these are activities characteristic of exploration in Marcia's model.) Such investigation requires planning and abstract thinking skills, both of which improve during the adolescent period. Clearly, psychosocial development and cognitive development are intrinsically linked.

*Everyday stories*

POLITICS AND PERSPECTIVES Justin will soon be old enough to vote in national elections. His parents vote according to their political party affiliation, and he has always assumed that he would do the same. But after he joins a political discussion group at his high school, he begins to form his own political views. Some of them are distinctly different from those of his parents, and he decides to volunteer for a candidate his parents do not support. At first, his parents claim that Justin is supporting the candidate simply to rebel against their views. He argues that they should look at each individual candidate and not vote based only on party affiliation. This initiates a discussion between them about the candidates' positions. The discussion helps Justin further analyze his views as well as those held by his parents.

## Ethnic and Racial Identity

Ethnicity and race are among the most conspicuous characteristics of identity. In the United States, this is especially true for adolescents of color (Kiang & Fuligni, 2009). *Ethnicity* can simply be a descriptive term, characterized by checking a box on a survey or some similar instrument. No doubt you have been asked to identify yourself on a survey, for example, as African American, Asian American, European American, or Hispanic/Latino. **Ethnic identity** is more complex. Its definition has two parts: one, the aspect of social identity that comes from membership in a particular ethnic group, and two, the importance of that membership to the individual (Phinney, 1992). Jean Phinney (1993, 2008) has studied ethnic identity extensively. Based on Erikson's theory of identity achievement, she has proposed a three-stage model of ethnic identity achievement. Phinney's model is shown in Table 16.1.

**ethnic identity** The social identity derived from membership in a particular ethnic group.

**Table 16.1** Phinney's Model of Ethnic Identity

| | | |
|---|---|---|
| Stage 1 | Unexamined ethnic identity | People in this stage haven't considered what it means to be part of a particular ethnic group. Instead, they tend to show a preference for the cultural values of the majority, or dominant culture. They may even have a negative view of their own ethnic group. |
| Stage 2 | Ethnic identity search | People in this stage are involved in learning about their ethnicity in terms of history, practices, and social movements. They show strong, and sometimes exclusive, affiliations with other members of the group. The experience of discrimination often pushes people of color in the United States into this stage. |
| Stage 3 | Ethnic identity achievement | People in this stage are self-confident about their ethnicity; they express ethnic pride and are secure in their view of the meaning of their own ethnicity. They show positive intergroup attitudes. |

**racial identity** The identity associated with membership in a group based on a socially constructed designation of race.

According to Phinney, the second stage—the stage of exploration—is crucial for adolescents as they develop a sense of ethnic identity. Ethnic identity is in turn associated with psychological health. Adolescents in stage 1 are more likely to show signs of depression. Those in the second or third stage are more likely to have positive psychological well-being (Quintana, 2007). The importance of a strong ethnic identity has been shown for adolescents from a range of ethnic groups. These include Hispanics (Umaña-Taylor, Gonzales-Bracken, & Guimond, 2009), Navajo and other American Indians (Jones & Galliher, 2007), Asian Americans (Kiang & Fuligni, 2009), and African Americans (Cross, 1995).

**Racial identity** is often related to ethnic identity. Note, though, that the two terms are not synonymous (Williams, Tolan, Durkee, Francois, & Anderson, 2012). People sometimes associate ethnicity with culture, and race with biology—associating, for example, race with skin color. But race is not defined by biology. Race is, in fact, a concept developed by society (Helms & Talleyrand, 1997). It is society that tends to treat people as if they belong to a particular race (Markus, 2008).

Adolescents who define themselves as white are not as likely as other adolescents to explore the meaning of their racial identity (Helms, 1995; Phinney, Jacoby, & Silva, 2007). They may even dismiss it as being unimportant. Janet Helms (1990) has proposed that whites begin to explore their racial identity through encounters with people of color. This process of exploration involves two general phases. The first begins with abandoning racism. The second involves defining a nonracist identity (Helms, 1990, 1995). (The stages are further described in Table 16.2.) By progressing through these stages (which only some people do), white adolescents and adults develop a sense of their own racial identity. For more on Janet Helms, see the following Focus On box.

Erin Patrice O'Brien/Getty Images

A strong ethnic identity in the Latino culture is reinforced through events such as the *quinceañera*, which celebrates a teen's 15th birthday.

## what if...?

Suppose you are part of an event-planning group in a multicultural club at your school. Several white students believe the group should sponsor fewer discussions about race. They claim that racism in our society is part of the past, not the present. They argue that they themselves were never members of groups that promoted racism. One of them says, "It's time for a color-blind society." How do you respond?

**Table 16.2** Helms's Model of Racial Identity in Whites

| | |
|---|---|
| **Phase 1: Abandonment of Racism** | |
| Contact | Individuals have contact (possibly limited) with people of color. They tend to dismiss the role of race, making comments such as, "I don't notice what race a person is." |
| Disintegration | Individuals experience a sense of guilt or shame about racism. They try to distance themselves from it by making comments such as, "It's not my fault that we have a history of racism in the United States." |
| Reintegration | Individuals become consciously aware of a white identity. They begin to acknowledge that being white gives them subtle privileges in U.S. culture. |
| **Phase 2: Definition of a Nonracist Identity** | |
| Pseudo-Independence | Individuals may affiliate with groups of people of color and look to individuals of color to define racism. |
| Immersion/Emersion | Individuals ask questions such as, "Who am I racially?" They attempt to determine what it means to be white. |
| Autonomy | Individuals understand and accept their own whiteness and can give up their privileged status as whites. |

Adolescents who are immigrants to the United States often live between two cultures. The culture of their families, and often their communities, may contrast with that of the larger society. These adolescents show four possible patterns of identification (Berry, 1990).

- *Integration:* strong identification with both cultures
- *Assimilation:* strong identification with the mainstream culture
- *Separation:* strong affiliation with the culture of origin
- *Marginalization:* weak identification with both cultures

## Focus On: Janet E. Helms

Janet E. Helms is a psychologist whose work focuses on issues of race, gender, and culture. Growing up in Kansas City, Missouri, she decided early in life to become a psychologist. "I decided—actually in second grade—that I would be a psychologist and work with autistic children, because I read about it in a magazine and that sounded like something good to do" (Carter, 1995, p. 73). But she did not end up working with children with autism. Instead she became a counseling psychologist. She is particularly interested in how people develop a sense of racial identity (Helms, 1995).

Helms herself is black. When asked how she became interested in racial identity in whites, she replied:

> Well, remember the accidents in life. It first started when I submitted an article on Black racial identity and the reviewer sent back comments that essentially said, "Well, why are you talking about Black identity? What about White identity? How do you know that White people don't have an identity?" . . . So I began to ask myself questions about whether or not White people did, in fact, think about their racial identity. . . . I began to think about that. And so I sent my trusty graduate student . . . out into the field to ask random White people whether or not they did develop White racial identities. Based on the answers that he was able to get from the people he interviewed, I began developing a model of how that might work for White people. . . . If you're going to study race, you need to study it as a psychological construct. . . . I presented the idea that White people have racial identities and that their racial identities would influence how they treated people of color. . . . I presented the notion of interactions, racial identity interactions—the notion that where I am [in racial identity development] and where you are [in racial identity development] influence how we relate to one another (Carter, 1995, pp. 78–79).

Courtesy of Boston College

Janet Helms's view that racial identity influences people's interactions with each other is one that many psychologists acknowledge. Many aspects of that identity begin to be formed during adolescence.

Integration seems to have the best result. In one study, researchers found that adolescents who identified strongly with both cultures showed more signs of positive well-being, such as self-esteem and school adjustment (Berry, Phinney, Sam, & Vedder, 2006). Adolescents who had experienced discrimination were more likely to show signs of separation or marginalization.

Recent research has focused on an issue termed "the immigrant paradox" (García Coll & Marks, 2012). This phrase refers to findings that first-generation immigrants to the United States fare better than their children and grandchildren do. The immigrant paradox applies to risky adolescent behaviors, as discussed in the feature Culture and the Immigrant Paradox.

## Culture and the Immigrant Paradox

Adolescents in second- and third-generation immigrant families engage in more risky behaviors than do first-generation immigrants (Bui, 2012). Such behaviors include, for example, taking part in violence and causing property damage. These behaviors relate to the so-called immigrant paradox—the finding that many first-generation immigrants fare better than those in the second and the third generations. The concept is paradoxical because we might expect generations who have been in the United States longer to fare better, not worse. After all, they have the benefit of resources like education, are more acculturated, and have better English skills.

David McNew/Getty Images

Studies have shown that first-generation immigrants tend to have greater success than their second- and the third-generation descendants.

How can we explain the immigrant paradox? Several explanations have been offered. First, in many cultures, children are expected to submit to parental authority (Lin & Liu, 1993). First-generation children are likely to agree to this submission. Later generations often challenge adult authority, at least partly because of peer pressure (Rumbaut, 2005). Peer pressure becomes more important for second- and third-generation adolescents. This pressure often distances them from their parents (Bui, 2012). Second, many immigrant families live in inner-city neighborhoods. Such neighborhoods may support adolescent subcultures that engage in risky behaviors. As they spend more time with peers, later-generation adolescents may come to find these groups attractive. Third, first- and later-generation adolescents select different frames of reference. Members of the first generation often compare their current life possibilities with their experiences in the country they left (Suárez–Orozco & Suárez–Orozco, 2001). As a result, they are optimistic about current possibilities. In contrast, second- and third-generation adolescents compare themselves with middle-class adolescents in the United States. They tend to see economic success as less accessible. This is especially true if they are in communities with poor-quality schools (Rumbaut, 2005).

The immigrant paradox does not necessarily apply to all immigrant groups, especially those with higher levels of education and income (García Coll & Marks, 2012). Many groups do face this problem, however. Thus, we as a society need to pay attention to it. We can do this by developing stronger schools, a wider range of job opportunities, and safer neighborhoods.

## Sexual Identity

We use the term *sexual identity* here to refer to a sense of self as heterosexual, bisexual, or homosexual (gay or lesbian). Adolescents who are gay, bisexual or transgender, often referred to as sexual minorities, have more difficulty developing a sexual identity than those who are heterosexual. This difficulty arises at least in part from the many messages they receive that society expects them to be heterosexual. Researchers have found that adolescents who are sexual minorities go through four stages of awareness and understanding of their sexual identity (Troiden, 1993):

1. **Sensitization.** They feel different from others but are not sure why.
2. **Self-recognition.** They experience inner turmoil and confusion because they recognize their attraction to those of the same sex or both sexes.
3. **Identity assumption.** They personally recognize their sexual identity, but at this point may not openly acknowledge their minority orientation.
4. **Commitment.** They publicly disclose their sexual orientation, personally accept it, and feel satisfied with it.

Researchers have also studied the ages at which gay, lesbian, and bisexual teens reach certain milestones of sexual identity (see Figure 16.3). In one study of 116 young people, the researchers found that most disclosed their sexual orientation in their mid to late teens. They were aware of their sexual orientation and experienced sexual contact at earlier ages, however (Maguen, Floyd, Bakeman, & Armistead, 2002).

Adolescents who are members of sexual minorities encounter a number of problems. They may face isolation from peers (Crowley, Harré, & Lunt, 2007), lack of support from family (Savin-Williams & Dubé, 1998), and victimization in school (Murdock & Bolch, 2005). All of these factors make their quest for identity even more difficult and put them at risk for psychological difficulties. For example, the number of suicide attempts is greater among adolescents with same-sex attractions and those uncertain about their sexual orientation than it is for heterosexual teens (Zhao, Montoro, Igartua, & Thombs, 2010). In fact, young people who are members of sexual minorities are 2 to 3 times more likely to attempt suicide (Centers for Disease Control, 2011). Disclosing their sexual orientation can be especially stressful to these young people. Understandably, they often fear rejection by parents and friends. In some cases, they find they need to develop a new circle of friends after disclosure (Bedard & Marks, 2010).

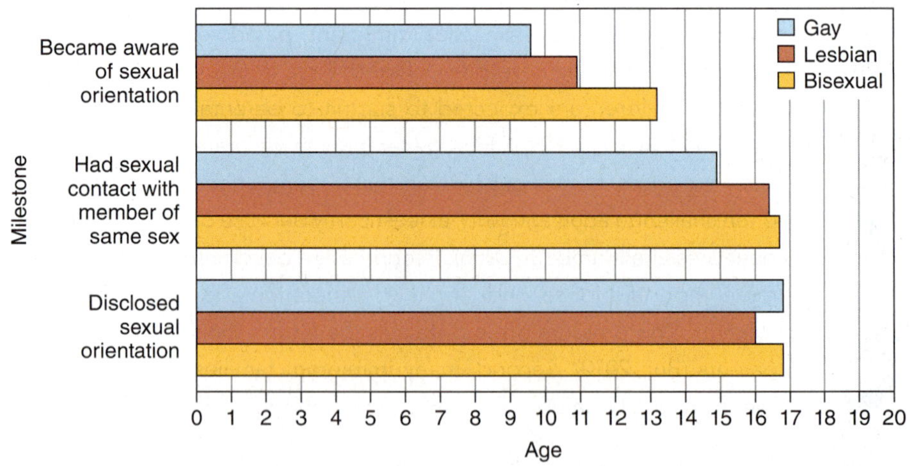


**FIGURE 16.3 Milestones of Sexual Identity for Sexual Minorities** In one study of adolescents who were members of sexual minorities, researchers found that most disclosed their sexual orientation in their mid to late teens, although they were aware of their sexual orientation and experienced sexual contact at earlier ages.
*Source:* Information from Maguen, Floyd, Bakeman, & Armistead, 2002.

As you can see from our discussion of ethnic, racial, and sexual identity, identity formation requires an understanding of the self on many dimensions. Thus, it is not surprising that identity achievement takes many years. In fact, some psychologists argue that it is seldom reached until early adulthood (Arnett, 2004). An important part of the process is the exploration that occurs during the adolescent years. One aspect of exploration involves changes in relationships with parents and peers. We turn to those relationships in the next section.

**autonomy** The sense of being a separate and independent individual, one capable of self-governance.

✓CHECK YOUR PROGRESS

1. What is the difference between identity achievement and identity diffusion?
2. How do Marcia's four patterns of identity achievement differ?
3. How does ethnic identity develop, according to Phinney?
4. What are some of the concerns of sexual minority youth?

## Relating to Others

**[ KEY QUESTION ] 2. What are important features of adolescents' relationships with their parents and their peers?**

Although adolescents grapple with issues of identity, they seldom do so in isolation. They are part of the family system, both contributing to it and benefiting from its support. They also are members of an increasingly complex peer network that includes friendships, groups, and romantic relationships. The way adolescents relate to others is important in determining their values and commitments. It also plays a role in their development of a sense of autonomy. We discuss the issues of adolescents' relationships with parents and with peers in this section.

### Adolescent–Parent Relationships

Not so long ago, psychologists viewed adolescence as a time when children needed to distance themselves aggressively from parents. As a result, adolescent-parent relationships were marked by a great deal of "storm and stress." Current views about this relationship are quite different. Many now believe that the key task for both adolescent and parent is to remain connected while the parent supports the adolescent's developing autonomy (Steinberg & Silk, 2002).

**Autonomy** is the sense of being a separate and independent individual. An autonomous person can govern himself or herself when making decisions about behaviors, activities, interests, and values. Adolescents' sense of autonomy grows as they become more independent, develop a more complex sense of self, and stretch their ability to self-monitor and self-regulate. The development of a sense of autonomy is considered central to healthy social and emotional well being.

How can parents support developing autonomy in their adolescents? Their continuing relationships with their children hold the key. Certain parenting styles promote high-quality relationships between parents and adolescents. These styles are marked by warmth, acceptance, emphasis on social responsibility, and gradual autonomy granting. You may recall from earlier chapters that Diana Baumrind (1991) discussed four parenting styles:

- *Authoritarian:* low levels of acceptance and warmth along with high levels of coercion and punishment.
- *Permissive:* high levels of acceptance and warmth along with low levels of control.
- *Authoritative:* high levels of acceptance and warmth along with moderate demands and control based on logical explanations.
- *Uninvolved:* low levels of acceptance and warmth along with low levels of control.

SW Productions/Getty Images

Authoritative parenting styles aid positive development in adolescents.

**transactional model** A model that emphasizes the bidirectional effects of parents and adolescents on each other.

You may also recall that authoritative styles are associated more with positive development than permissive, uninvolved, or authoritarian styles. This is as true for adolescents as for younger children (Steinberg, Blatt-Eisengart, & Cauffman, 2006).

## Attachment and Adolescent–Parent Relationships

When we discussed parents' relationships with infants and toddlers, we focused on the importance of attachment. According to attachment theory (Bowlby, 1969), attachment does not end as a child grows into an adolescent. Rather, attachment status—either secure or insecure—appears quite stable over time (Laursen & Collins, 2009). Adolescents who are securely attached to a parent show many advantages in psychosocial development over those who are not. They have more positive relationships with their friends, stronger social skills, and better abilities to compromise and negotiate disagreements with others (McElhaney, Allen, Stephenson, & Hare, 2009).

Although attachment remains important in adolescence, it does not remain unchanged. Three aspects of attachment have often been studied in adolescents:

- Seeking proximity to the attachment figure. ("Who is the person you miss most when you are not with him/her?")
- Considering the attachment figure to be a secure base. ("Who is the person you can always count on?")
- Using the attachment figure as a safe haven. ("Who is the person you most want to be with when you are feeling upset?")

© Jack Hollingsworth/Blend Images/Corbis

Adolescents frequently regard their mothers as a secure base of support throughout their development.

One study compared these three aspects of attachment during the early, middle, and late adolescent years (Markiewicz, Lawford, Doyle, & Haggart, 2006). The researchers found that adolescents in all three groups used mothers for a secure base, best friends for a safe haven, and romantic partners for proximity seeking. Thus, the function of attachment remains the same during adolescence, though its form looks quite different. Securely attached adolescents disengage somewhat from parents. Still, they find a way to maintain a connection with their parents and to feel they can count on them when they need to do so.

We should keep in mind that the adolescent is not the only one who changes during this period. Parents also are transformed as they acknowledge the physical, cognitive, and social development in their children. Another factor is that many parents of adolescents are in midlife. This life stage can present various personal challenges, such as stress related to career or job, and concerns about elderly parents (Miller, 2010). Given the multiple changes occurring for both parents and adolescents, it's easy to understand how each affects the other in complex ways.

The **transactional model** (Sameroff, 1975, 2009) captures the bidirectional effects of parent on adolescent and adolescent on parent. Each responds to the behavior of the other, and each response affects the other's behavior. Look at the example in Figure 16.4: Here, an adolescent's impulsivity leads him to yell at his parent. The parent responds by imposing a punishment. The overall result is an escalating series of negative encounters. This type of reciprocal hostility may eventually cause behavior problems or depressive symptoms in adolescents (Kim, Conger, Lorenz, & Elder, 2001; Laursen & Collins, 2009). Now look at the figure again, this time thinking about what might occur if either the adolescent or the parent responded in a less hostile, more moderate way. The outcome could be quite different, and much more positive.

## Adolescent–Parent Conflicts

Along with identity and autonomy development come inevitable conflicts between adolescents and parents. Conflicts do not necessarily result in poor outcomes, however, if the

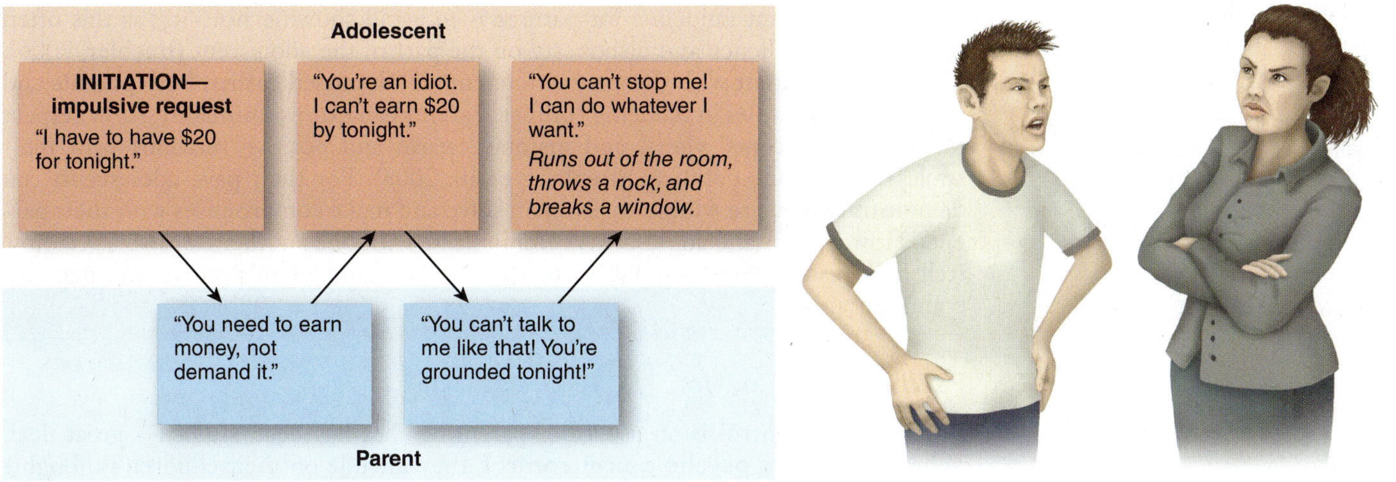


**FIGURE 16.4 An Example of the Transactional Model** In this illustration of the transactional model, an adolescent makes an impulsive request of his parent. A series of transactions follows, and the adolescent ends up damaging property. If either the parent or the adolescent had responded in a less hostile manner, the outcome would probably have been much more positive.

parent and adolescent learn to manage the conflicts and work toward a mutually acceptable resolution (Adams & Laursen, 2007). Many conflicts involve *bickering*, frequent petty arguments about everyday issues. Teens and parents bicker about chores and many other matters. Such bickering often peaks during the early teen years (Eisenberg et al., 2008). Fortunately, the number of conflicts between parents and children declines over the course of adolescence (Laursen, Coy, & Collins, 1998). Unfortunately, the negative intensity of the conflicts they do have increases (Smetana, Metzger, Gettman, & Campione-Barr, 2006).

Conflict levels between adolescents and parents vary based on gender and ethnicity (Cumsille, Darling, Flaherty, & Martínez, 2006). In one study, researchers asked ninth and twelfth graders to keep a diary of daily conflicts in their families (Chung, Flook, & Fuligni, 2009). The teens generally reported low levels of conflict with their parents. They reported more conflicts with mothers than with fathers, however, and girls reported more conflicts with both parents than did boys. Conflicts with parents tended to lead to emotional distress, especially for girls. Finally, adolescents from European American backgrounds reported more conflicts with parents than did those from Asian American backgrounds. Thus, based on the study, both culture and gender contribute to adolescent–parent conflicts.

Many conflicts between adolescents and parents center on differences of opinion over parental authority and personal freedom. That said, U.S. adolescents tend not to reject their parents' authority in all matters. They consider their friends, physical appearance, and leisure activities to be matters of personal choice. These choices are important to their sense of autonomy (Nucci, Killen, & Smetana, 1996). But they view parental authority as legitimate regarding issues involving morals, social conventions (such as politeness), and health and safety. Conflicts often occur where these activities and choices intersect (Smetana & Villalobos, 2009). This may happen, for instance, when friendships—a matter of personal choice—lead adolescents into unsafe behaviors—a matter of parental authority. These same general patterns of belief have been found in many countries, among them Chile and the Philippines (Darling, Cumsille, Peña-Alampay, & Coatsworth, 2009).

High levels of conflict, and their intensity, can result in poor parent–adolescent relationships, and stay with the adolescent into adulthood. Moreover, they can affect later relationships with romantic partners, making it more likely that the quality of these relationships will be poor as well (Overbeek, Stattin, Vermulst, Ha, & Engels, 2007). Clearly, then, it is important to ask what can be done to help reduce conflicts between parents and adolescents.

**psychological control** A type of control by which a person attempts to regulate the actions of another by using behaviors that intrude on the other person's thoughts and feelings about himself or herself.

One important guideline for parents is to avoid showing hostility, as this often results in disobedience and dishonesty on the part of the adolescent (Buehler, 2006). However, consistent with the transactional model discussed earlier, both parents and adolescents play roles in reducing conflict. Parents can express mutuality, show respect for their adolescents' views, and maintain warm and positive relations with their adolescents despite conflict (Eisenberg et al., 2008). For their part, adolescents can demonstrate they are willing to problem solve and make compromises with their parents. How parents and adolescents communicate with one another can also affect how well they resolve conflicts. Table 16.3 lists some examples of positive and negative communications.

## Psychological Control Parenting

Psychological control is an aspect of parenting that has been studied a great deal. When parents use **psychological control**, they intrude on their children's thoughts and feelings about themselves. Inducing guilt, shaming, and withdrawing love are examples of psychological control tactics (Barber, 1996). Adolescents exposed to these tactics may appear to go along with their parents' wishes. Such tactics have many negative effects, however. We see these effects during early, middle, and late adolescence (Barber, Stolz, & Olsen, 2005).

Psychological control interferes with adolescents' development of a secure sense of self (Soenens & Vansteenkiste, 2010) and with their ability to move toward greater autonomy and stronger identities (Luyckx, Soenens, Vansteenkiste, Goossens, & Berzonsky, 2007). It often forces them to act, think, or feel in a particular way, which

**Table 16.3** Examples of Positive and Negative Communications During Conflicts

| Type | Example |
|---|---|
| **Positive Communications** | |
| Offer praise/validation/endearment | "What a nice job you did with that." |
| Inject humor | "Maybe we could train the dog to take out the garbage." |
| Elicit opinion | "What do you think about that?" |
| Discuss own feelings | "It hurts my feelings when someone says things like that about me." |
| Discuss other's feelings | "How did you feel when I did that?" |
| Discuss emotions in general | "It's hard to decide when you have so many emotions." |
| Agree | "I agree with that thought." |
| **Negative Communications** | |
| **Type** | **Example** |
| Disagree/dispute/challenge | "You are totally wrong." |
| Put down/derogate | "You're an idiot. You don't know what you're talking about." |
| Use sarcasm/derisive humor | "If you're so smart, why do you act so stupid?" |
| Assert dominance/coerce | "You talk to me like that and you're grounded." |
| Interrupt | "Stop talking, listen to me." |
| Attempt to change subject/end or "stonewall" discussion | "I'm done. Forget any more discussion on this." |

*Source:* Based on information from Eisenberg et al., 2008.

**Table 16.4** Effects of Parental Psychological Control

| Parent's Behaviors | Adolescent's Reasoning | Effects on Psychosocial Development |
|---|---|---|
| Inducing guilt | "I'd better do what my parent says to avoid anxiety about being 'bad.'" | External compliance with parent's wishes, but lack of internal sense of integrity |
| Shaming | "I don't want my parents to be ashamed of me." | Hindered growth in identity and autonomy through lack of self-reliance |
| Withdrawing love | "I don't want my parents to stop loving me." | Feelings of inadequacy and fear of rejection by parents |

hinders their ability to become self-reliant (Soenens & Vansteenkiste, 2010). Adolescents exposed to psychological control tend to resent and feel rejected by their parents (Roth, Assor, Niemiec, Ryan, & Deci, 2009). They may also show symptoms of depression and antisocial behavior (Barber et al., 2005). Table 16.4 gives some examples of how parents' use of control can affect adolescents' reasoning and their eventual behavior and sense of well-being.

What about cultural differences? Some cultures use psychological control—especially guilt and shame—more often than others in parenting adolescents. Nevertheless, the negative effects of psychological control on autonomy have been found in a wide range of cultures (Wang, Pomerantz, & Chen, 2007).

## Adolescent–Peer Relationships

A well-known hallmark of the adolescent years is the growing importance of peer relationships. Compared with younger children, teens spend more time with peers, care more about peers' opinions, and have more complex relationships with peers (Brown & Larson, 2009). In a classic study, Robert Selman (1981) asked children and adolescents, "What makes a good friend?" He found that friendships during the middle school years are based largely on enjoying activities with peers who have similar interests. Friendships in the adolescent years involve new qualities of intimacy (Selman, Levitt, & Schultz, 1997). Recall from Chapter 15 that the ability to use abstractions improves during adolescence. Consistent with that development, adolescents often speak of their friendships in terms of abstract qualities, such as trust, faithfulness, and intimacy (Smetana & Villalobos, 2009).

One way to assess intimacy is to ask people about the emotional support they receive from friends and family. **Emotional support** refers to sharing feelings, concerns, sympathy, and acceptance (Willis & Shinar, 2000). In one study of children ages 9 to 18, early adolescents reported preferring to spend more time with their friends than with their parents. At the same time, they perceived their friends and parents as equally supportive. By midadolescence, they felt that friends provided more support than parents (Bokhorst, Sumter, & Westenberg, 2010).

### Gender Differences in Friendships

Boys' and girls' friendships during adolescence differ a great deal. Girls generally report receiving more emotional support from their friends than do boys (Bokhorst et al., 2010). Girls consistently have been found to also have more intense and intimate relationships with each other than boys do. And girls tend to value friendships in relation to their intimacy, closeness, and trust (Brown, 2004; Smetana & Villalobos, 2009).

Girls' friendships are not positive in every respect, however. Girls are also more likely than boys to use *relational aggression* to harm each other (although boys, too, sometimes use this form of aggression). Girls use relational aggression most during the early and middle adolescent years (Brown & Larson, 2009; Goldstein, Young, &

**emotional support** The sharing of feelings, concerns, sympathy, and acceptance with another.

© Ansgar Photography/Corbis

Females are more likely to use relational aggression than overt aggression during adolescence.

Boyd, 2008; Swearer, 2008). Furthermore, the use of this form of aggression is not restricted to girls in the United States. It is also found in more collectivist cultures, like Indonesia (French, Jansen, & Pidada, 2002).

As you may recall, relational aggression involves attempts to harm a friendship or socially exclude another person from a group. The techniques of relational aggression include spreading rumors (Crick & Grotpeter, 1995) and using nonverbal gestures like eye rolling to express disapproval (Galen & Underwood, 1997). Today, the use of social network websites and other electronic media allows such aggression to thrive without adult intervention (Subrahmanyam & Greenfield, 2008).

Engaging in relational aggression may enhance the status of a girl who uses it. Often, she is considered socially dominant—but at the expense of being well-liked (Cillessen & Borch, 2006). In contrast, girls who are the victims of this type of aggression may express feelings of loneliness and social anxiety (Storch & Masia-Warner, 2004). Unfortunately, the targets of relational aggression often internalize their experiences and come to blame themselves. This self-blame can result in a negative sense of self (Smetana & Villalobos, 2009).

## what if...?

Suppose you've volunteered to coach a girls' basketball team. Over the few weeks you've been coaching, you've noticed that one girl is often left out of the informal groups that form after practice. One day after practice, the team's co-captains tell you that they are sending her a text message. You hope the text might be an invitation for her to join them. But when you see the look of distress on her face when she reads the text message, you realize that it might have had a quite different purpose. You also know that other members of the team tend to go along with the wishes of the co-captains. What could you do to change the group dynamics and to support the girl who is being isolated, and possibly even bullied?

In contrast to girls' friendships, boys' friendships tend to focus on power, excitement, and agency (Rose, 2002). (*Agency* refers to the sense of oneself as an initiator of action.) We noted in Chapter 10 that boys use overt aggression more than girls do. Whereas both boys and girls use overt aggression less than they did in earlier periods, boys continue to use it more than girls, even in adolescence (Archer, 2004; Smith, Rose, & Schwartz-Mette, 2010). On the one hand, aggression among boys may simply be part of friendly competition. On the other hand, aggressive boys will single out other boys as a way of asserting power and dominance (Schneider, Woodburn, del Pilar Soteras del Toro, & Udvari, 2005).

As we've noted, boys' relationships involve less intimacy than those of girls. Some researchers have found that boys may avoid intimacy with each other in part because they fear being labeled homosexual (Martino & Pallotta-Chiarolli, 2003). Notably, boys' verbal aggression toward each other often centers on this highly enforced norm. Boys use antigay language to assert their own heterosexuality and masculinity, as well as to promote male bonding (Poteat, Kimmel, & Wilchins, 2011). In addition, boys who have been bullied because of gender nonconformity report that they have experienced more physical and verbal abuse than boys who are bullied for other reasons (Swearer, Turner, Givens, & Pollack, 2008). This aggression takes its toll. Boys who have experienced it have poorer psychological well-being than other boys, including higher levels of anxiety and depression (Swearer et al., 2008).

### Cliques and Crowds

**clique** A small group of peers, usually of 2 to 12 members, who are good friends and who are drawn together by similarities in various areas.

As adolescents become more involved with peer groups, they become active in cliques and crowds. A **clique** is a small group of peers, generally 2 to 12 in number, who are good friends (Brown, 2004). Cliques usually have a socially skilled leader and serve to provide mutual support to members. Adolescents are drawn together in cliques for various reasons. They tend to be attracted to others who are similar to themselves in such areas as academic interests, drug and alcohol use, sexual activity, and athletic ability. Other characteristics come into play as well. For example, hearing-impaired adolescents tend to form friendships and cliques with others who are hearing-impaired (Lerner, 2001). An adolescent may be a member of more than one clique at a time, depending on the setting—school, athletics, religious organizations, and neighborhood, for instance. In early adolescence, members of cliques are usually of the same gender, and then during midadolescence, mixed-gender groupings become more common.

A **crowd** is a larger group of friends and acquaintances, often created through the merging of several cliques. Whereas cliques are a source of close friendships, crowds enable a mixing of adolescents, so that new relationships evolve, often romantic relationships. Each crowd develops a particular reputation and public identity. During the early adolescent years, crowds are often large, and they differ from one another in only a few characteristics, such as social popularity. By midadolescence, crowds generally become smaller and more differentiated (Wentzel, 2001). As you may recall from your high school years, different crowds often have different labels, such as "brains," "jocks," "druggies," "nerds," and "loners" (Brown, 2004; Brown & Huang, 1995; Eckert, 1995). Each has a set of standards of behavior. Although these standards are rarely stated, members are well aware of them. The status of a specific group depends on the characteristics and culture of the setting. Being a "brain" gives a person high status in some high schools, for example, while in others it might be associated with low status. Being a member of a crowd can promote an individual's identity and social status. At the same time, it imposes certain limits, such as in selection of friends and activities.

**crowd** A large group of friends and acquaintances, often created through the merging of cliques.

© Loretta Hostettler/iStockphoto

Adolescents typically form friendships with those similar to themselves, as evident among these deaf and hard-of-hearing teens communicating with sign language.

## Romantic Relationships

Adolescents' same-sex peer networks remain about the same size throughout adolescence. In contrast, other-sex peer networks grow larger (Richards, Crowe, Larson, & Swarr, 1998). For heterosexual teens, the move from same-sex peer groups to groups that include both males and females can lead to romantic pairings. *Romantic relationships* are relationships that involve both sexuality and passion. As

© YAY Media AS/Alamy

Adolescents often are drawn to groups whose members display distinctive labels and standards of behavior.

**Table 16.5** Prevalence and Length of Adolescent Romantic Relationships

| Age | Report Having a Romantic Relationship | Average Length of the Relationship |
|---|---|---|
| 12 | 25% | A few weeks |
| 15 | 50% | 6 months |
| 18 | 70% | 1 year or more |

*Source:* Information from Connolly & McIsaac, 2009.

you can see in Table 16.5, such relationships increase in frequency and duration during adolescence.

As in other activities, adolescents vary in age when they first enter into romantic relationships (Carver, Joyner, & Udry, 2003; Furman, & Wehner, 1994). About 15 to 20% of adolescents have such relationships as early as age 11 or 12 (Connolly & McIsaac, 2009). These individuals are described as *early starters*. Early starters, especially girls, often entered puberty early, though other factors also play a role. Some researchers have found that insecure attachment to parents relates to early romantic relationships (Cooper, Shaver, & Collins, 1998). So does divorce, especially if there is continuing conflict between the parents (Chase-Lansdale, Cherlin, & Kiernan, 1995). In these situations, adolescents may be searching for intimate relationships that they fail to find in their families. When the romantic relationships of early starters involve sexual activity, problems may result. Early sexual intimacy can interfere with the development of a sense of identity (Connolly & McIsaac, 2009). It can also lead to risky sexual behavior and substance abuse. Both of these behaviors hinder healthy psychosocial development (Friedlander, Connolly, Pepler, & Craig, 2007).

Another 10% of adolescents are considered *late bloomers*. We know less about these adolescents than about their early-blooming counterparts. We do know, however, that often they are less embedded in their peer networks and have little emotional intimacy in their friendships (Davies & Windle, 2000). They may have certain temperamental traits, such as shyness, that make it harder for them to enter into romantic relationships (Caspi, Elder, & Bem, 1988). They also may have physical features, such as obesity, that make them less attractive to peers. Finally, they may have a chronic illness, such as diabetes, that sets them apart (Seiffge-Krenke, 2000).

Recall that we defined romantic relationships as including both sexuality and passion. Adolescents also report having sex outside of romantic relationships. "Hooking up" involves usually short-term sexual interactions (Manning, Giordano, & Longmore, 2006). Adolescents may also have "friends with benefits," friends with whom they share sexual relationships (Denizet-Lewis, 2004; Erlandsson, Jinghede Nordvall, Öhman, & Häggström-Nordin, 2013). Both of these types of sexual activity lack the intense feelings of love that is characteristic of romantic relationships. Research is beginning to uncover the negative effects of such relationships, especially for girls, whose social standing may suffer as a result of these activities (Grello, Welsh, & Harper, 2006; Stinson, 2010).

Researchers have discovered that romantic relationships in adolescents often go through typical patterns, or stages. Table 16.6 describes these stages. Adolescents engaging in a romantic relationship face a twofold challenge. On the one hand, they must develop emotional intimacy. On the other, they must maintain a separate and autonomous self outside of the relationship (Connolly & McIsaac, 2009).

**Table 16.6** Stages of Romantic Development

| | |
|---|---|
| Infatuation | Passionate feelings about and attraction to an individual, often discussed with the peer group |
| Affiliation | Interaction with the individual in a mixed-peer group |
| Intimacy | Shared disclosure and trust between two individuals in one-on-one situations |
| Committed | Compatible values and shared view of future |

*Source:* Information from Connolly & McIsaac, 2009.

Romantic relationships differ in quality. **Relationship quality** refers to how much partners show intimacy, affection, and nurturance to one another (Collins, Welsh, & Furman, 2009). Low-quality relationships are characterized by antagonism, unresolved conflict, and attempts to control the partner.

Early romantic relationships often involve conflicts. The results vary depending on how the partners react. Adolescents who believe that discussing differences is a healthy way of dealing with conflicts are often better at negotiating through them (Simon, Aikins, & Prinstein, 2008). In one study, researchers examined how adolescents dealt with conflicts in romantic relationships (McIsaac, Connolly, McKenny, Pepler, & Craig, 2008). They found that asking open-ended questions, compromising, and taking turns promoted better outcomes. In contrast, attacking verbally, dominating the conversation, creating distractions, and refusing to discuss the problem resulted in poorer outcomes.

© Roy Morsch/Age Fotostock

This teen couple faces the dual challenge of developing emotional intimacy between them while maintaining their own separate identities.

Boys and girls seem to be sensitive to different aspects of conflict. In one study, boys and girls viewed videotapes of their conflicts (Galliher, Welsh, Rostosky & Kawaguchi, 2004). They then rated their relationships. Girls rated their satisfaction higher for relationships that involved less conflict. Boys were more satisfied when they believed they could incorporate their girlfriends' points of view into joint decision making.

*Everyday stories*

LEARNING FROM CONFLICT Tamara and Juliana are discussing their relationships with their boyfriends. Tamara proudly claims that she and her boyfriend never argue. She says that either they agree with each other or she goes along with his ideas. Juliana says that she and her boyfriend often have conflicts, but they have found a way to work them out. She explains that each gives the other three minutes to describe his or her viewpoint without interruption. Then each has to summarize what the other said. This process, she says, has helped them resolve many differences.

Juliana and her boyfriend are using a technique that involves understanding the viewpoint of another by taking the other's perspective. Perspective taking helps adolescents improve their relationships. Consistently avoiding conflict can prevent the development of perspective-taking skills.

Conflict can end a relationship. When that occurs, depression can result. Depression in this situation is especially common for girls (Rizzo, Daley, & Gunderson, 2006) and for those whose partner initiated the breakup (Connolly & McIsaac, 2009). Some individuals have high **rejection sensitivity**. They tend to be anxious about rejection, to see rejection readily, and to overreact to it (Downey & Feldman, 2004). They may expect to be rejected, and they are generally less satisfied with their relationships (Ayduk, Downey, & Kim, 2001). They also experience more emotion-related violence in their relationships, and have lower self-esteem. Fortunately, their sensitivity tends to lessen with age—if they learn to regulate their emotional responses (Silvers et al., 2012). Interventions may be helpful for teens with high rejection sensitivity (Kerig, 2010; Romero-Canyas, Downey, Berenson, Ayduk, & Kang, 2010).

### ✓ CHECK YOUR PROGRESS

1. Describe the characteristics of attachment during adolescence.
2. What are some typical areas of conflict between adolescents and parents?
3. Why does parental psychological control often result in poor adolescent psychosocial development?
4. How do friendships differ for males and females during adolescence?
5. What do adolescents gain from high-quality romantic relationships?

**relationship quality** The extent to which partners show intimacy, affection, and nurturance.

**rejection sensitivity** The tendency to be anxious about rejection, to expect and perceive rejection readily, and to overreact to it.

**postconventional level** According to Kohlberg, the third and highest stage of moral development, which incorporates a belief in abstract principles and values, especially about human rights.

# Moral Development

**[ KEY QUESTION ] 3. How does moral development change during the adolescent period?**

Adolescent relationships involve basic issues of fair treatment of others. As we have mentioned, how individuals treat one another is a question of morality (Kant, 1785/1959). Notions of what is right and what is fair are central to moral development at any age. Adolescents, however, have cognitive advantages over younger children, as we have seen. They also have a wider range of experience in moral decision making. In this section, we first discuss how adolescents reason about justice. Then we turn to adolescent behaviors that support or violate their social relationships with others.

## Kohlberg's Stages of Moral Reasoning

| **Kohlberg's Stage Theory** |
|---|
| **Preconventional Stage** |
| **Conventional Stage:** Conform to social rules.<br>• Substage 3. Aim for interpersonal cooperation.<br>• Substage 4. Work to maintain social order. |
| **Postconventional Stage:** Base decisions on abstract moral principles.<br>• Substage 5. Consider the social contract and individual rights.<br>• Substage 6. Focus on universal principles. |

Moral reasoning involves the way a person justifies a moral decision. As mentioned in earlier chapters, Lawrence Kohlberg (1958, 1963, 1978) proposed a stage theory of moral development based on moral reasoning. He designed a series of imaginary moral dilemmas and asked children, adolescents and adults questions about them. He was not concerned about the actual decisions they reached. Rather, he was interested in the reasons they gave for their decisions. Based on these reasons, he developed a sequence of moral reasoning comprising three stages: preconventional, conventional, and postconventional (Crain, 2005).

Generally, very young children reason at the *preconventional stage*, as discussed in Chapter 10. During middle childhood, they enter the *conventional stage*, described in Chapter 13. Among adolescents, we find a range of levels of moral reasoning (Garmon, Basinger, Gregg, & Gibbs, 1996). Most teens are still at the conventional stage (Eisenberg, Morris, McDaniel, & Spinrad, 2009). Substage 3 is typical of the reasoning evident in adolescence. Some individuals move into substage 4 by the end of the adolescent period, while others progress to substage 5, which is at the **postconventional stage** (Gibbs, Basinger, Grime, & Snarey, 2007).

Table 16.7 contrasts Kohlberg's six stages with reference to one of his best-known dilemmas, the story of Heinz. In the story, Heinz's wife has cancer, but he cannot afford the only drug that might save her life. He is unable to borrow the money or buy the drug on credit. Finally, desperate, he steals the drug. The question is, should Heinz have broken the law to save his wife's life? Remember as you read the table that it is the respondent's reason for the answer, not the answer itself, that was important to Kohlberg.

By the end of adolescence, many individuals recognize their role as members of a society. Their moral decisions reflect this understanding. Consider the following scenario:

> *Imagine that a thousand people moved to an island in the Pacific, and set about building a community.... They are confronted by the tasks of forming a government and of developing laws and other modes of communal regulation (Adelson, Green, & O'Neil, 1969).*

Researchers presented this scenario to adolescents to discover their ideas about the purpose of laws. One 18-year-old boy responded, "Well, the main purpose [of the laws] would be just to set up a standard of behavior for people, for society living together, so that they can live peacefully and in harmony with each other" (Adelson et al., 1969, p. 328). This response shows abstract reasoning and awareness of the need for a social contract. Both are typical of substage 4, the second substage of the conventional stage.

Beyond the conventional stage is the postconventional stage of morality. Individuals in this stage base moral decisions on universal and abstract principles of human rights and justice. Such moral principles may or may not be in keeping with society's laws (Hedgepeth, 2005). Many people never reach this level, even in adulthood. A good example of moral reasoning at the postconventional stage is Martin Luther King, Jr. King called on universal principles of justice in his campaign to change laws of racial segregation.

**Table 16.7.** Kohlberg's Stages of Moral Reasoning Compared

| Stage and Substage | What Is Considered "Right" | Examples of Reasoning About the Heinz Dilemma |
|---|---|---|
| **Preconventional stage** | Persons at this level see morality as constructed by others. | |
| Substage 1. Obedience and punishment orientation | A person at this stage obeys rules to get rewards and avoid punishments. | Heinz should not steal the drug because it is wrong to steal. |
| Substage 2. Individualism and exchange | A person at this stage acts to exchange favors with others. Generally, someone at this stage has the view that "I will help you" so that in the future "you will help me." | Heinz should steal the drug because he needs his wife, and she will get better only if she has the drug. |
| **Conventional stage** | Persons at this level consider morality to be a matter of choosing "good" behavior as determined by the family, community, or society. | |
| Substage 3. Interpersonal relationships | A person at this stage acts to be seen as a "good boy" or "good girl." | It's okay for Heinz to steal the drug because, as a husband, it is his responsibility to take care of his wife. |
| Substage 4. Maintaining the social order | A person at this stage wants to make sure that society operates smoothly. | It's wrong for Heinz to steal the drug because if people stole whatever they wanted, there would be no sense of order in a society. |
| **Postconventional stage** | Persons at this level understand that a smoothly functioning society might not be a just one. Thus, they emphasize the importance of abstract principles and values, such as justice and human rights, and procedures for guaranteeing those rights. | |
| Substage 5. Social contract and individual rights | A person at this stage recognizes obligations to society's laws and operates according to a sense of hierarchy of principles. | It's wrong for Heinz to steal the drug, and he will need to pay for breaking society's law. Stealing the drug is acceptable, though, because his wife's right to life is more important than the druggist's right to property. |
| Substage 6. Universal principles | A person at this stage emphasizes that laws need to be based on universal principles of justice, such as equality of human rights and respect for the dignity of each person. If laws are found to be unjust, then the individual needs to act according to universal moral principles. | Heinz's wife should be saved because he needs to act on the guiding principle of preserving and respecting life. Heinz should not focus only on his wife's needs, however. He should organize to change the laws so that free medication is available for those who need it to live. |

*Source:* Based on Colby, Kohlberg, Gibbs, & Lieberman, 1983; Kohlberg, 1963, 1969, 1978.

Jim WEST/REPORT DIGITAL-REA/Redux

Teenagers who take advantage of opportunities to volunteer within their communities accelerate their moral development.

What do we know about individuals who are more—or less—advanced in moral reasoning? Both age and educational level are related to moral reasoning (Dawson, 2002). We noted earlier that most adolescents are in substage 3. Advances from substage 3 to substage 4 are sometimes associated with participation in community service and higher education (Gibbs et al., 2007). Such involvement advances moral reasoning by exposing individuals to diverse experiences. Often, these new experiences challenge immature and self-centered thinking about moral decisions. They also encourage adolescents to think more about abstract ideas, including social contracts and acting for the "common good." In contrast, juvenile offenders who are incarcerated tend to use lower levels of moral reasoning than other adolescents. This is the case across many countries and cultures, including China, England, Taiwan, Sweden, and the United States (Stams et al., 2006). Among juvenile offenders in the United States, researchers found that those showing higher levels of moral reasoning were less likely to commit crimes after being released (Leeman, Gibbs, & Fuller, 1993).

what if...?

High school students are often given many opportunities to engage in community service. They might sponsor a bake sale to collect money for a soup kitchen, volunteer at a homeless shelter, or conduct a drive to collect food for a food pantry. Do you think that such experiences might help adolescents advance in their moral development? Or do you think that only certain ones might be useful in this regard? What type of activities might be more likely to encourage adolescents to consider acting for the "common good"?

## Criticisms of Kohlberg's Theory

Kohlberg's theory has generated a great deal of research and discussion. It has also been criticized for a number of reasons. First, some investigators have pointed out that moral reasoning does not necessarily lead to moral behavior. For example, some studies indicate that even students who reason at the postconventional stage may cheat when given the opportunity (Hart, Burock, & London, 2003; Killen & Hart, 1995; Snarey, 1995).

Second, there are critics who argue that Kohlberg's theory has a Western bias. Thus, it may not be relevant to non-Western cultural groups. In certain cultures, for example, morality may be based less on systems of laws than on systems of personal relationships (Snarey, 1995). Kohlberg's system assumes a rights-based morality, which is based on balancing the rights of various members of society. Other cultures, though, support a duty-based morality (Shweder, Much, Mahapatra, & Park, 1997). Duties to family members, as well as to country, religion, or ethnic group, drive moral decision making in such cultures. Researchers who have studied moral reasoning within U.S. subcultures have found interesting cultural effects as well. In one study of African American adolescents, researchers assessed moral reasoning as it related to two value systems. *Afrocultural* values (that is, based on African cultures) were said to center on interdependence and spirituality. Competition and materialism were considered Anglo American values. Adolescents oriented toward Afrocultural values showed higher levels of moral reasoning (Woods & Jagers, 2003).

A third criticism of Kohlberg's theory relates to gender differences in moral development. A question raised in this regard is whether emphasizing rights and justice overlooks morality based on care for others. Carol Gilligan (1982) criticized Kohlberg's theory for neglecting the importance of the "ethic of care" in higher levels of moral reasoning. According to Gilligan's argument, abstract reasoning about justice represents a masculine ideal or stereotype. In contrast, an emphasis on care represents a feminine ideal or stereotype. In terms of Kohlberg's stages, those who emphasize care remain at the conventional stage and fail to advance to the post-conventional stage.

What does research have to say on this issue? Although few studies have uncovered large gender differences in moral development, some studies have found small differences. In a meta-analysis of 15 years of studies, males were found to have small advantages over females in research focusing on reasoning about justice. Females showed small advantages in studies involving the ethic of care (Jaffee & Hyde, 2000).

Carol Gilligan's initial criticism provoked deeper interest in dimensions of care as elements of moral dilemmas. "Care" here refers not just to relieving the suffering of others, but also to being responsive to others and having a sense of interdependence with others (Perry & McIntire, 1995). Current research indicates that, over time, individuals gradually change in their orientation toward caring for others. Children typically have an egocentric focus on their own needs. Young adolescents, especially females, tend to take a self-sacrificing approach. Finally, by late adolescence or adulthood, many individuals adopt a balanced view, one that weighs the needs of both self and others (Pratt, Skoe, & Arnold, 2004).

*Everyday stories*

REAL-LIFE MORAL DILEMMAS We frequently encounter moral dilemmas in everyday life. Such dilemmas seldom involve questions of life and death, as in the story of Heinz, described earlier. Rather, they typically raise questions about caring for another person, or about basic values such as honesty. On occasion, these issues may cause us conflict. Consider Mia and Janelle, who are good friends taking the same college course. Mia knows that Janelle has been under stress because of family problems. Consequently, Janelle has not been doing the course reading and is not prepared for the take-home midterm exam. The exam is given under an honor code, and both young women have agreed to the code. But while taking the exam, Janelle asks Mia to help her with some answers. Mia wants to help her friend, but she also wants to be true to the honor code. She wonders what she should do.

THE DEVELOPING BRAIN

## Moral Judgments

No single area of the brain governs moral judgments (Greene & Haidt, 2002). Several different brain circuits are involved, and these circuits change a great deal during early adolescence (Blakemore, 2012). Moral decisions and behaviors involve the social information-processing network, which is part of the *social brain,* discussed in Chapter 13. The brain regions and interconnections in this network are those most involved in the understanding of social information.

There is much evidence to support the idea that the prefrontal cortex is important in moral decision making (Eslinger et al., 2008). Studies tell us that areas of the prefrontal lobe are activated when people are asked to make moral decisions, for example (Harenski, Antonenko, Shane, & Kiehl, 2010). As you know, the prefrontal cortex develops significantly during adolescence (Burnett, Sebastian, Cohen Kadosh, & Blakemore, 2011). Research has shown differences in moral decision making that are consistent with these changes.

Let's consider an example, based on studies examining brain activity in participants who view scenarios in which someone is harmed. The harm is presented as either accidental or intentional. These studies show age differences in the brain's response to the scenarios. One part of the prefrontal cortex in particular (the ventromedial prefrontal cortex) shows increased activation with age, from childhood through early adolescence. This area is especially active during tasks that require emotional regulation (Wagner, & Heatherton, 2013). In contrast, activity in the amygdala, which is part of the limbic system, shows decreased activity with age (Decety, Michalska, & Kinzler, 2012). Together, these two areas of the brain indicate better functional connectivity during adolescence than during childhood, suggesting more interaction between them. Furthermore, this connectivity continues to expand during the adolescent period (Decety et al., 2012).

What do these findings mean? Recall that the prefrontal cortex is associated with, among other things, executive function. The limbic system is associated with emotion. It seems that, in responding to moral issues, adolescents depend more on executive function and less on automatic emotional responses than younger children do (Yurgelun-Todd, 2007).

Adolescent brain responses differ from those of adults during moral decision-making processes, as well. One area of difference again involves the prefrontal cortex. Recall that, in spite of great change during adolescence, this area is not fully developed until early adulthood (Blakemore, 2012; Yurgelun-Todd, 2007). Adolescent brains show greater activity in the prefrontal cortex than do adult brains when working on tasks requiring them to understand the intentions of others (Burnett, Thompson, Bird, & Blakemore, 2011).

Another area of difference is the *temporo-parietal junction* as shown in Figure 16.5. This region is associated with perspective taking and understanding the mental states of others. Adolescents show less activation in this region than adults when called on to evaluate the moral states of others, such as another person's intent to harm someone (Harenski, Harenski, Shane, & Kiehl, 2012). Similarly, young adolescents show less activation in the region than do older adolescents in situations that involve perspective taking and reciprocity (van den Bos, van Dijk, Westenberg, Rombouts, & Crone, 2010). (You are engaging in *reciprocity* when a person does something positive for you, and in return you

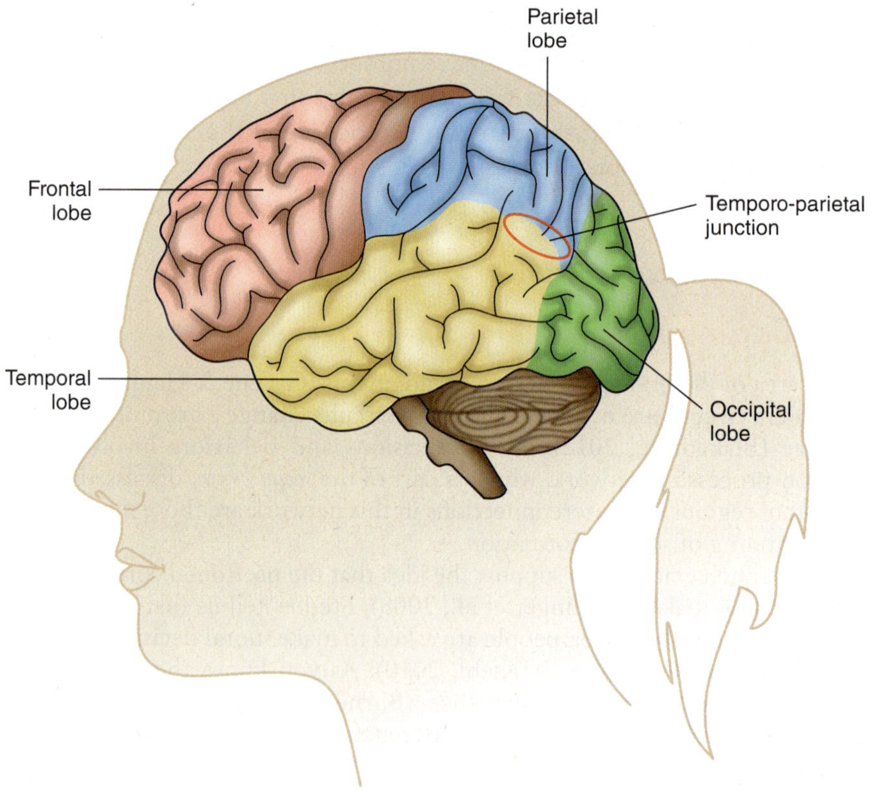


**FIGURE 16.5 The Connections between the Temporo-Parietal Junction and the Prefrontal Cortex** The temporo-parietal junction in the brain is associated with perspective taking and understanding the mental states of others—both important in moral decision making. During adolescence the connectivity between this brain region and the ventromedial prefrontal cortex becomes stronger. The ventromedial prefrontal cortex activates during emotional responses to moral situations such as reasoning through moral dilemmas.

do something positive for that person.) Perspective taking is often required in moral decision making. This is especially true in situations where we must determine whether another person intended harm and in situations that call for reciprocity.

## Prosocial and Antisocial Behavior

Recall from earlier chapters that when we engage in *prosocial behavior*, we act to benefit others (Carlo & Randall, 2001) without personal benefit and sometimes even at personal cost. When we engage in *antisocial behavior*, in contrast, we act to get what we want without concern for others. Both types of behavior change in adolescence.

### Prosocial Behavior in Adolescence

Adolescents often face dilemmas that require them to make prosocial decisions. They may, for example, need to decide whether to help someone when doing so means missing a favorite activity. How do they reason about such dilemmas? Nancy Eisenberg and her colleagues (Carlo, Eisenberg, & Knight, 1992; Eisenberg, Carlo, Murphy, & Van Court, 1995) have investigated this question. They developed a series of vignettes, along with a way of analyzing adolescents' responses to them, as a measure of prosocial reasoning. Here is a vignette based on those used by Eisenberg.

> *One day, Mary was going to a friend's party. On the way, she saw a girl who had fallen down and hurt her leg. The girl asked Mary to call her parents and to stay with her until they arrived to take her to the doctor. But if Mary did stay with her, she would be late to the party and miss having fun with her friends. What should Mary do?*

After hearing the vignette, participants were asked to rate the following list of responses on a scale from "greatly important" to "not important" (Eisenberg, Zhou, & Koller, 2001). Consider how these answers vary.

| **Responses** | **Reasoning** |
|---|---|
| "It depends on how much fun Mary expects the party to be." | This is an example of *hedonistic reasoning*, because it is based on the good Mary will get in the end. |
| "It depends on whether the girl really needs help." | This is an example of *needs-based reasoning*, because it focuses on the extent of other girl's needs. |
| "It depends on whether Mary's parents and friends will think she did the right or wrong thing." | This is an example of *approval-oriented reasoning*, which seeks approval for being "nice" or "good." |
| "It depends if Mary thinks she did the decent thing or not." | This is an example of *stereotypical reasoning*, which conforms to a person's stereotype about doing the right thing. |
| "It depends on how Mary would feel about herself if she helped or not." | This is an example of *internalized reasoning*, which involves living up to one's internalized and abstract values. |

As you might expect, individuals generally progress in their reasoning from hedonistic in childhood to internalized in late adolescence (Eisenberg et al., 2009). Needs-based reasoning shows a dramatic drop during late adolescence (ages 17 to 20). At the same time, internalized reasoning shows dramatic increases (Eisenberg, Cumberland, Guthrie, Murphy, & Shepard, 2005). In general, then, prosocial skills improve during adolescence, especially late adolescence. Are there gender differences consistent across the sexes? You may recall from earlier chapters that females have been found to be more prosocial than males. The answer is, these gender differences not only persist but increase during adolescence (Fabes, Carlo, Kupanoff, & Laible, 1999).

## Antisocial Behavior in Adolescence

We've seen that prosocial behaviors increase during adolescence. What about antisocial behaviors? For some adolescents, antisocial behaviors, such as violent and criminal activity, also increase during this period. There are many reasons why. One is that adolescents aren't as closely monitored by adults as are younger children. They also are more responsive to peer influences. The effects of peer influence are apparent between childhood and mid-adolescence, peaking at around age 14, with a slow decline thereafter (Steinberg & Silverberg, 1986).

The presence of peers makes adolescents more likely to seek immediate rewards. Sometimes, these rewards are associated with quite risky behaviors, such as gambling, using illegal substances, and driving carelessly. In one study, adolescents were given a hypothetical task in which they had to choose between having $200 today or $1,000 six months from today. In other words, they were asked to choose between an immediate reward and a delayed reward. The participants were randomly assigned to complete the task alone or with peers present. When peers were present, the adolescents showed a stronger preference for the immediate reward (O'Brien, Albert, Chein, & Steinberg, 2011). A combination of poor impulse control and an emphasis on sensation seeking are also common problems for adolescents. We discuss this issue in the accompanying Research Insights feature.

### Research Insights: Impulsivity and Reward Seeking

Willingness to take risks figures into much behavior that is considered antisocial in adolescents. One well-known psychologist, Laurence Steinberg, has proposed a two-system model of risk taking in adolescents (Steinberg, 2010): The "socioemotional system" is associated with reward-seeking behavior; the "cognitive control" system is associated with self-regulation and control. The two systems are not well synchronized during adolescence. Reward seeking often occurs with little self-regulation. This is especially true in situations involving peers (O'Brien et al., 2011).

Steinberg (2010) asked teens and young adults to fill out questionnaires about reward seeking and impulsivity. Items related to reward seeking included: "I like to have new and exciting experiences, even if they are a little frightening," and "I'll try anything once." Strong agreement with items like these is thought to indicate a strong desire to seek rewards through activities that provide varied and complex sensations. The impulsivity scale included questions such as: "I act on the spur of the moment." Individuals high in impulsivity are low in self-regulation.

Participants also completed a problem-solving task called the Tower of London, illustrated in Figure 16.6. The task required them to move one set of disks so that they formed the same pattern as another set of disks, but in as few moves as possible. Each disk can only be moved to a spindle next to it during a single turn. You can see how

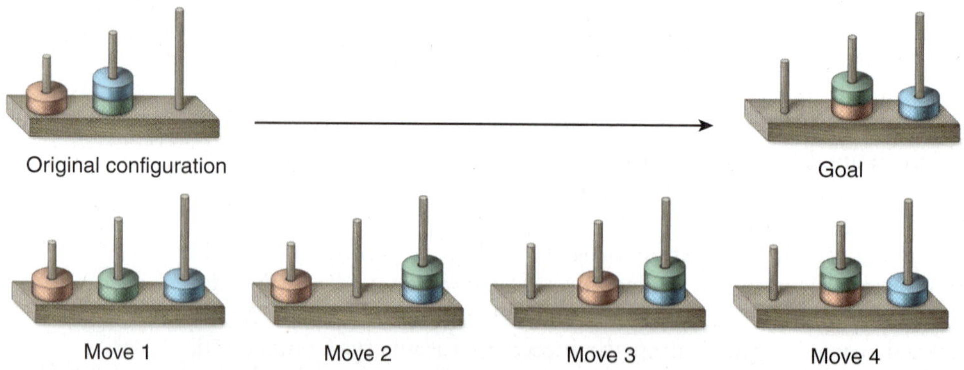


**FIGURE 16.6 The Tower of London Task** The Tower of London task involves forming a specified pattern (the goal configuration) by moving a set of disks from the original spindle to a different spindle creating the goal configuration in as few moves as possible. On any turn, a disk can only be moved to a spindle next to it. To complete the task successfully, a participant must plan ahead rather than act impulsively.

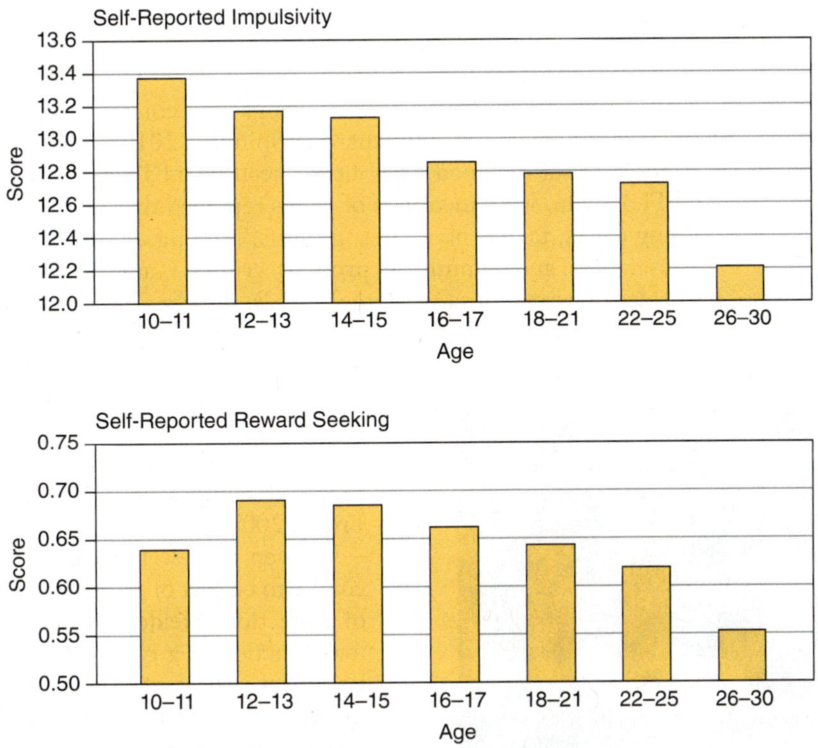


**FIGURE 16.7 Age Differences in Self-Reported Impulsivity and Reward Seeking** Laurence Steinberg found differences in the patterns of development of impulsivity and reward seeking behaviors. He proposed that reward-seeking behavior peaks during midadolescence, when impulsivity is declining but still high, explaining in part why adolescents are more inclined to take risks at this age. In these graphs impulsivity scores could range from 6 to 24 and reward-seeking scores could range from 0 to 1.

*Source:* Steinberg, L. (2010). A dual systems model of adolescent risk-taking. *Developmental Psychobiology, 52*, p. 220. Reprinted with permission of John Wiley & Sons, Inc.

succeeding at this task requires planning ahead rather than acting impulsively.

Steinberg found age differences in both impulsivity and reward-seeking tendencies. Impulsivity decreased from ages 10–11 to ages 26–30. Reward seeking increased from ages 10–11 to ages 12–15, and declined thereafter. Steinberg proposed that developmental timetables differ in these two areas. As a result, reward-seeking behavior peaks during midadolescence, when impulsivity is declining but still high (see Figure 16.7). Therefore, it is not surprising that middle adolescence is a period of heightened vulnerability to risk taking.

Under the power of peer influence, adolescents are more likely to behave as their peers do. If they align with a peer group that places great emphasis on risky behaviors, they may make bad decisions that involve breaking the law (Scott, & Steinberg, 2008). Shoplifting, stealing cars, illegal drug use, and underage drinking are typical delinquent behaviors of some teens. **Juvenile delinquency** refers to antisocial or illegal activity by people under the "age of majority." At this age, which is 18 under federal law and the laws of many states, individuals are adults in the eyes of the legal system.

Illegal activity is often associated with gangs. A **gang**, in this context, is a group of individuals with a shared sense of identity, often defined by their clothing, ethnicity, and territory. Gangs generally have a group leader and a hierarchy among members. They also have rules to guide members' behavior. These rules are designed to defend the honor or reputation of the group (Bouchard & Spindler, 2010). Much gang recruitment begins in middle school, at the beginning of adolescence (Johnstone, 1983), when individuals are beginning to wrestle with identity development. Most gang members are male (National Youth Gang Survey

**juvenile delinquency** Antisocial or illegal activity engaged in by those under the age of majority, which under federal law and in most states is 18.

**gang** A group of individuals with a common identity and orientation, who often participate in criminal activity.

Analysis, 2009). Only about 10% are female, so we know less about how females behave in gangs. Their activities are reportedly similar to those of males, however (Cyr & Decker, 2003).

Adolescents who belong to gangs may commit not only delinquent acts but also more serious crimes (Bouchard & Spindler, 2010). One group of researchers surveyed adolescents detained after being accused of illegal activity (Cyr & Decker, 2003). Those who were members of gangs reported that typical gang activities included selling drugs, taking part in gang fights, holding or carrying guns, setting up rival gang members, and committing property crimes. Gang violence accounts for 20% of homicides in large cities (McDaniel, 2012). Another interesting fact is that adolescent gang members are at least as likely to be victimized as well as to victimize others (Taylor, Freng, Esbensen, & Peterson, 2008). In a survey of eighth-grade students in 11 U.S. cities, 70% of adolescents who belonged to a gang reported being the victim of violence (such as assault or robbery). By comparison, 46% of those not involved in a gang reported being victims (Taylor, Peterson, Esbensen, & Freng, 2007).

© Ocean/Corbis

Adolescents in gangs are much more likely to take part in illegal activities, such as selling drugs and committing violent crimes.

Given this level of violence, why do many adolescents choose to be part of gangs? For some, gangs serve as a source of protection (Melde, Taylor, & Esbensen, 2009). They also may function as a type of family, with loyalty and bonding behaviors typical of a family unit (Petersen, 2000). Gang members have said that being part of a gang gave them feelings of worthiness, acceptance, and respect (Morris, 2012). The percentage of adolescents involved in gangs is 5 times greater in highly unstable neighborhoods (that is, neighborhoods where people move often) (Dupéré, Lacourse, Willms, Vitaro, & Tremblay, 2007). Gangs may play several roles for adolescents in such neighborhoods, including providing trust, support, and identity.

We have seen that gangs commit both delinquent acts and more serious crimes. Thus, it is not surprising that individuals who belong to gangs are more likely to be incarcerated, or imprisoned, than other adolescents. Apart from gang membership, however, incarceration rates of juveniles vary considerably based on ethnicity and gender (see Figure 16.8). Researchers have proposed various reasons for these differences.

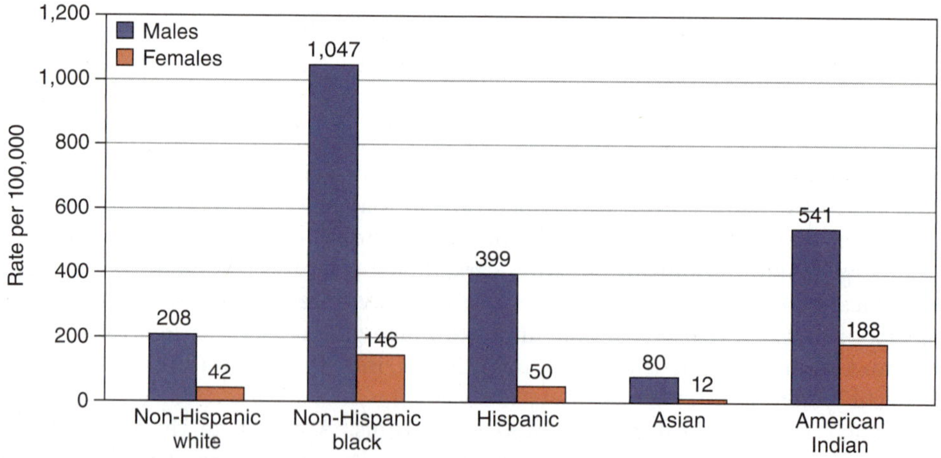


Note: These data come from the U.S. Census Bureau's Census of Juveniles in Residential Placement, which collects data from all juvenile residential custody facilities in the country. Rates are calculated per 100,000 juveniles ages 10 through the upper age of each state's juvenile court jurisdiction.

**FIGURE 16.8 Ethnic and Gender Differences in Incarceration Rates of Juveniles** Incarceration rates for juveniles vary considerably by race and ethnicity.
*Source:* Child Trends (2012). Juvenile Detention. Retrieved from www.childtrendsdatabank.org/?q=node/129.

As Figure 16.8 shows, people of color are arrested, convicted, and incarcerated in higher proportions than other groups. One explanation is that more police are present in minority neighborhoods than in mostly white neighborhoods. More police lead to more arrests. More arrests, combined with discrimination in the courts and the correctional system, lead to a disproportionate representation of people of color in the justice system (Piquero, 2008). Studies have been done that support the idea that the system is discriminatory. One meta-analysis of studies on race and sentencing, found that black adolescents were given stricter sentences than white adolescents who had committed the same crime and had the same prior record (Mitchell, 2005).

Females are much less likely than males to be involved in the correctional system. Nevertheless, female rates of incarceration are higher than they were three decades ago. In 1980, boys were 4 times as likely as girls to be arrested. Now they are only twice as likely, due to the rising number of female arrests (Cauffman, 2008). Furthermore, the prognosis for female offenders is worse than for male offenders. Female offenders often experience abuse, usually sexual abuse (Cauffman, 2008). Often, they have less ability to empathize with others (Broidy, Cauffman, Espelage, Mazerolle, & Piquero, 2003). Often, too, they have mental health problems. These difficulties have important implications for the intervention provided to adolescents in the juvenile justice system.

### Trying Juveniles as Adults Policy

Regardless of their developmental progress, adolescents in the United States become adults in the legal sense when they reach the age of majority. As defined previously, with respect to federal law and the laws of most states, that age is 18. At 18, adolescents can vote and, in most states, serve on juries, consent to medical treatment, and execute contracts (Woolard & Scott, 2009). At 18, they also can be tried and convicted as adults in federal courts and the courts of most states. Before they reach the age of majority, adolescents who have committed an offense generally enter the juvenile justice system, depending on the severity of the offense. This practice reflects the traditional belief that adolescents are still immature and can change. Based on this belief, the juvenile justice system emphasizes rehabilitation rather than punishment (Woolard & Scott, 2009).

The Juvenile Justice and Delinquency Prevention Act, Public Law 93–415, was passed in 1974. Its aim was to create a national unified program to deal with juvenile delinquency. Among other issues, the act differentiated status offenders from other offenders. *Status offenders* are juveniles whose offenses would not be considered criminal if they were older. Runaways, truants, and curfew violators are examples of status offenders. The act also called for the development of ways to keep juvenile offenders out of the juvenile corrections system. One alternative is to put them in community-based programs, instead of correctional facilities.

The act also supports the separation of adult from juvenile offenders. Separation is based on concerns that juveniles need different services than adults and that they should be protected from contact with adult offenders. However, under some circumstances, juveniles may be waived out of juvenile court and transferred to the adult system for trial. Much controversy exists over these transfers. Proponents maintain that, regardless of age, an offender should serve "adult time" for "adult crime" (Regnery, 1985). Opponents claim that placing juveniles in the adult system neglects important realities about their development. We've already seen that the psychosocial skills of adolescents are still developing. We've seen, too, that adolescents are often impulsive, susceptible to peer influence, and prone to engage in sensation-based reward seeking, especially in social situations. Many psychologists argue that for these reasons, adolescents should have less severe punishments and more interventions aimed at training and rehabilitation as a result of their acts than adults (Steinberg & Scott, 2010).

*John Neubauer/Photo Edit*

Before age 18, adolescent criminals are generally tried in the juvenile justice system, depending on the severity of their crime.

Individual states have taken various positions in addressing concerns about juvenile transfers. In general, transfers are determined based on the offender's age, the nature of the offense, and the offender's history of prior crimes. What about the extreme case in which being tried as an adult might expose the juvenile to the death penalty? In 2005, the U.S. Supreme Court considered this question in a landmark case, *Roper v. Simmons*. It ruled that imposing the death penalty on juveniles violates the Constitution's protection against cruel and unusual punishment.

**✓CHECK YOUR PROGRESS**

1. Describe Kohlberg's stages of moral reasoning.
2. What are the main criticisms of Kohlberg's theory?
3. How do adolescents differ from younger children in their prosocial reasoning?
4. Despite the dangers involved, why do some adolescents choose to be gang members?

# Risk and Resilience

**[ KEY QUESTION ] 4. What are some important risk factors and resilient processes that influence adolescent well-being?**

Most individuals move through adolescence successfully. Still, adolescents are at greater risk of developing psychological disorders than younger children. In fact, most mental health disorders begin in adolescence (Knopf, Park, & Mulye, 2008). We turn our attention in this section to the concepts of risk and resilience. **Risk factors** are characteristics or events that increase the probability of a poor outcome (Kraemer, Stice, Kazdin, Offord, & Kupfer, 2001). Note that risk increases the *probability* of a poor outcome. It does not guarantee that such an outcome will occur. Some individuals who are at risk are protected by their **resilience**, defined here as positive adaptation in the presence of risk factors (Compas & Reeslund, 2009; Luthar, 2006). In this section, we first consider depression and the risk factors that can make adolescents susceptible to this mental health disorder. Next, we look at eating disorders, which often first arise during the teen years. Finally, we look at programs to help adolescents achieve positive psychosocial development despite stress they may be under.

## Adolescent Depression

© Aurelia Angelica Marquis/iStockphoto

Depression is the most common psychological disorder among adolescents.

Depression is a *mood disorder*, a malady marked by a disabling disturbance in emotion. According to the *Diagnostic and Statistical Manual of Mental Disorders-5* (American Psychiatric Association, 2013), depression is characterized by feelings of sadness and loss of pleasure for two weeks or more. These feelings are often accompanied by feelings of worthlessness, sleep disturbances, weight changes, fatigue, inability to concentrate, irritability or listlessness, and recurrent thoughts of death. Clearly, depression is a serious concern. This is true not only because of its effects on the daily life of those suffering from it, but more so because it is associated with suicide and attempted suicide. As we explained in Chapter 14, suicide is one of the most frequent causes of death during the teen years. Depression is especially relevant to our discussion here because it is the most commonly occurring psychological disorder in adolescence (Hankin & Abela, 2005).

**WHEN SYSTEMS CONNECT**

### Risk Factors for Depression

**risk factors** Characteristics or events that increase the likelihood of a detrimental outcome.

**resilience** Positive adaptation despite the presence of risk factors.

Researchers have identified many risk factors for depression in adolescence, some of which are biological. Keep in mind that the neuroendocrine system is changing a great deal during the adolescent period. These changes relate to brain activity, which in turn relates to depression (Nelson, Leibenluft, McClure, & Pine, 2005). People with low brain activity of the neurotransmitters serotonin and norepinephrine are more likely to become depressed (El-Mansari et al., 2010). Individuals also have different levels of cortisol. You may recall that this hormone is secreted by the adrenal glands in response to novelty and stress. Increased levels of cortisol are often found in adolescents suffering from depression (Adam et al., 2010). These differences may be due to innate characteristics or result from early experiences, such as separation from parents or maltreatment.

In addition to biological changes, adolescents are undergoing cognitive changes having to do with self-evaluation and self-image. These cognitive factors are also related to depression. Aaron Beck, a psychologist who has studied how depressed persons think, proposed that they tend to view their experiences in a biased and negative way (Beck, 1967; Beck, Haigh, & Baber, 2012). They may, for example, repeatedly mull over their thoughts, causing them to experience the same negative pattern of feeling over and over (Rood, Roelofs, Bögels, & Alloy, 2010). Thus, a depressed teen might endlessly review in his mind an occasion that led him to believe others thought he "acted stupid." People who are depressed tend to focus on the negative aspects of their experiences, and in time come to feel hopeless about the future. They may also use illogical thinking, making arbitrary inferences based on little evidence. For example, a person with depression might interpret another person's words or facial expressions as sad even when others would not (Ridout et al., 2009; Ridout, Astell, Reid, Glen, & O'Carroll, 2003).

It is important to point out that not everyone who has risk factors for depression becomes depressed. To explain this phenomenon, researchers have proposed a **diathesis-stress model** of depression (Beck, 1967; Kercher & Rapee, 2009). Diathesis-stress models, like that shown in Figure 16.9, have two elements:

**diathesis-stress model** A model proposing that two elements, a predisposition (diathesis) to develop a disorder, and an environmental disturbance (stress), are necessary for a disorder to develop.

1. A predisposition, or *diathesis*, to develop a disorder (in this case, depression).
2. An environmental disturbance, or *stress*.

Both elements must generally be present for the disorder to develop. Thus, an adolescent at risk for depression is more likely to develop the disorder if she experiences a major stressful event, such as the death of a parent. Or she may become depressed in the face of multiple, less severe stressful events, such as having to change schools and move to a new neighborhood (Ge, Lorenz, Conger, Elder, & Simons, 1994; Graber & Sontag, 2009; Ingram & Luxton, 2005). In the diathesis-stress model, we again see the interplay between internal and external factors in development.

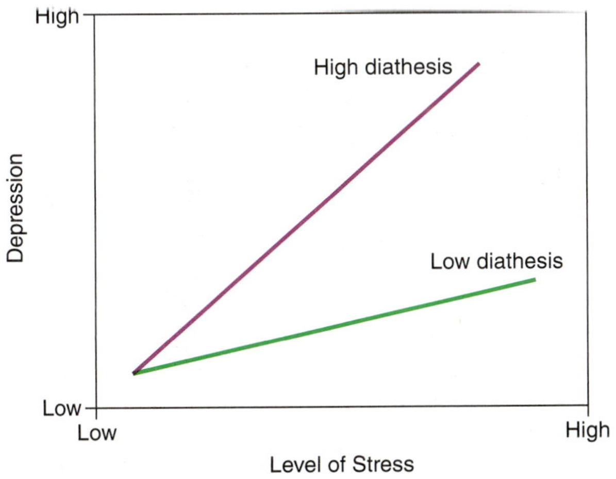


**FIGURE 16.9 The Diathesis-Stress Model for Depression** A diathesis, or predisposition, interacts with stress to produce different levels of depression in different people. An adolescent who has a high diathesis will likely show high levels of depression in response to high levels of stress. In contrast, an individual with a low diathesis will show only a modest increase in depression under similar circumstances.

Ted Foxx/Alamy

Family support can ameliorate some of the symptoms of depression.

## Incidence of Depression in Adolescents

Depression affects about 1 in 5 adolescents (Brent & Birmaher, 2002). At any one time, about 30% of adolescents report having depressive symptoms (Rushton, Forcier, & Schectman, 2002). Depression is the second leading cause of disability for individuals age 15 to 44 worldwide (World Health Organization, 2006). As already noted, it is the most commonly occurring disorder among adolescents (Hankin & Abela, 2005).

Girls have higher rates of depression than boys. This gender difference may be related to how girls experience puberty. In one study, researchers reported that girls who had persistent, negative views of their body image had experienced early puberty. These negative self-evaluations were in turn linked to depressive symptoms (Ohring, Graber, & Brooks-Gunn, 2002).

Depression rates in the United States also vary by ethnicity. Hispanic adolescents have higher rates (22%) than non-Hispanic white (18%), Asian American (17%), or African American (15%) (Saluja et al., 2004). A national survey found that the percentage of Hispanic adolescents likely to have felt sad or hopeless for at least two weeks (32.6%) is notably higher than that for black (24.7%) or non-Hispanic white (27.2%) adolescents (Centers for Disease Control, 2012). Researchers have attributed the unusually high level of stress for this group to many possible factors. Specifically, many Hispanic youths are first-generation immigrants, and they encounter many stressors caused by the family's decision to leave their country of origin. They may also be victims of discrimination, violence, and poor economic conditions. And if members of the family are undocumented or may be perceived as undocumented, Hispanic adolescents may live in fear of immigration raids. Despite these difficult life circumstances, support in the family and at school can ease the symptoms of depression for first-generation Hispanic adolescents (Potochnick & Perreira, 2010). The accompanying Research Insights feature discusses treatments for depression.

### what if...?

You have been mentoring a small group of high school students who are planning to apply to college. Over the course of several weeks, you notice that the mood of one of the students, Latisha, has changed. She used to be outgoing, energetic, and full of humor. Now she acts lethargic and disengaged from others in the group. When you ask her if she is feeling okay, she responds with a dispirited, "I guess so." You are worried that she may be coping with family problems or school problems, causing her to be depressed. You know that applying to college is putting more pressure on her. What are some ways you might be able to help her?

## Research Insights: Treatment for Adolescents with Depression

What are the most effective treatments for depression? Many studies have addressed this question. Few, however, have used randomized designs to test the most often recommended treatments. One that has is the Treatment for Adolescents with Depression Study (TADS). The TADS was a randomized study of 439 adolescents between 12 and 17 who had been diagnosed with depression (Treatment for Adolescents with Depression Team, 2009). The adolescents were randomly assigned to receive one of three treatments:

- Medication with an antidepressant (such as fluoxetine) that acts on neurotransmitters in the brain.
- Cognitive-behavioral therapy. This type of therapy is aimed at helping adolescents alter their thought processes by offering new interpretations and by challenging irrational thought patterns (Jungbluth & Shirk, 2009).
- A combination of medication and cognitive-behavioral therapy.

The investigators found that all three treatments produced improvements. Over the long run, though, it was the combination of treatments that proved most effective (Vitiello, 2009).

## Adolescent Eating Disorders

As discussed in Chapter 14, with adolescence comes many physical changes. Coinciding with these changes, young adolescents become increasingly aware of society's views of body image. Especially important today are views that promote thinness for females and muscle development for males (Sigel, 2009; Thompson, & Cafri, 2007). Young adolescents who believe their physical appearance falls short of society's ideals may try to change their appearance (Tyrka, Graber, & Brooks-Gunn, 2000). One common way they do this is to become intent on losing weight.

The Youth Risk Behavior Surveillance System (a national survey cited in Chapter 14) tells us that 62% of girls and 32% of boys had tried to lose weight during the 30 days before they took the survey (Centers for Disease Control, 2011). Losing weight is not necessarily a negative course of action, of course, especially in light of the high rates of overweight and obesity we noted in previous chapters. But when the goal is to lose weight immediately, adolescents put themselves at risk of developing an eating disorder. Behaviors that indicate an adolescent may be at risk include going without food for 24 or more hours, vomiting after eating, and using laxatives. Conversely, excessive eating can also result in habits leading to an eating disorder.

Eating disorders have been on the rise in the United States since the 1930s (Sigel, 2009). Estimates suggest that 5 to 6% of individuals have an eating disorder (Hudson, Hiripi, Pope, & Kessler, 2007). Among these individuals, adolescents outnumber adults 5 to 1. Eating disorders are more common among females than males. That said, the incidence among males is growing (Cafri, van den Berg, & Thompson, 2006; Woodside, Garfinkel, Lin, Goering, & Kaplan, 2001). Males today make up about 10% of those with eating disorders. Ethnic and racial differences exist as well, though eating disorders have been studied less among people of color than whites. Current reports, however, suggest that disorders that involve overeating occur more frequently among African Americans and Hispanics. Disorders involving undereating occur more frequently among non-Hispanic whites (Tallyrand, 2012).

There are several types of eating disorders, and so treatments for them differ (for more information go to http://www.nationaleatingdisorders.org/). One common disorder is **bulimia nervosa**. A person with bulimia nervosa engages in recurrent episodes of binge eating followed by purging, which is meant to make up for the binging. Purging behaviors include self-induced vomiting, use of laxatives, and/or excessive exercise. These practices can lead to abnormalities in the body's balance of sodium and potassium, which can lead to seizures or heart problems. Frequent self-induced vomiting can also damage tooth enamel. Treatment for bulimia usually involves nutrition therapy, as well as psychotherapy to address alternative ways to cope with stressors. Antidepressant medication is also prescribed to help some bulimics to change their binge and purge behaviors (Sysko, Sha, Wang, Duan, & Walsh, 2010).

Another type of eating disorder also features binge eating. A person with **binge eating disorder** typically eats an unusually large amount of food within a fairly short period of time but does not purge afterward. According to one definition, the person eats like this at least 2 times a week over a 6-week period, even when not feeling hungry (American Psychiatric Association, 2000; Pope et al., 2006). Excessive weight gain is one result of binge eating. Medication, such as antidepressants, combined with **cognitive-behavioral therapy**, have proven somewhat effective in treating this type of disordered eating (Grilo, Masheb, & Crosby, 2012).

The most severe type of eating disorder is **anorexia nervosa**, characterized by self-starvation and extreme weight loss. Early-maturing girls are at higher risk. So are girls who participate in certain activities that emphasize thin bodies, such as figure skating, ballet, and gymnastics (Becker, McDaniel, Bull, Powell, & McIntyre, 2012; Sigel, 2009). If left untreated, anorexia nervosa can disrupt major body functions. It can cause menstruation to stop, and lead to heart problems and decreased blood flow to the brain. Ultimately, it can cause death. Treatment often requires hospitalization,

**bulimia nervosa** An eating disorder marked by recurrent episodes of binge eating followed by behaviors to compensate for the binging, such as vomiting.

**binge-eating disorder** An eating disorder that is characterized by eating large amounts of food within a 2-hour period on a regular basis, at least 2 times a week over a 6-week period.

**cognitive-behavioral therapy** A type of intervention aimed at helping individuals alter irrational or distorted thought patterns.

**anorexia nervosa** An eating disorder characterized by self-starvation and excessive weight loss.

*BURGER/PHANIE/Photo Researchers, Inc.*

Adolescents with anorexia nervosa, the most severe type of eating disorder, have a distorted body image.

**cognitive dissonance theory** A psychological theory proposing that people experience psychological discomfort when there is inconsistency among their attitudes, beliefs, and behaviors.

to prevent malnutrition, especially in individuals whose weight is less than 75% of the ideal for their height. Medication for anxiety and depression, as well as family therapy, have also been found effective (Lock et al., 2010; Sigel, 2009). Anorexia is difficult to treat long term, however. Generally, only about 40 to 50% of those who receive treatment recover (Sigel, 2009).

Although the various eating disorders just described are associated with distinctive behaviors, they do have one factor in common: People with disordered eating patterns are dissatisfied with their bodies (Cole et al., 2012; Maxwell & Cole, 2012). Often, they do not perceive their bodies accurately. As proof of this, one group of researchers found that adolescents with eating disorders overestimated the size of their body parts, like waist and thighs, by 30% (Schneider, Frieler, Pfeiffer, Lehmkuhl, & Salbach-Andrae, 2009). Many adolescents whose body weight is appropriate see themselves as fat. In one study, 25% of normal-weight females and 8% of normal-weight males referred to themselves as overweight. How is it that their body perceptions are so inaccurate? The major predictor of such misperception was low self-esteem (Perrin & Boone-Heinonen, 2010).

*Everyday stories*

NEVER THIN ENOUGH Your good friend Sophia often talks about how fat she is. In fact, though, she is quite thin. At first, you thought she talked about her weight as a way to get people to comment on how thin she is. But over time you have come to realize that she is losing weight. You can see that her clothes don't fit her anymore, and you notice that she refuses to eat anything for lunch. When you mention this to her, she laughs it off: "I'll never be thin enough," she says. You also realize that Sophia doesn't see herself the same way as others do. She has a distorted body image.

Is there a way to prevent eating disorders? Programs that address the issue of appropriate body image have had some success. One type of program applies **cognitive dissonance theory**. This theory holds that people experience psychological discomfort when their attitudes, beliefs, and behaviors are inconsistent with one another (Festinger, 1957). In turn, the discomfort may motivate them to change their behaviors or their beliefs (Elliot & Devine, 1994).

How can we apply this theory to correcting a distorted body image? One program targets adolescents at risk for eating disorders because of their poor body image. Program participants critique the thin ideal of female attractiveness (Stice, Rohde, Durant, & Shaw, 2012; Stice, Shaw, Burton, & Wade, 2006). As part of the

*Simon Buratall/The New Times; Styling by Susan Joy*

Girls with distorted body images, often formed by comparing themselves to models in photos, as shown here, are at greater risk for developing eating disorders.

critiquing practice, they may be asked to write an essay about the costs of pursuing the thin ideal. Or they may role-play in an effort to convince one another not to pursue this ideal. The idea of these exercises is to revise their beliefs in order to change their behaviors. Participation in the exercises has been shown to result in a significant reduction in eating disorders among females from a range of ethnic groups (Rodriguez, Marchand, Ng, & Stice, 2008). More recently, an online version of this intervention has proved more effective than traditional approaches, such as giving adolescents a brochure to read about negative and positive body image (Stice et al., 2012).

**positive youth development** A strengths-based approach to understanding psychosocial development in adolescents.

## Positive Youth Development Practice

At one time, as we noted, adolescence was regarded primarily as a time of "storm and stress" (Hall, 1904). As a result, psychologists often focused their work on adolescent conflicts and problems. And although much research on psychosocial development in adolescents still concerns risky behaviors and mental illness, such as depression, studies today also pay attention to **positive youth development**. Psychologists Richard Lerner and Jacqueline Lerner have written a great deal on this subject (Lerner, 2007). They define positive youth development as a strengths-based approach to understanding psychosocial development. Rather than viewing adolescents as problems to be managed, this approach focuses on promoting adolescent resilience in the face of risks (Lerner, Almerigi, Thokos, & Lerner, 2005).

Positive youth development has emerged from *positive psychology*. This area of psychology is aimed at promoting individual happiness and well-being and understanding the characteristics that lead to positive experiences (Seligman, 2003). Positive youth development also reflects current interest in the role of activities that serve the common welfare. Teens' participation in such activities is sometimes termed "youth purpose" (Damon, 2008). Additionally, positive youth development focuses on adolescents' assets, or strengths (Benson, Leffert, Scales, & Blyth, 1998; Benson, Scales, Hamilton, & Sesma, 2006). The goals of positive youth development include the five characteristics described in Table 16.8.

The overall model of positive youth development is a systems model (Lerner, Lerner, von Eye, Bowers, & Lewin-Bizan, 2011). At the individual level, adolescents have certain strengths. Their immediate surroundings provide them with additional assets. They may receive support from family, schools, religious organizations, community organizations, and others, for example. The individual adolescent and his or her surroundings work together toward positive development. In turn, the adolescent's positive development benefits the surroundings. He or she is more likely to contribute positively to society and less likely to cause problems.

What kind of activities promote the five characteristics listed in Table 16.8? Several researchers have investigated this question. In particular, they have studied the effects of youth development programs such as Boy Scouts, Girl Scouts, and 4-H clubs. Such

**Table 16.8** Characteristics of Positive Youth Development

| | |
|---|---|
| *Competence* | A positive view of one's actions in social, academic, cognitive, health, and vocational areas |
| *Confidence* | An overall sense of positive self-worth and self-efficacy |
| *Connection* | Positive relationships with others and with institutions and organizations |
| *Character* | Respect for societal and cultural norms, a sense of right and wrong, and moral integrity |
| *Caring/compassion* | Sympathy and empathy for others |

*Source:* Information from Lerner, Phelps, Forman, & Bowers, 2009.

organizations enable adolescents to follow their own interests and to become friends with peers and adults with similar interests. In these contexts, they can explore numerous types of interests and define new aspects of their identity (Busseri & Rose-Krasnor, 2009). How effective are such organizations? In one study, researchers found that teens engaged in a range of organized out-of-school activities (such as Boy/Girl Scouts and church youth groups), as well as sports activities, showed higher levels on most aspects of positive youth development (Zarett et al., 2009). Another study found that participation in volunteer and community service activities predicted fewer problem behaviors and more positive behaviors in adolescents (Eccles, Barber, Stone, & Hunt, 2003).

Finally, a meta-analysis of studies on over 60 youth programs evaluated the effects of structured versus unstructured activities (Durlak & Weissberg, 2007; Durlak, Weissberg, & Pachan, 2010). Structured activities have these characteristics:

- They are aimed at achieving specific objectives.
- They include active learning and participation.
- They emphasize practice.
- They focus on the development of psychosocial or other skills.

One such structured program included a curriculum focused on decision-making skills (Tebes et al., 2007). Specifically, it featured a sequence of related steps, engaged adolescents in actively assessing their own approaches to decision making, and gave them opportunities to practice new skills. Such structured activities were found to better promote positive youth development than did unstructured activities.

Angela Rowlings/AP Photo

Structured activities, such as the Walk for Hunger shown here, promote positive youth development.

CHECK YOUR PROGRESS

1. What are the main risk factors for adolescent depression?
2. What are the most effective treatment options for adolescent depression?
3. Compare the characteristics of three major types of eating disorders.
3. Describe the five characteristics of positive youth development.
4. What are some out-of-school activities that promote positive youth development? How are they important to the development of positive psychosocial skills?

# CHAPTER SUMMARY

## The Development of the Self: Identity

**[ KEY QUESTION ] 1. How do adolescents develop a sense of identity?**

- According to Erikson, adolescents experiment with different roles and values to determine which fit them best. This experimentation, termed *identity crisis*, is one stage in Erikson's psychosocial theory of development.
- Marcia proposed four patterns of identity status for adolescents based on their exploration of and commitment to a set of goals, beliefs, and values: identity diffusion, in which neither an exploration nor a commitment has been made; identity foreclosure, in which a commitment has been made without an exploration; identity moratorium, in which an exploration is ongoing but a commitment has not been made; and identity achievement, in which both an exploration and a commitment have been made.
- Ethnic and racial identity are both important aspects of identity development. Phinney has proposed a general model of ethnic identity, which includes three stages: unexamined ethnic identity, ethnic identity search, and ethnic identity achievement. Helms has proposed a specific model of racial identity that applies to whites.
- Sexual identity also develops during adolescence. Research indicates that individuals who are members of sexual minorities often encounter difficulties, such as victimization, that put them at psychological risk.

## Relating to Others

**[ KEY QUESTION ] 2. What are important features of adolescents' relationships with their parents and their peers?**

- Parents need to support adolescents' developing sense of autonomy. As in earlier stages of development, authoritative parenting styles promote more positive psychosocial development during adolescence than do authoritarian, permissive or uninvolved styles.
- Secure attachment is important to adolescent psychosocial development. Adolescents often use their parents as a secure base, while friendships and romantic relationships gradually come to fulfill other functions of attachment, such as proximity seeking and finding a safe haven in which to share intimacy.
- Conflicts between adolescents and their parents often center on differences of opinion about parental authority and personal freedom. According to the transactional model, the behaviors of both parents and adolescents affect conflict and its resolution.
- Parental psychological control can be especially damaging to adolescents, hindering growth in identity, autonomy, and other aspects of psychosocial development, and resulting in resentment.
- Relationships with peers become increasingly important during the adolescent period. Girls have more intense and intimate relationships than boys. Both boys and girls express aggression in friendships, but boys show more overt aggression, whereas girls show more relational aggression.
- Romantic relationships become more common during the adolescent period, and most adolescents experience several romantic relationships during these years.

## Moral Development

**[ KEY QUESTION ] 3. How does moral development change during the adolescent period?**

- According to Kohlberg, most adolescents are in the conventional stage of moral development. They may progress from substage 3, when they are concerned with how they appear to others, to substage 4, when they are concerned with maintaining the social order. Some adolescents move into substage 5, when they focus their moral reasoning on social contracts and individual rights. Kohlberg's theory has been criticized for focusing more on moral reasoning than on moral actions, and for having a Western bias.
- Several brain circuits are related to moral decision making. The prefrontal cortex is important in moral reasoning, and this area is still developing during adolescence. The prefrontal cortex develops better connectivity with areas of the limbic system, especially the amygdala, during this period. In addition, the temporo-parietal junction shows increasing maturity. This area of the brain is associated with perspective taking and understanding the mental states of others.
- Prosocial behavior increases during adolescence, especially late adolescence. Antisocial behavior may also increase at this time, because of such factors as susceptibility to peer influence, poor impulse control, and emphasis on immediate reward. Antisocial behavior involving gang membership may result in encounters with the juvenile justice system.

## Risk and Resilience

**[ KEY QUESTION ] 4.** What are some important risk factors and resilient processes that influence adolescent well-being?

- Adolescents are more at risk of developing psychological disorders than younger children. Depression affects many adolescents and is related to brain activity involving neurotransmitters. Cognitive factors are also involved in depression.
- According to the diathesis-stress model, depression typically develops in those who have a biological predisposition to the disorder and have experienced a stressful event or series of events.
- Eating disorders are another area of risk for adolescents, especially females. Although there are different types of eating disorders, requiring distinctive treatments, most relate to poor body image.
- Many adolescents show evidence of resilience—that is, they develop positively in spite of encountering stressful events. Positive youth development focuses on the strengths of adolescents and on the activities and ecological factors that promote those strengths. Structured activities, in particular, help adolescents develop positive psychosocial skills.

# KEY TERMS

anorexia nervosa *621*
autonomy *599*
binge-eating disorder *621*
bulimia nervosa *621*
clique *604*
cognitive-behavioral therapy *621*
cognitive dissonance theory *622*
crowd *605*
diathesis-stress model *619*
emotional support *603*
ethnic identity *594*
gang *615*
identity *592*
identity achievement *593*
identity crisis *592*
identity diffusion *593*
identity foreclosure *593*
identity moratorium *593*
juvenile delinquency *615*
positive youth development *623*
postconventional level *608*
psychological control *602*
racial identity *595*
rejection sensitivity *607*
relationship quality *607*
resilience *618*
risk factors *618*
transactional model *600*

# CRITICAL THINKING QUESTIONS

1. **The Development of the Self: Identity.** Given the many different facets of identity that adolescents need to confront, analyze why an adolescent might show a pattern of identity diffusion in one aspect of identity and identity moratorium in another.
2. **Relating to Others.** Using the transactional model, formulate an example of how parental psychological control could affect the parent-adolescent relationship.
3. **Moral Development.** Explain why an adolescent may be more advanced in moral reasoning when presented with hypothetical moral dilemmas than when reacting to real-life situations that require making moral judgments.
4. **Risk and Resilience.** Construct an argument that explains why eating disorders are more prevalent among girls than boys.
5. **Cultural Perspectives.** Discuss various ways in which the immigrant paradox could be prevented from occurring in the future.

# REAL Development

## Psychosocial Development in Adolescence

In this module, you will be learning about the social development of adolescents.

In the first activity, you are a guidance counselor in training. The sex education awareness initiative you developed was so successful that the school district has decided to institute a new program to address other issues that are important to teens. The nurse and guidance counselor have asked you to observe interview sessions with Jenna and Mikayla. Using your knowledge of social development, you will analyze Jenna and Mikayla's responses.

In the second activity, you would like to offer parenting classes in the Washington school district. To begin the process you will review parenting research and then analyze your findings. You are interested in the qualities, techniques, and outcomes related to different parenting styles.

**WileyPLUS** Go to WileyPLUS to complete the *Real Development* activity.

# Milestones in Adolescence

## Ages 12–14

### Physical

- During the adolescent growth spurt, height and weight increase rapidly, along with muscle and bone growth; growth rate reaches its peak at about age 12 in girls and about age 14 in boys
- Primary sexual characteristics are associated with gonadarche, the maturation of the gonads—ovaries in females and testes in males
- Secondary sexual characteristics include the appearance of pubic hair, changes in voice, and, in girls, breast development
- Average age of menarche in girls is 12.5 years; boys experience puberty at about age 14
- Maturation of the different lobes of the brain proceeds in a somewhat patchwork fashion, called dissynchrony

© Mark Langridge/OJO Images/Getty Images

### Cognitive

- Begins to reason using logical necessity
- Has a receptive understanding of the academic language used in many subject areas
- Speed of processing information increases
- Working memory increases
- Can inhibit immediate incorrect responses across many trials
- Can use metacognitive skills to select appropriate learning strategies
- Reactive decision making can overtake deliberative decision making in the presence of peers

© CEFutcher/istock

### Psychosocial

- Likely to be in the process of initially investigating identity
- Often behaves as if there is an imaginary audience
- Continues to use mother as a secure base, but best friends become important as a safe haven when upset
- Girls likely to have more intense and intimate friendships than boys do
- Often belongs to same-gender cliques
- Moral reasoning is likely to be at the conventional stage

© Jack Hollingsworth/Blend Images/Corbis

- Likely to use hedonistic or needs-based reasoning when considering helping others
- Although impulsivity in decision making slowly declines, reward seeking increases

# Ages 15–18

## Physical

© TommL/iStockPhoto

- Girls stop growing about two years after the onset of menarche, whereas boys may continue to grow until age 18 or 20
- As the brain reorganizes, synapses that are not well developed are pruned and myelination of axons increases, creating a widespread network of integrated connections
- Temporal lobes and cerebellum reach maximum volume of gray matter at age 16–17; gray matter in prefrontal cortex may not reach this point until early 20s
- Needs 8.5 hours to 9.5 hours of sleep per night; becomes drowsy closer to midnight (three hours later than during childhood) and wakes up between 8 and 9 a.m.

© Getty Images/Purestock

## Cognitive

- Can apply hypothetical-deductive reasoning to solve many problems
- Acquires conceptual and, eventually, interpretive understanding of the academic language used in school-based academic subjects
- Processing speed reaches adult levels
- Working memory reaches adult levels
- Rational decision making improves but shows an optimistic bias

## Psychosocial

- Continues to search for identity, with racial, ethnic, and sexual identity become increasingly important
- Often acts from the perspective of a personal fable, believing self to be invincible
- Likely to engage in a romantic relationship and seek proximity to that partner
- Mixed-gender cliques become important
- Moral reasoning is likely to be at the later conventional stage, concerned with maintaining the social order
- Begins to use internalized reasoning when considering helping others
- Impulsivity and reward seeking in decision making decline

© Roy Morsch/Age Fotostock

# Glossary

## A

**5-2-1-0 program** A health promotion effort recommending 5 servings of fruit and vegetables daily, no more than 2 hours of television, 1 hour of physical activity, and 0 consumption of sugar-sweetened beverages.

**academic language** The language of a particular discipline; involves both terms and concepts important in that discipline.

**academic motivation** The effort taken to achieve academic goals; incorporates the overall value placed on school and commitments to educational pursuits.

**accommodation** A part of adaptation in which children change existing cognitive structures or create new ones to account for new experiences.

**acquired immunity** The immune system's response to specific pathogens that it has learned to identify.

**adolescence** A period of reorganization of the biological, psychological, social, and cognitive processes required for children to transform into young adults.

**adolescent growth spurt** A period of rapid increase in height, weight, and muscle mass; girls' growth spurt occurs between 12 and 14 years, and boys' between 14 and 16 years.

**Adrenarche** Maturation of the adrenal glands, which begins between the ages of 5 and 9; associated with the production and release of an adrenal hormone called *dehydroepiandrosterone (DHEA)*, an androgen.

**adult stem cells** These cells are undifferentiated cells that are found in mature tissues and organs, such as the brain, bone, and skin. The body can use these stem cells to renew and repair the specific tissues and organs in which the stem cells are located.

**affordances** Opportunities for exploration of an environment.

**alleles** Pairs of corresponding genes located at specific positions on specific chromosomes.

**allostatic load** The physiological cost of chronic stress.

**amniotic sac** A thin membrane arising from a cell mass within the blastocyst that completely surrounds the embryo/fetus and contains a protective fluid in which the embryo/fetus is immersed.

**analgesics** Drugs used to relieve pain and promote relaxation.

**anaphylaxis** A life-threatening allergic response requiring emergency treatment.

**androgens** A group of hormones produced by the adrenal gland. The hormone testosterone is responsible for the development of secondary male sexual characteristics, for example. Androgens also support bone growth in both sexes.

**anesthetics** Drugs that block sensation.

**animism** The belief that inanimate objects have life-like qualities such as thought, language and control of action.

**anorexia nervosa** An eating disorder characterized by self-starvation and excessive weight loss.

**anoxia** Lack of oxygen.

**anticipatory guidance** Guidance concerning what to expect and what to pay attention to during middle childhood; part of well-child visits.

**antisocial behavior** Actions that harm another person or a relationship.

**Apgar scale** An instrument used to assess the condition of newborn infants; it measures respiratory effort, heart rate, muscle tone, reflex irritability, and color.

**artificial insemination** A medical procedure in which sperm is introduced directly into a woman's cervical canal or uterus; the sperm may be from her partner or from a donor.

**assimilation** A part of adaptation in which children interpret their experiences in terms of existing cognitive structures.

**assisted reproductive technology (ART)** Any procedure in which both the male and female gametes—that is, the egg and sperm—are handled outside of the human body. ART does not refer to treatment that includes only the use of hormones that spur egg or sperm production.

**assisted vaginal delivery** Delivery done when spontaneous vaginal delivery is not possible. Forceps and vacuum extraction are the most common forms. Also called *instrumental delivery*.

**associative play** A form of play in which children engage in different activities but interact.

**asthma** An allergic condition that causes spasms of the airways in the lungs, making it difficult to breath.

**attachment** Lasting psychological connectedness between human beings.

**Attachment Q-Sort (AQS)** A measure of attachment behavior that can be used in clinic or home settings; it consists of a series of 75, 90 or 100 cards, each describing a specific behavioral characteristic of children between 12 and 48 months.

**attention** Selectively focusing on one source of information while ignoring others.

**attention deficit hyperactivity disorder (ADHD)** A disorder, often diagnosed during middle childhood, that involves hyperactivity and impulsivity, inattention, or both.

**authoritarian parenting** A type of parenting that attempts to control children through coercive demands and punishment accompanied by little warmth.

**authoritative parenting** A type of parenting that places demands on children through reasoning coupled with warmth.

**autism spectrum disorder** A group of developmental disorders that may be marked by deficits in social interaction, communication, and imagination, as well as repetitive and restricted patterns of interests and behaviors.

**automaticity** The ability to perform a well-learned task without much mental effort.

**autonomous orientation** In Piaget's theory, children's understanding that moral rules are established by humans and can change over time

**autonomy** The sense of being a separate and independent individual capable of self-governance.

## B

**Bayley Scales of Infant Development (BSID-III)** A widely used standardized test used to measure infant cognitive abilities, such as intelligence.

**Behaviorism** A theoretical orientation that emphasizes learning and focuses on observable behavior.

**bilingual education** The use of two languages in school for instruction.

**binge-eating disorder** An eating disorder that involves eating large amounts of food within a 2-hour period on a regular basis, at least 2 times a week over a 6-week period.

**Bioecological model** Bronfenbrenner's approach, in which the individual develops within and is affected by a set of nested environments, from the family to the entire culture.

**birth centers** Facilities typically established in or near conventional labor wards for the care of pregnant women who require little or no medical intervention during labor and birth.

**birth plan** A written outline of parents' wishes for labor and birth intended to help health-care providers know what parents want and expect.

**blastocyst** The name given to the embryo at about day 5 or 6 post-fertilization. It consists of three cell masses: the embryoblast, a hollow cavity that becomes the amniotic sac, and the trophoblast.

**body mass index (BMI)** A simple index of weight to height that is commonly used in classifying overweight and obesity.

**bonding theory** A theory suggesting that the period immediately after delivery is a sensitive period in the development of a close emotional bond between mother and child.

**Broca's area** An area in the front of the left hemisphere of the brain thought to be partially responsible for speech production.

**bulimia nervosa** An eating disorder that involves recurrent episodes of binge eating followed by behaviors to compensate for the binging, such as vomiting.

**bullying** Acts of verbal or physical aggression that are chronic and directed toward particular victims.

## C

**Case study** Detailed information gathered about a particular individual.

**categorization** The process of forming groups of similar objects; enables infants to effectively reduce the amount of information they must process, learn, and remember.

**central nervous system** The part of the nervous system that consists of the brain and the spinal cord.

**centration** The focusing of attention on one characteristic of an object or task to the exclusion of others.

**cephalocaudal** The direction of physical growth as it proceeds "from head to tail," with the greatest growth beginning at the top of the body and moving gradually downward.

**cerebral palsy (CP)** A group of permanent disorders in the development of movement and posture that are attributed to nonprogressive disturbances in the developing fetal or infant brain.

**cesarean delivery** A delivery in which the baby is surgically removed from the uterus through an incision in the mother's abdomen.

**child-directed speech** A style of speech typically used with infants, characterized by a higher-than-normal pitch, exaggerated intonation and rhythm, and simplified structure; also called *motherese or parentese.*

**chromosome** A strand of DNA containing a number of genes.

**Chronosystem** In Bronfenbrenner's bioecological model, changes in ecological systems that are caused by time.

**class inclusion** A description of objects or terms in which in smaller set can be conceptually grouped within a larger set.

**Classical conditioning** A type of learning in which a neutral stimulus (such as the sound of a bell) comes to evoke a response (such as salivation) originally evoked by a different stimulus (such as the presence of food).

**clique** A small group of peers, usually with 2 to 12 members, who are good friends and who are drawn together by similarities in various areas.

**co-construction** A term used to describe Vygotky's view that children construct knowledge using the assistance of others.

**code switching** A form of language alternation based on the context, usually referring to bilingual language use.

**cognitive dissonance theory** A psychological theory proposing that people experience psychological discomfort if there is inconsistency among their attitudes, beliefs, and behaviors.

**Cognitive domain** An area of development that involves patterns of change in children's intellectual abilities, including reasoning, learning, attention, memory, and language skills.

**cognitive operations** Internalized mental operations.

**cognitive-behavioral therapy** A type of intervention aimed at helping individuals change irrational or distorted thought patterns.

**collectivist cultures** Cultures in which the goals of the group are considered more important than the goals of individual.

**colostrums** A precursor to mature breast milk that consists primarily of enzymes, anti-infective agents, hormones, and growth factors

**concrete operations** Piaget's term to describe the thinking of 7- to 11-year-old children; logical thinking about physical, concrete objects.

**concussion** A brain injury caused a blow to the head or jaw, causing the soft tissue of the brain to bounce back and forth against the hard bone of the skull, causing bruising, tearing, or twisting of structures and blood vessels deep within the brain tissue.

**conservation** Realization that the essence of something remains the same even though surface characteristics change, characteristic of the cognitive operational stage.

**constraints model of motor development** Newell's idea that physical movements arise from the interactions of the individual body, the task prompting the need for movement, and the environment.

**constructivism** A view that children construct knowledge through interaction with objects and others.

**Continuity** The idea that development is a slow and steady process.

**conventional level** Kohlberg's second stage of moral development. Children at this stage conform to social rules in order to maintain social order.

**conventional transgressions** Actions that violate social norms but do not harm others.

**cooperative play** A form of play in which children interact while engaging in a common activity and with a common goal.

**coordinated school health program (CSHP)** A comprehensive program with eight interactive components designed to promote optimal health in children and their physical and social environments.

**coping** A person's active effort to manage stressful situations through the use of psychological resources.

**corticosteroids** A class of medications used to treat inflammation of soft tissues in a wide variety of chronic conditions, including asthma and other respiratory conditions, arthritis, and cancer.

**Critical period** A particular period of time in which a certain type of development must happen or it will not occur.

**Cross-sectional study** A study that compares groups of children of different ages at a single point in time.

**Cross-sequential study** A study that combines the cross-sectional and longitudinal approaches. In a cross-sequential study, two or more age groups are tested at two or more points in time.

**crowd** A large group of friends and acquaintances, often created through the merging of cliques.

**Culture** The customs, values, and traditions inherent in one's environment.

**cyberbullying** Bullying in which the bully uses e-mail, social media, or other forms of technology to attack victims.

## D

**decenter** The ability to focus on several aspects of an object or problem and relate them.

**deferred imitation** The ability to imitate after a delay; used to assess infants' memory and understanding.

**dental caries** Tooth decay.

**Denver Developmental Screening Test** An instrument used to assess the development of children between birth and 6 years of age.

**deoxyribonucleic acid (DNA)** The genetic material of cells; made of chemical building blocks called nucleotides arranged in a double-stranded helix, DNA contains all of the instructions needed to direct the activities of cells.

**Dependent variable** The variable that is measured to determine if it is affected by the independent variable in an experiment.

**Development** Change that is systematic, organized, and successive in character.

**developmental disabilities** Conditions that cause children's development to be delayed or different from that of other children their age; these conditions may be genetically based (such as Down syndrome) or may result from trauma or other causes.

**Developmental psychology** The field of psychology that is concerned with describing and understanding how people grow and change over their lifetimes.

**Developmental systems theory** A theory emphasizing reciprocal interactions between the individual and multiple levels of the individual's environment; work based on developmental systems theory examines interactions at four levels: genetic, neural, behavioral, and environmental.

**diathesis-stress model** A model proposing that two elements, a predisposition (diathesis) to develop a disorder and an environmental disturbance (stress), are necessary for a disorder to develop.

**differentiation** The process whereby physical structures become more specialized over time.

**Discontinuity** The view that development is characterized by abrupt changes in behavior; often associated with stage theories of development.

**discrete emotions theory** A theory holding that people are born with group of core emotions whose expression and recognition is fundamentally the same for all individuals in all cultures. These emotions are distinct from one another from a very young age, and each has its own neural, physiological, behavioral, and expressive features.

**disequilibrium** Occurs when the infant interacts with the environment and encounters something new and he experiences a discrepancy between his existing way of thinking and his ability to understand this novel experience or situation.

**disorganized attachment** Attachment that characterizes children who display confused and disorganized reactions to caregivers. In the Strange Situation, these children may simultaneously display contradictory behaviors, such as distress and avoidance, when reunited with caregivers and may appear dazed or depressed.

**distributive justice** Justice involving the way in which objects, rewards, and penalties can be distributed fairly.

**dizygotic twins** Twins who developed from two different eggs released and fertilized at the same time.

**domain-specific attributes** Particular areas of competence. Susan Harter has identified five domains that are important in middle childhood: physical appearance, scholastic competence, social acceptance, behavioral conduct, and athletic competence.

**dose-response effect** The relationship between the dosage of a substance, such as alcohol or radiation, and the result of exposure; usually, higher doses are associated with greater effects.

**doula** A nonmedical professional who provides women with physical and emotional assistance before, during, or after childbirth.

**Down syndrome** A condition that results from having an extra copy of chromosome 21; associated with mild to moderate mental retardation, motor impairment, heart defects, early onset of Alzheimer's disease, and childhood leukemia.

**dual-process model** A description of decision-making that involves two processes, one rapid and based on prior experience, the other slow and deliberative, using abstract reasoning.

**dynamic systems theory** A theory that describes motor development as a complex system of mutually interacting components in continuous interaction with each other.

## E

**Early Head Start** A nationwide, government-supported program that provides supports for low-income families with young children.

**early intervention programs** Statewide, integrated developmental services available to families with children up to three years of age whose healthy development is compromised.

**eclampsia** A medical emergency in which untreated symptoms of preeclampsia lead to maternal seizures and/or coma and even death of mother and baby. It may require immediate surgical delivery of the fetus.

**ectoderm** The outer germ layer of the blastocyst that develops into the nervous system (including the brain and spine), skin, nails, and hair, as well as the salivary, pituitary, and mammary glands.

**ectopic pregnancy** A condition in which the blastocyst phase of the embryo implants outside of the uterus, usually in the fallopian tube, where it cannot continue to develop. It quickly outgrows the space, resulting in pain and possibly rupture of the fallopian tube.

**effortful control** The voluntary restraining of a dominant response in order to use a more adaptive response.

**egocentric** Piaget's term for children's tendency to consider only their own perspective.

**egocentric speech** Piaget's term for children's tendency to talk to themselves out loud.

**egocentrism** Piaget's term used to describe the inability to distinguish one's own view from the viewpoints of others.

**Electra Complex** In psychoanalytic theory, a young girl's romantic love for her father and her corresponding feelings of competitiveness with her mother.

**electroencephalographs (EEGs)** Recordings of spontaneous electrical activity produced by the firing of neurons within the brain.

**electronic waste (e-waste)** Discarded electronic devices that contain mercury, lead, arsenic, and heavy metals.

**embryo** The name given to a developing human organism between the first cleavage of the single cell zygote into multiple cells and 8 weeks post-fertilization.

**embryoblast** The inner cell mass of the blastocyst, which is the developing human organism.

**embryonic period** The period of prenatal development starting at the beginning of week 3 and continuing through week 8; organogenesis takes place during the embryonic period.

**embryonic stem cells** Cells that result when, under the right conditions in a laboratory, the germ cells within the blastocyst can multiply without becoming differentiated into the three distinct germ layers. These cells are pluripotent, that is, they maintain the ability to become any somatic cell.

**emotional availability** The quality of emotional exchanges between two people focusing on their accessibility to each other and their ability to read and respond appropriately to one another's communications.

**emotional regulation** The process of adjusting our internal feeling states in order to achieve our goals.

**emotional support** The sharing of feelings, concerns, sympathy, and acceptance with another.

**empathy** An affective state that stems from the apprehension or comprehension of another's emotional state or condition.

**Enculturation** The transmission of culture across generations.

**endoderm** The innermost germ layer of the blastocyst that becomes the thyroid gland, bladder, lungs, and digestive system.

**English as a second language (ESL)** A program involving formal instruction in English.

**enzyme** A protein produced by human cells that function as biochemical catalysts, e.g., breaking down ingested food to use for energy.

**epiphyseal plate** The area at the end of long bones in the arms and legs where new bone grows during the growth spurt in height; also called the growth plate.

**ethnic identity** The social identity derived from membership in a particular ethnic group.

**Ethnography** A qualitative research approach that aims to capture the experiences and perspectives of the people being studied and to understand the meaning these people give to daily activities.

**ethnotheories** Parents' cultural beliefs about parenting practices that lead to positive child behaviors.

**event-related potentials (ERPs)** Measurements derived from EEGs that make it possible to relate the information from EEGs to the cognitive processes in which the brain is engaged.

**executive function** The capacity to regulate one's thinking and behavior.

**Exosystem** In Bronfenbrenner's bioecological model, a system in which the developing child is not actually present but which influences the child's development (for example, social policies created by the government).

**expectancy-value theory** A model describing the factors involved in an adolescent's selection of academic courses related to expectation for success and perception of task value.

**explicit memory** Conscious memory; permits recall and recognition of names, places, and events. Also called declarative memory.

**extremely low birthweight (ELBW)** Birthweight below 2 pounds 3 ounces (1,000 grams).

**extrinsic motivation** Behaviors that are motivated by external rewards or consequences.

## F

**failure to thrive** A diagnosis given to children who are consistently underweight or who fail to gain weight as expected.

**fast mapping** A process in which children learn a new word rapidly by forming a quick guess about their meaning.

**fetus** The human organism from about week 9 until birth.

**fine motor skills** Motor skills that involve use of the small muscles of the fingers and hands for activities such as grasping objects, holding, cutting, drawing, buttoning, and writing.

**food allergy** An immune response to a particular food.

**food desert** A geographic area, rural or urban, where residents have limited access to large supermarkets that sell a variety of foods.

**food insecurity** A condition that results from not having enough food or from not having enough food of sufficient nutritional quality

**food intolerance** Sensitivity to a particular food that does not result from an allergic reaction but occurs when a person's digestive system lacks the enzymes or microorganisms needed to digest the food.

**formal operations** The fourth stage of Piaget's theory of cognitive development; involves the ability to use abstract reasoning.

**frontal cortex** Brain region in which most conscious thinking takes place.

**functional magnetic resonance imaging (fMRI)** A form of magnetic resonance imaging (MRI) that registers blood flow to functioning areas of the brain; enables researchers to identify the regions of brain used to perform a particular task.

## G

**gametes** The cells of sexual reproduction: eggs, or ova, in females and sperm in males.

**gang** A group of individuals with a common identity and orientation, often involving criminal activity.

**gender constancy** The understanding that sex remains the same regardless of dress or actions.

**gender differences** Differences in behavior based on concepts of female and male.

**gender schema** The categories children develop to determine differences between males and females.

**gender stereotypes** The rigid determination of appropriate dress and actions based only on sex.

**gene** A segment of a DNA molecule; genes are the basic building blocks of inheritance.

**genome** The complete sequence of DNA, genes and chromosomes in a person.

**genotype** A person's genetic make-up as it was determined at the moment of fertilization.

**germinal period** The first two weeks of prenatal development from fertilization of the egg to the separation of the three germ layers of somatic cells, and including implantation of the blastocyst of the embryo into the uterine wall.

**gestational age** Age as measured in weeks from the first day of the mother's last menstrual cycle.

**glia** Cells in the nervous system that insulate neurons and hold them together.

**gonadarche** Development of primary sexual characteristics.

**goodness of fit** The match or mismatch in temperament and behavioral style between a child and caregivers.

**gross motor skills** Motor skills that involve use of the large muscles of the legs, arms, back, and shoulders, which are used in sitting, walking, running, jumping, and climbing.

**guided participation** Rogoff's term describing the process by which children actively acquire new skills and problem-solving capabilities through their participation in meaningful activities alongside parents, adults, or other more experienced companions.

## H

**habituation techniques** Indirect research techniques based on the tendency of babies to become bored with a familiar stimulus and look away from it and toward something less familiar.

**health literacy** The capacity to obtain, process, and understand basic health information and services needed to make appropriate health care decisions.

**health promotion** Incorporating healthy behaviors into daily life and avoiding known risks.

**hepatitis A** A bacterial infection spread through feces.

**herd immunity/community immunity** Group immunity that exists when 80 to 95% of the people in a community have been immunized against a disease.

**heteronomous orientation** In Piaget's theory, the young child's view that moral rules are ready-made.

**heterozygous** A condition in which an individual has a pair of nonidentical alleles at a particular position.

**homozygous** A condition in which an individual has a pair of identical alleles at a particular position.

**horizontal décalage** A term used by Piaget to describe children's tendency to understand certain types of conservation before other types.

**hostile aggression** Actions that have the intent of harming another.

**human papillomavirus** A virus, spread through sexual activity, that causes genital warts, which can cause cervical cancer in women later in life.

**hygiene hypothesis** A hypothesis that suggests the environments of Western children are unnaturally clean, dramatically decreasing their exposure to routine microorgnisms.

## I

**"I" self** That part of the self that thinks, makes judgments, realizes that it is separate from everything it sees, and controls the surrounding world.

**identity** An organized sense of self, which includes a sense of personal beliefs, goals, values, and commitments.

**identity achievement** According to Marcia, the status of an individual who has explored goals, values, and beliefs and made commitments to them.

**identity crisis** Erikson's term for the intense exploration of potential identities that characterizes adolescence.

**identity diffusion** According to Marcia, the status of an individual who has neither explored goals, values, and beliefs nor made commitments to them.

**identity foreclosure** According to Marcia, the status of an individual who has made commitments without exploration of goals, values, and beliefs.

**identity moratorium** According to Marcia, the status of an individual who is in the process of exploring goals, values, and beliefs but has not yet made commitments to them.

**imaginary audience** Adolescents' belief that they are the center of others' attention; a part of adolescent egocentricity.

**imitation** The ability to copy the actions of others.

**implicit memory** Automatic and unconscious memory. Also called procedural or nondeclarative memory.

**Imprinting** An innate form of rapid learning that involves attachment.

**in vitro fertilization (IVF)** The most commonly used assisted reproductive technology, in which sperm and egg cell are united in a petri culture dish.

**inclusive** With respect to a classroom or similar setting, including both children with disabilities and children without disabilities.

**Independent variable** The variable that a researcher expects to cause changes in the dependent variable.

**individualistic cultures** Cultures in which the goals of the individual are considered more important than the group goals.

**industry versus inferiority** The fourth of Erikson's psychosocial stages. Children become increasingly involved in activities important to their culture; those who do not engage successfully in such activities develop a sense of inferiority.

**Infant Health and Development Program (IHDP)** A program that provides support to families with infants who were born prematurely and at low birthweight.

**infant mortality rate** The death rate among babies in the first year of life.

**infant-directed speech** A special way of speaking that caretakers use to address infants; characterized by careful pronunciation, slow pacing, exaggerated intonation, and short sentences featuring much repetition.

**Information processing theory** A perspective that attempts to explain the mechanisms by which the human mind acquires, processes, retains, and comprehends information.

**initiative versus guilt** In Erikson's theory, the psychosocial conflict of the early childhood period; the child emerges with a sense of self that is largely either positive, based on feelings of satisfaction from successful initiations, or negative, based on feelings of guilt from perceived failures.

**inner speech** Vygotsky's term for the self-directed speech used when trying to guide behavior.

**insecure-avoidant attachment** Attachment that characterizes children who appear to avoid their caregivers. In the Strange Situation, such children are unresponsive to caregivers, are not distressed when they leave the room, and ignore them when they return.

**insecure-resistant attachment** Attachment that characterizes children who seek closeness to their caregivers but resist this closeness at the same time. In the Strange Situation, these children are distressed when their caregivers leave the room and make anxious contact with them when they return, showing both clinging behavior and resistance.

**instrumental aggression** Attempts to gain an object, privilege, or space without the intent of harming another.

**intellectual disabilities** Significant limitations both in intellectual functioning and in adaptive behavior, including everyday social and practical skills.

**intersubjectivity** A term used by Vygotksy for a process in which two individuals reach a shared understanding of a task or activity.

**intrinsic motivation** Behaviors that are motivated by interest or enjoyment of the activity itself.

**invented spelling** An unconventional type of spelling used by paying attention to the sounds of words.

**iron deficiency anemia** A condition caused by lack of iron in the blood; causes symptoms such as fatigue and decreased appetite.

## J

**juvenile delinquency** Antisocial or illegal activity engaged in by those under the age of majority, which under federal law and in most states is age 18.

## K

**kangaroo care** An intervention often used with preterm newborns in which the newborn is placed in skin-to-skin contact on the mother's breast to promote thermal regulation, breastfeeding, and bonding.

**kwashiorkor** The most common form of malnutrition; occurs when protein consumption does not meet the body's needs.

## L

**language acquisition device (LAD)** A hypothetical brain mechanism proposed to explain human acquisition of the syntactic structure of language.

**lanugo** Fine downy hair that covers the fetus in the womb beginning around 16 weeks. It insulates the fetus—which lacks body fat—and helps with body temperature regulation. It usually disappears by birth.

**lateralization** The extent to which certain brain functions are associated with either the right or left hemisphere of the brain.

**learning disabilities** Learning disabilities are neurological disorders that make it difficult to receive, process, store, and respond to information.

**limbic system** The brain system that governs emotion.

**literacy** The ability to read and write; the ability to read and write to relate effectively to a complex environment.

**Longitudinal study** A study that follows the same group of children over a substantial period of time.

**low birthweight (LBW)** Birthweight below 5 pounds 8 ounces (2,500 grams).

## M

**Macrosystem** In Bronfenbrenner's bioecological model, the outermost environmental level, consisting of the child's culture and society.

**malnutrition** The cellular imbalance between supply of nutrients and energy and the body's demand for them to ensure growth, maintenance, and specific functions.

**marasmus** The most severe form of malnutrition during early infancy; occurs when protein and energy consumption does not meet the body's needs.

**maturational theory** A theory of motor development proposing that motor behaviors develop in a relatively uniform sequence as the muscles and the brain mature. This approach assumes that motor behaviors are genetically predetermined and develop independently of experience.

**"me" self** That part of the self that is the object of the "I" self's thinking and judging.

**meiosis** The process of cell division in which gametes are formed; it results in four new cells, each containing 23 single chromosomes, each different from the parent cell, and all diffeent from one another.

**menarche** The beginning of menstruation in adolescent females.

**meningococcus** Bacterial meningitis, an acute infection of the brain and spinal fluid that spreads through casual contact with other persons.

**mesoderm** The germ layer between the ectoderm and endoderm that becomes the heart, circulatory and lymph systems, connective tissue, muscle, and bones.

**Mesosytem** In Bronfenbrenner's bioecological model, the relationship among microsystems (for example, the interactions between home and school).

**Microgenetic studies** Studies in which researchers observe the same children over a short period of time to document how their behavior is changing.

**micronutrients** Substances required by the body in very small amounts, such as vitamins and minerals.

**Microsystem** In Bronfenbrenner's bioecological model, the innermost environmental level (for example, home and school).

**midgrowth spurt** An increase in the rate of growth between ages 5 and 8.

**mirror neurons** Neurons that fire when an individual performs an action or when an individual observes someone else performing that action.

**mitosis** The process by which somatic cells duplicate themselves to promote growth and repair; mitosis results in genetically identical cells, each containing 46 chromosomes.

**monozygotic twins** Genetically identical twins who developed from the same fertilized egg.

**moral behavior** A disposition to do something on behalf of another person, or to behave in accord with a moral norm or standard bearing on human welfare or justice.

**moral development** Children's acquisition of society's standards regarding what is right and wrong and what is just and unjust.

**moral transgressions** Actions that aim to cause harm to another person.

**motor development** Increases in functional motor ability and changes in the quality of motor skills.

**motor milestones** Motor behaviors that emerge over time and are identified according to the average age at which children develop and demonstrate certain skills or physical attributes.

**muscular dystrophy (MD)** A broad term for a group of inherited diseases that cause muscle to degenerate and weaken.

**myelination** The process of laying down myelin sheaths to insulate the axons of neurons; it begins before birth and occurs in spurts throughout childhood.

**MyPlate** A guide to healthy eating from the United States Department of Agriculture.

## N

**natural childbirth** Childbirth that takes place without the use of anesthetics or other interventions.

**Nature** The biological factors, including genes, that contribute to development.

**neglected children** Children who are ignored when other children choose playmates.

**neonatal** Relating to the period from birth to one month.

**Neonatal Behavioral Assessment Scale (NBAS)** A neurobehavioral assessment scale that describes an infants' functioning in seven key areas: habituation, orientation, motor activity, range of state, regulation of state, autonomic functioning, and reflexes.

**neonatal intensive care unit (NICU)** Unit that specializes in the treatment of at-risk newborns.

**neonatal mortality rate** The death rate among newborns in the first 28 days of life.

**neo-Piagetian** A term given to developmental psychologists who elaborate on Piaget's theory by giving attention to additional aspects of cognition like memory.

**neurogenesis** The process of developing new neurons.

**neurons** Nerve cells; neurons have dendrites and axons through which they communicate with each other.

**neurotransmitters** Chemicals released into the synapse by neurons to enhance communication between neurons.

**newborn behavioral states** Behavioral patterns that recur and can be reliably recognized in newborns; the six states are deep sleep, light sleep, drowsiness, alert inactivity, alert activity, and crying.

**Nurture** The environmental factors and experiences that contribute to development.

## O

**obesity** Extreme overweight; in children, having a BMI above the 95th percentile.

**object exploration approach** An approach in which researchers observe infants' exploration and manipulation of objects to assess their learning and development.

**object permanence** The understanding that objects continue to exist even when they cannot be seen, heard, or touched.

**occipital cortex** Brain region that processes visual information.

**Oedipus Complex** In psychoanalytic theory, a young boy's romantic love for his mother and his corresponding hostility toward and fear of his father.

**Operant conditioning** A form of learning in which a behavior elicits certain consequences, which in turn make the behavior more or less likely to occur in the future.

**organogenesis** Development of major organ systems during the embryonic period, weeks 3–8 of prenatal development. By the end of week 8, 95% of major organs are complete.

**orthographic awareness** The awareness of the visual representation of words and their conventional spelling.

**otitis media** Inflammation of the middle ear.

**overregularization** A process by which children apply general rules of grammar even in cases where exceptions apply.

**overt aggression** Actions that harm another through physical injury or threats of physical injury.

**overweight** In children, having a BMI at or about the 85th percentile for age.

**oxytocin** A hormone secreted by the pituitary gland that stimulates the uterus to contract during and after labor and controls the production of milk in the mammary glands.

## P

**parallel play** A form of play in which children engage side by side in the same activity but do not interact.

**parietal cortex** Brain region that processes information about sensation.

**perception** The process of recognizing and interpreting objects and people through one or more of the senses.

**period of the fetus** The period of prenatal development that begins after organogenesis is 95% completed, at about week 9, and continues until birth.

**peripheral nervous system** The part of the nervous system that connects the central nervous system to sensory and other organs, muscles, blood vessels, and glands; it consists of the somatic nervous system and the autonomic nervous system.

**permissive parenting** A type of parenting that places few demands or limits on children and that often includes warmth.

**personal fable** Adolescents' belief about their own importance and uniqueness; a part of adolescent egocentricity.

**phenotype** The observable expression of a person's genotype.

**phonological awareness** The awareness that words are made up of sequences of sounds.

**Physical domain** An area of development that involves patterns of change in children's biology and health, including sensory abilities and motor skills.

**placenta** A structure formed when the trophoblast burrows into the lining of the uterus, joining the uterine mucous membrane with the membranes of the fetus. Substances ingested by the mother cross the placenta via the umbilical cord to the developing fetus, providing nourishment for its development.

**placenta abruptio** A life-threatening emergency condition in which the placenta peels away from the wall of the uterus, causing massive bleeding.

**placenta previa** A condition in which the placenta attaches low on the wall of the uterus, with the potential to cause bleeding late in pregnancy.

**popular children** children who are selected by many other children as potential playmates.

**popularity-by-decency** A type of popularity based on being kind and fun to be with.

**popularity-by-dominance** A type of popularity based on power.

**positive youth development** A strengths-based approach to understanding psychosocial development in adolescents.

**positron emission tomography (PET)** A test that uses a special camera and a radioactive chemical called a tracer to look at organs inside the body. The tracer is injected into a vein in the arm. As it moves through the body, it gives off tiny positively charged particles (positrons). A camera records the positrons and shows the results as pictures on a computer.

**postconventional level** According to Kohlberg, the third and highest stage of moral development, which involves a belief in abstract principles and values, especially about human rights.

**pragmatics** The use of appropriate rules of conversation.

**preconventional morality** Kohlberg's first stage of moral reasoning, in which children focus on obeying in order to gain rewards or avoid punishments.

**preeclampsia** A treatable medical condition that begins to develop after the 20th week of pregnancy, characterized by high blood pressure, protein in the urine, and sometimes swelling.

**premature infant** An infant born before 37 weeks' gestational age.

**preoperational** Piaget's second stage of development, generally occurring during ages 2 to 7 years, in which children begin to use symbols but still are not logical.

**primary prevention** A type of prevention that focuses on health promotion and the prevention of specific diseases and accidental injuries.

**primary sexual characteristics** Maturation of reproductive organs: ovaries, uterus, penis, and testes.

**primary, or basic, emotions** Emotions that can be seen from the beginning of infancy and that are assumed to be innate. They are often assumed to include joy, sadness, fear, anger, disgust, interest, surprise, and excitement.

**prosocial behavior** Actions that benefit another person or a relationship.

**proximodistal** The direction of physical growth as it proceeds "from near to far," from the central axis of the body outward to the periphery.

**pruning** The elimination of unused neural circuits, which streamlines neural processing and makes the remaining circuits work more quickly and efficiently.

**Psychoanalytic theory** Freud's view of personality development, which attributes it largely to unconscious sources in the human mind. Psychoanalytic theory includes the idea that children pass through five stages of psychosexual development that affect their adult personalities.

**psychological control** A type of control in which a person attempts to regulate another by using behaviors that intrude on the other's thoughts and feelings about himself or herself.

**Psychosocial domain** An area of development that involves patterns of change in children's personalities as well as their social and emotional skills, including relationships with others and the ability to regulate their own emotions.

**Psychosocial theory** Erikson's explanation of development, which focuses on the effects social influences. Erikson believed that individuals pass through eight stages of development. In each stage, they must resolve a crisis that determines their continuing healthy psychological development.

**puberty** The set of physical changes that signal the onset of reproductive maturation.

## Q

**Quasi-experiment** An experimental study in which participants are not randomly assigned to groups but in which one group is exposed to the manipulated variable of interest.

## R

**racial bullying** Bullying in which children are targeted because of their race or ethnicity.

**racial identity** The identity associated with membership in a group based on a socially defined view of race.

**Randomized controlled trial** An experimental study in which researchers randomly assign individuals to experimental and control groups and expose the experimental group to the manipulated variable of interest.

**reflexes** Unlearned involuntary movements or actions that are controlled by neural structures below the level of the cerebral cortex.

**rejected children** Children who are selected by many other children as those they do not want to play with.

**rejection sensitivity** The tendency to be anxious about rejection, to expect and perceive rejection readily, and to overreact to rejection.

**relational aggression** Actions that harm another by damaging a relationship.

**relationship quality** The extent to which partners show intimacy, affection, and nurturance.

**Reliability** The extent to which an instrument produces consistent measurements.

**resilience** Positive adaptation despite the presence of risk factors.

**response inhibition** A process that involves withholding an inappropriate motor or behavioral response.

**Rh incompatibility** A complication of pregnancy in which a mother who is Rh negative carries an Rh positive fetus; under certain conditions, antibodies in the mother's blood can attack the fetus's red blood cells.

**ribonucleic acid (RNA)** A single-stranded substance made of nucleotides that transcribes and translates instructions from DNA in order to make proteins.

**risk factors** Characteristics or events that increase the likelihood of a detrimental outcome.

## S

**scaffolding** Support that enables a child or novice to solve a problem, carry out a task, or achieve a goal that would be beyond his or her unassisted efforts.

**schemas** Organized patterns of thought which are continually being modified through assimilation and accommodation.

**school-based health center** A health clinic readily accessible to children and families operated as a partnership between the school and a community health organization.

**screening tests** Tests designed to identify certain harmful or potentially fatal disorders that are not otherwise apparent at birth.

**secondary emotions** Emotions that are not innate but that depend to some extent on cognitive development and self-awareness. They appear during the second year of life and include shame, embarrassment, guilt, envy and pride.

**secondary prevention** A type of prevention that focuses on detecting, diagnosing, and treating disease in the earliest stages and on halting the spread of communicable diseases by persons already infected.

**secondary sexual characteristics** External signs of sexual maturation, such as hair in the armpits, around the genitalia, and, in males, on the face and chest; growth and development of the penis (males) or breasts and labia (females).

**secure attachment** Attachment that characterizes children who use caregivers as a secure base from which to explore. In the Strange Situation, they are distressed when their caregivers leave the room but are happy and easily comforted when they return.

**self-concept** An individual's view of himself or herself in terms of traits, personality, and values.

**self-efficacy** Confidence in one's ability to organize and follow a course of action to solve a problem or accomplish a task.

**self-esteem** Judgments about one's own worth.

**self-regulation** A person's capacity to alter his or her behavior to adjust to social and situational demands.

**self-representations** Children's descriptions of themselves to themselves.

**semantics** The meaning of sentences or phrases within sentences.

**sensation** The detection and discrimination of sensory information.

**sense of self** The accumulation of knowledge about the self, such as beliefs regarding personality traits, physical characteristics, abilities, values, goals, and roles.

**Sensitive period** A time when a particular experience (or lack of it) has a profound effect on development.

**sensorimotor stage** Piaget's first stage of development, which lasts from birth to about the end of the second year; infants in this stage use senses and motor abilities to understand the world.

**seriation** The ability to arrange objects by increasing or decreasing characteristics, such as height or weight, typical of the concrete operational stage.

**sex differences** Biologically-based differences.

**sexually transmitted disease (STD)** One of a group of diseases caused by bacteria or viruses and transmitted between people during unprotected oral, genital, and anal sexual contact.

**social brain** Brain systems that combine to control various aspects of social processing.

**social comparison** The process of comparing one's own appearance, traits, abilities, and behaviors with those of others.

**social competence** The skills necessary for interacting with others.

**social dominance** Behavior intended to elevate or maintain social status.

**social information processing model** An information processing model that identifies the steps in perceiving and responding to social information.

**Social learning theory** Bandura's version of learning theory, which emphasizes the role of modeling, or observational learning, in behavior.

**social perspective taking** The ability to take the perspective of others in a social interaction.

**social referencing** The use of emotional cues from other people, such as facial expression and tone of voice, to regulate one's own emotional reactions.

**socialized speech** Piaget's term for children's ability to take into account the perspective of the listener.

**Sociocultural theory** Vygotsky's theory that children's cognitive growth depends on their interactions with adults and more knowledgeable peers, which in turn are based on broad cultural values.

**sociodramatic play** A type of symbolic play in which children enact social roles.

**somatic cells** Body cells, such as skin, muscle, bone, and so on.

**Stage theories** Theories proposing that development proceeds in a discontinuous manner; each stage is qualitatively different from the ones that precede and follow it.

**stage-environment fit** The relation between a person's developmental needs and the opportunities or constraints provided by the person's environment.

**stereotype threat** Fear that one's performance will conform to a stereotype.

**Strange Situation procedure** A laboratory procedure designed by Mary Ainsworth to capture individual differences in attachment; it involves separating infants and toddlers from their caregivers for brief periods and observing their responses when the caregivers return.

**sudden infant death syndrome (SIDS)** The most common cause of post-neonatal deaths in developed countries; commonly occurs during sleep while the babies are lying on their stomachs, although the actual mechanism of death is still unknown.

**symbolic play** A type of play in which a child uses one object to substitute for another.

**synapse** A tiny space between neurons, across which the neurons communicate.

**synaptogenesis** The process of synapse formation.

**syntax** The combination of words and phrases into meaningful sentences.

## T

**temperament** A set of inherited personality traits that are observable from the beginning of life and reflected in individual differences in reactivity and self-regulation in the domains of affect, activity, and attention.

**temporal cortex** Brain region that processes information about sound and is involved in consciously remembering past events and for facial recognition.

**teratogens** From *teras* for "monster" and *genesis* for "origin," any agent that can cause permanent damage to the embryo or fetus.

**tertiary prevention** A type of prevention that focuses on slowing the progress of a disease and limiting its disabling complications.

**The Newborn Behavioral Observations (NBO)** System based on the NBAS is used to sensitize parents to their newborn's capacities and individuality and to promote a positive relationship between parent and infant.

**theory of mind** Children's understanding of the mental states (i.e., "the minds") of themselves and others.

**theory of multiple intelligences** Gardner's theory that people have eight (possibly nine) separate intelligences: linguistic, musical, logical-mathematical, spatial, bodily-kinesthetic, interpersonal, intrapersonal, naturalistic, and (possibly) spiritual/existential.

**thought-mediated behavior** Behavior that is the result of thinking before acting in response to a situation.

**threshold effect** Related to the dose-response effect; the point of exposure below which no effect can be identified.

**transactional model** A model that emphasizes the bidirectional effects of parents and adolescents on each other.

**triarchic theory of intelligence** Sternberg's theory that intelligence is made up of three interacting elements: analytic intelligence, practical intelligence, and creative intelligence.

**tripartite model** A model that describes three roles that parents can play: interactive partner, direct instructor, and provider of opportunities.

**trophoblast** A cell mass within the blastocyst that becomes the placenta.

## U

**ultrasound** A noninvasive procedure in which part of the body is exposed to high-frequency sound waves from a machine, which produces real-time pictures of the inside of the body and helps physicians to diagnose problems.

**undernutrition** A type of malnutrition that results from insufficient food intake and repeated infectious diseases.

**uninvolved parenting** A type of parenting that places few demands on children and that provides them with little warmth.

## V

**vaccine** A substance used to stimulate the production of antibodies and provide immunity against one or several diseases.

**Validity** The extent to which an instrument measures what it claims to measure.

**vernix caseosa** An oily substance with dead skin cells that covers the fetus in the womb; thought to provide insulation and maintain body temperature. It usually disappears by birth.

**very low birthweight (VLBW)** Birthweight below 3 pounds 5 ounces (1,500 grams).

**viability** The ability of the fetus to survive outside the womb.

**violation-of-expectation method** A visual preference research method that assesses infants' ability to distinguish between an expected and an unexpected event.

**visual acuity** The ability to see detail clearly.

**visual preference procedures** Indirect research methods that use visual attention as a way of assessing the thought processes of babies and very young children.

## W

**Wernicke's area** An area in the brain thought to be partially responsible for language processing.

**white adipose tissue** White fat, in which excess calories are stored in the body. It is a complex and active endocrine organ that secretes enzymes, hormones, and adipokines.

**working memory** The part of the memory system where problems are actively worked on.

## Z

**zone of proximal development (ZPD)** Vygotsky's terms for the distance between a person's actual developmental level, as determined by independent problem solving, and the higher level of development that could be achieved under the guidance of an adult or a more capable peer.

**zygote** A single cell organism that results from the fertilization of an egg cell by a sperm; the fertilized egg.

# References


Abbeduto, L., Warren, S. F., & Conners, F. A. (2007). Language development in Down syndrome: From the prelinguistic period to the acquisition of literacy. *Mental Retardation and Developmental Disabilities Research Reviews, Special Issue on Down Syndrome, 13*(3), 247–261. doi:10.1002/mrdd.20158

Abramovitch, R., Corter, C., & Lando, B. (1979). Sibling interaction in the home. *Child Development, 50*, 997–1003.

Abrams, L., & Haney, W. (2004). Accountability and the grade 9 to 10 transition: The impact on attrition and retention rates. In G. Orfield (Ed.), *Dropouts in America: Confronting the graduation rate crisis* (pp. 181–205). Cambridge, MA: Harvard Publishing Group.

Acebo, C., Sadeh, A., Seifer, R., Tzischinsky, O., Hafer, A., & Carskadon, M. A. (2005). Sleep/wake patterns derived from activity monitoring and maternal report for healthy 1- to 5-year-old children. *Sleep, 28*(12), 1568–1577.

Ackerman, B., Izard, C., Kobak, R., Brown, E., & Smith, C. (2007). Relation between reading problems and internalizing behavior in school for preadolescent children from economically disadvantaged families. *Child Development, 78*, 581–596. doi:10.1111/j.1467-8624.2007.01015.x

Ackermann, H., Mathiak, K., & Riecker, A. (2007). The contribution of the cerebellum to speech production and speech perception: Clinical and functional imaging data. *The Cerebellum, 6*(3), 202–213. doi:10.1080/14734220701266742

Acredolo, L. P., Goodwyn, S. W., Horobin, K., & Emmons, Y. (1999). The signs and sounds of early language development. In L. Balter & C. Tamis-LeMonda (Eds.), *Child Psychology* (pp. 116–139). New York, NY: Psychology Press.

Adam, E. K., Doane, L. D., Zinbarg, R. E., Mineka, S., Craske, M. G., & Griffith, J. W. (2010). Prospective prediction of major depressive disorder from cortisol awakening responses in adolescence. *Psychoneuroendocrinology, 35*(6), 921–931. doi:10.1016/j.psyneuen.2009.12.007

Adams, M. J. (1990). *Beginning to read: Thinking and learning about print.* Cambridge, MA: MIT Press.

Adams, M. J., Trieman, R., & Pressley, M. (1998). Reading, writing, and literacy. In I. E. Sigel & K. Renninger (Eds.), *Handbook of child psychology: Vol. 4. Child psychology in practice* (5th ed., pp. 275–355). Hoboken, NJ: Wiley.

Adams, R. E., & Laursen, B. (2007). The correlates of conflict: Disagreement is not necessarily detrimental. *Journal of Family Psychology, 21*(3), 445–458. doi:10.1037/0893-3200.21.3.445

Adamson, L. B. (1996). *Communication development during infancy.* Boulder, CO: Westview.

Adelson, J., Green, B., & O'Neil, R. (1969). Growth of the idea of law in adolescence. *Developmental Psychology, 1*(4), 327–332. doi:10.1037/h0027705

Adolph, K. E. (2002a). Babies' steps make giant strides toward a science of development. *Infant Behavior and Development, 25*, 86–90. doi:10.1016/S0163–6383(02)00106–6

Adolph, K. E. (2002b). Learning to keep balance. In R. Kail (Ed.), *Advances in child development & behavior* (Vol. 30, pp. 1–40). Amsterdam, Netherlands: Elsevier.

Adolph, K. E. (2005). Learning to learn in the development of action. In J. Lockman, J. Reiser, & C. A. Nelson (Eds.), *Action as an organizer of perception and cognition during learning and development: Minnesota Symposium on Child Development* (Vol. 33, pp. 91–122). Mahwah, NJ: Erlbaum.

Adolph, K. E. (2008). Learning to move. *Current Directions in Psychological Science, 17*, 213–218.

Adolph, K. E., & Berger, S. E. (2006). Motor development. In W. Damon, & R. Lerner (Series Eds.) & D. Kuhn, & R. S. Siegler (Vol. Eds.), *Handbook of child psychology: Vol. 2: Cognition, perception, and language* (6th ed., pp. 161–213). Hoboken, NJ: Wiley.

Adolph, K. E., & Eppler, M. A. (2002). Flexibility and specificity in infant motor skill acquisition. In J. Fagan (Ed.), *Progress in infancy research* (Vol. 2, pp. 121–167). Mahwah, NJ: Erlbaum.

Adolph, K. E., & Robinson, S. R. (2013). The road to walking: What learning to walk tells us about development. In P. Zelazo (Ed.), *Oxford handbook of developmental psychology*. New York, NY: Oxford University Press.

Adolph, K. E., Karasik, L., & Tamis-LeMonda, C. S. (2010). Motor skills. In M. Bornstein (Ed.), *Handbook of cultural developmental science* (pp. 61–88). New York, NY: Taylor & Francis.

Adolph, K. E., Robinson, S. R., Young, J. W., & Gill-Alvarez, F. (2008). What is the shape of developmental change? *Psychological Review, 115*, 527–543. doi:10.1037/0033-295X.115.3.527

Adolph, K. E., Vereijken, B., & Denny, M. (1998). Learning to crawl. *Child Development, 69*, 1299–1312. doi:10.2307/1132267

Adolph, K. E., Vereijken, B., & Shrout, P. E. (2003). What changes in infant walking and why. *Child Development, 74*(2), 475–497. doi:10.1111/1467-8624.7402011

Aguiar, A., & Baillargeon, R. (2002). Developments in young infants' reasoning about occluded objects. *Cognitive Psychology, 45*(2), 267–336. doi:10.1016/S0010–0285(02)00005–1

Ahearn, W. H., & Tiger, J. H. (2013). *Behavioral approaches to the treatment of autism.* Washington, DC: American Psychological Association. doi:10.1037/13938-012

Ahlqvist, M., & Wirfalt, E. (2000). Beliefs concerning dietary practices during pregnancy and lactation: A qualitative study among Iranian women residing in Sweden. *Scandinavian Journal of Caring Sciences, 14*, 105–111. doi:10.1080/02839310050162334

Aidoo, M., Terlouw, D. J., Kolczak, M. S., McElroy, P. D., ter Kuile, F. O., Kariuki, S., . . . Udhayakumar, V. (2002). Protective effects of the sickle cell gene against malaria morbidity and mortality. *Lancet, 359*(9314), 1311–1312. doi:10.1016/S0140–6736(02)08273–9

Ainsworth, M. D. S., & Bowlby, J. (1991). An ethological approach to personality development. *American Psychologist, 46*, 331–341.

Ainsworth, M., Blehar, M., Waters, E., & Wall, S. (1978). *Patterns of attachment: A psychological study of the strange situation.* Hillsdale, NJ: Erlbaum.

Akhtar, N. (1999). Acquiring basic word order: Evidence for data–driven learning of syntactic structure. *Journal of Child Language, 26*(2), 339–356. doi:10.1017/S030500099900375X

Akinbami, L. J., Moorman, J. E., Garbe, P. L., & Sondik, E. J. (2009). Status of childhood asthma in the United States, 1980–2007. *Pediatrics, 123*(Supplement 3), S131–S145. doi:10.1542/peds.2008-2233C

Akinbami, L. J., Parker, J. D., & Merkle, S. (2010). Factors associated with school absence among children with symptomatic asthma, United States, 2002–2003. *Pediatric Allergy, Immunology, and Pulmonology, 23*(3), 191–200. doi:10.1089/ped.2010.0013

Alberts, A., Elkind, D., & Ginsberg, S. (2007). The personal fable and risk-taking in early adolescence. *Journal of Youth and Adolescence, 36*(1), 71–76. doi:10.1007/s10964–006–9144–4

Alderson, R. M., Rapport, M. D., Sarver, D. E., & Kofler, M. J. (2008). ADHD and behavioral inhibition: A re-examination of the stop-signal task. *Journal of Abnormal Child Psychology, 36*(7), 989–998. doi:10.1007/s10802–008–9230–z

Aldous, J., Mulligan, G. M., & Bjarnason, T. (1998). Fathering over time: What makes a difference? *Journal of Marriage and the Family, 60*, 809–820.

Aldridge, M. A., Stillman, R. D., & Bower, T. G. R. (2001). Newborn categorization of vowel-like sounds. *Developmental Science, 4*(2), 220–232. doi:10.1111/1467-7687.00167

Alink, L. R. A., Cicchetti, D., Kim, J., & Rogosch, F. A. (2012). Longitudinal associations among child maltreatment, social functioning, and cortisol regulation. *Developmental Psychology, 48*(1), 224–236. doi:10.1037/a0024892

Allard, E. (2008). Review of NABE review of research and practice, Volume 3. *International Journal of Bilingual Education and Bilingualism, 11*(1), 121–125. doi:10.2167/bebb153.0

Allen, S. E. M., & Crago, M. B. (1996). Early passive acquisition in Inuktitut. *Journal of Child Language, 23*(1), 129–155. doi:10.1017/S0305000900010126

Allen, S. M., & Hawkins, A. J. (1999). Maternal gatekeeping: Mother's beliefs and behaviors that inhibit greater father involvement in family work. *Journal of Marriage and the Family, 61*, 199–212.

Alliance for Excellent Education. (2010). *High school dropouts in America*. Retrieved from http://www.all4ed.org/files/GraduationRates_FactSheet.pdf

Alloway, T. P., Gathercole, S. E., & Pickering, S. J. (2006). Verbal and visuospatial short-term and working memory in children: Are they separable? *Child Development*, 77(6), 1698–1716. doi:10.1111/j.1467–8624.2006.00968.x

Alloway, T. P., Gathercole, S. E., Adams, A.–M., & Willis, C. (2005). Working memory abilities in children with special educational needs. *Educational and Child Psychology, 22*(4), 56–67.

Al-Namlah, A. S., Fernyhough, C., & Meins, E. (2006). Sociocultural influences on the development of verbal mediation: Private speech and phonological reading in Saudi Arabian and British samples. *Developmental Psychology, 42*(1), 117–131. doi:10.1037/0012-1649.42.1.117

Al-Qabandi, M., Gorter, J. W., & Rosenbaum, P. (2011). Early autism detection: Are we ready for routine screening? *Pediatrics, 128*(1):e211-7. doi:10.1542/peds.2010-1881.

Als, H., & McAnulty, G. (2011). The Newborn Individualized Developmental Care and Assessment Program (NIDCAP) with Kangaroo Mother Care (KMC): Comprehensive care for preterm infants. *Current Women's Health Reviews*, 7(3), 288–301. doi:10.2174/157340411796355216

Als, H., Duffy, F. H., McAnulty, G. B., Rivkin, M. J., Vajapeyam, S., Mulkern, R. V., . . . Eichenwald, E. C. (2004). Early experience alters brain function and structure. *Pediatrics, 113*(4), 846–857. doi:10.1542/peds.113.4.846

Als, H., Duffy, F., & McAnulty, G. B. (1988). The APIB: An assessment of functional competence in preterm and full-term newborns regardless of gestational age at birth: II. *Infant Behavior and Development, 11*, 319–331. doi:10.1016/0163–6383(88)90017–3

Als, H., Gilkerson, L., Duffy, F. H., McAnulty, G. B., Buehler, D. M., Vandenberg, K., & Jones, K. (2003). A three-center, randomized, controlled trial of individualized developmental care for very low birth weight preterm infants: Medical, neurodevelopmental, parenting, and caregiving effects. *Developmental and Behavioral Pediatrics, 24*(6), 399–408. doi:10.1097/00004703–200312000–00001

Als, H., Lawhon, G., Duffy, F. H., McAnulty, G. B., Gibes-Grossman, R., & Blickman, J. G. (1994). Individualized developmental care for the very low-birth-weight preterm infant: Medical and neurofunctional effects. *Journal of the American Medical Association, 272*(11), 853–858. doi:10.1001/jama.272.11.853

Als, H., Lester, B. M., Tronick, E. Z., & Brazelton, T. B. (1982). Manual for the assessment of preterm infants' behavior (APIB). In H. E. Fitzgerald, B. M. Lester, & M. W. Yogman (Eds.), *Theory and research in behavioral pediatrics* (pp. 65–132). New York, NY: Plenum Press.

Amato, P. R. (2010). Research on divorce: Continuing trends and new developments. *Journal of Marriage and the Family*, 72(3), 650–666. doi:10.1111/j.1741–3737.2010.00723.x

Amato, P. R., & Gilbreth, J. G. (1999). Nonresident fathers and children's well-being: A meta-analysis. *Journal of Marriage and the Family, 61*, 557–573.

American Academy of Audiology. (2010). *Clinical practice guidelines: Diagnosis, treatment and management of children and adults with central auditory processing disorder*.

American Academy of Neurology, Quality Standards Subcommittee. (1997). *Practice parameter: The management of concussion in sports.* Retrieved from http://www.aan.com/professionals/practice/guidelines/pda/Concussion_sports.pdf

American Academy of Pediatric Dentistry. (2010). *2010–11 Definitions, Oral Health Policies, and Clinical Guidelines.* Retrieved from http://www.aapd.org

American Academy of Pediatrics. (2011). *Caring for our children: National health and safety performance standards for out-of-home child care and early education programs* (3rd ed.). Elk Grove Village, IL: American Academy of Pediatrics.

American Academy of Pediatrics. (2011). *Energy drinks can harm children.* Retrieved from http://www.aap.org/en-us/about-the-aap/aap-press-room/Pages/Energy-Drinks-Can-Harm-Children.aspx

American Academy of Pediatrics, American Public Health Association, & National Resource Center for Health and Safety in Child Care and Early Education. (2002). *Caring for our children: National health and safety performance standards: Guidelines for out-of-home child care programs* (2nd ed.). Introduction. Retrieved from http://nrckids.org/CFOC

American Academy of Pediatrics, Committee on Fetus and Newborn, & American College of Obstetricians and Gynecologists, Committee on Obstetric Practice. (2006). The Apgar score. *Pediatrics, 117*(4), 1444–1447. doi:10.1542/peds.2006–0325.

American Academy of Pediatrics, Committee on Injury, Violence, and Poison Prevention, and Committee on Adolescence. (2006). The teen driver. *Pediatrics, 118*(6), 2570–2581. doi:10.1542/peds.2006–2830

American Academy of Pediatrics, Committee on Nutrition and the Council on Sports Medicine and Fitness. (2011). Sports drinks and energy drinks for children and adolescents: Are they appropriate? *Pediatrics, 127*(6), 1182–1189. doi:10.1542/peds.2011–0965

American Academy of Pediatrics, Committee on Public Education. (1999). Media education. *Pediatrics, 104*(2), 341–343.

American Academy of Pediatrics, Committee on Sports Medicine and Fitness and Committee on School Health. (2001/2007). Organized sports for children and preadolescents. *Pediatrics, 107*(6), 1459–1462.

American Academy of Pediatrics, Task Force on Infant Positioning and SIDS. (1992). Positioning and SIDS. *Pediatrics, 89*, 1120–1126.

American Academy of Pediatrics, Task Force on Sudden Infant Death Syndrome. (2011). Technical Report on SIDS and other sleep-related infant deaths: Expansion of recommendations for a safe infant sleeping environment. *Pediatrics, 128*(5), e1341–e1367. doi:10.1542/peds.2011–2285

American Academy of Pediatrics & American Academy of Family Physicians. (2004). Clinical practice guideline: Diagnosis and management of acute otitis media. *Pediatrics, 113*(5), 1451–1465.

American Association of Intellectual and Developmental Disabilities (AAIDD). (2013). Definition of intellectual disability. Retrieved from http://www.aaidd.org/content_100.cfm

American Association of Orthodontists. (2004). *The right time for an orthodontic check-up: No later than age 7.* Retrieved from http://www.braces.org/learn/upload/Problems-to-Watch-for-in-Growing-Children-APPROVED1.pdf

American College of Obstetricians and Gynecologists. (2000). Premenstrual syndrome: Clinical management guidelines for obstetrician-gynecologists. *ACOG Practice Bulletin, 15*, 1–9.

American College of Obstetricians and Gynecologists. (2008, February 6). ACOG news release. *Alcohol and pregnancy: Know the facts.* Retrieved from http://www.acog.org/from_home/publications/press_releases/nr02–06–08–1.cfm

American College of Obstetricians and Gynecologists. (2009). Induction of labor. *ACOG Practice Bulletin, No. 10.* Washington, DC: American College of Obstetricians and Gynecologists.

American Diabetes Association. (2008). Standards of medical care in diabetes. *Diabetes Care, 31* (Suppl. 1), S12–S54.

American Dietetic Association. (2011). *Pediatric Nutrition Care Manual, 2011 Edition.* Available by subscription from http://nutritioncaremanual.org/

American Psychiatric Association. (2000). *Diagnostic and statistical manual of mental disorders* (4th ed., text rev.). Washington, DC DC: Author.

American Psychiatric Association. (2013). *Diagnostic and statistical manual of mental disorders (5th ed.)*, Washington, DC: Author.

American Psychological Research Association. (2002). Ethical principles of psychologists and code of conduct. *American Psychologist, 57*, 1060–1073. doi:10.1037/0003–066X.57.12.1060

American Public Health Association. (2007). A call to action on breastfeeding: A fundamental public health issue. Retrieved from http://www.apha.org

American Society for Reproductive Medicine & Society for Assisted Reproductive Technology. (2006). *Guidelines on number of embryos transferred.* Retrieved from http://www.asrm.org/Media/Practice/Guidelines_on_number_of_embryos.pdf

American Society for Reproductive Medicine. (2003). *Age and fertility*. Retrieved from http://www.asrm.org/Patients/patientbooklets/agefertility.pdf

Anda, R. F., Felitti, V. J., Bremner, J. D., Perry, B. D., Dube, S. R., & Giles, W. H. (2006). The enduring effects of abuse and related experiences in childhood: A convergence of evidence from neurobiology and epidemiology. *European Archives of Psychiatry and Clinical Neuroscience, 256*, 174–186.

Anders, Y., Rossbach, EL, Weinert, S., Ebert, S., Kuger, S., Lehrl, S., & von Maurice, J. (2012). Home and preschool learning environments and their relations to the development of early numeracy skills. *Early Childhood Research Quarterly, 27*(2), 231–244. doi:10.1016/j.ecresq.2011.08.003

Anderson, C. A., Gentile D. A., & Buckley, K. A. (2007). *Violent videogame effects on children and adolescents: Theory, research, and public policy*. New York, NY: Oxford University Press.

Anderson, C. A., Shibuya, A., Ihori, N., Swing, E. L., Bushman, B. J., Sakamoto, A., . . . Saleem, M. (2010). Violent video game effects on aggression, empathy, and prosocial behavior in Eastern and Western countries: A meta-analytic review. *Psychology Bulletin, 136*, 151–173. doi:10.1037/a0018251

Anderson, D. R., & Pempek, T. A. (2005). Television and very young children. *American Behavioral Scientist, 48*(5), 505–522. doi:10.1177/0002764204271506

Anderson, P. J., Wood, S. J., Francis, D. E., Coleman, L., Anderson, V., & Boneh, A. (2007). Are neuropsychological impairments in children with early-treated phenylketonuria (PKU) related to white matter abnormalities or elevated phenylalanine levels? *Developmental Neuropsychology, 32*(2), 645–668. doi:10.1080/87565640701375963

Anderson, S. E., Dallal, G. E., & Must, A. (2003). Relative weight and race influence average age at menarche: Results from two nationally representative surveys of U.S. girls studied 25 years apart. *Pediatrics, 111*(4), 844–850.

Anderson, V. (2012). *Developmental social neuroscience and childhood brain insult: Theory and practice*. New York, NY: Guilford.

Andrade, S. E., Gurwitz, J. H., Davis, R. L., Chan, A., Finkelstein, J. A., Fortman, K., . . . Platt, R. (2004). Prescription drug use in pregnancy. *American Journal of Obstetrics and Gynecology, 191*, 398–407. doi:10.1016/j.ajog.2004.04.025

Andreassen, C., & Fletcher, P. (2007). *Early childhood longitudinal study, birth cohort (ECLS–B) Psychometric Report for the 2-Year Data Collection* (NCES 2007–084). Washington, DC: National Center for Education Statistics, Institute of Education Sciences, U.S. Department of Education.

Andrews, D. (2001). *Neuropsychology: From theory to practice*. New York, NY: Psychology Press.

Andriacchi, T. P., Andersson, G. B., Fermier, R. W., Stern, D., & Galante, J. O. (1980). A study of lower-limb mechanics during stair-climbing. *Journal of Bone and Joint Surgery, 62*(5), 749–757.

Anglin, J. M. (1993). Vocabulary development: A morphological analysis. *Monographs of the Society for Research in Child Development, 58*(10, Serial No. 238).

Anisfeld, M., Turkewitz, G., Rose, S. A., Rosenberg, F. R., Sheiber, F. J., Couturier-Fagan, D. A., & Sommer, I. (2001). No compelling evidence that newborns imitate oral gestures. *Infancy, 2*(1), 111–122. doi:10.1207/S15327078IN0201_7

Ansari, A., & Winsler, A. (2012). School readiness among low-income, Latino children attending family childcare versus centre-based care. *Early Child Development and Care, 182*(11), 1465–1485. doi:10.1080/03004430.2011.622755

Apgar, V. (1953). A proposal for a new method of evaluation of the newborn infant. *Current Researches in Anesthesia & Analgesia, 32*, 260–267.

Arbuthnot, K. (2009). The effects of stereotype threat on standardized mathematics test performance and cognitive processing. *Harvard Educational Review, 79*(3), 448–472.

Archer, J. (2004). Sex differences in aggression in real-world settings: A meta-analytic review. *Review of General Psychology, 8*(4), 291–322. doi:10.1037/1089–2680.8.4.291

Archer, J. (2006). Testosterone and human aggression: An evaluation of the challenge hypothesis. *Neuroscience & Biobehavioral Reviews, 30*(3), 319–345.

Archer, J., & Coyne, S. M. (2005). An integrated review of indirect, relational, and social aggression. *Personality and Social Psychology Review, 9*, 212–230. doi:10.1207/s15327957pspr0903_2

Ariff, K. M., & Beng, K. S. (2006). Cultural health beliefs in a rural family practice: A Malaysian perspective. *Australian Journal of Rural Health, 14*, 2–8. doi:10.1111/j.1440-1584.2006.00747.x

Armstrong, D. F. (2006). Neurodevelopment and chronic illness: Mechanisms of disease and treatment. *Mental Retardation and Developmental Disabilities Research Reviews, 12*, 168–173.

Arnett, J. J. (2000). Optimistic bias in adolescent and adult smokers and nonsmokers. *Addictive Behaviors, 25*(4), 625–632. doi:10.1016/S0306–4603(99)00072–6

Arnett, J. J. (2004). *Emerging adulthood: The winding road from the late teens through the twenties*. New York, NY: Oxford University Press.

Aron, A. R. (2008). Progress in executive-function research: From tasks to functions to regions to networks. *Current Directions in Psychological Science, 17*(2), 124–129. doi:10.1111/j.1467-8721.2008.00561.x

Arterberry, M., Cain, K. M., & Chopko, S. A. (2007). Collaborative problem solving in five-year-old children: Evidence of social facilitation and social loafing. *Educational Psychology, 27*(5), 577–596. doi:10.1080/01443410701308755

Artman, L., Cahan, S., & Avni-Babad, D. (2006). Age, schooling and conditional reasoning. *Cognitive Development, 21*(2), 131–145. doi:10.1016/j.cogdev.2006.01.004

Asher, S. R., & Hymel, S. (1986). Coaching in social skills for children who lack friends in school. *Social Work in Education, 8*(4), 205–218.

Asher, S., & McDonald, K. L. (2009). The behavioral basis of acceptance, rejection, and perceived popularity. In K. H. Rubin, W. Bukowski, & B. Laursen (Eds.), *The handbook of peer interaction, relationships, and groups* (pp. 232–248). New York, NY: Guilford.

Aslin, R. N. (2012). Infant eyes: A window on cognitive development. *Infancy, 17*, 126–140.

Aslin, R. N., & Schlaggar, B. L. (2006). Is myelination the precipitating neural event for language development in infants and toddlers? *Neurology, 66*(3), 304–305.

Association for Supervision and Curriculum Development. (2011). *Making the case for educating the whole child*. Alexandria, VA: Author.

Atance, C. M., & Jackson, L. K. (2009). The development and coherence of future-oriented behaviors during the preschool years. *Journal of Experimental Child Psychology, 102*(4), 379–391. doi:10.1016/j.jecp.2009.01.001

Atkinson, J. (2000). *The Developing Visual Brain*. Oxford, UK: Oxford University Press.

Auchus, R. J., & Rainey, W. E. (2004). Adrenarche—physiology, biochemistry, and human disease. *Clinical Endocrinology, 60*, 288–296.

Australian Institute of Family Studies (2005), *Growing up in Australia: The longitudinal study of Australian children: 2004 annual report*. Melbourne: Australian Government, Department of Families, Housing, Community Services and Indigenous Affairs. Retrieved from http:/-/-www.aifs.gov.au/-growingup/-pubs/-ar/-annualreport2004.html

Aviezer, O., Sagi, A., Joels, T., & Ziv, Y. (1999). Emotional availability and attachment representations in kibbutz infants and their mothers. *Developmental Psychology, 35*, 3, 811–821.

Ayala, R., Shu, T., & Tsai, L.-H. (2007). Trekking across the brain: The journey of neuronal migration. *Cell, 128*, 29–43. doi:10.1016/j.cell.2006.12.021

Ayduk, O., Downey, G., & Kim, M. (2001). Rejection sensitivity and depressive symptoms in women. *Personality and Social Psychology Bulletin, 27* (7), 868–877. doi:10.1177/0146167201277009

Ayoub, C., O'Connor, E., Rappolt-Schlichtmann, G., Raikes, H., Chazan-Cohen, R., & Vallotton, C. (2009). Losing ground early: Protection, risk and change in poor children's cognitive performance. *Early Childhood Research Quarterly, 24*, 289–305.

Bachman, J. G., Safron, D. J., Sy, S. R., & Schulenberg, J. E. (2003). Wishing to work: New perspectives on how adolescents' part-time work intensity is linked to educational disengagement, substance use, and other problem behaviours. *International Journal of Behavioral Development, 27*(4), 301–315. doi:10.1080/01650250244000281

Baddeley, A. D. (2001). Is working memory still working? *American Psychologist, 56*(11), 851–864. doi:10.1037/0003-066X.56.11.851

Baddeley, A. D. (2012). Working memory: Theories, models, and controversies. *Annual Review of Psychology, 63*, 1–29.

Baddeley, A. D., & Hitch, G. J. (1974). Working memory. In G. A. Bower (Ed.), *The psychology of learning and motivation: Advances in research and theory*. New York, NY: Academic Press.

Baddeley, A. D., Allen, R., & Hitch, G. J. (2010). Investigating the episodic buffer. *Psychologica Belgica, 50*(3–4), 223–243.

Badovinac, R. L., Werler, M. M., Williams, P. L., Kelsey, K. T., & Hayes, C. (2007). Folic acid-containing supplement consumption during pregnancy and risk for oral clefts: A meta-analysis. *Clinical and Molecular Teratology, 79*, 8–15. doi:10.1002/bdra.20315

Bae, Y., Choy, S., Geddes, C., Sable, J., & Snyder, T. (2000). *Trends in educational equity for girls and women* (NCES 2000–030). Washington, DC: U.S. Government Printing Office.

Bagner, D. M., Pettit, J. W., Lewinsohn, P. M., & Seeley, J. R. (2010). Effect of maternal depression on child behavior: A sensitive period? *Journal of the American Academy of Child & Adolescent Psychiatry, 49*(7), 699–707. doi:10.1097/00004583-201007000-00010

Bailey, T., Le Couteur, A., Gottesman, I., Bolton, P., Simonoff, E., Yuzda, E., & Rutter, M. (1995). Autism as a strongly genetic disorder: Evidence from a British twin study. *Psychological Medicine, 25*, 63–77.

Baillargeon, R. (1987). Object permanence in 3½- and 4½-month-old infants. *Developmental Psychology, 23*(5), 655–664.

Baillargeon, R. (2004). Infants' reasoning about hidden objects: Evidence for event-general and event-specific expectations. *Developmental Science*, 7(4), 391–424. doi:10.1111/j.1467-7687.2004.00357.x

Baillargeon, R. H., Morisset, A., Keenan, K., Normand, C. L., Jeyaganth, S., Boivin, M., & Tremblay, R. E. (2011). The development of prosocial behaviors in young children: Prospective population-based cohort study. *Journal of Genetic Psychology: Research and Theory on Human Development*, *172*(3), 221–251. doi:10.1080/00221325.2010.533719

Baillargeon, R., Kotovsky, L., & Needham, A. (1995). The acquisition of physical knowledge in infancy. In Sperber, D., Premack, D., & Premack, A. J. (Eds.), *Causal cognition: A multidisciplinary debate*. Symposia of the Fyssen Foundation (pp. 79–116). New York, NY: Clarendon/Oxford University Press.

Baird, A. A., Kagan, J., Gaudette, T., Walz, K. A., Hershlag, N., & Boas, D. A. (2002). Frontal lobe activation during object permanence: Data from near-infrared spectroscopy. *NeuroImage*, *16*, 1120–1126.

Baird, G., Pickles, A., Simonoff, E., Charman, T., Sullivan, P., Chandler, S., . . . Brown, D. (2008). Measles vaccination and antibody response in autism spectrum disorders. *Archives of Disease in Children*, *93*, 832–837. doi:10.1136/adc.2007.122937

Bakermans-Kranenburg, M. J., & van IJzendoorn, M. H., Kroonenberg, P. M. (2004). Differences in attachment security between African-American and white children: Ethnicity or socio-economic status. *Infant Behavior and Development*, *27*, 417–433.

Bakti, A., Baron-Cohen, S., Wheelwright, S., Connellan, J., & Ahluwalia, J. (2000). Is there an innate gaze module? Evidence from human neonates. *Infant Behavior & Development*, *23*, 223–229.

Balanced Budget Down Payment Act of 1996, Pub. L. No. 104–99 § 110 Stat. 26, 1996.

Bales, S. N. (2005). *Making the case for youth programs: The Minnesota research*. Washington, DC: FrameWorks Institute.

Bandstra, E. S., Morrow, C. E., Vogel, A. L., Fifer, R. C., Ofir, A. Y., Dausa, A. T., . . . Anthony, J. C. (2002). Longitudinal influence of prenatal cocaine exposure on child language functioning. *Neurotoxicology and Teratology*, *24*, 297–308. doi:10.1016/S0892-0362(02)00192-7

Bandura, A. (1973). *Aggression: A social learning analysis*. Oxford, UK: Prentice-Hall.

Bandura, A. (1977). *Social learning theory*. Oxford, UK: Prentice-Hall.

Bandura, A. (1986). *The social foundations of thought and action: A social cognitive theory*. Englewood Cliffs, NJ: Prentice Hall.

Bandura, A. (1997). *Self-efficacy: The exercise of control*. New York, NY: Freeman/Times Books/Henry Holt.

Bandura, A. (2006). Toward a psychology of human agency. *Perspectives on Psychological Science*, *1*(2), 164–180. doi:10.1111/ j.1745-6916.2006.00011.x

Bandura, A. (2008). An agentic perspective on positive psychology. In S. J. Lopez (Ed.), *Positive psychology: Exploring the best in people* (Vol. 1., pp. 167–196). Westport, CT: Greenwood Publishing Company.

Bandura, A., & Walters, R. (1963). *Social learning and personality development*. New York, NY: Holt, Rinehart, and Winston.

Bandura, A., Caprara, G. V., Barbaranelli, C., Gerbino, M., & Pastorelli, C. (2003). Role of affective self-regulatory efficacy in diverse spheres of psychological functioning. *Child Development*, *74*(3), 769–782. doi:10.1111/ 1467-8624.00567

Bandura, A., Ross, D., & Ross, S. A. (1961). Transmission of aggression through imitation of aggressive models. *The Journal of Abnormal and Social Psychology*, *63*(3), 575–582. doi:10.1037/ h0045925

Bangerter, A., & Heath, C. (2004). The Mozart effect: Tracking the evolution of a scientific legend. *British Journal of Social Psychology*, *43*, 605–623. doi:10.1348/0144666042565353

Baranov-Krylov, I. N., Kuznetsova, T. G., & Ratnikova, V. K. (2009). Attention parameters in visual search tasks in different age groups. *Neuroscience and Behavioral Physiology*, *39*(5), 481–487. doi:10.1007/s11055-009-9153-3

Barber, B. K. (1996). Parental psychological control: Revisiting a neglected construct. *Child Development*, *67*(6), 3296–3319. doi:10. 2307/1131780

Barber, B. K., Stolz, H. E., & Olsen, J. A. (2005). Parental support, psychological control, and behavioral control: Assessing relevance across time, culture, and method. *Monographs of the Society for Research in Child Development*, *70*(4), 1–137.

Barker, G., & Verani, F. (2008). Men's participation as fathers in the Latin American and Caribbean region: A critical literature review with policy considerations. Rio de Janeiro, Brazil: Promundo and Save the Children–Sweden. Retrieved from http://www.promundo.org.br

Barkley, R. A. (2011). Attention-deficit/hyperactivity disorder, self-regulation, and executive functioning. In K. D. Vohs & R. F. Baumesiter (Eds.), *Handbook of self-regulation: research, theory and application* (2nd ed., pp. 551–563). New York, NY: Guilford.

Barkley, R. A., Fischer, M., Smallish, L., & Fletcher, K. (2006). Young adult outcome of hyperactive children: Adaptive functioning in major life activities. *Journal of American Academy of Child and Adolescent Psychiatry*, *45*(2), 192–202. doi:10.1097/01.chi.0000189134.97436.e2

Barnard, W. M. (2004). Parent involvement in elementary school and educational attainment. *Children and Youth Services Review*, *26*, 39–62.

Barnett, W. S., Jung, K., Yarosz, D. J., Thomas, J., Hornbeck, A., Stechuk, R., & Burns, S. (2008). Educational effects of the Tools of the Mind curriculum: A randomized trial. *Early Childhood Research Quarterly*, *23*(3), 299–313. doi:10.1016/j.ecresq. 2008.03.001

Barnett, W. S., Lamy, C., & Jung, K. (2005). *The effects of state prekindergarten programs on young children's school readiness in five states*. New Brunswick, NJ: The National Institute for Early Education Research, Rutgers University.

Barnett, W. S., Yarosz, D. J., Thomas, J., Jung, K., & Blanco, D. (2007). Two-way and monolingual English immersion in preschool education: An experimental comparison. *Early Childhood Research Quarterly*, *22*, 277–293.

Baron-Cohen, S. (1995). *Mindblindness: An essay on autism and theory of mind*. Cambridge, MA: MIT Press.

Baron-Cohen, S., Ring, H. A., Bullmore, E. T., Wheelwright, S., Ashwin, C., & Williams, S. C. (2000). The amygdala theory of autism. *Neuroscience Biobehavioral Review*, *24*, 355–364.

Baron-Cohen, S., Tager-Flusberg, H., & Cohen, D. J. (Eds.). (1993). *Understanding other minds: Perspectives from autism*. Oxford, UK: Oxford University Press.

Baroody, A. J., & Li, X. (2009). Mathematics instruction that makes sense for 2- to 5-year olds. In E. L. Essa & M. M. Burnham (Eds.), *Informing our practice: Useful research on young children's development* (pp. 119–135). Washington, DC: NAEYC.

Barr, R. (2010). Transfer of learning between 2D and 3D sources during infancy: Informing theory and practice. *Developmental Review*, *30*(2), 128–154, doi:10.1016/j.dr.2010.03.001

Barr, R. G., Fujiwara, T. (2011). Crying in infants. In C. D. Rudolph, A. M. Rudolph, G. E. Lister, L. R. First, & A. A. Gershon (Eds.), *Rudolph's pediatrics* (22nd ed., pp. 318–321). New York, NY: McGraw–Hill.

Barr, R. G., Konner, M., Bakeman, R., & Adamson, L. (1991). Crying in !Kung San infants: A test of the cultural specificity hypothesis. *Developmental Medicine and Child Neurology*, *33*, 601–610.

Barr, R. G., Paterson, J. A., MacMartin, L. M., Lehtonen, L., & Young, S. N. (2005). Prolonged and unsoothable crying bouts in infants with and without colic. *Journal of Developmental and Behavioral Pediatrics*, *26*(1), 14–23.

Barr, R., & Hayne, H. (1999). Developmental changes in imitation from television during infancy. *Child Development*, *70*(5), 1067–1081. doi:10.1111/1467-8624.0007

Barr, R., & Hayne, H. (2003). It's not what you know, it's who you know: Older siblings facilitate imitation during infancy. *International Journal of Early Years Education*, *11*, 7–21.

Barr, R., Dowden, A., & Hayne, H. (1996). Developmental changes in deferred imitation by 6- to 24-month-old infants. *Infant Behavior & Development*, *19*(2), 159–170. doi:10.1016/S0163-6383(96)90015-6

Barr, R., Lauricella, A., Zack, E., & Calvert, S. L. (2010). Infant and early childhood exposure to adult-directed and child-directed television programming: Relations with cognitive skills at age four. *Merrill-Palmer Quarterly: Journal of Developmental Psychology*, *56*(1), 21–48. doi:10.1353/mpq.0.0038

Barr, R., Muentener, P., & Garcia, A. (2007). Age-related changes in deferred imitation from television by 6- to 8-month-olds. *Developmental Science*, *10*(6), 910–921.

Barrett, L. F. (2006). Are emotions natural kinds? *Perspectives on Psychological Science*, *1*(1), 28–58.

Barrett, L. F. (2009). Understanding the mind by measuring the brain: Lessons from measuring behavior. *Perspectives on Psychological Science*, *4*, 314–318.

Barrett, L. F., & Satpute, A. (2013). Large-scale brain networks in affective and social neuroscience: Towards an integrative architecture of the human brain. *Current Opinion in Neurobiology*, *23*, 1–12.

Barth, J. M., & Bastiani, A. (1997). A longitudinal study of emotion recognition and preschool children's social behavior. *Merrill-Palmer Quarterly, 43*(1), 107–128.

Bartlett, S. (2003). Water, sanitation and urban children: The need to go beyond "improved" provision. *Environment and Urbanization, 15*(2), 57–71. doi:10.1177/095624780301500220

Bartlett, S., Hart, R., Satterthwaite, D., de la Barra, X., & Missair, A. (1999). *Cities for children: Children's rights, poverty and urban management.* London, UK: Earthscan.

Basch, C. E. (2010). Healthier students are better learners: A missing link in school reforms to close the achievement gap. *Equity Matters: Research Review No. 6.* New York, NY: Columbia University.

Bass, L. E., & Warehime, M. N. (2011). Family structure and child health outcomes in the United States. *Sociological Inquiry, 81*(4), 527–548. doi:10.1111/j.1475-682X.2011.00391.x

Bateman, D. A., & Chiriboga, C. A. (2000). Dose-response effect of cocaine on newborn head circumference. *Pediatrics, 106*(3), E33. doi:10.1542/peds.106.3.e33

Bates, E., & Elman, J. L. (2000). The ontogeny and phylogeny of language: A neural network perspective. In S. Parker, J. Langer, & M. McKinney (Eds.), *Biology, brains, and behavior: The evolution of human development* (pp. 89–130). Santa Fe, NM: School of American Research Press.

Bates, J. E. (1987). Temperament in infancy. In J. D. Osoksky (Ed.), *Handbook of infant development* (pp. 1101–1149). New York, NY: Wiley.

Bates, J. E., Viken, R. J., Alexander, D. B., Beyers, J., & Stockton, L. (2002). Sleep and adjustment in preschool children: Sleep diary reports by mothers relate to behavior reports by teachers. *Child Development, 73*(1), 62–74.

Bates, J., Marvinney, D., Kelly, T., Dodge, K., Bennett, T., & Pettit, G. (1994). Childcare history and kindergarten adjustment. *Developmental Psychology, 30,* 690–700.

Bauer, C. R., Langer, J. C., Shankaran, S., Bada, H., Lester, B., Wright, L. L., . . . Verter, J. (2005). Acute neonatal effects of cocaine exposure during pregnancy. *Archives of Pediatric and Adolescent Medicine, 159,* 824–834. doi:10.1001/archpedi.159.9.824

Bauer, P. J. (2002). Long-term recall memory: Behavioral and neuro-developmental changes in the first 2 years of life. *Current Directions in Psychological Science, 11,* 137–141.

Bauer, P. J. (2004). Getting explicit memory off the ground: Step toward construction of a neuro-developmental account of changes in the first two years of life. *Developmental Review: Special Issue: Memory Development in the New Millennium, 24*(4), 347–373. doi:10.1016/j.dr.2004.08.003

Bauer, P. J. (2005). Developments in declarative memory: Decreasing susceptibility to storage failure over the second year of life. *Psychological Science, 16,* 41–47.

Bauer, P. J. (2006). Constructing a past in infancy: A neuro-developmental account. *Trends in Cognitive Science, 10*(4), 175–181. doi:10.1016/j.tics.2006.02.009

Bauer, P. J. (2007). Remembering the times of our lives: Memory in infancy and beyond. *The developing mind series.* Mahwah, NJ: Erlbaum.

Bauer, P. J., & Lukowski, A. F. (2010). The memory is in the details: Relations between memory for the specific features of events and long-term recall during infancy. *Journal of Experimental Child Psychology, 107*(1), 1–14. doi:10.1016/j.jecp.2010.04.004

Bauer, P. J., San Souci, P., & Pathman, T. (2010). Infant memory. *Wiley Interdisciplinary Reviews: Cognitive Science, 1,* 267–277.

Bauer, P. J., Wenner, J. A., Dropik, P. L., & Wewerka, S.S. (2000). Parameters of remembering and forgetting in the transition from infancy to early childhood. *Monographs of the Society for Research in Child Development. 65*(4), 1–204.

Bauer, P. J., Wiebe, S. A., Carver, L. J., Waters, J. M., & Nelson, C. A. (2003). Developments in long-term explicit memory later in the first year of life: Behavioral and electrophysiological indices. *Psychological Science, 14,* 629–635. doi:10.1046/j.0956–7976.2003.psci_1476.x

Bauer, P. J., Wiebe, S. A., Waters, J. M., & Bangston, S. K. (2001). Reexposure breeds recall: Effects of experience on 9-month-olds' ordered recall. *Journal of Experimental Child Psychology, 80*(2), 174–200. doi:10.1006/jecp.2000.2628

Baumard, N., Mascaro, O., & Chevallier, C. (2012). Preschoolers are able to take merit into account when distributing goods. *Developmental Psychology, 48*(2), 492–498. doi:10.1037/a0026598

Baumeister, R. R., Campbell, J. D., Krueger, J. J., & Vohs, K. D. (2005). Exploding the self-esteem myth. In S. O. Lilienfeld, J. Ruscio, & J. Steven, (Eds.), *Navigating the mindfield: A user's guide to distinguishing science from pseudoscience in mental health* (pp. 575–587). Amherst, NY: Prometheus Books.

Baumrind, D. (1967). Child care practices anteceding three patterns of preschool behavior. *Genetic Psychology Monographs, 75*(1), 43–88.

Baumrind, D. (1971). Current patterns of parental authority. *Developmental Psychology, 4*(1, Pt. 2), 1–103. doi:10.1037/h0030372

Baumrind, D. (1989). *Rearing competent children.* San Francisco, CA: Jossey-Bass.

Baumrind, D. (1991). The influence of parenting style on adolescent competence and substance use. *The Journal of Early Adolescence, 11*(1), 56–95.

Baverstock, K., & Dillwyn, W. (2006). The Chernobyl accident 20 years on: An assessment of the health consequences and the international response. *Environmental Health Perspectives, 114*(9), 1312–1317. doi:10.1289/ehp.9113

Baydar, N., & Brooks-Gunn, J. (1991). Effects of maternal employment and child care arrangements in infancy on preschoolers' cognitive and behavioral outcomes: Evidence from the children of the NLSY. *Developmental Psychology, 27,* 918–931.

Bayley, N. (1935). The development of motor abilities during the first three years. *Monographs for the Society of Research in Child Development, 1,* 1–26.

Bayley, N. (1969). *Bayley Scales of Infant Development.* New York, NY: Psychological Corporation.

Bayley, N. (1993). *Bayley Scales of Infant Development* (2nd ed.). New York, NY: Psychological Corporation.

Bayley, N. (2005). *Bayley Scales of Infant and Toddler Development* (3rd ed.). San Antonio, TX: Harcourt Assessment.

Bayliss, D. M., Jarrold, C., Baddeley, A. D., Gunn, D., & Leigh, E. (2005). Mapping the developmental constraints on working memory span performance. *Developmental Psychology, 41*(4), 579–597. doi:10.1037/0012–1649.41.4.579

Bear, M. F., Connors, B. W., & Paradiso, M. A. (2007). *Neuroscience: Exploring the brain* (3rd ed.). Philadelphia, PA: Lippincott Williams & Wilkins.

Bear, M., Connors, B., & Paradiso, M. (2007). *Neuroscience: Exploring the brain.* Philadelphia, PA: Lippincott Williams & Wilkins.

Bearison, D. J., Miniam, N., & Granowetter, L. (2002). Medical management of asthma and folk medicine in a Hispanic community. *Journal of Pediatric Psychology, 27*(4), 385–392.

Bearman, P. S., & Brückner, H. (2001). Promising the future: Virginity pledges and first intercourse. *American Journal of Sociology, 106*(4), 859–912.

Beasley, B., & Standley, T. C. (2002). Shirts vs. skins: Clothing as an indicator of gender role stereotyping in video games. *Mass Communication and Society, 5*(3), 279–293. doi:10.1207/S15327825MCS0503_3

Beaver, K. M. & Belsky, J. (2012). Gene-environment interaction and the intergenerational transmission of parenting: Testing the differential susceptibility hypothesis. *Psychiatric Quarterly, 83*(1), 29–40. doi:10.1007/s11126–011-9180–4

Beck, A. T. (1967). *Depression: Clinical, experimental, and theoretical aspects.* New York, NY: Harper & Row.

Beck, A. T., & Weishaar, M. E. (2008). Cognitive therapy. In R. J. Corsini, D. Wedding, & F. Dumont (Eds.), *Current psychotherapies* (pp. 263–294). Belmont, CA: Thomson Higher Education.

Beck, A. T., Haigh, E. A. P., & Baber, K. F. (2012). Biological underpinnings of the cognitive model of depression: A prototype for psychoanalytic research. *Psychoanalytic Review, 99*(4), 515–537. doi:10.1521/prev.2012.99.4.515

Becker, C. B., McDaniel, L., Bull, S., Powell, M., & McIntyre, K. (2012). Can we reduce eating disorder risk factors in female college athletes? A randomized exploratory investigation of two peer-led interventions. *Body Image, 9*(1), 31–42. doi:10.1016/j.bodyim.2011.09.005

Bedard, K. K., & Marks, A. K. (2010). Current psychological perspectives on adolescent lesbian identity development. *Journal of Lesbian Studies, 14*(1), 16–25. doi:10.1080/10894160903058857

Bedrova, E., & Leong, D. J. (1996). *Tools of the mind: The Vygotskian approach to early childhood education.* Upper Saddle River, NJ: Prentice-Hall.

Beer, J. S., & Ochsner, K. N. (2006). Social cognition: A multi-level analysis. *Brain Research, 1079*(1), 98–105. doi:10.1016/j.brainres.2006.01.0 02

Behar, D. M.,Villems, R., Soodyall, J., Blue-Smith, J., Pereira, L., Metspalu, E., . . . Genographic Consortium. (2008). The dawn of human matrilineal diversity. *American Journal of Human Genetics, 82*(5), 1130–1140.

Behrens, K. Y., Main, M., & Hesse, E. (2007). Mothers' attachment status as determined by the adult attachment interview predicts their 6-year-olds' reunion responses: A study conducted in Japan. *Developmental Psychology 43*(6), 1553–1567.

Beitel A., & Parke R. (1998). Paternal involvement in infancy: The role of maternal and paternal attitudes. *Journal of Family Psychology, 12*, 268–288.

Bekkers, R., & Wiepking, P. (2011). Accuracy of self-reports on donations to charitable organizations. *Quality & Quantity: International Journal of Methodology, 45*(6), 1369–1383. doi:10.1007/s11135-010-9341-9

Bell, E. R., Greenfield, D. B., & Bulotsky-Shearer, R. J. (2013). Classroom age composition and rates of change in school readiness for children enrolled in Head Start. *Early Childhood Research Quarterly, 28*(1), 1–10. doi:10.1016/j.ecresq.2012.06.002

Bell, M. A., & Fox, N. A. (1992). The relations between frontal brain electrical activity and cognitive development during infancy. *Child Development, 63*(5), 1142–1163.

Bell, M. A., & Wolfe, C. D. (2007). Changes in brain functioning from infancy to early childhood: Evidence from EEG power and coherence working memory tasks. *Developmental Neuropsychology, 31*(1), 21–38. doi:10.1080/87565640709336885

Bellagamba, F., Camaioni, L., & Colonnesi, C. (2006). Change in children's understanding of others' intentional actions. *Developmental Science, 9*(2), 182–188.

Belsky, J. (1986). Infant day care: A cause for concern? *Zero to Three, 6*, 1–9.

Belsky, J. (1990). Consequences of child care for children's development: A deconstructionist view. In A. Booth (Ed.), *Child care in the 1990s: Trends and consequences* (pp. 83–94). Hillsdale, NJ: Erlbaum.

Belsky, J., & Eggebeen, D. (1991). Early and extensive maternal employment and young children's socioemotional development: Children of the national longitudinal survey of youth. *Journal of Marriage and the Family, 53*, 1083–1110.

Belsky, J., Conger, R., & Capaldi, D. (2009). The intergenerational transmission of parenting: Introduction to the special section. *Developmental Psychology, 45*(5), 1201–1204. doi:10.1037/a0016245

Belsky, J., Steinberg, L., & Draper, P. (1991). Childhood experience, interpersonal development, and reproductive strategy: An evolutionary theory of socialization. *Child Development, 62*(4), 647–670.

Belsky, J., Steinberg, L., Houts, R. M., Friedman, S. L., DeHart, G., Cauffman, E., . . . NICHD Early Child Care Research Network. (2007). Family-rearing antecedents of pubertal timing. *Child Development, 78*(4), 1302–1321.

Belsky, J., Vandell, D. L., Burchinal, M., Clarke-Stewart, K. A., McCartney, K., Owen, M. T., & NICHD Early Child Care Research Network. (2007). Are there long-term effects of early child care? *Child Development, 78*, 681–701.

Bender, M. A., & Hobbs, W. (2003). Sickle cell disease. *Gene Reviews*. Retrieved from http://www.ncbi.nlm.nih.gov/bookshelf/br.fcgi?book=gene&part=sickle(pmid: 20301551)

Bendersky, M., Bennett, D., & Lewis, M. (2006). Aggression at age 5 as a function of prenatal exposure to cocaine, gender, and environmental risk. *Journal of Pediatric Psychology, 31*, 71–84. doi:10.1093/jpepsy/jsj025

Benes, F. M. (1994). Development of the corticolimbic system. In G. Dawson & K. W. Fischer (Eds.), *Human behavior and the developing brain*. New York, NY: Guilford.

Benetti, S., & Roopnarine, J. (2006). Paternal involvement with school-aged children in Brazilian families: Association with childhood competence. *Sex Roles, 55*, 669–678.

Benigno, J. P., Byrd, D. L., McNamara, J. P. H., Berg, K. W., & Farrar, J. M. (2011). Talking through transitions: Microgenetic changes in preschoolers' private speech and executive functioning. *Child Language Teaching and Therapy, 27*(3), 269–285. doi:10.1177/0265659010394385

Ben-Isaac, E., Schrager, S. M., Keefer, M., & Chen, A. Y. (2010). National profile of nonemergent pediatric emergency department visits. *Pediatrics, 125*(3), 454–459. doi:10.1542/peds.2009-0544

Benjet, C., & Kazdin, A. E. (2003). Spanking children: The controversies, findings and new directions. *Clinical Psychology Review, 23*(2), 197–224. doi:10.1016/S0272-7358(02)00206-4

Benson, J. B. (1993). Season of birth and onset of locomotion: Theoretical and methodological implications. *Infant Behavior and Development, 16*(1), 69–81. doi:10.1016/0163-6383(93)80029-8

Benson, P. L., Leffert, N., Scales, P. C., & Blyth, D. A. (1998). Beyond the "village" rhetoric: Creating healthy communities for children and adolescents. *Applied Developmental Science, 2*(3), 138–159. doi:10.1207/s1532480xads0203_3

Benson, P. L., Scales, P. C., Hamilton, S. F., & Sesma, A. (2006). Positive youth development: Theory, research, and applications. In R. M. Lerner & W. Damon (Eds.), *Handbook of child psychology: Vol. 1. Theoretical models of human development* (6th ed., pp. 894–941). Hoboken, NJ: Wiley.

Ben-Zur, H., & Reshef-Kfir, Y. (2003). Risk taking and coping strategies among Israeli adolescents. *Journal of Adolescence, 26*(3), 255–265. doi:10.1016/S0140–1971(03)00016–2

Beran, T., Ramirez-Serrano, A., Kuzyk, R., Fior, M., & Nugent, S. (2011). Understanding how children understand robots: Perceived animism in child-robot interaction. *International Journal of Human-Computer Studies, 69*(7–8), 539–550. doi:10.1016/j.ijhcs.2011.04.003

Berdan, L. E., Keane, S. P., & Calkins, S. D. (2008). Temperament and externalizing behavior: Social preference and perceived acceptance as protective factors. *Developmental Psychology, 44*, 957–968. doi:10.1037/0012-1649.44.4.957

Berg, C. J., Callaghan, W. M., Syverson, C. & Henderson, Z. (2010). Pregnancy-related mortality in the United States, 1998 to 2005. *Obstetrics & Gynecology, 116*(6), 1302–1309. doi:10.1097/AOG.0b013e3181fdfb11

Bergen, D. (2008). *Human development: Traditional and contemporary theories*. Upper Saddle River, NJ: Pearson/Prentice Hall.

Bergen, D., & Coscia, J. (2001). *Brain research and childhood education: Implications for educators*. Olney, MD: Association for Childhood Education International. Retrieved from the ERIC database (ED458943).

Berger, L. M., Hill, J., & Waldfogel, J. (2005). Maternity leave, early maternal employment and child health and development in the US. *Economic Journal, 115*, F29–F47.

Berger, S. E., Theuring, C. F., & Adolph, K. E. (2007). How and when infants learn to climb stairs. *Infant Behavior and Development, 30*(1), 36–49.

Bergeron, M. (2007). Improving health through youth sports: Is participation enough? *New Directions for Youth Development, 115*, 27–41.

Bergström, M., Kieler, H., & Waldenström, U. (2009). Effects of natural childbirth preparation versus standard antenatal education on epidural rates, experience of childbirth and parental stress in mothers and fathers: A randomised controlled multicentre trial. *British Journal of Obstetrics and Gynaecology, 116*(9), 1167–1176.

Berk, L. E., & Harris, S. (2003). Vygotsky, Lev. In L. Nadel (Ed.), *Encyclopedia of cognitive science*. London, UK: Macmillan Reference Ltd.

Berk, L. E., & Winsler, A. (1999). *Scaffolding children's learning: Vygotsky and early childhood education*. Washington, DC: National Association for the Education of Young Children.

Berk, L. E., Mann, T. D., & Ogan, A. T. (2006). *Make-believe play: Wellspring for development of self-regulation* (pp. 74–100). New York, NY: Oxford University Press, New York, NY.

Berkman, N. D., DeWalt, D. A., Pignone, M. P., Sheridan, S. L., Lohr, K. N., Lux, L., . . . Bonito, A. J. (2004). *Literacy and Health Outcomes. Evidence Report/TechnologyAssessment No. 87*. AHRQ Publication No. 04-E007-2. Rockville, MD: Agency for Healthcare Research and Quality.

Berndt, T. (2004). Friendship quality and social development. *Current Directions in Psychological Science, 11*(1), 7–10. doi:10.1111/1467-8721.00157

Bernier, A., Carlson, S., & Whipple, N. (2010). From external regulation to self-regulation: Early parenting precursors of young children's executive functioning. *Child Development, 81*(1), 326–339. doi:10.1111/j.1467-8624.2009.01397.x

Berry, J. W. (1990). Acculturation and adaptation: A general framework. In W. H. Holtzman & T. H. Bornemann (Eds.), *Mental health of immigrants and refugees* (pp. 90–102). Austin, TX: Hogg Foundation for Mental Health.

Berry, J. W., Phinney, J. S., Sam, D. L., & Vedder, P. (2006). Immigrant youth: Acculturation, identity, and adaptation. *Applied Psychology: An International Review, 55*(3), 303–332. doi:10.1111/j.1464-0597.2006.00256.x

Berthier, N., & Keen, R. (2006). Development of reaching in infancy. *Experimental Brain Research, 169*, 507–518. doi:10.1007/s00221-005-0169-9

Best, J. R., & Miller, P. H. (2010). A developmental perspective on executive function. *Child Development, 81*(6), 1641–1660. doi:10.1111/j.1467-8624.2010.01499.x

Betancourt, J. R., Green, A. R., King, R. K., Tan-McGrory, A., Cervantes, M., & Renfrew, M. (2009). *Improving quality and achieving equity:*

*A guide for hospital leaders.* Boston, MA: The Disparities Solutions Center.

Bhaskaram, P. (2002). Micronutrient malnutrition, infection and immunity: An overview. *Nutrition Review, 60*(5), S40–S45. doi:10.1301/00296640260130722

Bhutta, A. T., Cleves, M. A., Casey, P. H., Cradock, M. M., & Anand, K. J. (2002). Cognitive and behavioral outcomes of school-aged children who were born preterm: A meta-analysis. *The Journal of the American Medical Association, 288*(6), 728–737. doi:10.1001/jama.288.6.728

Bialystok, E. (2007). Acquisition of literacy in bilingual children: A framework for research. Language Learning, 57(Suppl. 1), 45–77. doi:10.1111/j.1467-9922.2007.00412.x

Bialystok, E., & Barac, R. (2012). Emerging bilingualism: Dissociating advantages for metalinguistic awareness and executive control. *Cognition, 122*(1), 67–73. doi:10.1016/j.cognition.2011.08.003

Bialystok, E., Craik, F. I. M., & Ryan, J. (2006). Executive control in a modified antisaccade task: Effects of aging and bilingualism. *Journal of Experimental Psychology: Learning, Memory, and Cognition, 32*(6), 1341–1354. doi:10.1037/0278-7393.32.6.1341

Bialystok, E., Majumder, S., & Martin, M. M. (2003). Developing phonological awareness: Is there a bilingual advantage? *Applied Psycholinguistics, 24*(1), 27–44.

Bialystok, E., McBride-Chang, C., & Luk, G. (2005). Bilingualism, language proficiency, and learning to read in two writing systems. *Journal of Educational Psychology*, 97(4):580–590.

Bigner, J. J., & Jacobsen, R. B. (1989). Parenting behaviors of homosexual and heterosexual fathers. In F. W. Bozett (Ed.), *Homosexuality and the family* (pp. 173–186). New York, NY: Harrington Park Press.

Bing, N. M., Nelson, W. M., & Wesolowski, K. L. (2009). Comparing the effects of amount of conflict on children's adjustment following parental divorce. *Journal of Divorce & Remarriage, 50*(3), 159–171. doi:10.1080/10502550902717699

Biringen, Z. (2000). Emotional availability: Conceptualization and research findings. *American Journal of Orthopsychiatry, 70*, 104–114.

Biringen, Z., & Robinson, J. (1991). Emotional availability: A reconceptualization for research. *American Journal of Orthopsychiatry, 61*, 258–271.

Birss, S. A. (2007). Transition to parenthood: Promoting the parent-infant relationship. In J. K. Nugent, C. H. Keefer, S. Minear, L. C. Johnson, & Y. Blanchard (Eds.). *Understanding newborn behavior and early relationships: The Newborn Behavioral Observations (NBO) system handbook* (pp. 27–49). Baltimore, MD: Paul H. Brookes.

Bishop-Josef, S. J., & Zigler, E. F. (2011). Play and Head Start. In S. J. Bishop-Josef & E. F. Zigler (Eds.), *Play in clinical practice: Evidence-based approaches* (pp. 293–317). New York, NY: Guilford.

Bitler, M., & Haider, S. (2009). *An economic view of food deserts in the United States.* Ann Arbor, MI: University of Michigan National Poverty Center.

Bjorklund, D. F., & Douglas, R. N. (1997). The development of memory strategies. In N. Cowan (Ed.), *The development of memory in childhood* (pp. 201–246). Hove, UK: Psychology Press/Erlbaum.

Bjorklund, D. F., & Rosenblum, K. E. (2002). Context effects in children's selection and use of simple arithmetic strategies. *Journal of Cognition and Development, 3*(2) 225–242. doi:10.1207/S15327647JCD0302_5

Bjornson, K. F., Song, K., Zhou, C., Coleman, K., Myaing, M., & Robinson, S. L. (2011). Walking stride rate patterns for children and youth. *Pediatric Physical Therapy, 23*(4), 354–363. doi:10.1097/PEP.0b013e3182352201

Black, R. E., Allen, L. H., Bhutta, Z. A., Caulfield, L. E., de Onis, M., Ezzati, M., . . . Rivera, J. (2008). Maternal and child undernutrition: Global and regional exposures and health consequences. *Lancet, 371*(9608), 243–260. doi:10.1016/S0140-6736(07)61690-0

Blackwell, L. S., Trzesniewski, K. H., & Dweck, C. S. (2007). Implicit theories of intelligence predict achievement across an adolescent transition: A longitudinal study and an intervention. *Child Development, 78*(1), 246–263. doi:10.1111/j.1467–8624.2007.00995.x

Blair, C. (2002). School readiness: Integrating cognition and emotion in a neurobiological conceptualization of children's functioning at school entry. *American Psychologist, 57*, 111–127.

Blake, S. M., Simkin, L., Ledsky, R., Perkins, C., & Calabrese, J. M. (2001). Effects of a parent-child communications intervention on young adolescents' risk for early onset of sexual intercourse. *Family Planning Perspectives, 33*(2), 52–61.

Blakemore, J. E. O. (2003). Children's beliefs about violating gender norms: Boys shouldn't look like girls, and girls shouldn't act like boys. *Sex Roles, 48*(9–10), 411–419. doi:10.1023/A:1023574427720

Blakemore, S. (2008). The social brain in adolescence. *Nature Reviews Neuroscience, 9*, 267–277. doi:10.1038/nrn2353

Blakemore, S. (2012). Imaging brain development: The adolescent brain. *NeuroImage, 61*(2), 397–406. doi:10.1016/j.neuroimage.2011.11.080

Blakemore, S. J., Burnett, S., & Dahl, R. E. (2010). The role of puberty in the developing adolescent brain. *Human Brain Mapping, 31*(6), 926–933.

Blakemore, S. J., Burnett, S., & Dahl, R. E. (2010). The role of puberty in the developing adolescent brain. *Human Brain Mapping, 31*(6), 926–933.

Blanchette, H. (2011). The rising cesarean delivery rate in America: What are the consequences? *Obstetrics & Gynecology, 118*(3), 687–690.

Blasi, A. (1983). Moral cognition and moral action: A theoretical perspective. *Developmental Review, 3*, 178–210. doi:10.1016/0273-2297(83)90029-1

Blass, E. M., & Shah, A. (1995). Pain-reducing properties of sucrose in human newborns. *Chemical Senses, 20*, 29–35. doi:10.1093/chemse/20.1.29

Blickstein, I. (2006). Does assisted reproduction technology, per se, increase the risk of preterm birth? *BJOG: An International Journal of Obstetrics & Gynecology, 113*(Suppl. 3), 68–71. doi:10.1111/j.1471–0528.2006.01126.x

Bloom, B., Cohen, R. A., & Freeman, G. (2011). Summary health statistics for U.S. children: National Health Interview Survey, 2010. *Vital Health Statistics, 10*(250). Retrieved from http://www.cdc.gov/nchs/data/series/sr_10/sr10_250.pdf

Bloom, D. (2010). Programs and policies to assist high school dropouts in the transition to adulthood. *Future of Children, 20*(1), 89–108. doi:10.1353/foc.0.0039

Bloom, P. (2010). The moral life of babies. *The New York Times Magazine.* Retrieved from http://www.nytimes.com/2010/05/09/magazine/09babies-t.html

Blum, D. (2010, February 5). Will science take the field? *The New York Times*, p. A25. Retrieved from http//www.nytimes.com/2010/02/05/opinion/05blum.html?_r=0

Blumenfeld, P., Modell, J., Bartko, W. T., Secada, W. G., Fredricks, J. A., Friedal, J., & Paris, A. (2005). School engagement of inner-city students during middle childhood. In C. R. Cooper, C. T. Garcia Coll, W. T. Bartko, H. Davis, & C. Chatman (Eds.), *Developmental pathways through middle childhood: Rethinking contexts and diversity as resources* (pp. 145–170). Mahwah, NJ: Erlbaum.

Blustein, D. L., Kenna, A. C., Gill, N., & DeVoy, J. E. (2008). The psychology of working: A new framework for counseling practice and public policy. *Career Development Quarterly, 56*(4), 294–308.

Boake, C. (2002). From the Binet-Simon to the Wechsler-Bellevue: Tracing the history of intelligence testing. *Journal of Clinical & Experimental Neuropsychology, 24*(3), 383–405.

Bodenheimer, T., Wagner, E. H., & Grumbach, K. (2002). Improving primary care for patients with chronic illness: The chronic care model part 2. *Journal of the American Medical Association, 288*, 1909–1914.

Bodrova, E., & Leong, D. J. (2003). *Learning and development of preschool children from the Vygotskian perspective.* New York, NY, US: Cambridge University Press.

Boersma, M., Kemner, C., de Reus, M. A., Collin, G., Snijders, T. M. Hofman, D., . . . van den Heuvel, M. P. (2013). Disrupted functional brain networks in autistic toddlers. *Brain Connectivity.* 3(1): 41–49. doi:10.1089/brain.2012.0127

Bogin, B. (1999). *Patterns of human growth* (2nd Ed.). Cambridge: Cambridge University Press.

Bogin, B., Smith, P., Orden, A. B., Varela Silva, M. I., & Loucky, J. (2002). Rapid change in height and body proportions of Maya American children. *American Journal of Human Biology, 14*, 753–761. doi:10.1002/ajhb.10092

Boice, J. D., Jr. (2006). Thyroid disease 60 years after Hiroshima and 20 years after Chernobyl. *Journal of the American Medical Association, 295*(9), 1060–1062. doi:10.1001/jama.295.9.1060

Bokhorst, C. L., Sumter, S. R., & Westenberg, P. M. (2010). Social support from parents, friends, classmates, and teachers in children and adolescents aged 9 to 18 years: Who is perceived as most supportive? *Social Development, 19*(2), 417–426. doi:10.1111/j.1467–9507.2009.00540.x

Bolli, R., Chugh, A. R., D'Amario, D., Loughran, J. H., Stoddard, M. F., Ikram, S., Beache, G., . . . Anversa, P. (2011). Cardiac stem cells in patients with ischaemic cardiomyopathy (SCIPIO): Initial results of a randomised phase 1 trial. *Lancet, 378*(9806), 1847–1857. doi:10.1016/S0140–6736(11)61590–0

Bonach, K. (2005). Factors contributing to quality coparenting: Implications for family policy. *Journal of Divorce & Remarriage, 43*(3–4), 79–104. doi:http:10.1300/J087v43n03_05

Bonder, B., Martin, L., & Miracle, A. W. (2002). *Culture in clinical care.* Thorofare, NJ: SLACK Incorporated.

Bonney, J. F., Kelley, M. L., & Levant, R. F. (1999). A model of fathers' behavioral involvement in child care in dual-earner families. *Journal of Family Psychology, 13*, 401–415.

Booth, J. L., & Siegler, R. S. (2008). Numerical magnitude representations influence arithmetic learning. *Child Development, 79*(4), 1016–1031. doi:10.1111/j.1467-8624.2008.01173.x

Bornstein, M. H. (1984). A descriptive taxonomy of psychological categories used by infants. In C. Sophian (Ed.), *Origins of cognitive skills* (pp. 313-338). Hillsdale, NJ: Erlbaum.

Bornstein, M. H. (1985). Colour-name versus shape-name learning in young children. *Journal Child Language, 12*(2), 387–393.

Bornstein, M. H. (2003). Parenting and child development: Intracultural and intercultural perspectives. In C. Poderico, P. Venuti, & R. Marcone (Eds.), *Diverse culture: Bambini diversi* (pp. 31–56). Rome, Italy: Unicopli.

Bornstein, M. H. (Ed.). (2002). *Handbook of parenting: Practical issues in parenting* (2nd ed., Vol. 5). Mahwah, NJ: Erlbaum.

Bornstein, M. H., Cote, L. R., Maital, S., Painter, K., Park, S., Pascual, L., . . . Vyte, A. (2004). Cross-linguistic analysis of vocabulary in young children: Spanish, Dutch, French, Hebrew, Italian, Korean, and American English. *Child Development, 75*(4), 1115–1139. doi:10.1111/j.1467-8624.2004.00729.x

Bornstein, M. H., Putnick, D. L., Heslington, M., Gini, M., Suwalsky, J. T. D., Venuti, P., de Falco, S., Giusti, Z., & Zingman de Galperín, C. (2008). Mother-child emotional availability in ecological perspective: Three countries, two regions, two genders. *Developmental Psychology, 44*, 666–680.

Bornstein, M. H., Tamis-LeMonda, C. S., Tal, J., Ludemann, P., Toda, S., Rahn, C. W., . . . Vardi, D. (1992). Maternal responsiveness to infants in three societies: The United States, France, and Japan. *Child Development, 63*(4), 808–821.

Borsato, G. N., & Padilla, A. M. (2008). Educational assessment of English-language learners. In L. A. Suzuki & J. G. Ponterotto (Eds.), *Handbook of multicultural assessment: Clinical, psychological, and educational applications* (pp. 471–489). Hoboken, NJ: Wiley.

Borst, G., Poirel, N., Pineau, A., Cassotti, M., & Houde, O. (2012). Inhibitory control efficiency in a Piaget-like class-inclusion task in school-age children and adults: A developmental negative priming study. *Developmental Psychology.* Advance online publication. doi:10.1037/a0029622

Bos, H. M. W., van Balen, F., & van den Boom, D. C. (2007). Child adjustment and parenting in planned lesbian-parent households. *American Journal of Orthopsychiatry*, 77, 38–48. doi:10.1037/0002–9432.77.1.38

Bottcher, L., & Dammeyer, J. (2012). Disability as a dialectical concept: Building on Vygotsky defectology. *European Journal of Special Needs Education*, 27(4), 433–446. doi:10.1080/08856257.2012.711958

Bouchard, M., & Spindler, A. (2010). Groups, gangs, and delinquency: Does organization matter? *Journal of Criminal Justice, 38*(5), 921–933. doi:10.1016/j.jcrimjus.2010.06.009

Bousha, D. M., & Twentyman, C. T. (1984). Mother-child interactional style in abuse, neglect, and control groups: Naturalistic observations in the home. *Journal of Abnormal Psychology, 93*(1), 106–114. doi:10.1037/0021-843X.93.1.106

Bowlby, J. (1951). Maternal care and mental health. *World Health Organization Monograph* (Serial No. 2).

Bowlby, J. (1958). The nature of the child's tie to his mother. *International Journal of Psychoanalysis, 39*, 350–371.

Bowlby, J. (1969). *Attachment and loss: Vol. 1. Attachment.* New York, NY: Basic Books.

Bowlby, J. (1973). *Attachment and loss: Vol. 2. Separation.* New York, NY: Basic Books.

Bowlby, J. (1980). *Attachment and loss: Vol. 3. Loss, sadness and depression.* New York, NY: Basic Books.

Bowlby, J. (1988). *A secure base: Parent-child attachment and healthy human development.* New York, NY: Basic Books.

Bowlby, J. (1989). *Secure and insecure attachment.* New York, NY: Basic Books.

Boyan, A., & Sherry, J. L. (2011). The challenge in creating games for education: Aligning mental models with game models. *Child Development Perspectives, 5*, 82–87. doi:10.1111/j.1750–8606.2011.00160.x

Boyce, P., Condon, J., Barton, J., & Corkindale, C. (2007). First-time fathers' study: Psychological distress in expectant fathers during pregnancy. *Australian and New Zealand Journal of Psychiatry, 41*, 718–725. doi:10.1080/00048670701517959

Boyer, C. B., Shafer, M. A., & Tschann, J. M. (1997). Evaluation of a knowledge- and cognitive-behavioral skills-building intervention to prevent STDs and HIV infection in high school students. *Adolescence, 32*(125), 25–42.

Boyland, E. J., Harrold, J. A., Kirkham, T. C., Corker, C., Cuddy, J., Evans, D., . . . Halford, J. C. G. (2011). Food commercials increase preference for energy-dense foods, particularly in children who watch more television. *Pediatrics, 128*(1), e93-e100. doi:10.1542/peds.2010–1859

Braddick, O., & Atkinson, J. (2011). Development of human visual function. *Vision Research 51*, 1588–1609. doi:10.1016/j.visres.2011.02.018

Bradford, K., & Hawkins, A. J. (2006). Learning competent fathering: A longitudinal analysis of marital intimacy and fathering. *Fathering, 4*(3), 215–234.

Bradley, B. S. (2010) Groupies R Us: Infants' surprising capacity for group-interaction. *Ab Initio International.* Retrieved from http://www.brazelton-institute.com/abinitio2010/art3.html

Branca, F., & Ferrari, M. (2002). Impact of micronutrient deficiencies on growth: The stunting syndrome. *Annuals of Nutrition and Metabolism, 46*, 8–17. doi:10.1159/000066397

Brandt, K., Perry, B., Seligman, S., Tronick, E. (2013). *Infant and early childhood mental health: Core concepts and clinical practice.* Arlington, VA: American Psychiatric Press.

Branum, A. M., & Lukacs, S. L. (2008). *Food allergy among U.S. children: Trends in prevalence and hospitalizations* (Data Brief No. 10). Hyattsville, MD: National Center for Health Statistics.

Braswell, G. S., & Callanan, M. A. (2003). Learning to draw recognizable graphic representations during mother-child interactions. *Merrill-Palmer Quarterly, 49*(4), 471–494. doi:10.1353/mpq.2003.0019

Braun, K. (2011). The prefrontal-limbic system: Development, neuroanatomy, function, and implications for socioemotional development. *Clinical Perinatology, 38*(4), 685–702.

Brazelton, T. B. (1973). Neonatal behavioral assessment scale. *Clinics in Developmental Medicine, No. 50.* London, UK: Heinemann Medical Books; Philadelphia, PA: Lippincott.

Brazelton, T. B. (1984). *Neonatal behavioral assessment scale* (2nd ed.). London, UK: Blackwell; Philadelphia, PA: Lippincott.

Brazelton, T. B. (1992). *Touchpoints: The essential reference: Your child's emotional and behavioral development.* Cambridge, MA: DaCapo Lifelong Books.

Brazelton, T. B. (2009). The role of the neonatal behavioral assessment scale: Personal reflections. In J. K. Nugent, B. J. Petrauskas, & T. B. Brazelton (Eds.), *The newborn as a person: Enabling healthy infant development worldwide.* Hoboken, NJ: Wiley.

Brazelton, T. B., & Nugent, K. (1995). *Neonatal behavioral assessment scale.* London, UK: Mac Keith Press.

Brazelton, T. B., & Nugent, J. K. (2011). *Neonatal behavioral assessment scale* (4th ed.). London, UK: Mac Keith Press.

Brazelton, T. B., Kozlowski, B., & Main, M. (1974). The origins of reciprocity: The early mother-infant interaction. In M. Lewis & L. A. Rosenblum (Eds.), *The effect of the infant on its caregiver* (pp. 49–76). New York, NY: Wiley.

Bredekamp, S., & Copple, C. (Eds.). (1997). *Developmentally appropriate practice in early childhood programs* (Rev. ed.). Washington, DC: NAEYC.

Brehmer, Y., Li, S., Müller, V., von Oertzen, T., & Lindenberger, U. (2007). Memory plasticity across the life span: Uncovering children's latent potential. *Developmental Psychology, 43*(2), 465–478. doi:10.1037/0012–1649.43.2.465

Brennan, K. A., & Shaver, P. R. (1995). Dimensions of adult attachment, affect regulation, and romantic relationship functioning. *Personality and Social Psychology Bulletin, 21*, 267–283.

Brenner, J. S. (2007). Overuse injuries, overtraining, and burnout in child and adolescent athletes. *Pediatrics, 119*(6), 1242–1245. doi:10.1542/peds.2007-0887

Brent, D. A., & Birmaher, B. (2002). Adolescent depression. *New England Journal of Medicine, 347*(9), 667–671. doi:10.1056/NEJMcp012249

Brent, R. L. (1999). Utilization of developmental basic science principles in the evaluation of reproductive risks from pre- and postconception environmental radiation exposures. *Teratology, 59*(4), 181. doi:10.1002/(SICI)1096-9926(199904)59:4<182:AID-TERA2>3.0.CO;2-H

Bretherton, I. (2000). Emotional availability: An attachment perspective. *Attachment and Human Development, 2*, 233–241.

Bricker, D., Squires, J., & Twombly, E. (2003). *The ASQTM:SE user's guide for the ages and stages questionnaires: Social-emotional behaviors.* Baltimore, MD: Paul H. Brookes.

Briggs, G. G., Freeman, R. K., & Yaffe, S. J. (2011). *Drugs in pregnancy and lactation: A reference guide to fetal and neonatal risk (9th ed.).* Philadelphia, PA: Lippincott Williams & Wilkins.

Bril, B., & Ledebt, A. (1998). Head coordination as a means to assist sensory integration in learning to walk. *Neuroscience and Biobehavioral Reviews, 22*, 555–563. doi:10.1016/S0149-7634(97)00044-4

Brinker, R. P., Seifer, R., & Sameroff, A. J. (1994). Relations among maternal stress, cognitive development, and early intervention in middle and low socioeconomic status infants with developmental disabilities. *American Journal on Mental Retardation, 98*, 463–480.

Brisk, M. E. (2006). *Bilingual education: From compensatory to quality schooling* (2nd ed.). Mahwah, NJ: Erlbaum.

Britton, C. (1996). Learning about "the curse": An anthropological perspective on experiences of menstruation. *Women's Studies International Forum, 19*(6), 645–653.

Brocato, D. E., Gentile, D. A., Laczniak, R. N., Maier, J. A., & Ji-Song, M. (2010). Television commercial violence: Potential effects on children. *Journal of Advertising, Special Issue on Advertising and Its Connection to Violence and Abuse, 39*(4), 95–107. doi:10.2753/JOA0091-3367390407

Brocki, K. C., & Bohlin, G. (2004). Executive functions in children aged 6 to 13: A dimensional and developmental study. *Developmental Neuropsychology, 26*(2), 571–593. doi:10.1207/s15326942dn2602_3

Brocki, K. C., & Bohlin, G. (2006). Developmental change in the relation between executive functions and symptoms of ADHD and co-occurring behavior problems. *Infant and Child Development, 15*(1), 19–40. doi:10.1002/icd.413

Broderick, C. B. (1993). *Understanding family process: The basics of family systems theory.* Newbury Park, CA: Sage.

Broerena, S., Murisa, P., Bouwmeestera, S., Field, A. P., & Voerman, J. S. (2011). Processing biases for emotional faces in 4- to 12-year-old non-clinical children: An exploratory study of developmental patterns and relationships with social anxiety and behavioral inhibition. *Journal of Experimental Psychopathology, 2*(4), 454–474.

Broidy, L. M., Nagin, D. S., Tremblay, R. E., Brame, B., Dodge, K. A. , Fergusson, D., . . . Vitaro, F. (2003). Developmental trajectories of childhood disruptive behaviors and adolescent delinquency: A six-site, cross-national study. *Developmental Psychology, 39*(2), 222–245. doi:10.1037/0012-1649.39.2.222

Broidy, L., Cauffman, E., Espelage, D. L., Mazerolle, P., & Piquero, A. (2003). Sex differences in empathy and its relation to juvenile offending. *Violence and Victims, 18*(5), 503–516. doi:10.1891/vivi.2003.18.5.503

Bronfenbrenner, U. (1977). Toward an experimental ecology of human development. *American Psychologist, 32*, 513–531. doi:10.1037/0003-066X.32.7.513

Bronfenbrenner, U., & Morris, P. (2006). The bioecological model of human development. In R. Lerner (Ed.), *Handbook of child psychology: Vol. 1. Theoretical models of human development* (pp. 793–828). Hoboken, NJ: Wiley.

Bronte-Tinkew, J., Carrano, J., Horowitz, A., & Kinukawa, A. (2008). Involvement among resident fathers and links to infant cognitive outcomes. *Journal of Family Issues, 29*(9), 1211–1244. doi:10.1177/0192513X08318145

Brooks-Gunn, J. (2005). Cause for celebration? Sustained effects of early childhood education. *NHSA Dialog, 8*(1), 1–4.

Brooks-Gunn, J., & Paikoff, R. L. (1993). "Sex is a gamble, kissing is a game": Adolescent sexuality and health promotion. In S. Millstein, A. Petersen, & E. Nightingale (Eds.), *Promoting the health of adolescents: New directions for the twenty-first century* (pp. 180–208). New York, NY: Oxford University Press.

Brooks-Gunn, J., Han, W. J., & Waldfogel, J. (2010). First-year maternal employment and child development in the first seven years [Monograph]. *Society for Research in Child Development, 75*(2).

Brooks-Gunn, J., Peterson, A. C., & Eichorn, D. (1985). The study of maturational timing effects in adolescence. *Journal of Youth and Adolescence, 14*, 149–161.

Brooks-Gunn, J., Rouse, C., & McLanahan, S. (2007). Racial and ethnic gaps in school readiness. In R. C. Pianta, M. J. Cox, & K. Snow (Eds.), *School readiness and the transition to kindergarten* (pp. 283–306). Baltimore, MD: Paul H. Brookes

Brooks-Gunn, J., Smith, J., Klebanov, P. K., Duncan, G. J., & Lee, K. (2003). The black-white test score gap in young children: Contributions of test and family characteristics. *Applied Developmental Science, 7*, 239–252.

Broughton, E. (2005). The Bhopal disaster and its aftermath: A review. *Environmental Health: A Global Access Science Source, 4*, 1–6. doi:10.1186/1476-069X-4-6

Brower, C., & Thompson, A. R. (2008). Hemophilia A. *Gene Reviews.* Retrieved from http://www.ncbi.nlm.nih.gov/bookshelf/br.fcgi?book=gene&part=hemo-a (pmid: 20301578)

Brown, A. M. (1990). Development of visual sensitivity to light and color vision in human infants: A critical review. *Vision Research, 30*, 1159–1188.

Brown, B. B. (2004). Adolescents' relationships with peers. In R. M. Lerner & L. Steinberg (Eds.), *Handbook of adolescent psychology* (2nd ed., pp. 363–394). Hoboken, NJ: Wiley.

Brown, B. B., & Huang, B. (1995). Examining parenting practices in different peer contexts: Implications for adolescent trajectories. In L. J. Crockett & A. C. Crouter (Eds.), *Pathways through adolescence: Individual development in relation to social contexts* (pp. 151–174). Hillsdale, NJ: Erlbaum.

Brown, B. B., & Larson, J. (2009). Peer relationships in adolescence. In R. M. Lerner & L. Steinberg (Eds.), *Handbook of adolescent psychology: Vol. 2. Contextual influences on adolescent development* (3rd ed., pp. 74–103). Hoboken, NJ: Wiley.

Brown, S. A., Arnold, D. H., Dobbs, J., & Doctoroff, G. L. (2007). Parenting predictors of relational aggression among Puerto Rican and European American school-age children. *Early Childhood Research Quarterly, 22*(1), 147–159. doi:10.1016/j.ecresq.2006.11.002

Browne, J. V., & Talmi, A. (2005). Family-based intervention to enhance infant-parent relationships in the neonatal intensive care unit. *Journal of Pediatric Psychology, 30*(8), 667–677. doi:10.1093/jpepsy/jsi053

Brownell, C., Nichols, S., Svetlova, M., Zerwas. S., & Ramani, G. (2010). The head bone's connected to the neck bone: When do toddlers represent their own body topography? *Child Development, 81*, 797–810.

Brownwell, C. A. (2013). Early development of prosocial behavior: Current perspectives. *Infancy, 18, 1*, 1–9. doi:10.1111/infa.12004.

Bruce, J., Lloyd, C., & Leonard, A. (with Engle, P., & Duffy, N.). (1995). *Families in focus: New perspectives on mothers, fathers and children.* New York, NY: Population Council.

Bruer, J. T. (2001). A critical and sensitive period primer. In D. B. J. Bailey, J. T. Bruer, F. J. Symons, & J. W. Lichtman (Eds.), *Critical thinking about critical periods* (pp. 3–26). Baltimore, MD: Brookes.

Bruner, J. (1962). Introduction. In L. S. Vygotsky, *Thought and language* (pp. v–x). Cambridge, MA: MIT Press.

Bruner, J. (1990). *Acts of meaning.* Cambridge, MA: Harvard University Press.

Bruner, J. S. (1985). *Child's talk: Learning to use language.* New York, NY: Norton.

Bruner, J. S., & Sherwood, V. (1975). Peek-a-boo and the learning of rule structures. In J. S. Bruner & K. Sylva (Eds.), *Play: Its role in development and evolution* (pp. 277–285). Harmondsworth, UK: Penguin.

Bruschweiler-Stern, N. (2009). Moments of meeting: Pivotal moments in mother, infant, father bonding. In J. K. Nugent, B. J. Petrauskas, & T. B. Brazelton (Eds). The newborn as a person: Enabling healthy infant development worldwide. Hoboken, NJ: Wiley (pp. 70–84).

Buchanan, C. M., Eccles, J. S., & Becker, J. B. (1992). Are adolescents the victims of raging hormones? Evidence for activational effects of hormones on moods and behavior at adolescence. *Psychological Bulletin, 111*(1), 62–107.

Buehler, C. (2006). Parents and peers in relation to early adolescent problem behavior. *Journal of Marriage and Family, 68*(1), 109–124. doi:10.1111/j.1741-3737.2006.00237.x

Buehler, D. M., Als, H., Duffy, F. H., McAnulty, G. B., & Liederman, J. (1995). Effectiveness of

individualized developmental care for low-risk preterm infants: Behavioral and electrophysiologic evidence. *Pediatrics, 96*(5), 923–932.
Buhimschi, C. S., & Weiner, C. P. (2009). Medications in pregnancy and lactation part 1: Teratology. *Obstetrics & Gynecology, 113*(1), 116–188. doi:10.1002/9780470691878.ch5
Bui, H. N. (2012). Immigrant generational status and delinquency in adolescence: Segmented assimilation and racial-ethnic differences. In C. García Coll & A. K. Marks (Eds.), *The immigrant paradox in children and adolescents: Is becoming American a developmental risk?* (pp. 135–158). Washington, DC: American Psychological Association.
Bulgren, J. A., Deshler, D. D., Schumaker, J. B., & Lenz, B. K. (2000). The use and effectiveness of analogical reasoning instruction in diverse secondary content classrooms. *Journal of Educational Psychology, 92*(3), 426–441. doi:10.1037/0022–0663.92.3.426
Bulotsky-Shearer, R. J., Manz, P. H., Mendez, J. L., McWayne, C. M., Sekino, Y., & Fantuzzo, J. W. (2012). Peer play interactions and readiness to learn: A protective influence for African American preschool children from low-income households. *Child Development Perspectives, 6*(3), 225–231. doi:10.1111/j.1750–8606.2011.00221.x
Burd-Sharps, S., Lewis, K., & Borges Martins, E. (2008). *The measure of America: American human development report, 2008–2009.* New York, NY: SSRC/Columbia University Press.
Burk, L. R., Armstrong, J. M., Park, J., Zahn-Waxler, C., Klein, M. H., & Essex, M. J. (2011). Stability of early identified aggressive victim status in elementary school and associations with later mental health problems and functional impairments. *Journal of Abnormal Child Psychology, 39*(2), 225–238. doi:10.1007/s10802–010–9454–6
Burnett, S., Sebastian, C., Cohen Kadosh, K., & Blakemore, S. (2011). The social brain in adolescence: Evidence from functional magnetic resonance imaging and behavioural studies. *Neuroscience and Biobehavioral Reviews, 35*(8), 1654–1664. doi:10.1016/j.neubiorev.2010.10.011
Burnett, S., Thompson, S., Bird, G., & Blakemore, S. (2011). Pubertal development of the understanding of social emotions: Implications for education. *Learning and Individual Differences, 21*(6), 681–689. doi:10.1016/j.lindif.2010.05.007
Burton, D. R. (2002). Antibodies, viruses and vaccines. *Nature Reviews Immunology, 2*, 706–713. doi:10.1038/nri891
Burton, L. M. (1992). Black grandparents rearing children of drug-addicted parents: Stressors, outcomes, and social service needs. *Gerontologist, 32*(6), 744–751.
Bus, A. G., & van IJzendoorn, M. H. (1999). Phonological awareness and early reading: A meta-analysis of experimental training studies. *Journal of Educational Psychology, 91*(3), 403–414.
Buss, A. H., & Plomin, R. (1975). *A temperament theory of personality development.* New York, NY: Wiley Interscience.
Buss, A. H., & Plomin, R. (1984). *Temperament: Early developing personality traits.* Hillsdale, NJ: Erlbaum.
Busseri, M. A., & Rose-Krasnor, L. (2009). Breadth and intensity: Salient, separable, and developmentally significant dimensions of structured youth activity involvement. *British Journal of Developmental Psychology, 27*(4), 907–933. doi:10.1348/026151008X397017
Bussey, K. (1999). Children's categorization and evaluation of different types of lies and truths. *Child Development, 70*(6), 1338–1347. doi:10.1111/1467-8624.00098
Byrne, B., & Fielding-Barnsley, R. (1995). Evaluation of a program to teach phonemic awareness to young children: A 2- and 3-year follow-up and a new preschool trial. *Journal of Educational Psychology, 87*(3), 488–503. doi:10.1037/0022-0663.87.3.488
Byrnes, J. P. (2005). Self-regulated decision-making in children and adolescents. In J. E. Jacobs & P. A. Klaczynski (Eds.), *The development of judgment and decision-making in children and adolescents* (pp. 5–38). Mahwah, NJ: Erlbaum.
Cabrera, N. J., Hutchens, R., & Peters, H. E. (2006). Introduction. In N. J. Cabrera, R. Hutchens, & H. E. Peters (Eds.), *From welfare to child care: What happens to young children when single mothers exchange welfare for work?* (pp. xiii–xxix). Mahwah, NJ: Erlbaum.
Cabrera, N. J., Tamis-LeMonda, C. S., Bradley, R. H., Hofferth, S., & Lamb, M. E. (2000). Fatherhood in the twenty-first century. *Child Development, 71*, 127–136.
Cabrera, N. J., West, J., Shannon, J. D., & Brookes-Gunn, J. (2006). Parental interactions with Latino infants: Variation by country of origin and English proficiency. *Child Development, 77*(6), 1190–1207.
Cabrera, N., & Garcia-Coll, C. (2004). Latino fathers: Uncharted territory in need of much exploration. In M. E. Lamb (Ed.), *The role of father in child development* (4th ed., pp. 98–120). Hoboken, NJ: Wiley.
Cafri, G., van den Berg., P., & Thompson, J. K. (2006). Pursuit of muscularity in adolescent boys: Relations among biopsychosocial variables and clinical outcomes. *Journal of Clinical Child and Adolescent Psychology, 35*(2), 283–291. doi:10.1207/s15374424jccp3502_12
Cahan, S., Greenbaum, C., Artman, L., Deluya, N., & Gappel-Gilon, Y. (2008). The differential effects of age and first grade schooling on the development of infralogical and logico-mathematical concrete operations. *Cognitive Development, 23*(2), 258–277. doi:10.1016/j.cogdev.2008.01.004
Cain, K., Oakhill, J., & Bryant, P. (2004). Children's reading comprehension ability: Concurrent prediction by working memory, verbal ability, and component skills. *Journal of Educational Psychology, 96*(1), 31–42. doi:10.1037/0022-0663.96.1.31
Caine-Bish, N. L., & Scheule, B. (2009). Gender differences in food preferences of school-aged children and adolescents. *Journal of School Health, 79*(11), 532–540.
Cairns, R. B., & Cairns, B. D. (2006). The making of developmental psychology. In W. Damon & R. Lerner (Eds.), *Handbook of child psychology* (6th ed., pp. 89–165). Hoboken, NJ: Wiley.
Caldera, Y. M. (2004). Paternal involvement and infant-father attachment: A Q-set study. *Fathering, 2*, 191–210.
Calvert, S. L., Rideout, V. J., Woolard, J. L., Barr, R. F., & Strouse, G. (2005). Age, ethnicity, and socioeconomic patterns in early computer use: A national survey. *American Behavioral Scientist, 48*(5), 590–607. doi:10.1177/0002764204271508
Cameron, N. (2006). *Human growth and development.* London, UK: Academic Press.
Cameron, N. (2007). Growth patterns in adverse environments. *American Journal of Human Biology, 19*(5), 615–621. doi:10.1002/ajhb.20661
Campbell, F. A., Ramey, C. T., Pungello, E., Sparling, J., & Miller-Johnson, S. (2002). Early childhood education: Young adult outcomes from the Abecedarian Project. *Applied Developmental Science, 6*(1), 42–57. doi:10.1207/S1532480XADS0601_05
Campos, J. J. (1983). The importance of affective communication in social referencing: A commentary on Feinman. *Merrill–Palmer Quarterly, 29*, 83–87.
Campos, J. J., & Sternberg, C. (1981). Perception, appraisal, and emotion: The onset of social referencing. In M. Lamb & L. Sherrod (Eds.), *Infant social cognition: Empirical and theoretical considerations* (pp. 273–314). Hillsdale, NJ: Erlbaum.
Campos, J. J., Anderson, D. I., Barbu-Roth, M. A., Hubbard, E. M., Hertenstein M. J., & Witherington, D. (2000). Travel broadens the mind. *Infancy, 1*, 149–219. doi:10.1207/S15327078IN0102_1
Campos, P. (2004). *The obesity myth: Why America's obsession with weight is hazardous to your health.* New York, NY: Penguin.
Camras, L. A., & Rappaport, S. (1993). Conflict behaviors of maltreated and nonmaltreated children. *Child Abuse & Neglect, 17*(4), 455–464. doi:10.1016/0145-2134(93)90020-6
Camras, L. A., & Sachs, V. B. (1991). Social referencing and caretaker expressive behaviour in a day care setting. *Infant Behaviour and Development, 14*, 27–36.
Camras, L. A., & Shutter, J. M. (2010). Emotional facial expressions in infancy. *Emotion Review, 2*(2), 120–129.
Canham, D. L., Bauer, L., Concepcion, M., Luong, J., Peters, J., & Wilde, C. (2007). An audit of medication administration: A glimpse into school health offices. *Journal of School Nursing 23*(1), 21–27.
Cantone, K. F. (2007). *Code-switching in bilingual children.* Dordrecht, Netherlands: Springer.
Cantrell, S. C., & Carter, J. C. (2009). Relationships among learner characteristics and adolescents' perceptions about reading strategy use. *Reading Psychology, 30*(3), 195–224. doi:10.1080/02702710802275397
Capaldi, D., Pears, K., Patterson, G., & Owen, L. (2003). Continuity of parenting practices across generations in an at-risk sample: A prospective comparison of direct and mediated associations. *Journal of Abnormal Child Psychology, 31*, 127–142. doi:10.1023/A:1022518123387
Capizzano, J., & Adams, G. (2004). Children in low-income families are less likely to be in center-based care. *Snapshots of America's Families III* (Report No. 16). Washington, DC: Urban Institute.

Carabin, H., Gyorkos, T. W., Soto, J. C., Joseph, L., Payment, P., & Collett, J. P. (1999). Effectiveness of a training program in reducing infections in toddlers attending day care centers. *Epidemiology, 10*(3), 219–227.

Cardno, A. G., & Gottesman, I. I. (2000). Twin studies of schizophrenia: From bow-and-arrow concordances to star wars Mx and functional genomics. American Journal of Medical Genetics, 97, 12–17. doi:10.1002/(SICI)1096-8628(200021)97:1<12::AID-AJMG3>3.3.CO;2-L

Carey, S. (1993). Speaking of objects, as such. In G. Harman (Ed.), *Conceptions of the human mind: Essays in honor of George A. Miller* (pp. 139–159). Hillsdale, NJ: Erlbaum.

Carey, S. (1999). Sources of conceptual change. In E. K. Scholnick, S. A. Nelson, P. H. Gelman, & P. H. Miller (Eds.), *Conceptual development: Piaget's legacy* (pp. 293–326). Mahwah, NJ: Erlbaum.

Carey, S. (2009). *The origin of concepts.* Oxford, UK: Oxford University Press.

Carlo, G., & Randall, B. A. (2001). Are all prosocial behaviors equal? A socioecological developmental conception of prosocial behavior. In F. Columbus (Ed.), *Advances in psychology research* (Vol. 3, pp. 151–170). Hauppauge, NY: Nova Science Publishers.

Carlo, G., Eisenberg, N., & Knight, G. P. (1992). An objective measure of adolescents' prosocial moral reasoning. *Journal of Research on Adolescence, 2*(4), 331–349. doi:10.1207/s15327795jra0204_3

Carlson, S. M. (2005). Developmentally sensitive measures of executive function in preschool children. *Developmental Neuropsychology, 28*(2), 595–616. doi:10.1207/s15326942dn2802_3

Carlson, V. J., & Harwood, R. L. (2003). Attachment, culture, and the caregiving system: The cultural patterning of everyday experiences among Anglo and Puerto Rican mother-infant pairs. *Infant Mental Health Journal, 24*(1), 53–73

Carlsson, B., Ahlstedt, S., Hanson, L. A., Lidin–Janson, G., Lindblad, B. S., & Sultana, R. (1976). *Escherichia coli* O antibody content in milk from healthy Swedish mothers from a very low socioeconomic group of a developing country. *Acta Paediatrica, 65*, 417–423.

Carmona, R. H. (2004). *Surgeon General's Statement on Community Water Fluoridation.* Retrieved from http://www.cdc.gov/fluoridation/fact_sheets/sg04.htm

Carpenter, D. O., Shen, Y., Nguyen, T., Le, L., & Lininger, L. L. (2001). Incidence of endocrine disease among residents of New York areas of concern. *Environmental Health Perspectives, 109*(6), 845–851. doi:10.2307/3454646

Carr, B. R. (1996). Fertilization, implantation, and endocrinology of pregnancy. In J. E. Griffin, & S. R. Ojeda, (Eds.), *Textbook of endocrine physiology* (3rd ed., pp. 223–243). Oxford, UK: Oxford University Press.

Carskadon, M. A., & Taylor, J. F. (1997). Public policy and sleep disorders. In M. R. Pressman & W. C. Orr (Eds.), *Understanding sleep: The evaluation and treatment of sleep disorders* (pp. 111–122). Washington, DC: American Psychological Association.

Carter, R. T. (1995). Pioneers of multicultural counseling: An interview with Janet E. Helms. *Journal of Multicultural Counseling and Development, 23*, 73–86.

Cartwright, K. B. (2012). Insights from cognitive neuroscience: The importance of executive function for early reading development and education. *Early Education and Development, 23*(1), 24–36. doi:10.1080/10409289.2011.615025

Carver, K., Joyner, K., & Udry, J. R. (2003). National estimates of adolescent romantic relationships. In P. Florsheim (Ed.), *Adolescent romantic relations and sexual behavior: Theory, research, and practical implications* (pp. 23–56). Mahwah, NJ: Erlbaum.

Carver, L. J., & Bauer, P. J. (1999). When the event is more than the sum of its parts: 9-month-olds' long-term ordered recall. *Memory,* 7(2), 147–174. doi:10.1080/741944070

Carver, L. J., & Bauer, P. J. (2001). The dawning of a past: The emergence of long-term explicit memory in infancy. *Journal of Experimental Psychology, 130*(4), 234–246. doi:10.1111/1467–7687.00116

Carver, L. J., & Vaccaro, B. G. (2007). 12-month-old infants allocate increased neural resources to stimuli associated with negative adult emotion. *Developmental Psychology, 43*, 54–69.

Case, R. (1991). *The mind's staircase: Exploring the conceptual underpinnings of children's thought and knowledge.* Hillsdale, NJ: Erlbaum.

Case, R., & Okamoto, Y. (1996). The role of central conceptual structures in the development of children's thought. *Monographs of the Society for Research in Child Development, 61*, 1–2, v–265.

Casey, B. J., Duhoux, S., & Cohen, M. M. (2010). Adolescence: What do transmission, transition, and translation have to do with it? *Neuron, 67*(5), 749–760. doi:10.1016/j.neuron.2010.08.033

Casey, B. M., McIntire, D. D., & Leveno, K. J. (2001). The continuing value of the Apgar score for the assessment of newborn infants. *New England Journal of Medicine, 334*(7), 467–471. doi:10.1056/NEJM200102153440701

Casey, B. M., Pezaris, E. E., & Bassi, J. (2012). Adolescent boys' and girls' block constructions differ in structural balance: A block-building characteristic related to math achievement. *Learning and Individual Differences, 22*(1), 25–36. doi:10.1016/j.lindif.2011.11.008

Casey, P. H., Whiteside–Mansell, L., Barrett, K., Bradley, R. H., & Gagus, R. (2006). Impact of prenatal and/or postnatal growth problems in low birth weight preterm infants on school-age outcomes: An 8-year longitudinal evaluation. *Pediatrics, 118*(3), 1078–1086. doi:10.1542/peds.2006–0361

Caspi, A., Elder, G. H., & Bem, D. J. (1988). Moving away from the world: Life-course patterns of shy children. *Developmental Psychology, 24*(6), 824–831. doi:10.1037/0012-1649.24.6.824

Caspi, A., McClay, J., Moffitt, T. E., Mill, J., Martin, J., Craig, I. W., . . . Poulton, R. (2002). Role of genotype in the cycle of violence in maltreated children. *Science, 297*, 851–853. doi:10.1126/science.1072290

Caspi, A., McClay, J., Moffitt, T. E., Mill, J., Martin, J., Craig, I. W., Taylor A., & Poulton, R. (2002). Role of genotype in the cycle of violence in maltreated children. *Science, 297*, 851–854.

Caspi, A., Sugden, K., Moffitt, T. E., Taylor, A., Craig, I. W., Harrington, H., . . . Poulton, R. (2003). Influence of life stress on depression: Moderation by a polymorphism in the 5-HTT gene. *Science, 301*(5631), 386–389. doi:10.1126/science.1083968

Cassidy, J., & Shaver, P. R. (Eds.). (1999). *Handbook of attachment: Theory, research, and clinical applications.* New York, NY: Guilford.

Cassidy, J., & Shaver, P. R. (Eds.). (2008). *Handbook of attachment: Theory, research, and clinical applications* (2nd ed.). New York, NY: Guilford.

Castle, J., Groothues, C., Bredenkamp, D., Beckett, C., O'Connor, T., Rutter, M., & the E.R.A. study team. (1999). Effects of qualities of early institutional care on cognitive attainment. *American Journal of Orthopsychiatry, 69*, 424–437.

Catalano, R. F., Berglund, M. L., Ryan, J. A., Lonczak, H. S., & Hawkins, J. D. (2004). Positive youth development in the United States: Research findings on evaluations of positive youth development programs. *The annals of the American Academy of Political and Social Science, 591*(1), 98–124. doi:10.1177/0002716203260102

Cattell, R. B. (1971). *Abilities: Their structure, growth, and action.* Oxford, UK: Houghton Mifflin.

Cauffman, E. (2008). Understanding the female offender. *Future of Children, 18*(2), 119–142. doi:10.1353/foc.0.0015

Caulfield, L. E., de Onis, M., Blössner, M., & Black, R. E. (2004). Undernutrition as an underlying cause of child deaths associated with diarrhea, pneumonia, malaria, and measles. *American Journal of Clinical Nutrition, 80*(1), 193–198.

Ceci, S. J., & Roazzi, A. (1994). The effects of context on cognition: Postcards from Brazil. In R. J. Sternberg & R. K. Wagner (Eds.), *Mind in context: Interactionist perspectives on human intelligence* (pp. 74–101). New York, NY: Cambridge University Press.

Ceci, S. J., Kulkofsky, S., Klemfuss, J. Z., Sweeney, C. D., & Bruck, M. (2007). Unwarranted assumptions about children's testimony accuracy. *Annual Review of Clinical Psychology, 3*, 311–328. doi:10.1146/annurev.clinpsy.3.022806.091354

Ceci, S. J., Papierno, P. B., & Kulkofsky, S. (2007). Representational constraints on children's suggestibility. *Psychological Science, 18* (6), 503–509. doi:10.1111/j.1467–9280.2007.01930.x

Cecil, K. M., Brubaker, C. J., Adler, C. M., Dietrich, K. N., Altaye, M., Egelhoff, J. C., . . . Lanphear, B. P. (2008). Decreased brain volume in adults with childhood lead exposure. *PLoS, 5*(5), e112. doi:10.1371/journal.pmed.0050112

Cédric, P., Koolschijn, M. P., & Crone, A. M. (2013). The neurocognitive development of performance monitoring. In K. C. Barrett, N. A. Fox, G. A. Morgan, D. J. Fidler, & L. A. Daunhauer (Eds.), *Handbook of self-regulatory processes in development: New directions and international perspectives* (pp. 199–214). New York, NY: Psychology Press.

Center for Family Policy & Research, University of Missouri (2013). *State of child welfare in America: 2011.* Retrieved from http://CFPR.missouri.edu/home.htm

Center on the Developing Child at Harvard University. (2007). *A science-based framework for early childhood policy: Using evidence to improve outcomes in learning, behavior and health for vulnerable children.* Retrieved from http://www.developingchild.harvard.edu

Center on the Developing Child at Harvard University. (2010). *The foundations of lifelong health are built in early childhood.* Retrieved from http://www.developingchild.harvard.edu

Centers for Disease Control and Prevention. (1999). Achievements in public health, 1900–1999: Healthier mothers and babies. *Morbidity and Mortality Weekly Review, 48*(38), 849–858. Retrieved from http://www.cdc.gov/mmwr/preview/mmwrhtml/mm4838a2.htm

Centers for Disease Control and Prevention. (2003). *BMI for children and teens.* Retrieved from http://www.cdc.gov/nccdphp/dnpa/bmi/bmi-for-age.htm

Centers for Disease Control and Prevention. (2003). QuickStats: Total fertility rates, by state—United States, 2003. *Morbidity and Mortality Weekly Review, 54*(49), 1262. Retrieved from http://www.cdc.gov/mmwr/preview/mmwrhtml/mm4847a1.htm

Centers for Disease Control and Prevention. (2004). *Sexually transmitted diseases surveillance 2004.* Retrieved from http://www.cdc.gov/std/stats04/syphilis.htm

Centers for Disease Control and Prevention. (2005). *Alcohol use and pregnancy.* Retrieved from http://www.cdc.gov/ncbddd/factsheets/FAS_alcoholuse.pdf

Centers for Disease Control and Prevention. (2006). *Teen pregnancy.* Retrieved from http://www.cdc.gov/reproductivehealth/AdolescentReproHealth

Centers for Disease Control and Prevention. (2007a). *Preventing smoking and exposure to secondhand smoke before, during, and after pregnancy.* Retrieved from http://www.cdc.gov/nccdphp/publications/factsheets/Prevention/pdf/smoking.pdf

Centers for Disease Control and Prevention. (2007b). *STDs and pregnancy: Fact sheet.* Retrieved from http://www.cdc.gov/std/pregnancy/STDs-and-pregnancy-fact-sheet-press.pdf

Centers for Disease Control and Prevention. (2007c). *Mother-to-child (perinatal) HIV transmission and prevention.* Retrieved from http://www.cdc.gov/hiv/topics/perinatal/resources/factsheets/pdf/perinatal.pdf

Centers for Disease Control and Prevention. (2007d). *National diabetes fact sheet.* Retrieved from http://www.cdc.gov/diabetes/pubs/pdf/ndfs_2007.pdf

Centers for Disease Control and Prevention. (2008). *Quick stats: Underage drinking.* Retrieved from http://www.cdc.gov/alcohol/quickstats/underage_drinking.htm

Centers for Disease Control and Prevention. (2010). *Cytomegalovirus (CMV) and congenital CMV infection.* Retrieved from http://www.cdc.gov/cmv/congenital-infection.html

Centers for Disease Control and Prevention. (2010a). *Teen drivers: Fact sheet.* Retrieved from http://www.cdc.gov/Motorvehiclesafety/Teen_Drivers/teendrivers_factsheet.html

Centers for Disease Control and Prevention. (2010b). *Heads up: Concussion in high school sports.* Retrieved from http://www.cdc.gov/concussion/HeadsUp/high_school.html

Centers for Disease Control and Prevention. (2011a). *Teen pregnancy at a glance: Improving the lives of young people and strengthening communities by reducing teen pregnancy.* Retrieved from http://www.cdc.gov/chronicdisease/resources/publications/aag/pdf/2011/Teen-Pregnancy-AAG-2011_508.pdf

Centers for Disease Control and Prevention. (2011b). *Sexually transmitted disease surveillance 2010.* Retrieved from http://www.cdc.gov/std/stats10/surv2010.pdf

Centers for Disease Control and Prevention. (2011c). National and state vaccination coverage among adolescents aged 13 through 17 years—United States, 2010. *Morbidity and Mortality Weekly Review, 60,* 1117–1123

Centers for Disease Control and Prevention. (2012). Prevalence of autism spectrum disorders. Autism and Developmental Disabilities Monitoring Network, 14 sites, United States, 2008. *MMWR Surveillance Summaries, 61*(3), 1–19.

Centers for Disease Control and Prevention. (2012). *Fetal alcohol spectrum disorders (FASDs).* Retrieved from http://www.cdc.gov/ncbddd/fasd/data.html

Centers for Disease Control and Prevention. (2012a). *Youth risk behavior surveillance—United States 2011.* Retrieved from http://www.cdc.gov/mmwr/pdf/ss/ss6104.pdf

Centers for Disease Control and Prevention. (2012b). *Youth risk behavior surveillance system: 2011 national overview.* Retrieved from http://www.cdc.gov/healthyyouth/yrbs/pdf/us_overview_yrbs.pdf

Centers for Disease Control and Prevention. (2012c). *Teen pregnancy graphics data descriptions, 1991–2009.* Retrieved from http://www.cdc.gov/TeenPregnancy/LongDescriptors.htm#PTP1

Centers for Disease Control and Prevention. (2012d). *HPV and men fact sheet.* Retrieved from http://www.cdc.gov/std/hpv/STD-Fact-HPV-and-men.htm

Centers for Disease Control and Prevention. (2012e). *Genital herpes fact sheet.* Retrieved from http://www.cdc.gov/std/herpes/std-fact-herpes.htm

Centers for Disease Control and Prevention. (2013). *Infertility.* Retrieved from http://www.cdc.gov/reproductivehealth/Infertility/index.htm

Centers for Disease Control. (1999). Achievements in public health, 1900-1999: Fluoridation of drinking water to prevent dental caries. *Morbidity and Mortality Weekly Review, 48*(12), 933–40.

Centers for Disease Control. (2000). Clinical growth charts. Retrieved from http://www.cdc.gov/growthcharts/

Centers for Disease Control. (2001). Recommendations for using fluoride to prevent and control dental caries in the United States. *Morbidity and Mortality Weekly Review, 50* (RR14), 1–42.

Centers for Disease Control. (2006). Vaccine preventable deaths and the global immunization vision and strategy, 2006–2015. *Morbidity and Mortality Weekly Review, 55*(18), 511–515.

Centers for Disease Control. (2007). Preventing smoking and exposure to secondhand smoke before, during, and after pregnancy. Retrieved from http://www.cdc.gov/nccdphp/publications/factsheets/Prevntion/pdf/smoking/pdf

Centers for Disease Control. (2008). Vaccines and immunizations: Statistics and surveillance 2008 Table Data. Retrieved from http://www.cdc.gov/vaccines/stats-surv/nis/data/tables_2008.htm

Centers for Disease Control. (2009). *Lead.* Retrieved from http://www.cdc.gov/nceh/lead/

Centers for Disease Control. (2010). *The association between school-based physical activity, including physical education, and academic performance.* Retrieved from http://www.cdc.gov/healthyyouth/health_and_academics/pdf/pa-pe_paper.pdf

Centers for Disease Control. (2010a). Deaths: Final Data for 2009. *National Vital Statistics Report, 60*(3). Retrieved from http://www.cdc.gov/nchs/data/dvs/deaths_2009_release.pdf

Centers for Disease Control. (2010b). Summary health statistics for U.S. Children: National Health Interview Survey, 2009. *Vital and Health Statistics Series 10, Number 247.*

Centers for Disease Control. (2011). *Coverage estimates for school entry vaccinations 2009–2010.* Retrieved from http://www2.cdc.gov/nip/schoolsurv/nationalAvg.asp

Centers for Disease Control. (2011). *Lesbian, gay, bisexual and transgender health.* Retrieved from http://www.cdc.gov/lgbthealth/youth.htm

Centers for Disease Control. (2012). *National action plan for child injury prevention: An agenda to prevent injuries and promote the safety of children and adolescents in the United States.* Retrieved from http://www.cdc.gov/safechild/pdf/National_Action_Plan_for_Child_Injury_Prevention.pdf

Ceponiene, R., Alku, P., Westerfield, M., Torki, M. & Townsend, J. (2005). ERPs differentiate syllable and nonphonetic sound processing in children and adults. *Psychophysiology, 42,* 391–406.

Chafen, J. J. S., Newberry, S. J., Riedl, J. A., Bravata, D. M., Maglione, M., Suttorp, M. J. J., . . . Shekelle, P. G. (2010). Diagnosing and managing common food allergies: A systematic review. *Journal of the American Medical Association, 303*(18), 1848–1856. doi:10.1001/jama.2010.582

Chaiklin, S. (2003). The zone of proximal development in Vygotsky's analysis of learning and instruction. In A. Kozulin, B. Gindis, V. S. Ageyev, & S. M. Miller (Eds.), *Vygotsky's educational theory in cultural context* (pp. 39–64). New York, NY: Cambridge University Press.

Chakrabarti, S., & Fombonne, E. (2001). Pervasive developmental disorders in preschool children. *Journal of the American Medical Association, 285,* 3093–3099.

Chall, J. S. (1979). The great debate: Ten years later, with a modest proposal for reading stages. In L. B. Resnick & P. A. Weaver (Eds.), *Theory and practice of early reading.* Hillsdale, NJ: Erlbaum.

Chall, J. S. (1983). *Stages of reading development.* New York, NY: McGraw–Hill.

Champagne, F. A., & Mashoodh, R. (2009). Genes in context: Gene-environment interplay and the origins of individual differences in behavior. *Current Directions in Psychological Science, 18*, 127–131.

Chandler, M. (Interviewer), & Steele, C. (Interviewee). (1999). *Secrets of the SAT: Interview with Claude Steele* [Interview Transcript]. Retrieved from http://www.pbs.org/wgbh/pages/frontline/shows/sats/interviews/steele.html

Chandra, A., Martinez, G. M., Mosher, W. D., Abma, J. C., & Jones, J. (2005). Fertility, family planning, and reproductive health of U.S. women: Data from the 2002 National Survey of Family Growth. *Vital Health Statistics, 23*(25). Retrieved from http://www.cdc.gov/nchs/data/series/sr_23/sr23_025.pdf

Chang, C., Lui, C., Wang, J., Huang, S., Lu, C., Chen, C., . . . Chang, W. (2010). Multiparametric neuroimaging evaluation of cerebrotendinous xanthomatosis and its correlation with neuropsychological presentations. BMC Neurology, 10, 1–8. doi:10.1186/1471-2377-10-59

Chang, H., Shelleby, E. C., Cheong, J., & Shaw, D. S. (2012). Cumulative risk, negative emotionality, and emotion regulation as predictors of social competence in transition to school: A mediated moderation model. Social Development, 21(4), 780–800. doi:10.1111/j.1467–9507.2011.00648.x

Chao, R. K. (2001). Extending research on the consequences of parenting style for Chinese Americans and European Americans. *Child Development, 72*(6), 1832–1843. doi:10.1111/1467-8624.00381

Chao, R. K., & Sue, S. (1996). Chinese parental influence and their children's school success: A paradox in the literature on parenting styles. In S. Lau (Ed.), *Growing up the Chinese way* (pp. 93–120). Hong Kong: Chinese University Press.

Charlesworth, W. R., & Kreutzer, M. A. (1973). Facial expressions of infants and children. In P. Ekman (Ed.), *Darwin and facial expression: A century of research in review* (pp. 91–138). New York, NY: Academic Press.

Charman, T., Swettenham, J., Baron-Cohen, S., Cox, A., Baird, G., & Drew, A. (1997). Infants with autism: An investigation of empathy, pretend play, joint attention, and imitation. *Developmental Psychology, 5*, 782–789.

Charo, R. A. (2007). Politics, parents, and prophylaxis—mandating HPV vaccination in the United States. *New England Journal of Medicine, 356*, 1905–1908. doi:10.1056/NEJMp078054

Chase-Lansdale, P. L., Cherlin, A. J., & Kiernan, K. K. (1995). The long-term effects of parental divorce on the mental health of young adults: A developmental perspective. *Child Development, 66*(6), 1614–1634. doi:10.2307/1131900

Chavkin, W. (2001). Cocaine and pregnancy—time to look at the evidence. *Journal of the American Medical Association, 285*(12), 1626–1628. doi:10.1001/jama.285.12.1626

Chawarska, K., Klin, A., & Volkmar, F. R. (2003). Automatic attention cueing through eye movement in 2-year-old children with autism. *Child Development, 74*, 1108–1122.

Chen, T. H., Chang, S. P., Tsai, C. F., & Juang, K. D. (2004). Prevalence of depressive and anxiety disorders in an assisted reproductive technique clinic. *Human Reproduction, 19*(10), 2313–2318. doi:10.1093/humrep/deh414

Chen, X., & French, D. C. (2008). Children's social competence in cultural context. *Annual Review of Psychology, 59*, 591–616. doi:10.1146/annurev.psych.59.103006.093606

Chen, Z., & Kaplan, H. (2001). Intergenerational transmission of constructive parenting. *Journal of Marriage and the Family, 63*, 17–31. doi:10.1111/j.1741-3737.2001.00017.x

Cherney, I. D., & Dempsey, J. (2010). Young children's classification, stereotyping and play behaviour for gender neutral and ambiguous toys. *Educational Psychology, 30*(6), 651–669. doi:10.1080/01443410.2010.498416

Chernoff, J., Flanagan, K. D., McPhee, C., & Park, J. (2007). *Preschool: First findings from the preschool follow-up of the early childhood longitudinal study, birth cohort (ECLS-B)* (NCES 2008–025). Washington, DC: National Center for Education Statistics, Institute of Education Sciences, US Department of Education.

Chess, S., & Thomas, A. (1989). Issues in the clinical application of temperament. In G. A. Kohnstamm, J. E. Bates, & M. K. Rothbart (Eds.), *Temperament in childhood.* (pp. 377–403). New York, NY: Wiley.

Chess, S., & Thomas, A. (1996). *Temperament: Theory and practice*. New York, NY: Guilford.

Cheung, C. S., & Pomerantz, E. M. (2012). Why does parents' involvement enhance children's achievement? The role of parent-oriented motivation. *Journal of Educational Psychology, 104*(3), 820–832. doi:10.1037/a0027183

Chichester, C. L., & Cairns, H. (2001). Grandparents and the care of children: The research evidence. In B. Broad (Ed.), *Kinship care: The placement choice for children and young people* (pp. 11–20). Dorset, UK: Russell House.

Child Trends DataBank. (2010). *Well-child visits 2000–2008: Analysis of the National Health Interview Surveys.* Retrieved from http://www.childtrendsdatabank.org/?q=node/85

Child Trends. (2012). *Children's early family experiences vary dramatically by mother's education and marital status.* Retrieved from http://www.childtrends.org/_pressrelease_page.cfm?LID=8A86AB63-CC76-4CF7-BFA7488368ED988D

Child, T. J., Henderson, A. M., & Tan, S. L. (2004). The desire for multiple pregnancies in male and female infertility patients. *Human Reproduction, 19*(3), 558–561. doi:10.1093/humrep/deh097

Children's Defense Fund (2005). State of America's Children, 2005. Retrieved from. http://www.childrensdefense.org/child-research-data-publications/data/state-of-americas-children-2005-report.html

Children's Defense Fund (2010). State of America's Children, 2010. Retrieved from. http://www.childrensdefense.org/child-research-data-publications/data/state-of-americas-children.pdf

ChildStats (2009). America' children: Key indicators of well-being. Retrieved from http://www.childstats.gov/americaschildren/glance.asp

Choi, H. J., Park, H. S., & Oh, J. Y. (2011). Cultural differences in how individuals explain their lying and truth-telling tendencies. *International Journal of Intercultural Relations, 35*(6), 749–766. doi:10.1016/j.ijintrel.2011.08.001

Chomsky, N. (1957). *Syntactic structures*. Oxford, UK: Mouton.

Chomsky, N. (1965). *Aspects of the theory of syntax*. Cambridge, MA: MIT Press.

Choudhury, S., Blakemore, S., & Charman, T. (2006). Social cognitive development during adolescence. *Social Cognitive and Affective Neuroscience, 1*(3), 165–174. doi:10.1093/scan/nsl024

Chrisler, J., & Caplan, P. (2002). The strange case of Dr. Jekyll and Ms. Hyde: How PMS became a cultural phenomenon and a psychiatric disorder. *Annual Review of Sex Research, 75*, 272–306.

Christakis, D. A., Zimmerman, F. J., DiGiuseppe, D. L., & McCarty, C. A. (2004). Early television exposure and subsequent attentional problems in children. *Pediatrics, 113*, 708–713.

Christopher, M. E., Miyake, A., Keenan, J. M., Pennington, B., DeFries, J. C., Wadsworth, S. J., . . . Olson, R. K. (2012). Predicting word reading and comprehension with executive function and speed measures across development: A latent variable analysis. *Journal of Experimental Psychology: General, 141*(3), 470–488. doi:10.1037/a0027375

Chronic Care: Self-Management Guideline Team, Cincinnati Children's Hospital Medical Center. (2007). *Evidence-based care guideline for chronic care self-management.* Retrieved from http://www.cincinnatichildrens.org/svc/alpha/h/health-policy/evbased/chronic-care.htm

Chua, H., Boland, J., & Nisbett, R. (2005). Cultural variation in eye movements during scene perception. *Proceedings of the National Academy of Sciences, 102*, 12629–12633. doi:10.1073/pnas.0506162102

Chugani, H. T., Muller, R.-A., & Chugani, D. C. (1996). Functional brain reorganization in children. *Brain and Development, 18*, 347–356.doi:org/10.1016/0387-7604(96)00032-0 http://dx.doi.org/10.1016/0387-7604(96)00032-0

Chumlea, W. C., Schubert, C. M., Roche, A. F., Kulin, H. E., Lee, P. A., Himes, J. H., & Shumei, S. S. (2003). Age at menarche and racial comparisons in U.S. girls. *Pediatrics, 111*(1), 110–113.

Chung, G. H., Flook, L., & Fuligni, A. J. (2009). Daily family conflict and emotional distress among adolescents from Latin American, Asian, and European backgrounds. *Developmental Psychology, 45*(5), 1406–1415.

Cicchetti, D., & Rogosch, F. A. (2001). The impact of child maltreatment and psychopathology on neuroendocrine functioning. *Development and Psychopathology, 13*(4), 783–804.

Cicchetti, D., & Rogosch, F. A. (2011). Interactive effects of corticotropin releasing hormone receptor 1, serotonin transporter linked polymorphic region, and child maltreatment on diurnal cortisol regulation and internalizing symptomatology. *Development and Psychopathology, 23*(4), 1125–1138. doi:10.1017/S0954579411000599

Cicchetti, D., & Toth, S. L. (2010). Child maltreatment: The research imperative and the exportation of results to clinical contexts. In B. M. Lester & J. D. Sparrow (Eds.), *Nurturing children and families: Building on the legacy of T. Berry Brazelton* (pp. 264–274). West Sussex, UK: Wiley–Blackwell.

Cicchetti, D., Rogosch, F. A., Gunnar, M. R., & Toth, S. L. (2010). The differential impacts of early physical and sexual abuse and internalizing problems on daytime cortisol rhythm in school-aged children. *Child Development, 81*(1), 252–269. doi:10.1111/ j.1467-8624.2009.01393.x

Cicchetti, D., Rogosch, F. A., Maughan, A., Toth, S. L., & Bruce, J. (2003). False belief understanding in maltreated children. *Development and Psychopathology. Special Issue: Experiments of Nature: Contributions to Developmental Theory, 15*(4), 1067–1091. doi:10.1017/S0954579403000440

Cicirelli, V. G. (1995). *Sibling relationships across the life span*. New York, NY: Plenum Press.

Ciesielski, K. T., Lesnik, P. G., Savoy, R. L., Grant, E. P., & Ahlfors, S. P. (2006). Developmental neural networks in children performing a categorical N-back task. *NeuroImage, 33*(3), 980–990. doi:10.1016/j.neuroimage.2006.07.028

Cillessen, A. H. N., & Borch, C. (2006). Developmental trajectories of adolescent popularity: A growth curve modeling analysis. *Journal of Adolescence, 29*(6), 935–959.

Clark, E. (1993). *The lexicon in acquisition*. New York, NY: Cambridge University Press.

Clark, N. M., Mitchell, H. E., & Rand, C. S. (2009). Effectiveness of educational and behavioral asthma interventions. *Pediatrics, 123*(Supplement 3), S185–S192. doi:10.1542/peds.2008-2233I

Clarke-Stewart, K. A. (1989). Infant day-care: Maligned or malignant? *American Psychology, 44*, 266–273.

Clarke-Stewart, K. A., & Allhusen, V. D. (2002). Nonparental caregiving. In M. H. Bornstein (Ed.), *Handbook of parenting: Vol. 3, Being and becoming a parent* (2nd ed., pp. 215–252). Mahwah, NJ: Erlbaum.

Clay, M. M. (2001). *Change over time in children's literacy development*. Portsmouth, NH: Heinemann.

Cleeton, E. R. (2001). Attitudes and beliefs about childbirth among college students: Results of an educational intervention. *Birth, 28*(3), 192–200. doi:10.1046/j.1523-536x.2001.00192.x

Clemens, D. H., & Sarama, J. (2007). Early childhood mathematics learning. In F. K. Lester. Jr. (Ed.), *Second handbook of research on mathematics teaching and learning* (pp. 461–555). New York, NY: Information Age.

Clifford, T. J., Campbell, M. K., Speechley, K. N., & Gorodzinsky, F. (2002). Infant colic: Empirical evidence of the absence of an association with source of early infant nutrition. *Archives of Pediatrics and Adolescent Medicine, 156*, 1123–1128.

Clifton, R. K., Perris, E. E., & McCall, D. D. (1999). Does reaching in the dark for unseen objects reflect representation in infants? *Infant Behavior & Development, 22*(3), 297–302. doi:10.1016/S0163–6383(99)00017–X

Coccia, M. E., & Rizzello, F. (2008). Ovarian reserve. *Annals of the New York Academy of Sciences, 1127*, 27–30. doi:10.1196/annals.1434.011

Cochran, M. (2007). *Finding our way: The future of American early care and education*. Washington, DC: Zero to Three.

Coe, D. P., Pivarnik, J. M., Womack, C. J., Reeves, M. J., & Malina, R. M. (2006). Effect of physical education and activity levels on academic achievement in children. *Medicine & Science in Sports & Exercise*, 1515–1519. doi:10.1249/01.mss.0000227537.13175.1b

Cohen Kadosh, R., Cohen Kadosh, K., Kaas, A., Henik, A., & Goebel, R. (2007). Notation-dependent and -independent representations of numbers in the parietal lobes. *Neuron, 52*(2), 307–314. doi:10.1016/j.neuron.2006.12.025

Cohen, A. (2009). Many forms of culture. *American Psychologist, 64*(3), 194–204. doi:10.1037/a0015308

Cohen, L. B. (2009). The evolution of human cognition: A personal account. *Infancy, 14*(4), 403–413.

Cohen, L. B., & Cashon, C. H. (2006). Infant cognition. In D. Kuhn, R. S. Siegler, R. W. Damon, & R. M. Lerner (Eds.), *Handbook of child psychology: Vol. 2, Cognition, perception, and language* (6th ed., pp. 214–251). Hoboken, NJ: Wiley.

Cohen-Bendahan, C. C. C., van de Beek, C., & Berenbaum, S. A. (2005). Prenatal sex hormone effects on child and adult sex-typed behavior: Methods and findings. *Neuroscience & Biobehavioral Reviews, Special Issue: Prenatal Programming of Behavior, Physiology and Cognition, 29*(2), 353–384. doi:10.1016/j.neubiorev. 2004.11.004

Colby, A., Kohlberg, L., Gibbs, J., & Lieberman, M. (1983). A longitudinal study of moral judgment. *Monographs of the Society for Research in Child Development, 48*(1–2). doi:10.2307/1165935

Cole, D. A., Cho, S., Martin, N. C., Youngstrom, E. A., March, J. S., Findling, R. L., . . . Maxwell, M. A. (2012). Are increased weight and appetite useful indicators of depression in children and adolescents? *Journal of Abnormal Psychology, 121*(4), 838–851. doi:10.1037/a0028175

Cole, M. (1999). *Culture in development*. In M. H. Bornstein & M. E. Lamb (Eds.), *Developmental psychology: An advanced textbook* (Vol. 4, pp. 73–123). Mahwah, NJ: Erlbaum.

Cole, M., & Packer, M. (2011). Culture in development. In M. E. Lamb and M. H. Bornstein (Eds.), *Social and personality development: An advanced textbook* (pp. 67–123). New York, NY: Psychology Press.

Cole, T. J. (2000). Secular trends in growth. *Proceedings of the Nutrition Society, 59*, 317–324. doi:10.1017/S0029665100000355

Coles, C. O., Platzman, K .A., Raskind–Hood, C. L., Brown, R. T., Falek, A., & Smith, I. E. (1997). A comparison of children affected by prenatal alcohol exposure and attention deficit hyperactivity disorder. *Alcoholism: Clinical and Experimental Research, 21*(1), 150–161. doi:10.1111/j.1530–0277.1997.tb03743.x

Collie, R., & Hayne, H. (1999). Deferred imitation by 6- and 9-month-old infants: More evidence for declarative memory. *Developmental Psychobiology, 35*(3), 83–90.

Collins, N. L., & Freeney, B. C. (2004). An attachment theory perspective on closeness and intimacy. In D. J. Mashek & A. Aron (Eds.), *Handbook of closeness and intimacy* (pp. 163–188). Mahwah, NJ: Erlbaum.

Collins, S. R., Garber, T., & Robertson, R. (2011). Realizing health reform's potential: How the Affordable Care Act is helping young adults stay covered [Commonwealth Fund Publication 1508(5)]. Retrieved from http://www.commonwealthfund.org/Publications/Issue_Briefs/2011/May/Helping_Young_Adults.aspx

Collins, W. A., Madsen, S. D., & Susman-Stillman, A. (2002). Parenting during middle childhood. In M. H. Bronstein (Ed.), *Handbook of parenting: Vol. 1. Children and parenting* (2nd ed., pp. 73–101). Mahwah, NJ: Erlbaum.

Collins, W. A., Welsh, D. P., & Furman, W. (2009). Adolescent romantic relationships. *Annual Review of Psychology, 60*, 631–652. doi:10.1146/annurev.psych.60.110707.163459

Collins, W., Maccoby, E., Steinberg, L., Hetherington, E., & Bornstein, M. (2000). Contemporary research on parenting: The case for nature and nurture. *American Psychologist, 55*, 218–232. doi:10.1037/0003–066X.55.2.218

Collishaw, S., Pickles, A., Messer, J., Rutter, M., Shearer, C., & Maughan, B., (2007). Resilience to adult psychopathology following childhood maltreatment: Evidence from a community sample. *Child Abuse & Neglect, 31*, 211–229.

Colombo, J. (1993). *Infant cognition: Predicting later intellectual functioning*. Belmont, CA: Sage.

Colombo, J., & Frick, J. E. (1999). Recent advances and issues in the study of preverbal intelligence. In M. Anderson (Ed), *The development of intelligence* (pp. 43–71). Hove, UK: Psychology Press/Taylor & Francis.

Colpin, H., & Bossaert, G. (2008). Adolescents conceived by IVF: Parenting and psychosocial adjustment. *Human Reproduction, 23*(12), 2724–2730. doi:10.1093/humrep/den297

Coltrane, S. (2001). Stability and change in Chicano men's family lives. In M. Kimmel & M. Messner (Eds.), *Men's lives* (5th ed., pp. 451–466). New York, NY: Macmillan.

Coltrane, S., Parke, R. D., & Adams, M. (2004). Complexity of father involvement in low-income Mexican American families. *Family Relations, 53*, 179–189.

Committee on Injury, Violence, and Poison Prevention. (2011). Child passenger safety. *Pediatrics, 127*(4): 788–793.

Commonwealth Fund Commission on Chronic Illness. (1957). *Chronic illness in the United States*. Cambridge, MA: Harvard University Press.

Compas, B. E. (2004). Process of risk and resilience during adolescence: Linking context and individuals. In R. M. Lerner & L. Steinberg (Eds.), *Handbook of adolescent psychology* (pp. 263–296). Hoboken, NJ: Wiley.

Compas, B. E., & Reeslund, K. L. (2009). Processes of risk and resilience during adolescence. In R. M. Lerner & L. Steinberg (Eds.), *Handbook of adolescent psychology: Vol. 1. Individual bases of adolescent development* (3rd ed., pp. 561–588). Hoboken, NJ: Wiley.

Compas, B. E., Connor-Smith, J. K., Saltzman, H., Thomsen, A. H., & Wadsworth, M. E.

(2001). Coping with stress during childhood and adolescence: Problem, progress, and potential in theory and research. *Psychological Bulletin, 127*(1), 87–127. doi:10.1037/0033-2909.127.1.87

Comstock, G., & Scharrer, E. (2006). Media and popular culture. In K. Renninger & I. Sigel (Eds.), *Handbook of child psychology: Vol. 4. Child psychology in practice* (pp. 817–863). Hoboken, NJ: Wiley.

Comstock, R. D., Collins, C. L., & McIlvain, N. M. (2012). *National high school sports-related injury surveillance study*. Columbus, OH: Center for Injury Research and Policy, Research Institute at Nationwide Children's Hospital.

Conboy, B. T., & Mills, D. L. (2006). Two languages, one developing brain: Event-related potentials to words in bilingual toddlers. *Developmental Science, 9*(1), F1–F12. doi:10.1111/j.1467-7687. 2005.00453.x

Conboy, B. T., Sommerville, J. A., & Kuhl, P. K. (2008). Cognitive control factors in speech perception at 11 months. *Developmental Psychology, 44*(5), 1505–1512. doi:10.1037/a0012975

Cone–Wesson, B. (2005). Prenatal alcohol and cocaine exposure: Influences on cognition, speech, language, and hearing. *Journal of Communication Disorders, 38*(4), 279–302.

Conger, R., Neppl, T., Kim, K., & Scaramella, L. (2003). Angry and aggressive behavior across three generations: A prospective, longitudinal study of parents and children. *Journal of Abnormal Child Psychology, 31*, 143–160. doi:10.1023/A:1022570107457

Connolly, J. A., & McIsaac, C. (2009). Romantic relationships in adolescence. In R. M. Lerner & L. Steinberg (Eds.), *Handbook of adolescent psychology: Vol. 2. Contextual influences on adolescent development* (3rd ed., pp. 104–151). Hoboken, NJ: Wiley.

Connor, C. M., Piasta, S. B., Fishman, B., Glasney, S., Schatschneider, C., Crowe, E., . . . Morrison, F. J. (2009). Individualizing student instruction precisely: Effects of child x instruction interactions on first graders' literacy development. *Child Development, 80*(1), 77–100. doi:10.1111/j.1467-8624.2008.01247.x

Cook, R., Golombok, S., Bish, A., & Murray, C. (1995). Disclosure of donor insemination: Parental attitudes. *American Journal of Orthopsychiatry, 65*(4), 549–559. doi:10.1037/h0079674

Cooper, M. L., Shaver, P. R., & Collins, N. L. (1998). Attachment styles, emotion regulation, and adjustment in adolescence. *Journal of Personality and Social Psychology, 74*(5), 1380–1397. doi:10.1037/0022-3514.74.5.1380

Cooper, R. P., & Aslin, R. N. (1990). Preference for infant-directed speech in the first month after birth. *Child Development, 61*(5), 1584–1595.

Corbett, S. S., & Drewett, R. F. (2004). To what extent is failure to thrive in infancy associated with poorer cognitive development? A review and meta-analysis. *Journal of Child Psychology and Psychiatry, 45*(3), 641–654. doi:10.1111/j.1469-7610.2004.00253.x

Corbit, C., & Carpenter, M. (2006). The nervous system game. *Science and Children, 43*(6), 26–29.

Cordero, J. F. (1993). The epidemiology of disasters and adverse reproductive outcomes: Lessons learned. *Environmental Health Perspectives, 101*(Suppl. 2), 131–136. doi:10.2307/3431386

Cornelius, M. D., & Day, N. L. (2000). The effects of tobacco use during and after pregnancy on exposed children. *Alcohol Research & Health, 24*(4), 242–249.

Corwyn, R. F., & Bradley, R. H. (1999). Determinants of paternal and maternal investment in children. *Infant Mental Health Journal, 20*, 238–256.

Côté, J. E. (2009). Identity formation and self-development in adolescence. In R. M. Lerner & L. Steinberg (Eds.), *Handbook of adolescent psychology: Vol. 1. Individual bases of adolescent development* (3rd ed., pp. 266–304). Hoboken, NJ: Wiley.

Côté, S. M., Petitclerc, A., Raynault, M. F., Xu, Q., Falissard, B., Boivin, M., & Tremblay, R. E. (2010). Short- and long-term risk of infections as a function of group child care attendance. *Archives of Pediatrics and Adolescent Medicine, 164*(12), 1132–1137. doi:10.1001/archpediatrics.2010.216

Couperus, J. W. (2011). Perceptual load influences selective attention across development. *Developmental Psychology, 47*(5), 1431–1439. doi:10.1037/a0024027

Courage, M. L., & Howe, M. L. (2002). From infant to child: The dynamics of cognitive change in the second year of life. *Psychological Bulletin, 128*(2), 250–277. doi:10.1037/0033-2909.128.2.250

Cowan, C. P., & Cowan, P. A. (2000). *When partners become parents: The big life change for couples*. Mahwah, NJ: Erlbaum.

Cowan, N. (2005). *Working memory capacity*. New York, NY: Psychology Press.

Cowie, H. (2011). Understanding why children and young people engage in bullying at school. In C. Barter & D. Berridge (Eds.), *Children behaving badly: Peer violence between children and young people* (pp. 33–45). West Sussex, UK: Wiley–Blackwell.

Cox, M., Owen, M. T., Henderson, V., & Margand, N. (1992). Prediction of infant-father and infant-mother attachment. *Developmental Psychology, 28*, 474–483.

Coyle, T. R., & Bjorklund, D. F. (1997). Age differences in, and consequences of, multiple- and variable-strategy use on a multitrial sort-recall task. *Developmental Psychology, 33*(2), 372–380. doi:10.1037/0012-1649.33.2.372

Coyne, S. M., Nelson, D., & Underwood, M. (2011). Aggression in children. In P. K. Smith & C. H. Hart (Eds.), *The Wiley–Blackwell handbook of childhood social development* (pp. 491–509). West Sussex, UK: Wiley.

Crain, W. (2000). *Theories of development: Concepts and applications* (4th ed). Upper Saddle River, NJ: Prentice Hall.

Crain, W. (2005). Kohlberg's stages of moral development. *Theories of development: Concepts and applications* (5th ed., pp. 151–173). Upper Saddle River, NJ: Pearson/Prentice-Hall.

Crick, N. R. (1997). Engagement in gender normative versus nonnormative forms of aggression: Links to social psychological adjustment. *Developmental Psychology, 33*(4), 610–617. doi:10.1037/0012-1649.33.4.610

Crick, N. R., & Dodge, K. A. (1994). A review and reformulation of social information-processing mechanisms of children's social adjustment. *Psychological Bulletin, 115*(1), 74–101. doi:10.1037/0033-2909.115.1.74

Crick, N. R., & Grotpeter, J. K. (1995). Relational aggression, gender, and social-psychological adjustment. *Child Development, 66*(3), 710–722. doi:10.2307/1131945.

Crockenberg, S. B. (1981). Infant irritability, mother responsiveness, and social support influences on the security of infant-mother attachment. *Child Development, 52*, 857–865.

Cronk, C., Crocker, A. C., Pueschel, S. M., Shea, A. M., Zackai, E., Pickens, G., & Reed, R. B. (1988). Growth charts for children with Down syndrome: 1 month to 18 years of age. *Pediatrics, 81*(1), 102–110.

Cross, W. E., Jr. (1995). Oppositional identity and African American youth: Issues and prospects. In W. D. Hawley & A. W. Jackson (Eds.), *Toward a common destiny: Improving race and ethnic relations in America* (pp. 185–204). San Francisco, CA: Jossey-Bass.

Crowley, C., Harré, R., & Lunt, I. (2007). Safe spaces and sense of identity: Views and experiences of lesbian, gay and bisexual young people. *Journal of Gay & Lesbian Psychotherapy, 11*(1–2), 127–143. doi:10.1300/J236v11n01_09

Crowley, M. J., Wu, J., Molfese, P. J., & Mayers, L. C. (2010). Social exclusion in middle childhood: Rejection events, slow-wave neural activity and ostracism distress. *Social Neuroscience, 5*(5–6), 483–495.

Cruse, A. (2004). *Meaning in language: An introduction to semantics and pragmatics* (2nd ed.). Oxford, England: Oxford University Press.

Cruz, J. R., Carlsson, B., Garcia, B., Gebre–Medhin, M., Hofvander, Y., Urrutia, J. J., & Hanson, L. A. (1982). Studies on human milk III. Secretory IgA quantity and antibody levels against *Escherichia coli* in colostrum and milk from underprivileged and privileged mothers. *Pediatric Research, 16*, 272–276.

Cryer, D., & Clifford, R. M. (2003). *Early childhood education and care in the USA*. Baltimore, MD: Paul H. Brookes.

Csibra, G., Kushnerenko, E., & Grossmann, T. (2008). Electrophysiological methods in studying infant cognitive development. In C. A. Nelson & M. Luciana (Eds.), *Handbook of developmental cognitive neuroscience* (2nd ed., pp. 247–262). Cambridge, MA: MIT Press.

Cummings, M. R. (2006). *Human heredity* (7th ed.). Belmont, CA: Thomson Brooks/Cole.

Cumsille, P., Darling, N., Flaherty, B. P., & Martínez, M. L. (2006). Chilean adolescents' beliefs about the legitimacy of parental authority: Individual and age-related difference. *International Journal of Behavioral Development, 30*(2), 97–106. doi:10.1177/0165025406063554

Cunningham, C. E., Cunningham, L. J., Ratcliffe, J., & Vaillancourt, T. (2010). A qualitative analysis of the bullying prevention and intervention recommendations of students in grades 5 to 8. *Journal of School Violence, 9*(4), 321–338. doi:10.1080/15388220.2010.507146

Cunningham, F. G., Leveno, K. J., Bloom, S. L., Hauth, J. C., Gilstrap, L. C., & Wenstrom,

K. D. (2005). *Williams obstetrics (22nd ed.)*. New York, NY: McGraw–Hill.

Curby, T. W., LoCasale-Crouch, J., Konold, T. R., Pianta, R. C., Howes, C., Burchinal, M., . . . Barbarin, O. (2009). The relations of observed pre-K classroom quality profiles to children's achievement and social competence. *Early Education and Development, 20*(2), 346–372. doi:10.1080/10409280802581284

Cuskelly, M., & Gunn, P. (2003). Sibling relationships of children with Down syndrome: Perspectives of mothers, fathers, and siblings. *American Journal on Mental Retardation, 108*(4), 234–244.

Cyr, J. L. S., & Decker, S. H. (2003). Girls, guys, and gangs: Convergence or divergence in the gendered construction of gangs and groups. *Journal of Criminal Justice, 31*(5), 423–433. doi:10.1016/S0047–2352(03)00048–5

D'Alli, R. E. (2009). Child and adolescent psychopharmacology. In W. B. Carey, A. C. Crocker, W. L. Coleman, E. R. Elias, & H. M. Feldman (Eds.), *Developmental-behavioral pediatrics* (4th ed., pp. 885–910). Philadelphia, PA: Saunders/Elsevier.

D'Angelo, S. L., & Omar, H. A. (2003). Parenting adolescents. *International Journal of Adolescent Medicine and Health, 15*(1), 11–19.

D'Hulst, C., & Kooy, R. F. (2009). Fragile X syndrome: From molecular genetics to therapy. *Journal of Medical Genetics, 46*(9), 577–584. doi:10.1136/jmg.2008.064667

Dacey, J. S., & Travers, J. F. (1999). *Human development across the lifespan* (4th ed.). New York, NY: McGraw–Hill.

Dacey, J., Travers, J., & Fiore, L. (2009). *Human development across the lifespan (7th ed.)*. New York, NY: McGraw-Hill.

Dahl, R. E. (2004). Adolescent brain development: A framework for understanding unique vulnerabilities and opportunities (keynote address). In *Adolescent brain development: Vulnerabilities and opportunities*. Symposium conducted at the New York Academy of Sciences, New York, NY.

Dahl, R. E. (2008). Biological, developmental, and neurobehavioral factors relevant to adolescent driving risks. *American Journal of Preventive Medicine, 35*(3S), S278–S284. doi:10.1016/j.amepre.2008.06.013

Dalenius, K., Brindley, P., Smith, B., Reinold, C., & Grummer-Strawn, L. (2012). *Pregnancy Nutrition Surveillance 2010 Report*. Atlanta, GA: U.S. Department of Health and Human Services, Centers for Disease Control and Prevention.

Dales, L., Hammer, S. J., & Smith, N. J. (2001). Time trends in autism and in MMR immunization coverage in California. *Journal of the American Medical Association, 285*(9), 1183–1185. doi:10.1001/jama.285.9.1183

Damasio, A. (2001). Fundamental feelings. *Nature, 413*, 781.

Damasio, A. (2005). Brain trust. *Nature, 435*, 571–572.

Damasio, A. R. (1994). *Descartes' error: Emotion, reason, and the human brain*. New York, NY: Random House.

Damasio, A. R. (1999). *The feeling of what happens: Body and emotion in the making of consciousness*. New York, NY: Harcourt Brace.

Damasio, A. R. (2003). *Looking for Spinoza: Joy, sorrow, and the feeling brain*. Orlando, FL: Harcourt.

Damasio, A. R. (2007). Neuroscience and ethics: Intersections. *American Journal of Bioethics, 7*(1), 3–7.

Damon, W. (1975). Early conceptions of positive justice as related to the development of logical operations. *Child Development, 46*, 301–312. doi:10.2307/1128122

Damon, W. (1980). Patterns of change in children's social reasoning: A two-year longitudinal study. *Child Development, 51*(4), 1010–1017. doi:10.2307/1129538

Damon, W. (1990). *The moral child: Nurturing children's natural moral growth*. New York, NY: Free Press.

Damon, W. (1996). *Greater expectations: Overcoming the culture of indulgence in our homes and schools*. New York, NY: Free Press.

Damon, W. (2008). *The path to purpose: Helping our children find their calling in life*. New York, NY: Free Press.

Damon, W., & Hart, D. (1988). *Self-understanding in childhood and adolescence*. New York, NY: Cambridge University Press.

Damon, W., & Lerner, R. M. (2008). The scientific study of child and adolescent development: Important issues in the field today. In W. Damon & R. M. Lerner (Eds.), *Child and adolescent development: An advanced course* (pp. 3–15). Hoboken, NJ: Wiley.

Daneman, M., & Carpenter, P. (1980). Individual differences in working memory and reading. *Journal of Verbal Learning and Verbal Behavior, 19*(4), 450–466. doi:10.1016/S0022–5371(80)90312–6

Daneman, M., & Green, I. (1986). Individual differences in comprehending and producing words in context. *Journal of Memory and Language, 25*(1), 1–18. doi:10.1016/0749–596X(86)90018–5

Daniels, A. S., Seacat, J. D., & Inglehart, M. R. (2009). Orthodontic treatment motivation and cooperation: A cross-sectional analysis of adolescent patients' and parents' responses. *American Journal of Orthodontics and Dentofacial Orthopedics, 136*, 780–787.

Danis, A., Pêcheux, M-G., Lefèvre, C., Bourdais, C., & Serres-Ruel, J. (2008). A continuous performance task in preschool children: Relations between attention and performance. *European Journal of Developmental Psychology, 5*(4), 401–418. doi:10.1080/17405620600866800

Dannemiller, J. L, & Freedland, R. L. (1991). Detection of relative motion by human infants. *Developmental Psychology, 27*, 67–78. doi:10.1037/0012–1649.27.1.67

Dapretto, M., Davies, M. S., Pfiefer, J. H., Scott, A. A., Sigman, M., Bookheimer, S. Y., & Iacoboni, M. (2006). Understanding emotions in others: Mirror neuron dysfunction in children with autism spectrum disorders. *Nature Neuroscience, 9*(1), 28–30.

Darling, N., Cumsille, P., Peña-Alampay, L., & Coatsworth, D. (2009). Individual and issue-specific differences in parental knowledge and adolescent disclosure in Chile, the Philippines, and the United States. *Journal of Research on Adolescence, 19*(4), 715–740. doi:10.1111/j.1532–7795.2009.00608.x

Darling-Hammond, L. (2006). No Child Left Behind and high school reform. *Harvard Educational Review, 76*(4), 642–667.

Darras, B. T., Korf, B. R., & Urion, D. K. (2008). Dystrophinopathies. *GeneReviews*. Retrieved from http://www.ncbi.nlm.nih.gov/books/NBK1119 (pmid: 20301298)

Darwin, C. (1859). *On the origin of species by means of natural selection, or the preservation of favoured races in the struggle for life*. London, UK: John Murray.

Darwin, C. R. (1872). *The expression of the emotions in man and animals*. London, UK: John Murray. Retrieved from http://darwin-online.org.uk/content/frameset?pageseq=1&itemID=F1142&viewtype=text.

Dasen, P. R. (1972). Cross-cultural Piagetian research: A summary. *Journal of Cross-Cultural Psychology, 3*(1), 23–40. doi:10.1177/002202217200300102

Davidhizar, R., & Giger, J. N. (2004). A review of the literature on care of clients in pain who are culturally diverse. *International Nursing Review, 51*(1), 47–55. doi:10.1111/j.1466–7657.2003.00208.x

Davidov, M., & Grusec, J. E. (2006). Untangling the links of parental responsiveness to distress and warmth to child outcomes. *Child Development, 77*(1), 44–58. doi:10.1111/j.1467-8624. 2006.00855.x

Davidson, M. C., Amso, D., Anderson, L. C., & Diamond, A. (2006). Development of cognitive control and executive functions from 4 to 13 years: Evidence from manipulations of memory, inhibition, and task switching. *Neuropsychologia, 44*(11), 2037–2078. doi:10.1016/j.neuropsychologia.2006.02.006

Davies, P. T., & Windle, M. (2000). Middle adolescents' dating pathways and psychosocial adjustment. *Merrill-Palmer Quarterly, 46*(1), 90–118

Davies, P. T., Sturge–Apple, M. L., Cicchetti, D., & Cummings, E. M. (2007). The role of child adrenocortical functioning in pathways between interparental conflict and child maladjustment. *Developmental Psychology, 43*(4), 918–930. doi:10.1037/0012–1649.43.4.918

Davies, S., Bishop, D., Manstead, A. S. R., & Tantam, D. (1994). Face perception in children with autism and Asperger's syndrome. *Journal of Child Psychology and Psychiatry, 35*(6), 1033–1057.

Davis, E. P., Bruce, J., Snyder, K., & Nelson, C. A. (2003). The X-trials: Neural correlates of an inhibitory control task in children and adults. *Journal of Cognitive Neuroscience, 15*(3), 432–443. doi:10.1162/089892903321593144

Davis, E. P., Buss, C., Muftuler, T., Head, K., Hasso, A., Wing, D.A., . . . Sandman, C.A. (2011). Children's brain development benefits from longer gestation. *Frontiers in Psychology, 2*, 1–7. doi:10.3389/fpsyq.2011.00001

Davis, M. (1992). The role of the amygdala in fear and anxiety. *Annual Review of Neuroscience, 15*, 353–375. doi:10.1146/annurev.ne.15.030192.002033.

Davis, R. N., Davis, M. M., Freed, G. L., & Clark, S. J. (2011). Fathers' depression related to positive and negative parenting behaviors with 1-year-old children. *Pediatrics, 127*(4), 612–618.

Davis-Kean, P. E., Huesmann, L. R., Jager, J., Collins, W. A., Bates, J. E., & Lansford, J. E. (2008). Changes in the relation of self-efficacy beliefs and behaviors across development. *Child Development, 79*(5), 1257–1269. doi:10.1111/j.1467–8624.2008.01187.x

Dawson, G., Meltzoff, A., Osterling, J., Rinaldi, J., & Brown, E. (1998). Children with autism fail to orient to naturally-occurring social stimuli. *Journal of Autism and Developmental Disorders*, *28*, 479–485.

Dawson, T. L. (2002). New tools, new insights: Kohlberg's moral reasoning stages revisited. *International Journal of Behavioral Development*, *26*, 154–166.

de Hevia, M. D. & Spelke, E. S. (2010). Number-space mapping in human infants. *Psychological Science*, *21*(5), 653–660. doi:10.1177/0956797610366091

De Lisi, R., & Wolford, J. L. (2002). Improving children's mental rotation accuracy with computer game playing. *The Journal of Genetic Psychology: Research and Theory on Human Development*, *163*, 272–282. doi:10.1080/00221320209598683

De Luca, B. M., Takano, K., Hinshaw, S. A., & Raisch, C. D. (2009). Are the "best" teachers in the "neediest" schools? An urban intradistrict equity inquiry. *Education and Urban Society*, *41*(6), 653–671. doi:10.1177/0013124509339265

de Onis, M., Onyango, A. W., Borghi, E., Siyam, A., Nishida, C., & Siekmann, J. (2007). Development of a WHO growth reference for school-aged children and adolescents. *Bulletin of the World Health Organization*, *85*(9), 649–732. doi:10.2471/BLT.07.043497

De Wolff, M. S., & van IJzendoorn, M. H. (1997). Sensitivity and attachment: A meta-analysis on parental antecedents of infant attachment. *Child Development*, *68*, 571–591.

Dean, B. B., Calimlim, B. M., Kindermann, S. L., Khandker, R. K., & Tinkelman, D. (2009). The impact of uncontrolled asthma on absenteeism and health-related quality of life. *Journal of Asthma*, *46*(9), 861–866. doi:10.3109/02770900903184237

Dearing, E., Kreider, H., & Weiss, H. B. (2008). Increased family involvement in school predicts improved child-teacher relationships and feelings about school for low-income children. *Marriage and Family Review*, *43*(3/4), 226–254. doi:10.1080/01494920802072462

Deary, I. J., Johnson, W., & Houlihan, L. M. (2009). Genetic foundations of human intelligence. *Human Genetics*, *126*(1), 215–232. doi:10.1007/s00439-009-0655-4

Deary, I. J., Penke, L., & Johnson, W. (2010). The neuroscience of human intelligence differences. *Nature Reviews in Neuroscience*, *11*, 201–211. doi:10.1038/nrn2793

Deater-Deckard, K., Atzaba-Poria, N., & Pike, A. (2004). Mother- and father-child mutuality in Anglo and Indian British families: A link with lower externalizing problems. *Journal of Abnormal Child Psychology*, *32*(6), 609–620. doi:10.1023/B:JACP.0000047210.81880.14

Deater-Deckard, K., Dodge, K. A., Bates, J. E., & Pettit, G. S. (1996). Physical discipline among African American and European American mothers: Links to children's externalizing behaviors. *Developmental Psychology*, *32*, 1065–1072.

Deater-Deckard, K., Petrill, S. A., Thompson, L. A., & DeThorne, L. S. (2005). A cross-sectional behavioral genetic analysis of task persistence in the transition to middle childhood. *Developmental Science*, *8*(3), F21–F26. doi:10.1111/j.1467-7687.2005.00407.x

DeCasper, A. J., & Fifer, W. P. (1980). Of human bonding: Newborns prefer their mothers' voices. *Science*, *208*(4448), 1174–1176. doi:10.1126/science.7375928

DeCasper, A. J., & Spence, M. J. (1986). Prenatal maternal speech influences newborns' perception of speech sounds. *Infant Behavior and Development*, *9*, 133–150. doi:10.1016/0163-6383(86)90025-1

DeCasper, A. J., & Spence, M. J. (1991). Auditorily mediated behavior during the perinatal period: A cognitive view. In M. J. S. Weiss & P. R. Zelazo (Eds.), *Newborn attention: Biological constraints and the influence of experience* (pp. 142–176). Norwood, NJ: Ablex.

DeCasper, A. J., Lecanuet, J. P., Busnel, M. C., Granier–Deferre, C., & Maugeais, R. (1994). Fetal reactions to recurrent maternal speech. *Infant Behavior and Development*, *17*(2), 159–164. doi:10.1016/0163-6383(94)90051-5

Decety, J., & Jackson, P. L. (2006). A social-neuroscience perspective on empathy. *Current Directions in Psychological Science*, *15*(2), 54–58. doi:10.1111/j.0963-7214.2006.00406.x

Decety, J., Michalaska, K. J., & Kinzler, C. D. (2012). The contribution of emotion and cognition to moral sensitivity: A neurodevelopmental study. *Cerebral Cortex*, *22*(1), 209–220. doi:10.1093/cercor/bhr111

Declercq, E., Menacker, F., & MacDorman, M. (2006). Maternal risk profiles and the primary cesarean rate in the United States, 1991–2002. *American Journal Public Health*, *96*(5), 867–872. doi:10.2105/AJPH.2004.052381

Dee, D. L., Li, R., Lee, C., & Grummer-Strawn, L. M. (2007). Associations between breastfeeding practices and young children's language and motor skill development. *Pediatrics*, *119*, S92–S98. doi:10.1542/peds.2006-2089N

Dehaene-Lambertz, G., Hertz-Pannier, L., & Dubois, J. (2006). Nature and nurture in language acquisition: Anatomical and functional brain-imaging studies in infants. *Trends in Neuroscience*, *29*(7), 367–373.

Delemarre-van de Waal, H. (2002). Regulation of puberty. *Best Practice & Research Clinical Endocrinology & Metabolism*, *16*(1), 1–12.

Dench, G., Ogg, J., & Thomson, K. (1999). The role of grandparents. In R. Jowell, J. Curtis, A. Park, & K. Thomson (Eds.), *British social attitudes: The 16th report*. Hampshire, UK: Ashgate.

Denham, S. A., Bassett, H., Mincic, M., Kalb, S., Way, E., Wyatt, T., & Segal, Y. (2012). Social-emotional learning profiles of preschoolers' early school success: A person-centered approach. *Learning and Individual Differences*, *22*(2), 178–189. doi:10.1016/j.lindif.2011.05.001

Denizet-Lewis, B. (2004, May 30). Friends, friends with benefits and the benefits of the local mall. *The New York Times*. Retrieved from http://209.157.64.200/focus/f-news/1144851/posts

Dennis, T. A., Hong, M., & Solomon, B. (2010). Do the associations between exuberance and emotion regulation depend on effortful control? *International Journal of Behavioral Development*, *34*(5), 462–472. doi:10.1177/0165025409355514

Dennis, T. A., O'Toole, L. J., & DeCicco, J. M. (2013). Emotion regulation from the perspective of developmental neuroscience. In K. C. Barrett, N. A. Fox, G. A. Morgan, D. J. Fidler, & L. A Daunhauer (Eds.), *Handbook of self-regulatory processes in development* (pp. 135–172). New York, NY: Psychology Press.

Denton, K., & West, J. (2002). Children's reading and mathematics achievement in kindergarten and first grade. *Education Statistics Quarterly*, *4*(1), 19–26.

Destin, M., & Oyserman, D. (2010). Incentivizing education: Seeing schoolwork as an investment, not a chore. *Journal of Experimental Social Psychology*, *46*(5), 846–849. doi:10.1016/j.jesp.2010.04.004

Devinsky, O., Morrell, M. J., & Vogt, B. A. (1995). Contributions of anterior cingulate cortex to behaviour. *Brain*, *118*, 279–306.

DeVoe, J. F., & Kaffenberger, S. (2005). *Student reports of bullying: Results from the 2001 School Crime Supplement to the National Crime Victimization Survey* (NCES 2005–310). Washington, DC: U.S. Department of Education, National Center for Education Statistics, U.S. Government Printing Office.

DeVries, M. W., & DeVries M. R. (1977). Cultural relativity of toilet-training readiness: A perspective from East Africa. *Pediatrics*, *60*(2), 170–177.

DeVries, R. (2000). Vygotsky, Piaget, and education: A reciprocal assimilation of theories and educational practices. *New Ideas in Psychology*, *18*, 187–213.

DeWals, P., Tairou, F., Van Allen, M. I., Uh, S–H., Lowry, B., Sibbald, B., . . . Niyonsenga, T. (2007). Reduction in neural-tube defects after folic acid fortification in Canada. *New England Journal of Medicine*, *357*(2), 135–142.

DeWalt, D. A., & Hink, A. (2009). Health literacy and child health outcomes: A systematic review of the literature. *Pediatrics*, *124*(Suppl. 3), S265–S274. doi:10.1542/peds.2009-1162B

Diamond, A. (2001). Prefrontal cortex development and development of cognitive functions. In N. J. Smelser and P. B. Baltes (Eds.), *International Encyclopedia of the Social and Behavioral Sciences* (pp. 11976–11982). Oxford, UK: Pergamon.

Diamond, A. (2006). The early development of executive functions. In E. Bialystok & F. Craik (Eds.), *Lifespan cognition: Mechanisms of change* (pp. 70–95). New York, NY: Oxford University Press.

Diamond, A. (2009). The interplay of biology and the environment broadly defined. *American Psychologist*, *45*(1), 1–8. doi:10.1037/a0014601

Diamond, A. (2011). Biological and social influences on cognitive control processes dependent on prefrontal cortex. *Progress in Brain Research*, *89*, 317–337.

Diamond, A. (2012). Activities and programs that improve children's executive functions. *Current Directions in Psychological Science*, *21*(5), 335–341.

Diamond, A., & Amso, D. (2008). Contributions of neuroscience to our understanding of cognitive development. *Current Directions in Psychological Science*, *17*, 136–141. doi:10.1111/j.1467-8721.2008.00563.x

Diamond, A., & Goldman-Rakic P. (1989). Comparison of human infants and rhesus monkeys on Piaget's A-not-B task: Evidence for dependence on dorsolateral prefrontal cortex. *Experimental Brain Research, 74*, 24–40.

Diamond, A., Barnett, W. S., Thomas, J., & Munro, S. (2007). Preschool program improves cognitive control. *Science, 318*(5855), 1387–1388. doi:10.1126/science.1151148

Diamond, A., Prevor, M. B., Callender, G., & Druin, D. P. (1997). Prefrontal cortex cognitive deficits in children treated early and continuously for PKU. *Monographs of the Society for Research in Child Development, 62*(4), 1–205. doi:10.2307/1166208

Diamond, K. E. (2001). Relationships among young children's ideas, emotional understanding, and social contact with classmates with disabilities. *Topics in Early Childhood Special Education, 21*(2), 104–113. doi:10.1177/027112140102100204

Diamond, K. E., & Hong, S. (2010). Young children's decisions to include peers with physical disabilities in play. *Journal of Early Intervention, 32*(3), 163–177. doi:10.1177/1053815110371332

Diamond, K. E., Hestenes, L. L., Carpenter, E. S., & Innes, F. K. (1997). Relationships between enrollment in an inclusive class and preschool children's ideas about people with disabilities. *Topics in Early Childhood Special Education, 17*(4), 520–536. doi:10.1177/027112149701700409

Dien, T. T. (1998). Language and literacy in Vietnamese American communities. In B. Perez (Ed.), *Sociocultural contexts of language and literacy* (pp. 123–161). Mahwah, NJ: Erlbaum.

Dietz, H. C. (2009). Marfan Syndrome. *GeneReviews*. Seattle, WA. Retrieved from http://www.ncbi.nlm.nih.gov/bookshelf/br.fcgi?book=gene&part=marfan (pmid: 20301510).

DiLalla, L. F., Thompson, L. A., Plomin, R., Phillips, K., Fagan, J. F., Haith, M. M., . . . Fulker, D. W. (1990). Infant predictors of preschool and adult IQ: A study of infant twins and their parents. *Developmental Psychology, 26*, 759–769.

Dilworth-Bart, J., Poehlmann, J., Hilgendorf, A. E., Miller, K., & Lambert, H. (2010). Maternal scaffolding and preterm toddlers' visual-spatial processing and emerging working memory. *Journal of Pediatric Psychology, 35*(2), 209–220. doi:10.1093/jpepsy/jsp048

Dixon, M., & Kaminska, Z. (2007). Does exposure to orthography affect children's spelling accuracy? *Journal of Research in Reading, 30*(2), 184–197. doi:10.1111/j.1467-9817.2007.00337.x

Dobbs, D. (2007). Big answers from little people. *Scientific American, 17*(2), 4–9.

Dobrowolski, S. F., Andersen, H. S., Doktor, T. K., & Andresen, B. S. (2010). The phenylalanine hydroxylase c.30C>G synonymous variation (p.G10G) creates a common exonic splicing silencer. *Molecular Genetics and Metabolism, 100*(4), 316–323. doi:10.1016/j.ymgme.2010.04.002

Dodge, K. A., Coie, J. D., & Lynam, D. (2006). Aggression and antisocial behavior in youth. In W. Damon & R. M. Lerner (Series Eds.) & N. Eisenberg (Vol. Ed.), *Handbook of child psychology: Vol. 3. Social, emotional, and personality development* (6th ed., pp. 719–788). Hoboken, NJ: Wiley.

Dodge, K. A., Pettit, G. S., Bates, J. E., & Valente, E. (1995). Social information-processing patterns partially mediate the effect of early physical abuse on later conduct problems. *Journal of Abnormal Psychology, 104*(4), 632–643. doi:10.1037/0021-843X.104.4.632

Dodge, K. A., Schlundt, D. C., Schocken, I., & Delugach, J. D. (1983). Social competence and children's sociometric status: The role of peer group entry strategies. *Merrill-Palmer Quarterly, 29*(3), 309–336.

Domar, A. (2009). *Psychological stress and infertility*. In C. Lockwood & T. Schwenk (Eds.), *UpToDate*. Waltham, MA: UpToDate. Retrieved from http://www.uptodate.com/contents/psychological-stress-and-infertility

Donenberg, G. R., Schwartz, R. M., Emerson, E., Wilson, H. W., Bryant, F. B., & Coleman, G. (2005). Applying a cognitive-behavioral model of HIV risk to youths in psychiatric care. *AIDS Education & Prevention, 17*(3), 200–216.

Donnelly, N., Cave, K., Greenway, R., Hadwin, J. A., Stevenson, J., & Sonuga-Barke, E. (2007). Visual search in children and adults: Top-down and bottom-up mechanisms. *The Quarterly Journal of Experimental Psychology, 60*(1), 120–136. doi:10.1080/17470210600625362

Doran, C. M., Hall, W. D., Shakeshaft, A. P., Vos, T., & Cobiac, L. J. (2010). Alcohol policy reform in Australia: What can we learn from the evidence? *Medical Journal of Australia, 192*(8), 468–470.

Dore, M. (2005). Child and adolescent mental health. In G. Mallon & P. Hess (Eds.), *Child welfare for the twenty-first century: A handbook of practices, policies and programs* (pp. 148–172). New York, NY: Columbia University Press.

Dotterer, A. M., McHale, S. M., & Crouter, A. C. (2009). The development and correlates of academic interests from childhood through adolescence. *Journal of Educational Psychology, 101*(2), 509–551. doi:10.1037/a0013987

Downey, G., & Feldman, S. I. (2004). Implications of rejection sensitivity for intimate relationships. In G. Downey & S. I. Feldman (Eds.), *The interface of social and clinical psychology: Key readings* (pp. 173–198). New York, NY: Psychology Press.

Drutz, J. E. (2010). Autism and chronic disease: Little evidence for vaccines as a contributing factor. In T. K. Duryea (Ed.), *UpToDate*. Waltham, MA: UpToDate.

Duchesne, S., & Ratelle, C. (2010). Parental behaviors and adolescents' achievement goals at the beginning of middle school: Emotional problems as potential mediators. *Journal of Educational Psychology, 102*(2), 497–507. doi:10.1037/a0019320

Dulude, D., Wright, J. & Belanger, C. (2000). The effects of pregnancy complications on the parental adaptation process. *Journal of Reproductive and Infant Psychology, 18*(1), 5–19.

Duncan, G. J., Dowsett, C. J., Claessens, A., Magnuson, K., Huston, A. C., Klebanov, P., . . . Japel, C. (2007). School readiness and later achievement. *Developmental Psychology, 43*(6), 1428–1446. doi:10.1037/0012-1649.43.6.1428

Dunfield, K. A., & Kuhlmeier, V. A. (2010). Intention-mediated selective helping in infancy. *Psychological Science, 21*, 523–527.

Dunifon, R. (2013). The influence of grandparents on the lives of children and adolescents. *Child Development Perspectives, 7*(1), 55–60.

Dunkle, M. C., & Nash, M. A. (1991). *Beyond the health room*. Washington, DC: Council of Chief State School Officers, Resource Center on Educational Equity.

Dunn, J. (1987). The beginnings of moral understanding: Development in the second year. In J. Kagan & S. Lamb (Eds.), *The emergence of morality in young children*. Chicago, IL: University of Chicago Press.

Dunn, J. (1988). *The beginnings of social understanding*. Cambridge, MA: Harvard University Press.

Dunn, J. (1993). *Young children's close relationships: Beyond attachment*. London, UK: Sage.

Dunn, J. (2003). Emotional development in early childhood: A social relationship perspective. In R. J. Davidson, K. R. Scherer, & H. H. Goldsmith (Eds.), *Handbook of affective sciences* (pp. 332–346). New York, NY: Oxford University Press.

Dunn, J. (2004). *Children's friendships: The beginnings of intimacy*. London, UK: Blackwell.

Dunn, J., & Dale, N. (1984). I a daddy: 2-year-olds' collaboration in joint pretend with sibling and with mother. In I. Bretherton (Ed.), *Symbolic play* (pp. 131–158). New York, NY: Academic Press.

Dunson, D. B., Baird, D. D., & Colombo, B. (2004). Increased infertility with age in men and women. *Obstetrics & Gynecology, 103*(1), 51–56. doi:10.1097/01.AOG.0000100153.24061.45

DuPaul, G. J., McGoey, K. E., & Mautone, J. A. (2003). Pediatric pharmacology and psychopharmacology. In M. Roberts (Ed.), *Handbook of pediatric psychology* (3rd ed., pp. 234–250). New York, NY: Guilford.

Dupéré, V., Lacourse, E., Willms, J. D., Vitaro, F., & Tremblay, R. E. (2007). Affiliation to youth gangs during adolescence: The interaction between childhood psychopathic tendencies and neighborhood disadvantage. *Journal of Abnormal Child Psychology, 35*(5), 1035–1045. doi:10.1007/s10802-007-9153-0

Duran, B. J., Dugan, T., & Weffer, R. (1998). Language minority students in high school: The role of language in learning biology concepts. *Science Education, 82*(3), 311–341. doi:10.1002/(SICI)1098-237X(199806)82:3 3.0.CO;2-F

Durbin, E. C. (2010). Validity of young children's self-reports of their emotion in response to structured laboratory tasks. *Emotion, 10*(4), 519–535. doi:10.1037/a0019008

Durieux-Smith, A., Fitzpatrick, E., & Whittingham, J. (2008). Universal newborn hearing screening: A question of evidence. *International Journal of Audiology, 47*(1), 1–10. doi:10.1080/14992020701703547

Durlak, J. A., & Weissberg, R. P. (2007). *The impact of after-school programs that promote personal and social skills*. Chicago, IL: Collaborative for Academic, Social, and Emotional Learning.

Durlak, J. A., Weissberg, R. P., & Pachan, M. (2010). A meta-analysis of after-school programs that seek to promote personal and social skills in children and adolescents. *American Journal of Community Psychology, 45*(3–4), 294–309. doi:10.1007/s10464–010–9300–6

Durston, S., & Casey, B. J. (2006). What have we learned about cognitive development from neuroimaging? *Neuropsychologia, 44*(11), 2149–2157. doi:10.1016/j.neuropsychologia.2005.10.010

Duvander, A-Z., & Andersson, G. (2006). Gender equality and fertility in Sweden: A study on the impact of the father's uptake of parental leave on continued childbearing. *Marriage and Family Review*, 39, 121–142.

Dweck, C. S. (1999). Caution: Praise can be dangerous. *American Educator, 23*(1), 1–5.

Dweck, C. S. (1999). *Self-theories: Their role in motivation, personality, and development*. New York, NY: Psychology Press.

Dyke, P., Mulroy, S., & Leonard, H. (2009). Siblings of children with disabilities: Challenges and opportunities. *Acta Paediatrica, 98*(1), 23–24. doi:10.1111/j.1651–2227.2008.01168.x

Dyson, A. H. (2003). *The brothers and sisters learn to write: Popular literacies in childhood and school cultures.* New York, NY: Teachers College Press.

Early, D. M., Barbarin, O., Bryant, D. M., Burchinal, M., Chang, F., Clifford, R. M., . . . Weaver, W. (2005). *Pre-kindergarten in eleven states: NCEDL's multi-state study of pre-kindergarten and study of state-wide early education programs (SWEEP)*. Chapel Hill, NC: National Center for Early Development and Learning.

Easterbrooks, A. E., & Biringen, Z. (2005). The emotional availability scales: Methodological refinements of the construct and clinical implications related to gender and at-risk interactions. *Infant Mental Health Journal, 26*, 291–294.

Easterbrooks, A., & Biringen, Z. (2000). Mapping the terrain of emotional availability and attachment. *Attachment and Human Development, 2*, 129–135.

Eccles, J. (2011). Gendered educational and occupational choices: Applying the Eccles et al. model of achievement-related choices. *International Journal of Behavioral Development, 35*(3), 195–201. doi:10.1177/0165025411398185

Eccles, J. S., & Roeser, R. W. (2009). Schools, academic motivation, and stage-environment fit. In R. M. Lerner & L. Steinberg (Eds.), *Handbook of adolescent psychology: Vol. 1. Individual bases of adolescent development* (3rd ed., pp. 404–434). Hoboken, NJ: Wiley.

Eccles, J. S., & Wigfield, A. (2002). Motivational beliefs, values, and goals. *Annual Review of Psychology, 53*(1), 109–132. doi:10.1146/annurev.psych.53.100901.135153

Eccles, J. S., Barber, B. L., Stone, M., & Hunt, J. (2003). Extracurricular activities and adolescent development. *Journal of Social Issues, 59*(4), 865–889. doi:10.1046/j.0022–4537.2003.00095.x

Eccles, J. S., Midgley, C., Wigfield, A., Buchanan, C. M., Reuman, D., Flanagan, C., & MacIver, D. (1993). Development during adolescence: The impact of stage-environment fit on young adolescents' experiences in schools and in families. *American Psychologist, 48*(2), 90–101.

Eckenrode, J., Campa, M., Luckey, D. W., Henderson, C. R., Cole, R., Kitzman, H., . . . Olds, P. L. (2010). Long-term effects of prenatal and infancy nurse home visitation on the life course of youths: 19-year follow-up of a randomized trial. *Archives of Pediatrics and Adolescent Medicine, 164*(1), 9–15.

Eckert, P. (1995). Trajectory and forms of institutional participation. In L. J. Crockett & A. C. Crouter (Eds.), *Pathways through adolescence: Individual development in relation to social contexts* (pp. 175–195). Hillsdale, NJ: Erlbaum.

Edelstein, B. L. (2002). Disparities in oral health and access to care: Findings of national surveys. *Ambulatory Pediatrics, 2*(2), 141–147. doi:10.1367/1539-4409(2002)002<0141:DIOHAA>2.0.CO;2

Edelstein, B. L., & Chinn, C. H. (2009). Update on disparities in oral health and access to dental care for America's children. *Academic Pediatrics, 9*(6), 415–419.

Edelstein, M. L., Abedi, M. R., & Wixon, J. (2007). Gene therapy clinical trials worldwide to 2007—an update. *The Journal of Gene Medicine, 9*(10), 833–842. doi:10.1002/jgm.1100

Edwards, C. P., Gandini, L., & Biovaninni, D. (1996). The contrasting developmental timetables of parents and preschool teachers in two cultural communities. In S. Harkness & C. M. Super (Eds.), *Parents' cultural belief systems. Their origins, expressions, and consequences* (pp. 270–288). New York, NY: Guilford.

Edwards, C., Gandini, L., & Forman, G. (Eds.) (1993). *The hundred languages of children: The Reggio Emilia approach to early childhood education*. Norwood, NJ: Ablex.

Edwin, H. K., Bird, J. A., Kulis, M., Laubach, S., Pons, L., Shreffler, W., . . . Burks, A. W. (2011). Sublingual immunotherapy for peanut allergy: Clinical immunologic evidence of desensitization. *Journal of Allergy and Clinical Immunology, 127*(3), 640–646. doi:10.1016/j.jaci.2010.12.1083

Ege, M. J., Mayer, M., Normand, A. C., Genuneit, J., Cookson, W., Phil, D., . . . von Mutius, E. (2011). Exposure to environmental microorganisms and childhood asthma. *The New England Journal of Medicine, 364*(8), 701–709.

Eggleston, P. A. (2007). The environment and asthma in US inner cities. *Chest, 132*(Suppl. 5), 782S–788S. doi:10.1378/chest.07-1906

Eggum, N. D., Eisenberg, N., Kao, K., Spinrad, T. L., Bolnick, R., Hofer, C., . . . Fabricius, W. V. (2011). Emotion understanding, theory of mind, and prosocial orientation: Relations over time in early childhood. *The Journal of Positive Psychology, 6*(1), 4–16. doi:10.1080/17439760.2010.536776

Eichenbaum, H., Yonelinas, A. R., & Ranganath, C. (2007). The medial temporal lobe and recognition memory. *Annual Review of Neuroscience, 30*, 123–152. doi:10.1146/annurev.neuro.30.051606.094328

Eimas, P. D, (1975). Auditory and phonetic coding of the cues for speech: Discrimination of the [r–l] distinction by young infants. *Perception & Psychophysics, 18*(5), 341–347. doi:10.3758/BF03211210

Eimas, P. D. (1975). Speech perception in early infancy. In L. B. Cohen & P. Salapatek (eds.), *Infant perception: From sensation to cognition* (Vol. 2, pp. 193–231). New York, NY: Academic Press.

Eimas, P. D., Sigueland, E. R., Jusczyk, R., & Vigorito, J. (1971). Speech perception in infants. *Science, 171*, 303–306.

Einspieler, C., Prechtl, F. R., Bos, A., Ferrari, F., & Coini, G. (2005). *Prechtl's method on the qualitative assessment of general movements in preterm, term and young infants. Clinics in developmental medicine* (No. 167). London, UK: Mac Keith Press.

Eisenberg, N. (2002). Empathy-related emotional responses, altruism, and their socialization. In R. J. Davidson & A. Harrington (Eds.). *Visions of compassion: Western scientists and Tibetan Buddhists examine human nature* (pp. 131–164). London, UK: Oxford University Press.

Eisenberg, N. (2006). Prosocial behavior. In N. Eisenberg (Ed.), *Children's needs III: Development, prevention, and intervention* (pp. 313–324). Washington, DC: National Association of School Psychologists.

Eisenberg, N., & Fabes, R. A. (1992). *Emotion, regulation, and the development of social competence*. Thousand Oaks, CA: Sage.

Eisenberg, N., & Fabes, R. A. (1998). Prosocial development. In W. Damon (Series Ed.) & N. Eisenberg (Vol. Ed.), *Handbook of child psychology: Vol. 3. Social, emotional, and personality development* (5th ed., pp. 701–778). New York, NY: Wiley.

Eisenberg, N., & Murphy, B. (1995). *Parenting and children's moral development*. Hillsdale, NJ: Erlbaum.

Eisenberg, N., & Spinrad, T. L. (2004). Emotion-related regulation: Sharpening the definition. *Child Development, 75*(2), 334–339. doi:10.1111/j.1467–8624.2004.00674.x

Eisenberg, N., & Valiente, C. (2002). Parenting and children's prosocial and moral development. In M. H. Bornstein (Ed.), *Handbook of parenting: Vol. 5. Practical issues in parenting* (pp. 111–142). Mahwah, NJ: Erlbaum.

Eisenberg, N., Carlo, G., Murphy, B., & Van Court, P. (1995). Prosocial development in late adolescence: A longitudinal study. *Child Development, 66*(4), 1179–1197. doi:10.2307/1131806

Eisenberg, N., Cumberland, A., Guthrie, I. K., Murphy, B. C., & Shepard, S. A. (2005). Age changes in prosocial responding and moral reasoning in adolescence and early adulthood. *Journal of Research on Adolescence, 15*(3), 235–260. doi:10.1111/j.1532–7795.2005.00095.x

Eisenberg, N., Fabes, R. A., & Spinrad, T. L. (2006). Prosocial development. In W. Damon & R. L. Lerner (Series Eds.) & N. Eisenberg (Vol. Ed.), *Handbook of child psychology: Vol. 3. Social, emotional, and personality development* (6th ed., pp. 646–718). Hoboken, NJ: Wiley.

Eisenberg, N., Fabes, R. A., Shepard, S. A., Guthrie, I. K., Murphy, B. C., & Reiser, M. (1999). Parental reactions to children's negative emotions: Longitudinal relations to quality of children's social functioning. *Child Development, 70*(2), 513–534. doi:10.1111/1467-8624.00037

Eisenberg, N., Fabes, R. A., Shepard, S. A., Murphy, B. C., Guthrie, I. K., Jones, S. (1997).

Contemporaneous and longitudinal prediction of children's social functioning from regulation and emotionality. *Child Development, 68*(4), 642–664. doi:10.2307/ 1132116

Eisenberg, N., Fabes, R. A., Shepard, S. A., Murphy, B. C., Guthrie, I. K., Jones, S., . . . Maszk, P. (1990). Empathy: Conceptualization, measurement, and relation to prosocial behavior. *Motivation and Emotion, 14*(2), 131–149. doi:10.1007/BF00991640

Eisenberg, N., Hofer, C., Spinrad, T. L., Gershoff, E. T., Valiente, C., Losoya, S. H., . . . Darling, N. (2008). Understanding mother-adolescent conflict discussions: Concurrent and across-time prediction from youths' dispositions and parenting. *Monographs of the Society for Research in Child Development, 73*(2), 1–147. doi:10.1111/j.1540–5834.2008.00470.x

Eisenberg, N., Morris, A. S., McDaniel, B., & Spinrad, T. L. (2009). Moral cognitions and prosocial responding in adolescence. In R. M. Lerner & L. Steinberg (Eds.), *Handbook of adolescent psychology: Vol. 1. Individual bases of adolescent development* (3rd ed., pp. 229–265). Hoboken, NJ: Wiley.

Eisenberg, N., Zhou, Q., & Koller, S. (2001). Brazilian adolescents' prosocial moral judgment and behavior: Relations to sympathy, perspective taking, gender-role orientation, and demographic characteristics. *Child Development, 72*(2), 518–534. doi:10.1111/ 1467–8624.00294

Eisenberger, N. I., & Lieberman, M. D. (2004). Why rejection hurts: A common neural alarm system for physical and social pain. *Trends in Cognitive Sciences, 8*, 294–300.

Ekman, P. (1984). Expression and the nature of emotion. In K. Scherer & P. Ekman (Eds.), *Approaches to emotion* (pp. 319–343). Hillsdale, NJ: Erlbaum.

Ekman, P. (1994). All emotions are basic. In P. Ekman & R. Davidson (Eds.), *The nature of emotion: Fundamental questions* (pp. 56–58). New York, NY: Oxford University Press.

Ekman, P. (2003). *Emotions revealed.* New York, NY: Times Books.

El Mansari, M., Guiard, B. P., Chernoloz, O., Ghanbari, R., Katz, N., & Blier, P. (2010). Relevance of norepinephrine-dopamine interactions in the treatment of major depressive disorder. *CNS Neuroscience & Therapeutics, 16*(3), e1–e17.

Eliot, L. (1999). *What's going on in there? How the brain and mind develop in the first five years of life.* New York, NY: Bantam.

Elkind, D. (1967). Egocentrism in adolescence. *Child Development, 38*(4), 1025–1034. doi:10. 2307/1127100

Elkind, D. (2007). *The power of play: How spontaneous imaginative activities lead to happier, healthier children.* Cambridge, MA: Da Capo Press.

Elkind, D. (2010, March 26). Playtime is over. *The New York Times*, p. A19.

Elliot, A., J., & Devine, P. G. (1994). On the motivational nature of cognitive dissonance: Dissonance as psychological discomfort. *Journal of Personality and Social Psychology, 67*(3), 382–394. doi:10.1037/0022–3514.67.3.382

Ellis, B. J. (2004). Timing of pubertal maturation in girls. *Psychological Bulletin, 130*, 920–958.

Ellis, B. J., & Essex, M. J. (2007). Family environments, adrenarche, and sexual maturation: A longitudinal test of a life history model. *Child Development, 78*(6), 1799–1817.

Elmore, R. F. (2009). Schooling adolescents. In R. M. Lerner & L. Steinberg (Eds.), *Handbook of adolescent psychology: Vol. 2. Contextual influences on adolescent development* (3rd ed., pp. 193–227). Hoboken, NJ: Wiley.

Elvedi–Gasparovic, V., Klepac–Pulanic, T., & Peter, B. (2006). Maternal and fetal outcome in elective versus emergency caesarean section in a developing country. *Collegium Antropologicum, 30*(1), 113–118.

Emde, R. N. (1980). Emotional availability: A reciprocal reward system for infants and parents with implications for prevention of psychosocial disorders. In P. M. Taylor (Ed.), *Parent-infant relationships* (pp. 87–115). Orlando, FL: Grune & Stratton.

Emde, R. N. (1983). The prerepresentational self and its affective core. *The Psychoanalytic Study of the Child, 38*, 165–192.

Emde, R. N. (1985). The affective self: Continuities and transformations from infancy. In J. D. Call, E. Galenson, & R. L. Tyson (Eds.), *Frontiers of infant psychiatry* (Vol. II, pp. 38–54). New York, NY: Basic Books.

Emde, R. N. (1998). Early emotional development: New modes of thinking for research and intervention. In J. G. Warhol (Ed.), *New perspectives in early emotional development* (pp. 29–45). New Brunswick, NJ: Johnson & Johnson Pediatric Institute.

Emde, R. N., & Easterbrooks, M. A. (1985). Assessing emotional availability in early development. In W. K. Frankenburg, R. N. Emde, & J. Sullivan (Eds.), *Early identification of the at-risk child: An international perspective* (pp. 79–102). New York, NY: Plenum.

Emde, R. N., Johnson, W., & Easterbrooks, M. A. (1987). The do's and don'ts of early moral development. In J. Kagan & S. Lamb (Eds.), *The emergence of morality in young children* (pp. 245–276). Chicago, IL: University of Chicago Press.

Emery, C. A. (2003). Risk factors for injury in child and adolescent sport: A systematic review of the literature. *Clinical Journal of Sports Medicine, 13*, 256–268.

Emery, N. J. (2000). The eyes have it: The neuroethology, function and evolution of social gaze. *Neuroscience & Biobehavioral Review, 24*, 581–604.

Emery, R. E. (1992). Family conflicts and their developmental implications: A conceptual analysis of meanings for the structure of relationships. In C. U. Shantz & W. W. Hartup (Eds.), *Conflict in child and adolescent development* (pp. 270–298). New York, NY: Cambridge University Press.

Emmett, P. M., & Rogers, I. S. (1997). Properties of human milk and their relationship with maternal nutrition. *Early Human Development, 49*, 27–28. doi:10.1016/S0378–3782 (97)00051–0

Emsellem, H. A., & Whiteley, C. (2006). *Snooze or lose: 10 "no war" ways to improve your teen's sleep habits.* Washington, DC: Joseph Henry Press and National Academies Press.

Engle, W. A., Tomashek, K. M., Wallman, C., & American Academy of Pediatrics, Committee on Fetus and Newborn. (2007). "Late-preterm" infants: A population at risk. *Pediatrics, 120*(6), 1390–1401. doi:10.1542/peds.2007–2952

English, A., & Park, M. J. (2012). *Access to health care for young adults: The Affordable Care Act is making a difference.* Chapel Hill, NC: Center for Adolescent Health & the Law; and San Francisco, CA: National Adolescent and Young Adult Health Information Center. Retrieved from http://www.adolescenthealth.org

Epstein, A. S. (2002, Summer). Helping preschool children become readers: Tips for parents. *High/Scope ReSource*, pp. 4–6.

Epstein, A. S., Schweinhart, L. J., & McAdoo, L. (1996). *Models of early childhood education.* Ypsilanti, MI: High/Scope Press.

Epstein, J. L. (1987). What principals should know about parent involvement. *Principal, 66*, 6–9.

Epstein, J. L. (1988). How do we improve programs for parental involvement? *Educational Horizons, 66*, 75–77.

Epstein, J. L. (2011). *School, family, and community partnerships: Preparing educators and improving schools* (2nd ed.). Philadelphia, PA: Westview Press.

Epstein, J. L., & Jansorn, N. R. (2004). School, family and community partnerships link the plan. *Education digest: Essential readings condensed for quick review, 69*(6), 19–23. Retrieved from http://search.proquest.com/docview/ 62072636?accountid=9673

Erickson, C. D., Splett, P. L., Mullett, S. S., Jensen, C., & Belseth, S. B. (2006). The healthy learner model for student chronic condition management—Part II: The asthma initiative. *Journal of School Nursing, 22*(6), 319–329.

Erikson, E. H. (1950). *Childhood and society.* New York, NY: Norton.

Erikson, E. H. (1959). *Identity and the life cycle.* New York, NY: Norton.

Erikson, E. H. (1968). *Identity: Youth and crisis.* Oxford, UK: Norton.

Erlandsson, K., Jinghede Nordvall, C., Öhman, A., & Häggström- Nordin, E. (2013). Qualitative interviews with adolescents about "friends-with-benefits" relationships. *Public Health Nursing, 30*(1), 47–57.

Ertas, N., & Shields, S. (2012). Child care subsidies and care arrangements of low-income parents. *Children and Youth Services Review, 34*(1), 179–185. doi:10.1016/j.childyouth. 2011.09.014

Escala, M. J., & Sánchez, J. C. (1977). Behavioral analysis applied to education: Liberation or domestication? *Revista Latinoamericana De Psicología, 9*(3), 397–407.

Eslinger, P. J., Robinson-Long, M., Realmuto, J., Moll, J., Deoliveira-Souza, R., Tovar-Moll, . . . Yang, Q. X. (2008) Developmental frontal lobe imaging in moral judgment: Arthur Benton's enduring influence 60 years later. *Journal of Clinical and Experimental Neuropsychology, 31*(2), 158–169. doi:10.1080/13803390802298064

Etaugh, C., Grinnell, K., & Etaugh, A. (1989). Development of gender labeling: Effect of age of pictured children. *Sex Roles, 21*(11–12), 769–773. doi:10.1007/BF00289807

Eugster, A., & Vingerhoets, A. J. (1999). Psychological aspects of in vitro fertilization: A review. *Social Science & Medicine, 48*(5), 575–589. doi:10.1016/S0277–9536(98)00386–4

Eun, B., Knotek, S. E., & Heining-Boynton, A. L. (2008). Reconceptualizing the zone of proximal development: The importance of the third voice. *Educational Psychology Review, 20*(2), 133–147. doi:10.1007/s10648-007-9064-1

Evans, G. W., & Schamberg, M. A. (2009). Childhood poverty, chronic stress, and adult working memory. *Proceedings of the National Academy of Sciences of the United States of America, 106*(16), 6545–6549. doi:10.1073/pnas.0811910106

Evans, G. W., Kim, P., Ting, A. H., Tesher, H. B., & Shannis, D. (2007). Cumulative risk, maternal responsiveness, and allostatic load among young adolescents. *Developmental Psychology, 43*(2), 341–351. doi:10.1037/0012-1649.43.2.341

Evans, G. W., Lepore, S. J., Shejwal, B. R., & Palsane, M. N. (1998). Chronic residential crowding and children's well-being: An ecological perspective. *Child Development, 69*(6), 1514–1523. doi:10.1111/j.1467-8624.1998.tb06174.x

Evans, J. St. B. T. (2003). In two minds: Dual processing accounts of reasoning. *Trends in Cognitive Sciences,* 7(10), 454–459. doi:10.1016/j.tics.2003.08.012

Evans, R. W. (2012). *Concussion and mild traumatic brain injury.* In M. J. Aminoff (Ed.), *UpToDate.* Waltham, MA: UpToDate.

Everitt, B. J., Cardinal, R. N., Parkinson, J. A., & Robbins, T. W. (2003). Impact of amygdala-dependent mechanisms of emotional learning. *Annals of New York Academy of Sciences, 985,* 233–250.

Eyer, D. E. (1992). *Mother-infant bonding: A scientific fiction.* New Haven, CT: Yale University Press.

Eyer, D. E. (1994). Mother-infant bonding: A scientific fiction. *Human Nature. 5*(1), 69–94.

Fabes, R. A., Carlo, G., Kupanoff, K., & Laible, D. (1999). Early adolescence and prosocial/moral behavior I: The role of individual processes. *Journal of Early Adolescence, 19*(1), 5–16. doi:10.1177/0272431699019001001

Fadiman, A. (1997). *The spirit catches you and you fall down: A Hmong child, her American doctors, and the collision of two cultures.* New York, NY: Farrar, Straus and Giroux.

Fadiman, A. (1998). *The spirit catches you and you fall down: A Hmong child, her American doctors, and the collision of two cultures.* New York, NY: Farrar, Straus and Giroux Paperbacks.

Fagan, J. F., & Detterman, D. K. (1992). The Fagan test of infant intelligence: A technical summary. *Journal of Applied Development Psychology. Special Issue: Does environment really contribute to healthy, quality life? 13*(2), 173–193.

Fagan, J. F., Holland, C. R., & Wheeler, K. (2007). The prediction from infancy of adult IQ and achievement. *Intelligence, 35*(3), 225–231. doi:10.1016/j.intell.2006.07.007

Fagot, B. I., & Leinbach, M. D. (1989). The young child's gender schema: Environmental input, internal organization. *Child Development, 60*(3), 663–672. doi:10.2307/1130731

Fair, D. A., Cohen, A. L., Dosenbach, N. U. F., Church, J. A., Meizen, F. M., Barch, D. M., . . . Schlaggar, B. L. (2008). The maturing architecture of the brain's default network. *PNAS, 105*(10), 4028–4032.

Falceto, O. G., Fernandes, C. L., Baratojo, C., & Giugliani, E. R. G. (2008). Factors associated with father involvement in infant care. *Rev Saúde Pública, 42*(6), 1–6.

Fang, Z., Schleppegrell, M. J., & Cox, B. E. (2006). Understanding the language demands of schooling: Nouns in academic registers. *Journal of Literacy Research, 38*(3), 247–273. doi:10.1207/s15548430jlr3803_1

Fannin, M. (2003). Domesticating birth in the hospital: "Family-centered" birth and the emergence of "homelike" birthing rooms. *Antipode, 35*(3), 513–535. doi:10.1111/1467-8330.00337

Fantuzzi, G. (2005). Adipose tissue, adipokines, and inflammation. *Journal of Allergy and Clinical Immunology, 115*(5), 911–919. doi:10.1016/j.jaci.2005.02.023

Fantz, R. L., & Miranda, S. B. (1975). Newborn infant attention to form of contour. *Child Development, 46,* 224–228. doi:10.1111/1467-8624.ep12189908

Farhat, T., Simons-Morton, B. G., Kokkevi, A., Van der Sluijs, W., Fotiou, A., & Kuntsche, E. (2012). Early adolescent and peer drinking homogeneity: Similarities and differences among European and North American countries. *Journal of Early Adolescence, 32*(1), 81–103. doi:10.1177/0272431611419511

Farrant, B. M., & Zubrick, S. R. (2012). Early vocabulary development: The importance of joint attention and parent-child book reading. *First Language, 32*(3), 343–364. doi:10.1177/0142723711422626

Farrant, B. M., Devine, T. A. J., Mayberry, M. T., & Fletcher, J. (2012). Empathy, perspective taking and prosocial behaviour: The importance of parenting practices. *Infant and Child Development, 21*(2), 175–188. doi:10.1002/icd.740

Farrell, A. E. (2011). *Fat shame: Stigma and the fat body in American culture.* New York, NY: New York University Press.

Farrey, T. (2008). *Game on.* New York, NY: ESPN Books.

Farrington, C. P., Miller, E., & Taylor, B. (2001). MMR and autism: Further evidence against a causal association. *Vaccine, 19*(27), 3632–3635. doi:10.1016/S0264-410X(01)00097-4

Farroni, T., Johnson, M. H., Menon, E., Zulian, L., Faraguna, D., & Csibra, G. (2005). Newborns' preference for face-relevant stimuli: Effects of contrast polarity. *Proceedings of National Academy of Sciences, 102,* 17245–17250.

Farver, J. A. M., Kim, Y. K., & Lee, Y. (1995). Cultural differences in Korean- and Anglo-American preschoolers' social interaction and play behaviors. *Child Development, 66*(4), 1088–1099. doi:10.2307/1131800

Farver, J. A. M., Xu, Y., Eppe, S., & Lonigan, C. (2006). Home environments and young Latino children's school readiness. *Early Childhood Research Quarterly, 21,* 196–212.

Fasih, T. (2008). *Linking educational policy to labor market outcomes.* Washington, DC: World Bank.

Fast, L. A., Lewis, J. L., Bryant, M. J., Bocian, K. A., Cardullo, R. A, Rettig, M., & Hammond, K. A. (2010). Does math self-efficacy mediate the effect of the perceived classroom environment on standardized math test performance? *Journal of Educational Psychology, 102*(3), 729–740. doi:10.1037/a0018863

FDA Drug Labeling Rule, 21, C.F.R. pt. 201.57 (2012). Retrieved from http://www.accessdata.fda.gov/scripts/cdrh/cfdocs/cfCFR/CFRSearch.cfm?fr=201.57

Feachem, R. G., & Koblinsky, M. A. (1984). Interventions for the control of diarrhoeal diseases among young children: Promotion of breast-feeding. *Bulletin of the World Health Organization, 62*(2), 271–291.

Feig, D. S., & Palda, V. A. (2002). Type 2 diabetes in pregnancy: A growing concern. *Lancet, 359,* 1690–1692. doi:10.1016/S0140-6736(02)08599–9

Feinman, S. (1982). Social referencing in infancy. *Merrill–Palmer Quarterly, 28,* 445–470.

Feiring, C., & Taska, L. S. (1996). Family self-concept: Ideas on its meaning. In B. Bracken (Ed.), *Handbook of self-concept* (pp. 317–373). New York, NY: Wiley.

Feldman, D. H. (2013). Cognitive development in childhood: A contemporary perspective. In R. M. Lerner, M. A. Easterbrooks, & J. Mistry (Eds.), *Handbook of psychology: Vol. 6. Developmental psychology* (2nd ed., pp. 197–213). Hoboken, NJ: Wiley.

Feldman, R. (2000). Parents' convergence on sharing and marital satisfaction, father involvement, and parent-child relationship at the transition to parenthood. *Infant Mental Health Journal, 21*(3), 176–191. doi:10.1002/1097-0355(200007)21:3.176::AID-IMHJ3,3.0.CO;2-4

Feldman, R., & Masalha, S. (2010). Parent-child and triadic antecedents of children's social competence: Cultural specificity, shared process. *Developmental Psychology, 46*(2), 455–467.

Feldman, R., Greenbaum, C. W., Mayes, L. C., & Erlich, H. S. (1997). Change in mother-infant interactive behavior: Relations to change in the mother, the infant, and the social context. *Infant Behavior and Development, 20,* 153–165.

Felliti, V. J., Anda, R. F., Nordbenberg, D., Williamson, A. M., Spitz, V., Edwards, . . . Marks, J. S. (1998). Relationship of childhood abuse and household dysfunction to many of the leading causes of death in adults: The adverse childhood experiences (ACE) study. *American Journal of Preventive Medicine, 14*(4), 354–360.

Feng, S., Fan, Y., Yu, Q., Lu, Q., & Tang, Y.-Y. (2008). The cerebellum connectivity in mathematics cognition. *BMC Neuroscience, 9*(Suppl. 1), 155. doi:10.1186/1471-2202-9-S1-P155

Ferguson, C. J., Garza, A., Jerabeck, J., Ramos, R., & Galindo, M. (2013). Not worth the fuss after all? Cross-sectional and prospective data on violent video game influences on aggression, visuospatial cognition and mathematics ability in a sample of youth. *Journal of Youth and Adolescence, 42*(1), 109–122. doi:10.1007/s10964-012—9803-6

Fergusson, D. M., Woodward, L. J., & Horwood, J. (1998). Maternal smoking during pregnancy and psychiatric adjustments in late adolescence. *Archives of General Psychiatry, 55,* 721–727.

Fergusson, E., Maughan, B., & Golding, J. (2008). Which children receive grandparental care and what effect does it have? *Journal*

*of Child Psychology and Psychiatry, 49*(2), 161–169. doi:10.1111/j.1469-7610.2007.01840.x
Fernald, A., & Cummings, A. (2003). *Ferguson's "clarification hypothesis" revisited: Does ID-speech facilitate word learning and word recognition by 18-month-olds?* Paper presented at the Biennial Meeting of the Society for Research in Child Development, Tampa, FL. Retrieved from http://www.srcd.org/
Fernald, A., & Simon, T. (1984). Expanded intonation contours in mothers' speech to newborns. *Developmental Psychology, 20*(1), 104–113.
Fernald, A., Taeschner, T., Dunn, J., Papoušek, N., de Boysson-Bardies, B., & Fukui, I. (1989). A cross-language study of prosodic modifications in mothers' and fathers' speech to preverbal infants. *Journal of Child Language, 16*(3), 477–501.
Fernell, E., Fagerberg, U. L., & Hellstrom, P. M. (2007). No evidence for a clear link between active intestinal inflammation and autism based on analyses of faecal calprotectin and rectal nitric oxide. *Acta Paediatrica, 96*(7), 1076–1079. doi:10.1111/j.1651-2227.2007.00298.x
Ferrari, F. (2011). New advances in the study of motor behavior. In T. B. Brazelton & J. Kevin Nugent, *The neonatal behavioral assessment scale* (4th ed.). London, UK: Mac Keith Press.
Ferrari, P. F., Visalberghi, E., Paukner, A., Fogassi, L., Ruggiero, A., & Suomi, S. (2006). Neonatal imitation in rhesus macaques. *PloS Biology, 4*, 1501–1508. doi:10.1371/journal.pbio.0040302
Ferry, A. L., Hespos, S. J., & Waxman, S. R. (2010). Categorization in 3- and 4-month old infants: An advantage of words over tones. *Child Development, 81*(2), 471–479.
Festinger, L. (1957). *A theory of cognitive dissonance*. Stanford, CA: Stanford University Press.
Field, T. (2009). The effects of newborn massage: United States. In J. K. Nugent, B. Petrauskas, & T. B. Brazelton (Eds.), *The newborn as a person: Enabling healthy infant development worldwide* (pp. 34–40). Hoboken, NJ: Wiley.
Field, T. M., Cohen, D., Garcia, R., & Greenberg, R. (1984). Mother-stranger face discrimination by the newborn. *Infant Behavior and Development*, 7(1), 19–25. doi:10.1016/S0163-6383(84)80019-3
Field, T. M., Hernandez-Reif, M., Diego, M., Feijo, L., Vera, Y., & Gil, K. (2004). Massage therapy by parents improves early growth and development. *Infant Behavior and Development, 27*, 435–442. doi:10.1016/j.infbeh.2004.03.004
Fields, R. D., Yu, C., & Nelson, P. G. (1991). Calcium, network activity, and the role of NMDA channels in synaptic plasticity in vitro. *Journal of Neuroscience, 11*, 134–136.
Fiese, B. H., & Schwartz, M. (2008). Reclaiming the family table: Mealtimes and child health and wellbeing. *Social Policy Report of the Society for Research in Child Development, 22*(4), 1–20.
Figert, A. E. (2005). Premenstrual syndrome as scientific and cultural artifact. *Integrative Physiological and Behavioral Science, 40*(2), 102–113.
Filippova, E., & Astington, J. W. (2010). Children's understanding of social-cognitive and social-communicative aspects of discourse irony. *Child Development, 81*(3), 913–928. doi:10.1111/j.1467-8624.2010.01442.x
Findlay, J. K., Gear, M. L., Illingworth, P. J., Junk, S. M., Kay, G., Mackerras, . . . Wilton, L. (2007). Human embryo: A biological definition. *Human Reproduction, 22*(4), 905–911.
Finkelstein, E. A., Trogdon, J. G., Cohen, J. W., & Dietz, W. (2009). Annual medical spending attributable to obesity: Payer- and service-specific estimates. *Health Affairs, 28*(5), w822–w831.
Finkelstein, J. (2000). Middle childhood: Physical and biological development. In A. Kazdin (Ed.), *Encyclopedia of psychology*, Vol 5. (pp. 220–225). Washington, DC: American Psychological Association.
Finnbogadóttir, H., Svalenius, E. C., & Persson, E. K. (2003). Expectant first-time fathers' experiences of pregnancy. *Midwifery, 19*(2), 96–105. doi:10.1016/S0266-6138(03)00003-2
Fire, A., Xu, S., Montgomery, M. K., Kostas, S. A., Driver, S. E., & Mello, C. C. (1998). Potent and specific genetic interference by double-stranded RNA in Caenorhabditis elegans. *Nature, 391*(6669), 806–811. doi:10.1038/35888
Fiscella, K. (2005). Race, genes and preterm delivery. *Journal of the National Medical Association, 97*(11), 1516–1526.
Fischer, K. W., & Bidell, T. (2006). Dynamic development of action and thought. In W. Damon & R. Lerner (Eds.), *Handbook of child psychology: Vol. 1. Theoretical models of human development* (6th ed., pp. 313–399). Hoboken, NJ: Wiley.
Fitch, W. T., Hauser, M. D., & Chomsky, N. (2005). The evolution of the language faculty: Clarifications and implications. *Cognition, 97*(2), 179–210. doi:10.1016/j.cognition.2005.02.005
Flavell, J. H. (1963). *The developmental psychology of Jean Piaget*. New York, NY: Van Nostrand.
Flavell, J. H. (1982). On cognitive development. *Child Development, 53*(1), 1–10. doi:10.2307/1129634
Flavell, J. H., Botkin, P. T., Fry C. L., Wright, J. W., & Jarvis, P. E. (1968). *The development of role-taking and communication skills in children*. New York, NY: Wiley.
Flavell, J. H., Everett, B. A., Croft, K., & Flavell, E. R. (1981). Young children's knowledge about visual perception: Further evidence for the Level 1–Level 2 distinction. *Developmental Psychology, 17*(1), 99–103. doi:10.1037/0012-1649.17.1.99
Flavell, J. H., Flavell, E. R., & Green, F. L. (1983). Development of the appearance–reality distinction. *Cognitive Psychology, 15*(1), 95–120. doi:10.1016/0010-0285(83)90005-1
Flavell, J. H., Miller, P. H., & Miller, S. A. (2002). *Cognitive Development* (4th ed.). Upper Saddle River, NJ: Prentice Hall.
Fletcher, R., Silberberg, S., & Galloway, D. (2004). New fathers' postbirth views of antenatal classes: Satisfaction, benefits, and knowledge of family services. *Journal of Perinatal Education, 13*, 18–26.
Flotte, T. (2007). Gene therapy: The first two decades and the current state-of-the-art. *Journal of Cellular Physiology, 213*(2), 301–305. doi:10.1002/jcp.21173
Flynn, E., & Siegler, R. (2007). Measuring change: Current trends and future directions in microgenetic research. *Infant and Child Development, 16*, 135–149. doi:10.1002/icd.502
Flynn, E., & Whiten, A. (2008). Imitation of hierarchical structure versus component details of complex actions, by 3- and 5-year-olds. *Journal of Experimental Child Psychology, 101*(4), 228–240. doi:10.1016/j.jecp.2008.05.009
Fogel, A. (1979). Peer vs. mother-directed behavior in 1- to 3-month-old infants. *Infant Behavior and Development, 2*, 215–226.
Fogel, A., Hsu, H., Shapiro, A. F., Nelson-Goens, G. C., & Secrist, C. (2006). Effects of normal and perturbed social play on the duration and amplitude of different types of infant smiles. *Developmental Psychology, 42*(3), 459–473. doi:10.1037/0012-1649.42.3.459
Fogel, A., Messinger, D. S., Dickson, K. L., & Hsu, H. (1999). Posture and gaze in early mother-infant communication: Synchronization of developmental trajectories. *Developmental Science*, 2, 325–332.
Foltz, C., Overton, W. F., & Ricco, R. B. (1995). Proof construction: Adolescent development from inductive to deductive problem-solving strategies. *Journal of Experimental Child Psychology, 59*(2), 179–195. doi:10.1006/jecp.1995.1008
Fombonne, E. (2009). Epidemiology of pervasive developmental disorders. *Pediatric Research, 65*, 591.
Fombonne, E., & Chakrabarti, S. (2001). No evidence for a new variant of measles-mumps-rubella-induced autism. *Pediatrics, 108*(4), e58. doi:10.1542/peds.108.4.e58
Fonagy, P. (2001). *Attachment theory and psychoanalysis*. New York, NY: Other Press.
Fordham, K., & Stevenson-Hinde, J. (1999). Shyness, friendship quality, and adjustment during middle childhood. *Journal of Child Psychology and Psychiatry, 40*(5), 757–768. doi:10.1111/1469-7610.00491
Forhan, S. E., Gottlieb, S. L., Sternberg, M. R., Xu, F., Datta, S. D., McQuillan, G. M., . . . Markowitz, L. E. (2009). Prevalence of sexually transmitted infections among female adolescents aged 14 to 19 in the United States. *Pediatrics, 124*, 1505–1512. doi:10.1542/peds.2009-0674
Forrest, J. D. (1993). Timing of reproductive life stages. *Obstetrics and Gynecology, 82*, 105–111. Retrieved from http://journals.lww.com/greenjournal/Abstract/1993/07000/Timing_of_Reproductive_Life_Stages.20.aspx
Fouts, H. N., Lamb, M. E., & Hewlett, B. S. (2004). Infant crying in hunter-gatherer cultures. *Behavioral and Brain Sciences, 27*(4), 462–463. doi:10.1017/S0140525X04260101
Fox, N. A. (1998). Critical importance of emotional development: Temperament and regulation of emotion in the first years of life [Supplement]. *Pediatrics 102*(5), 1230–1235.
Fox, N. A., & Bell, M. A. (1990). Electrophysiological indices of frontal lobe development: Relations to cognitive and affective behavior in human infants over the first year of life. In A. Diamond (Ed.), *The development and neural bases of higher cognitive functions* (pp. 677–698). New York, NY: New York Academy of Sciences Press.

Fox, N. A., & Calkins, S. D. (2003). The development of self-control of emotion: Intrinsic and extrinsic influences. *Motivation and Emotion*, *27*, 7–16. doi:10.1023/A:1023622324898

Fox, N. A., Henderson, H. A., Rubin, K., Calkins, S. D., & Schmidt, L. A. (2001). Continuity and discontinuity of behavioral inhibition and exuberance: Psychophysiological and behavioral influences across the first 4 years of life. *Child Development*, *72*, 1–21. doi:10.1111/1467-8624.00262

Fox, S. E., Levitt, P., & Nelson, C. A. (2010). How the timing and quality of early experiences influence the development of brain architecture. *Child Development*, *81*(1), 28–40. doi:10.1111/j.1467–8624.2009.01380.x

Frank, D. A., Augustyn, M., Knight, W. G., Pell, T., & Zuckerman, B. (2001). Growth, development, and behavior in early childhood following prenatal cocaine exposure: A systematic review. *Journal of the American Medical Association*, *285*(12), 1613–1625. doi:10.1001/jama.285.12.1613

Frankenburg, W. K., & Bresnick, B. (1998). *DENVER II Prescreening Questionnaire (PDQ II)*. Denver, CO: Denver Developmental Materials, Inc.

Franklin, A., & Davies, I. (2004). New evidence for infant colour categories. *British Journal of Developmental Psychology*, *22*, 349–377. doi:10.1348/0261510041552738

Frasier, S. D., & Rallison, M. L. (1972). Growth retardation and emotional deprivation: Relative resistance to treatment with human growth hormone. *Journal of Pediatrics*, *80*, 603–609. doi:10.1016/S0022–3476(72)80057–X

Freedman, D. G., & DeBoer, M. M. (1979). Biological and cultural differences in early child development. *Annual Review of Anthropology*, *8*, 579–600.

Freedman, D., Mei, Z., Srinivasan, S., Berenson, G., & Dietz, W. (2007). Cardiovascular risk factors and excess adiposity among overweight children and adolescents. *Journal of Pediatrics*, *150*, 12–17.

Freeze, R. A., & Lehr, J. H. (2009). *The fluoride wars: How a modest public health measure became America's longest-running political melodrama*. Hoboken, NJ: Wiley.

French, D. C., Jansen, E. A., & Pidada, S. (2002). United States and Indonesian children's and adolescents' reports of relational aggression by disliked peers. *Child Development*, *73*(4), 1143–1150. doi:10.1111/1467–8624.00463

Freud, S. (1940). *An outline of psychoanalysis*. New York, NY: Norton.

Freud, S. (1949). *An outline of psychoanalysis*. Oxford, UK: W. W. Norton.

Freud, S. (1964). An outline of psycho-analysis. In J. Strachey (Ed. and Trans.), *The standard edition of the complete psychological works of Sigmund Freud* (Vol. 23, pp. 141–207). London, UK: Hogarth Press. (Original work published 1940)

Freudenberg, N., & Ruglis, J. (2007). Reframing school dropout as a public health issue. *Preventing Chronic Disease*, *4*(4), A107.

Frey, K. S., & Ruble, D. N. (1990). *Strategies for comparative evaluation: Maintaining a sense of competence across the life span*. New Haven, CT: Yale University Press.

Friedlander, L. J., Connolly, J. A., Pepler, D. J., & Craig, W. M. (2007). Biological, familial, and peer influences on dating in early adolescence. *Archives of Sexual Behavior*, *36*(6), 821–830. doi:10.1007/s10508–006–9130–7

Frisch, R. E., & McArthur, J. W. (1974). Menstrual cycles: Fatness as a determinant of minimum weight for height necessary for their maintenance or onset. *Science*, *185*, 949–951.

Frith, C. D. (2007). The social brain? *Philosophical Transactions of the Royal Society Biological Sciences*, *362*(1480), 671–678.

Frith, U. (1989). Autism and "theory of mind". In C. Gillberg (Ed.), *Diagnosis and treatment of autism* (pp. 33–52). New York, NY: Plenum Press.

Froehlich, T. E., Lanphear, B. P., Auinger, P., Hornung, R., Epstein, J. N., Braun, J., Kahn, R. S. (2009). Association of tobacco and lead exposures with attention deficit/hyperactivity disorder. *Pediatrics*, *124*(6), e1054–e1063. doi:10.1542/peds.2009–0738

Fu, G., Cameron, C. A., Xu, F., Heyman, G., & Lee, K. (2007). Cross-cultural differences in children's choices, categorizations, and evaluations of truths and lies. *Developmental Psychology*, *43*(2), 278–293. doi:10.1037/0012–1649.43.2.278

Fulton, E., & Turner, L. A. (2008). Students' academic motivation: Relations with parental warmth, autonomy granting, and supervision. *Educational Psychology*, *28*(5), 521–534. doi:10.1080/01443410701846119

Furman, W., & Buhrmester, D. (1992). Age and sex differences in perceptions of networks of personal relationships. *Child Development*, *63*(1), 103–115. doi:10.2307/1130905

Furman, W., & Wehner, E. A. (1994). Romantic views: Toward a theory of adolescent romantic relationships. In R. Montemayor, G. R. Adams, & T. P. Gullotta (Eds.), *Personal relationships during adolescence* (Vol. 6, pp. 168–195). Thousand Oaks, CA: Sage.

Fuson, K. C. (1988). *Children's counting and concepts of number*. New York, NY: Springer-Verlag.

Gaertner, B. M., Spinrad, T. L., Eisenberg, N., & Greving, K. A. (2007). Parental childrearing attitudes as correlates of father involvement during infancy. *Journal of Marriage and Family*, *69*, 962–976.

Gagen, L., & Getchell, N. (2006). Using "constraints" to design developmentally appropriate movement activities for early childhood education. *Early Childhood Education Journal*, *34*(3), 227–232.

Galen, B. R., & Underwood, M. K. (1997). A developmental investigation of social aggression among children. *Developmental Psychology*, *33*(4), 589–600. doi:10.1037/0012–1649.33.4.589

Galinsky, E. (2006). *The economic benefits of high-quality early childhood programs: What makes the difference?* Washington, DC: Committee for Economic Development. Retrieved from http://familiesandwork.org/site/research/reports/ced.pdf

Gallagher, A., Levin, J., & Cahalan, C. (2002). GRE Research: Cognitive patterns of gender differences in mathematics admissions test. *ETS Report 02–19*. Princeton, NJ: Educational Testing Service.

Gallese, V., Rochat, M. J., & Berchio, C. (2013). The mirror mechanism and its potential role in autism spectrum disorder. *Developmental Medicine & Child Neurology*, *55*(1), 15–22. doi:10.1111/j.1469–8749.2012.04398.x

Galliher, R. V., Welsh, D. P., Rostosky, S. S., & Kawaguchi, M. C. (2004). Interaction and relationship quality in late adolescent romantic couples. *Journal of Social and Personal Relationships*, *21*(2), 203–216. doi:10.1177/0265407504041383

Galloway, J. C., & Thelen, E. (2004). Feet first: Object exploration in young infants. *Infant Behavior and Development*, *27*(1), 107–112. doi:10.1016/j.infbeh.2003.06.001

Galvan, A., Hare, T. A., Parra, C. E., Penn, J., Voss, H., Glover, G., & Casey, B. J. (2006). Earlier development of the accumbens relative to orbitofrontal cortex might underlie risk-taking behavior in adolescents. *Journal of Neuroscience*, *26*(25), 6885–6892.

Ganea, P. A., & Harris, P. L. (2010). Not doing what you are told: Early perseverative errors in updating mental representations via language. *Child Development*, *81*(2), 457–463.

Ganley, C. M., & Vasilyeva, M. (2011). Sex differences in the relation between math performance, spatial skills, and attitudes. *Journal of Applied Developmental Psychology*, *32*(4), 235–242. doi:10.1016/j.appdev.2011.04.001

Garaigordobil, M., & Berrueco, L. (2011). Effects of a play program on creative thinking of preschool children. *Spanish Journal of Psychology*, *14*(2), 608–618. doi:10.5209/rev_SJOP.2011.v14.n2.9

Garbarino, J. (1992). *Children and families in the social environment*. New York, NY: Aldine de Gruyter.

García Coll, C. T., Lamberty, G., Jenkins, R., McAdoo, H. P., Crnic, K., Wasik, B. H., & Vazquez García, H. (1996). An integrative model for the study of developmental competencies in minority children. *Child Development*, *67*(5), 1891–1914.

García Coll, C., & Marks, A. K. (2012). Introduction. In C. García Coll & A. K. Marks (Eds.). *The immigrant paradox in children and adolescents: Is becoming American a developmental risk?* (pp. 3–13). Washington, DC: American Psychological Association.

Gardner, D., & Shoback, D. (2011). *Greenspan's basic and clinical endocrinology*. New York, NY: McGraw–Hill.

Gardner, H. E. (1983). *Frames of mind: The theory of multiple intelligences*. New York, NY: Basic Books.

Gardner, H. E. (1993). *Multiple intelligences: The theory in practice*. New York, NY: Basic Books.

Gardner, H. E. (1999). *Intelligence reframed: Multiple intelligences for the 21st century*. New York, NY: Basic Books.

Gardner, H., & Traub, J. (2010). A debate on "multiple intelligences." *Cerebrum 2010: Emerging ideas in brain science* (pp. 34–61). Washington, DC: Dana Press. Retrieved from http://search.proquest.com/docview/622139888?accountid=9673

Gardner, H., Kornhaber, M. L., & Wake, W. K. (1996). *Intelligence: Multiple perspectives*. Orlando, FL: Harcourt Brace.

Gardner, M., & Steinberg, L. (2005). Peer influence on risk taking, risk preference, and risky decision making in adolescence and adulthood: An experimental study. *Developmental Psychology, 41*(4), 625–635. doi:10.1037/0012–1649.41.4.625

Garfield, C. F., & Fletcher, R. (2011). Sad dads: A challenge for pediatrics. *Pediatrics, 127*, 4.

Garmon, L. C., Basinger, K. S., Gregg, V. R., & Gibbs, J. C. (1996). Gender differences in stage and expression of moral judgment. *Merrill-Palmer Quarterly, 42*(3), 418–437.

Garn, S. M., & Haskell, J. A. (1959). Fat and growth during childhood. *Science, 130*, 1711–1712.

Garner, P. W., & Waajid, B. (2012). Emotion knowledge and self-regulation as predictors of preschoolers' cognitive ability, classroom behavior, and social competence. *Journal of Psychoeducational Assessment, 30*(4), 330–343. doi:10.1177/0734282912449441

Garon, N., Bryson, S. E., & Smith, I. M. (2008). Executive function in preschoolers: A review using an integrative framework. *Psychological Bulletin, 134*(1), 31–60. doi:10.1037/0033-2909.134.1.31

Garon, N., Bryson, S. E., & Smith, I. M. (2008). Executive function in preschoolers: A review using an integrative framework. *Psychological Bulletin, 134*(1), 31–60. doi:10.1037/0033-2909. 134.1.31

Garon, N., Bryson, S., & Smith, I. (2008). Executive function in preschoolers: A review using an integrative framework. *Psychological Bulletin, 134*(1), 31–60. doi:10.1037/0033–2909.134.1.31

Garrett, M., McElroy, A. M., & Staines, A. (2002). Locomotor milestones and babywalkers: Cross-sectional study. *British Medical Journal, 324*(7352), 1494. doi:10.1136/bmj.324.7352.1494

Gass, K., Jenkins, J., & Dunn, J. (2007). Are sibling relationships protective? A longitudinal study. *Journal of Child Psychology and Psychiatry, 48*(2), 167–175. doi:10.1111/j.1469–7610.2006.01699.x

Gathercole, S. E., & Pickering, S. J. (2000). Assessment of working memory in six- and seven-year-old children. *Journal of Educational Psychology, 92*(2), 377–390.

Gathercole, S. E., Pickering, S. J., Ambridge, B., & Wearing, H. (2004). The structure of working memory from 4 to 15 years of age. *Developmental Psychology, 40*(2), 177–190. doi:10.1037/0012-1649.40.2.177

Gathercole, S. E., Pickering, S. J., Knight, C., & Stegmann, Z. (2004). Working memory skills and educational attainment: Evidence from national curriculum assessments at 7 and 14 years of age. *Applied Cognitive Psychology, 18*(1), 1–16. doi:10.1002/acp.934

Gaudieri, P. A., Chen, R., Greer, T. F., & Holmes, C. S. (2008). Cognitive function in children with type 1 diabetes: A meta-analysis. *Diabetes Care, 31*(9), 1892–1897.

Gault-Sherman, M. (2012). It's a two-way street: The bidirectional relationship between parenting and delinquency. *Journal of Youth and Adolescence, 41*(2), 121–145. doi:10.1007/s10964–011–9656–4

Gauvain, M. (2001). *The social context of cognitive development*. New York, NY: Guilford.

Gauvain, M., & Parke, R. D. (2010). Socialization. In M. H. Bornstein (Ed.). *Handbook of cultural developmental science* (pp. 239–258). New York, NY: Psychology Press.

Gauvain, M., Perez, S. M., & Beebe, H. (2013). Authoritative parenting and parental support for children's cognitive development. In M. Gauvain, S. M. Perez, & M. Beebe (Eds.), *Authoritative parenting: Synthesizing nurturance and discipline for optimal child development* (pp. 211–233). Washington, DC: American Psychological Association.

Ge, X., Conger, R. D., & Elder, G. H. (2001). The relation between puberty and psychological distress in adolescent boys. *Journal of Research on Adolescence, 11*, 49–70.

Ge, X., Lorenz, F. O., Conger, R. D., Elder, G. H., & Simons, R. L. (1994). Trajectories of stressful life events and depressive symptoms during adolescence. *Developmental Psychology, 30*(4), 467–483.

Geary, D. C. (1996). Biology, culture, and cross-national differences in mathematical ability. In R. J. Sternberg & T. Ben-Zeev (Eds.), *The nature of mathematical thinking* (pp. 145–171). Hillsdale, NJ: Erlbaum.

Geary, D. C. (2006). Development of mathematical understanding. In D. Kuhn & R. S. Siegler (Eds.), *Handbook of child psychology: Vol. 2. Cognition, perception, and language* (6th ed., pp. 777–810). Hoboken, NJ: Wiley.

Geary, D. C. (2006). Development of mathematical understanding. In D. Kuhn & R. S. Siegler (Eds.), *Handbook of child psychology: Vol. 2. Cognition, perception, and language* (6th ed., pp. 777–810). Hoboken, NJ: Wiley.

Geary, D. C., Bow-Thomas, C. C., Liu, F., & Siegler, R. S. (1996). Development of arithmetical competencies in Chinese and American children: Influence of age, language, and schooling. *Child Development, 67*(5), 2022–2044. doi:10.2307/1131607

Gehring, U., Wijga, A. H., Brauer, M., Fischer, P., de Jongste, J. C., Kerkhof, M., . . . Brunekreef, B. (2010). Traffic-related air pollution and the development of asthma and allergies during the first 8 years of life. *American Journal of Respiratory and Critical Care Medicine, 181*(6), 596–603. doi:10.1164/rccm.200906-08580C

Geissbuehler, V., Stein, S., & Eberhard, J. (2004). Waterbirths compared to landbirths: An observational study of nine years. *Journal of Perinatal Medicine, 32*, 308–314.

Gelman, R. (1972). The nature and development of early number concepts. In H. W. Reese (Ed.), *Advances in child development and behavior* (Vol. 7, pp. 115–167). New York, NY: Academic Press.

Gelman, S. A., Taylor, M. G., & Nguyen, S. P. (2004). Mother-child conversations about gender. *Monographs of the Society for Research in Child Development, 69*(1), vii, 116–127. doi:10.1111/ j.1540-5834.2004.06901001.x

Gentile, D. A., Lynch, P. L., Linder, J. R., & Walsh, D. A. (2004).The effects of violent video game habits on adolescent hostility, aggressive behaviors, and school performance. *Journal of Adolescence, 27*, 5–22. doi:10.1016/j.adolescence.2003.10.002

Gentile, D. A., Mathieson, L. C., & Crick, N. R. (2011). Media violence associations with the form and function of aggression among elementary school children. *Social Development, 20*(2), 213–232. doi:10.1111/j.1467-9507.2010.00577

Gershoff, E. T. (2002). Corporal punishment by parents and associated child behaviors and experiences: A meta-analytic and theoretic review. *Psychological Bulletin, 128*(4), 539–579. doi:10.1037/0033-2909.128.4.539

Gershoff, E. T., Grogan-Kaylor, A., Lansford, J. E., Chang, L., Zelli, A., Deater-Deckard, K., & Dodge, K. A. (2010). Parent discipline practices in an international sample: Associations with child behaviors and moderation by perceived normativeness. *Child Development, 81*(2), 487–502. doi:10.1111/j.1467-8624.2009.01409.x

Gershoff, E. T., Lansford, J. E., Sexton, H. R., Davis-Kean, P., & Sameroff, A. J. (2012). Longitudinal links between spanking and children's externalizing behaviors in a national sample of white, black, Hispanic, and Asian American families. *Child Development, 83*(3), 838–843. doi:10.1111/j.1467–8624.2011.01732.x

Gerstadt, C. L., Hong, Y. J., & Diamond, A. (1994). The relationship between cognition and action: Performance of children 3½–7 years old on a Stroop-like day-night test. *Cognition, 53*(2), 129–153. doi:10.1016/0010-0277(94)90068-X

Gesell Institute of Child Development. (2010). *Gesell developmental observation (GDO)—revised*. Retrieved from http://www.gesellinstitute.org/pdf/2012-Gesell-Executive-Summary.pdf

Gesell, A. (1928). *Infancy and human growth*. New York, NY: Macmillan.

Gest, S., Rulison, K., Davidson, A., & Welsh, J. (2008). A reputation for success (or failure): The association of peer academic reputations with academic self-concept, effort, and performance across the upper elementary grades. *Developmental Psychology, 44*(3), 625–636.

Gestwicki, C. (2011). *Developmentally appropriate practice: Curriculum and development in early education* (4th ed.). Independence, KY: Wadsworth.

Gibbons, J., & Ng, S. H. (2004). Acting bilingual and thinking bilingual: An introduction. *Journal of Language and Social Psychology, 23*(1), 4–6. doi:10.1177/0261927X03260805

Gibbs, J. C., Basinger, K. S., Grime, R. L., & Snarey, J. R. (2007). Moral judgment development across cultures: Revisiting Kohlberg's universality claims. *Developmental Review, 27*(4), 443–500. doi:10.1016/j.dr.2007.04.001

Gibson, E. J. (2003). The world is so full of a number of things: On specification and perceptual learning. *Ecological Psychology, 15*(4), 283–288. doi:10.1207/s15326969eco1504_3

Gibson, E. J., & Schmuckler, M. A. (1989). Going somewhere: An ecological and experimental approach to development of mobility. *Ecological Psychology, 1*(1), 3–25. doi:10.1207/s15326969eco0101_2

Gibson, E. J., & Walk, R. D. (1960). The "visual cliff." *Scientific American, 202*(4), 64–71. doi:10.1038/scientificamerican0460–64

Gibson, J. J. (1979): *The ecological approach to visual perception*. Mahwah, NJ: Erlbaum.

Giedd, J. N., Blumenthal, J., Jeffries, N. O., Castellanos, F. X., Liu, H., Zijdenbos, A., . . . Rapoport, J. (1999). Brain development during childhood and adolescence: A longitudinal MRI study. *Nature and Neuroscience, 2*, 861–863.

Giesbrecht, G. F., Leadbeater, B. J., & MacDonald, S. W. S. (2011). Child and context characteristics in trajectories of physical and relational victimization among early elementary school children. *Development and Psychopathology, 23*(1), 239–252. doi:10.1017/S0954579410000763

Gilligan, C. (1982). *In a different voice: Psychological theory and women's development*. Cambridge, MA: Harvard University Press.

Gilliland, F. D. (2009). Outdoor air pollution, genetic susceptibility, and asthma management: Opportunities for intervention to reduce the burden of asthma. *Pediatrics, 123*(Suppl. 3), S168–S173. doi:10.1542/peds.2008-2233G

Ginsberg, H. P., & Opper, S. (1988). *Piaget's theory of intellectual development* (3rd ed.). Englewood Cliffs, NJ: Prentice Hall.

Ginsburg, G. S., & Bronstein, P. (1993). Family factors related to children's intrinsic/extrinsic motivational orientation and academic performance. *Child Development, 64*(5), 1461–1474. doi:10.2307/1131546

Ginsburg, H. P., Lee, J. S., & Boyd, J. S. (2008). Mathematics education for young children: What it is and how to promote it. *Social Policy Report: Giving Child and Youth Development Knowledge Away, 22*(1). Retrieved from http://www.srcd.org/spr.html

Gioia, K. A., & Tobin, R. M. (2010). Role of sociodramatic play in promoting self-regulation. In C. E. Schaefer (Ed.), *Play therapy for preschool children* (pp. 181–198). Washington, DC: American Psychological Association. doi:10.1037/12060-009

Giugliano, D. N., & Solomon, J. L. (2007). ACL tears in female athletes: A review. *Physical Medicine and Rehabilitation Clinics of North America, 18*(3), 417–438.

Gladwell, M. (2008). *Outliers: The story of success*. New York, NY: Little Brown.

Glantz, F. B. (2009). *Massachusetts family child care today: A report of the findings from the Massachusetts cost and quality study*. Wellesley, MA: Wellesley Centers for Women and Abt Associates.

Gleason, J. B., & Ratner, N. B. (2009). *The development of language* (7th ed.). Needham Heights, MA: Allyn & Bacon.

Gleitman, L. R., & Wanner, E. (1988). Current issues in language learning. In M. H. Bornstein & M. E. Lamb (Eds.), *Developmental psychology: An advanced textbook* (2nd ed., pp. 297–356). Hillsdale, NJ: Erlbaum.

Göbel, S. M., Shaki, S., & Fischer, M. H. (2011). The cultural number line: A review of cultural and linguistic influences on the development of number processing. *Journal of Cross-Cultural Psychology, 42* (4), 543–565. doi:10.1177/0022022111406251

Goble, P., Martin, C. L., Hanish, L. D., & Fabes, R. A. (2012). Children's gender-typed activity choices across preschool social contexts. *Sex Roles,* 67(7–8), 435–451. doi: 10.1007/s11199-012-0176-9

Godlee, F., Smith, J., & Marcovitch, H. (2011). Wakefield's article linking MMR vaccine and autism was fraudulent. *British Medical Journal, 342*(7788), 64–66. doi:10.1136/bmj.c7452

Gogtay N., Nugent T. F., Herman D. H., Ordonez, A., Greenstein D., Hayashi, K. M., . . . Thompson, P. M. (2006). Dynamic mapping of normal human hippocampal development. *Hippocampus, 16*(8), 664–672.

Gogtay, N., Giedd, J. N., Lusk, L., Hayashi, K. M., Greenstein, D., Vaituzis, A. C., . . . Thompson, P. M. (2004). Dynamic mapping of human cortical development during childhood through early adulthood. *Proceedings of the National Academy of Sciences, 101*(21), 8174–8179. doi:10.1073/pnas.0402680101

Gold, D. R., & Wright, R. (2005). Population disparities in asthma. *Annual Review of Public Health, 26,* 89–113. doi:10.1146/annurev.publhealth.26.021304.144528

Goldberg, A. E. (2010). *Lesbian and gay parents and their children: Research on the family life cycle*. Washington, DC: American Psychological Association.

Goldberg, S. (1977). Social competence in infancy: A model of parent-infant interaction. *Merrill–Palmer Quarterly, 23,* 163–177.

Goldberg, S. (1983). Parent-infant bonding: Another look. *Child Development, 54*(6), 1355–1382. doi:10.1111/1467-8624.ep12418472

Golden, N. H., & Shenker, I. R. (1992). Amenorrhea in anorexia nervosa: Etiology and implications. In M. P. Nussbaum & J. T. Dwyer (Eds.), *Adolescent nutrition and eating disorders* (pp. 503–518). Philadelphia, PA: Hanley & Belfus.

Goldin-Meadow, S. (2006). Nonverbal communication: The hand's role in talking and thinking. In R. M. Lerner & W. Damon (Eds.), *Handbook of child psychology:* Vol. 2. *Cognition, perception, and language* (6th ed., pp. 336–369). Hoboken, NJ: Wiley.

Goldsmith, H. H. (1989). Behavior-genetic approaches to temperament. In G. A. Kohnstamn, J. E. Bates, & M. K. Rothbart (Eds.), *Temperament in childhood.* New York, NY: Wiley.

Goldsmith, H. H., Lemery, K. S., Aksan, N., & Buss, K. A. (2000). Temperamental substrates of personality development. In V. J. Molfese & D. L. Molfese (Eds.), *Temperament and personality development across the lifespan* (pp. 1–32). Mahwah, NJ: Erlbaum.

Goldsmith, H. H., Lemery, K. S., Buss, K. A., & Campos, J. J. (1999). Genetic analyses of focal aspects of infant temperament. *Developmental Psychology, 35*(4), 972–985.

Goldstein, D. B. (2009). Common genetic variation and human traits. *New England Journal of Medicine, 360,* 1696–1698. doi:10.1056/NEJMp0806284

Goldstein, S. E., Young, A., & Boyd, C. (2008). Relational aggression at school: Associations with school safety and social climate. *Journal of Youth and Adolescence, 37*(6), 641–654. doi:10.1007/s10964-007-9192-4

Goleman, D. (2006). *Social intelligence: The new science of human relationships*. New York, NY: Bantam.

Golomb, C. (2004). *The child's creation of a pictorial world* (2nd ed.). Mahwah, NJ: Erlbaum.

Golombok, S. (2006). New family forms. In A. Clarke-Stewart & J. Dunn (Eds.), *Families count: Effects on child and adolescent development* (pp. 273–298). New York, NY: Cambridge University Press.

Golombok, S., Murray, C., Brinsden, P., & Abdalla, H. (1999). Social versus biological parenting: Family functioning and the socioemotional development of children conceived by egg or sperm donation. *Journal of Child Psychology and Psychiatry, and Allied Disciplines, 40*(4), 519–527. doi:10.1111/1469-7610.00470

Golub, M. S. (1996). Labor analgesia and infant brain development. *Pharmacology, Biochemistry, and Behavior. Special Issue: Neurobehavioral Teratology, 55*(4), 619–628. doi:10.1016/S0091-3057(96)00254-7

Gonder-Frederick, L. A., Zrebiec, J. F., Bauchowitz, A. U., Ritterband, L. M., Magee, J. C., Cox, D. J. & Clarke, W. L. (2009). Cognitive function is disrupted by both hypo- and hyperglycemia in school-aged children with type 1 diabetes: A field study. *Diabetes Care, 32*(6), 1001–1006.

Goodfellow, J., & Laverty, J. (2003). Grandparents supporting working families. *Family Matters, 66,* 14–19.

Goodman, J. F. (2002). Infant intelligence: Do we, can we, should we assess it? In C. R. Reynolds & R. W. Kamphaus (Eds.), *Handbook of psychological and educational assessment of children: Intelligence and achievement* (pp. 183–208). New York, NY: Guilford.

Gooren, E. M. J. C., van Lier, Pol A. C., Stegge, H., Terwogt, M. M., & Koot, H. M. (2011). The development of conduct problems and depressive symptoms in early elementary school children: The role of peer rejection. *Journal of Clinical Child and Adolescent Psychology, 40*(2), 245–253. doi:10.1080/15374416.2011.546045

Gopnik, A. (2009). Rational constructivisim: A new way to bridge rationalism and empiricism. *Behavioral and Brain Sciences, 32,* 208–209. doi:10.1017/S0140525X0900096X

Gormley, W. T., Jr., Gayer, T., Phillips, D., & Dawson, B. (2005). The effects of universal pre-K on cognitive development. *Developmental Psychology, 41*(6), 872–884. doi:10.1037/0012-1649. 41.6.872

Gottesman, I. I. (1963). Heritability of personality: A demonstration. *Psychological Monographs: General and Applied,* 77(9), 1–21. doi: 10.1037/h0093852

Gottesman, I. I. (1991). *Schizophrenia genesis: The origins of madness*. New York, NY: Freeman.

Gottlieb, G. (1997). *Synthesizing nature-nurture*. Mahwah, NJ: Erlbaum.

Gottlieb, G. (2002). Developmental-behavioral initiation of evolutionary change. *Psychological Review, 109*(2), 211–218.

Gottlieb, G. (2003). On making behavioral genetics truly developmental. *Human Development, 46*(6), 337–355. doi:10.1159/000073306

Gottlieb, G. (2007). Probabilistic epigenesis. *Developmental Science 10*(1), 1–11. doi:10.1111/j.1467-7687.2007.00556.x

Gottlieb, G., Wahlsten, D., & Lickliter, R. (2006). The significance of biology for human development: A psychobiological systems view. In W. Damon & R. Lerner (Series Eds.) & R. Lerner (Vol. Ed.), *Handbook of child psychology: Volume 1. Theoretical models of human development* (6th ed., pp. 210–257). Hoboken, NJ: Wiley.

Gottman, J. M., Katz, L. F., & Hooven, C. (1996). Parental meta-emotion philosophy and the emotional life of families: Theoretical models and preliminary data. *Journal of Family Psychology, 10*(3), 243–268. doi:10.1037/0893-3200.10.3.243

Gottman, J. M., Katz, L. F., & Hooven, C. (1997). *Meta-emotion: How families communicate emotionally*. Hillsdale, NJ: Erlbaum.

Gould, S. J. (1996). *The mismeasure of man*. New York, NY: Norton.

Graber, J. A., & Sontag, L. M. (2009). Internalizing problems during adolescence. In R. M. Lerner & L. Steinberg (Eds.), *Handbook of adolescent psychology: Vol. 1. Individual bases of adolescent development* (3rd ed., pp. 642–682). Hoboken, NJ: Wiley.

Graber, J. A., Lewinsohn, P. M., Seeley, J. R., & Brooks-Gunn, J. (1997). Is psychopathology associated with the timing of pubertal development? *Journal of American Academy of Child and Adolescent Psychiatry, 36*(12), 1768–1776.

Grady, J. S., Karraker, K., & Metzger, A. (2012). Shyness trajectories in slow-to-warm-up infants: Relations with child sex and maternal parenting. *Journal of Applied Developmental Psychology, 33*(2), 91–101. doi:10.1016/j.appdev.2011.11.002

Graham, S., & Williams, C. (2009). An attributional approach to motivation in school. In K. R. Wenzel & A. Wigfield (Eds.), *Handbook of motivation at school* (pp. 11–33). New York, NY: Routledge.

Gralinski, J. H., & Kopp, C. B., (1993). Everyday rules for behavior: Mothers' requests to young children. *Developmental Psychology, 29*(3), 573–584. doi:10.1037/0012–1649.29.3.573

Grant, S. F. A., Li, M., Bradfield, J. P., Kim, C. E., Annaiah, K., Santa, E., . . . Hakonarson, H. (2008). Association analysis of the FTO gene with obesity in children of Caucasian and African ancestry reveals a common tagging SNP. *PLoS ONE, 3*(3), e1746. doi:10.1371/journal.pone.0001746

Grantham-McGregor S., & Ani, C. (2001). A review of studies on the effect of iron deficiency on cognitive development in children. *Journal of Nutrition, 131*(2), 649S–668S.

Grassi-Oliveira, R., Ashy, M., & Stein, L. M. (2008). Psychobiology of childhood maltreatment: Effects of allostatic load? *Brazilian Review of Psychiatry, 30*(1), 60–68. doi:10.1590/S1516–44462008000100012

Gray, J. A. (1988). *The psychology of fear and stress* (2nd ed.). New York, NY: Cambridge University Press.

Graziano, P. A., Calkins, S. D., & Keane, S. P. (2010). Toddler self-regulation skills predict risk for pediatric obesity. *International Journal of Obesity, 34*(4), 633–641. doi:10.1038/ijo.2009.288

Grazzani, I., & Ornaghi, V. (2012). How do use and comprehension of mental-state language relate to theory of mind in middle childhood? *Cognitive Development, 27*(2), 99–111. doi:10.1016/j.cogdev.2012.03.002

Gredler, M. E. (2010). Understanding Vygotsky for the classroom: Is it too late? *Educational Psychology Review, 24*(1), 113–131. doi:10.1007/s10648-011-9183-6

Greenberger, E., & Steinberg, L. (1986). *When teenagers work: The psychological and social costs of adolescent employment*. New York, NY: Basic Books.

Greene, J., & Haidt, J. (2002). How (and where) does moral judgment work? *Trends in Cognitive Sciences, 6*(12), 517–523. doi:10.1016/S1364–6613(02)02011–9

Greenfeld, D. A. (2008). The impact of disclosure on donor gamete participants: Donors, intended parents, and offspring. *Current Opinions in Obstetrics and Gynecology, 20*(3), 265–268. doi:10.1097/GCO.0b013e32830136ca

Greenfield, P. M. (1991). Language, tools, and brain: The ontogeny and phylogeny of hierarchically organized sequential behavior. *Behavioral and Brain Sciences, 14*, 531–551. doi:10.1017/S0140525X00071235

Greenfield, P. M. (1997). You can't take it with you: Why abilities assessments don't cross cultures. *American Psychologist, 52*(10), 1115–1124. doi:10.1037/0003–066X.52.10.1115

Greenfield, P. M., Keller, H., Fuligni, A., & Maynard, A. E. (2003). Cultural pathways through universal development. *Annual Review of Psychology, 54*, 461–190.

Greenough, W., & Black, J. ( 1992). Induction of brain structure by experience: Substrates for cognitive development. In M. R. Gunnar & C. A. Nelson (Eds.), *Minnesota symposia on child psychology 24: Developmental behavioral neuroscience* (pp. 155–200). Hillsdale, NJ: Erlbaum.

Greer, F. R., Sicherer, S. H., Burks, W., & Committee on Nutrition and Section on Allergy and Immunology of the American Academy of Pediatrics. (2008). Effects of early nutritional interventions on the development of atopic disease in infants and children: The role of maternal dietary restriction, breastfeeding, timing of introduction of complementary foods, and hydrolyzed formulas. *Pediatrics, 121*, 183–191. doi:10.1542/peds.2007-3022

Gregg, P., Gutiérrez-Domènech, M., Waldfogel, J. (2007). The employment of married mothers in Great Britain, 1974–2000. *Economica, 74*(296), 842–864, doi:10.1111/j.1468-0335.2006.00574.xGregg et al. 2007

Gregg, V., Gibbs, J. C., & Basinger, K. S. (1994). Patterns of developmental delay in moral judgment by male and female delinquents. *Merrill-Palmer Quarterly, 40*(4), 538–553.

Grello, C. M., Welsh, D. P., & Harper, M. S. (2006). No strings attached: The nature of casual sex in college students. *Journal of Sex Research, 43*(3), 255–267. doi:10.1080/00224490609552324

Greskovich, J. F., & Macklis, R. M. (2000). Radiation therapy in pregnancy: Risk calculation and risk minimization. *Seminars in Oncology, 27*(6), 633–645.

Greven, C. U., Asherson, P., Rijsdijk, F. V., & Plomin, R. (2011). A longitudinal twin study on the association between inattentive and hyperactive-impulsive ADHD symptoms. *Journal of Abnormal Child Psychology, 39*(5), 623–632. doi:10.1007/s10802–011–9513–7

Grigorenko, E. L., Geissler, P. W., Prince, R., Okatcha, F., Nokes, C., Kenny, D. A., . . . Sternberg, R. J. (2001). The organization of Luo conceptions of intelligence: A study of implicit theories in a Kenyan village. *International Journal of Behavioral Development, 25*(4), 367–378. doi:10.1080/01650250042000348

Grilo, C. M., Masheb, R. M., & Crosby, R. D. (2012). Predictors and moderators of response to cognitive behavioral therapy and medication for the treatment of binge eating disorder. *Journal of Consulting and Clinical Psychology, 80*(5), 897–906. doi:10.1037/a0027001

Grimshaw, G. M., & Stanton, A. (2006). Tobacco cessation interventions for young people. *Cochrane Database of Systematic Reviews, 4* (Article No. CD003289). doi:10.1002/14651858.CD003289.pub4

Groen, G. J., & Parkman, J. M. (1972). A chronometric analysis of simple addition. *Psychological Review, 79*(4), 329–343. doi:10.1037/h0032950

Grolnick, W. S., & Pomerantz, E. M. (2009). Issues and challenges in studying parental control: Toward a new conceptualization. *Child Development Perspectives, 3*(3), 165–170. doi:10.1111/j.1750–8606.2009.00099.x

Grolnick, W. S., Friendly, R. W., & Bellas, V. M. (2009). Parenting and children's motivation at school. In K. R. Wenzel & A. Wigfield (Eds.), *Handbook of motivation at school. Educational psychology handbook series* (pp. 279–300). New York, NY: Routledge/Taylor & Francie.

Grossman, R., Johnson, M. H., Farroni, T., & Csibra, G. (2007). Social perception in the infant brain: Gamma oscillatory activity in response to eye gaze. *Social Cognitive and Affective Neuroscience, 2*(4), 284–291.

Grossmann, K. E., Grossmann, K., & Waters, E. (2006). *Attachment from infancy to maturity: The major longitudinal studies*. New York, NY: Guilford.

Gruber, H. E., & Vonèche, J. J. (Eds.). (1977). *The essential Piaget: An interpretive reference and guide*. New York, NY: Basic Books.

Gruchalla, R. S., Pongracic, J., Plaut, M., Evans, R., 3rd, Visness, C. M., Walter, M., . . . Mitchell, H. (2005). Inner city asthma study: Relationships among sensitivity, allergen exposure, and asthma morbidity. *Journal of Allergy and Clinical Immunology, 115*(3), 478–85. doi:10.1016/j.jaci.2004.12.006

Grundy, E., Murphy, M., & Shelton, N. (1999). Looking beyond the household: Intergenerational perspectives on living with kin and contacts with kin in Great Britain. *Population Trends, 97*, 19–27.

Grusec, J. E., Chapparo, M. P., Johnston, M., & Sherman, A. (2013). Social development and social relationships in middle childhood. In R. M. Lerner, A. Easterbrooks, & J. Mistry (Eds.), *Handbook of psychology: Vol. 6. Developmental psychology* (2nd ed., pp. 243–264). Hoboken, NJ: Wiley.

Guarino, C. M., Hamilton, L. S., Lockwood, J. R., Rathbun, A. H. (2006). *Teacher qualifications, instructional practices, and reading and mathematics gains of kindergartners* (NCES 2006-031). Washington, DC: U.S. Department of Education, National Center for Education Statistics.

Guilbert, T. W., Morgan, W. J., Zeiger, R. S., Mauger, D. T., Boehmer, S. J., Szefler, S. J., . . . Martinez, F. D. (2006). Long-term inhaled corticosteroids in preschool children at high risk for asthma. *The New England Journal of Medicine, 354*(19), 1985–97. doi:10.1056/NEJMoa051378

Gunderson, G. (1971). *The national school lunch program background and development*. Retrieved from http://www.fns.usda.gov/cnd/lunch/AboutLunch/ProgramHistory.htm

Gunnar, M. R., & Donzella, B. (2002). Social regulation of the cortisol levels in early human development. *Psychoneuroendocrinology, 27*, 199–220.

Gunnar, M. R., Fisher, P. A., & Early Experience, Stress and Prevention Network. (2006). Bringing basic research on early experience and stress neurobiology to bear on preventive interventions for neglected and maltreated children. *Developmental Psychopathology, 18*(3), 651–677. doi:10.1017/S0954579406060330

Gunnar, M., & Quevedo, K. (2007). The neurobiology of stress and development. *Annual Review of Psychology, 58*, 145–173. doi:10.1146/annurev.psych.58.110405.085605

Gunter, W. D., & Daly, K. (2012). Causal or spurious: Using propensity score matching to detangle the relationship between violent video games and violent behavior. *Computers in Human Behavior, 28*(4), 1348–1355. doi:10.1016/j.chb.2012.02.020

Günther, A. L. B., Remer, T., Kroke, A., and Buyken, A. E. (2007). Early protein intake and later obesity risk: Which protein sources at which time points throughout infancy and childhood are important for body mass index and body fat percentage at 7 y of age? *American Journal of Clinical Nutrition, 86*(6), 1765–1772.

Guo, J. J., Wade, T. J., Pan, W., & Keller, K. N. (2010). School-based health centers: Cost-benefit analysis and impact on health care disparities. *American Journal of Public Health, 100*(9), 1617–1623. doi:10.2105/AJPH.2009.185181

Gupta, R. S., Springston, E. E., Warrier, M. R., Smith, B., Kumar, R., Pongracic, J., & Holl, J. L. (2011). The prevalence, severity, and distribution of childhood food allergy in the United States. *Pediatrics, 128*(1), 9–17. doi:10.1542/peds.2011-0204

Guralnick, M. J. (2010). Early intervention approaches to enhance the peer-related social competence of young children with developmental delays: A historical perspective. *Infants & Young Children, 23*, 73–83. doi:10.1097/IYC.0b013e3181d22e14

Guralnick, M. J., Neville, B., Hammond, M. A., & Connor, R. T. (2007). The friendships of young children with developmental delays: A longitudinal analysis. *Journal of Applied Developmental Psychology, 28*(1), 64–79. doi:10.1016/j.appdev.2006.10.004

Gureasko-Moore, S., DuPaul, G. J., & White, G. P. (2007). Self-management of classroom preparedness and homework: Effects on school functioning of adolescents with attention deficit hyperactivity disorder. *School Psychology Review, 36*(4), 647–664.

Guthman, J. (2011). *Weighing in: Obesity, food justice and the limits of capitalism.* Berkeley, CA: University of California Press.

Guttentag, R. E., Ornstein, P. A., & Siemens, L. (1987). Children's spontaneous rehearsal: Transitions in strategy acquisition. *Cognitive Development, 2*(4), 307–326. doi:10.1016/S0885–2014(87)80010–2

Guttmacher Institute. (2006). *Facts on American teens' sexual and reproductive health*. Washington, DC: Author.

Guttmacher Institute. (2012). *Facts on American teens' sexual and reproductive health.* Retrieved from http://www.guttmacher.org/pubs/FB-ATSRH.html

Guyer, A. E., Choate, V. R., Pine, D. S., & Nelson, E. E. (2012). Neural circuitry underlying affective response to peer feedback in adolescence. *Social Cognitive and Affective Neuroscience*, 7(1), 81–92. doi:10.1093/scan/nsr043

Hack, M. H., Taylor, G., Drotar, D., Schluchter, M., Cartar, L., & Morrow, M. (2005). Function of extremely low birth weight children at school age: Poor predictive validity of the Bayley scales of infant development for cognitive development. *Pediatrics, 116*, 333–341.

Hack, M., & Fanaroff, A. A. (2000). Outcomes of children of extremely low birthweight and gestational age in the 1990s. *Seminars in Neonatology, 5*, 89–106. doi:10.1053/siny.1999.0001

Hack, M., Horbar, J. D., Malloy, M. H., Tyson, J. E., Wright, E., & Wright, L. (1991). Very low birth weight outcomes of the National Institute Child Health Development Neonatal Network. *Pediatrics, 87*(5), 587–597. doi:10.1016/0002–9378(95)90557–X

Hack, M., Klein, N. K., & Taylor, H. G. (1995). Long-term developmental outcomes of low birth weight infants. *The Future of Children, 5*(1), 176–196. doi:10.2307/1602514

Hack, M., Youngstrom, E. A., Cartar, L., Schluchter, M., Taylor, H. G., Flannery, D., . . . Borawski, E. (2004). Behavioral outcomes and evidence of psychopathology among very low birth infants at age 20 years. *Pediatrics, 114*(4), 932–940. doi:10.1542/peds.2003–1017–L

Hadad, B.-S., Maurer, D., & Lewis, T. L. (2011). Long trajectory for the development of sensitivity to global and biological motion. *Developmental Sciences, 14*(6), 1330–1339. doi:10.1111/j.1467–7687.2011.01078.x

Haflon, N., Regalado, M., Sareen, H., Inkelas, M., Reuland, C. H., Glascoe, F. P., & Olson, L. M. (2004). Assessing development in the pediatric office. *Pediatrics, 113*, 1926–1933.

Haflon, N., Stevens, G. D., Larson, K., Olson, L. M. (2011). Duration of a well-child visit: Association with content, family-centeredness, and satisfaction. *Pediatrics, 128*, 4, 657–664. doi:10.1542/peds.2011-0586

Hagan, J. F., Shaw, J. S., & Duncan, P. M. (Eds.) (2008). *Bright futures: Guidelines for health supervision of infants, children, and adolescents* (3rd ed.). Elk Grove Village, IL: American Academy of Pediatrics.

Hagenauer, G., & Hascher, T. (2010). Learning enjoyment in early adolescence. *Educational Research and Evaluation, 16*(6), 495–516. doi:10.1080/13803611.2010.550499

Hagerhed-Engman, L., Bornehag, C.-G., Sundell, J., & Aberg, N. (2006). Day-care attendance and increased risk for respiratory and allergic symptoms in preschool age. *Allergy, 61*(4), 447–453. doi:10.1111/j.1398-9995.2006.01031

Haith, M. M. (1998). Who put the cog in infant cognition? Is rich interpretation too costly? *Infant Behavior & Development, 21*(2), 167–179.

Hakvoort, E. M., Bos, H. M. W., Van Balen, F., & Hermanns, J. M. A. (2011). Postdivorce relationships in families, and children's psychosocial adjustment. *Journal of Divorce & Remarriage, 52*(2), 125–146. doi:http: 10.1080/10502556.2011.546243

Halberstadt, A. G., Denham, S. A., & Dunsmore, J. C. (2001). Affective social competence. *Social Development, 10*, 79–119.

Halfon, N., & Newacheck, P. W. (2010). Evolving notions of childhood chronic illness. *Journal of the American Medical Association, 303*(7), 665–666.

Halford, G. S., & Andrews, G. (2006). Reasoning and problem solving. In W. Damon & R. M. Lerner (Series Eds.) & D. Kuhn & R. S. Siegler (Vol. Eds.), *Handbook of child psychology: Vol. 2. Cognition, perception, and language* (6th ed., pp. 557–608). Hoboken, NJ: Wiley.

Halgren, E. (1992). Emotional neurophysiology of the amygdala within the context of human cognition. In J. P. Aggleton (Ed.), *The amygdala: Neurobiological aspects of emotion, memory, and mental dysfunction* (pp. 191–228). New York, NY: Wiley-Liss.

Halgunseth, L. C., Ispa, J. M., & Rudy, D. (2006). Parental control in Latino families: An integrated review in the literature. *Child Development, 77(5)*, 1282–1297.

Hall, G. S. (1893). *The content of children's minds entering school.* New York, NY: Kellogg.

Hall, G. S. (1904). *Adolescence: Its psychology and its relations to physiology, anthropology, sociology, sex, crime, religion, and education* (Vols. 1, 2). New York, NY: Appleton.

Halle, T., Forry, N., Hair, E., Perper, K., Wander, L., Wessel, J., & Vick, J. (2009). *Disparities in early learning and development: Lessons from the early childhood longitudinal study–birth cohort (ECLS–B).* Washington, DC: Child Trends.

Hallinan, M. T., & Kubitschek, W. N. (1999). Curriculum differentiation and high school achievement. *Social Psychology of Education, 3*(1–2), 41–62. doi:10.1023/A:1009603706414

Halpern, D. F., Benbow, C. P., Geary, D. C., Gur, R. C., Hyde, J. S., & Gernsbacher, M A. (2007). The science of sex differences in science and mathematics. *Psychological Science in the Public Interest, 8*(1), 1–51. doi:10.1111/j.1529–1006.2007.00032.x

Halpern-Felsher, B. (2009). Adolescent decision making: An overview. *Prevention Researcher, 16*(2), 3–7.

Hamilton, A. F. d. C. (2013). Reflecting on the mirror neuron system in autism: A systematic review of current theories. *Developmental Cognitive Neuroscience, 3*(1), 91–105. doi:10.1016/j.dcn.2012.09.008

Hamilton, B. E., Martin, J. A., & Sutton, P. D. (2004). Births: Preliminary data for 2003. *National Vital Statistics Reports, 53*(9), 1–17.

Hamilton, B. E., Martin, J. A., & Ventura, S. H. J. (2011) Births: Preliminary data for 2010. *National Vital Statistics Reports, 60*(2). Retrieved from http://www.cdc.gov/nchs/data/nvsr/nvsr60/nvsr60_02.pdf

Hamilton, B. E., Martin, J. A., & Ventura, S. J. (2010). Births: Preliminary data for 2009. *National Vital Statistics Reports, 59*(3), 1–19. Retrieved from http://www.cdc.gov/nchs/data/nvsr/nvsr59/nvsr59_03.pdf

Hamilton, B. E., Martin, J. A., & Ventura, S. J. (2012). Births: Preliminary data for 2011. *National Vital Statistics Reports, 61*(5). Retrieved from http://www.cdc.gov/nchs/data/nvsr/nvsr61/nvsr61_05.pdf

Hamlin, J. K., Ullman, T., Tenenbaum, J., Goodman, N., & Baker, C. (2013). The mentalistic basis of core social cognition: Experiments in preverbal infants and a computational model. *Developmental Science, 16*, *2*, 209–226.

Hamlin, J. K., Wynn, K., & Bloom, P. (2007). Social evaluation by pre-verbal infants. *Nature, 450*, 557–560.

Han, W. J. (2012). Bilingualism and academic achievement. *Child Development, 83*(1), 300–321.

Han, W. J., & Waldfogel, J. (2003). Parental leave: The impact of recent legislation on parents' leave-taking. *Demography, 40*(1), 191–200.

Han, W. J., Ruhm, C. J., & Waldfogel, J. (2009). Parental leave policies and parents' employment and leave-taking. *Journal of Policy Analysis and Management, 28*(1), 29–54.

Hankin, B. L., & Abela, J. R. Z. (2005). Depression from childhood through adolescence: A developmental vulnerability and stress perspective. In B. L. Hankin & J. R. Z. Abela (Eds.), *Development of psychopathology: A vulnerability-stress perspective* (pp. 245–288). Thousand Oaks, CA: Sage.

Hannah, M. E., & Midlarsky, E. (1999). Competence and adjustment of siblings of children with mental retardation. *American Journal on Mental Retardation, 104*(1), 22–37. doi:10.1352/0895–8017

Hannigan, J. H., & Randall, A. (2000). Alcohol in pregnancy and neonatal outcome. *Seminars in Fetal and Neonatal Medicine, 5*(3), 243–254. doi:10.1053/siny.2000.0027

Hare-Bruun, H. Nielsen, B. M., Kristensen, P. L., Møller, N. C., Togo, P., & Heirmann, B. L. (2011). Television viewing, food preferences and food habits among children: A prospective epidemiological study. *Biomedical Central Public Health, 11*, 311. Retrieved from http://www.biomedcentral.com/1471–2458/11/311

Harenski, C. L., Antonenko, O., Shane, M. S., & Kiehl, K. A. (2010). A functional imaging investigation of moral deliberation and moral intuition. *NeuroImage, 49*(3), 2707–2716. doi:10.1016/j.neuroimage.2009.10.062

Harenski, C. L., Harenski, K. A., Shane, M. S., & Kiehl, K. A. (2012). Neural development of mentalizing in moral judgment from adolescence to adulthood. *Developmental Cognitive Neuroscience, 2*(1), 162–173. doi:10.1016/j.dcn.2011.09.002

Harkness, S., & Super, C. M. (2005). Themes and variations: Parental ethnotheories in Western cultures. In K. H. Rubin & O.-B. Chung (Eds.), *Parental beliefs, parenting, and child development in cross-cultural perspective* (pp. 61–79). New York, NY: Psychology Press.

Harkness, S., & Super, C. P. (1996). *Parents' cultural belief systems: Their origin, expressions, and consequences*. New York, NY: Guilford.

Harkness, S., Zylicz, P. O., Super, C. M., Welles-Nyström, B., Bermudez, M. R., Bonichini, S., . . . Mavridis, C. J. (2011). Children's activities and their meanings for parents: A mixed-methods study of six Western cultures. *Journal of Family Psychology, 25*(6), 799–813. doi:10.1037/a0026204

Harlap, S., Kost, K., & Forrest, J. D. (1991). *Preventing pregnancy, protecting health: A new look at birth control choices in the United States*. New York, NY: Guttmacher Institute.

Harley, K., & Eskenazi, B. (2006). Time in the United States, social support, and health behaviors during pregnancy among women of Mexican descent. *Social Science and Medicine, 62*(12), 3048–3061. doi:10.1016/j.socscimed.2005.11.036

Harmon, R. J. (1981). Perinatal influences on the family: Some preventive implications. *Journal of Preventive Psychiatry, 1*(1), 132–139.

Harper, S., & Lynch, J. (2007). Trends in socioeconomic inequalities in adult health behaviors among U.S. states, 1990–2004. *Public Health Reports, 122*(2), 177–189.

Harris, P. L. (1995). Children's awareness and lack of awareness of mind and emotion. In D. Cicchetti & S. Toth (Eds.), *Rochester Symposium on Developmental Psychopathology: Vol. 6. Emotion, cognition and representation* (pp. 35–57). Rochester, NY: University of Rochester Press.

Harris, R., Nicoll, A. D., Adair, P. M., & Pine, C. M. (2004). Risk factors for dental caries in young children: A systematic review of the literature. *Community Dental Health, 21*(1), 71–85.

Harrison, A. C., & O'Neill, S. A. (2003). Preferences and children's use of gender-stereotyped knowledge about musical instruments: Making judgments about other children's preferences. *Sex Roles, 49*(7–8), 389–400. doi:10.1023/A:1025168322273

Hart, B., & Risley, T. R. (1995). *Meaningful differences in the everyday experience of young American children*. Baltimore, MD: Brooks.

Hart, B., & Risley, T. R. (2003). The early catastrophe: The 30 million word gap. *American Educator, 27*(1), 4–9.

Hart, D., Burock, D., & London, B. (2003). Prosocial tendencies, antisocial behavior, and moral development in childhood. In A. Slater & G. Bremner (Eds.), *Introduction to developmental psychology* (pp. 334–356). Oxford, UK: Blackwell.

Harter, S. (1985). *Self-perception profile for children*. Denver, CO: University of Denver.

Harter, S. (1990). *Causes, correlates, and the functional role of global self-worth: A life-span perspective*. New Haven, CT: Yale University Press.

Harter, S. (1998). The development of self-representations. In W. Damon & N. Eisenberg (Eds.), *Handbook of child psychology: Vol. 3. Social, emotional, and personality development* (5th ed.). New York, NY: Wiley.

Harter, S. (1999). *The construction of the self: A developmental perspective*. New York, NY: Guilford.

Harter, S. (2006). The self. In N. Eisenberg (Ed.), *Handbook of child psychology: Volume 3. Social, emotional, and personality development* (6th ed., pp. 505–570). Hoboken, NJ: Wiley.

Harter, S. (2012). *The construction of the self: Developmental and sociocultural foundations* (2nd ed.). New York, NY: Guilford.

Harter, S., & Pike, R. (1984). The pictorial scale of perceived competence and social acceptance for young children. *Child Development, 55*(6), 1969–1982. doi:10.2307/1129772

Hartmann, P. E., Rattigan, S., Saint, L., & Supriyana, O. (1985). Variation in the yield and composition of human milk. *Oxford Reviews of Reproductive Biology, 7*, 118–167.

Harvey, J. H., & Fine, M. A. (2010). *Children of divorce: Stories of loss and growth* (2nd ed.). New York, NY: Routledge.

Harwood, R. L., Miller, J. G., & Irizarry, N. L. (1995). *Culture and attachment: Perceptions of the child in context*. New York, NY: Guilford.

Haskins, R. (1985). Public school aggression among children with varying day-care experience. *Child Development, 56*, 689–703.

Hassan, A., Csemy, L. Rappo, M. A., & Knight, J. R. (2009). Adolescent substance abuse around the world: An international perspective. *Adolescent Medicine: State of the Art Reviews, 20*(3), 915–929.

Hasselhorn, M. (1992). Task dependency and the role of category typicality and metamemory in the development of an organizational strategy. *Child Development, 63*(1), 202–214. doi:10.1111/j.1467–8624.1992.tb03607.x

Hatano, G. (1993). *Commentary: Time to merge Vygotskian and constructivist conceptions of knowledge acquisition*. New York, NY: Oxford University Press.

Hauser-Cram, P., & Mitchell, D. M. (2013). Early childhood education. In K. R. Harris, S. Graham, and T. Urdan (Eds.), *Handbook of educational psychology, Vol. 3: Application of educational psychology to learning and teaching* (pp. 3–22). Washington, DC: American Psychological Association Press. doi:10.1037/13275-001

Hauser-Cram, P., & Steele, A. (2001). Parenting a child with mental retardation. In L. Balter (Ed.), *Parenthood in America: An encyclopedia*. Denver, CO: ABC–CLIO.

Hauser-Cram, P., Bronson, M. B., & Upshur, C. C. (1993). The effects of the classroom environment on the social and mastery behavior of preschool children with disabilities. *Early Childhood Research Quarterly, 8*, 479–497. doi:10.1016/S0885-2006(05)80081-X

Hauser-Cram, P., Cannarella, A., Tillinger, M., & Woodman, A. (2013). Disabilities and development. In R. M. Lerner, A. Easterbrooks, & J. Mistry (Eds.), *Handbook of psychology: Vol. 6. Developmental psychology* (2nd ed., pp. 547–569). Hoboken, NJ: Wiley.

Hauser-Cram, P., Durand, T. M., & Warfield, M. E. (2007). Early feelings about school and later academic outcomes of children with special needs living in poverty. *Early Childhood Research Quarterly, 22*(2), 161-172. doi:10.1016/j.ecresq.2007.02.001

Hauser-Cram, P., Krauss, M. W., & Kersh, J. (2009). Adolescents with developmental disabilities and their families. In R. M. Lerner & L. Steinberg (Eds.), *Handbook of adolescent psychology* (pp. 589–617). Hoboken, NJ: Wiley.

Hauser-Cram, P., Warfield, M. E., Krauss, M. W., Shonkoff, J. P., Upshur, C. C., & Sayer, A. (1999). Family influences on adaptive behavior in young children with Down syndrome. *Child Development, 70*, 979–989.

Hauser-Cram, P., Warfield, M. E., Shonkoff, J. P., & Krauss, M. W. (2001). Children with disabilities: A longitudinal study of child development and parent well-being. *Monographs of the Society for Research in Child Development, 66*, 1–131. doi:10.1111/1540-5834.00151

Haworth, C. M., Wright, M. J., Martin, N. W., Martin, N. G., Boomsma, D. I., Bartels, M., . . . Plomin, R. (2009). A twin study of the genetics of high cognitive ability selected from 11,000 twin pairs in six studies from four countries. *Behavioral Genetics, 39*(4), 359–370. doi:10.1007/s10519-009-9262-3

Hayne, H., Herbert, J., & Simcock, G. (2003). Imitation from television by 24- and 30-month olds. *Developmental Science, 6*(3), 254–261.

Haywood, K. M., & Getchell, M. (2009). *Lifespan motor development.* Champaign, IL: Human Kinetics.

Hazan, C., & Shaver, P. (1987). Romantic love conceptualized as an attachment process. *Journal of Personality and Social Psychology, 52*, 511–524.

Hazlett, H. C., Gu, H., McKinstry, R. C., Shaw, D. W. W., Botteron, K. N., Dager, S. R., . . . Paterson, S. J. (2012). Brain volume findings in 6-month-old infants at high familial risk for autism. *American Journal of Psychiatry. 169*(6): 601–608.

Health and Human Services (2011). *2011 Health and Human Services poverty guidelines.* Retrieved from http://aspe.hhs.gov/poverty/11poverty.shtml

Health Resources and Services Administration, U.S. Department of Health and Human Services. (2007). *Child health USA.* Retrieved from http://www.hrsa.gov/index.html

Heckhausen, J. (1987). Balancing for weaknesses and challenging developmental potential: A longitudinal study of mother-infant dyads in apprenticeship interactions. *Developmental Psychology, 23*(6), 762–770. doi:10.1037/0012-1649.23.6.762

Heckman, J. J., & Masterov, D. V. (2007). The productivity argument for investing in young children. *Applied Economics Perspectives and Policy, 29*(3), 446–493. doi:10.1111/j.1467-9353.2007.00359.x

Hedgepeth, E. (2005). Different lenses, different visions: Understanding moral views of stakeholders can help you promote a controversial program. *School Administrator, 62*(4), 36.

Hedges, L. V., & Nowell, A. (1995). Sex differences in mental scores, variability, and numbers of high-scoring individuals. *Science, 269*, 41–45. doi:10.1126/science.7604277

Hegland, S. M., & Rix, M. K. (1990). Aggression and assertiveness in kindergarten children differing in day care experiences. *Early Childhood Research Quarterly, 5*(1), 105–116.

Heim, C., & Nemeroff, C. B. (2001). The role of childhood trauma in the neurobiology of mood and anxiety disorders: Preclinical and clinical studies. *Biological Psychiatry, 49*, 1023–1039.

Heimann, M. (2010). Patterns of instability and change: Observations on regression periods in typically developing infants. In B. M. Lester & J. D. Sparrow (Eds.), *Nurturing children and their families* (pp. 95–106). Hoboken, NJ: Wiley–Blackwell.

Heird, W. C. (2007). Progress in promoting breast-feeding, combating malnutrition, and composition and use of infant formula, 1981–2006. *Journal of Nutrition, 137*, 499S–502S.

Helmerhorst, F. M., Perquin, D. A., Donker, D., & Keirse, M. J. (2004). Perinatal outcome of singletons and twins after assisted conception: A systematic review of controlled studies. *British Medical Journal, 328*(7434), 261. doi:10.1136/bmj.37957.560278.EE

Helms, J. E. (1990). *Black and white racial identity: Theory, research, and practice.* New York, NY: Greenwood Press.

Helms, J. E. (1995). An update on Helms's white and people of color racial identity models. In J. G. Ponterotto, J. M. Casas, L. A. Suzuki, & C. M. Alexander (Eds.), *Handbook of multicultural counseling* (pp. 181–198). Thousand Oaks, CA: Sage.

Helms, J. E., & Talleyrand, R. M. (1997). Race is not ethnicity. *American Psychologist, 52*(11), 1246–1247.

Helwig, C. C., & Turiel, E. (2002). *Children's social and moral reasoning.* Malden, MA: Blackwell.

Henderson, V. L., & Dweck, C. S. (1990). Motivation and achievement. In S. S. Feldman & G. R. Elliott (Eds.), *At the threshold: The developing adolescent* (pp. 308–329). Cambridge, MA: Harvard University Press.

Hepner, D. L., Harnett, M., Segal, S., Camann, W., Bader, A. M., & Tsen, L. C. (2002). Herbal medicine use in parturients. *Anesthesia and Analgesia, 94*, 690–693. doi:10.1097/00000539-200203000-00039

Hernandez-Reif, M., Field, T., & Diego, M. (2004). Touch perception in neonates. In T. Field (Ed.), *Touch and massage in early child development* (pp. 15–37). New Brunswick, Nova Scotia: Johnson & Johnson Pediatric Institute.

Hespos, S. J., & Ferry, A. L., & Rips, L. J. (2009). Five-month-old infants have different expectations for solids and liquids. *Psychological Science, 20*, 603–611. doi:10.1111/j.1467-9280.2009.02331.x

Hestenes, L. L., & Carroll, D. E. (2000). The play interactions of young children with and without disabilities: Individual and environmental influences. *Early Childhood Research Quarterly, 15*(2), 229–246. doi:10.1016/S0885-2006(00)00052-1

Hetherington, E. M. (1999). Should we stay together for the sake of the children? In E. M. Hetherington (Ed.), *Coping with divorce, single parenting and remarriage: A risk and resilience perspective* (pp. 93–116). Mahwah, NJ: Erlbaum.

Hetherington, E. M. (2006). The influence of conflict, marital problem solving and parenting on children's adjustment in nondivorced, divorced and remarried families. In A. Clarke-Stewart & J. Dunn (Eds.), *Families count* (pp. 203–237). New York, NY: Cambridge University Press.

Hetherington, E. M., & Kelly, J. (2002). *For better or for worse: Divorce reconsidered.* New York, NY: Norton.

Hetherington, S. E. (1990). A controlled study of the effect of childbirth classes on obstetric outcomes. *Birth, 17*(2), 86–90.

Heuther, S. E., & McCane, K. L. (2004). *Understanding pathophysiology.* St. Louis, MO: Mosby.

Heywood, A. H., Marshall, T., & Heywood, P. F. (1991). Motor development and nutritional status of young children in Madang, Papua New Guinea. *Papua New Guinea Medical Journal, 34*(2), 109–116.

Hickman, G. R., Bartholomew, M., Mathwig, J., & Heinrich, R. S. (2008). Differential developmental pathways of high school dropouts and graduates. *Journal of Educational Research, 102*(1), 3–14. doi:10.3200/JOER.102.1.3-14

Higgins, G. E., Piquero, N. L., & Piquero, A. R. (2011). General strain theory, peer rejection, and delinquency/crime. *Youth & Society, 43*(4), 1272–1297. doi:10.1177/0044118X10382032

Hildyard, K. L., & Wolfe, D. A. (2002). Child neglect: Developmental issues and outcomes. *Child Abuse & Neglect, 26*(6–7), 679–695. doi:10.1016/S0145-2134(02)00341-1

Hilgetag, C., & Barbasthis, H. (2009). Sculpting the brain. *Scientific American, 300*(2), 66–71.

Hill, D. J., Hosking, C. S., Zhie, C. Y., Leung, R., Baratwidjaja, K., Likura, Y., . . . Hsieh, K. H. (1997). The frequency of food allergy in Australia and Asia. *Environmental Toxicology and Pharmacology, 4*(1–2), 101–110. doi:10.1016/S1382-6689(97)10049-7

Hill, L. D., Gray, J. J., Carter, M. M., & Schulkin, J. (2005). Obstetrician-gynecologists' decision making about the diagnosis of major depressive disorder and premenstrual dysphoric disorder. *Journal of Psychosomatic Obstetrics and Gynaecology, 26*(1), 41–51.

Hill, P. D. (1991). The enigma of insufficient milk supply. *American Journal of Maternal Child Nursing, 16*(6), 312–316. doi:10.1097/00005721-199111000-00005

Hillis, D. S., Anda, R. F., Dube, S. R., Felitti, V. J., Marchbanks, P. A., & Marks, J. S. (2004). The association between adverse childhood experiences and adolescent pregnancy, long-term psychosocial consequences, and fetal death. *Pediatrics, 113*, 320–327. doi:10.1542/peds.113.2.320

Himmelsbach, A. (2009, March 9). First impressions can create unrealistic expectations for recruits. *The New York Times*, p. B–11.

Hinde, R. A., & Stevenson-Hinde, J. (1987). Interpersonal relationships and child development. *Developmental Review*, 7, 1–21.

Hinduja, S., & Patchin, J. W. (2010). Bullying, cyberbullying, and suicide. *Archives of Suicide Research, 14*(3), 206–221. doi:10.1080/13811118.2010.494133

Hjelmstedt, A., Widström, A. M., Wramsby, H., & Collins, A. (2004). Emotional adaptation following successful in vitro fertilization. *Fertility and Sterility, 81*(5), 1254–1264. doi:10.1016/j.fertnstert.2003.09.061

Hockenberry, M. J. (2003). *Wong's nursing care of infants and children.* St. Louis, MO: Mosby.

Hockenberry, M. J., Wilson, D., Winkelstein, M. L., & Kline, N. E. (Eds.). (2003). *Wong's nursing care of infants and children.* St. Louis, MO: Mosby.

Hodges, E. V. E., Boivin, M., Vitaro, F., & Bukowski, W. M. (1999). The power of friendship: Protection against an escalating cycle of peer victimization. *Developmental Psychology, 35*, 94–101. doi:10.1037/0012-1649.35.1.94

Hodnett, E. D., Stremler, R., Willan, A. R., Weston, J. A., Lowe, N. K., Simpson, K. R., . . . the SELAN Trial Group (2008). Effect on birth outcomes of a formalised approach to care in hospital labour assessment units: International, randomized, controlled trial. *British Medical Journal, 337*(7670), 618–622. doi:10.1136/bmj.a1021

Hoehl, S., & Striano, T. (2008). Neural processing of eye gaze and threat-related emotional facial expressions in infancy. *Child Development, 79*(6), 1752–1760.

Hoehl, S., Reid, V. M., Parise, E., Handl, A., Palumbo, L., & Striano, T. (2009). Looking at eye gaze processing and its neural correlates in infancy: Implications for social development and autism spectrum disorder. *Child Development, 80*(4), 968–985.

Hoehl, S., Wiese, L., & Striano, T. (2008). Young infants' neural processing of objects is affected by eye gaze direction and emotional expression. *PLoS ONE, 3*(6), 1–6.

Hoff, E. (2006). Language experience and language milestones during early childhood. In K. McCartney & D. Phillips (Eds.), *Blackwell handbook of early childhood development* (pp. 233–251). Malden, MA: Blackwell.

Hoffman, J., & Russ, S. (2012). Pretend play, creativity, and emotion regulation in children. *Psychology of Aesthetics, Creativity, and the Arts, 6*(2), 175–184. doi:10.1037/a0026299

Hoffman, S. D., & Maynard, R. A. (Eds.). (2008). *Kids having kids: Economic costs and social consequences of teen pregnancy (2nd ed.).* Washington, DC: Urban Institute Press.

Hoffmann, M. L. (1991). Empathy, social cognition, and moral action. In W. M. Kurtines & J. L. Gerwitz (Eds.), *Handbook of moral behavior and development: Vol. 1. Theory* (pp. 275–301). Hillsdale, NJ: Erlbaum.

Hoglund, W. L. G., Lalonde, C. E., & Leadbeater, B. J. (2008). Social-cognitive competence, peer rejection and neglect, and behavioral and emotional problems in middle childhood. *Social Development, 17*(3), 528–553. doi:10.1111/j.1467–9507.2007.00449.x

Homer, C. J. (2005). *Improving cultural competency in children's health care: Expanding perspectives.* Cambridge, MA: National Institute for Child Health Quality (NICHQ).

Hong, Y., Chiu, C., Dweck, C. S., Lin, D. M.–S., & Wan, W. (1999). Implicit theories, attributions, and coping: A meaning system approach. *Journal of Personality and Social Psychology,* 77(3), 588–599. doi:10.1037/0022–3514.77.3.588

Hongwanishkul, D., Happaney, K. R., Lee, W. S. C., & Zelazo, P. D. (2005). Assessment of hot and cool executive function in young children: Age-related changes and individual differences. *Developmental Neuropsychology, 28*(2), 617–644. doi:10.1207/s15326942dn2802_4

Hopkins, B., & Westra, T. (1989). Maternal expectations of their infants' development: Some cultural differences. *Developmental Medicine & Child Neurology, 31*(1), 384–390. doi:10.1111/j.1469–8749.1989.tb04008.x

Hornig, M., Briese, T., Buie, T., Bauman, M. L., Lauwers, G., Siemetzki, U., . . . Lipkin, W. I. (2008). Lack of association between measles virus vaccine and autism with enteropathy: A case-control study. *PLoS ONE, 3*(9), e3140. doi:10.1371/journal.pone.0003140

Hornik, R., & Gunnar, M. R. (1988). A descriptive analysis of infant social referencing. *Child Development, 59*, 626–634.

Hornik, R., Risenhoover, N., & Gunnar, M. R. (1987). The effects of maternal positive, neutral, and negative affective communication on infant responses to new toys. *Child Development, 58*, 937–944.

Horton, R. (2004). The lessons of MMR. *The Lancet, 363*(9411), 747–749. doi:10.1016/S0140-6736(04)15714-0

Horton, T. M., & Steuber, C. P. (2011). Overview of the outcome of acute lymphoblastic leukemia in children. In J. Park (Ed.), *UptoDate.* Waltham, MA: UptoDate.

Houde, O., Pineau, A., Leroux, G., Poirel, N., Perchey, G., Lanoe, C., . . . & Mazoyer, B. (2011). Functional magnetic resonance imaging study of Piaget's conservation-of-number task in preschool and school-age children: A neo-Piagetian approach. *Journal of Experimental Child Psychology, 110*(3), 332–346. doi:10.1016/j.jecp.2011.04.008

Houle, C. R., Leo, H. L., & Clark, N. M. (2010). A developmental, community and psychosocial approach to food allergies in children. *Current Allergy and Asthma Reports, 10*(5), 381–6. doi:10.1007/s11882-010-0123-1

Houston, D. M., Beer, J., Bergeson, T. R., Chin S. B., Pisoni, D. B., & Miyamoto, R. T. (2012). The ear is connected to the brain: Some new directions in the study of children with cochlear implants at Indiana University. *Journal of the American Academy of Audiology, 23*, 446–463.

Howe, N., Brody, M.-H., & Recchia, H. (2006). Effects of task difficulty on sibling teaching in middle childhood. *Infant and Child Development, 15*(5), 455–470. doi:10.1002/icd.470

Howe, N., Fiorentino, L., & Gariepy, N. (2003). Sibling conflict in middle childhood: Influence of maternal context and mother-sibling interaction over four years. *Merrill-Palmer Quarterly, 49*(2), 183–208.

Howell, K. K., Lynch, M. E., Platzman, K. A., Smith, G. H., & Coles, C. D. (2006). Prenatal alcohol exposure and ability, academic achievement, and school functioning in adolescence: A longitudinal follow-up. *Journal of Pediatric Psychology, 31*(1), 116–126. doi:10.1093/jpepsy/jsj029

Howes, C. (1992). *The collaborative construction of pretend.* Albany, NY: State University of New York Press.

Howes, C. (Ed.). (2003). *Teaching 4- to 8-year-olds: Literacy, math, multiculturalism, and classroom community.* Baltimore, MD: Brooks.

Howland, R. (2009). Evaluating the safety of medications during pregnancy and lactation. *Journal of Psychosocial Nursing and Mental Health Services, 47*(3), 19–22. Retrieved from http://www.jpnonline.com/showPdf.asp?rID=37911

Hoyert, D. L., Heron, M. P., Murphy, S. L., & Kung, H. (2006). Deaths: Final data for 2003. *National Vital Statistics Reports, 54*(13), 1–120.

Hoza, B., Vaughn, A., Waschbusch, D. A., Murray–Close, D., & McCabe, G. (2012). Can children with ADHD be motivated to reduce bias in self-reports of competence? *Journal of Consulting and Clinical Psychology, 80*(2), 245–254. doi:10.1037/a0027299

Hrdy, S. B. (1999). *Mother nature: A history of mothers, infants and natural selection.* New York, NY: Ballantine.

Hrdy, S. B. (2009). *Mothers and others: The evolutionary origins of mutual understanding.* Cambridge, MA: Belknap, Harvard University Press.

Hua, Z., & Dodd, B. (2006). *Phonological development and disorders in children: A multilingual perspective.* Tonawanda, NY: Multilingual Matters.

Huang, K. Y., O'Brien Caughy, M., Genevro, J. L., & Miller, T. L. (2005). Maternal knowledge of child development and quality of parenting among white, African-American and Hispanic mothers. *Journal of Applied Developmental Psychology, 26*, 149–170. doi:10.1016/j.appdev.2004.12.001

Hubert, N. C., Wachs, T. D., Peters-Martin, P., & Gandour, J. (1982). The study of early temperament: Measurement and conceptual issues. *Child Development, 53*, 571–600.

Hudson, J. A., & Sheffield, E. G. (1999). The role of reminders in young children's memory development. In L. Balter & C. S. Tamis-LeMonda (Eds.), *Child psychology: A handbook of contemporary issues* (pp. 193–214). New York, NY: Psychology Press.

Hudson, J. I., Hiripi, E., Pope, H. G., & Kessler, R. C. (2007). The prevalence and correlates of eating disorders in the national comorbidity survey replication. *Biological Psychiatry, 61*(3), 348–358. doi:10.1016/j.biopsych.2006.03.040

Hughes, C., & Graham, A. (2002). Measuring executive functions in childhood: Problems and solutions? *Child and Adolescent Mental Health,* 7(3), 131–142. doi:10.1111/1475-3588.00024

Hulin, M., Caillaud, D., & Annesi-Maeano, I. (2010). Indoor air pollution and childhood asthma: Variations between urban and rural areas. *International Journal of Indoor Environment and Health, 20*(6), 502–514. doi:10.1111/j.1600-0668.2010.00673.x

Hum, K. M., & Lewis, M. D. (2013). Neural mechanisms of emotion regulation in children: Implications for normative development and emotion-related disorders. In K. C. Barrett, N. A. Fox, G. A. Morgan, D. J. Fidler, & L. A. Daunhauer (Eds.), *Handbook of self-regulatory processes in development: New directions and international perspectives* (pp. 173–198). New York, NY: Psychology Press.

Human Genome Project. (2009). *Gene therapy.* Retrieved from http://www.ornl.gov/sci/techresources/Human_Genome/medicine/genetherapy.shtml

Human Genome Project. (2010). Genetic anthropology, ancestry, and ancient human migration. Retrieved from http://www.ornl.gov/sci/techresources/Human_Genome/elsi/humanmigration.shtml.

Humenick, S. S., Mederios, D., Wreschner, T. B., Walton, M. B., & Hill, P. D. (1994). The Maturation Index of Colostrum and Milk (MICAM): A measurement of breast milk maturation. *Journal of Nursing Measurement, 2*, 169–186.

Huntsinger, C. S., Jose, P. E., Krieg, D. B., & Luo, Z. (2011). Cultural differences in Chinese American and European American children's drawing skills over time. *Early Childhood Research Quarterly, 26*(1), 134–145.

Hurewitz, F., Brown-Schmidt, S., Thorpe, K., Gleitman, L. R., & Trueswell, J. C. (2000). One frog, two frog, red frog, blue frog: Factors affecting children's syntactic choices in production and comprehension. *Journal of*

*Psycholinguistic Research, 2*(6), 597–626. doi: 10.1023/A:1026468209238

Hurwitz, R. L., & Dean, A. L. (2011). Childhood lead poisoning: Clinical manifestations and diagnosis. In: D. H. Mahoney, M. B. Ewald, & J. E. Drutz (Eds.), *UpToDate*. Waltham, MA: UpToDate.

Hutman, T., Chela, M. K., Gillespie–Lynch, K., & Sigman, M. (2012). Selective visual attention at twelve months: Signs of autism in early social interactions. *Journal of Autism and Developmental Disorders, 42*(4), 487–498. doi:10.1007/s10803–01101262–5

Hutman, T., Rozga, A., DeLaurentis, A. D., Barnwell, J. M., Sugar, C. A., & Sigman, M. (2010). Response to distress in infants at risk for autism: A prospective longitudinal study. *Journal of Child Psychology and Psychiatry, 51*(9), 1010–1020. doi:10.1111/j.1469–7610.2010.02270.x

Huttenlocher, J., Vasileyva, M., Cymerman, E., & Levine, S. (2002). Language input and child syntax. *Cognitive Psychology, 45*(3), 337–374. doi:10.1016/S0010–0285(02)00500–5

Huttenlocher, P. R. (2002). Morphometric study of human cerebral cortex development. In P. R. Huttenlocher (Ed.), *Brain development: A reader* (2nd ed., pp. 117–128). Malden, MA: Blackwell.

Huttenlocher, P. R. (2002). *Neural plasticity: The effects of environment on the development of the cerebral cortex: Perspectives in cognitive neuroscience.* Cambridge, MA: Harvard University Press.

Huttenlocher, P. R. (2003). Basic neuroscience research has important implications for child development. *Nature Neuroscience, 6*, 541. doi: 10.1038/nn0603-541

Hwang, C. P., & Broberg, A. G. (1992). The historical and social context of child care in Sweden. In M. E. Lamb, K. J. Sternberg, C. P. Hwang, & A. G. Broberg (Eds.), *Child care in context: Cross-cultural perspectives* (pp. 27–54). Hillsdale, NJ: Erlbaum.

Hyde, M. L. (2005). Newborn hearing screening programs: Overview. *Journal of Otolaryngology, 34*(2), S70–S78.

Iacoboni, M. (2008). *Mirroring people: The new science of how we connect with others.* New York, NY: Farrar, Straus and Giroux.

Idjradinata, P., & Pollitt, E. (1993). Reversal of developmental delays in iron-deficient anemic infants treated with iron. *Lancet, 341*, 1–4.

Imada, T., Zhang, Y., Cheour, M., Taulu, S., Ahonen, A., & Kuhl, P. (2006). Infant speech perception activates Broca's area: A developmental magnetoencephalography study. *NeuroReport 17*, 957–962.

Ingram, R. E., & Luxton, D. D. (2005). Vulnerability-stress models. In B. L. Hankin & J. R. Z. Abela (Eds.), *Development of psychopathology: A vulnerability-stress perspective* (pp. 32–46). Thousand Oaks, CA: Sage.

Inhelder, B., & Piaget, J. (1958/1955). *The growth of logical thinking: From childhood to adolescence*. New York, NY: Basic Books. (Original work published 1955)

Inhelder, B., & Piaget, J. (1964). *The early growth of logic in the child: Classification and seriation.* New York, NY: Humanities Press.

Insel, T. (2010). Faulty circuits. *Scientific American, 302*(4), 44–51. doi:10.1038/scientificamerican0410–44

Institute for Clinical Systems Improvement (ICSI). (2008). *Routine prenatal care.* Bloomington, MN: Author. Retrieved from http://www.guideline.gov/summary/summary.aspx?doc_id=13010&nbr=006704&string=prenatal+AND+care

Institute of Medicine. (1998). *Dietary reference intakes: Thiamin, riboflavin, niacin, vitamin B6, folate, vitamin B12, pantothenic acid, biotin, and choline*. Washington, DC: National Academies Press.

Institute of Medicine. (2001). *Crossing the quality chasm.* Washington, DC: National Academies Press.

Institute of Medicine. (2002). *Is soccer bad for children's heads? Summary of the IOM workshop on neuropsychological consequences of head impact in youth soccer*. Washington, DC: National Academies Press.

Institute of Medicine. (2003). *Unequal treatment: Confronting racial and ethnic disparities in health care.* Washington, DC: National Academies Press.

Institute of Medicine. (2004). *Immunization safety review: Vaccines and autism.* Washington, DC: National Academies Press.

Institute of Medicine. (2005). *Preventing childhood obesity—health in the balance*. Washington, DC: National Academies Press.

Institute of Medicine. (2008). *Challenges and successes in reducing health disparities: Workshop summary.* Washington, DC: National Academies Press.

Institute of Medicine. (2008). *Nutrition standards and meal requirements for national school lunch and breakfast programs: Phase I. Proposed approach for recommending revisions.* Washington, DC: National Academies Press.

Institute of Medicine. (2009). *Depression in parents, parenting, and children*. Washington, DC: National Research Council and Institute of Medicine of the National Academies.

Insurance Institute for Highway Safety. (2009). *Fatality facts: Teenagers 2008*. Arlington, VA: Author.

Irwin, C. E., Jr., Adams, S. H., Park, M. J., & Newacheck, P. W. (2009). Preventive care for adolescents: Few get visits and fewer get services. *Pediatrics, 123*(4), e565–e572. doi:10.1542/peds.2008–2601

Isaacson, G. C. (2010). Overview of tympanostomy tube placement and medical care of children with tympanostomy tubes. In E. M. Friedman (Ed.), *UpToDate*. Waltham, MA: UpToDate.

Ishak, S., Tamis-LeMonda, C. S., & Adolph, K. E. (2007). Ensuring safety and providing challenge: Mothers' and fathers' expectations and choices about infant locomotion. *Parenting: Science and Practice*, 7(1), 57–68.

Isong, I. A., Zuckerman, K. E., Rao, S. R., Kuhlthau, K. A., Winickoff, J. P., & Perrin, J. M. (2010). Association between parents' and children's use of oral health services. *Pediatrics, 125*(3), 502–508. doi:10.1542/peds.2009-1417

Ispa, J. M., Fine, M. A., Halgunseth, L. C., Harper, S., Robinson, J., Boyce, L., & Brooks-Gunn, J. (2004). Maternal intrusiveness, maternal warmth, and mother-toddler relationship outcomes: Variations across low-income ethnic and language groups. *Child Development, 75*(6), 1613–1631.

Izard, C. E. (1971). *The face of emotion*. New York, NY: Appleton-Century-Crofts.

Izard, C. E. (1991). Perspectives on emotions in psychotherapy. In J. D. Safran & L. S. Greenberg (Eds.), *Emotion, psychotherapy, and change* (pp. 280–289). New York, NY: Guilford.

Izard, C. E. (1994). Innate and universal facial expressions: Evidence from developmental and cross-cultural research. *Psychological Bulletin, 115*(2), 288–299. doi:10.1037/0033–2909.115.2.288

Izard, C. E. (2009). Emotion theory and research: Highlights, unanswered questions, and emerging issues. *Annual Review of Psychology, 60*, 1–25. doi:10.1146/annurev.psych.60.110707.163539

Izard, C. E. (2011). Forms and functions of emotions: Matters of emotion-cognition interactions. *Emotion Review, 3*, 371–378.

Izard, C. E., Fantauazzo, C. A., Castle, J. M., Haynes, O. M., Rayias, M. F., & Putman, P. H. (1995). The ontogeny and significance of infants' facial expressions in the first 9 months of life. *Developmental Psychology, 31*(6), 997–1013. doi:10.1037/0012–1649.31.6.997

Izard, C. E., Woodburn, E. M., & Finlon, K. J. (2010). Extending emotion science to the study of discrete emotions in infants. *Emotion Review, 2*(2), 134–136. doi:10.1177/1754073909355003

Jacobson, J. L., & Jacobson, S. (2002, Winter). Effects of prenatal alcohol exposure on child development. *Alcohol Research and Health*, 282–286. Retrieved from http://pubs.niaaa.nih.gov/publications/arh26–4/282–286.htm

Jaffee, S. R., Caspi, A., Moffit, T. E., Dodge, K. A., Rutter, M., & Taylor, A. (2005). Nature × nurture: Genetic vulnerabilities interact with physical maltreatment to promote conduct problems. *Development and Psychopathology, 17*(1), 67–84. doi:10.1017/S0954579405050042

Jaffee, S., & Hyde, J. S. (2000). Gender differences in moral orientation: A meta-analysis. *Psychological Bulletin, 126*(5), 703–726. doi:10.1037/0033–2909.126.5.703

James, C. V., & Rosenbaum, S. (2001). Paying for quality care: Implications for racial and ethnic health disparities in pediatric asthma. *Pediatrics, 123*(Suppl. 3), S205–S210. doi:10.1542/peds.2008-2233

James, W. (1890). *The principles of psychology (Vol. I)*. New York, NY: Henry Holt.

James, W. (1890/1981). *Principles of psychology*. Cambridge, MA: Harvard University Press.

Janssen, P. A., Carty, E. A., & Reime, B. (2006). Satisfaction with planned place of birth among midwifery clients in British Columbia. *Journal of Midwifery and Women's Health, 51*(2), 91–97. doi:10.1016/j.jmwh.2005.10.012

Jedrychowski, W., Galas, A. S., Flaka, E., Jaceka, R., Penara, A., Spenglerb, J., & Pererac, F. P. (2007). Increased burden of respiratory disease in the first six months of life due to prenatal environmental tobacco smoke: Krakow birth cohort study. *Early Child Development and Care, 177*(4), 369–381. doi:10.1080/03004430500507719

Jenkins, J. S. (2001). The Mozart effect. *Journal of the Royal Society of Medicine, 94*, 170–172.

Jensen, A. R. (1969). How much can we boost IQ and scholastic achievement? *Harvard Educational Review, 39*(1), 1–123.

Jensen, A. R. (1998). *The g factor: The science of mental ability.* Westport, CT: Praeger.

Jeon, J., Victor, M., Adler, S. P., Arwady, A., Demmler, G., Fowler, K., . . . Cannon, M. J. (2006). Knowledge and awareness of congenital cytomegalovirus (CMV) among women. *Infectious Diseases in Obstetrics & Gynecology,* 1–7. doi:10.1155/IDOG/2006/80383

Jeong, M., Tashiro, M., Singh, L. N., Yamaguchi, K., Horikawa, E., Miyake, M., . . . Itoh, M. (2006). Functional brain mapping of actual car-driving using [18F]FDG-PET. *Annals of Nuclear Medicine, 20*(9), 623–628.

Jeynes, W. (2012). A meta-analysis of the efficacy of different types of parental involvement programs for urban students. *Urban Education, 47*(4), 706-742. doi:1177/0042085912445643

Jimerson, S. R. (1999). On the failure of failure: Examining the association between early grade retention and education and employment outcomes during late adolescence. *Journal of School Psychology, 37*(3), 243–272. doi:10.1016/S0022-4405(99)00005-9

Jimerson, S. R., Anderson, G. E., & Whipple, A. D. (2002). Winning the battle and losing the war: Examining the relation between grade retention and dropping out of high school. *Psychology in the Schools, 39*(4), 441–457. doi:10.1002/pits.10046

Johnson, A. (2013). Procedural memory and skill acquisition. In A. F. Healy & R. W. Proctor (Eds.), *Handbook of psychology: Vol. 4. Experimental psychology* (2nd ed., pp. 495–520). Hoboken, NJ: Wiley.

Johnson, C., Ferraina, S., Bianchi, L., & Caminiti, R. (1996). Cortical networks for visual reaching: Physiological and anatomical organization of frontal and parietal lobe arm regions. *Cerebral Cortex, 6*(2), 102–119. doi:10.1093/cercor/6.2.102

Johnson, D. E., Miller, L. C., Iverson, S., Thomas, W., Franchino, B., Dole, K., . . . Hostetter, M. K. (1992). The health of children adopted from Romania. *JAMA, 269*(16), 3446–3451. doi:10.1001/jama.1992. 03490240054036

Johnson, D. J., Jaeger, E., Randolph, S. M., Cauce, A. M., Ward, J., & National Institute of Child Health and Human Development Early Child Care Research Network. (2003). Studying the effects of early child care experiences on the development of children of color in the United States: Toward a more inclusive research agenda. *Child Development, 74*(5), 1227–1244. doi:10.1111/1467-8624.00604

Johnson, K. C., & Daviss, B. A. (2005). Outcomes of planned home births with certified professional midwives: Large prospective study in North America. *British Medical Journal, 330,* 1415–1419. doi:10.1136/bmj.330.7505.1416

Johnson, M. H. (2005). Sensitive periods in functional brain development: Problems and prospects. *Developmental Psychobiology, 46,* 287–292.

Johnson, M. H. (2007). The social brain in infancy: A developmental cognitive neuroscience approach. In D. Coch, K. W. Fischer, & G. Dawson (Eds.), *Human behavior, learning, and the developing brain: Typical development* (pp. 115–137). New York, NY: Guilford.

Johnson, M. H., Munakata, Y., & Gilmore, R. O. (2002). *Brain development and cognition.* Malden, MA: Wiley–Blackwell.

Johnson, M. H., Posner, M. I., & Rothbart, M. K. (1991). Components of visual orienting in early infancy: Contingency learning, anticipatory looking, and disengaging. *Journal of Cognitive Neuroscience, 3*(4), 335–344. doi:10.1162/jocn.1991.3.4.335

Johnson, M. J., Dziurawiec, S., Ellis, H., & Morton, J. (1991). Newborns' preferential tracking of face-like stimuli and its subsequent decline. *Cognition, 40,* 1–19.

Johnson, S. C., Dweck, C. S., Chen, F. S., Stern, H. L., Ok, S., & Barth, M. (2010). At the intersection of social and cognitive development: Internal working models of attachment in infancy. *Cognitive Science: A Multidisciplinary Journal, 34,* 807–825. doi:10.1111/j.1551-6709.2010.01112.x

Johnson, S. R. (1987). The epidemiology and social impact of premenstrual symptoms. *Clinical Obstetrics and Gynecology, 30,* 367–376.

Johnston, L. D., O'Malley, P. M., Bachman, J. G., & Schulenberg, J. E. (2008). Monitoring the future national results on adolescent drug use. *Overview of key findings, 2007* (NIH Publication No. 08–6418). Bethesda, MD: National Institute on Drug Abuse.

Johnston, M. V., Alemi, L., & Harum, K. H. (2003). Learning, memory, and transcription factors. *Pediatric Research, 53,* 369–374. doi:10.1203/01.PDR.0000049517.47493.E9

Johnstone, J. W. (1983). Recruitment to a youth gang. *Youth and Society, 14,* 281–300.

Jolles, D. D., Kleibeuker, S. W., Rombouts, S. A. R. B., & Crone, E. A. (2011). Developmental differences in prefrontal activation during working memory maintenance and manipulation for different memory loads. *Developmental Science, 14*(4), 713–724. doi:10.1111/j.1467-7687.2010.01016.x

Jolley, R. P. (2010). *Children and pictures: Drawing and understanding.* Hoboken, NJ: Wiley-Blackwell.

Jolly, M. C., Sebire, N., Harris, J. Robinson, S., & Regan, L. (2000). Obstetric risks of pregnancy in women less than 18 years old. *Obstetrics and Gynecology, 96*(6), 962–966. doi:10.1016/S0029-7844(00)01075-9

Jones, L. B., Rothbart, M. K., & Posner, M. I. (2003). Development of executive attention in preschool children. *Developmental Science, 6*(5), 498–504. doi:10.1111/1467-7687.00307

Jones, M. C. (1965). Psychological correlates of somatic development. *Child Development 36*(4), 899–911.

Jones, M. D., & Galliher, R. V. (2007). Ethnic identity and psychosocial functioning in Navajo adolescents. *Journal of Research on Adolescence, 17*(4), 683–696.

Jones, S. M., Pons, L., Roberts, J. L., Scurlock, A., Perry, T. T., Kulis, M., . . . Burks, A. W. (2009). Clinical efficacy and immune regulation with peanut oral immunotherapy. *The Journal of Allergy and Clinical Immunology, 124*(2), 292–300. doi:10.1016/j.jaci.2009.05.022

Jordan, B. (1993). *Birth in four cultures: A cross-cultural investigation of childbirth in Yucatan, Holland, Sweden and the United States* (4th ed.). Prospect Heights, OH: Waverland Press.

Joseph, R. (1992). The limbic system: Emotion, laterality, and unconscious mind. *Psychoanalytic Review, 79,* 405–456.

Joseph, R. (1999). Environmental influences on neural plasticity, the limbic system, emotional development, and attachment: A review. *Child Psychiatry and Human Development, 29*(3), 189–208.

Jungbluth, N. J., & Shirk, S. R. (2009). Therapist strategies for building involvement in cognitive-behavioral therapy for adolescent depression. *Journal of Consulting and Clinical Psychology,* 77(6), 1179–1184. doi:10.1037/a0017325

Just, M. A., Keller, T. A., & Cynkar, J. A. (2008). A decrease in brain activation associated with driving when listening to someone speak. *Brain Research, 1205,* 70–80. doi:10.1016/j.brainres.2007.12.075

Juvonen, J. (2006). Sense of belonging, social bonds, and school functioning. In P. A. Alexander & P. H. Winne (Eds.), *Handbook of educational psychology* (pp. 655–674). Mahwah, NJ: Erlbaum.

Kaback, M. M. (2006). Hexosaminidase A deficiency. *GeneReviews.* Retrieved from http://www.ncbi.nlm.nih.gov/bookshelf/br.fcgi?book=gene&part=tay-sachs (pmid: 20301397)

Kaczynski, K. J., Lindahl, K. M., Malik, N. M., & Laurenceau, J. P. (2006). Marital conflict, maternal and paternal parenting, and child adjustment: A test of mediation and moderation. *Journal of Family Psychology, 20,* 199–200.

Kagan, J. (1981). *The second year: The emergence of self-awareness.* Cambridge, UK: Cambridge University Press.

Kagan, J. (1998). Biology and the child. In W. Damon (Series Ed.) & N. Eisenberg (Vol. Ed.), *Handbook of Child Psychology: Vol. 3. Social, emotional, and personality development* (5th ed., pp. 177–235). New York, NY: Wiley.

Kagan, J. (2006). *An argument for mind.* New Haven, CT: Yale University Press.

Kagan, J. (2010). Temperament as sets of preparedness. In B. M. Lester & J. D. Sparrow (Eds.), *Nurturing children and families: Building on the legacy of T. Berry Brazelton* (pp. 164–174). West Sussex, UK: Wiley–Blackwell.

Kagan, J., & Snidman, N. (2004). *The long shadow of temperament.* Cambridge, MA: Harvard University Press.

Kagan, J., Snidman, N., & Arcus, D. (1998): Childhood derivatives of high and low reactivity in infancy. *Child Development, 69,* 1483–1493.

Kagan, J., Snidman, N., Kahn, V., & Towsley, S. (2007). The preservation of two infant temperaments into adolescence. *Monographs of the Society for Research in Child Development,* 72(2, Serial No. 287).

Kahn, M. (2002). *Basic Freud: Psychoanalytic thought for the 21st century.* New York, NY: Basic Books.

Kahneman, D. (2011). *Thinking, fast and slow.* New York, NY: Farrar, Straus and Giroux.

Kail, R. (2000). Speed of information processing: Developmental change and links to intelligence. *Journal of School Psychology, 38*(1), 51–61. doi:10.1016/S0022-4405(99)00036-9

Kail, R. (2002). Developmental change in proactive interference. *Child Development, 73*(6), 1703–1714. doi:10.1111/1467-8624.00500

Kail, R. V., & Ferrer, E. (2007). Processing speed in childhood and adolescence: Longitudinal models for examining developmental change. *Child Development, 78*(6), 1760–1770. doi:10.1111/j.1467-8624.2007.01088.x

Kaley, F., Reid, V., & Flynn, E. (2011). The psychology of infant colic: A review of current research. *Infant Mental Health Journal, 32*(5), 526–541. doi:10.1002/imhj.20308

Kandel, E. R. (2001). The molecular biology of memory storage: A dialogue between genes and synapses. *Science, 294*(5544), 1030–1038. doi:10.1126/science.1067020

Kandel, E. R. (2006). *In search of memory: The emergence of a new science of mind.* New York, NY: Norton.

Kann, L., Brener, N. D., & Wechsler, H. (2007). Overview and summary: School health policies and programs study 2006. *Journal of School Health,* 77(8), 385–397.

Kant, I. (1959). *Foundations of the metaphysics of morals* (L. W. Beck, Trans.). Indianapolis, IN: Bobbs-Merrill. (Original work published 1785)

Kaplowitz, P. B., Slora, E. J., Wasserman, R. C., Pedlow, S. E., & Herman-Giddens, M. E. (2001). Earlier onset of puberty in girls: Relation to increased body mass index and race. *Pediatrics, 108*(2), 347–353.

Kapoor, A., Dunn, E., Kostaki, A., Andrews, M. H., & Matthews, S. G. (2006). Fetal programming of hypothalamo-pituitary-adrenal function: Prenatal stress and glucocorticoids. *Journal of Physiology, 572*(Pt 1), 34–44. doi:10.1113/jphysiol.2006.105254

Karasik, L. B., Adolph, K. E., Tamis-Lemonda, C. S., & Bornstein, M. H. (2010). WEIRD walking: Cross-cultural research on motor development. *Behavioral and Brain Sciences, 33*(2–3), 95–96. doi:10.1017/S0140525X10000117

Karkach, A. S. (2006). Trajectories and models of individual growth. *Demographic Research, 15*(12), 347–400. doi:10.4054/DemRes.2006.15.12

Karmiloff-Smith, A. (2009). Nativism versus neuroconstructivism: Rethinking the study of developmental disorders. *Developmental Psychology, 45*(1), 56–63. doi:10.1037/a0014506

Kärnä, A., Voeten, M., Poskiparta, E., & Salmivalli, C. (2010). Vulnerable children in varying classroom contexts: Bystanders' behaviors moderate the effects of risk factors on victimization. *Merrill-Palmer Quarterly, 56*(3), 261–282. doi:10.1353/mpq.0.0052

Karpov, Y. V. (2005). *The Neo-Vygotskian approach to child development.* New York, NY: Cambridge University Press.

Kärtner, J., Keller, H., & Chaudhary, N. (2010). Cognitive and social influences on early prosocial behavior in two sociocultural contexts. *Developmental Psychology, 46*(4), 905–914. doi:10.1037/a0019718

Kattwinkel, J. (2013). Addressing high infant mortality in the developing world: A glimmer of hope. *Pediatrics, 131*(2), e579-e581. doi:10.1542/peds.2012-3171.

Kaufman, J., Plotsky, P. M., Nemeroff, C. B., & Charney, D. (2000). Effects of early adverse experiences on brain structure and function: Clinical implications. *Biological Psychiatry, 48,* 778–790.

Kavsek, M. (2004). Predicting later IQ from infant visual habituation and dishabituation: A meta-analysis. *Journal of Applied Developmental Psychology, 25*(3), 369–393.

Kawakami, K., Takai–Kawakami, K., Okazaki, Y., Kurihara, H., Shimizu, Y., & Yanaihara, T. (1997). The effect of odors on human newborn infants under stress. *Infant Behavior and Development, 20*(4), 531–535. doi:10.1016/S0163-6383(97)90041-2

Kawasaki, C., Nugent, J., Miyashita, H., Miyahara, H., & Brazelton, T. B. (1994). The cultural organization of infants' sleep. *Children's Environments, 11,* 135–141.

Kay, J. (2005). Crystallized intelligence versus fluid intelligence. *Psychiatry: Interpersonal & Biological Processes, 68*(1), 9–13. doi:10.1521/psyc.68.1.9.64189

Kaye, J. A., Melero-Montes, M., & Jick H. (2001). Mumps, measles, and rubella vaccine and the incidence of autism recorded by general practitioners: A time trend analysis. *British Medical Journal, 322*(7284), 460–463. doi:10.1136/bmj.322.7284.460

Kazui, M., Endo, T., Tanaka, A., Sakagami, H., & Suganuma, M. (2000). Intergenerational transmission of attachment Japanese mother-child dyads. *Japanese Journal of Educational Psychology, 48,* 323–332.

Keating, D. P. (2004). Cognitive and brain development. In R. M. Lerner & L. Steinberg (Eds.), *Handbook of adolescent psychology* (2nd ed., pp. 45–84). Hoboken, NJ: Wiley.

Keller, H. (2003). Socialization for competence: Cultural models of infancy. *Human Development, 46,* 288–311.

Keller, H. (2007). *Cultures of infancy.* Mahwah, NJ: Erlbaum.

Keller, H., Yovsi, R. D., Borke, J., Kärtner, J., Jensen, H., & Papaligoura, Z. (2004). Developmental consequences of early parenting experiences: Self-recognition and self-regulation in three cultural communities. *Child Development, 75,* 1745–1760.

Kellmann, P. J., & Arterberry, M. E. (2006). Infant visual perception. In W. Damon & R. M. Lerner (Series Eds.) & D. Kuhn & R. S. Siegler (Vol. Eds.), *Handbook of child psychology: Vol. 2. Cognition, perception, and language* (6th ed., pp. 109–160). Hoboken, NJ: Wiley.

Kellow, J. T., & Jones, B. D. (2008). The effects of stereotypes on the achievement gap: Reexamining the academic performance of African American high school students. *Journal of Black Psychology, 34*(1), 94–120. doi:10.1177/0095798407310537

Kelly, J. B. (2000). Children's adjustment in conflicted marriage and divorce: A decade review of research. *Journal of the American Academy of Child & Adolescent Psychiatry, 39*(8), 963–973. doi:10.1097/00004583-200008000-00007

Kelly, Y., Sacker, A., Schoon, I., & Nazroo, J. (2006). Ethnic differences in achievement of developmental milestones by 9 months of age: The millennium cohort study. *Developmental Medicine & Child Neurology, 48,* 825–830. doi:10.1111/j.1469-8749.2006.tb01230.x

Kennell, J. (2009). Parent-infant bonding and doula support. In J. K. Nugent, B. Petrauskas, & T. B. Brazelton (Eds.), *The newborn as a person: Enabling health infant development worldwide* (pp. 243–253). Hoboken, NJ: Wiley.

Kenward, B., & Dahl, M. (2011). Preschoolers distribute scarce resources according to the moral valence of recipients' previous actions. *Developmental Psychology, 47*(4), 1054–1064. doi:10.1037/a0023869

Keogh, B. K. (2002). *Temperament in the classroom: Understanding individual differences.* Baltimore, MD: Brookes.

Keough, L., Sullivan-Bolyai, S., Crawford, S., Schilling, L., & Dixon, J. (2011). Self-management of type 1 diabetes across adolescence. *Diabetes Educator, 37*(4), 486–500.

Kercher, A., & Rapee, R. M. (2009). A test of a cognitive diathesis-stress generation pathway in early adolescent depression. *Journal of Abnormal Child Psychology, 37,* 845–855. doi:10.1007/s10802-009-9315-3

Kerig, P. K. (2010). Relational dynamics as sources of risk and resilience in adolescent dating violence: Introduction and overview. *Journal of Aggression, Maltreatment, & Trauma, 19*(6), 585–586. doi:10.1080/10926771.2010.502074

Kesselring, T., & Muller, U. (2011). The concept of egocentrism in the context of Piaget's theory. *New Ideas in Psychology, 29*(3) 327–345. doi:10.1016/j.newideapsych.2010.03.008

Kestenbaum, R., & Nelson, C. A. (1990). The recognition and categorization of upright and inverted expressions by 7-month-old infants. *Infant Behavior and Development, 13,* 497–511.

Kester, J. D. (2001). Bandura: Beliefs, Bobo, and behavior. *APS Observer Online,* 14(6), 1–3. Retrieved from http:www.psychologicalscience.org/oberver/0701/keynote.html

Kiang, L., & Fuligni, A. J. (2009). Ethnic identity in context: Variations in ethnic exploration and belonging within parent, same-ethnic peer, and different-ethnic peer relationships. *Journal of Youth and Adolescence, 38*(5), 732–743. doi:10.1007/s10964-008-9278-7

Kiddoo, D., Klassen, T. P., Lang, M. E., Friesen, C., Russell, K., Spooner, C., & Vandermeer, B. (2006). *The effectiveness of different methods of toilet training for bowel and bladder control* (Evidence Report/Technology Assessment No. 147, AHRQ Publication No. 07-E003). Rockville, MD: Agency for Healthcare Research and Quality.

Killen, M., & Hart, D. (Eds.). (1995). *Morality in everyday life: Developmental perspectives.* New York, NY: Cambridge University Press.

Kim, J., & Cicchetti, D. (2010). Longitudinal pathways linking child maltreatment, emotion regulation, peer relations, and psychopathology. *Journal of Child Psychology and Psychiatry, 51*(6), 706–716. doi:10.1111/j.1469-7610.2009.02202.x

Kim, J.-Y., McHale, S. M., Crouter, A. C., & Osgood, D. W. (2007). Longitudinal linkages between sibling relationships and adjustment from middle childhood through adolescence. *Developmental Psychology, 43*(4), 960–973. doi:10.1037/0012-1649.43.4.960

Kim, K. J., Conger, R. D., Lorenz, F. O., & Elder, G. H. (2001). Parent-adolescent reciprocity in negative affect and its relation to early adult social development. *Developmental*

*Psychology, 37*(6), 775–790. doi:10.1037/0012-1649.37.6.775

Kim, P., Leckman, J. F., Mayes, L. C., Feldman, R., Wang, X., & Swain, J. E. (2010). The plasticity of human maternal brain: Longitudinal changes in brain anatomy during the early postpartum period. *Behavioral Neuroscience, 124*, 695–700.

Kim, Y. S., & Leventhal, B. (2008). Bullying and suicide: A review. *International Journal of Adolescent Medicine, 20*(2), 133–154. doi:10.1515/IJAMH.2008.20.2.133

Kimani, N. G. (2007). *Environmental pollution and impacts on public health: Implications of the Dandora Municipal Dumping Site in Nairobi, Kenya.* Nairobi, Kenya: United Nations Environment Programme.

Kim-Cohen, J., Caspi, A., Taylor, A., Williams, B., Newcombe, R., & Craig, I. W. (2006). MAOA, maltreatment, and gene-environment interaction predicting children's mental health: New evidence and a meta-analysis. *Molecular Psychiatry, 11*, 903–913.

King, A. (1998). Transactive peer tutoring: Distributing cognition and metacognition. *Educational Psychology Review, 10*(1), 57–74. doi:10.1023/A:1022858115001

King, K., & Fogle, L. (2006). Bilingual parenting as good parenting: Parents' perspectives on family language policy for additive bilingualism. *International Journal of Bilingual Education and Bilingualism, 9*(6), 695–712. doi: 10.2167/beb362.0

Kirby, M., Maggi, S., & D'Angiulli, A. (2011). School start times and the sleep-wake cycle of adolescents: A review and critical evaluation of available evidence. *Educational Researcher, 40*(2), 56–61. doi:10.3102/0013189X11402323

Kirkorian, H. L., Pempek, T. A., Murphy, L. A., Schmidt, M. E., & Anderson, D. R. (2009). The impact of background television on parent-child interaction. *Child Development, 80*(5), 1350–1359.

Kisilevsky, B. S., Hains, S. M. J., Jacquet, A. Y., Granier–Deferre, C., & Lecanuet, J. P. (2004). Maturation of fetal responses to music. *Developmental Science*, 7(5), 550–559. doi:10.1111/j.1467–7687.2004.00379.x

Kisilevsky, B. S., Pang, L. H., Hains, S. M. J. (2000). Maturation of human fetal responses to airborne sound in low- and high-risk fetuses. *Early Human Development, 58*(3), 179–195. doi:10.1016/S0378–3782(00)00075–X

Kitzinger, S. (1978). Pain in childbirth. *Journal of Medical Ethics, 4*(3), 119–121.

Klaus, M. H., & Kennell, J. H. (1981) *Parent-infant bonding.* St Louis, MO: Mosby.

Klaus, M. H., Jerauld, R., Kreger, N. C., McAlpine, W., Steffa, M., & Kennell, J. H. (1972). Maternal attachment: Importance of the first post-partum days. *New England Journal of Medicine, 286*(9), 460–463.

Klaus, M. H., Kennell, J. H., & Klaus, P. H. (1995). *Bonding: Building the foundations of secure attachment and independence.* Reading, MA: Addison–Wesley.

Kleberg, A., Westrup, B., & Stjernqvist, K. (2000). Developmental outcome, child behaviour and mother-child interaction at 3 years of age following Newborn Individualized Developmental Care and Intervention Program (NIDCAP) intervention. *Early Human Development, 60*, 123–135. doi:10.1016/S0378–3782(00)00114–6

Klein, J. D., & Committee on Adolescence of the American Academy of Pediatrics. (2005). Adolescent pregnancy: Current trends and issues. *Pediatrics, 116*, 281–286. doi:10.1542/peds.2005–0999

Klein, J. O., & Pelton, S. (2010). Acute otitis media in children: Epidemiology, pathogenesis, clinical manifestations, and complications. In S. L. Kaplan & E. M. Friedman (Eds.), *UpToDate*. Waltham, MA: UpToDate.

Klein, L. G., & Knitzer, J. (2006). *Effective preschool curricula and teaching strategies* (Pathways to Early School Success, Issue Brief No. 2). New York, NY: Columbia University, National Center for Children in Poverty.

Klein, M. C., Kaczorowski, J., Hearps, S. J., Tomkinson, J., Baradaran, N., Hall, W. A., McNiven, P., Brant, R., Grant, J., Dore, S., Brasset-Latulippe, A., Fraser, W. D. (2011). Birth technology and maternal roles in birth: Knowledge and attitudes of Canadian women approaching childbirth for the first time. *Journal of Obstetrics and Gynaecology Canada (JOGC), 33*(6), 598–608.

Kleiner, K. A. (1993). Developmental neurocognition: Speech and face processing in the first year of life. In B. de Boysson–Bardies, S. de Schonen, P. W. Jusczyk, P. McNeilage, & J. Morton, (Eds.), *NATO ASI series D: Behavioural and social sciences* (Vol. 69, pp. 103–108). New York, NY: Kluwer/Plenum.

Kliegman, R. M., Behrman, R. E., Jenson, H. B., & Stanton, B. F. (Eds.). (2007). *Nelson textbook of pediatrics* (18th ed.). Philadelphia, PA: Saunders Elsevier.

Klimes-Dougan, B., & Kistner, J. (1990). Physically abused preschoolers' responses to peers' distress. *Developmental Psychology, 26*(4), 599–602. doi:10.1037/0012-1649.26.4.599

Klin, A., & Jones, W. (2008). Altered face scanning and impaired recognition of biological motion in a 15-month-old infant with autism. *Developmental Science, 11*(1), 40–46.

Klin, A., Chawarska, K., Paul, R., Rubin, E., Morgan, T., Wiesner, L., & Volkmar, F. (2004). Autism in a 15-month-old child. *American Journal of Psychiatry, 161*, 1981–1988.

Klingberg, T. (2006). Development of superior frontal-intraparietal network for visuo-spatial working memory. *Neuropsychologia, 44* (11), 2171–2177. doi:10.1016/j.neuropsychologia.2005.11.019

Klinnert, M. D., Emde, R. N., Butterfleld, P., & Campos, J. J. (1986). Social referencing: The infant's use of emotional signals from a friendly adult with mother present. *Developmental Psychology, 22*, 427–432.

Klomek, A. B., Sourander, A., & Gould, M. (2010). The association of suicide and bullying in childhood to young adulthood: A review of cross-sectional and longitudinal research findings. *Canadian Journal of Psychiatry, 55*(5), 282–288.

Knafl, K., Breitmayer, B., Gallo, A., & Zoeller, L. (1996). Family response to childhood chronic illness: Description of management styles. *Journal of Pediatric Nursing, 11*(5), 315–326.

Knafo, A., & Plomin, R. (2006). Prosocial behavior from early to middle childhood: Genetic and environmental influences. *Developmental Psychology, 42*, 771–786. doi:10.1037/0012–1649.42.5.771

Knight, C. (1995). *Blood relations: Menstruation and the origins of culture.* New Haven, CT, and London, UK: Yale University Press.

Knopf, D., Park, M. J., & Paul Mulye, T. (2008). *The mental health of adolescents: A national profile, 2008.* San Francisco, CA: National Adolescent Health Information Center, University of California.

Kobayashi, H., & Kohshima, S. (1997). Unique morphology of the human eye. *Nature, 387*(6635), 767–768.

Kobayashi, H., & Kohshima, S. (2001). Unique morphology of the human eye and its adaptive meaning: Comparative studies on external morphology of the primate eye. *Journal of Human Evolution, 40*, 419–435.

Kobiella A., Grossman T., Reid, V., & Striano, T. (2008). The discrimination of angry and fearful facial expressions in 7-month-old infants: An event-related potential study. *Emotion and Cognition, 22*, 134–146.

Kochanska, G. (2001). Emotional development in children with different attachment histories: The first three years. *Child Development, 72*, 474–490.

Kochanska, G., Aksan, N., Prisco, T. R., & Adams, E. E. (2008). Mother-child and father-child mutually responsive orientation in the first 2 years and children's outcomes at preschool age: Mechanisms of influence. *Child Development, 79*(1), 30–44. doi:10.1111/j.1467-8624.2007.01109.x

Koenigs, M., Young, L., Adolphs, R., Tranel, D., Cushman, F., Hauser, M., & Damasio, A. (2007). Damage to the prefrontal cortex increases utilitarian moral judgements. *Nature, 446*, 908–911. doi:10.1038/nature05631

Kogan, M. D., Overpeck, M. D., Hoffman, H. J., & Casselbrant, M. L. (2000). Factors associated with tympanostomy tube insertion among preschool-aged children in the United States. *American Journal of Public Health, 90*(2), 245–250.

Kogan, N., & Carter, A. S. (1996). Mother-infant reengagement following the still-face: The role of maternal emotional availability in infant affect regulation. *Infant Behavior and Development, 19*, 359–370.

Kohlberg, L. (1958). *The development of modes of thinking and choices in years 10 to 16* (Unpublished doctoral dissertation). Chicago, IL: University of Chicago.

Kohlberg, L. (1963). *Moral development and identification.* In H. W. Stevenson, J. Kagan, C. Spiker, N. B. Henry, & H. G. Richey (Eds.), *Child psychology: The sixty-second yearbook of the National Society for the Study of Education, Part 1* (pp. 277–332). Chicago, IL: University of Chicago Press.

Kohlberg, L. (1969). Stage and sequence: The cognitive-developmental approach to socialization. In D. A. Golsin (Ed.), *Handbook of socialization theory and research* (pp. 347–480). Chicago, IL: Rand McNally.

Kohlberg, L. (1976). Moral stages and moralization: The cognitive-developmental approach.

In T. Lickona (Ed.), *Moral development and behavior: Theory, research and social issues* (pp. 31–53). New York, NY: Holt, Rinehart and Winston.

Kohlberg, L. (1978). Revisions in the theory and practice of moral development. In W. Damon (Ed.), *New directions for child development: Moral development*. New York, NY: Wiley.

Kohler, P. K., Manhart, L. E., & Lafferty, W. E. (2008). Abstinence-only and comprehensive sex education and the initiation of sexual activity and teen pregnancy. *Adolescent Health, 42*(4), 344–351.

Kolas, T., Saugstad, O. D., Daltveit, A. K., Nilsen, S. T., & Oian, P. (2006). Planned cesarean versus planned vaginal delivery at term: Comparison of newborn infant outcomes. *American Journal of Obstetrics and Gynecology, 195*(6), 1538–1543. doi:10.1016/j.ajog.2006.05.005

Kolb, R., & Fantie, B. (2008). Development of the child's brain and behavior. In C. R. Reynolds & E. Fletcher–Janzen (Eds.), *Handbook of clinical child neuropsychology* (pp. 19–46). New York, NY: Springer. doi:10.1007/978-0-387-78867-8_2

Kolobe, T. H. (2004). Childrearing practices and developmental expectations for Mexican–American mothers and the developmental status of their infants. *Physical Therapy, 84*, 439–453.

Konner, M. (2005). Hunter-gatherer infancy and childhood: The !Kung and others. In B. S. Hewlett & M. E. Lamb (Eds.), *Hunter-gatherer childhoods: Evolutionary, developmental and cultural perspectives* (pp. 19–64). Piscataway, NJ: Transaction Publishers.

Kontos, S., Howes, C., Shinn, M., & Galinsky, E. (1997). Children's experiences in family child care and relative care as a function of family income and ethnicity. *Merrill-Palmer Quarterly, 43*(3), 386–403.

Koob, A. (2009). *The root of thought: Unlocking glia—the brain cell that will help us sharpen our wits, heal injury, and treat brain disease.* Upper Saddle River, NJ: Pearson Education.

Koplin, J. J., Osborne, N. J., Wake, M., Martin, P. E., Gurrin, L. C., Robinson, M. N., . . . Allen, K. J. (2010). Can early introduction of egg prevent egg allergy in infants? A population-based study. *The Journal of Allergy and Clinical Immunology, 126*(4), 807–813. doi:10.1016/j.jaci.2010.07.028

Kopp, C. (1989). Regulation of distress and negative emotions: A developmental view. *Developmental Psychology, 25*(3), 343–354.

Kopp, C. B. (1992). Emotional distress and control in young children. *New Directions for Child Development, 55*, 41–56.

Kopp, C. B., & McCall, R. B. (1982). Predicting later mental performance for normal, at-risk, and handicapped infants. *Life Span Development and Behavior, 4*, 33–61.

Korn–Bursztyn, C. (2011). Nurturing development: Treating young children with autism spectrum disorder. In A. M. Bursztyn (Ed.), *Childhood psychological disorders: Current controversies* (pp. 87–101). Santa Barbara, CA: Prager/ABC–Clio.

Kovács, Á. M. (2009). Early bilingualism enhances mechanisms of false-belief reasoning. *Developmental Science, 12*(1), 48–54. doi:10.1111/j.1467-7687.2008.00742.x

Kovan, N., Chung, A., & Sroufe, A. (2009). The intergenerational continuity of observed early parenting: A prospective, longitudinal study. *Developmental Psychology, 45*, 1205–1213. doi:10.1037/a0016542

Koyama, M. S., Kelly, C., Shehzad, Z., Penesetti, D., Castellanos, F. X., & Milham, M. P. (2010). Reading networks at rest. *Cerebral Cortex, 20*(11), 2549–2559. doi:10.1093/cercor/bhq005

Kraemer, H. C., Stice, E., Kazdin, A., Offord, D., & Kupfer, D. (2001). How do risk factors work together? Mediators, moderators, and independent, overlapping, and proxy risk factors. *American Journal of Psychiatry, 158*(6), 848–856. doi:10.1176/appi.ajp.158.6.848

Kraemer, S. (2000). The fragile male. *British Medical Journal, 321*, 1609–1612. doi:10.1136/bmj.321.7276.1609

Kramer, M. S., Olivier, M., McLean, F. H., Dougherty, G. E., Willis, D. M., & Usher, R. H. (1990). Determinants of fetal growth and body proportionality. *Pediatrics, 86*(1), 18–26.

Kreider, R. M., & Ellis, R. (2011). *Number, timing and duration of marriages and divorces: 2009.* Washington, DC: U.S. Census Bureau. Retrieved from http://www.census.gov/prod/2011pubs/p70-125.pdf

Kreppner, J., Kumsta, R., Rutter, M., Beckett, C., Castle, J., Stevens, S., & Songua-Barke, E. J. (2010). Developmental course of deprivation-specific psychological patterns: Early manifestations, persistence to age 15, and clinical features. *Monographs of the Society for Research in Child Development, 75*(1). doi:10.1111/j.1540-5834.2010.00551.x

Kretch, K. S., & Adolph, K. E. (2013). Cliff or step? Posture-specific learning at the edge of a drop-off. *Child Development, 84*, 226–240.

Kreutzer, M. A., Leonard, C., & Flavell, J. H. (1975). An interview study of children's knowledge about memory. *Monographs of the Society for Research in Child Development, 40*(1), 1–60.

Kroger, J. (2004). *Identity in adolescence: The balance between self and other.* New York, NY: Routledge.

Kruger, A. C. (1993). Peer collaboration: Conflict, cooperation, or both? *Social Development, 2*(3), 165–182. doi:10.1111/j.1467-9507.1993.tb00012.x

Kuhl, P. K. (2004). Early language acquisition: Cracking the speech code. *Nature Reviews Neuroscience, 5*(11), 831–841.

Kuhl, P. K. (2007). Is speech learning "gated" by the social brain? *Developmental Science, 10*(1), 110–120. doi:10.1111/j.1467-7687.2007.00572.x

Kuhl, P. K. (2011). Who's Talking? *Science* 333, 529. doi:10.1126/science.1210277

Kuhl, P. K., & Damasio, A. (2012). Language. In E. R. Kandel, J. H. Schwartz, T. M. Jessell, S. Siegelbaum, & J. Hudspeth (Eds.), *Principles of neural science* (5th ed., pp. 1353–1372). New York, NY: McGraw–Hill.

Kuhl, P. K., Andruski, J. E., Chistovich, I. A., Chistovich, L. A., Kozhevnikova, E. V., Ryskina, V. L., Stolyarova, E. I., Sundberg, U., & Lacerda, L. (1997). Cross-language analysis of phonetic units in language addressed to infants. *Science, 277*(5326), 684–686. doi:10.1126/science.277.5326.684

Kuhn, D. (1992). Cognitive development. In M. H. Bornstein & M. E. Lamb (Eds.), *Developmental psychology: An advanced textbook* (pp. 211–272). Hillsdale, NJ: Erlbaum.

Kuhn, D. (2001). How do people know? *Psychological Science, 12*(1), 1–8. doi:10.1111/1467-9280.00302

Kuhn, D. (2008). Formal operations from a twenty-first century perspective. *Human Development, 51*(1), 48–55. doi:10.1159/000113155

Kuhn, D., Katz, J. B., & Dean, D. (2004). Developing reason. *Thinking & Reasoning, 10*(2), 197–219. doi:10.1080/13546780442000015

Kumsta, R., Kreppner, J., Rutter, M., Beckett, C., Castle, J., Stevens, S., & Sonuga-Barke, E. J. (2010). Deprivation-specific psychological patterns. *Monographs of the Society for Research in Child Development, 75*(1), 48–78. doi:10.1111/j.1540-5834.2010.00550.x

Kuntsche, E., Kuntsche, S., Knibbe, R., Simons-Morton, B., Farhat, T., Hublet, A., . . . Demetrovics, Z. (2011). Cultural and gender convergence in adolescent drunkenness: Evidence from 23 European and North American countries. *Archives of Pediatric and Adolescent Medicine, 165*(2), 152–158. doi:10.1001/archpediatrics.2010.191

Kunz, C., Rodriguez-Palmero, M., Koletzko, B., & Jensen, R. (1999). Nutritional and biochemical properties of human milk, Part 1: General aspects, proteins, and carbohydrates. *Clinics in Perinatology, 26*, 307–333.

Kuohung, W., & Hornstein, M. D. (2012). Evaluation of the infertile couple. In P. J. Snyder & W. F. Crowley (Eds.), *UpToDate*. Waltham, MA: UpToDate.

Kuppens, S., Grietens, H., Onghena, P., & Michiels, D. (2009). Associations between parental control and children's overt and relational aggression. *British Journal of Developmental Psychology, 27*(3), 607–623. doi:10.1348/026151008X345591

Kurinij, N., & Shiono, P. H. (1991). Early formula supplementation of breast-feeding. *Pediatrics, 88*, 745–750.

Kushnerenko, E., Ceponiene, R., Balan, P., Fellman, V., Huotilainen, R., & Näätänen, R. (2002). Maturation of the auditory event-related potentials during the first year of life. *NeuroReport: For Rapid Communication of Neuroscience Research, 13*(1), 47–51.

La Paro, K. M., & Pianta, R. C. (2001). Predicting children's competence in the early school years: A meta-analytic review. *Review of Educational Research, 70*(4), 443–484.

Lack, G. (2007). The concept of oral tolerance induction to foods. *The Journal of Allergy and Clinical Immunology, 59*, 63–72. doi:10.1159/000098513

Lack, G. (2008). Epidemiologic risks for food allergy. *The Journal of Allergy and Clinical Immunology, 121*(6), 1331–1336. doi:10.1016/j.jaci.2008.04.032http://www.jacionline.org/article/S0091-6749(08)00778-1/-article-footnote-1

Ladd, G. W., & Burgess, K. B. (1999). Charting the relationship trajectories of aggressive, withdrawn, and aggressive/withdrawn children during early grade school. *Child Development, 70*(4), 910–929. doi:10.1111/1467–8624.00066

Ladd, G. W., Herald-Brown, S. L., & Reiser, M. (2008). Does chronic classroom peer rejection predict the development of children's classroom participation during the grade school years? *Child Development, 79*(4), 1001–1005. doi:10.1111/j.1467–8624.2008.01172.x

LaGreca A. M., & Bearman, K. J. (2003). Adherence to pediatric treatment regimens. In J. L. Wallander, R. J. Thompson, A. Alriksson-Schmidt, & M. C. Roberts (Eds.), *Handbook of pediatric psychology* (3rd ed., pp. 119–140). New York, NY: Guilford Press.

Lamb, A. (2010). Everyone does it: Teaching ethical use of social technology. *Knowledge Quest, 39*(1), 62–67.

Lamb, M. E. (1983). Early mother-neonate contact and the mother-child relationship. *Journal of Child Psychology and Psychiatry and Allied Disciplines, 24*(3), 487–494. doi:10.1111/1469–7610.ep11358376

Lamb, M. E. (1987). *The father's role: Cross-cultural perspectives*. Hillsdale, NJ: Erlbaum.

Lamb, M. E. (1997). The development of father-infant relationships. In M. E. Lamb (Ed.), *The role of the father in child development* (3rd ed., pp. 104–120). New York, NY: Wiley.

Lamb, M. E. (1998). Fatherhood then and now. In A. Booth & A. C. Crouter (Eds.), *Men in families: When do they get involved? What difference does it make?* (pp. 47–52). Mahwah, NJ: Erlbaum.

Lamb, M. E. (2004). *The role of the father in child development*. Hoboken, NJ: Wiley.

Lamb, M. E., & Ahnert, L. (2006). Nonparental child care: Context, concepts, correlates, and consequences. In W. Damon & R. M. Lerner (Series Eds.) & K. A. Renninger & I. E. Sigel (Vol. Eds.), *Handbook of child psychology: Vol 4. Child psychology in practice* (6th ed., pp. 950–1016). Hoboken, NJ: Wiley.

Lamb, M. E., & Malloy, L. C. (2013). Child development and the law. In R. M. Lerner, A. Easterbrooks, & J. Mistry (Eds.), *Handbook of psychology: Vol. 6. Developmental psychology* (2nd ed., pp. 571–594). Hoboken, NJ: Wiley.

Lamb, M. E., Pleck, J. H., Charnov, E. L., & Levine, J. A. (1987). A biosocial perspective on paternal behavior and involvement. In J. Lancaster, J. Altmann, A. Rossi, & L. Sherrod (Eds.), *Parenting across lifespan: Biosocial dimensions* (pp. 111–142). Hawthorne, NY: Aldine de Gruyter.

Lamborn, S. D., Mounts, N. S., Steinberg, L., & Dornbusch, S. M. (1991). Patterns of competence and adjustment among adolescents from authoritative, authoritarian, indulgent, and neglectful families. *Child Development, 62*(5), 1049–1065. doi:10.2307/1131151

Lampl, M., Veldhuis, J. D., & Johnson, M. L. (1992). Saltation and stasis: A model of human growth. *Science, 258*(5083), 801–803. doi:10.1126/science.1439787

Lampman, C., & Phelps, A. (1997). College students' knowledge and attitudes and about cesarean birth. *Birth: Issues in Perinatal Care, 24*(3), 159–164. doi:10.1111/j.1523–536X.1997.tb00580.x

Landry, O., Russo, N., Dawkins, T., Zelazo, P. D., & Burack, J. A. (2012). The impact of verbal and nonverbal development on executive function in Down syndrome and Williams syndrome. *Journal on Developmental Disabilities, 18*(2) 26–35.

Landry, S. H., Miller-Loncar, C. L., Smith, K. E., & Swank, P. R. (2002). The role of early parenting in children's development of executive processes. *Developmental Neuropsychology, 21*(1), 15–41. doi:10.1207/S15326942DN2101_2

Landry, S. H., Smith, K. E., Swank, P. R., & Miller-Loncar, C. L. (2000). Early maternal and child influences on children's later independent cognitive and social functioning. *Child Development, 71*(2), 358–375. doi:10.1111/1467–8624.00150

Lansford, J. E., & Deater-Deckard, K. (2012). Childrearing discipline and violence in developing countries. *Child Development, 83*(1), 62–75. doi:10.1111/j.1467-8624.2011.01676.x

Lantz, P. M., Jacobson, P. D., Warner, K. E., Wasserman, J., Pollack, H. A., Berson, J., & Ahlstrom, A. (2000). Investing in youth tobacco control: A review of smoking prevention and control strategies. *Tobacco Control, 9*, 47–63.

Lapierre, M. A., Taylor Piotrowski, J., & Linebarger, D. L. (2012). Background television in the homes of US children. *Pediatrics, 130*, 5, 839–846. doi:10.1542/peds.2011-2581

Laplante, D., Orr, R., Neville, K., Vorkapich, L., & Sasso, D. (1996). Discrimination of stimulus rotations by newborns. *Infant Behavior and Development, 19*(3), 271–279. doi:10.1016/S0163–6383(96)90028–4

Lapsley, D. K. (2008). Moral self-identity as the aim of education. In L. P. Nucci & D. Narvaez (Eds.), *Handbook of moral and character education* (pp. 30–52). New York, NY: Routledge.

Larkby, C., & Day, N. (1997). The effects of prenatal alcohol exposure. *Alcohol Health & Research World, 21*(3), 192–198. Retrieved from http://www.hawaii.edu/hivandaids/The%20Effects%20of%20Prenatal%20Alcohol%20Exposure.pdf

Laski, E. V., & Siegler, R. S. (2007). Is 27 a big number? Correlational and causal connections among numerical categorization, number line estimation, and numerical magnitude comparison. *Child Development, 78*(6), 1723–1743. doi:10.1111/j.1467–8624. 2007.01087.x

Lattimore, K. A., Donn, S. M., Kaciroti, N., Kemper, A. R., Neal, C. R., Jr., & Vazquez, D. M. (2005). State of the art selective serotonin reuptake inhibitor (SSRI): Use during pregnancy and effects on the fetus and newborn: A meta-analysis. *Journal of Perinatology, 25*, 595–604. doi:10.1038/sj.jp.7211352

Laursen, B., & Collins, W. A. (2009). Parent-child relationships during adolescence. In R. M. Lerner & L. Steinberg (Eds.), *Handbook of adolescent psychology: Vol. 2. Contextual influences on adolescent development* (3rd ed., pp. 3–42). Hoboken, NJ: Wiley.

Laursen, B., Coy, K. C., & Collins, W. A. (1998). Reconsidering changes in parent-child conflict across adolescence: A meta-analysis. *Child Development, 69*(3), 817–832. doi:10.2307/1132206

Lavelli, M., & Fogel, A. (2005). Developmental changes in the relationship between the infant's attention and emotion during early face-to-face communication: The two-month transition. *Developmental Psychology, 41*(1), 265–280. doi:10.1037/0012–1649.41.1.265

Lay, K., Waters, E., & Park, K. A. (1989). Maternal responsiveness and child compliance: The role of mood as a mediator. *Child Development, 60*, 1405–1411. doi:10.2307/1130930

Layzer, J., Goodson, B. D., & Moss, M. (1993). *Life in preschool: Volume one of an observational study of early childhood programs for disadvantaged four-year-olds*. Cambridge, MA: Abt Associates.

Lazarus, R. S. (1991). *Emotions and adaptation*. New York, NY: Oxford University Press.

Lazarus, R. S., & Folkman, S. (1984). *Stress, appraisal, and coping*. New York, NY: Springer.

Lazarus, R., & Lazarus, B. (1994). *Passion and reason: Making sense of our emotions*. London, UK: Oxford University Press.

Leadbeater, B. J., & Hoglund, W. L. G. (2009). The effects of peer victimization and physical aggression on changes in internalizing from first to third grade. *Child Development, 80*(3), 843–859. doi:10.1111/j.1467–8624.2009.01301.x

Lear, J. G. (2007). Health at school: A hidden health care system emerges from the shadows. *Health Affairs, 26*(2), 409–419. doi:10.1377/hlthaff.26.2.409

Lebel, C., & Beaulieu, C. (2011). Longitudinal development of human brain wiring continues from childhood into adulthood. *Journal of Neuroscience, 31*(30), 10937–10947. doi:10.1523/JNEUROSCI.5302–10.2011

Lebra, T. S. (1984). *Japanese women: Constraint and fulfillment*. Honolulu, HI: University of Hawaii Press.

Lecanuet, J. (1996). Prenatal auditory experience. In I. Deliege & J. Sloboda (Eds.), *Musical beginnings: Origins and development of musical competence* (pp. 3–25). Oxford, UK: Oxford University Press.

Leckman, J. F., & Mayes, L. C. (1999). Preoccupations and behaviors associated with romantic and parental love: Perspectives on the origin of obsessive-compulsive disorder. *Child and Adolescent Psychiatry Clinics of North America, 8*(3), 635–665.

Lederberg, A. R., Schick, B., Spencer, P. E. (2013). Language and literacy development of deaf and hard-of-hearing children: Successes and challenges. *Developmental Psychology, 49*, 1, 15–30. doi:10.1037/a0029558

LeDoux, J. E. (1996). *The emotional brain*. New York, NY: Touchstone.

LeDoux, J. E. (2009). Emotional coloration of consciousness: How feelings come about. In L. W. Weiskrantz & M. Davies (Eds.), *Frontiers of consciousness* (pp. 69–130). New York, NY: Oxford University Press.

Lee, K., Xu, F., Fu, G., Cameron, C. A., & Chen, S. (2001). Taiwan and mainland Chinese and Canadian children's categorization and evaluation of lies and truth-telling: A modesty effect. *British Journal of Developmental Psychology, 19*, 525–542.

Lee, P. (1996). Cognitive development in bilingual children: A case for bilingual instruction in early childhood education. *Bilingual Research Journal, 20*(3–4), 499–522.

Lee, V. E., & Burkam, D. T. (2003). Dropping out of high school: The role of school organization and structure. *American Educational Research Journal, 40*(2), 353–393. doi:10.3102/00028312040002353

Leeman, L. W., Gibbs, J. C., & Fuller, D. (1993). Evaluation of a multi-component group treatment program for juvenile delinquents. *Aggressive Behavior, 19*(4), 281–292.

Lehmann, M., & Hasselhorn, M. (2012). Rehearsal dynamics in elementary school children. *Journal of Experimental Child Psychology, 111*(3), 552–560. doi:10.1016/j.jecp.2011.10.013

Lehr, C. A., Hansen, A., Sinclair, M. F., & Christenson, S. L. (2003). Moving beyond dropout towards school completion: An integrative review of data-based interventions. *School Psychology Review, 32*(3), 342–364.

Lemery, K. S., Goldsmith, H. H., Klinnert, M. D., & Mrazek, D. A. (1999). Developmental models of infant and childhood temperament. *Developmental Psychology, 35*, 189–204.

Lenroot, R. K., & Giedd, J. N. (2006). Brain development in children and adolescents: Insights from anatomical magnetic resonance imaging. *Neuroscience and Biobehavioral Reviews, 30*, 718–729. doi:10.1016/j.neubiorev.2006.06.001

Lenroot, R. K., & Giedd, J. N. (2011). Annual research review: Developmental considerations of gene by environment interactions. *Journal of Child Psychology and Psychiatry, 52*(4), 429–441. doi:10.1111/j.1469-7610.2011.02381.x

Lenroot, R. K., Gogtay, N., Greenstein, D. K., Wells, E. M., Wallace, G. L., Clasen, L. S., . . . Giedd, J. N. (2007). Sexual dimorphism of brain developmental trajectories during childhood and adolescence. *Neuroimage, 36*(4), 1065–1073.

Leong, A. (2006). The challenge of asthma in minority populations. In M. E. Gershwin & T. A. Albertson (Eds.), *Bronchial asthma: A guide for practical understanding and treatment* (pp. 357–384). Totowa, NJ: Humana Press.

Lerna, A., Esposito, D., Conson, M., Russo, L., & Massagli, A. (2012). Social-communicative effects of the Picture-Exchange Communication System (PECS) in autism spectrum disorders. *International Journal of Language & Communication Disorders, 47*(5), 609–617. doi:10.1111/j.1460–6984.2012.00172.x

Lerner, J. V., Phelps, E., Forman, Y., & Bowers, E. P. (2009). Positive youth development. In R. M. Lerner & L. Steinberg (Eds.), *Handbook of adolescent psychology: Vol. 1. Individual bases of adolescent development* (3rd ed., pp. 524–558). Hoboken, NJ: Wiley.

Lerner, R. M. (2001). Cliques. In J. V. Lerner, R. M. Lerner, & J. Finkelstein (Eds.), *Adolescence in America: Vol. 1. A–M* (pp. 126–127). Santa Barbara, CA: ABC–CLIO.

Lerner, R. M. (2002). *Concepts and theories of human development* (3rd ed.). Mahwah, NJ: Erlbaum.

Lerner, R. M. (2006). Developmental science, developmental systems, and contemporary theories of human development. In R. M. Lerner & W. Damon (Eds.), *Handbook of child psychology: Vol. 1. Theoretical models of human development* (6th ed., pp. 1–17). Hoboken, NJ: Wiley.

Lerner, R. M. (2007). *The good teen: Rescuing adolescence from the myth of the storm and stress year.* New York, NY: Stonesong Press.

Lerner, R. M. (2010). Applied developmental science: Definitions and dimensions. In V. Maholmes and C. G. Lomonaco (Eds.), *Applied research in child and adolescent development: A practical guide* (pp. 37–58). New York, NY: Psychology Press.

Lerner, R. M., Almerigi, J. B., Theokas, C., & Lerner, J. V. (2005). Positive youth development A view of the issues. *The Journal of Early Adolescence, 25*(1), 10–16. doi:10.1177/0272431604273211

Lerner, R. M., Easterbrooks, M. A., & Mistry, J. (2013). *Developmental science across the life span: An introduction* (pp. 3–17). Hoboken, NJ: Wiley.

Lerner, R. M., Lerner, J. V., von Eye, A., Bowers, E. P., & Lewin-Bizan, S. (2011). Individual and contextual bases of thriving in adolescence: A view of the issues. *Journal of Adolescence, 34*(6), 1107–1114. doi:10.1016/j.adolescence.2011.08.001

Leroy, F., Glasel, H., Dubois, J., Hertz-Pannier, L., Thirion, B., Mangin, J. F., & Dehaene-Lambertz, G. (2011). Early maturation of the linguistic dorsal pathway in human infants. *Journal of Neuroscience, 31*(4), 1500–1506.

Leslie, L., Gordon, J. N., Lambros, K., Premji, K., Peoples, J., & Gist, K. (2005). Addressing the developmental and mental health needs of young children in foster care. *Developmental and Behavioral Pediatrics, 26*(2), 140–151.

Lester, B. M., & Lagasse, L. L. (2010). Children of addicted women. *Journal of Addictive Diseases, 29*(2), 259–276. doi:10.1080/10550881003684921

Lester, B. M., & Sparrow, J. (Eds.). (2010). *Nurturing children and families: Building on the legacy of T. Berry Brazelton.* Hoboken, NJ: Wiley.

Lester, B. M., LaGasse, L. L., & Seifer, R. (1998). Cocaine exposure and children: The meaning of subtle effects. *Science, 282* (5389), 633–634. doi:10.1126/science.282.5389.633

Lester, B. M., Tronick, E. Z, & Brazelton, T. B. (2004). The neonatal intensive care unit network neurobehavioral scale procedures. *Pediatrics, 113*(3), 641–667.

LeVine, R. A. (2010). The six cultures study: Prologue to a history of a landmark project. *Journal of Cross-Cultural Psychology, 41*(4), 513–521.

LeVine, R. A., & Norman, K. (2001). The infant's acquisition of culture: Early attachment reexamined in anthropological perspective. In C. C. Moore & H. F. Matthews (Eds.), *The psychology of cultural experience* (pp. 83–104). New York, NY: Cambridge University Press.

LeVine, R. A., Dixon, S., LeVine, S., Richman, A., Leiderman, P. H., Keefer, C. H., & Brazelton, T. B. (1994). *Child care and culture: Lessons from Africa.* Cambridge, UK: Cambridge University Press.

Levinson, S. C. (1983). *Pragmatics.* Cambridge, UK: Cambridge University Press.

Levy, S. E., Mandell, D. S., & Schultz, R. T. (2009). Autism. *Lancet, 374* (9701), 1627–1638. doi:10.1016/S0140-6736(09)61376-3

Levy, Y., Broides, A., Segal, N., & Danon, Y. L. (2003). Peanut and tree nut allergy in children: Role of peanut snacks in Israel? *Allergy, 58*(11), 1206–1207. doi:10.1046/j.1398-9995.2003.00307.x

Levy-Shiff, R. (1994). Individual and contextual correlates of marital change cross the transition to parenthood. *Developmental Psychology, 30*, 591–601.

Lewis, B. A., Singer, L. T., Short, E. J., Minnes, S., Arendt, R., Weishampel, P., . . . Min, M. O. (2004). Four-year language outcomes of children exposed to cocaine in utero. *Neurotoxicology and Teratology, 26*(5), 617–627. doi:10.1016/j.ntt.2004.06.007

Lewis, C. C. (1995). *Educating hearts and minds: Reflections on Japanese preschool and elementary education.* Cambridge, UK: Cambridge University Press.

Lewis, M. (2000). Self-conscious emotions: Embarrassment, pride, shame, and guilt. In M. Lewis & J. M. Haviland-Jones (Eds.), *Handbook of emotions* (2nd ed., pp. 623–636). New York, NY: Guilford.

Lewis, M., & Brooks-Gunn, J. (1979). *Social cognition and the acquisition of self.* New York, NY: Plenum Press.

Lewis, M., & Carmody, D. P. (2008). Self-representation and brain development. *Developmental Psychology 44*(5), 1329–1334. doi:10.1037/a0012681

Lewis, M., & Ramsey, D. (2002). Cortisol response to embarrassment and shame. *Child Development, 73*, 1034–1045. doi:10.1111/1467-8624.00455

Lewis, M., Takai-Kawakami, K., Kawakami, K., & Sullivan, M. W. (2010). Cultural differences in emotional responses to success and failure. *International Journal of Behavioral Development, 34*(1), 53–61. doi:10.1177/0165025409348559

Lewkowicz, D. J., & Hansen-Tift, A. M. (2012). Infants deploy selective attention to the mouth of a talking face when learning speech. *Proceedings of the National Academy of Sciences, 109*(5), 1431–1436. doi:10.1073/pnas.1114783109

Li, J. (2011). Cultural frames of children's learning beliefs. In L. A Jensen (Ed.), *Bridging cultural and developmental approaches to psychology: New syntheses in theory, research, and policy* (pp. 26–48). New York, NY: Oxford University Press.

Li, J., & Fischer, K. W. (2004). Thoughts and emotions in American and Chinese cultural beliefs about learning. In D. Y. Dai & R. Sternberg (Eds.), *Motivation, emotion, and cognition: Integrative perspectives on intellectual functioning and development* (pp. 385–418). Mahwah, NJ: Erlbaum.

Li, W., Farkas, G., Duncan, G. J., Burchinal, M. R., & Vandell, D. L. (2012). Timing of high-quality child care and cognitive, language, and preacademic development. *Developmental Psychology.* Advance online publication. doi:10.1037/a0030613

Li, Y., Dai, Q., Jackson, J. C., & Zhang, J. (2008). Overweight is associated with decreased cognitive functioning among school-age children and adolescents. *Obesity, 16*(8), 1809–1815. doi:10.1038/oby.2008.296

Lieberman, A. F., & Zeanah, C. H. (1995). Disorders of attachment in infancy. *Child and Adolescent Psychiatric Clinics of North America, 4*, 571–587.

Lieberman, E., Lang, J. M., Frigoletto, Jr., F., Richardson, D. K., Ringer, S. A., & Cohen, A. (1997). Epidural analgesia, intrapartum fever, and neonatal sepsis evaluation. *Pediatrics, 99*(3), 415–419. doi:10.1542/peds.99.3.415

Lieberman, J. A., & Sicherer, S. H. (2010). The diagnosis of food allergy. *American Journal of Rhinology & Allergy, 24*(6), 439–43. doi:10.2500/ajra.2010.24.3515

Lifter, K., Foster-Sanda, S., Arzamarski, C., Briesch, J., & McClure, E. (2011). Overview of play: Its uses and importance in early intervention/early childhood special education. *Infants & Young Children, 24*(3), 225–245. doi:10.1097/IYC.0b013e31821e995c

Lillas, C., & Turnbull, J. (2009). *Infant/child mental health, early intervention, and relationship-based therapies: A neurodevelopmental framework for interdisciplinary practice.* New York, NY: Norton.

Lim, G., & Fortaleza, K. (2000). Overcoming challenges in newborn hearing screening. *Journal of Perinatology, 20*(8, Part 2), S138–S142.

Lin, C., & Liu, W. (1993). Intergenerational relationships among Chinese immigrants from Taiwan. In H. P. McAdoo (Ed.), *Family ethnicity: Strength in diversity* (pp. 271–286). Newbury Park, CA: Sage.

Linares, T., Singer, L. T., Kirchner, L., Short, E. J., Min, M. O., Hussey, P., & Minnes, S. (2006). Mental health outcomes of cocaine-exposed children at 6 years of age. *Journal of Pediatric Psychology, 31*(1) 85–97. doi:10.1093/jpepsy/jsj020

Lind, S. E., & Bowler, D. M. (2010). Impaired performance on see-know tasks amongst children with autism: Evidence of specific difficulties with theory of mind or domain-general task factors? *Journal of Autism and Developmental Disorders, 40*(4), 479–484. doi:10.1007/s10803-009-0889-y

Linebarger, D. L., & Walker, D. (2005). Infants' and toddlers' television viewing and language outcomes. *American Behavioral Scientist, 48*, 624–645. doi:10.1177/0002764204271505

Lippman, A., Melnychuk, R., Shimmin, C., & Boscoe, M. (2007). Human papillomavirus, vaccines and women's health: Questions and cautions. *Canadian Medical Association Journal, 177*(5), 484–487. doi:10.1503/cmaj.070944

Lipton, J. S., & Spelke, E. S. (2003). Origins of number sense: Large-number discrimination in human infants. *Psychological Science, 14*(5), 396–401. doi:10.1111/1467-9280.01453

Liszkowski, U., Carpenter, M., Striano, T., & Tomasello, M. (2006). Twelve- and 18-month-olds point to provide information for others. *Journal of Cognition and Development*, 7, 173–187.

Litonjua, A. A., & Weiss, S. T. (2010). Epidemiology of asthma. In P. J. Barnes (Ed.), *UpToDate.* Waltham, MA: UpToDate.

Little, S. E. (2006). Cost of transferring one through five embryos per in vitro fertilization cycle from various payor perspectives. *Obstetrics & Gynecology, 108*(3), 593–601. doi:10.1097/01.AOG.0000230534.54078.b3

Liu, S., Liston, R. M., Joseph, K. S., Heaman, M., Sauve, R., & Kramer, M. S., for the Maternal Health Study Group of the Canadian Perinatal Surveillance System. (2007). Maternal mortality and severe morbidity associated with low-risk planned cesarean delivery versus planned vaginal delivery at term. *Canadian Medical Association Journal, 176*(4), 455–460.

Livingston, G., & Parker, K. (2010). Since the start of the great recession, more children raised by grandparents. Pew Research Social & Demographic Trends. Retrieved from http://www.pewsocialtrends.org/2010/09/09/since-the-start-of-the-great-recession-more-children-raised-by-grandparents/

Lobo, M., & Galloway, J. C. (2008). Postural and object-oriented experiences advance early reaching, object exploration, and means–end behavior. *Child Development, 79*, 6, 1869–1890.

Lock, J., Le Grange, D., Agras, W. S., Moye, A., Bryson, S. W., & Jo, B. (2010). Randomized clinical trial comparing family-based treatment with adolescent-focused individual therapy for adolescents with anorexia nervosa. *Archives of General Psychiatry, 67*(10), 1025–1032. doi:10.1001/archgenpsychiatry.2010.128

Loehlin, J. C., Horn, J. M. & Ernst, J. L. (2007). Genetic and environmental influences on adult life outcomes: Evidence from the Texas Adoption Project. *Behavioral Genetics, 37*(3), 463–476. doi:10.1007/s10519-007-9144-5

Loewenstein, G. F., Weber, E. U., Hsee, C. K., & Welch, N. (2001). Risk as feelings. *Psychological Bulletin, 127*(2), 267–286. doi:10.1037/0033-2909.127.2.267

Lohmander, L. S., Östenberg, A. Englund, M., & Roos, H. (2004). High prevalence of knee osteoarthritis, pain, and functional limitations in female soccer players twelve years after anterior cruciate ligament injury. *Arthritis and Rheumatism, 50*(10), 3145–3152.

London, M. L., Ladewig, P. W., Ball, J. W., & Bindler, R. C. (2003). *Maternal, newborn and child nursing: Family centered care.* Upper Saddle River, NJ: Prentice Hall.

Lonigan, C. J., Burgess, S. R., & Anthony, J. L. (2000). Development of emergent literacy and early reading skills in preschool children: Evidence from a latent-variable longitudinal study. *Developmental Psychology, 36*(5), 596–613. doi:10.1037/0012-1649.36.5.596

Lopez, A., Dietz, V. J., Wilson, M., Navin, T. R., & Jones, J. L. (2000). Preventing congenital toxoplasmosis. *Morbidity and Mortality Weekly Review, 49*, 57–75. Retrieved from http://www.cdc.gov/mmwr/preview/mmwrhtml/rr4902a5.htm

López, M. G., & Tashakkori, A. (2006). Differential outcomes of two bilingual education programs on English language learners. *Bilingual Research Journal 30*(1), 123–145.

Lorenz, K. (1965). *Evolution and the modification of behavior.* Chicago, IL: University of Chicago Press.

Losh, M., Martin, G. E., Klusek, J., Hogan–Brown, A. L., & Sideris, J. (2012). Social communication and theory of mind in boys with autism and fragile X syndrome. *Frontiers in Psychology, 3*, 1–12. doi:10.3389/fpsyg.2012.00266

Lovas, G. S. (2005). Gender and patterns of emotional availability in mother-toddler and father-toddler dyads. *Infant Mental Health Journal, 26*, 327–353.

Lovell, M. R., Collins, M. W., Iverson, G. L., Johnston, K. M., & Bradley, J. P. (2004). Grade 1 or "ding" concussions in high school athletes. *American Journal of Sports Medicine, 32*(1), 47–54.

Lowery, R. M., Sabis-Burns, D., & Anderson-Brown, S. (2008). Book buddies: Kindergartners and fifth graders explore books together. *Dimensions of Early Childhood, 36*(3), 31–37.

Lowry, R., Wechsler, H., Galuska, D. A., Fulton, J. E., & Kann, L. (2002). Television viewing and its associations with overweight, sedentary lifestyle, and insufficient consumption of fruits and vegetables among U.S. high school students: Differences by race, ethnicity, and gender. *Journal of School Health*, 72, 413–421.

Lozoff, B., & Georgieff, M. K. (2006). Iron deficiency and brain development. *Seminars in Pediatric Neurology, 13*, 158–165. doi:10.1016/j.spen.2006.08.004

Lozoff, B., De Andraca, I., Castillo, M., Smith, J. B., Walter, T., & Pino, P. (2003). Behavioral and developmental effects of preventing iron-deficiency anemia in healthy full-term infants. *Pediatrics, 112*(4), 846–854.

Lucas, P., Arai, L., Baird, J., Kleijnen, J., Law, C., & Roberts, H. (2007). A systematic review of lay views about infant size and growth. *Archives of Disease in Childhood, 92*, 120–127.

Luciana, M., & Nelson, C. A. (1998). The functional emergence of prefrontally-guided working memory systems in four- to eight-year-old children. *Neuropsychologia, 36*(3), 273–293. doi:10.1016/S0028-3932(97)00109-7

Lucido, F. (2000). The influence of bilingualism on English reading scores. *Reading Improvement, 37*(2), 87–91.

Ludlow, J. P., Evans, S. F., & Hulse, G. (2004). Obstetric and perinatal outcomes in pregnancies associated with illicit substance abuse. *Australian and New Zealand Journal of Obstetrics and Gynecology, 44*(4), 301–306. doi:10.1111/j.1479–828X.2004.00221.x

Luebbe, A. M., Kiel, E. J., & Buss, K. A. (2011). Toddlers' context-varying emotions, maternal responses to emotions, and internalizing behaviors. *Emotion, 11*(3), 697–703. doi:10.1037/a0022994

Luke, B., & Brown, M. B. (2007). Elevated risks of pregnancy complications and adverse outcomes with increasing maternal age. *Human Reproduction, 22*(5), 1264–1272. doi:10.1093/humrep/del522

Lumeng, J. C., Cabral, H. J., Gannon, K., Heeren, T., & Frank, D. A. (2007). Prenatal exposures to cocaine and alcohol and physical growth patterns to age 8 years. *Neurotoxicology and Teratology, 29*, 446–457.

Luna, B., Garver, K. E., Urban, T. A., Lazar, N. A., & Sweeney, J. A. (2004). Maturation of cognitive processes from late childhood to adulthood. *Child Development, 75*(5), 1357–1372. doi:10.1111/j.1467–8624.2004.00745.x

Luna, B., Padmanabhan, A., & O'Hearn, K. (2010). What has fMRI told us about the development of cognitive control through adolescence? *Brain and Cognition, 72*(1), 101–113. doi:10.1016/j.bandc.2009.08.005

Luna, B., Paulsen, D. J., Padmanabhan, A., & Geier, C. (2013). The teenage brain: Cognitive control and motivation. *Current Directions in Psychological Science, 22*(2), 94–100. doi:10.1177/0963721413478416

Luna, B., Thulborn, K. R., Munoz, D. P., Merriam, E. P., Garver, K. E., Minshew, N. J., . . . Sweeney, J. A. (2001). Maturation of widely distributed brain function subserves cognitive development. *NeuroImage, 13*, 786–793.

Luo, Y., & Baillargeon, R. (2005). When the ordinary seems unexpected: Evidence for incremental physical knowledge in young infants. *Cognition, 95*, 297–328. doi:10.1016/j.cognition.2004.01.010

Lupien, S. J., King, S., Meaney, M. J., & McEwen, B. S. (2000). Child's stress hormone levels correlate with mother's socioeconomic status and depressive state. *Biological Psychiatry, 48*(10), 976–980. doi:10.1016/S0006–3223(00)00965–3

Lupien, S. J., McEwen, B. S., Gunnar, M. R., & Heim, C. (2009). Effects of stress throughout the lifespan on brain, behaviour and cognition. *Nature Reviews Neuroscience, 10*, 434–445. doi:10.1038/nrn2639

Lupton, C., Burd, L., & Harwood R. (2004). Cost of fetal alcohol spectrum disorders. *American Journal of Medical Genetics, 127*C(1), 42–50. doi:10.1002/ajmg.c.30015

Luria, A. (1966). *Higher cortical functions in man*. Oxford, UK: Basic Books.

Luthar, S. S. (2006). Resilience in development: A synthesis of research across five decades. In D. Cicchetti & D. J. Cohen (Eds.), *Developmental psychopathology: Vol. 3. Risk, disorder, and adaptation* (2nd ed., pp. 739–795). Hoboken, NJ: Wiley.

Luyckx, K., Soenens, B., Vansteenkiste, M., Goossens, L., & Berzonsky, M. D. (2007). Parental psychological control and dimensions of identity formation in emerging adulthood. *Journal of Family Psychology, 21*(3), 546–550. doi:10.1037/0893–3200.21.3.546

Lynch, V., Phong, S., Kenney, G., & Macri, J. (2010). *Uninsured children: Who are they and where do they live?* Washington, DC: Robert Wood Johnson Foundation. Retrieved from http://www.rwjf.org/files/research/67668.pdf

Macchi Cassia, V., Turati, C., & Simion, F. (2004). Can a nonspecific bias toward top-heavy patterns explain newborns' face preference? *Psychological Science, 15*(6), 379–383. doi:10.1111/j.0956–7976.2004.00688.x

Maccoby, E., & Martin, J. (1983). Socialization in the context of the family: Parent-child interaction. In P. H. Mussen (Series Ed.) & E. M. Hetherington (Vol. Ed.), *Handbook of child psychology: Vol. 4. Socialization, personality, and social development* (4th ed., pp. 1–101). New York, NY: Wiley.

MacDorman, M. F., & Mathews, T. J. (2008). *Recent trends in infant mortality in the United States (National Center for Health Statistics Data Brief No. 9)*. Hyattsville, MD: National Center for Health Statistics.

Machaalani, R., & Waters, K. A. (2008). Neuronal cell death in the sudden infant death syndrome brainstem and associations with risk factors. *Brain, 131*(1), 218–228. doi:10.1093/brain/awm290

MacKenzie, M. J., Nicklas, E., Waldfogel, J., & Brooks-Gunn, J. (2012). Corporal punishment and child behavioural and cognitive outcomes through 5 years of age: Evidence from a contemporary urban birth cohort study. *Infant and Child Development, 21*(1), 3–33. doi:10.1002/icd.758

MacMahon, B. (1973). *Age at menarche: United States* (Department of Health, Education and Welfare Publication Number 74-1615). Rockville, MD: National Center for Health Statistics.

Macnamara, J. T. (1966). *Bilingualism and primary education: A study of Irish experience*. Edinburgh, Scotland: Edinburgh University Press.

MacWhinney, B. (2005). Language development. In M. H. Bornstein & M. E. Lamb (Eds.), *Developmental science: An advanced textbook* (5th ed., pp. 359–387). Mahwah, NJ: Erlbaum.

Madsen, K. M., Hviid, A., Vestergaard M., Schendel, D., Wohlfhart, A., Thorsen, P., . . . Melbye, M. (2002). A population-based study of measles, mumps, and rubella vaccination and autism. *New England Journal of Medicine, 347*, 1477–1482. doi:10.1056/NEJMoa021134

Madsen, K. M., Lauritsen, M. B., Pedersen, C. B., Thorsen, P., Plesner, A., Andersen, P. H., & Mortensen, P. B. (2003). Thimerosal and the occurrence of autism: Negative ecological evidence from Danish population-based data. *Pediatrics, 112*(3), 604–606

Maehr, M. L., & Zusho, A. (2009). Achievement goal theory: The past, present, and future. In K. R. Wenzel, & A. Wigfield (Eds.), *Handbook of motivation at school* (pp. 77–104). New York, NY: Routledge/Taylor & Francis.

Maestripieri, D. (2001). Is there mother-infant bonding in primates? *Developmental Review, 21*(1), 93–120. doi:10.1006/drev.2000.0522

Magnuson, K. A., Sexton, H. R., Davis–Kean, P. E., & Huston, A. C. (2009). Increases in maternal education and young children's language skills. *Merrill-Palmer Quarterly, 55*(3), 319–350.

Maguen, S., Floyd, F. J., Bakeman, R., & Armistead, L. (2002). Developmental milestones and disclosure of sexual orientation among gay, lesbian, and bisexual youths. *Journal of Applied Developmental Psychology, 23*(2), 219–233. doi:10.1016/S0193–3973(02)00105–3

Maguire, M. J., White, J., & Brier, M. R. (2011). How semantic categorization influences inhibitory processing in middle-childhood: An event-related potentials study. *Brain and Cognition, 76*(1), 77–86. doi:10.1016/j.bandc.2011.02.015

Mahler, M., Pine, F., & Bergman, A. (1975). *The psychological birth of the human infant*. New York, NY: Basic Books.

Main, M., & Solomon, J. (1990). Procedures for identifying infants as disorganized/disoriented during the Ainsworth strange situation. In M. T. Greenberg, D. Cicchetti, & E. M. Cummings (Eds.), *Attachment in the preschool years* (pp. 121–160). Chicago, IL: University of Chicago Press.

Majdandzic, M., & van den Boom, D. C. (2007). Multimethod longitudinal assessment of temperament in early childhood. *Journal of Personality, 75*, 121–167.

Majnemer, A., & Barr, R. G. (2006). Association between sleep position and early motor development. *Journal of Pediatrics, 149*(5), 623–629. doi:10.1016/j.jpeds.2006.05.009

Makela, A., Nuorti, J. P., & Peltola, H. (2002). Neurologic disorders after measles-mumps-rubella vaccination. *Pediatrics, 110*(5), 957–963. doi:10.1542/peds.110.5.957

Malaguzzi, L. (1993). For an education based on relationships. *Young Children, 49*, 9–12.

Malina, R. M., Bouchard, C., & Bar-Or, O. (2004). *Growth, maturation and physical activity* (2nd ed.). Champaign, IL: Human Kinetics.

Malti, T., Gummerum, M., Keller, M., & Buchmann, M. (2009). Children's moral motivation, sympathy, and prosocial behavior. *Child Development, 80*(2), 442–460. doi:10.1111/j.1467–8624.2009.01271.x

Mandler, J. M., (2000). Perceptual and conceptual processes in infancy. *Journal of Cognition and Development, 1*(1), 3–36. doi:10.1207/S15327647JCD0101N_2

Mandler, J. M. (2004). Thought before language. *Trends in Cognitive Sciences, 8*(11), 508–513. doi:10.1016/j.tics.2004.09.004

Mandler, J. M. (2006). Actions organize the infant's world. In K. Hirsh-Pasek & R. M. Golinkoff (Eds.), *Action meets word: How children learn verbs* (pp. 111–133). New York, NY: Oxford University Press.

Mandler, J. M., & McDonough, L. (1993). Concept formation in Infancy. *Cognitive Development, 8*, 291–318.

Mandler, J. M., & McDonough, L. (1995). Long-term recall of event sequences in infancy. *Journal of Experimental Child Psychology, 59*, 457–474.

Manning, W. D., Giordano, P. C., & Longmore, M. A. (2006). Hooking up: The relationship contexts of "nonrelationship" sex. *Journal of Adolescent Research, 21*(5), 459–483. doi:10.1177/0743558406291692

Maratsos, M. (2000). More overregularizations after all: New data and discussion on Marcus, Pinker, Ullman, Hollander, Rosen, & Xu. *Journal of Child Language, 27*(1), 183–212. doi:10.1017/S0305000999004067

March of Dimes. (2007). *Birth defects: Cerebral palsy*. Retrieved from http://www.marchofdimes.com/baby/birthdefects_cerebralpalsy.html

March of Dimes. (2008). *Preterm birth overview*. Retrieved from http://www.marchofdimes.com/peristats

March of Dimes. (2009). *Prematurity: Personal stories*. Retrieved from http://www.marchofdimes.com/mission prematurity.html

March of Dimes. (2009a). *Prenatal care*. Retrieved from http://www.marchofdimes.com/pnhec/159_513.asp.

March of Dimes. (2009b). *Complications of pregnancy*. Retrieved from http://www.marchofdimes.com/pnhec/188.asp.

Marchetta, C. M., Denny, C. H., Floyd, L., Cheal, N. E., Sniezek, J. E., & McKnight–Eily, L. R. (2012). Alcohol use and binge drinking among women of childbearing age—United States, 2006–2010. *Morbidity and Mortality Weekly, 61*(28), 534–538.

Marchman, V. A., Saccuman, C., & Wulfeck, B. (2004). Productive use of the English past tense in children with focal brain injury and specific language impairment. *Brain and Language, 88*(2), 202–214. doi:10.1016/S0093-934X(03)00099-3

Marcia, J. E. (1980). Identity in adolescence. In J. Adelson (Ed.), *Handbook of adolescent psychology* (pp. 159–187). New York, NY: Wiley.

Marcovitch, S., & Zelazo, P. D. (1999). The A-not-B error: Results from a logistic meta-analysis. *Child Development, 70*(6), 1297–1313.

Marcovitch, S., Cesaroni, L., Roberts, W., & Swanson, C. (1995). Romanian adoption: Parents' dreams, nightmares, and realities. *Child Welfare Journal, 74*(5), 993–1017.

Marcus, G. F., Pinker, S., Ullman, M., Hollander, M., Rosen, T. J., & Xu, F. (1992). Overregularization in language acquisition. *Monographs of the Society for Research in Child Development, 57*(4), i–182. doi:10.2307/1166115

Markiewicz, D., Lawford, H., Doyle, A. B., & Haggart, N. (2006). Developmental differences in adolescents' and young adults' use of mothers, fathers, best friends, and romantic partners to fulfill attachment needs. *Journal of Youth and Adolescence, 35*(1), 127–140. doi:10.1007/s10964–005–9014–5

Markowitz, M. (2007). Lead poisoning. In R. M. Kliegman, *Nelson Textbook of Pediatrics* (18th ed.). Philadelphia, PA: Saunders Elsevier.

Markus, H. R. (2008). Pride, prejudice, and ambivalence: Toward a unified theory of race and ethnicity. *American Psychologist, 63*(8), 651–670. doi:10.1037/0003–066X.63.8.651

Markus, H. R., & Kitayama, S. (1991). Culture and the self: Implications for cognition, emotion, and motivation. *Psychological Review, 98*(2), 224–253. doi:10.1037/0033-295X.98.2.224

Markus, H. R., & Kitayama, S. (1991). Culture and the self: Implications for cognition, emotion, and motivation. *Psychological Review, 98*(2), 224–253. doi:10.1037/0033–295X.98.2.224

Markus, H., & Hamedani, M. (2007). Sociocultural psychology: The dynamic interdependence among self systems and social systems. In S. Kitayama & D. Cohen (Eds.), *Handbook of cultural psychology* (pp. 3–39). New York, NY: Guilford.

Markus, H., & Kitayama, S. (1991). Culture and the self: Implications for cognition, emotion, and motivation. *Psychological Review, 98*, 224–253.

Marsh, H. W., & Kleitman, S. (2005). Consequences of employment during high school: Character building, subversion of academic goals, or a threshold? *American Educational Research Journal, 42*(2), 331–369. doi:10.3102/00028312042002331

Marsh, L. E., & Hamilton, D. C. (2011). Dissociation of mirroring and mentalising systems in autism. *NeuroImage, 56*(3), 1511–1519. doi:10.1016/j.neuroimage.2011.02.003

Marshall, N. A., & Shibazaki, K. (2012). Instrument, gender, and musical style associations in young children. *Psychology of Music, 40*(4), 494–507. doi:10.1177/0305735611408996

Martin, C. L., DiDonato, M. D., Clary, L., Fabes, R. A., Kreiger, T., Palermo, F., & Hanish, L. (2012). Preschool children with gender normative and gender non-normative peer preferences: Psychosocial and environmental correlates. *Archives of Sexual Behavior, 41*(4), 831–847. doi:10.1007/s10508–012–9950–6

Marshall, N. L., Creps, C. L., Burstein, N. R., Cahill, K. E., Robeson, W. W., Wang, S. Y., . . . Glantz, F. B. (2003). *Family child care today: A report of the findings of the Massachusetts cost/quality study*. Wellesley, MA: Wellesley Centers for Women.

Martin, J. A., Hamilton, B. E., Sutton, P., Ventura, S., Menacker, F., Kirmeyer, S., & Mathews T. J. (2009). Births: Final data for 2006. *National Vital Statistics Reports, 57*(7), 1–102. Retrieved from http://www.cdc.gov/nchs/data/nvsr/nvsr57/nvsr57_07.pdf

Martin, J. A., Hamilton, B. E., Ventura, S. J., Osterman, M. J. K., Wilson, E. C. & Mathews, T. J. (2012). Births: Final data for 2010. *National Vital Statistics Report, 61*(1). Retrieved from http://www.cdc.gov/nchs/data/nvsr/nvsr61/nvsr61_01.pdf

Martin, J. A., Hamilton, B. E., Ventura, S. J., Osterman, M. J. K., Kirmeyer, S., Mathews, T. J., & Wilson, E. C. (2011). Births: Final data for 2009. *National Vital Statistics Reports, 60*(1). Hyattsville, MD: National Center for Health Statistics.

Martinez, G. M., Chandra, A., Abma, J. C., Jones, J., & Mosher, W. D. (2006). Fertility, contraception, and fatherhood: Data on men and women from cycle 6 (2002) of the National Survey of Family Growth. *Vital and Health Statistics, 23*(26). Hyattsville, MD: National Center for Health Statistics.

Martinez, G. M., Copen, C. E., & Abma, J. C. (2011). Teenagers in the United States: Sexual activity, contraceptive use, and childbearing, 2006–2010 National Survey of Family Growth. *Vital and Health Statistics, 23*(31). Hyattsville, MD: National Center for Health Statistics.

Martino, S. C., Elliot, M. N., Colling, R. L., Kanuse, D. E., & Berry, S. H. (2008). Virginity pledges among the willing: Delays in first intercourse and consistency of condom use. *Journal of Adolescent Health, 43*(4), 341–348.

Martino, W., & Pallotta-Chiarolli, M. (2003). *So what's a boy? Addressing issues of masculinity and schooling*. Maidenhead, UK: Open University Press.

Martin-Rhee, M. M., & Bialystok, E. (2008). The development of two types of inhibitory control in monolingual and bilingual children. *Bilingualism: Language and Cognition, 11*(1), 81–93. doi:10.1017/S1366728907003227

Martins, M. A., & Silva, C. (2006). The impact of invented spelling on phonemic awareness. *Learning and Instruction, 16*(1), 41–56. doi:10.1016/j.learninstruc.2005.12.005

Martland, H. S. (1928). Punch drunk. *Journal of the American Medical Association, 91*(15), 1103–1107. doi:10.1001/jama.1928.02700150029009

Martorell, R., Rivera, J., Kaplowitz, H., & Pollitt, E. (1992). Long-term consequences of growth retardation during early childhood. In M. Hernandez & J. Argente, (Eds.), *Human growth: Basic and clinical aspects* (pp. 143–149). Amsterdam, Netherlands Elsevier.

Marván, M. L., Vacio, A., García-Yáñez, & Espinosa-Hernádez, G. (2007). Attitudes toward menarche among Mexican preadolescents. *Women & Health 46*(1), 7–23.

Mastropieri, M. A., & Scruggs, T. E. (1998). Constructing more meaningful relationships in the classroom: Mnemonic research into practice. *Learning Disabilities Research & Practice, 13*(3), 138–145.

Masur, E. F., McIntyre, C. W., & Flavell, J. H. (1973). Developmental changes in apportionment of study time among items in a multitrial free recall task. *Journal of Experimental Child Psychology, 15*(2), 237–246. doi:10.1016/0022–0965(73)90145–8

Mathews, T. J., & Hamilton, B. E. (2009). *Delayed childbearing: More women are having their first child later in life* (National Center for Health Statistics Data Brief No. 21). Hyattsville, MD: National Center for Health Statistics. Retrieved from http://www.cdc.gov/nchs/data/databriefs/db21.pdf

Mathews, T. J., & MacDorman, M. F. (2012). Infant mortality statistics from the 2008 period linked birth/infant death data set. *National Vital Statistics Report, 60*(5). Retrieved from http://www.cdc.gov/nchs/data/nvsr/nvsr60/nvsr60_05.pdf

Mathieson, K., & Banerjee, R. (2010). Preschool peer play: The beginnings of social competence. *Educational and Child Psychology, 27*(1), 9–20.

Matson, J. L., & Kozlowski, A. M. (2010). The increasing prevalence of autism spectrum disorders. *Research in Autism Spectrum Disorders, 5*(1), 418–425. doi:10.1016/j.rasd.2010.06.004

Matson, J. L., Tureck, K., Turygin, N., Beighley, J., & Rieske, R. (2012). Trends and topics in early intensive behavioral interventions for toddlers with autism. *Research in Autism Spectrum Disorders, 6*(4), 1412–1417. doi:10.1016/j.rasd.2012.02.010

Matsui, E. C., Eggleston, P. A., Buckley, T. J., Krishnan, J. A., Breysse, P. N., Rand, C. S., & Diette, G. B. (2006). Household mouse allergen exposure and asthma morbidity in inner-city preschool children. *Annals of Allergy, Asthma & Immunology, 97*(4), 514–20. doi:10.1016/S1081-1206(10)60943-X

Matthews, C. E., Chen, K. Y., Freedson, P. S., Buchowski, M. S., Beech, B. M., Pate, R. R., & Troiano, R. P. (2008). Amount of time spent in sedentary behaviors in the United States, 2003–2004. *American Journal of Epidemiology, 167*, 875–881. doi:10.1093/aje/kwm390

Mattson, S., & Smith, J. E. (Eds.). (2010). *Core curriculum for maternal-newborn nursing* (4th ed.). Philadelphia, PA: Elsevier Saunders.

Matusov, E., & Hayes, R. (2000). Sociocultural critique of Piaget and Vygotsky. *New Ideas in Psychology, 18*(2–3), 215–239. doi:10.1016/S0732-118X(00)00009-X

Mauras, N., Rogol, A. D., Haymond, M. W., & Veldhuis, J. D. (1996). Sex steroids, growth hormone, insulin-like growth factor-1: Neuroendocrine and metabolic regulation in puberty. *Hormone Research, 45*(1–2), 74–80.

Maury, E. & Brichard, S. M. (2010). Adipokine dysregulation, adipose tissue inflammation and metabolic syndrome. *Molecular and Cellular Endocrinology, 314*(1), 1–16. doi:10.1016/j.mce.2009.07.031

Mautone, J. A., Marshall, S. A., Costigan, T. E., Clarke, A. T., & Power, T. J. (2012). Multidimensional assessment of homework: An analysis of students with ADHD. *Journal of Attention Disorders, 16*(7), 600–609. doi:10.1177/1087054711416795

Maxwell, M. A., & Cole, D. A. (2012). Development and initial validation of the adolescent responses to body dissatisfaction measure. *Psychological Assessment, 24*(3), 721–737. doi:10.1037/a0026785

May, A. L., Kuklina, E. V., & Yoon, P. W. (2012). Prevalence of cardiovascular disease risk factors among U.S. adolescents, 1999–2008. *Pediatrics, 129*(6), 1035–1041. doi:10.1542/peds.2011–1082.

May, P. A., Gossage, J. P., Kalberg, W. O., Robinson, L. K., Buckley, D. Manning, M., & Hoyme, H. E. (2009). Prevalence and epidemiologic characteristics of FASD from various research methods with an emphasis on recent in-school studies. *Developmental Disabilities Research Reviews, 15*(3), 176–192.

Mayberry, L., Affonso, D. Shibuya, J., & Clemmens, D. (1999). Integrating cultural values, beliefs, and customs into pregnancy and postpartum care: Lessons learned from a Hawaiian public health nursing project. *The Journal of Perinatal & Neonatal Nursing, 13*(1), 15–26.

Mayer, K. (2009). Emerging knowledge about emergent writing. In E. L. Essa & M. M. Burnham (Eds.), *Informing our practice: Useful research on young children's development* (pp. 111–118). Washington, DC: NAEYC.

Mayer, R. E. (2003). Memory and information processes. In W. M. Reynolds & G. E. Miller (Eds.), *Handbook of Psychology: Vol. 7. Educational Psychology* (pp. 47–57). Hoboken, NJ: Wiley.

Maynard, A. E., & Greenfield, P. M. (2003). Implicit cognitive development in cultural tools and children: Lessons from Maya Mexico. *Cognitive Development, 18*(4), 489–510. doi:10.1016/j.cogdev.2003.09.005

Mayo Clinic. (2009). *Infertility*. Retrieved from http://www.mayoclinic.com/health/infertility

Mayo Clinic. (2011). *Sex education: Talking to your teen about sex*. Retrieved from http://www.mayoclinic.com/health/sex-education/CC00032

Mayo Clinic. (2012). *Prenatal vitamins: Why they matter, how to choose*. Retrieved from http://www.mayoclinic.com/health/prenatal-vitamins/PR00160/METHOD=print

Mayson, T. A., Harris, S. R., & Bachman, C. L. (2007). Gross motor development of Asian and European children on four motor assessments: A literature review. *Pediatric Physical Therapy, 19*, 148–153. doi:10.1097/PEP.0b013e31804a57c1

Mazur, A., & Booth, A. (1998). Testosterone and dominance in men. *Behavioral and Brain Sciences, 21*, 353–363.

McAnulty, G., Duffy, F. H., Kosta, S., Weisenfeld, N. I., Warfield, S., Butler, S. C., Alidoost, M., Holmes-Bernstein, J., Robertson, R., Zurakowski, D., Als, H. (2013). School-age effects of the newborn individualized developmental care and assessment program for preterm infants with intrauterine growth restriction: Preliminary findings. *BMC Pediatrics, 13*, 25. doi:10.1186/1471-2431-13-25

McCall, R. B. (1981). Nature-nurture and the two realms of development: A proposed integration with respect to mental development. *Child Development, 52*(1), 1–12.

McCall, R. B., Appelbaum, M. I., & Hogarty, P. S. (1973). Developmental changes in mental performance. *Monographs of the Society for Research in Child Development, 38*(3, Serial No. 150), 1–83.

McCandliss, B., Beck, I. L., Sandak, R., & Perfetti, C. (2003). Focusing attention on decoding for children with poor reading skills: Design and preliminary tests of the Word Building intervention. *Scientific Studies of Reading*, 7(1), 75–104. doi:10.1207/S1532799XSSR0701_05

McCarthy, C. (2013). Pediatricians and television: It's time to rethink our messaging and our efforts. *Pediatrics, 131, 3*, 589–590.

McCartt, A. T., Hellinga, L. A., & Braitman, K. A. (2006). Cell phones and driving: Review of research. *Traffic Injury Prevention*, 7, 89–106.

McCarty, M. E., & Keen, R. (2005). Facilitating problem-solving performance among 9- and 12-month-old infants. *Journal of Cognition and Development, 6*, 209–228. doi:10.1207/s15327647jcd0602_3

McCoog, I. J. (2007). Integrated instruction: Multiple intelligences and technology. *The Clearing House: A Journal of Educational Strategies, Issues and Ideas, 81*(1), 25–28. doi:10.3200/TCHS.81.1.25–28

McCormick, M. C. (1993). Has the prevalence of handicapped infants increased with improved survival of the very low birth weight infant? *Clinics in Perinatology, 20*, 263–277.

McCrory, P., Meeuwisse, W., Johnston, K., Dvorak, J., Aubry, M., Molloy, M., & R. Cantu, R. (2009). Consensus statement on concussion in sports—3rd international conference on concussion in sport, held in Zurich, November 2008. *Journal of Neuroscience, 16*, 755–763.

McDaniel, D. D. (2012). Risk and protective factors associated with gang affiliation among high-risk youth: A public health approach. *Injury Prevention, 18*(4), 253–258. doi:10.1136/injuryprev-2011–040083

McDonald, J. L., & Roussel, C. C. (2010). Past tense grammaticality judgment and production in non-native and stressed native English speakers. *Bilingualism: Language and Cognition, 13*(4), 429–448. doi:10.1017/S1366728909990599

McDonald, S., Murphy, K., Beyene, J., & Ohlsson, A. (2005). Perinatal outcomes of in vitro fertilization twins: A systematic review and meta-analyses. *American Journal of Obstetrics and Gynecology, 193*(1), 141–152. doi:10.1016/j.ajog.2004.11.064

McDonough, L., & Mandler, J. M. (1994). Very long-term recall in infants: Infantile amnesia reconsidered. *Memory, 2*, 339–352.

McDowell, D. J., & Parke, R. D. (2009). Parental correlates of children's peer relations: An empirical test of a tripartite model. *Developmental Psychology, 45*(1), 224–235. doi:10.1037/a0014305

McElhaney, K. B., Allen, J. P., Stephenson, J. C., & Hare, A. L. (2009). Attachment and autonomy during adolescence. In R. M. Lerner & L. Steinberg (Eds.), *Handbook of adolescent psychology: Vol. 1. Individual bases of adolescent development* (3rd ed., pp. 358–403). Hoboken, NJ: Wiley.

McEwen, B. S. (2004). Protection and damage from acute and chronic stress. *Annals of the New York Academy of Sciences, 1032, 1e7*. doi:10.1196/annals.1314.001

McEwen, B., & Lasley, E. N. (2002). *The end of stress as we know it*. Washington, DC: National Academies Press.

McEwen, B., & Wingfield, J. C. (2003). The concept of allostasis in biology and biomedicine. *Hormones and Behavior, 43*(1), 2–15. doi:10.1016/S0018–506X(02)00024–7

McFadyen, B. J., & Winter, D. A. (1988). An integrated biomechanical analysis of normal stair ascent and descent. *Journal of Biomechanics, 21*(9), 733–744. doi:10.1016/0021–9290(88)90282–5

McGarrigle, J., & Donaldson, M. (1974). Conservation accidents. *Cognition, 3*(4), 341–350. doi:10.1016/0010-0277(74)90003-1

McGee, G., Brakman, S. V., & Gurmankin, A. (2001). Gamete donation and anonymity. *Human Reproduction, 16*(10), 2033–2038. doi:10.1093/humrep/16.10.2033

McGraw, M. B. (1932). From reflex to muscular control in the assumption of an erect posture and ambulation in the human infant. *Child Development, 3*(4), 291–297. doi:10.2307/1125356

McGuffin, P., Riley, B., & Plomin, R. (2001). Genomics and behavior: Toward behavioral genomics. *Science, 16*(291), 1232–1249. doi:10.1126/science.1057264

McGuiness, T. M. (2007). Dispelling the myth of bullying. *Journal of Psychosocial Nursing and Mental Health Services, 45*(10), 19–22.

McHale, S. M., & Crouter, A. C. (1996). The family contexts of children's sibling relationships. In G. H. Brody (Ed.), *Sibling relationships: Their causes and consequences* (pp. 173–196). Westport, CT: Ablex.

McHale, S. M., Dariotis, J. K., & Kauh, T. J. (2003). Social development and social relationships in middle childhood. In R. M. Lerner, M. A. Easterbrooks, & J. Mistry (Eds.), *Handbook of psychology: Vol. 6. Developmental Psychology* (pp. 241–265). Hoboken, NJ: Wiley.

McIsaac, C., Connolly, J., McKenny, K. S., Pepler, D., & Craig, W. (2008). Conflict negotiation and autonomy processes in adolescent romantic relationships: An observational study of interdependency in boyfriend and girlfriend effects. *Journal of Adolescence, 31*(6), 691–707. doi:10.1016/j.adolescence.2008.08.005

McKay, A. (2006). Trends in teen pregnancy rates from 1996–2006: A comparison of Canada, Sweden, USA and England/Wales. *Canadian Journal of Human Sexuality, 19*(1–2), 43–52.

McKenna, J. J., & McDade, T. (2005). Why babies should never sleep alone: A review of the co-sleeping controversy in relation to SIDS, bedsharing and breast feeding. *Paediatric Respiratory Reviews, 6*, 134–152. doi:10.1016/j.prrv.2005.03.006

McLachlan, H., & Waldenstrom, U. (2005). Childbirth experiences in Australia of women born in Turkey, Vietnam, and Australia. *Birth: Issues in Perinatal Care, 32*(4), 272–282. doi:10.1111/j.0730–7659.2005.00370.x

McLaughlin, K. A., Zeanah. C. H., Fox, N. A., & Nelson, C. A. (2012). Attachment security as a mechanism linking foster care placement to improved mental health outcomes in previously institutionalized children. *Journal of Child Psychology & Psychiatry, 53*(1), 46–55.

McLoyd, V. C., & Smith, J. (2002). Physical discipline and behavior problems in African American, European American, and Hispanic children: Emotional support as a mediator. *Journal of Marriage & Family, 64*, 40–53.

McMahon, C. A., Boivin, J., Gibson, F. L., Hammarberg, K., Wynter, K., Saunders, D., & Fisher, J. (2011). Age at first birth, mode of conception and psychological well-being in pregnancy: Findings from the parental age and transition to parenthood Australia (PATPA) study. *Human Reproduction, 26*(6), 1389–1398.

McMahon, S. D., Wernsman, J., & Rose, D. S. (2009). The relation of classroom environment and school belonging to academic self-efficacy among urban fourth- and fifth-grade students. *Elementary School Journal, 109*(3), 267–281. doi:10.1086/592307

McManus, B., & Nugent, J. K. (2011). Feasibility study of early intervention provider confidence following a neurobehavioral intervention for high-risk newborns. *Journal of Reproductive and Infant Psychology, 29*(4), 395–403. doi:10.1080/02646838.2011.623228

McManus, B., & Nugent, J. K. (2012). A neurobehavioral intervention incorporated into a state early intervention program is associated with higher perceived quality of care among parents of high-risk newborns. *Journal of Behavioral Health Services & Research*, 1–8. doi:10.1007/s11414-012-9283-1

McMorris, B. J., & Uggen, C. (2000). Alcohol and employment in the transition to adulthood. *Journal of Health and Social Behavior, 41*(3), 276–294.

McPherson, M., Arango, P., Fox, H., Lauver, C., McManus, M., Newacheck, P., . . . & Strickland, B. (1998). A new definition of children with special health care needs. *Pediatrics, 102*(1), 137–140.

McWayne, C. M., Cheung, K., Wright, L. E. G., Hahs-Vaughn, D. L. (2012). Patterns of school readiness among head start children: Meaningful within-group variability during the transition to kindergarten. *Journal of Educational Psychology, 104*(3) 862–878. doi:10.1037/a0028884

Meaney, M. (2010). Epigenetics and the biological definition of gene X environment interactions. *Child Development, 81*, 41–79. doi:10.1111/j.1467–8624.2009.01381.x

Meeus, W. (2003). Parental and peer support, identity development and psychological well-being in adolescence. *Psychology: The Journal of the Hellenic Psychological Society, 10*(2–3), 192–201.

Meeus, W. (2011). The study of adolescent identity formation 2000–2010: A review of longitudinal research. *Journal of Research on Adolescence, 21*(1), 75–94. doi:10.1111/j.1532–7795.2010.00716.x

Mehta, M. A., Golembo, N. I., Nosarti, C., Colvert, E., Mota, A., Williams, S. C. R., . . . Sonuga-Barke, E. J. S. (2009). Amygdala, hippocampal and corpus callosum size following severe early institutional deprivation: The English and Romanian Adoptees Study Pilot. *Journal of Child Psychology and Psychiatry, 50*(8), 943–951.

Melde, C., Taylor, T. J., & Esbensen, F. (2009). "I got your back": An examination of the protective function of gang membership in adolescence. *Criminology: An Interdisciplinary Journal, 47*(2), 565–594. doi:10.1111/j.1745–9125.2009.00148.x

Melnyk, B. M., Feinstein, N. F., & Fairbanks, E. (2002). Evidence-based practice. Effectiveness of informational/behavioral interventions with parents of low birth weight (LBW) premature infants: An evidence base to guide clinical practice. *Pediatric Nursing, 28*, 511–516.

Meltzer, H. (1989). Serotonergic dysfunction in depression. *British Journal of Psychiatry, 8*, S25–S31.

Meltzer, L. (2010). *Promoting executive function in the classroom*. New York, NY: Guilford.

Meltzer, L., & Krishnan, K. (2007). Executive function difficulties and learning disabilities: Understandings and misunderstandings. In L. Meltzer (Ed.), *Executive function in education: From theory to practice* (pp. 77–105). New York, NY: Guilford.

Meltzoff, A. N. (1988). Infant imitation and memory: Nine-month olds in immediate and deferred tests. *Child Development, 59*, 217–225.

Meltzoff, A. N. (1990). The implications of cross-modal matching and imitation for the development of representation and memory in infants. In A. Diamond (Ed.), *The development and neural bases of higher cognitive functions* (pp. 1–37). New York, NY: New York Academy of Science.

Meltzoff, A. N. (1995). What infant memory tells us about infantile amnesia: Long-term recall and deferred imitation. *Journal of Experimental Child Psychology, 59*, 497–515.

Meltzoff, A. N., & Moore, M. K. (1977). Imitation of facial and manual gestures by human neonates. *Science, 198*(4312), 75–78. doi:10.1126/science.198.4312.75

Meltzoff, A. N., & Moore, M. K. (1983). Newborn infants imitate adult facial gestures. *Child Development, 54*(3), 702–709. doi:10.1111/1467–8624.ep8598223

Meltzoff, A. N., & Moore, M., K. (1994). Imitation, memory, and the representation of persons. *Infant Behavior & Development, 17*(1), 83–99. doi:10.1016/0163–6383(94)90024–8

Meltzoff, A. N., Kuhl, P. K., Movellan, J., & Sejnowski, T. J. (2009). Foundations for a new science of learning. *Science, 325*, 284–288.

Mendez, M. A., & Adair, L. S. (1999). Severity and timing of stunting in the first two years of life affect performance on cognitive tests in late childhood. *Journal of Nutrition, 129*, 1555–1562.

Menon, M., Tobin, D. D., Corby, B. C., Menon, M., Hodges, E., & Perry, D. (2007). The developmental costs of high self-esteem for antisocial children. *Child Development, 78*(6), 1627–1639. doi:10.1111/j.1467–8624.2007.01089.x

Menyuk, P., & Brisk, M. E. (2005). *Language development and education: Children with varying language experiences*. New York, NY: Palgrave Macmillan.

Mercer, S. H., Nellis, L. M., Martinez, R. S., & Kirk, M. (2011). Supporting the students most in need: Academic self-efficacy and perceived teacher support in relation to within-year academic growth. *Journal of School Psychology, 49*(3), 323–338. doi:10.1016/j.jsp.2011.03.006

Mercuri, E., Baranello, G., Domenico, M. M. R., Cesarini, L., & Ricci, D. (2007). The development of vision. *Early Human Development, 83*(12), 795–800.

Merin, N., Young, G. S., Ozonoff, S., & Rogers, S. J. (2007). Visual fixation patterns during reciprocal social interaction distinguish a subgroup of 6-month-old infants at risk for autism from comparison infants. *Journal of Autism and Developmental Science, 37*(1), 108–121. doi:10.1007/s10803-006-0342-4

Mervis, C. B. (2009). Language and literacy development of children with Williams syndrome. *Topics in Language Disorders, 29*(2), 149–169. doi:10.1097/TLD.0b013e3181a72044

Mervis, C. B., & Rosch, E. (1981). Categorization of natural objects. *Annual Review of Psychology, 32*, 89–115.

Messias, D., & DeJoseph, J. (2007). The personal work of a first pregnancy: Transforming identities, relationships, and women's work. *Women & Health, 45*(4), 41–64. doi:10.1300/J013v45n04_03

Metcalfe, J., & Finn, B. (2013). Metacognition and control of study choice in children. *Metacognition and Learning, 8*(1), 19–46. doi:10.1007/s11409-013-9094-7

Metcalfe, J., & Mischel, W. (1999). A hot/cool system analysis of delay of gratification:

Dynamics of willpower. *Psychological Review, 106*(1), 3–19. doi:10.1037/0033-295X.106.1.3

Mezulis, A., Hyde, J. S., & Clark, R. (2004). Father involvement moderates the effect of maternal depression in infancy on child behavior problems. *Journal of Family Psychology, 18*, 575–588.

Mick, E., Biederman, J., Faraone, S. V., Sayer, J., & Kleinman, S. (2002). Case-control study of attention-deficit hyperactivity disorder and maternal smoking, alcohol use and drug use during pregnancy. *Journal of the American Academy of Child & Adolescent Psychiatry, 41*(4), 378–385. doi:10.1097/00004583-200204000-00009

Mikami, A. Y., Boucher, M. A., & Humphreys, S. K. (2005). Prevention of peer rejection through a classroom-level intervention in middle childhood. *Journal of Primary Prevention, 26*(1), 5–23. doi:10.1007/s10935-004-0988-7

Mikami, A. Y., Lerner, M. D., Griggs, M. S., McGrath, A., & Calhoun, C. D. (2010). Parental influence on children with attention-deficit/hyperactivity disorder: II. Results of a pilot intervention training parents as friendship coaches for children. *Journal of Abnormal Child Psychology, 38*(6), 737–749. doi:10.1007/s10802-010-9403-4

Mikkola, K., Ritari, N., Tommiska, V., Salokorpi, T., Lehtonen, L., Tammela, O., . . . Fellmann, V. (2005). Neurodevelopmental outcome at 5 years of age of a national cohort of extremely low birth weights infants who were born in 1996–1997. *Pediatrics, 116*(6), 1391–1400. doi:10.1542/peds.2005-0171

Milgrom, P., Zero, D. T., & Tanzer, J. M. (2009). An examination of the advances in science and technology of prevention of tooth decay in young children since the Surgeon General's Report on Oral Health. *Academic Pediatrics, 9*(6), 404–409. doi:10.1016/j.acap.2009.09.001

Miller, A. (2012). Children today are more imaginative than in the 1980s, study suggests. *Monitor on Psychology, 43*(8), 12.

Miller, B. C. (2002). Family influences on adolescent sexual and contraceptive behavior. *The Journal of Sex Research, 39*(1), 22–26.

Miller, J. W., Naimi, T. S., Brewer, R. D., & Jones, S. E. (2007). Binge drinking and associated health risk behaviors among high school students. *Pediatrics, 119*, 76–85.

Miller, K. F., Kelly, M., & Zhou, X. (2005). Learning mathematics in China and the United States: Cross-cultural insights into the nature and course of preschool mathematical development. In J. I. D. Campbell (Ed.), *Handbook of mathematical cognition* (pp. 163–178). New York, NY: Psychology Press.

Miller, K. S., Levin, M. L., Whitaker, D. J., & Xu, X. (1998). Patterns of condom use among adolescents: The impact of mother-adolescent communication. *American Journal of Public Health, 88*(10), 1542–1544.

Miller, P. H. (1990). The development of strategies of selective attention. In D. F. Bjorklund (Ed.), *Children's strategies: Contemporary views of cognitive development* (pp. 157–184). Hillsdale, NJ: Erlbaum.

Miller, P. H. (2002). *Theories of developmental psychology* (4th ed.). New York, NY: Worth.

Miller, P. J., Wang, S., Sandel, T., & Cho, G. E. (2002). Self-esteem as folk theory: A comparison of European American and Taiwanese mothers' beliefs. *Parenting: Science and Practice, 2*, 209–239. doi:10.1207/s15327698jfc0604_2

Miller, S. A. (1988). Parents' beliefs about children's cognitive development. *Child Development, 59*, 259–285. doi:10.1111/1467-8624.ep8588509

Miller, S. R., Tserakhava, V., & Miller, C. J. (2011). "My child is shy and has no friends: What does parenting have to do with it?" *Journal of Youth and Adolescence, 40*(4), 442–452. doi:101007/s10964-010-9550-5

Miller, T. W. (2010). Life stress and transitions in the life span. In T. W. Miller (Ed.), *Handbook of stressful transitions across the lifespan* (pp. 3–17). New York, NY: Springer.

Mills, C., Stephan, S. H., Moore, E., Weist, M. D., Daly, B. P., & Edwards, M. (2006). The president's New Freedom Commission: Capitalizing on opportunities to advance school-based mental health services. *Clinical Child and Family Psychology Review, 9*, 149–161.

Minagawa-Kawai, Y., Matsuoka, S., Dan, I., Naoi, N., Nakamura, K., & Kojima, S. (2009). Prefrontal activation associated with social attachment: Facial-emotion recognition in mothers and infants. *Cerebral Cortex, 19*(2), 284–292.

Minde, K. (2000). The assessment of infants and toddlers with medical conditions and their families. In J. Osofsky & H. Fitzgerald (Eds.), *Handbook of infant mental health* (Vol. 2). New York, NY: Wiley.

Mindell, J. A., Sadeh, A., Kohyama, J., & Hwei How, T. P. (2010). Parental behaviors and sleep outcomes in infants and toddlers: A cross-cultural comparison. *Sleep Medicine, 11*, 393–399.

Minozzi, S., Amato, L., Vecchi, S., & Davoli, M. (2008). Maintenance treatments for opiate-dependent pregnant women. *Cochrane Database of Systematic Reviews, 2*. doi:10.1002/14651858.CD006318.pub2

Minuchin, P. (1985). Families and individual development: Provocations from the field of family therapy. *Child Development, 56*, 289–312. doi:10.1111/1467-8624.ep7251588

Minuchin, P. (1988). Relationships within the family: A systems perspective on development. In R. A. Hinde & J. Stevenson-Hinde (Eds.), *Relationships within families: Mutual influences* (pp. 7–26). New York, NY: Oxford University Press.

Mitchell, J. F., Sundberg, K. A., & Reynolds, J. H. (2009). Spatial attention decorrelates intrinsic activity fluctuations in macaque area V4. *Neuron, 63*(6), 879–888. doi:10.1016/j.neuron.2009.09.013

Mitchell, J. J., & Scriver, C. R. (2007). Phenylalanine hydroxylase deficiency. *GeneReviews*. Retrieved from http://www.ncbi.nlm.nih.gov/bookshelf/br.fcgi?book=gene&part=pku (pmid: 20301677)

Mitchell, O. (2005). A meta-analysis of race and sentencing research: Explaining the inconsistencies. *Journal of Quantitative Criminology, 21*(4), 439–466. doi:10.1007/s10940-005-7362-7

Mitsis, E. M. Halperin, J. M., & Newcorn, J. H. (2000). Serotonin and aggression in children. *Current Psychiatry Reports, 2*, 95–101.

Miur, I. T., Okamoto, Y., Kim, C. C., Steere, M., & Fayol, M. (1993). First graders' cognitive representation of number and understanding of place value: Cross-national comparisons—France, Japan, Korea, Sweden, and the United States. *Journal of Educational Psychology, 85* (1), 24–30. doi 10.1037/0022-0663.85.1.24

Mofenson, L., Taylor, A. W., Rogers, M., Campsmith, M., Ruffo, N. M., Clark, J., . . . Sansom, S. (2006). Achievements in public health: Reduction in perinatal transmission of HIV infection—United States, 1985–2005. *Morbidity and Mortality Weekly Review, 55*(21), 592–597. Retrieved from http://www.cdc.gov/MMWR/preview/mmwrhtml/mm5521a3.htm

Moffitt, T. E., & Caspi, A. (2007). Evidence from behavioral genetics for environmental contributions to antisocial conduct. In J. Grusec & P. Hastings (Eds.), *Handbook of socialization* (pp. 96–123). New York, NY: Guilford.

Moll, L. C. (1990). *Vygotsky and education*. Cambridge, UK: Cambridge University Press.

Monahan, K. C., Lee, J. M., & Steinberg, L. (2011). Revisiting the impact of part-time work on adolescent adjustment: Distinguishing between selection and socialization using propensity score matching. *Child Development, 82*(1), 96–112. doi:10.1111/j.1467-8624.2010.01543

Mondloch, C. J., & Lewis, T. L. (1999). Face perception during early infancy. *Psychological Science, 10*(5), 419–422. doi:10.1111/1467-9280.00179

Monk, C. S., Webb, S. J., & Nelson, C. A. (2001). Prenatal neurobiological development: Molecular mechanisms and anatomical change. *Developmental Neuropsychology, 19(2)*, 211–236.

Monrad, M. (2007). *High school dropout: A quick stats fact sheet*. Retrieved from http://www.betterhighschools.org/docs/NHSC_DropoutFactSheet.pdf

Monteiro, C. A., Levy, R. B., Claro, R. M., de Castro, I. R. R., & Cannon, G. (2010). Increasing consumption of ultra-processed foods and likely impact on human health: Evidence from Brazil. *Public Health Nutrition, 14*(1), 5–13. doi:10.1017/S1368980010003241

Montgomery, D. E., Anderson, M., & Uhl, E. (2008). Interference control in preschoolers: Factors influencing performance on the day-night task. *Infant and Child Development, 17*(5), 457–470. doi:10.1002/icd.559

Moon, C., Cooper, R. P., & Fifer, W. (1993). Two-day-olds prefer their native language. *Infant Behavior and Development, 16*, 495–500. doi:10.1016/0163-6383(93)80007-U

Moore, K. I., & Persaud, T. V. N. (2003). *Before we are born* (6th ed.). Philadelphia, PA: Elsevier Saunders.

Moore, M. K., & Meltzoff, A. N. (2004). Object permanence after a 24-hr delay and leaving the locale of disappearance: The role of memory, space and identity. *Developmental*

*Psychology, 40*(4), 606–620. doi:10.1037/0012-1649.40.4.606

Morelli, G. A., Rogoff, B., & Angelillo, C. (2003). Cultural variation in young children's access to work or involvement in specialised child-focused activities. *International Journal of Behavioral Development, 27*(3), 264–274. doi:10.1080/ 01650250244000335

Morelli, G. A., Rogoff, B., Oppenheim, D., & Goldsmith, D. (1992). Cultural variation in infants' sleeping arrangements: Questions of independence. *Developmental Psychology, 28*, 604–613.

Morokuma, S., Doria, V., Ierullo, A. Kinukawa, N., Fukushima, K., Nakano, H., . . . Papageorghioul, A. T. (2008). Developmental change in fetal response to repeated low-intensity sound. *Developmental Science 11*(1), 47–52. doi:10.1111/j.1467-7687.2007.00646.x

Morra, S., Gobbo, C., Marini, Z., & Sheese, R. (2008). *Cognitive development: Neo-Piagetian Perspectives*. New York, NY: Taylor & Francis Group/Erlbaum.

Morris, E. J. (2012). Respect, protection, faith and love: Major care constructs identified within the subculture of selected urban African American adolescent gang members. *Journal of Transcultural Nursing, 23*(3), 262–269. doi:10.1177/1043659612441014

Morrissey, T. W., Lekies, K. S., & Cochran, M. M. (2007). Implementing New York's universal pre-kindergarten program: An exploratory study of systemic impacts. *Early Education and Development, 18*(4), 573–596. doi:10.1080/10409280701681649

Morrow, L. M. (2005). *Literacy development in the early years: Helping children read and write* (5th ed.). Boston, MA Pearson/Allyn & Bacon.

Morse, S. B., Zheng, H., Tang, Y., Roth, J. (2009). Early school-age outcomes of late preterm infants. *Pediatrics, 123*(4), e622.

Mortensen, E. L., Michaelsen, K. F., Sanders, S. A., & Reinisch, J. M. (2002). The association between duration of breastfeeding and adult intelligence. *Journal of the American Medical Association, 287*(18), 2365–2371.

Morton, J., & Johnson, M. H. (1991). CONSPEC and CONLERN: A two-process theory of infant face recognition. *Psychological Review, 98*(2), 164–181. doi:10.1037/0033-295X.98.2.164

Mosher, W. D., & Jones, J. (2010). Use of contraception in the United States: 1982–2008. *Vital and Health Statistics, 23*(29). Retrieved from http://www.cdc.gov/NCHS/data/series/sr_23/sr23_029.pdf

Mosher, W. D., Chandra, A., & Jones, J. (2005). Sexual behavior and selected health measures: Men and women 15–44 years of age, United States, 2002. Advance data from *Vital and Health Statistics, 362*.

Mosier, C. E., & Rogoff, B. (1994). Infants' instrumental use of their mothers to achieve their goals. *Child Development, 65*(1), 70–79. doi:10.1111/j.1467-8624.1994.tb00735.x

Moskowitz, S. M., Chmiel, J. F., Sternen, D. L., Cheng, E., & Cutting, G. R. (2008). *CFTR-related disorders. GeneReviews.* Retrieved from http://www.ncbi.nlm.nih.gov/bookshelf/br.fcgi?book=gene&part=cf(pmid:20301428)

Moss, M. (2013, February 20). The extraordinary science of addictive junk food. *The New York Times Sunday Magazine*. Retrieved from http://www.nytimes.com/2013/02/24/magazine/the-extraordinary-science-of-junk-food.html?pagewanted=all&_r=0

Mouradian, W. E., Wehr, E., & Crall, J. J. (2000). Disparities in children's oral health and access to dental care. *Journal of the American Medical Association, 284*(2), 2625–2631. doi:10.1001/jama.284.20.2625

Moyle, J. J., Fox, A. M., Arthur, M., Bynevelt, M., & Burnett, J. R. (2007). Meta-analysis of neuropsychological symptoms of adolescents and adults with PKU. *Neuropsychology Review, 17*(2), 91–101. doi:10.1007/s11065-007-9021-2

Muir, D., & Field, J. (1979). Newborn infants orient to sounds. *Child Development, 50*, 431–436. doi:10.1111/1467-8624.ep12421745

Mulder, E. J., Robles deMedina, P. G., Huizink, A. C., Van Den Bergh, B. R., Buitelaar, J. K., & Visser, G. H. (2002). Prenatal maternal stress: Effects on pregnancy and the (unborn) child. *Early Human Development, 70*(1–2), 3–14.

Mullen, E. M. (1995). *Mullen Scales of Early Learning* (AGS ed.). Circle Pines, MN: American Guidance Service Inc.

Muller, U., Kerns, K. A., & Konkin, K. (2012). Test-retest reliability and practice effects of executive function tasks in preschool children. *The Clinical Neuropsychologist, 26*(2), 271–287. doi:10.1080/13854046.2011.645558

Müllerová, D. & Kopecký, J. (2007). White adipose tissue: Storage and effector site for environmental pollutants. *Physiological Research, 56*, 375–381.

Mullins, T. L. K., Zimet, G. D., Rosenthal, S. L., Morrow, C., Ding, L., Shew, M., . . . Kahn, J. A. (2012). Adolescent perceptions of risk and need for safer sexual behaviors after first human papillomavirus vaccination. *Archives of Pediatric and Adolescent Medicine, 166*(1), 82–88. doi:10.1001/archpediatrics.2011.186.

Mullis, I. V. S., Martin, M. O., Gonzalez, E. J., & Kennedy, A. M. (2003). PIRLS 2001 international report: IEA's study of reading literacy achievement in primary schools. Chestnut Hill, MA: Boston College. Retrieved from http://timss.bc.edu/pirls2001.html

Munakata, Y. (2006). Information processing approaches to development. In D. Kuhn & R. S. Siegler (Eds.), *Handbook of child psychology: Vol. 2. Cognition, perception, and language* (6th ed., pp. 426–463). Hoboken, NJ: Wiley.

Murdock, T. B., & Bolch, M. B. (2005). Risk and protective factors for poor school adjustment in lesbian, gay, and bisexual (LGB) high school youth: Variable and person-centered analyses. *Psychology in the Schools, 42*(2), 159–172. doi:10.1002/pits.20054

Murphy, K., McKone, E., & Slee, J. (2003). Dissociations between implicit and explicit memory in children: The role of strategic processing and the knowledge base. *Journal of Experimental Child Psychology, 84* (2), 124–165.

Murray, C. J. L., & Frenk, J. (2010). Ranking 37th—measuring the performance of the U.S. health care system. *New England Journal of Medicine, 362*, 98–99.

Myers, B. J. (1984). Mother-infant bonding: The status of this critical-period hypothesis. *Developmental Review, 4*(3), 240–274. doi:10.1016/S0273-2297(84)80007-6

Myowa-Yamakoshi, M., Tomonaga, M., Tanaka, M., & Matsuzawa, T. (2004). Imitation in neonatal chimpanzees (Pan troglodytes). *Developmental Science*, 7(4), 437–442. doi:10.1111/j.1467-7687.2004.00364.x

Nachtigall, R. D., Becker, G., Quiroga, S. S., & Tschann, J. M. (1998). The disclosure decision: Concerns and issues of parents of children conceived through donor insemination. *American Journal of Obstetrics & Gynecology, 178*(6), 1165–1170. doi:10.1016/S0002-9378(98)70318-7

Nag, M. (1994, September 10). Beliefs and practices about food during pregnancy. *Economic and Political Weekly*, 2427–2438.

Nagy, E. (2006). From imitation to conversation: The first dialogues with human neonates. *Infant and Child Development 15*(3), 223–232. doi:10.1002/icd.460

Nagy, E., & Molnar, P. (1994). Homo imitans or homo provocans? *International Journal of Psychophysiology, 18*(2), 128.

Nagy, E., & Molnar, P. (2004). Homo imitans or homo provocans? Human imprinting model of neonatal initiation. *Infant Behavior and Development, 27*(1), 54–63. doi:10.1016/j.infbeh.2003.06.004

Nagy, E., Liotti, M., Brown, S., Waiter, G., Bromiley, A., Trevarthen, C., & Bardos, G. (2010). The neural mechanisms of reciprocal communication. *Brain Research, 1353*, 159–167. doi:10.1016/j.brainres.2010.07.066

Nagy, W. E., & Scott, J. A. (2000). Vocabulary processes. In M. L. Kamil, P. B. Mosenthal, P. D. Pearson, & R. Barr (Eds.), *Handbook of reading research, Vol. III* (pp. 269–284). Mahwah, NJ: Erlbaum.

Nation, M., Crusto, C., Wandersman, A., Kumpfer, K., Seybolt, D., Morrissey-Kane, E., & Davino, K. (2003). What works in prevention: Principles of effective prevention programs. *American Psychologist, 58*(6–7), 449–456.

National Association for the Education of Young Children. (2009). Position statements of NAEYC. Retrieved from http://www.naeyc.org/positionstatements

National Association of School Nurses [NASN]. (2006). *Issue brief: School nursing management of students with chronic health conditions.* Silver Spring, MD: Author.

National Association of School Nurses [NASN]. (2010). *Position statement: Caseload assignments.* Silver Spring, MD: Author.

National Association of School Nurses [NASN]. (2011). *Position statement: Medication administration in the school setting.* Silver Spring, MD: Author.

National Campaign to Prevent Teen Pregnancy. (2011). *Counting it up: The public costs of teen childbearing: Key data*. Retrieved from http://www.thenationalcampaign.org/costs/pdf/countingit-up/key-data.pdf

National Cancer Institute. (2012). *Cervical cancer prevention (PDQ®)*. Retrieved from http://www.cancer.gov/cancertopics/pdq/prevention/cervical/Patient

National Center for Education Statistics. (2011). *Student reports of bullying and cyber-bullying: Results from the 2009 School Crime Supplement to the National Crime Victimization Survey*. Retrieved from http://nces.ed.gov/whatsnew/commissioner/remarks2011/09_22_2011.asp

National Center for Health Statistics. (2006). *Trends in the Health of Americans chartbook.* Hyattsville, MD: Author. Retrieved from http://www.cdc.gov/nchs/data/hus/hus06.pdf

National Center for Health Statistics. (2007). *Trends in the health of Americans chartbook.* Hyattsville, MD: Author. Retrieved from http://www.cdc.gov/nchs/data/hus/hus07.pdf#025

National Center for Health Statistics. (2008). *2004 period linked birth/infant death data* (Prepared by the March of Dimes Perinatal Data Center). Retrieved from http://www.marchofdimes.com/peristats/Peristats.aspx

National Center for Health Statistics. (2009). *Health, United States, 2009*. Hyattsville, MD: Author. Retrieved from http://www.cdc.gov/nchs/data/hus/hus09.pdf

National Center for Health Statistics. (2010). *Health, United States, 2009*. Hyattsville, MD: Author. Retrieved from http://www.cdc.gov/nchs/data/hus/hus09.pdf

National Center for Health Statistics. (2012). *Health, United States, 2011: With special feature on socioeconomic status and health*. Hyattsville, MD: Author. Retrieved from http://www.cdc.gov/nchs/data/hus/hus11.pdf

National Center for Injury Prevention and Control. (2011). *Fatal injury and leading causes of death reports for 2010*. Atlanta, GA: Centers for Disease Control and Prevention. Search of database for all years and ages is available at http://webappa.cdc.gov/sasweb/ncipc/leadcaus10_us.html

National Council on the Developing Child. (2004). *Young children develop in an environment of relationships* (Working Paper No. 1). Retrieved from http://www.developingchild.harvard.edu

National Fragile X Foundation. (2010). *What is Fragile X?* Retrieved from http://www.nfxf.org/html/what.htm

National Geographic Society. (n.d.). *The Genographic Project.* Retrieved from https://genographic.nationalgeographic.com/genographic/index.html

National Health and Medical Research Council of the Australian Government. (2007). *A systematic review of the efficacy and safety of fluoridation.* ISBN Online: 1864964154

National Highway Traffic Safety Administration. (2008). *Graduated driver licensing system*. Washington, DC: U.S. Department of Transportation, National Highway Traffic Safety Administration.

National Highway Traffic Safety Administration. (2010). *Fatality analysis reporting system (FARS), 2009*. Washington, DC: U.S. Department of Transportation, National Highway Traffic Safety Administration, National Center for Statistics and Analysis.

National Human Genome Research Institute. (2005). The use of racial, ethnic, and ancestral categories in human genetics research. *American Journal of Human Genetics, 77*(4): 519–532. doi:10.1086/491747

National Human Genome Research Institute. (2009). *DNA, genes and genomes.* Retrieved from http://www.genome.gov

National Institute of Allergy and Infectious Diseases. (2004). *HIV Infection in infants and children*. Retrieved from http://www.niaid.nih.gov/factsheets/hivchildren.htm

National Institute of Allergy and Infectious Diseases. (2010a). *Food allergy: An overview* (U.S. Department of Health and Human Services National Institutes of Health Publication No. 11-5518). Retrieved from http://www.niaid.nih.gov/topics/foodallergy/documents/foodallergy.pdf

National Institute of Allergy and Infectious Diseases. (2010b). *Guidelines for the diagnosis and management of food allergy in the United States: Summary of the NIAID-Sponsored Expert Panel Report* (U.S. Department of Health and Human Services National Institutes of Health Publication No. 11-7700). Retrieved from http://www.niaid.nih.gov/topics/foodAllergy/clinical/Documents/FAGuidelinesExecSummary.pdf

National Institute of Arthritis and Musculoskeletal and Skin Diseases. (2009). *Sports injuries.* Retrieved from http://www.niams.nih.gov/Health_Info/Sports_Injuries/child_sports_injuries.asp#most

National Institute of Child Health and Human Development [NICHD]. (2010). *Facts about Down Syndrome.* Retrieved from http://www.nichd.nih.gov/publications/pubs/downsyndrome.cfm#DownSyndrome

National Institute of Child Health and Human Development Early Child Care Research Network. (1997). Child care in the first year of life. *Merrill-Palmer Quarterly, 43*(3), 340–360.

National Institute of Child Health and Human Development Early Child Care Research Network. (2000). Characteristics and quality of child care for toddlers and preschoolers. *Applied Developmental Science, Special Issue: The Effects of Quality Care on Child Development, 4*(3), 116 135. doi:10.1207/S1532480XADS0403_2

National Institute of Child Health and Human Development Early Child Care Research Network. (2002). Child-care structure → process → outcome: Direct and indirect effects of child-care quality on young children's development. *Psychological Science, 13*(3), 199–206. doi:10.1111/1467-9280.00438

National Institute of Child Health and Human Development Early Child Care Research Network. (2005). Duration and developmental timing of poverty and children's cognitive and social development from birth to third grade. *Child Development, 76*(4), 795–810. doi:10.1111/j.1467-8624.2005.00878.x

National Institute of Child Health and Human Development Early Child Care Research Network & Duncan, G. J. (2003). Modeling the impacts of child care quality on children's preschool cognitive development. *Child Development, 74*(5), 1454–1475. doi:10.1111/1467-8624.00617

National Institute of Mental Health. (2008). *Attention deficit hyperactivity disorder (ADHD)* (NIH Publication No. 08–3572). Retrieved from http://www.nimh.nih.gov/health/publications/attention-deficit-hyperactivity-disorder/complete-index.shtml

National Institute of Neurological Disorders and Stroke (NINDS). (2006). *Cerebral Palsy: Hope through research*. (NIH Publication No. 06–159). Retrieved from http://www.ninds.nih.gov/disorders/cerebral_palsy/detail_cerebral_palsy.htm

National Institute on Alcohol Abuse and Alcoholism (NIAAA). (2006). Underage drinking: Why do adolescents drink, what are the risks, and how can underage drinking be prevented? *Alcohol Alert, 67*. Rockville, MD: Author. Retrieved from http://pubs.niaaa.nih.gov/publications/AA67/AA67.pdf

National Institute on Alcohol Abuse and Alcoholism (NIAAA). (2009). A developmental perspective on underage alcohol use. *Alcohol Alert, 78*. Rockville, MD: Author. Retrieved from http://pubs.niaaa.nih.gov/publications/AA78/AA78.pdf

National Institute on Deafness and Other Communication Disorders. (2002). Otitis media (ear infection) (National Institutes for Health Publication No. 974216). Bethesda, MD: Author.

National Institute on Drug Abuse (2010). *Cocaine: Abuse and addiction* (NIH Publication Number 10–4166). Washington, DC: U.S. Department of Health and Human Services.

National Institute on Drug Abuse. (2008). *InfoFacts: Steroids (anabolic-androgenic)*. Retrieved from http://www.nida.nih.gov/Infofacts/steroids.html

National Institutes of Health Consensus Development Conference Statement. (2010). Vaginal birth after cesarean: New insights March 8–10, 2010. *Obstetrics & Gynecology, 115*(6), 1279–1295.

National Institutes of Health. (2009). *Stem cells.* Retrieved from http://stemcells.nih.gov/info

National Institutes of Health. (2011). *Federal Policy. Stem Cell Litigation*. Retrieved from http://stemcells.nih.gov/policy

National Research Council. (2009). *Mathematics learning in early childhood: Paths toward excellence and equity.* Washington, DC: National Academies Press.

National Research Council and Institute of Medicine. (2004). *Children's health: The nation's wealth.* Washington, DC: National Academies Press.

National Research Council and Institute of Medicine. (2007). *Challenges in adolescent health care: Workshop report*. Washington, DC: National Academies Press.

National Research Council Committee on Educational Interventions for Children with Autism. (2001). *Educating children with autism.* Washington, DC: National Academies Press.

National Safety Council. (2010). *Understanding the distracted brain*. Retrieved from http://www.nsc.org/safety_road/Distracted_Driving/Documents/Dstrct_Drvng_White_Paper_Fnl(5-25-10).pdf

National Scientific Council on the Developing Child. (2005). *Excessive stress disrupts the architecture of the developing brain* (Working Paper No. 3). Retrieved from http://www.developingchild.harvard.edu

National Youth Court Center. (2010). *I joined teen court to help others like it helped me*. Retrieved from http://youthcourt.net/wp-content/uploads/2010/05/success_stories1.pdf

National Youth Gang Survey Analysis. (2009). *Gender of gang members*. Retrieved from http://www.nationalgangcenter.gov/survey-analysis/demographics

Natsuaki, M. N., Ge, X., Reiss, D., & Neiderhiser, J. M. (2009). Aggressive behavior between siblings and the development of externalizing problems: Evidence from a genetically sensitive study. *Developmental Psychology, 45*(4), 1009–1018. doi:10.1037/a0015698

Nazzi, T., Floccia, C., & Bertoncini, J. (1998). Discrimination of pitch contours by neonates. *Infant Behavior and Development, 21*(4), 779–784. doi:10.1016/S0163–6383(98)90044–3

Needelman, H., Jackson, B., McMorris, C., & Roberts, H. (2008). Referral for early intervention services in late premature infants with a NICU experience. *Journal of Neonatal-Perinatal Medicine, 1*, 169–174.

Neild, R. C. (2009). Falling off track during the transition to high school: What we know and what can be done. *Future of Children, 19*(1), 53–76.

Nelson, C. (1995). The ontogeny of human memory: A cognitive neuroscience perspective. *Developmental Psychology, 31*, 723–738.

Nelson, C., Morse, P., & Leavitt, L. (1979). Recognition of facial expressions by seven-month-old infants. *Child Development, 50*, 1239–1242.

Nelson, C. A. (2004). What do studies of face processing tell us about trajectories of development? A commentary on Cashon and Cohen. *Journal of Cognition and Development, 1*, 131–135. doi:10.1207/s15327647jcd0501_13

Nelson, C. A. (2011). Neural development and lifelong plasticity. In D. P. Keating (Ed.), *Nature and nurture in early development* (pp. 45–69). New York, NY: Cambridge University Press.

Nelson, C. A., & Luciana, M. (2008). *Handbook of Developmental Cognitive Neuroscience* (2nd ed.). Cambridge, MA: MIT Press.

Nelson, C. A., & McCleery, J. P. (2008). Use of event-related potentials in the study of typical and atypical development. *Journal of the American Academy of Child & Adolescent Psychiatry, 47*(11), 1252–1261. doi:10.1097/CHI.0b013e318185a6d8

Nelson, C. A., Bos, K., Gunnar, M. R., & Sonuga-Barke, E. J. S. (2011). Children without permanent parents: Research, practice, and policy: V. The neurobiological toll of early human deprivation. *Monographs of the Society for Research in Child Development, 76*(4), 127–146. doi:10.1111/j.1540–5834.2011.00630.x

Nelson, C. A., De Hann, M., & Thomas, K. M. (2006). *Neuroscience of cognitive development: The role of experience and the developing brain.* Hoboken, NJ: Wiley.

Nelson, C. A., Furtado, E. A., Fox, N. A. & Zeanah, C. H. (2009). The deprived human brain. *American Scientist, 97*, 222–229.

Nelson, C. A., Thomas, K. M., & de Haan, M. (2006). Neural bases of cognitive development. In D. Kuhn & R. S. Siegler (Eds.), *Handbook of child psychology: Vol. 2. Cognition, perception, and language* (6th ed., pp. 3–57). Hoboken, NJ: Wiley.

Nelson, C. A., Thomas, K. M., & de Haan, M. (2006). *Neuroscience of cognitive development: The role of experience and the developing brain.* Hoboken, NJ: Wiley.

Nelson, C. A., Zeanah, C. H., Fox, N. A., Marshall, P. J., Smyke, A., & Guthrie, D. (2007). Cognitive recovery in socially deprived young children: The Bucharest early intervention project. *Science, 318*, 1937–1940.

Nelson, C. A., Zeanah, C. H., Fox, N., Marshall, P. J., Smyke, A. T., & Guthrie, D. (2008). Letter to the editor. *Science, 319*, 1336–1337.

Nelson, C. H., & de Haan, M. (1996). Neural correlates of infants' visual responsiveness to facial expressions of emotion. *Developmental Psychobiology, 29*(7), 577–595.

Nelson, D. B., Grisso, J. A., Joffe, M. M., Brensinger, C., Shaw, L., & Datner, E. (2003). Does stress influence early pregnancy loss? *Annals of Epidemiology, 13*(4), 223–229. doi:10.1016/S1047–2797(02)00419–2.

Nelson, E. E., Leibenluft, E., McClure, E., & Pine, D. S. (2005). The social re-orientation of adolescence: A neuroscience perspective on the process and its relation to psychopathology. *Psychological Medicine, 35*(2), 163–174. doi:10.1017/S0033291704003915

Nelson, K. (1977). Facilitating children's syntax acquisition. *Developmental Psychology, 13*(2), 101–107. doi:10.1037/0012–1649.13.2.101

Nelson, K. (1986). *Event knowledge: Structure and function in development.* Hillsdale, NJ: Erlbaum.

Nelson, K. E., Welsh, J. A., Trup, E. M. V., & Greenberg, M. T. (2011). Language delays of impoverished preschool children in relation to early academic and emotion recognition skills. *First Language, 31*(2), 164–194. doi:10.1177/0142723710391887

Nelson, K., & Fivush, R. (2000). The socialization of memory. In E. Tulving & F. Craik (Eds.), *The Oxford handbook of memory* (pp. 283–296). London, UK: Oxford University Press.

Nelson, K., & Gruendel, J. (1986). Children's scripts. In K. Nelson (Ed.), *Event knowledge: Structure and function in development* (pp. 21–46). Hillsdale, NJ: Erlbaum.

Nelson, K., & Gruendel, J. M. (1981). Generalized event representations: Basic building blocks of cognitive development. In M. E. Lamb & A. L. Brown (Eds.), *Advances in development psychology* (Vol. 1, pp. 131–158). Hillsdale, NJ: Erlbaum.

Neppl, T., Conger, R., Scaramella, L., & Ontai, L. (2009). Intergenerational continuity in parenting behavior: Mediating pathways and child effects. *Developmental Psychology*, 45, 1241–1256. doi:10.1037/a0014850

Nestle, M. (2007). *Food politics: How the food industry influences nutrition and health* (2nd ed.). Berkeley, CA: University of California Press.

Neubauer, A., Gawrilow, C., & Hasselhorn, M. (2012). The watch-and-wait task: On the reliability and validity of a new method of assessing self-control in preschool children. *Learning and Individual Differences, 22*(6) 770–777. doi:10.1016/j.lindif.2012.05.006

Neumann, E., McCloskey, M. S., & Felio, A. C. (1999). Cross-language positive priming disappears, negative priming does not: Evidence for two sources of selective inhibition. *Memory & Cognition, 27*(6), 1051–1063. doi:10.3758/BF03201234

Neveus, T., Eggert, P., Evans, J., Macedo, A., Rittig, S., Tekgül, S., . . . Robson, L. (2010). Evaluation of and treatment for monosymptomatic enuresis: A standardization document from the International Children's Continence Society. *The Journal of Urology, 183*, 441–447. doi:10.1016/j.juro.2009.10.043

Nevo, E., & Breznitz, Z. (2013). The development of working memory from kindergarten to first grade in children with different decoding skills. *Journal of Experimental Child Psychology, 114*(2) 217–228. doi:10.1016/jjecp.2012.09.004.

New, R. (2000). The Reggio Emilia approach: It's not an approach—it's an attitude. In J. Roopnarine & J. Johnson (Eds.), *Approaches to early childhood education*. Columbus, OH: Merrill.

Newell, K. (1986). Constraints on the development of coordination. In M. G. Wade & H. T. A. Whiting (Eds.), *Motor development in children: Aspects of coordination and control* (pp. 341–360). Amsterdam, Netherlands: Martinus Nijhoff.

Newport, E. L. (1990). Maturational constraints on language learning. *Cognitive Science, 14*, 11–28. doi:10.1207/s15516709cog1401_2

Newport, E. L., & Aslin, R. N. (2004). Learning at a distance: I. Statistical learning of non-adjacent dependencies. *Cognitive Psychology, 48*, 127–162.

Newton, E., & Jenvey, V. (2011). Play and theory of mind: Associations with social competence in young children. *Early Child Development and Care, 181*(6), 761–773. doi:10.1080/03004430.2010.486898

Newton, X. (2010). End-of-high-school mathematics attainment: How did students get there? *Teachers College Record, 112*(4), 1064–1095.

Ng, F. F., Pomerantz, E. M., & Lam, S. (2007). European American and Chinese parents' responses to children's success and failure: Implications for children's responses. *Developmental Psychology, 43*(5), 1239–1255. doi:10.1037/0012-1649.43.5.1239

NICHD Early Child Care Research Network (2004). Trajectories of physical aggression from toddlerhood to middle childhood. *Monographs of the Society for Research in Child Development, 69*(4), 1–143. doi:2004-22480-001

Nicolson, S., Judd, F., Thomson-Salo, F., & Mitchell, S. (2013). Supporting the adolescent mother-infant relationship: Preliminary trial of a brief perinatal attachment intervention. *Archives of Womens Mental Health*. doi:10.1007/s00737-013-0364-9

Nielsen, G. L., Sorensen, H. T., Larsen, H., & Pedersen, L. (2001). Risk of adverse birth outcome and miscarriage in pregnant users of non-steroidal anti-inflammatory drugs: Population-based observational study and

case-control study. *British Medical Journal, 332*, 266–270. doi:10.1136/bmj.322.7281.266
Nielsen, M., Simcock, G., & Jenkins, L. (2008). The effect of social engagement on 24-month-olds' imitation from live and televised models. *Developmental Science, 11*(5), 722–731. doi:10.1111/j.1467–7687.2008.00722.x
Nielsen-Bohlman, L., Panzer, A. M., & Kindig, D. A. (2004). Institute of Medicine Committee on Health Literacy. *Health literacy: A prescription to end confusion.* Washington, DC: National Academies Press.
Nigro, G., Adler, S. P., La Torre, R., & Best, A. M. (2005). Passive immunization during pregnancy for congenital cytomegalovirus infection. *New England Journal of Medicine 353*, 1350–1362. doi:10.1056/NEJMoa043337
Nikapota, A. D. (2002). Cultural and ethnic issues in service provision. In M. Rutter & E. Taylor (Eds.), *Child and adolescent psychiatry* (4th ed., pp. 1146–1157). Oxford, UK: Blackwell.
Ninio, A., & Snow, C. E. (1996). *Pragmatic development.* Boulder, CO: Westview Press.
Nisbett, R. (2007). A psychological perspective—past, present, and future. In S. Kitayama & D. Cohen (Eds.), *Handbook of cultural psychology* (pp. 837–844). New York, NY: Guilford.
Nisbett, R. E. (2005). Heredity, environment, and race differences in IQ: A commentary on Rushton and Jensen. *Psychology, Public Policy, and Law, 11*(2), 302–310. doi:10.1037/1076–8971.11.2.302
Nisbett, R. E. (2009). *Intelligence and how to get it: Why schools and culture count.* New York, NY: Norton.
No Child Left Behind (NCLB) Act of 2001, 20 U.S.C.A. § 6301 *et seq.* (2001).
Nomura, Y., Wickramaratne, P. J., Pilowsky, D. J., Newcorn, J. H., Bruder-Costello, B., Davey, C., . . . Weissman, M. N. (2007). Low birth weight and risk of affective disorders and selected medical illness in offspring at high and low risk for depression. *Comprehensive Psychiatry, 48*, 470–478. doi:10.1016/j.comppsych.2007.04.005
Nord, M., Coleman-Jensen, A., Andrews, M., & Carlson, S. (2010). *Household Food Security in the United States, 2009* (E 108, Department Economic Research Service).
Norenzayan, A., Choi, I., & Peng, K. (2007). Perception and cognition. In S. Kitayama & D. Cohen (Eds.), *Handbook of cultural psychology* (pp. 569–594). New York, NY: Guilford.
Nsamenang, A. B. (1992). *Human development in cultural context: A third-world perspective.* Newbury Park, CA: Sage.
Nucci, L. P., Killen, M., & Smetana, J. G. (1996). Autonomy and the personal: Negotiation and social reciprocity in adult-child social exchanges. *New Directions for Child and Adolescent Development, 73*, 7–24. doi:10.1002/cd.23219967303
Nugent, J. K. (1985). *Using the NBAS with infants and their families.* White Plains, NY: March of Dimes Birth Defects Foundation.
Nugent, J. K. (1991). Cultural and psychological influences on the father's role in infant development. *Journal of Marriage and the Family, 53*(2), 475–485.
Nugent, J. K. (1994). Cross-cultural research in child development: Implications for clinicians. *Zero to Three, 15*(2), 1–8.
Nugent, J. K., & Alhaffer, D. (2006). The NBO and the March of Dimes NICU Family Support program: The effects of the NBO as an educational and emotional support system for parents of premature infants. Retrieved from http://www.brazelton-institute.com/abinitio2006summer/art5.htm
Nugent, J. K., & Brazelton, T. B. (2000). Preventive infant mental health: Uses of the Brazelton scale. In J. Osoksky & H. E. Fitzgerald (Eds.), *WAIMH handbook of infant mental health* (Vol. 2, pp. 159–202). New York, NY: Wiley.
Nugent, J. K., Blanchard, Y., & Stewart, J. S. (2008). Supporting parents of premature infants: An infant-focused family-centered approach. In D. Brodsky & M. A. Ouellette (Eds.), *Primary care of the premature infant* (pp. 255–267). New York, NY: Elsevier.
Nugent, J. K., Keefer, C. H., Minear, S., Johnson, L., & Blanchard, Y. (2007). *Understanding newborn behavior and early relationships: The newborn behavioral observations (NBO) system handbook.* Baltimore, MD: Brookes.
Nugent, J. K., Lester, B. M., & Brazelton, T. B. (Eds.). (1989). *The cultural context of infancy: Vol. 1. Biology, culture and infant development.* Norwood, NJ: Ablex.
Nugent, J. K., Lester, B. M., & Brazelton, T. B. (Eds.). (1991). *The cultural context of infancy: Vol. 2. Multicultural and Interdisciplinary Approaches to Parent-Infant Relations.* Norwood, NJ: Ablex.
Nugent, J. K., Petrauskas, B. J., & Brazelton, T. B. (Eds.). (2009). *The newborn as a person: Enabling health infant development worldwide.* Hoboken, NJ: Wiley.
Nulman, I., Rovet, D., Altman, D., Bradley, C., Einarson, T., & Koren, G. (1994). Neurodevelopment of adopted children exposed in utero to cocaine. *Canadian Medical Association Journal, 151*, 1591–1597.
Nutbeam, D. (2000). Health literacy as a public health goal: A challenge for contemporary health education and communication strategies into the 21st century. *Health Promotion International, 15*, 259–67. doi:10.1093/heapro/15.3.259
Nyborg, H. (2004). Multivariate modeling of testosterone-dominance associations. *Behavioral and Brain Sciences, 27*, 155–159.
O'Brien, L., Albert, D., Chein, J., & Steinberg, L. (2011). Adolescents prefer more immediate rewards when in the presence of their peers. *Journal of Research on Adolescence, 21*(4), 747–753. doi:10.1111/j.1532–7795.2011.00738.x
O'Donnell, K., O'Connor, T. G., & Glover, V. (2009). Prenatal stress and neurodevelopment of the child: Focus on the HPA axis and role of the placenta. *Developmental Science, 32*(4), 285–292. doi:10.1159/000216539
O'Grady, W. (2005). *How children learn language.* Cambridge, UK: Cambridge University Press.
Oakes, L. M., & Madole, K. L. (2003). Principles of developmental change in infants' category formation. In D. H. Rakison & L. M. Oakes (Eds.), *Early concept and category development: Making sense of the blooming, buzzing confusion* (pp. 132–158). New York, NY: Oxford University Press.
Oberman, L. M., & Ramachandran, V. S. (2007). The simulating social mind: The role of the mirror neuron system and simulation in the social and communicative deficits of autism spectrum disorders. *Psychological Bulletin, 133*(2), 310–327. doi:10.1037/0033-2909.133.2.310
Oberman, L. M., Hubbard, E. M., McCleery, J. P., Altschuler, E. L., Ramachandran, V. S., & Pineda, J. A. (2005). EEG evidence for mirror neuron dysfunction in autism spectrum disorders. *Cognitive Brain Research, 24*, 190–198.
Oddy, W. H. (2012). Infant feeding and obesity risk in the child. *Breastfeeding Review, 20*(2), 7–12.
Odell, C., O'Hara, K., Kiel, S., & McCullough, K. (2007). Emergency management of seizures in the school setting. *Journal of School Nursing, 23*, 158–165. doi:10.1177/10598405070230030601
Odom, S. L., Vitztum, J., Wolery, R., Lieber, J., Sandall, S., Hanson, M. J., . . . Horn, E. (2004). Preschool inclusion in the United States: A review of research from an ecological systems perspective. *Journal of Research in Special Education Needs, 4*(1), 17–49. doi:10.1111/J.1471-3802. 2004.00016.x
Odom, S., Zercher, C., Li, S., Marquart, J., Sandall, S., & Brown, W. (2006). Social acceptance and rejection of preschool children with disabilities: A mixed-methods analysis. *Journal of Educational Psychology, 98*, 807–823. doi:10.1037/0022-0663. 98.4.807
Offit, P. A., Quarles, J., Gerber, M. A., Hackett, C. J., Marcuse, E. K., Kollman, T. R., . . . Landry, S. (2002). Addressing parents' concerns: Do multiple vaccines overwhelm or weaken the infant's immune system? *Pediatrics, 109*(1), 124–129. doi:10.1542/peds.109.1.124
Ogbu, J. U. (1994). Racial stratification and education in the United States: Why inequality persists. *Teachers College Record, 96*(2), 264–298.
Ogden, C. L., Carroll, M., & Flegal, K. (2008). High body mass index for age among U.S. children and adolescents, 2003–2006. *Journal of the American Medical Association, 299*(20), 2401–2405.
Ogden, C. L., & Carroll, M. (2010). *Prevalence of obesity among children and adolescents: United States, trends 1963–1965 through 2007–2008.* Hyattsville, MD: National Center for Health Statistics. Retrieved from http://www.cdc.gov/nchs/data/hestat/obesity_child_07_08/obesity_child_07_08.pdf
Ogden, C. L., Carroll, M. D., Curtin, L. R., Lamb, M. M., & Flegal, K. M. (2010). Prevalence of high body mass index in U.S. children and adolescents, 2007–2008. *Journal of the American Medical Association, 303*, 242–249.
Ogden, C. L., Carroll, M. D., Kit, B. K., & Flegal, K. M. (2012a) *Prevalence of obesity in the United States, 2009–2010* (Data Brief No. 82). Hyattsville, MD: National Center for Health Statistics. Retrieved from http://www.cdc.gov/nchs/data/databriefs/db82.pdf
Ogden, C. L., Carroll, M. D., Kit, B. K., & Flegal, K. M. (2012b). Prevalence of obesity and trends in body mass index among U.S. children

and adolescents, 2009–2010. *Journal of the American Medical Association, 307*(5), 483–490. doi:10.1001/jama.2012.40

Oh, W., Rubin, K. H., Bowker, J. C., Booth-LaForce, C., Rose-Krasnor, L., & Laursen, B. (2008). Trajectories of social withdrawal from middle childhood to early adolescence. *Journal of Abnormal Psychology, 36*(4), 553–566. doi:10.1007/s10802–007–9199–z

Ohgi, S., Fukuda, M., Moriuchi, H., Kusumoto, T., Akiyama, T., Nugent, J. K., & Saitoh, H. (2002). Comparison of kangaroo care and standard care: Behavioral organization, development, and temperament in healthy, low-birth-weight infants through 1 year. *Journal of Perinatology, 22*, 374–379. doi:10.1038/sj.jp.7210749

Ohring, R., Graber, J. A., & Brooks-Gunn, J. (2002). Girls' recurrent and concurrent body dissatisfaction: Correlates and consequences over 8 years. *International Journal of Eating Disorders, 31*(4), 404–415. doi:10.1002/eat.10049

Ojeda, S. R. (1996). Female reproductive function. In J. E. Griffin, & S. R. Ojeda (Eds.), *Textbook of endocrine physiology* (3rd ed., pp. 164–200) Oxford, UK: Oxford University Press.

Okagaki, L., & Sternberg, R. J. (1993). Parental beliefs and children's school performance. *Child Development, 64*(1), 36–56. doi:10.2307/1131436

Olds, D., Henderson, C. R., Cole, R., Eckenrode, J., Kitzman, H., Luckey, D., . . . Powers, J. (1997). Long-term effects of nurse home visitation on children's criminal and antisocial behavior: Fifteen-year follow-up of a randomized controlled trial. *JAMA, 280*, 1238–1244.

Olesen, V., & Woods, N. F. (Eds.). (1986). *Culture, society, and menstruation.* Washington, DC: Hemisphere Publishing.

Oller, D. K., & Eilers, R. E. (Eds.). (2002). *Language and literacy in bilingual children.* Clevedon, UK: Multilingual Matters.

Oller, D. K., Cobo-Lewis, A. B., & Eilers, R. E. (1998). Phonological translation in bilingual and monolingual children. *Applied Psycholinguistics, 19*(2), 259–278. doi:10.1017/S0142716400010067

Olson, D. R. (2012). Commentary on "How do use and comprehension of mental-state language relate to theory of mind in middle childhood?" by I. Grazzani and V. Ornaghi. *Cognitive Development, 27*(2), 112–113. doi:10.1016/j.cogdev.2012.02.001

Olson, K. R., & Dweck, C. S. (2009). Social cognitive development: A new look. *Child Development Perspectives, 3*(1), 60–65. doi:10.1111/j.1750–8606.2008.00078.x

Olthof, T. (2012). Anticipated feelings of guilt and shame as predictors of early adolescents' antisocial and prosocial interpersonal behaviour. *European Journal of Developmental Psychology, 9*(3), 371–388. doi:10.1080/17405629.2012.680300

Onchwari, G., & Keengwe, J. (2011). Examining the relationship of children's behavior to emotion regulation ability. *Early Childhood Education Journal, 39*(4), 279–284. doi:10.1007/s10643-011-0466-9

Online Mendelian Inheritance in Man (OMIM). (2012). *Melanocortin1 receptor* (MIM No. 155555). Baltimore, MD: Johns Hopkins University. Retrieved from http://www.ncbi.nlm.nih.gov/omim/

Online Mendelian Inheritance in Man (OMIM). (2013). *Down syndrome* (MIM No. 190685). Baltimore, MD: Johns Hopkins University. Retrieved from http://www.ncbi.nlm.nih.gov/omim/

Online Mendelian Inheritance in Man (OMIM). (2013). *Fragile X mental retardation syndrome* (MIM No. 300624). Baltimore, MD: Johns Hopkins University. Retrieved from http://www.ncbi.nlm.nih.gov/omim/

Online Mendelian Inheritance in Man (OMIM). (2013). *Schizophrenia* (MIM No. 181500). Baltimore, MD: Johns Hopkins University. Retrieved from http://www.ncbi.nlm.nih.gov/omim/

Opfer, J. E., & Siegler, R. S. (2004). Revising preschoolers' *living things* concept: A microgenetic analysis of conceptual change in basic biology. *Cognitive Psychology, 49*, 301–332. doi:10.1016/j.cogpsych.2004.01.002

Orfield, G. (2004). Losing our future: Minority youth left out. In G. Orfield (Ed.), *Dropouts in America: Confronting the graduation rate crisis* (pp. 1–11). Cambridge, MA: Harvard University Press.

Organisation for Economic Co-operation and Development (2006). *The Program for International Student Assessment (PISA).* Retrieved from http://www.oecd.org/dataoecd/15/13/39725224.pdf

Organization of Teratology Information Specialists. (2003). *Ibuprofen and pregnancy.* Retrieved from http://www.otispregnancy.org/pdf/Ibuprofen.pdf

Organization of Teratology Information Specialists. (2010). *Cocaine and pregnancy.* Retrieved from http://www.otispregnancy.org/files/cocaine.pdf

Orpinas, P., & Horne, A. M. (2006). *Bullying prevention: Creating a positive school climate and developing social competence.* Washington, DC: American Psychological Association.

Osgood, D. W., Wilson, J. K., O'Malley, P. M., & Bachman, J. G. (1996). Routine activities and individual deviant behavior. *American Sociological Review, 61*(4), 635–655. doi:10.2307/2096397

Osofsky, H. J., & Osofsky, J. D. (2010). Understanding and helping traumatized infants and families. In B. M. Lester & J. D. Sparrow (Eds.), *Nurturing children and families: Building on the legacy of T. Berry Brazelton* (pp. 254–263). West Sussex, UK: Wiley–Blackwell.

Osofsky, J. D., & Lieberman, A. F. (2011). A call for integrating a mental health perspective into systems of care for abused and neglected infants and young children. *American Psychologist, 66*(2), 120–128.

Osterhout, L., Poliakov, A., Inoue, K., McLaughlin, J., Valentine, G., Pitkanen, I., . . . Hirschensohn, J. (2008). Second-language learning and changes in the brain. *Journal of Neurolinguistics, 21*(6), 509–521. doi:10.1016/j.jneuroling.2008.01.001

Ostrov, J. M., & Crick, N. R. (2007). Forms and functions of aggression during early childhood: A short-term longitudinal study. *School Psychology Review, 36*(1), 22–43.

Ouellette, G., & Sénéchal, M. (2008). Pathways to literacy: A study of invented spelling and its role in learning to read. *Child Development, 79*(4), 899–913. doi:10.1111/j.1467-8624.2008. 01166.x

Over, H., Carpenter, M. (2013). The social side of imitation. *Child Development Perspectives, 7, 1*, 6–11.

Overbeek, G., Stattin, H., Vermulst, A., Ha, T., & Engels, R. C. M. E. (2007). Parent-child relationships, partner relationships, and emotional adjustment: A birth-to-maturity prospective study. *Developmental Psychology, 43*(2), 429–437. doi:10.1037/0012-1649.43.2.429

Overton, W. (2006). Developmental psychology: Philosophy, concepts, methodology. In R. Lerner (Ed.), *Handbook of child psychology: Vol. 1. Theoretical models of human development* (6th ed., pp. 18–88). Hoboken, NJ: Wiley.

Overton, W. F. (1998). Developmental psychology: Philosophy, concepts, and methodology. In R. M. Lerner & W. Damon (Eds.), *Handbook of child psychology: Vol. 1. Theoretical models of human development* (5th ed., pp. 107–188). New York, NY: Wiley.

Overton, W. F. (Ed.). (1990). *Reasoning, necessity, and logic: Developmental perspectives.* Hillsdale, NJ: Erlbaum.

Owen, D., Andrews, M. H., & Matthews, S. (2005). Maternal adversity, glucocorticoids and programming of neuroendocrine function and behaviour. *Neuroscience and Biobehavior Review, 29*(2), 209–26. doi:10.1016/j.neubiorev.2004.10.004

Owens, R. E. (2011). *Language development: An introduction* (8th ed.). Boston, MA: Allyn & Bacon.

Ozonoff, S., Young, G. S., Carter, A., Messinger, D., Yirmiya, N., Zwaigenbaum, L., Bryson, S., Carver, L. J., Constantino, J. N., Dobkins, K., Hutman, T., Iverson, J. M., Landa, R., Rogers, S. J., Sigman, M., Stone, W. L. (2011). Recurrence risk for autism spectrum disorders: A baby siblings research consortium study. *Pediatrics, 128*(3), 488–495. doi:10.1542/peds.2010–2825

Pachter, L. M., & Dworkin, P. H. (1997). Maternal expectations about normal child development in four cultural groups. *Archives of Pediatrics Adolescent Medicine, 151*, 1144–1150.

Pachter, L. M., Weller, S. C., Baer, R. D., de Alba Garcia, J. E. G., Trotter, R. T., Glazer, M., & Klein, R. (2002). Variation in asthma beliefs and practices among mainland Puerto Ricans, Mexican Americans, Mexicans and Guatamelans. *Journal of Asthma, 39*(2), 119–134.

Padilla-Walker, L. M., Carlo, G., Christensen, K. J., & Yorgason, J. B. (2012). Bidirectional relations between authoritative parenting and adolescents' prosocial behaviors. *Journal of Research on Adolescence, 22*(3), 400–408. doi:10.1111/j.1532-7795.2012.00807.x

Paik, H. (2001). The history of children's use of electronic media. In D. Singer & J. Singer (Eds.), *Handbook of children and the media* (pp. 7–28). Thousand Oaks, CA: Sage.

Palfrey, J. S., Hauser-Cram, P., Bronson, M. B., Warfield, M. E., Sirin, S., & Chan, E. (2005). The Brookline Early Education Project: A 25-year follow-up study of a family-centered early health and development intervention. *Pediatrics, 116*, 144–152. doi:10.1542/peds.2004-2515

Palinscar, A. S., & Brown, A. L. (1984). Reciprocal teaching of comprehension-fostering and comprehension-monitoring activities. *Cognition and Instruction, 1*(2), 117–175. doi:10.1207/s1532690xci0102_1

Palkovitz, R. (1997). Reconstructing "involvement": Expanding conceptualizations of men's caring in contemporary families. In A. J. Hawkins & W. J. Doherty (Eds.), *Generative Fathering* (pp. 200–217). London, UK: Sage.

Palkovitz, R. (2002). *Involved fathering and men's adult development: Provisional balances.* Mahwah, NJ: Erlbaum.

Palladino, D. K., & Helgeson, V. S. (2012). Friends or foes? A review of peer influence on self-care and glycemic control in adolescents with type 1 diabetes. *Journal of Pediatric Psychology, 37*(5), 591–603. doi:10.1093/jpepsy/jss009

Palmer, D., Berg, C. A., Wiebe, D. J., Beveridge, R. M., Korbel, C. D., Upchurch, R., . . . Donaldson, D. L. (2004). The role of autonomy and pubertal status in understanding age differences in maternal involvement in diabetes responsibility across adolescence. *Journal of Pediatric Psychology, 29*(1), 35–46.

Pan, B. A., & Snow, C. E. (1999). The development of conversation and discourse skills. In M. Barrett (Ed.), *The development of language* (pp. 229–249). Hove, UK: Psychology Press.

Pan, B. A., Rowe, M. L., Singer, J. D., & Snow, C. E. (2005). Maternal correlates of growth in toddler vocabulary production in low-income families. *Child Development, 76*(4), 763–782. doi:10.1111/1467-8624.00498-i1

Pan, H. W. (1994). *Children's play in Taiwan.* Albany, NY: State University of New York Press.

Parade, S. H., Supple, A. J., & Helms, H. M. (2012). Parenting during early childhood predicts relationship satisfaction in young adulthood: A prospective longitudinal perspective. *Marriage & Family Review, 48*(2), 150–169. doi:10.1080/01494929.2011.629078

Paris, S. G., & Paris, A. H. (2006). Assessments of early reading. In W. Damon & R. M. Lerner (Series Eds.) & K. A. Renninger & I. E. Sigel (Vol. Eds.), *Handbook of child psychology: Vol. 4. Child psychology in practice* (6th ed., pp. 48–74). Hoboken, NJ: Wiley.

Park, M. J., Adams, S. H., & Irwin, C. E. (2011). Health care services and the transition to young adulthood: Challenges and opportunities. *Academic Pediatrics, 11*(2), 115–122.

Parke, R. D. (1996). *Fatherhood.* Cambridge, MA: Harvard University Press.

Parke, R. D. (2002). Fathers and families. In M. H. Bornstein (Ed.), *Handbook on parenting* (2nd ed., Vol. 3, pp. 27–73). Mahwah, NJ: Erlbaum.

Parke, R. D., & Buriel, R. (2006). Socialization in the family: Ethnic and ecological perspectives. In R. Lerner (Ed.), *Handbook of child psychology: Vol. 3. Social, Emotional, and Personality Development* (6th ed., pp. 429–504). Hoboken, NJ: Wiley.

Parke, R. D., Burks, V. M., Carson, J. L., Neville, B., & Boyum, L. A. (1994). Family-peer relationships: A tripartite model. In R. D. Parke & S. G. Kellam (Eds.), *Exploring family relationships with other social contexts* (pp. 115–145). Hillsdale, NJ: Erlbaum.

Parke, R., & Brott, A. (1999). *Throwaway dads: The myths and barriers that keep men from being the fathers they want to be.* Boston, MA: Houghton Mifflin.

Parke, R., & Clarke-Stewart, A. (2011). *Social development.* Hoboken, NJ: Wiley.

Parker, A. K. (2009). Elementary organizational structures and young adolescents' self-concept and classroom environment perceptions across the transition to middle school. *Journal of Research in Childhood Education, 23*(3), 325–339. doi:10.1080/02568540909594664

Parpal, M., & Maccoby, E. E. (1985). Maternal responsiveness and subsequent child compliance. *Child Development, 56*, 1326–1334. doi:10.2307/1130247

Parsons, J. T., Siegel, A. W., & Cousins, J. H. (1997). Late adolescent risk-taking: Effects of perceived benefits and perceived risks on behavioral intentions and behavioral change. *Journal of Adolescence, 20*(4), 381–392. doi:10.1006/jado.1997.0094

Parten, M. B. (1932). Social participation among pre-school children. *The Journal of Abnormal and Social Psychology, 27*(3), 243–269. doi:10.1037/h0074524

Pasalich, D. S., Livesey, D. J., & Livesey, E. J. (2010). Performance on Stroop-like assessments of inhibitory control by 4- and 5-year-old children. *Infant and Child Development, 19*(3), 252–263. doi:10.1002/icd.667

Pascalis, O. & Kelly, D. J. (2009). The origins of face processing in humans: Phylogeny and ontogeny. *Perspectives on Psychological Science, 4*(2), 200–209.

Passow, S., Müller, M., Westerhausen, R., Hugdahl, K., Wartenburger, I., Heekeren, H. R., . . . Li, S. (2012). Development of attentional control of verbal auditory perception from middle to late childhood: Comparisons to healthy aging. *Developmental Psychology.* Advance online publication. doi:10.1037/a0031207

Pasterski, V., Golombok, S., & Hines, M. (2011). Sex differences in social behavior. In P. K. Smith & C. H. Hart (Eds.), *The Wiley–Blackwell handbook of childhood social development* (pp. 281–298). West Sussex, UK: Wiley-Blackwell.

Patchin, J. W., & Hinduja, S. (2011). Traditional and nontraditional bullying among youth: A test of general strain theory. *Youth & Society, 43*(2), 727–751. doi:10.1177/0044118X10366951

Pathman, T., Samson, Z., Dugas, K., Cabeza, R., & Bauer, P. J. (2011). A "snapshot" of declarative memory: Differing developmental trajectories in episodic and autobiographical memory. *Memory, 19*(8), 825–835. doi:10.1080/09658211.2011.613839

Patient Protection and Affordable Care Act of 2010, Pub. L. No. 111–148 § 124 Stat. 119 (2010). Retrieved from http://www.gpo.gov/fdsys/pkg/PLAW-111publ148/pdf/PLAW-111publ148.pdf

Patrick, H., & Nicklas, T. A. (2005). A review of family and social determinants of children's eating patterns and diet quality. *Journal of the American College of Nutrition, 24*(2), 83–92.

Patrick, K., Spear, B., Holt, K., & Sofka, D. (2001). *Bright futures in practice: Physical activity.* Washington, DC: National Center for Education in Maternal and Child Health.

Paul, C., & Thomson-Salo, F. (2013). *The baby as subject: Clinical studies in infant-parent therapy.* London, UK: Karmac.

Paul, D. B. (1997). *The history of newborn phenylketonuria screening in the U.S.* In N. A. Holtman & M. S. Watson (Eds.), *Promoting safe and effective genetic testing in the United States: Final report of the task force on genetic testing.* Washington, DC: National Institutes of Health-Department of Energy Working Group on Ethical, Legal, and Social Implications of Human Genome Research. Retrieved from http://www.genome.gov/10002397

Paus, T. (2009). Brain development. In R. M. Lerner & L. Steinberg (Eds.), *Handbook of adolescent psychology: Vol. 1. Individual bases of adolescent development* (3rd ed., pp. 95–115). Hoboken, NJ: Wiley.

Paus, T. (2010). Growth of white matter in the adolescent brain: Myelin or axon? *Brain and Cognition, 72*(1), 26–35.

Pavlov, I. (1927). *Conditioned reflexes.* London, UK: Oxford University Press.

Pears, K. C., & Fisher, P. A. (2005). Emotion understanding and theory of mind among maltreated children in foster care: Evidence of deficits. *Development and Psychopathology, 17*(1), 47–65. doi:10.1017/S0954579405050030

Pearson, J. L. Hunter, A. G., Ensminger, M. E., & Kellam, S. G. (1990). Black grandmothers in multigenerational households: Diversity in family structure and parenting involvement in the Woodlawn community. *Child Development, 61*, 434–442.

Pedlow, R., Sanson, A., Prior, M., & Oberklaid, F. (1993). Stability of maternally reported temperament from infancy to 8 years. *Developmental Psychology, 2*, 998–1007.

Pelchat, D., Lefebvre H., & Perreault, M. (2003). Differences and similarities between mothers' and fathers' experiences of parenting a child with a disability. *Journal of Child Health Care, 7*(4), 231–247.

Pelphrey, K. A., & Carter, E. J. (2008). Charting the typical and atypical development of the social brain. *Development and Psychopathology, 20*(4), 1081–1102. doi:10.1017/S0954579408000515

Penn, A. H., Altshuler, A. E., Small, J. W., Taylor, S. F., Dobkins, K. R., & Schmid-Schönbein, G. W. (2012). Digested formula but not digested fresh human milk causes death of intestinal cells in vitro: Implications for necrotizing enterocolitis. *Pediatric Research, 72*(6), 560–567. doi:10.1038/pr.2012.125

Perez, S. M., & Gauvain, M. (2009). Mother-child planning, child emotional functioning, and children's transition to first grade. *Child Development, 80*(3), 776–791. doi:10.1111/j.1467-8624.2009.01297.x

Perinatal HIV Guidelines Working Group. (2009). *Public Health Service Task Force recommendations for use of antiretroviral drugs in pregnant HIV-infected women for maternal health and interventions to reduce perinatal HIV transmission in the United States* (pp. 1–90). Retrieved from http://aidsinfo.nih.gov/ContentFiles/PerinatalGL.pdf

Perlman, S. B., & Pelphrey, K. A. (2010). Regulatory brain development: Balancing emotion and cognition. *Social Neuroscience, 5*(5–6), 533–542. doi:10.1080/17470911003683219

Perner, J., & Wimmer, H. (1985). "John *thinks* that Mary *thinks* that . . . : Attribution of second-order beliefs by 5- to 10-year-old children. *Journal of Experimental Child Psychology, 39*, 437–471.

Perrin, E. M., Boone-Heinonen, J., Field, A. E., Coyne-Beasley, T., & Gordon-Larsen, P. (2010). Perception of overweight and self-esteem during adolescence. *International Journal of Eating Disorders, 43*(5), 447–454.

Perrin, J. M. (2008). Prevention and chronic health conditions among children and adolescents. *Ambulatory Pediatrics, 8*, 271–272.

Perrin, J. M., Bloom, S. R., & Gortmaker, S. L. (2007). The increase of childhood chronic conditions in the United States. *Journal of the American Medical Association, 297*(24), 2755–2759.

Perry, C. M., & McIntire, W. G. (1995). Modes of moral judgment among early adolescents. *Adolescence, 30*(119), 707–715.

Perry, S. E., Wilson, D., Hockenberry, M. J., & Lowdermilk, D. L. (2005). *Maternal child nursing care.* New York, NY: Elsevier Health Sciences.

Petalas, M. A., Hastings, R. P., Nash, S., Dowey, A., & Reilly, D. (2009). "I like that he always shows who he is": The perceptions and experiences of siblings with a brother with autism spectrum disorder. *International Journal of Disability, Development and Education, 56*(4), 381–399. doi:10.1080/10349120903306715

Petanjek, Z., Judaš, M., Šimic, G., Rašin, M. R., Uylings, H. B. M., Rakic, P., & Kostović, I. (2011). Extraordinary neoteny of synaptic spines in the human prefrontal cortex. *PNAS Proceedings of the National Academy of Sciences of the United States of America, 108*(32), 13281–13286. doi:10.1073/pnas.1105108108

Peters, C., Kantaris, X., Barnes, J., & Sutcliffe, A. (2005). Parental attitudes toward disclosure of the mode of conception to their child conceived by in vitro fertilization. *Fertility and Sterility, 83*(4), 914–919. doi:10.1016/j.fertnstert.2004.12.019

Petersen, R. D. (2000). Definitions of a gang and impacts on public policy. *Journal of Criminal Justice, 28*(2), 139–149. doi:10.1016/S0047-2352(99)00036-7

Petersen, S. E., & Posner, M. I. (2012). The attention system of the human brain: 20 years after. *Annual Review of Neuroscience, 35*, 73–89. doi:10.1146/annurev-neuro-062111-150525

Peterson, C. C., Wellman, H. M., & Liu, D. (2005). Steps in theory-of-mind development for children with deafness or autism. *Child Development, 76*(2), 502–517. doi:10.1111/j.1467-8624.2005.00859.x

Petitto, L. A., Berens, M. S., Kovelman, I., Dubins, M. H., Jasinska, K., & Shalinksy, M. (2012). The "perceptual wedge hypothesis" as the basis for bilingual babies' phonetic processing advantage: New insights from fNIRS brain imaging. *Brain and Language, 121*(2), 130–143. doi:10.1016/j.bandl.2011.05.003

Petrill, S. A., & Deter-Deckard, K. (2004). The heritability of general cognitive ability: A within-family adoption design. *Intelligence, 32*(4), 403–409. doi:10.1016/j.intell.2004.05.001

Phillips, D. C., & Kelly, M. E. (1975). Hierarchical theories of development in education and psychology. *Harvard Educational Review, 45*(3), 351–375.

Phinney, J. S. (1992). The multigroup ethnic identity measure: A new scale for use with diverse groups. *Journal of Adolescent Research*, 7(2),156–176.doi:10.1177/074355489272003

Phinney, J. S. (1993). A three-stage model of ethnic identity development in adolescence. In M. E. Bernal & G. P. Knight (Eds.), *Ethnic identity: Formation and transmission among Hispanics and other minorities* (pp. 61–79). Albany, NY: State University of New York Press.

Phinney, J. S. (2008). *Ethnic identity exploration in emerging adulthood.* New York, NY: Analytic Press/Taylor & Francis Group.

Phinney, J. S., & Baldelomar, O. A. (2011). Identity development in multiple cultural contexts. In L. A. Jensen (Ed.), *Bridging cultural and development approaches to psychology: New syntheses in theory, research, and policy* (pp. 161–186). Oxford, UK: Oxford University Press.

Phinney, J. S., Jacoby, B., & Silva, C. (2007). Positive intergroup attitudes: The role of ethnic identity. *International Journal of Behavioral Development, 31*(5), 478–490. doi:10.1177/0165025407081466

Piaget, J. (1926). *The language and thought of the child.* (M. Warden, Trans.). Oxford, UK: Harcourt & Brace. (Original work published 1923).

Piaget, J. (1929). *The child's conception of the world.* Oxford, UK: Harcourt, Brace.

Piaget, J. (1952). *The origins of intelligence in children.* New York, NY: International Universities Press.

Piaget, J. (1952/1936). *The origins of intelligence in children.* (Original work published 1936). New York, NY: International Universities Press.

Piaget, J. (1954). *The construction of reality in the child.* New York, NY: Basic Books.

Piaget, J. (1962). *Play, dreams, and imitation in childhood* (C. Gattegno & F. M. Hodgson, Trans.). New York, NY: Norton. (Original work published 1945).

Piaget, J. (1965) *The child's conception of number.* New York, NY: Norton.

Piaget, J. (1965). *The moral judgment of the child.* New York, NY: Free Press.

Piaget, J. (1966). Moral feelings and judgments. In H. E. Gruber & J. J. Vonèche (Eds.), *The essential Piaget* (pp. 154–158). New York, NY: Basic Books.

Piaget, J. (1969). *The language and thought of the child.* Cleveland, OH: Meridian Books.

Piaget, J. (1973). *The child and reality: Problems of genetic psychology.* New York, NY: Grossman.

Piaget, J. (2008). Intellectual evolution from adolescence to adulthood. *Human Development, 51*(1), 40–47. (Original work published 1972). doi:10.1159/000112531

Picariello, M. L., Greenberg, D. N., & Pillemer, D. B. (1990). Children's sex-related stereotyping of colors. *Child Development, 61*(5), 1453–1460. doi:10.2307/1130755

Pierce, K., Carter, C., Weinfeld, M., Desmond, J., Hazin, R., Bjork, R., Gallagher, N. (2011). Detecting, studying, and treating autism early: The one-year well-baby check-up approach. *Journal of Pediatrics. 159*(3): 458–465.

Pietromonaco, P. R., Feldman, Barrett, L., & Powers, S. A. (2006). Adult attachment theory and affective reactivity and regulation. In D. K. Snyder, J. A. Simpson, & J. N. Hughes (Eds.), *Emotion regulation in couples and families: Pathways to dysfunction and health* (pp. 57–74). Washington, DC: American Psychological Association.

Pignotti, M. S., & Donzelli, G. (2008). Perinatal care at the threshold of viability: An international comparison of practical guidelines for the treatment of extremely preterm births. *Pediatrics, 121*, e193–e198. doi:10.1542/peds.2007-0513

Pike, A., Coldwell, J., & Dunn, J. (2005). Sibling relationships in early/middle childhood: Links with individual adjustment. *Journal of Family Psychology, 19*(4), 523–532. doi:10.1037/0893-3200.19.4.523

Pike, A., Kretschmer, T., & Dunn, J. (2009). Siblings—friends or foes? *Psychologist, 22*(6), 494–496.

Pillow, B. H. (2002). Children's and adults' evaluation of the certainty of deductive inferences, inductive inferences, and guesses. *Child Development, 73*, 779–792. doi:10.1111/1467-8624.00438

Pillow, B. H., Pearson, R. M., Hecht, M., & Bremer, A. (2010). Children's and adults' judgments of the certainty of deductive inferences, inductive inferences, and guesses. *Journal of Genetic Psychology, 171*(3), 203–217. doi:10.1080/00221320903300403

Pin, T., Eldridge, B., & Galea, M. P. (2007). A review of the effects of sleep position, play position, and equipment use on motor development in infants. *Developmental Medicine & Child Neurology, 49*, 858–867. doi:10.1111/j.1469-8749.2007.00858.x

Pinderhughes, E. E., Dodge, K. A., Bates, J. E., Pettit, G. S., & Zelli, A. (2000). Discipline responses: Influences of parents' socioeconomic status, ethnicity, beliefs about parenting, stress, and cognitive-emotional processes. *Journal of Family Psychology, 14*(3), 380–400. doi:10.1037/0893-3200.14.3.380

Pinker, S. (1984). *Language learnability and language development.* Cambridge, MA: Harvard University Press.

Pinker, S. (1994). *The language instinct.* New York, NY: Morrow.

Pinker, S., & Jackendoff, R. (2005). The faculty of language: What's special about it? *Cognition, 95*(2), 201–236. doi:10.1016/j.cognition.2004.08.004

Pinto, A. I., Pessanha, M., Aguiar, C. (2013). Effects of home environment and center-based child care quality on children's language, communication, and literacy outcomes. *Early Childhood Research Quarterly, 28*(1), 94–101. doi:10.1016/j.ecresq.2012.07.001

Pintrich, P. R. (2000). Multiple goals, multiple pathways: The role of goal orientation in learning and achievement. *Journal of Educational Psychology, 92*(3), 544–555. doi:10.1037/0022–0663.92.3.544

Piquero, A. R. (2008). Disproportionate minority contact. *Future of Children, 18*(2), 59–79. doi:10.1353/foc.0.0013

Piquero, A. R., Farrington, D. P., & Blumstein, A. (2003). The criminal career paradigm. *Crime and Justice, 30,* 359–506.

Pitcher, E. G., & Prelinger, E. (1963). *Children tell stories: An analysis of fantasy.* New York, NY: International Universities Press.

Pitchford, N. J., & Mullen, K. T. (2005). The role of perception, language, and preference in the developmental acquisition of basic color terms. *Journal of Experimental Child Psychology, 90*(4), 275–302. doi:10.1016/j.jecp.2004.12.005

Pleck, J. H., & Masciadrelli, B. P. (2004). Paternal involvement by U.S. residential fathers: Levels, sources and consequences. In M. E. Lamb (Ed.), *The role of the father in child development* (4th ed., pp. 222–271). Hoboken, NJ: Wiley.

Plomin, R., & Saudino, K. J. (1994). Quantitative genetics and molecular genetics. In J. E. Bates & T. D. Wachs (Eds.), *Temperament: Individual differences at the interface of biology and behavior* (pp. 143–171). Washington, DC: American Psychological Association.

Plomin, R., & Spinath, F. M. (2004). Intelligence: Genetics, genes, and genomics. *Journal of Personality and Social Psychology, 86*(1), 112–129. doi:10.1037/0022–3514.86.1.112

Plomin, R., DeFries, J. C., McClearn, G. E., & McGuffin, P. (2007). *Behavioral genetics* (5th ed.). New York, NY: Worth.

Pluess, M., & Belsky, J. (2010). Differential susceptibility to parenting and quality childcare. *Developmental Psychology, 46,* 379–390. doi:10.1037/a0015203

Pollak, S. D., & Sinha, P. (2002). Effects of early experience on children's recognition of facial displays of emotion. *Developmental Psychology, 38*(5), 784–791. doi:10.1037/0012-1649.38.5.784

Pollak, S. D., Cicchetti, D., Hornung, K., & Reed, A. (2000). Recognizing emotion in faces: Developmental effects of child abuse and neglect. *Developmental Psychology, 36*(5), 679–688. doi:10.1037/0012-1649.36.5.679

Pollak, S. D., Cicchetti, D., Klorman, R., & Brumaghim, J. T. (1997). Cognitive brain event-related potentials and emotion processing in maltreated children. *Child Development, 68*(5), 773–787. doi:10.1111/j.1467–8624.1997.tb01961.x

Pollan, M. (2008). *In defense of food: An eater's manifesto.* New York, NY: Penguin.

Pollet, S. L. (2009). A nationwide survey of programs for children of divorcing and separating parents. *Family Court Review, 47*(3), 523–543. doi:10.1111/j.1744–1617.2009.01271.x

Pollitt, E. (2000). Developmental sequel from early nutritional deficiencies: Conclusive and probability judgments. *Journal of Nutrition, 130,* 350–353.

Pollitt, E., Gorman, K. S., Engle, P. L., Martorell, R., & Rivera, J. (1993). Early supplementary feeding and cognition: Effects over two decades. *Monographs of the Society for Research in Child Development, 58*(7), 1–99. doi:10.1111/1540–5834.ep9411130984

Pomerantz, E. M., Moorman, E. A., & Litwack, S. D. (2007). The how, whom, and why of parents' involvement in children's academic lives: More is not always better. *Review of Educational Research, 77*(3), 373–410. doi:10.3102/003465430305567

Pomerleau, A., Malcuit, G., Chicoine, J. F., Seguin, R., Belhumeur, C., Germain, P., . . . Jeliu, G. (2005). Health status, cognitive and motor development of young children adopted from China, East Asia, and Russia across the first 6 months after adoption. *International Journal of Behavioral Development, 29,* 445–457. doi:10.1177/01650250500206257

Pope, H. G., & Katz, D. L. (1998). Affective and psychotic symptoms associated with anabolic steroid use. *American Journal of Psychiatry, 145*(4), 487–490.

Pope, H. G., Kouri, E. M., & Hudson, M. D. (2000). Effects of supraphysiologic doses of testosterone on mood and aggression in normal men: A randomized controlled trial. *Archives of General Psychiatry, 57*(2), 133–140.

Pope, H. G., Lalonde, J. K., Pindyck, L. J., Walsh, T., Bulik, C. M., Crow, S. J., . . . Hudson, J. I. (2006). Binge eating disorder: A stable syndrome. *American Journal of Psychiatry, 163*(12), 2181–2183. doi:10.1176/appi.ajp.163.12.2181

Popkin, B. M., Adair, L., Akin, J. S., Black, R., Briscoe, J., & Flieger, W. (1990). Breast-feeding and diarrheal morbidity. *Pediatrics, 86*(6), 874–882.

Popper, K. R. (1962). *Conjectures and refutations.* New York, NY: Basic Books.

Population Council (2001). The unfinished transition: Gender equity: Sharing the responsibilities of parenthood (Population Council Issues Paper). Retrieved from http://www.popcouncil.org/publications/issues_papers/transition_4.html

Porter, C. L., Hart, C. H., Yang, C., Robinson, C. C., Olsen, S. F., Zeng, Q., & Olsen, J. A. (2005). A comparative study of child temperament and parenting in Beijing, China and the western United States. *International Journal of Behavioral Development, 29*(6), 541–551. doi:10.1080/01650250500147402

Porter, R. H., & Winberg, J. (1999). Unique salience of maternal breast odors for newborn infants. *Neuroscience and Biobehavioral Reviews, 23*(3), 439–449. doi:10.1016/S0149–7634(98)00044–X

Porter, T., Paulsell, D., Del Grosso, P., Avellar, S., Hass, R., & Vuong, L. (2010). *A review of the literature on home-based child care: Implications for future directions.* Washington DC: Office of Planning, Research and Evaluation, Administration for Children and Families, U.S. Department of Health and Human Services. Retrieved from http://www.acf.hhs.gov/programs/opre/cc/supporting_quality/reports/lit_review/lit_review.pdf

Posada, G., Gao, Y., Wu, F., Posada, R., Tascon, M., Schoelmerich, A., . . . Synnevaag, B. (1995). The secure-base phenomenon across cultures: Children's behavior, mothers' references, and experts' concepts [Monograph]. *Society for Research in Child Development, 60*(2–3, Serial No. 244), 27–48.

Posner, M. I., & Rothbart, M. K. (2000). Developing mechanisms of self-regulation. *Development and Psychopathology, 12,* 427–441. doi:10.1017/S0954579400003096.

Posner, M. I., & Rothbart, M. K. (2007). *Educating the human brain.* Washington, DC: American Psychological Association.

Posner, M. I., Rothbart, M. K., Sheese, B. E., & Tang, Y. (2007). The anterior cingulate gyrus and the mechanism of self-regulation. *Cognitive, Affective, & Behavioral Neuroscience,* 7(4), 391–395. doi:10.3758/CABN.7.4.391.

Poteat, V. P., Kimmel, M. S., & Wilchins, R. (2011). The moderating effects of support for violence beliefs on masculine norms, aggression, and homophobic behavior during adolescence. *Journal of Research on Adolescence, 21*(2), 434–447. doi:10.1111/j.1532–7795.2010.00682.x

Poti, J. M., & Popkin, B. M. (2011). Trends in energy intake among US children by eating location and food source, 1977–2006. *Journal of the American Dietetic Association, 111*(8), 1156–1164.

Potochnick, S. R., & Perreira, K. M. (2010). Depression and anxiety among first-generation immigrant Latino youth: Key correlates and implications for future research. *Journal of Nervous and Mental Disease, 198*(7), 470–477. doi:10.1097/NMD.Ob013e318le4cc24

Powell, D. R. (2006). Families and early childhood interventions. In W. Damon & R. Lerner (Series Eds.) & K. A. Renninger & I. E. Sigel (Vol. Eds.), *Handbook of child psychology: Vol. 4. Child psychology in practice* (6th ed., pp. 548–591). Hoboken, NJ: Wiley.

Powell, L. M., Chaloupka, F., & Bao, Y. (2007). The availability of fast-food and full-service restaurants in the United States: Associations with neighborhood characteristics. *American Journal of Preventive Medicine, 33*(4S), S240–S245. doi:10.1016/j.amepre.2007.07.005

Powell, L. M., Slater, S., Mirtcheva, D., Bao, Y. & Chaloupka, F. (2007). Food store availability and neighborhood characteristics in the United States. *Preventive Medicine, 44,* 198–95. doi:10.1016/j.ypmed.2006.08.008

Powner, M. W., Gerland, B., & Sutherland, J. D. (2009). Synthesis of activated pyrimidine ribonucleotides in prebiotically plausible conditions. *Nature, 459,* 239–242. doi:10.1038

Prado, A., Piovanotti, M., & Vieira, M. (2007). Concepções de pais e mães sobre comportamento paterno real e ideal. *Psicologia em Estudo, Maringá, 12*(1), 41–50.

Prasad, A. S. (1998). Zinc deficiency in humans: A neglected problem. *Journal of the American College of Nutrition, 17*(6), 542–543.

Prat, C. S. (2013). The neural basis of language faculties. In R. J. Nelson & S. J. Y. Mizumori (Eds.). *Handbook of psychology: Vol. 3. Behavioral neuroscience* (2nd ed., pp. 595–619). Hoboken, NJ: Wiley.

Pratt, M. W., Skoe, E. E., & Arnold, M. L. (2004). Care reasoning development and family socialisation patterns in later adolescence: A longitudinal analysis. *International Journal of Behavioral Development, 28*(2), 139–147. doi:10.1080/01650250344000343

President's New Freedom Commission on Mental Health. (2003). *Achieving the promise: Transforming mental health care in America, final report*. Rockville, MD: U.S. Department of Health and Human Services.

Pressley, M., & Hilden, K. R. (2006). Cognitive strategies: Production deficiencies and successful strategy instruction everywhere. In D. Kuhn & R. Siegler (Eds.), *Handbook of child psychology: Vol. 2. Cognition, perception, and language* (6th ed., pp. 511–556). Hoboken, NJ: Wiley.

Pressman, L., Pipp-Siegel, S., Yoshinaga-Itano, C., & Deas, A. (1999). The relation of sensitivity to child expressive language gain in deaf and hard-of-hearing children whose care givers are hearing. *Journal of Deaf Studies and Deaf Education, 4*(4), 294–304.

Prevatt, F., & Kelly, F. D. (2003). Dropping out of school: A review of intervention programs. *Journal of School Psychology, 41*(5), 377–395. doi:10.1016/S0022–4405(03)00087–6

Prevor, M. B., & Diamond, A. (2005). Color-object interference in young children: A Stroop effect in children 3½–6½. *Cognitive Development, 20*(2), 256–278. doi:10.1016/j.cogdev.2005.04.001

Price, C. S., Thompson, W. W., Goodson, B., Weintraub, E., Croen, L. A., Hinrichsen, V. L., . . . DeStefano, F. (2010). Prenatal and infant exposure to thimerosal from vaccines and immunoglobulins and risk of autism. *Pediatrics, 126*(4), 656–664. doi:10.1542/peds.2010-0309

Price, M. (2009). The nativists are restless. *Monitor on Psychology, 40*(9), 42–43.

Primakoff, P., & Myles, D. G. (2002). Penetration, adhesion and fusion in mammalian sperm-egg interaction. *Science, 296*, 2183–2185. doi:10.1126/science.1072029

Prior, M., Smart, D., Sanson, A., & Oberklaid, F. (2001). Longitudinal predictors of behavioural adjustment in pre-adolescent children. *Australian and New Zealand Journal of Psychiatry, 35*(3), 297–307. doi:10.1046/j.1440–1614.2001.00903.x

Prock, L., & Rappaport, L. (2009). Attention and deficits of attention. In W. B. Carey, A. C. Crocker, W. L. Coleman, E. R. Elias, & H. M. Feldman (Eds.), *Developmental-behavioral pediatrics* (4th ed., pp. 524–534). Philadelphia, PA: Saunders/Elsevier.

Public Broadcasting Corporation. (2009). *The Venus of Willendorf: Exaggerated beauty*. Retrieved from http://www.pbs.org/howartmadetheworld/episodes/human/venus/#

Puffer, E., Schatz, J., & Roberts, C. W. (2007). The association of oral hydroxyurea therapy with improved cognitive functioning in sickle cell disease. *Child Neuropsychology, 13*, 142–154. doi:10.1080/09297040600584626

Puhl, R. M., & Heuer, C. A. (2010). Obesity stigma: Important considerations for public health. *American Journal of Public Health, 100*, 1019–1028.

Puhl, R. M., & Latner, J. D. (2007). Stigma, obesity, and the health of the nation's children. *Psychological Bulletin, 133*(4), 557–580.

Puma, M., Bell, S., Cook, R., Heid, C., & Lopez, M. (2005). *Head Start Impact Study: First year findings*. Washington, DC: U.S. Department of Health and Human Services, Administration for Children and Families.

Purnell, L. D. (2009). *Culturally competent health care* (2nd ed.). Philadelphia, PA: F. A. Davis.

Puroila, A., Estola, E., & Syrjala, L. (2012). Does Santa exist? Children's everyday narratives as dynamic meeting places in a day care centre context. *Early Child Development and Care, 182*(2), 191–206. doi:10.1080/03004430.2010.549942

Purves, D., Augustine, G. J., Fitzpatrick, D., Hall, W. C., Lamantia, A. S., & White, L. E. (Eds.). (2012). *Neuroscience* (5th ed.). Sunderlund, MA: Sinauer.

Putallaz, M., & Gottman, J. M. (1981). An interactional model of children's entry into peer groups. *Child Development, 52*(3), 986–994. doi:10.2307/1129103

Pye, C., & Quixtan Poz, P. (1988). Precocious passives (and antipassives) in Quiché Mayan. *Papers and Reports on Child Language Development, 27*, 71–80.

Quinn, D. M., & Spencer, S. J. (2001). The interference of stereotype threat with women's generation of mathematical problem-solving strategies. *Journal of Social Issues, 57*(1), 55–71. doi:10.1111/0022–4537.00201

Quinn, P. C. (2010). The acquisition of expertise as a model for the growth of cognitive structure. In S. P. Johnson (Ed.), *Neoconstructivism: The new science of cognitive development* (pp. 252–273). New York, NY: Oxford University Press.

Quinn, P. C. (2011). Born to categorize. In U. Goswami (Ed.), *Wiley–Blackwell handbook of childhood cognitive development* (2nd ed., pp. 129–152). Oxford, UK: Wiley–Blackwell.

Quinn, P. C., & Bhatt, R. S. (2012). Grouping by form in young infants: Only relevant variability promotes perceptual learning. *Perception, 41*, 1468–1476.

Quinn, P. C., & Eimas, P. D. (1996). Perceptual organization and categorization. In C. Rovee-Collier & L. Lipsitt (Eds.), *Advances in infancy research* (Vol. 10, pp. 1–36). Norwood, NJ: Ablex.

Quinn, P. C., & Eimas, P. D. (1998). Evidence for a global categorical representation of humans by young infants. *Journal of Experimental Child Psychology, 69*(3), 151–174. doi:10/1006/jecp.1998.2443

Quintana, S. M. (2007). Racial and ethnic identity: Developmental perspectives and research. *Journal of Counseling Psychology, 54*(3), 259–270. doi:10.1037/0022–0167.54.3.259

Raeburn, P. (2005, August 14). A second womb. *The New York Times Magazine*.

Raghubar, K. P., Barnes, M. A., & Hecht, S. A. (2010). Working memory and mathematics: A review of developmental, individual difference, and cognitive approaches. *Learning and Individual Differences, 20*(2), 110–122. doi:10.1016/j.lindif.2009.10.005

Rägo, L., & Santoso, B. (2008). Drug regulation: History, present and future. In C. J. van Boxtel, B. Santoso, and I. R. Edwards (Eds.), *Drug benefits and risks: International textbook of clinical pharmacology* (2nd ed., pp. 65–77). Amsterdam, Netherlands: IOS Press.

Raichle, M. E. (2010). The brain's dark energy. *Scientific American, 302*(3), 44–49. doi:10.1038/scientificamerican0310–44

Rakison, D. H., & Oakes, L. M. (2003). *Early category and concept development: Making sense of the blooming, buzzing confusion* (pp. 132–158). New York, NY: Oxford University Press.

Ramani, G. B., & Siegler, R. S. (2008). Promoting broad and stable improvements in low-income children's numerical knowledge through playing number board games. *Child Development, 79*(2), 375–394. doi:10.1111/j.1467-8624.2007.01131.x

Ramey, C. T., & Ramey, S. L. (2004). Early learning and school readiness: Can early intervention make a difference? *Merrill–Palmer Quarterly, 50*(4), 471–491. doi:10.1353/mpq.2004.0034

Ramey, C., Ramey, S., & Lanzi, R. (2006). Children's health and education. In W. Damon & R. Lerner (Series Eds.) & K. Renninger & I. Sigel (Vol. Eds.), *Handbook of child psychology: Volume 4. Child psychology in practice* (6th ed., pp. 864–892). Hoboken, NJ: Wiley.

Ramsden, S., Richardson, F. M., Goulven, J., Thomas, M. S. C., Ellis, C., Shakeshaft, C., . . . Price, C. J. (2011). Verbal and nonverbal intelligence changes in the teenage brain. *Nature, 479*(7371), 113–116. doi:10.1038/nature10514

Rankinen, T., Zuberi, A., Chagnon,Y. C., Weisnagel, S. J., Argyropoulos, G., Walts, B, . . . Bouchard, C. (2006). The human obesity gene map: The 2005 update. *Obesity, 14*, 529–644. doi:10.1038/oby.2006.71

Ratey, J. J. (2001). *A user's guide to the brain: Perception, attention, and the four theaters of the brain*. New York, NY: Pantheon.

Rathunde, K., & Csikszentmihalyi, M. (2006). The developing person: An experiential perspective. In R. M. Lerner & W. Damon (Eds.), *Handbook of child psychology: Vol. 1. Theoretical models of human development* (6th ed., pp. 465–515). Hoboken, NJ: Wiley.

Rathvon, N. (2004). *Early reading assessment: A practitioner's handbook*. New York, NY: Guilford Press.

Rautava, P., Erkkola R., & Sillanpaa, M. (1991). The outcomes and experiences of first pregnancy in relation to the mother's childbirth knowledge: The Finnish family competence study. *Journal of Advanced Nursing, 16*, 1226–1232.

Raver C. C. (2002). Emotions matter: Making the case for the role of young children's emotional development for early school readiness. *Social Policy Report, XVI* (3), 3–18.

Ravid, D., & Berman, R. A. (2010). Developing noun phrase complexity at school age: A text-embedded cross-linguistic analysis. *First Language, 30*(1), 3–26. doi:10.1177/0142723709350531

Ream, R. K. (2003). Counterfeit social capital and Mexican-American underachievement. *Educational Evaluation and Policy Analysis, 25*(3), 237–262. doi:10.3102/01623737025003237

Recchia, H. E., Howe, N., Ross, H. S., & Alexander, S. (2010). Children's understanding and production of verbal irony in family conversations. *British Journal of Developmental Psychology, 28*(2), 255–274. doi:10.1348/026151008X401903

Reddy, C. C., Collins, M. W., & Gioia, G. A. (2008). Adolescent sports concussion. *Physical Medicine & Rehabilitation Clinics of North America, 19*(2), 247–269.

Reece, E. A. (2008). Perspectives on obesity, pregnancy and birth outcomes in the United States: The scope of the problem. *American Journal of Obstetrics and Gynecology, 198*(1), 23–27. doi:10.1016/j.ajog.2007.06.076

Reed, M. S. (2009). Educational assessment. In W. B. Carey, A. C. Crocker, W. L. Coleman, E. R. Elias, & H. M. Feldman (Eds.), *Developmental-behavioral pediatrics* (4th ed., pp. 811–827). Philadelphia, PA: Saunders/Elsevier.

Reese, L., Garnier, H., Gallimore, H., & Goldenberg, C. (2002). Longitudinal analysis of the antecedents of emergent Spanish literacy and middle-school English reading achievement of Spanish-speaking students. *American Educational Research Journal*, 7(3), 633–662.

Reese, M. A. (2002). Best practices: TRIO student support services and upward bound [Brochure]. Retrieved from http://www.educ.uidaho.edu/bestpractices

Regalado, M., & Halfon, N. (1998). Parenting: Issues for the pediatrician. *Pediatric Annals, 27*(1), 31–37.

Regnery, A. S. (1985). Getting away with murder: Why the juvenile justice system needs an overhaul. *Policy Review, 34*, 65–72.

Reid, R., Trout, A. L., & Schartz, M. (2005). Self-regulation interventions for children with attention deficit/hyperactivity disorder. *Exceptional Children, 71*(4), 361–377.

Reissig, C. J., Strain, E. C., & Griffiths, R. R. (2009). Caffeinated energy drinks: A growing problem. *Drug and Alcohol Dependence. 99*(1–3), 1–10. doi:10.1016/j.drugalcdep.2008.08.001

Repacholi, B. M., & Meltzoff, A. N. (2007). Emotional eavesdropping: Infants selectively respond to indirect emotional signals. *Child Development, 78*(2), 503–521.

Rest, J. R. (1979). *Development in judging moral issues*. Minneapolis, MN: University of Minnesota Press.

Retraction. (2010). Retraction—ileal-lymphoid-nodular hyperplasia, non-specific colitis, and pervasive developmental disorder in children. *Lancet, 375*(9713), 445. doi:10.1016/S0140-6736(10)60175-4

Revai, K., Dobbs, L. A., Nair, S., Patel, J. A., Grady, J. J., & Chonmaitree, T. (2007). Incidence of acute otitis media and sinusitis complicating upper respiratory tract infection: The effect of age. *Pediatrics, 119*(6), e1408–e1412. doi:10.1542/peds.2006-2881

Reyna, V. F., & Farley, F. (2006). Risk and rationality in adolescent decision making: Implications for theory, practice, and public policy. *Psychological Science in the Public Interest*, 7(1), 1–44. doi:10.1111/j.1529–1006.2006.00026.x

Reynolds, A. J., Ou, S., & Topitzes, J. W. (2004). Paths of effects of early childhood intervention on educational attainment and delinquency: A confirmatory analysis of the Chicago Child-Parent Centers. *Child Development, 75*(5), 1299–1328. doi:10.1111/j.1467–8624.2004.00742.x

Rezaie, R., Simos, P. G., Fletcher, J. M., Juranek, J., Cirino, P. T., Li, Z., . . . Papanicolaou, A. C. (2011). The timing and strength of regional brain activation associated with word recognition in children with reading difficulties. *Frontiers in Human Neuroscience, 5*, 1–12. doi:10.3389/fnhum.2011.00045

Rheingold, H. L. (1982). Little children's participation in the work of adults, a nascent prosocial behavior. *Child Development, 53*(1), 114–125.

Richards, M. H., Crowe, P. A., Larson, R., & Swarr, A. (1998). Developmental patterns and gender differences in the experience of peer companionship during adolescence. *Child Development, 69*(1), 154–163. doi:10.2307/1132077

Richardson, F. M., Thomas, M. S. C., Filippi, R., Harth, H., & Price, C. J. (2010). Contrasting effects of vocabulary knowledge on temporal and parietal brain structure across lifespan. *Journal of Cognitive Neuroscience, 22*(5), 943–954. doi:10.1162/jocn.2009.21238

Richert, R. A., Robb, M. B., Fender, J. G., & Wartella, E. (2010). Word learning from baby videos. *Archives of Pediatrics & Adolescent Medicine, 164*, 432–437.

Richman, A. L., LeVine, R. A., New, R. S., Howrigan, G. A., Welles-Nystrom, B., & LeVine, S. (1988). Maternal behavior to infants in five cultures. In R. A. LeVine, P. M. Miller, & M. M. West (Eds.), *Parental behavior in diverse societies* (pp. 81–98). San Francisco, CA: Jossey-Bass.

Richman, A., Miller, P., & Levine, R. (1992). Cultural and educational variations in maternal responsiveness. *Developmental Psychology, 28*(4), 614–621.

Rideout, V. J., & Hamel, E. (2006). *The media family: Electronic media in the lives of infants, toddlers, preschoolers and their parents.* Menlo Park, CA: Kaiser Family Foundation.

Rideout, V. J., Foehr, U. G., & Roberts, D. F. (2010). *Generation M2: Media in the Lives of 8- to 18-Year Olds*, Menlo Park, CA: Kaiser Family Foundation.

Rideout, V. J., Vandewater, E. A., & Wartella, E. A. (2003). *Zero to six: Electronic media in the lives of infants, toddlers, and preschoolers.* Menlo Park, CA: Kaiser Family Foundation.

Ridout, N., Astell, A. J., Reid, I. C., Glen, T., & O'Carroll, R. E. (2003). Memory bias for emotional facial expressions in major depression. *Cognition and Emotion, 17*(1), 101–122. doi:10.1080/02699930302272

Ridout, N., Dritschel, B., Matthews, K., McVicar, M., Reid, I. C., & O'Carroll, R. E. (2009). Memory for emotional faces in major depression following judgement of physical facial characteristics at encoding. *Cognition and Emotion, 23*(4), 739–752. doi:10.1080/02699930802121137

Rieder, C., & Cicchetti, D. (1989). Organizational perspective on cognitive control functioning and cognitive-affective balance in maltreated children. *Developmental Psychology, 25*(3), 382–393. doi:10.1037/0012-1649.25.3.382

Ripa, L. W. (1993). A half-century of community water fluoridation in the United States: Review and commentary. *Journal of Public Health Dentistry, 53*(1), 17–44. doi:10.1111/j.1752-7325.1993.tb02666.x

Rivers, I., Poteat, V. P., & Noret, N. (2008). Victimization, social support, and psychosocial functioning among children of same-sex and opposite-sex couples. *Developmental Psychology, 44*(1), 127–134. doi:10.1037/0012–1649.44.1.127

Rivers, S. E., Reyna, V. F., & Mills, B. (2008). Risk taking under the influence: A fuzzy-trace theory of emotion in adolescence. *Developmental Review, 28*(1), 107–144. doi:10.1016/j.dr.2007.11.002

Rizzo, C. J., Daley, S. E., & Gunderson, B. H. (2006). Interpersonal sensitivity, romantic stress, and the prediction of depression: A study of inner-city, minority adolescent girls. *Journal of Youth and Adolescence, 35*(3), 469–478. doi:10.1007/s10964–006–9047–4

Rizzolatti, G., & Craighero, L. (2004). The mirror-neuron system. *Annual Review of Neuroscience, 27*, 169–192. doi:10.1146/annurev.neuro.27.070203.144230

Robaey, P., Dobkin, P., Leclerc, J–M., Cyr, F., Sauerwein, C., & Théorêt, Y. (2000). A comprehensive model of the development of mental handicap in children treated for acute lymphoblastic leukemia: A synthesis of the literature. *International Journal of Behavioral Development, 24*(1), 44–58.

Robbers, M. L. P. (2011). Families in society. *Journal of Contemporary Social Services, 92*(2), 169–175. doi:10.1606/1044–3894.4100

Robert Wood Johnson Foundation. (2009). *The negative impact of sugar-sweetened beverages on children's health*. Retrieved from http://www.rwjf.org/files/research/20091203herssb.pdf

Robert Wood Johnson Foundation, Bridging the Gap. (2010). *Availability of competitive foods and beverages: New findings from U.S. elementary schools* [Research brief]. Retrieved from http://www.bridgingthegapresearch.org

Robert Wood Johnson Foundation, Commission to Build a Healthier America. (2009). *Beyond health care: New directions to a healthier America.* Retrieved from http://www.commissiononhealth.org

Robin, L., Dittus, P., Whitaker, D., Crosby, R., Ethier, K., Mezoff, J., . . . Pappas-Deluca, K. (2004). Behavioral interventions to reduce incidence of HIV, STD, and pregnancy among adolescents: A decade in review. *Journal of Adolescent Health. 34*(1), 3–26.

Robins, R. W., & Trzesniewski, K. H. (2005). Self-esteem development across the lifespan. *Directions in Psychological Science, 14*, 158–162. doi:10.1111/j.0963–7214.2005.00353.x

Rochat, P. (2003). Five levels of self-awareness as they unfold early in life. *Consciousness and Cognition, 12*, 717–731.

Roche, A. F. (1979). Secular trends in human growth, maturation, and development. *Monographs of the Society for Research in Child Development, 44*(3–4), 3–27.
Rodriguez, R., Marchand, E., Ng, J., & Stice, E. (2008). Effects of a cognitive dissonance-based eating disorder prevention program are similar for Asian American, Hispanic, and White participants. *International Journal of Eating Disorders, 41*(7), 618–625. doi:10.1002/eat.20532
Roebroeck, M. E., Jahnsen, R., Carona, C., Kent, R. M., & Chamberlain, M. A. (2009). Adult outcomes and lifespan issues for people with childhood-onset physical disability. *Developmental Medicine & Child Neurology, 51*(8), 670–678. doi:10.1111/j.1469–8749.2009.03322.x
Roeser, R. W., Eccles, J. S., & Sameroff, A. J. (1998). Academic and emotional functioning in early adolescence: Longitudinal relations, patterns, and prediction by experience in middle school. *Development and Psychopathology, 10*(2), 321–352. doi:10.1017/S0954579498001631
Roeser, R. W., Peck, S. C., & Nasir, N. S. (2006). Self and identity processes in school motivation, learning, and achievement. In P. A. Alexander & P. H. Winne (Eds.), *Handbook of educational psychology* (pp. 391–424). Mahwah, NJ: Erlbaum.
Rogers, V. W., & Motyka, E. (2009). 5-2-1-0 goes to school: A pilot project testing the feasibility of schools adopting and delivering healthy messages during the school day. *Pediatrics, 123*, S272–S276. doi:10.1542/peds.2008–2780E
Roggman, L. A., Boyce, L. K., Cook, G. A., & Cook, J. (2002). Getting dads involved: Predictors of father involvement in Early Head Start and with their children. *Infant Mental Health, 23*, 62–78.
Rogoff, B. (1990). *Apprenticeship in thinking: Cognitive development in social context.* New York, NY: Oxford University Press.
Rogoff, B. (2003). *The cultural nature of human development.* New York, NY: Oxford University Press.
Rogoff, B., Correa–Chavez, M., & Silva, K. G. (2011). Cultural variation in children's attention and learning. In M. A. Gernsbacher, R. W. Pew, L. M. Hough, & J. R. Pomerantz (Eds.), *Psychology and the real world: Essays illustrating fundamental contributions to society* (pp. 154–163). New York, NY: Worth.
Rogoff, B., Mistry, J. J., Goncu, A., & Mosier, C. (1993). Guided participation in cultural activity by toddlers and caregivers. *Monographs of the Society for Research in Child Development, 58*(7, Serial No. 236).
Roid, G. H. (2003). *Stanford-Binet Intelligence Scales* (5th ed.). Itasca, IL: Riverside.
Roisman, G. I., & Fraley, R. C. (2012). A behavior-genetic study of the legacy of early caregiving experiences: Academic skills, social competence, and externalizing behavior in kindergarten. *Child Development, 83*(2), 728–742. doi:10.1111/j.1467-8624.2011.01709.x
Rolstad, K., Mahoney, K., & Glass, G. V. (2005). The big picture: A meta-analysis of program effectiveness research on English language learners. *Educational Policy, 19*(4), 572–594.
Romans, S. E., Martin, J. M., Gendall, K., & Herbison, G. P. (2003). Age of menarche: The role of some psychosocial factors. *Psychological Medicine, 33*, 933–939.
Romeo, R. D., & McEwen, B. (2006). Stress and the adolescent brain. *Annals of the New York Academy of Sciences, 1094*, 202–214.
Romero-Canyas, R., Downey, G., Berenson, K., Ayduk, O., & Kang, N. J. (2010). Rejection sensitivity and the rejection-hostility link in romantic relationships. *Journal of Personality, 78*(1), 119–148. doi:10.1111/j.1467–6494.2009.00611.x
Rood, L., Roelofs, J., Bögels, S. M., & Alloy, L. B. (2010). Dimensions of negative thinking and the relations with symptoms of depression and anxiety in children and adolescents. *Cognitive Therapy and Research, 34*(4), 333–342. doi:10.1007/s10608–009–9261–y
Roopnarine, J. L., & Johnson, J. E. (2005). *Approaches to early childhood education* (4th ed.). Upper Saddle River, NJ: Pearson.
Roopnarine, J. L., Fouts, H. N., Lamb, M. E., & Lewis-Elligan, T. Y. (2005). Mothers' and fathers' behaviors toward their 3- to 4-month-old infants in lower, middle, and upper socioeconomic African American families. *Developmental Psychology, 41*(5), 723–732.
*Roper v. Simmons*, 543 U.S. 551 (2005).
Ropper, A. H., & Samuels, M. A. (2009). *Adams and Victor's principles of neurology* (9th ed.). Columbus, OH: McGraw–Hill.
Roscoe, R. D., & Chi, M. T. H. (2007). Understanding tutor learning: Knowledge-building and knowledge-telling in peer tutors' explanations and questions. *Review of Educational Research*, 77(4), 534–574. doi:10.3102/0034654307309920
Rose, A. J. (2002). Co-rumination in the friendships of girls and boys. *Child Development, 73*(6), 1830–1843. doi:10.1111/1467–8624.00509
Rose, L. T., & Fischer, K. W. (2009). Dynamic systems theory. In R. A. Shweder, T. R. Bidell, A. C. Dailey, S. Dixon, P. J. Miller, & J. Modell (Eds.), *The child: An encyclopedic companion* (pp. 264–265). Chicago, IL: University of Chicago Press.
Rose, S. A., & Feldman, J. F. (1990). Infant cognition: Individual differences and developmental continuities. In J. Colombo & J. W. Fagen (Eds.), *Individual differences in infancy: Reliability, stability, prediction* (pp. 229–245). Hillsdale, NJ: Erlbaum.
Rose, S. A., & Tamis-LeMonda, C. S. (1999). Visual information processing in infancy: Reflections on underlying mechanisms. In L. Balter & C. S. Tamis-LeMonda (Eds.), *Child psychology: A handbook of contemporary issues* (pp. 64–84). Philadelphia, PA: Psychology Press.
Rose, S. A., Feldman, J. F., & Jankowski, J. J. (2005). Recall memory in the first three years of life: A longitudinal study of preterms and full-terms. *Developmental Medicine and Child Neurology, 47*, 653–659 doi:10.1111/j.1469-8749.2005.tb01049.x
Rosenbaum, J. E. (2001). *Beyond college for all: Career paths for the forgotten half.* New York, NY: Russell Sage Foundation.
Rosenbaum, J. E. (2006). Reborn a virgin: Adolescents' retracting of virginity pledges and sexual histories. *American Journal of Public Health, 96*(6), 1098–1103.
Rosenbaum, J. E. (2009). Patient teenagers? A comparison of the sexual behavior of virginity pledgers and matched nonpledgers. *Pediatrics, 123*(1), e110–e120.
Rosenberg, J. (2002). Neonatal death risk: Effect of prenatal care is most evident after term birth. *Perspectives on Sexual and Reproductive Health, 34*(5), 270–272.
Rosenberg, J., Pennington, B. F., Willcutt, E. G., & Olson, R. K. (2012). Gene by environment interactions influencing reading disability and the inattentive symptom dimension of attention deficit/hyperactivity disorder. *Journal of Child Psychology and Psychiatry, 53*(3), 243–251. doi:10.1111/j.1469–7610.2011.02452.x
Rosenberg-Lee, M., Barth, M., & Menon, V. (2011). What difference does a year of schooling make? Maturation of brain response and connectivity between 2nd and 3rd grades during arithmetic problem solving. *NeuroImage, 57*(3), 796–808. doi:10.1016/j.neuroimage.2011.05.013
Rosenstein, D., & Oster, H. (1997). Differential facial responses to four basic tastes in newborns. In P. Ekman & E. L. Rosenberg (Eds.), *What the face reveals: Basic and applied studies of spontaneous expression using the Facial Action Coding System (FACS). Series in affective science* (pp. 302–327). New York, NY: Oxford University Press.
Rostad, A. M., Nyberg, P., & Sivberg, B., (2008). Predicting developmental deficiencies at the age of four based on data for the first seven months of life. *Infant Mental Health Journal, 29*(6), 588–608. doi:10.1002/imhj.20194
Roth, G., Assor, A., Niemiec, C. P., Ryan, R. M., & Deci, E. L. (2009). The emotional and academic consequences of parental conditional regard: Comparing conditional positive regard, conditional negative regard, and autonomy support as parenting practices. *Developmental Psychology, 45*(4), 1119–1142. doi:10.1037/a0015272
Roth, W.-M., & Thom, J. S. (2009). The emergence of 3D geometry from children's (teacher-guided) classification tasks. *Journal of the Learning Sciences, 18*(1), 45–99. doi:10.1080/10508400802581692
Rothbart, M. K., & Bates, J. E. (1998). *Temperament.* Hoboken, NJ: Wiley.
Rothbart, M., & Bates, J. (2006). Temperament. In N. Eisenberg, W. Damon, & L. M. Richard (Eds.), *Handbook of child psychology: Vol. 3. Social, emotional, and personality development* (6th ed., pp. 99–166). Hoboken, NJ: Wiley.
Rothbaum, F., Weisz, J., Pott, M., Miyake, K., & Morelli, G. (2000). Attachment and culture: Security in the United States and Japan. *American Psychologist, 55*(10), 1093–1104.
Rouse, C. E., Brooks-Gunn, J., & McLanahan, S. (2005). Introducing the issue. *The Future of Children, 15*(1), 5–14. doi:10.1353/foc.2005.0010
Rovee, C. K., & Rovee, D. T. (1969). Conjugate reinforcement of infant exploratory behavior. *Journal of Experimental Child Psychology, 8*(1), 33–39

Rowe, R., Maughan, B., Worthman, C., Costello, E. J., & Angold, A. (2004). Testosterone, antisocial behavior, and social dominance in boys: Pubertal development and biosocial interaction. *Biological Psychiatry, 55*(5), 546–552.

Rowland, R. (1985). The social and psychological consequences of secrecy in artificial insemination by donor (AID) programmes. *Social Science and Medicine, 21*(4), 391–396. doi:10.1016/0277-9536(85)90219-9

Rowland, T. (2005). *Children's exercise physiology.* Champaign, IL: Human Kinetics.

Rubin, E. M., Lucas, S., Richardson, P., Rokhsar, D., Pennacchio, L. (2004). Finishing the euchromatic sequence of the human genome. *Nature, 431*, 931–945. doi:10.1038/nature03001

Rubin, K. H., & Burgess, K. B. (2002). Parents of aggressive and withdrawn children. In M. H. Bornstein (Ed.), *Handbook of parenting: Vol. 1. Children and parenting* (2nd ed., pp. 383–418). Mahwah, NJ: Erlbaum.

Rubin, K. H., Bukowski, W. M., & Parker, J. G. (2006). Peer interactions, relationships, and groups. In N. Eisenberg (Ed.), *Handbook of child psychology: Vol. 3. Social, emotional, and personality development* (6th ed., pp. 571–645). Hoboken, NJ: Wiley.

Rubin, K. H., Bukowski, W., & Parker, J. G. (1998). Peer interactions, relationships, and groups. In W. Damon & N. Eisenberg (Eds.), *Handbook of child psychology: Vol. 4. Social, emotional, and personality development* (5th ed., pp. 619–700). New York, NY: Wiley.

Rubin, K. H., Bukowski, W., Parker, J., & Bowker, J. C. (2008). Peer interactions, relationships, and groups. In W. Damon & R. Lerner (Eds.), *Developmental psychology: An advanced course.* Hoboken, NJ: Wiley.

Rubin, K. H., Cheah, C., & Menzer, M. (2010). Peers. In M. H. Bornstein (Ed.), *Handbook of cultural developmental science* (pp. 223–237). New York, NY: Psychology Press.

Rubin, K. H., Coplan, R. J., & Bowker, J. C. (2009). Social withdrawal in childhood. *Annual Review of Psychology, 60*, 141–171. doi:10.1146/annurev.psych.60.110707.163642

Rubin, K. H., Coplan, R., Chen, X., Bowker, J., & McDonald, K. L. (2011). Peer relationships in childhood. In M. H. Bornstein & M. E. Lamb (Eds.), *Developmental science: An advanced textbook* (6th ed., pp. 519–570). Hoboken, NJ: Wiley.

Ruble, D. N., & Frey, K. S. (1991). *Changing patterns of comparative behavior as skills are acquired: A functional model of self-evaluation.* Hillsdale, NJ: Erlbaum.

Ruble, D. N., Martin, C. L., & Berenbaum, S. A. (2006). Gender development. In W. Damon & R. M. Lerner (Series Eds.) & N. Eisenberg (Vol. Ed.), *Handbook of child psychology: Vol. 3. Social, emotional, and personality development* (6th ed., pp. 858–932). Hoboken, NJ, Wiley.

Ruble, D. N., Taylor, L. J., Cyphers, L., Greulich, F. K., Lurye, L. E., & Shrout, P. E. (2007). The role of gender constancy in early gender development. *Child Development, 78*(4), 1121–1136. doi:10.1111/j.1467-8624.2007.01056.x

Rudd, R. E., Anderson, J. E., Oppenheimer, S., & Nath, C. (2007). Health literacy: An update of medical and public health literature. In J. P. Comings, B. Garner, & C. Smith (Eds.), *Review of adult learning and literacy* (Vol. 7, pp. 175–203). Mahwah, NJ: Erlbaum.

Rudolf, M. C. J., & Logan, S. (2005). What is the long-term outcome for children who fail to thrive? A systematic review. *Archive of Disease in Childhood, 90*, 925–931. doi:10.1136/adc.2004.050179

Ruebush, M. (2009). *Why dirt is good: 5 ways to make germs your friends.* New York, NY: Kaplan.

Rueda, M. R., Checa, P., & Combita, L. M. (2012). Enhanced efficiency of the executive attention network after training in preschool children: Immediate changes and effects after two months. *Developmental Cognitive Neuroscience, 2*(Suppl. 1), S192–S204. doi:10.1016/j.dcn.2011.09.004

Rueda, M. R., Posner, M. I., & Rothbart, M. K. (2005). The development of executive attention: Contributions to the emergence of self-regulation. *Developmental Neuropsychology, 28*(2), 573–594. doi:10.1207/s15326942dn2802_2

Rueda, M. R., Rothbart, M. K., McCandliss, B. D., Saccomanno, L., & Posner, M. (2005). Training, maturation, and genetic influences on the development of executive function. *Proceedings of the National Academy of Sciences of the United States of America, 102*(41), 14479–80. Retrieved from http://www.pnas.org/cgi/doi/10.1073/pnas.0506897102 (doi:10.1073/pnas.0506897102)

Rueda, M. R., Rothbart, M. K., Saccomanno, L., & Posner, M. I. (2007). Modifying brain networks underlying self-regulation. In D. Romer & E. F. Walker (Eds.), *Adolescent psychopathology and the developing brain: Integrating brain and prevention science* (pp. 401–419). New York, NY: Oxford University Press. doi:10.1093/acprof:oso/9780195306255.003.0018

Rueda, R. (2005). Searching for the grand unifying theory: Reflections on the field of LD. *Learning Disability Quarterly, 28*(2), 168–170. doi:10.2307/1593620.

Ruffman, T., Slade, L., & Redman, J. (2005). Young infants' expectations about hidden objects. *Cognition, 97*, B35–B43. doi:10.1016/j.cognition.2005.01.007

Ruhm, C. J. (1997). Is high school employment consumption or investment? *Journal of Labor Economics, 15*(4), 735–776.

Ruhm, C. J. (2000). Parental leave and child health. *Journal of Health Economics, 19*(6), 931–960.

Rumbaut, R. (2005). Children of immigrants and their achievement: The roles of family, acculturation, social class, ethnicity, and school contexts. In R. D. Taylor (Ed.), *Addressing the achievement gap: Theory informing practice* (pp. 21–59). Greenwich, CT: Information Age.

Rushton, J. L., Forcier, M., & Schectman, R. M. (2002). Epidemiology of depressive symptoms in the national longitudinal study of adolescent health. *Journal of the American Academy of Child & Adolescent Psychiatry, 41*(2), 199–205. doi:10.1097/00004583-200202000-00014

Rushton, J. P., & Jensen, A. R. (2005). Thirty years of research on race differences in cognitive ability. *Psychology, Public Policy, and Law, 11*(2), 235–294. doi:10.1037/1076-8971.11.2.235

Russ, S. W. (2009). Pretend play, emotional processes, and developing narratives. In S. W. Russ (Ed.), *The psychology of creative writing* (pp. 247–263). New York, NY: Cambridge University Press. doi:10.1017/CBO9780511627101.017

Russ, S. W., & Dillon, J. A. (2011). Changes in children's pretend play over two decades. *Creativity Research Journal, 23*(4) 330–338. doi:10.1080/10400419.2011.621824

Russell, K. F., Vandermeer, B., & Hartling, L. (2011). Graduated driver licensing for reducing motor vehicle crashes among young drivers (Article No. CD003300). *Cochrane Database Systematic Reviews, 5*(10).

Russell, S., & Joyner, K. (2001). Adolescent sexual orientation and suicide risk: Evidence from a national study. *American Journal of Public Health, 91*, 1276–1281.

Rusyniak, D. E., Arroyo, A., Acciani, J., Froberg, B., Kao, L., & Furbee, B. (2010). Heavy metal poisoning: Management of intoxication and antidotes. *Molecular, Clinical, and Environmental Toxicology, 100*, 365–396. doi:10.1007/978-3-7643-8338-1_11

Rutter, M. (1990). Psychosocial resilience and protective mechanisms. In J. Rolf, A. S. Masten, D. Cicchetti, K. H. Nuechterlein, & S. Weintraub (Eds.), *Risk and protective factors in the development of psychopathology* (pp. 181–214). New York, NY: Cambridge University Press.

Rutter, M. (2000). Genetic studies of autism: From the 1970s into the millennium. *Journal of Child Psychology & Psychiatry, 28*, 3–14.

Rutter, M. (2002). Nature, nurture, and development: From evangelism through science toward policy and practice. *Child Development, 73*(1), 1–21.

Rutter, M. (2006). *Genes and behavior: Nature-nurture interplay explained.* London, UK: Malden Blackwell.

Rutter, M. (2006). *Genes and development.* Oxford, UK: Blackwell.

Rutter, M. (2006). The psychological effects of early institutional rearing. In P. J. Marshall & N. A. Fox (Eds.), *The developmental of social engagement: Neurobiological perspectives. Series in affective science* (pp. 355–391). New York, NY: Oxford University Press.

Rutter, M., & English and Romanian Adoptees (ERA) Study Team (1998). Developmental catch-up, and deficit, following adoption after severe global early privation. *Journal of Child Psychology and Psychiatry, 39*(4), 465–476. doi:10.1017/S0021963098002236

Rutter, M., & O'Connor, T. G. (2004). Are there biological programming effects for psychological development? Findings from a study of Romanian adoptees. *Developmental Psychology, 40*(1), 81–94. doi:10.1037/0012-1649.40.1.81

Rutter, M., & Rutter, M. (1993). *Developing minds.* New York, NY: Basic Books.

Rutter, M., Beckett, C., Castle, J., Colvert, E., Kreppner, J., Mehta, M., . . . Sonuga-Barke, E. (2007). Effects of profound early institutional deprivation: An overview of findings from a UK longitudinal study of Romanian adoptees. *European Journal of Developmental Psychology, 4*(3), 332–350. doi:10.1080/17405620701401846

Rutter, M., Kim-Cohen, J., & Maughan, B. (2006). Continuities and discontinuities in psychopathology between childhood and adult life. *Journal of Child Psychology and Psychiatry, 47*(3–4), 276–295.

Rutter, M., Moffit, T. E., & Caspi, A. (2006). Gene-environment interplay and psychopathology: Multiple varieties but real effects. *Journal of Child Psychology and Psychiatry, 47*(3–4), 226–261.

Ryan, K. E., & Ryan, A. M. (2005). Psychological processes underlying stereotype threat and standardized math test performance. *Educational Psychologist, 40*(1), 53–63. doi:10.1207/s15326985ep4001_4

Ryan, R. M., & Deci, E. L. (2000a). Intrinsic and extrinsic motivations: Classic definitions and new directions. *Contemporary Educational Psychology, 25*(1), 54–67. doi:10.1006/ceps.1999.1020

Ryan, R. M., & Deci, E. L. (2000b). Self-determination theory and the facilitation of intrinsic motivation, social development, and well-being. *American Psychologist, 55*(1), 68–78. doi:10.1037/0003–066X.55.1.68

Ryan, R. M., Martin, A., & Brooks-Gunn, J. (2006). Is one good parent good enough? Patterns of mother and father parenting and child cognitive outcomes at 24 and 36 months. *Parenting: Science and Practice, 6*, 211–228.

Ryan, S. (2007). Parent-child interaction styles between gay and lesbian parents and their adopted children. In F. Tasker & J. J. Bigner (Eds.), *Gay and lesbian parenting: New directions* (pp. 105–132). Washington, DC: American Psychological Association.

Ryder, N., & Leinonen, E. (2003). Use of context in question answering by 3-, 4- and 5-year-old children. *Journal of Psycholinguistic Research, 32*(4), 397–415. doi:10.1023/A:1024847529077

Saar, M. (2007). Sports participation outside school in total physical activity of children. *Perceptual and Motor Skills, 105*(2), 559–562.

Saarni, C. (1997). Emotional competence and self-regulation in childhood. In C. Saarni (Ed.), *Emotional development and emotional intelligence: Educational implications* (pp. 35–69). New York, NY: Basic Books.

Saarni, C., Campos, J. J., Camras, L., & Witherington, D. (2006). Emotional development: Action, communication, and understanding. In N. Eisenberg (Ed.), *Handbook of child psychology: Vol. 3. Social, emotional, and personality development* (6th ed., pp. 226–299). Hoboken, NJ: Wiley.

Sacchetti, P., Sousa, K. M., Hall, A. C., Liste, I., Steffensen, K. R., Theofilopoulos, S., . . . Arenas, E. (2009). Liver X receptors and oxysterols promote ventral midbrain neurogenesis in vivo and in human embryonic stem cells. *Cell Stem Cell, 5*(4), 409–419. doi:10.1016/j.stem.2009.08.019

Sacks, B., & Buckley, S. J. (2003). Motor development for individuals with Down syndrome: An overview. *Down Syndrome Issues and Information, 2*(4), 131–141. doi:10.3104/9781903806173

Sacks, O. (1985). *The man who mistook his wife for a hat.* New York, NY: Simon & Schuster.

Safe Kids. (2011). *Sport and recreation safety fact sheet.* Retrieved from http://www.safekids.org

Sagi, A., & Hoffmann, M. L. (1976). Empathic distress in the newborn. *Developmental Psychology, 12*(2), 175–176.

Saigal, S., Hoult, L. A., Streiner, D. L., Stoskopf, B. L., & Rosenbaum, P. L. (2000). School difficulties at adolescence in a regional cohort of children who were extremely low birth weight. *Pediatrics, 105*(2), 325–331. doi:10.1542/peds.105.2.325

Salariya, E. M., Easton, P. M. & Cater, J. I. (1978). Duration of breast-feeding after early initiation and frequent feeding. *Lancet, 2*, 1141–1143. doi:10.1016/S0140–6736(78)92289–4

Saleem, M., Anderson, C. A., & Gentile, D. A. (2012). Effects of prosocial, neutral, and violent video games on children's helpful and hurtful behaviors. *Aggressive Behavior, 38*(4), 281–287. doi:10.1002/ab.2142

Saluja, G., Iachan, R., Scheidt, P., Overpeck, M., Sun, W., & Giedd, J. (2004). Prevalence of and risk factors for depressive symptoms among young adolescents. *Archives of Pediatric and Adolescent Medicine, 158*, 760–765.

Sameroff, A. (1975). Transactional models in early social relations. *Human Development, 18*, 65–79.

Sameroff, A. (2009). The transactional model. In A. Sameroff (Ed.), *The transactional model of development: How children and contexts shape each other* (pp. 1–21). Washington, DC: American Psychological Association.

Sameroff, A. (2010). A unified theory of development: A dialectic integration of nature and nurture. *Child Development, 81*(1), 6–22. doi:10.1111/j.1467–8624.2009.01378.x.

Sameroff, A. J., & Chandler, M. J. (1975). Reproductive risk and the continuum of caretaking casualty. In F. D. Horowitz, E. M. Hetherington, S. Scarr-Salapatek, & G. M. Siegel (Eds.), *Review of child development research* (pp. 187–244). Chicago, IL: University of Chicago Press.

Sameroff, A. J., & Fiese, B. H. (2000).Transactional regulation: The developmental ecology of early intervention. In J. P. Shonkoff & S. J. Meisels (Eds.), *Handbook of early childhood intervention* (pp. 135–159). New York, NY: Cambridge University Press.

Sameroff, A. J., & Haith, M. M. (Eds.). (1996). *The five- to seven-year shift: The age of reason and responsibility.* Chicago, IL: University of Chicago Press.

Sampson, H. A. (2004). Update on food allergy. *The Journal of Allergy and Clinical Immunology, 113*, 805–819. doi:10.1016/j.jaci.2004.03.014

Sampson, H. A., & Ho, D. (1997). Relationship between food-specific IgE concentration and the risk of positive food challenges in children and adolescents. *The Journal of Allergy and Clinical Immunology, 100*(4), 444–451. doi:10.1016/S0091-6749(97)70133-7

Sampson, P. D., Streissguth, A. P., Bookstein, F. L., & Barr, H. M. (2000). On categorizations in analyses of alcohol teratogenesis. *Environmental Health Perspectives, 108*(Suppl. 3), 421–428. doi:10.2307/3454531

Sampson, P. D., Streissguth, A. P., Bookstein, F. L., Little, R. E., Clarren, S. K., Dehaene, P., . . . Graham, J. M., Jr. (1997). Incidence of fetal alcohol syndrome and prevalence of alcohol-related neurodevelopmental disorder. *Teratology, 56*, 317–326. doi:10.1002/(SICI)1096–9926(199711)56:5<317::AID–TERA5>3.0.CO;2–U

Sander, L. (2009, January 15). Under new NCAA rule, 7th-grade basketball players are "prospective athletes." *Chronicle of Higher Education.* Retrieved from http://chronicle.com/article/Under-New-NCAA-Rule-7th-Gr/42251

Sander, M. C., Werkle-Bergner, M., Gerjets, P., Shing, Y. L., & Lindenberger, U. (2012). The two-component model of memory development, and its potential implications for educational settings. *Developmental Cognitive Neuroscience, 2*(Suppl. 1), S6–S77. doi:10.1016/j.dcn.2011.11.005

Sanders, L., & Buckner, E. B. (2006). The Newborn Behavioral Observations (NBO) system as a nursing intervention to enhance engagement in first-time mothers: Feasibility and desirability. *Pediatric Nursing, 32*(5), 455–459.

Sandler, I., Miles, J., Cookston, J., & Braver, S. (2008). Effects of father and mother parenting on children's mental health in high- and low-conflict divorces. *Family Court Review, 46*(2), 282–296. doi:10.1111/j.1744–1617.2008.00201.x

Sanford, B., & Weber, P. C. (2010). Etiology of hearing impairment in children. In G. C. Isaacson (Ed.), *UpToDate.* Waltham, MA: UpToDate.

Santelli, J., Sandfort, T., & Orr, M. (2008). Transnational comparisons of adolescent contraceptive use: What can we learn from these comparisons? *Archives of Pediatrics & Adolescent Medicine, 162*(1), 92–94.

Sarkadi, A., Kristiansson, R., Oberklaid, F., & Bremberg, S. (2008). Fathers' involvement and children's developmental outcomes: A systematic review of longitudinal studies. *Acta Pædiatrica, 97*, 153–158.

Sarrazin, J., & Cyr, F. (2007). Parental conflicts and their damaging effects on children. *Journal of Divorce & Remarriage, 47*(1–2), 77–93. doi:10.1300/J087v47n01_05

Satin, A. J., Leveno, K. J., Sherman, M. L., Reedy, N. J., Lowe, T. W., & McIntire, D. D. (1994). Maternal youth and pregnancy outcomes: Middle school versus high school age groups compared with women beyond the teen years. *American Journal of Obstetrics and Gynecology, 171*, 184–187.

Savin-Williams, R. C., & Diamond, L. (2004). Sex. In R. M. Lerner & L. Steinberg (Eds.), *Handbook of adolescent psychology* (2nd ed., pp. 189–231). Hoboken, NJ: Wiley.

Savin-Williams, R. C., & Dubé, E. M. (1998). Parental reactions to their child's disclosure of a gay/lesbian identity. *Family Relations: An Interdisciplinary Journal of Applied Family Studies, 47*(1), 7–13. doi:10.2307/584845

Savoca, M. R., Evans, C. D., Wilson, M. E, Harshfield, G. A., & Ludwig, D. A. (2004). The association of caffeinated beverages with blood pressure in adolescents. *Archives of Pediatric and Adolescent Medicine, 158*, 473–477.

Sax, L. (2005). *Why gender matters: What parents and teachers need to know about the emerging science of sex differences*. New York, NY: Doubleday.

Sayer, L. C. (2006). Economic aspects of divorce and relationship dissolution. In L. C. Sayer (Ed.), *Handbook of divorce and relationship dissolution* (pp. 385–406). Mahwah, NJ: Erlbaum.

Scanlon, D. M., & Vellutino, F. R. (1996). Prerequisite skills, early instruction, and success in first-grade reading: Selected results from a longitudinal study. *Mental Retardation and Developmental Disabilities Research Reviews, 2*(1), 54–63. doi:10.1002/(SICI)1098-2779(1996)2:13.0.CO;2-X

Scarr, S. (1992). Developmental theories for the 1990s: Development and individual differences. *Child Development, 63*(1), 1–19. doi:10.1111/j.1467–8624.1992.tb03591.x

Scarr, S. (1996). How people make their own environments: Implications for parents and policy makers. *Psychology, Public Policy, and Law, 2*(2), 204–228. doi:10.1037//1076–8971.2.2.204

Scarr, S., & McCartney, K. (1983). How people make their own environments: A theory of genotype greater than environment effects. *Child Development, 54*(2), 424–435. doi:10.2307/1129703

Schaal, B., Tremblay, R., Soussignan, R., & Sussman, E. (1996). Male testosterone linked to high social dominance but low physical aggression in early adolescence. *Journal of the American Academy of Child & Adolescent Psychiatry, 35*(10), 1322–1330.

Schacter, D. L. (1992). Understanding implicit memory: A cognitive neuroscience approach. *American Psychologist, 47*(7), 559–569.

Schacter, D. L., & Scarry, E. (2000). *Memory, brain, and belief.* Cambridge, MA: Harvard University Press.

Schaffir, J. (2007). Do patients associate adverse pregnancy outcomes with folkloric beliefs? *Archives of Womens' Mental Health, 10*(6), 301–304. doi:10.1007/s00737–007–0201–0

Schalet, A. (2004). Must we fear adolescent sexuality? *Medscape General Medicine, 6*(4), 44. Retrieved from http://www.medscape.com/viewarticle/494933

Schatz, J., & McClellan, C. B. (2006). Sickle cell disease as a *neurodevelopmental* disorder. *Mental Retardation and Developmental Disabilities Research Reviews, 12*, 200–207. doi:10.1002/mrdd.20115

Scheers, N. J., Rutherford, G. W., & Kemp, J. S. (2003). Where should infants sleep? A comparison of risk for suffocation of infants sleeping in cribs, adult beds, and other sleeping locations. *Pediatrics, 112*, 883–889. doi:10.1542/peds.112.4.883

Schickendanz, J. (1999). *Much more than the ABC's*: The early stages of reading and writing. Washington, DC: NAEYC.

Schilling, L. S., Knafl, K. A., & Grey, M. (2006). Changing patterns of self-management in youth with type I diabetes. *Journal of Pediatric Nursing, 21*(6), 412–424.

Schleepen, T. M. J., & Jonkman, L. M. (2012). Children's use of semantic organizational strategies is mediated by working memory capacity. *Cognitive Development, 27*(3), 255-260. doi:10.1016/j.cogdev.2012.03.003

Schmahmann, J. D., & Caplan, D. (2006). Cognition, emotion and the cerebellum. *Brain, 129*(2), 290–291. doi:10.1093/brain/awh729

Schmakel, P. O. (2008). Early adolescents' perspectives on motivation and achievement in academics. *Urban Education, 43*(6), 723–749. doi:10.1177/0042085907311831

Schmidt, L. (2009). Social and psychological consequences of infertility and assisted reproduction: What are the research priorities? *Human Fertility, 12*(1), 14–20. doi:10.1080/14647270802331487

Schmidt, M. E., Rich, M., Rifas-Schiman, S., Oken, E., & Taveras, E. (2009). Television viewing in infancy and child cognition at 3 years of age in a US cohort. *Pediatrics, 123*(3), 370–375.

Schmitt, K. L., & Anderson, D. R. (2002). Television and reality: Toddlers' use of visual information from video to guide behavior. *Media Psychology, 4*, 51–76. doi:10.1207/S1532785XMEP0401_03

Schneider, B. H. (1992). Didactic methods for enhancing children's peer relations: A quantitative review. *Clinical Psychology Review, 12*(3), 363–382. doi:10.1016/0272–7358(92)90142–U

Schneider, B. H., Woodburn, S., del Pilar Soteras del Toro, M., & Udvari, S. J. (2005). Cultural and gender differences in the implications of competition for early adolescent friendship. *Merrill-Palmer Quarterly, 51*(2), 163–191. doi:10.1353/mpq. 2005.0013

Schneider, N., Frieler, K., Pfeiffer, E., Lehmkuhl, U., & Salbach-Andrae, H. (2009). Comparison of body size estimation in adolescents with different types of eating disorders. *European Eating Disorders Review, 17*(6), 468–475. doi:10.1002/erv.956

Schneider, W. (2002). Memory development in childhood. In G. Mazzoni & T. O. Nelson (Eds.), *Blackwell handbook of childhood cognitive development* (pp. 236–256). Malden, MA: Blackwell. doi:10.1002/9780470996652.ch11

Schneider, W., & Lockl, K. (2002). The development of metacognitive knowledge in children and adolescents. In T. J. Perfect & B. L. Schwartz (Eds.), *Applied metacognition* (pp. 224–257). New York, NY: Cambridge University Press.

Schore, A. N. (1996). The experience-dependent maturation of a regulatory system in the orbital prefrontal cortex and the origin of developmental psychopathology. *Development and Psychopathology, 8*, 59–87. doi:10.1017/S0954579400006970

Schore, A. N. (2000). Attachment and the regulation of the right brain. *Attachment & Human Development, 2*(1), 23–47.

Schumacher, R., Hamm, K., Goldstein, A., & Lombardi, J. (2006). *Starting off right: Promoting child development from birth in state early care and education initiatives.* Washington, D.C.: Center for Law and Social Policy. Retrieved from http://www.clasp.org/admin/site/publications_states/files/0316.pdf

Schunk, D. H. (2012). *Learning theories: An educational perspective* (6th ed.). Boston, MA. Allyn & Bacon.

Schunk, D. H., & Pajares, F. (2009). Self-efficacy theory. In K. R. Wenzel & A. Wigfield (Eds.), *Handbook of motivation at school* (pp. 35–53). New York, NY: Routledge/Taylor & Francis.

Schupp, H. T., Cuthbert, B. N., Bradley, M. M., Hillman, C. H., Hamm, A. O., & Lang, P. J. (2004). Brain processes in emotional perception: Motivated attention. *Cognition and Emotion, 18*, 593–611.

Schwartz, D. A. (2009). Gene-environment interactions and airway disease in children. *Pediatrics, 123*(Suppl. 3), S151–S159. doi:10.1542/peds.2008-2233E

Schwarz, A. (2010, September 24). Congress considers concussion protections. *The New York Times*, p. B11. Retrieved from http://www.nytimes.com/2010/09/24/sports/football/24concussion.html

Schweinhart, L. J., Barnes, H. V., & Weikart, D. P. (1993). Significant benefits: The High/Scope Perry Preschool study through age 27. *Monographs of the High/Scope Educational Research Foundation, 10*, Yypsilanti, MI: High/Scope Press.

Schweinhart, L. J., Montie, J., Xiang, Z., Barnett, W. S., Belfield, C. R., & Nores, M. (2005). Lifetime effects: The High/Scope Perry Preschool study through age 40. *Monographs of the High/Scope Educational Research Foundation, 14.* Yypsilanti, MI: High/Scope Press.

Scott, E. S., & Steinberg, L. (2008). Adolescent development and the regulation of youth crime. *Future of Children, 18*(2), 15–33. doi:10.1353/foc.0.0011

Scott, L. S. (2011). Mechanisms underlying the emergence of object representations during infancy. *Journal of Cognitive Neuroscience, 23*, 2935–2955.

Scott, L. S., & Monesson, A. (2010). Experience dependent neural specialization during infancy. *Neuropsychologia, 48*, 1857–1861.

Scott, L. S., & Nelson, C. A. (2006). Featural and configural face processing in adults and infants: A behavioral and electrophysiological investigation. *Perception, 35*(8), 1107–1128. doi:10.1068/p5493

Scott-Little, C., Kagan, S. L., & Frelow, V. S. (2006). Conceptualization of readiness and the content of early learning standards: The intersection of policy and research. *Early Childhood Research Quarterly, 21*(2), 153–173. doi:10.1016/j.ecresq.2006.04.003

Scrimsher, S., & Tudge, J. (2003). The teaching/learning relationship in the first years of school: Some revolutionary implications of Vygotsky's theory. *Early Education and Development, Special Issue: Vygotskian Perspectives in Early Childhood Education, 14*(3), 293–312. doi:10.1207/s15566935eed1403_3

Scruggs, T. E., & Mastropieri, M. A. (2000). The effectiveness of mnemonic instruction for students with learning and behavior problems: An update and research synthesis. *Journal of Behavioral Education, 10*(2–3), 163–173. doi:10.1023/A:1016640214368

Segall, M. H., Dasen, P. R., Berry, J. W., & Poortinga, Y. H. (1999). *Human behavior in global perspective: An introduction to cross-cultural psychology*. Needham Heights, MA: Allyn & Bacon.

Seifert, S. M., Schaechter, J. L., Hershorin, E. R., & Lipshultz, S. E. (2011). Health effects of energy drinks on children, adolescents, and young adults. *Pediatrics, 127*(3), 511–528. doi:10.1542/peds.2009–3592

Seiffge-Krenke, I. (2000). Diversity in romantic relations of adolescents with varying health status: Links to intimacy in close friendships. *Journal of Adolescent Research, 15*(6), 611–636. doi:10.1177/0743558400156001

Selby, J. M. & Bradley, B. S. (2003). Infants in groups: A paradigm for the study of early social experience. *Human Development, 46*, 197–221.

Seligman, M. (1970). On the generality of the laws of learning. *Psychological Review*, 77, 406–418. doi:10.1037/h0029790

Seligman, M. E. P. (2003). Positive psychology: Fundamental assumptions. *Psychologist, 16*(3), 126–127.

Selman, R. L. (1976). Social-cognitive understanding: A guide to educational and clinical practice. In T. Lickona (Ed.), *Moral development and behavior: Theory, research, and social issues* (pp. 299–316). New York, NY: Holt, Rinehart, & Winston.

Selman, R. L. (1980). *The growth of interpersonal understanding: Developmental and clinical analyses*. New York, NY: Academic Press.

Selman, R. L. (1981). The child as a friendship philosopher. In S. R. Asher & J. M. Cottman (Eds.), *The development of children's friendships*. New York, NY: Cambridge University Press.

Selman, R. L., Levitt, M. Z., & Schultz, L. H. (1997). The friendship framework: Tools for the assessment of psychosocial development. In R. L. Selman, C. L. Watts, & L. H. Schultz (Eds.), *Fostering friendship: Pair therapy for treatment and prevention* (pp. 31–52). Hawthorne, NY: Aldine de Gruyter.

Seminara, S. B., Messager, S., Chatzidaki, E. E., Thresher, R. R., Acierno, J. Jr., Shagoury, J. K. . . . Colledge, W. H. (2004). The GPR54 gene as a regulator of puberty. *Obstetrical & Gynecological Survey, 59*(5), 351–353.

Seo, K.-H., & Ginsburg, H. P. (2004). What is developmentally appropriate in early childhood mathematics education? Lessons from new research. In D. H. Clements, J. Samara, & A.-M. DiBiase (Eds.), *Engaging young children in mathematics: Standards for early childhood mathematics education* (pp. 91–104). Hillsdale, NJ: Erlbaum.

Sepkoski, C. M., Lester, B. M., Ostheimer, G. W., & Brazelton, T. B. (1992). The effects of maternal epidural anesthesia on neonatal behavior during the first month. *Developmental Medicine and Child Neurology, 34*(12), 1072–1080.

Servin, A., Nordenström, A., Larsson, A., & Bohlin, G. (2003). Prenatal androgens and gender-typed behavior: A study of girls with mild and severe forms of congenital adrenal hyperplasia. *Developmental Psychology, 39*(3), 440–450. doi: 10.1037/0012-1649.39.3.440

Setlik, J., Bond, G. R., & Ho, M. (2009). Adolescent prescription ADHD medication abuse is rising along with prescriptions for these medications. *Pediatrics, 124*, 875–880. doi: 10.1542/peds.2008–0931

Setti, A., & Caramelli, N. (2007). Inhibition and language pragmatic view in redundant data problem solving. *Cognitive Development, 22*(3), 299–309. doi:10.1016/j.cogdev.2006.12.002.

Shanahan, M. J., & Flaherty, B. P. (2001). Dynamic patterns of time use in adolescence. *Child Development*, 72(2), 385–401. doi:10.1111/1467–8624.00285

Shankaran, S., Lester, B. M., Das, A., Bauer, C. R., Bada, H. S., Lagasse, L., & Higgins, R. (2007). Impact of maternal substance abuse during pregnancy on childhood outcome. *Seminars in Fetal & Neonatal Medicine, 12*(2), 143–50. doi:10.1016/j.siny.2007.01.002

Shannon, J. D., Tamis-LeMonda, C. S., & Cabrera, N. (2006). Fathering in infancy: Mutuality and stability between 6 and 14 months. *Parenting: Science & Practice, 6*, 167–188.

Shatz , M., & Gelman, R. (1973). The development of communication skills: Modifications in the speech of young children as a function of the listener. *Monographs of the Society for Research in Child Development, 37*, 1–38. doi:10.2307/1165783

Shaw, A., & Olson, K. R. (2012). Children discard a resource to avoid inequity. *Journal of Experimental Psychology, 141*(2), 382–395. doi:10.1037/a0025907

Shaw, P., Kabani, N. J., Lerch, J. P., Eckstrand, K., Lenroot, R., Gogtay, N., . . . Wise, S. P. (2008). Neurodevelopmental trajectories of the human cerebral cortex. *The Journal of Neuroscience, 28*(14), 3586–3594.

Shaywitz, S. (2003). *Overcoming dyslexia: A new and complete science-based program for reading problems at any level*. New York, NY: Knopf.

Shearer, B. (2004). Multiple intelligences theory after 20 years. *Teachers College Record, 106*(1), 2–16. doi:10.1111/j.1467–9620.2004.00312.x

Sheffield, E. G., & Hudson, J. A. (2006). You must remember this: Effects of video and photograph reminders on 18-month-olds' event memory. *Journal of Cognition & Development*, 7(1), 73–93. doi:10.1207/s15327647jcd0701_4

Sheffield, J. S., Butler–Koster, E. L., Casey, B. M., McIntire, D. D., & Leveno, K. J. (2002). Maternal diabetes mellitus and infant malformations. *Obstetrics and Gynecology, 100*, 925–930. doi:10.1016/S0029–7844(02)02242–1

Shelov, S., & Altmann, T. (2009). *Caring for your baby and young child: Birth to age 5* (5th ed.). Elk Grove Village, IL: American Academy of Pediatrics.

Shepard, R., & Trudeau, F. (2008). Research on the outcomes of elementary school physical education. *Elementary School Journal, 108*(3), 251–264.

Sherman, D. K., Hartson, K. A., Binning, K. R., Purdie-Vaughns, V., Garcia, J., Taborsky-Barba, S., . . . Cohen, G. L. (2013). Deflecting the trajectory and changing the narrative: How self-affirmation affects academic performance and motivation under identity threat. *Journal of Personality and Social Psychology, 104*(4), 591–618. doi:10.1037/a0031495

Shing, Y. L., Lindenberger, U., Diamond, A., Li, S., & Davidson, M. C. (2010). Memory maintenance and inhibitory control differentiate from early childhood to adolescence. *Developmental Neuropsychology, 35*(6), 679–697. doi:10.1080/87565641.2010.508546

Shinskey, J. L., & Munakata, Y. (2003). Are infants in the dark about hidden objects? *Developmental Science, 6*(3). doi:273–282 10.1111/1467–7687.00283

Shonkoff, J. P., & Bales, S. N. (2011). Science does not speak for itself: Translating child development research for the public and its policymakers. *Child Development, 82*(1), 17–32.doi:10.1111/j.1467-8624.2010.01538.x

Shonkoff, J. P., & Phillips, D. A. (2000). *From neurons to neighborhoods: The science of early childhood development*. Washington, DC: National Academies Press.

Shonkoff, J. P., Boyce, W. T., & McEwen, B. S. (2009). Neuroscience, molecular biology, and the childhood roots of health disparities: Building a new framework for health promotion and disease prevention. *Journal of the American Medical Association, 301*, 2252–2259. doi:10.1001/jama.2009.754

Shope, J. T. (2007). Graduated driver licensing: Review of evaluation results since 2002. *Journal of Safety Research, 38*, 165–175.

Shortridge, K. F., Lawton, J. W. M., & Choi, E. K. K. (1990). Protective potential of colostrum and early milk against prospective influenza viruses. *Journal of Tropical Pediatrics, 36*, 94–95.

Shostak, M. (1981). *Nisa: The life and words of a !Kung Woman*. Cambridge, MA: Harvard University Press.

Shults, R. A. (2004). Child passenger deaths involving drinking drivers—United States, 1997–2002. *Morbidity & Mortality Weekly Report, 53*(4), 77–79.

Shweder, R. A., Much, N. C., Mahapatra, M., & Park, L. (1997). The "big three" of morality (autonomy, community, divinity) and the "big three" explanations of suffering. In A. M. Brandt & P. Rozin (Eds.), *Morality and health* (pp. 119–169). Florence, KY: Taylor & Frances/Routledge.

Sibley, A., Sheehan, M., & Pollard, A. J. (2012). Assent is not consent. *Journal of Medical Ethics: Journal of the Institute of Medical Ethics, 38*(1), 3–3. doi:10.1136/medethics-2011-100317

Sicherer, S. H., & Sampson, H. A. (2010). Food allergy. *The Journal of Allergy and Clinical Immunology, 125*(Suppl. 2), S116–125. pmid: 20042231

Siegal, M., Iozzi, L., & Surian, L. (2009). Bilingualism and conversational understanding in young children. *Cognition, 110*(1), 115–122. doi:10.1016/j.cognition.2008.11.002

Siegel, A. C., & Burton, R. V. (1999). Effects of baby walkers on motor and mental development in human infants. *Journal of Developmental and Behavioral Pediatrics, 20*(5), 355–361.

Siegel, D. (2001). Toward an interpersonal neurobiology of the developing mind: Attachment relationship, "mindsight," and neural integration. *Infant Mental Health Journal, 22*(1–2), 67–94.

Siegel, J. M., Yancy, A. K., Aneshensel, C. S., & Schuler, R. (1999). Body image, perceived pubertal timing, and adolescent mental health. *Journal of Adolescent Health, 25*, 155–165.

Siegler, R. S. (1995). How does change occur: A microgenetic study of number conservation. *Cognitive Psychology, 28*(3), 225–273. doi:10.1006/cogp.1995.1006

Siegler, R. S., & Alibali, M. W. (2004). *Children's thinking* (4th ed.). Upper Saddle River, NJ: Prentice Hall.

Siegler, R. S., & Booth, J. L. (2004). Development of numerical estimation in young children. *Child Development, 75*(2), 428–444. doi:10.1111/j.1467-8624.2004.00684.x

Siegler, R. S., & Jenkins, E. A. (1989). *How children discover new strategies*. Hillsdale, NJ: Erlbaum.

Siegler, R. S., & Shrager, J. (1984). Strategy choice in addition and subtraction: How do children know what to do? In C. Sophian (Ed.), *Origins of cognitive skills* (pp. 229–293). Hillsdale, NJ: Erlbaum.

Sigal, A. B., Wolchik, S. A., Tein, J., & Sandler, I. N. (2012). Enhancing youth outcomes following parental divorce: A longitudinal study of the effects of the new beginnings program on educational and occupational goals. *Journal of Clinical Child and Adolescent Psychology, 41*(2), 150–165. doi:10.1080/15374416.2012.651992

Sigal, A., Sandler, I., Wolchik, S., & Braver, S. (2011). Do parent education programs promote healthy postdivorce parenting? Critical distinctions and a review of the evidence. *Family Court Review, 49*(1), 120–139. doi:10.1111/j.1744-1617.2010.01357.x

Sigel, E. (2009). Disordered eating behaviors: Anorexia nervosa and bulimia nervosa. In W. B. Carey, A. Crocker, W. L. Coleman, E. R. Elias, & H. M. Feldman (Eds.), *Developmental-behavioral pediatrics* (4th ed., pp. 569–581). Philadelphia, PA: Saunders.

Sigman, M., Mundy, P., Sherman, T., & Ungerer, J. (1986). Social interactions of autistic, mentally retarded and normal children with their caregivers. *Journal of Child Psychology & Psychiatry, 27*, 647–669.

Silk, J. S., Morris, A. S., Kanaya, T., & Steinberg, L. (2003). Psychological control and autonomy granting: Opposite ends of a continuum or distinct constructs? *Journal of Research on Adolescence, 13*(1), 113–128. doi:10.1111/1532-7795.1301004

Silveri, M. M., Tzilos, G. K., & Yurgelun-Todd, D. A. (2008). Relationship between white matter volume and cognitive performance during adolescence: Effects of age, sex and risk for drug use. *Addiction, 103*(9), 1509–1520. doi:10.1111/j.1360-0443.2008.02272.x

Silvers, J. A., McRae, K., Gabrieli, J. D. E., Gross, J. J., Remy, K. A., & Ochsner, K. N. (2012). Age-related differences in emotional reactivity, regulation, and rejection sensitivity in adolescence. *Emotion, 12*(6), 1235–1247. doi:10.1037/a0028297

Silverstein, J., Klingensmith, G., Copeland, K., Plotnick, L., Kaufman, F., Laffel, L., . . . Clark, N. (2005). Care of children and adolescents with type 1 diabetes: A statement of the American Diabetes Association. *Diabetes Care, 28*(1), 186–212.

Silverstein, M., & Ruiz, S. (2006). Breaking the chain: How grandparents moderate the transmission of maternal depression to their grandchildren. *Family Relations, 55*, 601–612.

Simcock, G & DeLoache, J. (2006). Get the picture? The effects of iconicity on toddlers' re-enactment from picture books. *Developmental Psychology, 42*, 1352–1357.

Simcock, G., & Dooley, M. (2007). Generalization of learning from picture books to novel test conditions by 18- and 24-month-old children. *Developmental Psychology, 43*(6), 1568–1578. doi:10.1037/0012-1649.43.6.1568

Simkin P. (1991). Just another day in a woman's life? Women's long-term perceptions of their first birth experience. Part I. *Birth, 18*(4), 203–210.

Simkin, P. (1992). Just another day in a woman's life? Part II: Nature and consistency of women's long-term memories of their first birth experiences. *Birth 19*(2), 64–81

Simkin, P., Bolding, A., & Keppler, A. (2010). *Pregnancy, childbirth, and the newborn* (4th ed.). New York, NY: Simon & Schuster.

Simmering, V. R. (2012). The development of visual working memory capacity during early childhood. *Journal of Experimental Child Psychology, 111*(4), 695–707. doi:10.1016/j.jecp.2011.10.007

Simon, V. A., Aikins, J. W., & Prinstein, M. J. (2008). Romantic partner selection and socialization during early adolescence. *Child Development, 79*(6), 1676–1692. doi:10.1111/j.1467-8624.2008.01218.x

Simonson, C., Barlow, P., Dehennin, N., Sphel, M., Toppet, V., Murillo, D., & Rozenberg, S. (2007). Neonatal complications of vacuum-assisted delivery. *Obstetrics & Gynecology, 109*(3), 626–633.

Simos, P. G., Fletcher, J. M., Sarkari, S., Billingsley, R. L., Denton, C., & Papanicolaou, A. C. (2007). Altering the brain circuits for reading through intervention: A magnetic source imaging study. *Neuropsychology, 21*(4), 485–496. doi:10.1037/0894-4105.21.4.485

Simpson, W. J. (1957). A preliminary report on cigarette smoking and the incidence of prematurity. *Obstetrical & Gynecological Survey, 12*(6), 868–869.

Singer, J., & Hornstein, J. (2010). The touchpoints approach for early childhood care and education providers. In B. M. Lester & J. D. Sparrow (Eds.), *Nurturing children and families: Building on the legacy of T. Berry Brazelton* (pp. 288–299). West Sussex, UK: Wiley-Blackwell.

Singer, L. T., Minnes, S., Short, E., Arendt, R., Farkas, K., Lewis, B., . . . Kirchner, L. (2004). Cognitive outcomes of preschool children with prenatal cocaine exposure. *Journal of the American Medical Association, 291*(20), 2448–2456. doi:10.1001/jama.291.20.2448

Sintov, N. D., & Prescott, C. A. (2011). The influence of social desirability and item priming effects on reports of proenvironmental behavior. *Ecopsychology, 3*(4), 257–267. doi:10.1089/eco.2011.0043

Sisson, S. B., Church, T. S., Martin, C. K., Tudor-Locke, C., Smith, S. R., Bouchard, C., . . . Katzmarzyk, P. T. (2009). Profiles of sedentary behavior in children and adolescents: The U.S. national health and nutritional examination survey, 2001–2006. *International Journal of Pediatric Obesity, 4*(4), 353–359. doi:10.3109/17477160902934777

Skinner, B. F. (1953). *Science and human behavior*. New York, NY: Macmillan.

Skinner, B. F. (1974). *About behaviorism*. New York, NY: Knopf.

Skinner, B. F. (1983). *A matter of consequences*. New York, NY: Knopf.

Skinner, D., Bailey, D. B., Correa, V., & Rodriguez, P. (1999). Narrating self and disability: Latino mothers' construction of identities vis-à-vis their child with special needs. *Exceptional Children, 65*(4), 481–495.

Slaby, R. G., & Frey, K. S. (1975). Development of gender constancy and selective attention to same-sex models. *Child Development, 46*(4), 849–856. doi:10.2307/1128389

Slade, A. (2002). Keeping the baby in mind: A critical factor in perinatal mental health. *Zero to Three, 22*(6), 10–16.

Slater, A. (1995). Individual differences in infancy and later IQ. *Journal of Child Psychology and Psychiatry, 36*(1), 69–112.

Slater, A., Morison, V., Town, C., & Rose, D. (1985). Movement perception and identity constancy in the new-born baby. *British Journal of Developmental Psychology, 3*(3), 211–220. doi:10.1111/j.2044-835X.1985.tb00974.x

Small, M. (1998). *Our babies, ourselves: How biology and culture shape the way we parent*. New York, NY: Anchor Books.

Smetana, J. G. (2006). *Social-cognitive domain theory: Consistencies and variations in children's moral and social judgments*. Mahwah, NJ: Erlbaum.

Smetana, J. G., & Braeges, J. L. (1990). The development of toddler's moral and conventional judgments *Merrill-Palmer Quarterly, 36*(3), 329–346.

Smetana, J. G., & Villalobos, M. (2009). Social cognitive development in adolescence. In R. M. Lerner & L. Steinberg (Eds.), *Handbook of adolescent psychology: Vol. 1. Individual bases of adolescent development* (3rd ed., pp. 187–228). Hoboken, NJ: Wiley.

Smetana, J. G., Metzger, A., Gettman, D. C., & Campione-Barr, N. (2006). Disclosure and secrecy in adolescent-parent relationships. *Child Development, 77*(1), 201–217. doi:10.1111/j.1467-8624.2006.00865.x

Smetana, J. G., Rote, W. M., Jambon, M., Tasopoulos-Chan, M., Villalobos, M., & Comer, J. (2012). Developmental changes and individual differences in young children's moral judgments. *Child Development, 83*(2), 683–696. doi:10.1111/j.1467- 8624.2011.01714.x

Smith, A. J., Jordan, J. A., Flood, M. F., & Hansen, D. J. (2010). Social skills interventions. In A. J. Smith, J. A. Jordan, M. F. Flood, & D. J. Hansen (Eds.), *Practitioner's guide to empirically based measures of social skills* (pp. 99–115). New York, NY: Springer.

Smith, B. H., Barkley, R. A., & Shapiro, C. J. (2006). Attention-deficit/hyperactivity disorder. In E. J. Mash & R. A. Barkley (Eds.), *Treatment of childhood disorders* (3rd ed., pp. 65–136). New York, NY: Guilford.

Smith, D. G., Xiao, L., & Bechara, A. (2012). Decision making in children and adolescents: Impaired Iowa gambling task performance in early adolescence. *Developmental Psychology, 48*(4), 1180–1187. doi:10.1037/a0026342

Smith, I. M. & Bryson, S. E. (1994). Imitation and action in autism: A critical review. *Psychological Bulletin, 116(2)*, 259–273.

Smith, M. J., Schmidt, P. J., & Rubinow, D. R. (2003). Operationalizing DSM-IV criteria for PMDD: Selecting symptomatic and asymptomatic cycles for research. *Journal of Psychiatric Research, 37*(1), 75–83.

Smith, R. J. H., Bale J. F., Jr., & White, K. R. (2005). Sensorineural hearing loss in children. *Lancet, 365*(9462), 879–890. doi:10.1016/S0140-6736(05)71047-3

Smith, R. L., Rose, A. J., & Schwartz-Mette, R. A. (2010). Relational and overt aggression in childhood and adolescence: Clarifying mean-level gender differences and associations with peer acceptance. *Social Development, 19*(2), 243–269. doi:10.1111/j.1467–9507.2009.00541.x

Smyke, A., Zeanah, C., Fox, N., Nelson, C., & Guthrie, D. (2010). Placement in foster care enhances quality of attachment among young institutionalized children. *Child Development, 81*(1), 212–223.

Snarey, J. (1995). In a communitarian voice: The sociological expansion of Kohlbergian theory, research, and practice. In W. Kurtines & J. Gewirtz (Eds.), *Moral development: An introduction*. (pp. 109–133). Boston, MA: Allyn & Bacon.

Snarey, J., & Samuelson, P. (2008). Moral education in the cognitive developmental tradition: Lawrence Kohlberg's revolutionary ideas. In L. P. Nucci & D. Narvaez (Eds.), *Handbook of moral and character education* (pp. 53–79). New York, NY: Routledge.

Snow, C. E. (2010). Academic language and the challenge of reading for learning about science. *Science, 328*(5977), 450–452. doi:10.1126/science.1182597

Snow, C. E., & Kang, J. Y. (2006). Becoming bilingual, biliterate, and bicultural. In W. Damon & R. M. Lerner (Series Eds.) & K. A. Renninger & I. E. Sigel (Vol. Eds.), *Handbook of child psychology: Vol. 4. Child psychology in practice* (6th ed., pp. 75–102). Hoboken, NJ: Wiley.

Society for Adolescent Medicine. (2004). Confidential health care for adolescents: Position paper of the Society for Adolescent Medicine. *Journal of Adolescent Health, 35*(2), 160–167.

Society for Research in Child Development. (2007). *SRCD ethical standards for research with children*. Retrieved from http://www.srcd.org/ethicalstandards.html

Soderqvist, S., Nutley, S. B., Peyrard-Janvid, M., Matsson, H., Humphreys, K., Kere, J., & Klingberg, T. (2012). Dopamine, working memory, and training induced plasticity: Implications for developmental research. *Developmental Psychology, 48*(3), 836–843. doi:10.1037/a0026179

Soenens, B., & Vansteenkiste, M. (2010). A theoretical upgrade of the concept of parental psychological control: Proposing new insights on the basis of self-determination theory. *Developmental Review, 30*(1), 74–99. doi:10.1016/j.dr.2009.11.001

Soken, N., & Pick, A. (1999). Infants' perceptions of dynamic affective expressions: Do infants distinguish specific expressions? *Child Development, 70*, 1275–1282.

Sokol, R. J., Delaney-Black, V., & Nordstrom, B. (2003). Fetal alcohol spectrum disorder. *Journal of the American Medical Association, 290*(22), 2996–2999. doi:10.1001/jama.290.22.2996

Sokolove, M. (2008, May 11). The uneven playing field. *The New York Times Magazine*. Retrieved from http://www.nytimes.com/2008/05/11/magazine/11Girls-t.html?pagewanted=all

Solomon, N. M. (2002). *Girls' participation in sports: An important tool in teen pregnancy prevention. Policy brief.* Los Angeles, CA: California Women's Law Center.

Solomons, G., & Solomons, H. C. (1975). Motor development in Yucatecan infants. *Developmental Medicine & Child Neurology, 17*, 41–46. doi:10.1111/j.1469–8749.1975.tb04955.x

Somerville, L. H., & Casey, B. J. (2010). Developmental neurobiology of cognitive control and motivational systems. *Current Opinions in Neurobiology, 20*(2), 236–241. doi:10.1016/j.conb.2010.01.006

Sommerfield, A. J., Deary, I. J., McAulay, V., & Frier, B. M. (2003). Short-term, delayed, and working memory are impaired during hypoglycemia in individuals with type 1 diabetes. *Diabetes Care, 26*(2), 390–396.

Sood, B., Delaney-Black, V., Covington, C., Nordstrom-Klee, B., Ager, J., Templin, T., . . . Sokol, R. (2001). Prenatal alcohol exposure and childhood behavior at age 6 to 7 years: I. dose-response effect. *Pediatrics, 108*, e34. doi:10.1542/peds.108.2.e34

Sorce, J. F., Emde, R. N., Campos, J. J., & Klinnert, M. D. (1985). Maternal emotional signaling: Its effect on the visual cliff behavior of 1-year-olds. *Developmental Psychology, 21*(1), 195–200.

Sorkhabi, N. (2005). Applicability of Baumrind's parent typology to collective cultures: Analysis of cultural explanations of parent socialization effects. *International Journal of Behavioral Development, 29*(6), 552–563. doi:10.1080/01650250500172640

Sosa, R., Kennell, J., Klaus, M., Robertson, S., & Urrutia, J. (1980). The effect of a supportive companion on perinatal problems, length of labor, and mother-infant interaction. *New England Journal of Medicine, 303*(11), 597–600.

Sowell, E. R., Thompson, P. M., & Toga, A. W. (2007). Mapping adolescent brain maturation using structural magnetic resonance imaging. In D. Romer & E. F. Walker (Eds.), *Adolescent psychopathology and the developing brain* (pp. 55–84). New York, NY: Oxford University Press.

Sowell, E. R., Thompson, P. M., Leonard, C. M., Welcome, S. E., Kan, E., & Toga, A. W. (2004). Longitudinal mapping of cortical thickness and brain growth in normal children. *Journal of Neuroscience, 24*(38), 8223– 8231.

Spargo, J. (1906). *The bitter cry of the children*. Chicago, IL: Quadrangle Books.

Spear, L. (2007). The developing brain and adolescent-typical behavior patterns: An evolutionary approach. In D. Romer & E. F. Walker (Eds.), *Adolescent psychopathology and the developing brain:* (pp. 9–30). New York, NY: Oxford University Press.

Spearman, C. (1927). *The nature of intelligence and the principles of cognition* (2nd ed.). Oxford, UK: Macmillan.

Spector, R. E. (2009). *Cultural diversity in health and illness* (7th ed.). Upper Saddle River, NJ: Pearson/Prentice Hall.

Spelke, E. S. (1991). Physical knowledge in infancy: Reflections on Piaget's theory. In S. Carey & R. Gelman (Eds.), *The epigenesis of mind: Essays on biology and cognition* (pp. 133–169). Hillsdale, NJ: Erlbaum.

Spelke, E. S. (1998). Nativism, empiricism, and the origins of knowledge. *Infant Behavior & Development, 21*(2), 181–200. doi:10.1016/S0163–6383(98)90002–9

Spelke, E. S., & Kinzler, K. D. (2007). Core knowledge. *Developmental Science, 10*(1), 89–96. doi:10.1111/j.1467–7687.2007.00569.x

Spelke, E. S., & Newport, E. L. (1998). Nativism, empiricism, and the development of knowledge. In W. Damon & R. M. Lerner (Eds.), *Handbook of child psychology: Vol. 1. Theoretical models of human development* (5th ed., pp. 275–340). Hoboken, NJ: Wiley.

Spelke, E. S., Breinlinger, K., Macomber, J., & Jacobson, K. (1992). Origins of knowledge. *Psychological Review, 99*(4), 605–632. doi:10.1037/0033–295X.99.4.605

Spelke, E. S., Gilmore, C. K., & McCarthy, S. (2011). Kindergarten children's sensitivity to geometry in maps. *Developmental Science, 14*(4), 809–821. doi:10.1111/j.1467-7687.2010.01029.x

Spence, M. J., & Freeman, M. S. (1996). Newborn infants prefer the maternal low-pass filtered voice, but not the maternal whispered voice. *Infant Behavior and Development, 19*(2), 199–212. doi:10.1016/S0163–6383(96)90019–3

Spencer, S. J., Steele, C. M., & Quinn, D. M. (1999). Stereotype threat and women's math performance. *Journal of Experimental Social Psychology, 35*(1), 4–28. doi:10.1006/jesp.1998.1373

Sperling, G. (1960). The information available in brief visual presentations. *Psychological Monographs: General and Applied, 74*(11), 1–29. doi:10.1037/h0093759

Spiers, H. J., & Maguire, E. A. (2007). Neural substrates of driving behavior. *NeuroImage, 36*(1–3), 245–255. doi:10.1016/j.neuroimage.2007.02.032.

Spinrad, T., Eisenberg, N., Cumberland, A., Fabes, R., Valiente, C., Shepard, S., & Guthrie, I. K. (2006). Relation of emotion-related regulation to children's social competence: A longitudinal study. *Emotion, 6*(3), 498–510.

Spörer, N., & Brunstein, J. C. (2009). Fostering the reading comprehension of secondary school students through peer-assisted learning: Effects on strategy knowledge, strategy use, and task performance. *Contemporary Educational Psychology, 34*(4), 289–297. doi:10.1016/j.cedpsych.2009.06.004

Spörer, N., Brunstein, J. C., & Kieschke, U. (2009). Improving students' reading comprehension skills: Effects of strategy instruction and reciprocal teaching. *Learning and Instruction, 19*(3), 272–286. doi:10.1016/j.learninstruc.2008.05.003

Spoth, R., Greenberg, M., & Turrisi, R. (2008). Preventive interventions addressing underage drinking: State of the evidence and steps toward public health impact. *Pediatrics, 121*(Suppl. 4), S311–S336. doi:10.1542/peds.2007–2243E

Spratt, E. G., Friedenberg, S., LaRosa, A., Bellis, M. D., Macias, M. M., Summer, A. P., . . . Brady, K. T. (2012). The effects of early neglect on cognitive, language, and behavioral functioning in childhood. *Psychology, 3*(2), 175–182. doi:10.4236/psych.2012.32026

Spritz, B. L., Sandberg, E. H., Maher, E., & Zajdel, R. T. (2010). Models of emotion skills and social competence in the Head Start classroom. *Early Education and Development, 21*(4), 495–516. doi:10.1080/10409280902895097

Squire, L. R., & Knowlton, B. J. (1995). Memory, hippocampus, and brain systems. In M. S. Gazzaniga (Ed.), *The cognitive neurosciences* (pp. 825–837). Cambridge, MA: MIT Press.

Squire, L. R., Stark, C. E., & Clark, R. E. (2004). The medial temporal lobe. *Annual Review of Neuroscience, 27*, 279–306. doi:10.1146/annurev.neuro.27.070203.144130

Squire, L. R., Wixted, J. T., & Clark, R. E. (2007). Recognition memory and the medial temporal lobe: A new perspective. *National Review of Neuroscience, 8*(11), 872–883. doi:10.1038/nrn2154.

Squires, D. (2010). *International profiles of health care systems: Australia, Canada, Denmark, England, France, Germany, Italy, The Netherlands, New Zealand, Norway, Sweden, Switzerland, and the United States.* Washington, DC: Commonwealth Fund.

Squires, J., Bricker, D., Twombly, E., Yockelson, S., Schoen Davis, M., & Kim, Y. (2002). *Ages & stages questionnaires: Social-emotional: A parent-completed, child-monitoring system for social-emotional behaviors.* Baltimore, MD: Brookes.

Srivastava, A. K., Kesavachandran, C. N., & Kumar, S. (2011). Evaluating risks of acquired clinical vulnerability among subjects exposed to e-waste. *Reviews of Environmental Contamination and Toxicology, 214*, 1–14. doi:10.1007/978-1-4614-0668-6_1

Sroufe, L. A. (2005). Attachment and development: A prospective, longitudinal study from birth to adulthood. *Attachment & Human Development*, 7(4): 349–367.

Sroufe, L. A., & Waters, E. (1977). Attachment as an organizational construct. *Child Development, 48*, 1184–1199.

Sroufe, L. A., Egeland, B., Carlson, E., & Collins, W. A. (2005). *The development of the person: The Minnesota study of risk and adaptation from birth to adulthood.* New York, NY: Guilford.

St. Lawrence, J. S., Brasfield, T. L., Jefferson, K. W., Alleyne, E., O'Bannon, R. E., & Shirley, A. (1995). Cognitive-behavioral intervention to reduce African American adolescents' risk for HIV infection. *Journal of Consulting and Clinical Psychology, 63*(2), 221–237.

Staff, J., Messersmith, E. E., & Schulenberg, J. E. (2009). Adolescents and the world of work. In R. M. Lerner & L. Steinberg (Eds.), *Handbook of adolescent psychology: Vol. 2. Contextual influences on adolescent development* (3rd ed., pp. 270–313). Hoboken, NJ: Wiley.

Stams, G. J., Brugman, D., Deković, M., van Rosmalen, L., van der Laan, P., & Gibbs, J. C. (2006). The moral judgment of juvenile delinquents: A meta-analysis. *Journal of Abnormal Child Psychology, 34*(5), 697–713. doi:10.1007/s10802–006–9056–5.

Statler, A., & Hornstein, J. (2009). The touchpoints approach. In J. K. Nugent, B. Petrauskas, & T. Berry Brazelton (Eds.), *The newborn as a person: Enabling health development worldwide.* Hoboken, NJ: Wiley.

Stattin, H., & Magnusson, D. (1990). *Pubertal maturation in female development.* Hillsdale, NJ: Erlbaum.

Stearns, E., & Glennie, E. J. (2006). When and why dropouts leave high school. *Youth & Society, 38*(1), 29–57. doi:10.1177/0044118X05282764

Steelandt, S., Thierry, B., Broihanne, M., & Dufour, V. (2012). The ability of children to delay gratification in an exchange task. *Cognition, 122*(3), 416–425. doi:10.1016/j.cognition.2011.11.009

Steele, C. M. (1997). A threat in the air: How stereotypes shape intellectual identity and performance. *American Psychologist, 52*(6), 613–629. doi:10.1037/0003–066X.52.6.613

Steele, C. M., & Aronson, J. (1995). Stereotype threat and the intellectual test performance of African Americans. *Journal of Personality and Social Psychology, 69*(5), 797–811. doi:10.1037/0022–3514.69.5.797

Steele, C. M., Spencer, S. J., & Aronson, J. (2002). Contending with group image: The psychology of stereotype and social identity threat. In M. P. Zanna (Ed.), *Advances in experimental social psychology* (Vol. 34, pp. 379–440). San Diego, CA: Academic Press.

Steenbergen, B., Marteniuk, R., & Kalbfleisch, L. (1995). Achieving coordination in prehension: Joint freezing and postural contributions. *Journal of Motor Behavior, 27*, 333–348.

Steffenburg, S., Gillberg, C., Hellgren, L., Andersson, L., Gillberg, I. C., Jakobsson, G., Bohman, M. (1989). A twin study of autism in Denmark, Finland, Iceland, Norway and Sweden. *Journal of Child Psychology and Psychiatry, 30*(3), 405–416.

Stegelin, D. A. (2005). Making the case for play policy: Research-based reasons to support play-based environments. *Young Children, 60*(2), 76–85.

Stein, M. T., Kennell, J. H., & Fulcher, A. (2004). Benefits of a doula present at the birth of a child. *Journal of Developmental & Behavioral Pediatrics, 25* (Suppl. 5), S89–S92. doi:10.1097/00004703–200410001–00018

Stein, M., Federspiel, A., Koenig, T., Wirth, M., Strik, W., Wiest, R., . . . Dierks, T. (2012). Structural plasticity in the language system related to increased second language proficiency. *Cortex, 48*(4), 458–465.

Steinberg, L. (2010). A behavioral scientist looks at the science of adolescent brain development. *Brain and Cognition, 72*(1), 160–164. doi:10.1016/j.bandc.2009.11.003

Steinberg, L. (2010). A dual systems model of adolescent risk-taking. *Developmental Psychobiology, 52*, 216–224. doi:10.1002/dev.20445

Steinberg, L., & Scott, E. (2010). Should juvenile offenders ever be sentenced to life without the possibility of parole? *Human Development, 53*, 53–54.

Steinberg, L., & Silk, J. S. (2002). Parenting adolescents. In M. H. Bornstein (Ed.), *Handbook of parenting: Vol. 1. Children and parenting* (2nd ed., pp. 103–133). Mahwah, NJ: Erlbaum.

Steinberg, L., & Silverberg, S. B. (1986). The vicissitudes of autonomy in early adolescence. *Child Development, 57*(4), 841–851. doi:10.2307/1130361

Steinberg, L., Blatt-Eisengart, I., & Cauffman, E. (2006). Patterns of competence and adjustment among adolescents from authoritative, authoritarian, indulgent, and neglectful homes: A replication in a sample of serious juvenile offenders. *Journal of Research on Adolescence, 16*(1), 47–58. doi:10.1111/j.1532–7795.2006.00119.x

Steinberg, L., Cauffman, E., Woolard, J., Graham, S., & Banich, M. (2009). Are adolescents less mature than adults? Minors' access to abortion, the juvenile death penalty, and the alleged APA "flip-flop." *American Psychologist, 64*(7), 583–594. doi:10.1037/a0014763

Steiner, J. E. (1979). Human facial expressions in response to taste and smell stimulation. *Advances in Child Development and Behavior, 13*, 257–295.

Stern, D. N. (1974). Mother and infant at play: The dyadic interaction involving facial, vocal, and gaze behaviors. In M. Lewis & L. A. Rosenblum (Eds.), *The effect of the infant on its caregiver* (Vol. 1, pp. 187–213). New York, NY: Wiley.

Stern, D. N. (1985). *The interpersonal world of the infant.* New York, NY: Basic Books.

Stern, D. N. (1995). *The motherhood constellation.* New York, NY: Basic Books.

Sternberg, R. J. (2003). Our research program validating the triarchic theory of successful intelligence: Reply to Gottfredson. *Intelligence, 31*(4), 399–414. doi:10.1016/S0160–2896(02)00143–5

Sternberg, R. J. (2007a). Intelligence and culture. In S. Kitayama & D. Cohen (Eds.), *Handbook of cultural psychology* (pp. 547–568). New York, NY: Guilford.

Sternberg, R. J. (2007b). Who are the bright children? The cultural context of being and acting intelligent. *Educational Researcher, 36*(3), 148–155. doi:10.3102/0013189X07299881

Sternberg, R. J. (2009a). Toward a triarchic theory of human intelligence. In J. C. Kaufman & E. L. Grigorenko (Eds.), *The essential*

*Sternberg: Essays on intelligence, psychology, and education* (pp. 33–70). New York, NY: Springer.

Sternberg, R. J. (2009b). The theory of successful intelligence. In J. C. Kaufman & E. L. Grigorenko (Eds.), *The essential Sternberg: Essays on intelligence, psychology, and education* (pp. 71–100). New York, NY: Springer.

Stevens, C., & Bavelier, D. (2012). The role of selective attention on academic foundations: A cognitive neuroscience perspective. *Developmental Cognitive Neuroscience, 2*(Suppl. 1), S30–S48. doi:10.1016/j.dcn.2011.11.001

Stevens, C., Harn, B., Chard, D. J., Currin, J., Parisi, D., & Neville, H. (2013). Examining the role of attention and instruction in at-risk kindergarteners: Electrophysiological measures of selective auditory attention before and after an early literacy intervention. *Journal of Learning Disabilities, 46*(1), 73–86. doi:10.1177/0022219411417877

Stevens, C., Lauinger, B., & Neville, H. (2009). Differences in the neural mechanisms of selective attention in children from different socioeconomic backgrounds: An event-related brain potential study. *Developmental Science, 12*(4), 634–646. doi:10.1111/j.1467-7687.2009.00807.x

Stevens, E., Blake, J., Vitale, G., & MacDonald, S. (1998). Mother-infant object involvement at 9 and 15 months: Relation to infant cognition and early vocabulary. *First Language, 18*(53), 203–222.

Stevens, G., Mascarenhas, M., & Mathers, C. (2009). Global health risks: Progress and challenges. *Bulletin of the World Health Organization, 87*(9), 646. doi:10.2471/BLT.09.070565

Stevens, J. (2004, January 20). Canada appeals for positive role models. *The Daily Orange*. Retrieved from http://www.dailyorange.com

Stevenson, H., Hofer, H., & Randel, B. (2000). Middle childhood and schooling. In A. Kazdin (Ed.), *Encyclopedia of psychology* (pp. 229–234). Washington, DC: American Psychological Association.

Stevens-Smith, D. (2006). Balancing with the brain in mind. *Teaching Elementary Physical Education, 17*(50), 28–33.

Stice, E., Rohde, P., Durant, S., & Shaw, H. (2012). A preliminary trial of a prototype Internet dissonance-based eating disorder prevention program for young women with body image concerns. *Journal of Consulting and Clinical Psychology, 80*(5), 907–916. doi:10.1037/a0028016

Stice, E., Shaw, H., Burton, E., & Wade, E. (2006). Dissonance and healthy weight eating disorder prevention programs: A randomized efficacy trial. *Journal of Consulting and Clinical Psychology, 74*(2), 263–275. doi:10.1037/0022-006X.74.2.263

Stiles, J., & Lernigan, T. L. (2010). The basics of brain development. *Neuropsychology Review, 20*, 327–348. doi:10.1007/s11065-010-9148-4

Stinson, R. D. (2010). Hooking up in young adulthood: A review of factors influencing the sexual behavior of college students. *Journal of College Student Psychotherapy, 24*, 98–115. doi:10.1080/87568220903558596

Stipek, D., Recchia, S., & McClintic, S. (1992). Self-evaluation in young children. *Monographs of the Society for Research in Child Development, 57* (No. 1, Serial No. 226). doi:10.2307/1166190

Storch, E. A., & Masia-Warner, C. (2004). The relationship of peer victimization to social anxiety and loneliness in adolescent females. *Journal of Adolescence, 27*(3), 351–362. doi:10.1016/j.adolescence.2004.03.003

Strachan, D. P. (1989). Hay fever, hygiene and household size. *British Medical Journal, 299*(6710), 1259–1260. doi:10.1136/bmj.299.6710.1259

Strain, P. S., & Cordisco, L. K. (1994). LEAP Preschool. In S. Harris & J. Handleman (Eds.), *Preschool education programs for children with autism* (pp. 225–252). Austin, TX: PRO-ED.

Strassberg, Z., Dodge, K. A., Pettit, G. S., & Bates, J. E. (1994). Spanking in the home and children's subsequent aggression toward kindergarten peers. *Development and Psychopathology, 6*(3), 445–461. doi:10.1017/S0954579400006040

Strassman, F. (1992). The function of menstrual taboos among the Dogon: Defense against cuckoldry? *Human Nature, 3*(2), 89–131.

Strata, P. (2009). David Marr's theory of cerebellar learning: 40 years later. *Journal of Physiology, 587*(23), 5519–5520. doi:10.1113/jphysiol.2009.180307

Stratton, K., Wilson, C. B., & McCormick, M. (Eds.). (2001). *Immunization safety review: Measles-mumps-rubella vaccine and autism*. Washington, DC: National Academies Press.

Straus, M. A. (2001). *Beating the devil out of them: Corporal punishment in American families and its effects on children*. Piscataway, NJ: Transaction Press.

Straus, M. A., & Stewart, J. H. (1999). Corporal punishment by American parents: National data on prevalence, chronicity, severity, and duration in relation to child and family characteristics. *Psychology Review, 2*, 55–70. doi:10.1023/A:1021891529770

Strauss, M. S., & Curtis, L. E. (1984). Development of numerical concepts in infancy. In C. Sophian (Ed.), *The 18th Annual Carnegie Symposium on Cognition: Origins of Cognitive Skills* (pp. 131–155). Hillsdale, NJ: Erlbaum.

Streisand, R., Swift, E., Wickmark, T., Chen, R., & Holmes, C. S. (2005). Pediatric parenting stress among parents of children with type 1 diabetes: The role of self-efficacy, responsibility, and fear. *Journal of Pediatric Psychology, 30*(6), 513–521.

Streissguth, A. P. (1993). Fetal alcohol syndrome in older patients. *Alcohol and Alcoholism, 2*, 209–212.

Streissguth, A. P., Bookstein, F. L., & Barr, H. M. (1996). A dose-response study of the enduring effects of prenatal alcohol exposure: Birth to 14 years. In H. L. Spohr & H. C. Steinhausen (Eds.), *Alcohol, pregnancy, and the developing child* (pp. 141–168). Cambridge, UK: Cambridge University Press.

Strelau, J. (1998). *Temperament: A psychological perspective*. New York, NY: Plenum.

Striano, T., Kopp, F., Grossmann, T., & Reid, V. M. (2006). Eye contact influences neural processing of emotional expressions in 4-month-old infants. *Social Cognitive and Affective Neuroscience, 1*(2), 87–95.

Strom, R. E., & Boster, F. J. (2007). Dropping out of high school: A meta-analysis assessing the effect of messages in the home and in school. *Communication Education, 56*(4), 433–452. doi:10.1080/03634520701413804

Strong, W. B., Malina, R. M., Blinkie, C. J. R., Daniels, S. R., Dishman, R. K., Gutin, B., . . . Trudeau, F. (2005). Evidence-based physical activity for school-aged youth. *Journal of Pediatrics, 146*, 732–737.

Strozer, J., Juszczak, L., & Ammerman, A. (2010). *2007–2008 national school-based health care census*. Washington, DC: National Assembly on School-Based Health Care.

Stuart, M. J., & Nagel, R. L. (2004). Sickle cell disease. *Lancet, 364*(9442), 1343–1360. doi:10.1016/S0140-6736(04)17192-4

Stubbs, M. L. (2008). The menstrual cycle and adolescent health. *Annals of the New York Academy of Science, 1135*, 58–66.

Stupica, B., Sherman, L. J., & Cassidy, J. (2011). Newborn irritability moderates the association between infant attachment security and toddler exploration and sociability. *Child Development, 82*(5), 1381–1389.

Suárez-Orozco, C., & Suárez-Orozco, M. M. (2001). *Children of Immigration*. Cambridge, MA: Harvard University Press.

Subcommittee on Attention-Deficit/Hyperactivity Disorder, Steering Committee on Quality Improvement and Management, Wolraich, M., Brown, L., Brown, R. T., DuPaul, G., Earls, M., . . . Visser, S. (2011). ADHD: Clinical practice guideline for the diagnosis, evaluation, and treatment of attention-deficit/hyperactivity disorder in children and adolescents. *Pediatrics, 128*(5), 1007.

Subrahmanyam, K., & Greenfield, P. (2008). Online communication and adolescent relationships. *Future of Children, 18*(1), 119–146. doi:10.1353/foc.0.0006

Substance Abuse Prevention, Substance Abuse and Mental Health Services Administration [SAMHSA]. (2007). *Reach to Teach: Educating elementary and middle school children with fetal alcohol spectrum disorders* (DHHS Pub. No. SMA-4222). Rockville, MD: SAMHSA. Retrieved from http://fasdcenter.samhsa.gov/documents/Reach_To_Teach_Final_011107.pdf

Suggs, W. (2001). Title IX has done little for minority female athletes—because of socioeconomic and cultural factors, and indifference. *Chronicle of Higher Education 48*(14), A35–A37.

Sullivan, M. W., Carmody, D. P., & Lewis, M. (2010). How neglect and punitiveness influence emotion knowledge. *Child Psychiatry and Human Development, 41*(3), 285–298. doi:10.1007/s10578-009-0168-3

Sunderam, S., Chang, J., Flowers, L., Kulkarni, A., Sentelle, G., Jen, G., & Macaluso, M. (2009). Assisted reproductive technology surveillance—United States, 2006. *Surveillance Summaries, 58*(SS05), 1–25.

Supekar, K., Musen, M., & Menon, V. (2009). Development of large-scale functional brain networks in children. *PLoS Biology, 7*(7), 1–15. doi:10.1371/journal.pbio.1000157

Super, C. M., & Harkness, S. (2009). The developmental niche of the newborn in rural

Kenya. In J. K. Nugent, B. Petrauskas, & T. B. Brazelton (Eds.), *The newborn as a person: Enabling healthy infant development worldwide* (pp. 85–97). Hoboken, NJ: Wiley.

Supple, A. J., Ghazarian, S. R., Peterson, G. W., & Bush, K. R. (2009). Assessing the cross-cultural validity of a parental autonomy granting measure: Comparing adolescents in the United States, China, Mexico, and India. *Journal of Cross-Cultural Psychology, 40*(5), 816–833. doi:10.1177/0022022109339390

Susman, E. J., & Rogol, A. (2004). Puberty and psychological development. In R. M. Lerner & L. Steinberg (Eds.), *Handbook of adolescent psychology* (2nd ed., pp. 15–44). Hoboken, NJ: Wiley.

Sutherland, K. E., Altenhofen, S., & Biringen, Z. (2012). Emotional availability during mother-child interactions in divorcing and intact married families. *Journal of Divorce & Remarriage, 53*(2), 126–141. doi:10.1080/10502556.2011.651974

Suzman, S. M. (1985). Learning the passive in Zulu. *Papers and Reports on Child Language Development, 24*, 131–137.

Swanson, H. L., & Sachse-Lee, C. (2001). Mathematical problem solving and working memory in children with learning disabilities: Both executive and phonological processes are important. *Journal of Experimental Child Psychology, 79*(3), 294–321. doi:10.1006/jecp.2000.2587

Swearer, S. M. (2008). Relational aggression: Not just a female issue. *Journal of School Psychology, 46*, 611–616. doi:10.1016/j.jsp2008.08.001

Swearer, S. M., Turner, R. K., Givens, J. E., & Pollack, W. S. (2008). "You're so gay!" Do different forms of bullying matter for adolescent males? *School Psychology Review, 37*(2), 160–173.

Sweeten, T. L., Posey, D. J., Shekhar, A., & McDougle, C. J. (2002). The amygdala and related structures in the pathophysiology of autism. *Pharmacology, Biochemistry, and Behavior, 71*, 449–455.

Swidey, N. (2010, November 1). Why an iPhone could actually be good for your 3-year-old. *Boston Globe Magazine*, pp. 19–22.

Swinburn, B. A., Sacks, G., Hall, K. D., McPherson, K., Finegood, D. T., Moodie, M. L., & Gortmaker, S. L. (2011). The global obesity pandemic. *Lancet, 378*(9793), 804–814.

Sysko, R., Sha, N., Wang, Y., Duan, N., & Walsh, B. T. (2010). Early response to antidepressant treatment in bulimia nervosa. *Psychological Medicine, 40*(6), 999–1005. doi:0.1017/S0033291709991218

Szekely, E., Tiemeier, H., Arends, L. R., Jaddoe, V. W. V., Hoffman, A., Verhulst, F. C., & Herba, C. M. (2011). Recognition of facial expressions of emotions by 3-year-olds. *Emotion, 11*(2), 425–435. doi:10.1037/a0022587

Tager-Flusberg, H. (1999). A psychological approach to understanding the social and language impairments in autism. *International Review of Psychiatry, 11*, 325–334. doi:10.1080/ 09540269974203

Tager-Flusberg, H. (2010). The origins of social impairment in autism spectrum disorder: Studies of infants at risk. *Neural Networks, 23*(8–9), 1072–1076. doi:10.1016/j.neunet.2010.07.008

Tager-Flusberg, H. (2012). The origins of social impairments in autism spectrum disorder: Studies of infants at risk. *Journal of the Academy of Child and Adolescent Psychiatry, 51*(3), 249–260.

Tager-Flusberg, H., & Zukowski, A. (2009). Putting words together: Morphology and syntax in the preschool years. In J. Berko Gleason & N. Ratner (Eds.), *The development of language* (7th ed., pp. 139–185). Boston, MA: Allyn & Bacon.

Takahashi, K. (1986). Examining the strange situation procedure with Japanese mothers and 12-month-old infants. *Developmental Psychology, 22*, 265–270.

Takanishi, R., & Kauerz, K (2008). PK inclusion: Getting serious about a P–16 education system. *Phi Delta Kappan, 89*(7), 480–447.

Talge, N. M., Holzman, C., Wang, J., Lucia, V., Gardiner, J., & Breslau, N. (2010). Late-preterm birth and its association with cognitive and socioemotional outcomes at 6 years of age. *Pediatrics, 126*(6), 1124.

Talleyrand, R. M. (2012). Disordered eating in women of color: Some counseling considerations. *Journal of Counseling & Development, 90*(3), 271–280. doi:10.1002/j.1556-6676.2012.00035.x

Talwar, V., & Lee, K. (2008). Social and cognitive correlates of children's lying behavior. *Child Development, 79*(4), 866–881. doi:10.1111/j.1467-8624.2008.01164.x

Tamis-LeMonda, C. S., Shannon, J. D., Cabrera, N. J., & Lamb, M. E. (2004). Fathers and mothers at play with their 2- and 3-year olds: Contributions to language and cognitive development. *Child Development, 75*(6), 1806–1820.

Tanaka, S. (2005). Parental leave and child health across OECD countries. *Economic Journal, 115*(501), F7–F28.

Tanner, J. M. (1978). *Foetus into man.* Cambridge, MA: Harvard University Press.

Tanner, J. M. (1987). Growth as a mirror of the condition of society: Secular trends and class distinctions. *Pediatrics International, 29*(1), 96–103. doi:10.1111/j.1442-200X.1987.tb00015.x

Tanner, J. M. (1991). *Foetus into man.* Cambridge, MA: Harvard University Press.

Tanner, J. M., & Cameron, N. (1980). Investigation of the mid-growth spurt in height, weight and limb circumferences in single-year velocity data from the London 1966–1967 growth survey. *Annals of Human Biology, 7*(6), 565–577.

Tanner, J. M., Healy, M., & Cameron, N. (2001). *Assessment of skeletal maturity and prediction of adult height.* Philadelphia, PA: Saunders.

Tapert, S. R., Caldwell, L., & Burke, C. (2004/2005). Alcohol and the adolescent brain. *Alcohol Research and Health, 28*(4), 205–212.

Taras, H. (2005). Physical activity and student performance at school. *Journal of School Health, 75*(6), 214–218.

Tarullo, A. R., Mliner, S., & Gunnar, M. R. (2011). Inhibition and exuberance in preschool classrooms: Associations with peer social experiences and changes in cortisol across the preschool year. *Developmental Psychology, 47*(5), 1374–1388. doi:10.1037/a0024093

Tarullo, A. R., Obradović, J., & Gunnar, M. R. (2009). Self-control and the developing brain. *Zero to Three, 29*(3), 31–37.

Tasker, F., & Patterson, C. J. (2007). Research on gay and lesbian parenting: Retrospect and prospect. In F. Tasker & J. J. Bigner (Eds.), *Gay and lesbian parenting: New directions* (pp. 9–34). Washington, DC: American Psychological Association.

Taubes, G. (2011). *Why we get fat and what to do about it.* New York, NY: Alfred A. Knopf.

Tayie, F., & Powell, C. (2012). Sex differences in the association between prenatal smoking and decreased birthweight, and intensive health care of the neonate. *Behavioral Medicine, 38*(4), 138–142. doi:10.1080/08964289.2012.703977

Taylor, B., Miller, E., Farrington, P., Petropoulos, M., Favot-Mayaud, I., Li, J., & Waight, P. A. (1999). Autism and measles, mumps, and rubella vaccine: No epidemiologic evidence for a causal association. *Lancet, 353*(9169), 2026–2029. doi:10.1016/S0140-6736(99)01239-8

Taylor, T. J., Freng, A., Esbensen, F., & Peterson, D. (2008). Youth gang membership and serious violent victimization: The importance of lifestyles and routine activities. *Journal of Interpersonal Violence, 23*(10), 1441–1464. doi:10.1177/0886260508314306

Taylor, T. J., Peterson, D., Esbensen, F., & Freng, A. (2007). Gang membership as a risk factor for adolescent violent victimization. *Journal of Research in Crime and Delinquency, 44*(4), 351–380. doi:10.1177/0022427807305845

Tebes, J. K., Feinn, R., Vanderploeg, J. J., Chinman, M. J., Shepard, J., Brabham, T., . . . Connell, C. (2007). Impact of a positive youth development program in urban after-school settings on the prevention of adolescent substance use. *Journal of Adolescent Health, 41*(3), 239–247. doi:10.1016/j.jadohealth.2007.02.016

Tenenbaum, J. B., Kemp, C., Griffiths, T. L., and Goodman, N. D. (2011). How to grow a mind: Statistics, structure, and abstraction. *Science, 331*(6022), 1279–1285

Terrion, J. L. (2006). Building social capital in vulnerable families: Success markers of a school-based intervention program. *Youth & Society, 38*(2), 155–176. doi:10.1177/0044118X05282765

Tessier, R., Cristo, M. B., Velez, S., Giron, M., Nadeau, L., Figueroa de Calume, Z., . . . Charpak, N. (2003). Kangaroo mother care: A method for protecting high-risk, low-birth-weight and premature infants against developmental delay. *Infant Behavior & Development, 26*(3), 384–397. doi:10.1016/S0163–6383(03)00037–7

Teunisse, J. P., & de Gelder, B. (1994). Do autistics have a generalized face processing deficit? *International Journal of Neuroscience, 77*(1–2), 1–10.

Thelen, E. (1995). Motor development: A new synthesis. *American Psychologist, 50*(2), 79–95. doi:10.1037/0003-066X.50.2.79

Thelen, E., & Smith, L. B. (1994). *A dynamic systems approach to the development of cognition and action.* Cambridge, MA: MIT Press.

Thelen, E., & Smith, L. B. (2006). Dynamic systems theories. In W. Damon & R. Lerner (Series Eds.) & D. Kuhn & R. S. Siegler (Vol. Eds.), *Handbook of child psychology: Vol 1. Theoretical Models of Human Development* (6th ed., pp. 258–312). Hoboken, NJ: Wiley.

Thelen, E., & Spencer, J. P. (1998). Postural control during reaching in young infants: A dynamic systems approach. *Neuroscience and Biobehavioral Review, 22*(4), 507–514. doi:10.1016/S0149–7634(97)00037–7

Thiessen, E. D., & Saffran, J. R. (2003). When cues collide: Use of stress and statistical cues to word boundaries by 7- to 9-month-old infants. *Developmental Psychology, 39*(4), 706–716. doi:10.1037/0012–1649.39.4.706

Thomaes, S., Reijntjes, A., Orobio de Castro, B., Bushman, B. J., Poorthuis, A., & Telch, M. J. (2010). I like me if you like me: On the interpersonal modulation and regulation of preadolescents' state of self-esteem. *Child Development, 81*(3), 811–825. doi:10.1111/j.1467–8624.2010.01435.x

Thomas, A., & Chess, S. (1977). *Temperament and development.* New York, NY: Brunner/Mazel.

Thomas, A., Chess, S., Birch, H. G., Hertzig, M. E., & Korn, S. (1963). *Behavioral individuality in early childhood.* New York, NY: New York University Press.

Thomas, D. G., Grant, S. L., & Aubuchon-Endsley, N. L. (2009). The role of iron in neurocognitive development. *Developmental Neuropsychology, 34*(2), 196–222.

Thomas, F., Renaud, F., Benefice, E., De Meeüs, T., & Guegan, J. F. (2001). International variability of ages at menarche and menopause: Patterns and main determinants. *Human Biology, 73*(2), 271–290.

Thomas, K., & Thomas, J. (2008). Principles of motor development for elementary school physical education. *Elementary School Journal, 108*(13), 181–195.

Thomas, M., & Johnson, M. H. (2008). New advances in understanding sensitive periods in brain development. *Current Directions in Psychological Science, 17*, 1–5. doi:10.1111/j.1467–8721.2008.00537.x

Thomas, R., & Perera, R. (2006). School-based programmes for preventing smoking (Article No. CD001293). *Cochrane Database of Systematic Reviews, 3.* doi:10.1002/14651858.CD001293.pub2

Thomas, W. P., & Collier, V. P. (2002). *A national study of school effectiveness for language minority students' long-term academic achievement.* Retrieved from http://www.crede.ucsc.edu/research/llaa/1.1_final.html

Thompson, J. K., & Cafri, G. (Eds). (2007). *The muscular ideal: Psychological, social, and medical perspectives.* Washington, DC: American Psychological Association.

Thompson, R. A. (1994). Emotion regulation: A theme in search of definition. In N. A. Fox (Ed.), The development of emotion regulation: Biological and behavioral considerations. *Monographs of the Society for Research in Child Development, 59*(2–3, Serial No. 240).

Thompson, R. A. (1997). Sensitivity and security: New lessons to ponder. *Child Development, 68*(4), 595–597.

Thompson, R. A. (2000a). The legacy of early attachments. *Child Development, 71*(1), 145–152.

Thompson, R. A. (2000b). Childhood anxiety disorders from the perspective of emotion regulation and attachment. In M. W. Vasey & M. R. Dadds (Eds.), *The developmental psychopathology of anxiety* (pp. 160–182). Oxford, UK: Oxford University Press.

Thompson, R. A. (2006). The development of the person: Social understanding, relationships, conscience, self. In W. Damon & R. M. Lerner (Series eds.) & N. Eisenberg (Vol. Ed.), *Handbook of child psychology: Vol. 3. Social, emotional, and personality development* (6th ed., pp. 24–98). Hoboken, NJ: Wiley.

Thompson, R. A. (2011). The emotional child. In D. Cicchetti & G. I. Roisman (Eds.), *Minnesota Symposia on Child Psychology: Vol. 36. The origins and organization of adaptation and maladaptation* (pp. 13–54). Hoboken, NJ: Wiley.

Thompson, R. A. (2012). Changing societies, changing childhood: Studying the impact of globalization on child development. *Child Development Perspectives, 6*(2), 187–192. doi:10.1111/j.1750-8606.2012.00234.x

Thompson, R. & Newton, E. (2013). Baby altruists? Examining the complexity of prosocial motivation in young children. *Infancy, 18, 1*, 120–133. doi:10.1111/j.1532-7078.2012.00139.x

Thompson, T. L., & Zerbinos, E. (1995). Gender roles in animated cartoons: Has the picture changed in 20 years? *Sex Roles, 32* (9–10), 651–673. doi:10.1007/BF01544217

Thomson, N. R., & Jones, E. F. (2005). Children's, adolescents', and young adults' reward allocations to hypothetical siblings and fairness judgments: Effects of actor gender, character type, and allocation pattern. *Journal of Psychology, 139*, 349–367. doi:10.3200/JRLP.139.4.349-368

Thurstone, L. L. (1938). *Primary mental abilities.* Chicago, IL: University of Chicago Press.

Tierney, A. L., Gabard-Durnham, L., Vogel-Farley, V., Tager-Flushing, H., & Nelson, C. A. (2012). Developmental trajectories of resting EEG power: An endophenotype of autism spectrum disorder. *PLoS One,* 7(6): e39127. doi:10.1371/journal.pone.0039127

Tillman, C., Eninger, L., Forssman, L., & Bohlin, G. (2011). The relation between working memory components and ADHD symptoms from a developmental perspective. *Developmental Neuropsychology, 36*(2), 181–198. doi:10.1080/87565641.2010.549981

Tinanoff, N., & Palmer, C. A. (2000). Dietary determinants of dental caries and dietary recommendations for preschool children. *Journal of Public Health Dentistry, 60*(3), 197–206. doi:10.1111/j.1752-7325.2000.tb03328.x

Tobler, N. S., Roona, M. R., Ochshorn, P., Marshall, D. G., Streke, A. V., & Stackpole, K. M. (2000). School-based adolescent drug prevention programs: 1998 meta-analysis. *Journal of Primary Prevention, 20*(4), 275–336.

Todd, R. M., & Lewis, M. D. (2008). Self-regulation in the developing brain. In J. Reed & J. Warner-Rogers (Eds.), *Child neuropsychology: Concepts, theory, and practice* (pp. 285–315). Oxford, UK: Wiley-Blackwell.

Tolchinsky, L. (2006). The emergence of writing. In C. A. MacArthur, S. Graham, & J. Fitzgerald (Eds.), *Handbook of writing research* (pp. 83–95). New York, NY: Guilford.

Tolman, D. (2002). *Dilemmas of desire: Teenage girls talk about sexuality.* Cambridge, MA: Harvard University Press.

Tomasello, M. (2003). *Constructing a language: A usage-based theory of language acquisition.* Cambridge, MA: Harvard University Press.

Tomasello, M. (2006). Acquiring linguistic constructions. In W. Damon & R. M. Lerner (Series Eds.) & D. Kuhn & R. S. Siegler (Vol. Eds.), *Handbook of child psychology: Vol. 2. Cognition, perception, and language* (6th ed., pp. 255–298). Hoboken, NJ: Wiley.

Tomasello, M. (2007). Cooperation and communication in the 2nd year of life. *Child Development Perspectives, 1*(1), 8–12.

Tomasello, M. (2009). *Why we cooperate.* Cambridge, MA: MIT Press.

Tomkins, S. S. (1962). *Affect imagery and consciousness.* New York, NY: Springer.

Tomkins, S. S. (1984). Affect theory. In K. R. Scherer, & P. Ekman (Eds.), *Approaches to emotion* (pp. 163–196). Hillsdale, NJ: Erlbaum.

Tomonaga, M., Tanaka, M., Matsuzawa, T., Myowa–Yamakoshi, M., Kosugi, D., . . . Bard, K. A. (2004). Development of social cognition in infant chimpanzees (Pantroglodytes): Face recognition, smiling, gaze, and the lack of triadic interactions. *Japanese Psychological Research, 46*, 227–235. doi:10.1111/j.1468–5584.2004.00254.x

Tompkins, G. (2003). *Literacy for the 21st century.* Upper Saddle River, NJ: Prentice Hall.

Tomporowski, P. D., Davis, C. L., Miller, P. H., & Naglieri, J. A. (2008). Exercise and children's intelligence, cognition and academic achievement. *Educational Psychology Review, 20*(2), 111–131. doi:10.1007/s10648–007–9057–0

Tong, V. T., Jones, J. R., Dietz, P. M., D'Angelo, D., & Bombard, J. M. (2009). Trends in smoking before, during, and after pregnancy—Pregnancy Risk Assessment Monitoring System (PRAMS), United States, 31 Sites, 2000–2005. *Morbidity and Mortality Weekly Review, 58*(SS04), 1–29.

Toomela, A. (1999). Drawing development: Stages in the representation of a cube and a cylinder. *Child Development, 70*(5), 1141–1150. doi:10.1111/1467-8624.00083

Topping, K. J. (2005). Trends in peer learning. *Educational Psychology, 25*(6), 631–645. doi:10.1080/01443410500345172

Topping, K. J. (2006). Building reading fluency: Cognitive, behavioral, and socioemotional factors and the role of peer-mediated learning. In S. J. Samuels & A. E. Farstrup (Eds.), *What research has to say about fluency instruction* (pp. 106–129). Newark, DE: International Reading Association.

Torgesen, J. K., & Mathes, P. G. (2000). *A basic guide to understanding, assessing and teaching phonological awareness.* Austin, TX: Pro-Ed.

Torpy, J. M., Lynm, C., & Glass, R. M. (2004). Malnutrition in children. *Journal of the*

*American Medical Association, 292*(5), 648. doi:10.1001/jama.292.5.648

Toth, S. L., Rogosch, F. A., Manly, J. T., & Cicchetti, D. (2006). The efficacy of toddler-parent psychotherapy to reorganize attachment in the young offspring of mothers with major depressive disorder: A randomized preventive trial. *Journal of Consulting and Clinical Psychology, 74*(6), 1006–1016.

Tottenham, N., Hare, T. A., Quinn, B. T., McCarry, T. W., Nurse, M., Gilhooly, T., . . . Casey, B. J. (2010). Prolonged institutional rearing is associated with atypically large amygdala volume and difficulties in emotion regulation. *Developmental Science, 13*(1), 46–61. doi:10.1111/j.1467-7687.2009.00852.x

Tough, P. (2008). *Whatever it takes: Geoffrey Canada's quest to change Harlem and America*. Boston, MA: Houghton Mifflin.

Towner, D. R., & Ciotti, M. C. (2007). Operative vaginal delivery: A cause of birth injury, or is it? *Clinical Obstetrics & Gynecology, 50*(3), 563–581.

Tran, H. (1999). Antenatal and postnatal maternity care for Vietnamese women. In P. Rice (Ed.), *Asian mothers, western birth* (2nd ed., pp. 61–76). Melbourne, Australia: Ausmed Publishing.

Trautner, H. M., Ruble, D. N., Cyphers, L., Kirsten, B., Behrendt, R., & Hartmann, P. (2005). Rigidity and flexibility of gender stereotypes in childhood: Developmental or differential? *Infant and Child Development, 14*(4), 365–381. doi:10.1002/icd.399.

Travers, B. E., & Travers, J. F. (2008). *Children's literature: A developmental perspective*. Hoboken, NJ: Wiley.

Trawick-Smith, J., & Dziurgot, T. (2011). "Good-fit" teacher-child play interactions and the subsequent autonomous play of preschool children. *Early Childhood Research Quarterly, 26*(1), 110–123. doi:10.1016/j.ecresq.2010.04.005

Treatment for Adolescents with Depression Study (TADS) Team. (2009). The treatment for adolescents with depression study (TADS): Outcomes over 1 year of naturalistic follow-up. *American Journal of Psychiatry, 166*, 1141–1149. doi:10.1176/appi.ajp.2009.08111620

Treiman, R. (1993). *Beginning to spell: A study of first grade children.* New York, NY: Oxford University Press.

Tremblay, R. E. (2000). The development of aggressive behavior during childhood: What have we learned in the past century? *International Journal of Behavioral Development, 24*(2), 129–141. doi:10.1080/016502500383232

Tremblay, R., Schaal, B., Boulerice, B., Arnseault, L., Soussignan, R., Paquette, D., & Laurent, D. (1998). Testosterone, physical aggression, dominance, and physical development in early adolescence. *International Journal of Behavioral Development, 22*(4), 753–777.

Trevarthen, C. (2003). Infant psychology is an evolving culture. *Human Development, 46*(4), 233–246. doi:10.1159/000070372

Trevarthen, C., & Aitken, K. J. (2001). Infant intersubjectivity: Research, theory, and clinical applications. *Journal of Child Psychology and Psychiatry and Allied Disciplines, 42*, 3–48.

Trevathan, W. R. (1984). Factors influencing the timing of initial breastfeeding in 954 out-of-hospital births. *Medical Anthropology, 8*, 302–307.

Triandis, H. (2007). Culture and psychology: A history of the study of their relationship. In S. Kitayama & D. C. Vohen (Eds.), *Handbook of cultural psychology* (pp. 59–76). New York, NY: Guilford.

Troiden, R. R. (1993). *The formation of homosexual identities*. New York, NY: Columbia University Press.

Trollet, C., Athanasopoulos, T., Popplewell, L., Malerba, A., & Dickson, G. (2009). Gene therapy for muscular dystrophy: Current progress and future prospects. *Expert Opinion on Biological Therapy, 9*(7), 849–866. doi:10.1517/14712590903029164

Tronick, E. (2007). *The Neurobehavioral and Social-Emotional Development of Infants and Children*. New York, NY: Norton.

Tronick, E. Z. (1989). Emotions and emotional communication in infants. *American Psychologist, 44*(2), 112–119.

Tronick, E. Z. (2003). Emotions and emotional communication in infants. In J. Raphael–Leff (Ed.), *Parent-infant psychodynamics: Wild things, mirrors & ghosts* (pp. 35–53). London and Philadelphia: Whurr Publishers.

Tronick, E. Z. (2009). *The neurobehavioral and social-emotional development of infants and children.* New York, NY: Norton.

Tronick, E. Z., Als, H., & Brazelton, T. B. (1980). Monadic phases: A structural descriptive analysis of infant-mother face-to-face interaction. *Merrill-Palmer Quarterly, 26*, 3–24.

Troseth, G. K. (2003). TV guide: Two-year-old children learn to use video as a source of information. *Developmental Psychology, 39*(1), 140–150. doi:10.1037/0012–1649.39.1.140

Troseth, G. K., & DeLoache,. J. S. (1998). The medium can obscure the message: Young children's understanding of video. *Child Development, 69*(4), 950–965.

True, M. M., Pisani, L., & Oumar, F. (2001). Infant-mother attachment among the Dogon of Mali. *Child Development, 72*(5), 1451–1466.

Tsang, J. M., Dougherty, R. F., Deutsch, G. K., Wandell, B. A., & Ben–Shachar, M. (2009). Frontoparietal white matter diffusion properties predict mental arithmetic skills in children. *Proceedings of the National Academy of Sciences of the United States of America, 106*(52), 22546–22551. doi:10.1073/pnas.0906094106

Tulving, E. (1972). Episodic and semantic memory. In E. Tulving & W. Donaldson (Eds.), *Organization of memory* (pp. 382–403). New York, NY: Academic Press.

Tulving, E. (2002). Episodic memory: From mind to brain. *Annual Review of Psychology, 53*(1), 1–25. doi:10.1.1146/annurev.psych.53.100901.135114

Tunks, K. W., & Giles, R. M. (2009). Writing their words: Strategies for supporting young authors. *Young Children, 64*(1), 22–25.

Turk-Browne, N. B., Scholl, B. J., & Chun, M. M. (2008). Babies and brains: Habituation in infant cognition and functional neuroimaging. *Frontiers in Human Neuroscience, 2*(16), 1–11. doi:10.3389/neuro.09.016.2008

Turkle, S. (2011). *Alone together: Technology and the reinvention of intimacy and solitude.* New York, NY: Basic Books.

Turner, R. B. (2009). The common cold. In G. L. Mandell, J. E. Bennett, & R. Dolin (Eds.), *Principles and Practice of Infectious Diseases* (7th ed., pp. 809–814). Philadelphia, PA: Elsevier Churchill Livingstone.

Tyrka, A. R., Graber, J. A., & Brooks-Gunn, J. (2000). The development of disordered eating: Correlates and predictors of eating problems in the context of adolescence. In A. R. Tyrka, J. A. Graber, & J. Brooks-Gunn (Eds.), *Handbook of developmental psychopathology* (2nd ed., pp. 607–624) Dordrecht, Netherlands: Kluwer Academic Publishers.

Tyson, K., Darity, W., & Castellino, D. R. (2005). It's not "a black thing": Understanding the burden of acting white and other dilemmas of high achievement. *American Sociological Review, 70*(4), 582–605. doi:10.1177/000312240507000403UNESCO

U.S. Census Bureau. (2000). *Statistical abstract of the United States: 2000.* Washington, DC: Government Printing Office.

U.S. Census Bureau. (2003). *Married couple and unmarried-partner households: 2000.* Retrieved from http://www.Census.gov/prod/2003pubs/censr-5.pdf

U.S. Centers for Disease Control and Prevention. (2008, October 15). CDC releases new infant mortality data. Retrieved from http://www.cdc.gov/media/pressrel/2008/r081015.htm

U.S. Centers for Disease Control and Prevention. (2010). National Center for Health Statistics. Retrieved from http://www.cdc.gov/nchs/vitalstats.htm

U.S. Department of Agriculture & U.S. Department of Health and Human Services. (2010). *Dietary guidelines for Americans, 2010* (7th ed.). Washington, DC: U.S. Government Printing Office. Retrieved from http://www.dietaryguidelines.gov

U.S. Department of Agriculture & U.S. Department of Health and Human Services. (2011). *Dietary guidelines for Americans, 2010* (7th ed.). Washington, DC: U.S. Government Printing Office. Retrieved from http://www.dietaryguidelines.gov

U.S. Department of Agriculture. (2009). *Access to affordable and nutritious food: Measuring and understanding food deserts and their consequences: Report to Congress.* Rockville, MD: U.S. Department of Health and Human Services. Retrieved from: http://www.ers.usda.gov/publications/ap/ap036/

U.S. Department of Agriculture. (2010). *National School Lunch Program.* Retrieved from http://www.fns.usda.gov/cnd

U.S. Department of Agriculture. (2011). *MyPlate.* Retrieved from http://www.ChooseMyPlate.gov

U.S. Department of Agriculture. (2012). Nutrition standards in the national school lunch and school breakfast programs (Final rule). *Federal Register,* 77(17), 4088–4167. Retrieved from http://www.gpo.gov/fdsys/pkg/FR-2012-01-26/pdf/2012-1010.pdf

U.S. Department of Education, National Center for Education Statistics (2008). *The nation's report card: Writing 2007, national assessment of educational progress at grades 8 and 12*. Washington, DC: Author.

U.S. Department of Education, National Center for Education Statistics. (2011). *The condition of education 2011* (NCES 2011–033).

U.S. Department of Health and Human Services, Center for the Evaluation of Risks to Human Reproduction. (2003). *Rubella*. Retrieved from http://cerhr.niehs.nih.gov/common/rubella.html

U.S. Department of Health and Human Services, Health Resources and Services Administration. (2010). *The registered nurse population: Findings from the 2008 national sample survey of registered nurses*. Retrieved from http://bhpr.hrsa.gov/healthworkforce/rnsurveys/rnsurveyfinal.pdf

U.S. Department of Health and Human Services, Health Resources and Services Administration, Maternal and Child Health Bureau (2009). *Prenatal services*. Rockville, MD: Author. Retrieved from http://www.mchb.hrsa.gov/programs/womeninfants/prenatal.html

U.S. Department of Health and Human Services, Health Resources and Services Administration, Maternal and Child Health Bureau (2013). *Child Health USA 2012*. Rockville, MD: Author. Retrieved from http://mchb.hrsa.gov/chusa12/hsfu/pages/pc.html

U.S. Department of Health and Human Services, Office on Women's Health. (2010). *Pregnancy and medicines*. Retrieved from http://www.womenshealth.gov/publications/our-publications/fact-sheet/pregnancy-medicines.cfm#c

U.S. Department of Health and Human Services, National Institute on Drug Abuse. (2009). *NIDA InfoFacts: Prescription and over-the-counter medications*. Retrieved from http://www.drugabuse.gov/PDF/Infofacts/PainMed09.pdf

U.S. Department of Health and Human Services. (1979). *Healthy People: the Surgeon General's Report on Health Promotion and Disease Prevention*. Washington, DC: U.S. Government Printing Office.

U.S. Department of Health and Human Services. (2001). *The Surgeon General's call to action to prevent and decrease overweight and obesity*. Rockville, MD: Author.

U.S. Department of Health and Human Services. (2008). Physical activity guidelines for Americans. Retrieved from http://www.healthypeople.gov/2020/topicsobjectives2020/overview.aspx?topicId=33

U.S. Department of Health and Human Services. (2010a). Oral health. In *Healthy people 2010: Objectives for improving health* (Vol. 2, Objective 21). Retrieved from http://www.healthypeople.gov

U.S. Department of Health and Human Services. (2010b). Child Maltreatment 2008. Washington, DC: U.S. Government Printing Office. Retrieved from http://www.acf.hhs.gov/programs/cb/stats_research/index.htm#can

U.S. Department of Health and Human Services. (2011). *Child health USA 2011*. Rockville, MD: Author. Retrieved from http://mchb.hrsa.gov/publications/childhealthusa.html

U.S. Food and Drug Administration, Center for Devices and Radiological Health. (2007). *Title 21—Food and Drugs. Chapter I—Food and Drug Administration, Department of Health and Human Services. Subchapter C—Drugs: General. Part 201—Labeling*. Rockville, MD: Author. Updated April 1, 2012. Retrieved from http://www.accessdata.fda.gov/scripts/cdrh/cfdocs/cfcfr/CFRSearch.cfm?fr=201.57

Uccelli, P., & Páez, M. M. (2007). Narrative and vocabulary development of bilingual children from kindergarten to first grade: Developmental changes and associations among English and Spanish skills. *Language, Speech, and Hearing Services in Schools, 38*(3), 225–236. doi:10.1044/0161-1461(2007/024)

Umaña-Taylor, A. J., Gonzales-Backen, M. A., & Guimond, A. B. (2009). Latino adolescents' ethnic identity: Is there a developmental progression and does growth in ethnic identity predict growth in self-esteem? *Child Development, 80*(2), 391–405. doi:10.1111/j.1467–8624.2009.01267.x

Umbel, V. M., Pearson, B. Z., Fernández, M. C., & Oller, D. K. (1992). Measuring bilingual children's receptive vocabularies. *Child Development, 63*(4), 1012–1020. doi:10.2307/1131250

Underhill, K., Montgomery, P., & Operario, D. (2008). Abstinence-plus programs for HIV infection prevention in high-income countries (Article No. CD007006). *Cochrane Database of Systematic Reviews 23*(1).

UNESCO Institute for Statistics. (2010). *Out-of-school adolescents*. Retrieved from http://www.uis.unesco.org/Library/Documents/out%20of%20school%20adol_en.pdf

United Nations Children's Fund (UNICEF). (2003). *Delivering essential micronutrients: Iron*. Available from: http://www.unicef.org/nutrition/index_iron.html

United Nations Children's Fund (UNICEF). (2007). *Progress for children: A world fit for children statistical review*. Retrieved from www.unicef.org/progressforchildren/2007n6/index_41503.htm

United Nations Children's Fund (UNICEF). (2009). *Diarrhea: Why children are still dying and what can be done*. Available from: http://whqlibdoc.who.int/publications/2009/9789241598415_eng.pdf

United Nations Children's Fund (UNICEF). (2009). *Low birthweight incidence by country (2000–2007)*. Retrieved from http://www.childinfo.org/low_birthweight_profiles.php

United Nations Children's Fund (UNICEF). (2010). *Progress for children: Achieving the Millennial Development Goals with equity. No. 9*. New York, NY: UNICEF.

United Nations Children's Fund (UNICEF). (2007). *Child poverty in perspective: An overview of child well-being in rich countries* (Report Card 7). Florence, Italy: UNICEF Innocenti Research Centre.

United Nations Millennium Development Goals Report. (2008). Retrieved from http://www.un.org/millenniumgoals/reports.shtml

United Nations Standing Committee on Nutrition. (2010). Progress in nutrition: 6th report on the world nutrition situation. Retrieved from http://www.unscn.org

Upchurch, D. M., Lillard, L. A., Aneshensel, C. S., & Li, N. (2002). Inconsistencies in reporting the occurrence and timing of first intercourse among adolescents. *Journal of Sex Research. 39*(3), 197–206.

Urion, D. K. (2009). Diagnostic methods for disorders of the central nervous system. In W. B. Carey, A. C. Crocker, W. L. Coleman, E. R. Elias, & H. M. Feldman (Eds.), *Developmental-behavioral pediatrics* (4th ed., pp. 836–840). Philadelphia, PA: Saunders.

Ursache, A., Blair, C., Stifter, C., Voegtline, K. (2013). Emotional reactivity and regulation in infancy interact to predict executive functioning in early childhood. *Developmental Psychology, 49, 1*, 127–137. doi:10.1037/a0027728

Usher, J. A., & Neisser, U. (1993). Childhood amnesia and the beginning of memory for four early life events. *Journal of Experimental Psychology, 122*(2), 155–165.

Uskul, A. K. (2004). Women's menarche stories from a multicultural sample. *Social Science & Medicine 59*, 667–679.

Vaillancourt, T., McDougall, P., Hymel, S., & Sunderani, S. (2010). Respect or fear? The relationship between power and bullying behavior. In S. R. Jimerson, S. M. Swearer, & D. L. Espelage (Eds.), *Handbook of bullying in schools: An international perspective* (pp. 211–222). New York, NY: Routledge/Taylor & Francis.

Vaish, A., & Striano, T. (2004). Is visual reference necessary? Contributions of facial versus vocal cues in 12-month-olds' social referencing behavior. *Developmental Science*, 7, 261–269.

Vakil, S., Freeman, R., & Swim, T. J. (2003). The Reggio Emilia approach and inclusive early childhood programs. *Early Childhood Education Journal, 30*, 187–192.

Valiente, C., Eisenberg, N., Fabes, R. A., Shepard, S. A., Cumberland, A., & Losoya, S. H. (2004). Prediction of children's empathy-related responding from their effortful control and parents' expressivity. *Developmental Psychology, 40*(6), 911–926. doi:10.1037/ 0012-1649.40.6.911

Valiente, C., Swanson, J., & Lemery-Chalfant, K. (2012). Kindergartners' temperament, classroom engagement, and student-teacher relationship: Moderation by effortful control. *Social Development, 21*(3), 558–576. doi:10.1111/j.1467-9507.2011.00640.x

Vallotton, C. D., Harewood, T., Ayoub, C. A., Pan, B., Mastergeorge, A. M., & Brophy-Herb, H. (2012). Buffering boys and boosting girls: The protective and promotive effects of Early Head Start for children's expressive language in the context of parenting stress. *Early Childhood Research Quarterly, 27*, 695–707. doi:10.1016/j.ecresq.2011.03.001

Van Cleave, J., Gortmaker, S. L., & Perrin, J. M. (2010). Dynamics of obesity and chronic

health conditions among children and youth. *Journal of the American Medical Association, 303*(7), 623–630. doi:10.1001/jama.2010.104
van Cleave, J., Gortmaker, S. L., & Perrin, J. M. (2010). Dynamics of obesity and chronic health conditions among children and youth. *Journal of the American Medical Association, 303*(7), 623–630. doi:10.1001/jama.2010.104
Van de Vijver, F. J. R., & Brouwers, S. A. (2009). Schooling and basic aspects of intelligence: A natural quasi-experiment in Malawi. *Journal of Applied Developmental Psychology, 30*(2), 67–74. doi:10.1016/j.appdev.2008.10.010
Van de Walle, G. A., Carey, S., & Prevor, M. (2000). Bases for object individuation in infancy: Evidence from manual search. *Journal of Cognition and Development, 1*(3), 249–280. doi:10.1207/S15327647JCD0103_1
van den Boom, D. C. (1994). The influence of temperament and mothering on attachment and exploration: An experimental manipulation of sensitive responsiveness among lower-class mothers with irritable infants. *Child Development, 65*(5), 1457–1477. doi:10.1111/j.1467–8624.1994.tb00829.x
van den Boom, D. C. (1997). Sensitivity and attachment: Next steps for developmentalists. *Child Development, 68*(4), 592–594. doi:10.1111/j.1467–8624.1997.tb04219.x
van den Bos, W., van Dijk, E., Westenberg, M., Rombouts, S. A. R. B., & Crone, E. A. (2010). Changing brains, changing perspectives: The neurocognitive development of reciprocity. *Perspectives in Psychological Science, 22*(1), 60–70. doi:10.1016/j.conb.2007.03.009
van den Oord, E. J. C., Rispens, J., Goudena, P. P., & Vermande, M. (2000). Some developmental implications of structural aspects of preschoolers' relations with classmates. *Journal of Applied Developmental Psychology, 2*(6), 619–669. doi:10.1016/S0193-3973(00)00057-5
van Heuven, W. J. B., & Dijkstra, T. (2010). Language comprehension in the bilingual brain: FMRI and ERP support for psycholinguistic models. *Brain Research Reviews, 64*(1), 104–122. doi:10.1016/j.brainresrev.2010.03.002
van Honk, J., Schutter, D., Hermans, E., & Putnam, P. (2004). Testosterone, cortisol, dominance, and submission: Biologically prepared motivation, no psychological mechanisms involved. *Behavioral and Brain Sciences, 27*(1), 160–161
Van Hoorn, J. L., Nourot, P. M., Scales, B., & Alward, K. R. (2006). *Play at the center of the curriculum* (4th ed.). Upper Saddle River, NJ: Merrill.
van IJzendoorn, M. H., & Sagi, A. (1999). Cross-cultural patterns of attachment: Universal and contextual dimensions. In J. Cassidy & P. Shaver (Eds.), *Handbook of attachment theory and research* (pp. 713–734). New York, NY: Guilford.
van IJzendoorn, M. H., & Sagi, A. (2001). Cultural blindness or selective inattention? *American Psychologist, 56*, 824–825.
van IJzendoorn, M. H., & Sagi-Schwartz, A. (2008). Cross-cultural patterns of attachment: Universal and contextual dimensions. In J. Cassidy & P. Shaver (Eds.), *Handbook of attachment* (2nd ed., pp. 880–905). New York, NY: Guilford.
van IJzendoorn, M. H., Vereijken, C. M. J. L., Bakermans-Kranenburg, M. J., & Riksen-Walraven, J. M. (2004). Assessing attachment security with the attachment Q-Sort: Meta-analytic evidence for the validity of the observer AQS. *Child Development, 75*(4).
Van Leihenhorst, L., Gunther, M. B., Op de Macks, Z. A., Rombouts, S. A., Westenberg, P. M., & Crone, E. A. (2010). Adolescent risky decision-making: Neurocognitive development of reward and control regions. *NeuroImage, 51*(1), 345–355. doi:10.1016/J.Neuroimage.2010.02.038
Van Riper, M. (2000). Family variables associated with well-being in siblings of children with Down syndrome. *Journal of Family Nursing, 6*(3), 267–286. doi:10.1177/107484070000600305
Van, D. B., Cohen, M. X., Kahnt, T., & Crone, E. A. (2012). Striatum-medial prefrontal cortex connectivity predicts developmental changes in reinforcement learning. *Cerebral Cortex, 22*(6), 1247–1255. doi:10.1093/cercor/bhr198
Vandell, D. L., & Corasaniti, M. A. (1990). Variations in early child care: Do they predict subsequent social, emotional, and cognitive differences? *Early Childhood Research Quarterly, 5*, 555–572.
Vanhaesebrouck, P., Allegaert, K., Bottu, J., Debauche, C., Devlieger, H., Docx, M. . . ., Van Reempts, P. (2004). The EPIBEL Study: Outcomes to discharge from hospital for extremely preterm infants in Belgium. *Pediatrics, 114*(3), 663–675. doi:10.1542/peds.2003-0903-L
Vann, J. J. C., Finkle, J., Ammerman, A., Wegner, S., Skinner, A. C., Benjamin, J. T., & Perrin, E. M. (2011). Use of a tool to determine perceived barriers to children's healthy eating and physical activity and relationships to health behaviors. *Journal of Pediatric Nursing, 26*, 404–415. doi:10.1016/j.pedn.2010.10.011
Varga, M. E., Pavlova, O. G., & Nosova, S. V. (2010). The counting function and its representation in the parietal cortex in humans and animals. *Neuroscience and Behavioral Physiology, 40*(2), 185–196. doi:10.1007/s11055–009–9238–z
Vassar College. (2005). *Julia Lathrop in the Vassar Encyclopedia*. Retrieved from http://vcencyclopedia.vassar.edu/alumni/julia-lathrop.html
Vaughn, B. E., & Waters, E. (1990). Attachment behavior at home and in the laboratory: Q-sort observations and strange situation classifications of one-year-olds. *Child Development, 61*, 1965–1973.
Vaughn, B. E., Kopp, C. B., & Krakow, J. B. (1984). The emergence and consolidation of self-control from eighteen to thirty months of age: Normative trends and individual differences. *Child Development, 55*(3), 990–1004.
Veenstra, R., Lindenberg, S., Munniksma, A., & Dijkstra, J. K. (2010). The complex relation between bullying, victimization, acceptance, and rejection: Giving special attention to status, affection, and sex differences. *Child Development, 81*(2), 480–486. doi:10.1111/j.1467–8624.2009.01411.x
Veldhuis, J. D., Roemmich, J. N., & Rogol, A. D. (2000). Gender and sexual maturation contrasts in the neuroregulation of growth hormone secretion in prepubertal and late adolescent male and females. *Journal of Clinical Endocrinology and Metabolism 85*, 2385–2394.
Vellutino, F. R., Fletcher, J. M., Snowling, M. J., & Scanlon, D. M. (2004). Specific reading disability (dyslexia): What have we learned in the past four decades? *Journal of Child Psychology and Psychiatry, 45*(1), 2–40. doi:10.1046/j.0021-9630.2003.00305.x
Ventura, S. J., Curtin, S. C., & Abma, J. C. (2012). Estimated pregnancy rates and rates of pregnancy outcomes for the United States, 1990–2008. *National Vital Statistics Report, 60*(7). Hyattsville, MD: National Center for Health Statistics. Retrieved from http://www.cdc.gov/nchs/data/nvsr/nvsr60/nvsr60_07.pdf
Verkerk, G., Jeukens–Visser M., Houtzager B., Koldewijn K., van Wassenaer A., Nollet F., & Kok J. (2012). The infant behavioral assessment and intervention program in very low birth weight infants: Outcome on executive functioning, behaviour and cognition at preschool age. *Early Human Development, 88*(8), 699–705.
Villar, J., Valladares, E., Wojdyla, D., Zavaleta, N., Carroli, G., Velazco, A., . . . Faundes, A. (2006). Caesarean delivery rates and pregnancy outcomes: The 2005 WHO global survey on maternal and perinatal health in Latin America. *Lancet, 367*(9525), 1819–1829. doi:10.1016/S0140–6736(06)68704–7
Visser, B. A., Ashton, M. C., & Vernon, P. A. (2006). Beyond *g*: Putting multiple intelligences theory to the test. *Intelligence, 34*(5), 487–502. doi:10.1016/j.intell.2006.02.004
Vitiello, B. (2009). Treatment of adolescent depression: What we have come to know. *Depression and Anxiety, 26*(5), 393–395. doi:10.1002/da.20572
Volkmar, F. R., Lord C., Bailey, A., Schultz, R. T., & Klin, A. (2004). Autism and pervasive developmental disorders. *Journal of Child Psychology and Psychiatry, 45*(1), 1–36. doi:10.1046/j.0021- 9630.2003.00317.x
Volling, B. L. (2003). Sibling relationships. In M. H. Bornstein, L. Davidson, C. L. M. Keyes, & K. A. Moore. (Eds.), *Well-being: Positive development across the life course* (pp. 205–220). Mahwah, NJ: Erlbaum.
Volling, B. L., Blandon, A. Y., & Gorvine, B. J. (2006). Maternal and paternal gentle guidance and young children's compliance from a within-family perspective. *Journal of Family Psychology, 20*, 514–525.
von Kodolitsch, Y., Raghunath, M., & Nienaber, C. A. (1998). Marfan syndrome: Prevalence and natural course of cardiovascular manifestations. *Zeitschrift für Kardiologie [Journal for Cardiology], 87*(3), 150–160.
Von Korff, M., Gruman, J., Schaefer, J. K., Curry, S. J., & Wagner, E. H. (1997). Collaborative management of chronic illness. *Annals of Internal Medicine, 127*, 1097–1102.

von Salisch, M. (2008). Themes in the development of emotional regulation in childhood and adolescence and a transactional model. In M. Vandekerckhove, C. von Scheve, S. Ismer, S. Jung, & S. Kronast (Eds.), *Regulating emotions: Social necessity and biological inheritance* (pp. 146–167). Malden, MA: Blackwell.

Von Suchodoletz, A., Trommsdorff, G., & Heikamp, T. (2011). Linking maternal warmth and responsiveness to children's self-regulation. *Social Development, 20*(3), 486–503. doi:10.1111/j.1467-9507.2010.00588.x

Voyer, D., Voyer, S., & Bryden, M. P. (1995). Magnitude of sex differences in spatial abilities: A meta-analysis and consideration of critical values. *Psychological Bulletin, 117*(2), 250–270. doi:10.1037/0033–2909.117.2.250

Vygotsky, L. (1934/1986). *Thought and language* (rev. ed.). Cambridge, MA: MIT Press.

Vygotsky, L. (1962). *Thought and language*. Cambridge, MA : MIT Press. doi:10.1037/11193–000

Vygotsky, L. S. (1978). *Mind in society: The development of higher psychological processes*. Cambridge, MA: Harvard University Press.

Vygotsky, L. S. (1986). *Thought and language* (rev. ed.). Cambridge, MA: MIT Press.

Vygotsky, L. S. (1987). *Thinking and speech* (N. Minick, Trans). New York, NY: Plenum Press.

Waddington, C. H. (1957). *The strategy of the genes*. New York, NY: Macmillan.

Wagner, D. D., & Heatherton, T. F. (2013). Self-regulatory depletion increases emotional reactivity in the amygdala. *Social Cognitive and Affective Neuroscience, 8*(4), 410–417.

Wagner, E. (1998). Chronic disease management: What will it take to improve care for chronic illness? *Effective Clinical Practice, 1*(1), 2–4.

Wagner, E., & MacColl Institute for Healthcare Innovation Center for Health Studies Group Health Cooperative. (2007, December 10). *Redesigning chronic illness care: The chronic care model. A national program of the Robert Wood Johnson Foundation.* Paper presented at the Institute for Healthcare Improvement National Forum, Orlando, FL. Retrieved from http://www.improvingchroniccare.org

Wahl, K., & Metzner, C. (2012). Parental influences on the prevalence and development of child aggressiveness. *Journal of Child and Family Studies, 21*(2), 344–355. doi:10.1007/s10826–011–9484–x

Wahlsten, D. (1994). The intelligence of heritability. *Canadian Psychology, 35*(3), 244–259. doi:10.1037/0708-5591.35.3.244

Wahlstrom, D., White, T., & Luciana, M. (2010). Neurobehavioral evidence for changes in dopamine system activity during adolescence. *Neuroscience of Biobehavior Review, 34*(5), 631–648. doi:10.1016/j.neubiorev.2009.12.007

Wai, J., Cacchio, M., Putallaz, M., & Makel, M. C. (2010). Sex differences in the right tail of cognitive abilities: A 30-year examination. *Intelligence, 38*(4), 412–423. doi:10.1016/j.intell.2010.04.006

Wainryb, C., Brehl, B. A., & Matwin, S. (2005). Being hurt and hurting others: Children's narrative accounts and moral judgments of their own interpersonal conflicts. *Monographs of the Society for Research in Child Development, 70*(3), 1–114. doi:10.1111/j.1540-5834.2005.00350.x

Wakefield, A. J., Murch, S. H., Anthony, A., Linell, J., Casson, D. M., Malik, M., . . . Walker-Smith, J. A. (1998). Ileal-lymphoid-nodular hyperplasia, non-specific colitis, and pervasive developmental disorder in children. *Lancet, 351*(9103), 637–641. doi:10.1016/S0140-6736(97)11096-0

Wald, L. (1915). *The house on Henry Street*. New York, NY: Holt.

Walden, T. A. (1991). Infant social referencing. In J. Garber & K. A. Dodge (Eds.), *The development of emotion regulation and dysregulation* (pp. 69–88). Cambridge, UK: Cambridge University Press.

Walden, T. A., & Baxter, A. (1989). The effects of context and age on social referencing. *Child Development, 60*, 1511–1518.

Walden, T., Lemerise, E., & Smith, M. C. (1999). Friendship and popularity in preschool classrooms. *Early Education and Devel-opment. Special Issue: Early Peer Relationships, 10*(3), 351–371. doi:10.1207/s15566935eed1003_7

Waldenstrom, U., & Schytt, E. (2008). A longitudinal study of women's memory of labour pain: From 2 months to 5 years after the birth. *British Journal of Obstetrics and Gynaecology: An International Journal of Obstetrics and Gynaecology, 116*(4), 577–583. doi:10.1111/j.1471–0528.2008.02020.x

Waldfogel, J. (2006). Early childhood policy: A comparative perspective. In K. McCartney & D. Phillips (Eds.), *The handbook of early childhood development* (pp. 576–594). London, UK: Blackwell.

Walker, L. J., Hennig, K. H., & Krettenauer, T. (2000). Parent and peer contexts for children's moral reasoning development. *Child Development, 71*, 1033–1048. doi:10.1111/1467–8624.00207

Wallach, H. R., & Matlin, M. W. (1992). College women's expectations about pregnancy, childbirth, and infant care: A prospective study. *Birth: Issues in Perinatal Care, 19*(2), 202–207. doi:10.1111/j.1523–536X.1992.tb00403.x

Waller, J., Marlow, L. A. V., & Wardle, J. (2006). Mothers' attitudes towards preventing cervical cancer through human papillomavirus vaccination: A qualitative study. *Cancer Epidemiology, Biomarkers & Prevention, 15*, 1257. doi:10.1158/1055–9965.EPI–06–0041

Walsh, M. E., & Barrett, J. G. (2005). The roots of violence and aggression. In K. Thies & J. F. Travers (Eds.), *The handbook of human development for health care professionals*. Sudbury, MA: Jones & Bartlett.

Walton, G. E., Armstrong, E. S., & Bower, T. G. R. (1998). Newborns learn to identify a face in eight/tenths of a second? *Developmental Science, 1*(1), 79–84. doi:10.1111/1467–7687.00016

Walton, G. E., Bower, N. J. A., & Bower, T. G. R. (1992). Recognition of familiar faces by newborns. *Infant Behavior & Development, 15*(2), 265–269. doi:10.1016/0163–6383(92)80027–R

Wang, J., & Barrett, K. C. (2013). Mastery motivation and self-regulation during early childhood. In K. C. Barrett, N. A. Fox, G. A. Morgan, D. J. Fidler, & L. A. Daunhauer (Eds.), *Handbook of self-regulatory processes in development: New directions and international perspectives* (pp. 337–380). New York, NY: Psychology Press.

Wang, Q., Pomerantz, E. M., & Chen, H. (2007). The role of parents' control in early adolescents' psychological functioning: A longitudinal investigation in the United States and China. *Child Development, 78*(5), 1592–1610. doi:10.1111/j.1467–8624.2007.01085.x

Wang, S., Baillargeon, R., & Brueckner, L. (2004). Young infants' reasoning about hidden objects: Evidence from violation-of-expectation tasks with test trials only. *Cognition, 93*(3), 167–198. doi:10.1016/j.cognition.2003.09.012

Wang, S., Baillargeon, R., & Paterson, S. (2005). Detecting continuity violations in infancy: A new account and new evidence from covering and tube events. *Cognition, 95*, 129–173, doi:10.1016/j.cognition.2002.11.001

Wang, Y., & Beydoun, M. A. (2007). The obesity epidemic in the United States—gender, age, socioeconomic, racial/ethnic, and geographic characteristics: A systematic review and meta-regression analysis. *Epidemiologic Reviews, 29*(1), 6–28. doi:10.1093/epirev/mxm007

Wang, Y.-L., Brown, S. A., & Horner, S. D. (2010). School-based lived experiences of adolescents with type 1 diabetes: A preliminary study. *Journal of Nursing Research, 18*(4), 258–265. doi:10.1097/JNR.0b013e3181fbe107

Wang, Z., Deater-Deckard, K., Cutting, L., Thompson, L. A., & Petrill, S. A. (2012). Working memory and parent-rated components of attention in middle childhood: A behavioral genetic study. *Behavior Genetics, 42*(2), 199–208. doi:10.1007/s10519–011–9508–8

Ward, C. D., Phillips, P. M., & Cooper, R. P. (1998). Lack of preference for the paternal face in four-month-olds. *Infant Behavior and Development, 21*, 743. doi:10.1016/S0163–6383(98)91956–7

Warneken, F., & Tomasello, M. (2006). Altruistic helping in human infants and young chimpanzees, *Science, 311*(5765), 1301–1303.

Warneken, F., & Tomasello, M. (2007). Helping and cooperation at 14 months of age. *Infancy, 11*(3), 271–294.

Warneken, F., & Tomasello, M. (2009).The roots of human altruism. *British Journal of Psychology, 100*, 455–471.

Wartella, E., Richert, R. A., & Robb, M. B. (2010). Babies, television, and videos: How did we get here? *Developmental Review, 30*(2), 116–127. doi:10.1016/j.dr.2010.03.008

Wason, P. C. (1968). Reasoning about a rule. *Quarterly Journal of Experimental Psychology, 20*(3), 273–281. doi:10.1080/14640746808400161

Waszak, F., Li, S., & Hommel, B. (2010). The development of attentional networks: Cross-sectional findings from a life span sample. *Developmental Psychology, 46*(2), 337–349. doi:10.1037/a0018541

Watamura, S. E., Donzella, B., Alwin, J., & Gunnar, M. R. (2003). Morning-to-afternoon increases in cortisol concentrations for infants and toddlers at childcare: Age

differences and behavioral correlates, *Child Development 74*(4), 1006–1020.
Waterhouse, L. (2006). Multiple intelligences, the Mozart effect, and emotional intelligence: A critical review. *Educational Psychologist, 41*(4), 207–225. doi:10.1207/s15326985ep4104_1
Waters, E. (1987). *Attachment Q-set* (Version 3). Retrieved from http://www.johnbowlby.com
Waters, E., Matas, L., & Sroufe, L. A. (1975). Infants' reactions to an approaching stranger: Description, validation, and functional significance of wariness, *Child Development, 46*, 348–356.
Waters, E., Weinfield, N. S., & Hamilton, C. E. (2000). The stability of attachment security from infants to adolescence and early adulthood: General discussion, *Child Development, 71*(3), 703–706.
Waters, S., Virmani, E., Thompson, R. A., Meyer, S., Raikes, A., & Jochem, R. (2010). Emotion regulation and attachment: Unpacking two constructs and their association. *Journal of Psychopathology and Behavioral Assessment 32*, 37–47.
Watkins, P. L., Farrell, A. E., & Hugmeyer, A. D. (2012). Teaching fat studies: From conception to reception. *Fat Studies, 1*(2), 180–194.
Watson, J. (1930). *Behaviorism*. New York, NY: Norton.
Wattendorf, D. J., & Muenke, M. (2005). Fetal alcohol spectrum disorders. *American Family Physician, 72*(2), 279–282, 285.
Weatherston, D. J. (2000, October/November). The infant mental health specialist. *Zero to Three*, pp. 3–10.
Wechsler, D. (1958). *The measurement and appraisal of adult intelligence*. Baltimore, MD: Williams & Wilkins.
Weimer, A. A., Sallquist, J., & Bolnick, R. R. (2012). Young children's emotion comprehension and theory of mind understanding. *Early Education and Development, 23*(3), 280–301. doi:10.1080/10409289.2010.517694
Weinraub, M. (1984). *Children in context: Preparing for the development of our greatest natural resource?* Washington, DC: American Psychological Association.
Weis, J. P. (2004). Contemporary literacy skills. *Knowledge Quest, 32*(4), 12–15.
Weiss, H. B., Kreider, H., Lopez, M. E., & Chatman, C. M. (Eds.). (2005). *Preparing educators to involve families: From theory to practice.* Thousand Oaks, CA: Sage.
Weiss, K. B., Sullivan, S. D., & Lytle, C. S. (2000). Trends in the cost of illness for asthma in the United States, 1985–1994. *Journal of Allergy and Clinical Immunology, 106*(3), 493–499. doi:10.1067/mai.2000.109426
Weiss, S. T. (2002). Eat dirt: The hygiene hypothesis and allergic diseases. *New England Journal of Medicine, 347*, 930–931. doi:10.1056/NEJMe020092
Weissmann, M. M., Warner, V., Wickramatne, P. J., & Kandel, D. B. (1999). Maternal smoking during pregnancy and psychopathology in offspring followed to adulthood. *Journal of American Academy of Child and Adolescent Psychiatry, 38*, 892–899.
Weitzman, M., Byrd, R. S., Aligne, C. A., & Moss, M. (2002). The effects of tobacco exposure on children's behavioral and cognitive functioning: Implications for clinical and public health policy and future research. *Neurotoxicology and Teratology, 24*(3), 397–406. doi:10.1016/S0892–0362(02)00201–5
Welder, A. N., & Graham, S. A. (2006). Infants' categorization of novel objects with more or less obvious features. *Cognitive Psychology, 52*(1), 57–91. doi:10.1016/j.cogpsych.2005.05.003
Wells, S. (2002). *The journey of man: A genetic odyssey*. New York, NY: Random House.
Wen, S. W., Liu, S., Kramer, M. S., Marcoux, S., Ohlsson, A., Sauve, R., & Liston, R. (2001). Comparison of maternal and infant outcomes between vacuum extraction and forceps deliveries. *American Journal of Epidemiology, 153*(2), 103–107. doi:10.1093/aje/153.2.103
Wentzel, K. R. (2001). Peer groups. In J. V. Lerner, R. M. Lerner, & J. Finkelstein (Eds.), *Adolescence in America: Vol. 1. A–M* (pp. 489–493). Santa Barbara, CA: ABC–CLIO.
Werker, J. F., & McLeod, P. J. (1989). Infant preference for both male and female infant-directed talk: A developmental study of attentional and affective responsiveness. *Canadian Journal of Psychology, 43*(2), 230–246.
Werner, E. E. (1972). Infants around the world: Cross-cultural studies of psychomotor development from birth to two years. *Journal of Cross-Cultural Psychology, 3*, 111–134. doi:10.1177/002202217200300201
Werner, E., & Smith, R. (1992). *Overcoming the odds: High-risk children from birth to adulthood.* New York, NY: Cornell University Press.
Wertsch, J. V. (1984). The zone of proximal development: Some conceptual issues. *New Directions for Child Development, 23*, 7–18. doi:10.1002/cd.23219842303
Westbury, C., & Dennett, D. C. (2000). Mining the past to construct the future: Memory and belief as forms of knowledge. In D. L. Schacter & E. Scarry (Eds.), *Memory, brain, and belief* (pp. 11–32). Cambridge, MA: Harvard University Press.
Westermann, G., Thomas, M. S. C., & Karmiloff-Smith, A. (2011). Neuroconstructivism. In G. Westermann, M. S. C. Thomas, & A. Karmiloff-Smith (Eds.), *The Wiley-Blackwell handbook of child cognitive development* (2nd ed., pp. 723–747). Hoboken, NJ: Wiley-Blackwell.
Weyer, M., & Sandler, I. N. (1998). Stress and coping as predictors of children's divorce-related ruminations. *Journal of Clinical Child Psychology, 27*(1), 78–86. doi:10.1207/s15374424jccp2701_9
Whitaker, D. J., Miller, K. S., & Clark, L. F. (2000). Reconceptualizing adolescent sexual behavior: Beyond did they or didn't they? *Family Planning Perspectives, 32*(3), 111–117.
Whitaker, R. C., Wright, J. A., Pepe, M. S., Seidel, K. D., & Dietz, W. H. (1997). Predicting obesity in young adulthood from childhood and parental obesity. *New England Journal of Medicine, 337*, 869–873. doi:10.1056/NEJM199709253371301
White, R. W. (1959). Motivation reconsidered: The concept of competence. *Psychological Review, 66*(5), 297–333. doi:10.1037/h0040934
Whiteman, S. D., McHale, S. M., & Crouter, A. C. (2011). Family relationships from adolescence to early adulthood: Changes in the family system following firstborns' leaving home. *Journal of Research on Adolescence, 21*(2), 461–474. doi:10.1111/j.1532-7795.2010.00683.x
Whiting, B. B., & Whiting, J. W. (1975). *Children of six cultures: A psycho-cultural analysis.* Oxford, UK: Harvard University Press.
WHO Multicentre Growth Reference Study Group. (2006). WHO Child Growth Standards based on length/height, weight and age. *Acta Paediatrica Supplement, 450*, 76–85.
Widen, S. C., & Russell, J. A. (2003). A closer look at preschoolers' freely produced labels for facial expressions. *Developmental Psychology, 39*(1), 114–128. doi:10.1037/0012-1649.39.1.114
Wiebe, S. A., Sheffield, T. D., & Espy, K. A. (2012). Separating the fish from the sharks: A longitudinal study of preschool response inhibition. *Child Development, 83*(4), 1245–1261. doi:10.1111/j.1467-8624.2012.01765.x
Wieczorek-Deering, D., Greene, S., Nugent, J. K., & Graham, R. (1991). Categories of attachment and their determinants in an Irish urban sample. *Irish Journal of Psychology, 12*(2), 216–234.
Wigfield, A., & Cambria, J. (2010). Students' achievement values, goal orientations, and interest: Definitions, development, and relations to achievement outcomes. *Developmental Review, 30*(1), 1–35. doi:10.1016/j.dr.2009.12.001
Wilbur, R. (1979). *American sign language and sign system.* Baltimore, MD: University Park Press.
Wilcox, T., Stubbs, J., Hirshkowitz, A., & Boas, D. A. (2012). Functional activation of the infant cortex during object processing. *NeuroImage, 62*(3), 1833–1840. doi:10.1016/j.neuroimage.2012.05.039
Wilde, E. A., McCauley, S. R., Hunger, J. V., Bigler, E. D., Chu, A., Wang, Z., . . . Levin, H. S. (2008). Diffusion tensor imaging of acute mild traumatic brain injury in adolescents. *Neurology, 70*(12), 948–955.
Wilkinson, D. L., Magora, A., Garcia, M., & Khurana, A. (2009). Fathering at the margins of society: Reflections from minority, crime-involved fathers. *Journal of Family Issues, 30*(7), 945–967. doi:10.1177/0192513X09332354
Wilkinson, K. M., Ross, E., & Diamond, A. (2003). Fast mapping of multiple words: Insights into when "the information provided" does and does not equal "the information perceived." *Journal of Applied Developmental Psychology, 24*(6), 739–762. doi:10.1016/j.appdev.2003.09.006
Williams, D. R., Sternthal, M., & Wright, R. J. (2009). Social determinants: Taking the social context of asthma seriously. *Pediatrics, 123*(Suppl. 3), S174–S184. doi:10.1542/peds.2008-2233H
Williams, J. H. G. (2008). Self-other relations in social development and autism: Multiple roles for mirror neurons and other brain bases. *Autism, 1*(2), 73–90.
Williams, J. L., Tolan, P. H., Durkee, M. I., Francois, A. G., & Anderson, R. E. (2012). Integrating racial and ethnic identity research

into developmental understanding of adolescents. *Child Development Perspectives, 6*(3), 304–311.

Williams, K. D., & Jarvis, B. (2006). Cyberball: A program for use in research on interpersonal ostracism and acceptance. *Behavior Research Methods, 38*(1), 174–180. doi:10.3758/BF03192765

Williams, S. T., Mastergeorge, A. M., & Ontai, L. L. (2010). Caregiver involvement in infant peer interactions: Scaffolding in a social context. *Early Childhood Research Quarterly, 25*(2), 251–266. doi:10.1016/j.ecresq.2009.11.004

Willis, T. A., & Shinar, O. (2000). Measuring perceived and received social support. In S. Cohen, L. G. Underwood, & B. H. Gottlieb (Eds.), *Social support measurement and intervention* (pp. 86–135). New York, NY: Oxford University Press.

Willoughby, T., Adachi, P. J. C., & Good, M. (2012). A longitudinal study of the association between violent video game play and aggression among adolescents. *Developmental Psychology, 48*(4), 1044–1057. doi:10.1037/a0026046

Wilson, B. J. (2006). The entry behavior of aggressive/rejected children: The contributions of status and temperament. *Social Development, 15*(3), 463–479. doi:10.1111/j.1467-9507. 2006.00351.x

Wilson, B. J., Petaja, H., & Mancil, L. (2011). The attention skills and academic performance of aggressive/rejected and low aggressive/population children. *Early Education and Development, 22*(6), 907–930. doi:10.1080/10409289.2010.505258

Wilson, K. R., Havighurst, S. S., & Harley, A. E. (2012). Tuning in to kids: An effectiveness trial of a parenting program targeting emotion socialization of preschoolers. *Journal of Family Psychology, 26*(1), 56–65. doi:10.1037/a0026480

Wilson, S., & Durbin, C. E. (2010). Effects of paternal depression on fathers' parenting behaviors: A meta-analytic review. *Clinical Psychology Review, 30*, 167–180.

Winberg, J. (2005). Mother and newborn baby: Mutual regulation of physiology and behavior: A selective review. *Developmental Psychobiology, 47*, 217–229.

Winch, P. J., Alam, M. A., Akther, A., Afroz, D., Ali, N. A., Ellis, A. A., . . . Rahman Seraji, M. (2005). Local understandings of vulnerability and protection during the neonatal period in Sylhet District, Bangladesh: A qualitative study. *Lancet, 366*(9484), 478–485. doi:10.1016/S0140–6736(05)66836–5

Winner, E. (1989). *Adult-level performance by the average child: Chinese children's drawings.* Paper presented at Society for Research in Child Development, Kansas City, MO, April 1989.

Winnicott, D. (1960). The theory of the parent-child relationship. *International Journal of Psychoanalysis, 41*, 585–595.

Winsler, A., & Naglieri, J. (2003). Overt and covert verbal problem-solving strategies: Developmental trends in use, awareness, and relations with task performance in children aged 5 to 17. *Child Development, 74*(3), 659–678. doi:10.1111/1467-8624.00561

Winsler, A., Fernyhough, C., & Montero, I. (Eds.). (2009). *Private speech, executive functioning, and the development of verbal self-regulation.* New York, NY: Cambridge University Press. doi:10.1017/CBO9780511581533

Winsler, A., Madigan, A. L., & Aquilino, S. A. (2005). Correspondence between maternal and paternal parenting styles in early childhood. *Early Childhood Research Quarterly, 20*(1), 1–12. doi:10.1016/j.ecresq.2005.01.007

Wittmer, D. S., & Peterson, S. H. (2006). *Infant and toddler development and responsive program planning.* Upper Saddle River, NJ: Pearson.

Wojslawowicz Bowker, J. C., Rubin, K. H., Burgess, K. B., Booth-LaForce, C., & Rose-Krasnor, L. (2006). Behavioral characteristics associated with stable and fluid best friendship patterns in middle childhood. *Merrill-Palmer Quarterly, 52*(4), 671–693. doi:10.1353/mpq.2006.0000

Wolchik, S. A., Wilcox, K. L., Tein, J., & Sandler, I. N. (2000). Maternal acceptance and consistency of discipline as buffers of divorce stressors on children's psychological adjustment problems. *Journal of Abnormal Child Psychology, 28*(1), 87–102. doi:/10.1023/A:1005178203702

Wolf, M. S., Wilson, E. A. H., Rapp, D. N., Waite, K. R., Bocchini, M. V., Davis, T. C., & Rudd, R. E. (2009). Literacy and learning in health care. *Pediatrics, 124*(Suppl. 3), S275–S281. doi:10.1542/peds.2009-1162C

Wolff, J. J., Gu, H., Gerig, G., Elison, J. T., Styner, M., Gouttard, S., . . . Piven, J. (2012). Differences in white matter fiber tract development present from 6 to 24 months in infants with autism. *American Journal of Psychiatry, 169*(6), 589–600. doi:10.1176/appi.ajp.2011.11091447

Wolff, J. M., & Crockett, L. J. (2011). The role of deliberative decision making, parenting, and friends in adolescent risk behaviors. *Journal of Youth and Adolescence, 40*(12), 1607–1622. doi:10.1007/s10964–011–9644–8

Wolff, P. H. (1959). Observations on newborn infants. *Psychosomatic Medicine, 221*, 110–118.

Wolff, P. H. (1987). *The development of behavioral states and the expression of emotions in early infancy: New proposals for investigation.* Chicago, IL: University of Chicago Press.

Wolfson, A. R., & Carskadon, M. A. (1998). Sleep schedules and daytime functioning in adolescents. *Child Development, 69*(4), 875–887.

Woltering, S., & Lewis, M. D. (2009). Developmental pathways of emotion regulation in childhood: A neuropsychological perspective. *Mind, Brain, and Education, 3*(3), 160–169. doi: 10.1111/j.1751-228X.2009.01066.x

Women in Congress. (2009). *Jeannette Rankin.* Retrieved from http://womenincongress.house.gov/member-profiles/profile.html?intID=202

Wong, S., Chan, K., Wong, V., & Wong, W. (2002). Use of chopsticks in Chinese children. *Child: Care, Health and Development, 28*(2), 157–161. doi:10.1046/j.1365-2214.2002.00256.x

Wood, R. (2011). *The natural history of childhood food allergy.* In S. Schirer (Ed.), *UpToDate.* Waltham, MA: UpToDate.

Woods, L. N., & Jagers, R. J. (2003). Are cultural values predictors of moral reasoning in African American adolescents? *Journal of Black Psychology, 29*(1), 102–118. doi:10.1177/0095798402239231

Woodside, D. B., Garfinkel, P. E., Lin, E., Goering, P., & Kaplan, A. S. (2001). Comparisons of men with full or partial eating disorders, men without eating disorders, and women with eating disorders in the community. *American Journal of Psychiatry, 158*(4), 570–574. doi:10.1176/appi.ajp.158.4.570

Woolard, J. L., & Scott, E. (2009). The legal regulation of adolescence. In R. M. Lerner & L. Steinberg (Eds.), *Handbook of adolescent psychology: Vol. 2. Contextual influences on adolescent development* (3rd ed., pp. 345–371). Hoboken, NJ: Wiley.

Wooldridge, M. B., & Shapka, J. (2012). Playing with technology: Mother-toddler interaction scores lower during play with electronic toys. *Journal of Applied Developmental Psychology, 335*(5), 211–218. doi:10.1016/j.appdev.2012.05.005

Woollett, A. (1986). The influence of older siblings on the language environment of young children. *British Journal of Developmental Psychology, 4*, 235–245.

Working Group on ELL Policy. (2011). *Improving educational outcomes for English Language Learners: Recommendations for the reauthorization of the Elementary and Secondary Education Act.* Retrieved from http:ellpolicy.org/esea

World Health Organization. (n.d.). *Genomic Resource Centre: Genes and human disease.* Retrieved from http://www.who.int/genomics/public/geneticdiseases/en/index2.html

World Health Organization. (2000). *Obesity: Preventing and managing the global epidemic* (WHO technical report series 894). Geneva, Switzerland: Author.

World Health Organization. (2003). *Obesity and overweight: Facts* (Report on global strategy on diet, physical activity and health). Geneva, Switzerland: Author. Retrieved from http://www.who.int/dietphysicalactivity/media/en/gsfs_obesity.pdf

World Health Organization. (2005). *2004 Global immunization data.* Geneva, Switzerland: Author. Retrieved from http://www.who.int/immunization_monitoring/data/GlobalImmunizationData.pdf

World Health Organization. (2006). *Disease control priorities related to mental, neurological, developmental and substance abuse disorders.* Geneva, Switzerland: Author.

World Health Organization. (2009). *The WHO child growth standards.* Retrieved from http://www.who.int/childgrowth/en/

World Health Organization. (2010). *World health statistics 2010.* Geneva, Switzerland: Author.

Worthman, C. M., & Panter-Brick, C. (2008). Homeless street children in Nepal: Use of allostatic load to assess the burden of childhood adversity. *Developmental Psychopathology, 20*(1), 233–255. doi:10.1017/S0954579408000114

Wright, J. C., Huston, A. C., Scantlin, R., & Kotler, J. (2001). The early window project: "Sesame Street" prepares children for school. In S. M. Fisch & R. T. Truglio (Eds.), *"G" is for "growing": Thirty years of research on children and Sesame Street* (pp. 97–114). Mahwah, NJ: Erlbaum.

Wright, R. J., Mitchell, H., Visness, C. M., Cohen, S., Stout, J., Evans, R., & Gold, D. R. (2004). Community violence and asthma morbidity: The inner-city asthma study. *American Journal of Public Health, 94*(4), 625–632. doi:10.2105/AJPH.94.4.625

Wrightson, A. S. (2007). Universal newborn hearing screening. *American Family Physician, 75*(9), 1349–1352.

Wynn, K., Bloom, P., & Chiang, W. (2002). Enumeration of collective entities by 5-month-old infants. *Cognition, 83*(3), B55–B62. doi:10.1016/S0010–0277(02)00008–2

Wyshak, G., & Frisch, R. E. (1982). Evidence for a secular trend in age of menarche. *New England Journal of Medicine, 306*(17), 1033–1035.

Xing, X., Zhang, Y., & Wang, M. (2011). Intergenerational transmission of corporal punishment: Mediating effects of parents' attitudes toward corporal punishment. *Chinese Journal of Clinical Psychology, 19*(6), 827–829.

Xu, F., Bao, X., Fu, G., Talwar, V., & Lee, K. (2010). Lying and truth-telling in children: From concept to action. *Child Development, 81*(2), 581–596. doi:10.1111/j.1467–8624.2009.01417.x

Xu, R. J. (1996). Development of the newborn GI tract and its relation to colostrum/milk intake: A review. *Reproduction, Fertility, and Development, 8*(1), 35–48. doi:10.1071/RD9960035

Yagmurlu, B., & Altan, O. (2010). Maternal socialization and child temperament as predictors of emotion regulation in Turkish preschoolers. *Infant and Child Development, 19*(3), 275–296. doi:10.1002/icd.646

Yaman, A., Mesman, J., van IJzendoorn, M. H., & Bakermans-Kranenburg, M. J. (2010). Parenting and toddler aggression in second-generation immigrant families: The moderating role of child temperament. *Journal of Family Psychology, 24*(2), 208–211. doi:10.1037/a0019100

Yazdanbakhsh, M., Kremsner, P. G., & van Ree, R. (2002). Allergy, parasites, and the hygiene hypothesis. *Science, 296*(5567), 490–494. doi:10.1126/science.296.5567.490

Yeung, D. Y. L., Tang, C. S., & Lee, A. (2005). Psychosocial and cultural factors influencing expectations of menarche: A study on Chinese premenarcheal teenage girls. *Journal of Adolescent Research 20*(1), 118–135.

Yeung, W. J., Sandberg, J. F., Davis-Kean, P. E., & Hofferth, S. L. (2001). Children's time with fathers in intact families. *Journal of Marriage and the Family, 63*, 136–154.

Yin, S. H., Johnson, M., Mendelsohn, A. L., Abrams, M. A., Sanders, L. E., & Dreyer, B. P. (2009). The health literacy of parents in the United States: A nationally representative study. *Pediatrics, 124*, S289–S298. doi:10.1542/peds.2009-1162E

Yirmiya, N., Gamliel, I., Pilowsky, T., Feldman, R., Baron-Cohen, S., & Sigman, M. (2006). The development of siblings of children with autism at 4 and 14 months: Social engagement, communication, and cognition. *Journal of Child Psychology and Psychiatry, 47*(5), 511–523.

Yoshinaga-Itano, C. (1999). Universal newborn hearing screening, assessment, and intervention. *The Hearing Journal, 52*, 11–21.

Young, J. M., & Hauser-Cram, P. (2006). Mother-child interaction as a predictor of mastery motivation in children with disabilities born preterm. *Journal of Early Intervention, 28*(4), 252–263. doi:10.1177/105381510602800402

Young, J., & Fleming, P. J. (1998). Reducing the risks of SIDS: The role of the pediatrician. *Paediatrics Today, 6*, 41–48.

Younger, B. A., & Fearing, D. D. (2000). A global-to-basic trend in early categorization: Evidence from a dual-category habituation task. *Infancy, 1*(1), 47–58. doi:10.1207/S15327078IN0101_05

Youth Risk Behavior Surveillance Systems. (2010). *Trends in the prevalence of selected risk behaviors and obesity for all students, national YRBS: 1991–2009*. Retrieved from http://www.cdc.gov/healthyyouth/yrbs/pdf/us_summary_all_trend_yrbs.pdf

Youth Risk Behavior Surveillance Systems. (2012). *Youth Risk Behavior Surveillance Systems: 2011 national overview*. Retrieved from http://www.cdc.gov/healthyyouth/yrbs/pdf/us_overview_yrbs.pdf

Yu, C. K. H., Teoh, T. G., & Robinson, S. (2006). Obesity in pregnancy. *British Journal of Obstetrics and Gynecology, 113*, 1117–1125. doi:10.1111/j.1471–0528.2006.00991.x

Yuill, N. (2009). The relation between ambiguity understanding and metalinguistic discussion of joking riddles in good and poor comprehenders: Potential for intervention and possible processes of change. *First Language, 29*(1), 65–79. doi:10.1177/0142723708097561

Yurgelun-Todd, D. (2007). Emotional and cognitive changes during adolescence. *Current Opinion in Neurobiology, 17*(2), 251–257. doi:10.1016/j.conb.2007.03.009

Zahn-Waxler, C., Robinson, J., & Emde, R. (1992). The development of empathy in twins. *Developmental Psychology, 28*, 1038–1047.

Zahn-Waxler, C., Schiro, K., Robinson, J. L., Emde, R., & Schmitz, S. (2001). Empathy and prosocial patterns in young MZ and DZ twins: Development and genetic and environmental influences. In R. N. Emde & J. K. Hewitt (Eds.), *Infancy to early childhood* (pp. 141–162). New York, NY: Oxford University Press.

Zarrett, N., Fay, K., Li, Y., Carrano, J., Phelps, E., & Lerner, R. M. (2009). More than child's play: Variable- and pattern-centered approaches for examining effects of sports participation on youth development. *Developmental Psychology, 45*(2), 368–382. doi:10.1037/a0014577

Zeanah, C. H., & Boris, N. W. (2000). Disturbances and disorders of attachment in early childhood. In C. H. Zeanah (Ed.), *Handbook of infant mental health* (2nd ed., pp. 353–368). New York, NY: Guilford.

Zelazo, P. D., & Frye, D. (1998). Cognitive complexity and control: II. The development of executive function in childhood. *Current Directions in Psychological Science, 7*(4), 121–126. doi:10.1111/1467–8721.ep10774761

Zelazo, P., Carlson, S., & Kesek, A. (2008). The development of executive function in childhood. In C. A. Nelson & M. Luciana (Eds.), *Handbook of developmental cognitive neuroscience* (2nd ed., pp. 553–574). Cambridge, MA: MIT Press.

Zentner, M., & Bates, J. E. (2008). Child temperament: An integrative review of concepts, research programs, and measures. *European Journal of Developmental Science, 2*(1–2), 7–37.

Zeskind, P. S., & Gingras, J. L. (2006). Maternal cigarette-smoking during pregnancy disrupts rhythms in fetal heart rate. *Journal of Pediatric Psychology, 31*(1), 5–14. doi:10.1093/jpepsy/jsj031

Zhang, L., Chen, L., & Fang, F. (2011). The adaptation of dynamic test using the Inventory of Piaget's Developmental Task (IPDT): An initial validation and application. *Acta Psychologica Sinica, 43*(9), 1075–1086.

Zhang, W., Liu, X., & Song, H. (2010). The influence of "hot" executive function on the verbal working memory of attention deficit hyperactivity disorder (ADHD) and reading disability (RD) children. *Acta Psychologica Sinica, 42*(3), 415–422. doi:10.3724/SP.J.1041.2010.00415

Zhang, X., & Kramer, M. S. (2012). The rise in singleton preterm births in the USA: The impact of labour induction. *British Journal of Obstetrics and Gynaecology, 119*(11), 1309–1315.

Zhao, Y., Montoro, R., Igartua, K., & Thombs, B. D. (2010). Suicidal ideation and attempt among adolescents reporting "unsure" sexual identity or heterosexual identity plus same-sex attraction or behavior: Forgotten groups? *Journal of the American Academy of Child & Adolescent Psychiatry, 49*(2), 104–113. doi:10.1097/00004583-201002000–00004.

Zigler, E. F., & Muenchow, S. (1992). *Head Start: The inside story of America's most successful educational experiment.* New York, NY: Basic Books.

Zigler, E., & Syfco, S. J. (2004). Moving Head Start to the states: One experiment too many. *Applied Developmental Science, 8*(1), 51–55.

Zill, N., Resnick, G., Kim, K., O'Donnell, K., Sorongon, A., McKay, R., . . . D'Elio, M. A. (2003). *Head Start FACES 2000: A whole-child perspective on program performance.* Washington, DC: U.S. Department of Health and Human Services.

Zimmer, C. (2008). The search for intelligence. *Scientific American, 299*(4), 68–75. doi:10.1038/sceintificamerican1008–68

Zimmerman, F. J., Christakis, D. A., & Meltzoff, A. N. (2007). Associations between media viewing and language development in children under age 2 years. *Journal of Pediatrics, 151*(4), 364–368. doi:10.1016/j.jpeds.2007.04.071

Zosuls, K. M., Ruble, D. N., Tamis-LeMonda, C. S., Shrout, P. E., Bornstein, M. H., & Greulich, F. K. (2009). The acquisition of gender labels in infancy: Implications for gender-typed play. *Developmental Psychology, 45*(3), 688–701. doi:10.1037/a0014053

Zucker, E., & Howes, C. (2009). Respectful relationships: Socialization goals and practices among Mexican mothers. *Infant Mental Health Journal, 30*(5), 501–522.

Zukow-Goldring, P. (2002). Sibling caregiving. In M. H. Bornstein (Ed.), *Handbook of parenting: Vol. 3. Being and becoming a parent* (pp. 253–286). Mahwah, NJ: Erlbaum.

Zurer Pearson, B. (2008). *Raising a bilingual child*. New York, NY: Random House.

Zwaigenbaum, L., Bryson, S., Rogers, T., Roberts, W., Brian, J., & Szatmari, P. (2005). Behavioral manifestation of autism in the first year of life. *International Journal of Developmental Neuroscience, 23*, 143–152.

Zwiers, J. (2007). Teacher practices and perspectives for developing academic language. *International Journal of Applied Linguistics, 17*(1), 93–116. doi:10.1111/j.1473-4192.2007.00135.x

Zwiers, J. (2008). *Building academic language: Essential practices for content classrooms, grades 5–12*. San Francisco, CA: Jossey-Bass.

# Name Index

*Note:* italic *n* indicates caption or note following table, figure, or illustration.

## B

## C

## I

## M

## N

## S

## Z

# Subject Index

*Note:* Italic *f* and *t* denote figures and tables, respectively.

## F

## G

## I

## N

## Q



## R



## S

## T

## W



## Y



## Z